THE OXFORD HANDBOOK OF

MODERN IRISH POETRY

THE OXFORD HANDBOOK OF

MODERN

IRISH POETRY

Edited by
FRAN BREARTON
and
ALAN GILLIS

OXFORD
UNIVERSITY PRESS

OXFORD
UNIVERSITY PRESS

Great Clarendon Street, Oxford, OX2 6DP,
United Kingdom

Oxford University Press is a department of the University of Oxford.
It furthers the University's objective of excellence in research, scholarship,
and education by publishing worldwide. Oxford is a registered trade mark of
Oxford University Press in the UK and in certain other countries

British Library Cataloguing in Publication Data
Data available

Library of Congress Cataloging in Publication Data
Data available

ISBN 978-0-19-956124-7

Printed and bound in Great Britain by
CPI Group (UK) Ltd, Croydon, CRO 4YY

This book is dedicated to the memory of Michael Allen (1935–2011), tutor, friend, and inspiration.

Acknowledgements

We are grateful to the following for permission to reproduce copyright material: AP Watt Ltd on behalf of Gráinne Yeats for quotations from the poems of W.B. Yeats; David Higham Associates for quotations from Louis MacNeice's poems; John Coffey for permission to quote from poems by Brian Coffey; the Estate of Thomas MacGreevy for permission to quote from MacGreevy's poems; Faber and Faber Ltd for permission to quote from the poems of Samuel Beckett, Seamus Heaney, and Paul Muldoon; Carcanet Press Ltd for quotations from Thomas Kinsella, Sinead Morrissey, and Justin Quinn; Random House Group Ltd for quotations from Leontia Flynn and Michael Longley; quotations from poems by Ciaran Carson, Alan Gillis, Vona Groarke, Medbh McGuckian, Derek Mahon, John Montague, Nuala ní Dhomhnaill, and David Wheatley are reproduced by kind permission of The Gallery Press, Loughcrew, Oldcastle, Co. Meath, Ireland; we are grateful to Bloodaxe Books for permission to quote from Brendan Kennelly, *Familiar Strangers: New & Selected Poems* and Caitriona O'Reilly, *The Nowhere Birds* and *The Sea Cabinet*; thanks to Wild Honey Press, Shearsman Books, and the authors for permission to quote from the works of Geoffrey Squires, Trevor Joyce, Maurice Scully, and Catherine Walsh. Every effort has been made to trace copyright holders, and any omissions will be rectified at the earliest opportunity.

PREFACE

....

Irish poetry has travelled some distance in terms of its critical profile over the last hundred years. It was once subsumed by critics into English poetry (although with an Arnoldian tolerance of its Celtic 'otherness'); later, Yeats and Joyce were the exemplars of international modernism. By the 1960s, studies of 'Anglo-Irish Poetry' in its own right began to emerge; by the 1980s, as Irish Studies became increasingly institutionalized in the academy, and as the rise to fame of Heaney and a generation of poets from the North of Ireland brought Irish poetry to international audiences in a way not seen since Yeats, 'Irish poetry' became a subject of academic study on an extraordinary scale. The 1980s, for instance, saw the publication of studies by Robert Garratt (*Modern Irish Poetry*, 1986), Dillon Johnston (*Irish Poetry After Joyce*, 1985), and Edna Longley (*Poetry in the Wars*, 1986), a critical interest that has only increased in the decades that have followed. Irish writing has become, almost, a 'centre' against which other anglophone writings define themselves.

'Poetry' and 'Ireland' have also developed, in recent decades, an extraordinary critical, cultural, and touristic synonymity. Poetry itself is obviously implicated in the development of nationalism in Ireland and with the 'Irish story'; poetry (even, in the case of Heaney, the poet) can become a national symbol—one of Ireland's major exports. At the same time, writers who exhibit a healthy scepticism towards the idea of an 'Irish tradition' and a willingness to bite the hand that feeds (the very marketability of 'Irish identity') have, ironically, continually served to reinvigorate an Irish poetic tradition in part through their felt unease with the label of 'Irish poet'.

In one sense, to tell the history of poetry in Ireland over the last 130 years is also, chronologically, to tell some of the complex history of the island of Ireland, and part of the aim here is to situate the poetry in its sociopolitical contexts. Yet whatever 'Irish poetry' is, it has never, at its best, been merely the product of history. The dialogues between poets and poems, other cultures, other art forms, the two-way workings of influence, all serve to complicate the story of Irish poetry. The premise of this handbook, therefore, is neither wholly thematic nor straightforwardly literary-historical. While the broad structure moves from Yeats to the present day, within that narrative are sections unconfined to historical period or event.

One of the ways in which discussions of 'Irish poetry' can prove misleading is the extent to which 'Irish' becomes a non-permeable category. In reality, to draw a circle around Irish poetry is, if not an artificial, then certainly a necessarily limiting enterprise. Whatever we mean by Irish poetry, it cannot be understood without reference to its broader context in the anglophone poetry world, nor without reference to a lively Irish language poetic tradition. For practical reasons not every dialogue, nor every cultural exchange, can be pursued here, but the essays point towards key intersections in and beyond these islands in ways paradigmatic of a network of contexts and influences reaching far beyond the scope of this book.

Ironically, perhaps, poetry itself is not the major achievement of the Irish Literary Revival (Yeats's contribution aside), which lay more obviously in the theatre, although some coverage is given here to the work of relatively minor poets in the years of the Revival. The First World War is a period in which quarrels emerge that colour debates about Irish poetry not only through the 1920s, but into the present day. The 'Easter 1916' poets bring to the fore debates about poetry and nation; Yeats's formalism is in dialogue with exponents of modernist experimentation in both Britain and Ireland—MacGreevy and Devlin among them; and if exile is most obviously identified with Joyce and Beckett as novelist and playwright respectively, the contribution of these writers to the development of Irish poetry should not be underestimated either. The broadly chronological areas that follow in this book, from the 1930s to the 1990s, allow scope for in-depth coverage of the century's key poetic voices, from the refashioning of Yeats's Ireland on the part of poets such as MacNeice, Kavanagh, and Clarke, through to the controversially titled 'Northern Renaissance'.

By far the most critical attention in Irish poetry criticism to date, aside of that given to Yeats, has been devoted to the work of the 'Northern generation' (or generations) of Heaney, Longley, Mahon, Muldoon, McGuckian, and Carson, and to a predominantly lyric mode. Whilst acknowledging ways in which the emergence of this generation is not separable from Ireland's own 'troubled' history, there is also a recognition that this forms only part of a more complex poetic landscape in Ireland as a whole. The thematic sections interspersed throughout the book—chapters on women's poetry, religion, translation, painting, music, romanticism—allow for comparative studies of poets north and south across the century. Central to the guiding spirit of this project is discussion of poetic form, and an exploration of the generic diversity of poetry in Ireland—its various manipulations, reinventions, and sometimes repudiations of tradition.

To bring a project like this through to the present day is to flirt dangerously with Bloomian predictions. At the beginning of a new century, however, there is a case for suggesting, not that Irish poetry is once again undergoing something of a revival, but that it remains, as it has always been, a vibrant, provocative, and influential presence in and beyond these islands.

FB and AG
Belfast and Edinburgh, December 2011

CONTENTS

PART VII POETRY AND POLITICS: THE 1970s AND 1980s

PART VIII CULTURAL LANDSCAPES

List of Contributors

Shane Alcobia-Murphy is Senior Lecturer at the University of Aberdeen. He is the author of *Governing the Tongue in Northern Ireland* (2005) and *Sympathetic Ink: Intertextual Relations in Northern Irish Poetry* (2006). He has edited a number of collections of essays, including *The Poetry of Medbh McGuckian* (2010).

Jonathan Allison is Associate Professor of English at the University of Kentucky and was formerly director of the W. B. Yeats Summer School. His edition of *Letters of Louis MacNeice* was published by Faber in 2010.

Fran Brearton is Reader in English at Queen's University Belfast. She is the author of *The Great War in Irish Poetry* (2000) and *Reading Michael Longley* (2006). She recently co-edited (with Edna Longley) *Incorrigibly Plural: Louis MacNeice and his Legacy* (2012).

Matthew Campbell teaches modern literature at the University of York. He has published on Romantic, Victorian, and contemporary poetry from Britain as well as Ireland, and is the editor of *The Cambridge Companion to Contemporary Irish Poetry* (2003) and *The Voice of the People: Writing the European Folk Revival, 1761–1914* (2012).

Heather Clark is the author of *The Ulster Renaissance: Poetry in Belfast 1962–1972* (2006), which won the Donald Murphy Prize and the Robert Rhodes Prize from the American Conference for Irish Studies, and *The Grief of Influence: Sylvia Plath and Ted Hughes* (2011). She is Professor of Literature at Marlboro College in Vermont.

Catriona Clutterbuck lectures in the School of English, Drama, and Film at University College Dublin. Her research interests centre on contemporary Irish poetry and gender in Irish writing. She has published essays on Derek Mahon, Eavan Boland, Thomas Kinsella, Eiléan Ní Chuilleanáin, Medbh McGuckian, Brian Friel, Anne Devlin, Lady Gregory, and Charles J. Kickham, as well as on the critical and cultural contexts of Irish poetry.

Neil Corcoran is Emeritus Professor at the University of Liverpool, where he was King Alfred Professor of English Literature until 2010. He previously taught at the universities of Sheffield, Swansea, and St Andrews. His publications include studies of Seamus Heaney and Elizabeth Bowen and, most recently, *Shakespeare and the Modern Poet* (2010).

Gerald Dawe is Associate Professor and Fellow of Trinity College Dublin. His collections of poetry include *Lake Geneva* (2003), *Points West* (2008), and *Selected Poems*

(2012). His other publications include *The Proper Word: Collected Criticism* (2007) and the anthology, *Earth Voices Whispering: Irish Poetry of War 1914–1945* (2008).

Eric Falci is an Assistant Professor of English at the University of California, Berkeley. His monograph, *Continuity and Change in Irish Poetry, 1966–2010*, will be published by Cambridge University Press.

Leontia Flynn is research fellow in the Seamus Heaney Centre for Poetry, Queen's University Belfast. Her most recent collection, *Profit & Loss* (2011), was shortlisted for the T. S. Eliot Prize, and her study of Medbh McGuckian's poetry will be published by Irish Academic Press in 2012.

Kit Fryatt is a Lecturer in English at Mater Dei Institute of Education, a college of Dublin City University, where with colleagues she coordinates the activities of the Irish Centre for Poetry Studies.

Miriam Gamble is Lecturer in English at The University of Edinburgh. Her first collection, *The Squirrels Are Dead* (2010), won a Somerset Maugham Award in 2011; she has also received the Eric Gregory Award, the Ireland Chair of Poetry Bursary Award, and the Vincent Buckley Poetry Prize.

Alan Gillis is Lecturer in English at the University of Edinburgh, and editor of *Edinburgh Review*. He has published three collections of poems with the Gallery Press: *Somebody, Somewhere* (2004), *Hawks and Doves* (2007), and *Here Comes the Night* (2010). He has been shortlisted for the *Irish Times* Poetry Now Award, the T. S. Eliot Prize, and has won The Rupert and Eithne Strong Award for best first collection in Ireland. As a critic he is author of *Irish Poetry of the 1930s* (2005), and has co-edited *Critical Ireland* (2001) and *The Edinburgh Guide to Studying English Literature* (2010).

John Goodby is a Senior Lecturer in English at Swansea University. He is the co-editor of the *Angel Exhaust* special issue on avant-garde Irish poetry (1999) and author of *Irish Poetry since 1950: From Stillness into History* (2000). He is currently editing a new, centenary edition of the collected poems of Dylan Thomas for publication in 2014. His own recent poetry includes the collection *Illennium* (2010) and a contribution to *The Forward Book of Best Poems of the Decade* (2011).

Warwick Gould FRSL is Professor of English Literature at the University of London, where he is Director of the Institute of English Studies in the School of Advanced Study. He has been editor of *Yeats Annual* since 1983 and has co-edited *The Secret Rose, Stories by W. B. Yeats: A Variorum Edition* (1981), *Modernist Writers and the Marketplace* (1996), *The Collected Letters of W. B. Yeats*, volume II (1997), *Writing the Lives of Writers* (1998), and Yeats's *Mythologies* (2005).

Jim Haughey teaches English at Anderson University in Anderson, South Carolina. He is the author of *The First World War in Irish Poetry* (2002), and has published essays on

Francis Ledwidge, James Joyce, William Trevor, Seamus Heaney, Michael Longley, and Christina Reid.

Hugh Haughton was born in Cork and is Professor in the Department of English and Related Literatures, York. He is the author of *The Poetry of Derek Mahon* (2007) and co-editor (with Valerie Eliot) of the first two volumes of *The Letters of T. S. Eliot* (2009).

Rui Carvalho Homem is Professor of English at the University of Oporto, Portugal. He is the author of *Shakespeare and the Drama of Alterity* (in Portuguese; 2003) and *Poetry and Translation in Northern Ireland: Dislocations in Contemporary Writing* (2009). He has published extensively on Irish poetry, early modern English drama, and word-and-image studies. He also works as a literary translator.

Dillon Johnston is the founder and former director of the Wake Forest University Press, the major publisher of Irish poetry in North America. He is the author of *Irish Poetry After Joyce* (1985; rev. 1997), *Poetic Economies of England & Ireland, 1912–2000* (2001), and essays on British and Irish literature. With Guinn Batten he is co-author of the Irish poetry section of the *Cambridge History of Irish Literature* (2006). He teaches at Washington University in St Louis.

Maria Johnston is Christopher Tower Lecturer in Poetry in the English Language at Christ Church College, Oxford. She is a regular reviewer of contemporary poetry and has recently co-edited with Philip Coleman *Reading Pearse Hutchinson* (2011).

Damien Keane is currently an Assistant Professor in the Department of English at the State University of New York at Buffalo. His research broadly deals with the sociological relations of sound technologies, printed matter, and institutional formations, and he is nearing completion of a manuscript entitled *Ireland and the Problem of Information*.

Elmer Kennedy-Andrews is Professor of English Literature at the University of Ulster, Coleraine. His books include *The Poetry of Seamus Heaney: All the Realms of Whisper* (1988), *The Art of Brian Friel* (1995), *The Poetry of Seamus Heaney: A Reader's Guide to Essential Criticism* (2000), *Fiction and the Northern Ireland Troubles: (De-)Constructing the North* (2003), and *Writing Home: Poetry and Place in Northern Ireland 1968–2008* (2008). He has edited and contributed to critical collections on *Seamus Heaney* (1992), *Contemporary Irish Poetry* (1992), *The Poetry of Derek Mahon* (2002), *Irish Fiction Since the 1960s* (2006), *Paul Muldoon* (2006), and *Ciaran Carson* (2009). He is currently working on a study of Northern Irish Poets and America, and a book on The Jew in Irish Literature.

Richard Kirkland is Professor of Irish Literature in the Department of English, King's College London. He has published extensively on twentieth-century Irish culture.

Edward Larrissy is Head of School and Chair in Poetry in the School of English, Queen's University Belfast. He was educated at Oxford, and has taught previously at

Warwick, Keele, and Leeds. His special interests are in the poetry of Britain and Ireland in the Romantic and modern periods, and in the relationship between the Romantic period and the twentieth century. His books include *Reading Twentieth-Century Poetry: The Language of Gender and Objects* (1990), *Yeats the Poet: The Measures of Difference* (1994), *Blake and Modern Literature* (2006), and *The Blind and Blindness in Literature of the Romantic Period* (2007). He is also the editor of, among other things, *W. B. Yeats: The Major Works* (2001) in the Oxford World's Classics series. He is a Member of the Royal Irish Academy.

Edna Longley is Professor Emerita at Queen's University Belfast. Her books include *The Living Stream: Literature and Revisionism in Ireland* (1994), *Poetry & Posterity* (2000), and *Edward Thomas: The Annotated Collected Poems* (2008).

John McAuliffe has published three collections of poems with the Gallery Press: *A Better Life* (2002), *Next Door* (2007), and *Of All Places* (2011). He is Senior Lecturer in Creative Writing and Modern Literature at the University of Manchester, where he is also co-director of the Centre for New Writing.

Gail McConnell completed a doctorate at Queen's University Belfast in 2010 and currently teaches part-time in the School of English. Her research examines how theology shapes subjectivity, language, and poetic form in modern British and Irish poetry.

Peter McDonald is Christopher Tower Student and Tutor in Poetry in the English Language at Christ Church, Oxford. His books include *Mistaken Identities: Poetry and Northern Ireland* (1997), *Serious Poetry: Form and Authority from Yeats to Hill* (2002), *The Collected Poems of Louis MacNeice* (2007), and *Sound Intentions: The Workings of Rhyme in Nineteenth-Century Poetry* (2012). He has published five volumes of poetry, as well as his *Collected Poems* (2012). He is currently editing a three-volume edition of *The Complete Poems of W. B. Yeats* for the Longman Annotated Poets series.

Peter Mackay is originally from the Isle of Lewis. He completed a PhD on the poetry of Seamus Heaney and William Wordsworth at Trinity College Dublin, has lectured at Trinity on Scottish Literature, and has worked as a Research Fellow at Queen's University Belfast. His monograph *Sorley MacLean* was published by RIISS in 2010; he has also co-edited *Modern Irish and Scottish Poetry* (2011), and has published a pamphlet of poems, *From Another Island* (2010). He currently works as a Broadcast Journalist for BBC Alba.

Steven Matthews is Professor of English at Oxford Brookes University. He is the author of several books, including *Irish Poetry: Politics, History, Negotiation: The Evolving Debate, 1969 to the Present* (1997); *Yeats as Precursor* (2000); and *Les Murray* (2001). He has edited the *Contexts* series of monographs for Arnold, a series to which he has contributed the volume on *Modernism* (2004). He is also currently editor of the *Sourcebooks* series for Palgrave, for which his volume on *Modernism* appeared in 2008. His *T. S. Eliot and Early Modern Literature* will appear from Oxford University Press in 2012. A volume of poetry, *Skying*, is due from Waterloo Press, also in 2012.

Michael O'Neill is a Professor of English at Durham University. Recent publications include, as editor, *The Cambridge History of English Poetry* (2010).

Aodán Mac Póilin was born in Belfast in 1948, where he lives in an Irish-speaking community. He is director of ULTACH Trust, a cross-community Irish language organization and has published translations of poetry and prose from Irish, and articles on literature, cultural and linguistic politics, language planning, and broadcasting. He is co-editor of *Styles of Belonging: The Cultural Identities of Ulster* (1992) and *Ruined Page: New Selected Poems of Padraic Fiacc* (1994), and editor of *The Irish Language in Northern Ireland* (1997). He is currently working on a bilingual anthology of Gaelic prose.

Justin Quinn is Associate Professor at both the University of Western Bohemia and the Charles University. His most recent critical book is the *Cambridge Introduction to Modern Irish Poetry* (2008). He also translates poetry from the Czech (above all Petr Borkovec and Bohuslav Reynek). At present he is working on a book about transnational poetry.

Jahan Ramazani is Edgar F. Shannon Professor of English at the University of Virginia. He is the author of *Yeats and the Poetry of Death* (1990), *Poetry of Mourning: The Modern Elegy from Hardy to Heaney* (1994), a finalist for the National Book Critics Circle Award, and *The Hybrid Muse: Postcolonial Poetry in English* (2001). He also wrote *A Transnational Poetics* (2009), winner of the Harry Levin Prize of the ACLA. He co-edited the most recent editions of *The Norton Anthology of Modern and Contemporary Poetry* (2003) and *The Twentieth Century and After* in *The Norton Anthology of English Literature* (2006, 2012).

John Redmond is a Senior Lecturer in Creative Writing at the University of Liverpool. He has written two books of poems, a poetry writing handbook, and has recently edited the *Selected Poems of James Liddy* (2011). His critical study of twentieth-century British poetry, *Poetry and Privacy*, will be published by Seren in 2012.

Stephen Regan is Professor of English at Durham University. His publications include *The Politics of Pleasure: Aesthetics and Cultural Theory* (1992), *Philip Larkin: The New Casebook* (1997), *The Eagleton Reader* (1998), *The Nineteenth-Century Novel: A Critical Reader* (2001), and *Irish Writing 1789–1939: An Anthology of Irish Literature in English* (2004). He has written essays on the work of modern Irish poets, including W. B. Yeats, Louis MacNeice, and Seamus Heaney, and has edited George Moore's *Esther Waters* for Oxford World's Classics (2012).

Susan Schreibman is The Long Room Hub Senior Lecturer in Digital Humanities at Trinity College Dublin. Dr Schreibman is the Founding Editor of the web-based projects *The Thomas MacGreevy Archive* and *Irish Resources in the Humanities*. Her publications include *Collected Poems of Thomas MacGreevy: An Annotated Edition* (1991), *A Companion to Digital Literary Studies* (2008), and *A Companion to Digital Humanities* (2004). She is currently working on a biography of Thomas MacGreevy.

Paul Simpson is a Professor of English Language in the School of English at Queen's University Belfast. He is best known for his books and articles in stylistics and critical linguistics, and his publications in this area include *Language, Ideology and Point of View* (1993), *Language through Literature* (1996), and *Stylistics* (2004), all published by Routledge. He is the co-editor of *Language, Discourse and Literature* (2007) and has edited the PALA journal *Language and Literature* (2003–9). *On the Discourse of Satire* was published by Benjamins in 2003, while his co-authored textbook *Language and Power* appeared in 2009. He is currently developing a monograph on the pragmatics of verbal humour.

Tom Walker is the Ussher Lecturer in Irish Writing at Trinity College Dublin. He has published articles on several aspects of the work of Louis MacNeice and is currently completing a monograph on the poet's relationship with the Irish poetry of his time.

David Wheatley is Senior Lecturer at the University of Hull. He is the author of four collections of poetry with Gallery Press, and for many years edited the poetry journal *Metre* with Justin Quinn. He has edited the poetry of James Clarence Mangan, also for Gallery Press (2003), and Samuel Beckett's *Selected Poems* for Faber and Faber (2009), and reviews regularly for *The Guardian*, *TLS*, *LRB*, and other journals. His poetry has been awarded several prizes, including the Rooney Prize for Irish Literature and the Vincent Buckley Poetry Prize, and features in the *Penguin Book of Irish Poetry* (2010).

PART I

POETRY AND THE REVIVAL

CHAPTER 1

....

RECOVERING ANCIENT
IRELAND

....

MATTHEW CAMPBELL

AFTER a century-long sojourn with the Tuatha de Danaan in Tír na nÓg and a further two hundred years attempting to get back to Ireland, Yeats's Oisin arrived back from his wanderings appalled to see what had become of the once-heroic people he had known:

> Making way from the kindling surges, I rode on a bridle-path
> Much wondering to see upon all hands, of wattles and woodwork made,
> Your bell-mounted churches, and guardless the sacred cairn and the rath,
> And a small and a feeble populace stooping with mattock and spade,
>
> Or weeding or ploughing with faces a-shining with much-toil wet;
> While in this place and that place, with bodies unglorious, their chieftains stood,
> Awaiting in patience the straw-death, croziered one, caught in
> your net: Went the laughter of scorn from my mouth like the roaring
>   of wind in a wood.
>
> And because I went by them so huge and so speedy with eyes so bright,
> Came after the hard gaze of youth, or an old man lifted his head:
> And I rode and I rode, and I cried out, 'The Fenians hunt wolves in the night,
> So sleep thee by daytime.' A voice cried, 'The Fenians a long time are dead.'[1]

The Wanderings of Oisin was Yeats's first published book, and it asked its first readers in 1889 to make at least two connections on reading the poem and coming across the declaration of the death of the Fenians.

As one of the tyros of Irish literary revival, Yeats might have asked first that he be seen finally to reclaim the Ossianic for Irish literature. After more than a century of controversy over the authorship and authenticity of the fragments presented by Scottish author James Macpherson as a rediscovered Scottish epic, Ossian was now uncontestably Oisin,

---

[1] W. B. Yeats, 'The Wanderings of Oisin', *The Variorum Edition of the Poems of W. B. Yeats*, ed. Peter Allt and Russell K. Alspach (Basingstoke: Macmillan, 1956), 58–9.

bard-warrior of the Fianna who were the followers of Fionn MacCumhaill and not Macpherson's Fingal.[2] A more pressing connection in 1889 would have been the association of these Fianna with the latter-day Fenians, the Irish Republican Brotherhood, who were a militant political grouping involved in violent agitation since the 1860s, including assassinations and bombings in Dublin and in England. Yeats may have wanted readers to recognize the returning Fenian John O'Leary in the figure of Oisin, imprisoned and exiled by the British but returned to Ireland peacefully to inspire a cultural revival among a younger generation of Irish writers. R. F. Foster has said that for Yeats, O'Leary's return in 1885 was that of 'a voice from a heroic past', and O'Leary 'pressed Samuel Ferguson's work (epic poems such as *Congal* [1872] and 'Conary' [1880]) on the young acolyte, who then discovered the repositories of legends in volumes produced by the Royal Irish Academy and the Irish Texts Society'.[3]

The passage from Yeats's long poem also alludes fairly precisely to other contested political and poetic matter. In the immediate terms of late nineteenth-century Irish politics, one concern is with the unfinished business after the defeat of the Home Rule bill of 1886, as well as with the Irish Churches, which were about to turn on the Irish nationalist leader of the day, Charles Stewart Parnell. For Yeats, the Christian, and particularly Catholic influence is one of a set of polarities in an Irish history caught in versions of antiquity that vacillated between Christian and pagan. These polarities invigorated the matter of an ongoing cultural revival, itself exchanging the Ossianic and the Churches, the epic and the domestic, the cultured and the philistine. Oisin sees that Ireland has been converted by St Patrick, and the poem ends with Yeats's version of the famous debates between the two, which appear in a number of extant manuscripts from early scribal historiography, re-collected by scholars such as Standish Hayes O'Grady in the revival of Irish antiquarianism from the eighteenth into the nineteenth century.[4] The story is of the transition between pagan and Christian: the cairn and the rath are guardless, the wattle and woodwork churches ring bells, the people are no longer warriors but farmers, and they await a 'straw-death', caught in the net of the 'croziered one', Patrick. This is no obvious anti-Christianity from the young Yeats. By his mid-twenties he was saturated in Rosicrucianism and theosophy as much as the extraordinary retelling of Irish history he had encountered in Ferguson or in the work of Hayes O'Grady's cousin and fellow antiquary, Standish James O'Grady. The younger O'Grady's *History of Ireland: The Heroic Period* (1872) told of a continuity in Irish history, positing an integrated Irish

[2] James Macpherson, *The Poems of Ossian*, ed. Howard Gaskill (Edinburgh: Edinburgh University Press, 1996).

[3] R. F. Foster, *W. B. Yeats: A Life*, vol. I: *The Apprentice Mage, 1865–1914* (Oxford: Oxford University Press, 1997), 42, 44. See also R. F. Foster, 'Oisin Comes Home', in *Words Alone: Yeats and his Inheritances* (Oxford: Oxford University Press, 2011), 129–73.

[4] For a Victorian overview of knowledge of the Oisin/St Patrick dialogue poems, see Standish Hayes O'Grady's introduction to his *Transactions of the Ossianic Society* publication, *The Pursuit after Diarmuid O Dhuibhne, and Grainne etc* (Dublin: O'Daly, 1857), 15–36, and in particular his versified translation of the conversation between Oisin and Patrick, 'The Lamentation of Oisin after the Fenians', 230–93. Oisin asks the saint's forgiveness at the end of the dialogue.

'race' succeeding down from the first Milesian invasion. According to Yeats, this work did 'more than anything else to create that preoccupation with Irish folk-lore and legend and epic which is called the Irish literary movement', and all the more exciting in that it 'retold nearly every great legend, and traced the links that bound them one to another in a chaotic but vehement and lyrical prose'.[5]

The Wanderings of Oisin is in one way not a primary recovery of an ancient Ireland: it is, rather, a re-recovery or retelling of contested historical matter. If its subject matter is ancient, then it is a story that tells of the loss and rediscovery of one sort of ancient Ireland, which was partly the matter of conjecture based on archaeological record and partly reconstructed from fragments of myth and history collected from scattered manuscripts. In one sense, this is an Irish history made from myth, the Ireland of Newgrange and Tara, the Red Branch knights and the Fianna. If that Ireland represented some sort of Golden Age, then for other Irish writers and historians of the nineteenth century it gave way to another with a rather more full historical record, the early Christian Ireland which followed it. In a succession of great scribal collections, such as the seventeenth-century *Annals of the Four Masters*, this history emphasized the tradition and stability of a feudal system of High Kings and archbishops, the integration of Church and Brehon Law, and a culture in which the bard was pre-eminent. The seven-volume John O'Donovan translation of the *Annals* was one of the greatest projects of the mid-Victorian Royal Irish Academy, although the result looks at times as if it is little more than a copious listing of dates and genealogies.

As is common in Irish historiography, debate even over dates themselves can be furious. The contemporary historian Tom Bartlett settles on the first authentic date in Irish history: AD 431 marked the appointment of Palladius as bishop of a presumably already-Christian Ireland. If what occurred before that date is then 'pre-history', Bartlett tells us that one of Europe's oldest man-made structures, Newgrange, possibly dates from 3800 BC.[6] If that level of antiquity lies beyond the accurate reach of Victorian or modern historiography, imaginative attempts were needed to recover it. Standish James O'Grady wrote romance fictions based on his recreation of Irish mythology, but it is Irish poetry that has occupied these various gaps in the historical tale. O'Grady's lesson about Irish epic to such as Yeats was that 'To all great nations their history presents itself under the aspect of poetry.'[7] If succeeding poets have thankfully never wholly succeeded in reviving the bardic, the poetry does move between myth and fact in ways that have variously enlightened and limited its development.

The keenness of Irish poets to recover this ancient material is in one way linked with the emergence of a distinctively Irish-English poetry in the nineteenth century, poetry that sought epic material to match its post-Romantic interest in the ballad and lyric. To speak of 'ancient Ireland' or 'old Ireland' is in many ways to engage with a poetic or

---

[5] W. B. Yeats, *Uncollected Prose*, ed. John P. Frayne, 2 vols. (London: Macmillan, 1970), I, 367.

[6] Thomas Bartlett, *Ireland: A History* (Cambridge: Cambridge University Press, 2010), 1–3.

[7] Standish James O'Grady, *History of Ireland: The Heroic Period*, 2 vols. (London: Sampson Low, 1878), II, 40.

imaginative concept as much as a historical or social one. Through various metaphoric constructions, between viewing history as a continuous national tale which neverthe-less suffered various disruptions, or as a disconnected series of synchronous or anachro-nistic re-imaginings, the poetic recovery of a seemingly lost past has remained for the last 150 years or so a matter for singular obsession in Irish poetry. That recovery also pro-vided a number of options for a poetic tradition that was caught in its way between refin-ing, translating, and then perpetuating the authenticity which tradition represented, as well as the challenge to the authentic in the need to innovate or experiment both within and outwith its formal prescriptions.

Yeats's version of the Ossianic mixes the mythical with theosophical fancy and con-temporary politics, happily shifting between natural and supernatural histories. It sug-gests a model of an imaginative apprehension of the past through which the present might be understood, and this conception persisted through the succeeding century. To take just one example, which makes a similar move from contemporary history back to a conjectural anthropology: in 1975, in 'Funeral Rites', Seamus Heaney imagined a funeral procession of those who had died in the Northern Irish 'Troubles' of the late twentieth century, travelling through a landscape marked by Viking and British invasions to Newgrange. It is written as if it were a return along the umbilical cord to a point of origin for historical birth at a site for burial of the dead. Antiquity must authenticate a violent present:

> Now as news comes in
> of each neighbourly murder
> we pine for ceremony,
> customary rhythms:
>
> the temperate footsteps
> of a cortège, winding past
> each blinded home.
> I would restore
>
> the great chambers of Boyne,
> prepare a sepulchre
> under the cupmarked stones.[8]

Heaney's fantasy of the serpent of the funeral making its way through a fairly precise geo-graphical journey, from Derry or Belfast to Newgrange on the River Boyne, through Cú Chulainn's Gap of the North and returning via Strangford and Carlingford Loughs, is matched by a historical journey which is less precise. It comes in and out of the focus of myths and dates, but it marked various recent deaths on its first publication in 1975. In its progress the poem travels back a notional six millennia to the megalithic burial cairn via the fjords named by Vikings over the centuries of their invasions at the turn of the second millennium AD, and then past the site of the battle in which King William defeated King James on 12 July 1690 (a date actually altered from 1 July on the old Julian calendar).

---

[8] Seamus Heaney, *North* (London: Faber, 1975), 7.

The pining for 'ceremony,/customary rhythms' is a function of an elegiac poetry which is aware that it is fulfilling a place in a succession or even a sequence of reiterated losses which may be typical of Irish poetry's engagement with antiquity. Up to the writing of Heaney and after, the notion of ancient Ireland is tied up with that of an island of antiquity, presenting both a geographical and argumentative ground for its aspiration to be a singular and sovereign political entity. As Thomas Davis told the readers of *The Nation* newspaper in 1845, advocating the need for collecting a specifically Irish literature:

> This country of ours is no sand bank, thrown up by some recent caprice of earth. It is an ancient land, honoured in the archives of civilisation, traceable into antiquity by its piety, its valour, and its sufferings. Every great European race has sent its stream to the river of the Irish mind. Long wars, vast organisations, subtle codes, beacon crimes, leading virtues and self-mighty men were here. If we live influenced by wind and sun and tree and not by the passion and deeds of the past, we are a thriftless and a hopeless people.[9]

For Davis and his fellow 'Young Irelanders', the nationalist conception of antiquity was at first an English-language version of the Irish sean-Éireann, or 'Old Ireland'. This place existed in a reasonably elastic time, strung across various possible starting points or staging posts, dating back before the defeat of King James (1691) or the battles of Kinsale (1601) or Clontarf (1014), or even the island of saints and scholars that Yeats's Oisin would greet with such anger.

By the nineteenth century, 'Old Ireland' could fulfil a similar function in nostalgia as olde or merry England. But in the songs and lyrics of the diaspora the phrase denotes a place which has rather more definitively been left behind. The poet Timothy Daniel Sullivan, writer of 'God Save Ireland' for the Fenian Manchester Martyrs (publicly executed in 1867), editor of *The Nation* and later Parnellite Home Rule MP, might have expressed something typical in his imagining of the plight of the post-Famine emigrant in one of his 1861 'Songs of the Backwoods'. It was later collected as 'Dear Old Ireland' and begins:

> Deep in Canadian woods we've met,
> From one bright island flown;
> Great is the land we tread, but yet
> Our hearts are with our own.
> And ere we leave this shanty small,
> While fades the Autumn day:
> We'll toast old Ireland,
> Dear old Ireland,
> Ireland, boys, hurra![10]

[9] Thomas Davis, 'The Library of Ireland', in *Thomas Davis: Selections from his Prose and Poetry*, ed. T. W. Rolleston (Dublin: Talbot Press, 1914), 357.
[10] Timothy Daniel Sullivan, 'Dear Old Ireland', in *A Treasury of Irish Poetry in the English Tongue*, ed. Stopford Brooke and T. W. Rolleston (New York: Macmillan, 1915), 236–8.

In the same year, *The New York Leader* printed Walt Whitman's 'Old Ireland', a poem that had opened with a vision of 'an ancient sorrowful mother/Once a queen', mourning the loss of a child to emigration:

> Yet a word ancient mother,
> You need crouch there no longer on the cold ground with forehead between
>   your knees,
> O you need not sit there veil'd in your old white hair so dishevel'd,
> For know you the one you mourn is not in that grave,
> It was an illusion, the son you love was not really dead,
> The Lord is not dead, he is risen again young and strong in another country,
> Even while you wept there by your fallen harp by the grave,
> What you wept for was translated, pass'd from the grave,
> The winds favor'd and the sea sail'd it,
> And now with rosy and new blood,
> Moves to-day in a new country.[11]

It is unfortunate that Whitman succumbed to a number of clichés grasped from Young Ireland versions of Jacobite *aisling* poetry as well as to the demands of his vast New York Irish-American readership: two million had entered the US and Canada between 1820 and 1860; 260,450 Irish-born people lived in New York in 1860, more than the then population of Dublin.[12] It is only the very newness of America, however, that provides succour to the loss of old Ireland—and perhaps to the quality of the poem.

If the populist sentiments of the homesick cling too much to the idea of 'Old Ireland', then the notion of 'Ancient Ireland' has served longest for Irish poets, since it contains within it strong suggestions of the feudalism and hierarchy of centuries of civilization. At the very least it served as a direct counterpart to the concept that had sustained a historiography of 'Ancient Britain' and the 'Ancient Britons' since the seventeenth century, reinvigorated in the age of Romanticism with some Celtic colouring by William Wordsworth or William Blake or Matthew Arnold.[13] Despite the mischief that Arnold might have sown in his 1865 *Lectures on Celtic Literature* by suggesting that the pre-Norman Ancient Britons and the Ancient Irish were substantially the same Celtic people, as an aristocratic concept, the recovery of the Ossianic was added to by one function it served for Macpherson in the 1760s: that was to mourn the loss of the legitimate but Catholic line of the British monarchy after the defeat of King James at Aughrim in 1691. Revised for the nineteenth-century ideology of nationalism by the Young Ireland writers of the 1840s, Jacobite nostalgia for the loss of a Catholic king was translated into the secular republicanism they had inherited from their United Irishman predecessors.

A poet associated with Young Ireland, yet by no means entirely of the party, James Clarence Mangan tried his hand at the anthemic in his 'Irish National Hymn' printed in

[11] Walt Whitman, *The Complete Poems*, ed. Francis Murphy (Harmondsworth: Penguin, 1975), 388.
[12] See Jay P. Dolan, *The Irish Americans: A History* (New York: Bloomsbury Press, 2008), 82.
[13] See Wordsworth's visions of the ancient Britons and Stonehenge in *The Prelude* and *The Excursion*, Blake's *Jerusalem*, and Arnold's *Lectures on Celtic Literature*. See also my 'Wordsworth and the Druids', *Proceedings of the British Academy*, vol. 162 (London: British Academy, 2009), 211–42.

1848 in John Mitchel's *United Irishman*, a newspaper which showed the increasing radicalization of the Young Irelanders in the latter years of the Irish Famine:

> O Ireland! Ancient Ireland!
>   Ancient! yet for ever young!
> Thou our mother, home and sire-land—
>   Thou at length hast found a tongue—
>   Proudly thou, at length,
>   Resistest in triumphant strength.
> Thy flag of freedom floats unfurled;
>   And as that mighty God existeth,
>   Who giveth victory when and where He listeth,
> Thou yet shalt wake and shake the nations of the world.[14]

When he is writing by rote or, more likely, for a commission, Mangan can affect the hysterical. But there is interest even in his moments of doggerel: 'resistest', 'existeth/He listeth', 'wake and shake'. The move from 'Ancient Ireland' to 'nations of the world' is still freighted with allusion and in-joke. The failed leader of a rebellion of 1803, the executed Robert Emmet, stands behind the notion of a silenced Ireland finding its tongue and taking its place among the nations of the world.[15] Along with the antiquarians like O'Donovan with whom he had worked in the 1830s on the Ordinance Survey project, and who were subsequently grouped around the Royal Irish Academy, Mangan would have suspected that ancient Ireland may have been more a place of provincial kingdoms than an integrated nation with a continuous history ruptured only by colonization. But he also knew, along with Davis, that the same nation-building or decolonizing processes that the other states of Europe had gone through, or were still going through under the modernizing pressure of their various nationalisms, were also constructed on the imagined communities of a shared antiquity along with language change and disputes over revealed religion: 'And as that mighty God existeth,/Who giveth victory when and where He listeth'.

The second stanza, however, turns the poem round in quite unexpected ways:

> For this dull world still slumbers.
>   Weetless of its wants or loves,
> Though, like Galileo, numbers
>   Cry aloud, 'It moves! it moves!'
>   In a midnight dream
>   Drifts it down Time's wreckful stream—
> All march, but few descry the goal,
>   O Ireland! be it thy high duty
>   To teach the world the might of Moral Beauty,
> And stamp God's image truly on the struggling soul.

---

[14] James Clarence Mangan, 'Irish National Hymn', *Selected Writings*, ed. Sean Ryder (Dublin: UCD Press, 2004), 290–1.

[15] For one of numerous historical accounts of the significance of Emmet's speech, see Bartlett, *Ireland: A History*, 245.

To go from an ancient Ireland restored through divine intervention to the words of Galileo ('"It moves! it moves!"') is progress towards a modernity of a sort. The Catholic Mangan alludes to Galileo's supposed muttering of the heresy of Copernicus that the Inquisition had forced him to recant, that it is the earth that moves and that an immove-able God-created world is thus not at the centre of the Universe.[16] For Mangan to suggest that the astronomical movement of the earth is analogous to the movement of national history is one thing. Further to suggest that history is an indiscriminate process of ruin ('Drifts it down Time's wreckful stream'), which might be redeemed by another history where it is the duty of Ireland in her mighty moral beauty to 'stamp God's image truly on the struggling soul', is entirely another thing again. This brings physics into the Hegelian dialectic that Mangan would have read in the German poetry he translated through the 1830s and 1840s, and into the Carlylean anti-utilitarianism that so influenced his Young Ireland contemporaries. There is also a penitent residue of Mangan's own strange Catholicism going on in the background. Ancient and modern circle each other in an interrelationship that envisages a revolutionary moment emerging out of the national wreck of Famine. Unusually enough for Mangan, who frequently published pseudony-mously, 'Irish National Hymn' was credited to him on its first publication in May 1848, and it ended with an italicized invocation of the prophetic note, 'these words come from *one whom some have called a Seer*'. The prophecy had small import: the debacle of the failed Young Ireland rising at Ballingarry, which occurred just two months later, was to result in another of the deportations of the insurgent from Victorian Ireland.

In Mangan, and to a lesser extent in Davis, Ireland's very ancientness was the basis of an authenticated emergent republicanism, and an enabling of a modernity of artistic form and subject matter, as much as political or constitutional change. Their contem-porary, the poet Samuel Ferguson, was yoked together with Davis and Mangan by Yeats in one of his own early radical moments, the 1892 poem 'To Ireland in the Coming Times'. For Ferguson, ancient Ireland is a conservative category, which establishes in tradition a sense of continuity and order as well as adding stability to a hierarchical state. Between Mangan and Ferguson a fissure of a sort opens up in Irish poetry, one that may be seen to this day, in which two types of formalism compete for conflicting political and cultural purposes over the same historical and poetic material. If Mangan's proclamation that 'Mannerism is a grand thing'[17] suggests an innovative strain in an Irish poetry open to international influences, which travels through James Joyce, Samuel Beckett, Thomas Kinsella, and Trevor Joyce, Ferguson's liberal-conservative development of a self-consciously Hiberno-English poetic diction and prosody might have found itself happier when influencing Yeats or Austin Clarke or Patrick Kavanagh or Seamus Heaney. And it is an argument over the ancient, between an insistence on its deliberate defamiliarization and an urge to keep rewriting it as pragmatically relevant, which marks this distinction. In Mangan's great poem written as Famine took hold in

---

[16] See Sean Ryder's note in Mangan, *Selected Writings*, 477.
[17] Mangan, 'An Extraordinary Adventure in the Shades', *Selected Writings*, 367.

1846, 'A Vision of Connaught in the Thirteenth Century', time is allowed to wreck the dream of an integrated Gaelic and Catholic Arcadia, recreated from the point of view of a German visionary. Yet the Arcadian had still been allowed for the first three stanzas of a poem willing to suggest that this might not all be mere old Irish nostalgia. Either way, ancient gives way to modern when it is overcome with historical or empirical fact: ' "It moves! it moves!" '

Ferguson's way is maybe not that distinct, even if he was of another party. The initially recreant character of Lomna Dubh in 'Conary', a blank-verse retelling of a tale from the Ulster cycle of myths, argues for an order based on custom. The reasons are imminent atrocity: the ambush and murder of King Conary and his household with the aid of witchcraft and treachery. Lomna expresses the reasons for his cold feet thus:

> 'We gave thee licence,' Lomna said,—'and I
> Grieve that we gave it, yea, or took the like,—
> To take a plunder; but we gave thee not
> Licence to take the life, the soul itself
> Of our whole nation, as you now would do.
> For, slay our reverend sages of the law,
> Slay him who puts the law they teach in act;
> Slay our sweet poets, and our sacred bards,
> Who keep the continuity of time
> By fame perpetual of renowned deeds;
> Slay our experienced captains who prepare
> The youth for martial manhood, and the charge
> Of public freedom, as befits a state
> Self-governed, self-sufficing, self-contained;
> Slay all that minister our loftier life,
> Now by this evil chance assembled here,
> You leave us but the carcass of a state,
> A rabble ripe to rot, and yield the land
> To foreign masters and perpetual shame.'[18]

This can be read two ways, either as an argument against colonization or as an argument for the preservation of union within a benign, albeit imperial, Victorian British state.[19] Either way, it takes a broadly Burkean line on the legitimacy conferred on systems of government by traditions of political stability and cultural confidence. The poet/bard nestles happily in that list of the good things about King Conary's contested reign, in the midst of the law, the army, and religion. Revolution, if that is what the act of Lomna's confederates is to be, will destroy the 'continuity of time' conferred by the bard's retelling of 'renowned deeds', leaving a carcass, a rabble, and 'perpetual shame'. Lomna's arguments for moderation go unheeded and he commits suicide.

[18] Samuel Ferguson, *Poems* (Dublin: McGee, 1880), 81.
[19] Compare Peter Denman, *Samuel Ferguson: The Literary Achievement* (Gerrards Cross: Colin Smythe, 1990), 155ff, and Colin Graham, *Ideologies of Epic: Nation, Empire and Victorian Epic Poetry* (Manchester: Manchester University Press, 1998).

The act of terror does happen in 'Conary': although it is rendered in the past, the burning of a house and the entrapment of family within would have held resonances for those accustomed to tales of agrarian outrage, such as that memorably recreated by William Carleton in his 1830 story 'Wildgoose Lodge'. Such motivation as Ferguson gives to the brothers who carry out the murder is merely vengeance, and that had been the motive of Carleton's ribbonmen as well. But William Allingham's *Laurence Bloomfield in Ireland*, a long poem in couplets from the 1860s that also turns on an act of terror—the assassination of a land agent—seeks motivation from 'Old Ireland' itself. An impressionable young farmer, Neal Doran, finds that poetry and song tell him all he has not been taught in school:

> With this, Old Ireland's glories, and her wrongs,
> Her famous dead, her landscapes, and her songs,
> Were fever'd fancy's beverage,—things well known
> Mingled with names and dreams confus'dly shown.
> Poetic visions hover'd; every page
> For Erin's glory, every fireside sage
> Whose *shanahus* a brooding audience drew,
> Were pleasant to his soul, and gospel-true.
> Since dumb her school-books upon Ireland's tale,
>
> . . .
>
> But better thus, than dry and dusty live,
> Devoid of all th' ancestral past can give,
> And every human touch from hill and shore
> Being blotted out, let memory claim no more
> In this her ancient realm, than where, exiled,
> The shepherd sadly tracks th' Australian wild.[20]

Neal joins the local ribbon lodge, although the fact of assassination does enable him to see the error of his ways. Nevertheless, a passage such as the one above appears to argue that it is irrelevant whether the facts of the past be correct or not as long as they exist in memory, recovered or false, at home or in emigration. A native of Ballyshannon in Donegal, Allingham had been settled as a poet and journalist in England for some time, but John O'Leary published lengthy extracts from the poem in the Fenian newspaper, *The Irish People*.

Allingham's is a liberal unionist solution to pressing political issues of social instability and long-held grievance. If he ultimately doesn't replace fact with myth, his solution, of celebrating an ancient past while practising model landlordism, was to receive short shrift both among his Irish contemporaries and in the history that was to unfold after the poem's publication. In Oscar Wilde's *The Importance of Being Earnest*, Lady Bracknell's question 'What are your politics?' is answered by Jack: 'Well, I am afraid I really have none. I am a liberal unionist.'[21] But if Allingham's version of Irish history,

---

[20] William Allingham, *Laurence Bloomfield in Ireland* (London: Longman, 1864), VI, 21–40.
[21] Oscar Wilde, *The Importance of Being Earnest*, in *Plays* (Harmondsworth: Penguin, 1954), 267.

and through it one solution of 'the Irish problem', ultimately spoke more to an English bourgeois audience than the readers of *The Irish People*, it did amount to one argument for the value of the ancient. It is one version of that staple of Irish fictions, the Big House, transformed through its rediscovered *noblesse oblige* into the enlightened educative mode of the late-Victorian United Kingdom. Once the land agitation has subsided due to Bloomfield's enlightened reforms, we are allowed a peek into his study:

> Here a soft blaze of flow'rs in full daylight,
> There, ivied casement, shadowing aright
> The mournful relics of the secret Past,
> Waifs, liftings, from that ocean deep and vast,
> The thought and work of many a vanish'd race;
> The life of ancient Erin you may trace
> In Druid's torque, moon-horn'd, of thinnest gold
> Square bell that to St. Patrick's preaching toll'd,
> Cups, coins, and fibulæ, and ogham-stones,
> Spears, axes, arrow-heads, of flint or bronze.
> Whatever knowledge (at the best but small)
> Of such is extant, Laurence knows it all,
> And sometimes to his neighbours far and near
> Imparts in modest lecture, short and clear,
> On things Hibernian; chiefly those around,—
> The Giant's Grave, the Fort, the Fairy-Mound,
> The crumbling Abbey-wall, the Round-Tower gray,
> Still rising smooth and firm as on the day
> Its taper cap received the topmost stone;
> The mountain Carn, to distant counties shown;
> The Norman-English Keep on river brink;
> His light firm hand connecting link with link
> Of Irish history, so that none complain
> To find it gall them like a rusty chain.[22]

Allingham's experiment, not just with Irish liberalism but with a social or realist mode of poetry, comes more from the novel than Irish or English nineteenth-century poetry. Ferguson's 'Conary' would be more recognizable to the readers of the Arthurian or Norse romances rewritten by Alfred Tennyson or William Morris or Richard Wagner, as Northern European myth refashioned for late-Romantic audiences drawn to the glamour of supposedly less civilized, more violent ancestors. The word 'glamour', a Scots word that is a corruption of the word 'gramarye', or French *grimoire* meaning 'magic' or 'enchantment', is recorded by the *Oxford English Dictionary* in Walter Scott's novels and in Tennyson's *Idylls of the King*. But it also belongs to Standish O'Grady, as a feature shown when the apparently plain or simple surface of the old manuscript poems copied out in the monasteries shrugs off the 'scholastic' criticism apparent in their collation and revision and reveals something of the true spirit of the pre-Christian originals:

---

[22] Allingham, *Laurence Bloomfield*, IX, 204–27.

…we feel, oftentimes, a sudden weirdness, a strange glamour shoots across the poem when the tale seems to open for a moment into mysterious depths, druidic secrets veiled by time, unsunned caves of thought, indicating a still deeper range of feeling, a still lower and wider reach of imagination.

For O'Grady, the success of Macpherson was that he had felt this glamour, and that it had emerged into the literary sublime in the recreation of the hoax. Macpherson's greatest asset was his very freedom both from fact and from authenticity:

Thus released from the curb of history, he gave free rein to the imagination, and in the conventional literary language of sublimity, gave full expression to the feelings that arose within him, as to him, pondering over those ballads, their gigantesque element developed into a greatness and solemnity, and their vagueness and indeterminateness into that misty immensity and weird obscurity which, as constituent factors in a poem, not as background, form one of the elements of the false sublime.[23]

This might be 'chaotic but vehement and lyrical prose', as Yeats would have it, but it also has much to say for the persistence of the Longinian 'false sublime' in subsequent poetic versions of what the Celtic might be.

The gigantesque, solemnity, vagueness, obscurity—O'Grady's strange aesthetic categories of glamour or even weirdness—all are allowed to comport with the falseness or the bogus nature of poetic creativity in this late flowering of the literary sublime. It persists into Yeats's last poems and plays and beyond, either in *The Death of Cuchulain* or 'Cuchulain Comforted', and in 'Under Ben Bulben', in 1939:

> Many times man lives and dies
> Between his two eternities,
> That of race and that of soul,
> And ancient Ireland knew it all.
> Whether man dies in his bed
> Or the rifle knocks him dead,
> A brief parting from those dear
> Is the worst man has to fear.
> Though grave-diggers' toil is long,
> Sharp their spades, their muscles strong,
> They but thrust their buried men
> Back in the human mind again.[24]

Whatever the knowledge of ancient Ireland, it is something excavated from history and it gives a momentary apprehension of the synchronous, which O'Grady had also granted to Macpherson. Memory, be it race memory or soul memory, is not allowed to die.

Yeats's talk of the eternities of 'race' and 'soul' has been slow to leave Irish poetry, as his contemporaries and inheritors still insisted on revisiting this particular site of memory.

---

[23] O'Grady, *History of Ireland*, II, 45–6.
[24] Yeats, *Variorum Poems*, 637.

Samuel Beckett's remains a rare voice of complaint against 'the antiquarians, delivering with the altitudinous complacency of the Victorian Gael the Ossianic goods'.[25] His response though is no more than frustration: in *Murphy*, the character Neary can only head-butt the non-existent thighs of the statue of Cú Chulainn in the General Post Office in Dublin.[26] In the same novel Beckett produced a wicked caricature of the poet Austin Clarke under the guise of the poet turned mental nurse Austin Ticklepenny. Clarke's breakdown in times of revolution and civil war had been real enough, even though his earliest solution had been to revisit 'the Ossianic goods'. His 1925 collection, *The Cattledrive in Connaught*, rewrote both the Ulster cycle and the Gaelic poetry of the seventeenth and eighteenth centuries for the uncertainty that followed Civil War. It was a collection concerned to create, through a synthetic formalism, a post-revival version of what his MA thesis supervisor, the executed 1916 leader Thomas MacDonagh, called 'the Irish Mode'. This was an Irish version of the new vernacular poetry that was being written across 1920s Europe from various regional modernisms. As we have seen, the empirical and the innovative can move across apparent poetic categories between the likes of Mangan and Allingham, but Clarke attempted to bring them back into the old Irish material, as ancient matter for contemporary unease.

In the midst of poems working deliberate anachronisms of the mythic and the contemporary, the seemingly gnomic lyric 'The Lost Heifer' expresses an Irish-mode synchrony of myth and ballad symbolism against the landscape of a post-war Ireland:

> When the black herds of the rain were grazing,
> In the gap of the pure cold wind
> And the watery hazes of the hazel
> Brought her into my mind,
> I thought of the last honey by the water
> That no hive can find.
>
> Brightness was drenching through the branches
> When she wandered again,
> Turning the silver out of dark grasses
> Where the skylark had lain,
> And her voice coming softly over the meadow
> Was the mist becoming rain.[27]

On the one hand this is a version of the 'Drimin Donn Dhilis', the sweet brown cow of the Jacobite song of eviction and homelessness. Among numerous English versions, Samuel Ferguson had translated it in 1834. The placing of allusion to the song in a volume which contained versions of other material to do with cattle—that is, the story of the *Táin Bó Cuailgne* or the cattle raid of Maeve, Queen of Connacht in the Ulster cycle—invokes the war that ended in the death of Cú Chulainn.

---

[25] Samuel Beckett [as Andrew Belis], 'Recent Irish Poetry' (1934), in *Irish Writing in the Twentieth Century*, ed. David Pierce (Cork: Cork University Press, 2000), 378.

[26] Beckett, *Murphy* (London: Faber, 2009).

[27] Austin Clarke, *Collected Poems*, ed. R. Dardis Clarke (Manchester: Carcanet, 2008), 120.

In putting at least two versions of a recovered antiquity beside each other, Clarke creates something beyond even incongruity or anachronism: he seeks the synchronous notion of myth worked up from a Yeats-influenced symbolist aesthetic. This is gently ushered into the false sublime with a prosodic structure replicating the 'wandering', 'evasive' rhythms of the English-language Irish-mode verse so recently described by MacDonagh, and for which MacDonagh acknowledges the example of Yeats. And it also infuses that sonic indeterminacy with the stock-in-trade of European symbolist poetry, synaesthesia, confusing subject and object, noun and verb. In the first line, is it rain or herds which are grazing? In the next, what is the gap between cold wind and a watery hazel? Are the words 'hazes' and 'hazel' in anything other than sonic relation, required merely to do the job of assonantal or cross-rhyme with 'grazing'? In the second stanza, how can brightness drench? And at the end, how is a voice 'mist becoming rain'? In one way this is an empirical nonsense. In another it is about 'becoming' itself, a world of blur and vagueness, of a loss on the verge of sensible utterance, a historical moment which has as yet revealed itself only as aftermath. For the critic Nicholas Allen, the period of civil war from 1921 to 1924 produced many versions of such aftermath along with a modernism hitherto unnoticed in Irish literature and art. Introducing a discussion of Beckett's early work, he invokes a temporality which includes 'the contingencies of the not yet, the perhaps and the never has been'. Shifted into the materiality of the historical moment, the period following that of revolution, 'the state is revealed as made, not given, a compromise between influences that exercise the full weight of recent authority in executions, imprisonment and censorship'. It might not seem to, but Clarke's version of ancient Ireland, like those of others before him, was lost in this 'made, not given' state of affairs.[28]

The aftermath of ancient Ireland has yet to come. Poets and novelists like Louis MacNeice or Beckett may have felt at mid-century that talk of mythic or symbolist figures from the past, be they Cú Chulainn or Cathleen Ni Houlihan, meant a dangerously atavistic streak in Irish culture, in which 'each one in his will/Binds his heirs to continuance of hatred'.[29] Subsequent revivals of Irish poetry have nevertheless returned to its example. John Montague's *Rough Field* (1972) recycles a poem from the late 1950s into its sequence concerned with a place immanent with history resurfacing in violence. The past is the present, and not only in memory:

> Ancient Ireland, indeed! I was reared by her bedside,
> The rune and the chant, evil eye and averted head,
> Fomorian fierceness of family and local feud.
> Gaunt figures of fear and of friendliness,
> For years they trespassed on my dreams,

---

[28] Nicholas Allen, *Modernism, Ireland and Civil War* (Cambridge: Cambridge University Press, 2009), 113.

[29] Louis MacNeice, *Autumn Journal* 'Canto XVI', *Collected Poems*, ed. Peter McDonald (London: Faber, 2007), 139.

> Until once, in a standing circle of stones,
> I felt their shadows pass
> Into that dark permanence of ancient forms.[30]

Perhaps neither Yeats nor Clarke would allow the word 'permanence' to attach to those standing stones, but they still promulgate dreams of the timeless.

From Trevor Joyce to Seamus Heaney, presenting contrasting versions of the early-Christian ascetic Sweeney,[31] to Thomas Kinsella or Ciaran Carson, Irish poets continue to return to differing versions of ancient golden ages, saints and scholars, or the erstwhile Ossianic. Given the contemporary use such versions must assume, this has become one poetic and linguistic proving ground. To end just with continuing versions of the Ulster cycle, the challenge is in groping towards command over notoriously violent texts. Kinsella's *Táin* might not have foretold the return of violence to the part of Ireland in which the saga was set, as he was working on it through the 1960s, but when published in 1969 it could only have a powerful relevance. Carson's 2007 version might have been fashioned in a time of peace. His translations of the old Irish verse within the tale gather a stark direct-ness much removed from Clarke's deliberate vaguenesses, but still aware of modernist precedent. He carries through the intensification of the imagist lyric of the early twentieth century, and the recurring obsession in Irish poetry with the minute proprieties of forms such as the haiku:

ravens gnaw	men's necks	blood-gushes
fierce fray	hacked flesh	battle-drunk
men's sides	blade-struck	war-torn
raking fingers	battle-brave	men of Crúachan
ruination	bodies crushed	underfoot
long live Ulster	woe to Ireland	
woe to Ulster	long live Ireland[32]	

This is the song of the Morrigan, sung before the battle that will lead to the death of the hero, Cú Chulainn. Traditionally appearing as a crow, she perches on the shoulder of the statue of Cú Chulainn in the General Post Office. If she is not a figure for the sovereignty of Ireland, she may be associated with its internecine struggles, its lurches back into the indistinctness of various civil and uncivil wars.

The Irish-language poet Nuala Ní Dhomhnaill has invoked both the Morrigan and the fury of Queen Maeve to do battle with the timidity of the men of Ireland, often more preoccupied than they should be with symbolic rather than more earthly matter. It is a satiric version of myth, which still persists in turning to the horror of a past from which poetry cannot avert its eyes:

---

[30] John Montague, 'Like Dolmens Round my Childhood', in *The Rough Field* [1972] (Dublin: Dolmen, 1979), 16–17.

[31] Trevor Joyce, *The Poems of Sweeney Peregrine* (Dublin: New Writers' Press, 1976), and Seamus Heaney, *Sweeney Astray* (London: Faber, 1983).

[32] Ciaran Carson, *The Táin* (London: Penguin, 2007), 197.

Is í an bhadbh í,   She is the hooded crow
ar foluain os cionn an tslua.   hovering over the crowd.
Priocann sí na súile   She picks the eyes
as na leanaí sa chliabhán.   from kids in cots.
Is í an scréachán í,   She is the screecher,
éan búistéara;   the butcher-bird:
beidh do chuid fola   your blood will be in pools
ina logaibh faoi do chosa;   under your feet
beidh do chuid feola   your flesh
ar crochadh   will hang
ina spólaí fuara   in cold joints
ó cruacha stíl   from meat hooks
mura bhfuil an méid sin   if it's not already so—
déanta cheana   because it's not just on your statue
mar ní ar do dhealbh   in the G.P.O.
in Ard-Oifig an Phoist amháin   I see her sitting
a chím í suite   on your shoulder
ar do ghualainn,   Cú Chulainn.[33]
a Chú Chulainn.

To say that such a recovery of the ancient has been multiform in the last century and a half might be stating the obvious. As Ní Dhomhnaill rewrites this Irish myth for the purposes of feminist satire, she is just as likely to re-inhabit fairy tale or the figure of the mermaid. Hers is an Irish version of the retelling of the feminist tale in myth, as evinced by Liz Lochhead or Carol Ann Duffy or Angela Carter in Scotland and England. The Irish version is maybe not that singular, and if ancient Ireland provides one source of material for Irish poets, male or female, then so do Homer or Dante for Heaney or Carson, as they had done for Joyce or Beckett before them. In Carson's hands, though, one of the things the *Táin* becomes is a tale of place, or the naming of places. It is filled full of etymologies and translations, as its epic material lends heroism to the everyday locations of Louth and Down, as if the farmlands and rivers and mountains claim knowledge from antiquity. It is an alternative history of a sort, an arbitrary, perhaps factitious

[33] Nuala Ní Dhomhnaill, 'An Mhór-Ríon ag Cáiseamh na Baidhbhe le Cú Chulainn'/'The Great Queen Berates the Badbh Cú Chulainn', *Rogha Dánta/Selected Poems*, trans. Michael Hartnett (Dublin: Raven Arts, 1988), 122–5.

account of naming. But it is also one source of the authenticity required from antiquity. For Ní Dhomhnaill to invoke Maeve and the Morrigan as she does establishes another version of authenticity turned to fiction for the purposes of poetry.

CHAPTER 2

....

YEATS AND SYMBOLISM

....

WARWICK GOULD

I

....

In 'The Symbolism of Poetry' (1900) Yeats declares that:

> All writers, all artists of any kind, in so far as they have had any philosophical or critical power, perhaps just in so far as they have been deliberate artists at all, have had some philosophy, some criticism of their art; and it has often been this philosophy, or this criticism, that has evoked their most startling inspiration, calling into outer life some portion of the divine life, or of the buried reality...[1]

Such writerly self-consciousness takes its origins in Yeats's thinking as controversialist, essayist, scholar, interpreter, occultist. Yeats's early poetry, particularly that of *The Wind Among the Reeds* (1899), is frequently termed 'symbolist', a word that can seem frustratingly vague. Yeats identifies a 'continuous *indefinable* symbolism' as the 'substance of all style', and claims that the 'element of evocation, of suggestion' in writing had come to preoccupy writers working in opposition to the nineteenth-century 'scientific movement'.[2] Ernest Jones later thought that the word 'symbolism' in its widest sense 'comprise[d] almost the whole development of civilisation'.[3] And the word also invokes French *symboliste* poetry, of which the monolingual Yeats had little direct knowledge.[4]

---

[1] W. B. Yeats, *Early Essays: The Collected Works of W. B. Yeats*, vol. IV, ed. Richard J. Finneran and George Bornstein (New York: Scribner, 2007), 114.

[2] Ibid., emphasis added.

[3] Ernest Jones, 'The Theory of Symbolism', quoted in René Wellek, 'What is Symbolism?', in *The Symbolist Movement in the Literature of European Languages*, ed. Anna Balakian (Budapest: Akademiai Kiado, 1982), 17.

[4] Yeats wrote, in a letter to Ernest Boyd, February 1915: 'Of the French symbolistes I have never had any detailed or accurate knowledge.' See *The Collected Letters of W. B. Yeats*, general ed. John Kelly (Oxford: Oxford University Press [InteLex Electronic Edition]), 2002 (*CL InteLex*), no. 2,603.

Yeats's essay responded to Arthur Symons's *The Symbolist Movement in Literature*.[5] Symons, in turn, took his point of departure from Thomas Carlyle's remark in *Sartor Resartus* (1831): 'It is in and through Symbols that man, consciously or unconsciously lives, works, and has his being: those ages, moreover, are accounted the noblest which can best recognise symbolical worth, and prize it highest.'[6] Whether or not Yeats at the time was familiar with the whole chapter on 'Symbols' in *Sartor Resartus*, or whether its thought was simply 'in the air' in conversations with his father and Symons, is not known. But he would have agreed that '[i]n the Symbol...there is ever, more or less distinctly and directly, some embodiment and revelation of the Infinite; the Infinite is made to blend itself with the Finite, to stand visible, and as it were, attainable there.'[7] Carlyle writes '[b]y Symbols, accordingly, is man guided and commanded', and claims 'the Universe is but one vast Symbol of God', asking 'what is man himself but a Symbol of God; is not all that he does symbolical; a revelation...of the mystic god-given force that is in him...?'[8] Carlyle also expressed a Shelleyan idea of the Poet as Legislator:

> Highest of all Symbols are those wherein the Artist or Poet has risen into Prophet, and all men can recognize a present God, and worship the same: I mean religious Symbols....A Hierarch, therefore, and Pontiff of the World will we call him, the Poet and inspired Maker; who, Prometheus-like, can shape new Symbols...we account him Legislator and wise who can so much as tell when a Symbol has grown old, and gently remove it.[9]

Symbolism as the underlying poetic mode brings forty-six pages of notes to sixty-two pages of poems in *The Wind Among the Reeds*. These:

> elaborate essays...[on] Irish faery lore & mythology...made out of quite new material...will probably make most of the critics spend half of every review in complaining that I have written very long notes about very short poems. I am in hopes however that others will forgive me the poems for the sake of the valuable information in the notes.[10]

[5] Arthur Symons, *The Symbolist Movement in Literature* (London: William Heinemann, 1899). Symons dedicated this book to Yeats, who '*more than any one else, will sympathise with what I say in it, being yourself the chief representative of that movement in our country*', p. v. Arthur Symons inscribed Yeats's copy of the book on 5 March 1900, the actual day of publication.

[6] Ibid., 3. Cf. Thomas Carlyle, *Sartor Resartus: The Life and Opinions of Herr Teufelsdröckh in Three Books* (London: Chapman and Hall, Ltd., 1831, rpt. 1869), Book 3, ch. iii ('Symbols'), 215. Carlyle's frontispiece portrait identifies this edition (not in Yeats's library) as the one read by Yeats in the 1880s, as it reminded him of Dr George Sigerson (see W. B. Yeats, *Memoirs*, ed. Denis Donoghue, [London: Macmillan, 1972], 53). Brian John's *Supreme Fictions: Studies in the Work of William Blake, Thomas Carlyle, W. B. Yeats and D. H. Lawrence* (Montreal and London: McGill-Queen's, 1974) does not explore Yeats's reading of Carlyle, but suggests that Symons and Yeats held the same view of him: Yeats's debt to Carlyle is 'more considerable than [Yeats] would wish to admit': see 80, n.5.

[7] Carlyle, *Sartor Resartus*, 213; cited in Symons, *Symbolist Movement*, 4–5.

[8] Carlyle, *Sartor Resartus*, 217.

[9] Ibid., 213.

[10] W. B. Yeats, *The Collected Letters of W. B. Yeats, II, 1896–1900*, ed. Warwick Gould, John Kelly, and Deirdre Toomey (Oxford: Clarendon Press, 1997), 305.

'Symbolist' in Symons's title, however, names a French, and increasingly international, artistic movement. *Symbolisme* historicized, as René Wellek suggests, is a series of concentric circles moving forwards and back from a French coterie of the 1880s—Jean Moréas had published (and then renounced) his manifesto, '*Le Symbolisme*', in *Le Figaro* by 18 September 1886—and comprehends the phase in French writing and other arts from Baudelaire to Valéry and its international repercussions in the work of artists such as Ibsen, Wagner, George, and Rilke.[11]

For Yeats, Symbolism as method rather than movement also characterized the English-language forerunners of that French movement. His narrator in the 1896 *Savoy* text of *Rosa Alchemica* remembers:

> that mood which Edgar Poe found in a wine-cup, and how it passed into France and took possession of Baudelaire, and from Baudelaire passed to England and the Pre-Raphaelites, and then again returned to France, and still wanders the world, enlarging its power as it goes, awaiting the time when it shall be, perhaps, alone, or, with other moods, master over a great new religion, and an awakener of...fanatical wars...and forget the wine-cup where it was born.[12]

II

Yeats first met Symons in January 1891 at the Rhymers' Club in London, and Yeats shared Symons's rooms in Fountain Court between October 1895 and February 1896.[13] When the compositional chronology of Yeats's *Ideas of Good and Evil* (1903) is unscrambled, Symbolism and how it might play in Ireland proves a major theme. But in the autumn of 1898, reference to Symons was designedly suppressed when Yeats sought to 'keep people awake' during the gap between the end of the 1798 centennial celebrations until the December announcement of the inaugural Irish Literary Theatre for the following May.[14] He orchestrated a mock debate in the Dublin *Daily Express*, which, under the new management of Horace Plunkett and on the demise of *United Ireland*, had become the fighting Irish paper of the day. He urged the editor, T. P. Gill, to get Lionel Johnson, 'John Eglinton' (W. K. Magee), George Russell (A. E., *sic*, at this time), and

---

[11] Wellek, 'What is Symbolism?', 28.

[12] W. B. Yeats, *The Secret Rose, Stories by W. B. Yeats: A Variorum Edition* (Basingstoke: Macmillan, 1992), 143–4. Yeats withdrew the passage from *The Secret Rose* (London: Lawrence & Bullen, 1897), probably because of Irish suspicion of his occult leanings. Eliot devoted *From Poe to Valéry* (New York: Harcourt, Brace & Co., 1948) to this chain of influence.

[13] W. B. Yeats, *The Collected Letters of W. B. Yeats, I, 1865–1895*, ed. John Kelly and Eric Domville (Oxford: Clarendon Press, 1986), 239. Symons replaced Lionel Johnson as Yeats's leading 'decadent' Rhymers' Club friend when Johnson's drinking became problematical. See also Denis Donoghue, 'Yeats: The Question of Symbolism', in *The Symbolist Movement in the Literature of European Languages*, ed. Balakian, 279–93.

[14] Yeats, *Collected Letters*, II, 239.

William Larminie to write for its new Saturday literary spread. Yeats wrote: 'I want to excite general interest in Irish legends & in the Irish literary attitude in Dublin this month, as a preliminary to the publication of our dramatic project in December.... I hope for a deal of literary stir'.[15]

The debate began with John Eglinton's question 'What should be the Subjects of a National Drama?' on 18 September 1898. In Eglinton's view, Irish 'folk-lore and antiquities ... obstinately refuse to be taken up out of their old environment and be transplanted into the world of modern sympathies'. The 'proper mode of treating them', he averred, was a 'forgotten mythopoeic secret'. The Irish, like the Jews in Renan's view, tended to look backward, whereas the Saxon 'believes in the present, and, indeed, it belongs to him'. The 'consolations of history' had to be renounced in favour of 'a national drama or literature [which] must spring from a native interest in life and its problems and a strong capacity for life among the people. If these do not, or cannot exist, there cannot exist a national drama or literature.' Eglinton then hinted darkly, 'In London and Paris they seem to believe in theories and "movements," and to regard individuality as a noble but "impossible" savage; and we are in some danger of being absorbed into their error', before concluding with the nativist sentiment: 'Some of our disadvantages are our safeguards.'[16]

With these remarks, the premeditated public controversy, as planned by Yeats, suddenly turned into a profound, multilateral dispute with more opinions than protagonists. On 24 September, Yeats responded to Eglinton on behalf of the great passions of 'ancient legends', citing Dante, Homer, and Shakespeare:

> All great poets ... speak to us of the hopes and destinies of mankind in their fullness; because they have wrought their poetry out of the dreams that were dreamed before men became so crowded upon one another, and so buried in their individual destinies and trades, that every man grew limited and fragmentary. If you were to take out of poetry the personages and stories and metaphors that first, it may be, visited the shepherds and hunters, who lived before men tilled the ground, not merely its substance but its language would crumble into nothing.[17]

For Yeats, Standish O'Grady, and others, the Irish legends were *dinnshenchas*: 'Our legends are always associated with places, and not merely every mountain and valley, even every strange stone and little coppice has its legend, preserved in written or unwritten tradition.' 'The Irish romantic movement' had 'arisen out of this tradition' and 'should always', claimed Yeats, 'be haunted by places', striving to 'make Ireland, as Ireland and all other lands were in ancient times, a holy land to her own people'.[18]

Eglinton, responding to Yeats on 8 October, proposed 'two conceptions of poetry, mutually antagonistic': the Wordsworthian, 'able to confer on even common things

---

[15] Ibid., 282.

[16] John Eglinton; W. B. Yeats[;] A. E.; W. Larminie, *Literary Ideals in Ireland* (London: T. Fisher Unwin; Dublin: Daily Express Office, 1899), 11–13.

[17] W. B. Yeats, 'A Note on National Drama', 24 September 1898, *Literary Ideals in Ireland*, 17–19.

[18] Ibid., 19.

the radiance of the imagination'; and, the other, an aesthetic conception, 'to which those who are rather in sympathy with art than with philosophy are inclined, regard[ing] the poet as passive to elect influences and endowing old material with new form'. If Finn and Cuchulain were to appear once more in literature, Eglinton argued, they 'must be expected to take up on their broad shoulders something of the weariness and fret of our age'.[19]

On 29 October, Yeats returned to Eglinton's distinction between Wordsworthian and 'aesthetic' schools of poetry. Where Eglinton favoured the realist orientation of Wordsworthian poetry, Yeats greatly favoured the Idealist 'aesthetic', invoking A. H. Hallam in a non-French, anti-Arnoldian retro-formation of his own symbolical tradition, and countering Eglinton's preference. In so doing, Yeats grandly declared that 'the great movement of our time' consisted of the 'renewal of belief'. He wrote: 'I believe that all men will more and more reject the opinion that poetry is "a criticism of life", and be more and more convinced that it is a revelation of a hidden life'.[20] He concluded:

> I believe...that the difference between good and bad poetry is not in its preference for legendary, or for unlegendary subjects, or for a modern or for an archaic treatment, but in volume and intensity of its passion for beauty, and in the perfection of its workmanship; and that all criticism that forgets these things is mischievous, and doubly mischievous in a country of unsettled opinion.[21]

For all that, however, it was Yeats's broader call upon 'the best intellects of our day' that must have confirmed Eglinton's fears. These best intellects included, according to Yeats, not only the Belgian Emile Verhaeren but also 'Count Villiers de L'Isle Adam, the principal founder of the *symbolist movement*' (my emphasis).[22] Of Villiers, Yeats tells us, 'M. Remy de Gourmont has written, "He opened the doors of the unknown with a crash, and a generation has gone through them to the infinite"'.[23] But with the term 'symbolist movement' now uttered in Dublin's best paper, Yeats had opened Ireland with a crash to

---

[19] John Eglinton, 'National Drama and Contemporary Life?', first published (confusingly) as 'What should be the Subjects of a National Drama' (*Daily Express*, 8 October 1898): see *Literary Ideals in Ireland*, 24–26. Eglinton's 'broad shoulders' with their Keatsian 'weariness...and...fret' supplied Yeats's image of the arts, the 'shoulders' of which were 'about to take upon their shoulders the burdens that have fallen from the shoulders of priests, and to lead us back upon our journey by filling our thoughts with the essences of things, and not with things' (*Early Essays*, 141–2). Yeats's essays can only fully be read if re-immersed in such contexts as gave rise to their rhetoric.

[20] W. B. Yeats, 'John Eglinton and Spiritual Art', *Literary Ideals in Ireland*, 36; W. B. Yeats, *Early Articles and Reviews, Collected Works*, vol. IX, ed. John P. Frayne and Madeleine Marchaterre (New York: Scribner, 2004), 421–2. On A. H. Hallam's influence, see below n.108.

[21] Yeats, *Literary Ideals in Ireland*, 37; *Early Articles and Reviews*, 42–122.

[22] Yeats, *Literary Ideals in Ireland*, 32; *Early Articles and Reviews*, 419.

[23] Yeats, *Literary Ideals in Ireland*, 32; *Early Articles and Reviews*, 419. Yeats reused the quotation 'from memory' in his 1897 review of Maeterlinck's *Aglavaine and Sélysette* in *The Bookman* (September 1897): see *Early Articles and Reviews*, 350, 600, n.1. That review and 'Mr. Arthur Symons's New Book' (i.e., *Amoris Victima*; see *Early Articles and Reviews*, 332–5) were reused in 'The Autumn of the Flesh': see *Literary Ideals in Ireland*, 69–75, and *Early Essays*, 139–42 and 408. Yeats is unlikely to have engaged closely with Rémy de Gourmont's *Le Livre des masques* (1895): the quotation was surely provided by Symons.

the very 'theories and "movements" ' imported from Paris via London that Eglinton had feared. Dublin Nativism was under threat.

In response, on 5 November, Eglinton widened his distinction between the poetry of thought (Wordsworth, Tennyson, Browning) and that of artifice (Coleridge, D. G. Rossetti, Swinburne), disavowing 'the symbolists' as decadents: Villiers with his objection to the sun and to daylight, and Verlaine who, Eglinton claimed, 'hated to hear the laugh of a healthy man'. 'Art...for the sake of art', Eglinton warned, 'may achieve the occult triumphs of the symbolist school, but humanity will return its indifference in kind, and leave [such art] to the dignity and consolation of "unpopularity" '.[24]

Russell duly entered the fray on 12 November, misquoting Yeats's 'The Rose of the World':

> For these red lips, with all their mournful pride,
> Troy passed away in one high funeral gleam
> And Usna's children died. [sic]

but without naming the poet. He commented:

> These dreams, antiquities, traditions, once actual, have passed from the world of sense into the world of memory and thought; and time, it seems to me, has not taken away from their power nor made them more remote from sympathy, but has rather purified them by removing them from earth unto heaven .... they have now the character of symbol, and, as symbol, are more potent than history.[25]

Unsurprisingly, Russell provided, on Yeats's side, the mystic and the historic argument for symbolism. He claimed: 'Modern literature...grows more subjective year after year', and that 'Yeats, in common with an ever-increasing number of thoughtful men' had adopted a 'transcendental philosophy'. 'To regain that spiritual consciousness with its untrammelled ecstasy' was 'the hope of every mystic' and such an 'ecstasy' was 'the poetic passion'. Eglinton, according to Russell, had been 'misled as to Mr Yeats's position by an unfamiliarity with the symbols which the poet employs in his subtle and mystic art'.[26] Russell further claimed: 'Yeats, in common with other literary men, is trying to ennoble literature by making it religious rather than secular, by using his art for the revelation of another world rather than to depict this one'.[27]

Yeats had himself sent a response to Eglinton on 8 November, but Gill spiked it. 'You did quite right to leave my letter out', Yeats told Gill: widening the controversy was more important than trumping Eglinton.[28] Yet Yeats's piece was, in fact, the first draft of what became 'The Symbolism of Poetry' in 1900. In this, Yeats argues that the 'something new'

---

[24] John Eglinton, 'Mr. Yeats and Popular Poetry', *Literary Ideals in Ireland*, 45.
[25] A. E., 'Literary Ideals in Ireland', *Literary Ideals in Ireland*, 50–1. Lines 2–5 of Yeats's poem are quoted, with l. 3 omitted: see *The Variorum Edition of the Poems of W. B. Yeats*, ed. Peter Allt and Russell K. Alspach (Basingstoke: Macmillan, 1956), 111.
[26] A. E., 'Literary Ideals in Ireland', 53.
[27] Ibid., 53–4.
[28] Yeats, *Collected Letters*, II, 302.

added to old legends by the imagination of the writer comes not (as Eglinton seemed to believe) from ' "his age" and "personality" and the "facts of life" ' but from 'an ideal world entered by the soul in moments of exaltation'. Yeats continues:

> It is this issue in some form that has divided the spiritualist from the materialist in all controversies about the foundations of life, and it is always this issue, in some form, that divides the 'symbolist' critic, from the critic, whose principles of criticism were shaped during the scientific movement of the middle of the century. John Eglinton sees that this is the issue.... The school of poetry which I admire, believes that the subjects of poetry are ideal, and so far above 'the normal human consciousness' <and> that they are invisible and imperceptible to it, and that the poet can only express them, or rather bring the 'normal human consciousness' into <this> their presence, by combining the images and things he has seen with his mind's eye or his body's eye, into an ideal harmony. He combines images and things into patterns, and chants a melancholy or resolute music, which affect the minds of his readers much as the ceremonial dance and the ceremonial music in the forest affected the ancient priests and priestesses.[29]

Even Russell's 'mystic' response could not match Yeats's candour about the 'magic' involvement of the poet with the ideal world in moments of exaltation. Had Eglinton seen those words it would have been surprising had he not asked just how this engagement took place in the act of composition, and it might have been interesting to see how far Yeats would divulge, in an Irish context, the private principles soon clarified in 'Magic' (1901). For the moment he held the English word 'symbolist' in inverted commas as a matter of moral hygiene. ' "Symbolist" ', used twice in this abandoned essay, is used in only 16 of the 1,128 occurrences of 'symbol' or its compounds in the searchable corpus of Yeats's oeuvre.[30] By contrast, the uses of 'symbolical', are distinct, as in his description of Villiers' *Axël* as a 'Symbolical Drama', and Althea Gyles as a 'Symbolical Artist' whose work heralds the coming of 'Symbolical Art'.[31]

At this point in the debate, William Larminie intervened to point out that Yeats inclined 'more than is quite safe to the theories of the French poets [which] whether they learned of the existence of such a thing as "magic" from England, or discovered it for themselves, have driven the theory of it to lengths undreamt of in England. Nothing, they say, should be named, everything suggested'.[32] Larminie also outed Symons as the London authority behind this debate, the poems quoted in Symons's valedictory 'Stéphane Mallarmé' reminding him of 'homeopathic soup'—as 'rich and nutritious' as a *Punch* recipe for broth made from the drumstick of a robin's leg.[33] 'Mere weariness and

---

[29] Ibid., 296.

[30] Thirteen usages describe individuals such as W. T. Horton, Keats, and Edward Calvert ('fragmentary symbolists'), Blake and Wagner, a system such as that in Yeats's *A Vision* (1937), or name Symons's book.

[31] *Early Articles and Reviews*, 234, 423. Certain poems, lines, or images by Keats, Tennyson, Browning, and Rossetti were also described by Yeats as 'symbolic' (*Collected Letters, II*, 296).

[32] William Larminie, 'Legends as Material for Literature', *Literary Ideals in Ireland*, 58.

[33] *Fortnightly Review*, 64, n.s. (November 1898), 677–85, and reprinted in *The Symbolist Movement in Literature* (1899). For the misquoted passages, see 12–89.

vacuity come of the aimless ransacking of the dictionary to find words which "may cap-
ture and recapture sudden fire"', he sneered. Were a 'consummation' of time imminent,
art would 'probably cease to be necessary'.[34]

The rhetoric of 'The Autumn of the Flesh', Yeats's published rebutter to both Russell
and Larminie, was 'flung up' from the 'hidden tides' of the controversy, necessarily less
easy to understand once that essay had been divorced from the controversy and revised
for *Ideas of Good and Evil* as 'The Autumn of the Body'.[35] Taking its title from Russell's
vision of a spiritual 'ecstasy' as prevailing over the *fin de siècle* 'lust of the flesh', 'The
Autumn of the Flesh' came on 3 December. Russell had claimed that though a mystic
'had been for a hundred years absorbed in the lust of the flesh, the lust of the eyes, and
the pride of life, in the moment he … attained to spiritual vision and ecstasy he … c[a]me
to his true home, to his true self', and Yeats, as a modern mystical writer was 'trying to
ennoble literature by making it religious rather than secular, by using his art for the rev-
elation of another world'.[36]

Yeats acknowledged his kinship with writers 'struggling, all over Europe' against 'the
picturesque and declamatory', against 'externality' brought into literature by 'a time of
scientific and political thought'; and he defended what he saw as the marked propensity
of the French writers to work in movements. He saw the differences between Villiers and
Flaubert as a categorical shift from 'old romanticism' to 'new'.[37] In this, perhaps his most
extraordinary essay before *Per Amica Silentia Lunae*, Yeats without naming the Symbolist
movement adumbrates its potential apocalypse: the arts 'lie dreaming of things to come',
as incipient belief transcended the many things that positive science, the interpreter of
exterior law, has always denied: 'communion of mind with mind in thought and without
words, foreknowledge in dreams and in visions, and the coming amongst us of the dead,
and of much else'.[38] Yeats continued:

> We are, it may be, at a crowning crisis of the world, at the moment when man is
> about to ascend … the stairway he has been descending from the first days … . Man
> has wooed and won the world, and has fallen weary, and not, I think, for a time, but
> with a weariness that will not end until the last autumn, when the stars shall be
> blown away like withered leaves. … The arts are, I believe, about to take upon their
> shoulders the burdens that have lain upon the shoulders of priests, and to lead us
> back upon our journey by filling our thoughts with the essences of things, and not
> with things.[39]

Quoting Symons's new essay on Mallarmé, Yeats set out a manifesto for an 'ever more
arduous search for an almost disembodied ecstasy', for an art that will permit new long

---

[34] William Larminie, *Literary Ideals in Ireland*, 65.
[35] Yeats, 'The Autumn of the Flesh', *Literary Ideals in Ireland*, 69–75, at 69; revised and retitled in
Ideas of Good and Evil (London: A. H. Bullen, 1903), 296–305: see *Early Essays*, 139–42.
[36] A. E., 'Literary Ideals in Ireland', in *Literary Ideals in Ireland*, 53–4.
[37] Yeats, *Literary Ideals in Ireland*, 69–70; *Early Essays*, 139.
[38] Yeats, *Literary Ideals in Ireland*, 72; *Early Essays*, 140–1.
[39] Yeats, *Literary Ideals in Ireland*, 72–4; *Early Essays*, 141–2.

poems with themes drawn from such subjects as the return of Ulysses, which will be 'the signature, or symbol of a mood of the divine imagination'.[40]

All this was too much for Russell. His concluding salvo, 'Nationality and Cosmopolitanism in Literature', on 10 December turned against the Decadence which, from Rossetti onwards, he had never liked and which he now symbolized as a 'crimson figure undergoing a dark crucifixion'. Russell argued that whereas psychic maladies which attack all races when their civilization grows old had to be reflected in art, 'in Ireland we are not yet sick with this sickness'.[41] By contrast, an Irish national art would express a 'peculiar ideal…nobler than that which the cosmopolitan ideal suggests'.[42] Vaguely asserting that this 'ideal of Ireland grows from mind to mind', and 'assume[s] the character of a sacred land', he misappropriated Yeats's 'And still the thoughts of Ireland brood/Upon her holy quietude'[43] and drowned it in a sentimental flood of cliché about Tir-na-noge, the 'inner Ireland', the 'Land of the Living Heart'.[44] Russell cast a plague on the houses of both Yeats and Eglinton, affecting to preside with a high-minded mystical superiority. Advocating a path for Irish literature 'wind[ing] spirally upwards to a mountain-top of our own which may in future be the Meru to which many worshippers will turn', he borrowed Yeats's stairway metaphor (in which lay the essence of his new cyclical theory of history).[45]

Yeats then discouraged Eglinton from writing yet another article so that Gill could 'close the correspondence' with Russell's article and 'publish the whole in a pamphlet'.[46] But this does not imply that Yeats found Russell's arguments conclusive. Lofty and (it must be said) wafty, Russell's final article could not conceal the differences that had emerged in the visionary experiments he and Yeats had undertaken in developing Yeats's Celtic Mystical Order. 'Strained' relations were now publicized by Russell's busyness behind the scenes. He confided to Lady Gregory that he had himself 'carefully fomented the discussion on both sides', finding 'a little private joy in doing this as I have long been battered by Yeats on one side and Eglinton on the other…I have stood aside while they went for each other'.[47] Yeats later wrote of their differences, and he was extraordinarily generous in his unpublished Autobiography:

> [Russell] saw constantly before him in vision an extraordinary world, the nature spirits as he believed, and I wished him to record all as Swedenborg had recorded, and submit his clairvoyance to certain tests. This seemed to him an impiety, and perhaps the turning towards it of the analytic intellect checked his gift, and he

---

[40] Yeats, *Literary Ideals in Ireland*, 74–5; *Early Essays*, 142.

[41] A. E., *Literary Ideals in Ireland*, 80.

[42] Ibid., 82.

[43] Yeats, *Variorum Poems*, 138v.

[44] A. E., *Literary Ideals in Ireland*, 84.

[45] Ibid., 87.

[46] Yeats, *Collected Letters*, II, 313.

[47] Quoted in ibid., 302, n.3. Russell considered *The Savoy* as 'all "mud from a muddy spring"' produced by 'people with a sexual mania like Beardsley, Symons or that ruck', but saw Yeats's 'Rosa Alchemica' in the same journal as 'a most wonderful piece of prose…a book sustained at that level throughout would be one of the greatest things in literature' (ibid., 59, n.2).

became extremely angry; and my insistence on understanding symbolically what he took for literal truth increased his anger.[48]

In a word, the 1898 *Literary Ideals in Ireland* discussion of French Symbolism exposed Yeats's Magic in Ireland, where it was as suspect as Russell's yogibogeybox Mysticism was harmless.

III

Yeats had been in Belfast and Dublin in November 1893 when Paul Verlaine stayed with Arthur Symons in Fountain Court in London. Symons and probably W. E. Henley had provided introductions to Verlaine and Mallarmé when Yeats went to Paris in early February 1894, to stay with Moina and MacGregor Mathers, ostensibly for 'a quiet dream with the holy Kabala'.[49] Yeats wrote to Mallarmé on his last Saturday before presenting himself, on the Sunday afternoon, proffering Verlaine's name and their faint kinship as co-contributors to Henley's *National Observer*. Mallarmé, however, was in England. According to his daughter, Geneviève, Madame Mallarmé 'a mimé' his absence in England to this 'espèce d'Anglais...ne sachant pas un mot de français'.[50] If Yeats was, as Donoghue suggests, 'slow in attending to the sounds emanating from France', it was because he could not *hear* them.[51] Nor was it provinciality that held him from the heart of the Symbolist movement. In 1895–6 conversations with Symons in Fountain Court widened his awareness; but, deaf to the relation between sound and meaning (crucial for Mallarmé), Yeats could only say, vaguely, 'nor shall I ever know how much my practice and theory owe to the passages that he read me from Catullus and from Verlaine and Mallarmé'.[52]

Yeats visited Paris primarily to stay with MacGregor Mathers. In 1890, Mathers had initiated Yeats into the Hermetic Order of the Golden Dawn. Four years later, Mathers offered a *vade mecum* to the Rose Croix occultism of Stanislaus de Guaïta, and there Yeats found international confirmation of the symbolical theories and practices he had developed for himself. Yeats had read (or tried to read) Villiers' *Axël* as 'a sacred book'. Maud Gonne, who had helped him to translate some key passages, accompanied him to the first night of the play on 26 February 1894:

---

[48] Yeats, *Memoirs*, 130–1.
[49] Yeats, *Collected Letters, I*, 379.
[50] As cited from Mallarmé's *Correspondance*, III, 235, in Yeats, *Collected Letters, 1*, 381, n. 3.
[51] 'In comparison with Joyce, Pound, and Eliot, he was provincial in that respect: he was...notably sluggish in his reception of the French poets, and...would hardly have made the effort but for the stimulation offered by Symons's company...what Yeats learned of Continental literature, either from Symons or anyone else, was slight; he was already half-way toward Symbolist procedures by instinct, as the early poems show'. Donoghue, 'Yeats: The Question of Symbolism', 279–80.
[52] W. B. Yeats, *Autobiographies: The Collected Works of W. B. Yeats*, vol. III, ed. William H. O'Donnell and Douglas N. Archibald (New York: Scribner, 1999), 246.

Before I went to Paris in 1894 I had read with great difficulty, for I had little French—
almost as learned men read newly-discovered Babylonian cylinders—the *Axel* of
Villiers de l'Isle-Adam. That play seemed all the more profound, all the more beauti-
ful, because I was never quite certain that I had read a page correctly.... [I]t was
about those things that most occupied my thought.... It did not move me because I
thought it a great masterpiece, but because it seemed part of a religious rite, the
ceremony perhaps of some secret Order wherein my generation had been
initiated.[53]

Axël endorsed his own occultism, which had shaped his own theory of Symbolism, less
an affair of sounds or poetic technique, but of belief, of evocation not suggestion, as his
review of the performance suggested.[54] In 1925 he wrote of it: 'I was in the midst of one of
those artistic movements that have the intensity of religious revivals in Wales and are
such a temptation to the artist in his solitude.' '[S]entence after sentence' of his 'revivalist
thoughts' now 'le[ft him] a little ashamed'.[55]

IV

An unambiguous clue to the root-tip of Yeats's thought is found in 'A Symbolic Artist
and the Coming of Symbolic Art', his essay for *The Dome* of December 1898 on the work
of Althea Gyles, the designer of the symbolical covers of *The Secret Rose* (1897), *Poems*
(1899), and *The Wind Among the Reeds*.[56] He, Russell, and Gyles had lived in the 'house-
hold', a theosophical commune at 3 Ely Place, Dublin, in 1891, and the influence of this
'conventual house' was formative. '[A] religious philosophy which has changed many
ordinary people into ecstatics and visionaries' was developed. Despite the danger that 'a
passion for symbol' could take the place of 'the old interest in life', Yeats saw Gyles's inspi-
ration as 'a wave of a hidden tide that is flowing through many minds in many places,
creating a new religious art and poetry'.[57]

Under Russell's guruship ('the most subtle and spiritual poet of his generation,
and a visionary who may find room beside Swedenborg and Blake'), their belief sys-
tems moved in an inherently unstable theosophical kaleidoscope of Indian,
Christian cabbalistic, and Celtic symbols and keywords (such as 'mirror' and

---

[53] W. B. Yeats, *Prefaces and Introductions: The Collected Works of W. B. Yeats*, vol. VI, ed.
William H. O'Donnell (New York: Macmillan, 1988), 156.

[54] Yeats, *Early Articles and Reviews*, 234–7.

[55] Yeats, *Prefaces and Introductions*, 157.

[56] Yeats, *Early Articles and Reviews*, 423. Symons was probably the first to note that the latter book's
'symbolism extends to the cover, where reeds are woven into a net to catch the wandering sounds',
'Mr Yeats as Lyric Poet', *Saturday Review* 87 (6 May 1899), 553–4; rpt. with revision in Arthur Symons,
Studies in Prose and Verse (London: J. M. Dent, 1904), 231.

[57] Yeats, *Early Articles and Reviews*, 424–9. The 'hidden tide' recurs in the opening sentence of
'The Autumn of the Flesh': see above n. 35.

'lamp'[58]), all worthy of digression. One such keyword is 'mood', which Yeats uses 397 times in his searchable canon. Sometimes it is indistinguishable from the aesthetic currency of Walter Pater's conclusion to *Studies in the History of the Renaissance*, 'some mood of passion or insight or intellectual excitement',[59] or from Wilde's 'mystery of moods'.[60] By contrast to mood as *intimité* of subjective experience, Yeats extracts 'The Moods' from its original 1895 context to form an entire essay in *Ideas of Good and Evil*:

> Literature differs from explanatory and scientific writing in being wrought about a mood, or a community of moods, as the body is wrought about an invisible soul. . . . It seems to me that these moods are the labourers and messengers of the Ruler of All, the gods of ancient days still dwelling on their secret Olympus, the angels of more modern days ascending and descending upon their shining ladder; and that argument, theory, erudition, observation, are merely what Blake called 'little devils who fight for themselves', illusions of our visible passing life, who must be made serve the moods, or we have no part in eternity . . . the imaginative artist . . . belongs to the invisible life, and delivers its ever new and ever ancient revelation. . . . The only restraint he can obey is the mysterious instinct that has made him an artist, and that teaches him to discover immortal moods in mortal desires, an undecaying hope in our trivial ambitions, a divine love in sexual passion.[61]

The editors of *Early Essays* are silent on the concept of the 'Moods' as 'messengers of . . . the gods'. Yeats was responding to Pater, who had referred, in *The Renaissance*, to 'those old pagan gods still going to and fro on the earth, under all sorts of disguises'. Pater introduced these old pagan gods when discussing the 'spirit of rebellion and revolt against the moral and religious ideas of the time', which he discerned in 'a medieval Renaissance'.[62] Pater's image alludes to Satan in the Book of Job (1:7), but he explicitly associates these 'decayed gods' with Heinrich Heine's *Gods in Exile*: 'decayed gods' redundified by the coming of Christianity.[63] Most frequently, Yeats articulated his idea of Moods in terms of Irish folklore, with special reference to fairies. These fairies, he

---

[58] For Solomon's lamp see *Prefaces and Introductions*, 156, and for Villiers's 'words behind which glimmered a spiritual and passionate mood, as a flame glimmers behind the dusky blue and red glass in an Eastern lamp' see *Early Essays*, 139. Villiers's 'Sacred Book' gives rise to the lamp motif again in Yeats's memories of Tulira Castle: see *Autobiographies*, 246–7. M. H. Abrams takes his title, *The Mirror and the Lamp* (1953), from Yeats's Preface to *The Oxford Book of Modern Verse*: See *Prefaces and Introductions*, 198.

[59] Walter Pater, *The Renaissance: Studies in Art and Poetry, the 1893 Text*, ed. Donald L. Hill (Berkeley and Los Angeles: University of California Press, 1980), 188.

[60] Oscar Wilde, *The Complete Letters of Oscar Wilde*, ed. Merlin Holland and Rupert Hart-Davis (London: Fourth Estate, 2000), 272.

[61] Yeats, 'The Moods', *Early Essays*, 143. This first appeared as the opening paragraph of 'Irish National Literature: Contemporary Prose Writers', *The Bookman*, August 1895 (see *Early Articles and Reviews*, 270–6). For Blake's 'devils' see *The Works of William Blake, Poetic, Symbolic, and Critical*, eds. E. J. Ellis and W. B. Yeats (London: Quaritch, 1893), vol. III, 66.

[62] Pater, *The Renaissance: Studies in Art and Poetry, the 1893 Text*, 18.

[63] Ibid., 19, 24, 93.

asserted, changed their shape 'with their moods—symbolizing or following the feelings of the moment':

> The peasants say they are fallen angels who were too good to be lost, too bad to be saved, and have to work out their time in barren places of the earth. An old Irish authority—*the Book of Armagh*—calls them gods of the earth, and quite beyond any kind of doubt many of them were long ago gods in Ireland.[64]

In a *Celtic Twilight* essay, 'The Golden Age', Yeats is in a train nearing Sligo, and reminisces: 'The last time I had been there something was troubling me, and I had longed for a message from those beings or bodiless moods, or whatever they be, who inhabit the world of spirits'.[65] This message had come, Yeats writes, in the form of a complex, symbolical dream. When 'Invoking the Irish Fairies', Yeats and Florence Farr in 1892 experienced a 'terrible warfare' between two kingdoms of fairies:

> It is that contest of the minor forces of good and evil which knows no hour of peace but goes on everywhere and always. The fairies are the lesser spiritual moods of that universal mind, wherein every mood is a soul and every thought a body. Their world is very different from ours, and they can but appear in forms borrowed from our limited consciousness, but nevertheless, every form they take and every action they go through, has its significance and can be read by the mind trained in the correspondence of sensuous form and supersensuous meaning.[66]

'[T]he Great Moods...are alone immortal, and the creators of mortal things...every Mood is a being that wears, to mortal eyes, the shape of' the Celtic gods.[67] Such had been the moods in early texts of 'The Wisdom of the King'. In the proem to *The Celtic Twilight* (1893):

> *Time drops in decay*
> *Like a candle burnt out,*
> *And the mountains and woods*
> *Have their day, have their day;*
> *But, kindly old rout*
> *Of the fire-born moods,*
> *You pass not away.*[68]

This proem prepares us for Paddy Flynn, the 'Teller of Tales', who knew:

> of no less ample circumstance than did Homer himself. Perhaps the Gaelic people shall by his like bring back again the ancient simplicity and amplitude of the imagination. What is literature but the expression of moods by the vehicle of symbol and

---

[64] Yeats, 'Irish Fairies, Ghosts, Witches etc.', *Lucifer* 15 January 1889, *Early Articles and Reviews*, 81.

[65] W. B. Yeats, *Mythologies*, ed. Warwick Gould and Deirdre Toomey (Basingstoke: Palgrave Macmillan, 2005), 69.

[66] Yeats, 'Invoking the Irish Fairies', *The Irish Theosophist* (October 1892); *Early Articles and Reviews*, 184.

[67] Yeats, *The Secret Rose Variorum*, 31.

[68] Yeats, *Mythologies*, 433.

incident? And are there not moods which need heaven, hell, purgatory, and faeryland for their expression, no less than this dilapidated earth? Nay, are there not moods which shall find no expression unless there be men who dare to mix heaven, hell, purgatory, and faeryland together, or even to set the heads of beasts to the bodies of men, or thrust the souls of men into the heart of rocks?[69]

It also prepares us for the encounter whereby Yeats, George and Lucy Pollexfen met the Queen of the Faeries at Rosses Point, as described in 'Regina, Regina Pigmeorum, Veni', when Yeats asked her 'whether she and her people were not '"dramatisations of our moods"'. Creditably, the Queen of the Faeries told Yeats that this was not her department. He pressed her on 'her purpose in the universe', which 'only seemed to puzzle her. At last she appeared to lose patience, for she wrote this message for me upon the sands— the sands of vision—"Be careful, and do not seek to know too much about us." '[70] Yeats had posed the obverse of a question that, in the 1890s, he frequently asked. Did the Moods operate as a *Zeitgeist*? What then of the individual creative mind's role in their influence upon humanity and history?

In attempting to outline Blake's 'Symbolic System' in *The Works of William Blake Poetic, Symbolic, and Critical*, which he had edited with Edwin Ellis in 1893, he had written 'The Necessity of Symbolism' by late June 1891, followed by 173 pages of exposition of 'The Symbolic System', the 'greater part' of which is Yeats's.[71] His mystical line of enquiry, via Boehme's 'signatures', insists that the 'chief difference between the metaphors of poetry and the symbols of mysticism is that the latter are woven together into a complete system'.[72] Starting from Blake's *There is No Natural Religion* and *All Religions are One*, which meditates on the 'universal Poetic Genius', Yeats claims:

> Sometimes the mystical student, bewildered by the different systems, forgets for the moment that the history of moods is the history of the universe, and asks where is the final statement—the complete doctrine. The universe is itself that doctrine and statement. All others are partial, for it alone is the symbol of the infinite thought which is in turn symbolic of the universal mood we name God.[73]

Spiritual change is related to what Blake calls the 'Spirit of Prophesy' or 'reception of the poetic genius':

> This poetic genius or central mood in all things is that which creates all by affinity— worlds no less than religions and philosophies. First, a bodiless mood, and then a

---

[69] Ibid., 441.

[70] Ibid., 36–7.

[71] 'I also wrote a very important essay called "The Necessity of Symbolism" for the Book on Blake & went through it with Ellis & made suggested alterations', he told Katharine Tynan (*Collected Letters, 1*, 252). See Ian Fletcher, 'The Ellis-Yeats-Blake Manuscript Cluster', *Book Collector* 21:1 (1972), 7–294. For Yeats's May 1900 note on authorship, see Allan Wade, *A Bibliography of the Writings of W. B. Yeats* (London: Rupert Hart-Davis, 1968), 241.

[72] [W. B. Yeats], 'The Necessity of Symbolism', in *The Works of William Blake: Poetic, Symbolic, and Critical, I*, 238.

[73] Ibid., 239.

surging thought, and at last a thing. This triad is universal in mysticism, and corresponds to Father, Son, and Holy Spirit.[74]

Comparing Swedenborgian, Kabalistic, Theosophical, and Blakean systems, Yeats continues:

> [a]s mood differs from mood, and emotion from emotion, not by discrete but by continuous degrees, it will be seen that there is something common to them all—a mood that goes through all the moods...[w]hen...we allow our imagination to expand away from this egotistic mood, we become vehicles for the universal thought and merge in the universal mood....The 'genius' within us...only becomes peaceful and free when it grows one with 'the poetic genius'—the universal mood.[75]

That 'universal mood' seems the collective of the 'rout' in the proem to *The Celtic Twilight*, immanent amid the Tennysonian 'decay and fall' of all things. Revising it as 'The Moods' for *The Wind Among the Reeds*, Yeats asks:

> What one in the rout
> Of the fire-born moods
> Has fallen away?[76]

Change itself is caused by the decay of the Moods themselves, a foretaste of a cyclical theory of history. A 1924 note to 'The Friends of the People of Faery' recalls gyres in Swedenborg's Spiritual Diary, and Blake's 'Jacob's Ladder' as 'an ascending gyre'.[77] The Moods, 'the messengers of the Ruler of All, the angels ascending and descending upon their shining ladder', come and go in two-way traffic, microcosmic and macrocosmic intermediaries, like Blake's angels.

V

'The Moods' is entirely congruent with Yeats's theory of the Moods, set out in *Rosa Alchemica* in the April 1896 issue of Symons's *Savoy* magazine. That story not only contains the idea that the Symbolist movement itself is a 'mood which Edgar Poe found in a wine cup', a contemporary *Zeitgeist*, but also lays out, under the guise of fiction, what I take to be Yeats's central belief projection of the relation between the moods and symbolical thinking. In the neophyte explanation of the beliefs of the Order of the Alchemical Rose, the key doctrine is that of:

> the independent reality of our thoughts, which was...the doctrine from which all true doctrines rose. If you imagine, [the book] said, the semblance of a living being, it is at once possessed by a wandering soul, and goes hither and thither working

---

[74] Ibid., 241.
[75] Ibid., 241–3.
[76] Yeats, *Variorum Poems*, 142.
[77] Yeats, *Mythologies*, 81, 298. Yeats could not have seen this watercolour before 1906.

good or evil…and gave many examples, received, it said, from many gods. Eros had taught them how to fashion forms in which a divine soul could dwell and whisper what it would into sleeping minds; and Ate, forms from which demonic beings could pour madness, or unquiet dreams, into sleeping blood; and Hermes…and Aphrodite…and all divinities alike had revealed…that all minds are continually giving birth to such beings, and sending them forth to work health or disease, joy or madness. If you would give forms to the evil powers, it went on, you were to make them ugly, thrusting out a lip with the thirsts of life, or breaking the proportions of a body with the burdens of life; but the divine powers would only appear in beautiful shapes, which are but, as it were, shapes trembling out of existence, folding up into a timeless ecstasy, drifting with half-shut eyes into a sleepy stillness. The bodiless souls who descended into these forms were what men called the moods; and worked all great changes in the world; for just as the magician or the artist could call them when he would, so they could call out of the mind of the magician or the artist, or if they were demons, out of the mind of the mad or the ignoble, what shape they would, and through its voice and its gestures pour themselves out upon the world. In this way all great events were accomplished; a mood, a divinity, or a demon, first descending like a faint sigh into men's minds and then changing their thoughts and their actions until hair that was yellow had grown black, or hair that was black had grown yellow, and empires moved their border, as though they were but drifts of leaves. The rest of the book contained symbols of form, and sound, and colour, and their attribution to divinities and demons, so that the initiate might fashion a shape for any divinity or any demon, and be as powerful as Avicenna among those who live under the roots of tears and of laughter.[78]

Yeats's obsession with the Moods in the 1890s—his use of that term declines after *Ideas of Good and Evil*[79]—emphasized how artistic labour could refine and increase their potency, 'perfecting earthly power and perception until they are so subtilised that divine power and divine perception descend to meet them, and the song of earth and the song of heaven mingle together'. In William Allingham's verse, 'the Immortal Moods, which are so impatient of rhetoric…found…the one perfect ritual fashioned for their honour by Irish hands'.[80] 'Once a symbolism has possessed the imagination of large numbers of men it becomes, as I believe, an embodiment of disembodied powers, and repeats itself in dreams and visions, age after age,' writes Yeats in the 1899 notes to *The Wind Among the Reeds*.[81] The Moods, then, are a collective symbol for the involuntary networking power of symbolism itself.

Where did all this occultation leave the impressionable impressionist, Arthur Symons? When the morality of his *London Nights* (1896) was attacked, he drafted a new preface for the second (1897) edition, signed and dated 'Rosses Point, Sligo, 2 *September* 1896'. It was 'laughable' to commend or condemn:

[78] Ibid., 186–7.
[79] There are thirteen usages in that volume, twenty-seven in his occasional prose to 1897, with only nine thereafter.
[80] Yeats, *Early Articles and Reviews*, 313, 266.
[81] Yeats, *Variorum Poems*, 810.

this or the other passing caprice of our wisdom or our folly as a due or improper subject for the 'moment's monument' of a poem! It is as if you were to say to me, here on these weedy rocks of Rosses' Point, where the grey sea passes me continually, flinging a little foam at my feet, that I may write of one rather than another of these waves, which are not more infinite than the moods of men.

The moods of men!...whatever has once been a mood of mine, though it has been no more than a ripple on the sea, and had no longer than that ripple's duration, I claim the right to render, if I can in verse.[82]

Yeats at first had been 'repelled' by Symons, who 'with a superficial deduction I suppose from the chapter in Marius called "Animula Vagula"...saw nothing in literature but a series of impressions'. Clearly still stuck in Paterian moods, Symons sought '[m]usic halls and amorous adventure' to supply 'vivid impressions for his verse', while Yeats, unctuous in such matters, 'knew the greatest kind of literature is passion. I sought passion, religious passion above all, as the greatest good of life, and always cherished the secret hope of some mysterious initiation. He thought to spend his life, in so far as it was an artistic life, in making the silver mirror without speck, and I thought to see it fused and glowing.'[83]

VI

Symons, though respectful of Mysticism, had no head for ritual magic or evocation, so essential to Yeats for composition. Yet Symons saw, diffidently, that Yeats's 'renewal of belief' was 'the great movement of our time'. In the March 1900 dedication to *The Symbolist Movement in Literature*, he swept Yeats's '*own Irish movement your own poetry and A.E.'s poetry*' into the pan-European movement '*in the most intimate sense*'. Acknowledging his difficulties with mysticism:

> I speak often in this book of Mysticism, and that I, of all people, should venture to speak, not quite as an outsider, of such things, will probably be a surprise to many. It will be no surprise to you, for you have seen me gradually finding my way, uncertainly but inevitably, in that direction which has always been your natural direction.[84]

Symons conceded his own loyalty to Paterian impressionism being '*so meshed about with the variable and too clinging appearances of things, so weak before the delightfulness of earthly circumstance*'.[85]

In the 1899 edition, Symons gives just eight pages to a theory of symbolism before grazing amongst *symbolistes*—Nerval, Villiers, Rimbaud, Verlaine, Laforgue, Mallarmé,

---

[82] Arthur Symons, *London Nights*, MS., Princeton.
[83] Yeats, *Memoirs*, 36.
[84] Symons, *Symbolist Movement*, vi.
[85] Ibid.

Huysmans, Maeterlinck. He writes: 'What distinguishes the Symbolism of our day from the Symbolism of the past is that it has now become conscious of itself...a literature in which the visible world is no longer a reality, and the unseen world no longer a dream'.[86]

Though Symons's influence is undeniable—his 1908 edition was a turning point for T. S. Eliot—in the context of Yeats's own rather more arduous writings on Symbolism the book is as disappointing as its constituent pieces were illuminating. Overwhelmed by Pater, Symons's final paragraph follows the cadence of Pater's famous conclusion.[87] Death, Pater's 'last curiosity', Symons's 'final uncertainty', remains, but, with a little help from Plotinus (probably via Yeats), Symons contrives to look at the real world and its distractions as mere 'shadows through which we have our shadowy passage':

> as we realise the identity of a poem, a prayer, or a kiss, in that spiritual universe which we are weaving for ourselves...it is at least with a certain relief that we turn to an ancient doctrine, so much more likely to be true because it has so much the air of a dream. On this theory alone does all life become worth living, all art worth making, all worship worth offering. And because it might slay as well as save, the freedom of its sweet captivity might so easily become deadly to the fool, because that is the hardest path to walk in where you are told only, walk well; it is perhaps the only counsel of perfection which can ever really mean much to the artist.[88]

This listless refusal to endorse Yeats's religious view of art capitulates to decadent impressionism. Following the consequences of Yeats's *mythos*, Symons was not ready to renounce serpent charmers and the delights of the music halls for the mystic way.[89]

VII

By 29 March 1900, Yeats was writing 'The Symbolism of Poetry', 'a rather elaborate thing—about four times as long as I expected',[90] stiffening his earlier writings on the subject, notably 'The Symbolism of Painting' (1898), while responding to reviews of *The Wind Among the Reeds* with some 'philosophy, some criticism of...art'.[91] Symons read

---

[86] Ibid., 5–6.

[87] Cf. the opening of its five-page conclusion ('Our only chance, in this world, of a complete happiness') with Pater's 'For our one chance...' and 'Well, the doctrine of Mysticism, with which all this symbolical literature has much to do, of which it is all so much the expression, presents us not with a guide for conduct, not with a plan for our happiness, not with an explanation of any mystery, but with a theory of life which makes us familiar with mystery, and which seems to harmonise these instincts which make for religion, passion, and art, freeing us at once from a great bondage' with Pater's own concluding sentences (*The Renaissance*, 190).

[88] Symons, *Symbolist Movement*, 174–5.

[89] Yeats, *Memoirs*, 97.

[90] Yeats, *Collected Letters*, II, 506; *Early Essays*, 113–21. A few days earlier he had written a brief explanatory note for *The Shadowy Waters* to *North American Review*, which concluded 'the more one explains the more one narrows the symbols' (*Collected Letters*, II, 502).

[91] Yeats, *Early Essays*, 114.

Yeats's manuscript and thought it 'among the best things [he had] done'.[92] Yeats placed this essay in the April 1900 *Dome*, and, 'because it has been dedicated to me', Yeats was able to say of Symons's 'subtle book' that 'I cannot praise [it] as I would'.[93] He was in fact disappointed with the book that had appeared just one month before. He read it 'very carefully' and 'found it curiously vague in its philosophy'. Symons had 'not really thought about it & contradicts himself sometimes almost in the same sentence, but there is a great deal of really very fine criticism'.[94]

Yeats was never comfortable in Symons's international *symboliste* pantheon. Creative divisions in English and Irish poetic traditions were both his difficulty and opportunity: in a provincial way, a national way, an occult way, he had become a *symbolical* writer, and his own strange theories of the Moods, and of the independent reality of our thoughts, were self-grounded.[95] He had for a time thought that art was 'tribeless, nationless, a blossom gathered in No Man's Land',[96] but in March 1896 he had told Henri Davray, the translator of 'Rosa Alchemica': 'I want you to understand that I am an Irish poet, looking to my own people for my ultimate best audience & trying to express the things that interest them & which will make them care for the land in which they live'.[97]

Symons's dedication made difficulties for Yeats in Ireland. Reviewing *The Shadowy Waters*, W. P. Ryan claimed that '[a]t times Mr Yeats seems desirous of illustrating in poetry some of the things which Mr Arthur Symons set so delicately and yet so unconvincingly in prose in "The Symbolist Movement in Literature" '.[98] Symons had come to Symbolism through Decadence. 'Symbolist' conferred French dignity and high seriousness upon the Decadent project of Paterian impressionism whereby literature would be a 'new and beautiful and interesting disease'.[99] Yeats had come to Symbolism via Irish folklore; the manuscripts of Blake, the occult interpretation of his work, and attempts to relate it to the systemic mysticisms of Swedenborg and Boehme; theosophical studies of symbols and their practical employment in divinatory systems; and his investigations of

[92] Yeats, *Collected Letters, II*, 512. On 5 April 1900 Yeats and Symons met to discuss 'The Symbolism of Poetry' (ibid., 506, 512, n.13).

[93] Yeats, *Early Essays*, 113.

[94] Yeats, *Collected Letters, II*, 506.

[95] Yeats argued that Symons's 'provincialism was curable, mine incurable', in *Autobiographies*, 148.

[96] Yeats, *Early Essays*, 151.

[97] Yeats, *Collected Letters, II*, 15.

[98] (*Freeman's Journal*, 1 January 1901, 7: see Yeats, *Collected Letters of W. B. Yeats, Vol. III: 1901–1904*, ed. John Kelly and Ronald Schuchard (Oxford: Clarendon Press 1994), 11, n.6. Even before Yeats's arrival in America in 1903, the New York *Independent* of 12 November 1903 had disapproved of his latest work and voiced a suspicion 'that the Irish revival is nothing, after all, but another form of decadence'. This unsigned article 'may well have been' by Paul Elmer More who, in the New York *Evening Post* on 12 December detected 'failure and decay, rather than…mastery and growth' in Yeats's successive works. '[T]he real kinship of Mr. Yeats's present style is with that of Arthur Symons, himself a disciple of the French decadents; only one must add in justice that no taint of moral degeneration has appeared in the Irish writer – and that is much to concede to a decadent' (*Collected Letters, III*, 498, n.2).

[99] Arthur Symons, 'The Decadent Movement in Literature', *Harper's New Monthly Magazine*, November 1893, 858–9. *The Symbolist Movement in Literature* grew from this essay.

similar systems among the Hermetic Students of the Golden Dawn, and for his own Celtic Mystical Order. Yeats discovered his provinciality at the hands of Symons, but also discovered how controversial was his 'heteredox' mysticism in Nativist Ireland even before the publication of *The Wind Among the Reeds* in April 1899. French Symbolism focused that unpopularity.[100]

In the upper room of the Cheshire Cheese all were ephebes. We have no good model for influence in such a *cenâcle*.[101] Nevertheless, Yeats was his own man as a poetic thinker by the time he wrote 'The Moods' in 1895. Expounding the system of a precursor poet, he heeded Blake's warning that the only way to avoid enslavement by the systems of others was to create one's own. To these heady influences he added his own experiments with theosophical thought; his work with the Tattvas; his visionary activities; the syllabus of that alternative university, the Order of the Golden Dawn; his engagement in and management of visionary explorations in the attempt to create rituals for his Celtic Mystical Order; his scrying and his mescalin and hashish experiments.

These activities suggest a mind all too experimental, knocking very determinedly at the 'doors of perception'.[102] That is why an Irish poet ambitious in a London culture distinguished himself from the prevailing decadent Impressionists and came to be aligned by their leader with the European Symbolists. We should not, I think, weigh the European *symboliste* achievement as *prima facie* superior because international. To register Yeats's absolute distinctiveness as a symbolical thinker is to begin to ask awkward questions about the nature of international esteem. For Denis Donoghue:

> Yeats started out as a Symbolist and ended as something else... there were scruples which prevented him from making his entire art with Symons and the Symbolists: the scruple was present, more often than not, right from the start, even though it was suppressed.[103]

Yeats was an occult believer. Symons only briefly believed that it might be a good thing to find out about belief, while Yeats survived the Symbolist appellation that Symons had thrust upon him. Down off those stilts, he remained a symbolical writer for the rest of his life, turning after *The Wind Among the Reeds* to Irish mythological narrative, a path adumbrated in 'The Autumn of the Body'. Turning symbolical techniques to 'concrete' writing 'about himself', 'he gained in power' from 'what he lost in mystery.[104]

---

[100] Yeats, *Collected Letters*, III, 71.

[101] Harold Bloom's model of influence operates between the strong, living poet and the mighty dead: see *The Anxiety of Influence* (New York: Oxford University Press, 1973). For T. S. Eliot, 'immature poets imitate' while 'mature poets steal', *Selected Essays* (London: Faber and Faber, 1951), 182.

[102] William Blake, 'The Marriage of Heaven and Hell, Plate 14: see David V. Erdman (ed.), *The Poetry and Prose of William Blake* (New York: Doubleday & Company, 1965), 39. Denis Donoghue, however, argues in 'Yeats: The Question of Symbolism' that Yeats's 'mind was not, in fact, experimental; it knew only too well what it liked and was not disposed towards novelties of perception', in *The Symbolist Movement*, ed. Balakian, 279.

[103] Ibid., 284.

[104] C. M. Bowra, *The Heritage of Symbolism* (London: Macmillan, 1943), 218.

VIII

'The Symbolism of Poetry' is unforthcoming on the subject of the 'call[ing] down among us of certain disembodied powers' by the 'pre-ordained energies' of sounds, colours, and forms.[105] 'Magic', quietly published in the *Monthly Review* (September 1901), grew from a split within the Order of the Golden Dawn, and offered Yeats's personal belief:

> in the practice and philosophy of what we have agreed to call magic, in what I must call the evocation of spirits, though I do not know what they are, in the power of creating magical illusions, in the visions of truth in the depths of the mind when the eyes are closed; and I believe in three doctrines, which have, as I think…been the foundations of nearly all magical practices. These doctrines are:
>
> (1) That the borders of our mind are ever shifting, and that many minds can flow into one another, as it were, and create or reveal a single mind, a single energy.
> (2) That the borders of our memories are as shifting, and that our memories are a part of one great memory, the memory of Nature herself.
> (3) That this great mind and great memory can be evoked by symbols.[106]

The non-chronological deployment of contents in *Ideas of Good and Evil* promotes this essay such that Yeats allows us to read all of his developing thought on Symbolism armed with those three principles. His purpose is well served by that decision, invisible unless the intricate history of his writings is reassembled. Musing on the visions he and Mathers had had, Yeats offers us a clue as to why 'all knowledge is biography' and why the subsequent poetry of a symbolical writer had to be biographical:

> In coming years I was to see and hear of many such visions, and though I was not to be convinced, though half convinced once or twice, that they were old lives, in an ordinary sense of the word life, I was to learn that they have almost always some quite definite relation to dominant moods and moulding events in this life. They are, perhaps, in most cases…symbolical histories of these moods and events, or rather symbolical shadows of the impulses that have made them, messages as it were out of the ancestral being of the questioner.[107]

On reading a draft of an essay by C. M. Bowra in 1935, Yeats commented:

> I don't think I was really much influenced by French Symbolism. My development was different but…I found I could not explain it, or even that it might make everybody hostile. When Symons talked to me about the Symbolistes, or read me passages from his translations of Mallarme, I seized upon everything that at all resembled my own thought; here at last was something I could talk about. My symbolism came from actual experiments in vision, made by my friends or myself in the

---

[105] Yeats, *Early Essays*, 115–16.
[106] Ibid., 25.
[107] Ibid., 30.

society which called itself 'The Hermetic Students', and continually I talked ever by myself and those friends. I felt that those investigations were private, and felt also, and indeed still feel, that one can only explain oneself if one draws one's illustrations from accepted schools of thought.[108]

[108] Yeats, CL Intelex 6239, to Maurice Bowra, 31 May (1935), '....Furthermore I felt that unaccepted schools, however profound, are incomplete <and isolated> because isolated from the rest of knowledge. There was however one book which influenced me very greatly, it had just been edited by [Richard] Le Gallienne, it was the younger Hallam's essay on Tennyson. It was only the first half of the essay which influenced me, and in that he defined what he called "aesthetic poetry". By "aesthetic poetry" he meant exactly what the French mean by "pure poetry". It may interest you that an English critic was probably the first to make that <discovery> definition...I am full of curiosity about certain of the writers you are studying, Stephan George for instance. Ignorant of languages I have always had to get much of my knowledge from such books as yours. A single quotation is sometimes an illumination.'

CHAPTER 3

....

YEATS, CLARKE, AND THE IRISH POET'S RELATIONSHIP WITH ENGLISH

....

MICHAEL O'NEILL

I

....

In 'A General Introduction for My Work' (written in 1937), after raging against the 'persecution' suffered by 'The "Irishry"', and acknowledging that 'there are moments when hatred poisons my life and I accuse myself of effeminacy because I have not given it adequate expression', W. B. Yeats confronts directly the dualities central to his poetry and his identity, reflecting on his predicament as a consciously 'Irish' poet who writes in English:

> Then I remind myself that though mine is the first English marriage I know of in the direct line, all my family names are English, and that I owe my soul to Shakespeare, to Spenser and to Blake, perhaps to William Morris, and to the English language in which I think, speak, and write, that everything I love has come to me through English; my hatred tortures me with love, my love with hate. I am like the Tibetan monk who dreams at his initiation that he is eaten by a wild beast and learns on waking that he himself is eater and eaten.[1]

Inevitably, as this passage makes clear, the Irish poet's relationship with English cannot extricate itself from his or her relationships with 'Englishness' and 'Irishness'. 'My hatred tortures me with love, my love with hate': the chiastic formulation is typically alert to the entangling in one another of opposites. Earlier, in a prose work based on a lecture entitled 'The New Ireland', Yeats defended the satirical and realistic thrust of works produced

---

[1] W. B. Yeats, *The Major Works*, ed. Edward Larrissy [1997] (Oxford: Oxford University Press, 2001), 384–5.

by Irish writers in the twentieth century, works such as James Joyce's *Ulysses*, in terms that anticipate the closing comment of the quotation above: 'We had passed through an initiation like that of the Tibetan ascetic, who staggers half dead from a trance, where he has seen himself eaten alive and not yet learned that the eater was himself.'[2] By the time of 'A General Introduction for My Work', composed a few years later, Yeats had learned that, in his relationship with his Anglo-Irish identity, he was himself 'eater and eaten'. The phrasing suggests that the contradictory pulls of which Yeats was aware in his Anglo-Irish identity assume, for him, a larger significance: cultures, like individuals, are places of intersection, intense, rivalrous sites where creativity and destruction co-exist.

Seamus Deane would have us regard Yeats's agonizing in 'A General Introduction for My Work' as displaying 'the pathology of literary unionism'.[3] But it is less 'literary unionism' than awareness of literary division to which Yeats bears witness. His reluctance to resolve too quickly tensions associated with identity, to side too promptly or ever finally with either side of his Anglo-Irish status, is one reason why his poetry and criticism possess endurance and imaginative stamina. These qualities are evident in his later embrace of the 'Anglo-Irish solitude' he found in Augustus John's portrait of him, 'an outlawed solitude' that was Protestant, and took its self-fashioning bearings from a strikingly individualist notion of the legacy bequeathed by eighteenth-century Irish writers and thinkers such as Jonathan Swift.[4] 'I declare,' he writes in 'Blood and the Moon', constructing a consciously embattled phase of his Anglo-Irish identity, 'This winding, gyring, spiring treadmill of a stair is my ancestral stair;/That Goldsmith and the Dean, Berkeley and Burke have travelled there'.[5] Consuming his dreams, he is driven forward to shape others, through a poetry that 'declares' and yet always travels in 'gyring, spiring' and intricate motions, experimenting with forms that reflect a continual awareness of dialectical disturbance; so, Helen Vendler interprets the complex dealings with sonnet convention in 'The Second Coming' as promoting awareness of the fact that 'The poem rebels, in an almost "Irish" way, against the English Enlightenment models of a progressive philosophy of history.'[6] For Marjorie Howes, Yeats's 'Anglo-Irish poems', such as 'Meditations in Time of Civil War', depict a 'version of nationality that is splendidly vulnerable...and that flaunts its origins in arbitrary acts of will'.[7] Certainly words such as 'English' and 'Irish', and their cognates and associated formations, have a habit of consuming any stable identification in Yeats's work.

---

[2] W. B Yeats, *The Variorum Edition of the Poems of W. B. Yeats*, ed. Peter Allt and Russell K. Alspach (Basingstoke: MacMillan, 1956), 835. See also Terence Brown, *The Life of W. B. Yeats* (Oxford: Blackwell, 1999), 339.

[3] Quoted in Brown, *Life of W. B. Yeats*, 379.

[4] Ibid., 331.

[5] Yeats, *Variorum Poems*, 480–2.

[6] Helen Vendler, *Our Secret Discipline: Yeats and Lyric Form* (Oxford: Oxford University Press, 2007), 173.

[7] Marjorie Howes, *Yeats's Nations: Gender, Class, and Irishness* (Cambridge: Cambridge University Press, 1996), 130.

II

Influences on Yeats's sense of being an Irish poet writing in English include, according to 'A General Introduction for my Work', the 'old Fenian leader John O'Leary'. O'Leary gave Yeats the poems of Thomas Davis, the Young Ireland poet, and 'said they were not good poetry but had changed his life when a young man'. Yeats is terse in old age about his lack of respect for the artistic achievement of the Young Ireland poets, but they affected his attitude towards subject matter since he 'admired' the fact the poets were 'not separated individual men; they spoke or tried to speak out of a people to a people; behind them stretched the generations'.[8] Poems such as Davis's 'A Nation Once Again' are an important element in what Thomas Kinsella speaks of as 'a kind of literary nationalism…strengthened…with…great gifts of particularity and drama' in the early Yeats.[9] Davis yearned for a time when he 'might see/Our fetters rent in twain,/And Ireland, long a province, be/A Nation once again'.[10] Yeats's 'fitful Danaan rhymes' in 'To Some I have Talked with by the Fire' involve a displaced contest fought by 'the embattled flaming multitude/Who rise, wing above wing, flame above flame,/And, like a storm, cry the Ineffable Name'.[11] That 'Ineffable Name' resonates with esoteric suggestions but it also hints at the new Ireland that Yeats was imagining.

Davis, indeed, is a writer whom Yeats subtly deployed in his explorations of what it meant to be an Irish writer composing in English. In 1910 he was able, in a charged meditation, both to praise the Young Ireland poet for living a 'life' that 'had the moral simplicity which can give to actions the lasting influence that style alone can give to words' and to criticize him for transmitting 'ideas and images' whose relatively coarse populist appeal means that they lacked 'rich personal experience', 'patience of study', and 'delicacy of sense'.[12] In 'September 1913', Yeats alludes to Davis's 'The Green above the Red' with its roll call of heroes. Davis wrote: 'Sure 'twas for this Lord Edward died, and Wolf [sic] Tone sunk serene—/Because they could not bear to leave the Red above the Green'.[13] Yeats, writing out of the conviction that intervention in the Lane Gallery controversy was urgent since Ireland's 'history' was 'now plastic'[14] and that such intervention was doomed to fail given the nature of his audience, calls Davis to mind as he asks, in 'September 1913': 'For this Edward Fitzgerald died,/And Robert Emmet and Wolfe Tone,/All that delirium of the brave?' But Yeats gives to Davis's lines two ironizing twists: the first in that he annuls a sense of connection between 'Romantic Ireland' and

---

    [8] Yeats, *Major Works*, 380.
    [9] Thomas Kinsella, ed., *The New Oxford Book of Irish Verse* (Oxford: Oxford University Press, 1986), p. xxvii.
    [10] Quoted from Kinsella, ed., *New Oxford Book of Irish Verse*, 305.
    [11] Yeats, *Variorum Poems*, 136–7.
    [12] Quoted in R. F. Foster, *W. B. Yeats: A Life*, vol. 1: *The Apprentice Mage: 1865–1914* (Oxford: Oxford University Press, 1997), 418–19.
    [13] Ibid., 496, and, for the quotation from Davis, 620.
    [14] Ibid., 494.

the present in the very question, 'For this...?'; the second in that in 'All that delirium of the brave' he cannot but concede that the heroes of the past might have been acting blindly or madly, even though one might read such a construction as the belief of those against whom Yeats aims his polemic. Sorrowing over the loss of 'Romantic Ireland', Yeats also implies his own distance from the martyrological clichés he seems to invoke.[15]

Thomas MacDonagh took exception to 'Danaan' as an example of Yeats's made-up Gaelicisms, and his rebuke reminds us of the poet's frequent discovery that in seeking to write a new poetry for a nation yet to be born, Yeats's audience would often be one that he would himself have to dream into existence.[16] The poet who in 'The Fisherman' writes 'in scorn' of an 'audience' asserts a freedom to work within his own terms: terms which concede and celebrate the fact that they involve 'Imagining' 'A man who does not exist,/A man who is but a dream'.[17] There, Yeats's rhythms assume a lilt of driving confidence that counterpoints the scepticism of the paraphrasable content. The poem makes us aware that the Anglo-Irish poet, whilst likely to brood upon a past that can hardly avoid being mythologized, is, through the longing to escape the treacherous contradictions of the present, always likely to be drawn, however sardonically, to the utopian.

Yeats's early poetry stands at a haunting remove from the Irish myths he celebrates in English. In 'The Celtic Element in Literature' (1902) he asserted his belief that 'the Irish legends move among known woods and seas, and have so much of a new beauty, that they may well give the opening century its most memorable symbols'.[18] Yet he had to endure charges of so-called 'West-Britonism' brought against him by uncompromising nationalists, even as a younger Yeats had not been above abusing others for belonging to 'the shoddy society of "West Britonism"'.[19] His own self-positioning in relation to debates about 'De-Anglicization' and the Irish language shows a twisting complexity that runs parallel with his gyring political views about Ireland. Wearing his neo-Fenian garb, he attacked Gavan Duffy in the 1890s battle over the nature of a new Irish Literary Club on account of Duffy's 'old quarrel with John Mitchel'.[20] More circumspectly, he asked in 1892 whether it might be possible to 'build a national tradition, a national literature which shall be none the less Irish in spirit from being English in language?'[21] But his distaste for modes of uncompromising nationalism would also make itself increasingly felt in the years to come.

MacDonagh's sneer at the figure of 'Clooth-na-Bare' in 'The Hosting of the Sidhe' ('The word *clooth* is not Irish; it has no meaning'[22]) is only a subtler version of the view

---

[15] Yeats, *Variorum Poems*, 289–90.

[16] Thomas MacDonagh, *Literature in Ireland: Studies Irish and Anglo-Irish* (London: Fisher Unwin, 1916), 51.

[17] Yeats, *Variorum Poems*, 347–8.

[18] Yeats, *Major Works*, 378.

[19] See Foster, *W. B. Yeats: A Life*, vol. 1, 235, 53.

[20] The phrase is T. W. Rolleston's, quoted in Foster, *W. B. Yeats: A Life*, vol. 1, 124.

[21] Quoted in Declan Kiberd, *Inventing Ireland: The Literature of the Modern Nation* (London: Jonathan Cape, 1995), 155. See also Kiberd's chapter on 'Deanglicization' [*sic*] in this work for a sympathetic and suggestive overview of the thought of Douglas Hyde, the movement's great champion, 136–54.

[22] MacDonagh, *Literature in Ireland*, 51.

that Yeats's evocation of 'Irish legends' was self-serving or hostile to the interests of the true 'Gael'. An account of Yeats's reading of 'The Hosting of the Sidhe' at the Poetry Bookshop in London around 1912 is relevant in this context:

> From the workshop next door came the muffled beat of the gold-beaters' mallets. A ripple of expectation ran through the packed audience, then a deep expectant hush as the poet stood silent for a moment framed in the candlelight against the dark curtain, a tall dark romantic figure with a dreamy, inward look on his pale face. He began softly, almost chanting, 'The Hosting of the Sidhe', his silvery voice gradually swelling up to the final solemn finale.[23]

Was the London audience in the presence of genuine poetic magic or pseudo-Celtic hocus-pocus? Did those 'gold-beaters' belong to the 'pavements grey' ('The Lake Isle of Innisfree') of the empire's capital city? Or were they proleptic attendant spirits from Yeats's own future city of the imagination, Byzantium? The 'tall romantic figure' who was arguably taking in his audience was always taking them on, too. 'The Hosting of the Sidhe' confronted its readers or listeners with a spellbinding chant that proclaimed the value and intensity of a culture whose very place names and mythological figures would puzzle as well as intrigue an ear trained on, say, Tennyson's *Idylls of the King*:

> The host is riding from Knocknarea
> And over the grave of Clooth-na-Bare;
> Caoilte tossing his burning hair,
> And Niamh calling *Away, come away:*
> *Empty your heart of its mortal dream...*[24]

Clooth-na-Bare may be a form of cod Gaelic, but its three syllables effectively estrange; and if, like the rest of the poem, they confront the rational mind with a species of esoteric, supposedly 'Celtic' lore, Yeats's strongest desire is to suggest that such lore is itself a particular example of the 'passions and beliefs of ancient times' by which literature must be 'constantly flooded', if it is not to dwindle 'to a mere chronicle of circumstance, or passionless phantasies, and passionless meditations'.[25] Caoilte and Niamh—warrior and beautiful woman—are Yeats's Irish versions of Achilles and Helen, in touch with the universal, or, at any rate, international, even as they link literature with nationality. Niamh's hypnotizing, energized 'calling' cries out against its apparent escapism; it bids the reader *'Empty your heart of its mortal dream'*, rebuking attachment to the world, but also passionately if implicitly advocating a staunchly anti-materialist, anti-commercial ethic. In doing so, her words, unworldly as they may seem, pose a challenge to the British government from which Yeats would receive a Civil List pension and also to all government. It is not a poem that is designed to appease any nascent Sinn Fein aspirations, blowing, as it does, with its own cold, unlamenting loneliness from a desolate place within the poet's consciousness.

---

[23] Foster, *W. B. Yeats: A Life*, vol. 1, 474.
[24] Yeats, *Variorum Poems*, 140–1.
[25] Yeats, *Major Works*, 376.

It does evoke a collective force in its reference to the 'sidhe', the faery people of the wind, at once embodiments of occult powers supplying the poet with necessary, dangerous inspiration and spectral armies in the air: 'The host is rushing 'twixt night and day,/ And where is there hope or deed as fair?' From the long perspective of Yeats's entire career, the poem intimates that the closest the poet might come to fulfilment of cultural hope or satisfactory political action is in a poetic utterance such as itself. We tread carefully in *The Wind among the Reeds* (1899) because we tread on the poet's dreams of an Ireland yet to be, but an Ireland dependent for that future on the continued life of 'sweet everlasting Voices'[26] from the Irish past: voices that communicate in English, but English used in an 'Irish way'.

In 'Nineteen Hundred and Nineteen',[27] *The Tower* (1928) spirals out of the sacred city of Byzantium towards which it sails in the volume's opening poem and into the violent chaos of recent Irish history. Yeats confronts what the poem presents as a seemingly inevitable conflict: seemingly inevitable in that revivalist aspirations and Anglo-Irish accommodations seem now to be so many futile 'pretty dreams'. Taking as his local instantiation of conflict the guerrilla warfare between the Irish Republican Army and the Black and Tans, Yeats articulates one of his most artistically poised and terrifying visions of apocalypse, captured in the central line, 'Herodias' daughters have returned again', where 'returned again' captures the stealthy, nightmarish fact of recurrence recurring. Herodias's daughters ride on the wind, manifestations of the hosting of the Sidhe at their most haunting.

In a poem about returns, it is a grimly appropriate irony that Yeats should return to his former poetic self. Whereas the Sidhe in the earlier poem serve as befitting emblems of resistance to any 'mortal dream', Herodias' daughters represent the succumbing of the mortal world to forces best explained for Yeats through references to an early fourteenth-century witch and her incubus. Earlier Celtic images had been the ground for a new vision that would redefine Matthew Arnold's attribution of magic to the Celtic. Arnold's comment (for example) that 'The Celt is not melancholy, as Faust or Werther are melancholy, from "a perfectly definite motive," but because of something about him "unaccountable, defiant and titanic"' provokes a double response in Yeats. He quotes and writes of such remarks in 'The Celtic Element in Literature': 'it is well to consider them a little, and see where they are helpful and where they are hurtful', offsetting this diplomatic balance with a sudden revelation of what is at stake in the attempt to wrest the power of naming from a well-meaning but unwittingly patronizing ally: 'If we do not, we may go mad some day, and the enemy root up our rose-garden and plant a cabbage-garden instead.'[28]

When the world did go mad, Yeats concedes and reacts indomitably against 'the despotism of fact' by still keeping the 'folk tradition' to the fore, but making it the vehicle for a vision of nightmare.[29] The tripled sestets of the last section of 'Nineteen Hundred and

---

[26] 'The Everlasting Voices', *Variorum Poems*, 141.
[27] Ibid., 428–33.
[28] Yeats, *Major Works*, 370.
[29] Ibid., 370, 373.

Nineteen' revolve round and round as they bring before us a revelation of where the dream of a new Irish culture inflecting itself through English had reached. Yeats opens the section with a cool, even laconic control as, we are half-persuaded, the images well up from *Spiritus Mundi*: 'Violence upon the roads: violence of horses'. It is that second 'violence' that connects the world of modern atrocities 'upon the roads' to a 'tumult of images', at the centre of which are the 'horses' ridden by 'Herodias' daughters'. The sequence's predecessor, 'Meditations in Time of Civil War',[30] similarly moves between the brutally factual—'Last night they trundled down the road/That dead young soldier in his blood'—and the poet's inner phantasmagoria, dominated by what, there, more self-deprecatingly, he calls 'The half-read wisdom of daemonic images'. Herodias' daughters have stepped out of the shadows of Mallarméan Symbolism and Wildean Decadence to insist on their relevance to the modern. And yet, amidst the rubble of hopes and the destruction of dreams, poetic form, in the shape of sturdily withstanding yet continually modified structures, asserts a value still available to the poet in his 'ghostly solitude'. Yeats's project, at the heart of his Anglo-Irish poetic identity, of welding the present to the past, refashioning both in the same act, finds an objective correlative in his ability to find imaginative (if little other) 'purpose in the labyrinth of the wind'.

That labyrinthine wind serves as an image of Yeats's powerfully appalled vision of history as its plot had unfolded itself in his own country. If a labyrinth implies entrance into criss-crossing pathways of allegiance and hatred, the wind that composes its being implies a force at odds with human constructions. Its manifestations in this final section deal a blow to the emblem of adversity that Yeats has shaped in the third section of the sequence. There, Yeats accepts with haughty grandeur ('I am satisfied with that') the comparison of 'solitary soul' and 'swan'; he accepts it only if the image enacts his need for a visualized drama corresponding to the tensions he experiences as a 'solitary' figure facing historical chaos, a drama that would present him with 'The wings half spread for flight,/The breast thrust out in pride/Whether to play, or to ride/Those winds that clamour of approaching night'. Such an image of 'pride' is itself 'troubled', and the 'winds' that the 'solitary soul' might 'ride' have the stanza's final words as they 'clamour of approaching night'.

By the close of the section, the solitary individual, refigured in a less haughty fashion when Yeats refers to his 'laborious life', has given way to a more collective helplessness: Yeats is part of a community (which includes the Anglo-Irish helpers of his youthful dreams) that 'now/That winds of winter blow/Learn that we were crack-pated when we dreamed'. The 'laborious' uses of 'that' imply a painful process of adjusting to facts; 'crack-pated' recalls the idiom of Shakespeare's Fool in *King Lear*. The word rebukes not only the dreams of a new, harmonious Ireland but also the section's earlier assumption of a heroic posture (in the image of the swan ready 'to ride/Those winds that clamour of approaching night'). The 'winds of winter' turn into 'that foul storm' in the fifth section, and thence into the 'labyrinth of the wind' that the poet calls up, is caught up in, confronts, and from which, at the close, he seeks to win some clarity of vision when the final

---

[30] Yeats, *Variorum Poems*, 417–27.

sestet begins, 'But now wind drops…' . If all that emerges is the shambling figure of Robert Artisson, the sense of a lonely power at work in the poet's 'secret meditation' is unsubduable.

In its interplay between its sections, between other poems in *The Tower*, and between earlier poems such as 'The Hosting of the Sidhe', the final section of 'Nineteen Hundred and Nineteen' shows in action what Yeats means by speaking of the poet as engaged in a continual remaking of the self. This remaking flaunts, in post-Wildean fashion, a range of performative possibilities. But, more centrally, it is a condition enjoined on Yeats by his struggle to explore what it means to be 'Anglo-Irish', a struggle evident in an earlier poem, 'To Ireland in the Coming Times'.[31] This poem, originally published under the more explicitly self-justifying and therefore self-betraying title 'Apologia to Ireland in the Coming Days', begins by asserting the poet's wish for brotherhood with '*a company/That sang, to sweeten Ireland's wrong,/Ballad and story, rann and song*'. The lines speak of Yeats's desire to be part of a larger poetic '*company*' and to connect his work to the traditional genres mentioned in the last line, including the Irish '*rann*', or 'verse'. But just as '*rann*' is both part of the poem's diction and consciously alienated from it, so Yeats is alert to the dialectic involved in longing for kinship, a dialectic that involves apartness, one half-conceded in the opening line's conditional tense: '*Know, that I would accounted be*'. Roy Foster understandably reads the poem as 'a manifesto' that fused 'occultism and advanced nationalism', but if the poem 'announced [Yeats's] arrival as a frankly political poet',[32] it invites us to read it as a manifesto that is self-searching and inward, one that is exploring as well as expounding what it might mean to be a 'political poet'. The poem shifts from appeal—'*Nor may I less be counted one/With Davis, Mangan, Ferguson*'—to a mode of address that is at once competitively assertive ('*My rhymes more than their rhyming tell/Of things discovered in the deep,/Where only body's laid asleep*'), and aimed at an audience yet to be brought into being: '*I cast my heart into my rhymes,/That you, in the dim coming times,/May know how my heart went with them/After the red-rose-bordered hem*'. The poetry seeks to unite Yeats's occult explorations, '*things discovered in the deep*', with a new Irish national consciousness imaged by the rose. But its sinuous, at times slightly convoluted syntax bears witness to the difficulty of satisfying all parties and impulses.

Yeats's occultism tugs itself back into the mainstream of the Romantic visionary tradition when in '*only body's laid asleep*' he echoes Wordsworth's evocation in 'Lines Written a Few Miles above Tintern Abbey' of the state in which 'we are laid asleep/In body, and become a living soul'.[33] But it un-anchors itself from the Wordsworthian in the next line's reference to '*elemental creatures*', originally '*elemental beings*'. The change from '*beings*' to '*creatures*' feels like a puckish revolt against high Romantic vision in favour of a dancingly light Rosicrucianism that brings Pope's *The Rape of the Lock* to mind. Yet its high

---

[31] Ibid., 137–9.
[32] *W. B. Yeats: A Life: 1*, 122, 123.
[33] Quoted in *William Wordsworth: The Major Works*, Oxford Authors, ed. Stephen Gill (1984; Oxford: Oxford University Press, 2000), 131–5.

spirits refuse to settle for the mock-heroic. Yeats is restlessly assertive in relation to a multifaceted English poetic tradition. At the same time he is impishly if gravely confident of his superiority as a poet to the Irish tradition in which he positions himself. Ultimately, his is a perilously liminal and solitary space, one in which his greatest poetry would often flourish. The wording of '*my heart went with them*' implies that the poet was led by his feelings to follow '*them*', but when one tries to gloss '*them*' a short-circuiting occurs that leads us back to '*my rhymes*' rather than, say, Davis, Mangan, Ferguson, even as that latter possibility is not wholly cancelled.

Anglo-Irish poetry comes fully of age in Yeats's 'Easter, 1916'.[34] This poem about the birth of 'A terrible beauty' treats the reincarnation of 'Romantic Ireland' as a force to be reckoned with, not simply in nationalist myth, but in the midst of Dublin's 'grey/ Eighteenth-century houses'. The tortuous publication history of the poem may tell a complex story of rival allegiances. Whenever it was published it would have troubled the minds of those longing for simplified positions. Maud Gonne—'No I don't like your poem, it isn't worthy of you & above all it isn't worthy of the subject'—managed to illuminate the poem's excellence in the act of articulating her blindness to it.[35] The poem itself contrives to be impassioned and doubting, eloquently honouring the 'sacrifice' made by the patriots while hinting that the lure of sacrifice can only too easily turn a heart to stone.

That Yeats has Gonne in mind as he plots his ambivalent responses to an event that would decisively alter the nature of Irish history makes her dismissal of the poem more complexly ironic. Terence Brown sees Gonne as the poem's 'presiding spirit' and relates the implied image of 'the stone of the fanatic heart' to Yeats's earlier journal comment that 'Women, because the main event of their lives has been a giving of themselves, give themselves to an opinion as if [it] were some terrible stone doll.' Before making this remark, Yeats has just given cautious approval to the fact that 'Maud Gonne writes that she is learning Gaelic.'[36] Gonne's fervent nationalism, the poem might make us feel as a subtext, is a terrifying, sublime muse of history working on and through figures such as Padraic Pearse and James Connolly. If Con Markiewicz is a screen-figure for Gonne ('That woman's days were spent/In ignorant good-will'), she is calculatedly denied the force that Yeats senses at work in history. It is, for the poet and poem, as though events were being shaped in accord with and 'Transformed utterly' by a power that is mesmerically close to an incarnation of Gonne's will to change.

The poem is coerced by events to acknowledge the triumph of Gonne's vision and to imply the limits of the poet's earlier ironizing critique of his fellow Dubliners as living 'where motley is worn'. Yet 'Easter, 1916' realizes, too, the limits of simple celebration: its defence of the 'living stream' against the troubling 'stone' of sacrifice suggests a preference for an idea of being Irish that avoids the impassioned extremes of the revolutionary

---

[34] Yeats, *Variorum Poems*, 391–4.

[35] Quoted from *The Poems of W. B. Yeats*, ed. Michael O'Neill (London: Routledge, 2004), 35.

[36] Brown, *Life of W B. Yeats*, 231, and *Memoirs: Autobiography—First Draft, Journal*, ed. Denis Donoghue (London: Macmillan, 1972), which is quoted in Brown, 231.

extremist; and its hedging of bets even as the poem builds to a final climax is striking. 'England may keep faith/For all that is done and said' reminds Yeats's readers that Home Rule had been granted in law if not put into effect (because of the First World War), and casts doubt, too, on the absolute accuracy of the deeds and words of those who mistrust England. It is the passage in the poem that most clearly speaks of Yeats's divided allegiances, or indeed his allegiance to the fact of division. George Cusack has recently applied Hazard Adams's idea of 'antitheticality' to Yeats's drama and his wish to 'resist all political agendas, thereby providing a constant impetus for change and preventing any ideology from gaining complete dominance': the passage Cusack quotes from Adams argues suggestively in relation to Yeats's Blakean mode of thought that 'To grasp antitheticality is to grasp that there are three sides to every argument' and that Yeats wished to 'maintain continual active tension with the negations current in culture'.[37]

Yeats maintains a 'continual active tension' of this kind in 'Easter 1916' by positioning himself with troubled, impassioned awareness between modes and idioms. 'For England may keep faith/For all that is done and said' cleverly reverses the usual phrase 'said and done', a phrase which implies that the talking is now over; Yeats sounds as though he is repeating this idea, but 'done and said' implies the impulse to go on speaking about the Rising after it has happened, suggesting that many more words will be uttered about its politico-historical significance. Moreover, the revision from the first printing's 'For all she had done and said'[38] tilts the line in the direction of a more detached perspective, since it concedes the possibility of incomplete utterance and action from others beside 'England' (the 'she' of the first printing). At the same time, Yeats is able to strike, or seemingly strike, a boldly nationalist note in 'Wherever green is worn', but only after he has dealt the 'dream' wounds that are the more penetrating for being inflicted in a spirit of near-reverent compassion: 'We know their dream; enough/To know they dreamed and are dead;/And what if excess of love/Bewildered them till they died?' Yeats's Anglo-Irish ambivalences come to a focus in and run their course between those two uses of 'know': the first rational and detached from, the second emotionally entangled in, the 'dream'. And the attempt to allay questioning in 'enough/To know' works only for a moment. The next impulse is to pose a 'what if' question which prompts a double response: namely that, for the revolutionaries to be 'Bewildered', 'makes no odds' and 'matters a great deal'. Louis MacNeice, a poet whose own career plays with antinomies in a way that links and contrasts with Yeats's practice, hears the tone of these lines as 'slightly patronizing and at the same time envious'.[39] His comment attunes itself shrewdly to the play of tones in the original. Yeats struggles to do justice to those who sacrificed themselves for a 'dream' (much as he was only too aware a poet might) and not to be wholly caught up in an event that may 'after all' have

---

[37] George Cusack, *The Politics of Identity in Irish Drama: W. B. Yeats, Augusta Gregory and J. M. Synge* (New York: Routledge, 2009), 44. Hazard Adams is quoted on the same page from his 'Yeats and Antithetical Nationalism', in *Yeats's Political Identities: Selected Essays*, 309–24, ed. Jonathan Allison (Ann Arbor: University of Michigan Press, 1996), 311.

[38] Yeats, *Variorum Poems*, 394.

[39] Louis MacNeice, *The Poetry of W. B. Yeats* [1941] (London: Faber, 1967), 118.

been 'needless'. What MacNeice implicitly allows for is a refusal by the poem to cede prec-
edence to history as some supposed objective reality, and in his dealings with the chal-
lenges and burdens of writing an Anglo-Irish poetry Yeats never loses sight of the
significance of his belief that 'Active virtue, as distinguished from the passive acceptance
of a code, is . . . theatrical, consciously dramatic, the wearing of a mask'.[40]

III

Alan Gillis has written trenchantly of Austin Clarke as the author of poems 'coiling
around the schism between reason and faith until they choke', noting that, for all its air
of escapist archaism, Clarke's 'Irish mode was meant as a modernizing force'.[41] Clarke,
indeed, engages with his version of the Anglo-Irish predicament in tormented, and, *pace*
the scorn of Samuel Beckett who caricatures the poet in *Murphy*, compelling ways.[42]
Writing in English, Clarke brings to bear on his use of language the full weight of his
apprehension of Irish history and culture. He found inspiration in 'the Celtic
Romanesque era' and his poetry is distinguished by its adaptation of Gaelic metrical
forms, including subtle patternings of sound and rhymes that often avoid accentual
chimes, tricking the ear to expressive effect.[43] A Clarke poem builds its artistic identity
around the beauty to be found in dissonance; it is rarely other than a system of latent
disharmonies richly yet frustratedly yearning for a final aesthetic and experiential
harmony.

Clarke's response to the poetry of the Irish Literary Revival, especially that written by
Yeats, was complicated; he admired its escape 'from the mighty law and order of English
poetry into [a] shadowy, irresponsible world of delicate rhythm and nuance', but he felt
that it finally retreated from the Irish subject matter which he wished to address, partic-
ularly what he called 'the drama of racial conscience'. Central to this 'drama', for Clarke,
was the struggle between sexual instinct (occasionally the source of joy, more often of
anguish) and regulatory control, and between different modes of Catholic Christianity,
varying in their degree of tolerance and intolerance.[44] The drama is at the heart of
Pilgrimage (1929), a volume that explores subjects from the Irish past that have 'imagi-
native parallels for his own time'.[45] It is a volume that seeks, as does much of Clarke's

---

[40] Yeats, *Major Works*, 413–14.
[41] Alan Gillis, *Irish Poetry of the 1930s* (Oxford: Oxford University Press, 2005), 87, 80.
[42] By 'Anglo-Irish' in Clarke's case, I refer to the fact that he is an Irish poet writing in English. The
use of the same term in relation to Yeats refers to the same predicament, but it carries with it a further
political and historical charge, suggesting the poet's eventual if never uncomplicated siding with the
so-called 'Protestant Ascendancy'.
[43] Austin Clarke, *Collected Poems*, ed. R. Dardis Clarke (Manchester: Carcanet, 2008), 541.
[44] Quoted from Maurice Harmon, *Austin Clarke: A Critical Introduction* (Dublin: Wolfhound Press,
1989), 19, 60.
[45] Ibid., 60.

poetry in different ways, to answer his own question in a letter to Seamus O'Sullivan: 'Yeats, in transforming himself into a world poet, has left the Irish Revival baby on the doorstep, and the question is what are we to do with it'?[46]

The repressive attitude to sexuality enjoined by monastic Catholicism internalizes itself in the speaker of 'Celibacy', a poem in *Pilgrimage*, an effect reinforced through the chime between the end of one line and the middle of the next: 'I groaned/On the flagstone of help/To pluck her from my body'.[47] Yet if this self-torture seems the agonized or satirized default position of many poems, Clarke can glimpse momentary healings of the wound of division. In the same collection he offers, in 'The Planter's Daughter', a delicate marriage between the 'beauty' of the woman and the admiration of the community. He does so in a lyric that sings with a grave simplicity, relishing its vowel music: 'few in the candlelight/Thought her too proud,/For the house of the planter/is known by the trees'.[48] The heavy stresses interspersed with lilting trisyllabic feet create their own upbeat version of the locked-in tensions characteristic of Clarke's more sombre, self-manacled poetry.

Here a release is imagined; the 'Men that had seen her' may have been 'silent', but the echoic chiming of 'silent' with 'planter' and 'went' prepares us for the joyous flutter of exclamatory eloquence with which the poem concludes: 'And O she was the Sunday/In every week'. If ever a poem interceded between and conciliated opposites, 'the planter's daughter' and 'a crowd', privilege and lack of privilege, beauty and ordinariness, even, however precariously, the colonial and the colonized, it is this one. Comparable if austere strains of celebration are at work in 'Aisling', also from *Pilgrimage*, though this poem draws from its female muse, seen in poetic vision, an altogether less comforting message about the possibility of dwelling. She tells of 'peace', gathered 'Companies', and 'storytelling', but also of 'strangers' who 'leave upon the oar', and she induces in the poet a premonition of his alienated status: 'O must I wander/Without praise, without wine, in rich strange lands?'[49] The ending leaves the poet on Irish soil ('the coldness of Mount Brandon'), but it brings home to him his role as steward of an Irish mode deserted by its presiding muse: 'the secret woman left me'.

Clarke's Anglo-Irish muse was frequently at odds with the pieties of the Irish Free State, and he has fun in later work at the expense of, say, the Christian Brother who, in 'Another Protestant Insult' (1968): 'Half-doored himself in surprise before he could say a Hail Mary,/As he backed from an opened page, exclaiming in rage, "Another/Protestant insult to Our Lady"'.[50] Clarke is alive to betrayals, let-downs, hyprocrisies, the grubby compromises that banish ideals. But he is also the poet of the 'rich strange lands' of modernity's commerce with the past, in pursuit of the liberating, not restricting, 'Sunday/In every week'. This pursuit is interlaced with irony, to be sure, in a poem such

---

[46] Ibid., 76.
[47] Clarke, *Collected Poems*, 153.
[48] Ibid., 169.
[49] Ibid. 170–1.
[50] Ibid. 467–9.

as 'Martha Blake' (1938), a work in which the very sound arrangements bring out, as Donald Davie has brilliantly shown, a complexity of response. Davie argues that Clarke 'feels along with Martha Blake the whole way; and the only sign that he is also detached from her, feeling for her and about her as well as with her (feeling for instance that she does not understand how spiritual experience *must* be mediated through the senses) is in the calculated harshness with which from time to time the cadence is blocked from providing the reader with the pleasure it has led him to expect.'[51]

This judgement is superbly attuned to Clarke's practice. However, one might wish to place the tonal emphasis slightly differently. The poem's irony subdues itself. Yes, there is a flaring of the near-satirical at the close, when Martha is said to be 'ignorant of all the rest,/The hidden grace' of ordinariness.[52] Yet the poem has the grace to concede the authenticity of her delight in the Eucharist. Davie's reading is more certain in its assumption that Martha does not understand 'how spiritual experience *must* be mediated through the senses' than is warranted by Clarke's glimpse of a reconciliation between sense and spirit. In the following lines 'lying' implies critique, but the Crashaw-like exuberance of the writing momentarily puts chary detachment out of countenance, without putting it wholly to flight. Here, as in his greatest poetry, Clarke sees experience as riddled by the divisions that are part of his Anglo-Irish predicament, but the impulse to celebrate is only half-blocked by his ironizing intelligence: 'Her soul is lying in the Presence/Until her senses, one/By one, desiring to attend her,/Come as for feast...'. Irony is evident, as it is even more so in the later 'Martha Blake at Fifty-One', where the poem's 'last breath', like the woman's, is 'disappointed'.[53] But the earlier poem, in particular, refuses merely to dismiss Martha's experience, and is alive to the significance of the rhyme between 'Presence' and 'senses'.

In 'The Flock at Dawn' (1960) Clarke writes with the satirically embittered yet virtuosic anxiety typical of the poetry he published towards the end of his career, asserting: 'The English language/Was loopholed here for centuries.'[54] The surprising 'loopholed' implies the 'loophole' through which Irishness, that elusive category, revealed itself. Yet the following 'But' suggests that the colonizing genius of Spenser (the 'Edmund' who 'jumped the wave-tops') resulted in a shaming defeat for Irish literature: 'We lost', Clarke continues, 'in that war of words. The syllables /Which measure all delight; mouth-exile. Scansion's /Our darling fondled over sea.'[55] It is typical of Clarke to fight that lost 'war of words' over again in a poetry that enacts, in its assonantal savouring, both a pleasure in words and a bitter awareness of 'mouth-exile'.

If poetry is made from the quarrel with the self, Clarke's poetry thrives on its torn and riven relationship with its own medium. English is reworked through his sonic elaborations to declare the presence within it of an estranged Irish muse and music. His notes to

[51] Donald Davie, 'Austin Clarke and Padraic Fallon', *Poetry Nation* 3 (1974), 89.

[52] Clarke, *Collected Poems*, 184–5.

[53] Ibid., 269–74.

[54] Ibid., 229–31.

[55] For discussion of Clarke's technique and his attempt to fight against the 'mouth-exile' experienced by Irish poets, see Harmon, *Austin Clarke*, 21–7.

his poetry reveal his nuanced allegiance to the ideas of Thomas MacDonagh, whom he worked with at University College Dublin and replaced, albeit for a short-lived period, after MacDonagh was executed following the Easter Rising. 'Assonance,' Clarke comments in a note to *Pilgrimage*, 'more elaborate in Gaelic than in Spanish poetry, takes the clapper from the bell of rhyme....Unfortunately the internal patterns of assonance and consonance in Gaelic stanzas are so intricate that they can only be suggested in another language.'[56] The note reclaims Gaelic poetry from obscurity and endows it with scholarly prestige, but it does so in the spirit of elegy, and with the strong suggestion that the writer is going against the grain in writing in English.

In 'Vanishing Irish' (1955) the title's adjective implies the process of losing rather than the fact of loss, and the poem is more affecting for not straightforwardly dwelling on loss; it is principally the past tense of the opening that alerts us to the poem's concern with cultural attrition as a result of linguistic 'vanishing': 'Poverty drew lip down and yet there was laughter /In that raggedness of ours. Blind Raftery, /Who knew man's charges are both long and short, /Clapped heat to the touch-hole of the mighty mortar /Once.'[57] The language is packed and requires unpacking, even as it maintains what Gillis calls 'a po-faced surface.'[58] One might wish to point to the effect, at once intimate and unforthcoming, created by the conspiratorial use of 'ours', or indeed, by the dislocating rhyming (the first syllable of 'laughter' picked up by the first syllable of 'Raftery') as a result of which a straggling sense of incompleteness accompanies the forceful echoic thump: it is as though Clarke were finding an equivalent in sound for the assertion made of Raftery—true, too, one feels, of (and for) the twentieth-century poet—that 'His only belongings were longings'. Typical of Clarke also is the compressed and punning metaphor involved in 'charges'. These charges might be explosive when delivered by a 'mighty mortar'. Twinning with that meaning is the notion of a political or revolutionary 'charge', induced perhaps after 'charges'—of oppressive government, say—had been levelled. But ghosting the word is the sense of 'charges' as 'wards', those one is charged to look after, bringing into play the filial and ancestral obligations felt by and imposed on a poet who might be thinking, as possibly 'Blind Raftery' was, of his legacy for later poets, his 'charges'.

'Vanishing Irish' affects because it is in stubborn, inward turmoil. Clarke may know of Raftery's 'longings', semi-rhyming them with 'Hugs, squeezes, kisses, a hundred thousand strong', turning longing into an erotic desire for kinship with all the details of experience offered by his country. But he asks immediately, 'And how can I tell of his journey?' The Blind Raftery, who 'made the song' that Yeats draws on for quasi-Homeric if embittered inspiration in 'The Tower', has become, for Clarke, both a double and an opaque other. How can he tell of his journey since it is too painfully close to the bone and too distant, unrecapturable when spoken of outside a language, Gaelic, in which Clarke is not writing and that his audience is not reading?[59] 'Our silence now/Is beyond the aim of

---

[56] Clarke, *Collected Poems*, 544.
[57] Ibid., 204.
[58] Gillis, *Irish Poetry of the 1930s*, 78.
[59] Yeats, *Variorum Poems*, 411.

words and telltale frowned on', he comments wryly. Yet the wryness is not without a positive dimension, bringing out how in a Clarke poem each new impulsion of phrasing and verbal trickery can redirect. Here 'Our silence' takes on the status of a near-absolute, the Anglo-Irish poet's equivalent of a word-defeating Logos, as well as pointing towards absolute loss. It releases, though, an impish, exilic humour: so, 'telltale frowned on' uses English words, but the idiom is crankily and jauntily at odds with mainstream English speech. It is as though the phrase were alluding to the fragmentary survival of the past through oral culture, with its 'telltale' recollections, and mimicking those who 'frowned on' the residue of Raftery's culture.

Irish, then, is 'vanishing', not quite vanished; its persistence as a cultural force is both near-fiction and obdurate if nostalgic longing, a doubling mirrored by the poem's mixture of arch wit and avoidance of respectability, and manifest in the last six lines' sudden eruption of down-at-mouth, darkly comic energy. The lines begin 'Somewhere, the last of our love-songs found a refuge'. If they locate this refuge 'Perhaps in the hall of Rhadamanthus', stern and unbending judge of the dead, they revitalize the last love song's post-mortal life in the image of 'the comeback of its fol-de-rol/Skipping around the monstrous, unseen columns', and grant it freedom 'from our burden of bad thoughts and gloating'. Our 'burden' suggests a different, anxiety-laden poetry, and it is the excellence of the poem to convey such a burden through its own burdened rhetoric and rhyming, yet to unshackle itself from its own imposed chains.

For Clarke, the Yeatsian bequest was an early source of inspiration and a subsequent prompt for often though not solely embattled opposition. At the same time Clarke makes fine poetry out of his ability to check the impulse to quarrel with Yeats. After all, the poets had, if not 'one sap and one root',[60] then a shared awareness of the need to tap into two saps and two roots. Yeats's experimentations with rhythm in 'The Lake Isle of Innisfree' won Thomas MacDonagh's approval as a poem that resisted 'English' scansion and demanded to be read 'as if it were a line of prose, only with that beauty of vibration in the voice which goes with the fine grave words of poetry'.[61] MacDonagh and Clarke recognized, with whatever reservations, a forerunnner in Yeats.

Clarke's 'In the Savile Club' (1968) mimics the senior poet's high self-regard as 'he stood, respectful, for a few/Moments before himself', the line-ending tumbling into an abyss of implicit bathos.[62] But for all its digs and subversions the poem suggests a fascination with Yeats's poetry, its ability to emerge resiliently from 'Reality' with 'exquisite/Love lyrics'. That resilience finds an echo in Clarke's own wincing verve and sardonic, weighted buoyancy, and offers a pointer towards the enduring significance of poems that dwell always in two places at once. In 'The Echo at Coole', Clarke subtly reprises his themes of alienation, doubt, and commitment to poetry as he recalls a visit to Coole.[63] The 'catalpa' celebrated by Yeats had put forth 'blooms that had lost their seed/And

---

[60] Ezra Pound, 'A Pact', *Selected Poems* (London: Faber, 1948), 97.
[61] MacDonagh, *Literature in Ireland*, 67–8.
[62] Clarke, *Collected Poems*, 396–8.
[63] Ibid., 398–9.

names in lengthy Latin': an emblem, perhaps, of Irish poetic losses sustained at the hands of an imperial tongue.

Yet Yeats is more than a magnificent wrong turning; he also makes poetry possible for his successors, who in their turn work to complete or take in new directions what Clarke calls his predecessor's 'unfinished/Poem'. Clarke ingeniously responds to lines that Yeats wrote for a draft of 'A Prayer for my Daughter', 'printed by Jon Stallworthy in *Between the Lines*'.[64] He constructs an updated Renaissance echo-poem that asks, among other things, 'how can I be certain my way is right?', a question earning the answer '*Write*'. The answer is both enabling and indicative of a lonely quest. It implies that there is no alternative to the dilemma of being an Irish poet who writes in English than to continue to explore that dilemma in writing. For both writers, though they wear their rue with a difference, lamenting and unlamenting song derives from the awareness that, as Yeats puts it with definitive clarity in 'A General Introduction for My Work', 'Gaelic is my national language, but it is not my mother tongue.'[65]

---

[64] Ibid., 553.
[65] Yeats, *Major Works*, 385.

PART II

THE POETRY OF WAR

PART II

THE POETICS
OF WAR

CHAPTER 4

....

'THE ROSES ARE TORN':
IRELAND'S WAR POETS

....

JIM HAUGHEY

I

....

For most of the twentieth century, a general drawing-down of blinds prevailed over Ireland's role in the First World War. While Northern Irish unionists commemorated the 36th (Ulster) Division's service to Crown and Empire, across the border, nationalists, eager to promote their own myth of origin, found it politically inexpedient to acknowledge the sacrifices of the thousands of Irishmen who served in the British Army during the conflict. And so began the Great Amnesia whereby the memory of Ireland's war dead was effectively expunged from public memory.[1]

Despite the recent resurgence of interest in Ireland's Great War experience, relatively little has been written about the country's wartime poetry. Subsumed under the misty retrospect of the Irish Literary Revival or tidied away as a minor tributary of Georgian verse, serious study of Ireland's Great War poets has been further handicapped by the misguided notion that war poetry in general is little more than 'a vulgar...version of history'.[2] Of course, Yeats didn't help matters either when he famously pronounced his 'distaste for certain poems written in the midst of the Great War'.[3] The key word here is 'distaste': Yeats didn't so much object to 'war poetry', only war poetry that did not appeal

---

[1] A forgotten war memorial for a forgotten war dead: through years of neglect, the National War Memorial at Islandbridge came to resemble an Ozymandian 'wreck' until renovation in the late 1980s. An official re-dedication didn't take place until July 2006. Though the Memorial lists the total number of Irish war casualties at 49,400, recent estimates favour a more conservative figure of around 35,000.

[2] Edna Longley blames this fallacy on 'modernist-based or -biased criticism'. See *Poetry in the Wars* (Newcastle: Bloodaxe, 1986), 12.

[3] See W. B. Yeats, ed., 'Introduction', in *The Oxford Book of Modern Verse 1892–1935* (Oxford: Clarendon Press, 1936), p. xxxiv.

to his personal aesthetic, an aesthetic more compatible with the heroic ideals of traditional martial verse.

Consequently, as of writing, only two books have been published on Irish poetry of the First World War. Though more preoccupied with how the war is re-imagined in the work of major poets like Yeats, Graves, MacNeice, Mahon, Heaney, and Longley, Fran Brearton's *The Great War in Irish Poetry* (2000) provides an authoritative assessment of how 'Irish involvement in the Great War was, and has remained, a problematical subject', while also noting the 'contradiction' that soldier poets like Francis Ledwidge and Tom Kettle 'sensed in their positions as soldiers in the British Army and Irish writers sympathetic to the nationalist cause'.[4] Meanwhile my own book, *The First World War in Irish Poetry* (2002), surveys the work of over thirty Irish poets in an attempt to understand how Irish war poetry helped shape Irish war memory.[5] But scholars venturing beyond this rather small enclosure of war poetry studies will soon find themselves embarked on a bibliographical treasure hunt,[6] for aside from biographical sketches and commemorative ephemera, most of what has been written about Ireland's Great War poets tends to focus on their engagement with the national question,[7] their representation of the 'conflicting elements in the Irish inheritance',[8] or their deflection of 'the actual experience of war' as a way to cope with a growing sense of 'alienation'.[9] As we shall see, though, deflection and alienation form only a part of the Irish response.

Love of country was the most recurrent theme in the popular war poetry written throughout Europe between 1914 and 1918. Patriotism narcotized the great and the not-so-great, as even poets like Rilke opted for the grand gesture in their early war verse. For many, though, the war offered an opportunity for personal or ideological redemption. Idealization of duty and heroism accompanied lofty Christian imperatives. Recreations of ambrosial pasts and edifying visions of future utopias flooded the public imagination. However, while English war poets sought refuge in pre-war sureties as a way to cope with the conflict's unparalleled horror, the divisive and contentious nature of Irish pre-war memory ruled out any similar consolatory retrospect for Irish war poets. In the absence of a mutually agreed history, Irish war poets looked to landscape,

---

[4] Fran Brearton, *The Great War in Irish Poetry: W. B. Yeats to Michael Longley* (Oxford: Oxford University Press, 2000), 4, 20.

[5] Jim Haughey, *The First World War in Irish Poetry* (London: Associated University Presses, 2002).

[6] Among the more insightful commentaries about the impact of the war on Irish culture is Edna Longley's *The Living Stream: Literature and Revisionism in Ireland* (Newcastle: Bloodaxe, 1994), where she examines how memory of the Easter Rising and the Battle of the Somme has been 'processed by state ideologies', 69. Tilling similar ground, D. G. Boyce explores how memory of the war still plays a role in 'the forging of Irish identities'. See *The Sure Confusing Drum: Ireland and the Great War* (Swansea: University College of Swansea, 1993), 24.

[7] See Declan Kiberd's 'The Great War in Irish Memory', *Inventing Ireland: The Literature of the Modern Nation* (London: Jonathan Cape, 1995).

[8] Seamus Heaney, 'Introduction', in *Francis Ledwidge: Selected Poems*, ed. Dermot Bolger (Dublin: New Island Books, 1992), 19. Terence Brown, 'Writing the War: Our War', in *Ireland and the Great War*, ed. John Horne (Dublin: Royal Irish Academy, 2008), 236–7.

[9] Brown, 'Writing the War: Our War', 236–7.

to redemptive suffering, and to political idealization to create a meta-narrative they hoped could transcend Ireland's religious and political fault lines. But even their modes of speech reveal tensions between subject and expression as the traditional idioms of martial poetry struggle to articulate the indescribable. Nestled among blocs of pastoral rumination or figurative excess, arguments frequently surface with little forewarning. Indeed, contradictory viewpoints often appear in close proximity within the same poem: war is glorified while its suffering is condemned; violence is deplored yet the cause it serves is upheld. The war also provides a platform to air other grievances, both private and public, thus producing a war poetry that can be intensely personal as well as thematically universal.

II

Such tensions are rife in the work of Francis Ledwidge. 'I saw horrors there that must have made the soul of Dante envious,' he wrote in a letter home from the front to his friend Paddy Healy.[10] Yet few of these 'horrors' feature directly in his war poetry, and when he does engage the war, he often oscillates between pro- and anti-war platitude, between reverence for and distrust of the heroic ideal. Such incongruities form inter-changeable parts of his sensibility and identity.

The war, in certain respects, proved a distraction to Ledwidge as a poet, because his preferred subject was the landscape of his native County Meath. This predilection for rural idealism has led some to conclude that his language was 'simply unequipped to describe the horror of the Somme.'[11] Such claims, though, tend to conflate war poetry with reportage, and Ledwidge was not concerned with simply being a reporter. Instead, his poetry is preoccupied by what he wishes to see. This desire to transcend the detritus of war suffuses his war poetry with deflection, pastoral antithesis, metaphoric backdrop, and political ambiguity.

In his letters, Ledwidge appeared to share most of his fellow soldiers' attitudes toward the war: the sense of duty, the call of destiny, the self-assurances that the cause was a just one. But the sentiments expressed in his war poems tend to be more ambivalent. 'Soliloquy', for example, embodies some of the contradictions we now associate with Ledwidge's view of the war.[12] A syntactic *trompe l'oeil*, the poem begins like a wistful bil-dungsroman ('When I was young I had a care/Lest I should cheat me of my share...'), settles us into passive reader mode with its childhood retrospect, then shifts quickly to

[10] Quoted in Hubert Dunn, *The Minstrel Boy: Francis Ledwidge, and the Literature of His Time, Including Six Previously Unpublished Poems* (Dublin: Booklink, 2006), 175.

[11] Dermot Bolger, ed., *The Ledwidge Treasury: Selected Poems of Francis Ledwidge* (Dublin: New Island, 2007), 104.

[12] Francis Ledwidge, *The Complete Poems*, ed. Liam O'Meara (Newbridge, Kildare: Goldsmith Press, 1997), 238.

condemnation. Far from offering redemption or glory, the war assumes an adversarial role but not in the guise we customarily expect (pointless death). Instead, Ledwidge ponders what posterity has in store for him:

> And now I'm drinking wine in France
> The helpless child of circumstance.
> To-morrow will be loud with war,
> How will I be accounted for?

Animated by shifting moods and a peeling away of received ideals, the last lines repeat the pattern of sounding the customary platitude only to repudiate it: 'a soldier's heart,/Is greater than a poet's art/And greater than a poet's fame/A little grave that has no name/Whence honour turns away in shame.' Omitted from the early editions of the *Complete Poems*, presumably because of its repudiation of the martial code, that final line not only confronts the 'old Lie' but also points toward the inadequacy of allegory as 'honour' is reduced to the status of superficial ornamentation.

The Victorians may have lost their enthusiasm for nature as a 'moral/ethical force', but nature for Ledwidge, like his Romantic forebears, is frequently associated with 'positive attributes'.[13] In 'A Soldier's Grave', he embraces nature as guide, nurturer, and final refuge: 'And where the earth was soft for flowers we made/A grave for him that he might better rest.'[14] Flowers crowd Ledwidge's war poems like the 'floral tributes brought to the dead by Theocritan and Virgilian elegy'.[15] Paul Fussell notes that besides providing an imaginative escape, pastoral was 'a way of invoking a code to hint by antithesis at the indescribable'.[16] Antithesis, however, is not Ledwidge's only preoccupation here. There is also empathy for the dead: 'So, Spring shall come and leave it sweet arrayed,/And there the lark shall turn her dewy nest'. Larks, Fussell reminds us, 'were evidence that ecstasy was still an active motif in the universe'.[17] Yet Ledwidge seems less concerned with abstract motifs. For him, the lark signifies the regenerative power of nature.

The ameliorative powers of pastoral are further invoked in one of Ledwidge's last poems. 'Home' reads like just another homesick eclogue.[18] We are in the company of birds again ('A burst of sudden wings at dawn') as Ledwidge's favoured octosyllabics evoke a dream-like cadence. Inversions ('wood-way dim') and alliterations ('mist and murmurings') varnish the poem with Parnassian decorum, but the last four lines disturb the pastoral dreaminess:

> This is a song a robin sang
> This morning on a broken tree,
> It was about the little fields
> That call across the world to me.

---

[13] Bernard Richards, *English Poetry of the Victorian Period, 1830–1890* (London: Longman, 1988), 130.
[14] Ledwidge, *Complete Poems*, 236.
[15] Richards, *English Poetry of the Victorian Period*, 130.
[16] Paul Fussell, *The Great War and Modern Memory* (Oxford: Oxford University Press, 1975), 235.
[17] Ibid., 242.
[18] Ledwidge, *Complete Poems*, 257.

Decamping to more consoling pastures (an act of emotional as well as aesthetic transference), Ledwidge replaces in his mind's eye the ravaged Belgian countryside (the 'broken tree') with memories of an Irish Elysium ('the little fields'). Nature is not so much admired as it is appropriated; visual reinterpretation serves as an act of personal as well as artistic reclamation.

The bloodlines of Ledwidge's war poetry are not exclusively rooted in landscape tradition. He is also capable of evoking the gravitas of classical epic. In 'War', personification endows the poem with narrative immediacy:

> I am love and Hate and the terrible minds
> Of vicious gods, but more am I,
> I am the pride in the lover's eye,
> I am the epic of the sea.[19]

Like Rupert Brooke, '[who] welcomed the coming of war as a chance to escape the depression and mess of his private life', Ledwidge linked his war to the classical age.[20] War is a purgative agent. Its pageantry and drama elevate history to myth, but the literary self-consciousness (Homeric echoes) suggests an aesthetic fidelity also.

At times, Ledwidge is obsessed with *his* place in history, particularly Irish history. Noteworthy for its Gaelic versification (internal rhymes like 'morn'/'thorn'), poetic suffixes ('lamenting inly'/'queenly'), a stylistic tic typical of Parnassian beauty, and standard nationalist tropes, 'The Dead Kings' employs myth and pastoral to link Ireland's Celtic past to the Easter Rebellion:

> And I, too, told the kings a story
> Of later glory, her fourth sorrow:
> There was a sound like moving shields
> In high green fields and the lowland furrow.

Wistful longings for an Irish Arcadia give way to the sound of war:

> And one said: 'A loud tramp of men
> We'll hear again at Rosnaree.'
> A bomb burst near me where I lay.
> I woke, 'twas day in Picardy.[21]

Ledwidge felt regret about the Rising. He struggled to resolve his nationalist sympathies with his British soldier's uniform. He lost friends. He felt politically disconnected. These last two lines form an ironic epilogue. None of the compensatory self-assurances of a Brookean 'foreign field' suffice. Ledwidge anticipates his own historical obsolescence.

Many of his war poems reveal a preoccupation with a broken aesthetic. Images of pastoral decay serve as stand-ins for the war's destruction. In 'Autumn Evening in Serbia', the very language itself seems jaded: 'From the bend of the briar/The roses are torn,/And

---

[19] Ibid., 209.
[20] Paul Delany, *The Neo-Pagans: Friendship and Love in the Rupert Brooke Circle* (London: Macmillan, 1987), 28.
[21] Ledwidge, *Complete Poems*, 230.

the folds of the wood tops/Are faded and worn.'[22] Torn roses, broken trees, implication, and deflection: beauty is transitory, but the desire for transcendence implies that ugliness is transitory also.

Ledwidge's war poems locate oases of coherency and tranquillity, celebrating the restorative powers of pastoral as a salve against the war. But the war also sharpens perception, engendering identity through parochial intimacy. His most effective technique of deflection is achieved in poems that are, on the surface, the least concerned with the war. In 'To One Who Comes Now and Then',[23] written a week before he was killed by shellfire near Ypres (31 July 1917), Ledwidge's tribute to a personal friendship retrospectively takes on greater significance. The war dead speak, imploring us from their soon-to-be constructed avenues of commemorative masonry to always remember:

> Come often, friend; with welcome and surprise
> We'll greet you from the sea or from the town;
> Come when you like and from whatever skies
> Above you smile or frown.

III

In his elegy for Lady Gregory's son, Robert ('In Memory of Major Robert Gregory'), Yeats's eulogistic description of the dead Irish airman ('Our Sidney and our perfect man'), seems most appropriate when describing Tom Kettle. Nationalist politician, intellectual, poet, Kettle was an eyewitness to German atrocities in Belgium in 1914 and believed unequivocally that the war was a just one. Participating in recruitment drives after he received his commission in the Royal Dublin Fusiliers, Kettle reminded his audiences that he was fighting not for King and Country but for a 'free Ireland in a united Europe'.[24] When he was killed during the 10th (Irish) Division's assault on Ginchy in September 1916, he had already predicted his own historical oblivion: 'These men [leaders of the Easter Rising] will go down in history as heroes and martyrs; and I will go down—if I go down at all—as a bloody British officer'.[25]

Like Ledwidge, Kettle is regarded as an historical enigma, someone who transcends Ireland's traditional political divisions. If his reputation as a war poet depended on what he wrote before he left for the front, though, there would be little to commend as most of these poems feature the high-mindedness, swinging rhythms, and imperialist rhetoric of Kiplingesque jingoism.[26] But when he sets affectation aside, Kettle has something

---

[22] Ibid., 153.

[23] Ibid., 256.

[24] Roger McHugh, 'Thomas Kettle and Francis Sheehy-Skeffington', in *The Shaping of Modern Ireland*, ed. Conor Cruise O'Brien (Toronto: University of Toronto Press, 1960), 137.

[25] Quoted in J. B. Lyons, *The Enigma of Tom Kettle: Irish Patriot, Essayist, Poet, British Soldier, 1880–1916* (Dublin: Glendale Press, 1983), 293.

[26] Kettle and Stephen Gwynn published some of their own poems along with a selection of traditional ballads in their co-edited book, *Battle Songs for the Irish Brigades* (Dublin: Maunsel, 1915).

important to say, and nowhere is this more evident than in his best war poem, the son-
net, 'To my Daughter, Betty, the Gift of God'.[27]

In the octet, Kettle writes with one eye on posterity: 'You'll ask why I abandoned you,
my own,/And the dear heart that was your baby throne,/To dice with death.' The sestet
provides the answer:

> So here, while the mad guns curse overhead,
> And tired men sigh with mud for couch and floor,
> Know that we fools, now with the foolish dead,
> Died not for flag, nor King, nor Emperor,
> But for a dream, born in a herdsman's shed,
> And for the secret Scripture of the poor.

In the space of six lines, Kettle takes us from the terror of the front (the haunting per-
sonification of 'the mad guns') to the Christian altruism of that beautiful final sentiment.
In response to poet Padraic Colum's charge that Kettle fought for the wrong cause,
Kettle's wife Mary responded that her husband 'died most nobly for the cause of Irish
Nationality, in dying for the cause of European honour'.[28] But the note of self-depreca-
tion ('we fools') suggests that Kettle, despite his attempt to ennoble the war by proclaim-
ing it as a struggle to save civilization, knew he would be harshly judged by the nationalist
version of Irish history. Combining self-eulogy with historical resignation, Kettle lays a
wreath not just for his own brand of nationalism but for all mankind.

IV

The typical trench poem possesses 'a strong element of the shock-horror style...and a
hammer-blow final line that takes a conventional stab at patriotism'.[29] But many trench
poems are anything but anti-patriotic. Instead, homesickness, 'cheerful endurance', and
a general 'grumbling' about life at the front tend to be the most recurring preoccupa-
tions.[30] Nowhere are these sentiments more visibly displayed than in the poetry of sol-
dier-poet Patrick MacGill, whose 1917 collection *Soldier Songs* frequently delivers 'what
Home expects', where 'things are sanitised and rhythms are persistently cheery'.[31]

Ironically MacGill's literary reputation rests more on his wartime novels, which have
been praised for 'their scathing account of his [war] experiences'.[32] During the war, he
served with the London Irish Rifles but remained 'skeptical about the goal of the war'

---

[27] Tom Kettle, *Poems and Parodies* (London: Duckworth, 1916), 15–16.

[28] Mary Kettle, 'Introduction', *The Ways of War* (New York: Scribner's, 1917), 6.

[29] G.W. Stephen, 'The War Poets: Time for a New View?', *Agenda* 22 (1984–5), 146.

[30] George Parfitt, *English Poetry of the Great War: Contexts and Themes* (London: Harvester
Wheatsheaf, 1990), 61.

[31] Ibid., 68.

[32] Hal May, ed., 'MacGill Patrick', *Contemporary Authors* 116 (Detroit: Gale, 1986), 295.

and critical of those 'who had provoked [the] conflict', yet these reservations seldom surface in his war poetry.[33] For the most part, MacGill plays cheerleader, a role he acted out in 'public recitals of his writing, heralded by pipes of the London Irish regiment, to tug the heartstrings of his audiences'.[34] In his preface to *Soldier Songs*, he freely admits that his poems have 'no import' other than to give 'expression to the soldier's soul'.[35] Not surprisingly, then, MacGill documents the war as a recognizable narrative, but his 'attitude' doesn't always differ 'from that of the more reflective war poets, such as Owen, Sassoon, and Rosenberg'.[36]

MacGill was wounded at the Battle of Loos in 1915, and despite his poetry's often breezy emotional disengagement, combat experience did chasten to some extent his tendency to euphemize front-line trauma. In 'Before the Charge', his snapshot of pre-combat anxiety reminds us how time goes slow in hell:

> The night is still and the air is keen,
> Tense with menace the time crawls by,
> In front is the town and its homes are seen,
> Blurred in outline against the sky.[37]

Fear cloaks nature with a sinister malevolence: 'The dead leaves float in the sighing air,/ The darkness moves like a curtain drawn...'. The fateful resignation of the final line ('We charge at dawn') concludes the poem with a disturbing sense of the inevitable.

Though frequently laden with stale poeticisms, MacGill's language occasionally surprises, as in the imagistic precision of 'The Star-Shell' where he describes a falling flare:

> A moment's brightness in the sky,
> To vanish at a breath,
> And die away as soldiers die
> Upon the wastes of death.[38]

The waste and futility of war are neatly conceptualized in this striking simile (the fragile flame that is the soldiers' lives compared to the dissolving sparks), and the lines move from reportage to statement without the attendant rhetorical fussiness of most anti-war poetry.

Another soldier poet who shares both Ledwidge and MacGill's sense of a broken aesthetic is Lord Dunsany. Better known as a writer of fantasies, Dunsany published only two war poems during the conflict, neither of which conforms to the typical features of trench poetry. 'Songs from an Evil Wood', written shortly after he was posted to France, is virtually a found poem. In a letter to his wife Beatrice, Dunsany marvelled at the starry

[33] Myles Dungan, '*They Shall Not Grow Old*': *Irish Soldiers and the Great War* (Dublin: Four Courts Press, 1997), 129.

[34] Hugh Cecil, *The Flower of Battle: How Britain Wrote the Great War* (South Royalton, Vermont: Steerforth Press, 1996), 231.

[35] Patrick MacGill, *Soldier Songs* (London: Herbert Jenkins, 1917), 10.

[36] Robert Greacen, '"Taking the Derry Boat": Patrick MacGill, Novelist', *Eire-Ireland* 16 (1981), 97.

[37] MacGill, *Soldier Songs*, 52.

[38] Ibid., 110.

night lit by a heavy barrage: the 'scarlet' colour of the horizon 'so amazing that it almost made the poem itself,' he wrote.[39] The gothic setting (dark forest) and supernatural figures seem loosely allegorical. But Dunsany forces the reader to see the greater significance of these events:

> They are all abroad to-night
> And are breaking the hills with their brood,
> And the birds are all asleep,
> Even in Plugstreet Wood.[40]

Behind the nightmare pastoral lies an unsettling acceptance that these horrors have occurred before and will again.

The other poem Dunsany published during the war was the Italian sonnet 'A Dirge of Victory', which, with its timely sense of epilogue, appeared in *The Times* on Armistice Day, 11 November 1918. The significance of the title (coupling lament with triumph) becomes clear when we realize that the poem does not celebrate victory but rather elegizes those who did not live to see the peace:

> Lift not thy trumpet, Victory, to the sky
> Nor through battalions nor by batteries blow,
> But over hollows full of old wire go,
> Where armed dregs of war, the long-dead lie
> With wasted iron that the guns passed by
> When they went eastward like a tide at flow.[41]

'[H]ollows full of old wire': for Paul Fussell this conflation of landscape with the detritus of war serves as a type of pastoral irony whereby the 'desirable' is contrasted with the 'actual'.[42] In Dunsany's hands, though, there is no consolation via pastoral antithesis. The landscape is forever blighted by the 'long-dead'; no impulse from a 'vernal wood' can soak up the blood memory. The only victory is that the war is over:

> The deep mud burned under the thermite's breath,
> And winter cracked the bones that no man heeds:
> Hundreds of nights flamed by: the seasons passed.
> And thou hast come to them at last, at last!

That optimistic last line, with its straining epizeuxis ('at last, at last'), seems misplaced given the generally gloomy historical perspective that drapes heavily over the poem. For Dunsany, erasing the past is as endemic to the Irish experience as commemorating it. His prediction that history would not be kind to the Irish war dead (the 'bones that no man heeds') proved prophetic in 1979 (and even more brutally so a few years later with the bombing of the Cenotaph in Enniskillen in 1987) when the graves of veterans who had died in the First and Second World Wars were vandalized in Belfast City Cemetery

[39] Quoted in Mark Amory, *Lord Dunsany: A Biography* (London: Collins, 1972), 133.
[40] Lord Dunsany, *Fifty Poems* (London: G. P. Putnam's, 1929), 11–13.
[41] Ibid., 15.
[42] Fussell, *The Great War*, 237–8.

by people who believed these old dead soldiers wore the wrong uniform and died for the wrong cause. To prevent further desecration, the headstones had to be stacked away like discarded building supplies in a dank storage shed in Belfast's Lady Dixon Park.

V

At first glance, C. S. Lewis's verdict on the war seems casual and callous. He wrote: 'It is too cut off from the rest of my experience and often seems to have happened to someone else. It is even in a way unimportant.'[43] And when he does feel obliged to recall it, the details he selects amount to little more than comfortable distillations. When remembering the 'first bullet' that whizzed over his head, he opts for classical allusion: ' "This is War. This is what Homer wrote about." '[44] Lewis's reluctance to revisit his war experiences could be a way of coping with lingering war neuroses, but such reticence also pervades his war poetry.

Unlike Ledwidge and Kettle who served with Irish regiments, Lewis, after attending public school in England, enlisted in the University Officers' Training Corps while a student at Oxford, and eventually became 'commissioned as a Second Lieutenant in the Somerset Light Infantry'.[45] And like many of these other classically educated young men, he arrived in the trenches with a classical view of history where warfare, while horrible, was still heroic.

Most of the poems in his first collection, *Spirits in Bondage* (1919), were written during the war, and Lewis initially appears to have been somewhat ambivalent about their reception, especially by his regiment: he adopted a pseudonym (Clive Hamilton) for fear the other officers and men would 'talk about "our b[lood]y lyrical poet again" when [he] made a mistake'.[46]

The volume's main themes are the 'malevolence of nature' and 'the remoteness and essential goodness of God', but the poems also express a desire to 'escape from the suffering…to the comfort of a romantic paradise'.[47] In this way, the collection reads like an extended pastoral elegy littered with dichotomies: beauty/ugliness; idealism/cynicism; hope/resignation; innocence/experience. Loosely categorized as Romantic with 'topical references' to the war to 'anchor them in the twentieth century',[48] most of these war poems were written before Lewis became a committed Christian. Consequently, they dramatize a quest for a dream world that prefigures his later predilection for the alternate realities of Narnia and Perelandra.

---

[43] C. S. Lewis, *Surprised by Joy* (New York: Harcourt, 1955), 196.

[44] Ibid., 196.

[45] Ibid., 186, 188.

[46] Walter Hooper, 'Preface', in C. S. Lewis, *Spirits in Bondage* [1919] (New York: Harvest, 1984), p. xxxv.

[47] Peter J. Schakel, *Reason and Imagination in C. S. Lewis: A Study of 'Till We Have Faces'* (Grand Rapids, Michigan: Eerdmans, 1984), 93–4.

[48] Chad Walsh, *The Literary Legacy of C. S. Lewis* (New York: Harcourt, 1979), 36.

Not surprisingly, Lewis's war poetry is suffused with archaic language: 'Long leagues on either hand the trenches spread/And all is still.../The pale, green moon is riding overhead'. It's tempting to read these lines, taken from a poem called 'French Nocturne', as an attempt to heroicize the war.[49] The language seems more appropriate to the field at Agincourt. But Lewis treats any overt reference to the war like an unwelcome anachronism: 'There comes the buzzing plane: and now, it seems/Flies straight into the moon. Lo! where he steers/Across the pallid globe and surely nears/In that white land some harbour of dear dreams!' Showing little interest in making an ideological statement about the war, Lewis applies the language of medieval romance to mitigate any threat the war may present to his aesthetic.

In 'Apology', however, he questions the utility of writing heroic verse at all: 'Is it good to tell old tales of Troynovant/Or praises of dead heroes, tried and sage,/Or sing the queens of unforgotten age...?/How should I sing of them?'[50] The past as antidote to the present offers cold comfort when confronted by war's ugliness. In the last lines, the speaker wakes from a dream to learn that 'The East is pale and cold'. Romantic symbols unhitch themselves from their customary connotative moorings: 'No hope is in the dawn, and no delight.' This shift from a reassuring landscape to one of menace is a typically Romantic trope, as Lewis questions not only the martial code with its genuflections toward glory, honour, and sacrifice, but also the very language of heroic poetry, which seems hopelessly outmoded when burdened with the task of describing the front.

In terms of what it has to say about the war, 'Death in Battle' appears to be little more than an extended escapist meditation, but the poet pleads to be liberated from a private hell that is as much mental as it is physical. The first of the six quatrains (complete with envelope rhyme) embrace the standard Romantic notion of Death as release:

> Open the gates for me,
> Open the gates of the peaceful castle, rosy in the West,
> In the sweet dim Isle of Apples over the wide sea's breast,
> Open the gates for me![51]

Lewis acknowledged his proclivity 'toward things pale, remote, and evanescent; the water-colour world of Morris, the leafy recesses of Malory, the twilight of Yeats'.[52] The 'Death' noted in the title suggests an Owenesque conceit whereby the speaker enters some 'dark tunnel' which he hopes will lead to 'dewy upland places in the garden of God', far from the 'men cursing in fight' and their 'brutal, crowded faces...'. The war's indignities intensify the hunger for aesthetic release. Poetic periphrases ('rosy in the west', 'sweet dim isle', 'end of day') reveal a painterly passion for allegory. Like a sixteenth-century navigator intrigued by a blank spot on a Mercator map, the speaker finds solace in the mystical rather than the actual. Technically, the poem demonstrates Lewis's fondness for metrical variation, taking risks with the fourteen-syllable line (that staple of

[49] Lewis, *Spirits in Bondage*, 4.
[50] Ibid.,12.
[51] Ibid., 74.
[52] Lewis, *Surprised by Joy*, 198.

sixteenth-century verse) to stretch out the emotional freight. But the studied literariness may have also been a way to 'suppress the unpleasant memories'.[53]

With their Romantic aspirations, narrative leaps, ominous sunsets, and bitterly resigned endings, Lewis's war poems conform to the traditions of canonical war poetry as he invokes 'past myths' to address 'present horrors'.[54] Yet if Owen sees the martyrdom of Christ in the soldiers' suffering, Lewis sees a 'malicious deity' at work.[55] In this regard, the war shaped the writer Lewis was to become. It forced him to channel the knowledge gained from his vast reading into an ongoing critical inquiry about good and evil and man's relationship with his creator. The war may have destroyed the faith of many of its survivors, but for Lewis, it seems to have inspired a hunger for belief.

VI

Even though women's war poetry provides a voice for those not directly involved in the fighting, 'a privileging of the male voice and the experience of combat still persists'.[56] But these other voices do present a fuller picture of the war's impact and help counterbalance the explicit and implicit ideologies that permeate soldier poetry. Certainly serious study of women's war poetry has been hampered by its alleged passivity, its second-hand reportage, its prescriptive treatment of grief. Women war poets, we are led to believe, were too preoccupied with mourning, patriotic sentiment, and recruitment rhetoric. When anti-war sentiment was expressed, the objection was rarely ideological: war itself was not so much contested as its repercussions were.

The distinction for Ireland's most prolific war poet goes to Katharine Tynan, who published four volumes of poetry during the war.[57] Described as a '"grief counsellor" for countless correspondents'[58] because most of her war poems were 'written on the occasion of the death of someone she did not know personally',[59] Tynan elegized lost lovers and golden boys, and consoled bereaved mothers. Despite their formulaic quality, these poems remind us that not all the suffering occurred at the front.

Tynan's most recurring subject is motherhood, a topic she understood only too well with two sons on active duty. There is a wistfulness about what might have been;

[53] Don King, C. S. Lewis, Poet: The Legacy of his Poetic Impulse (Kent, Ohio: Kent State University Press, 2001), 54.

[54] Ibid., 75.

[55] Ibid., 77.

[56] Janis Stout, Coming out of War: Poetry, Grieving and the Culture of the World Wars (Tuscaloosa: University of Alabama Press, 2005), 59.

[57] Katharine Tynan, Flower of Youth: Poems in War Time (London: Sidgwick & Jackson, 1915), The Holy War (London: Sidgwick & Jackson, 1916), Late Songs (London: Sidgwick & Jackson, 1917), and Herb O'Grace: Poems in War Time (London: Sidgwick & Jackson, 1918).

[58] Hugh Cecil, The Flower of Battle, 332.

[59] Ann Connerton Fallon, Katharine Tynan (Boston: Twayne, 1979), 95.

religious consolation is doled out as a universal panacea; women feature as symbolic representations of nation and empire; and anti-German sentiment sometimes reaches hysteric levels. No doubt this 'anguished complicity' in getting behind the war effort was also due to a vicarious fascination with heroic death, a fate largely denied women,[60] and in her most famous war poem, 'Flower of Youth', Tynan reflects popular sentiment with her pro-war justifications.[61] Those who make the ultimate sacrifice receive their heavenly reward.[62] Grief is worn as a badge of honour. Read against the grain, the poem's orthodox Victorian sentiments (sentimentality, artifice, idealism, the invigorating power of nature) demonstrate how antithesis can work both ways: in this case, the attempt to transcend the obscenity of war is magnified by the poet's consolatory overreach. The euphemistic window dressing reminds us of the falsity of artifice:

> Heaven's thronged with gay and careless faces,
> New-waked from dreams of dreadful things,
> They walk in green and pleasant places
> And by the crystal water-springs
> Who dreamt of dying and the slain,
> And the fierce thirst and the strong pain.

With its Blakean echoes ('England's green and pleasant land') and cautious optimism, Tynan's war elegy acquires a certain degree of ornamentation as she tries to envision what heaven must look like. Death is part of some holy plan:

> They run and leap by a clear river
> And of their youth they have great joy.
> Oh, if the sonless mothers weeping,
> And widowed girls could look inside
> The glory that hath them in keeping
> Who went to the Great War and died,
> They would rise and put their mourning off,
> And say: 'Thank God, he has enough!'

Tynan elides 'distinctions between classes, religions, and types'.[63] Instead of the customary patriarchal order, authority emanates 'from the maternal role'.[64] But while the poem's prescriptive quality breaks the sacerdotal link between artist and craft, Tynan uses poetry to begin the process of healing and acceptance. Judged by such standards, her war poetry is more therapeutic than ideological.

---

[60] Janet Montefiore, ' "Shining Pins and Wailing Shells": Women Poets and the Great War', in *Women and World War 1: The Written Response*, ed. Margaret Goldman (London: Macmillan, 1993), 53, 55.

[61] Katharine Tynan, *Flower of Youth: Poems in War Time*, 54–5.

[62] Fallon, *Katharine Tynan*, 93.

[63] Donna L. Potts, 'Irish Poetry and the Modernist Canon: A Reappraisal of Katharine Tynan', in *Border Crossings: Irish Women Writers and National Identities*, ed. Kathryn Kirkpatrick (Tuscaloosa, University of Alabama Press, 2000), 84.

[64] Ibid.

Winifred Letts did not enjoy the same widespread wartime readership as Katharine Tynan, but while most of her war poems express the same patriotic sentiments and general air of optimism, Letts periodically adopts the ironic mode to question the received platitudes of pro patria. She published two collections of poetry during the war (*Hallow'een and Poems of the War* in 1916 and *The Spires of Oxford and Other Poems* in 1917), and her work as a nurse, first with the Voluntary Aid Detachment (VAD) and later with the Almeric Paget Military Massage Corps, sharpened her better war poems with an immediacy and particularity that transcend the generalized impressions of most war verse.

In 'What Reward?' we encounter neither consolatory tone nor lofty imperative.[65] Instead, Letts's subjects are the shell shocked, the mentally debilitated, those for whom death might have been a better alternative:

> One has his glory,
> One has found his rest.
> But what of this poor babbler here
> With chin sunk on his breast?
> Flotsam of battle,
> With brain bemused and dim,
> O God, for such a sacrifice
> Say, what reward for him?

Pity, bitterness, resignation: such responses did not exclusively belong to the 'dominant male voices'.[66] Each stanza forms a rhetorical question, but because the reader cannot provide an adequate answer, an air of complicity envelops the poem. Question becomes statement as the speaker teases out the compensatory ironies of 'glory' and 'rest' before outrage gives way to disillusionment ('O God'). Unlike Tynan, who resorts to spiritual recourse to make sense of the indefensible, Letts leaves us only with loaded questions.

Another poem, 'Screens (In a Hospital)',[67] shifts the focus away from the war wounded to examine how the war affected those whose job it was to cure and to care:

> They put the screens about his bed;
> We might not play the gramophone,
> And so we played at cards instead
> And left him dying there alone.

Emotional and physical fatigue serve as a general anaesthetic, effecting an immunity to suffering. Detachment serves as a survival mechanism. One can only take so much.

A Union Jack is 'spread upon' the dead soldier when 'he goes away'. Death is transmuted, a flag buried, flesh becomes metonym: the dead soldier becomes his country. The final lines match Sassoon for irony and sardonic understatement:

---

[65] Winifred Letts, *The Spires of Oxford* (New York: E. P. Dutton, 1917), 23.

[66] Nosheen Khan, *Women's Poetry of the Great War* (Lexington: University Press of Kentucky, 1988), 124–5.

[67] Letts, *The Spires of Oxford*, 21.

> He'll want those three red screens no more,
> Another man will get his bed,
> We'll make the row we did before
> But—Jove!—I'm sorry that he's dead.

Letts is at her best when she tackles the casualties largely left out of the official narrative. Over three hundred British soldiers were executed during the war for 'desertion or cowardice'.[68] In 'The Deserter', she describes the execution of a soldier who refused to kill. Most war poems pay tribute to the dead or wounded, but Letts ponders the irony of a man killed because he refused to kill:

> There was a man,—don't mind his name,
> Whom Fear had dogged by night and day.
> He could not face the German guns
> And so he turned and ran away.
> But who can judge him, you or I?
> ...
> The shots rang out and down he fell,
> An English bullet in his heart.
> An English bullet in his heart!
> But here's the irony of life,—
> His mother thinks he fought and fell
> A hero, foremost in the strife.
> So she goes proudly; to the strife
> Her best, her hero son she gave.
> O well for her she does not know
> He lies in a deserter's grave.[69]

The Unknown Soldier becomes the unknown deserter. Letts cautions us not to 'judge' this man but to reconsider what it means to be heroic: perhaps true honour resides 'not in the carrying out of duty but in its humane dereliction'.[70]

Pacifism had its advocates, too. Active in the Irish suffrage movement, Eva Gore-Booth described herself as an 'extreme' pacifist.[71] For her, the war was a denial of God's dominion. Though some of her war poems are marked by a language clogged with trite figurative images and opaque mystical ponderings, they challenge the gender-centrism of the ruling patriarchy. Her 1917 collection, *Broken Glory*, as its title suggests, addresses 'the full horror at militarism, the triumph of mindless aggression and the loss of Christ'.[72] During the war, Gore-Booth travelled throughout Britain visiting prisoners of war and attending courts martial and tribunals on behalf of conscientious objectors as a 'watcher' or 'prisoner's friend'.[73] In 'The Tribunal', she portrays such proceedings as nothing more than ritualistic bullying:

---

[68] Geoff Dyer, *The Missing of the Somme* (London: Phoenix Press, 1994), 53.
[69] Letts, *The Spires of Oxford*, 30.
[70] Dyer, *The Missing of the Somme*, 54.
[71] Gifford Lewis, *Eva Gore-Booth and Esther Roper: A Biography* (London: Pandora, 1988), 163.
[72] Ibid., 143.
[73] Khan, *Women's Poetry of the Great War*, 101.

> Before six ignorant men and blind
> Reckless they rent aside
> The veil of Isis in the mind...
> Men say they shirked and lied.[74]

Gore-Booth's theosophical leanings underpin many of her war poems which are domi-nated by a faith in mankind's potential perfectibility as she embraces all faith traditions: 'For the Hidden One in every heart,/Lost star in the world's night,/Fire that burns in the soul of art,/The Light within the Light...'. Not surprisingly she rarely engages the war directly. A habitual mollifier, she advocates spiritual truth as the universal cure for all suffering.

Despite her spiritual leanings, Gore-Booth did not see the war as a Christian crusade. In 'Dreams', she indicts those who have brought civilization to its knees:

> German or French or English, words most vain
> To that which knows not any nation's pride,
> Whose pity is as all men's sorrow wide,
> Folded about our broken world of pain.

She also refused to conscript her voice to the rival factions in Irish politics. She did not compromise her beliefs to avoid public condemnation as anti-German sentiment grew strident. She was that rare combination of poet and activist. For her the protest was in the poetry.

VII

AE (George Russell) shared Gore-Booth's pacifist sympathies, though he was 'firmly on the side of the allies'.[75] During the war he privately published *The Gods of War* (1915), a collection of anti-war poems left out of the early editions of his *Collected Poems* because he believed them to be too preachy. And preachy they can be. Warmongers castigated, man's innate brutality condemned, when AE is not voicing concerns about the war, he finds solace in God's omnipotence.

In 'Battle Ardour', the adrenaline rush of aerial combat transmogrifies the act of war-fare into something elemental and infinite:

> Unto what heaven wends this wild ecstasy?
> Is the fired spirit light from his wings,
> Self being outcast, as the diver flings
> His garment so that every limb be free?[76]

---

[74] Eva Gore-Booth, *Poems of Eva Gore-Booth* (London: Longmans, Green, 1929), 527–8.

[75] Henry Summerfield, *That Myriad-minded Man: A Biography of George William Russell 'A.E.', 1867–1935* (Totowa, New Jersey: Rowan and Littlefield, 1975), 169.

[76] Ibid., 239.

War beguiles with its spectacle and stagecraft. The aesthetic of death appals and appeals.

The war also provided the occasion to address Ireland's political fractiousness. For Declan Kiberd, AE 'wrote the only significant poem of the time to lament the Irishmen who died in both conflicts [the war and the Easter Rebellion]'.[77] The poem to which he refers, 'To the Memory of Some I Knew Who are Dead and Who Loved Ireland', attempts to defuse unionist and nationalist enmities by proffering an olive branch in the shape of a One Ireland solution where the 'modern Irish', as AE describes them in an accompanying letter submitted along with the poem for publication, are a people comprised of 'many races'.[78] Cross-cutting between eulogistic overtures to the Easter Rising and the war, he assembles an heroic catalogue (Pearse, MacDonagh, Kettle, Connolly), attempting to do what history cannot: construct an imagined Ireland where all traditions like 'One river, born from many streams,/ Roll in one blaze of blinding light'. The desire to locate a common ground is undermined by the fear that even the act of commemoration will become divisive. As noted earlier, history would vindicate such fears as the memory of the thousands of Irishmen who fought in the Great War would be condemned to the 'Great Oblivion'.[79]

VIII

Though Ireland's war poets embraced the popular pro- and anti-war sentiments that characterized the 'generic British response',[80] they also shared the same sense of 'idealization, abstraction, [and] remoteness from reality' as their German counterparts.[81] Assigning definitive stages of development to Irish war poetry proves problematic, however, as poets register a range of notes rather than follow any discrete patterns of response. That they regarded the war as adversarial to their art is borne out in their repeated attempts to create alternative landscapes of memory, their studied lyricism serving as an aesthetic prophylaxis to combat the disagreeable. For soldier poets like Ledwidge and Kettle, for whom the concept of nation was a muddied affair, the annulment of the personal in favour of a national identity proved equally challenging. Retreating into the Pastoral or climbing onto the cross of self-sacrifice, their war poetry ultimately reveals the 'complex reality of [their] country'.[82]

But at their best, these poets offer a range of responses that often more accurately reflect their contemporary public's attitudes toward the war than the canonical poetry of

---

[77] Kiberd, *Inventing Ireland*, 240.

[78] Both poem and letter were published in the *Irish Times* in December 1917.

[79] F. X. Martin, '1916: Myth, Fact, and Mystery', *Studia Hibernica* 7 (1967), 68.

[80] David Goldie, 'Was There a Scottish War Literature? Scotland, Poetry, and the First World War', in Tim Kendall, ed., *The Oxford Handbook of British and Irish War Poetry* (Oxford: Oxford University Press, 2007), 154.

[81] Patrick Bridgwater, *The German Poets of the First World War* (London and Sydney: Croom Helm, 1985), 15.

[82] Gerald Dawe, 'Francis Ledwidge: A Man of His Time', *Irish Times* (31 July 2004), 11.

protest. And while these poets might have benefited from the general public's insatiable appetite for war verse, the fact that they continued to employ nineteenth-century language and prosody demonstrates how changes in poetry do not occur along neat, parallel lines but rather that varieties of poetry continue to be written and read long after the critics pronounce them dead. Most importantly, Ireland's war poets retain their faith that poetry matters and that it matters even more in wartime. It certainly mattered to Francis Ledwidge. In one of his last poems, he was still asking questions of his art: 'can the lark forget the cloud/When poppies shroud the seeded furrow?'[83] For Ledwidge, and for all war poets, the answer will always be no.

[83] Ledwidge, 'The Lanawn Shee', *The Complete Poems*, 258.

CHAPTER 5

'PLEDGED TO IRELAND': THE POETS AND POEMS OF EASTER 1916

GERALD DAWE

THE English composer Arnold Bax (1883–1953), who had lived in Ireland during the early years of the twentieth century, was much taken by W. B. Yeats's poetry of the period. Spending time in Glencolmcille, County Donegal, and later on, from 1911 to 1913, in Dublin, he met with 'AE', among others, and was influenced greatly by the revivalist and mystical strands of the Celtic renaissance. He took on the name of 'Dermot O'Byrne' and published poems under that pseudonym, contributing to *The Irish Review*, one of the nationalist cultural outlets, whose co-founders included Thomas MacDonagh and editor Joseph Mary Plunkett. Both men would become signatories of the Proclamation of the Irish Republic which Padraic Pearse, another of the signatories, proclaimed, as president of the Provisional government, outside the General Post Office in Dublin's main thoroughfare, O'Connell Street, on Monday, 24 April 1916.

O'Byrne supported the 1916 Rising in a series of poems, *A Dublin Ballad and Other Poems*, printed and announced for publication in 1918. The collection, however, was banned by the British censor in Ireland, although copies were informally distributed and the work became known, particularly for the sentiment of the title poem, and others such as 'Martial Law in Dublin', 'Shells at Oranmore, April 1916', and 'In Memoriam My Friend Patrick H. Pearse (*Ruler of Ireland for one Week*)'. The poems are unequivocally pro-nationalist and critical of the local popular response to the Rising which had initially been at best quizzical, but at worst hostile to the actions of those Irish Volunteers who had taken over several locations in Dublin as acts of insurrectionary defiance against continuing British rule in Ireland:

> And when the devil's made us wise
> Each in his own peculiar hill,
> With desert hearts and drunken eyes

> We're free to sentimentalize
> By corners where the martyrs fell.[1]

By all accounts the 'drunken eyes' and the freedom to 'sentimentalize' the actions of the rebellious Volunteers that Easter week in 1916 had happened within a year or so of the prisoners being released from gaols in Britain, the momentum having begun with the execution of the leading figures of the rebellion, including three poets generally referred to as 'The 1916 poets'—Thomas MacDonagh, Padraic Pearse, and Joseph Mary Plunkett.[2] Bax/O'Byrne is quite explicit in 'The Irish Mail (Paddington)' about how he viewed the British soldiers whom he had encountered on their way to suppress the Rising:

> My dream and ache I shouldered through
> A mob of Khaki men and blue.
>
> Red brutish faces smeared with sweat
> Surged up like evil masks to set
> Their hideousness to hound away
> The wistful wonder of the day.
>
> They mixed lewd talk of girls with beer;
> One tattooed monster with a leer
> Began to sentimentalize
> About some Kathleen's arms and eyes.[3]

The pastoral poet, Francis Ledwidge—Meath-born county council worker, trade union activist, and fervent nationalist—had been injured at the front and was on a convalescent leave back in Ireland in 1916 prior to rejoining his unit of the Royal Inniskilling Fusiliers stationed in Derry. He walked through Dublin in the aftermath of the destruction of the General Post Office (GPO)—the insurgents' headquarters)—and through the main boulevards of the city, as debris from the ruins still smouldered:

> In Dublin he mingled with the crowds who gathered in O'Connell Street every day to stare at the still-smoking ruins. The newspaper reports of the devastation said that from the Pillar to the quays on both sides, all the buildings were gone, leaving only a mass of rubble. The walls and portico were all that was left of the Post Office, but from the gutted interior smoke was still rising into the air. The Imperial Hotel opposite had also been demolished, but the name in gilt letters still remained on the front wall. The Metropole Hotel and the whole block of which it formed part had disappeared, leaving a debris of bricks and stones. The statues of Nelson and O'Connell remained intact.[4]

---

[1] Dermot O'Byrne, 'A Dublin Ballad—1916', *A Dublin Ballad and Other Poems: Poetry Booklets Two* (Dublin: The Candle Press, 1918), 7.

[2] Desmond Ryan, ed., *The 1916 Poets* [1963] (Dublin: Gill & Macmillan, 1995).

[3] 'The Irish Mail (Paddington)', *Dermot O'Byrne/Arnold Bax Poems*, ed. Lewis Foreman (London: Thames Publishing, 1979), 61. The poem carries the note: 'From MS. Previously unpublished'.

[4] Alice Curtayne, *Francis Ledwidge: A Life of the Poet* (Dublin: New Island Books, 1998), 157.

Later Ledwidge wrote this brief elegy:

> A noble failure is not vain,
> But hath a victory its own.
> A bright delectance from the slain
> Is down the generations thrown.
>
> And, more than Beauty understands,
> Has made her lovelier here, it seems.
> I see white ships that crowd her strands,
> For mine are all the dead men's dreams.[5]

Ledwidge knew, and was known by, the poet-leaders of the Rising, and after the execution of Plunkett and MacDonagh he would write their elegies. In the case of MacDonagh, Ledwidge's tribute was inscribed with the image of the yellow bittern, from Cathal Buidhe MacGilla Ghunna's 'An Bunan Buidhe'. That poem MacDonagh had translated into English from its original Irish:

> It's not for the common birds that I'd mourn
>   The black-bird, the corn-crake, or the crane,
> But for the bittern that's shy and apart
>   And drinks in the marsh from the lone bog-drain.
> Oh! If I had known you were near your death,
>   While my breath held out I'd have run to you,
> Till a splash from the Lake of the Son of the Bird
>   Your soul would have stirred and waked anew.[6]

In his tribute to the executed poet, Ledwidge associates the desolate sense of loss with the fleeting recognition which saw the yellow bittern, along with the March weather and astringent landscape, as images of lonely perseverance that would become identified in Irish public consciousness with both poets' early and violent deaths:

> He shall not hear the bittern cry
> In the wild sky where he is lain,
> Nor voices of the sweeter birds
> Above the wailing of the rain.[7]

The sense of sacrifice is also conveyed in Ledwidge's honouring of Joseph Mary Plunkett's wife, Mary Gifford, who had married her ailing fiancé on the night before his execution by firing squad. Gifford, whose sister was MacDonagh's wife, was from a middle-class Protestant background, and had converted to the highly charged mystical Catholicism of her aesthete husband-to-be, who had himself been a student of MacDonagh's,

---

[5] Ibid., with note 'Unpublished poem in Dunsany Papers', 157. Subsequently reprinted under the title 'O'Connell Street', in *The Complete Works of Francis Ledwidge*, ed. Alice Curtayne (London: Martin Brian & O'Keeffe, 1974, reprinted Dublin: Poolbeg Press, 1998), 154.

[6] Thomas MacDonagh, 'The Yellow Bittern', in *The 1916 Poets*, ed. Ryan, 80.

[7] Francis Ledwidge, 'Thomas MacDonagh', *The Complete Poems*, ed. Liam O'Meara (Newbridge, Kildare: Goldsmith Press, 1997), 175.

learning Irish for university matriculation. In Ledwidge's poem, the aristocratic lifestyle of the Plunkett family (Joseph Mary's father was a papal count) is subsumed in the telling address to the woman at the 'heart' of the bloody execution. In effect the execution becomes the symbol of the Rising and this motif would in turn become the conventional meaning of *what* had happened, rather than why and/or how:

> We see you not as one of us
> Who so lament each little thing,
> You profit more by honest loss,
> Who lost so much, than song can sing.
>
> This you have lost, a heart which bore
> An ideal love, an ideal shame,
> And earned this thing, for evermore
> A noble and a splendid name.[8]

For a solder-poet engaged in the killing fields of the First World War, Ledwidge was caught painfully in the middle, as his loyalties, both emotional and political, were drawn into intense conflict by the executions in May, and by his own return to active service in December 1916.[9] The following year Ledwidge, who was the same age as Plunkett but from the other end of the social spectrum, was killed in action.

According to one of the leading authorities on the Rising, Max Caulfield, the third and best known of the poet-leaders, Padraic Pearse, had not only the political legacy of the Volunteers' actions on his mind the very night before his execution; he also was concerned about safeguarding his poetic legacy. In a much-quoted letter to his beloved mother, Pearse, enclosing his final poem, subsequently published under the title, 'The Mother' ('We suffer in their coming and their going;/And tho' I grudge them not, I weary, weary/Of the long sorrow—and yet I have my joy:/My sons were faithful and they fought')[10] instructs 'My dearest Mother':

> I have written two papers about financial affairs and one about my books which I want you to get. With them are a few poems which I want added to the poems in MS. in my book case. You asked me to write a little poem which would seem to be said by you about me. I have written it, and a copy is in Arbour Hill barracks with other papers.[11]

In case there was any dispute about the role he played as president of the putatively named and proclaimed new Irish Republic, Pearse states that he has 'just received Holy Communion' and that 'except for the great grief of parting from you [his mother]', he is 'happy'—'This is the death I should have asked for if God had given me the choice of all deaths—to die a soldier's death for Ireland and for freedom.'[12]

---

[8] 'To Mrs Joseph Plunkett', *Complete Poems*, ed. O'Meara, 221. See 'The Dead Kings', 'At Currabwee', 'Thro' Bogac Ban', and 'Dreams', which also deal with the aftermath of the Rising and the fate of the leaders.

[9] Curtayne, *Francis Ledwidge*, 168.

[10] 'The Mother', in *The 1916 Poets*, ed. Ryan, 20.

[11] Max Caulfield, *The Easter Rebellion* [1963] (Dublin: Gill & Macmillan, 1995), 285.

[12] Ibid., 285.

Meanwhile, it is the desire for a 'soldier's death', inspired by his love for 'Ireland' and 'for freedom', which provoked George Russell ('AE') to write to the *Irish Times* a long letter. In it he sets out his views on the looming conflict *in* Ireland when the First World War will come to an end, and when the Irish soldiers fighting at the front will return home to share the island with those who had fought against the British troops during Easter Week. Russell's letter links the events of April with what he sees as a New Ireland struggling for life and self-expression: 'We are a new people, and not the past, but the future, is to justify this new nationality.' In what might seem to be a surprisingly forward-looking and radical view for one of the founders of the Celtic Revival, Russell states:

> I believe that new character far more than the spirit of the ancient race, was the ferment in the blood of those who brought about the astonishing enterprise of Easter week. Pearse himself, for all his Gaelic culture, was sired by one of the race he fought against. He might stand in that respect as a symbol of the new race which is springing up.[13]

Anatomizing the new situation emerging in Ireland in 1917–18, Russell's understanding of 'our political differences' finds its focus in the concluding paragraph of the letter and in the tribute-poem which he appends, 'To the Memory of Some I knew who are Dead and who loved Ireland', subsequently published under the title, 'Salutation'. The poem, in seven stanzas, devotes alternate stanzas to those who fought and died in The First World War (Alan Anderson, Thomas Kettle, the nationalist MP and academic, and Willie Redmond), along with those executed in May (Thomas MacDonagh, James Connolly, and Padraic Pearse): 'your dream, not mine,/But yet the thought for this you fell/Has turned life's water into wine'. The concluding stanza seeks a poetic reconciliation between the contending historical forces of nationalism and of unionism in an image of mystical revelation:

> Here's to you men I never met
>   Yet hope to meet behind the veil,
> Thronged on some starry parapet
>   That looks down upon Innisfail,
> And see the confluence of dreams
>   That clashed together in our night,
> One river, born from many streams,
>   Roll in one blaze of blinding light.[14]

The First World War and the Easter Rising merge into one inclusive metaphor of a common afterlife, a notion of glorious posterity and posthumous triumph which underpins much of the poetry by and about Easter 1916.

Thomas MacDonagh, who, unlike the other two poet-leaders was a married man with a young family (his son Donagh was born in 1912, his daughter Barbara in 1915), was

---

[13] 'The New Nation: Letter from Mr. George Russell', *Irish Times* (19 December 1917), 6.

[14] The poem is included, with many others quoted in this essay, in *Earth Voices Whispering: An Anthology of Irish War Poetry 1914–1945*, ed. Gerald Dawe (Belfast: Blackstaff, 2008), 19–21.

refused a visit by his wife on the eve of his execution by firing squad. MacDonagh had been, first, a teacher and then assistant headmaster at Pearse's St Enda's school for boys, and latterly a university lecturer in English at University College Dublin, where he had met Eoin MacNeill, professor of early Irish history and a senior figure of the Volunteer movement (and, incidentally, great-uncle of the acclaimed Belfast novelist Brian Moore). In the fragment of his court-martial speech which Max Caulfield reprints in *The Easter Rebellion*, MacDonagh reveals a little of the intellectual roots that inspired him, and others, to challenge the overarching military power of the British Empire.

'It would not be seemly,' he states, 'for me to go to my doom without trying to express, however inadequately, my sense of the high honour I enjoy in being of those predestined in this generation to die for the cause of Irish freedom'.[15] Turning his attention to members of the court martial, MacDonagh quotes from Horace (*Odes*: III.ii.13) the now infamous axiom:

> You will, perhaps, understand this sentiment, for it is one to which an Imperial poet of a bygone age bore immortal testimony: 'Tis sweet and glorious to die for one's country'. You would all be proud to die for Britain, your Imperial patron, and I am proud and happy to die for Ireland, my glorious Fatherland.[16]

On 3 May, Pearse and MacDonagh—along with Thomas Clarke, one of the last links with the Fenian chain of republican insurrection—were executed, and the following day at dawn, Plunkett, Pearse's brother Willie, commandant Edward Daly, and Michael O'Hanrahan were dispatched by firing squad. Further executions in Dublin, and the hanging of Roger Casement in Pentonville Gaol, London, brought the number of executions to sixteen. In their wake an increasing sense of revulsion, awe, and fascination grew with what the leaders of the revolt—middle-class intellectuals in the main—had set in train. It was a mood that was both quite specific and local to Ireland, but which also contained within it the ultimate seeds of separation from British rule of a substantial majority of the population of Ireland, and it marked too the beginning of the end for the British Empire as a world power.

For those who had been very much a social and cultural part of that imperial society in Ireland, the role played by one of the leading families, the Gore-Booths of Sligo, must have provoked more than bewildered amusement. When young, both girls of the family, Eva and Con (or Constance) had beguiled W. B. Yeats, who met them first in Sligo in 1894. Thirty years later, after their deaths within a year of each other, Yeats had battened on to the aftermath of the Rising, and the role Constance had played in the Rising, as second-in-command in the Irish Citizen's Army action, seizing the College of Surgeons, St Stephen's Green (for which she was court-martialled and sentenced to death) as the

---

[15]   Caulfield, *The Easter Rebellion*, 286.

[16]   Ibid., 286. MacDonagh's use of the phrase contrasts with Wilfred Owen's in his famous war poem, 'Dulce Et Decorum Est', drafted while Owen was recovering from shell shock in Craiglockhart Hospital in the first half of October 1917. Owen sees the sacrifice of the trenches as 'the cud/Of vile, incurable sores on innocent tongues', and the famous Latin tag is for him 'The old Lie'. See *The Collected Poems of Wilfred Owen* (London: Chatto & Windus, 1963), 55.

symbolic fulcrum of change. Yeats's poem, 'In Memory of Eva Gore-Booth and Con Markiewicz', laments the impact both politics and political violence has had upon the sisters in contrast to the demeanour and classical setting of their meetings in one of the 'big houses' to which Yeats was drawn:

> The light of evening, Lissadell,
> Great windows open to the south,
> Two girls in silk kimonos, both
> Beautiful, one a gazelle.[17]

The characteristic Yeatsian turn, 'But', reveals the change that time has wrought and the 'Conspiring among the ignorant' which is the grubbiness of 'politics':

> But a raving autumn shears
> Blossom from the summer's wreath;
> The older is condemned to death,
> Pardoned, drags out lonely years
> Conspiring among the ignorant.
> I know not what the younger dreams –
> Some vague Utopia – and she seems,
> When withered old and skeleton-gaunt,
> An image of such politics.[18]

Con's sister Eva, a feminist and activist on trade-union and social rights,[19] was also a poet and responded to the events of 1916, in particular to the obvious distress and worry over her sister's death sentence (commuted to life imprisonment; she was released from gaol in June 1917) in a cluster of poems including 'Easter Week', 'Heroic Death, 1916', 'To Constance—in Prison', 'Christmas Eve In Prison', 'To C.M. on her Prison Birthday', 'Roger Casement', and 'Comrades'. The characteristic note is elegiac as she laments the failed Rising in terms of its heroism and the tragic sacrifice of young life, while the nobility of the cause (a recurrent theme through the poetry of 1916) is not contaminated by the reality of violence or the actuality of war. This is 'Easter Week':

> Grief for the noble dead
> Of one who did not share their strife
> And mourned that any blood was shed,
> Yet felt the broken glory of their state,
> Their strange heroic questionings of Fate
> Ribbon with gold the rags of this our life.[20]

---

[17] W. B. Yeats, *The Variorum Edition of the Poems of W. B. Yeats*, ed. Peter Allt and Russell K. Alspach (Basingstoke: Macmillan, 1956), 475.

[18] Ibid.

[19] In his poem 'The Subjection of Women', Austin Clarke makes a particular point of naming the women involved in the Rising and who subsequently became activists in trade-union rights, social-health and feminist causes, including Countess Markiewicz, Helena Moloney, Louie Bennett, Eva Gore-Booth, and Dr Kathleen Lynn, 'who founded/A hospital for sick babes, foundlings'. See Austin Clarke, *Collected Poems*, ed. R. Dardis Clarke (Manchester: Carcanet, 2008), 431–2.

[20] Eva Gore-Booth, *Selected Poems* (London: Longmans, Green and Co., 1933), 76.

The religious colouring of the poem—'blood', 'broken glory', 'ribbon with gold'—is matched by Gore-Booth's sense of the political significance of the events unfolding *after* the Rising. In a poem addressed to her sister in prison, she asks what 'time' has 'to do with thee' who is 'free in a prison cell' and answers:

> Nay on that undreamed judgement day,
> When on the old world's scrap-heap flung,
> Powers and empires pass away,
> Radiant and unconquerable
> Though shalt be young.[21]

The apocalyptic note of prophetic righteousness, of an ideal world beyond this, pervades much of the poetry written out of the Easter Rising. It is typical of the poetry which the three poet-leaders wrote themselves in the years leading up to the Rising.

In his astute and comprehensive reading of the poetry of Pearse, MacDonagh, and Plunkett, 'The Messianic Ideal', Richard J. Loftus identifies the main literary influences and metaphorical tropes of each of the three poets, along with the ideological pulses which they share as nationalist activists. He writes: 'All three were, by their own claim, "visionary" poets, and the ideals, if one may call them that, which they celebrate in their verse, are meant to invoke a spiritual vision that is not only personal—although for each it is that, to be sure—but also national and racial.'[22] In Loftus's view, the recurrent modes of the '1916 poets' include a cult of primitivism, an ideal of simplicity, the use of old Celtic sagas, the inheritance of heroic Gaelic tradition in writing, and the Roman Catholic religious traditions of saintliness, sacrifice, and martyrdom. Declan Kiberd has remarked that these selfsame energies yearned for 'expression but the forms preferred by England, however well-intentioned, just did not fit'. He goes on to make the point that there was 'remarkably little anti-English sentiment in the writings of the Easter rebels for all that':

> Many of them revered particular English poets—Pearse admired and even imitated Wordsworth; MacDonagh wrote a fine thesis on Thomas Campion and devoted his very last class at University College Dublin to the virtues of Jane Austen, before marching out to prepare for insurrection; and Joseph Plunkett learned much from Francis Thompson. What they rejected was not England but the British imperial system, which denied expressive freedom to its colonial subjects.[23]

It is hardly surprising, bearing this view in mind, that the 1916 literature of apocalypse merges with a mysticism not uncommon in the *fin de siècle* writing of the period. In the variations of Pearse's poetry in English, his translations from Irish, and in his writing in Irish, 'his theme, imagery and even rhythm', according to Loftus, have their sources in the Old Testament, such as in his much-anthologized poem, 'The Rebel', which opens:

---

[21] 'To C.M. on her Prison Birthday', Gore-Booth, *Selected Poems*, 78.

[22] Richard J. Loftus, *Nationalism in Modern Anglo-Irish Poetry* (Madison and Milwaukee: University of Wisconsin Press, 1964), 132.

[23] Declan Kiberd, '1916: The Idea and the Action', in *Modern Irish Writers and the Wars*, ed. Kathleen Devine (Gerrards Cross: Colin Smythe, 1999), 27.

> I am come of the seed of the people, the people that sorrow,
> That have no treasure but hope,
> No riches laid up but a memory
> Of an Ancient glory.[24]

Similarly MacDonagh, a keen student of English and European literature,[25] was well versed in literary form and particularly in the Symbolist movement. His poetry is marked by conventional images of the time, such as the rose. This functions as both 'a symbol of Christ' but also 'in the tradition of Irish protest literature—which MacDonagh knew well—[it] has yet another meaning as a symbol for the Irish nation',[26] as in the following poem on the birth of his daughter, 'Barbara Born 24th March 1915':

> When the life of the cities of Europe goes
> The way of Memphis and Babylon,
> In Ireland still the mystic rose
> Will shine as it of old has done.
>
> O rose of Grace! O rare wild flower,
> Whose seeds are sent on the wings of Light!
> O secret rose, our doom, our dower,
> Black with the passion of our night;
>
> Be bright again in the heart of this child,
> In peace, in trembling joy made known![27]

Both Pearse and MacDonagh also wrote plays, and the dramatic voice is at the centre of their poetic manner, addressing the reader in the tone and demeanour of a rebel leader and martyr sorrowfully departing this life. In Plunkett, whose poetry is probably the best known of the trio, the intent lyricism imitates an impersonal 'bardic' voice of posthumous, transcendent love:

> The blackbird now with psalter clear
> Sings the ritual of the day
> And the lark with bugle gay
> Blows reveille to the morn,
> Earth and heaven's latest born.[28]

According to William Irwin Thompson's study, *The Imagination of an Insurrection: Dublin 1916*, of 'all the poet and poetic figures who took part in the literary insurrection of 1916', Plunkett was 'the most mysterious, and so little is known about him that he is likely to remain the least understood of all the rebel leaders'.[29] Nevertheless, Thomas

---

[24] 'The Rebel', *The 1916 Poets*, ed. Ryan, 22.
[25] See MacDonagh's *Literature in Ireland: Studies Irish & Anglo-Irish* (Dublin: The Talbot Press, 1916).
[26] Loftus, *Nationalism in Modern Anglo-Irish Poetry*, 148.
[27] 'Barbara', *The 1916 Poets*, ed. Ryan, 114.
[28] 'See the Crocus' Golden Cup', *The 1916 Poets*, ed. Ryan, 172.
[29] William Irwin Thompson, *The Imagination of an Insurrection: Dublin 1916: A Study of an Ideological Movement* (New York: Oxford University Press, 1967), 131.

MacDonagh's son, Donagh, describes Plunkett as '[p]ale, delicate, with weak eyes…yet no man to be ignored in any company'. He continues:

> Born in 1887, he was educated at Catholic University School, Belvedere and Stoneyhurst, spent many years abroad in search of health which the damp air of Ireland could never give him. He was a mystic whose inspiration was in St John of the Cross and St Catherine of Siena, a poet of sensibility and grace and at last an enthusiastic organizer of revolution.[30]

The spectacular nature of life's simplicity, as each of the three men firstly anticipate and then face the battle and imminent death, is scored throughout their poems, such as in Pearse's four-line poem, 'Christmas 1915', which is both plea and war-cry:

> O king that was born
> To set bondsmen free,
> In the coming battle,
> Help the Gael![31]

Or in MacDonagh's 'The Poet Captain', which concludes:

> …they chose for leader a stern sure man
> That looked not back on the waste of story:
> For his country he fought in the battle's van,
> And he won her peace and he won her glory.[32]

Poems are dedicated to loved ones, mothers, wives, children, friends, comrades—all those who will be left behind to mourn and, by implication, to take up the struggle. The idea of commemoration, such a systemic part of Irish poetry in Irish and transcribed into Irish poetry in English during the nineteenth century, finds its most recognizable form in several poems W. B. Yeats wrote in response to Easter 1916 and also in his play, *The Dreaming of the Bones* (1919). As he remarks in 'Easter 1916', Yeats knew several of those involved in the leadership who were behind the Rising and whom he had 'met…at close of day':

> Coming with vivid faces
> From counter or desk among grey
> Eighteenth-century houses.[33]

These are the rebels who in colonial Dublin of once-great Anglo-Irish 'Eighteenth-century houses' will transform themselves and their society because of a dream and 'excess of love' for their country, against which Yeats voices a question that had been on many people's minds after the executions about the intentions of the British administration and the pre-Rising promises for a form of Irish Home Rule:

---

[30] Donagh MacDonagh, 'Plunkett and MacDonagh', in *Leaders and Men of the Easter Rising: Dublin 1916*, ed. F. X. Martin (New York: Cornell University Press, 1967) 168–9. See also Plunkett's sister Geraldine's 'Foreword', *The Poems of Joseph Mary Plunkett* (London: T. Fisher Unwin, 1916).
[31] *The 1916 Poets*, ed. Ryan, 23.
[32] Ibid., 72.
[33] Yeats, *Variorum Poems*, 391–2.

> Was it needless death after all?
> For England may keep faith
> For all that is said and done.

In the Irish ballad tradition of singing the praises of a named individual, townland, or place, Yeats recites the names of those to whom he has previously referred—'That woman' (Constance Markiewicz), 'This man' (Pearse), 'This other' (MacDonagh), and so on—culminating in the refrain:

> I write it out in a verse –
> MacDonagh and MacBride
> And Connolly and Pearse[34]

The executions took place in the first week in May, and a week later Yeats wrote to Lady Gregory, his most trusted confidante, that he had 'no idea that any public event could so deeply move me—and I am despondent about the future'.[35] That he was working on his poem 'Easter 1916' through the summer at Maud Gonne's house on the Normandy coast during one of the most lethal offensives taking place at the Somme, and that he reputedly could hear artillery in the distance, might have added to his despondency.[36] It is also true, as Nicholas Grene reminds us, 'for all that ["Easter 1916"] is a public poem on a public event, announced as such in its very title, up to the end of the last stanza [it] works in the characteristic Yeatsian mode of overheard reverie, in which we watch and only half-comprehend the poet conjuring up an inner landscape'.[37]

In other contemporaneous poems of his, such as 'Sixteen Men Dead', 'The Rose Tree', and 'On a Political Prisoner', and in later work (for instance his two poems on 'Roger Casement'), Yeats is drawn back to both the *dramatis personae* of the tragic events as well as the specific locale of the Rising. In 'The O'Rahilly' (January 1937) Yeats alludes to one of the well-known casualties of the Rising and of 'the death he met':

> Stretched under a doorway
> Somewhere off Henry Street;
> They that found him found upon
> The door above his head
> 'Here died the O Rahilly
> R.I.P.' writ in blood.
>   *How goes the weather?*[38]

In the anonymous voice of a ballad-singer,[39] Yeats circumvents the need to understand or analyse the meaning and implications of 1916 by simply presenting how he imagines

---

[34] Ibid., 394.

[35] 'To Lady Gregory: 11 May 1916', in *W. B. Yeats: The Major Works*, ed. Edward Larrissy (Oxford: Oxford University Press, 2001), 463.

[36] Caulfield, *The Easter Rebellion*, 345.

[37] Nicholas Grene, *Yeats's Codes* (Oxford: Oxford University Press, 2008), 37.

[38] Yeats, *Variorum Poems*, 585.

[39] For the political ballad tradition in Ireland see Eimear Whitfield, 'Another Martyr for Old Ireland: The Balladry of Revolution', in *Revolution? Ireland 1917–1923*, ed. David Fitzpatrick (Dublin: Trinity History Workshop, 1990), 60–8.

the popular tradition (which had been such a critically enabling release in Yeats's own early writing). He would commemorate the foolhardy bravery of The O'Rahilly, co-founder and director of Armaments of the Irish Volunteers, killed in action in a street adjacent to the GPO,[40] and also, famously, toyed with the notion towards the end of his life that he himself, by writing an inflammatory play *Cathleen Ni Houlihan* (1902), had played an imagined part in the Rising:

> I lie awake night after night
> And never get the answers right.
> Did that play of mine send out
> Certain men the English shot?[41]

Notwithstanding the unanswerable question, the reality was that, luckily enough for Yeats, he could view the question from a perspective (in 1938) of having survived the brutal if short-lived war of independence, the civil war, and the partition of the country, and had played a role as senator in the newly established Parliament of the Irish Free State. As Europe moved towards the Second World War, the legacy of 1916 would remain a bone of contention in both states of the partitioned island of Ireland—a source of inspiration for some and calumny for others.

To northerner John Hewitt the event glowed in his memory by proxy. As a 'boy of nine' he hears his teacher's account of:

> 'The abandoned motor cars, the carcasses
> Of army horses littering the street...'
> No more remains of all that he must have told them
> Of that remote, ambiguous defeat.[42]

It is a 'defeat' which Hewitt reinterprets through his understanding of the post-1968 Troubles in Northern Ireland: 'the fierce infection pulses/in the hot blood of half our ghetto-youth', with the 'angled rifles' of snipers and bombs left in doorways and in 'unattended cars'. As a much younger, and more idealistic poet, Hewitt also sings the praises of James Connolly whom he had heard as a six-year-old 'address a Labour crowd'—which places the event probably in 1913 when Connolly was living in Belfast and working as a trade-union activist—and felt 'very proud'.[43]

The legacy which Cork-born Patrick Galvin identifies in his 'A Day of Rebellion' is much more immediate and much more jaundiced. It is as if for all the hope engendered and pride restored by the events of 1916, precious little new has actually come to pass as a result of the sacrifices that, ideologically located in 1916, are viewed by one of those born after the events had taken place:

---

[40] See the account in Caulfield, *The Easter Rebellion*, 255–9.

[41] Yeats, 'The Man and the Echo', in *Variorum Poems,* 632.

[42] 'Nineteen Sixteen, or the Terrible Beauty', in *The Collected Poems of John Hewitt*, ed. Frank Ormsby (Belfast: Blackstaff, 1991), 204.

[43] Hewitt, 'In Memory of James Connolly', in *Collected Poems*, ed. Ormsby, 443–4.

> Softly
> As if the world might break with moving
> They walked over the bodies of the dead
> The flag is burning on the GPO
> Now tell me where all good Christians go?[44]

It was to the myth of 1916 that other poets responded. C. Day Lewis registers the allure and dramatic idealism in two poems of remembrance—one on the fiftieth anniversary of the Rising[45] and the second, 'Remembering Con Markiewicz', which sees her as the embodiment of the fatal hopefulness of 1916:

> Fanatic, bad actress, figure of fun –
> She was called each. Ever she dreamed,
> Fought, suffered for a losing side, it seemed
> (The side which always at last is seen to have won),
> *Oh fiery shade and unvexed bone.*
> Remember a heart impulsive, gay and tender,
> Still to an ideal Ireland and its real poor alive.
> When she died in a pauper bed, in love
> All the poor of Dublin rose to lament her
> *A nest is made, an eagle flown.*[46]

It is his typically unflinching gaze that shows Thomas Kinsella to be the key witness to what happened to the mystique, mythology, and ideological use of the 1916 Rising and its executed leaders in post-independent Ireland of the 1940s and 1950s. 'Nightwalker' alludes to the aftermath of the struggle for independence and the bloody internecine conflict that ensued after British withdrawal. As seen from governmental offices in the 1950s, the long poem dramatizes an Ireland on the cusp of dramatic social change with the abandonment, effectively, of the Sinn Fein policies of economic and cultural separatism as once espoused by the leaders of the Rising and pursued, ostensibly, by their political inheritors of the new state:

> Among us, behind locked doors, the ministers
> Are working, with a sureness of touch found early
> In the nation's birth – the blood of enemies
> And brothers dried on their hide long ago.
> Dragon old men, upright and stately and blind,
> Or shuffling in the corridor finding a key,
> Their youth cannot die in them; it will be found
> Beating with violence when their bodies rot.[47]

---

[44] Patrick Galvin, *New and Selected Poems* (Cork: Cork University Press, 1996), 124.

[45] C. Day Lewis, 'Kilmainham Jail: Easter Sunday 1966', in *The Complete Poems* (London: Sinclair-Stevenson Ltd, 1992), 661–2.

[46] Ibid., 664.

[47] Thomas Kinsella, 'Nightwalker', *Poems 1956–1973* (Mountrath: Dolmen Press, 1980), 105. This passage is excised from the latest version of 'Nightwalker' in Thomas Kinsella, *Collected Poems 1956–2001* (Manchester: Carcanet, 2001).

In an earlier poem, 'A Country Walk', Kinsella registers the shock of recognizing *where* the original selflessness and national cultural energy had ended up, from 'A trench coat playground' to 'a gombeen jungle':

> – armed in hate –
> Brother met brother in a modern light,
> They turned the bloody corner, knelt and killed,
> Who gather still at Easter round his grave,
> Our watchful elders.[48]

But as the narrator of the poem proceeds on his country walk and turns another corner, the imagined figure of the nationalist fighter of Easter 1916, the soldier in the war of independence and the scabrous civil war, recedes into the actual world of the here and now:

> The sombre monuments
> That bear their names: MacDonagh & McBride
> Merchants; Connolly's Commercial Arms...[49]

The high idealism and bloody struggles of the past have turned by the quirk of historical fate back into Yeats's dismal 'Paudeen' fumbling in the greasy till of commercialism.[50] So much for the terrible beauty and the transformation of tragic gaiety which Yeats had seen at play in the heroic generation of leaders of 1916. Those passions had become by Kinsella's generation either a mark of bitter irony (as in 'A Country Walk') or a distant shadow such as the note of poignant romantic loss recollected in John Montague's 'Herbert Street Revisited'.

A poem about the break-up of Montague's marriage, the dramatic setting shifts in and out of focus in both time and place:

> A pony and donkey cropped flank
> By flank under the trees opposite;
> Short neck up, long neck down,
> As Nurse Mullen knelt by her bedside
> To pray for her lost Mayo hills,
> The buried bodies of Easter Volunteers.[51]

As Montague revisits the early years of married life in 'this Dublin Georgian street', his younger fellow northern poet Paul Muldoon revisits in '7 Middagh Street' Yeats's rhetorical question about his play *Cathleen Ni Houlihan* and the role it may or may not have played in inspiring those who took part in the Easter Rising. 'As for his crass, rhetorical/posturing', Muldoon asserts:

---

[48] Kinsella, *Poems 1956–1973*, 55–6. The 'trench coat' was early on identified with the IRA; 'gombeen' means a devious grasping individual who seeks to benefit materially at other people's expense.
[49] Ibid., 56.
[50] See Yeats, 'September 1913' and 'Paudeen', *Variorum Poems*, 289, 291.
[51] John Montague. 'Herbert Street Revisited', *Collected Poems* (Oldcastle: Gallery, 1995), 111.

> ...'Did that play of mine
> send out certain men (*certain* men?)
>
> the English shot...?'
> the answer is 'Certainly not'.
>
> If Yeats had saved his pencil-lead
> would certain men have stayed in bed?
>
> For history's a twisted root
> with art its small, translucent fruit
>
> and never the other way round.[52]

Questions abound as well as 'what ifs' about the Easter Rising and its political and cultural significance. Yeats, for one, seemed incapable of letting go of the event and right up to his own death in 1939 he was still asking himself and his putative reader about the meaning of 1916:

> When Pearse summoned Cuchulain to his side,
> What stalked through the Post office? What intellect,
> What calculation, number, measurement replied?[53]

While in the third part of 'Three Songs to the One Burden' he recalls the Abbey actor, Sean Connolly (no relation of James), who 'Close to the City Hall...' died, and concludes with the resoundingly unresolved image:

> And yet who knows what's yet to come
> For Patrick Pearse had said
> That in every generation
> Must Ireland's blood be shed.
> *From mountain to mountain ride the fierce horsemen.*[54]

James Stephens's 'verdict' on the leaders of 1916, that 'they were good men—men, that is, who willed no evil',[55] is, according to Charles Townshend, an apt reflection:

No person living was worse off for having known Thomas MacDonagh, for example. And most of Ireland's intellectual elite had known him, even if not all had admired him. Ireland's greatest writer, W. B. Yeats, worried that 'I know most of the Sinn Fein leaders & the whole thing bewilders me Conolly [sic] is an able man & Thomas MacDonough [sic] both able & cultivated'. (Pearse he had 'long looked upon a man made dangerous by the Vertigo of Self Sacrifice', who had 'moulded himself on Emmett [sic]'.)[56]

However, in his introduction to the anthology *Goodbye Twilight*, published twenty years after the Rising, poet, editor, and radical left-wing activist Leslie H. Daiken remarked upon the 'upcoming generation' who were responding to the 'messianic grandiloquence'

---

[52] Paul Muldoon, *Poems 1968–1998* (London: Faber, 2001), 178.
[53] Yeats, 'The Statues', *Variorum Poems*, 611.
[54] Ibid., 608.
[55] James Stephens, *The Insurrection in Dublin* [1916] (Gerrard's Cross: Colin Smythe, 1992), 89.
[56] Charles Townshend, *Easter 1916: The Irish Rebellion* (London; Penguin, 2006), 309.

of the 1916 poets in the only way they saw possible: by rejecting politics and distancing themselves from the country and its recent history:

> The cultured studentry fostered pessimism. Futility, or more often an inconsequential groping in the dark for a new bourgeois aesthetic, drove the more sensitive poets away from 'politics' (i.e. Ireland: and all its problems) to Paris, where the soul of Joyce ever presides as a source of inspiration to all through-going isolationists. Thither, with Thomas MacGreevy as a vanguard, trekked younger men like Samuel Beckett, Denis Devlin, and Brian Coffey; driven by the psychology of escape, then become a cult, across the wastelands of interiorization, and technical experiment, they eventually found a mecca in a sort of essentially-celtic [sic] surrealism—as far from Ireland as they could get, in art.[57]

It is, however, difficult not to agree with Charles Townshend's contemporary view, that while 'the power of martyrdom' is the power to 'prohibit compromise', the 'symbolic effect of the event of Easter 1916' was to 'burst the limits of what could be imagined'[58]—a view corroborated by Monk Gibbon in his autobiography, *Inglorious Soldier*. Poet and First World War soldier, Gibbon was on medical leave from the front, when he witnessed the turmoil as it unfolded in Dublin during that fateful week, including the execution of the leading pacifist intellectual Francis Sheehy-Skeffington by command of Captain Bowen-Colhurst, a deranged army officer, an incident which would have a profound and lasting effect on Gibbon's life.[59] *Inglorious Soldier* also describes Gibbon's own journey as a young soldier, a minister's son, carrying with him at the front the poems of Thomas MacDonagh—an image that reveals something of the actual complex nature of the time in which many of these men and women lived and in which their poems were first written and published.[60] Gibbon also expresses the opinion which, in hindsight, it is difficult to deny, that the execution of the Rising leaders, 'shots from khaki-uniformed firing parties', 'did more to create the Republic of Ireland than any shot fired by a Volunteer in the course of Easter week'.[61]

---

[57] Leslie H. Daiken, 'Introduction', *Goodbye Twilight: Songs of the Struggle in Ireland* (London: Lawrence and Wishart, 1936), pp. xi, xii.

[58] Townshend, *Easter 1916*, 355.

[59] Captain J. Bowen-Colhurst, a member of the well-known Ascendancy family who owned Blarney Castle, was a veteran of the Boer War and had been at the retreat from Mons in the First World War. He was formally court martialled for the murder and found guilty but insane, and incarcerated in Broadmoor Criminal Asylum where he remained for eighteen months before emigrating to Canada on a full pension until his death in 1966.

[60] Monk Gibbon, *Inglorious Soldier* (London: Hutchinson, 1968), 171.

[61] Ibid., 71.

CHAPTER 6

....

W. B. YEATS: POETRY
AND VIOLENCE

....

EDNA LONGLEY

THE words 'violence' and 'violent' recur in Yeats's poetry: Maud Gonne teaching 'to ignorant men most violent ways' ('No Second Troy'); 'Violence upon the roads: violence of horses/...evil gathers head' ('Nineteen Hundred and Nineteen'); 'Even the wisest man grows tense/With some sort of violence/Before he can accomplish fate,/Know his work or choose his mate' ('Under Ben Bulben'); 'a man/Violent and famous' ('Cuchulain Comforted'). The more positive inflections occur during the 1930s, but ambiguity already surfaces for scrutiny in 'Ancestral Houses' (1921), the poem that begins 'Meditations in Time of Civil War':

> O what if levelled lawns and gravelled ways
> Where slippered Contemplation finds his ease
> And Childhood a delight for every sense,
> But take our greatness with our violence?[1]

In these quotations 'violence' also shifts between historical and psychic eruptions; and between the overlapping spheres of politics, war, sexuality, and creativity. Both 'violence' and 'violent' appear rarely enough to suggest that Yeats deploys them with great deliberation. But they shadow other words at the points where passion might become uncontrollable (rage, hatred, bitterness, fury); where verbal violence might have material effects ('angry wind', 'intemperate speech'); where blood 'dims' or 'stains' or 'make[s] a right Rose Tree'; where frenzy or madness looms. The phantasmal finale of 'Meditations in Time of Civil War' blurs the boundary between the poetic matrix and murderous events in the outer world: 'Frenzies bewilder, reveries perturb the mind;/Monstrous familiar images swim to the mind's eye.'[2]

---

[1] W. B. Yeats, *The Variorum Edition of the Poems of W. B. Yeats*, ed. Peter Allt and Russell K. Alspach (Basingstoke: Macmillan, 1956), 256, 432–3, 638, 634, 418.

[2] Ibid., 405, 506, 402, 482, 396, 426.

In 'Yeats and Violence', Michael Wood argues that Yeats's sequence 'Nineteen Hundred and Nineteen' (1921) depicts the 'breaking of a vast illusion [the illusion of progress] as having violence at its heart, and indeed as possible only through violence'.[3] If, here and elsewhere, Yeats anticipates later twentieth-century horrors, an issue debated by Wood, it is partly because his poetry *as poetry* has been forced to engage so comprehensively with violence. 'Easter, 1916' pivots on an oxymoron in which violence shocks Romantic and aesthetic premises, shocks poetry: 'A terrible beauty is born'.[4] This chapter's main focus will be the poems by Yeats that mention 'violence', along with five others that present a violence-suffused scenario: 'Easter, 1916', 'The Rose Tree', 'The Second Coming', 'Crazy Jane Grown Old Looks at the Dancers', and 'Blood and the Moon'. All the poems are also reflexively occupied with 'poetry and violence'.

Violence was always potentially on Yeats's poetic horizon after he abandoned the decorative 'rose of battle', woven into his 1890s incantations, for structures that internalized the conflicts of his life and times, and for a conflict-based vision of history. Here chickens and eggs (experience, poetic practice, aesthetic theory, philosophy) are hard to unscramble. Writing on Yeats's 'Anger Management, 1898–1913', Adrian Frazier suggests that the psychic wounds inflicted by Maud Gonne, when Yeats learned that she had long been someone else's lover, conditioned his increasingly angry public interventions.[5] Certainly, personal and political anger merge in 'No Second Troy' (1908), which, as Frazier notes, 'blames' Gonne, while feigning not to do so:

> Why should I blame her that she filled my days
> With misery, or that she would of late
> Have taught to ignorant men most violent ways,
> And hurled the little streets upon the great,
> Had they but courage equal to desire?
> What could have made her peaceful with a mind
> That nobleness made simple as a fire,
> With beauty like a tightened bow, a kind
> That is not natural in an age like this...?[6]

'Desire' spans the erotic and the revolutionary; 'bow' links Blakean sexual symbolism with Amazonian aggression; and 'violent' reverberates beyond its ostensible noun by displacing covert anger onto 'ignorant men' (as Yeats had been ignorant) who lack the courage of their convictions or emotions. The poem's final rhetorical question 'Was there another Troy for her to burn?' evokes a Homeric conflagration of sex, politics, and violence that implicitly consumes the speaker: Yeats as the betrayed Menelaus. A trail runs from 'No Second Troy' to 'Leda and the Swan' (1922), where the rape that begets Helen symbolizes the violent forces that drive history. To connect sex and violence at a less

---

[3] Michael Wood, 'Yeats and Violence', *London Review of Books* 30, 16 (14 August 2008), 22; and see Wood, *Yeats and Violence* (Oxford: Oxford University Press, 2010).

[4] Yeats, *Variorum Poems*, 394.

[5] Adrian Frazier, 'Anger management, 1898–1913', in *W. B. Yeats in Context*, ed. David Holdeman and Ben Levitas (Cambridge: Cambridge University Press, 2010), 35–45.

[6] Yeats, *Variorum Poems*, 256.

mythic level, Yeats seems to have needed the persona of Crazy Jane. In 'Crazy Jane Grown Old Looks at the Dancers' (1929) 'he wound her coal-black hair/As though to strangle her'; while 'she.../Drew a knife to strike him dead'. For Jane, consummation and violence are one: 'They had all that had their hate'. This 'Frankie and Johnny' fantasia, with its refrain '*Love is like the lion's tooth*', originated in a dream, hence in the unconscious, and perhaps in Yeats's greatest sexual passion. He glosses the poem as 'Blake's old thought "sexual love is founded upon spiritual hate"'.[7]

Ireland gave Yeats more objective cause for 'spiritual hate':

> Irish things...make life nearly unendurable. The feeling is nearly always the same: a consciousness of energy, of certainty, and of transforming power stopped by a wall, by something one must either submit to or rage against helplessly. It often alarms me; is it the root of madness? So *violent* it is, and all the more because I seldom lose my temper in the ordinary affairs of life. (January 1909, italics mine)

Yeats claims, however, that 'style' and 'mask' have enabled him to 'subdue a kind of Jacobin rage', to turn 'petulant combativeness' into 'self-possession'. He asks: 'Is not one's art made out of the struggle in one's soul? Is not beauty a victory over oneself?'[8] In 'No Second Troy', 'tightened bow' reflexively figures the verbal muscle developed by the need to reckon with 'violent ways' or feelings: to reconceive Gonne *qua* Muse. 'Beauty' is not yet 'terrible', but it comes within a few lines of 'violence'. In 'Crazy Jane Grown Old' the dance, one of Yeats's key symbols for poetry, assumes an archetypal guise. The poem's folk elements are integral to its suggestion that violence lurks at the root of sexuality, love, emotion. The (equally disturbing) reflexive corollary is that to grasp this may be to heighten poetic intensity:

> Did he die or did she die?
> Seemed to die or died they both?
> God be with the times when I
> Cared not a thraneen for what chanced
> So that I had the limbs to try
> Such a dance as there was danced—
> *Love is like the lion's tooth.*[9]

Friedrich Nietzsche might have applauded '[s]uch a dance'. Nietzsche, who first impressed Yeats in the early 1900s, and who preceded him in conceiving style as self-mastery or mask, had given violence an intellectual glamour: 'You say it is the good cause that hallows even war? I tell you: it is the good war that hallows every cause....Not your pity but your bravery has saved the unfortunate up to now.'[10] For Otto Bohlmann, Nietzsche 'clearly confirmed or stimulated Yeats's approach to rationality, to the

[7] Ibid., 514; W. B. Yeats, *The Letters of W. B. Yeats*, ed. Allan Wade (London: Rupert Hart-Davis, 1954), 758.

[8] W. B. Yeats, *W. B. Yeats: Memoirs*, ed. Denis Donoghue (London: Macmillan, 1972), 138, 156–7.

[9] Yeats, *Variorum Poems*, 514–15.

[10] Friedrich Nietzsche: *Thus Spoke Zarathustra*, ed. R. J. Hollingdale (Harmondsworth: Penguin, 1962), 74.

attributes and morality of the hero, to the conflict of self and soul, to the cyclical nature of history'.[11] Michael Valdez Moses, too, considers Nietzsche's influence 'especially profound and enduring'.[12] Yet in 1903 Yeats 'did not go all the journey with [Nietzsche]'; and it can be hard to determine what he owes directly to him; what to Nietzsche's broader presence in the Zeitgeist; what to kindred elements in William Blake: '[Nietzsche's] thought flows always, though with an even more violent current, in the bed Blake's thought has worn'.[13] And, while both Nietzsche and Yeats surfed post-Romantic currents whereby the aesthetic reaction against nineteenth-century bourgeois morality faced the shocks of modernity, Yeats had to absorb worse shocks than did Nietzsche (d.1900). Nietzsche's model of 'This world [as] the will to power', based on a spectacular charge by Prussian cavalry during the Franco-Prussian War (1870–1), was never shattered by the Great War.[14] Fluctuating Irish contexts also affect Yeats's poetic mediations of rationality, heroism, interior conflict, and historical cycles. So we must ask where an individual poem positions itself vis-à-vis violent phenomena: a matter of overall 'voice' rather than 'speaker'. We must also ask whether Yeatsian intensity can overdose on violence, perhaps in circumstances that cause his admiration for Nietzsche to resurface. There is a line, which Nietzsche's philosophy crosses, between grasping the urges at the root of human nature, and making them the basis for thought or action.

The poems that Yeats wrote after the Easter Rising (1916) qualify Maud Gonne's quasi-Nietzschean joy: 'tragic dignity has returned to Ireland'. Yeats's phrase is 'tragic, heroic lunacy', and he sifts a complex mix of violent events: passive-aggressive self-sacrifice; civil mayhem (the—often forgotten—deaths of non-combatants); brutal retaliation (the execution of the Rising's leaders).[15] The speaker of 'Easter, 1916' explicitly wonders: 'Was it needless death after all?' 'After all', the UK government had promised Home Rule when the war was over. For Yeats, one awkward issue is that the Rising can be seen as partly inspired by tropes that the Irish Literary Revival had set in motion. Subtending his 1916 poems is the question that his late poem, 'The Man and the Echo', poses more bluntly as regards his play *Cathleen ni Houlihan* (1902): 'Did that play of mine send out/Certain men the English shot?'[16] Closer to the Rising, Yeats obliquely distinguishes or extricates his own poetics from two violence-promoting traditions: first, the Irish nationalist ballad patented by the cultural politics of Young Ireland in the mid-nineteenth century; second, blood-and-soil Romanticism, then feeding ideals of 'sacrifice' on both sides of the Great War, and conditioned in Ireland (as in Poland and some other European countries) by Catholicism. 'Easter, 1916' is a revisionist ballad that questions sacrifice and

---

[11] Otto Bohlmann, *Yeats and Nietzsche* (London: Macmillan, 1982), 2–3.

[12] Michael Valdez Moses, 'Nietzsche', in *Yeats in Context*, ed. Holdeman and Levitas, 267.

[13] John Kelly and Ron Schuchard, *Collected Letters of W. B. Yeats*, vol. 3, *1901–1904* (Oxford: Clarendon Press, 1994), 335; George Bornstein and Richard J. Finneran, eds., *W. B. Yeats: Early Essays* (New York: Scribner, 2007), 97.

[14] See Bohlmann, *Yeats and Nietzsche*, 35.

[15] Wade, ed., *Letters of W. B. Yeats*, 613; John Kelly, ed., *Collected Letters of W. B. Yeats* (InteLex Electronic Edition, 2002)—henceforward *CL InteLex*—2945.

[16] Yeats, *Variorum Poems*, 383.

destabilizes the kind of refrain on which patriotic assurance depends (e.g. 'A nation once again'). At the end of the poem, Yeats juxtaposes 'A terrible beauty is born' with the refrain of an anti-British ballad ('The Wearing of the Green'), and with a third refrain, 'changed utterly', which implies that the only assurance about Ireland's future is its violent origin:

> I write it out in a verse –
> MacDonagh and MacBride
> And Connolly and Pearse
> Now and in time to be,
> Wherever green is worn,
> Are changed, changed utterly:
> A terrible beauty is born.

'Easter 1916' is a first-person poem in which the speaker argues with himself and with history. This brings speaker close to 'voice', but the overall dynamics include tensions at the level of image and rhythm as to whether the balance sheet of violence tilts towards life or death. The dead leaders' ironically 'vivid faces' are set against 'grey/Eighteenth-century houses'; the 'stone' of ideology against 'the living stream'. The latter image becomes kinetic in the rhythms of a life-affirming catalogue: 'The rider, the birds that range/From cloud to tumbling cloud,/Minute by minute they change'.[17] In 'The Rose Tree', Yeats disclaims authorship of the Rising by delegating the poem to a dialogue between two executed leaders, Padraic Pearse and James Connolly. The poem ends with Pearse asserting the necessity for blood sacrifice (Yeats had worried about his 'Vertigo of self-sacrifice'): 'There's nothing but our own red blood/Can make a right rose tree.' Here Yeats evokes—but, crucially, does not invoke—a Eucharistic symbolic act that has disempowered his own symbols, along with 'moderate opinion'.[18] If 'Easter, 1916' recognizes that events have sidelined its author, 'The Rose Tree' ventriloquizes on the margin: its underlying voice either holding violence at a distance or held at a distance by violence.

'The Second Coming' (1919) also positions itself to the side of violent events. The speaker figures as a commentator ('The best lack all conviction, while the worst/Are full of passionate intensity') or, at best, a mediumistic prophet: 'Surely some revelation is at hand'. Poetry itself is seemingly sidelined since 'the worst' have expropriated 'passionate intensity'. The poem's reflexive dimension seems relevant to its climax:

> …a vast image out of *Spiritus Mundi*
> Troubles my sight: somewhere in sands of the desert
> A shape with lion body and the head of a man,
> A gaze blank and pitiless as the sun,
> Is moving its slow thighs…
>   …now I know
> That twenty centuries of stony sleep
> Were vexed to nightmare by a rocking cradle,

---

[17] Ibid., 391–4.
[18] Ibid., 396; *CL InteLex*, 2935, 3002.

> And what rough beast, its hour come round at last,
> Slouches towards Bethlehem to be born?[19]

There is a critical tendency to detach the apocalyptic 'rough beast' from its poetic hinterland and its verbal nuances: to see it as free-standing or free-slouching. For instance, Bohlmann cites Nietzsche apropos Yeats's own inexact gloss ('a brazen winged beast that I associated with laughing ecstatic destruction'): 'The beast's "lion body" recalls Zarathustra's picture of the "*laughing lions*" that will come for his "higher ones, stronger ones, triumphanter ones"'.[20] Yet the man-animal in the poem appears neither 'ecstatic' nor positively leonine (contrast '*Love is like the lion's tooth*'). The millennial cycles schematized in *A Vision* (1925), which help Yeats to account for historical turbulence, do not determine his poetry's response to particular events. The 'widening gyre' in the first line of 'The Second Coming' is a framework, not a theme; the last line completes complex dynamics. For Ben Levitas, these dynamics incline towards the 'civilised self-examination', which is civilization's guard 'against the sublimation of its immanent brutalities'.[21] Or perhaps Yeats makes poetry a site of resistance to what Wood calls 'a new degree of uncontrollable violence and a new realm of impunity'.[22] The beast, an Antichrist, may also embody anti-poetry. At the very least, the voice of 'The Second Coming' reclaims 'intensity' from violence.

Where crisis tests a poet's resources, the particularity of that crisis matters. The Easter Rising and the Great War both play into 'The Second Coming'; but what immediately 'troubles [Yeats's] sight' is the Russian Revolution of 1917. This seems to have clinched his perception that 'Mere anarchy is loosed upon the world/The blood-dimmed tide is loosed'. The French Revolution (to which the Russian was routinely compared) and Edmund Burke's *Reflections on the Revolution in France* add historical depth to the sense of extremity. The poem's drafts contain the words 'Burke', 'mobs', 'murderer', and the cancelled line: 'And there's no Burke to cry aloud, no Pitt'.[23] Yeats's horror at the fate of the Romanoffs has been under-noted. 'Crazy Jane on the Mountain' (1938) remains horrified: 'A King had some beautiful cousins,/But where are they gone?/Battered to death in a cellar,/And he stuck to his throne'.[24]

'The Second Coming' echoes words and phrases in Burke's *Reflections*. 'The ceremony of innocence is drowned' parallels his most famous 'cry': 'the age of chivalry is gone'. 'Ceremony', also a motif in the closely related poem 'A Prayer for My Daughter', evokes royalty: Yeats never uses the word so conspicuously again. The *Reflections* were triggered by a sermon in which Richard Price, a politically radical Unitarian minister, had likened the French Revolution to the birth of Christ and quoted *Nunc Dimittis*. Burke ripostes: 'a

---

[19] Yeats, *Variorum Poems*, 401–2.
[20] Bohlmann, *Yeats and Nietzsche*, 178–9.
[21] Ben Levitas, 'War, 1914–1923', in *Yeats in Context*, ed. Holdeman and Levitas, 52.
[22] Wood, 'Yeats and Violence', 24.
[23] See Jon Stallworthy, *Between the Lines: Yeats's Poetry in the Making* (Oxford: Clarendon Press, 1963), 17–20.
[24] Yeats, *Variorum Poems*, 628.

saint and apostle, who may have *revelations* of his own...may incline to think it pious and decorous to compare [the Revolution] with the entrance into the world of the Prince of Peace...announced by the voice of angels to the quiet *innocence* of shepherds' [italics mine]. Further, Burke's portrayal of revolutionary women as crazed Bacchantes (the 'Theban and Thracian orgies, acted in France') connects with images of female violence in 'Nineteen Hundred and Nineteen' and 'A Prayer for My Daughter', and with the latter's female counter-image: 'How but in custom and in ceremony/Are innocence and beauty born?'[25] This symbolic birth also offsets 'terrible beauty' and 'rough beast'. Burke's presence in 'The Second Coming' suggests that 'Surely some revelation is at hand' need not be taken straight. Like the dispersed oxymoron of 'beast' and 'Bethlehem', the line may reprise what Conor Cruise O'Brien calls Burke's 'peculiar kind of furious irony'.[26] In 'If I Were Four and Twenty' (1919), a neo-Burkean essay that attacks the violent tendency of Marxist thought, Yeats uses the words 'beast' and 'loose' and refers to early Christianity: 'Logic is loose again, as once in Calvin and Knox...or in Christianity itself in its first raw centuries, and because it must always draw its deductions from what any dolt can understand, the wild beast cannot but destroy mysterious life'.[27]

Yeats seems much less appalled by the Great War. Perhaps, like the Easter Rising, the assassination of individual royals brought 'terror' and 'beauty' more vividly together than did mass death on the Western Front. Yeats denied that the war directly concerned him: 'the most expensive outbreak of insolence and stupidity the world has ever seen'; 'I shall keep the neighbourhood of the seven sleepers of Ephesus, hoping to catch their comfortable snores till bloody frivolity is over.'[28] His tone is not that in which Wilfred Owen anatomizes 'futility'. Yet critics have increasingly looked behind such denials—or denial. Fran Brearton concludes: 'Yeats's self-presentation is in many respects deceptive; the war influences his thinking, and it is a presence, if a shadowy one, in his poetry.'[29] At a practical level, Yeats lived much in England during the war, dodged air raids, and got caught up in wartime politics (as in his campaigning against Irish conscription). Further, as Ben Levitas notes, discussion of Yeats and the Great War now belongs to a historiographical context in which Ireland itself 'is understood as inevitably caught up in the wider war'.

Yeats's own manoeuvring understands this. Levitas calls his professed 'neutrality' both 'an obvious and politic position' and 'a delicate compromise between the split National and Irish Volunteer movements'.[30] That is, constitutional nationalists

[25] Frank M. Turner, ed., Edmund Burke: *Reflections on the Revolution in France* (New Haven and London: Yale University Press, 2003), 61; Yeats, *Variorum Poems*, 406.

[26] Edmund Burke, *Reflections on the Revolution in France*, ed. Conor Cruise O'Brien (Harmondsworth: Penguin, 1969), 43.

[27] W. B. Yeats: *Later Essays: The Collected Works of W. B. Yeats*, vol. V, ed. William O'Donnell (New York: Scribner), 44.

[28] Quoted in R. F. Foster, *W. B. Yeats: A Life*, vol. 2, *The Arch-Poet* (Oxford: Oxford University Press, 2003), 5; Yeats, *Letters*, ed. Wade, 600.

[29] Fran Brearton, *The Great War in Irish Poetry* (Oxford: Oxford University Press, 2000), 45.

[30] Levitas, 'War, 1914–1923', 46–7.

encouraged Irish involvement in the war; republicans did not. Nevertheless, both the opportunist Rising and its military suppression were shaped by wartime conditions. Hence the balancing act of 'An Irish Airman Foresees his Death' (1918): one of Yeats's three elegies for Major Robert Gregory. Here Gregory is made to say, 'Those that I fight I do not hate,/Those that I guard I do not love', and to claim a Nietzschean heroic-aesthetic rather than patriotic motive: 'A lonely impulse of delight/Drove to this tumult in the clouds'.[31] In positioning itself far above Great War violence, and in preserving Yeats's nationalist credentials, 'An Irish Airman' ignores the fact that Gregory was an Irish unionist and British patriot. In January 1921 Yeats refused to attend a memorial 'Warriors' Day' because: 'A Tribute from me would lack all sincerity. Though I might try to think of men, who served in France or Italy with a good conscience & who now perhaps need help, I would think instead of other ex-service men called "Auxiliary police" who in my own country rob & murder without hindrance'.[32] Yeats chooses not to 'think of' the many Irishmen who had served in the war, some of whom had received a rough welcome home from republicans.[33]

Yet 'An Irish Airman' has to mention the war: 'this tumult in the clouds'. And Yeats's allusion to the Auxiliaries (recruited from former servicemen to assist the Royal Irish Constabulary during the Anglo-Irish War, 1919–21) exemplifies how, to quote Brearton, European and Irish wars are 'inextricably linked' in his mind as in reality.[34] In 1918, indeed, Yeats planned a lecture on 'English War poetry & Irish Rebellion Poetry'.[35] Political caution killed this project, but it may have helped him, in 'Nineteen Hundred and Nineteen', to synthesize the violent conflicts of the years 1914 to 1921: 'All men are dancers and their tread/Goes to the barbarous clangour of a gong'. The sequence's original title, 'Thoughts upon the Present State of the World', declares Yeats's intended scope; his final title datelines millennial cycles, post-war Europe, and the start of the Anglo-Irish War. His global thoughts were locally sparked by an Auxiliary atrocity that had left 'the mother, murdered at her door,/To crawl in her own blood'. This has all the more impact for being the only direct impression of violence. But violence pervades the sequence in mutating symbolic guises: vandalized art, wind or 'foul storm', 'barbarous clangour', animal ferocity: 'We, who seven years ago/Talked of honour and of truth,/Shriek with pleasure if we show/The weasel's twist, the weasel's tooth'. The final section condenses previous images of cumulative violence (or cumulative dismay) into a symbolic whirlwind, another surreal 'revelation':

> Violence upon the roads, violence of horses;
> Some few have handsome riders, are garlanded
> On delicate sensitive ear or tossing mane,

---

[31] Yeats, *Variorum Poems*, 328.

[32] *CL InteLex*, 3850.

[33] See Peter Hart, *The IRA and its Enemies: Violence and Community in Munster, 1916–1923* (Oxford: Clarendon Press, 1998).

[34] Brearton, *Great War in Irish Poetry*, 49.

[35] *CL InteLex*, 3436.

> But wearied running round and round in their courses
> All break and vanish, and evil gathers head:
> Herodias' daughters have returned again,
> A sudden blast of dusty wind and after
> Thunder of feet, tumult of images,
> Their purpose in the labyrinth of the wind;
> And should some crazy hand dare touch a daughter
> All turn with amorous cries, or angry cries,
> According to the wind, for all are blind.
> But now wind drops, dust settles; thereupon
> There lurches past, his great eyes without thought
> Under the shadow of stupid straw-pale locks,
> That insolent fiend Robert Artisson
> To whom the love-lorn Lady Kyteler brought
> Bronzed peacock feathers, red combs of her cocks.[36]

'Nineteen Hundred and Nineteen' is a Great War poem in the terms of Yeats's retrospect: 'established things were shaken by the Great War'.[37] For Michael Wood, this shaken establishment includes 'liberal England; all the Irish people who hoped for a non-violent progression to independence...all the inheritors of the Enlightenment...all the believers in some sort of moral progress running alongside the 19th century's manifest advances in science and technology'.[38] Yet Yeats's 'we' is not situated outside violence. It has a share in human beastliness, in 'The weasel's twist, the weasel's tooth'. This makes the sequence more bleakly pessimistic than 'The Second Coming'. Even the aesthetic domain, like ideals of governance and Enlightenment, has now been overwhelmed by 'evil'. The first section begins: 'Many ingenious lovely things are gone'. In the last section, no function of mind seems able to withstand a 'violence' portrayed as 'mindless' by definition. The term 'apocalyptic nihilism' (coined by Michael Ignatieff) applies to the irresistible 'blindness', 'anger', and 'stupidity' of evil's female and male incarnations: 'Herodias' daughters'/'Robert Artisson'.

Herodias' status as Salome's mother fits the ironical way in which Yeats uses images from, and of, 1890s aestheticism to figure art's impotence ('delicate sensitive ear') or transposes them into the present: Oscar Wilde's *Salome* acquires a new violent currency. But Herodias was also the object of a medieval witch-cult, which fits with the allusion to a reputed Irish witch, Lady Alice Kyteler—Artisson being her 'familiar'. Yeats had written of some Irish fairies: '[The Sidhe] journey in whirling winds, the winds that were called the dance of the daughters of Herodias in the Middle Ages'.[39] Like other motifs in 'Nineteen Hundred and Nineteen' (violent horses, nightmare), witchcraft recalls *Macbeth*, with its theme of spiritual debasement or damnation. Kyteler's submission to Artisson, aristocracy and art ('bronzed') being debased too, again takes 'anarchy' further

---

[36] Yeats, *Variorum Poems*, 428–33.
[37] Yeats, 'Modern Poetry', *Later Essays*, 94–5.
[38] Wood, 'Yeats and Violence', 22.
[39] Yeats, *Variorum Poems*, 800.

than in 'The Second Coming'. This last revelation, which concentrates all the rest, may portend another monstrous birth ('lurches' echoes 'slouches') or parody the ideal marriage imagined in 'A Prayer for My Daughter'. While the voice of the sequence can sound despairingly elegiac, its finale shows that 'furious irony' still braces Yeats's critique. Stripped of illusion rather than disillusioned, his poetry faces 'the growing murderousness of the world'.[40]

Yet the speaker of 'Ancestral Houses' wonders whether 'greatness' and 'violence' might be interdependent: 'O what if levelled lawns and gravelled ways...But take our greatness with our violence?' In a sequence that 'meditates' on the Irish Civil War of 1922, 'violence' may be a way of highlighting the raw energy required to 'create the institutions of a new nation...all our slow growing coral' amid internecine struggle.[41] And not only in Ireland: the sequence's wider orbit is post-war chaos and reconstruction in a 'shaken' Europe where ancestry, inheritance, continuity, and tradition have been thrown into various sociopolitical melting pots. And while Yeats tends to favour the 'ancestral', his desire to be involved (and for the Literary Revival to be involved) in Ireland's future keeps him open to new sources of energy. Cyclical history, too, assumes a more benign aspect in a perspective that sees every civilization as beginning in violence and ending in decadence. 'Ancestral Houses' posits that 'the inherited glory of the rich' may be 'some marvellous empty sea-shell' rather than a 'fountain' that 'rains down life'. At a reflexive level, these dialectics implicate poetry and Yeats's capacity for artistic self-renewal: 'Some violent bitter man, some powerful man/Called architect and artist in that they,/ Bitter and violent men, might rear in stone/The sweetness that all longed for night and day'. This proposes that the founding energies of art, as well as society, have something to do with 'violence', 'bitterness', and 'power'.[42]

Actual Civil War violence tests such a hypothesis. In 'The Stare's Nest by My Window', the sixth (penultimate) poem, violence first occurs offstage: 'somewhere/A man is killed or a house burned'; then, centre stage: 'Last night they trundled down the road/That dead young soldier in his blood'. The effect echoes Great War poems. Is this Yeats's Civil War Unknown Soldier? The Irish Civil War, which killed over a thousand people, had an ideological basis in the terms of the 1921 Treaty that ended the Anglo-Irish War. Anti-Treaty republicans, led by Eamon de Valera, thought that the pro-Treatyites, who formed the Provisional government (and would govern as Cumann na nGaedheal until 1932), had compromised the principle of Irish self-determination by agreeing to dominion status.[43] Yeats, unlike Maud Gonne, supported the Treaty, but held 'both sides...responsible for this whirlpool of hate'.[44] In the fifth poem, 'The Road at My Door', where the speaker meets pro-Treaty and anti-Treaty combatants, he neutrally 'envies' what they have in common: their immersion in action. In 'The Stare's Nest' the factual images of

---

[40]   Yeats, *Autobiographies* (London: Macmillan, 1955), 192.
[41]   *CL InteLex*, 4342.
[42]   Yeats, *Variorum Poems*, 417–18.
[43]   See Bill Kissane, *The Politics of the Irish Civil War* (Oxford: Oxford University Press, 2005).
[44]   *CL InteLex*, 4100.

death are framed by a symbolic refrain that pleads for all-embracing reconstruction: 'O honey-bees,/Come build in the empty house of the stare.' The speaker also tracks violence to its sources in ideology: 'We had fed the heart on fantasies,/The heart's grown brutal from the fare'. This rephrases Voltaire's 'Those who can make you believe absurdities can make you commit atrocities.' From one angle, 'Meditations' marks poetry's ultimate sidelining. In both its material and symbolic aspect, Yeats's west-of-Ireland tower is on the margins. But, from another angle, poetry sidelines the war. More overtly than in 'The Second Coming' or 'Nineteen Hundred and Nineteen', Yeats speaks as a poet. Reflexive images—'My House', 'My Table', 'My Descendants', 'My Door', 'My Window'—occupy the foreground.[45]

'Meditations' dramatizes the way in which this imaginative locus is challenged by the forces ranged against every constructive enterprise: against poetry, artworks, social architecture, cultural capital like that accumulated by the Revival. As in 'Nineteen Hundred and Nineteen', the survival of 'monuments' is in question. But Civil War violence has brought this question nearer home (as house-symbolism) and required some answers. It has made new demands on Yeats's poetry: on the resistance it exemplifies and figures. The sequence's interest in men of action ('Some violent bitter man', civil-warriors, the 'man-at-arms' who 'founded' the tower) marks a self-goading concern with masculinity. Yeats's most hopeful symbol for poetry (in the third poem) is a Japanese gift, 'a changeless sword', which 'may moralise/My days out of their aimlessness' because it fuses art with power. The sword reappears in the final poem as 'A glittering sword out of the east': but now as an ambiguous sign in another revelatory phantasmagoria dominated by 'Monstrous familiar images'. These include 'The rage-driven, rage-tormented, and rage-hungry troop'. Here Yeats stylizes civil war as mutual savagery: 'Trooper belabouring trooper, biting at arm or at face,/Plunges, towards nothing'. The poet-speaker, the would-be man of action, himself feels the pull of 'rage-driven' violence, of apocalyptic nihilism. 'All that senseless tumult' tempts him to cry, meaninglessly, 'For vengeance on the murderers of Jacques Molay'. In the last stanza, however, he 'shuts the door' on images and dialectics that remain unresolved. To enter the tower's interior is to tilt the scale towards poetry ('abstract joy') rather than the public world ('something that all others understand or share'). Yet poetic interiority has again been invaded by that world: by a new violence-induced—or perhaps violence-inducing—need to defend or define poetry's own values.[46]

Yeats was still completing 'Meditations' when, in December 1922, he was appointed to the Irish Senate. This public turn more directly exposed him, along with any latent ambiguity about violence, to violent realities, including state-violence, state-vengeance: the government officially executed seventy-seven anti-Treaty 'Irregulars'. Meanwhile the houses of thirty-seven senators were burned down, and Yeats's Dublin house was put under armed guard. 'Blood and the Moon' (1927) is an oblique elegy for Kevin O'Higgins,

---

[45] Yeats, *Variorum Poems*, 423–5.
[46] Ibid., 421, 426–7.

Minister for Justice and a zealous proponent of the executions policy, who was assassi-
nated in July 1927. Despite getting less attention than 'Easter, 1916', 'Blood and the Moon'
is an equally significant, if not equally good, political poem. The assassination of
O'Higgins, a personal friend, once again brought violence close to home and to poetry.
Yeats called him a 'martyred intellectual', and expected (wrongly) that his martyrdom
would equal Pearse's.[47] In 'Parnell's Funeral' (1933) he is still mourning O'Higgins as the
first Irish government's 'sole statesman'.[48] This contrasts with Conor Cruise O'Brien's
account of O'Higgins as 'ruthless and implacable'. O'Brien quotes his notorious words,
'if necessary seven hundred and seventy-seven', and places Yeats's regard for O'Higgins
in evidence that Yeats 'was as near to being a Fascist as the conditions of his own country
permitted'.[49] Yeats shows his regard by making this Catholic politician a kind of honor-
ary Protestant. That is, he identifies him with qualities for which, in reaction to the
diminished clout of the southern Irish Protestant minority, he had started to idealize
eighteenth-century Ascendancy Ireland. The second section of 'Blood and the Moon'
announces that 'Goldsmith and the Dean [Swift], Berkeley and Burke' belong to Yeats's
(and presumably O'Higgins's) 'ancestral stair'. In the first section, the tower's exterior
also takes on a new symbolic aspect:

> Blessed be this place,
> More blessed still this tower;
> A bloody, arrogant power
> Rose out of the race
> Uttering, mastering it,
> Rose like these walls from these
> Storm-beaten cottages...[50]

Neither 'bloody' nor 'arrogant' has the negative vibe one might expect. Similarly, Yeats
prefaces the entry of Goldsmith et al. by linking 'utterance' with other kinds of 'mastery'.

'Blood', so directly seen in 'the mother murdered' or the 'dead young soldier', has
acquired metaphorical connotations. It colours 'race' and 'power'. It represents Irish his-
tory as a blood-struggle. 'Parnell's Funeral' would later configure myth, 'sacrifice', 'ani-
mal blood', 'popular rage', and communal scapegoating in a manner that corresponds to
René Girard's analysis in *Violence and the Sacred* (1972). The second section of 'Blood
and the Moon' refers to Swift's 'blood-sodden breast' (Swift's blood reappears, 'enriched'
by 'bitterness', in 'Parnell's Funeral'), and associates him with 'The strength that gives our
blood and state magnanimity of its own desire'. This euphemistically implies that
O'Higgins, a 'strong man', displayed Swiftian strength in his policy of executions. The
speaker himself seems about to cry out for 'vengeance on the murderers of Kevin
O'Higgins'. Yet the poem's third and fourth sections ponder 'blood' and 'stain' in a way

---

[47] Letter to O'Higgins's widow, *CL InteLex*, 5012.

[48] Yeats, *Variorum Poems*, 543.

[49] Conor Cruise O'Brien, 'Passion and Cunning: An Essay on the Politics of W. B. Yeats', *Passion and
Cunning: Essays on Nationalism, Terrorism & Revolution* (New York: Simon and Schuster, 1988), 34, 41.

[50] Yeats, *Variorum Poems*, 480.

that eventually positions the pure 'moon' of imagination above violence. The 'blood of innocence' is said to have 'left no stain' on the moonlit tower, even though its historical ground has been 'blood-saturated' by 'Soldier, assassin, executioner' for motives that include 'abstract hatred'. The exclamation 'Odour of blood on the ancestral stair!' (O'Higgins's death) is followed by frustration that stops short of vengeance: 'And we that have shed none must gather there/And clamour in drunken frenzy for the moon.' 'Blood and the Moon' is a psychodrama in which desire for violent retaliation nearly fractures the psyche. 'Frenzy' ebbs in the final section, which concludes with the speaker attaching 'the stain of blood' to 'power'; whereas 'no stain/Can come upon the visage of the moon/When it has looked in glory from a cloud.'

The voice of 'Blood and the Moon' is sometimes dominated by the speaker's declarative rage; sometimes polarized between the titular symbols; sometimes nuanced by subtler effects of word and image. It is the latter that stop it from being a cry for vengeance: 'anger management' once again. The calming last lines ('no stain' etcetera), which cleanse some stains from the poem itself, have their origin in a passage where poetic complexity re-emerges as attention to minutiae: 'Upon the dusty, glittering windows cling,/And seem to cling upon the moonlit skies,/Tortoiseshell butterflies, peacock butterflies'. The oxymoron, 'dusty, glittering', poises the 'dusty wind' of 'Nineteen Hundred and Nineteen' against the 'glittering sword' of 'Meditations'. Repeated words ('cling', 'butterflies') also contribute to a zen-like moment.[51]

Does Yeats credit O'Higgins with not having 'shed blood'? Or is his career covered by power's necessary 'strength' and 'stain of blood'? Do 'blood' and 'moon' ultimately polarize politician and poet—also as aspects of Yeats himself? His letters to Maud Gonne in the last months of 1927 are relevant to the poem, and to subsequent poems that implicate violence. Here he defends capital punishment ('your own church has again & again—in the Papal states—confirmed sentences of death'); and denies that his support for tough measures, which 'protect many harmless people', involves 'hatred'.[52] Ten years later he would write: 'If human violence is not embodied in our institutions [i.e., a proper Irish army] the young and old [will not give them] their loyalty. A government is legitimate because some instinct has compelled it to take life in defence of its laws and its shores.'[53] To Gonne he says: 'Today I have one settled conviction "create, draw a firm strong line & hate nothing what ever not even … Satan himself". I hate many things but I do my best'; 'Balzac … made authoritative government (government which can, at need, be remorseless, as in his "Catherine des Medicis") interesting in my eyes—that is what I mean by the "strong line", a line drawn upon the fluctuating chaos of human nature.'[54] In fact, the letters draw a stronger line than do any of Yeats's poems to date. He had himself noticed that, in 'Leda and the Swan' (1922), 'bird and lady took such possession of the scene' as to eradicate his political template for the poem: a 'movement from above … preceded by

[51] Ibid., 481–2.
[52] CL InteLex, 5039, 5035.
[53] Yeats, 'On the Boiler', Later Essays, 241.
[54] CL InteLex, 5033, 5035.

some violent annunciation'.[55] One object of this essay is to counter the tendency to read Yeats's later politics back into his earlier poetry; and, indeed, into later poems that resist his own opinions. From 1916 to 1927 Yeats's imagination was tested by a series of catastrophic events, diverse but interlinked: events in which he was often personally concerned; events that placed his poems in a shifting relation to violence; events that caused poetry itself to be at issue and at stake.

During the last twelve years of his life, Yeats was more likely to write poems in which voice and violence converge. A notorious example occurs in 'Three Songs to the Same Tune' (1933–4), where a fictional patriot sings 'good strong blows are delights to the mind'. The songs derive from Yeats's brief flirtation with Ireland's nearest equivalent to any kind of fascist movement: Eoin O'Duffy's Blueshirts. The Blueshirts were formed owing to fears that de Valera, who had come to power democratically in 1932, would not respect the state's institutions. These fears proved groundless, and Yeats himself developed some admiration for de Valera. When he published 'Three Songs', he explained or excused them thus: 'In politics I have but one passion and one thought, rancour against all, who, except under the most dire necessity, disturb public order: a conviction that public order cannot long persist without the rule of educated and able men ....Some months ago that passion laid hold on me with the *violence* which unfits the poet for all politics but his own [italics mine].'[56] 'Authoritative government' (Mussolini, not Hitler) attracted Yeats primarily because, as a writer and a Protestant, he relied on elitism to secure his influence in Ireland. Perhaps, too, with actual violence no longer on his doorstep, he indulged hatreds, as of 'this filthy modern tide', which in others he might have dubbed 'abstract'. 'Rage' is among the souped-up stimuli that his later Muse sometimes required.[57] 'Crazy' and 'mad', too, cross over from the other side of the equation.

Meanwhile Nietzschean heroics, with their repudiation of 'pity', come back into the picture. 'Crazy Jane on the Mountain' fantasizes about a 'violent' Cuchulain avenging the Romanoffs.[58] Another example is Yeats's infamous omission of Wilfred Owen from his *Oxford Book of Modern Poetry* (1936) on the grounds that 'passive suffering is not a theme for poetry'. His contrasting praise of Oliver St John Gogarty's 'gay, stoical...heroic song' alludes to an incident in which Gogarty escaped from assassins by swimming across the Liffey. Yeats's celebration here of 'swashbucklers, horsemen, swift indifferent men' is hardly the voice of 'Nineteen Hundred and Nineteen' or 'Meditations in Time of Civil War'.[59] 'Under Ben Bulben' (1938) is a different matter:

> You that Mitchel's prayer have heard,
> 'Send war in our time O Lord!'
> Know that when all words are said
> And a man is fighting mad,

[55] Yeats, *Variorum Poems*, 828.
[56] See Foster, *W. B. Yeats: A Life*, vol. 2, 478.
[57] Yeats, 'The Statues', *Variorum Poems*, 611; 'The Spur', ibid., 591.
[58] Ibid., 628.
[59] W. B. Yeats, ed., *The Oxford Book of Modern Verse* (Oxford: Clarendon Press, 1936), pp. xxxiv, xv.

Something drops from eyes long blind,
He completes his partial mind...
Even the wisest man grows tense
With some sort of violence
Before he can accomplish fate,
Know his work or choose his mate.[60]

The more Yeats's poetry prefers declaration to dialectics, the more it draws a strong line, the less he transmutes 'human violence' into intensity or complexity. In 'Under Ben Bulben' the 'completion' sealed by 'some sort of violence' comes over as simplification. This is felt in the speaker's hectoring tone, a coarsening of texture, over-emphatic rhymes and rhythms. Instead of envying the devil for having all the best tunes, as 'Blood and the Moon' seems to do, Yeats has taken to devising war-tunes of his own—and thus does violence to his poetic voice.

But this is only sometimes the case. 'The Man and the Echo' (1938), which ends with 'Man' being 'distracted' by a 'stricken' rabbit's cry, is a painful self-interrogation that asks whether Yeats's life and work have ever had violent consequences: 'Did that play of mine...?' 'Long-legged Fly' (1937–8) invokes Nietzschean heroes (Julius Caesar, Michael Angelo), but in rhythms that defuse violence by rendering power as creative concentration: '*Like a long-legged fly upon the stream,/His mind moves upon silence.*'[61] Nietzsche's presence in 'Lapis Lazuli' (1936) may be more problematic. His concept of 'tragic joy' informs the relative postures of art and history, ultimately personified by the carved 'Chinamen' whom the poem brings to life: 'On all the tragic scene they stare./One asks for mournful melodies.'[62] For Michael Valdez Moses, 'Lapis Lazuli' 'can be viewed as a painful instance of Yeats's ethically irresponsible and politically misguided response to the growing threats of fascism and a wider war in Europe'. 'Any defence,' he says, 'rests on an implicit acceptance of the Nietzschean view that the highest duty of the artist is to transform the violence and cruelty of human existence into an object worthy of aesthetic and philosophic contemplation.'[63] For John Lyon, there is no defence: the poem's 'artifice...piled upon artifice...plays on the reader, and on the troubled Thirties world in which its first readers must live, a sick and inhumane joke or trick or contrivance'.[64] But 'Lapis Lazuli' is neither a transcription of Nietzsche nor a simple regression to the 1890s. The layering of art form within art form and the long view of violence ('Old civilisations put to the sword') mark a deliberate stylization that—presciently—asks what art should do when history becomes extreme. 'Lapis Lazuli' resembles Shakespeare's last plays more than the tragedies to which it alludes—'There struts Hamlet, there is Lear'—or perhaps Prospero behind the scenes. Yeats's 1920s sequences had confronted huge destruction, the imperative of reconstruction, and their meaning for poetry. He may

---

[60] Yeats, *Variorum Poems*, 638.
[61] Ibid., 617.
[62] Ibid., 567.
[63] Moses, 'Nietzsche', 273–4.
[64] John Lyon, 'War, Politics, and Disappearing Poetry: Auden, Yeats, Empson', in *The Oxford Handbook of British and Irish War Poetry*, ed. Tim Kendall (Oxford: Oxford University Press, 2007), 293.

have earned the right to say: 'All things fall and are built again,/And those who build them again are gay'—no mere declaration, but heard as diminuendo and crescendo in the poem's rhythms. One of Yeats's will-and-testament poems, 'Lapis Lazuli' involves a retrospect on 'poetry and violence'. It suggests the multifarious legacy he left to other poets (not only Irish) who might be similarly tested.

His last poem to mention 'violence' is a deathbed poem. Yeats wrote 'Cuchulain Comforted' in January 1939:

> A man that had six mortal wounds, a man
> Violent and famous, strode among the dead;
> Eyes stared out of the branches and were gone.
>
> Then certain Shrouds that muttered head to head
> Came and were gone. He leant upon a tree
> As though to meditate on wounds and blood...

The uncanny atmosphere reflects the poem's origins in a dream, although the dream itself was partly shaped by Dante's *Inferno*. Hence terza rima and the Dantesque detail of Cuchulain meeting a 'shade', who tells him: 'Your life will grow much sweeter if you will/ Obey our ancient rule and make a shroud.'[65] This underworld or unconscious is also shaped/shaded by Yeats's own poems, including earlier meditations on 'wounds and blood'. At one level, the '[v]iolent and famous' Cuchulain represents the later Yeats: the finished mask of 'one that ruffled in a manly pose/For all his timid heart' ('Coole Park, 1929').[66] Since the shades are 'timid'—'[c]onvicted cowards all'—they may represent the self to whom Cuchulain is anti-self. Roy Foster sees Yeats's projected afterlife as a bit of a comedown: 'banishment to the company of outcasts'.[67] Yet, mirroring the chthonic collaboration of both selves, the poem's rhythm is extraordinarily 'comforting' or assuaging, as in the climax: 'They sang, but had nor human tunes nor words,/Though all was done in common as before;//They had changed their throats and had the throats of birds.'[68] This metamorphosis, which has the pulse of a resurrection, symbolizes Yeats's posterity more mysteriously than does the golden bird of 'Sailing to Byzantium'. Moreover, the fact that Cuchulain 'meditates' and sews a shroud turns the hero into a poet as opposed to the poet envying the hero. Perhaps the Yeatsian unconscious has gone back to basics. The scenario recalls two early poems: 'Fergus and the Druid' (1892), where a king prefers 'dreams' to his crown; 'Adam's Curse' (1901), where 'stitching and unstitching' figures poetic craft.[69] In his final meditation on 'wounds and blood', Yeats seems to make poetry a matter of life and death. The poem's strange course, from 'mortal wounds' to 'the throats of birds', implies that poetry can do something different from other responses to violence, however marginal, 'outcast', or downcast it may appear. It cannot really respond with its own violence. It cannot redeem. Yet it can absorb and, in some sense, transfigure.

---

[65] Yeats, *Variorum Poems*, 634.
[66] Ibid., 489.
[67] Foster, W. B. *Yeats: A Life*, vol. 2, 648.
[68] Yeats, *Variorum Poems*, 635.
[69] Ibid., 102, 204.

PART III

MODERNISM AND TRADITIONALISM

CHAPTER 7

....

YEATS, ELIOT, AND
THE IDEA OF TRADITION

....

EDWARD LARRISSY

I

....

To compare Yeats and Eliot enhances one's sense of Yeats's relationship to critical and aesthetic tendencies which were in varying degrees operative, from the 1890s onwards, in Ireland, Britain, America, and continental Europe. Bringing Eliot into the picture gives one a better sense of the extent to which they shared a context, and adds definition to the distinctiveness of what each achieved. Central to what they shared, at least at the beginning of the period, is a felt need to respond to the innovations of French Symbolism, especially as interpreted by a work well known to both, Arthur Symons's *The Symbolist Movement in Literature*.[1] Each of them sought to convey a state of mind, or mood, in terms of symbol and association, in ways that would transfer feeling to the reader without the need for otiose discursiveness. A problem each shares is that of relating what is, in its essentials, a modern picture of the mind to tradition.

It is surely better to speak, as Patrick Keane does in the title of his book, of *Yeats's Interactions with Tradition* than, as F. A. C. Wilson does in the title of his, simply of *Yeats and Tradition*.[2] Yet even 'interaction' does not do justice to the complexity of any writer's relationship with past writers and thinkers, and Yeats was an extraordinarily learned and widely read poet. One of a number of things he learnt from Blake, I suspect, was the confidence to make what influenced him his own. Rather as alchemical or Neoplatonic symbols are in Blake changed both as individual items and by virtue of their role in his

---

[1] Arthur Symons, *The Symbolist Movement in Literature* (London: Heinemann, 1899). See the discussions in Terence Brown, *The Life of W. B. Yeats*, 2nd edn. [1999] (Oxford: Blackwell, 2001), 71–3; and in Peter Ackroyd, *T. S. Eliot* (London: Hamish Hamilton, 1984), 33–4.

[2] Patrick J. Keane, *Yeats's Interactions with Tradition* (Columbia: University of Missouri Press, 1987); F. A. C. Wilson, *W. B. Yeats and Tradition* (London: Gollancz, 1958).

system, so when Yeats asks, in 'Coole Park and Ballylee, 1931', 'What's water but the generated soul?', he is indeed drawing upon *The Cave of the Nymphs*, an allegorical interpretation of Homer by the Neoplatonic philosopher Porphyry.[3] Yet the deftly realized natural setting provides a context in this mutable world, not in the Neoplatonic realm of Forms. And the reflections of the speaker ironize the reference to Porphyry: 'Another emblem there!' An ironic Neoplatonist then? That would scarcely be interesting enough for Yeats. Rather, the reference to Porphyry becomes involved in a meditation about the poet's store of images, and the kind of society that thinks in images—one whose loss, as the poem goes on to remind us, might be regretted by a 'last Romantic'.

But even to stress Yeats's creative appropriations does not go far enough. His eventual repertoire of points of reference, including Blake, Shelley, Burke, Swift, Neoplatonic philosophy, and Nietzsche, is as strong-minded a re-ordering as Eliot's. Yeat's promotion of this kind of list is not as powerful and effective as was Eliot's promotion of the Metaphysical poets; but there are ways in which Yeats, in like manner, reordered tradition for readers as well as for himself.

Yeats's essay 'Poetry and Tradition', written in 1907, was originally published in 1908 as 'Poetry and Patriotism' in a booklet called *Poetry and Ireland* from the Cuala Press.[4] There were in fact two essays in this booklet, the other, also called 'Poetry and Tradition', being by Lionel Johnson. Of course, poets' critical ideas change over time, but Yeats's essay belongs to a period of transition in his thought and poetic style, and contains elements that link his earlier and later career. The original title of the essay, and the fact that Johnson's essay accompanied it (for he is also one of the 'last Romantics'), remind one of the link between poetry and social traditions evoked in 'Coole Park and Ballylee, 1931'. And indeed, the essay brings together 'the romantic conception of Irish Nationality' promoted by John O'Leary on the one hand;[5] and, on the other, a prescription for good poetry, which is related to that 'romantic conception':

> When Lionel Johnson, and Katharine Tynan, and I myself began to reform Irish poetry we thought to keep unbroken the thread running up to Grattan which John O'Leary had put into our hands, though it might be our business to explore new paths of the labyrinth. We sought to make a more subtle rhythm, a more organic form than that of the older poets who wrote in English, but always to remember certain ardent ideas and high attitudes of mind which were to our imagination the nation itself, so far as a nation can be summarised in the intellect.[6]

I want first to look at Romanticism: what idea of Romantic poetry is being promoted, and what are the links between this and nation. Eliot is openly critical of Romantic theory and practice, but is still in thrall to both—not in the same way that Yeats was, but still

---

[3] W. B. Yeats, *The Variorum Edition of the Poems of W. B. Yeats*, ed. Peter Allt and Russell K. Alspach (Basingstoke: Macmillan, 1956), 490–2.

[4] W. B. Yeats and Lionel Johnson, *Poetry and Ireland* (Dublin: Cuala Press, 1908).

[5] W. B. Yeats, *Early Essays: The Collected Works of W. B. Yeats*, vol. IV, ed. Richard J. Finneran and George Bornstein (New York: Scribner, 2007), 180.

[6] Ibid., 181.

in a manner that reveals a shared intellectual environment in the early twentieth cen-
tury. I shall then go on to consider the implications of another phrase that does not
appear in the extract above, but is important in Yeats's essay: namely, 'country spiritism'
(his phrase for the belief of the Irish country people in the supernatural), which is the
form in which his esoteric interests make their appearance here. As for Eliot, he was far
more interested in the esoteric than readers have yet generally recognized, and the inter-
est illuminates his own sense of the sacred. Finally, I shall make Yeats's comments on
Grattan and O'Leary the occasion for a reflection on the idea of culture in Yeats and
Eliot.

II

The aesthetic point about 'a more subtle rhythm, a more organic form' merits attention.
For without the help of phrases such as this, we might be inclined to wonder whether
Yeats's 'romantic conception' of nationality has much to do with that vast, various, and
perplexing 'ism', Romanticism in the arts. And indeed, it is not clear that Yeats does use
that word as a contemporary literary critic would use it. Yet it seems equally clear that he
is indeed referring, when he speaks of the qualities of poetry, to things he can find in
some Romantic poets, especially Blake and Shelley. In this, he was engaged in helping to
remake readers' sense of what was the best early nineteenth-century poetry.

Recently, the advent of the various new historicisms, and the move to rediscover forgot-
ten women poets, have prompted derision of the Romantic-period canon of the 'big six'
male poets: Blake, Wordsworth, Coleridge, Byron, Shelley, and Keats. Yet Blake had taken
a long time to achieve this eminence, arguably a position at which he did not securely
arrive until at least the 1960s, chiefly as a result of the influence in that period of Northrop
Frye. That Blake should ever have set off on this path is a result of the efforts of nineteenth-
century poets and critics such as the Rossetti brothers and of Swinburne, whose biography
of Blake appeared in 1868. But Yeats's assistance was particularly effective. Whatever one
may think of the rigour and reliability of the three-volume *Works of William Blake* that
Yeats brought out in 1893 with Edwin Ellis, it is easily the most serious and comprehensive
edition to have appeared until then.[7] And Yeats's advocacy expressed itself in other ways:
through essays, reviews, and through references to Blake in a variety of texts which are
primarily on other subjects. For example, it is clear from Yeats's 1900 essay on 'The
Symbolism of Poetry' that when he there speaks of 'organic rhythms and words as subtle,
as complex, as full of mysterious life, as the body of a flower or of a woman', he is in part
thinking of Blake's poetry, for he offers the admission that this poetry may sometimes be
'obscure or ungrammatical as in some of the best of the Songs of Innocence and

---

[7] Edwin John Ellis and W. B. Yeats, eds, *The Works of William Blake, Poetic, Symbolic and Critical*, 3
vols. (London: Bernard Quaritch, 1893).

Experience.[8] This, indeed, is the only example of any poetry to be found in that important concluding section. The only other actual poet mentioned is Tennyson, exponent of 'that brooding over scientific opinion that so often extinguished his central flame'.[9]

When Yeats was a young man, not only were Tennyson and Browning in the ascendant, but people still remembered that, in the so-called Romantic period, there had been poets called Thomas Campbell and Samuel Rogers; and that, apart from having been a novelist, Walter Scott was a renowned poet. They still read Felicia Hemans; recalled the names of poems by Southey; and still read (and listened to) Thomas Moore. Yeats evoked this lost world in his essay 'What is "Popular Poetry"?' But it was not lost then, as the word 'popular' indicates: 'Longfellow, and Campbell, and Mrs Hemans, and Macaulay in his *Lays*, and Scott in his longer poems are the poets of a predominant portion of the middle class.'[10] In the 1890s people even remembered Macpherson's *Ossian*: it may be recalled that, in *The Countess Kathleen and Various Legends and Lyrics* (1893), the poem that in subsequent collections was renamed by Yeats as 'The Rose of Battle' was called 'They Went Forth to the Battle but they always fell'—a slight misquotation from Macpherson's 'Cath-Loda' (1763). Little of this idea of the Romantic period survives into the twentieth century. Yeats's generation, partly guided by the pre-Raphaelites, wished to move poetry away from declamation, discursiveness, otiose description, towards subtle but intense presentation and embodiment: Blake moved up in their estimation and Hemans down. In doing this, they created the Romantic period as we know it—or used to know it. This Romantic period—complete with the 'big six'—did not exist until this process had begun, and Yeats was more influential than many of his contemporaries in instigating it.

I have used the example of Yeats's Blake because it is the most striking and indubitable success of his promotional activities. So well was this activity recognized by his contemporaries that it actually gives one a better idea of T. S. Eliot's literary politicking if one reads the latter's essay on Blake alongside some of his less charitable remarks about Yeats. In that essay, notwithstanding Blake's 'peculiar honesty', his efforts were for Eliot vitiated by his construction of an eccentric mythology.[11] As for the early Yeats, 'he was very much fascinated by self-induced trance states, calculated symbolism, mediums, theosophy, crystal-gazing and hobgoblins. Golden apples, archers, black pigs and such paraphernalia abounded.'[12] The essay on Blake is in part an attempt to discourage tendencies that were alive in the still widely distributed works of early Yeats, and which might be perpetuated by critics such as John Middleton Murry. Murry was one of the chief targets of Eliot's criticism. His flaw was to promote an expressivist view of poetry, which encouraged the notion of the poet as a personality with an original message that might require an idiosyncratic mythology.[13]

---

[8] Yeats, *Early Essays*, 120.
[9] Ibid.
[10] Ibid., 7.
[11] T. S. Eliot, *The Sacred Wood: Essays on Poetry and Criticism* [1921] (London: Methuen, 1928), 151, 157–8.
[12] T. S. Eliot, *The Use of Poetry and the Use of Criticism* [1933] (London: Faber, 1964).
[13] Edward Larrissy, *Blake and Modern Literature* (Basingstoke: Palgrave Macmillan, 2006), 34–6.

To understand Yeats's use of the word 'romantic', one needs also to grasp the connection he makes between a certain style of Romanticism and the 'romantic conception of Irish nationality'. The most instructive point to grasp concerns the ethical. To see why this is so, it may be worth standing back from the question at hand to remark on the acuteness, the sensitivity, of Yeats's conscience and the associated capacity for remorse: 'not a day/But something is recalled,/My conscience or my vanity appalled'[14] 'Did that play of mine send out/Certain men the English shot?'[15] Of course, the very title of *Responsibilities* is an ethical term. When, in 'Poetry and Tradition', Yeats speaks of 'certain ardent ideas and high attitudes of mind', he is not being vague and precious. Rather, he is trying to express the way in which the ethical is mediated through the aesthetic. The epigraphs to *Responsibilities*, rightly considered, offer a concise and memorable clue to this aspect of Yeats's thought. There are two of them: 'In dreams begins responsibility' (said to come from an 'Old Play'); and, from Khoung Feu Tseu (i.e. Confucius), this: 'How am I fallen from myself, for a long time now/I have not seen the Prince of Chang in my dreams.'[16] We should read the two quotations together—ideogrammatically, one might say. The statement that responsibility begins in dreams sounds potentially dubious, like a piece of the most degraded Romanticism. But the explanation is provided in the second quotation. The Prince of Chang was a ruler of exemplary rectitude. If we see images of good persons in our dreams, then we are setting out on the path to responsibility. Images offer the affective example of something we could become, of someone we could imitate or follow. One might wish to die for a cause espoused by a person encountered in such a dream; but Yeats cannot believe that anyone would die for an abstract moral or political treatise. This is one of the distinctions upon which the 'change' in 'Easter 1916' hinges. When the leaders of the rebellion are shot, they cease to be associated with the fruitless, opinionated argument personified by Constance Markievicz: 'Her nights in argument/Until her voice grew shrill.'[17] Having turned themselves into martyrs by the sacrifice of their lives, they have also turned themselves into images, and will garner loyalty, devotion, and sacrifice to their cause.

The last two stanzas of 'Among School Children' offer a meditation which concludes with an apostrophe to the organic union of life and form;[18] but while this is not intended to elucidate an ethical concept, it is certainly relevant to our discussion, for Yeats shows in *Responsibilities* and elsewhere that, in like manner, moral responsibility should come to imbue a life rather than coerce it from without. Such an idea goes right back to the early essay on 'The Symbolism of Poetry', published in 1900: 'Those formulas and generalisations, in which a hidden sergeant has drilled the ideas of journalists, and through them the ideas of all but all the modern world, have created in their turn a forgetfulness like that of soldiers in battle.'[19] Forgetfulness: this is reminiscent of 'How am I fallen from

---

[14] Yeats, 'Vacillation', *Variorum Poems*, 501.

[15] Yeats, 'The Man and the Echo', ibid., 632. On Yeats and remorse, see Peter McDonald, *Serious Poetry: Form and Authority from Yeats to Hill* (Oxford: Oxford University Press, 2002), 17–50.

[16] Yeats, *Variorum Poems*, 269.

[17] Ibid., 392.

[18] Ibid., 445–6.

[19] Yeats, *Early Essays*, 113.

myself.' In the Romantic tradition of poetry which Yeats helped to create by remoulding the past, he thought that he had found the techniques which would act upon his readers' minds in the service of an ethically informed idea of the Irish nation. Thus, in 'To Ireland in the Coming Times' he says 'Nor may I less be counted one/With Davis, Mangan, Ferguson' because he imbued his work with esoteric symbols 'and things discovered in the deep/Where only body's laid asleep'—that is, in the world of dreams.[20]

Eliot's remaking of tradition does not align itself with Romanticism. When, towards the end of 'Tradition and the Individual Talent', he rejects every item in Wordsworth's definition of poetry ('emotion recollected in tranquillity'), he is only confirming an implication the reader has grasped from the start. We have been told that it is not the intensity of 'the emotions' that counts, but 'the intensity of the artistic process'; that 'the poet has not a "personality" to express, but a particular medium'.[21] The conception of the 'medium', of the results of the 'artistic process', can be concisely illustrated by reference to Eliot's notorious essay on 'Hamlet and his Problems', where he claims that the character of Hamlet lacks artistic inevitability because the play does not present us with an 'objective equivalent to his feelings'.[22] Therefore we cannot make sense of the feelings. The general formula for successful art is couched in terms of the 'objective correlative': 'The only way of expressing emotion in the form of art is by finding an "objective correlative"; in other words, a set of objects, a chain of events, which shall be the formula of that *particular emotion*; such that when the external facts, which must terminate in sensory experience are given, the emotion is immediately evoked.'[23] The task of the artist is to confect the work of art in such a way that it conveys the feeling, without further reference to what the artist feels about the feeling: that would bring in 'personality'. In the early 1920s, Eliot's prime example of poetry that is successful in this regard is that of the Metaphysicals. He derives a description of the poet's mind from the work of Donne, and what that work shows about the way Donne thought. The 'ordinary man's experience', says Eliot, 'is chaotic, irregular, fragmentary. The latter falls in love, or reads Spinoza, and these two experiences have nothing to do with each other, or with the noise of the typewriter or the smell of the cooking; in the mind of the poet these experiences are always forming new wholes.'[24] In other words, we have here an example of a potential objective correlative. The 'set of objects', 'the chain of events', are here constituted by falling in love, reading Spinoza, the noise of the typewriter, and the smell of cooking.

The essay on 'The Metaphysical Poets' adds further implications, however. First, there is the emphasis on unifying thought and feeling: 'A thought to Donne was an experience; it modified his sensibility.'[25] In the formula above, the phrase about 'reading Spinoza' being unified with experiences like falling in love, or the smell of the cooking, is meant to indicate how this might look in a modern context. Secondly, this kind of unification

---

[20] Yeats, *Variorum Poems*, 138.
[21] Eliot, *Sacred Wood*, 55–6.
[22] Ibid., 101.
[23] Ibid., 100.
[24] T. S. Eliot, *Selected Prose of T. S. Eliot*, ed. Frank Kermode (London: Faber, 1975), 64.
[25] Ibid.

has become difficult since the early seventeenth century: 'In the seventeenth century a dissociation of sensibility set in, from which we have never recovered.'[26] That is to say, thought, feeling, and sensation have become dissociated, such that the language of feeling is detached from the experiences which, prior to the dissociation, had given it body: Eliot is, indeed, offering a history of poetic style and language simultaneously with a history of sensibility. But this history is not quite as anti-Romantic as it might look at first glance. Whatever the modernist character of Eliot's emphasis on the 'process' and the 'medium', it is also the case that the conveying of 'feeling' remains a central artistic aim; and this is a Romantic imperative. It is not a prime characteristic of classical and neo-classical theories, which are essentially mimetic. The aim of uniting thought and feeling was central to the work of Romantic poets such as Wordsworth, Coleridge, Shelley, and Keats. Indeed, Eliot's desiderata for good poetry (one might even include the reference to Spinoza) sound like a recipe for the early Coleridge's deliberately associative (and significantly titled) 'Conversation Poems'. If one remembers Keats's concept of 'negative capability', instead of insisting on Romantic 'egotism', one can entertain the possibility of a Romantic precursor for Eliot's 'impersonality'. A telling piece of evidence is to be found in the extent to which Eliot's preparation for the 1926 Clark Lectures, the ostensible subject of which was the Metaphysical poets, involved a consideration of the critical ideas of Keats and Coleridge.[27]

It is sometimes said that Eliot derived the idea of 'dissociation of sensibility' from Rémy de Gourmont's 'The Problem of Style', and Eliot himself claimed de Gourmont as a prime influence on his thinking in the Preface to the second edition of *The Sacred Wood*.[28] Certainly, the latter's formulation is strikingly similar to Eliot's:

> If, to the visual memory, the writer joins the emotive memory, and if he has the power, in evoking a material spectacle, of recovering the emotional state which that spectacle had aroused in him, then he possesses, even if he is ignorant, the whole art of writing.[29]

The notion of 'recovering' an emotional state is derived from the concept of 'association of ideas', a fact confirmed when de Gourmont invokes the British Empiricists, specifically Hobbes and Locke, in support of his contention that 'Sensation is the basis of everything, of the moral and intellectual life as well as the physical life.'[30] Unfortunately, the 'dissociating intelligence' has obscured this fact.[31] The remark on sensation should be read as unifying it with the moral and intellectual life, as well as offering a high valuation of it. We are by no means far from the mental universe inhabited by the early Wordsworth and Coleridge: in

[26] Ibid.
[27] Edward Lobb, *T. S. Eliot and the Romantic Critical Tradition* (London: Routledge and Kegan Paul, 1981), 60–92.
[28] Eliot, *Sacred Wood*, p. viii.
[29] Rémy de Gourmont, *Selected Writings*, ed. and trans. Glenn S. Burne (Ann Arbor: University of Michigan Press, 1966), 114.
[30] Ibid., 123.
[31] Ibid., 119.

the Preface to *Lyrical Ballads*, the former claimed that poetry exhibits 'the manner in which we associate ideas in a state of excitement'.[32] Before Coleridge took up the study of Kant, during the period when much of his most original work was accomplished, he was an enthusiast of the philosophers Hartley and Berkeley. Both Coleridge and Wordsworth in the 1790s were experimenting with innovative ways of representing mental process in poetry by looking to empiricist psychology for guidance. Suggesting a like debt, Keats, memorably, yearned for 'a Life of Sensations rather than of Thoughts!' It seems unlikely that the Keats who wrote the Odes meant by this that he yearned for an existence bordering on unconsciousness: he will have meant something like 'intuitive perceptions through the senses'.[33] Eliot's historiography also has more in common with the Romantics than might at first appear. Keats preferred the Elizabethan to the Miltonic, and Coleridge preferred the Elizabethan and Jacobean to the dominant Augustan school of the eighteenth century.

However, there is no correlative in Eliot's poetry for the overt moral seriousness of Yeats's middle and later periods. This is because Eliot starts by depicting consciousness, and ends by connecting that consciousness to a religious framework, by which stage morality is subordinated to faith. Yeats, however, still believes in action and personality, perhaps because there is a national tradition to renew: as Steven Matthews says, 'the nation is still awaiting the emergence of distinctive individual and cultural *personality*'.[34] Since Yeats's sense of tradition is involved in the struggle for nationhood, and for the creation of a national literature, he cannot leave the personality that acts and chooses outside the realm of art.

III

If we are to differentiate the ideas about tradition held by Yeats and Eliot, it will not do to see one as Romantic and the other as classical, even though it is essential to distinguish between the nature of their indebtedness to Romanticism. However, in order to be able to do that with any degree of accuracy, there are other unexpected points of convergence which need to be assessed. A major point of difference between Yeats and Eliot used to be seen as residing in their attitudes to esotericism. Yeats joined the Hermetic Order of the Golden Dawn, toyed with Theosophy, attended seances, and ultimately produced, with the assistance of his wife, a major occult synthesis, *A Vision*. Eliot, on the other hand, wrote satirically of Madame Blavatsky and the 'Seven Sacred Trances'; and in *The Waste Land* disguised her, equally satirically, as Madame Sosostris, 'the wisest woman in Europe,/With a wicked pack of cards'.[35] This is usually taken as a straightforwardly dismissive reference

---

[32] William Wordsworth and Samuel Taylor Coleridge, *Lyrical Ballads, and Other Poems, 1797–1800*, ed. James Butler and Karen Green (Ithaca, NY: Cornell University Press, 1992), 14.

[33] W. W. Beyer, quoted in Lobb, *T. S. Eliot and the Romantic Critical Tradition*, 66.

[34] Steven Matthews, *Yeats as Precursor: Reading in Irish, British and American Poetry* (Basingstoke: Palgrave Macmillan, 2000), 10.

[35] T. S. Eliot, *The Complete Poems and Plays* (London: Faber, 1969), 44, 62.

to the way in which ideas of the sacred can be corrupted and vulgarized. Yet this descrip-
tion occurs in a poem which acknowledges its indebtedness to Jessie L. Weston's book
From Ritual to Romance (1920). And this was by no means merely a work of speculative
anthropology. Weston was a member of the occultist Quest Society, founded in 1897 by
G. R. S. Mead, who had been Madame Blavatsky's London secretary between 1889 and her
death in 1891.[36] In her book, Weston acknowledges her debt to Mead in exploring 'the mys-
terious border-land between Christianity and Paganism'.[37] Leon Surette claims, in his *The
Birth of Modernism,* that she saw in the Grail legend 'an occult tradition that has secretly
maintained itself since antiquity'.[38] This does not negate the qualification Eliot enters
against occultism. Rather, it reveals a different attitude to the legacy of the Grail legend,
Eliot seeing it as a myth of spiritual renewal which was given its truest form in the Christian
narrative. As Leon Surette says, 'His subsequent decision to convert to orthodox
Christianity clearly separates him from the occult movement, but it does not negate a com-
mon ground of interest'.[39] The common ground of interest lies in the perception of a simi-
larity between the truths conveyed by ancient myths and those conveyed by Christianity.
But this would sound rather bland if one did not notice that Eliot thought ancient truths
contained the potential for the renewal of civilization by means of a profound conversion,
one which went beyond notional assent to a credo, or the personal experience of belief:
one which involved a whole way of life, and the rituals and imagery that linked it to the rest
of society, and sustained it emotionally as well as intellectually. These are the points of con-
vergence between magical and Christian practice.

In this light, it is by no means surprising to find that the passage from *Burnt Norton*
about 'the still point' and 'the dance' is indebted to Charles Williams's description of the
magical dance of the Tarot in his novel *The Greater Trumps* (1932).[40] Williams, an
Anglican, best remembered now for his association with C. S. Lewis and J. R. R. Tolkien,
was for a while a member of the Salvator Mundi Temple of the Fellowship of the Rosy
Cross. He was a good friend of Evelyn Underhill, who managed to combine an Anglican
faith with membership of the Golden Dawn. Williams's influence, as Grover Smith has
shown, is also to be seen in Eliot's play *The Cocktail Party,* first performed in 1949. Here
the visionary moments, and the ideas of initiation and sacrifice, especially as undergone
by a young woman (Celia), are influenced by the magical shamanism of Williams's nov-
els.[41] As for *Four Quartets,* there is another influence upon them which in Eliot's mind
appears to have been inseparable from esotericism: that of Blake. When Eliot was writ-
ing *East Coker,* Blake 'kept getting into' it.[42] The *Quartets* are in part related to the four

---

[36] Leon Surette, *The Birth of Modernism: Ezra Pound, T. S. Eliot, W. B. Yeats and the Occult*
(Montreal: McGill-Queen's University Press, 1993), 17.
[37] Ibid., 234.
[38] Ibid.
[39] Ibid., 240.
[40] Helen Gardner, *The Composition of Four Quartets* (London: Faber, 1978), 85.
[41] Grover Smith, 'Eliot and the Shamans', in *T. S. Eliot at the Turn of the Century,* ed. Marianne
Thormählen (Lund: Lund University Press, 1994), 166, 174–8.
[42] Quoted in Gardner, *The Composition of Four Quartets,* 18.

traditional elements;[43] and this was also true both of Blake's Four Zoas and, according to occultists, of the four Tarot suits.

Yeats's interest in the esoteric has an opposite tendency to that of Eliot. Where Eliot finds in Christianity the apotheosis and spiritualization of ancient rituals of fertility and renewal, including magical ones, Yeats sees Christianity as one more example of those rituals—and one which often mistakenly sought to involve them in a life-denying purpose. In Yeats's essay on 'Poetry and Tradition' his interest in the esoteric appears first as 'country spiritism'—the belief of the Irish country people in spirits and the fairies. This phrase is then connected with the possibility of 'a new philosophy of spiritism coming to a seeming climax in the work of Frederic Myers, and in the investigations of uncounted obscure persons', which could 'change the country spiritism into a reasoned belief that would put its might into all the rest. A new belief seemed coming.'[44] The idea of changing 'country spiritism' into 'reasoned belief' is fairly obvious code for the activities of occultists such as Yeats himself. And such activities have the added attraction of validating Yeats's own Irish background. R. F. Foster has demonstrated the strong tradition of occultism in certain Anglo-Irish circles.[45] And I myself have pointed out the Rosicrucian tradition of the inner orders of Freemasonry, a fairly pervasive institution of Irish Protestant society.[46] It is this tradition which provides Yeats's early symbolism of Rose and Cross, and arguably much else besides.

Eliot had a point. Yeats desires a tradition that derives its strength from a religion, or something very like it; but it will have hobgoblins and golden apples. Yeats could admire Dante quite as much as Eliot did for the strength and richness of the framework that medieval Catholicism lent to his poetry. But despite the Christian imagery occasionally to be found in Various Legends and Lyrics and in The Wind Among the Reeds, and despite his acquaintance with Anna Kingsford, Yeats does not have in mind even an esoteric Christian revival.[47] As W. J. McCormack says, 'Yeats's relationship to Church or doctrine was never close, despite his grandfather's holy orders. The incarnation took its place in his philosophy of history, as if he were a comparativist, not a believer.'[48] Rather, he thinks of his magical practices and esoteric beliefs as, among other things, akin to what the Druids did and thought: 'And ancient Ireland knew it all,' as he states in 'Under Ben Bulben'.[49] It was Eugene O'Curry, comparing the Druids to the Magi, who had explained that Druidism was 'that form of the Eastern philosophy or religion which prevailed in

[43] Ibid.

[44] Yeats, Early Essays, 182.

[45] R. F. Foster, 'Protestant Magic: W. B. Yeats and the Spell of Irish History', Paddy and Mr Punch: Connections in Irish and English History (London: Allen Lane, 1993), 212–32.

[46] Edward Larrissy, Yeats the Poet: The Measures of Difference (Hemel Hempstead: Harvester, 1994), 17–22.

[47] Anna Kingsford's works were collected in The Credo of Christianity and Other Addresses and Essays on Esoteric Christianity and Some Letters by Edward Maitland, ed. Samuel Hopgood Hart (London: John M. Watkins, 1916). This book was in Yeats's library.

[48] W. J. McCormack, Blood Kindred: W. B. Yeats: The Life, The Death, The Politics (London: Pimlico, 2005), 112.

[49] Yeats, Variorum Poems, 637.

early ages in our own as well as other western nations.'[50] Yeats's own Anglo-Irish class could, however, offer a truer understanding of ancient Druid truths than that which was open to his Catholic compatriots, by virtue of the opportunities it offered for occult learning.

Yet it will be worth pausing and reflecting on the way in which the supernatural actually makes itself felt in Yeats. In the 1890s, he thought of poetry in terms indissociable from magic:

> All sounds, all colours, all forms, either because of their pre-ordained energies or because of long association, evoke indefinable and yet precise emotions, or, as I prefer to think, call down among us certain disembodied powers, whose footsteps over our hearts we call emotions; and when sound, and colour, and form are in a musical relation, a beautiful relation to one another, they become as it were one sound, one colour, one form, and evoke an emotion that is made out of their distinct evocations and yet is one emotion.[51]

He proceeds to call the evoked emotion 'a god', though elsewhere in this period it may be a 'mood'. Yeats's evocation of the supernatural is far more tentative and subtle than, say, Blake's invented mythology in his prophetic books. The symbolist language has been toned down by the time Yeats writes 'Poetry and Tradition', but the effect of the words he uses there—'a subtle rhythm, a more organic form'—is certainly not such as to encourage clunking mythological machinery. Yeats's own development of the idea of organic form is towards a style of representing the mind in motion: in other words, it is a development of the representation of association of ideas pioneered by Wordsworth and Coleridge. It is this which underlies the meditative manner of a poem such as 'Coole Park and Ballylee', even allowing the poet to break in on his own thoughts: 'Another emblem there!' The best-known—or most notorious—example of this effect in Yeats is to be found in the second section of the poem 'The Tower', where the speaker recalls his story of Red Hanrahan encountering an old man who shuffles cards which he is able to enchant into a pack of hounds pursuing a hare. Yeats remembers that Hanrahan follows them 'towards—/O towards I have forgotten what—enough!' And consider how the second section of the poem begins: Yeats presents himself pacing upon the battlements, staring out at the landscape, calling up 'Images and memories'. We start with 'Beyond that ridge lived Mrs French'.[52] The centrality of association of ideas to Yeats's method has been most clearly advanced by Cairns Craig, though he gives to the archetypes in Anima Mundi a secondary role, whereas I think it is better to see Yeats's chains of association in the mundane memory as leading up to the Great Memory.[53] There is nothing especially surprising, from everything else we know about Yeats, in an account which sees his con-

[50] Eugene O'Curry, *On the Manners and Customs of the Ancient Irish*, 3 vols. (London: Williams and Norgate, 1873), II, 179.

[51] Yeats, *Early Essays*, 115–16.

[52] Yeats, *Variorum Poems*, 410–12.

[53] Cairns Craig, *Yeats, Eliot, Pound and the Politics of Poetry* (London: Croom Helm, 1982), 36–9, 78–82.

servative philosophy as combining the valuing of loved association with the belief in a realm of supernatural forms to which the Anglo-Irish magus has access.

IV

'The Tower' contains the famous lines about Yeats's pride in his Anglo-Irish Protestant inheritance:

> The pride of people that were
> Bound neither to Cause nor to State,
> Neither to slaves that were spat on,
> Nor to the tyrants that spat,
> The people of Burke and of Grattan...[54]

The remark about Grattan in the essay on 'Poetry and Tradition' puts the Anglo-Irish tradition in an unexpected light: 'we thought to keep unbroken the thread running up to Grattan which John O'Leary had put into our hands'.[55] It is not obvious that there is a strong kinship between the kinds of Irish independence espoused respectively by Grattan and O'Leary, nor indeed that there is a thread such as Yeats describes. Of course, Yeats has another fact in mind: O'Leary was inimical to the kind of sectarianism which would deprive Grattan, or indeed Burke, of the right to be regarded as fully Irish. As he says in a lecture of 1886:

> ... you should never be content to take on trust such of our great writers as have spoken to you through the English language. You must give your days and nights to our Swifts, Goldsmiths, Berkeleys, Burkes.... To be sure, you will be told by narrow-minded or ignorant people that there is little that is Irish about all or most of them. But if you begin by freeing yourself from narrow-mindedness, you have made a great (perhaps the greatest) step towards freeing yourself also from ignorance.[56]

Yeats finds in this open-mindedness of O'Leary evidence of a form of nobility that is held in common by him and Grattan. He describes how he is seeking to encourage in Ireland a critique of modern society and its modes of thought similar to that offered by Morris and Ruskin in England. One also infers, then, the appeal to a type of nobility that scorns calculation and utility. At the same time, one does have to register his urge to unify the divisions of Ireland. In this essay, there may be an elegiac note of regret at the fading of this ideal Ireland from people's minds, but the ideal Ireland would possess this profound unity.

---

[54] Yeats, *Variorum Poems*, 414.
[55] Yeats, *Early Essays*, 181.
[56] John O'Leary, quoted in Donald T. Torchiana, *W. B. Yeats and Georgian Ireland* (Evanston, Illinois: Northwestern University Press, 1966), 108n.

Yeats was to develop this unity across the traditions most explicitly and sharply in his later years. This development was partly spurred by his knowledge of Frank O'Connor's translations of Irish poetry into English. The first stanza of Yeats's 'The Curse of Cromwell', from *New Poems* (1938), runs thus:

> You ask what I have found, and far and wide I go:
> Nothing but Cromwell's house and Cromwell's murderous crew,
> The lovers and the dancers are beaten into the clay,
> And the tall men and the swordsmen and the horsemen, where are they?
> And there is an old beggar wandering in his pride—
> His fathers served their fathers before Christ was crucified.[57]

The line on 'the lovers and the dancers' who are 'beaten into the clay' is a reference to O'Connor's translation of the anonymous poem in Irish, 'Cad a dhéanfamaid feasta gan adhmad', known as 'Kilcash'.[58] The poem laments the collapse of the Gaelic order and refers to the earl, the lady, and the people being beaten into the clay. The lines about Christ's crucifixion, however, derive from another of O'Connor's translations, this time from Egan O'Rahilly's early eighteenth-century poem to which he gives the title 'Last Lines'.[59] The translation ends thus: 'I shall go after the heroes, aye, into the clay/My fathers followed theirs before Christ was crucified.' Yeats means the present tense of his poem to refer to his own day: the curse of Cromwell continues, and it is a legacy, he thinks, of vile modernity. This is the spirit in which he can adopt the voice of a last representative of the Gaelic order. In 'Under Ben Bulben' we have the lines from 'Kilcash' about being beaten into the clay again, pressed into a service of a sketch of the unified matter of Ireland:

> Sing the peasantry, and then
> Hard-riding country gentlemen...
> Sing the lords and ladies gay
> That were beaten into the clay
> Through seven heroic centuries.[60]

Here, the Protestant with a horse joins the Gaelic earls in a compound image of that ideal Ireland adumbrated in 'Poetry and Tradition'. It is as if Yeats were to say that in history, as in life, nothing can be sole or whole that has not been rent. This is entailed by the necessary brokenness and imperfection of existence, something he learnt to understand from Nietzsche's philosophy of tragic affirmation, and something from which Ireland should learn.

'The Curse of Cromwell' can prompt one to explore another, parallel, line of thought: one which leads into areas that lie close to Eliot's historiography. For if 'money's rant is on', as Yeats there claims, that is because he thinks the seventeenth century initiates the modern era of bourgeois scientific materialism.[61] It must

---

[57] Yeats, *Variorum Poems*, 580.
[58] See the translation by Frank O'Connor collected in *The Penguin Book of Irish Verse*, ed. Brendan Kennelly (Harmondsworth: Penguin, 1970), 69–70.
[59] Ibid., 74–5.
[60] Yeats, *Variorum Poems*, 639–40.
[61] Ibid., 580.

therefore have been tempting to identify the contagion in literature, and consider some such literary-historical thesis as Eliot advances with his 'dissociation' theory. And indeed, this is what Yeats does. His friend Herbert Grierson had sent him his new edition of Donne in 1912, and Yeats had replied that he now understood Donne, and had noticed that 'the more precise and learned the thought the greater the beauty, the passion'.[62] It is some years since T. R. Henn drew out the implications of this admiration, but there is no reason to dissent from what he then said: 'From Donne [Yeats] learnt much in his technique from 1912 onwards, but it seems probable that he found other precedents in that life; the fusion of intense religious experience with sensuality; the obsession of the tomb-haunter, the concern with apparitions and strong ghosts; poetry which set, for the first time in English poetry, the full theme of *Odi et Amo*'.[63] Yeats kept up with Grierson's work, and in 1922 we find him writing to say that the anthology, *Metaphysical Lyrics and Poems of the Seventeenth Century* (1921), which he had evidently been promised, had not yet arrived.[64] This is the same anthology that prompted Eliot's great review-article, 'The Metaphysical Poets'. Prior to this, Yeats had been imitating stanza forms derived from Abraham Cowley, as Thomas Parkinson has pointed out: 'the form of "In Memory of Major Robert Gregory" was taken from Cowley's "Ode on the Death of Mr William Hervey" and used again in "A Dialogue of Self and Soul" and part II of "The Tower". The stanza form of "The Mother of God" also came from Cowley'.[65] There is no reason to think that Yeats preferred Cowley to Donne. Indeed, as we shall see, if anything the evidence seems to point in the opposite direction. But looking for an appropriate form in which to commemorate Robert Gregory, it was natural to consider whether an elegiac ode, such as Cowley's on William Hervey, would offer a fruitful model. More generally, what Yeats found in the poets of the early to mid-seventeenth century, apart from the union of thought and passion, is the capacity that Grierson ascribes to Donne in the introduction to his anthology: '[Donne] is one of the first masters, perhaps *the* first, of the elaborate stanza or paragraph in which the discords of individual lines or phrases are resolved in the complex and rhetorically effective harmony of the whole group of lines'.[66] But even so, if we are to consider the case of the forms borrowed from Cowley, Yeats is by no means subservient, displaying a characteristic hesitation between a relatively loose effect and relative formality: thus, as Helen Vendler says, discussing Yeats's use of the Cowley stanza, 'In the later work of Yeats, as . . . in "The Tower",

[62] W. B. Yeats, *The Letters of W. B. Yeats*, ed. Allan Wade (London: Rupert Hart Davis, 1954), 570.

[63] T. R. Henn, *The Lonely Tower: Studies in the Poetry of W. B. Yeats* [1950] (London: Methuen, 1965), 40. See also Steven Matthews, 'Yeats's "Passionate Improvisations": Grierson, Eliot, and the Byronic Integration of Yeats's Later Poetry', 127–41, *English* 49 (2000), 129–30.

[64] Yeats, *Letters*, ed. Wade, 693; Herbert J. C. Grierson, ed., *Metaphysical Lyrics and Poems of the Seventeenth Century* (Oxford: Clarendon Press, 1921).

[65] Thomas Parkinson, *W. B. Yeats: The Later Poetry* (Berkeley: University of California Press, 1964), 199. Yeats might have had to hand Cowley's *Poems*, ed. A. R. Waller (Cambridge: Cambridge University Press, 1905). Closer in time is Cowley's *Essays and Selected Verse*, ed. J. M. Attenborough (London: Walter Scott, 1915).

[66] Grierson, ed, *Metaphysical Lyrics and Poems*, p. xxiii.

apparent lexical and syntactic informality obscures a strict formality of stanza-construction.'[67]

Cowley has other uses for Yeats than the mere provision of stanza forms. Yeats devises little historical narratives in which Cowley plays a significant part. The best known of these occurs in the historiographical sections of *A Vision*, both versions: the 1937 edition simply repeats the 1925 one: 'The gyre ebbs out in order and reason, the Jacobean poets succeed the Elizabethan, Cowley and Dryden the Jacobean as belief dies out.'[68] This does not sound very promising. But matters are not so clear-cut. In his 1926 Introduction to a translation of Merriman's *The Midnight Court,* Yeats notes that Merriman has Venus call on 'Ovid, Virgil, Tibullus, Cowley, Waller.'[69] Here Cowley figures as a champion of love. In the Introduction to *Wheels and Butterflies* (1934), looking back on his early 'romantic' affiliations, Yeats recalled how 'I acknowledged, being a romantic, no verse between Cowley and Smart's *Song to David,* no prose between Sir Thomas Browne and the *Conversations* of Landor.'[70] But on which side of the dividing line did Cowley lie? In his essay on Louis Lambert, published in 1934, Yeats makes it clear that Cowley was always approved: 'Here and there in Blake, in Keats, in Blunt, in Browning…there is a deep masculine resonance, that comes, I think, from a perfect accord between intellect and blood, lacking elsewhere since the death of Cowley.'[71] These are the terms in which Eliot praised metaphysical poetry, and in which Yeats had also praised Donne, supported by an historical thesis reminiscent of Eliot's. For Yeats, the early seventeenth century would have had the added attraction that it was the period of the great Rosicrucian synthesis of Robert Fludd (1574–1637) and his associates.[72]

It fits with this historical thesis that for Yeats this age, and more especially what came before it, displayed a unity of culture. In *Autobiographies,* recalling the tale of Dante hearing 'a common man sing some stanza from the *Divine Comedy*', he mused: 'Had not Europe shared one mind and heart, until both mind and heart began to break into fragments a little before Shakespeare's birth?'[73] A page or so later he asks, 'must I reverse the cinematograph?' He is writing of his life from 1887 to 1891, and having replied to this question in the affirmative, offers his celebrated thoughts on how he might write a new

---

[67] Helen Vendler, *Our Secret Discipline: Yeats and Lyric Form* (Oxford: Oxford University Press, 2007), 294.

[68] W. B. Yeats, *A Vision: An Explanation of Life Founded Upon the Writings of Giraldus and Upon Certain Doctrines Attributed to Kusta Ben Luka* (London: T. Werner Laurie, 1925), 205; W. B. Yeats, *A Vision* (London: Macmillan, 1937), 295.

[69] W. B. Yeats, *Prefaces and Introductions: The Collected Works of W. B. Yeats,* vol. VI, ed. William H. O'Donnell (New York: Macmillan, 1988), 160.

[70] W. B. Yeats, *Wheels and Butterflies* (London: Macmillan, 1934), 7.

[71] W. B. Yeats: *Later Essays: The Collected Works of W. B. Yeats,* vol. V, ed. William O'Donnell (New York: Scribner), 128.

[72] William Wynn Westcott, the prime mover in the formation of the Golden Dawn, was the author of *In Memory of Robert Fludd: an address to the Rosicrucians assembled at Bearstead, in Kent, on September 14, 1907* (London: Societas Rosicruciana in Anglia, 1907).

[73] W. B. Yeats, *Autobiographies: The Collected Works of W. B. Yeats,* vol. III, ed. William H. O'Donnell and Douglas N. Archibald (New York: Scribner, 1999), 165.

mythological poetry, with 'Patrick or Columcille, Oisin or Finn, in Prometheus' stead;
and instead of Caucasus Cro-Patrick or Ben Bulben'.[74] For '[h]ave not all races had their
first unity from a mythology that marries them to rock and hill?'[75] Yeats's early Celticism
is conceived as a way of overcoming modern alienation in Ireland, and despite his later
appreciation of the intellectual and creative achievements of Georgian Ireland, 'Under
Ben Bulben' shows him attempting to unify those achievements with the Celtic world in
a society loosely defined as pre-Cromwellian.

Eliot also desires unity of culture: as he put it in *Notes Towards the Definition of Culture*
(1948), 'no culture can appear or develop except in relation to a religion'; while at the
same time, 'there is an aspect in which we can see religion as the *whole way of life* of a
people, from birth to grave, from morning to night and even in sleep'.[76] The inclusion of
the word 'sleep' is another reminder of Eliot's ideal of the immersion of the whole self in
culture and religious faith—the aspect of his thinking that makes his interest in occult
traditions and practices more understandable. This essay from the late 1940s marks the
final evolution of Eliot's concept of 'the mind of Europe', to which he had first referred in
Tradition and the Individual Talent. For the individual born in Britain, the tradition has
to be European. The mind of Europe changes, but 'abandons nothing *en route*...does
not superannuate Shakespeare, or Homer, or the rock drawing of the Magdalenian
draughtsmen'.[77] By the time he came to write *After Strange Gods* (1934), the 'mind of
Europe', at first apparently open to the archaic and the primitive, had as David Moody
points out, become 'in effect the Christian mind'.[78] An important prompt to this devel-
opment was a consideration of the poetry of Dante, who in the essay included in *The
Sacred Wood* was already said to benefit from 'a mythology and a theology which had
undergone a more complete absorption into life than those of Lucretius'.[79] As Lucy
McDiarmid points out, 'All these poets [Yeats, Eliot, Auden] attempted, in the thirties, to
"plunge [the work of art] back into social life" through the "applied arts of literature"'.[80]
Dante might not at first sight seem the most likely representative of such an immersion,
yet as we have noted, both poets see him as produced by an organically unified culture,
and Yeats goes so far as to suggest that his works might be sung by a 'common man'.

The organically conceived mental processes which provided the material for early
Yeats and Eliot—Yeats's 'moods', Eliot's 'images' of which 'the soul is constituted'[81]—
make for better poetry than the 'opinion' or 'personality' of much nineteenth-century

[74] Ibid., 166–7.

[75] Ibid., 167.

[76] T. S. Eliot, *Christianity and Culture: The Idea of a Christian Society and Notes towards the Definition of Culture* (New York: Eliot Press, 2008), 100, 103.

[77] Eliot, *Sacred Wood*, 51.

[78] A. David Moody, 'The Mind of Europe in T. S. Eliot', in *T. S. Eliot at the Turn of the Century*, ed. Thormählen, 19.

[79] Eliot, *Sacred Wood*, 163.

[80] Lucy McDiarmid, *Saving Civilization: Yeats, Eliot and Auden Between the Wars* (Cambridge: Cambridge University Press, 1984), 66, quoting from Yeats's 'Pages from a Diary Written in 1930', in W. B. Yeats, *Explorations* (London: Macmillan, 1962), 300.

[81] Eliot, *Complete Poems and Plays*, 23.

poetry. They offer an opportunity for poetry to rediscover strengths lost since the seventeenth century. Yet they remain an index of the modern, isolated consciousness unless reconnected to a cultural framework. For Yeats, the chains of association lead upwards to the realm of archetypal images in *Anima Mundi*, a knowledge vouchsafed to the Anglo-Irish magus; for Eliot the themes and patterns of life are shown redeemed in the Christian narrative, which is, so to speak, a spiritualized version of the old myths of rebirth, of which we find traces in our daily lives.

CHAPTER 8

IRISH POETIC MODERNISM: PORTRAIT OF THE ARTIST IN EXILE

SUSAN SCHREIBMAN

ON or about 1 May 1925, Thomas MacGreevy, ex-British civil servant (Department of the Admiralty and the Irish Land Commission) and ex-British army officer (Royal Field Artillery), began to write poetry. Although MacGreevy had begun to make a name for himself in Dublin as a commentator on Irish cultural life with one or two short stories published in the small magazines that had sprung up in Dublin in the years immediately prior to and following Irish independence, it was not until he emigrated to London in May 1925 that he began to write poetry seriously.

Exile is not just a physical condition, but a mental state. It is an estrangement from one's home and one's homeland, one's history, family, and friends. Denis Devlin achieved it serving in the newly-established Irish state as an employee of the Department of Foreign Affairs; Samuel Beckett was able to achieve it thanks to the small income he received upon his beloved father's death; George Reavey seemed to be in permanent exile, being born in Belarus to a Northern Irish father and a Polish mother, calling nowhere home, except perhaps New York City late in life.

Irish poetic modernism is a story of poets and poetry in exile. Indeed, Irish modernism is a story of exile: Joyce left Dublin in 1904, never to return except for two brief visits in 1909 and 1912, and throughout his life Yeats had long periods of residence outside Ireland. Of the five poets to be discussed in this article, Samuel Beckett, Brian Coffey, Denis Devlin, Thomas MacGreevy, and George Reavey, only MacGreevy returned permanently to Ireland—and it took an act of war to help him make that decision. Their work is still too often considered marginal to the canon of Irish poetry. In many ways this is not surprising: Ireland, nearly 100 years after independence, still struggles with categories of Irishness, admitting select definitions of who belongs, and who does not; of what writing represents the people and the nation. I will argue here that the writing of these men, who were, to paraphrase Wallace Stevens's acute observation on MacGreevy, eager to be at the heart of their times, represents an important and too frequently ignored extended Irish community. Their writing gives voice to the hopes and dreams, the frustrations and alienation of the generations of Irish who emigrated because of economic or social conditions: to seek a better life, for adventure, or for political reasons. Their writing, through its engagement with other cultures, sought to expand a national self-understanding. But all too frequently it was dismissed as marginal. In poem after poem their work captures the struggle of loss and attainment and the inner conflict of embracing the unfamiliar, until, as Brian Coffey quoting Laura Riding writes, 'wherever the soul gives in to flesh/without a struggle is home'.[1]

The aesthetic and political formation of the writers under discussion here takes place, as T. S. Eliot writes in *Four Quartets*, during the 'the years of *l'entre deux guerres*'.[2] It was a time of economic instability, a time when the belief of the avant garde that its *isms*—Futurism, Imagism, Vorticism—could change the world had been shattered. The world was changed, not by words, but by the devastation of war. Ireland experienced the 1914–18 war differently from other European states. At first the Irish rate of enlistment in the Great War was slightly lower, but still comparable to other parts of the British Isles.[3] The 1916 Rising changed this. At first the Irish public viewed the Rising negatively: many families, particularly amongst Dublin's working poor, had sons and husbands, brothers and uncles serving with the British forces. But upon the hasty court martial and execution of the Rising's leaders less than an week after the Irish surrender, public opinion turned against the European war, leaving those who had enlisted prior to the event branded traitors to the Republican cause. Ireland's experience of war did not end with the Armistice, but extended through the Anglo-Irish War (which began January 1919), immediately followed by a Civil War (which ended May 1923). Indeed, the establishment of the Irish state in 1922 occurred in the same year as the publication of both Joyce's *Ulysses* and T. S. Eliot's *The Waste Land*. As Terence Brown has argued, the Irish socio-cultural construction can be viewed as an experiment as revolutionary and symbolic as these two works of high modernism.[4]

This is the world that Coffey, Beckett, Reavey, and Devlin, born 1905, 1906, 1907, and 1908, respectively, inherited. The greats of modernism were already great; some on the cusp of greatness had died in the war and would haunt the next generation as absent presences. Although they had not participated in the pre-war avant-garde belief that a regenerative social order would arise phoenix-like from the ashes of revolutionary change, they shared with that generation the post-war sense of *ennui* and a belief in a bleaker future. These particular writers, however, did experience the danger and sacrifice of a revolutionary ideal in the birth of the Irish Free State. Beckett recalled his horror in witnessing the destruction of Dublin in 1916 from the Dublin Mountains as flames

---

[1] Brian Coffey, *Poems and Versions 1929–1990* (Dublin: Dedalus, 1991), 72.

[2] T. S. Eliot, *Four Quartets* (London: Faber, 1944), 21.

[3] Keith Jeffery, *Ireland and the Great War* (Cambridge: Cambridge University Press, 2000), 6.

[4] Terence Brown, 'Ireland, Modernism and the 1930s', in *Modernism and Ireland: The Poetry of the 1930s*, ed. Patricia Coughlan and Alex Davis (Cork: Cork University Press, 1995), 24.

from the capital lit the night sky;[5] and Devlin would have overheard plans for revolution as a boy in his father's pub in Parnell Street, which was a favourite gathering place for Michael Collins and his associates during the struggle for independence. One of Devlin's last poems, 'The Tomb of Michael Collins', harks back to this time recalling the loss of childhood innocence and the betrayal of an ideal.

Although these five men never resided in the same place at the same time, except briefly in Paris in 1933, they sought each other out, read, published, promoted, and reviewed each other's work. The most often quoted and concise statement on how their work differed from other Irish poetry of the time is contained in Beckett's August 1934 article in *The Bookman* entitled 'Recent Irish Poetry' (published under the pseudonym Andrew Belis). This is the nearest Beckett got to throwing down the literary gauntlet, placing himself squarely in the middle of ongoing Irish cultural debates. The article is the work of a young man (he was twenty-eight) surveying his peers and finding many of them lacking. He marked a line in the literary sand and divided his fellow poets into the 'antiquarians and others'. The antiquarians, although in the majority, he dismissed, as 'delivering with the altitudinous complacency of the Victorian Gael the Ossianic goods'.[6] The others, which he noted Yeats described as 'the fish that lie gasping on the shore, suggesting that they might at least learn to expire with the air',[7] comprise, in the first instance, MacGreevy, who he describes as an 'independent', bridging the generations between Yeats and Beckett's own. Beckett argued that MacGreevy's writing was not a 'flight from self-awareness' but embodied a self-perception facing into 'inarticulate earth and inscrutable heaven'.[8] He reserves, however, the most praise for his contemporaries Coffey and Devlin, who he writes are 'without question the most interesting of the youngest generation of Irish poets',[9] constituting, as Beckett then believed, 'the nucleus of a living poetic in Ireland'.[10]

Beckett's critique, according to Devlin, 'raised a storm'. Devlin, who was living in Dublin when the article was published (Beckett and MacGreevy were in London), witnessed the fallout, as he wrote to MacGreevy in a letter of 31 August:

> It appears Yeats was furious; it appears that Austin Clarke is vindictive by nature and will pursue Sam to his grave; it appears Seamas [sic] O'Sullivan thought he might have been mentioned at least; and my domestic bull Higgins voyez-moi ce type amazed me by being glad 'he got off so lightly'. I was flattered by what he wrote of me and through his agency a poem has been taken by the Bookman.[11]

Beckett's article fuelled an ongoing debate in Irish letters about who best represented contemporary Irish poetry. Almost a year prior to Beckett beginning the article, James

---

[5] Anthony Cronin, *The Last Modernist: Samuel Beckett* (New York: Harper Collins, 1997), 36.
[6] Samuel Beckett, *Disjecta: Miscellaneous Writings and a Dramatic Fragment* (London: John Calder, 1983), 70.
[7] Ibid., 70.
[8] Ibid., 74.
[9] Ibid., 75.
[10] Ibid., 76.
[11] TCD MS 8112/5.

Stephens had been planning a publication of an anthology of Irish writing by members of the newly-formed Irish Academy of Letters for the New York publisher Methuen & Co. In June 1933, Stephens sent letters to members of the Academy asking for contributions. Two months later Devlin wrote to MacGreevy, 'Won't Stephens' Irish anthology be absurd without us four?'[12]

The Irish Academy of Letters was first mooted by W. B. Yeats in 1928 as a 'rallying-point for dissident intellectuals' to combat the newly introduced Censorship of Publication Bill, 1928, referred to in Dáil debates as the Evil Literature Bill.[13] The organization was not formed, however, until 1933 when Yeats began renewed efforts to see it established. Although the criteria for membership was that writers be Irish and living in Ireland, Pádraic Colum was asked (he accepted) as well as Joyce (he refused), with Yeats assuring the latter that 'all the writers here who are likely to form our Council are students of your work'.[14] Although the first members of the Academy included the *crème de la crème* of Irish literati (including AE, Austin Clarke, Pádraic Colum, St John Ervine, F. R. Higgins, Frank O'Connor, Seán O'Faoláin, Liam O'Flaherty, Seumas O'Sullivan, Lennox Robinson, George Bernard Shaw, Edith Somerville, and James Stephens), there were no students of Joyce amongst them. Stephens's publication would have been critical in bringing to an American audience what was presumed to be the best of contemporary Irish writing.

Indeed, Stephens's letter to potential contributors stressed the historical importance of the volume.[15] (Although the volume was submitted to Methuen in September 1935, events conspired against its publication. Almost a year after the manuscript was submitted, several key authors, including Yeats, Shaw, and O'Flaherty, failed to contribute texts, and the anthology's sponsor, Methuen Director E. V. Lucas, passed away three years later, causing the project to languish.) Devlin was acute in observing that without the work of Beckett, Coffey, MacGreevy, and himself, an important voice associated with the avant garde was excluded. Thus despite the confidence of Beckett's convictions, what he termed a 'living tradition' was not to take root in Ireland.

MacGreevy, some five years earlier, made a not unrelated observation to Beckett's. His claim, far from being embraced, represented a minority opinion. MacGreevy, who by 1929 was living in Paris and acting as amanuensis to Joyce during the writing of *Work in Progress* (published as *Finnegans Wake)* found himself defending Joyce's literary project as Seán O'Faoláin, one of Ireland's chief critics of the text, dismissed it as striking 'at the inevitable basis of language, universal intelligibility'. O'Faoláin continued: 'Yet no genuine student of literature can dare be unfamiliar with it: it is one of the most interesting and pathetic literary adventures I know, pathetic chiefly because of its partial success'.[16]

---

[12] TCD MS 8112/2.

[13] R. F. Foster, *W. B. Yeats: A Life*, vol. II: *The Arch-Poet, 1915–39* (Oxford, Oxford University Press, 2003), 375.

[14] Ibid., 448.

[15] James Stephens, *Letters of James Stephens with an Appendix Listing Stephens' Published Writings*, ed. Richard J. Finneran (London: Macmillan, 1974), 374–5.

[16] Seán O'Faoláin, ' "Anna Livia Plurabelle": Letter to the Editor of the *Irish Statesman*', 5 January 1929, 355.

A row erupted in the pages of the *Irish Statesman* with MacGreevy defending Joyce's work. Far from being a partial success, MacGreevy countered, the text was not only deeply rooted in literary and Catholic traditions, it pushed those traditions to *an* (as opposed to *the*) ultimate limit. If *Ulysses* could be read as a modern equivalent of Dante's *Inferno*, then this new work could be read as a *Purgatorio* in which not only the characters, but language itself, is in a state of flux. Here the characters are in time (as opposed to eternity); mobile, not stationary, moving towards a new consciousness committed to social salvation. MacGreevy closes the letter to the editor with what can only be described as an exhausted plea to the disbelievers to be 'at least respectful enough to a very great writer to cease attributing dubious æsthetic motives as previously they attributed dubious moral motives to him'.[17] MacGreevy's defence of Joyce also found its voice in poetry. 'For an Irish Book, 1929' was published a short time later in *transition* (edited by Eugene Jolas), which was also serializing *Work in Progress*:

> A rich fig tree
> The large leaves lovely to see
> The fruits delicious to taste
>
> It was manured with a dung of English literature
> And a slag of Catholic theology
> But these have been tried elsewhere
> Here the earth was fertile
> The root strong
> The gardener knew how to entrap the sun
> And to anticipate the listing
> Of even the gentlest wind.[18]

The published title of the text obscured (as so many of MacGreevy's titles did) the poem's biographical and temporal rooting. An earlier draft of the poem was entitled 'On Reading Joyce', which was later simplified to 'Re Joyce'.[19]

While these poets, by and large, did not find a receptive audience at home for their work, they found outlets and champions in the little magazines abroad and the formidable editors who ran them: in addition to *transition*, there was T. S. Eliot's *The Criterion*, Harriet Monroe's *Poetry*, and Samuel Putnam's *The New Review*. Several journals in Ireland also accepted their work. George Russell (AE) was particularly open to publishing MacGreevy's poems in the *Irish Statesman* (he published some half dozen before they appeared in book form), while the *Dublin Magazine* published poems by Beckett, Devlin, and MacGreevy.

Perhaps the most important statement on the work of this new generation was Putnam's two-volume anthology *The European Caravan*, subtitled *An Anthology of the New Spirit in European Literature: Part 1. France, Spain, England and Ireland.* Jacob

---

[17] Thomas MacGreevy, ' "Anna Livia Plurabelle": Letter to the Editor of the *Irish Statesman*', 16 February 1929, 475–6. Accessed 1 October 2009, the *Thomas MacGreevy Archive* (www.macgreevy.org).

[18] Thomas MacGreevy, *Collected Poems of Thomas MacGreevy: An Annotated Edition*, ed. Susan Schreibman (Dublin: Anna Livia Press, 1991), 61.

[19] TCD MS 7989/1/96.

Bronowski edited the England and Ireland section that included poems by Beckett and MacGreevy (other authors in the English/Irish section include Richard Aldington, W. H. Auden, Lyle Donaghy, T. S. Eliot, HD, James Joyce, D. H. Lawrence, Dorothy Richardson, Geoffrey Taylor, and Virginia Woolf), with Reavey translating many poems from the Russian for a second volume which never appeared. By the 1930s avant-garde post-war writing was seen to be inherently different from that written before the war: there was, as Bronowski argued, a greater preoccupation with style under the influence of the 'experimental and psychological' writing of James Joyce and Marcel Proust.[20] Interestingly, the motivation for this volume bears similarities to Stephens's in that both were to introduce contemporary (European and Irish, respectively) writing to an American audience. *The European Caravan*, published by New York's Brewer, Warren & Putnam in 1931, sought to capture 'the spiritual chaos, marked by the seeming breakdown of reality itself'. Here the work of Beckett and MacGreevy, who by 1931 were firmly established in avant-garde circles in Paris, was central to the 'after-War spirit in European literature'.[21]

Yet it was not until George Reavey founded the Littéraire Européen (European Literary Bureau) and the Europa Press (in 1932 and 1935 respectively) that book-length publication of Beckett's, Coffey's, and Devlin's work became possible. The Littéraire Européen also provided a small but steady income for the writers Reavey represented (including Beckett, Coffey, and Devlin) via commissions for translations.[22] His motivation in establishing the Europa Press was to provide a vehicle for his peers who he felt were being unfairly rejected by English publishers. Moreover, Reavey did not stop at publishing fine limited editions of texts that would be attractive to collectors, but in the spirit of other avant-garde publications, brought writers and artists together to create a synthesis of expression impossible via one medium alone. He did this mainly through the offices of Stanley William Hayter, one of the greatest printmakers of the twentieth century. Hayter's Paris studio, Atelier 17, was considered one of the most influential art studios of the time. Here he worked with contemporary artists including Miró, Picasso, and Kandinsky to encourage their exploration of printmaking as a medium. Reavey's own volume, *Nostradam* (1935), and his translation by Pierre Charnay, *Signes d'Adieu* (1935), were illustrated by Hayter and Roger Viellard respectively. Beckett, in contrast to his later collaborations with artists, opted not to have any illustrations for *Echo's Bones*, which was published by the Europa Press in 1935.

By any standard, Reavey's list of authors for the Europa series is impressive. Besides publishing his own and Beckett's collections, Reavey published collections by Devlin (*Intersessions* in 1937) and Coffey (*Third Person* in 1938). Reavey also hoped to publish a

[20] Jacob Bronowski, 'Introduction' to the England and Ireland section of *The European Caravan* (New York: Brewer, Warren & Putnam, 1931), 432.

[21] Samuel Putnam, Foreword to *The European Caravan* (New York: Brewer, Warren & Putnam, 1931), p. v.

[22] Sandra O'Connell, 'Brian Coffey and George Reavey: A Friendship of Lasting Importance', in *Other Edens: The Life and Work of Brian Coffey*, ed. Benjamin Keatinge and Aengus Woods (Dublin: Irish Academic Press 2009), 49.

volume by MacGreevy. However, a year earlier Heinemann had brought out MacGreevy's *Poems* and he had not enough new texts for a second collection. There were also volumes from Paul Eluard and Charles Henri Ford. A collection of short stories by Dylan Thomas was accepted (*The Burning Baby*), but the printers refused to set it as they felt it contained obscene passages.

Thus the nucleus of a poetic tradition that Beckett was so sure would take hold in Ireland in 1934, by and large passed Irish poetry by. Just as Yeats and Joyce had done a generation earlier, Beckett, Coffey, Devlin, and MacGreevy left Ireland for Paris and London to find intellectual and creative homes that they could not find in the newly-established Free State. Their poetry owed more to T. S. Eliot than Thomas Davis, and to French Symbolism than Irish mythology. The work of all these poets drew deeply from a Christian ethos. Yet it was MacGreevy's dissatisfaction with the emerging alliance between Church and State in creating a rigidly narrow definition of Irish national identity that caused him in 1925 to quit his position as Assistant Organising Librarian for the Carnegie United Kingdom Trust (a position he had held since 1921) and make a new life in London.

MacGreevy, a generation older than the others, was born in 1893 in Tarbert, County Kerry. He was a participant in many of the events his younger colleagues experienced second hand. He joined the Civil Service at the age of sixteen as a Boy Clerk, and worked his way up to a Second Division Clerk in the Department of the Admiralty in London. When war broke out his work was considered essential to the war effort and at first he escaped conscription. When it became clear that he would be released from the Civil Service, he was advised to join the army as an officer. As a Second Lieutenant in the Royal Field Artillery, he witnessed the unspeakable; but like so many other writers and artists of his generation, he was compelled to reshape the unspeakable into art.

Coffey once described Devlin as a poet of distance, but the same can be said of MacGreevy's work.[23] This tempered reflection inserts a space not only between the poet and his poems, but between poem and reader. Coffey describes it as a sense of 'reserve' that 'infuses a poet's work with a quality of monumental stability'.[24] The first piece in *Poems* (1934), MacGreevy's only collection of poetry published in his lifetime (in both London and New York), is indicative of this liminal space:

> I labour in a barren place,
> Alone, self-conscious, frightened, blundering;
> Far away, stars wheeling in space,
> Around my feet, earth voices whispering.[25]

'Nocturne', with its four lightly echoing lines, recalls both the musical form inspired by the night, as well as Whistler's famous series of enigmatic paintings in which he recalls a scene from memory resulting in a pared-down vision of focal points as opposed to a

---

[23] Brian Coffey, 'Denis Devlin: Poet of Distance', in *Place, Personality and the Irish Writer*, ed. Andrew Carpenter (Gerrards Cross: Colin Smythe, 1977), 137.

[24] Coffey, 'Denis Devlin: Poet of Distance', 142.

[25] MacGreevy, *Collected Poems*, ed. Schreibman, 1.

realistic portrait. MacGreevy's poem, composed a decade after the event, is equally impressionistic: he utilizes the most primeval elements of earth and sky to convey the sense of hopelessness and isolation, frustration and horror, of war. For MacGreevy, the space between this 'bitch of a world' and inscrutable heaven is the place poetry occupies.

This liminal space is also expressed in one of Coffey's earliest poems, 'Yuki-Hira', dedicated to the poet's parents. It was used as a Christmas card in 1933 while Coffey was living in Paris.[26] Two years later he sent MacGreevy a manuscript entitled *Image at the Cinema* which he intended to submit to the Europa Press. The manuscript is in itself a production consisting of typed and handwritten poems written on small sheets of crosshatched paper each mounted on a larger sheet, along with published poems extracted from journals also mounted on the larger folios. The collection (which was never published) consisted of eighteen poems, the last being 'Yuki Hira'. The poem was not included in *Third Person*, but it is the first poem Coffey reprinted in his 1991 collection *Poems and Versions 1929–1990*:

> Came then His command
> that I take the mountain road, go
> through the last village....
>
> Dawn, the chrysanthemums in my garden,
> my house in my garden, my life, there.
> My mother weeping gently
> grey hair was blown by the autumn wind.
> My father stood to bless me genuflecting,
> stood as an ancestor would, with steady eyes.
> Knelt at my feet my wife, covered my feet
> with her hair, the wind had fallen, her hair
> in her sorrow drawn, curled on the path.[27]

In following 'His command' the narrator journeys to a space filled with abandonment and vacancy, compelled to leave the presence of loved ones who reassure him of the reality of his surroundings to travel to a distant land in which his only occupation is to 'drag water-pails on the shore'.

This sense of estrangement from one's self, one's surroundings, from one's God, is a frequent theme in Irish poetic modernism. Many of MacGreevy's poems construct social spaces in an attempt to recover what would otherwise be repressed or forgotten. In 'The Six Who Were Hanged', MacGreevy recounts his participation in a public event outside Mountjoy Gaol on 14 January 1921, in which six Republican prisoners are hanged within its walls. Outside there is a densely packed crowd of some twenty thousand people who stand praying and signing hymns. As the bell tolls for each prisoner being hanged, the murmur of the chanting of the Rosary rises to a pitch as the crowd, overpowered by emotion, drop to their knees to pray.[28] MacGreevy, aware of his own

---

[26] TCD MS 8110/8.
[27] Coffey, *Poems and Versions*, 13.
[28] Dorothy Macardle, *The Irish Republic* (London: Corgi, 1968), 391.

impotence, and the futility of the praying crowd ('What, these seven hundred years,/Has Ireland had to do/With the morning star?'), physically removes himself:

> Tired of sorrow,
> My sorrow, their sorrow, all sorrow,
> I go from the hanged,
> From the women,
> I go from the hanging;
> Scarcely moved by the thought of the two to be hanged,
> I go from the epilogue.[29]

The conclusion of MacGreevy's poem captures a sense of alterity, a space beyond consolation. Some twenty-five years later, Denis Devlin attempted to find an epilogue to another devastating European war in a remote corner of Ireland. He had spent the war years in the United States as a diplomat from a neutral country, First Secretary to the Consulate General in New York, before being posted to the Legation in Washington DC. It was while he was serving in Washington that Devlin met the French poet Alexis Leger, or St John Perse—also a diplomat, who later was to receive the Nobel Prize— who during the Second World War held the post of advisor to the Library of Congress. Although twenty-one years Devlin's senior, the two established both an admiration for each other's work and a friendship. Leger remained poetically silent until after coming to Washington. Of the poems that ended the exile—'Exil', 'Pluies' ('Rains'), 'Neiges' ('Snows'), and 'Poème à l'Etrangère'—'Rains' and 'Snows' were published by the *Swanee Review* in 1945, with translations by Devlin. Leger's familiarity with exile, with the eternal exile of the human condition itself, would have been instantly recognizable to Devlin whose own poetry circled back upon these same themes. Perhaps because of a concomitant sensibility, the work of the poet who wrote 'On too many frequented shores have my footsteps been washed away before the day' inspired Devlin in such a way that he is still regarded as one of the finest translators of Leger's verse into English.[30]

For Devlin, as perhaps for Leger, language itself became the one solid substance. Devlin was impelled to find in the 'impalpable community of language': a home he could not locate in any specific time or place.[31] When he returned to Ireland after the war Devlin sought out a place to take stock beyond the quotidian. Following in the footsteps of generations of pilgrims to St Patrick's Purgatory at Lough Derg, he, alongside a motley throng—the 'poor in spirit on their rosary rounds'; the 'jobbers with their whiskey-

---

[29] MacGreevy, *Collected Poems*, ed. Schreibman, 9.

[30] St-John Perse, 'Exile', *Exile and Other Poems*, trans. Denis Devlin (New York: Pantheon Books, 1953), reprinted in Denis Devlin, *Collected Poems of Denis Devlin*, ed. J. C. C. Mays (Dublin: Dedalus, 1989), 226.

[31] Stan Smith, '"Precarious Guest": The Poetry of Denis Devlin', in *Modernism and Ireland*, ed. Coughlan and Davis, 232.

angered eyes; the 'pink bank clerks'; and 'invalids on penitential feet'—wills himself into becoming part of a world he has left.[32] 'Lough Derg', the title poem of his second collection (published in 1946), begins with an ironic observation on neutral Ireland: 'With mullioned Europe shattered, this Northwest,/Rude-sainted isle would pray it whole again'. 'Lough Derg' is Devlin's attempt to find redemption in communal prayer rooted to place. He is surrounded by those for whom 'All is simple and symbol'; the 'incomprehended rendered fabulous'.[33] The implication is that Devlin no longer has access to this world: as he writes in an early draft of the poem, 'the misunderstood is fabled mystery'.[34] Like MacGreevy, Devlin concedes by the end of the poem: 'We pray to ourself. The metal moon, unspent/Virgin eternity sleeping in the mind,/Excites the form of prayer without content'.[35]

Devlin's last, great poetic sequence, *The Heavenly Foreigner* (first published in 1950 in *Poetry Ireland*, and reprinted posthumously in 1967 in an annotated and edited edition by Brian Coffey) consists of eleven poems, each named after a city. It is a sequence rooted in place, albeit eleven places to which the poet no longer has access, except in memory. It is a poem of ghosts, of leavetakings, of absences:

> In the memory, years interweave: they do not follow one another
> Like jealous ambassadors in the Mayor's procession.
> All the years flow from a hundred streets
> Intemperately towards the mansion.[36]

Nor does the poet have access to time:

> Time does not stretch ahead of me
> As if I might unroll my scroll on it
> But it is volumed round me, thick with echoes, things
> I cannot see throughout.[37]

The sequence is dedicated to the 'face of one I loved and one befriended'. In the introduction to the 1967 edition Coffey hints that the abiding presence is that of a single woman but does not give further details.[38] The beloved, the anima, is addressed in each of the cities, nevertheless, she is epiphanic. She is missed opportunities, moments beyond grasp ('the sense escaped me'), reminding the poet of 'Such things so and so many years ago' which cause time and place to dissolve: 'The already is my present unresolved.'[39]

---

[32] Devlin, 'Lough Derg', *Collected Poems*, ed. Mays, 132.
[33] Ibid., 132–5.
[34] NLI MS 33,760/2/3.
[35] Devlin, *Collected Poems*, ed. Mays, 135.
[36] Denis Devlin, *The Heavenly Foreigner* (Dublin: Dolmen Editions, 1967), 30.
[37] Ibid., 31.
[38] Ibid., 8.
[39] Ibid., 31.

There is, however, another presence in the poem: 'Something there was other/Always at my elbow'.[40] This other is reminiscent of the presence Robert Shackleton and his team felt while on an expedition to the South Pole, as used by T. S. Eliot in *The Waste Land*: 'the third who walks always beside you'.[41] In Eliot's version the other is a Christ figure, 'Gliding wrapt in a brown mantle, hooded'.[42] In Devlin's poem, the other pulls him back, 'So well I can be faithful to a ghost'[43] until in the penultimate poem the poet exclaims: 'O Heavenly Foreigner! Your price is high'.[44] The last poem in the sequence is entitled 'Notre Dame de Paris'. It is a poem about that most final of exiles: 'We are pulled up short by death.../Our hands make the final signal on the same high-voltage wire'.[45] The world, at last, dematerializes: 'And there's only a light smoke in my hands'.[46]

The unfinished, the incomplete, the time wasted, 'On too many frequented shores have my footsteps been washed away before the day', waiting for wars to end and the trepidation of new beginnings filled with anything but hope, is a recurring motif in Irish poetic modernism; as in Beckett's enigmatic poem 'Dieppe' in which the narrator turns 'towards the lights of old'.[47]

Perhaps Brian Coffey's most poignant statement on the condition of exile is *Missouri Sequence*, dated 1962 but begun a decade earlier after a long poetic silence. As he wrote to MacGreevy in July 1950: 'Poetry is again filling my private thoughts, after some years, and I may perhaps get a chance to do some verses'.[48] On a cold winter's evening in January 1953, Coffey finished the sequence. He sent MacGreevy an early typescript: a meditation on this juncture in his life, his renewed friendship with MacGreevy, and the pain of the realization that one's wishes for oneself in youth may become the reality of what one achieves in middle age.[49] The occasion for the poem was the resignation of his post as lecturer of philosophy at St Louis University in Missouri, which necessitated that he and his family leave the United States after a five-year residency. The text marks a time of crisis in Coffey's personal and professional life, his midway of life's journey, although Coffey's dark forest is the harsh, flat central plains of the United States where ice storms sweep down from Canada and the Irish dead lie peacefully in a graveyard a few miles from his home.

Missouri never becomes home to the narrator (although his children boast American twangs and help the neighbours at harvest time). The ordinariness of the local, still exotic to the poet, permeates the text: tree-frogs, couch-grass, butterflies, beetles, Whip-poor-Will, cicadas. It is here, as a stranger in a strange land, that he finds his path has been lost. Coffey, unlike Beckett, Devlin, or MacGreevy, was not a willing expatriate. It

---

[40] Ibid., 35.
[41] T. S. Eliot, *The Waste Land*, ed. Michael North (New York: Norton, 2001), 17.
[42] Ibid., 17.
[43] Devlin, *Heavenly Foreigner*, 21.
[44] Ibid., 36.
[45] Ibid., 38.
[46] Ibid., 37.
[47] Samuel Beckett, *Collected Poems in English and French* (London: John Calder, 1977), 49.
[48] TCD MS 8110/35.
[49] TCD MS 8110/41.

was probably more a matter of chance than design, and this sense of rejection and exclusion is palpable. This affective evocation is somewhat anomalous in Coffey's oeuvre, as is the poem's entire framework: it is narrative as opposed to lyrical, clearly autobiographical, temporally fixed, and geographically determined. Its relatively plain, unexperimental, syntactically simple use of language is a departure for Coffey. It is as if, in this instance, to create meaning, the poem required fixed temporal and spatial coordinates, a narrative to establish these coordinates, and a reader/listener who 'will hear me out'.[50] Thomas MacGreevy, to whom the first poem in the sequence, 'Nightfall, Midwinter, Missouri', is dedicated, is that listener.

The first stanzas establish a series of bounded spaces: the interior where the warm rooms protect the family from the storm outside; the mare in her barn; the impassable road disallowing anyone or anything to cross. These contrasts provoke others: the warmth of family home to the warmth of a homeland lost; the pull of the past stronger than the feelings of belonging to the present; the distance, physical and emotional, between his children full of life in Missouri and his dying mother in Ireland. Not only in the third stanza is the road impassable, but so is memory, and the poem is an attempt to reclaim what has been lost. The poem can thus be read as a meditation on home: physically, conceptually, socially. Its central tension is a system of opening and closing, of being isolated and at the same time penetrable. For the narrator, the very act of embracing the home that has been established in exile excludes him from the one left behind.

For Coffey, home is a site of conflict: 'Pain it was to come,/pain it will be to go': a phrase he repeats several times.[51] The Irish home the narrator dreams of, he realizes, is an illusion: 'Return home take on while I dream it/the fictive form of heaven on earth'.[52] The home established in exile in the United States must now be abandoned, and with the relocation to the United Kingdom, there is another exclusion, another departure, another loss.

Coffey was, in many ways, an economic migrant. He and his family were free to visit Ireland; economic circumstances made it impossible for them to stay. Thus the Ireland of the poet's imagination bears very little resemblance to its economic and social reality. Rather, it takes on the status of a representational space; a poetically imagined symbolic evocation:[53]

> yet I am charmed
> by the hills behind Dublin,
> those white stone cottages,
> grass green as no other green is green,
> my mother's people, their ways[54]

---

[50] Coffey, *Poems and Versions*, 70.
[51] Ibid., 72.
[52] Ibid., 71.
[53] Andrew Thacker, *Moving Through Modernity: Space and Geography in Modernism* (Manchester: Manchester University Press, 2003), 20.
[54] Coffey, *Poems and Versions*, 70.

Each of the poem's sections takes its inspiration from the seasons, and each is dedicated to an individual important to Coffey. The first section, 'Nightfall, Midwinter, Missouri', is dedicated (as already noted) to MacGreevy; the second section, 'March, Missouri', to Leonard Eslick, a colleague at St Louis University; 'Muse, June, Related', to the memory of Denis Devlin; and the final section, 'Missouri, Midsummer, Closure', to Bridget, his wife. About halfway through the first section, Coffey addresses MacGreevy directly:

> Dear Tom, in Ireland,
> you have known
> the pain between
> its fruiting and the early dream
> and you will hear me out.[55]

And MacGreevy does, knowing too well the angst caused by the place one must leave and the place one cannot live. But the love of Ireland is reciprocal—it mourns for her exiles: 'there is a love of Ireland/withering for Irishmen'.[56]

'Does it matter where one dies', Coffey asks, 'supposing one knows how?'[57] Does it matter that Irish souls have 'gone back to God from Byrnesville', the small hamlet where Coffey lived in Missouri. 'The truth is,' Coffey later concedes, 'where the cross is not/the Christian does not go.'[58] Here Coffey responds to one of the preoccupations in MacGreevy's poetry: that of the place of death. In MacGreevy's poem 'Recessional', the poet, standing at the edge of the waterfall in Engelbergeraa, Switzerland (where the eponymous character in Henry James's *Roderick Hudson* spends his final days) ponders:

> Supposing I drowned now,
> This tired, tiresome body,
> Before flesh creases further,
> Might, recovered, go fair,
> To be laid in Saint Lachtin's,
> Near where once,
> In tender, less glaring, island days
> And ways
> I could hear—
> Where listeners still hear—
> That far-away, dear
> Roar
> The long, silvery roar
> Of Mal Bay.[59]

Saint Lachtin is the site of a disused church on the outskirts of Tarbert, County Kerry, where MacGreevy's maternal family are buried. An earlier draft contained the line

---

[55] Ibid., 70.
[56] Ibid., 70.
[57] Ibid., 70.
[58] Ibid., 71.
[59] Thomas MacGreevy, *Collected Poems*, ed Schreibman, 41.

'Where kindred still hear', rather than 'Where listeners still hear'. The revision distances MacGreevy from his own story. Coffey, on the other hand, is preoccupied with his:

> Yet we must leave America,
> bitter necessity no monopoly
> of Irish soil.
> It was pain once to come,
> It is pain now to go.[60]

While Beckett's poetry is filled with paths deliberately not taken, the poems do not contain the angst of Coffey's choices. Of Beckett's early poems, only a tiny handful can be located in Ireland. 'Enueg I' is one of these. Written, most probably, in response to Peggy Sinclair's ultimately fatal tuberculosis, it makes a mockery of 'celtic self-importance':

> Above the mansions the algum-trees
> the mountains
> my skull suddenly
> clot of anger
> skewered aloft strangled in the cang of the wind
> bites like a dog against its chastisement.[61]

Not only does the narrator traverse the city on 'ruined feet' but the city itself oozes decay: 'the livid canal', 'a dying barge', 'a stillborn evening turning a filthy green'.

This is an Ireland easy to leave. There is none of Coffey's romantic yearnings or MacGreevy's nostalgia. Many of Beckett's poems that deal with home are raw and personal; of the poems published in *Echo's Bones*, several are about his father's death in 1933, such as 'Malacoda': 'thrice he came/the undertaker's man/impassable behind his scutal bowler'.[62]

Perhaps it is Denis Devlin who, in a poem written not long before his untimely death in 1959, comes closest to reconciling the life of the exile. The first section of his 'Memoirs of a Turcoman Diplomat' begins:

> Evenings ever more willing lapse into my world's evening,
> Birds, like Imperial emblems, in their thin, abstract singing,
> Announce some lofty Majesty whose embassies are not understood.[63]

Here, there is no abstract or empty space, no longing for an unattainable place. This evening in a foreign city belongs to the foreigner who can read the signs to which the natives no longer have access:

> The woman who passes by, sideways, by your side:
> There was one you loved for years and years
> Suddenly the jaw is ugly, the shoulders fall,
> Provoking but resentment, hardly tears.[64]

---

[60] Coffey, *Poems and Versions*, 71.
[61] Beckett, *Collected Poems*, 10.
[62] Ibid., 26.
[63] Devlin, *Collected Poems*, ed. Mays, 295.
[64] Ibid., 295.

Towards the end of his life, Devlin reconciled his lives as diplomat and poet, recovering a sense of belonging felt possibly only in childhood:

> These are the Four Green Fields we loved in boyhood,
> There are some reasons it's no loss to die for:
> Even it's no loss to die for having lived;
> It is inside our life the angel happens
> Life, the gift that God accepts or not[65]

Soon after hearing about Devlin's death, Coffey (living in London) wrote to MacGreevy (in Dublin):

> It was very sad to hear of the death of Denis. Moya [Devlin's sister] sent me a wire on the day he died, and an earlier letter of Don's [Devlin's brother] and one even earlier of Denis's had prepared me for the rest. I thought a lot about those days in Paris when we were all together, surprised to find how close it all was to my heart, as if of yesterday—one's best times timeless or unaging rather. I have always been sad about the accidents that scattered us, when as it seemed, we could have been more 'useful' at home. I am in fact still quite unreconciled to the role of foreigner here, exile from there and so on, at this late hour. Moya tells me it was a gentle and orderly going out, as he liked things.[66]

Brian Coffey was the last of his peers to pass away, in the spring of 1995, aged eighty-nine. He outlived Devlin by thirty-six years, MacGreevy by twenty-eight, Reavey by nineteen, and Beckett by six. The burst of creativity that began with *Missouri Sequence* continued throughout his life, and his Menard Press (established in the attic of his house) published his own and the work of those he valued, in limited editions of beautifully crafted books. Coffey lived to see a small renaissance of interest in the poetry of the friends of his youth: Michael Smith's *Lace Curtain* sought to bring to a wider public their poetry in issues of the journal published from the late 1960s through the 1970s; J. C. C. Mays' edition of Devlin's *Collected Poems* appeared in 1989; my edited and annotated edition of MacGreevy's poems was published in 1991, as was Coffey's own selection of his poetry.

Coffey's palpable longing for home would never be expressed as directly in his later poetry as it was in *Missouri Sequence*. Yet a fluidity of identity, a disappearance of the real, and a sense of hybridity permeate the work of all these writers. Home did not become a place of fixed coordinates, a geo-referenced point that can be located on Google maps. Rather, home became the narration, created not on fixity but on instability, on the shores where there remain no physical traces of the writers' presence.

---

[65] Ibid., 283.
[66] TCD MS 8110/43.

CHAPTER 9

··

SAMUEL BECKETT: EXILE AND EXPERIMENT

··

DAVID WHEATLEY

In October 1937, after almost a decade of toing and froing between Ireland and various European elsewheres, Samuel Beckett left Dublin for Paris with the intention of settling there definitively. Forced to return to Ireland almost immediately to give evidence in the libel action his uncle 'Boss' Sinclair had brought against Oliver St John Gogarty, Beckett was ridiculed in court as a 'bawd and blasphemer' from Paris, an experience that can only have confirmed to him the rightness of his earlier decision.[1] He would never again live in Ireland, but complete disentanglement from the land of his birth proved elusive. The presence of his mother and brother in Ireland occasioned regular return visits, and even after his adoption of French, later works strongly rooted in his Irish beginnings (*All That Fall, Company*) were drafted in English rather than his adoptive second language. Irish philistinism remained an irritant in the form of book-bannings—Beckett himself imposed a ban on performances of his work in Ireland as a protest at clerical censorship of the Dublin Theatre Festival in 1958—but with his Nobel Prize win in 1969 came a belated rediscovery of Beckett's Irishness and an incorporation of the writer into the iconography of the Irish cultural tourist industry.

The scholarly fruits of this re-absorption have ranged from the solidly argued (the photo-archive of Eoin O'Brien's *The Beckett Country*) to the fanciful and outright fantastical (Declan Kiberd's comparison of the voice in the dark in *Company* to 'the process of composition...carried out by the Gaelic *filí*', and the Gaelic palimpsests of Paul Muldoon's *To Ireland, I*).[2] Beckett the poet represents a special case again. His reception as a poet can be roughly periodized as follows. The early career, complete with the ritual denunciation of all or almost all things Irish in 'Recent Irish Poetry' (1934), culminates

---

[1] James Knowlson, *Damned to Fame: The Life of Samuel Beckett* (London: Bloomsbury, 1996), 280.

[2] Eoin O'Brien, *The Beckett Country: Samuel Beckett's Ireland* (Monkstown: The Black Cat Press, in association with London: Faber, 1986); Declan Kiberd, *Inventing Ireland: The Literature of the Modern Nation* (London: Jonathan Cape, 1995), 535; Paul Muldoon, *To Ireland, I* (Oxford: Clarendon Press, 2000).

in the publication of *Echo's Bones* in 1935, to little or no reaction; George Reavey's Europa Press ceases publication in 1939 and the book is not reprinted until *Poems in English* in 1961. Meanwhile Beckett has begun to publish poetry in French, though he does not gather this work into book form until *Poèmes* in 1968. The first real revival of interest in his work (in English) comes from the group associated with the New Writers' Press, founded in Dublin by Michael Smith and Trevor Joyce in 1967.[3] Although this group reject the professional Irishness, as they saw it, of the dominant mainstream, their championing of Beckett's poetry nevertheless takes place under the banner of a specifically Irish modernism, a narrative that receives academic consecration in the 1995 essay collection *Modernism and Ireland: The Poetry of the 1930s*. While the poetry has attracted other loyal readers, such as Marjorie Perloff and Derek Mahon, there is no consensus as to whether it properly belongs in the Anglo-American modernist tradition, the Irish subset thereof, or the broader church of Irish poetry in general; as recently as 2005 Dillon Johnston and Guinn Batten could declare that 'the jury is still out and demanding further evidence' on Beckett's poetic achievement.[4]

If the Irish modernist reading is now the official counter-history to the previous Revivalist narrative of the 1930s, there are good reasons for dissenting from it. First of all, there is its implication that the 1930s yoked Beckett and his contemporaries together in an abiding *esprit de corps*, when, as Patrick Crotty notes, it was not a decade in which any of the writers vaunted as 1930s Irish modernists 'did his best or most characteristic work,'[5] not to mention the far from critical attitude to his contemporaries to be gleaned from Beckett's letters during these years (he described Denis Devlin's 'Bacchanal' to MacGreevy as 'very very bad... When he gets metaphysical it is awful').[6] In a persuasive reading of Beckett and his contemporaries, Alan Gillis stresses not just their political and religious but aesthetic differences too.[7] This 1930s Irish modernist narrative account also risks privileging his Irishness at the expense of the liberating effect on Beckett of beginning to compose seriously in French, a process that begins with the twelve poems of 1938–9 first published after the war in *Les Temps modernes*. Equally, if the contemporary Irish poet most beholden to the influence of Beckett's poetry is Derek Mahon, his apparent distance from the 1930s modernist style has long sanctioned a neglect of the cross-fertilizing elements in the MacNeice and Beckett lines of the Irish poetic family tree, or stranded them behind a North-South picket fence.[8]

[3] Trevor Joyce, 'New Writers' Press: The History of a Project', in *Modernism and Ireland: The Poetry of the 1930s*, ed. Patricia Coughlan and Alex Davis (Cork: Cork University Press, 1995), 276–306.

[4] Dillon Johnston and Guinn Batten, 'Contemporary Poetry in English: 1940–2000', in *The Cambridge History of Irish Literature*, vol. 2, ed. Margaret Kelleher and Philip O'Leary (Cambridge: Cambridge University Press, 2006), 365.

[5] Patrick Crotty, 'The Irish Renaissance, 1890–1940: Poetry in English', in *The Cambridge History of Irish Literature*, vol. 2, ed. Kelleher and O'Leary, 99.

[6] Samuel Beckett, letter to MacGreevy, 21 September 1937, *The Letters of Samuel Beckett 1929–1940*, ed. Martha Dow Fehsenfeld and Lois More Overbeck (Cambridge: Cambridge University Press, 2009), 549.

[7] Alan Gillis, *Irish Poetry of the 1930s* (Oxford: Oxford University Press, 2005), 96–140.

[8] A comparative reading of Beckett and Mahon can be found in Stephen Watt, *Beckett and Contemporary Irish Writing* (Cambridge: Cambridge University Press, 2009).

Even at its apparently furthest from Ireland, then, Beckett's work is capable of surpris-
ing us with a sudden flaring up of origins, as in one of the addenda to *Watt*: 'for all the
good that frequent departures out of Ireland had done him, he might just as well have
stayed there'.[9] With or without explicit reference to Ireland, the pattern of *exitus-reddi-
tus*, departure and return, forms a central paradigm in Beckett's work, with its abun-
dance of doomed escape attempts, dead ends, and journeys that double back on
themselves. In the late prose text 'The Way', we find this paradigm being enacted in the
most literal manner:

> The way wound up from foot to top and thence on down another way. On back
> down. The ways crossed midway more and less. A little more and less than midway
> up and down. The ways were one-way. No retracing the way up back down nor back
> up the way down. Neither in whole from top or foot nor in part from on the way.
> The one way back was on and on was always back.[10]

The journey suggests an infinity symbol, whose circuitous nature recalls the Heraclitean
paradox used by T. S. Eliot as an epigraph to *Four Quartets* ('*Hodos ano kato mia kai hote*', where
'*hodos ano kato*' denotes a path leading upwards and downwards at once).[11] Beckett's poetry
too is full of such issueless ways. What dooms his journeys to their endless circularity,
I wish to argue, is the absence of any meaningful point of arrival and, correspondingly,
the loss of any recognizable starting point too, otherwise 'home'. As the poet tells himself
in 'Serena III': 'hide yourself not in the Rock keep on the move/keep on the move'.[12]
Physically, and more than physically, these are poems of exile: from Ireland, self, love,
and language, and not just the English language, as the poems' claustrophobic intensity
is not visibly diminished by Beckett's embrace of French. Though the Beckett speaker
frequently aspires to a loss of self, he does so very much on his own terms. 'One is no
longer oneself', the narrator of *First Love* says of the troubling experience of sexual
desire:

> and it is painful to be no longer oneself, even more painful if possible than when one
> is. For when one is one knows what to do to be less so, whereas when one is not one
> is any old one irredeemably. What goes by the name of love is banishment, with now
> and then a postcard from the homeland...[13]

The route to the non-self lies through the self, perhaps in the same contradictory way
that 'on' is 'back' and 'back' is 'on' in 'The Way'. Beckett's 1935 collection, *Echo's Bones and
Other Precipitates*, commemorates two lovers overtaken by extremes of self and non-self,

---

[9] Samuel Beckett, *Watt*, ed. C. J. Ackerley (London: Faber, 2009), 217.

[10] Samuel Beckett, 'The Way', in *Company, Ill Seen Ill Said, Worstward Ho, Stirrings Still*, ed. Dirk Van
Hulle (London: Faber, 2009), 125.

[11] *Heraclitus: Fragments: A Text and Translation with a Commentary*, ed. T. M. Robinson (Toronto:
University of Toronto Press, 1987), 40. Robinson translates the fragment as 'A road up (and) down (is)
one and the same (road)'.

[12] Samuel Beckett, *Selected Poems, 1930–1989*, ed. David Wheatley (London: Faber, 2009), 29.

[13] Samuel Beckett, 'First Love', *The Complete Short Prose, 1929–1989*, ed. S. E. Gontarski (New York:
Grove Press, 1995), 31.

Narcissus and Echo, the former devoured by all-engrossing self-love, the second spurned by him and condemned to waste away to stone. Beckett praised Thomas MacGreevy in 1934 as an 'existentialist in verse',[14] and as one who explores the modernist 'breakdown of the object' and 'rupture of the lines of communication'.[15] *Echo's Bones* too can be seen as partaking of the 1930s existential moment. To read these poems as pitting a hostile and loathed external world against a privileged and febrile consciousness, however, would be to oversimplify: what is self and what is other in these poems is often far from imme-diately apparent. If the poet's mood is saturnine and his surroundings dark and mina-tory, establishing where cause and effect lie may be as quixotic as looking for 'up' and 'down' on our Heraclitean infinity symbol.

A more challenging approach is to see the poems and their settings as pulsing surfaces of back-and-forth currents and counter-currents. For example, though Beckett appears to trade on the Romantic pathetic fallacy in a poem such as 'Enueg I', overlaying the Dublin landscape with his disaffected humour, the poem can be read as switching, or rewiring, the expected polarity of inside and outside, subjective and objective. Consider its opening:

> Exeo in a spasm
> tired of my darling's red sputum
> from the Portobello Private Nursing Home
> its secret things
> and toil to the crest of the surge of the steep perilous bridge
> and lapse down blankly under the scream of the hoarding
> round the bright stiff banner of the hoarding
> into a black west
> throttled with clouds.
>
> Above the mansions the algum-trees
> the mountains
> my skull sullenly
> clot of anger
> skewered aloft strangled in the cang of the wind
> bites like a dog against its chastisement.[16]

Here and throughout the poem the mind is passive, invaded and overthrown by the vio-lence of nature (the skull 'strangled in the cang of the wind', 'the mind annulled/wrecked in wind', 'in my skull the wind going fetid'), while the landscape, both animate and inan-imate, teems with human traits and motives ('the scream of the hoarding', 'the tattered sky like an ink of pestilence', 'the fingers of the ladders hooked over the parapet'). In a let-ter to MacGreevy of 8 September 1934, Beckett expressed his admiration for Paul Cézanne's treatment of landscape, which refuses Romantic concepts of interanimating sympathy and understanding: 'Cézanne appears to have been the first to see landscape &

---

[14] Samuel Beckett, 'Recent Irish Poetry', in *Disjecta: Miscellaneous Writings and a Dramatic Fragment* (London: John Calder, 1983), 74.
[15] Ibid., 70.
[16] Beckett, *Selected Poems*, 14.

state it as material of a strictly peculiar order, incommensurable with all human expression whatever.' Of Jacob van Ruysdael's *Entrance to the Forest* he comments: 'there is no entrance anymore nor any commerce with the forest, its dimensions are its secrets & it has no communication to make'.[17]

We are thus confronted, from the outset, with impasse. Yet as forms of paralysis go, this is an impasse that is also an advance, as Beckett seeks to move beyond the formulaic Revivalism lampooned in 'Recent Irish Poetry'. Mention of Beckett's early criticism alongside his poetry helps to frame this paradox: how is it that Beckett can offer so confidently in his prose to 'Make it New' only to run aground continually in poems described by Gillis as 'hung on the page like pulverized linguistic corpses that can signify only pain, angst, futility, and ultimately nothing'?[18] The answer lies in the peculiar temporal rhetoric of the modernism he preaches, which, as in Osip Mandelstam's 'On the Nature of the Word', should not be mistaken for a form of progressivism ('The theory of progress in literature represents the crudest, most repugnant form of academic ignorance',[19] the Russian poet declares.). Beckett is not proposing to lead Irish poetry incrementally towards self-betterment: he fast-forwards straight to the *ne plus ultra* of eternal newness. As Paul de Man has written, 'Modernity exists in the form of a desire to wipe out whatever came earlier, in the hope of reaching at last a point that could be called a true present',[20] a 'true present' that would be quasi-Messianic if it did not instantly miscarry. (Beckett's Messiahs, it hardly needs pointing out, have a tendency not to keep their appointments.)

Gillis reminds us of the discussion of time in *Proust* and Beckett's refusal of what he calls the 'vulgarity of a plausible concatenation'[21] in favour of obsessive fragmentation, breakdown, and paralysis. But there is a way out of this. Even as Beckett's poems fail to reach the condition of pure subjectivity he finds in Proust, which would unlock the way to a resurrection from the deathly grip of Habit, they throw up a 'series of partial annexations'[22] or (in reference to the Proustian narrator's obsession with Albertine) a *'pictorial multiplicity',*[23] in the manner of Marcel Duchamp's *Nu descendant un escalier*, displacing onto the spatial axis the failed attempts at unity on the axis of time. This imbues many of the poems of *Echo's Bones* with the character of stop-motion photography, as though a shutter were separating one sensation from the next. (Photography as metaphor appealed sufficiently to Beckett for him to devote a whole poem to it in 'Rue de Vaugirard', mixing light and shade—'expose la plaque aux lumières et aux ombres'—to produce the epiphanic image, which he represents as a photographic negative—'un négatif irrécusable'.)

---

[17] Beckett to MacGreevy, 8 September 1934, *Letters of Samuel Beckett, 1929–1940*, 222.

[18] Gillis, *Irish Poetry of the 1930s*, 121.

[19] Osip Mandelstam, 'On the Nature of the Word', *The Collected Critical Prose and Letters*, ed. Jane Gary Harris, trans. Jane Gary Harris and Constance Link (London: Collins Harvill, 1991), 119.

[20] Paul de Man, 'Literary History and Literary Modernity', *Blindness and Insight: Essays in the Rhetoric of Contemporary Criticism* (Minneapolis: University of Minnesota Press, 1983), 148.

[21] Samuel Beckett, *Proust and Three Dialogues* (London: John Calder, 1965), 81–2.

[22] Ibid., 18.

[23] Ibid., 47.

'Enueg I' too synthesizes light and shade, moving from the 'black west' of its opening stanza to the white arctic landscapes of its closing lines, but is hardly a voyage of enlightenment. Each of its sections brings the impasse between the ego and its surroundings to a moment of crisis, but rather than force a resolution the poem dissolves the scene and starts afresh. The cityscape of the opening stanza shuts down in a vision of the 'black west'; the mountains on the horizon are relinquished in a 'clot of anger'; connection with nature at closer quarters, along the canal bank, curdles in images of lurid decay; a conversation with a young boy cuts to the jungles of Sumatra; predatory nature dethrones poetic consciousness; and one last avenue of social rather than alienated individual experience, a group of thirsty hurling fans, triggers two final gestures of disavowal and disconnection. Patricia Coughlan has found an 'unwelcome wholeness of perspective' forced on the observing self by the journey convention of this poem,[24] but as the narrator of *Dream of Fair to Middling Women* might plead: 'the only unity in this story is, please God, an involuntary unity'.[25] Wholeness and the self appear mutually incompatible, brushing against each other only to tear forcefully apart.

Any involuntary or provisional unity achieved by the poem finds its most authentic expression in its jump-cut transitions, and our sensation of the sudden and baffling distances we cover in following them. This is the fissuring of the word surface on which Beckett theorized to Axel Kaun in 1937, freeing the 'something or nothing' that lurks behind to seep through.[26] Gaston Bachelard has explored the implications of language lying athwart the zones of being and non-being and, in a chapter of *The Phenomenology of Space* on 'The Dialectics of Outside and Inside', finds promise as well as paralysis in the penumbra of ever-'shifting thresholds'. He characterizes the 'being of man' as:

> ...the being of a *surface*, of the surface that separates the region of the same from the region of the other.... [O]n the surface of being, in that region where being wants to be both visible and hidden, the movements of opening and closing are so numerous, so frequently inverted, and so charged with hesitation, that we could conclude on the following formula: man is half-open being.[27]

'Enueg I' is full of such comings and goings and if the speaker's physical displacement is imagined as the poem's horizontal axis, at any point in the narrative it opens onto different temporal and intertextual thresholds. The 'secret things' of line four derive from *Inferno*, III:21. 'Algum-trees' are from the Book of Chronicles, where Solomon orders them brought from Lebanon, and while their exact identity remains conjectural (much to Denis Devlin's puzzlement when Beckett showed him the poem in manuscript),[28] the similarity to *algos*, the Greek for 'pain', ratchets up the poem's theme of ubiquitous

[24] Patricia Coughlan, ' "The Poetry is Another Pair of Sleeves": Beckett, Ireland and Modernist Lyric Poetry', in *Modernism and Ireland*, ed. Coughlan and Davis, 196.

[25] Samuel Beckett, *Dream of Fair to Middling Women* (Monkstown: Black Cat Press, 1992), 132.

[26] Beckett to Axel Kaun, 9 July 1937, *Letters of Samuel Beckett, 1929–1940*, 518.

[27] Gaston Bachelard, *The Phenomenology of Space*, trans. Maria Jolas (Boston: Beacon Press, 1969), 222.

[28] Beckett to MacGreevy, 9 October 1933, *Letters of Samuel Beckett, 1929–1940*, 166.

dolour. I have referred to Heraclitus, and the appearance of Democritus here (his prefatory epithet 'wearish' comes courtesy of Burton's *Anatomy of Melancholy*) completes that pseudo-couple of pre-Socratic Greeks. The 'still flagrant rafflesia' is a reference to Max Nordau's *Degeneracy*, on which Beckett took notes, the implication of stench and corruption linking uncomfortably with the crimson 'sputum' of the tubercular beloved in the poem's second line. The borough of Chapelizod introduces a Joycean context, and the elevation of the sweaty heroes' beverages to the Hellenic dignity of nepenthe and moly permits a rare crossover in Beckett from Gaelic to classical mythology. (Nepenthe and moly are, respectively, a drug of forgetfulness and a charm used against Circe's enchantments; 'Moly' was also the original title for the uncollected early poem 'Yoke of Liberty'.) And finally, the poem's concluding four lines are a straight borrowing from Arthur Rimbaud's 'Barbare'. Here then is not just a pictorial multiplicity, but an arrangement of the textual surface as a series of intertextual overlaps, 'opening and closing' onto a space somewhere between Beckett's and the poem's various sponsor-influences.

In *Being and Time* Martin Heidegger employs 'thrownness' (*Geworfenheit*) to characterize the state of unhoused Being ('the "*thrownness*" of this entity into its "there"'),[29] and the poems of *Echo's Bones* dwell repeatedly on love as a manifestation of this exile-from-self. The techniques I have applied to 'Enueg I' yield a similar dividend of progress-through-breakdown when applied to one of the most erotically suggestive and tender poems in the collection, 'Alba'. Disjunction remains a given. First, the woman 'shall be here', and 'shall establish' 'the white plane of music' before morning (readers of *Murphy* will recall its hero's use of 'music' as a code word for sex). The prospect of the woman's presence cannot be endured without some more self-defence than the poem has thus far provided, and in its final stanza Beckett issues a series of masochistic, pre-emptive cancellations that nullify the possibility of any encounter, shifting also from the future of 'shall' to the peremptory present ('there is no sun'). For all the pyrotechnics of this subjective collapse, 'Alba' retains an eerie poise and beauty that place it among the very best of Beckett's poems:

> who though you stoop with fingers of compassion
> to endorse the dust
> shall not add to your bounty
> whose beauty shall be a sheet before me
> a statement of itself drawn across the tempest of emblems
> so that there is no sun and no unveiling
> and no host
> only I and then the sheet
> and bulk dead[30]

'Sanies I' mixes an even more troublesome female into the mix, the poet's mother. In *Molloy*, a meditation on love jumps erratically from Molloy's love interests to his mother

---

[29] Martin Heidegger, *Being and Time*, trans. John Macquarrie and Edward Robinson (Oxford: Blackwell, 1962), 174.

[30] Beckett, *Selected Poems*, 19.

and ribald anality ('But is it true love, in the rectum?'),[31] and here too the pleasure of fundamental stimulation by his bicycle on a day trip to North Dublin ('all heaven in the sphincter') triggers a series of free associations that move from his parents' marriage and his birth to present erotic fantasies. The association of his birth with 'Spy Wedsday', when Judas betrayed Christ, suggests the injustice of the poet's expulsion into the world, and the comparison of 'pain drawn like a cork' to a 'glans' offers a psychosexual twist, where one might have expected a popping, celebratory champagne cork instead, though 'buckets of fizz' duly turn up too. Mrs Rochester in *Jane Eyre* is the most famous of mad or unpresentable women in modern literature relegated to out-of-the-way nooks and crannies, but in Beckett the unmentionable mother frequently *is* the cranny to which the speaker would ideally like to withdraw ('ah to be back in the caul now with no trusts'). Female confinement is not confined to the poet either: the short story 'Fingal', from *More Pricks Than Kicks*, also features a trip to Portrane, in which an old man assures Belacqua that Dean Swift kept a 'motte' in a local tower,[32] a Hibernicism that echoes the 'Madame de la Motte' of 'Sanies II'.

Love is banishment, the narrator of *First Love* declared, and in its very first sentence that novella proposed an equation between love (or marriage at least) and the death of the father. *First Love* extracts much Freudian farce from its narrator's inability to emerge from his deep grief for his father and channel his sexuality into less morbid outlets. The next poem in *Echo's Bones*, 'Sanies II', is one long masochistic fantasy, complete with bamboo-wielding prostitute, but here too there are currents of sexual dysfunction and anxiety. The poet envisages 'Sparkling beestings for me', 'beestings' being the first milk given by an animal that has recently given birth. This has the advantage, for the speaker, of downgrading the mother to animal status (and 'Serena II' will feature a whelping Kerry Blue bitch), but also puns on 'bee-stings', given the preceding images of pain, not to mention the presence of a prick in the form of that 'glans'. In 'Love and Lethe', from *More Pricks Than Kicks*, the unprepossessing Ruby Tough bears 'marks in her nether lip where she could persuade no bee to sting her any more'.[33] Parental sexual intercourse being the ultimate primal scene the poet cannot face, he adds the prick-like bee-stings to his baggage of sexual anxiety before introducing his love interest in the poem's last section.

Before he does this, the cyclist-poet signals his sexual unease again by describing his appearance as 'clipped like a pederast'. *More Pricks Than Kicks* makes much of Belacqua's fantasies of willing cuckoldry and impotence, and when the love interest arrives the poet pointedly dismounts rather than the more active opposite:

> I see main verb at last
> her whom alone in the accusative
> I have dismounted to love
> gliding towards me dauntless nautch-girl on the face of the waters

---

[31] Samuel Beckett, *Molloy* (Paris: Olympia Press, 1955), 76.
[32] Samuel Beckett, *More Pricks Than Kicks* (London: Calder & Boyars, 1970), 34.
[33] Ibid., 96.

Psychosexual readings of this kind can easily go too far, as when Lawrence Harvey finds a pair of women's breasts in the bicycles 'curved handlebars'.[34] To Roger Little the entire poem is in any case too bogged down in Freudian obliquity to be an unqualified success ('The profound obligation to self has not yet found projections and a manner which simultaneously recognize his obligation to the reader.')[35] The poem concludes on the word 'home', recommending the nautch-girl 'cadge a lift' to the 'cob of [her] web' in Holles Street maternity hospital. The self-exile sketched in *First Love* speaks of the pain of being 'no longer oneself', but in 'Sanies I' it is the moment of becoming oneself that is traumatic, in the womb with which the poem hysterically connects any hint of the erotic. If this is 'home', it has become overdetermined to the point of uninhabitability, and if frantic identifications with the womb of home are the theory, the neurotic shortfall of exile remains the practical reality.

Set in London, 'Serena I' upgrades its own ruminations on exile to a form of species anxiety. Beckett's periods of residence in London in the 1930s were not the happiest, and 'Serena I' seethes with strangled rage. The 1974 poem 'Something there' ends with a vision of a mysterious presence 'somewhere out there' ('something/not life/necessarily'), but where the escape into the 'irreducible inorganic singleness' of the 'mineral' that Beckett found in the painting of Jack Yeats epitomized ultimate release,[36] the animal kingdom of Regent's Park Zoo, too, provides a relief from the burden of the human, all-too-human. 'Serena I' toys with a polytheistic vision ('all things full of gods'), but few of the zoo animals Beckett views appear very divine. Bored and mangy, 'they stare out across monkey-hills the elephants/Ireland',[37] the imagined glimpse of the poet's home-land (rather than the weaver-bird's or boa constrictor's) suggesting Beckett believes he too is staring out from a zoo-like confinement. The separated line 'ah father father that art in heaven' (though the poem predates the death of William Beckett in 1933) under-lines the sense of exile through grief and abandonment that is also such a feature of *First Love*. The cityscape of the stanza beginning 'I surprise me moved by the many a funnel hinged' parallels another prose text, Celia's walk by Battersea Bridge in *Murphy*, though where the latter evinces sympathy for the plight of a shivering Chelsea pensioner, here the mass of passers-by are a 'canaille', one of whom is a 'guttersnipe' for asking to see the poet's narcissistic accessory, his 'Mirror'. Bliss is passing incognito and incommunicado or, better again, being rid of one's humanity altogether. The final eight lines of 'Serena I' prefigure the French poem 'La Mouche':

> my brother the fly
> the common housefly
> sidling out of darkness into light

---

[34] Lawrence Harvey, *Samuel Beckett: Poet & Critic* (Princeton: Princeton University Press, 1970), 143.

[35] Roger Little, 'Beckett's Poems and Verse Translations, or: Beckett and the Limits of Poetry', in *The Cambridge Companion to Samuel Beckett*, ed. John Pilling (Cambridge: Cambridge University Press, 1994), 191.

[36] Beckett to Cissie Sinclair, 14 August 1937, *Letters of Samuel Beckett, 1929–1940*, 535–6.

[37] Beckett, *Selected Poems*, 25.

fastens on his place in the sun
whets his six legs
revels in his planes his poisers
it is the autumn of his life
he could not serve typhoid and mammon[38]

The Irish modernist context for the poems of *Echo's Bones* is at least established if debatable, but contexts become entirely scarcer on the ground when we consider Beckett's later poetry, in English and French. He had translated Paul Eluard, André Breton, and René Crevel, and signed the 'Poetry is Vertical' manifesto in the literary journal *transition*, but it makes little sense to speak of Beckett's French poetry as surrealist. A more meaningful framework is its contribution to carrying Beckett over the threshold to the full literary bilingualism soon to find expression in the great post-war fiction and drama. Paris in the 1930s abounded in *émigré* poets and writers (the Uruguayan Jules Supervielle, the Lithuanian-Russian Oscar Venceslas de Lubicz Miłosz, and the Belgian Henri Michaux), some of whom, such as Beckett's Romanian friend-to-be E. M. Cioran, had also taken refuge in French from their native tongues.

'Je ne peux pas sortir je suis dans un pays sans traces', Beckett writes in the 1947 poem 'bon bon il est un pays',[39] returning us in updated form to our earlier dialectic of breakthrough and paralysis. The experience of writing in French may have disposed of Beckett's Irish imbroglios, but it has already hatched fresh prisons of its own. Neither self nor other offers any refuge, as in 'ainsi a-t-on beau' with its lament at being 'enfermé chez soi enfermé chez eux'. *Echo's Bones* took its title from a myth in which the act of perception is subsumed by the omnipresent image of the self (Narcissus confronting his reflection), and in the French poems also (the previously mentioned 'Rue de Vaugirard', 'Arènes de Lutèce' with its optical illusions) the visual field is often a focus for the 'vigilant coenaesthesia'[40] in which these poems attempt to outstare the deadening effects of habit. In his reading of Beckett's poetry Alan Gillis quotes Osip Mandelstam, a poet Beckett rated highly,[41] and in Mandelstam's 1922 essay 'Nature of the Word' he anatomizes the symbolist poetics and the impasse of exhaustion to which they lead:

> Perception is demoralized. Nothing is real, genuine. Nothing is left but a terrifying quadrille of 'correspondences', all nodding to one another. Eternal winking. Never a clear word, nothing but hints and reticent whispers. The rose nods to the girl, the girl to the rose. No one wants to be himself.[42]

Where Symbolism figures and tropes the object as something always other than itself, Mandelstam stresses its integrity as a verbal utensil or icon: 'a complex composite of

[38] Ibid., 26.

[39] Ibid., 53.

[40] Samuel Beckett, 'Tal Coat', *Proust and Three Dialogues*, 101.

[41] 'Oh, he's a *fine* poet!'—quoted in Anne Atik, *How It Was: A Memoir of Samuel Beckett* (London: Faber, 2001), 121.

[42] Mandelstam, 'On the Nature of the Word', 128.

phenomena…a candle burning inside a paper lantern'.[43] Beckett for his part had little enthusiasm for the arch-Symbolist Stéphane Mallarmé, preferring the more unruly Rimbaud, and in his German letter of 1937 he rejects the 'forest of symbols' of Charles Baudelaire's *Correspondences*, whose officious 'birds of interpretation…are never silent'.[44] Beckett's French poems too are complex verbal artefacts, but the abandonment of his candlestick by the hare in the second-last *mirlitonnade* ('à bout de songes un bouquin') suggests they are happy to go without the artificial lighting foreseen by Mandelstam.

While Beckett's French poems of the 1930s and 1940s form distinct groups, it is with a much later sequence that I wish to conclude. 'Dichten = condensare', according to Ezra Pound,[45] and modern poetry scarcely comes in a more condensed form than that of the *mirlitonnades* (1978). The play *Not I* dates from 1972, but in the *mirlitonnades* Beckett goes one step further, avoiding any use at all of the first-person pronoun. A scattering of third-person pronouns and a solitary 'tu' in the second-last word of the sequence aside, these are poems that approximate to Maurice Blanchot's idea of *le neutre*. Beckett's friend B. S. Johnson rejected narrative linearity by publishing a novel in a box (*The Unfortunates*, 1969), its chapters unbound, and the composition history of the *mirlitonnades* reveals a similar amoeba-like resistance to the tyranny of the spine. As ghosts, many of its animating presences can manage perfectly well without a backbone:

> rentrer
> à la nuit
> au logis
> allumer
>
> éteindre voir
> la nuit voir
> collé à la vitre
> le visage[46]

Illumination is forever in short supply in late Beckett (for Mark Nixon, 'The most important word in Beckett's late texts, poetic and otherwise, is "faint"'),[47] but at least from *Lessness* on, the late texts are full of trace elements in the visual field that might signal the encounter with the non-self at last, assuming they are more than daydreams. Demanding to be not just seen but 'ill seen', these traces resemble the painterly technique of anamorphosis, where a random-seeming smudge, as in the distorted skull in Hans Holbein's *The Ambassadors*, unexpectedly comes into focus and reveals its centrality to the composition. Consequently, another feature of late Beckett is the watcher figure, as in 'fin fond du néant':

---

[43] Ibid., 129.

[44] Beckett to Axel Kaun, 9 July 1937, *Letters of Samuel Beckett, 1929–1940*, 519.

[45] Ezra Pound, *An ABC of Reading* (London: Faber, 1951), 36.

[46] Beckett, *Selected Poems*, 70. In my translation: 'back home/at night/on with the light//extinguish see/the night see/pressed to the window/the face'.

[47] Mark Nixon, '"Unutterably Faint": Beckett's Late English Poetry', in *Fulcrum: An Annual of Poetry and Aesthetics* 6 (2007), 518.

> fin fond du néant
> au bout de quelle guette
> l'oeil crut entrevoir
> remuer faiblement
> la tête le calma disant
> ce ne fut que dans ta tête[48]

The verb 'entrevoir' prefigures the assonating vowels of 'comment dire' ('vouloir croire entrevoir quoi'), and places us again in an in-between space. The line 'lueurs lisières' returns to the non-identity at the heart of identity, the non-self of the self. Forty years earlier Beckett had felt 'enfermé chez soi enfermé chez eux', but an extra twist of no's knife now cancels the self in which one might feel at home or not:

> lueurs lisières
> de la navette
> plus qu'un pas s'éteignent
> demi-tour remiroitent
>
> halte plutôt
> loin des deux
> chez soi sans soi
> ni eux[49]

The 'navette' of the second line might recall Job, who thought his days swifter than a 'weaver's shuttle' (Job 7:6), but the weaving metaphor shows that constant back-and-forth movement need not be random or unproductive. A 'selvedge' is the self-finished edge of a fabric, and the locus of the self throughout these poems is both on-edge and on its own edge. As a relief from this condition, not just in his poetry, but in Beckett's late prose and drama too, there is an ever-stronger compulsion to measure out time and space, whether through drily mathematical accounts of his settings (*The Lost Ones, Imagination Dead Imagine*), step-counting (*Footfalls*), or attempts to measure the speaker's lifespan. The *mirlitonnades* oblige on this last count:

> somme toute
> tout compte fait
> un quart de milliasse
> de quarts d'heure
> sans compter
> les tempts morts[50]

The process becomes self-referential in 'écoute-les', as the poem describes it own doling-out in words (a theme to which Beckett will return one last time in 'comment dire'/'what

---

[48] Beckett, *Selected Poems*, 72 ('far end of void/after what watch/eye thought it saw/the head feebly stir/calmed him saying/all in the head').

[49] Ibid., 75 ('flashes edgings/of the shuttle/take more than a step fade/about-turn shine like new//halt rather/far from each/by your self selfless/out of their reach').

[50] Ibid., 71 ('all said and done/game over amounts/to a quarter billion/quarter hours gone/not including/extra time').

is the word'). The tic of instant self-cancellation we saw in 'chez soi sans soi' is repeated in the insistence that words are added to words ('les mots/aux mots') without a word ('sans mot'):

> écoute-les
> s'ajouter
> les mots
> aux mots
> sans mot
> les pas
> aux pas
> un à
> un[51]

After the first two lines the poem is all in monosyllables, and just as *Happy Days* contains an implied third act in which the sand has engulfed Winnie, these poems yearn for the ultimate leave-taking from self and language, as in the tiny 'd'où':

> d'où
> la voix qui dit
> vis
>
> d'une autre vie[52]

The commanding voice comes from within, while remaining alien to the self, or if it is the self, speaks from the depths of our un-self-knowing and self-estrangement. This is the voice that tells us: 'vis' ('live'), which the stanza-break then fine-tunes to 'd'une autre vie'. What we are living is not life; life is 'une autre vie', not ours.

One way in which Beckett has continued to live a life not his is in the work of subsequent Irish poets. The most consistently Beckettian of contemporary Irish poets, in temperament if not always technique, is Derek Mahon. Mahon frequently references Beckett in his work ('An Image from Beckett', 'Exit Molloy'), and has produced versions of the *mirlitonnades* ('Burbles'). The *mirlitonnades* correspond closely in date to Mahon's sequence 'Light Music', from *Poems 1962–1978*, in which he abdicates his usual stanza forms for something more evanescent. While Mahon inclines far more to an aesthetic of epiphany and recuperation than his mentor (it is hard to imagine Beckett describing a farm bathed in sunlight 'as if singled out/for benediction'), there are moments at which the Northern Irish poet's vision of entropy coincides with the older writer's familiar scenes of 'grandeur and desolation',[53] as in 'Elpenor' with its echo of Beckett's 'Dieppe':

> Edacity in the palace
> and in the sandy timber
> of my crumbling monument,

---

[51] Ibid,. 74 ('listen to them/add up/words/upon words/without a word/step/upon step/one by/one').

[52] Ibid., 94 ('whence/the voice that says/live//another life').

[53] Beckett, 'First Love', *Complete Short Prose, 1929–1989*, 90.

> its lengthening shadow
> pointing towards home.[54]

Mahon is one of two Irish poets compared to Beckett by Stephen Watt in *Beckett and Contemporary Irish Writing*; the other is Paul Muldoon. Beckett's increasing presence in Muldoon's work from around this time (Mary Farl Powers was a published scholar.) has emphatically not coincided with a drive towards minimalism (even his haiku sequences have a mini-epic flavour to them). In *Emblements* Powers uses the image of a worm-eaten cankered potato, suggestive of the Irish great famine but also, in retrospect, of the assault on the artist's body by the cancer that would kill her in 1992. To Stephen Watt, Beckett's relationship to Muldoon mirrors that of a parasite and its host, with Beckett the worm of grief in the elegist's breast, forever confronting him with an implacable death's head. Muldoon is left:

> trying to make sense of the '*quaquaqua*'
> of that potato-mouth; that mouth as prim
> and proper as it's full of self-opprobrium[55]

Muldoon's example shows that there is more to a creative dialogue with Beckett than affecting stump-like one-stress lines carefully combed free of all social-realist detail. But no less a proof of affinity transcending slavish imitation is the Beckettian transformation that another Northern Irish poet, Ciaran Carson, wrought on his style in his 2003 collection *Breaking News*. Nothing in *The Irish for No* or *Belfast Confetti* prepares us for the radical fragmentation on show in the feedback-like effects of a poem such as 'Spin Cycle 2':

> gun-gun
>
> ear-plugs in
>
> blank-blank[56]

A writer unjustly overlooked by Watt is Thomas Kinsella; and while the nationalist framework to Kinsella's understanding of Irish writing is alien to Beckett (one thinks of his letter to MacGreevy protesting his 'chronic inability to understand...a phrase like "The Irish People"'),[57] this is not to detract from the powerful affinities between Beckett's poetry and any number of Kinsella sequences, from *Nightwalker* and *One* to later work such as *Godhead* and *Littlebody*:

> The waves are alive, arguing among themselves,
> hurrying in disorder between two stillnesses:
>
> out beyond the first stir of unrest

[54] Derek Mahon, *Poems 1962–1978* (Oxford: Oxford University Press, 1979), 96.

[55] Paul Muldoon, *Poems 1968–1998* (London: Faber, 2001), 336, and Stephen Watt, *Beckett and Contemporary Irish Writing*, 144–61.

[56] Ciaran Carson, *Breaking News* (Oldcastle: Gallery, 2003), 40. For more on *Breaking News*, see David Wheatley, ' "Pushed next to nothing": Ciaran Carson's *Breaking News*', in *Ciaran Carson: Critical Essays*, ed. Elmer Kennedy-Andrews (Dublin: Four Courts Press, 2009), 45–65.

[57] Beckett to MacGreevy, 31 January 1938, *Letters of Samuel Beckett, 1929–1940*, 599.

at a depth without light;

and in the last lap of salt water stopped at my foot,
discovering the first thought of withdrawal.[58]

While the Irish-language tradition is also alien to Beckett, his influence on Kinsella suggests subterranean links to the crystalline economy of early Irish lyrics. A final writer deserving of mention, and also with connections to the tradition of the early Irish lyric, is Trevor Joyce. His 2007 gathering *What's in Store* features a large number of through-composed sequences and translations from Irish and other languages, but while Joyce's work privileges process and incompletion over achieved lyric fullness, it is more readily hospitable than Beckett's to Platonic abstraction ('the ideal form/exists/in imagination/only').[59] An approach to the emotions allows Joyce's work to register more turbulence, but if the poet's instinct is to be rid of the self, the route to this unburdening proceeds by way of untidy sloughing rather than orderly sublimation:

> Heart
>   to ash
>   exhausted
> settles
>   in a ruined
>   house.
> Say, why
>   should I
>   experience
> nostalgia
>   for the forms
>   of men?
> How,
>   rid now
>   of all familiar
> fixes,
>   slough
>   my self?[60]

Ultimately, however, attempts to trace a school of Beckett in contemporary Irish poetry risk incoherence on the most basic level. 'The artist who stakes his being is from nowhere, has no kith', Beckett insisted in 'Homage to Jack B. Yeats'.[61] The aesthetic of exile that drives his work makes a nowhere of Ireland, England, or France, but firmly rules out the option of our becoming too at-home in these existential no-man's-lands by

---

[58] Thomas Kinsella, 'High Tide: Amagansett', *Collected Poems* (Manchester: Carcanet, 2001), 335.
[59] Trevor Joyce, *What's in Store: Poems 2000–2007* (Dublin: New Writers' Press, 2007), 224.
[60] Ibid., 170.
[61] Beckett, 'Homage to Jack B. Yeats', *Disjecta*, 149.

circling back ('the one way back was on and on was always back'), time and again, to the bleak and unredeemed particularity of this fetid Dublin cityscape, this dying London fly, this disappointed lover's bed. The fearless experimenter launches himself with theatrical bravado only for his poems to bog down in chronic failure and paralysis. Or, to turn this reading inside out, the poems bog down in chronic failure and paralysis and still contrive to vindicate their author's experimental bravado in a peerlessly realized vision of boredom, horror, and glory.

CHAPTER 10

....

VOICE AND VOICEPRINTS: JOYCE AND RECENT IRISH POETRY

....

DILLON JOHNSTON

> What is the voice? I said.
> A closed-tube resonator, like the canal of the ear,
> You said. The vocal column begins in the vocal folds,
> Which pucker like lips on the mouthpiece of a saxophone.
> Every voice can be voiceprinted like a musical score....
>
> Ciaran Carson, 'Second Take'.[1]

I

....

On a business trip from Trieste to Dublin, late in 1909, James Joyce told fellow writer Pádraic Colum 'I am not a poet'.[2] Although at that moment Joyce was an entrepreneur, returning to Dublin to establish the city's first motion-picture theatre, his status as an emerging writer was based on his poetry, a chapbook of thirty-six brief lyrics published as *Chamber Music* in 1907. Colum interpreted his friend to mean that he could 'put more of himself into prose' and that the lyrics now seemed jejune to Joyce. Colum speculated further, and others have followed him, that the lyrics are not poems proper but songs to be sung, most being delicate imitations of Elizabethan/Cavalier harpsichord or lute

---

[1] Ciaran Carson, *For All We Know* (Oldcastle: Gallery, 83).
[2] Mary and Padraic Colum, *Our Friend James Joyce* (New York: Doubleday, 1958), 82–3.

songs by Shakespeare, Dowland, Nashe, Jonson, and others, many of whose lyrics Joyce knew by heart.

Although this repertory of early monocular love lyrics and his competence as a musician gave Joyce a topic and a model for his early poetry, he would soon alter the speaker's role, by admitting other narrators, even unspecified speakers, or doubling perspective to allow for parallactic sightings, sometimes even unreliable readings which may lead to uncertain conclusions. Although Joyce's masterful innovations in narration, which would significantly impact upon recent Irish poetry as well as prose, occurred mostly in his prose, these experimental narrations began a stealthy emergence in Joyce's poetry, where narrative doubling or duplicity is generally ignored, and apparent narrative uniformity is read as the poet's voice, or even his 'voiceprint'.

Writing in 1982, Seamus Heaney assumed a majority view when he suggested that we approach Joyce's poems as refined music: 'at a slight aesthetic distance, with a connoisseur's awareness'. Heaney continued: 'And that, in fact, seems to be the way Joyce himself appreciated poetry.... It is poetry as the handmaiden of music, as evocation, invitation to dream.... It would seem that Joyce aimed for such a response when he wrote his own verse.'[3] As have many other readers, Heaney offers faint praise for these lyrics or for the even thinner volume *Pomes Pennyeach*, thirteen poems on disparate subjects, bundled together for publication in 1926. He turns instead to Joyce's two Swiftian broadsides, 'Gas from a Burner' and 'The Holy Office', endorsing Stanislaus Joyce's youthful prediction that 'ruthlessness, not delicacy, would be the keynote of my brother's work'.[4] However, so much of what these two broadsides accomplish is achieved in the fiction, and excepting Thomas Kinsella's caustic, effective satire *Butcher's Dozen*, few recent Irish poets vent such savage indignation.

In the development of Irish poetry over the last half-century, it may seem inexplicable that so many poets have valued the legacy of the novelist Joyce, at best a poet in his youth, over that of Yeats, Ireland's—and perhaps for a full century the globe's—major poet. It is worthwhile to remind ourselves how Joyce differed from Yeats in many regards, such as: (1) his preference for cities (not the colonial capital London, but Dublin and continental cities) and for urban over rural landscapes; (2) his fascination with etymologies, translation, puns, and other wordplay; (3) his attention to bodies and incarnation over abstractions, which grew in part from his early steeping in Catholicism; (4) his adaptation of Aristotle rather than Plato; (5) his interest in space, public and private, as well as what is now called 'deep space' and its indivisibility from time; and (6) his strong, shaping interest in music. These differences distilled into concerns over narration and found expression in narrative strategies, including point of view, identity of narrators, tone, and voice. Perhaps more than he attracted imitators or devotees, Joyce seems to offer solutions for younger poets confronting some similar problems, perhaps especially the issue of who

---

[3] Seamus Heaney, *Finders Keepers: Selected Prose, 1971–2001* (London: Faber, 2002), 389.
[4] Quoted in ibid., 390.

speaks in poems when the poet falls silent and yields his narrative role to characters or unidentified interlocutors.[5]

Although as a young man Joyce would distinguish himself from other university ephebes by taking as models European masters such as Ibsen, Hauptmann, and Flaubert, Yeats was, nevertheless, among his earliest literary heroes. Joyce's first collection of poems, now lost, was entitled *Moods*, most likely inspired by Yeats's essay entitled 'The Moods' (1895) which began: 'Literature differs from explanatory and scientific writing in being wrought about a mood, or a community of moods, as the body is wrought about an invisible soul.'[6] Early in the next century, however, Joyce began distancing himself from the powerful influence of Yeats, first in 'The Day of the Rabblement' where he criticizes Yeats's 'treacherous instinct of adaptability' in his leadership of what Joyce saw as the popular and politicized Irish Literary Theatre.[7] Then, in 1902, Joyce introduced himself to Yeats before berating him for his involvement with 'politics, folklore ... [and] the historical setting of events', according to Richard Ellmann's frequently cited narration of this encounter.[8] Yeats continued to support and encourage Joyce, as is evident in a letter following their Dublin meeting: 'Your technique in verse is much better than the technique of any young Dublin man I have met during my time. ... I will do anything for you I can.'[9] He must have felt at times that Joyce was masticating, rather than merely biting, the hand that fed him, but Yeats continued to help Joyce, writing to the Royal Literary Fund at Pound's prompting to recommend the impoverished writer for a grant. Whereas Yeats particularly praised Joyce's fiction, he also included poetry as part of Joyce's 'most beautiful gift'. For example, he cites the 'poem on the last page of his *Chamber Music* which will, I believe, live. It is a technical and emotional masterpiece.'[10]

Among the three dozen poems in this cycle about lost love, the most frequently cited of Joyce's lyrics is this closing lyric which begins: 'I hear an army charging upon the land,/And the thunder of horses plunging',[11] apparently echoing the opening of a Yeats poem: 'I hear the Shadowy Horses, their long manes a-shake,/Their hoofs

---

[5] In early readings of Joyce, pioneering critics such as Hugh Kenner called attention to the complexities of Joyce's narration: see especially Kenner, *Joyce's Voices* (London: Faber, 1978). In my own book, *Irish Poetry After Joyce* (Notre Dame: University of Notre Dame Press, 1985), I argued that Joyce's complex narration—his point of view, tone, unassigned narration—was a major influence on recent Irish poetry. (Some of my argument is revisited in this essay.) Meanwhile, Declan Kiberd has argued incisively that 'Joyce's *Ulysses* is a text without any final authority', in *Inventing Ireland: The Literature of the Modern Nation* (London: Jonathan Cape, 1995), 339. More recently, David Butler made a case for Joyce's influence on recent Irish poetry, specifically regarding Ciaran Carson's *The Twelfth of Never* (Oldcastle: Gallery, 1998). See ' "Slightly Out of Synch": Joycean Strategies in Ciaran Carson's *The Twelfth of Never*', in *Irish University Review*, 33:2 (Autumn/Winter 2003), 337–55.

[6] W. B. Yeats, *Essays & Introductions* (New York: Macmillan, 1961), 195.

[7] James Joyce, *Occasional, Critical, and Political Writing*, ed. Kevin Barry (Oxford: Oxford University Press, 2000), 51.

[8] Richard Ellmann, *James Joyce* (Oxford: Oxford University Press, 1982), 102.

[9] Ibid., 104.

[10] Ibid., 391.

[11] James Joyce, *Poems and Shorter Writings* (London: Faber, 1991), 48.

heavy with tumult, their eyes glimmering white'.[12] In 1913, Ezra Pound would single out Joyce's poem as an example of his imagist poetry, although, as Walton Litz concedes, 'Joyce was never a part of the movement… [but] his early literature had led him to many of the conclusions articulated by Pound'.[13] Other critics, such as William York Tindall, invite us to consider similarities between Joyce's tidal setting and George Meredith's concluding stanza in the Victorian poet's sequence *Modern Love* (1862):[14]

> In tragic hints here see what evermore
> Moves dark as yonder midnight ocean's force,
> Thundering like ramping hosts of warrior horse
> To throw that faint thin line upon the shore![15]

Interlinked by assonantal *o*'s, Meredith's poem suggests the profound depths of the unconscious that fetches up on the narrow margin of the conscious mind. Joyce evokes some of this psychological seascape in his middle stanza:

> They cry unto the night their battle-name:
> I moan in sleep when I hear afar their whirling laughter.
> They cleave the gloom of dreams, a blinding flame,
> Clanging, clanging upon the heart as upon an anvil.[16]

The mysterious shibboleths of the invading hosts, each shouting his *nom de guerre*, the speaker's dream-response, the synaesthetic metaphors of a blinding flame that cleaves and clangs as if forging the conclusion of *A Portrait of the Artist*, all suggest the powerful surge of the unconscious. The next line describing the amphibian host, like Sir Gawain's adversary 'shaking in triumph their long, green hair', may seal the poem in a suggestive but irrational undisclosure.

Litz asserts that this concluding poem from *Chamber Music* demonstrates that the visual effects of Joyce's youthful work are dependent upon what T. S. Eliot named the 'auditory imagination', which grows from 'his [Joyce's] own love for music and understanding of musical technique'.[17] Among the songs Joyce learned by heart and sang as party pieces at the Sheehy's, and at the homes of other friends, or otherwise especially admired, Elizabethan lyrics may have been his favourites. The editors of an edition of *Chamber Music*, both esteemed critics, offer what may seem extravagant praise: 'The poems are reminiscent of Elizabethan and Cavalier poetry in their lyric quality. They express their traditional idealism with a refined elegance and technical skill, reminding

---

[12] W. B. Yeats, 'He bids his Beloved be at Peace', *The Variorum Edition of the Poems of W. B. Yeats*, ed. Peter Allt and Russell K. Alspach (Basingstoke: MacMillan, 1956), 154.

[13] A. Walton Litz, *The Art of James Joyce* (New York: Oxford University Press, 1964), 53.

[14] James Joyce, *Chamber Music*, ed. William York Tindall, with Introduction and Notes (New York: Columbia University Press, 1954), 225.

[15] George Meredith, 'Modern Love', in *Victorian Poetry: An Annotated Anthology*, ed. Francis O'Gorman (Oxford: Blackwell, 2004), 349.

[16] James Joyce, *Poems and Shorter Writings*, 48.

[17] Litz, *The Art of James Joyce*, 63.

us not only of Ben Jonson but of Tom Moore in their fluency.'[18] Among the few other critics who ardently admire Joyce's imitations, Myra Russel asserted, nearly three decades ago:

> [T]o be musical and Elizabethan is a very remarkable achievement. And if some of the poems fall short, it is hardly surprising when we consider how high the standards were.... The Elizabethans intrigued and enticed him.... The strong connecting links suggest that these are the lyrics with which Joyce's poems should be compared, not those of his own day.[19]

Russel would require an impossible reading, seeing clearly through the contemporary screen, not hearing the quaintness of older English, not acknowledging Borges's point that replicating *Don Quixote* word for word in the twentieth century would produce for our contemporaries a work of literature far different from Cervantes' novel. Imitation and allusion frequently result in pastiche, as in lyric XIV, which Joyce had designated as the sequence's climax. In his notes to *Chamber Music*, Tindall identifies borrowings from the 'Song of Solomon' in lyrics XIII and XXXIV, but especially in lyric XIV, where the lover anticipates consummation: 'My dove, my beautiful one,/Arise, arise!/.../The odorous winds are weaving/A music of sighs:/Arise, arise,/My dove, my beautiful one!'[20] We might add that in early-modern Christendom, 'Song of Solomon' was read allegorically as sanctioned erotica. Often quoted, it attracted deliberate and unconscious parody, so in Joyce's borrowings we may be as likely to hear the rude mechanicals at play in *A Midsummer Night's Dream* ('Asleep my love/What dead my dove?/O Pyramus, arise!') as the borrowed love lyrics of Solomon.[21] With his head filled also with Yeats, Thomas Moore, Walter Pater, the detested Tennyson ('The Lady of Shalott', 'Mariana'), Irish ballads, and other Victorian lyrics, pastiche seems inevitable.

Most critics have been more dismissive, as was G. W. Stonier in 1936: 'We may take *Chamber Music* and *Pomes Pennyeach* as the attempt at "the Attic note", by way of the English classicists, Jonson and Dryden. They are curiously perfect, dead little poems.'[22] More recently, Vicki Mahaffey reaches a succinct judgement concerning Joyce's short works, namely his poems, *Giacomo Joyce*, and *Exiles*:

> First, and most damagingly, they are humourless.... Secondly, they are spare, denuded of the variable styles and elaborate contexts that make *Ulysses* and *Finnegans Wake* seem inexhaustible. Finally, they are easily dismissed as immediately derivative of both Joyce's experiences and his reading.[23]

---

[18] A. Norman Jeffares and Brendan Kennelly, *James Joyce: The Poems in Verse and Prose* (London: Kyle Cathie Ltd, 1992), 1.

[19] Myra Russel, 'The Elizabethan Connection: The Mission Score of James Joyce's *Chamber Music*', in *James Joyce Quarterly* 18:2 (Winter 1981), 146.

[20] Joyce, *Poems and Shorter Writings*, 26.

[21] William Shakespeare, *A Midsummer Night's Dream*, Act Five, Scene One.

[22] G. W. Stonier, 'Leviathan', *The New Statesman and Nation* 12 (10 October 1936), 551–2. Reprinted in *James Joyce: A Literary Reference*, ed. A. Nicholas Fargnoli (New York: Carroll & Graf, 2001).

[23] Vicki Mahaffey, 'Joyce's Shorter Works', in *The Cambridge Companion to James Joyce*, ed. Derek Attridge (Cambridge: Cambridge University Press, 1990), 185.

The two volumes of poems cannot be redeemed from such accurate, authoritative criticism, but we may attend here to some overlooked issues in these poems that remain unresolved to challenge or even influence the next generations of poets. From nearly the beginning of his career as a writer of prose poems and poems in verse, Joyce was concerned with the question of the narrative voice: who is the primary or exclusive speaker in the poem? How is tone controlled? From what angle and with what scope are the images and actions of the poem envisioned?

Mahaffey suggests that these issues of narration are ignored by Joyce or oversimplified in the poems in *Chamber Music*. She writes: 'There is only one voice in *Chamber Music*, that of an alternately idealistic and sensual young lover who desires to enter his beloved's chamber. As her room, heart, and womb, this space is warm and inviting'. But after lyric XIV, she adds, the space declines toward being manifest as the tomb, where the two become, in lyric XXX, 'grave lovers'. Mahaffey suggests that the 'smallness of the poems' structure, together with the fact that they are all sung by the same voice', induces a claustrophobic reading. She may mean simply that the characters share a vocabulary and syntax and, therefore, are not clearly distinctive.[24] Without identifying the narrator, the sequence opens with music: 'Strings in the earth and air/Make music sweet;/Strings by the river where/The willows meet'.[25] The second lyric introduces the woman as pianist and sets the mood in darkening colours. In the third lyric, the narrator addresses the 'lonely watcher of the skies' whom we take to be the woman although identities are not clearly determined. Harps play to personified Love, and the winds offer a choral response. This lyric is laden with prefixes, *un-*, *un-*, *re-*, *over-*, *un-*, which tend to qualify or undercut narrative statements.[26] Lyric IV begins with an imperative for the woman not only to hear 'One who is singing by your gate', an aperture like her chamber that suggests various interpretations, but also to suspend daydreams and to identify the singer as himself:

> O bend no more in revery
>   When he at eventide is calling,
> Nor muse: Who may this singer be
>   Whose song about my heart is falling?
> Know you by this, the lover's chant,
>   'Tis I that am your visitant.[27]

As the genre of song varies—calling, soft song, chant—the identity of the speaker emerges from third to first person, with the consequence that narration—point of view, tone, voice—becomes problematic in this lyric and, eventually, in the sequence.

---

[24] Ibid., 194.
[25] Joyce, *Poems and Shorter Writings*, 13.
[26] Ibid., 15.
[27] Ibid., 16.

II

During the gestation of the lyrics in *Chamber Music*, between 1900 and 1903, Joyce also developed in prose a series of brief prose-snapshots which he called 'epiphanies' rather than the more conventional 'prose poems'. Gaining some gravity through its sacred associations, this term meant for Joyce 'a sudden spiritual manifestation, whether in the vulgarity of speech or of gesture or in a memorable phase of the mind itself'.[28] The epiphany could be dramatic, exposing the obtuseness or insipidity of minor characters in fiction, or lyrical, recording an elevated, radiant moment in the musings of the author or the first-person narrator. Joyce once thought to contrast his poet-hero with his society in the novel *Stephen Hero* by inserting the epiphanies at intervals. For example, Epiphany XXII conveys both vulgarity of speech and Stephen's judgement when his friend McCann offers condolences for the death of Stephen's sister:

> – I was sorry to hear of the death of your sister…sorry we didn't
>   know in time…to have been at the funeral.
> Stephen released his hand gradually and said:
> – O, she was very young…a girl.
> McCann released his hand at the same rate of release, and
> said:
> – Still…it hurts.

By the time he had cobbled together much of his novel *Stephen Hero*, Joyce must have recognized that the epiphanies could not function effectively as observations presented directly to the reader—as mini-dramas—but that they required authorial explanation, so Joyce added: 'The acme of unconvincingness seemed to Stephen to have been reached at that moment.'[29]

Joyce would soon doubt the credibility of the monocular viewpoint and the authoritative voice which he found the epiphanies required when they were employed in his fiction. In *Stephen Hero*, Joyce's protagonist had unfolded his concept of *epiphany* in a peripatetic monologue with his straight-man Cranly whom he told 'that the clock of the Ballast Office was capable of an epiphany': 'I will pass it time after time.…It is only an item in the catalogue of Dublin's street furniture. Then all at once I see it and I know at once what it is: epiphany'.[30] In *A Portrait of the Artist As A Young Man*, Stephen develops his concept and integrates it into his aesthetic, but he abandons the term *epiphany* and even mocks it in *Ulysses*.

In place of the term *epiphany* Joyce came to prefer the term *parallax*, which is introduced into *Ulysses* by Bloom, standing before the Ballast Office clock, the site in *Stephen Hero* of Stephen's controversial explanation of *epiphany*. *Parallax* initially was an

---

[28] James Joyce, *Stephen Hero*, ed. John J. Slocum, Herbert Cahoon, and Theodore Spencer (New York: New Directions, 1963), 211.

[29] Ibid., 169.

[30] Ibid., 211.

astronomer's method of locating a celestial body by measuring the apparent shift in the position of the body when sighted from two points of view, or from the same observation point at two different times. Critics have recognized that these methods of determining 'geocentric' parallax have their analogues in the multiple points of view in *Ulysses*. The term can be applied to the way the reader must 'locate' Stephen and, especially, Bloom from a number of partial or even inaccurate sightings. *Parallax* implies not the incompleteness of any one character, as Ellmann has suggested, but 'the incompleteness of any one viewpoint within the novel, as well as being a strategy for involving the reader in the search for meaning'.[31] As Hugh Kenner concluded, 'Reality, Joyce learned early, does not answer to the "point of view", the monocular vision, the single ascertainable tone.'[32] Joyce came to realize that historical validity depended on an authority of judgment and imagination that no person could legitimately claim. Consequently, Joyce leads the shift from a single point of view to a more dramatic form of narration in which the reader arrives at judgements formerly proclaimed by the narrator. As no insignificant by-product of this narrative shift, Joyce suggests to Irish poets a way of freeing their vision from historical determinism, which has had a killing hold on the Irish consciousness.

Although Joyce's ideas of point of view may influence his poetic progeny, his attention to the related concept of *voice* may be a more valuable legacy. In his other thin book of poetry, published in 1927, he raises the issue of *voice* in his opening poem. Of this chapbook Mahaffey writes: 'As the title suggests *Pomes Pennyeach* are not worth much individually; ... they are musical, nostalgic, and markedly sentimental'.[33] Although they lack the sequential narrative suggested in *Chamber Music*, a few individual poems rise above the earlier poems, especially in the complex ways they explore, and address the problem of, narration. The volume opens with 'Tilly', a title that suits the chapbook's lightly mocking commercial title but which otherwise remains enigmatic. It refers to an extra amount thrown in for good measure after purchase, that which makes, for example, the butcher's or the baker's dozen. We might expect a poet's tilly to be the last poem in this volume of thirteen, but here it serves as a prologue. The poem opens: 'He travels after a winter sun' although we cannot yet distinguish this *he* from anyone else who walks the earth. With the second line, we know he is a drover, herding cattle into a winter sunset north of Cabra, Joyce's suburban residence in 1904:

> Urging the cattle along a cold red road,
> Calling to them, a voice they know,
> He drives his beasts above Cabra.[34]

The second stanza resumes with 'a voice' which 'tells them home is warm./They moo and make brute music with their hoofs./He drives them with a flowering branch before him,/

[31] Quoted in Johnston, *Irish Poetry After Joyce*, 34.
[32] Kenner, *Joyce's Voices*, 83.
[33] Mahaffey, 'Joyce's Shorter Works', 197.
[34] Joyce, *Poems and Shorter Writings*, 51.

Smoke pluming their foreheads.' The poem closes by contrasting two voices, the drover's voice of pastoral poetry, bringing comfort and cohesion, and a voice of violated nature:

> Boor, bond of the herd,
> Tonight stretch full by the fire!
> I bleed by the black stream
> For my torn bough!

Because in the closing two lines the referent is so powerfully and memorably disturbing, we recognize the 'torn bough' as an allusion to 'this grove of pain' in Canto XIII of *The Inferno of Dante* where a suicide, metamorphosed into a tree, cries: ' "Why do you dismember me?"/Blood bubbled out of it. "Why have you torn/me?" the trunk began to weep again.'[35] In Joyce's poem, the drover, not unlike the mountain man at the conclusion of *A Portrait*, lives harmoniously, if brutishly, in nature. The other, more Joycean, voice expresses the modern poet's alienation from, and disharmony within, nature.[36]

Joyce's engagement with voice and with questions of narration differ from Yeats's practice but also from attitudes toward self and voice in some contemporary poetry such as that of Seamus Heaney. Yeats's concept of the mask—his effort to create 'cold and passionate' poems contrary to his warm-blooded, romantic nature—introduces an antithetical voice but rarely contributes to multivocal poems. Although Yeats constructs poems as dialogues and creates dramatic characters such as Crazy Jane, Ribh, and Cuchulain, he remains a lyric, rather than a dramatic, poet.

Except in some of his epiphanies, Joyce seems disinclined to speak in his own, or any, uniform voice, or to employ phrases that seem familiarly Joycean. Previously read for decades as hard-edged realism, *Dubliners* has divulged its secrets of narration to contemporary scholars. Referring to a revisionary reading of 'Eveline' by Hugh Kenner, Margot Norris writes: 'My own readings of the *Dubliners* stories repeatedly produce many such "hidden stories" concealed by the narrative voice.'[37]

Readers of *A Portrait* understand that the story is often told through a third-person narration shaped by Stephen's thoughts, memories, and expectations as he builds a bridge between youthful expectations and experience, especially those based on events in public spaces. Early in the novel, his anticipation of relief from his stressful schooldays takes the general heading 'Going home for the holidays!' He looks forward to conveyance in the 'cars' and then, perhaps in anticipation of home baking, to the 'long, long chocolate train with cream facings'. Although he fashions this future vacation on memories from prior furloughs, in his keen anticipation he emphasizes the incremental and teleological aspects of the journey: 'The telegraph poles were passing, passing. The train went on and on. It knew.'[38] Briefer than the Bible's succinct 'Jesus wept', Stephen's 'It knew'

---

[35] Ciaran Carson, trans., *The Inferno of Dante Alighieri* (London: Granta, 2002), 85.

[36] Joyce may be locating the second voice beside the *Duibh-linn*, an early name for Dublin according to P. W. Joyce in *Irish Place Names* (Dublin: Appletree Press, 1984), 53.

[37] Margot Norris, 'The Perils of "Eveline"', *Suspicious Readings of Joyce's Dubliners* (Philadelphia: University of Pennsylvania Press, 2003). Reprinted in James Joyce, *Dubliners* (New York: Norton, 2006), 284.

[38] James Joyce, *A Portrait of the Artist As A Young Man*, ed. Seamus Deane (London: Penguin, 1992), 18.

indicates a collaboration between the homeward-bound Stephen and his steam-driven conveyance.

Years later, when Stephen accompanies his father to Cork, the train allows for a contrast between Stephen's creativity and his father's. Waking from a dream, he composes an original poem-prayer—addressee unknown—'to fit the insistent rhythm of the train; and silently, at intervals of four seconds, the telegraph poles held the galloping notes of the music between punctual bars'. Then, lodged in the hotel, Stephen listened as 'his father's voice festooned the strange sad happy air'.[39] The contrasting songs, suspended within two representations of musical bars—the restrained measure of the telegraph poles and the jollier festoons—suggest the greater gravity of Stephen's artistic impulse, while we can understand that the even more secret telegrams conveyed by elaborate rhythms are borne by these wires.

Among his father's old Cork acquaintants, Stephen meets in a pub a man identified by the narrator as 'a brisk old man' and named by Simon Dedalus as Johnny Cashman. Although we know his full name and he is addressed by other topers as Johnny and Johnny Cashman, the narrator adopts Stephen's condescension toward the man by addressing him—eight times within less than two pages—as 'the little old man'.[40] As in this case, narration in the novel is often a vector resulting from the pull of Stephen's opinions or observations and those of a third-person narrator, although this rarely transpires in a uniform manner. As the novel progresses, Stephen assumes more of the narrative burden, with his lectures on aesthetics and his composition of the villanelle giving him a dominant portion of the narration. Finally, with the shift to the diary conclusion, the novel becomes exclusively a portrait rather than a painterly title consistent with a fuller cast of scholar-artists as, for example, in Raphael's *The School of Athens* or Rembrandt's *The Anatomy Lesson*.

Whereas much of *A Portrait* transpires in Stephen's mind and in private spaces, we also see Stephen in public spaces such as the playing fields, lecture hall, school assembly, national library, night-town, and in horse-drawn cars, trains, and trolleys. The capaciousness of *Ulysses*, however, allows for more numerous settings. In his radically fresh rereading of this novel, Declan Kiberd has written:

> Although *Ulysses* is a book of privacies and subjectivities, an astounding number of its scenes are set in public space—libraries, museums, bars, cemeteries, and most of all the streets. Its characters enjoy the possibilities afforded by those streets for random, unexpected meetings. And it is this very openness to serendipity which allows Joyce to renew his styles and themes with each succeeding episode.[41]

As frequently as interior monologue or stream of consciousness, Joyce employs free indirect discourse or what Hugh Kenner termed 'the Uncle Charles Principle', in which the narration yields momentarily to be tinctured by the idioms or insights of one

---

[39] Ibid., 92–4.
[40] Ibid., 100–1.
[41] Declan Kiberd, *Ulysses and Us: The Art of Everyday Living* (London: Faber, 2009), 12.

character or another.[42] Because 'The Wandering Rocks' episode of *Ulysses* provides us with the greatest array of Dubliners and the widest distribution of narrative responsibilities, we might allow several examples from that episode to represent shifting points of view across the entire novel. These examples will be illustrative as we turn to narration in some contemporary Irish poems.

On the day of Paddy Dignam's funeral, which draws our hero Leopold Bloom from the privacy of kitchen, bedroom, and jakes into the public space of the Dublin streets, shops, horse-drawn conveyance, and Glasnevin Cemetery, and then upon his public rounds, Dignam Junior sets forth in his new public role as the orphaned firstborn of a deceased alcoholic father. In an effort to understand and come to live with the most private human experience of death, Master Dignam assumes family errands, turning to the public spheres of the Dublin streets, the evening newspaper, and mass entertainment. He takes a special interest in a much-publicized high-stakes boxing match with 'the two puckers stripped to their pelts and putting up their props', a match which he soon discovers, like his father's abusive life, has slipped into the past: 'May the twentysecond. Sure, the blooming thing is all over.'[43] Young Dignam's idiom, which infests the narrative, suggests more strongly than an omniscient narrator's assertion that the son will follow the father's course in life, perhaps even into the afterlife, staged incongruously but briefly in Barney Kiernan's pub.

Here, the match undergoes an oral replay, and Paddy Dignam himself makes an appearance, but only to inhabit one of the parodic balloons or aneurisms that at various moments inflate in the arteries of the Cyclops narrative and interrupt the 'realistic' narration.[44] Nauseous—perhaps seasick from 'waves of volupcy'—Paddy requests from his otherworldly abode buttermilk to settle his stomach.[45] Three episodes later in the Circe episode, Paddy, who declares himself on the path of prālăyā, transmigrates as a scorbutic dog who, discommoded by the need for a toilet, seeks 'a lamp. I must satisfy an animal need. That buttermilk didn't agree with me.'[46] Neither Paddy's presence nor his urgencies in these two separated episodes are witnessed by other characters, as either exaggerations of their experience or hallucinations from repressed experience. They function as private utterances, available to readers but unavailable to characters who 'live in the narrative' rather than in the crawlspaces or priest holes adjacent to, but hidden from, the novel's public spaces.

Of course, Joyce's narrative strategies are not limited to free indirect discourse or longer stretches of interior monologue. Joyce employs a variety of narrative manoeuvres, such as juxtaposing two images or statements rather than insinuating a narrative event through a character's singular language. For example, the fourth section of 'The Wandering Rocks' finds the Dedalus sisters at home, hungry and awaiting the possible sale of some of Stephen's books in order to feed themselves. When Katey lifts the lid on a

[42] Kenner, *Joyce's Voices*, 15.
[43] James Joyce, *Ulysses*, ed. Hans Gabler (New York: Random House, 1986), 206.
[44] Ibid., 261–2.
[45] Ibid., 248.
[46] Ibid., 386.

steaming stovetop kettle, she finds not sustenance but boiling shirts, presumably the girls' dutiful meeting of their ne'er-do-well father's requirement that he keep up appearances. Nearly three hundred lines further into 'The Wandering Rocks', Lenehan characterizes a charity dinner for the Glencree reformatory featuring the Lord Mayor and other local celebrities as a 'Boiled shirt affair' which for the privileged reader, but for neither character nor narrator, links wayward, imprisoned youth and the undernourished but labouring Dedalus girls through this brief notice of a sumptuous fundraiser.[47]

Part of the pleasure of rereading Joyce arises from such discoveries, but controversy sometimes develops over temporarily insoluble cruxes in the novel. For example, many critics believe that in the seventy lines of late-night exchange between the returning Bloom and the bedridden Molly, Leopold requests breakfast in bed and, according to some, thereby begins to restore his masculinity. Molly does muse on the request, highly unusual for the domesticated Poldy, three times during her monologue, but the breakfast order becomes more haute cuisine and less credible with each mention. It seems likely that in Bloom's entrance to sleep through an incantation derived from the pantomime *Sinbad the Sailor*—'Going to dark bed there was a square round Sinbad the Sailor roc's auk's egg in the night of the bed of all the auks of the rocs of Darkinbad the Brightdayler'—Molly heard simply a request for a breakfast of eggs in bed.[48] If so, the narration can be charged neither to Molly nor to Bloom. In the last eighty lines of the 'Ithaca' episode, he is designated only as 'the narrator', but he has yielded to fatigue from his twenty-hour day as the narrator disappears into himself.

Joyce's last word on narrative reticence may be Stephen Dedalus's priestly posture in *A Portrait*. Imagining his role as priest during Mass, Stephen 'shrank from the dignity of celebrant because it displeased him to imagine that all the vague pomp should end in his own person'. In administering communion, he preferred 'to stand aloof from the altar, forgotten by the people'.[49] Later, in a frequently quoted passage, Stephen extends this reticence to the artist who, 'like the god of the creation remains within or behind or beyond or above his handiwork, invisible, refined out of existence'.[50]

III

Only some Irish poets follow Joyce in dispensing with a dominant voice, while adopting a parallactic point of view and a multivocal narration, not as primary legatees so much as inheritors of these complex narrative strategies. For example, Brendan Kennelly, in a prefatory note to his long poem *Cromwell*, characterizes his book's narrator as 'not a voice' but 'many voices'.[51] To address the incipient stages of the Troubles, in *The Rough*

---

[47] Ibid., 192.
[48] Ibid., 607.
[49] Joyce, *A Portrait of the Artist*, 171–2.
[50] Ibid., 233.
[51] Brendan Kennelly, *Cromwell* (Dublin: Beaver Row Press, 1983), 1.

Field, John Montague fashions a narrative collage in which the poet's own voice is interspersed with fragments of sectarian tracts, old newspaper clippings, family letters, lines from ballads, and other bits of local history.[52] In his succinctness, Thomas Kinsella's narrative voice is distinctive, yet in the satiric *Butcher's Dozen* he gives voice to the victims of Bloody Sunday in Derry. He also assumes the voice of legendary figures from *Lebor Gabàla Érinn*. He opens *A Technical Supplement* with the voice of the cartographer William Petty, and throughout his poetry he frequently assumes the viewpoint of the Joycean *flaneur*, occasionally yielding to other voices en route, so that the identity of the narrator cannot always be taken for granted.[53]

As in stories such as 'Eveline', where Joyce employs 'free indirect discourse', narration in Eiléan Ní Chuilleanáin's poetry is often the enigma to be resolved or, at least, recognized. For a relatively straightforward example, in 'River, with Boats', we open with two stanzas of tactile, auditory, and visual imagery from the perspective of a room that offers a view of a river. In the final stanza, the tidal river lifts a boat to the level of the room's window, and the perspective reverses: 'The window is blocked/By the one framed eye/ Of a tethered coaster/.../And the faces of the mariners/Crowd at the glass...' It then flips again: '...like fishes', the viewer becoming the viewed becoming the viewer.[54] Ní Chuilleanáin shares with Joyce a multilingualism and a commitment to translation. By contrast, Eavan Boland remains remote from such interests, much closer to Yeats than to Joyce, sharing with the former a lyrical voice and a frequent use of first-person narration, what she calls 'the difficult "I" of perception'.[55]

At least in his early poetry, Seamus Heaney was intent on 'finding a voice', by which he meant getting 'your own feeling into your own words', words that 'have the feel of you about them'.[56] In the title poem of *Station Island* (1984) a Joycean interlocutor is advising the Heaney character to 'swim/out on your own and fill the element/with signatures on your own frequency,/echo soundings, searches, probes, allurements'.[57] Because Paul Muldoon does not share Heaney's advocacy of a single, sincere voice, we might believe he is merely chalking the court to compete with Heaney. However, Muldoon's statement to an interviewer in 2004 seems to align him with Stephen Dedalus, and perhaps with Joyce. Asked how it felt 'to discover...[his] own voice', Muldoon responded: 'I don't know if I've ever found a voice. In fact, I'm rather sceptical of that idea having any currency. Each poem demands its own particular voice.' Muldoon then echoes Stephen's statement about anticipating priestly Eucharistic duties, when he says, 'What I'm interested in is the emptying of the self, and the giving over of oneself to the power

[52] John Montague, *Collected Poems* (Oldcastle: Gallery, 1995).

[53] Thomas Kinsella, *Collected Poems, 1956–2001* (Manchester: Carcanet, 2001).

[54] Eiléan Ní Chuilleanáin, *Selected Poems* (Oldcastle: Gallery, 2008), 55. See Dillon Johnston, 'Secrecy and Sensuality in Ní Chuilleanáin's Baroque Art', in *Gender and Sexuality in Modern Ireland*, ed. Anthony Bradley and Maryann Gialanella Valiulis (Amherst: University of Massachusetts Press, 1997), 188.

[55] Eavan Boland, *Object Lessons* (Manchester: Carcanet, 1995), 178.

[56] Heaney, *Finders Keepers*, 16.

[57] Seamus Heaney, *Station Island* (London: Faber, 1984), 94.

beyond and within us',[58] although Muldoon might here and there still manipulate the reader.

It is very probable that Muldoon shares Stephen Dedalus's belief in the absent author. In practice we can sometimes identify a consistent narrative voice, comprised of off-the-wall rhymes, references, or voice-overs juxtaposing history and popular culture, infanti-lized refrains, esoteric vocabulary, quaint sex, and a masterful command of poetic forms and prosodic effects. For example, the opening stanzas of his elegy to the singer-song-writer Warren Zevon and to Muldoon's sister Maureen, both cancer fatalities, employ terza rima while spanning sub-cultures and centuries:

> I want you to tell me if, on Grammy night, you didn't get one hell of a kick
>   out of all those bling-it-ons in their bulletproof broughams,
>   all those line managers who couldn't manage a line of coke,
>
> all those Barmecides offering beakers of barm—
>   if you didn't get a kick out of being as incongruous
>   there as John Donne at a junior prom.[59]

In a certain sense, however, none of this voice is reliably himself. In his poems, paterfa-milias Muldoon often steps onstage as the Trickster—generative, protean, and rarely manageable.

These final pages can illustrate how Joyce's narrative strategies influence a recent poetic volume—Ciaran Carson's *For All We Know* (2009). As David Butler has shown, Joyce's influence on one volume, Carson's earlier sonnet sequence *The Twelfth of Never* (1998), goes beyond narration.[60] Carson, indeed, may be the most urban of all Irish poets after Joyce. In a recent interview, Carson said:

> Joyce has always interested me, as much for his rendering of the music of the city—sounds of traffic, printing shops, cutlery in restaurants, songs, fragments of speech—as for any overarching narrative, more *Ulysses*, perhaps, than *Dubliners*. I love his delight in the particular, and I'm sure it lies behind many of my own attempts to render the actuality of things.[61]

Beyond urban life, Carson shares with Joyce a Catholic upbringing, a thorough practical and theoretical knowledge of music, multilingual interest and expertise in various lan-guages, a frequently unsheathed satirical blade, and a grounding in storytelling. Carson's verse novel or fiction-as-a-poetic-sequence is comprised of seventy lyrics mostly of seven couplets (or one sonnet) each. The lyrics' thirty-five titles repeat in the same order in the book's second half. Although the poems under the titles change, each poem in the second round usually conveys some variation on the earlier one. The story is told by

---

[58] Paul Muldoon, Interview with James S. F. Wilson, 'The Art of Poetry LXXXVII', *The Paris Review* 169 (Spring 2004), 78–9.
[59] Paul Muldoon, 'Sillyhow Stride', *Horse Latitudes* (London: Faber, 2006), 95.
[60] Butler, '"Slightly Out of Synch"'.
[61] Elmer Kennedy-Andrews, 'For all I Know: Ciaran Carson in Conversation with Elmer Kennedy-Andrews', *Ciaran Carson: Critical Essays*, ed. Elmer Kennedy-Andrews (Dublin: Four Courts Press, 2009), 20.

lovers—Nina and Gabriel (a name borrowed from Joyce's 'The Dead'?)—a French performer/scholar of music and an Irish journalist. They meet first in Belfast and then in Paris, Dresden, Berlin, and other European cities.

The story, which closes after a summary of Nina's death in a car crash in Nevers, France, is shadowy but poignant and arresting in itself. Carson's title is borrowed from a popular blues song of the last mid-century recorded by Billie Holiday, Aretha Franklin, and others, including Nina Simone, who may well have provided the first name for Carson's heroine. As did 'The Lass of Aughrim' in 'The Dead' and many songs and espe-cially arias from operas in *Ulysses*, the lyrics haunt the narratives. The brevity of love is reinforced by the title and by verses that complete the refrain—'... this may only be a dream'; 'we come and go like ripples on a stream', 'Tomorrow may never come'—as well as by poignant Carsonic word-music. As death closes their love, so the story haunting Gabriel assumes characteristics of the fugue, endlessly extended, with two voices in counterpoint. (We might recall that in the 'Sirens' episode of *Ulysses* the narrator remains oblivious to the fugal structure that forces him to repeat and contradict his narrative and to mutter apologetically, 'As said before...'.[62]

So, we are offered a love story, but more precisely a *noirish* epistemological thriller, in which the principal mystery is the variable identity of the narrator and the origin of emotions and events. Beyond that we contend with the unreliability of language in itself and across linguistic divides, with shifts in narrative modes (such as folktale, catalogues of commodities, Troubles or Cold-War fiction, film noir), with a partially cyclical story, whether fugal or in a single-track recurrence of the narrative events, and, finally, with alternative systems and paradigms.

In the same interview, which anticipated publication of *For All We Know*, Carson speaks of his fascination with poems by Paul Celan that venture 'into a world which seems to use language to go beyond language, or beyond our normal understanding of it' to 'things inexpressible in ordinary language'. His next statement delivers us at the door of this poetic volume:

> Besides that aesthetic, I'm drawn more to mysticism than dogmatism. 'The cloud of unknowing'. In my case the logical outcome of Catholicism seems to have been agnosticism, or atheism. Or at least not knowing, as indicated by the title of the book of poems... *For all we know*.[63]

Some closer attention to a few of these seventy lyrics can remind us that 'not knowing', when distinguished from disbelief or nihilism, can still lead to an aesthetic appreciation of complexity and pattern and to an advanced wonder rather than a full understanding. Much as lines from arias recur as leitmotifs in *Ulysses*, macaronic lines, some from pop-ular lyrics, recur frequently to convey themes. The opening poem, 'Second Time Round', begins in French:

---

[62] Joyce, *Ulysses*, Episode 11, lines 569, 764, and throughout.
[63] Kennedy-Andrews, 'Ciaran Carson in Conversation with Elmer Kennedy-Andrews', *Ciaran Carson: Critical Essays*, 16.

> *Ce n'est pas comme le pain de Paris.* There's no stretch in it,
> you said. It was our anniversary, whether first or last.
>
> It's the matter of the texture. Elasticity.[64]

While bread is the primary topic, internal rhyme, '*last*' and '*Elasticity*', insinuates a link between flexibility, reflexivity, and the duration of the couple's companionship. Although the speaker is 'grappling/with his partner's language', this division could be overcome:

> Then slowly, slowly we would draw in *on one* an*oth*er
> until everything was implicated like *wool* sp*ool*ed
>
> from my *yawn*ing hands as you *wound* the *yarn* into a ball.
> For how many seasons have we circled *round* each other[65]

The assonance of *ow, on, oth,* and the internal rhyme of *wound/round,* help coax the lovers toward closure. In eye-rhyme, w*ool* sp*ool*ed, the lovers are implicated, their tale literally folded together. The dilation of *yawning* precedes the wind-up of 'yarn into a ball/…we circled round each other'. When we return to this poem after concluding the book, the account of their first love-making takes on an elegiac tone:

> *La nuit s'approche,* you said, and then I saw the parish church
> below the Alps of those three words, and snow falling, a bell
> tolling as their farewells dimmed into the gathering dusk.
>
> Our two candles were guttering by now. We climbed the stair
> and found ourselves spreadeagled on the patchwork double quilt[66]

The lines compose a little symphony of sound, 'chamber music', if you will, that reminds us that these memories are ensconced and, as with the poems' early daguerreotype, immobilized in art. The quilt, made by Nina's old-maid aunts during the Second World War, not only covers the couple's private intimacies but also represents an overview of their public space in Paris: 'parks, avenues, cemeteries, temples, impasses, arcades'; 'you once thought the quilt was Paris, the *quartiers* demarcated by pattern and colour'.[67] In the book's final lyric, we are reminded that the quilt also contains 'staggered repeats', a synchronic pattern that recurs, but with variation, and that has its analogues in music and visual art: 'as the fugue must reiterate its melodic fragments/in continuously unfinished tapestries of sound'.

The strange phrasing in the opening lyric—'and found ourselves'—either accelerates the linear narrative or accentuates a past moment, as if the future couple were overseeing their anterior selves. Nina's repetition of the opening phrase of the book's epigraph—*La nuit s'approche*—reinforces the notion that this climactic moment, and all that follows

---

[64] Carson, *For All We Know*, 15.
[65] Ibid.
[66] Ibid.
[67] Ibid., 37, 47.

including Nina's death, has already transpired. As readers we face the major challenge of identifying the narrator as he/she varies within and between the poems. The poem usually opens with Gabriel handing over the narration to Nina, who seems to have most of the lines. If she is already deceased, however, her statements may be seen as Gabriel's recollections, drawn up from the borehole of grief. So many lines address the complexity of language—of storage, transmission, and translation, not merely from one national language to another but also between spoken and written words—that we are forewarned to be cautious in identifying narrators.

Whereas some of the exchanges are extra-vocal—'Everything was in the way you said a thing, your manner/and your mannerisms, even the way you cocked your head/spoke volumes'[68]—many of the spoken lines are disembodied, as in a dream or over a telephone: 'I remember the first time you telephoned me, you said./*Telephoned*, I said, isn't that terribly old-fashioned?' Then, remembering the coin-operated phone, the narrator asks:

> Is that you? Yes, you say, it's me, didn't you know my voice?
> You know what the voice is? you said. What is the voice? I said.
>
> A closed-tube resonator, like the canal of the ear,
> you said. The vocal column begins in the vocal folds,
>
> which pucker like lips on the mouthpiece of a saxophone.
> Every voice can be voiceprinted like a musical score
>
> and can be used to prove you did a crime of which you spoke.
> That's why I knew your voice then. And you're speaking in it now.[69]

One might argue that, as with this poem's technical definition of voice, an encyclopaedic erudition pervades Carson's poems and becomes his voice. Yet this definition of voiceprint seems more like a parody than language 'intimately connected with the poet's natural voice', which was Heaney's prescription for *voice*.[70] In reviewing *For All We Know* for *Poetry Ireland*, Barra Ó Seaghdha wrote that 'Carson is liberated from the burden of a personal voice'; poems 'do not present themselves as the emanation of a personality'.[71] Conscious of the issue, Carson makes this central to his narrative, as in 'Second Take'. By forgoing a 'natural voice', Carson may be exchanging a fiduciary relation between narrator and audience for one of mystery, encryption, and suspension of certitude. As in Joyce's fiction, readers' discoveries reside in the language chosen rather than in the assertions expressed by an authorial voice. As Carson 'refines himself out of existence', in

---

[68] Ibid., 105.

[69] Ibid., 83.

[70] Barra Ó Seaghdha, 'Ciaran Carson', *Poetry Ireland Review* 94 (July 2008), 84.

[71] *Chambers Dictionary* defines *voiceprint* as 'a visual representation of speech indicating frequency, amplitude and duration'. Going online to 'Technabob', we can discover a commercialization of *voiceprint* unwittingly closer to Carson's satiric purpose: 'It seems like virtually anything can be turned into art. While the spoken word can be art in the form of poetry and song, it's not often that it's something that you can physically see. After all, a voice is something heard, not seen. However, with *Voiceprints*, you can display a visual reresentation of your spoken words.'

Joyce's terms, his personality 'impersonalizes itself', with voiceprints adhering, if they exist, to the narrators and characters rather than to the author.

Recalling that we're discussing only a few cases of Joyce's relation to his poetic descendants, we can recognize, generally, that suspending the personal voice, or mixing it with more dramatic modes and methods of narration, may free poets to undertake other innovations. Constructions such as Carson's *noirish* verse novel can be more elaborate than autobiographical or confessional poetry usually permits. From the multiple narrators and narrative modes refracted through the various planes of Joyce's language in *Ulysses* and *Finnegans Wake*, his poetic successors may inherit the even greater gift of a more audacious invention, a fearlessness to undertake the truly ambitious work.

PART IV

....

MID-CENTURY IRISH POETRY

....

CHAPTER 11

....

PATRICK KAVANAGH'S 'POTENTIALITIES'

....

KIT FRYATT

THE Dublin literary periodical *Envoy* ceased publication in July 1951. On the back pages of its final issue it ran the last of Patrick Kavanagh's regular 'Diary' articles, a version of a talk given earlier that year at University College Dublin, entitled 'Literature in the University'. Though the magazine had been relatively short-lived, it was important to the poet, giving him regular income and the chance to voice developing attitudes to art and society. Kavanagh sometimes claimed his work for *Envoy* played a part in his 1950s poetic renovation, though it preceded by a number of years the serious illness and convalescence which he came to regard as a rebirth.

Envoy cultivated a reputation for distrust of nationalist introspection and cherished Irish institutions. Kavanagh's contributions were irascible even by the standards of a magazine which frequently voiced exasperation with its milieu, and they were relished by many readers more for bracing ill-temper than argument. He was never, as his biographer Antoinette Quinn notes, 'given to consecutive reasoning'.[1] 'Literature in the University' is characteristically jumpy and declamatory, its single-sentence paragraphs offering a close parallel to Kavanagh's spoken manner. Like much of his prose it is opinionated, but when interesting it is characteristically so: what seems initially mere provocation, through sometimes tortuous associative development, becomes less easily dismissible.

Kavanagh cheerfully suggests that the university might be of best use to the poet in ensuring a ready supply of supine devotees to his genius (he was fond of opining, and repeats the sentiment in 'Literature in the University', that women serve much the same purpose):

> This willingness to admire the good would be a real function of a university; and out of it good would come, and release for the admirers.

---

[1] Antoinette Quinn, *Patrick Kavanagh: A Biography* [2001] (Dublin: Gill and Macmillan, 2003), 352.

It may be said outright what is implicit in my theme—that you cannot learn to be a genius either in a university or out of it.

It might be that universities open a man's mind to his own potentialities, but if the potentialities are there it is almost certain that they will find a way out; they will burst a road. I scarcely believe in the theory of the 'mute inglorious Milton'. There might well be mute Bowens or Priestleys or Blundens, but hardly a Milton, a Shakespeare, an Auden.[2]

Kavanagh associated Gray's 'Elegy Written in a Country Churchyard', a poem he learnt as a schoolboy, with anxiety about achievement.[3] Here he seems drawn to its figure for wasted promise through a Miltonic concern with ambition and arrogance. 'Admire' is a favourite verb of Milton's, employed in many different contexts in the poems, though perhaps most memorably in mock-heroic scenes of diabolic wonderment in *Paradise Lost*.[4] Kavanagh's genius, it may be said, has 'a mind not to be changed by place or time';[5] while 'either in a university or out of it' returns us to the articulation of similar ideas by Christopher Marlowe's Mephistopheles, almost invariably invoked as an editorial note to Satan's boasts of eschatological self-sufficiency.[6]

The unwieldy word 'potentialities' extends the mood of mock-pomposity. 'Potentiality', though nearly synonymous with 'potential', seems a more abstract quality still, a sense reflected in the *Oxford English Dictionary*'s definition: 'an instance of the latent capacity for development; a person, thing, etc., in which the quality of having potential is embodied'. It is an older word than we might imagine—the *OED* records first usage in 1587—but it seems always to have surfaced in scholarly discourse: the *OED* citations are taken from works of doctrinal theology, philosophy, psychology, linguistics, and reference. The few literary uses recorded are either negative, referring to lost potential, or are exactly synonymous with a now rare sense of 'potential', the state of actually having power. No poetic use is cited.

Kavanagh's ballad 'If Ever You Go to Dublin Town', written at around the same time as 'Literature in the University', uses 'potentiality' to suggest both scholarly fustian and squandered talent:

> I saw his name with a hundred others
> In a book in the library;
> It said he had never fully achieved
> His potentiality.[7]

The preceding stanza enjoins the reader of a future century to 'Sniff for my personality/ Is it vanity's vapour now?', while the next and last asserts, 'He knew that posterity has no

---

[2] Patrick Kavanagh, 'Literature in the University' (1951), *A Poet's Country: Selected Prose*, ed. Antoinette Quinn (Dublin: Lilliput Press, 2003), 233.

[3] See the late poem, 'The Poet's Ready Reckoner', in Patrick Kavanagh, *Collected Poems*, ed. Antoinette Quinn (London: Penguin, 2004), 251–5.

[4] See John Milton, *Paradise Lost*, I, l.731; II, l.677; VI, l.498.

[5] Ibid., I, l.253.

[6] Christopher Marlowe, *Dr Faustus*, I, iii, l.76–7.

[7] Kavanagh, *Collected Poems*, 193.

use/For anything but the soul'. Here 'potentiality' is intermediary between 'personality' and 'posterity'—it is how the first makes a claim on the second, and how the latter judges the former. In turn, the plosive trio is associated with the insubstantial—both negatively valued 'vanity's vapour' and the 'soul', the lonely and lofty 'spirit' of genius.

Patrick Kavanagh's 'potentiality', the extent to which he achieved or failed it, is the subject of this essay. His background was such as to make deep anxiety about and considerable pride in literary achievement all but inevitable. He was born in Mucker, a townland in the parish of Inniskeen, County Monaghan, on 21 October 1904. His father, James Kavanagh, was the illegitimate son of a schoolmaster—the poet refers to the stigma of bastardy on occasion, always obliquely—who worked from the family home as a cobbler. His mother Bridget, a former barmaid, managed the household and the livestock which provided its subsidiary income. His parents were frugal and hard-working, ambitious to buy and farm their own land. They bought a five-acre farm in 1910; by the 1920s the Kavanaghs were among the more prosperous small farmers in their district. Patrick was the third child and eldest son of a family of nine—his only brother, Peter, was twelve years his junior. As heir to business and farm, Patrick was in some ways spoilt, and would all his life demand attention and adulation, particularly from women. His clumsiness and dreamy laziness, meanwhile, attracted ire from his parents and employers. He attended the National (primary) school in nearby Kednaminsha from 1909 to 1918. The education he received there, which was always catechetical in form and usually so in content, did not engage his interest, but he had a good memory, a knack for arithmetic, and enjoyed learning poems by heart. He remembered school anthologies with affection, as an early stimulus to poetic enthusiasm, though he also recognized early the danger of derivativeness for the autodidact poet, registering it in a squib of the 1930s, 'The Weary Horse', in which the nag 'language vitiate' has 'the blank look' of 'a Victorian book/In a modern school'.[8] However, he proved not to be academically gifted in a way which might have given him the chance of a scholarship to secondary school, and his formal education finished before he was fourteen years old.

Having no particular talent for his father's trade, Kavanagh spent most of the years between the end of his schooling and the beginnings of his literary career in the late 1930s working on the family farms. The monotony of farmwork and the embarrassment of impecunious dependence are conjured in the narrative poem *The Great Hunger* (1942) and the novel *Tarry Flynn* (1948). His 1938 memoir *The Green Fool*, though lighter in tone than the 1940s work, does not gloss over the emotional and material privation of rural Irish life to anything like the extent that the author's subsequent repudiations of it might suggest.

Kavanagh found it difficult to remember how a childish pleasure in learning poetry became a desire to write it:

> And that was me in that virginal time before I had ever thought of writing a verse. A
> strange time, difficult to visualize, for a man who afterwards became so deeply involved

---

[8] Ibid., 28.

in verse. How strange a thing like that happens to a man. He dabbles in something and does not realize that it is his life. There is nothing deliberate or conscious about my beginnings. It all happened like an accident. With most other verse writers of whom I have read there was usually a literary background or some roots somewhere.[9]

The assertion seems truthful and likely: moments of literary vocation are convenient for biographical narrative but in reality rare. But it is also strategic, allowing Kavanagh to deny responsibility for his poetic ambition, to forget the humiliations which accompany the pursuit of experience. The potent road-burster has a proudly submissive streak, willing poetry to overwhelm him so he need not humble himself by courting it. He declares himself rootless, in contrast to those with 'a literary background', inverting a notion of peasant autochthony to which he had always a vexed response.

Kavanagh's early productivity was of a scale which might well prompt forgetfulness of his pre-poetic life. He wrote voluminously, but attained publishable quality only occasionally. Success of a sporadic and unpredictable kind is to be expected of the poet teaching himself to write; it characterized Kavanagh's career, however, long after his literary apprenticeship concluded. His discovery in 1925 of AE's *Irish Statesman* introduced him to modern literature; in 1930 the journal published 'Ploughman', which became Kavanagh's *entrée* to writerly circles. In December 1931 he walked to Dublin dressed in patched working clothes to meet AE, affectations which he was to regret as the actions of a 'gobshite',[10] but which demonstrate his early appreciation of the value of iconic gesture. He was yet to strike such memorable poses in verse; 'Ploughman' makes far less impact than an encounter with the ploughman. The four-quatrain poem alternates trimeter and dimeter lines, each presenting a contrast: green lea against brown clay, 'silvery gull' and 'brazen crow', 'tranquillity' and 'ecstasy', earth against sky. The first three stanzas become progressively abstract, the fourth returns in resolution to the soil: 'I find a star-lovely art/ In a dark sod'. Kavanagh's uncertain command of verbal music might be gauged by the fact that the poem as originally published did not include 'dark', which was AE's suggestion.

'Ploughman' achieved sufficient currency to be chosen as the title poem for Kavanagh's first collection, *Ploughman and Other Poems* (1936). It is representative of, and rather more accomplished than, most of the volume's poems, but does not suggest the direction of the poet's subsequent development. Indeed, only one poem in *Ploughman* does so: 'Inniskeen Road: July Evening'. This sonnet, quite unlike the other pieces in *Ploughman*, specifies the social life, 'the wink-and-elbow language of delight', which the poet forgoes in the process of developing his own suggestive idiom, his vocabulary of poetic pleasure.[11] 'Inniskeen Road' marks a significant achievement because of its reflective quality: the poet excluded from the 'codes' and nudges of revellers on their way to a barn dance will make of their speech a flexible poetic vernacular. The closing couplet

[9] Kavanagh, 'School Book Poetry', *A Poet's Country*, 270.
[10] Letter to Peter Kavanagh, 19 January 1949, quoted in Quinn, *Patrick Kavanagh*, 70.
[11] Kavanagh, *Collected Poems*, 15. For 'Ploughman' see *Collected Poems*, 6-7, and Quinn, *Patrick Kavanagh*, 68.

sees him master of his newly burst road, if uncertain how to proceed along it: 'A road, a mile of kingdom, I am king/Of banks and stones and every blooming thing.' Similar oscillations between potency and anxiety mark the decade between the publication of this collection and Kavanagh's next trade collection, *A Soul for Sale* (1947).

'Shancoduff', which might also be considered an early success, though it underwent much revision before finding the form in which it is best known, and long remained uncollected, describes Reynolds' Farm, the smallholding that was Kavanagh's particular responsibility from its purchase in 1925. (It became his property in a formal sense only in 1938, however, when Bridget Kavanagh transferred the deeds in the hope that he would marry and settle there.) Its celebration of bleak beauty ends in characteristic anxiety, as the poet overhears cattle-drovers disparage the 'hungry hills', implicitly ascribing their barrenness to the farmer's literary pursuits. 'Shancoduff', like 'Inniskeen Road', manipulates literary tropes while conceding little to elevated diction or intertextual reference. 'The every blooming thing' of 'Inniskeen Road' and the 'three perishing calves' of 'Shancoduff' are more self-conscious than Kavanagh's later poetic colloquialisms, but vital compared to the stiff pastoral of his other 1930s work; the allusions in both poems— to Alexander Selkirk (Defoe's inspiration for Robinson Crusoe) and Lot's wife respectively—are determinedly accessible.

Nonetheless, 'Shancoduff' comments coherently and subtly on its own historical moment. The sublime, a source of power for the poet, signifies only poverty for the drover whose pragmatic words dominate the last stanza. In the poem, as printed in the *Dublin Magazine* in 1937, the drovers are 'cattle-smugglers', making their interest less professional than predatory, and suggesting again the anxiety which always animates and disturbs proprietorial pomp in Kavanagh. 'I hear,' responds the poet, 'and is my heart not badly shaken?'[12] As with some of Yeats's rhetorical questions, the reader is tempted to answer impertinently. 'Shancoduff' incorporates the drover's un- or pre-Romantic values to assert an uninterrupted Romanticism, but it does so in terms which require no theorization or annotation. Attention to the ordinariness of Kavanagh's language obliges us to acknowledge that in his best poems it is accompanied by a more than ordinary capacity for self-awareness.

An analogous facility is evident in *The Green Fool*, the fictionalized autobiography that Kavanagh was later to repudiate. The book was written to requirement and reviewed favourably as refreshing comic-realist relief from solemn Revivalist idealization of the 'peasant'. The commission made good use of Kavanagh's talents at this stage in his career: his delight in explication was indulged by the necessity to gloss rural customs for urban audiences; the same audience's demand for entertainment checked his propensity to hector. However, even sympathetic accounts of *The Green Fool* find something distasteful in its light-touch impressionism and its marketability to the readership which had enthusiastically consumed translations of Blasket Island autobiography.[13] If Kavanagh was writing primarily for his London patrons, he was doing so with a competence and

---

[12] Ibid., 21.
[13] See Quinn, *Patrick Kavanagh*, 87–105.

confidence that militated against servility and which, moreover, outstripped anything he had managed in verse. The short, anecdotal chapters have the authoritative movement of good poems, the dialogue's liveliness is matched by its likeliness, and the exposition of rural custom is unexploitative. His delineation of the mutual invisibility of the popular culture of his experience and the Irish Revivalism expected by many of his readers is valuable in a literary-historical sense, though not reliable in autobiographical detail; it is lightly handled, while not yet disfigured by the misrepresentation and resentment that would come to overwhelm his remarks on the subject. If *The Green Fool* is unambitious, it is remarkably well executed.

The book's withdrawal, following a vindictive libel action by Oliver St John Gogarty, is to be regretted, as is Kavanagh's subsequent conviction that it was 'dreadful', written 'under the evil aegis of the so-called Irish Literary Revival' and 'stage-Irish' in conception.[14] That conflation of Revivalism with stage-Irishry is characteristic of Kavanagh's fractious attitude to the writers of the generation preceding his own. His prejudices represent something like an inversion of those of the major Revival writers: where they install the claims of cultural nationalism above those of religious difference, Kavanagh is bitterly anti-nationalist and ferociously sectarian. His impatience with the class system which made him an object of interest as a 'farmer-poet' curiously parallels the social privilege that legitimized Revival interventions in folk culture. To call Kavanagh a kind of 'anarchist', as Anthony Cronin does,[15] is to occlude his conservative and timid aspect, but his inconsistencies are sufficiently numerous and blatant to suggest strategic rejection of coherent thought on the subject of a national literature. On Yeats, in particular, he found it necessary to express an array of mutually incompatible opinions.

Yeats's unrivalled dominance of twentieth-century Irish poetry created a vacancy— at least as far as literary journalism and publishers' marketing departments are concerned—for his successor. Kavanagh was the most likely candidate in his generation and made repeated applications for the position by denying Yeats's greatness or his Irishness, or more usually, both. Vulgarized accounts of the theory of poetry proposed by Harold Bloom in *The Anxiety of Influence* (1973) have kept the notion of Yeats as disabling precursor current in more scholarly contexts too. Bloomian ideas are of limited use in dealing with an Irish generation which arguably produced no 'strong' poet, while a psychological paradigm runs the risk of mystifying rather then illuminating Kavanagh's hostile attitude to Yeats, which he attributed frankly to 'spite'.[16] Such an admission, though it was made for effect at a gathering of academics who had bored him, renders superfluous any analysis of his simple put-downs, among which we might group 'W. B. Yeats', which was, piquantly enough but wholly coincidentally, the last poem Kavanagh published. When Kavanagh aimed at more than curmudgeonliness, he articulated reservations which are widely shared among general readers if not among

[14] Kavanagh, 'Self-Portrait', *A Poet's Country*, 306.
[15] Anthony Cronin, *Dead As Doornails: A Chronicle of Life* [1976] (Oxford: Oxford University Press, 1986), 92.
[16] Quinn, *Patrick Kavanagh*, 430.

scholars: unease with Yeats's doctrines of deliberate artifice, impatience with his prostra-
tion before Anglo-Ireland, distrust of his intellectual charlatanism.[17] Kavanagh's sectar-
ian prejudice and his anti-nationalism collide spectacularly whenever he considers
Yeats's Irishness: in a marvellously ambivalent 1962 account, he contrives to chide Yeats
both for being a Protestant 'outsider' and for creating a national myth in which Catholics
as different in temperament and purpose as Patrick Pearse and Frank O'Connor could
invest energy. 'In the end he became a stage Anglo-Irishman,' Kavanagh wrote in his
contribution to the *Irish Times* Centenary Supplement.[18] The phrase at once suggests
Kavanagh's contempt for Abbey Theatre sentimentalizations of the peasantry and his
horror at Yeats's disregard for the authentic.

Theatricality and authenticity are crucial to one very important exception to the
remarks above, a poem in which it might be argued Kavanagh displays features (albeit
somewhat deflected) of a Bloomian ephebe: *The Great Hunger*. The long poem was writ-
ten when Kavanagh was in close contact with Frank O'Connor, who co-edited with Sean
Ó Faoláin the Dublin literary periodical *The Bell*. O'Connor was centrally important to
the publication and reception of *The Great Hunger*, praising it in the issue of *Horizon* in
which extracts first appeared under the title of 'The Old Peasant', and using his influence
as a member of the editorial board of Cuala Press to have the poem published as a
limited-edition chapbook.

The poems that Kavanagh published in *The Bell* in 1940 and 1941 represent an enor-
mous advance in competence on *Ploughman*—the poet's immense compositional effort
of the late 1930s, which produced half a dozen manuscript collections, was at last show-
ing results. 'Stony Grey Soil', 'A Christmas Childhood', and 'Art McCooey', which
appeared in the six months between October 1940 and April 1941, form a triad on the
subject of potential. The iambs and anapaests of 'Stony Grey Soil' create a lumbering
rhythm that matches the poem's subject of rural gaucheness and emotional impoverish-
ment while repudiating Yeatsian wavering. The metaphor of 'soil' or clay for that which
suppresses joy and creativity in the countryman had been part of Kavanagh's poetic
stock for some time: here, however, it becomes particular as the poet names 'Mullahinsha,
Drummeril, Black Shanco' in what might be called, with an apology to the later
Kavanagh, a 'hate-act and its pledge'.[19] 'Stony Grey Soil' enumerates the ways in which
'potentialities' are retarded: self-deception, cowardice, a paradoxical worship of ugly
pragmatism at the expense of 'beauty, love and truth'. Its deliberate clumsiness bears wit-
ness to the partial success of that retardation; its audacious play with register ('O stony
grey soil of Monaghan/You burgled my bank of youth!') shows the poet bursting his
road towards the territory of self-satire.[20]

'A Christmas Childhood' is a poem of origins, of the conditions instrumental in devel-
oping a lyric sense. Poetry requires both the sonic and the semantic, so a passer-by

---

[17] Kavanagh, 'William Butler Yeats' and 'George Moore's Yeats', *A Poet's Country*, 178–81, 182–5.
[18] Kavanagh, *A Poet's Country*, 178, 185.
[19] Kavanagh, *Collected Poems*, 38–9; see also 217.
[20] Ibid.

speaks approvingly of the poet's father's skill as a musician: "'Can't he make it talk—/the melodion" [sic]', and the child-poet makes primal attempts at signifying—six notches in the doorpost to represent his age—to its accompaniment. Juxtaposing the local and the archetypal is a verbal matter: 'Cassopeia was over/Cassidy's hanging hill'—the poem is psychologically acute in that the similar sound of the names of constellation and neighbour is just the sort of coincidence that might strike a six-year-old as mysteriously meaningful.[21]

'Art McCooey' is explicitly a poem of retrospection: from the perspective of 'Donnybrook in Dublin ten years later' the speaker 'recover[s]' an earlier self, the peasant 'empire builder' carting manure to his 'foreign possessions'.[22] Kavanagh moved to Dublin permanently in 1939, and except for some periods of convalescence in later life, returned to Monaghan only occasionally. A cinematic fade which signals a temporal and geographical shift anticipates similar effects in *The Great Hunger* and the masterly lyric 'Kerr's Ass': 'The steam rising from the load is still/Warm enough to thaw my frosty fingers'.[23] The title suggests another form of retrospection, rare in Kavanagh's work: an allusion to Ireland's Gaelic traditions. Art McCooey, or MacCumhaigh (1738–1773), a labourer and gardener, lived not far from Inniskeen, in Creggan, County Armagh. Around two dozen of MacCumhaigh's poems survive; all in Irish, many lament the fall of the Gaelic social order, while the best known, 'Ag Úir Chill an Chreagáin' ('In Creggan Churchyard'), is an *aisling* notable for its touching, naive manner and lack of Jacobite-inspired hope. Kavanagh's choice of title has been read as a 'programmatic' rejection of Anglo-Ireland and the Revival and an acknowledgement of MacCumhaigh as a 'literary ancestor'.[24] Given that Kavanagh boasted no proficiency in Irish, scorned attempts to revive the language for everyday and literary purposes and was crudely impatient with nostalgia for Gaelic Ireland, the line of descent is distinctly murky, and the opportunism of the gesture militates against its effectiveness as a snub to Revivalism. In a much later essay, Kavanagh found fault with MacCumhaigh's whimsy and lack of specificity.[25] But the apolitical texture of MacCumhaigh's poems, in which satire and lament resolve into pathos or fantasy, finds a parallel, curiously enough, in both the idea of 'mute inglorious Milton', in which Kavanagh professes not to believe, and his individualistic assertion that 'potentialities' cannot be constrained by social or educational deprivation. Kavanagh, like his eighteenth-century predecessor, situates his protests in the realm of the aesthetic, not within political structures.

'Art McCooey' anticipates in lyric and comic mode concerns which in *The Great Hunger* are elaborated as tragedy and drama: the emotional, sexual, and intellectual privation which characterized the lives of Irish small farmers at mid-century. The social and economic reasons for such extreme constraint of personal freedom, and its role in

---

[21] Ibid., 39–41.

[22] Ibid., 41–3.

[23] Ibid.

[24] Antoinette Quinn, 'Patrick Kavanagh's Parish Myth', in *Tradition and Influence in Anglo-Irish Poetry*, ed. Terence Brown and Nicholas Grene (Basingstoke: Macmillan, 1989), 106.

[25] Kavanagh, 'On Poetry', *A Poet's Country*, 258.

prolonging the depopulation of the Irish countryside, are treated in depth by historians,[26] and with specific reference to Kavanagh, by the chapter on *The Great Hunger* in Quinn's biography.[27] 'Art McCooey' summarizes the problem in eight lines. The poet meets a neighbour who has been disappointed in courtship:

> We wove our disappointments and successes
> To patterns of a town-bred logic
> 'She might have been sick…' 'No, never before,
> A mystery, Pat, and they all appear so modest.'
>
> We exchanged our fool advices back and forth:
> 'It could easily be their cow was calving,
> And sure the rain was desperate that night…'
> Somewhere in the mists a light was laughing.[28]

Without leaving the mode of lyric reminiscence for something more exegetical, these few lines allude to a remarkable number of the conditions which by the 1940s had diminished and demoralized Irish rural communities. A century's social change has destroyed traditional modes of managing sexual behaviour, leaving the poet and his interlocutor at the mercy of 'town-bred logic', garnered presumably from the censored popular press and cinema. The potential excuse of a calving cow, however, reminds the reader that the speakers—tied to their smallholdings—have not even the dubious freedoms of consumer culture as compensation for the loss of established *mores*. A lingering misogyny— 'they all appear so modest'—almost immediately checks a sentimental view of those traditional customs. Stranded between modernity and archaism, and suffering the worst of each, the poet and his neighbour become self-defeatingly timid, mocked by an *ignis fatuus* cloaked in Revivalist mist.

However, 'Art McCooey' reaches a conclusion quite different from that of *The Great Hunger* on the artistic consequences of emotional and social retardation:

> Wash out the cart with a bucket of water and a wangel
> Of wheaten straw. Jupiter looks down.
> Unlearnedly and unreasonably poetry is shaped,
> Awkwardly but alive in the unmeasured womb.[29]

Potency is signified openly by the patriarchal presence of Jupiter and anti-intellectual defiance, but also implicitly in the ironic claim of awkward, 'unmeasured' composition. 'Art McCooey', with hardly a misstep in its adaptation of Hiberno-English vernacular to well-turned lyric pastoral, continues Kavanagh's progress along the road first burst on a July evening in Inniskeen.

---

[26] For a concise account, see Joseph Lee, *The Modernisation of Irish Society 1848–1918* (Dublin: Gill and Macmillan, 1973), 1–20.

[27] Quinn, *Patrick Kavanagh*, 165–91.

[28] Kavanagh, *Collected Poems*, 42.

[29] Ibid., 43.

Except for its excursions into free indirect style, *The Great Hunger* is voiced by a more detached speaker, and its account of the effects of deprivation is more pessimistic, more likely, and yet also, perhaps, more amenable to elegiac sentimentality of the 'mute inglorious Milton' variety. Standing 'between the plough handles', the protagonist Patrick Maguire 'sees/At the end of a long furrow his name signed/Among the poets, prostitutes';[30] a little later in the poem's seasonal movement, though the passage belongs earlier in Maguire's life story, we are told, 'Nobody will ever know how much tortured poetry the pulled weeds on the ridge wrote/Before they withered in the July sun.'[31] Given the unpatronizing care with which Kavanagh elsewhere delineates Maguire's intellectual capacities and interests, these glimpses of him as *poète maudit* seem out of place if not ridiculous. Maguire is not unreflective, but (as we might expect) lacks the leisure to pursue his thoughts; he is self-aware enough to know the limits of his knowledge, an 'undergraduate' in his community's 'university', the pub.[32] Kavanagh's characterization of him as a bohemian *manqué* makes little sense except as part of *The Great Hunger*'s synthetic attitude to forms of creativity, its persistent conflation of potency and potential. The metaphor which follows the image of withered weeds is less remarkable than some commentators have suggested, since it draws on the ancient convention by which the soul (*anima*, a feminine noun in Latin) is personified as a woman, but it is nonetheless a significant inversion of the creative confluence of masculine and feminine power which concludes 'Art McCooey': 'Nobody will ever read the wild, sprawling, scrawling mad woman's signature,/The hysteria and the boredom of the enclosed nun of his thought.'[33]

The poem's figuration of the body is unisexual also, returning repeatedly to the image of parted legs, in which the reader might perceive a submerged allusion to King Lear's 'unaccommodated man ... poor, bare, fork'd animal'.[34] Early in the poem Maguire is seen with his head 'hanging between wide-apart/Legs' of his plough-shafts, a uxorious gesture from the 'man who made a field his bride', albeit one disrupted by the Cerberean presence of his dog and horse between the same shafts.[35] The girls of the parish sit 'on the grass banks of lanes/Stretch-legged and lingering staring' at men too timid to make a pass at them; conversely, Maguire's unmarried sister Mary Anne finds herself 'straddle-legged' across life, 'One leg in hell and the other in heaven/And between the purgatory of middle-aged virginity'.[36] Mrs Maguire's uncomfortable accommodation of sexual 'Nature' to repressive, superstitious Catholicism prompts another recurrence: 'He listened to the lie that is a woman's screen/Around a conscience when soft thighs are

---

[30] Ibid., 68.
[31] Ibid., 76.
[32] Ibid., 77–8.
[33] Ibid., 76.
[34] William Shakespeare, *King Lear*, III.iv, 106–8.
[35] Kavanagh, *Collected Poems*, 64–6.
[36] Ibid., 76, 78.

spread.'[37] Maguire spreads his own legs to masturbate over the hearth,[38] and is metaphorically bisected by his mother's harsh tongue: 'It cut him up the middle till he became more woman than man,/And it cut through to his mind before the end.'[39] This more direct allusion to *King Lear*—'I am cut to th'brains'[40]—supports the suggestion that Kavanagh drew on the play's concern with the absolute material basis of human existence in composing *The Great Hunger*. The effect of the poem's many 'fork'd animal' images is of an obsessive focus on the generative organs, deflected to 'thighs' and 'legs' by the demands of cynical Respectability, but so minutely as to render the evasion pointless.[41]

Lost potential is the master theme of *The Great Hunger*: Kavanagh never fulfilled his own potential more completely than in writing about his powerless, directionless namesake. Quinn points to the autobiographical content of the poem, and the contemporaneous, unfinished 'Why Sorrow?', which the poet later mined for 'Father Mat' and the lyric 'The Long Garden'.[42] Maguire, and to a lesser extent, the priest-protagonist of the more fragmented works, is a shadow-self, the countryman that the poet could have become or remained, had he not urbanized and impoverished himself—both Maguire and Father Mat are financial successes compared to their perpetually indigent creator. That Kavanagh should achieve poetic success in writing about a failed alter ego has its ironic aspect, which Declan Kiberd seizes upon to link him (somewhat factitiously) with Beckett.[43] The difference between these near-contemporaries is more illuminating than any similarity: Beckettian failure is more total than anything Kavanagh contemplated, discouraging of any notion of 'potentiality'. Even the relatively elaborate and somewhat sentimental world of *Waiting for Godot* (1956) could never accommodate 'God the Father in a tree/The Holy Spirit is the rising sap/And Christ...the green leaves'.[44] *The Great Hunger* focuses on 'potentiality' to the exclusion of reflection upon its necessarily negative quality: achievement replaces and obliterates it; all that which we are prone to call 'potential' is in some sense wasted potential. Nor does Kavanagh question, as Beckett does, that fulfilment itself might be a logical fallacy, an error born of our imprisonment in temporality.

Implicitly, however, the poem does recognize that potential is necessarily abstract, and it begins to act upon the principles of concretion and particularity which underpin Kavanagh's later work. His statements of the presence of God 'in the bits and pieces of Everyday' can sometimes militate against their explicit intentions—that 'Everyday' is itself an abstraction is emphasized by the capital letter.[45] More significant are the links he draws between abstraction and lack of courage or potency:

---

[37] Ibid., 73.

[38] Ibid., 72.

[39] Ibid., 78.

[40] Shakespeare, *King Lear*, IV.v, 189.

[41] Kavanagh, *Collected Poems*, 69.

[42] Quinn, *Patrick Kavanagh*, 164.

[43] Declan Kiberd, 'Underdeveloped Comedy: Patrick Kavanagh', *Irish Classics* (London: Granta, 2000), 590–1.

[44] Kavanagh, *Collected Poems*, 68.

[45] Ibid., 72.

> Once one day in June when he was walking
> Among his cattle in the Yellow Meadow
> He met a girl carrying a basket –
> And he was then a young and heated fellow.
> Too earnest, too earnest! He rushed beyond the thing
> To the unreal. And he saw Sin
> Written in letters larger than John Bunyan dreamt of.[46]

A flight to the conceptual is the intellectual equivalent of premature ejaculation: far from indicating maturity, it reveals a mind stranded in the anxieties and obsessions of adolescence. Addiction to abstraction is, for Kavanagh, not just a peasant's emotional problem, but a national disease. His prose returns again and again to the damage done to Irish culture by the 'idea of Ireland as a spiritual entity'.[47] He blames Protestant writers in particular for elevating Irishness to an abstraction. That this is prejudiced and unfair is beyond doubt, but it explains the otherwise puzzling interpolation of Bunyan—philoprogenitive and not exercised by sexual morality to the exclusion of other principles governing Christian conduct, the seventeenth-century writer seems otherwise anomalous in this context. For Kavanagh, abstraction—moral or national—is a Protestant malady which Catholics have foolishly adopted and allowed to flourish: a reversal, at least in part, of the Protestant prejudice which depicts Catholicism as abstruse and scholastic. Kavanagh's case against Higgins as a peddler of nationalist illusion rests on the Protestant poet's supposed envy of the organic national identity conferred by Catholicism: Kavanagh is ultimately reluctant to concede that even the loathed 'spiritual entity' might be a Protestant creation. Nonetheless, a connection between Protestantism and spurious abstraction might illuminate the puzzling simile by which Mrs Maguire is likened to 'a Protestant spire'.[48] She, we learn a little later in the poem, cynically uses the institutionalized abstractions of religious form to conceal her heathenish trust in natural impulse. But her son is duped by the 'screen', as Kavanagh's contemporaries were by cultural nationalism, and 'took it as the literal truth'.[49]

The Great Hunger is not itself free from the contagion—personifications appear even where the poet is at pains to reject the melodrama of an abstract understanding of fulfilment. Maguire watches children picking flowers and reflects that rather than have 'life's truth singly', bloom by bloom, he desires an:

> Absolute envased bouquet –
> All or nothing. And it was nothing. For God is not all
> In one place, complete and labelled like a case in a railway store
> Till Hope comes in and takes it on his shoulder –[50]

---

46 Ibid., 70.
47 Kavanagh, *A Poet's Country*, 181.
48 Kavanagh, *Collected Poems*, 67.
49 Ibid., 73.
50 Ibid., 72.

An adroit use of free indirect style means that the railway porter Hope can both demonstrate the terminal nature of Maguire's enthralment by abstract thought, and the poet's continued struggle to resist it with quotidian figuration.

Kavanagh's trust in particularity as a source of poetic power became near to absolute, and too often, absolutist. The sporadic nature of his achievement shows the limits of such trust in minutiae and mundanity, though when he allows a political charge to galvanize a poem, as in his elegy for the socialist activist James Larkin (1876–1947), the result is energetic and refreshing. 'Lough Derg', also written in 1942, is more explicitly sociological than *The Great Hunger*. It emerged from Kavanagh's reportage on pilgrimages for the *Irish Independent* and the Catholic weekly *The Standard*. The poem contains autobiographical matter of interest: for example, as Quinn notes, Kavanagh 'smuggle[s]' into it the prehistory of his sexual experience—the 'convent schoolgirl' with whom he lost his virginity had been sexually abused by a priest.[51] But the lyric's origins in features journalism are apparent: more documentary than poem, its language remains mostly lifeless and Kavanagh's ambivalence about the value of the pilgrimage manifests itself in confusion rather than fruitful tension. It might seem that the failure of 'Lough Derg' to offer a microcosmic account of mid-century Irish life validates Kavanagh's celebrated confidence in the local and specific, which in his best-known polemic he theorizes as the 'parochial':

> Parochialism and provincialism are direct opposites. The provincial has no mind of his own; he does not trust what his eyes see until he has heard what the metropolis— towards which his eyes are turned—has to say on the subject. This runs through all activities.
>
> The parochial mentality on the other hand never is in any doubt about the social and artistic validity of his parish. All great civilisations are based on parochialism— Greek, Israelite, English.... In Ireland we are inclined to be provincial, not parochial, for it requires a great deal of courage to be parochial. When we do attempt having the courage of our parish we are inclined to go false and to play up to the larger parish on the other side of the Irish Sea. In recent times we have had two great Irish parishioners—James Joyce and George Moore.[52]

Kavanagh's 1948 novel *Tarry Flynn* differs from *The Green Fool* in that it has shed provincial anxiety about comprehensibility to and reception by metropolitan or non-Irish readers. The result is a text secure in idiom and adept in the creation of atmosphere, but underpowered in terms of narrative, and indeed, overall direction. To employ a Hiberno-English phrase, *Tarry Flynn* is 'country cute': shrewd, alert to nuance, but constrained by received ideas and repetitive focus. It does not play up to those readers from larger parishes across the Irish Sea or Atlantic Ocean, but neither does it make a compelling case for their attention.

Critics have, in any case, tended to place unwarranted faith in Kavanagh's formula, which read in context leads to the suspicion that it was concocted for that gleefully

[51] Quinn, *Patrick Kavanagh*, 81.
[52] Kavanagh, 'Parochialism and Provincialism', *A Poet's Country*, 237.

anglophile provocation: 'Greek, Israelite, English'. Not only did he keep an eye turned towards various metropoli in the interests of income and self-promotion; he was sensitive of his standing among the artistic urban bourgeoisie, a touchiness demonstrated by his libel action against the journal *The Leader* in 1954. It is perhaps telling of more than Kavanagh's ambiguous relationship to the establishment—telling of something in Irish poetry's relation to power—that this libel case ultimately led to the Taoiseach, John A. Costello, acting as Kavanagh's sponsor and employment agent.[53]

Similarly, it is possible to overstate the importance of Kavanagh's long convalescence after a successful treatment for lung cancer, to which he attributed a personal renaissance. The years 1955 and 1956 were undoubtedly creative ones for the poet, but the deliberate casualness which he presented as a new development was anticipated in *The Great Hunger*. His memorable metaphor for productive carelessness, playing 'a true note on a dead slack string',[54] is present, albeit not yet positively valued, in the 1942 poem as 'October playing a symphony on a slack wire paling'.[55] Nor does the doctrine of slackness represent any real diminution of anxiety about 'potentiality', though in the later work its expression is less overt.

The strongest single lyric of Kavanagh's later career is, however, directly related to his illness and recovery. 'The Hospital' is doctrinaire in its insistence on the poet's duty as Adamic namer, but it contrives to unite colloquial diction with a certain altitude: 'Naming these things is the love-act and its pledge/For we must record love's mystery without claptrap,/Snatch out of time the passionate transitory.'[56] Under the rubric of 'claptrap', the reader suspects, falls Yeatsian naming of the 'Easter 1916' variety, but behind the generative metaphor of 'love-act and its pledge' we sense the presence of that poem's domestic simile for the poet's public role: 'murmuring name upon name/as a mother names her child', Kavanagh adding to it his perennial masculinist concern with potency.[57] The paradox of 'snatching' and preserving the 'transitory', meanwhile, articulates the elusiveness of potential: fulfil it, and it disappears. Occasionally, Kavanagh's later work also explores the dangers of 'not-caring'. 'Living in the Country', written about a prolonged stay in Monaghan in 1959, contains this notably proleptic reflection:

> Oddly enough I begin to think of St Francis
> ...
> Was he an old fraud, a non-poet
> Who is loved for his non-ness
> Like any performer?[58]

[53] Costello, out of office at the time of the trial, acted for *The Leader*. His efficient and somewhat brutal cross-examination of Kavanagh won the case for the defendant, but he felt remorse when the poet became seriously ill shortly afterwards, and used his influence to secure him an extra-mural lectureship at University College Dublin. For a full account, see Quinn, *Patrick Kavanagh*, 325–41.

[54] Kavanagh, *A Poet's Country*, 315.

[55] Kavanagh, *Collected Poems*, 64.

[56] Ibid., 217.

[57] W. B. Yeats, *The Variorum Edition of the Poems of W. B. Yeats*, ed. Peter Allt and Russell K. Alspach (Basingstoke: Macmillan, 1956), 394.

[58] Kavanagh, *Collected Poems*, 234.

'Living in the Country', of mostly indifferent quality, works through bitter self-pity to a tantalizing flash of pastoral lyricism: 'Except that it was August evening under whitethorn/And early blackberries', asserting, in the self-reflexive manner familiar since 'Inniskeen Road: July Evening', that the poet is not yet quite null.[59]

But it is impossible to deny that Kavanagh has been loved for his 'non-ness', and for what he is not. Most egregious among the many claims upon him must be that of Irish nationalism, closely followed by that of the sentimental 'spirituality' that has inflected parts of the practice of the post-Vatican II Catholic Church. The latter is least explicable on the basis of glutinous exercises such as 'Advent',[60] while the former seems a triumph of wish-fulfilment over all available evidence. If we can discount the sympathetic interest shown him by John Betjeman and Cyril Connolly, and accept Kavanagh's claim that he was 'never much considered by the English critics', then we must also admit that Irish criticism tends to overvalue him.[61] Such penetrating critical accounts as Seamus Heaney's, for example, which detail generously Kavanagh's enabling effects on a greater talent, have been adduced to inflate the older poet's achievement.[62] Kavanagh's service to Irish poetry in freeing it from the pieties of cultural nationalism and Yeatsian high-talk is inestimable, but he proved unable, except in a handful of poems, to serve his own potentiality. It has been left to posterity—in Ireland, pre-eminently represented by Seamus Heaney and Paul Durcan—to explore possibilities revealed but not exploited by this extraordinary poetic personality.[63]

[59] Ibid., 235.

[60] Ibid., 110–11.

[61] Kavanagh, *A Poet's Country*, 302.

[62] Seamus Heaney, 'Patrick Kavanagh', *Preoccupations: Selected Prose 1968–1978* (London: Faber, 1980), and 'The Placeless Heaven: Another Look at Kavanagh', *The Government of the Tongue* (London: Faber, 1988).

[63] See Paul Durcan's suite of poems beginning with 'Surely My God is Kavanagh', *Greetings to Our Friends in Brazil* (London: Harvill, 1999), 127–42; also, for a discussion of Durcan on Kavanagh, see *Patrick Kavanagh*, ed. Stan Smith (Dublin: Irish Academic Press, 2009), 3.

CHAPTER 12

···

MACNEICE AMONG HIS IRISH CONTEMPORARIES: 1939 AND 1945

···

TOM WALKER

I

···

The presence of this essay in this collection signals the degree to which the work of Louis MacNeice has found a central place in accounts of twentieth-century Irish poetry. Such has been the emphasis on locating MacNeice among Irish concerns, by critics including Terence Brown, Edna Longley, and Peter McDonald, that Richard Danson Brown has recently sought to recover 'the English MacNeice'.[1] Danson Brown's study, *Louis MacNeice and the Poetry of the 1930s* (2009), sets about this recovery by considering MacNeice's poems of the 1930s among those of his English contemporaries Stephen Spender, C. Day Lewis, and W. H. Auden. The question of MacNeice's Englishness, however, is put to one side as Danson Brown implicitly shows that MacNeice's identity is less important than what his poems do, by exploring how they respond to similar historical pressures in distinctive yet dialogic ways to the poems of these contemporaries. But this approach also reflects back on the way in which MacNeice's place within Irish literature has been constructed. For although his Irish identity has often been discussed, as yet little is known about how MacNeice's poems actually relate to the work of his Irish contemporaries.

In 1974 Derek Mahon claimed that MacNeice 'had no place in the intellectual history of modern Ireland'—presumably to make his own recovery of MacNeice as an influence all the more striking.[2] But much has come to light since that complicates such poetical

---

[1] Richard Danson Brown, *Louis MacNeice and the Poetry of the 1930s* (Tavistock: Northcote House, 2009), 6–7.

[2] Derek Mahon, 'MacNeice in England and Ireland', in *Time Was Away: The World of Louis MacNeice*, ed. Terence Brown and Alec Reid (Dublin: Dolmen Press, 1974), 113–14.

positioning. Terence Brown has drawn attention to MacNeice's (mostly frustrated) attempts to become involved in Ireland's 'intellectual history', which include his seventeen-month term as poetry editor of the Dublin literary periodical *The Bell*.[3] Edna Longley and Gillian McIntosh have both investigated how MacNeice, together with writers such as John Hewitt, W. R. Rodgers, Sam Hanna Bell, and Sam Thompson, played a part in promoting a more progressive politics in Northern Ireland.[4] MacNeice did not, unlike W. B. Yeats or Seán O'Faoláin, take a central role in 'the intellectual history of modern Ireland', but he was not a Joycean exile either. Moreover, the biographical and epistolary record questions Mahon's view that MacNeice's contemporaries 'were not Frank O'Connor, Denis Johnston and Patrick Kavanagh, but Cyril Connolly, Noel Coward and William Empson'.[5] MacNeice was familiar with many Irish writers and their work, including Mahon's three examples. Johnston and MacNeice, who both spent the Second World War working for the BBC, were friends. During the summer of 1945, for instance, Johnston stayed with MacNeice and his family in County Mayo, where they were taking an extended holiday.[6] MacNeice knew O'Connor, writing to Laurence Gilliam (his boss in the BBC Features Department) on visiting Dublin in 1945 that: 'The Dublin intelligentsia are more disgruntled than ever; Frank O'Connor says the only Irish landscape he likes is Kilkenny because it reminds him of England.' He also admired O'Connor's work, mentioning in another letter to Gilliam having read 'nearly all Frank O'Connor's stories' and commenting 'I think he's extremely good'; he had earlier praised O'Connor's 'excellent translations' of Irish-language poetry.[7] MacNeice's and Kavanagh's paths crossed too. Only fragments survive of Kavanagh's 'The Ballad of the Palace Bar', but it recorded a row that broke out in Dublin in 1939 when Austin Clarke insulted MacNeice, according to Kavanagh, with the words: 'Let him go back and labour for Faber and Faber'. While in 1960, MacNeice produced a reading of Kavanagh's 'The Great Hunger', with an introduction by the author, for BBC radio.[8]

But this knowledge of MacNeice's involvement in mid-twentieth-century Irish cultural life has yet to translate into a sense of how his poems engaged with the work of his Irish contemporaries. Rather, in current accounts of Irish literary history, MacNeice is partly seen as belonging to Irish literary tradition through his successful grappling with the legacy of Yeats, which is most prominent in his 1941 study *The Poetry of W. B. Yeats*, but also recurs in Yeatsian allusions throughout his work. For example, in an account of

---

[3] Terence Brown, 'MacNeice's Ireland, MacNeice's Islands', in *Literature and Nationalism*, ed. Vincent Newey and Ann Thompson (Liverpool: Liverpool University Press, 1991), 225–38. MacNeice is listed as poetry editor of *The Bell* from January 1946 until May 1947.

[4] Edna Longley, 'Progressive Bookmen: Left-wing Politics and Ulster Protestant Writers', *The Living Stream: Literature and Revisionism in Ireland* (Newcastle: Bloodaxe, 1994), 107–29; Gillian McIntosh, *The Force of Culture: Unionist Identities in Twentieth-Century Ireland* (Cork: Cork University Press, 1999), 180–219.

[5] Mahon, 'MacNeice in England and Ireland', 113.

[6] Jon Stallworthy, *Louis MacNeice* (London: Faber, 1995), 336.

[7] MacNeice to Lawrence Gilliam, 12 June [1945] and 14 July [1945], BBC Written Archives, LI/285/2; Louis MacNeice, *The Poetry of W. B. Yeats* (Oxford: Oxford University Press, 1941), 49.

[8] Antoinette Quinn, *Patrick Kavanagh: A Biography* (Dublin: Gill and Macmillan, 2001), 127, 394–5.

the Yeatsian succession that also considers the work of Kavanagh, Clarke, and F. R. Higgins, Edna Longley identifies MacNeice as the only poet 'both to receive Yeats dialectically and to develop the Yeatsian dialectic'.[9] Besides his interest in Yeats's work, MacNeice's position in Irish literary tradition is also strongly associated with his posthumous identification as an influence by several more recent Northern Irish poets, including Mahon, Michael Longley, and Paul Muldoon. As Fran Brearton argues, these Northern Irish poets 'have become the lens through which [MacNeice] is viewed', having retrospectively reformed the literary canon to bring his 'reputation to rest in Ireland'.[10]

Such is the strength of this conception of MacNeice, as a homeless outsider posthumously assimilated into Irish culture by contemporary Northern Irish poetry, that literary history risks being distorted to make his career better fit within such a narrative. For instance, Elmer Kennedy-Andrews's recent study of Northern Irish poetry since 1968 casts MacNeice in the familiar role of enabling precursor. In characterizing him as a 'nomad' later appropriated by Northern Irish poets, Kennedy-Andrews presents him as 'living in a limbo between England and Ireland' and 'migrating between the North and the South of Ireland'—an overwrought way of saying that MacNeice lived in England but visited friends and family in both the North and South of Ireland. But this is followed by the observation that 'for some fellow poets' MacNeice 'does not qualify as an "Irish" poet at all', illustrated by the apparent fact that he 'goes unrepresented in both Montague's and Kinsella's anthologies of Irish poetry'.[11] But MacNeice's work does appear in John Montague's *Faber Book of Irish Verse* (1974) and Thomas Kinsella's *New Oxford Book of Irish Verse* (1986). Indeed, MacNeice's poetry was also included in the original 1958 *Oxford Book of Irish Verse*, edited by Donagh MacDonagh and Lennox Robinson, and Faber and Faber's 1949 anthology *Contemporary Irish Poetry*, edited by Robert Greacen and Valentin Iremonger, complicating somewhat any account of MacNeice's rescue from literary 'limbo'.

Heather Clark identifies the appropriation of MacNeice by Longley, Mahon, and Muldoon as a self-empowering act of genealogy: 'By collectively establishing MacNeice as the doyen of Northern Irish poetry, by promoting a selective canon, and by "rewriting" many of his ideological and philosophical concerns in their own work... they have placed him at the beginning of a line of an inheritance which is, by right, theirs.'[12] As an example of this strategic identification, Clark points to Muldoon's use of 'Tendencies in Modern Poetry', a 1939 BBC radio broadcast by MacNeice and F. R. Higgins, as an

[9] Edna Longley, '"It is time that I wrote my will": Anxieties of Influence and Succession', in *Yeats Annual No. 12. That Accusing Eye: Yeats and His Irish Readers*, ed. Warwick Gould and Edna Longley (Basingstoke: Macmillan, 1996), 156.

[10] Fran Brearton, *The Great War in Irish Poetry: W. B. Yeats to Michael Longley* (Oxford: Oxford University Press, 2000), 147.

[11] Elmer Kennedy-Andrews, *Writing Home: Poetry and Place in Northern Ireland 1968–2008* (Cambridge: D. S. Brewer, 2008), 37.

[12] Heather Clark, *The Ulster Renaissance: Poetry in Belfast 1962–1972* (Oxford: Oxford University Press, 2006), 133.

introduction to his *Faber Book of Contemporary Irish Poetry* (1986)—notorious for its inclusion of only ten poets, seven of whom are from the North. During the exchange, Higgins asserts the superiority of modern Irish over English poetry, which he attributes to Irish poets' possession of an unbroken 'racial rhythm'—by which Higgins means a connection to some form of shared 'belief emanating from life, from nature, from revealed religion, and from the nation'. A sceptical MacNeice asks if this 'racial rhythm' is more important for the poet than any 'extra-national rhythms', observing that: 'On those premises there is more likelihood of good poetry appearing among the Storm Troopers of Germany than in the cosmopolitan communities of Paris or New York.' Higgins defiantly agrees that 'in some respects I actually believe so' and reminds MacNeice that 'you as an Irishman, cannot escape from your blood, nor from our blood-music that brings the racial character to mind'.[13] In using this exchange, as Clark argues: 'Muldoon's implication is, obviously, that MacNeice is the more enlightened of the two; Higgins's ideas about "racial character" sound almost fascist in hindsight.' The 'enabling example' of MacNeice's scepticism towards concepts such as 'racial blood-music' offers Muldoon licence for his own 'distance and irony' in relation to the Troubles.[14] Muldoon presents MacNeice as standing at the beginning of a tradition in Irish poetry that has questioned the inward-looking poetic nationalism espoused by Higgins, a tradition that implicitly includes Muldoon and those few poets who were included in his anthology.

But this version of MacNeice presents only a partial picture, revealing as much about Muldoon's self-fashioning in response to the pressures of Northern Ireland in the mid-1980s as it does about MacNeice's response towards Higgins in the late 1930s. MacNeice's and Higgins's on-air confrontation actually marked the beginning of a friendship between the poets. In a letter written soon after the exchange, MacNeice reported: 'Higgins after denouncing me for 24 hours for having de-Irishised myself asked me if I'd like to belong to the Irish Academy of letters. I said yes.'[15] That same year, the two poets engaged in another broadcast, 'A Literary Night Out', this time on Radio Éireann, that aimed to reproduce 'the salty, sensitive, exuberant talk of the Dublin literary pub', but which their producer Roibeárd Ó Faracháin (the poet Robert Farren) viewed as a failure: 'poor Fred Higgins and poor Louis MacNeice, both good poets, both men of mind, could not at that time even half-master the very special business of largely impromptu live broadcasting'.[16] Higgins died in 1941 but his memory stayed with MacNeice who, in 1953, proposed a radio feature on his life and work to the BBC, describing his personality as 'an extraordinary blend of delicacy and Falstaffianism'.[17] In his long poem *Autumn Sequel* (1954), he memorialized Higgins, under the pseudonym 'Reilly', as a figure

---

[13] Broadcast on 11 July 1939, printed as: F. R. Higgins and Louis MacNeice, 'Tendencies in Modern Poetry', *Listener* 22, no. 550 (27 July 1939), 185–6.

[14] Clark, *The Ulster Renaissance*, 138–9.

[15] MacNeice to Eleanor Clark, 16 July [1939], *Letters of Louis MacNeice*, ed. Jonathan Allison (London: Faber, 2010), 250–1.

[16] Roibeárd Ó Faracháin, 'Some Early Days in Radio', in *Written on the Wind: Personal Memories of Irish Radio*, ed. Louis McRedmond (Dublin: Radio Telefís Éireann, 1976), 40.

[17] MacNeice to BBC Features Organizer, 21 January 1953, Bodleian Library, MacNeice Papers.

analogous to Dylan Thomas: 'I knew one other poet who made his choice/To sing and die, a meticulous maker too'.[18] And in 1962 he recollected that 'in the late Thirties I came to know Yeats's disciple, the late F. R. Higgins, who thought I was lacking in "singing robes" but seemed pleased to let me beguile him away from the Abbey Theatre when he was supposed to be rehearsing the company; we used to meet other poets'.[19]

II

During the summer of 1939, MacNeice was involved in thinking about Ireland and its poetry through his research for *The Poetry of W. B. Yeats*. But he was also physically in Ireland. Following on from the broadcast with Higgins, which took place in Belfast in July, he returned to Ireland with his friend Ernst Stahl in mid-August, visiting Dublin and staying with his family, who had rented a holiday home in Cushendun, County Antrim, before heading west. MacNeice and Stahl were in Galway on 1 September when news arrived that Germany had invaded Poland and they promptly drove to Dublin, from where Stahl travelled on to England.[20] But MacNeice stayed, spending the next day drinking with Dublin's literati who, as he recollects in his posthumously published memoir *The Strings are False* (1965), 'hardly mentioned the war but debated the correct version of Dublin street songs'.[21] He then remained in Ireland for several months, moving between Belfast and Dublin, before travelling to the United States in January 1940.[22]

This was the longest sustained period of time that MacNeice had spent in Ireland since his childhood. Critical accounts have focused on his ambivalent attitude to the war at the time: in a surviving letter from November 1939, he frankly wondered 'if' it was his war, and he only finally returned to England from America to join the war effort at the end of 1940.[23] But MacNeice's five months in Ireland represent more than just a phase in a longer interlude of indecisiveness. Putting his later choices to one side, it is clear that he was not just in Ireland, but becoming involved in its cultural life. *The Strings are False* mentions meeting the painter Jack Yeats and the former Irish revolutionary turned author Ernie O'Malley in Dublin, and the artist George McCann in Belfast.[24] McCann and his wife, the artist Mercy Hunter, went on to provide a link between MacNeice and Belfast's cultural circles for the rest of his life; part of the time he and his family spent in

---

[18] Louis MacNeice, *Collected Poems*, ed. Peter McDonald (London: Faber, 2007), 455.

[19] Louis MacNeice, 'Under the Sugar Loaf', *New Statesman* 63, no. 1633 (29 June 1962), 948–9.

[20] Stallworthy, *Louis MacNeice*, 258–9.

[21] Louis MacNeice, *The Strings are False: An Unfinished Autobiography* (London: Faber, 1965), 212. In his notes for the memoir, MacNeice lists Higgins, Brinsley Macnamara, and Seamus O'Sullivan as his Dublin drinking companions on 2 September. Louis MacNeice, [Notebook of] varied notes, c.1939, Harry Ransom Humanities Research Centre, (MacNeice, L.), Misc., Hanley II.

[22] Stallworthy, *Louis MacNeice*, 267.

[23] MacNeice to E. R. Dodds, 19 November [1939], *Letters of Louis MacNeice*, ed. Allison, 366–7; Stallworthy, *Louis MacNeice*, 285–6.

[24] MacNeice, *The Strings Are False*, 213–15.

Mayo in the summer of 1945 was at O'Malley's home.[25] This was also the period in which he beguiled Higgins 'away from the Abbey Theatre...to meet other poets.'[26] MacNeice even submitted a play to the Abbey in 1939, though it was never performed.[27] He was not only in Belfast and Dublin but also involved in the literary life of both cities, and the effects of thinking about Yeats while drinking with Ireland's literati can be traced in his poetry from the turn of the decade.

The sequence 'The Coming of War', written during August and September 1939, was first published in Dublin in the 1940 Cuala Press volume *The Last Ditch*. It offers a diary-like account of MacNeice's response to the developing international situation leading up to the declaration of war, mediated through his experience of travelling through different parts of Ireland. But as originally printed, before later being cut, it also engages extensively with modern Irish poetry, exploring Ireland not only as a place but also as a set of poetic possibilities in the face of the imminent conflict.[28] Several of the sequence's poems clearly engage with the work of Yeats. For instance, McDonald notes that the opening poem, 'Dublin', recalls Yeats's 'Easter, 1916' through its metre, 'its imagery of stone and water, and its equivocal attitude to the historical characters who harden into figures of national myth ("O'Connell, Grattan, Moore")'.[29] Richard Danson Brown also points to Yeatsian parallels in the sequence's seventh poem, later retitled 'Galway', which is 'haunted by Yeats's cadence' and 'anticipates MacNeice's reading of Yeats's refrain poems' in *The Poetry of W. B. Yeats*.[30] But as 'The Coming of War' unfolds, it is not only Yeats's poetical terrain that is explored.

In the fifth poem the speaker, having been in Northern Ireland, is travelling to the west of Ireland:

> Running away from the War,
> Running away from the red
> Pillar-box and the stamps
> Bearing George's head.[31]

These opening lines, through their insistent repetition, ballad-like (abcb) alternating rhymes ('red' and 'head'), and use of simple three- and four-stress rhythms, partly inhabit the world of song and cast a kind of spell, driving the poem beyond the signs of Britishness in Ulster that are a reminder of the imminent war. Initially, the metre of this

---

[25] Stallworthy, *Louis MacNeice*, 394, 335.

[26] MacNeice, 'Under the Sugar Loaf', 948–9.

[27] Stallworthy, *Louis MacNeice*, 266–7. *Blacklegs: A Play* [1939] was eventually printed in *Oxford Poetry* 4, no. 1 (Spring 2000).

[28] MacNeice, *Collected Poems*, 680–6. The sequence was originally made up of ten poems in *The Last Ditch* (Dublin: Cuala Press, 1940). It was shortened to seven poems (omitting II, IV, and V) when reprinted in *Plant and Phantom* (London: Faber, 1941), and retitled 'The Closing Album' and cut to five poems (omitting VIII and IX) for *Collected Poems 1925–1948* (London: Faber, 1949).

[29] Peter McDonald, *Louis MacNeice: The Poet in his Contexts* (Oxford: Clarendon Press, 1991), 100.

[30] Richard Danson Brown, 'Neutrality and Commitment: MacNeice, Yeats, Ireland and the Second World War', *Journal of Modern Literature* 28:3 (Spring 2005), 118.

[31] MacNeice, *Collected Poems*, 683.

song-like poem is faintly militaristic, as the poem marches to the beat of 'the drum' in the 'Black North' from which the speaker is escaping. But its thumping beat is subtly undermined by the Irish place names, 'Dungannon', 'Augher', 'Clogher', in the poem's third stanza. The point of rhythmic stress becomes less pronounced and the resulting wavering, dreamy rhythm finds a mimetic correlative in the poet's final admission that he is hoping to escape by hiding his 'head/In the clouds of the West'.

This association between escapism from the war, the West of Ireland, and a less urgent kind of poetic rhythm is further underlined in the sequence's sixth poem. It recasts the preceding poem's rhyme scheme into an altogether more relaxed metre, as the country-side of Sligo and Mayo is leisurely described:

> In Sligo the country was soft; there were turkeys
> > Gobbling under sycamore trees
> And the shadows of clouds on the mountains moving
> > Like browsing cattle at ease.[32]

Indeed, on arriving in the West, MacNeice adopts a set of distinctively Irish poetic pro-cedures in this transformed ballad-like stanza. The setting, the meandering rhythm, and the rhyme scheme all recall the verse of the Irish literary revival and its aftermath, including the early poetry of F. R. Higgins, such as 'Old Galway' from his 1925 collection *Island Blood*:

> Far in a garden's wreckage,
> > Stark in the wind-cleared moon,
> Grandees on wave-green marble
> > Of Connemara stone,
> Gleam down the courtly pavings,
> > Where windfalls are strewn –
> Tripping steps led by the stringsmen
> > Thumbing an old tune.[33]

MacNeice's poem also shares Higgins's musically rich use of assonance: in its opening stanza, the vowel sound in the first line's 'soft' returns in the second line's 'gobbling', a pattern then repeated in the third and fourth lines with 'clouds' and 'browsing'; and a similar pattern can be seen in 'Old Galway' between 'garden's', 'stark', 'marble', and 'Connemara'. Through such patterns of assonance, Higgins's verse loosely attempts to reproduce the formal procedures of Irish-language poetry in English-language poetry. In particular, Higgins in 'Old Galway' seems to be mimicking the Great Quatrain, *Rannaigecht Mór*, which in terms of its principal rhyme scheme 'may not seem to differ essentially from the popular English ballad measure', but does differ through complex patterns of internal rhyme and consonance.[34] Furthermore, in using a wavering sense of rhythmic stress, Higgins is following the poet and Easter 1916 rebel leader Thomas

---

[32] Ibid.

[33] F. R. Higgins, *Island Blood* (London: John Lane, 1925), 15–16.

[34] Charles W. Dunn, 'Celtic', in *Versification: Major Language Types*, ed. W. K. Wimsatt (New York: Modern Language Association, 1972), 139.

MacDonagh's contention in *Literature in Ireland* (1916) that 'the Irish Mode' in English-language poetry is differentiated by 'a tendency to give, in certain poems, generally of short rhyming lines, almost equal stress value to all the syllables, a tendency to make the line the metrical unit'.[35]

But Higgins's 'Irish Mode', like the West of Ireland it so often depicts, does not offer an enduring route of escape from the coming war for MacNeice. In this sixth poem in the sequence portents of death intrude upon this 'soft' western setting and Irish song-like verse:

> And pullets pecking the flies from around the eyes of heifers
>   Sitting in farmyard mud
> Among hydrangeas and the falling ear-rings
>   Of fuschias red as blood.

Besides the hints at violence in the description of the 'pullets pecking the flies' and the 'fuschias red as blood', the very rhyme between 'mud' and 'blood' evokes First World War poems such as Wilfred Owen's 'Apologia pro Poemate Meo'. It suggests that even Irish poetry may not be able to escape the impact of the impending re-run of that earlier conflict. In the next stanza, the speaker turns from this disquieting scene to picturesque descriptions of Mayo's 'tumbledown walls'. But when night falls at the close of the poem, the turfstacks rise ominously 'against the darkness/Like the tombs of nameless kings'. Sligo and Mayo flicker 'from milkmaid pastoral...to less Arcadian prospects', as Edna Longley suggests.[36] But particular Irish poetic possibilities, Higgins's style, and the Irish literary revival's preoccupation with the Irish West are also inhabited and challenged by these hints of coming death. This Irish mode's escapism in the current historical circumstances is undermined in a complex response to Higgins's accusation that 'as an Irishman' MacNeice cannot escape from his 'blood-music'.[37]

That he should fleetingly put on Higgins's singing robes points to the education MacNeice received at this time, partly through Higgins, about the stylistic particularities of modern Irish verse. This is apparent in the section of *The Poetry of W. B. Yeats* in which MacNeice compares Yeats to his Irish successors. He praises the craft of several Irish poets, including Seumas O'Sullivan, Padraic Colum, Joseph Campbell, Frank O'Connor, Austin Clarke, and Higgins. This is a product not only of the positive influence of Yeats, he argues, but also of the example of early Irish verse's use of 'assonance, alliteration and internal rhymes'. He also cites approvingly MacDonagh's 'account of Anglo-Irish poetry as a genre distinct from English poetry' due to the 'more uniform stress over the syllables' in its rhythms. But as well as this delineation of the Irish mode, MacNeice makes certain critical judgements. He argues that 'Colum and Campbell can at times be accused of facile prettiness'. In contrast, 'early Irish poetry appears to have combined two virtues usually divorced, to have been unusually elaborate in pattern and

---

[35] Thomas MacDonagh, *Literature in Ireland: Studies Irish and Anglo-Irish* (Dublin: Talbot Press, 1916), 73.

[36] Edna Longley, *Louis MacNeice: A Critical Study* (London: Faber, 1988), 25.

[37] Higgins and MacNeice, 'Tendencies in Modern Poetry', 186.

at the same time to have been direct and clear-cut'. He also praises O'Connor and
Higgins, in his later verse, for having realized, under the influence of J.M. Synge, 'that it
is more important for their poetry to be strong than to be pretty'.[38] Within this effort to
forge an Irish mode in English-language poetry, MacNeice is attempting to differentiate
between a strain that he views as somewhat romantic and a more matter-of-fact, hard,
and direct poetry, which is both truer to the manner of early Irish lyric and more aes-
thetically successful. This relates to his earlier discussion in the study of how 'in trying to
avoid the materialism of the Saxon', Yeats had 'misrepresented the genius of the Gael' by
following Matthew Arnold's famous conception of the Celts as in revolt against 'the des-
potism of fact'. MacNeice argues that 'this is not borne out by early Irish poetry', citing
MacDonagh's description of Irish lyric as 'clear', 'direct', 'gem-like', and 'hard', as well as
the materialism, cruelty, and 'hardness' found in O'Connor's translations from the Irish,
such as this quatrain from 'Devil, Maggot and Son':

> Three things seek my death,
>   Hard at my heels they run –
> Hang them, sweet Christ, all three –
>   Devil, maggot and son.[39]

The ninth poem in 'The Coming of War' moves towards this hard and direct version
of the Irish mode. Recasting the same ballad-like (abcb) quatrain once again, it operates
in ironic counterpoint to the sixth poem's air of escapism and 'pretty' descriptions of
landscape. But in its first and last quatrains, the poem also undercuts its own initial pret-
tiness, 'the sky is a lather of stars', with the recognition in the repeated, Yeats-like, refrain
that nothing 'can drive the war away'. Furthermore, in the middle quatrain, the land-
scape itself is suddenly oppressive: 'The black horns of the headlands/Grip my gullet
tight'.[40] A bleaker mode has been found in which to face up honestly to the war now at
hand. The sequence has travelled from the point at which the speaker was trying to run
'away from the War', to this admission that the war cannot be driven away, and part of its
journey has been through the literary territory of contemporary Ireland, subtly inhabit-
ing its locations and techniques.

III

The start of the Second World War had found MacNeice not only in Ireland but among
its writers, and the period at the end of the war was somewhat similar. On 5 April 1945
the poet and his family travelled to Northern Ireland to stay with his stepmother outside
Carrickfergus. MacNeice returned to London for a few weeks at the end of April, but

---

[38] MacNeice, *The Poetry of W. B. Yeats*, 208–13.
[39] MacNeice, *The Poetry of W. B. Yeats*, 47–9; Frank O'Connor, *The Fountain of Magic* (London:
Macmillan, 1939), 32.
[40] MacNeice, *Collected Poems*, 685.

then rejoined his family and they stayed in Ireland until the beginning of September.[41] The trip started out as a working holiday, as MacNeice had been given the 'job of grooming new writers' in Belfast and writing several radio scripts for the BBC.[42] But as his letters to his boss Laurence Gilliam show, this holiday was extended into a longer sabbatical, as in mid-June he decamped to Achill Island, County Mayo, for a couple of months.[43]

The sabbatical proved to be highly productive. MacNeice wrote *The Dark Tower*, one of his finest radio plays, and several of his poems about Ireland have their roots in the period. These form a loose sequence at the centre of his 1948 volume *Holes in the Sky*, which McDonald has labelled as 'MacNeice's Achill Poems'.[44] But while some of these poems clearly respond to this setting in the West of Ireland, it is also significant that during this period MacNeice was spending time in Northern Ireland and in the company of its writers, several of whom he was 'grooming' for the BBC. One of these was the poet W. R. Rodgers, who a year later moved to London to share an office with him. Another was the fiction writer Sam Hanna Bell, who became a radio producer in Belfast. Hanna Bell later recollected that the three of them had been drinking together in a Belfast pub when the news arrived of the bombing of Hiroshima.[45] This had taken place on 6 August 1945, so MacNeice must have left his family in Achill and travelled back to Belfast for at least a few days. Such a detail of his day-to-day movements points to his exposure to the city's literary life during the summer of that year—an exposure reflected in the poems he wrote.

Part of this literary life included involvement in *Lagan*, the periodical started in 1943 by Sam Hanna Bell, John Hewitt, and John Boyd. In the first issue's editorial, Boyd, who also went on to work as a producer for BBC Northern Ireland, declared that the magazine aimed to foster a literary tradition springing 'out of the life and speech of this province'.[46] MacNeice contributed a poem, 'The Godfather', to the fourth and final number of *Lagan* in 1946, which also contained extracts from Rodgers's first radio script, 'The City Set on a Hill', that MacNeice had produced in Belfast in November 1945.[47] Rodgers's piece, a portrait of Armagh, was very much in tune with the regionalist agenda of *Lagan*, which had been stridently reiterated by Hewitt (a close friend of Rodgers) in an essay entitled 'The Bitter Gourd: Some Problems of the Ulster Writer' that had been published in the 1945 issue. Hewitt argued that the Ulster writer 'must be a *rooted* man, must carry the native tang of his idiom like the native dust on his sleeve; otherwise he is an airy

[41] Stallworthy, *Louis MacNeice*, 332–3.

[42] Laurence Gilliam, BBC Features Department memo, 3 August 1945, BBC Written Archives, LI/285/2.

[43] MacNeice to Laurence Gilliam, 12 June [1945] and 14 July [1945], BBC Written Archives, LI/285/2.

[44] Peter McDonald, ' "This mirror of wet sand": Louis MacNeice's Achill Poems', *Agenda* 43, no. 2–3 (2008), 46–57. A loose sequence of poems seems to run from 'Littoral' to 'Western Landscape', all of which are dated 1945 (and some more specifically as June or July 1945). MacNeice, *Collected Poems*, 259–67.

[45] Barbara Coulton, *Louis MacNeice in the BBC* (London: Faber, 1980), 78.

[46] John Boyd, 'Introduction', *Lagan* 4 (1946), 6.

[47] Louis MacNeice, 'The Godfather', and W. R. Rodgers, 'Armagh: The City Set on a Hill', *Lagan* 4 (1946), 19, 13–18.

internationalist'.[48] MacNeice would appear to be that very 'airy internationalist', and in the Irish poems in *Holes in the Sky* he complicates the very possibility of being 'a *rooted* man'.

Near the beginning of the loose sequence is 'Carrick Revisited', which links the present poet to the past child:

> Here are the new villas, here is a sizzling grid
> But the green banks are as rich and the lough as hazily lazy
> And the child's astonishment not yet cured.[49]

But instead of offering anything as straightforward as roots, this 'topographical frame' unsettles the speaker's sense of connection, as he reflects on the complications of time and location. Small distances are opened up between the child he was and the place this was, and the man and place they have become. The poet was and still is surprised to be in Carrickfergus, which both is and is not the place where he was raised. A 'random chemistry of soil and air' has 'determined largely' the 'channels' of his 'dreams', but these memories do not straightforwardly form the poet's self. Rather they further a sense of dislocation from the past as they 'peer' at him from the shelf he has put them on and are only 'half-heard through boarded time'.[50] In the 'The Bitter Gourd', Hewitt had asserted that:

> I do not mean that a writer ought to live and die in the house of his fathers. What I do mean is that he ought to feel that he belongs to a recognisable focus in place and time. How he assures himself of that feeling is his own affair. But I believe he must have it. And with it, he must have *ancestors*. Not just of the blood, but of the emotions, of the quality and slant of mind.[51]

In certain respects the speaker in 'Carrick Revisited' appears to be directly heeding Hewitt's call, as he examines the extent to which he feels he 'belongs to a recognisable focus in place and time'. But the speaker finds that he cannot assure himself of a sense of belonging. Carrickfergus and the past with which it is associated, rather than offering a point of stability, undermine the self's unity, as MacNeice complicates Hewitt's assertions by teasing out some of their philosophical difficulties in the context of the facts of his own experience.

A change in perspective in the penultimate stanza of 'Carrick Revisited', which looks back towards MacNeice's 'ancestors', further emphasizes the instability of this site of his roots:

> Torn before birth from where my fathers dwelt,
> Schooled from the age of ten to a foreign voice,
> Yet neither western Ireland nor southern England

[48] John Hewitt, 'The Bitter Gourd: Some Problems of the Ulster Writer', *Lagan* 3 (1945); repr. in *Ancestral Voices: The Selected Prose of John Hewitt*, ed. Tom Clyde (Belfast: Blackstaff, 1987), 115.
[49] MacNeice, *Collected Poems*, 261–2.
[50] Ibid.
[51] Hewitt, 'The Bitter Gourd', 116.

Cancels this interlude; what chance misspelt
May never now be righted by my choice.[52]

MacNeice's father and mother were originally from the west of Ireland; his father's family had left Omey Island in Connemara in a sectarian dispute when he was thirteen.[53] So MacNeice's early childhood in Carrick is framed by a deeper sense of dislocation originating in his family's roots in the Irish west, as well as his own schooling in England. He has 'ancestors', just not ones whose 'recognisable focus in place' straightforwardly matches his own. This forms a further riposte to Hewitt's regionalist tenets, centred around the realities of 'chance' and 'choice', as MacNeice reverses the prestige conferred on roots by implying that he regards his roots in Carrickfergus as something of a mistake. By contrast, in Hewitt's 'Townland of Peace', published in *The Bell* in 1944, the speaker recollects 'walking in the county' of his 'kindred', and this landscape facilitates an encounter with his 'father's father' who 'ran these roads/a hundred years ago'.[54] Whereas MacNeice's own memories of Carrickfergus are estranged, peering at him from a shelf, Hewitt un-self-consciously connects with his family's past presence in this landscape, when his grandfather moves 'beside him' as a comforting quasi-ghost. The identification between Hewitt's sense of self, his family, and the landscape is presented as straightforward, stretching from his grandfather's time to the present; but in several respects it is merely imagined.

MacNeice's final image for his childhood 'interlude' in 'Carrick Revisited' is 'a belated rock in the red Antrim clay'. This echoes a similar image in Hewitt's 'Once Alien Here', first published, like 'The Bitter Gourd', in the 1945 issue of *Lagan*.[55] The poem again reimagines the lives of Hewitt's ancestors: 'Once alien here my fathers built their house'. The speaker juxtaposes these settlers with the native Irish who 'gave the rain-pocked stone a meaning', but then appropriates this meaning in stone to proclaim himself as now a part of this landscape. That his ancestors are buried 'in Ulster clay' and that Ulster's 'rock' is 'native' to his thought underpins his attempt to 'seek a native mode to tell/our stubborn wisdom individual'. But MacNeice reworks Hewitt's imagery of 'clay' and 'rock' in 'Carrick Revisited'. Rather than an identity underpinned by his ancestor's buried in this clay, or the region's rocks forming a part of his 'native' thought, MacNeice's childhood 'interlude' is itself a 'belated rock in the red Antrim clay'. In fact, this childhood is the poet's only ancestor in the Antrim earth: resistant and aloof to that present self in its stone-like state; 'belated' in that, contrary to Hewitt's schema of belonging, it does not make him a 'native' and is not native to his thought.

This dialogue with Hewitt appears to continue in 'The Strand'. It offers an imaginary encounter with MacNeice's dead father:

---

[52] MacNeice, *Collected Poems*, 262.

[53] David Fitzpatrick, "'I will acquire an attitude not yours'': Was Frederick John MacNeice a Home Ruler, and Why Does This Matter?', *Field Day Review* 4 (2008), 140–55.

[54] John Hewitt, 'Townland of Peace', *The Bell* 9, no. 1 (October 1944), 10–12; repr. in *Collected Poems of John Hewitt*, ed. Frank Ormsby, 642–3.

[55] John Hewitt, 'Once Alien Here', *Lagan* 3 (1945), 5; repr. in *Collected Poems of John Hewitt*, 20–1.

> ...my steps repeat
>
> Someone's who now has left such strands for good
> Carrying his boots and paddling like a child,
> A square black figure whom the horizon understood –
>
> My father.[56]

Rather than moving beside him as a friendly ghost, MacNeice's father is more complexly an echo in the poet's own reflection in a 'mirror of wet sand'. The son is mirroring the father but at an unbridgeable remove. However, the poem is not merely dismissing the kind of relationship with one's ancestors or the landscape that Hewitt's work promotes. It is exploring the limits of such relationships: 'the horizon understood' his father; the western Irish landscape formed him, such that he 'kept something in him solitary and wild'; and the mountains on Achill 'fulfilled him'. But although the poem evokes the relationship of MacNeice's father with the landscape and, in terms of the poet's own memory, the landscape has become a synecdoche for his father, the possibility of this relationship being open to MacNeice, as his father's son, is not present.

Even his father was only a 'visitor', and whereas it is the ghost of his father that haunts this poem, it is MacNeice who is rendered ghostly through his inability fully to belong in the west of Ireland. His only claim to keeping 'something in him' of this place is through the memory of a father who himself only carried 'something' of this place. The usual ghostly roles are reversed, as is mutedly echoed in the poem's form, with the *terza rima* recalling the *Divine Comedy*, in that it is Dante who is rendered ghostly to the figures he encounters in the afterlife. To turn back to Hewitt, the poem again uncovers complications as regards a regionalist agenda through an exploration of MacNeice's personal circumstances. Hewitt decrees in 'The Bitter Gourd' that a poet should 'have a native place'. But in 'The Strand', as in 'Carrick Revisited', what might have been that place turns out to be a source of further estrangement.[57] In contrast to Hewitt's 'Once Alien Here', we might label MacNeice's two poems 'Once Native Here' or even 'Never Native Here'.

Finally, at the end of the loose sequence in 'Western Landscape', MacNeice sets out to honour the site of his father's actual and his own wished-for roots. The landscape's implied indifference in 'The Strand' is here more explicitly stated. Whatever we desire, our 'affinity' with this place's 'light and line' is merely temporary; 'cloud and rock' are only relevant if they form part of the poet's 'permanence'. At the poem's end the speaker tries to reconcile himself to this reality:

> ...let me, if a bastard
> Out of the West by urban civilization
> (Which unwished father claims me – so I must take
> What I can before I go) let me who am neither Brandan
> Free of all roots nor yet a rooted peasant
> Here add one stone to the indifferent cairn...

---

[56] MacNeice, *Collected Poems*, 263.
[57] Hewitt, 'The Bitter Gourd', 115.

> With a stone on the cairn, with a word on the wind, with a prayer in
>   the flesh let me honour this country.[58]

The speaker's desire for attachment confronts the fact that he is a visitor, who can merely offer something 'in token' to this place. But looking at 'Western Landscape' in the context of MacNeice's exposure to Belfast's literary milieu in the summer of 1945 gives a word like 'rooted' a specific historical weight, related to the regionalist ideas put forward by Northern Irish writers during the period. As Brearton suggests, MacNeice in this poem is undermining 'Hewitt's dictum' that the Ulster writer must be 'a *rooted* man', by showing that he both might not be able to be 'rooted' and yet still might wish to add his tribute to the 'indifferent' landscape.[59] So that while set in the west, the poem implicitly tests some of regionalism's underlying principles. Edna Longley comments more generally of these 'Achill Poems' that their 'western landscapes function as a topography for metaphysical inquiry'.[60] But these metaphysical inquiries closely relate to the work Hewitt and others in Northern Ireland were attempting to get poetry to perform in the mid-1940s. During this period at the end of the Second World War, MacNeice was once again not only in Ireland but among its poets, and his poems make their way in implicit dialogue with the poetry and pronouncements of his Irish contemporaries.

[58] MacNeice, *Collected Poems*, 267.
[59] Brearton, *The Great War in Irish Poetry*, 132.
[60] Longley, *Louis MacNeice*, 32.

CHAPTER 13

···

THE POETICS OF PARTITION: POETRY AND NORTHERN IRELAND IN THE 1940s

···

RICHARD KIRKLAND

If, as we are told, every second person in Dublin has written a play, then it would appear that every second Belfastman—in the University district at any rate—has written a slim volume of poetry!

Editorial, *The Northman*, 1941[1]

Up in the North they are determined to produce a native culture or 'lose a fall'.

Patrick Kavanagh, 1948[2]

A plausible, if not uncontroversial, contention is that the history of poetry in the northern part of Ireland during the twentieth century shapes itself into three revivals, or what Michael Longley has termed 'a sequence of energetic spurts', 'prolonged but never continuous'.[3] The first, in the early years of the century, existed as part of a cultural revival more usually characterized as concentrated in drama and performance, but was distinguished by such poetry as Moira O'Neill's *Songs of the Glens of Antrim* (1900), Joseph Campbell's and Herbert Hughes's *Songs of Uladh* (1904), and Ethna Carbery's *The Four Winds of Eirinn* (1902). This work was distinctive in its adaptation of Celtic Revivalist poetic modes to specifically Ulster material (most obviously in its depictions of County Down, the Glens of Antrim, and County Donegal) and recent scholarship has revealed the significance of its artistic and cultural achievement. The third revival is usually identified as emerging during the mid to late 1960s with Belfast as its hub, and was

---

[1] Unsigned, 'Editorial: Modern Irish Poetry', *The Northman* X, no. 3 (Autumn 1941), 33.
[2] Patrick Kavanagh, 'Poetry in Ireland Today', *The Bell* XVI, no. 1 (April 1948), 41.
[3] Michael Longley, 'Poetry', *Causeway: The Arts in Ulster*, ed. Michael Longley (Belfast: Arts Council of Northern Ireland, 1971), 95.

focused on what was, by any account, a remarkable constellation of individual talents, most obviously Seamus Heaney, Derek Mahon, Michael Longley, Paul Muldoon, and Medbh McGuckian. Again, after a prolonged period of critical scepticism that resisted the identification of these talents as a movement, recent research has more clearly identified the totality of the poetic achievement that allows it to be seen as a 'renaissance'.[4]

The second of the three Northern poetic revivals is the subject of this essay and was, by comparison, a more troubled, if equally vigorous, affair. Its onset coincided with the beginning of the Second World War, or what the Queen's University of Belfast magazine, *The New Northman*, called 'the present eruption of Nazi frightfulness',[5] and was championed most energetically by the young student poet and critic Robert Greacen. Other significant poets involved were Roy McFadden and John Gallen, and, in a slightly more semi-detached way, John Hewitt, May Morton, and W. R. Rodgers. It was a period of obsessive coterie building, anthology compiling, and manifesto drafting, and had, according to Greacen, 'an exhilarating tang', which 'led to perhaps more good work than might have been expected in the circumstances'.[6] As with many provincial cultural revivals, a certain iconoclasm was important to its self-definition. Described by the contemporary writer John Boyd as 'poets and controversialists',[7] Greacen and McFadden (along with Gallen), according to Terence Brown, 'vigorously eschewed the weight of convention in preference for exuberant, romantic avant-garde self-examination'.[8] Brown's perception accords with Greacen's own estimation of the group which, as he notes in his autobiography *Even Without Irene*:

> incurred dislike in some quarters (especially among their immediate and somewhat Marxist-oriented Elders) and [had] a reputation for a certain arrogance. Who were they to set themselves up? They were 'angry young men' long before the catchphrase had been invented. What was worse, they had assumed a strangely non-committal political attitude in the middle of a war which was, so we were told, being fought to ensure the survival of civilised human values. It was all very reprehensible.[9]

Greacen, who was the last surviving figure of this Revival, died in 2008 and so it is perhaps a good time to revisit the movement and assess both its successes and (perhaps more interestingly) the reasons why it failed to establish any significant legacy. Certainly one of the more notable elements of the movement was its limited timeframe. Although McFadden and Hewitt would go on to produce a substantial body of work over the course of their lives, the period of poetic activity in the 1940s was for all of these writers remarkably contained. For instance, after 1948's *The Undying Day*, Greacen would not publish another collection until 1975; McFadden's *The Heart's Townland* of 1947 would

[4] Heather Clark, *The Ulster Renaissance: Poetry in Belfast 1962–1972* (Oxford: Oxford University Press, 2006).

[5] Editorial, *The New Northman* VIII, no. 2 (Summer 1940), 25.

[6] Robert Greacen, *Even Without Irene: An Autobiography* (Belfast: Lagan, 1995), 140.

[7] John Boyd, *The Middle of My Journey* (Belfast: Blackstaff, 1990), 24.

[8] Terence Brown, *Northern Voices: Poets from Ulster* (Dublin: Gill & Macmillan, 1975), 129.

[9] Greacen, *Even Without Irene*, 140–1.

not gain a successor until 1971; and after *No Rebel Word* of 1948, Hewitt would have no further major collection until the 1960s. More remarkably still, Rodgers—whose dramatic success during the 1940s was something of a phenomenon—was effectively finished as a poet after his collection *Europa and the Bull* from 1952. Hewitt and McFadden at least would continue to publish in magazines and journals during this long hiatus, but the cessation of full collections indicates in itself a change in the poetic weather. One persuasive way of understanding this shift is provided by John Wilson Foster, who groups these poets under the label of 'Ulster neo-Romantics', and notes that, as such, they could hardly flourish in an environment soon to be dominated by the vigorously anti-Romantic Movement poets of the 1950s. For this reason, they had to keep 'their heads down for a quarter of a century until the Movement was no longer recognisable as such'.[10] Only when it was safe to re-emerge would they then hesitatingly make a return.

As the 'neo-Romantics' label suggests, these poets were bound together not just by period and geography. The close textual interrelationships that they formed were symptomatic of a particular orientation towards language, experience, and history that at some level was shaped in relation to a nascent idea of Northern Ireland and its political and cultural institutions. In this, their work exhibits something of the condition identified by the critic Robert Farren in 1948 when he observed that 'Partition has now become spiritual in some of those who live in the six counties'.[11] For these poets at least, the internalization implied by the idea of partition as a 'spiritual' condition involved a turning away in disgust from the contingencies of Irish politics and the concomitant articulation of a form of progressive liberalism. Such national issues were, in turn, understood as strictly residual, locked in the past, and of no relevance to a Northern Ireland whose future was perceived, for better or worse, as internationalist. As McFadden's 'In Ireland Now' from 1942 despaired: 'In Ireland now, at autumn, by frugal fires,/We strive to lock the present out with the closed door/And night-slammed windows'.[12] As the poem goes on to observe in a telling manner: 'Mechanised malice has split the sacred veils/Of yesterday's *Sinn Fein*'. In many ways this stance would become a provincial version of the fetishization of the modern found in much English poetry of the 1930s, but it also demanded the repudiation of other, more local, concerns. In an article for *Poetry Ireland* from 1948, Greacen located the regionalism of poetry in the North as both a reaction against the 'more vague and meaningless extremes of the "internationalism" of the "Thirties"' and (I think more significantly) a rejection of 'the Cathleen ni Houlihan tradition or "the mist that does be upon the bog"'.[13] While slightly glib (and certainly

---

[10] John Wilson Foster, *Colonial Consequences: Essays in Irish Literature and Culture* (Dublin: Lilliput, 1991), 79.

[11] Robert Farren, *The Course of Irish Verse in English* (London: Sheed and Ward, 1948), 168. Farren's qualification of this statement is also worth pausing over: 'But all that we mean by Ireland is holding them from absorption into English poetry; and if the grip can be seen in Hewitt it has all but succeeded entirely with Rodgers. A markedly Irish temperament and a love of the Irish country keep him with the covey.'

[12] Roy McFadden, Alex Comfort, and Ian Serraillier, *Three New Poets* (Billericay: Grey Walls Press, 1942), 21–2.

[13] Robert Greacen, 'A Note on Two Ulster Poets', *Poetry Ireland* 2 (July 1948), 12.

potentially antagonistic), this dislike of what he goes on to term 'Gaelic influences' constitutes one of the key ways in which the movement self-identified. In an editorial (probably also by Greacen) for *The Northman* in 1941 this mode of Irish poetry is dismissed as nothing more than 'clique-writing about Cathleen ni Houlihan and Brian Boru',[14] while for McFadden, 'the insistence on the past, on the duty of conforming with the Gaelic mode, is enough to frustrate and weary the most vigorous of us'.[15] In turn, Hewitt noted that Ulster poets 'show no interest in or capacity for utilising the "Irish" mode.... Briefly I can only say that for most of the Ulster poets Irish has never been the folk tongue, that assonance falls strangely upon our ears, that we think Wordsworth a better poet than Mangan.'[16]

As Hewitt's blanket-definition refusal of the 'Irish mode' suggests, there were all kinds of selective suppressions involved in this stance. Indeed as some of Hewitt's later poetry would acknowledge directly, the self-conscious need to modernize the poetic language articulated by this group was in response, whether stated or not, to the exhausted poetics of the Celtic twilight and the constituency it claimed to speak for. Just as the persistent theme of this earlier mode was historical and political grievance, so its suppression in the poets of the 1940s indicates a silence that could also speak of guilt. As McFadden, perhaps the first of these poets along with Rodgers to recognize the limitations of this position, ultimately noted of Partition, 'my generation had been born on one side of that wall and it required a conscious effort to dig through to an "Irish tradition"'.[17] Unlike later Ulster poetry, however, digging would not be one of the distinctive metaphors of this revival. Instead the poems and manifestos proclaim an almost frantic need to keep looking forward, to handle the past only through quotation, and to herald the new in as many ways as possible. In the poetry of Greacen, Hewitt, and Rodgers especially, this desire was made manifest through a notably declarative mode; a form of address that Foster identifies in Rodgers' collection *Awake! And Other Poems* as an 'apocalyptic voice... rebuking, admonitory, euphoric, evangelical',[18] as in his 'Directions to a Rebel':

> Rise from table! rush from hall! O do not
> Acquiesce in their toadying truths, refuse
> To sing their subsidised praises, or borrow
> Their easy loans; these are the open traps
> For apathy: boot and batter them.[19]

One of the more powerful effects of this voice is the manner in which it establishes itself as normative. In other words, its absolute certainty asserts itself as the only possible way

---

[14] Unsigned, 'Editorial: Modern Irish Poetry', *The Northman* X, no. 3 (Autumn 1941), 33.

[15] Roy McFadden and Geoffrey Taylor, 'Poetry in Ireland: A Discussion', *The Bell* 6, no. 4 (1943), 343.

[16] John Hewitt, 'Poetry and Ulster: A Survey', *Poetry Ireland*, no. 8 (January 1950), 7.

[17] Sarah Ferris, '"One who stayed": An Interview with Roy McFadden', *Irish Studies Review*, no. 17 (Winter 1996/7), 22.

[18] John Wilson Foster, '"The Dissidence of Dissent": John Hewitt and W. R. Rodgers', *Colonial Consequences*, 125.

[19] W. R. Rodgers, *Awake! and Other Poems* (London: Secker & Warburg, 1941), 48.

of addressing a particular topic. Indeed, it is worth noting that one of the most profound ways in which the generation of Northern poets that emerged in the late 1960s would differ from the poets of the 1940s was in their problematizing of this mode of declaration.

The movement, then, set its face to the future, rejected the past, and frequently expressed a desire to break with what was understood as a tradition of artistic mediocrity in the North. Indeed just as the rhetorical momentum of many revivals is reliant on an identification of a preceding period of general malaise, a landscape of underachievement against which the pyrotechnics of the new movement can be contrasted, so this Revival too had to clear a space for itself. In 1941 Rodgers famously described Belfast as 'a backwater of literature out of sight of the running stream of contemporary verse',[20] while for Hewitt in 1944, it was no less than a 'Sahara of the arts'.[21] Greacen was more forthright again:

> Since the generation of Joseph Campbell and AE, until the late thirties, there was an almost complete blank in poetic utterance and in drama. No middle generation of quality had arisen to whom the younger writer could look for guidance, not to speak of inspiration. This indeed was perhaps to a certain extent advantageous, as elsewhere the slightly older generation acts frequently as a brake on new talent.[22]

Greacen overstates his case, but certainly the need for renewal was in the air, and the weight of inherited tradition could be disabling. Consider, for instance, the manner in which the Belfast-born poet Maurice J. Craig's early poem 'Black Swans', from the start of the decade, labours under a Yeatsean influence so profound that it borders on parody:

> As we, for a foretaste,
> Watch, sleeping in its savage bed
> Some lithe, destructive beast
> That having travelled far, has fed.[23]

Perhaps the most obvious means of contesting this kind of recycling was to invest in the idea of a more distinctively local mode, and it is for this reason that the ideological engine of the Belfast revival became a commitment to regionalism. It is beyond the scope of this essay to discuss in detail the extent of the regionalist movement in Ulster during this period, but it is worth considering briefly why as a body of ideas it proved attractive. As Tom Clyde notes in a perceptive essay, regionalism emerged because of a 'complex web of international, national, regional, and personal factors', the most important of which was the onset of the Second World War and the manner in which

---

[20] Rodgers, *Awake! and Other Poems*, n.p.

[21] Roy McFadden, 'No Dusty Pioneer: A Personal Recollection of John Hewitt', in *The Poet's Place: Ulster Literature and Society: Essays in Honour of John Hewitt, 1907–1987*, ed. Gerald Dawe and John Wilson Foster (Belfast: Institute of Irish Studies, 1991), 171.

[22] Brown, *Northern Voices*, 128.

[23] Maurice J. Craig, *Black Swans* (Dublin: Gayfield, 1941), n.p.

this event isolated Northern Ireland from the rest of the island.[24] Concomitantly, the influx of foreign—mostly American—troops into the Province led to a greater awareness of a distinct cultural and regional identity, a perception reinforced by the government's establishment of the Council for the Encouragement of Music and the Arts (CEMA) in 1943. Alongside this, and crucial to Clyde's argument, is a perception that the war had cast into stark relief both the inherent problems of nationalism as a foundational element of identity and the dangers of an over-centralized state. That regionalism might offer some answer to such anxieties, while also speaking to the seemingly intractable terms of Northern Ireland's partitioned and sectarian public realm, made it a potentially alluring system of ideas. Other factors were less profound but equally significant. Clyde notes that the government's request to the Orange Order to tone down the triumphalism of their annual celebrations may have led to an illusory sense that some of the old hatreds were lessening, while the considerable poetic success of Louis MacNeice and (especially) Rodgers in Britain allowed for the identification of what appeared to be a distinctly Ulster literary sensibility. That said, it is still important to recognize that most historians and critics of regionalism in Northern Ireland during this time agree that its meaning and effect was elided, ambiguous, and discontinuous. Indeed, ultimately regionalism was a phenomenon located almost entirely within the realm of culture and its superstructural institutions, and was rarely found elsewhere. Clyde's assertion that, after all, 'not a single local politician embraced the Regionalist cause', is telling.[25]

Poetic regionalism, however, was a different, and perhaps more plausible, project. Heather Clark has usefully identified the typical content of such poetry in the North as 'place names, idiomatic speech, rural or working-class dictions, and translations from Irish legends'.[26] The poets of the 1940s certainly made much use of such topics, but it was perhaps in their attitude towards this material that the regionalist agenda was most clearly identifiable. Alongside the turn to the local, the particular, and the ideal of a lived tradition, poetic regionalism involved a quite distinctive orientation towards the past, a questioning of ethno-sectarian myths of communal history, and the creation of new languages in a deliberately self-conscious manner. As this suggests, the vitality of such a belief system was willed into existence through seemingly endless statements of definition, credo, and principle. As such, the theoretical superstructure of regionalism could not be separated from the poems it justified, and indeed sometimes the two modes would merge. When in 1948 Greacen noted that 'for an excellent statement of the regional position as it affects the Six County writer the reader should refer to Hewitt's *Overture for Ulster Regionalism*', it is easy to mistake the fact that he is referring to a poem.[27] Similarly one might note the dogmatism of

---

[24] Tom Clyde, 'A Stirring in the Dry Bones: John Hewitt's Regionalism', *The Poet's Place*, ed. Dawe and Foster, 250.

[25] Clyde, 'A Stirring in the Dry Bones', 257.

[26] Clark, *The Ulster Renaissance*, 114.

[27] Robert Greacen, 'A Note on Two Ulster Poets', 12.

McFadden's regionalist collection *The Heart's Townland* from 1947 with its overly confident command to 'go and find the tartan of your clan./Then all your rhymes will ring, your metres span.'[28]

Perhaps the key early event in the creation of these revival energies was Greacen's assumption from 1940 of the editorship of the Queen's University magazine, *The Northman* (temporarily renamed *The New Northman* during this period), with his 'true and resourceful ally' Gallen.[29] With a desire to make the magazine 'into a journal of reasonable literary quality',[30] Greacen steered it away from what he condemned in his opening editorial as its previous 'odd assortment of highbrowism, pedantry, and pseudo-classicism'[31] and towards the publication of both local and national creative writers. The boldness of the strategy was obvious and its major achievement was, in Brown's words, 'to hold power for just long enough for the assumptions and practice of the English New Apocalypse poets to receive an airing in wartime Belfast'.[32] That said, the hijacking of the magazine for literature was, perhaps, a mixed blessing. Before the editorship of Greacen and Gallen, *The Northman* had been a reasonably lively, politically engaged journal that considered itself, with some justification, to be 'practically the only independent publication in Northern Ireland'.[33] Alongside articles on contemporary politics and the threat to Northern Ireland posed by the imminent global conflict, it published such unlikely features as a series of essays on the United Irishmen. In this context, and particularly in light of the Second World War, the editors' 'strangely non-committal political attitude'[34] was unfortunate, and was exacerbated by the manner in which their turn towards the literary involved the over-promotion of their own work (alongside that of McFadden's). Certainly it is possible to have some sympathy with the views of the playwright St John Ervine, who, in the Spring 1941 issue, criticized this change in direction, lamented *The Northman*'s turn away from politics, and accused the editors of publishing 'feeble imitations of sour and disgruntled "modern" poems' and stories 'which seem to have been written by persons who were begotten and born in underground urinals'.[35]

After a couple of years the two poets were, in Greacen's words, 'ousted from the editorship'[36] and *The Northman* reverted to something close to what it had been before their stewardship. Their tenure had been controversial, but it was also clear that the magazine would always have a very limited reach. The struggle for quality submissions was unceasing, and at one point, only six students held subscriptions to the magazine out of a student body of 2,500. It was clear that any poetic revival in Belfast during this time would have to emerge without the nourishment of the city's major educational institution, a

---

[28] Roy McFadden, 'Directions for a Journey', *The Heart's Townland* (London: Routledge, 1947), 34.
[29] Robert Greacen, 'John Gallen: An Appreciation', *The Northman* XV, no. 3 (Summer 1947), 14.
[30] Greacen, *Even Without Irene*, 141.
[31] Editorial, *The New Northman* VIII, no. 3 (Winter 1940–1), 44.
[32] Brown, *Northern Voices*, 129.
[33] Unsigned, 'Prognostication', *The New Northman* VII, no. 3 (Autumn 1939), 88.
[34] Greacen, *Even Without Irene*, 141.
[35] St John Ervine, letter, *The New Northman* IX, no. 1 (Spring 1941), 7.
[36] Greacen, *Even Without Irene*, 141.

point emphasized by John Hewitt in his important essay 'The Bitter Gourd: Some Problems of the Ulster Writer' in 1945.[37] Despite this indifference, Greacen would frequently mythologize his period as editor. It was a time, he insisted, when the 'Ulster renascence' was proclaimed with a 'deep sincerity'. As he observed, 'we had done with the sham writing and slavish imitation of third-rate minor work that for too long had posed as characteristically *Ulster*. In the midst of the holocaust, some of us saw, if for an instant only, the vision splendid.'[38] In 1950 Hewitt was to advance a similar perspective, observing that a diet of 'the fine rice of the Apocalyptics rather than the coarse barley of the Ards' had 'turned the university magazine from being a compendium of club reports into a coterie journal, lively, experimental, provocative, utterly irrelevant.'[39]

The pamphlet *Poems from Ulster*, edited by Greacen in 1942, is typical of the early energy and idealism of this group. Bearing a dramatic image by Leslie Owen Baxter of a bird rising over the dome of Belfast City Hall with a looming red hand in the background, its cover spoke of a poetry renaissance which was both rooted in Northern Ireland while seeking to be transcendent of it. The poets anthologized were recognizably of *The Northman* coterie and included Craig, Gallen, McFadden, and Alex Comfort, while Greacen's introduction set out to clear a space for the new poetry in terms that deliberately invited controversy. As he proclaimed, with the onset of the war:

> a sea of silence swamped the vociferous *litterati* who had told us so often of their devotion to the extreme Left. The minor of these poets took either to alcohol or to academic philosophy: the elder writers, who still clung to star-and-daisy verse, began a we-told-you-so whispering campaign, and sat tight, waiting for young men, like those presented in this anthology, to begin the reaction.[40]

In these terms the young poets were inheritors of a 'legacy of lies, shams, deceptions, compromise and half-truths', caught up in and forced to respond to 'the holocaust of brutality and murder and destruction that has soaked into the core of what is regarded as our civilisation.'[41]

Predictably perhaps, Ervine again rose to Greacen's bait and responded furiously to *Poems from Ulster*. In a letter to Greacen that was published in *The Northman* he accused the poets of 'wilful obscurity', an inability to punctuate ('You are worse, in this respect, than women novelists, and, God knows, they're pretty awful'), and asserted that the preface was merely 'trotting out that stale stuff about the world the selfish unimaginative old men have bequeathed to young men'. He saved his most venomous attack for McFadden's contribution:

> I notice that Mr. McFadden is terribly upset about Belgium's starving children. Why Belgium's particularly? Was he upset enough to get out of his leather chair? Forgive

---

[37] John Hewitt, *Ancestral Voices: The Selected Prose of John Hewitt* (Belfast: Blackstaff, 1987), 117–18.
[38] Robert Greacen, 'Yesterday and To-morrow', *The Northman* XIV, centenary edition (Winter 1945), 28.
[39] John Hewitt, 'Poetry and Ulster: A Survey', 6.
[40] Robert Greacen, ed., *Poems from Ulster* (Belfast: Erskine Mayne, 1942), 3.
[41] Ibid.

me if I seem impatient with people who are so busy telling others what to do, that they have no time to do anything themselves. I'm distrustful of heart-bleeders. I've noticed that people with hot heads often have cold feet.[42]

The object of this vitriol, McFadden's 'Poem', illustrates well some of the ambivalence and hesitancy implicit to *The Northman* coterie's attitude to the war. It opens:

> Sitting futile in a room,
> While Belgium's starving children,
> Pouch-eyed, brow-puckered, humourless,
> Shrivel into premature age,
> My head is heavy with my sins and the sins of my brothers.
>
> The square white table and the painted china,
> The yawning ten o'clock fire and the grumbling clock,
> Blend into a bleeding dagger of accusation
> That pricks my heart and my head with a hundred wounds.[43]

Perhaps because of its unpromising beginning the poem cannot develop beyond the contemplation of its own helplessness, its pity forever bleeding into self-pity. Indeed such is its despair that even a turn towards an ironic understanding of its own complacencies—a technique that would be frequently utilized by Derek Mahon later in the century—is an impossibility. Instead, trapped in the circularity of his own declarative impotence, the poet finds himself 'pinioned between fat arms of a leather chair' unable to do anything more than fetishize his own futility. Ervine's disdain was intemperate but understandable.

Greacen, at least, was encouraged by the experience of *Poems from Ulster*, and in 1944 was to publish another selection by himself, Bruce Williamson, and Valentin Iremonger called, with a polemicist's eye, *On the Barricades*. Described in *Even Without Irene* as 'a selection of our most militant poems',[44] *On the Barricades* was as controversial as its title promised, declaring itself as 'proof of a new vitality in Irish writing, a vitality the older generations will not acknowledge. Here [the authors] raise, and defend, their first barricades against the low standards, facile half-truths and lack of integrity that have for too long rotted the Anglo-Irish spirit'.[45] The initially mystifying terms of this denunciation make more sense in the context of Greacen's recent relocation to Dublin, and might bear the imprint of Michael McLaverty's warning to the young poet that the city was a 'trap for the writer who would squander his energies and ideas in tavern talk'.[46] Either way the message managed to be both declaratory and yet muddled. Typical of this, and the most notable poem in the pamphlet, was Greacen's 'Dialogue in the Storm', in which an artist figure engages in dialogue with a hostile crowd who doubt both his vocation and

---

[42] St John Ervine, 'St John Ervine on *Poems from Ulster*', *The Northman* XI, no. 1 (Winter 1941–2), 2.

[43] Quoted in *Poems from Ulster*, ed. Greacen, 19.

[44] Greacen, *Even Without Irene*, 152.

[45] Robert Greacen, Bruce Williamson, and Valentin Iremonger, eds., *On the Barricades* (Dublin: New Frontiers Press, 1944), n.p.

[46] Greacen, *Even Without Irene*, 143.

purpose. Eventually the Artist wins them over to the extent that the 'Chorus from the Crowd' declare:

> We are many, they are few,
> Our hearts beat strong
> And we'll try to do
> What's good for each.
> We are many, they are few,
> We'll win the day,
> When we're sure of what we do.

To which the Artist responds:

> *Yes, comrades, now you're speaking true*
> You'll win when you're sure of the things you do.
> And the earth shall move in your hand,
> *And the earth shall lie in your palm.*[47]

It is fair to note that Greacen was only twenty-four when he wrote 'Dialogue in the Storm', but nevertheless its indebtedness to what were already the worst clichés of the overtly 'committed' poetry of the 1930s suggest its obsolescence was inbuilt. In 1950 Hewitt observed that Greacen was 'always in a hurry, scarcely taking the time to let the mood crystallise, or to work over his verses'. As a result, the poems 'do not as yet cohere, do not add up, as it were'.[48] Hewitt's judgement was strict but ultimately not unfair.

Another important factor in the poetic revival of this time was the influence of the group who would gather in Campbell's Coffee House opposite City Hall on Donegal Square West during the late 1930s and through the 1940s, a coterie of liberal thinkers which included Greacen, McFadden, Morton, and Hewitt. Decorated with murals painted by the local illustrator and cartoonist Rowell Friers,[49] the top floor of Campbell's presented a bohemian aspect and was, in Greacen's words, 'an island of tolerance in our bitterly divided community'.[50] Certainly Campbell's range of talents was diverse and came from the realms of artists and writers, institutional life, and the public realm. According to Boyd, Denis Ireland (essayist and general wit), William Conor (painter), and Richard Rowley (poet and publisher) 'ruled the roost',[51] while figures such as Joe Tomelty (playwright and actor), Sam Hanna Bell, F. L. Green (novelist and author of *Odd Man Out*, a thriller that features a memorable caricature of John Hewitt),[52] and Jimmy Vitty (librarian at the Linenhall Library) were also frequent attendees. McFadden records that MacNeice was also a visitor, though this can only have been sporadically.[53]

---

[47] Quoted in *On the Barricades*, ed. Greacen et al., 7–12. Reprinted in Greacen's *The Undying Day* (London: Falcon Press, 1948), 48–54.

[48] Hewitt, 'Poetry and Ulster: A Survey', 8.

[49] Rowel Friers, *Drawn From Life: An Autobiography* (Belfast: Blackstaff, 1994), 135.

[50] Greacen, *Even Without Irene*, 146.

[51] Boyd, *The Middle of My Journey*, 23.

[52] See Sarah Ferris's *Poet John Hewitt, 1907–1987 and Criticism of Northern Irish Protestant Writing* (Lampeter: Edwin Mellon Press, 2002), 123–30, for a very full discussion of this representation.

[53] Roy McFadden, *Collected Poems: 1943–1995* (Belfast: Lagan, 1996), 339.

Critical opinions about the importance of Campbell's differ. While for Patricia Craig the café maintained a 'decent standard of liberalism'[54] in a city often portrayed as inimical to such values, Sarah Ferris has dismissed its conversation as 'desultory'.[55] Significantly perhaps, the views of those who attended are more uniform. Alongside Greacen's idealized 'island of tolerance', Friers (the possessor of a 'caustic' tongue according to McFadden)[56] remembers the café as a 'meeting place worthy of Dr Johnson',[57] while, less hyperbolically, the journalist James Kelly recalls the conversation as 'lively, sometimes ribald, covering the theatre, the arts, politics and newspapers'.[58] Boyd notes a general sympathy towards Marxism and the Left Book Club as part of its character,[59] while Greacen states that the conversation was 'crisp, wryly humorous in the throwaway Northern fashion. It tends towards practicality rather than abstraction'.[60] Either way, the liberalism of the top floor did not extend throughout the café. The ground floor, as Kelly remembers, was the domain of the extreme Protestant loyalist Norman Porter and his friend at the time, a young Ian Paisley.[61] In this way the stratification of Campbell's represented in microcosm the stratification of Ulster politics.

Some of the atmosphere of Campbell's is recreated in McFadden's poem 'Coffee at Crumble's' from 1979, which presents the 'coffee-culture, biscuit chat' of 'Derek Walsh' (Ireland), 'Dan Armour' (Jack Louden), and 'Maynard Chatterton' (Rowley).[62] Lost 'in soft and settled self-esteem' as they rehearse their familiar anecdotes, McFadden's vision of Campbell's recognizes its bohemian aspect but also its complacency and terminal provincialism. As such it is a location that is inimical to art, and the young poet who finds himself there is advised to 'prepare your exit to the street'. That said, and despite McFadden's retrospective dismissal, Campbell's certainly allowed younger Ulster writers to connect with an earlier generation of local artists, and this was important in a province prone to cultural amnesia. Perhaps in this way Campbell's real significance lay not in what it was, but rather what it was not—an enclave from the perceived bigotry that was seen to typify so much of life elsewhere in the city.

Ultimately the Campbell's group would relocate to the Chalet d'Or in Fountain Lane where the remnants of the coterie would continue to gather through the 1950s and 1960s. Indeed Friers recalls seeing Hewitt there in 1987, 'his eyes drooped as if he were dozing', and thinking him 'the last of that coffee set which was born round the corner in Campbell's'.[63] Perhaps the most enduring memorial to the group is Greacen's *Northern*

---

[54] Patricia Craig, 'The Liberal Imagination in Northern Irish Prose', in *Returning to Ourselves: Second Volume of Papers from the John Hewitt International Summer School*, ed. Eve Patten (Belfast: Lagan, 1995), 142.

[55] Ferris, *Poet John Hewitt, 1907–1987*, 20.

[56] McFadden, 'No Dusty Pioneer', 172.

[57] Friers, *Drawn From Life*, 123.

[58] James Kelly, *Bonfires on the Hillside: An Eyewitness Account of Political Upheaval in Northern Ireland* (Belfast: Fountain Publishing, 1995), 149.

[59] Boyd, *The Middle of My Journey*, 23.

[60] Greacen, *Even Without Irene*, 146.

[61] Kelly, *Bonfires on the Hillside*, 151.

[62] McFadden, *Collected Poems*, 132–5.

[63] Friers, *Drawn From Life*, 141.

Harvest: An Anthology of Ulster Writing from 1944, a collection which found room for most of its talents including Ireland, Harry Morrow, Hewitt, Boyd and Rowley. As with much of his polemicizing during this period, Greacen's introduction placed what he termed 'the new awakening in Ulster Writing' in the context of the onset of war and noted the 'widespread interest which that renascence has aroused'. Perhaps for this reason the collection can be read as an expression of cultural unionism both in its contrast of the distinctly reserved characteristics of the 'Northern Irish' with the 'exuberant, colourful and, above all, voluble make-up of our fellow-Irishmen South and West of the Border', and its desire to 'win a sympathetic audience in Great Britain'.[64]

Campbell's and the office of the *Northman* at Queen's were not the only meeting places for writers in Belfast during this time. Greacen notes the importance of regular meetings at the flat of Sam Hannah Bell and Bob Davidson on Saturday afternoons, while Friers recalls frequent gatherings at Hewitt's flat, 18 Mount Charles, a less ribald group than at Campbell's and one that included such figures as the painters Alicia Boyle, John Luke, and Colin Middleton.[65] At these events, according to McFadden, 'Jungian allusions pervaded the room like the persistent aroma of herbal tobacco'.[66] Alongside these, *Lagan*, the literary journal founded by John Boyd and Bob Davison in 1943, played an important role in publishing local writers under the rubric of what it termed in its first editorial 'an Ulster literary tradition', although its brevity (according to Hewitt it 'struck rough water and sank' in 1946)[67] and limited market (the final issue only sold 500 copies) suggests that if there was an Ulster poetic renaissance it was one of writing not reading. It was through these outlets that the process of coterie formation took place, and the value of this was immense for writers who had been previously isolated. As Clyde has noted, Hewitt as a poet felt himself almost totally alone for nearly fifteen years until he met the young McFadden, and it is clear that the importance of establishing a creative community was one he felt keenly: 'serious workers in any craft have the responsibility of solidarity', he wrote in a letter to McFadden in 1943.[68] Hewitt and 'the other poet', as Hewitt called McFadden, certainly had things in common, although their differences were also significant.[69] McFadden has noted that they were both 'of the Left', 'shared a preference for decentralised Government', and 'had a feeling for place and tradition'. On the other hand, he has been careful to record that Hewitt did not share his 'belligerently anti-militarist' views, and contrasts Hewitt's Ulster regionalism with his own youthful 'romantic Irishness'.[70] According to McFadden, Hewitt wanted him to be a 'lieutenant in an Ulster Regionalist Crusade', and was disappointed by his reluctance fully to assume such a role.[71]

---

[64] Robert Greacen, ed., *Northern Harvest: An Anthology of Ulster Writing* (Belfast: Derek MacCord, 1944), n.p.

[65] Greacen, *Even Without Irene*, 143.

[66] McFadden, 'No Dusty Pioneer', 175.

[67] Hewitt, 'Poetry and Ulster: A Survey', 6.

[68] McFadden, 'No Dusty Pioneer', 171.

[69] Clyde, 'A Stirring in the Dry Bones', 253.

[70] McFadden, 'No Dusty Pioneer', 169.

[71] Ibid., 176.

Perhaps the ultimate coterie poem of this period is Hewitt's 'Roll Call'. Written in 1942 and published in *Lagan*, it was originally meant to be part of the *Freehold* sequence but was subsequently omitted, and eventually reappeared in Frank Ormsby's magisterial 1991 *Collected Poems of John Hewitt*. 'Roll Call', in Hewitt's words, lists 'those Ulstermen I considered representative of the best values of my Region',[72] and included, among others, descriptions of Middleton, Luke, McLaverty, and the regional geographer Estyn Evans. Of the poets, perhaps the most interesting portrait is that of Rodgers:

> that still man I have praised, whose hanging pipe
> and tweedy gestures cover up the press
> and hurtling force of his bold images
> that crash his words together till they break
> with harsh new light that strikes us wide awake;
> I owe his thought much thanks but not his style.[73]

In itself the inclusion of Rodgers is significant if only because, according to Foster, Rodgers' 'self-advertising Irishness dismayed Greacen and the Ulster poets, even though they too were wartime neo-Romantics'.[74] That Hewitt includes him as one of his 'comrades' in the poem indicates, then, a certain desire for inclusivity, although the crushing qualification of 'I owe his thought much thanks but not his style' also indicates that this had strict limits. According to McFadden, Hewitt was jealous of the success of Rodgers' breakthrough collection *Awake!* in 1941, but 'he had overcome his resentment with the realisation that he had his own style, whatever the fashion of the day preferred'.[75]

The next poet summoned by Hewitt's poem, a young McFadden, is less problematic, and is described as 'the grave lad with the disconcerting smile/the countrytown solicitor whose verse touches new riches'. 'We marvel one so young can be so wise', Hewitt goes on to observe with a touch of condescension. In a similar manner Morton is then dismissed as 'that fine woman with the gentle skill/for roses, words and friendship most of all'. Hewitt's mention is brief but nevertheless important because it indicates something of the extent to which Morton has since been overlooked as part of the Ulster poetry movement during this time. Originally from Limerick, Morton was secretary, and later chairperson, of the Belfast branch of PEN, a friend of the Hewitts and McFadden, and a frequenter of Campbell's. Her first collection *Dawn and Afterglow* was dominated by an erotically charged delight in the Ulster countryside which, as in 'Mountain Mist', could reach moments of ecstatic contemplation:

> Maiden of the mountain mist,
> Stooping boldly to be kissed
> When the young and ardent sun
> First pursues you – half in fun,

---

[72] John Hewitt, *The Collected Poems of John Hewitt*, ed. Frank Ormsby (Belfast: Blackstaff, 1991), 657.
[73] Ibid., 486–9.
[74] Foster, *Colonial Consequences*, 64.
[75] McFadden, 'No Dusty Pioneer', 177.

> Wherefore snatch your robe of grey
> From his grasp, and haste away
> When his passion's hot desire
> Follows you with lips of fire?[76]

Morton's later *Masque in Maytime* from 1948 was a more ambitious affair again. An attempt, according to the jacket blurb, to 'capture the colour and rhythm, the accompanying music and the underlying theme of a natural ballet produced on an Ulster landscape by the caprice of the Ulster climate', the poem describes a May dawn in a fever of sexual imagery ('Faster, faster grows the measure,/Life is rhythm and love is pleasure') that culminates in a climax of fervour:

> Held in an ecstasy of golden dream
> the trees, enchanted, stand. The amorous sun,
> long fingers warm as quivering heart-strings stretched
> from out life's burning core, now claims the morn
> with benediction that is part embrace.[77]

This climax is followed by the brutality of a storm which threatens to destroy the trees and plants: 'Bride-plant, dishevelled in her pain,/Is beaten to the earth again!'[78] J. N. Browne has described Morton's poetry as typified by 'a buoyancy',[79] and in its overt eroticism and oversprung rhythms it seems to derive from the same wellspring of feeling from which Rodgers' nature poetry would also draw. If nothing else, the comparison demonstrates how Rodgers' work was less *sui generis* than it can now sometimes appear.

By the time that the poetic movement in the North was becoming recognized, it was actually losing momentum. Greacen had left for Dublin in 1943 without completing his degree at Queen's, *Lagan* closed in 1946, and McFadden's *The Heart's Townland* of 1947 was both the climax of his engagement with a Hewitt-inspired regionalism and his final collection for a generation. This is not to suggest that there was not continuing poetic activity in Belfast through the late 1940s, but rather to note that it was activity that was increasingly wary of attaching itself to a movement, let alone a revival. Indeed even as early as 1945 Hewitt was 'declaring against the word "renascence"' in 'The Bitter Gourd'.[80] In 1948 McFadden and Barbara Hunter initiated *Rann*—'A Quarterly of Ulster Poetry' as its subtitle defined itself. The journal ran for twenty issues and had its successes, although the decision in only the second issue to change its subtitle to 'an Ulster Quarterly of Poetry 'was a small but indicative alteration.'[81] McFadden eventually abandoned *Rann* after five years because of 'tiredness, not need of cash or an increased circulation.'[82]

---

[76] May Morton, *Dawn and Afterglow* (Belfast: Quota Press, 1936), 27.

[77] May Morton, *Masque in Maytime* (Lisburn: Lisnagarvey Press, 1948), 9.

[78] Morton, *Masque in Maytime*, 11.

[79] Sam Hanna Bell, et al., eds., *The Arts in Ulster: A Symposium* (London: George G. Harrap, 1951), 148.

[80] Hewitt, 'The Bitter Gourd', 108.

[81] For more on the shifting fortunes of *Rann* see Frank Shovlin's *The Irish Literary Periodical, 1923–1958* (Oxford: Oxford University Press, 2004).

[82] McFadden, 'No Dusty Pioneer', 174.

Another important marker of changing times was Hewitt's essay 'Poetry and Ulster: A Survey', published in *Poetry Ireland* in 1950. Prompted by the publication of a number of anthologies of Irish poetry that contained significant proportions of work by Ulster poets, the article was both a celebration of the achievements of Northern poets through the 1940s and a valediction for a period that was passing. Significantly, despite the creative communion he had felt with McFadden and others, the essay returned Hewitt again to his theme of creative isolation, his belief that the Ulster poet 'is of necessity a lonely figure'. For this reason, as the essay asserts, there is 'no such thing as Ulster Poetry.... We simply have poets of Ulster Birth.'[83] It was almost as if Hewitt's critical unconscious was anticipating the creatively barren poetic period of the 1950s, a time that Greacen would describe as a poetic 'wilderness'.[84]

Looking back at the poetic activity of the 1940s from the perspective of 1999, Greacen observed:

> I am not sure that this did amount to a renaissance, although at the time I would have wanted it to be and I probably thought that it was. Possibly that was wishful thinking. We should have shared concerns about living in a divided community and exploring [sic] how this could be resolved in terms of decent human relationships.[85]

The simplicity of this statement is compelling, and despite the achievements of the time, it is ultimately hard to argue against its appraisal. It is not that the Belfast poets of the 1940s failed to identify the problems of aesthetics, culture, and politics that poetry in the North had to face during this period. Indeed the need for creative renewal was often powerfully felt and articulated. Unfortunately, however, it is in their ultimate failure to refashion these antinomies that their interest now resides. In a review of McFadden's early collection *Flowers for a Lady* from 1945, Grizel Christie remarked presciently: 'Mr McFadden is undoubtedly a poet with something to say, but as one reads through this volume one is tempted to ask whether there is any necessity to say it so often and in such similar terms.'[86] Christie's dismissal might stand as the epitaph for the movement as a whole. Indeed, it would not be until the arrival of the generation of Northern poets that followed in the 1960s that the contradictions of identity that Greacen, McFadden, and Hewitt identified could be resolved through a poetry that was less dogmatic, less sure of where it stood and what side it was on. To express this differently, it was a matter of letting back into the poetry something that these writers had suppressed: the matter of Ireland.

[83] Hewitt, 'Poetry and Ulster: A Survey', 5.
[84] John Brown, *In the Chair: Interview with Poets from the North of Ireland* (Cliffs of Moher: Salmon Press, 2002), 10.
[85] Ibid., 6.
[86] Grizel Christie, Reviews, *The Northman* XIV, 1 (Autumn 1945), 28.

CHAPTER 14

DISTURBING IRISH POETRY: KINSELLA AND CLARKE, 1951–1962

JOHN McAULIFFE

I

The 1950s were a transitional period for Irish poets and publishers. Existing journals and publishers went out of business early in the decade. When Thomas Kinsella reflected in 'The Irish Writer' (1966) on his sense of a writer's isolation, he referred to his contemporaries, with a characteristic mix of objectivity and humour, as 'a scattering of incoherent lives. It will seem on a bad day that there are a few madmen and hermits, and nothing more. I can learn nothing from them except that I am isolated.'[1] How accurate is Kinsella's sense of the Irish 1950s, a time which proved a template for his existential and Darwinian sense of a writing life? Irish poets were generally published in England: Louis MacNeice and Donagh MacDonagh published with Faber, which had also published Robert Greacen and Valentin Iremonger's anthology of modern Irish poetry in 1949. Patrick Kavanagh was variously published in London by Macmillan, Longman, and, later, O'Brian and O'Keefe, but during the 1950s his sole book publication was printed on his brother Peter's hand press. Austin Clarke had begun his career by publishing with Maunsel in Dublin in 1917 and his 1936 *Collected Poems* had been published by Allen and Unwin in London and Macmillan in New York. But by 1950 he was publishing small editions of his one-act plays at his home, a venture he named the Bridge Press. In 1951 the journals *Envoy* and *Poetry Ireland* had ceased publication; in 1952 Kavanagh and his brother would launch *Kavanagh's Weekly*, which lasted thirteen issues; *The Bell* rarely published poems in the years before it closed in 1954. The peculiarly private and

---

[1] Thomas Kinsella, 'The Irish Writer' (1966), in *Davis, Mangan, Ferguson? Tradition and the Irish Writer*, ed. W. B. Yeats and Thomas Kinsella (Dublin: Dolmen, 1970), 57.

unworldly situation of Irish poetry publication would change in the Lemass years, but the transition generated formative and disturbing work. In particular, the defining narrative of twentieth-century Irish poetry, the coordination and sometimes explosive rebalancing of past and present, is reimagined by Clarke and Kinsella in different ways that owe much to their experience of writing and publishing poems at a time when Irish culture can be characterised as insular and impoverished, and when—for poets—the complexity of Yeats's legacy and example became more apparent.

II

Why had Irish poetry become so inconspicuous and private an enterprise in the Republic? Primarily, Ireland's post-war condition was not conducive to new initiatives. After the short-lived influx of Marshall Plan aid, the devaluation of sterling and then the punt, in 1949, intensified already existing isolationist tendencies in the new state. Brian Girvin argues that 'at the end of the second world war, Eire entered an isolationist phase from which it did not emerge until the 1960s at the earliest.... This insularity closed Ireland off from developments in the outside world and affected virtually every aspect of the society, including culture, economic policy and diplomacy.'[2] Kinsella remembers another defining feature of that decade: 'My contemporaries—only recently left school—leaving the country, emigration the only apparent opportunity.'[3] Economic hardship calcified the already narrow cultural sphere. Girvin and, before him, Donal O Drisceoil have analysed how the Irish state used censorship during and after the Second World War. O Drisceoil notes the particular case of Frank O'Connor, and how the state pursued him, not only banning his fiction and poetry but effectively barring him from freelance work at RTE after he published his 1942 *Horizon* essay, 'The Future of Irish Literature'.[4] Censorship would continue to act as an informing context for older and new writers throughout the 1950s and 1960s. Girvin notes how this situation worsened in the 1950s due to 'the composition of the Censorship Board (which was dominated by the Knights of Columbanus) [and] the campaign against evil literature initiated by Archbishop McQuaid, [a Knight himself, as was the Chair of the Censorship Board, William Magennis] and driven by the Knights', which typified 'an embattled state fearful of Church intervention and ready to meet its concerns'.[5] Girvin reports one concrete effect of this consolidation of cultural power: 'Between 1950 and 1954, the Censorship Board banned twice as many books as were censored between 1930 and 1945.'[6]

---

[2] Brian Girvin, 'Church, State and the Moral Community', in *The Lemass Era: Politics and Society in the Ireland of Sean Lemass*, ed. Brian Girvin and Gary Murphy (Dublin: UCD Press 2005), 125.

[3] Thomas Kinsella, 'The Dolmen Press', in *The Dolmen Press*, ed. Maurice Harmon (Dublin: Lilliput, 2001), 138.

[4] Donal O Drisceoil, *Censorship in Ireland 1939–1945: Neutrality, Politics and Society* (Cork: Cork University Press, 1996). 212.

[5] Girvin, 'Church, State and the Moral Community', 140.

[6] Ibid., 134.

By the 1950s, then, commercial publishers, popular journals, and distributors drew the attention of the Censorship Board. Liam Miller's return to Dublin in 1951 transformed that situation for Irish poetry. Trained as an architect in London in the 1940s, Miller had witnessed and been impressed by a literary ecosystem where small presses coexisted and competed with more established presses. In 1951, on his return, contemporary poetry and its associated public outlets seemed hardly to exist,[7] and Miller saw the foundation and continuation of the Dolmen Press not in business terms, but as part of his enthusiasm for the literary world and for printing as an art in itself.[8] Working initially with an Adana flatbed press with Caslon type, Miller published a ballad poem by Sigerson Clifford, *Travelling Tinkers*. Clifford's sequence is derived from the itinerary poems of Austin Clarke's first mature book, *The Cattle Drive in Connaught* (1926), although it inflects Clarke's democratic vistas with a more predictable and tragic opposition between a pure past and a corrupt contemporary moment. The book sold out after he launched it, with a sure sense of his market, at Puck Fair in Killorglin; Miller followed it with another success—a booklet of Christmas carols. In 1952 Miller was loaned a larger press and a font of Bodoni type by Cecil and Blanaid Salkeld, with which he published the first work of Thomas Kinsella, the poet with whom his press would come to be most strongly identified.

That publication, of a single subsequently uncollected poem titled 'The Starlit Eye', is significantly different in quality and content.[9] Initially, the poem's most striking aspect is its subject matter, a sexual encounter on a recognizably modern beach, composed in confident rhyming lines which do not engage with the prevailing modes of Irish poetry. Its phrasing already seems definitive and would soon be seen as typical: 'The breathing sea in Dublin Bay', 'The girl's patient, cool content', 'Night grows around our satisfaction.' The poem's small-press context is surely what enabled the more daring lines which follow:

> I quickly put the question whether
> blood should be put down on the bright
> and starlit eye be closed up tight
> before the judicial blink of a ship

Kinsella used the small press to publish poems, under the radar of official cyclopean cultural attitudes to art, which describe love and sexuality in a recognizably modern Dublin setting. Encouraged by the lack of official attention, Dolmen next published David Marcus's version of Brian Merriman's bawdy *The Midnight Court*, mindful that Frank O'Connor's earlier version had been banned. Miller also worked to consolidate the press by commissioning translations of medieval Irish poems by Kinsella, and by publishing illustrated excerpts from the Bible. But if Miller sometimes published work which was at home with the collusively Catholic tenor of Lemass and de Valera's Ireland, Kinsella's Dolmen work continued to disturb received ideas about 'Irish poetry'.

---

[7] John Montague writes 'They were not in print' in his memoir of Irish poets in the 1950s, 'Scylla and Charybdis', in *Flowing, Still: Irish Poets on Irish Poetry*, ed. Pat Boran (Dublin: Dedalus, 2009), 44.

[8] Maurice Harmon, ed., *The Dolmen Press* (Dublin: Lilliput, 2001); Liam Miller, *Dolmen XXV: An Illustrated Bibliography of the Dolmen Press 1951–1976* (Dublin: Dolmen, 1976).

[9] Thomas Kinsella, *The Starlit Eye* (Dublin: Dolmen, 1952).

In 1953 Miller also inaugurated Kinsella's long and revolutionary engagement with the canon of poetry in Irish when he commissioned the poet to translate 'St Patrick's Breastplate' (or 'The Deer's Cry'). Kinsella remembers that initial translation commission as 'an awakening from the Irish language, national and pure in heart, as I had known it until then'.[10] His version of 'St Patrick's Breastplate', his first effort at translation, later set to music by Brian Boydell, is notably fresh and distinctive in its response to the familiar prayer: its opening lines address God as 'the Macrocosm-Maker' in terms that would be familiar to readers of *Astounding Science Fiction*.[11] Dolmen's initial success also allowed Miller to publish more work by younger writers. Just as Miller had envisaged, it led to a renewal of poetry in Ireland, a renewal which Dolmen may be said to have instigated, just as new alternative small presses like the Marvell Press in England and, more commercially (it was attached to the eponymous San Francisco bookshop), City Lights in America, which discovered and promoted work by striking new voices who were unable to find editorial support at the larger publishing houses; City Lights also published unconventional works which reacted against their conservative and censorious cultural context.

Dolmen's first editions of Kinsella's poems are original not just in their choice of material but in how they approach that material. Like the work of other Dolmen poets Richard Murphy and Richard Weber, they respond, not to W. B. Yeats, but to W. H. Auden and early T. S. Eliot. In particular, Kinsella's first two Dolmen books imitate Auden's formal finish and omnivorous confidence in his ability to weld together different kinds of material ('As I roved out impatiently/Good Friday with my bride/To drink in the rivered Ringwood/ The draughty season's pride' begins 'In the Ringwood'); the poems also reach at times for Eliot's authoritatively weary and sometimes summary tone ('O Rome thou art, at coffee break, O Rome/Thou also art a town of staring clerks'; and 'A cigarette, the moon, a sigh/Of educated boredom, greet/A curlew's lingering threadbare cry', from 'Baggot Street Deserta').[12] Recognizably postmodern, the poems of Kinsella's first two books with their glancing or contemporary recontextualization of Irish material, served notice of a new life in Irish poetry. One consequence of Dolmen's success was that Liam Miller became acquainted with Austin Clarke, helping the older poet to set the type on his Bridge Press publications initially but soon beginning to print them under the Dolmen imprint.

III

Austin Clarke's publication history reflected his complex and tortuous biography. His early work had met short-lived acclaim in London, but his persistent and cautious

---

[10] Harmon, *The Dolmen Press*, 142.

[11] Thomas Kinsella, *St Patrick's Breastplate* (Dublin: Dolmen, 1954). Kinsella refers to his long enthusiasm for science fiction in his brilliant, studied memoir of Seán Ó Riada in Kinsella, *Peppercanister Poems 1972–1978* (Salem: Wake Forest University Press, 1979), 147–57.

[12] Thomas Kinsella, *Collected Poems* (Manchester: Carcanet, 2001), 16, 20, 11.

espousal of a particularly elaborate and intermittently allegorical version of the Gaelic mode had been criticized in Ireland since the publication of his first book in 1917. Joseph Campbell initially identified Clarke's tendency to overdecorate his lines; by 1930, when Clarke was living and publishing in the southeast of England, his poems began to integrate contemporary and mythological material, offering an idealized historical critique of the new state, but Padraic Colum argued that his emphasis on Gaelic forms would limit his development; in 1934 Samuel Beckett referred to the poems as 'antiquarian'.[13] The 1936 *Collected Poems*, published in London and New York, would be his last such publication for twenty-five years. On his return to Dublin, Clarke was unable to find a publisher for his 1938 collection, *Night and Morning*, which he privately published with the Orwell Press. He produced verse drama in the Irish mode for the next eighteen years, which he self-published, with London publication by Norgate and Williams. In 1949 a modernizing writer like Sean O Faolain could write that Clarke had 'exhausted the usefulness' of the Gaelic forms,[14] and Patrick Kavanagh could group Clarke with Robert Farren and others as Paddy Irish Mist in 'The Paddiad'. Clarke, however, persisted. In a 1946 essay on contemporary poetry in *The Bell*, he wrote: 'Irish poetry has its own problems, and they are not those of contemporary England. We have to move on slowly, inch by inch, carrying our merry and doleful past with us.'[15] In 1951 he published a short, dutiful account of Irish poetry, funded by The Cultural Relations Committee of Ireland, which focused on Yeats's example and on poets who continued to draw on the Irish Literary Revival's grand narratives; it dismissed modern or 'modernistic' writers and mentioned no younger poets.

But a major shift occurs in Clarke's work a decade later. While Kinsella had found ways of writing poems free of traditional Irish expectations, when Clarke began to write poems again in the mid-1950s, publishing them himself under the Bridge Press imprint, the 'merry and doleful' past took on a revitalizing, purely formal force: that shift is certainly related to the changed method of publishing his poems in the 1950s. Now, Clarke's conservatism began to assume a different character, a character which would attract much notice from modernist poets and critics. Although the satires and later poems are even more ingrained and informed, syllable by syllable and half-line by half-line, by patterns imported from a wide variety of Irish-language models, that archaism is now shaping material with which it had no obvious or natural connection. The jarring effect was suddenly much easier to relate to modernist exemplars: the 1955 publication of *Ancient Lights* was welcomed by Dublin-based younger writers including Donald Davie, Denis Donoghue, and John Montague. Subtitled *Poems and Satires: First Series*, the short book declared Clarke's intentions to continue as he had recommenced, and was followed in the same series by *Too Great a Vine* and *The Horse Eaters* in 1957 and 1960. These poems initially surprised their Dublin readers by responding so directly to the cultural climate,

---

[13] Lorraine Ricigliano, *Austin Clarke: A Reference Guide* (New York: G. K. Hall, 1993), 18, 28, 30.
[14] Quoted in ibid., 43.
[15] Austin Clarke, 'Poetry in Ireland To-day', *Reviews and Essays of Austin Clarke*, ed. Gregory Schirmer (Gerrards Cross: Colin Smythe, 1995), 108.

one characterized by Clarke in 1950 as 'stagnating from censorship and materialism'.[16] However, their continuation of earlier concerns, both stylistically and thematically, was made clear when Clarke collected these three series of poems and satires for the Dolmen Press *Later Poems* in 1961, pointedly including alongside them the poems of *Pilgrimage* (1929) and *Night and Morning* (1938). He was thereby emphasizing continuities rather than the rupture and new development which are the most remarkable features of the 1950s satires, and encouraging critics instead to read the work on his own defensive (and misleading) technical terms.

Clarke's newly ironic use of his Gaelic formal models may be traced to two historical factors which complicated his ideas about his work: the Censorship Act (1929) and the death of Yeats in 1939. Clarke's first experience of censorship occurred when the state banned *The Bright Temptation* (1932), a light and comic historical novel which might now be classed as teen fiction. It was an experience that seems to have daunted and energized him, further estranging him from the new State. That year, Yeats nominated him as a founder member of the Irish Academy of Letters. Clarke saw the new organization as a means of assuming a Yeatsian prominence in the new state, and a way of challenging government policy on censorship, a matter which preoccupied him in his writing too. It is no coincidence that his poems and prose become increasingly tangled and polysemous. It may be best illustrated in an overtly teasing passage from one of his memoirs, *A Penny in the Clouds*, when he writes about a London affair with an artist's younger wife:

> Soon I would be playing quoits with Avril on happy afternoons, rolling a thin golden hoop with her, kissing her shoulder as she bent to feather the dart which she took from my quiver, or chasing blissfully with her after uncatchable butterflies.[17]

The sexual encounter with Avril (also described in similarly contorted terms in the 1962 poem 'From a Diary of Dreams') is not so much told slant as encoded, and Clarke obviously enjoys and even exults in the ingenuity of his concealments and elusiveness. Censorship seemed to demand this kind of writing and it, as much as his use of Irish language sound patterns, seemed finally to allow Clarke to modulate his work in a way that would distinguish him from Yeats and the more conventional Celticism of his own early work.

However, Clarke still saw the authority of Yeats's example and moulded an idea of the poet which was national *and* marginal, Irish rather than modern. Where Kinsella approached Yeats through Eliot's modernist and Auden's postmodern responses to his national poetry, Clarke's obsessive interest in Yeats is rarely diluted by other influences. Evident early on, an emulous and partial version of Yeats emerges: Steven Matthews notes that Clarke even uses his obituary for Yeats as the occasion for a self-portrait as successor, concluding, 'the artistic tradition of the literary revival has not been broken'.[18] Matthews also captures the productive confusion at the heart of Clarke's response to

---

[16] Quoted in Ricigliano, *Austin Clarke: A Reference Guide*, 46.

[17] Austin Clarke, *A Penny in the Clouds* (Dublin: Routledge and Kegan Paul, 1968), 180.

[18] Steven Matthews, *Yeats as Precursor: Readings in Irish, British and American Poetry* (Basingstoke: Macmillan, 2000), 50.

Yeats, which resulted in a distinctive new aesthetic based on a 'radical splitting of genres, satire and symbolic resolution'.[19] Clarke's contrary, pied forms, then, are founded on his changed use of Irish material, his yoking together of scandalous subject matter and revered forms.

In spite of its innovations, as noted above, Clarke insisted that his new work in the 1950s and 1960s partook of the 'unbroken' tradition of the Literary Revival, and it may be that this insistence led Kinsella to his famous opposing formula of Ireland's broken and dual traditions, a formula which offers a more convincing context for understanding the radical, critical nature of Clarke's later work.[20] That is, Clarke's 1950s 'satires and poems' are less obviously evidence of a combined Irish tradition than they are the product of their disenchanted post-war, post-Yeatsian moment. The poems rarely fit their material and their formal obligations together. Clarke revisits earlier, more temperate dialogues between nation (or nature) and Church in 'The Blackbird of Derrycairn':

> Stop, stop and listen for the bough top
> Is whistling and the sun is brighter
> Than God's own shadow in the cup now![21]

This poem, which Clarke initially wrote for the 1942 radio play, *As the Crow Flies*, famously exhibits Clarke's use of Irish language assonance and rhyme patterns, but it also suggests how his poems begin to hinge on, rather than papering over, the tensions between past and present. The intricate sound patterns highlight the awkwardness and forced phrasing of this particular mixed marriage. The third line's image of 'cup now' undermines its echo of 'shadow' and 'bough top'. Clarke's attention to sound and his related interest in punning define his late style, but the extremity of his focus on these aspects of a poem comes at the expense of cadence and image. The same problem affects each stanza, although its famous closing lines, where the internal rhymes force an unlikely verb into place, intimate that the 'song', the formal structure of the poem, is no end in itself, but part of a larger, scholarly art: 'But knowledge is found among the branches./Listen! The song that shakes my feathers/Will thong the leather of your satchels.'

Such moments of clarity and insight occur elsewhere too, but by the 1955 publication of *Ancient Lights*, which includes this slightly out of place 1942 lyric, Clarke was drawing on Irish forms to describe contemporary urban life, thereby reversing the earlier work's use of traditional forms to describe traditional Irish material. Clarke now grounds the best of the poems' epiphanies in complex, social settings which frame and ironize them. In the much-discussed title poem, 'Ancient Lights', cinematic images combine with puns and idiomatic phrasing.[22] Although critics have picked away at the obscurity of its narrative, there is unusual fluency and range in its discursive stanzas, and its celebration of a

---

[19] Ibid., 52.
[20] Thomas Kinsella, *The Dual Tradition: An Essay on Poetry and Politics in Ireland* (Manchester: Carcanet, 1995).
[21] Austin Clarke, *Collected Poems*, ed. R. Dardis Clarke (Manchester: Carcanet, 2008), 203.
[22] Ibid., 199.

child's discovery of his own power and agency, 'hail[ing] the skies' to save a sparrow, and then witnessing a visionary flood: 'I heard/From shore to shore the iron gratings/Take half our heavens with a roar.' The poem's secure narrative voice acts as a foil to its punning ('shore' for 'gutter', 'heavens' for Church'), slippery syntax (that interpolated 'shore to shore') and sometimes obscure images, offering a convincing vision of a more natural, less encumbered street (and country).

Elsewhere Clarke's poems are confined (too closely) by the language and norms of their 1950s subjects: clever, button-pressing satires like 'Marriage' and 'Celebrations' subject the language of contemporary public rhetoric to grotesque, satirical transformations, flinging obscenities at the hypocritical Vatican flag in one, identifying marriage with shame and contraception ('Aye, there's the rub!') in the other.[23] 'Three poems about children' uses pious talk about Limbo—'Has not a Bishop declared/That flame-wrapped babes are spared/Our life-time of temptation?'—to extrapolate a Swiftian argument for infanticide: 'Those children, charred in Cavan,/Passed straight through Hell to Heaven.'[24] These poems are fierce and full of feeling, but they too force the language into odd phrases. For every apt allusion there is a dud phrase or place-holder that jars or distracts the reader's attention. In this last poem, why *straight* in 'passed straight through'? In 'Celebrations', why *again* in 'Let ageing politicians pray/Again, hoardings recount our faith'? How does that first line's plainness fit with the hardworking pun on 'hoardings recount' (which refers to how 'posters remember', but also how 'financial savings tell' our faith)? And how does any of this fit with the allusion to Justice *and* William Blake's robin redbreast in the next line: 'The blindfold woman in a rage'? Clarke's satires are marred by such unevennesses, fireworks alongside damp squibs, puns alongside coinages ('God only knows what treasury/Uncrams'). Some poems collapse under the pressure of such combinations and nothing is left but the impression of a vague and righteous fury, which documents and indicts the nationalist, isolationist society it depicts. These less successful poems' rough, disjunctive turns, Latinate vocabulary, and terrible material act as a critique of any imaginative purity attendant on Gaelic forms. However, the misplaced critical emphasis on Clarke's technique, a recurring and unfortunately dominant feature of Clarke criticism, misses the narrative power and particularity of the arguments made in poems like 'Ancient Lights'.[25]

Clarke followed *Ancient Lights* by publishing two further books, also in editions of 200 copies, also subtitled 'Poems and Satires'. *Too Great a Vine* begins with 'Usufruct', a legal term which the poem glosses in relation to the decision of Clarke's mother to will her son's home to the Church on his death. It is followed by 'Abbey Theatre Fire', which not only savages Yeats as a rhetorician and mythologizer but seems to identify him with Clarke's mother, stripping the son of his rightful inheritance. Other satires are more

---

[23] Ibid., 196, 195.

[24] Ibid., 196.

[25] See John McAuliffe, 'Against Irish Studies: Reading Austin Clarke and his Critics', in *New Voices in Irish Criticism*, ed. P. J. Mathews (Dublin: Four Courts, 2000), 255–60. For a more recent example of this approach see Sir Christopher Ricks's 'Introduction' to Clarke's *Collected Poems*, pp. xii–xxiv.

obscure and many of the later short poems seem exhausted by their subjects. They rail against norms, but now that the peculiar norms of 1950s Ireland have largely disappeared, the poems often seem like out-of-date medicine. They lack the bracing imagination of change and discovery evident in 'Ancient Lights', and are often piecemeal, internally inert, monotonous, and insufficient in their development.

The shifting of the burden of the past to a formal level is less strictly observed in the long poems, which are not so crabbed in their construction. 'Beyond the Pale', for instance, receives two dense pages of annotation by W. J. McCormack in his edition of Clarke's *Selected Poems*, and some lines are still obscure to that editor.[26] The less effective 'The Loss of Strength' uses an awkwardly regular Spenserian stanza shape: each stanza is twelve lines long and ends with a short summary six-syllable statement which encourages Clarke both to pad some lines with details *and* to import the sermonizing pedantry of the satires. The poem does have its moments, and local and historical specificity do not limit their pertinence:

> Gelignite has blown up
> Too much: yet on the Hill of Allen
> The blasters are at work. Gallon
> By gallon our roads go on. Stonecrushers
> Must feed them. Fionn hunted here, Oisin
> Complained of age. I think of rushed bones,
> Bogland, in furnaces, grown greener[27]

In 'The Flock at Dawn' from *The Horse Eaters* (the third of the 'Poems and Satires' series), Clarke's specificity, his insistence on historical particularity, makes his attack on rich religious orders almost but not quite applicable to the credit crunch of 2009:

> Our monks reside in eighteenth-century mansions
> Now. Hell-fire rakes have spirited these heirs.
> Always in debt to banks, they plan more buildings,
> Made reckless by the vow of poverty,
> Pile up the sums that burning souls have willed
> To them in clock-tower, high walls, such debris;
> Teach alms to gamble, while agents share the kitty.[28]

These Bridge Press pamphlets, republished by the Dolmen Press as *Later Poems* in 1961, may fairly be said to comprise a disturbing and innovative collection. Alan Gillis writes of Clarke's earlier work that it 'critiques the State not because of its coercive repression, but because it constitutes a corruption of the national purity it is meant to embody... he remains drawn, as an artist, to organicist modalities, scared off by the indeterminate vulnerability of the alternatives'.[29] Although Clarke doggedly insists in the 1950s on

---

[26] Austin Clarke, *Selected Poems*, ed. W. J. McCormack (London: Penguin, 1991), 242–4.
[27] Clarke, *Collected Poems*, 218.
[28] Ibid., 231.
[29] Alan Gillis, *Irish Poetry of the 1930s* (Oxford: Oxford University Press, 2005), 94.

foregrounding his allegiance to a Gaelic mode, there is nothing antiquarian or idealized in the jagged, disjunctive particularities of these later poems and satires. Perhaps their formal emphasis eased Clarke's work into the renewed discussion of post-Yeatsian Ireland which occurred in the 1960s. Yet it is not their reference to residual forms of Irish poetry but their obvious modernity, their emphasis on reason, and their immersion in the emerging culture of independent Ireland, which anticipates the turning tide of 1960s Ireland. Seamus Deane may overstate the case when he sees in them evidence that 'Clarke is a startling example of the salutary effects which flow from the *abandonment* [my italics] of unexamined and therefore misunderstood myths and systems',[30] but Clarke's later work, homemade at the Bridge Press rather than produced for the larger, international houses where he had so often performed the role of representative Irish poet, is more riven by the postcolonial reality of the Irish Republic and more representative of its realities than is his early work or the work of his contemporaries.

IV

If Clarke's first series of poems and satires respond to their contemporary context on its own terms, Thomas Kinsella's third collection, *Downstream*, published in 1962 by Dolmen, in England by Oxford University Press and in the US by Knopf, continues to draw on a wider range of technical and imaginative resources. Its international success, also an indication of the ways in which Irish society and business were emerging from the isolation of the Emergency, begins with a prologue, in tetrameter couplets, which neatly parodies clichés about poets' 'alertness when it comes to beer/an affectation that their ear/for music is a little weak', which it opposes to the poet's actual domestic situation as the occasion of inspiration: 'Suddenly—or as I lend/A hand about the house, or bend/Low above an onion bed/– Memory stumbles in the head'.[31] These lines and this transition easily fit into the Movement aesthetic associated with Kingsley Amis and Donald Davie. Indeed, much of *Downstream* enacts those poets' realism and kitchen-sink anger with the idealizing and pretentiousness of earlier poetry.

However, Kinsella's prologue suggests that he would not be content to contribute to what Auden called a poetry of disenchantment, and that he would discover a more allegorical mode (as had Auden), counteracting the realism of the Movement and the romanticism of their predecessors. The poem's closing fourteen-line stanza is different, more abstract, and less comfortable with simply stating the objection to rhetoric than Movement poets. It ends with a parade of abstractions, 'Helped along by blind Routine,/ Futility flogs a tambourine...', which seems also to parody the closing lines of the title poem of *Another September*, his second book ('Truth, Justice, such figures').[32] The mix of

---

[30] Seamus Deane, 'Literary Myths of the Revival: A Case for their Abandonment', in *Myth and Reality in Irish Literature*, ed. Joseph Ronsley (Waterloo: Wilfrid Laurier University Press, 1977), 323.
[31] Thomas Kinsella, '*I wonder whether one expects...*', *Downstream* (Dublin: Dolmen, 1962), 9–10.
[32] Kinsella, *Collected Poems*, 20.

Movement satire and Auden-like allegory is typical of the entire collection, situating its contemporary scenes in a larger, poetic system than a particularly Irish context: 'Wedding Morning', for instance, observes 'the chatter of champagne,/The poised photographer, the flying veil,/The motors crowded on the squandered lawn', before concluding 'Down the bright gravel stroll the families/With Blood, the trader, profiting in their peace.'[33] The first section of *Downstream* presents a series of portraits, each of which follows a similar procedure, first seeing their subject clearly and without illusion, then using them to serve or illustrate a larger point, the caged monkey of 'Charlie'—'its neck,/Weary and slack with prison, came erect/And Jacob's glittering eye peered out upon us'—a process repeated in the more ostensibly personal portraits of Dick King and Maura in 'Dick King' and 'Cover her face'.[34]

Kinsella's established method is powerful and effective, as in 'The Laundress'. This poem typically refuses to identify the poet as an elevated figure with a higher calling. Instead the poem unpredictably and unglamorously identifies an expectant mother and worker as an artist figure 'stitch[ing] a linen sheet', her work on the white sheet not dissimilar to the naturally changing, seasonal fields of France, 'land that would spread white/When she would reach her term'.[35] The title initially seems to miss the poem's larger themes, its vaguely French and Flanders setting which suggests a reference to the First World War, and the fact of its subject's pregnancy, on which the poem turns. The third stanza coordinates these two private and public worlds in a way that exemplifies Kinsella's arrangement of his material in *Downstream*:

> As the fish disturbs the pond
> And sinks without a stain
> The heels of ripeness fluttered
> Under her apron.[36]

Kinsella chooses an unusual image to describe the personal and private experience of feeling the baby kicking, an image 'without a stain', a phrase which extends the innocence of the poem's eponymous subject, the mother who cleans and repairs the (presumably stained) sheets while seated at an open door. An allegorical network of innocence and experience seems to loom, then, over the particular, actual description. The verb 'disturbs' further complicates how we respond to the poem, alluding as it does to W. B. Yeats's 'Easter 1916', which famously imagines the 1916 rebels as 'a stone that disturbs the living stream'. Yeats's poem is also written in a three-beat line, and it too imagines a kind of pietà in which the poet's role is 'To murmur name upon name,/As a mother names her child'. Kinsella, though, resists Yeats's poem's explicit, and explicitly Irish, argument about historical change, and concludes instead with an emblematic and pastoral stanza, whose emphatic rhymes reflect the cyclical, unchanging seasonal world they describe:

---

[33] Kinsella, *Downstream*, 14.

[34] Ibid., 17.

[35] Ibid., 13–14. The pregnant laundress may allude also to the Magdalene Laundries' reliance on unmarried mothers for unpaid labour.

[36] Ibid.

> The sower plumps his acre,
> Flanders turns to the heat,
> The winds of Heaven winnow
> And the wheels grind the wheat.
> She searched in the basket
> And fixed her ruffled sheet.[37]

The conscious, deliberate retreat from history as progress or development in 'The Laundress' suggests Kinsella's antagonistic engagement with 'Easter 1916', but the density of the poem's reference and its adroit formal independence are very different from the ways in which Clarke, Kavanagh, and others wrote about Yeats.

Kinsella's antagonism to Lemass's republic is, of course, just as informed as Clarke's. Kinsella worked in the Department of Finance during the period that he wrote his first three books, and his perspective is clearly and satirically defined in 'A Country Walk', whose narrator mixes intense introspection with a scissoring gaze at the streets and roads he walks:

> Around the corner, in an open square,
> I came upon the sombre monuments
> That bear their names: MacDonagh & McBride,
> Merchants; Connolly's Commercial Arms[38]

'A Country Walk' develops themes evident in the landscapes of 'In the Ringwood' and 'King John's Castle' from *Another September* (1956). Kinsella's meditation on Irish history is, as is the case throughout *Downstream*, more inflected with allegory than the earlier poems. The 'Country' of the title puns on the geography and history which the poem conflates, moving between a keenly described actual walk ('I swung the gate shut with a furious sigh') and snapshot portraits of a nation in historical crisis—scenes which involve, in chronological order, the 'crossed swords' of Irish epic, 'the first Normans', 'knot-necked Cromwell', and those who 'answered the Phantom Hag/Tireless Rebellion' in 1798 and 1916.[39] At its conclusion, however, Kinsella retreats from the historical world, from the idea that human agency or nation effect meaningful change, insisting instead on its own dark, sexual pastoral whose jangling of uneasy terms seem themselves like a liberation:

> *Venit Hesperus.*
> In green and golden light; bringing sweet trade.
> The inert stirred. Heart and tongue were loosed:
> "The waters hurtle through the flooded night…"[40]

The long title poem, 'Downstream', continues to shift away from any emphasis on a national poetry, using another 'non-native' form, terza rima, and immediately picking up on the closing line of 'A Country Walk' when it begins:

[37] Ibid.
[38] Ibid., 48.
[39] Ibid., 46–7.
[40] Ibid.

> The West a fiery complex, the East a pearl,
> We gave our frail skiff to the hungry stream,
> Ruffling the waters. Caught on a running swirl
>
> Our gunwale dipped and steadied on the seam
> Of calm and current. I raised my chin to zip
> My jacket on the Cantos[41]

The poem's importance has been noted by all of Kinsella's critics, from Thomas Dillon Redshaw's initial exegesis of its drafts to Brian John, Dillon Johnston, Andrew Fitzsimons, and Alex Davis's accounts of its subsequent redrafting.[42] The poem and book's publication were accompanied by the publication of the *Dolmen Miscellany of Irish Writing*, edited by Kinsella and John Montague. It included work by younger prose writers, such as John McGahern and Aidan Higgins, and attempted, as do Kinsella's poems, to represent modernity rather than Ireland. The brief editorial summarizes the impatience of a generation with the aspirational nationalism of its predecessors: 'The main link between them however is their obvious desire to avoid the forms of "Irishism".'[43] Kinsella's poem does more than 'avoid the forms of 'Irishism'. Sometimes criticized for its 'literary' language—the Yeatsian swan, the Stygian river, and jewelled sun—the poem's achievement is in fact bound up with its sophisticated, critical use of existing literary tropes. Unlike Clarke's career-long interest in the itinerary poem, whose emphasis is predominately documentary, Kinsella foregrounds the journey's literariness as a subject of the poem, something announced with those Cantos into which the poem dips as surely as its river. As in 'A Country Walk', the longer form allows Kinsella to use Irish and mythological material more explicitly and extensively than he had previously done, without collapsing the poem into the existing models for using that material. In all of its revised guises, the poem moves easily between the physical and metaphysical world, present and past, but without the sometimes cumbersome stage machinery of his country walk. It registers, with what now seems characteristic immediacy, a simultaneous grasp on psychological, mythological, and actual frames of reference.

Downstream's success and the support of T. K. Whitaker in the Department of Finance enabled Kinsella to take a sabbatical in 1962, which allowed him to increase his commitment to a revisionist translation of Irish-language poetry. In San Francisco and then Boston, he researched *The Táin*'s surviving texts and its critical contexts.[44] This particular translation project is very different to those of the Revival and its inheritors (including Clarke) who attempt to carry across the original's rhymes and assonance.

---

[41] Ibid., 50.

[42] Thomas Dillon Redshaw, 'The Wormwood Revisions', *Eire-Ireland* 6:2 (Summer 1971), 111-56; Brian John, *Reading the Ground: The Poetry of Thomas Kinsella* (Washington DC: Catholic University Press, 1996); Dillon Johnston, *Irish Poetry after Joyce* [1985] (Syracuse: Syracuse University Press, 1997); Andrew Fitzsimons, *The Sea of Disappointment: Thomas Kinsella's Pursuit of the Real* (Dublin: UCD Press, 2008); Alex Davis, 'Thomas Kinsella and the Pound Legacy: His Jacket on the "Cantos"', 38–53, *Irish University Review* 31 (2001).

[43] John Montague and Thomas Kinsella, eds., *The Dolmen Miscellany of Irish Writing* (Dublin: Dolmen, 1962), prefatory page.

[44] Harmon, *The Dolmen Press*, 146.

Kinsella's version is better seen in the context of modern and contemporary approaches to grammars of myth: to how Eliot drew on *The Golden Bough*, how Auden drew on Icelandic sagas, and Ted Hughes on Shakespeare's versions of classical mythology, as well as to the more popular, Jungian myth criticism of Joseph Campbell and Northrop Frye. Maria Tymoczko sums up its success:

> [I]n a sense his translation was thus a brilliant argument about the medieval tale [and] represents early Irish culture in a remarkably perspicuous manner. Kinsella's translation is racy—verbally, sexually, scatologically—and irreverent, reflecting qualities that Yeats and Synge and others valued in Irish culture and Irish literature, and that Joyce and Flann O'Brien perpetuated. The translation was startling and shocking at the time he published it: it was both dislocating and exhilarating to see an unapproachable story that had always been treated with piety and reverence actually appeal to modern sensibilities.[45]

The importance of Kinsella's translation work for Dolmen, as well as the early work's interest in allegory, also undermine critical accounts which insist Kinsella's work may be broken down into early and American periods. Andrew Fitzsimons's recent book on Kinsella makes an excellent case for the continuities in his work, and sees in *Downstream* many of the interests which preoccupy Kinsella in the Peppercanister poems, but he does not make the link between Kinsella's work on *The Táin* and his original poetry of that period. Kinsella's Peppercanister poems owe as much to his experience as a translator of medieval poetry as they do to his interest in William Carlos Williams and Ezra Pound.[46] The translation work, stemming from Miller's initial commission, has been almost coterminous with his publishing career. As Kinsella collated the heterogeneous materials that make up *The Táin* (in the definitive form in which we now know it), he was beginning to write longer poems and sequences whose interest in the contexts of poetry—in how poems are written, read, and understood—are shaped by his research *and* by his hands-on experience of setting and publishing his first poems,[47] as surely as Clarke's increasingly 'lecherous and anti-clerical'[48] work was encouraged by the freedom afforded him by small-press publication.

V

In 'The Irish Writer', the 1966 paper with which this essay began, Thomas Kinsella looked back at his experience of writing poems in an isolated state whose cultural sphere was

---

[45] Maria Tymoczko, 'Retranslating *The Táin*', in *Irish Literary Supplement* (Autumn 2009), 11.

[46] Dillon Johnston notes that at a rare 1997 reading, Kinsella seemed comfortable with the idea of a split in his work and 'spoke of Auden's early influence and said that he "left the ghost of Auden in the distance" in the course of translating the Táin'; see Johnston, *The Poetic Economies of England and Ireland, 1912–2000* (Basingstoke: Palgrave, 2001), 131.

[47] Dillon Johnston perceptively analyses this area of Kinsella's 1970s sequences in *Irish Poetry after Joyce*, 53–68.

[48] John Montague's phrase, quoted in Johnston, *Poetic Economies*, 140.

confined and policed, and wrote sceptically about the possibility of a modern, national art: 'It is not as though literature or national life were a corporate, national investigation of a corporate, national experience—as though a nation were a single animal, with one complex artistic feeler.'[49] He and Austin Clarke made new kinds of poems in that context, one refusing to shoulder or foreground the traditional baggage of Irish poets, the other finding new ways to use and ventriloquize that material. In succeeding decades, Clarke's late narrative poems would continue to shock, disturbing received ideas about gender and sexuality, just as much as his satires attacked the clerical state.[50] Each successive volume of Kinsella's Peppercanister sequences continues to deepen and refract how we read them and their predecessors. He continues to publish in intermittent instalments with Dedalus in Dublin and subsequently in book form with Carcanet in Manchester and Wake Forest in the US. The momentum of his poems and the trajectory of his life in America have exceeded many of the enabling designs and ideas which powered his great 1970s collections, but the poet's birthplace and initial experience of the Second World War, the Emergency and its isolating aftermath, still remain vital to an understanding of his work. Their example, and their different ranges of form and subject, are evident in the work of poets who subsequently worked and, sometimes, published in Dublin or with Dolmen, including Michael Hartnett whose movement between satire, the lyric, narrative poems, and versions of the Tao, Lorca, and O Bruadair, draw on distinctive elements of Clarke's and Kinsella's work. And the contrast between Kinsella and Clarke, too often understated, is very evident in Hartnett's least consistent work, *A Farewell to English*, which seeks to conflate their explorations of new ways to write and arrange past and present moments.

Clarke and Kinsella are two of a generation of poets whose work developed or changed during a period when they worked without an established publishing house, and had a hands-on relation to seeing their poems into print. Patrick Kavanagh's celebratory sonnets were initially published on a hand press, which is itself now part of the Kavanagh Archive at University College Dublin. While Dolmen's archive resides in Wake Forest University, the actual printing press was removed to Dingle by an employee who used it to set up the Hawthorne Press, which has since been reconstituted as Púca Press by its Swiss artist-designer and owner. Her first production, *Allagar na gCloch/Stone Chat* (2006) matched photographs of Kerry walls with accompanying texts, using images of the stones as starting points for retelling local history and myth. This was a conjunction of past and present that Dolmen's publications often shared, but Dolmen's most wide-ranging and influential achievements were works by Clarke and Kinsella which were more interested in disturbing any straightforward continuity between individual, contemporary moments and a community's history.

---

[49] Kinsella, *Davis, Mangan, Ferguson*, 66.
[50] See Ed Madden, *Tiresian Poetics: Modernism, Sexuality, Voice 1888–2001* (Madison: Fairleigh Dickinson University Press, 2008), 218–54.

CHAPTER 15

....

MEMORY AND STARLIGHT IN LATE MACNEICE

....

JONATHAN ALLISON

In January 1920, Louis MacNeice wrote to his stepmother in Carrickfergus that he had had the unusual experience, while travelling to school at Sherborne, of sitting alone in the dark in a third-class carriage. His train from Fleetwood to Euston had been delayed, which meant that he had missed his train from Waterloo to Sherborne and had had to take a later train at 5 p.m. which 'stopped at nearly every station'.[1] Consequently, the journey (which today takes over two hours to complete) was conducted in the growing darkness of the January evening. Due to his isolation in the darkened carriage, the stars appeared very vivid in the cloudless sky, which he could see clearly through the window. This was casually mentioned at the time ('At Fleetwood discovered that McCammonds were in 1st class carriage so had to go in 3rd class one by myself. Saw stars from train to Sherborne'), but as he later recalled the incident (or an incident very similar to this) in *The Strings Are False*, it came to have a deeper significance than is acknowledged in the letter home: 'In January 1921 I found myself wonderfully alone in an empty carriage in a rocking train in the night between Waterloo and Sherborne. Stars on each side of me; I ran from side to side of the carriage checking the constellations.'[2] In writing his unfinished autobiography, MacNeice has presumably misremembered the year of the incident, but he seems to be clearly referring to the moment of unwonted isolation in the train as described in the letter of 21 January 1920. In letters written in the ensuing days after this journey, he mentions that the boys at school have recently seen 'Pegasus and Andromeda' from the dormitory window, and that they are reading about astronomy.[3] One or two books were circulating, including Sir Robert Ball's *Star-Land: Being Talks*

[1] FLM (Frederick Louis MacNeice) to GBM (Georgina Beatrice MacNeice), 21 January 1920, *Letters of Louis MacNeice*, ed. Jonathan Allison (London: Faber, 2010), 39.
[2] Louis MacNeice, *The Strings Are False: An Unfinished Autobiography*, ed. E. R. Dodds (London: Faber, 1965), 78.
[3] FLM to GBM, 25 January 1920, *Letters*, 39.

with Young People about the Wonders of the Heavens (1889), which MacNeice read with some interest at the time.[4] Ball was a popular lecturer and his book was written in a very accessible style, designed for an educated, juvenile audience. Having just recently made the journey from Carrickfergus, and usually alert to things Hibernian, as his schoolboy letters attest, it would not have escaped MacNeice's attention that the author held the title 'Royal Astronomer of Ireland', clearly printed below his name on the title page. In his poem 'Star Gazer', from his final, posthumously published volume, *The Burning Perch* (1963), MacNeice returns to this memory as described in *The Strings Are False*, and he mentions that he had read 'in the textbooks' how vast the distance was between earth and the stars, a distance so great that the furthest astral light was very old indeed, and probably originated at a date prior to his own birth, if not indeed much earlier: 'I had read in the textbooks/How very far off they were, it seemed their light/Had left them (some at least) long years before I was.'[5] In his chapter on the stars, in a sub-section called 'The Distance of the Stars', Ball discusses this particular point in some detail, in a manner that bears a striking resemblance to MacNeice's observation:

> Among the stars which we can see in our telescopes, we feel confident there must be many from which the light has taken hundreds of years, or even thousands of years, to arrive here. When, therefore, we look at such objects, we see them, not as they are now, but as they were ages ago; in fact, a star might have ceased to exist for thousands of years, and still be seen by us every night as a twinkling point in our great telescopes.
>
> Remembering these facts, you will, I think, look at the heavens with a new interest. There is a bright star, Vega or Alpha Lyrae, a beautiful gem, but so far off that the light from it which we now see started before many of my audience were born.[6]

The general point was presumably well-known by junior astronomers, although it seems likely that Ball's articulation of the idea had become part of the poet's mental furniture at about this time, when reading *Star-Land*, following swiftly upon this unusual experience on the train. Striving to convey to his young readers the vastness of astronomical distances, Ball reaches for the image of an immensely long railway line stretching from London to Alpha Centauri: 'The length of the railway, of course, we have already stated: it is twenty billions of miles. So I am now going to ask your attention [*sic*] to the simple question as to the fare which it would be reasonable to charge for the journey.'[7] There is perhaps a particular interest here for the twelve-year-old MacNeice, so recently arrived from the train to Sherborne, in which the unusual coincidence of rail travel and stargazing became so deeply impressed that it was recalled with considerable enthusiasm not only when writing his memoirs in 1940, but again when writing a lyric poem in 1963. Although the speaker is very far from being 'breathless', 'Star-gazer' is constructed as

---

[4] FLM to GBM, 1 February 1920, *Letters*, 41.

[5] Louis MacNeice, *Collected Poems*, ed. Peter McDonald (London: Faber, 2007), 607.

[6] Robert Ball, *Star-Land: Being Talks with Young People about the Wonders of the Heavens* (London: Cassell and Company, 1889), 315.

[7] Ibid., 316.

two complete sentences, with a perfect coincidence of syntax and stanza worthy of the later Yeats, and the alternating longer and shorter lines capture the fluency and immediacy of the speaker's voice. Beginning with the notably precise figure of 'forty-two years' (which I have suggested may not be wholly accurate), the voice interrupts itself with an apparently careless but actually carefully placed parenthetic aside, capturing the spontaneity of the poet's thoughts, and self-deprecatingly halting the flow of the utterance, while challenging the monumental formality which may be implied by a phrase like 'Forty-two years ago'. Some of the speaker's emotion is conveyed through the occurrence of rather emphatic verbs—'darting', 'catch', 'punched', and 'excited'—while his heightened feeling is further suggested by the phrase 'intolerably bright', as though the experience is almost unendurably pleasurable and nearly impossible to assimilate: in that sense, it's a moment in which the visible, like some terrible beauty, appears both radiant and objectionable:

> Forty-two years ago (to me if to no one else
> The number is of some interest) it was a brilliant starry night
> And the westward train was empty and had no corridors
> So darting from side to side I could catch the unwonted sight
> Of those almost intolerably bright
> Holes, punched in the sky, which excited me partly because
> Of their Latin names...[8]

In the second stanza, the speaker registers distance from the boy's youthful exuberance, as conveyed by the word 'remembering', emphasizing his role as the narrator who proposes to draw from this memory some larger point. The parenthetic qualifying phrase '(some at least)' in the ninth line of the first stanza, like the phrase 'some of them at least' in the eleventh, suggests the making of distinctions, trying to avoid rapture, and asserting a reasonable tone. The more regular, modulated pentameter lines also contribute to the effect of control which he affects with 'I mark' in stanza two, as he tries to assert some kind of conclusion. Taking the point made by Ball and other astronomers about the age of astral light, the speaker imagines a future in which humans have become extinct. The space following the half-line 'Anyone left alive' offers a momentary silence in response to that surprising phrase, and the concluding lines return somewhat indulgently but nonetheless poignantly to the memory of the boy on the train, whose 'admiration' is made to seem the more valuable, almost redemptive, in contrast with that apocalyptic thought.

MacNeice had described the poems of *The Burning Perch* to Allen Tate as 'all thumbnail nightmares', and various critics have discussed the nightmare imagery and logic deployed in the late poems.[9] John Press speaks of 'bad dreams, nightmarish journeys and scenes where everything is in flux' as typical of the late MacNeice, and Peter McDonald writes: 'On the whole, it is darkness rather than light which is pervasive in MacNeice's late poetry, and nightmare rather than dream which is its dominant

---

[8] MacNeice, *Collected Poems*, 607.
[9] FLM to AT, 2 August 1963, *Letters*, 701.

element.'[10] The nightmare element in 'Star-gazer' surfaces most strongly with the thought of human extinction that emerges in response to the notion of astronomical distance and time, which has the effect of making human life seem almost insignificant; but the theme of dreams and nightmare (or, as Press points out, sinister or incoherent encounters, with the illogical structure of dream) recurs in poems not only in *The Burning Perch* but in *Visitations*. Of the figure in 'The Burnt Bridge', for instance, we are told 'the more he dreamt [he] was the more alone' and in 'House on a Cliff' the central figure 'talks at cross/Purposes, to himself, in a broken sleep'. In 'Dreams in Middle Age' MacNeice writes 'Sooner let nightmares whinny'.[11] And the word 'nightmare' is explicitly introduced again in the dedicatory poem of *The Burning Perch*: 'To Mary'.

MacNeice had left his wife Hedli Anderson in 1961, and in late 1962 he moved into a house on Stocks Road, Aldbury, with his lover, the actress Mary Wimbush, who worked for the BBC. He had previously dedicated several volumes 'To Hedli' (*Springboard*, 1944, *Collected Poems 1925–1948*, 1949, and *Visitations*, 1957)[12] but the dedication in *The Burning Perch* was addressed to Wimbush, in which he begins his pledge to her by begging her forgiveness for the nightmare vision he presents to her, a vision which, it is implied, has suffused his imagination:

> To Mary
> Forgive what I give you. Though nightmare and cinders,
> The one can be trodden, the other ridden,
> We must use what transport we can. Both crunching
> Path and bucking dream can take me
> Where I shall leave the path and dismount
> From the mad-eyed beast and keep my appointment
> In green improbable fields with you.[13]

The poem opens with the word 'Forgive', almost a confession of guilt and of personal limitation. All he can give is 'nightmare and cinders' although they are not insuperable obstacles: one can be ridden (nightmares), the other trodden upon. If 'cinders' might suggest the faded or extinguished embers of a fiery passion (or moment of creativity) now dormant, or if treading on them might suggest a pilgrimage or some kind of penitential journey, we might recall that taking walks on the cinder path with his governess near the Rectory were among the poet's earliest memories ('We called it the Cinder Path because it was made of cinders, it put your teeth on edge to walk on it'),[14] so perhaps it is not surprising that so many childhood memories emerge in this volume; nor is it surprising that 'nightmare' is often associated here with childhood memory and experience. 'We must use what transport we can,' he claims (whether cinder path or nightmare ride), and there is perhaps the hope they may be transported together within or through

---

[10] John Press, *Louis MacNeice* (London: British Council and Longmans, Green & Co., 1965), 40; Peter McDonald, *Louis MacNeice: The Poet in his Contexts* (Oxford: Clarendon, 1991), 187.

[11] MacNeice, *Collected Poems*, 514, 516, 496.

[12] See MacNeice, *Collected Poems*, 212, 301, 494.

[13] Ibid., 576.

[14] MacNeice, *Strings Are False*, 49.

the poems. His promise to dismount from the horse of imagination or of bad dream implies his desire to control it and to avoid becoming absorbed by it. Getting off the path or off his ride signals a certain determination to assert his will over the circumstances in which they are embroiled, and sounds all the more assertive for the contrast with those poems in the late verse in which he seems to be on a train ride he can neither control nor terminate. The green fields seem 'improbable' because he realizes the elusiveness if not impossibility of the idyllic; because the self is qualified by memory, and his dreams are tinged by nightmare. The green fields in fact seem to echo the evocation in 'The Introduction' of a lovers' 'grave glade', changing by the end of the poem to a 'green grave', which again suggests the close proximity between life and death, or between dream and nightmare, within the poet's imagination.[15]

A poem like 'After the Crash' takes the nightmare theme in a slightly different direction, in which the protagonist is neither in a dream nor having one, but is unable to remember the events surrounding a fatal accident in which he was involved. He understands that time has passed only by observing the hemlock that has grown all over the asphalt around him, and by seeing or imagining the damage done to his crash helmet and his hand, implying the multiple injuries he himself has sustained. MacNeice himself was involved with Mary Wimbush in a car crash in 1961, but the poem is cast in the third person, and the protagonist's perceptions are presented with a surreal, hallucinatory quality. There are references to signals bouncing back from the moon, to the hens, and the small, blind cats, and of course the hemlock overgrowing the asphalt, suggesting that a very long time indeed has passed.

We are told that 'life seemed still going on' and are told that 'he came to', but in what sense he awoke ('came to') is not clear, since suddenly he has a vision of the scales in the sky as fatally balanced, and he has clearly missed his chance to experience the process of death, being dead, though nightmarishly aware of that fact: 'And knew in the dead, dead calm/It was too late to die.'[16] The figure as it were wakes up to the knowledge that it is too late to die. To return to the image from 'To Mary' of dismounting his ride, in order to join his beloved, there are numerous poems, including 'After the Crash', in which dismounting is not an option, in which stopping the death-bound train is impossible.

Like 'Star-gazer', the poem 'Soap Suds', which immediately follows the dedicatory poem, focuses on the relationship between past and present, and on the contrast between moments in childhood (vividly recalled), and an adulthood which affords the ambivalent pleasures of long recall and the grief of knowing what has been lost. The poem's faintly comical, bubbly title almost sounds like a phrase from a period commercial advertisement, but there is a fruitful contrast between the title and the meditation on memory, origins, and home which the poem offers. It begins with a Proustian recollection of a childhood memory triggered by the smell of a bar of soap: as Jon Stallworthy notes, 'In a Proustian day-dream, "Soap Suds" take the place of *madeleine*.'[17] The opening

---

[15] MacNeice, *Collected Poems*, 593.
[16] Ibid., 585–6.
[17] Jon Stallworthy, *Louis MacNeice* (London: Faber, 1995), 453.

phrase 'This brand of soap' conveys the impression that the speaker is pointing to an object which the reader too can observe, suggesting a sense of dramatic immediacy and intimacy.[18] At the same time, the hand holding the soap is also the hand holding the pen with which he is writing the poem, hence both soap and pen are agents for conveying the memory and for setting the scene. As the speaker recalls the big house he visited when he was eight, he has a vision through the bathroom walls of a croquet lawn on which he tapped a ball through croquet hoops—an imaginative way of following the speaker's trail back to childhood, represented by the reverse movement of the ball going back through the hoops, 'To rest at the head of a mallet held in the hands of a child.' Long, flowing lines allow the casual speaking voice to tell his story unhindered and follow its every fantastic, extraordinary twist and turn as the ball 'skims forward':

> Through hoops where no hoops were and each dissolves in turn
> And the grass has grown head-high and an angry voice cries Play!
> But the ball is lost and the mallet slipped long since from the hands
> Under the running tap that are not the hands of a child.[19]

As D. B. Moore writes, 'there is a sense of failure, an almost hysterical effect of time telescoping' through the croquet hoops.[20] The telescoping of time, the measuring of the distance from the past to the present is suggested by the image of 'tower with a telescope' (also an image of surveillance and power); in the second stanza, the 'faded globes' suggest the relics of the ages, while conveying also the notion of faded maps of territories over which the owners no longer assert control:

> And these were the joys of that house: a tower with a telescope;
> Two great faded globes, one of the earth, one of the stars;
> A stuffed black dog in the hall; a walled garden with bees;
> A rabbit warren; a rockery; a vine under glass; the sea.

The stuffed dog is a nightmarishly mummified remnant of a beloved family pet, a museum specimen, the black dog of death. It is a pathetic image of what Dan Davin calls 'nature morte': 'For Louis there was always something sinister about libraries and museums: however the scholar in him might value them, in his poetry they tend to symbolize nature morte, life dead and so susceptible of control, the immortal shrivelled to the immortelle.'[21] And 'the vine under glass', while doubtless of interest to a child, is something vital and alive which has been controlled and made into an object of the scientific gaze. By contrast, the last in the series of 'joys' is the untamed and protean sea, 'To which he has now returned'—a redemptive moment in an otherwise funereal and deadening scene. As a voice cries out, the ball is tapped. In its acoustic variety and richness ('crack, a great gong booms') and its use of hyphenated phrasing ('dog-dark'), the line is reminiscent of Dylan Thomas—as also in the awareness of time passing and of the inevitability

---

[18] MacNeice, Collected Poems, 577.
[19] Ibid.
[20] D. B. Moore, The Poetry of Louis MacNeice (Leicester: Leicester University Press, 1972), 197.
[21] Dan Davin, Closing Times (London: Oxford University Press, 1975), 57.

of death. The gong, as ever in MacNeice, suggests both the objective passing of time and the speaker's feelings of apprehension at that fact. By contrast to the sound of a moment in time being marked by a gong, the following long line—'Skims forward through the hoop and then through the next and then . . .'—suggests (or enacts) the movement of the ball over the lawn and through time. The use of repeated conjunctions ('and') suggests movement and flow, as the line's fluency imitates the ball's smooth movement over the grass. Indeed, the dynamism of the line contrasts strikingly with the rather static, poised list of objects (the catalogued 'joys' of the house) a few lines earlier. The poem moves full circle on itself, and as Stallworthy remarked: 'Again there is sunlight on the garden and, as the train wheels had revolved once at the perimeter of the Rectory garden, the ball revolves—it and the globes and the gong (all linked by their common adjective *great*) reinforcing the circular movement of the poem.'[22]

'Soap Suds' is set in the home—Seapark, near Carrickfergus—of MacNeice's step-uncle, Thomas MacGregor Greer, a well-known leading Unionist figure in the area, with close ties to the Larne gunrunning of 1914 and to local recruitment for the UVF and for the 36th (Ulster) Division which fought at the Somme. Indeed, his success in the latter venture earned him plaudits from Edward Carson, as conveyed in a letter of 12 July 1916.[23] (The poet recalls visiting Seapark when he was eight, after September 1915, when Thomas Greer's influence on Unionist politics, particularly the movement to resist Home Rule, was at its height.) MacNeice was of course a visitor, not a resident of this house, and nor was he a member of the class which is traditionally associated with such houses. His father's second marriage was to Beatrice Greer, and the Greer family was a prominent linen family, members of an Ulster Protestant ascendancy, with properties in Tullylagan (County Tyrone) as well as in Regent's Park and Hampshire. The opening lines of MacNeice's greatest poem, *Autumn Journal*, are in fact set in another house owned by a branch of the Greers, in Hampshire: 'Close and slow, summer is ending in Hampshire,/Ebbing away down ramps of shaven lawn where close-clipped yew/Insulates the lives of retired generals and admirals'.[24] There is perhaps a relished irony for the poet in setting himself in such locations, and one of MacNeice's touchstones was the poetry of Yeats, whose idealized, elegiac representation of the big houses of the Anglo-Irish were integral to his poetics. The self-elegiac fantasy of 'Soap Suds' is linked to an elegiac presentation of the house itself, with its faded globes and relics, although it is not clear what redemptive values he finds there, if any. The poem closes shockingly, with the acceleration of time and the transformation of the child's hands to those of the adult speaker, who is washing his wrinkled hands under the running tap. The running water, not unlike the moving ball in the poem, signifies the unstoppable force of time pressing forward to certain death. The grass, now grown 'head-high', echoes the overgrown hemlock in 'After the Crash', and everything, as in that poem, has turned to nightmare. MacNeice's poems about time depend crucially upon the representation of memory in order to achieve

[22] Stallworthy, *Louis MacNeice*, 453.
[23] MacNeice, *Letters*, 58, n.5.
[24] MacNeice, *Collected Poems*, 101.

their effects, whereby he conveys the sense of accelerated time as like a train, or fast-flowing water, or indeed a horse over which one can have no control and from which he cannot dismount.

I began by considering MacNeice's journey by boat and train from Ireland to England and thence to Euston, Waterloo, and Sherborne, a journey he made regularly during his period of attendance at Sherborne preparatory school. When he attended Marlborough College and later Oxford, similar kinds of trajectory had to be negotiated at the beginning and end of each term, and it is hardly surprising, perhaps, that sea and train travel became important tropes in his work for the rest of his life. As several critics have pointed out, and as several of his poems imply, the movement of train or bus in his writing becomes a metaphor for the passage of time, as does the movement of the croquet ball through hoops in 'Soap Suds'. In 'Star-gazer', the journey from Waterloo to Sherborne coincides with an extraordinarily vivid sighting of stars, which in turn leads the speaker to think about the voyage of astral light over vast stretches and billions of miles of space and time. The fact that Robert Ball would use train travel as an apparently far-fetched illustration for space travel suggests the centrality of train travel in British culture at that time, while also affording MacNeice an unusual opportunity to meld together the experiences of watching the skies and travelling by railway in this powerfully speculative lyric poem of the early 1960s. He was interested at various stages of his life in quest poems, Celtic immram and the Norse saga, although few of his later poems, while occasionally using travel as a poetic trope, betray great interest in those forms. Having said that, we see in the later lyrics a tendency to view memory itself as a kind of journey imagined in spatial terms, like the croquet ball passing through hoops, and to view intimacy as a sort of journey, whether as nightmare or as treading the cinder path—both of which are images that have origins in earliest childhood.

In the Clark Lectures given in the last year of his life, and published as *Varieties of Parable*, MacNeice begins by exploring the definition of 'parable' as given by the *Oxford English Dictionary*. It can mean 'any saying or narration in which something is expressed in terms of something else'. Also, it adds, 'any kind of enigmatical or dark saying'. He continues:

> This should certainly cover the whole range of my specimens from the *Faerie Queene*, which Spenser himself described as a 'dark conceit', to *The Ancient Mariner*, *Waiting for Godot*, *Pincher Martin* or the poems of Edwin Muir....But to counter the 'dark saying' of the dictionary, I should like to anticipate some of my later remarks and state baldly here that one very valuable kind of parable, and particularly so today, is the kind which on the surface may not look like a parable at all. This is a kind of double-level writing, or, if you prefer it, sleight-of-hand. It has been much used by poets and one could make out a case that all worthwhile poetry involves something of the sort.[25]

---

[25] Louis MacNeice, *Varieties of Parable* (Cambridge: Cambridge University Press, 1963), 2–3.

MacNeice's fascination with parable at this time is suggestive for a reading of the later work. He is interested in expanding the definition of the genre in various directions, and he expressed distaste for narrow definitions of the term, such as restricting it to the parables of the New Testament, for instance. In poems such as the ones we have considered above, there is clearly an interest in 'double-level writing' and 'sleight-of-hand', which MacNeice wishes to attribute to parable, and it is quite likely that in *The Burning Perch* the poet was aiming for the narrative simplicity, compression, and intensity of parable, as he defines the term.

PART V

POETRY AND THE ARTS

CHAPTER 16

....

MODERN IRISH POETRY
AND THE VISUAL ARTS:
YEATS TO HEANEY

....

NEIL CORCORAN

I

....

Despite the best efforts of Kingsley Amis ('nobody wants any more poems about . . . paint-ings'),[1] modern poetry's engagement with the visual arts has been constant since the 'imagism' of the early twentieth century in which modernism first conceived itself, and conceived of itself, as painterly in its very self-definition. Ekphrasis—poetry about vis-ual representations—has been endemic to modern poetry and has attracted a large body of critical and theoretical activity. Modern Irish poetry, initiated by Yeats, has the rela-tionship almost programmed into its DNA. The son of a painter and the brother of a great painter, Yeats himself trained briefly in an art school. He frequently makes refer-ence to painting and sculpture in both his poetry and prose, and he opened his *Oxford Book of Modern Verse* with a 'free verse' lineation of Walter Pater's famous passage on *La Gioconda* in *The Renaissance*. 'Only by putting it in free verse,' says Yeats, 'can one show its revolutionary importance'; but the extremely undistinguished verse resulting may be allowed instead to indicate Yeats's sense of the inextricability of poetry and painting in the foundational aesthetics of modernity.[2]

He is fascinated early by the Pre-Raphaelites, notably Dante Gabriel Rossetti, painter and outstanding ekphrastic sonneteer; he is permanently interested in Blake; the paint-ers of the Quattrocentro figure in several major poems; he is converted by Hugh Lane to the French Impressionists; in *A Vision* he compares his system-making to Wyndham Lewis's cubes and Brancusi's ovoids; and in that book's 'Dove or Swan' chapter he reads

---

[1] Quoted in *Poetry of the 1950s*, ed. D. J. Enright (Tokyo: The Kenkyusha Press, 1955), 17.
[2] W. B. Yeats, ed., *The Oxford Book of Modern Verse* (Oxford: Oxford University Press, 1936), p. viii.

historical process through the history of sculpture. He rarely writes purely ekphrastic poems: 'On a Picture of a Black Centaur by Edmund Dulac' only appears to be an exception, since the image it evokes is in fact composite, and the poem is therefore an example of what John Hollander usefully calls 'notional ekphrasis'.[3] Poignantly, however, 'A Bronze Head' in *Last Poems*, Yeats's final poem on Maud Gonne, takes off from Lawrence Campbell's painted bronze plaster cast in Dublin's Municipal Gallery. A genuine ekphrastic poem, its mimetic image of 'a bird's round eye/Everything else withered and mummy-dead' outstares many of the more sparing images of Gonne in Yeats's work, a terrible counterpart to those representing her as a Pre-Raphaelite beauty.[4]

Even if not generally ekphrastic, however, certain of Yeats's poems, among them some of his greatest, are so intimately involved with the visual arts as to provoke from critics a language of the painterly and sculptural. Such poems as 'Leda and the Swan' (which introduces 'Dove or Swan'), 'Lapis Lazuli', 'Sailing to Byzantium', 'Among School Children', 'Under Ben Bulben', and 'Long-legged Fly' are weightily pondered responses to the visual and testamentary to its pre-existing plastic power in ways variously admiring and competitive. Such poems invite readings of that agonistic kind characteristic of contemporary theorists of ekphrasis who tend to perceive the relationship between *poesis* and *pictura* as a combination of iconophilia and iconophobia.

The relationship between 'Leda and the Swan', for instance, and the image of Michelangelo's which is probably its most significant source would appear a prime case, even an allegory, of what James A. W. Heffernan reads as the 'paragonal' (from Leonardo's *paragone*) and gendered nature of ekphrasis, its posing of a relationship between language gendered as male and visual representation gendered as female. Furthermore, when Heffernan characterizes the dynamic and obstetric nature of ekphrasis, in which the poem narrativizes the 'pregnant moment' of the visual representation, he is using terms almost demanded by Yeats's magnificently perturbing, volcanically dynamic sonnet of divine violation and gestation and their eventual consequence in the catastrophe of 'the burning roof and tower/And Agamemnon dead'.[5] The poem realizes, as ekphrasis often does, but not often with such power, the potent linguistic energy inherent in the stasis of the pictorial image, and it electrifies the stillness of the image into a linguistic object no longer still but, like the swan's 'great wings' of its opening line, 'beating still'. 'The Tragic Theatre', an essay of 1910, proves that Yeats understands all of this theoretically as well as creatively when he says, with reference to Titian and medieval Chinese painting, and with a superb confidence of discrimination, that 'it seems at times as if the graphic art, unlike poetry which sings the crisis itself, were the celebration of waiting'.[6] At such moments,

[3] See John Hollander, *The Gazer's Spirit: Poems Speaking to Silent Works of Art* (Chicago: University of Chicago Press, 1995), *passim*.

[4] W. B. Yeats, *The Variorum Edition of the Poems of W. B. Yeats*, ed. Peter Allt and Russell K. Alspach (Basingstoke: Macmillan, 1956), 618–19.

[5] See James A. W. Heffernan, *Museum of Words: The Poetics of Ekphrasis from Homer to Ashbery* (Chicago: University of Chicago Press, 1993), *passim*.

[6] W. B. Yeats, *Essays and Introductions* (London: Macmillan, 1961), 244.

when the magnificence of Yeats's prose virtually matches that of his greatest poetry, he himself sings the crisis of representation to which any act of ekphrasis may give rise.

Not only does Yeats write poems prominently preoccupied with the visual arts, and poems which enact the opportunities of the ekphrastic, in some of the most excruciated ways, but he also writes, in 'The Municipal Gallery Revisited', one of the great poems of the institution in which the visual arts are validated and made universally available by modernity. Published in book form in the same year, 1938, as Auden's 'Musée des Beaux Arts', the other great poem of the modern museum, it offers the conception of the public gallery as the church of a secular modernity: the domain of commemoration, the pre-server of the values of a community or a state, the site of reverence and the opportunity for transcendence.

The gallery's paintings as Yeats evokes them transform the revolutionary Ireland of his immediate past into permanent testamentary image and do so by painting 'an Ireland/The poets have imagined, terrible and gay'.[7] Here Yeats is fantasizing a kind of reverse ekphrasis in which the paintings reconfigure poetry. But of course many paint-ings do originate in poetry: J. M. W. Turner's *The Golden Bough*, which deeply impressed Yeats in his youth, is a notable instance. Since the concept of tragic gaiety figures so largely in Yeats's work, and since the word 'terrible' resounds so memorably in the refrain of 'Easter, 1916', he must, himself, be one of the poets who have enablingly imagined the Ireland of these painters; perhaps even the only one. The relationship between poetry and painting is a competitive agon here, then, in which the poet makes himself pre-eminent and victorious, but it is also reciprocal. The reciprocity enables a form of self-transcendence for this poet, who has of course known the sitters for many of the gallery's portraits. So that the poem's famous final lines—'Think where man's glory most begins and ends/And say my glory was I had such friends'—themselves transform the desire for fame, which might seem arrogance or vainglory, into a splendour and effulgence retaining something of the aura of the word 'glory' in Christian theology. This is an exhilarating reversal of the emotion and the gesture which the paintings initially pro-voke in the ageing poet ('Heart smitten with emotion I sink down'); and at its close 'The Municipal Gallery Revisited' assumes the language of theological transformation to enact what is virtually a secular theophany. The gallery of modern art, 'this hallowed place', becomes the scene of worldly redemption, which is what painting and sculpture are, at their most intense and exalted, for W. B. Yeats; and the poem, like the gallery itself, takes on the aspect of the monumental. Doing so, it becomes in Irish literature, to steal a phrase from Seamus Heaney's 'The Settle Bed', an 'un-get-roundable weight'.[8]

Yeats's poems involving the visual arts might indeed seem formidably un-get-roundable to his successors, particularly if we agree with James Heffernan that ekph-rasis is doubly paragonal in that it stages a contest not only between word and image but also between one poet and another.[9] Derek Mahon in fact has a poem in *Harbour Lights*

[7] Yeats, *Variorum Poems*, 602.
[8] Seamus Heaney, *Seeing Things* (London: Faber, 1991), 28.
[9] Heffernan, *Museum of Words*, 23.

(2005) entitled 'Lapis Lazuli' and dedicated, as Yeats's poem of the same title is, to Harry Clifton, although we must assume that Mahon's dedicatee is a different man and poet.[10] This appears to parade the inevitability of the relationship with Yeats while at the same time deflecting it with an elegant literary joke. In fact, however, engagements with the visual in Irish poetry after Yeats seem to me to reveal no deep anxiety about him and neither are they inevitably agonistic, despite much ekphrastic theory. The spirit of poetry bloweth where it listeth, and relations between poetry and painting may signal many things other than the competitive: the genuinely tributary, the cooperative, the self-reflexive, the self-identifying, the tutelary.[11] The other is not always rival. Even so, the competitive is clearly sometimes involved too.

II

Among the generation with the awkward task of succeeding Yeats, Louis MacNeice, Brian Coffey, and Padraic Fallon all wrote poems related to the visual arts. MacNeice has his own gallery poem, 'The National Gallery', celebrating the return of its paintings to London after the war, which also views the gallery as a species of human or worldly redemption, 'our lop-sided instincts and customs atoned for here': the final line prays that the newly opened windows might let in the air to 'Purge our particular time-bound unliving lives, rekindle a pentecost in Trafalgar Square'.[12] Such emotion must be understood in the immediately post-war context of *Holes in the Sky* (1948), and is consonant with many other literary Christian and quasi-Christian productions of the time, but it inevitably seems a little portentous now. MacNeice's poem of the early 1930s, 'Nature Morte', more memorably epitomizes Jean-Baptiste-Siméon Chardin in its final couplet in a way congruent with the metaphysical aura sometimes taken on by ordinary objects in his poems too. This is ekphrasis as self-reflexive, therefore, perhaps almost self-parodistically so when in Chardin, we are told, 'the appalling unrest of the soul/Exudes from the dried fish and the brown jug and the bowl'.[13]

Brian Coffey's 'Painterly', subtitled 'Remembering Chagall', reads some unspecified images by the painter as the register of his love for and admiration of a woman and of Coffey's love for and admiration of Chagall himself:

> Nicotiana open where
> he has been drawn to
> to see her open eyes

[10] Derek Mahon, *Harbour Lights* (Oldcastle: Gallery, 2005), 24–5.
[11] In thinking about the possibilities of ekphrasis I am indebted to Elizabeth Bergmann Loizeaux's *Twentieth-Century Poetry and the Visual Arts* (Cambridge: Cambridge University Press, 2008).
[12] Louis MacNeice, *Collected Poems*, ed. Peter McDonald (London: Faber, 2007), 258–9.
[13] Ibid., 23.

> silence then deep eyes
> silence hers silence his[14]

This lapidary telegraphese seems alert to the ethics of ekphrasis in which the poet who presumes to give a voice to the silence of the painter's image acknowledges his presumption as the interruption of a kind of contractual silence between painter and subject. The painter, Coffey writes, 'nor ever would loose his care/to keep her self selfsame/secret living veiled'.[15] The paradox is that, in speaking on behalf of the painter or the painting, the poet is inevitably exposing the secret to language, giving voice to a silent image, so that an act of admiration is also an act of violation; which is precisely not what this poem figures Chagall doing with his subject in the painting's devoted act of 'care'.

The poet of the immediately post-Yeatsian generation most preoccupied with the visual arts, however, is Padraic Fallon. Fallon is extremely uneven, even within individual poems, but the earlier of two poems called 'Lakshmi', on a statue of the Hindu goddess, is an exception. The poet concentrates with awe on the 'dangerous bronze figure', a composite of erotic and spiritual revelation, from a culture altogether other than his own. Fallon imagines the lotus on which the goddess stands as the graceful growth of Hindu culture itself: 'there was/Dancing here that folded into a lotus'.[16] A poem of admiration, entrancement and allure, 'Lakshmi' offers an instance of Irish ekphrasis as an interiorization of otherness, Fallon reading himself out of his own cultural heritage and assumptions in a way exemplary in the inward-turned Ireland of the mid-twentieth century.

As such, this poem joins hands with work by a much-travelled younger-generation poet, John Montague, whose early sequence 'Cultural Centre: *Musée Imaginaire*' is subscribed 'New Haven, 1954' and whose title picks up the phrase made current by André Malraux in *Les Voix du Silence* (1951) as an index of modernity's relationship with art in the 'museum without walls'.[17] The 'cultural centre' of the title is knowingly alert also to the further transformations undergone by the new democratizing of the institution of the gallery represented by the more community-inclined or demotic ideology of such 'centres'. Hence the four sections of the poem are entitled as 'rooms' I to III and an 'entrance hall'. These are the shared spaces of hitherto quite distinct, and distinctive, cultures: a Catalan crucifixion and a many-handed Indian god; a Botticelli-derived virgin and a Japanese mountain; a canvas figuring 'slaughtered forms' and a 'complete abstraction'. The image of the 'minatory' crucifix hangs over the whole, however, and meets, in the final lines, the 'minute harmless god of silver plate' hanging at the waist of a 'tiny nun' taking her class on a cultural visit; and the poem ends with her standing 'possessively beneath/The lean, accusing, Catalan crucifix'.[18]

---

[14] Brian Coffey, *Poems and Versions 1929–1990* (Dublin: Dedalus, 1991), 208.

[15] Ibid.

[16] Padraic Fallon, *Collected Poems* (Oldcastle: Gallery, 1990), 143.

[17] André Malraux, *Les Voix du Silence* (Paris: Gallimard, 1951); *The Voices of Silence: Man and His Art*, trans. Stuart Gilbert (New York: Doubleday, 1953).

[18] John Montague, *Collected Poems* (Oldcastle: Gallery, 1995), 204–5.

This is the poem of an Irish Catholic, or ex-Catholic, taking countenance of the facts of both cultural relativism and religious desuetude. The nun's assumption of possession is undercut by the diminution of the force of the traditional Catholic image at her waist, by her diminutive size, and by the accusation of the Catalan image, product of a culture of deep belief and awe responsive to great human suffering. But it too, by being transposed here, has become cultural object rather than religious icon; and the fiercely numinous power discovered in it by this once Catholic poet will become less and less available to, and less readable by, an increasingly secular society. This is a haunted poem, index of a transitional moment in Irish modernity, uncertain of its own emotion and allegiances and of what might constitute its own 'cultural centre', of what might any longer suffice in the imaginary museum of the Irish Catholic imagination.

Appropriately, then, Montague has also written an outstanding ekphrastic poem on an image in Bruges by the early Renaissance Netherlandish painter Gerard David. A prose poem in the volume *Tides* (1971) with the ominous title 'Coming Events', which seems deeply to have internalized Auden's 'Musée des Beaux Arts', it is the only ekphrastic poem Montague has written and one of the very few prose poems. Genre and form are appropriately matched, as the unemphatic register of his distinguished prose examines David's image of a man being almost decorously flayed, with the torturers, the onlookers, and even the victim himself displaying little emotion. The poem's final sentence, with its playing on the cliché of being 'led to admire', is responsive in its understated insouciance, leaving the poem's real work to be done by the discrepancy between this sentence and its title: 'The whole scene may be intended as an allegory of human suffering but what the line of perspective leads us to admire is the brown calfskin of the principal executioner's boots.'[19] 'Coming events', then: but also a complement to Auden's 'how everything turns away/Quite leisurely from the disaster'—including, of course, the implicated viewer of the image too.[20]

III

Michael Longley, like both Derek Mahon and Seamus Heaney, has an early poem dedicated to the Northern Irish painter Colin Middleton. He also has an elegy for Gerard Dillon, the Belfast painter who, in Longley's memorial trope, has become 'a room full of self-portraits', in what seems a variant of Auden's trope in his elegy for Yeats that the poet after death has 'become his admirers'.[21] Dillon is also commemorated by some attributes of the Catholic Belfast of his origins, 'The shawls of factory workers,/A blind drawn on the Lower Falls', although many of his paintings in fact take Connemara for their

[19] Ibid., 244.
[20] W. H. Auden, 'Musée des Beaux Arts', *Collected Poems*, ed. Edward Mendelson [1976] (London: Faber, 1991), 179.
[21] Ibid., 247.

subject.[22] Longley's poem celebrates not just the dead painter, then, but the decencies and probities of the place and community which nurtured him. In 1973, when it appeared in *An Exploded View*, whose punning title is drawn from the visual arts, this must have seemed a decent gesture of its own, a tactfully understated signal of rapprochement in a city exploding in sectarian division.

Longley's persistent interest in the visual arts is manifest in various ways: he has collaborated with painters on limited editions, including *Patchwork* with Jim Allen in 1981 and *Out of the Cold* with his daughter Sarah Longley in 1999—about whose own work he has a poem in *Snow Water* (2004), 'Primary Colours'—and he has written entries for exhibition catalogues.[23] In one of these, for the Northern Irish painter Felim Egan in 1996, he evokes the painter's canvases and methods by quoting both John Ashbery and Emily Dickinson; reading paintings through poems, therefore. When he says that Egan's 'rich tonalities depend on a frugality of means' he may well be supplying a phrase appropriate to his own work too, and in fact his note concludes by quoting a phrase from his poem 'Stilts'—'playthings for the soul'—as also appropriate to Egan, and then going on to quote a stanza.[24] We could hardly have a clearer indication of the way in which a poet reading a painter is also reading himself. Longley writes: 'Purged of rhetoric, Beckettian almost, earthy and yet ethereal, his is a pianissimo world where whimsy swells into vision.'[25] Not Beckettian, maybe: but the other terms apply, especially to the poem which gives its title to Longley's 1976 volume, *Man Lying on a Wall*.

'Man Lying on a Wall' is an ekphrastic poem written as a 'homage to L. S. Lowry', which takes his well-known painting of that title as its subject. The poem has its whimsical element, as it speculates on the poem's geometry and imagines that the man lying without the support of the wall would be a kind of miracle or conjuring trick. This seems psychologically acute about what we actually do, sometimes, in front of paintings, as we separate out formal from material properties by tracing shapes, proportions, the squares and triangles of geometrical observation behind the work's production. The Lowry painting is likely to promote such speculation since its spare, precise means emphasize the geometry of the repeated brick rectangles of the wall itself and of chimney, clock tower, and cigarette pointing upwards into what Longley accurately calls 'the enormous weight of the sky'. But the poem then turns from formal speculation to the actual image:

> It is difficult to judge whether or not
> He is sleeping or merely disinclined
> To arrive punctually at the office

---

[22] Michael Longley, 'In Memory of Gerard Dillon', *Collected Poems* (London: Jonathan Cape, 2006), 70.

[23] Michael Longley, *Patchwork*, with drawings by Jim Allen (Oldcastle: Gallery, 1981); *Out of the Cold: Drawings and Poems for Christmas*, with Sarah Longley (Belfast: Abbey Press, 1999); 'Primary Colours', *Collected Poems*, 300; *Causeway: The Arts in Ulster* (Belfast: Arts Council of Northern Ireland, 1971).

[24] Michael Longley, 'Stilts', *Collected Poems*, 102.

[25] http://www.felimegan.ie/longley.html.

> Or to return home in time for his tea.
> He is wearing a pinstripe suit, black shoes
> And a bowler hat: on the pavement
> Below him, like a relic or something
> He is trying to forget, his briefcase
> With everybody's initials on it.[26]

Fran Brearton reads this poem as congruent with the volume's preoccupations with alternative and divided selves and with 'moments of self-conscious fictionality', and she elegantly says that it is a poem 'inspired by [a work] of art and self-consciously about the workings of art'.[27] This is true, and the poem takes its place in the history of ekphrastic self-reflexivity: but it is more peculiar than this too. Inspired by the Lowry image, which is among his most famous, the poem nevertheless misreads it or mistakes it. The man in Lowry is not wearing a pinstripe suit, but a black jacket and brown trousers, and he is not wearing a hat. In addition, it is also not at all difficult to judge whether he is sleeping or not since his left eye, which we can clearly see, is wide open. Longley has either misremembered the painting or deliberately varied it for the purposes of his poem. He has, in other words, made it his own. But this is what all ekphrastic poets do with paintings, even if usually not by so manifestly altering the original image.

Longley also makes it his own when the poem's originating whimsy culminates, if not in 'vision', then in that thing into which this poet's work often wanders, a form of ramifyingly peculiar rumination which raises more questions than it is ever likely to answer. In those lines which have a faintly Larkinesque cadence, why is the briefcase like a relic, exactly, or something he is trying to forget? We assume that it has everybody's initials on it because everybody has their relics and their things they wish to forget. But that detail too is one final appropriation of the painting's actuality since, very strikingly, the initials on the briefcase in the painting are LSL—Lowry's own, of course. By obliterating them and replacing them with everybody's, Longley is also replacing them with his own, assuming possession of the painting in the way he assumes possession of Lowry's title for his book. This poem may therefore be read almost as an emblem of one possibility of ekphrasis.

When Longley writes an ekphrastic poem about his own portrait by Edward McGuire, 'Sitting for Eddie', he makes its signal element the fact that McGuire gets the colour of his eyes wrong. This must have been galling, and the poem refers to 'crazed arguments' with the painter on the matter.[28] McGuire could also be regarded though as trumping the strange mistake, if it is that, which Longley makes about Lowry's painting. Poems and paintings, and perhaps paintings and people too when people are their subject, need not correspond and be equivalent.

---

[26] Longley, *Collected Poems*, 107.
[27] Fran Brearton, *Reading Michael Longley* (Tarset: Bloodaxe, 2006), 117, 120.
[28] Longley, *Collected Poems*, 198.

IV

Derek Mahon is probably the most thoroughgoing ekphrastic poet in Irish writing between Yeats and Heaney. His poem for Colin Middleton, 'A Portrait of the Artist' (first published as 'Van Gogh among the Miners' in his first book, *Night-Crossing*, in 1968), ventriloquized for Van Gogh, finds a brilliant image for the way the aesthetics of his art are a mode of humanistically displaced evangelical Christianity when the painter projects his future work as 'Setting fierce fire to the eyes/Of sunflowers and fishing boats,/Each one a miner in disguise'.[29] There is an intensity of empathy in this, which is Mahon's for Van Gogh, as well as Van Gogh's for the miners, and the displacement of Protestant evangelicalism by the alternative luminosity of art clearly has implications close to home for this poet born into Protestant working-class Belfast; and his subsequent volumes offer many further readings of himself into painters and paintings including, outstandingly, Edvard Munch, Paolo Uccello, Pieter de Hooch, and William Scott. 'Art Notes' in *Life on Earth* (2008) is a sequence of nine ekphrastic poems, including the evocation of work by Edward Hopper, René Magritte, and Howard Hodgkin;[30] and his 1982 volume, *The Hunt By Night*, is entitled after the great painting by Uccello in the Ashmolean in Oxford.

Mahon's finest achievement as an ekphrastic poet, also published in that book, is 'Courtyards in Delft'. Subtitled 'Pieter de Hooch, 1659', it evokes a painting in the National Gallery (although Mahon's plural title suggests that other de Hooch canvases may impinge upon it too). The first three stanzas suggest what de Hooch's image appears to exclude—knowingly, since it prominently foregrounds a pail and broom. In Mahon's reading even the trees have their 'trim composure'; and the regularity of the poet's stanzaic shapes is a formal mimesis of composure too. Not only the literal dust and dirt are swept out of the image, however: so is the complicating mess of love and sex which in other paintings—by de Hooch himself, and by Vermeer, for instance, in images sometimes tense with secret or as yet unrealized narratives—might be emblematized by spinet-playing, 'lewd fish', and a bird about to fly its cage. However, Mahon's poem says of the painting's image that 'this is life too': the routine housewifely care of seventeenth-century Delft has been unforgettably memorialized by de Hooch, made 'vividly mnemonic' in pictorial afterlife. And the poem 'Courtyards in Delft' is admiringly, scrupulously atttentive to this.

But its penultimate stanza suddenly turns from an evocation of the painting to the poet's personal pronoun:

> I lived there as a boy and know the coal
> Glittering in its shed, late-afternoon
> Lambency informing the deal table,

---

[29] Derek Mahon, *New Collected Poems* (Oldcastle: Gallery, 2011), 25.
[30] Ibid., 299–307.

The ceiling cradled in a radiant spoon.
I must be lying low in a room there,
A strange child with a taste for verse,
While my hard-nosed companions dream of fire
And sword upon parched veldt and fields of rain-wept gorse.[31]

This is a recognition scene which comes as a genuine shock, as Mahon literalizes, as it were, the metaphor of reading oneself into a painting, crossing the working-class Belfast of his childhood with the courtyards of seventeenth-century Delft in a quite unpredictable piece of deft analogizing. One obvious element of the analogy is reticently withheld: that both cultures are Protestant and, indeed, that they are directly linked through the presence of 'King Billy', William of Orange, in Northern Irish Protestant iconology. Clearly enough, however, what Mahon is recognizing in the de Hooch is that cleanliness which is next to godliness in Protestant virtue. In fact, although Mahon doesn't say so, the painting prominently includes, in the form of a written tablet above its arch, a piece of homiletic advice recommending patience and meekness.[32] Another element of analogy, however—that both are engaged in, or products of, imperial venture—is insinuated by the word 'veldt', which summons the open spaces of South Africa in which the men of seventeenth-century Holland were building their empire while women such as those depicted in the painting kept the homes clean. What de Hooch's painting ultimately excludes is the 'fire' of imperial plunder, of imperialism as Protestant moral obligation; and what lies just behind Mahon's poem is the conflagration of Northern Ireland at the time of its writing, the violence of which the 'hard-nosed companions' of his childhood dream in a Belfast of barely contained sectarian suppressions and repressions.

In Mahon's 1999 *Collected Poems* the final stanza is jettisoned; most unfortunately, in my view.[33] In *The Hunt By Night* version the repressed violence finally returns with, as it were, a vengeance. Dutch imperialism goes on the march when 'the pale light of that provincial town/Will spread itself like ink or oil/Over the not yet accurate linen/Map of the world', and the exclusionary stasis of de Hooch's image is galvanized into narrative consequence when the poem's final lines voice a desire that is the clamour of domestic repression itself: 'If only now the Maenads, as of right,/Came smashing crockery, with fire and sword,/We could sleep easier in our beds at night.'[34] The apparently demented paradox remembers, no doubt, the subsequent history of South Africa, but is also tuned to the post-1960s frequencies of Northern Irish atrocity and outrage. The poem is therefore almost as perturbed in its sense of inevitable consequence as Yeats's 'Leda and the Swan'; and Mahon's relationship to de Hooch is manifestly agonistic as well as admiring, a potently revisionary piece of ekphrastic deconstruction.

---

[31]   Derek Mahon, *The Hunt by Night* (Oxford: Oxford University Press, 1982), 9–10.

[32]   See Peter C. Sutton, *Pieter de Hooch, 1629–1684* (New Haven: Yale University Press, 1998), 124.

[33]   In fact, the stanza does not exist in the poem's first appearance: Derek Mahon, *Courtyards in Delft* (Oldcastle: Gallery, 1981); it was then added to the version in *The Hunt by Night*; but was subsequently dropped from the version in Mahon's *Selected Poems* [1990] (London: Penguin, 1991) and has never reappeared in any edition since.

[34]   Mahon, *The Hunt by Night*, 10.

'Like ink or oil': like, therefore, the medium of poetry and the medium of painting. Reading himself into the painting as a 'strange child with a taste for verse', Mahon is also self-reflexively crossing his own nascent poetry with de Hooch's painting. The child lying low—hiding out, biding his time—will eventually emerge as the poet who, in the act of reading a painting with powerful originality, will get his place and time into perspective; into, in fact, the long perspectives of artistic representation. In poetry of deftly understated implication, Mahon here writes, then, ekphrasis as a form of historical analogy, discernment, and critique.

He also writes a characteristic poetry of light. Glittering coal and radiant spoon are, in these lines, 'vividly mnemonic' too; and 'Lambency informing the deal table' is richly ambivalent. 'Lambency' is light shining softly like a flame, but may also mean the brilliant and delicate play of wit or fancy. Derek Mahon, by using the word in the first sense, is operating in the second. 'Inform' means to give a shape to, which the light in a painting may do to a table, but which we don't usually conceive of light as doing to an actual table. So the implicit transferral of the actually remembered table of childhood into a painted representative of itself—as it is, now, also, a poetic one—may be regarded as an ultimate form of ekphrasis, and 'Courtyards in Delft' becomes not only an ekphrastic poem but a painterly one too.

V

Seamus Heaney's relations with the visual arts are apparent from the beginning. In addition to his Colin Middleton poem in *Death of a Naturalist* (1966),[35] one of several painterly coordinates shared with Longley and Mahon, he has a poem called 'Bogland' in *Door into the Dark* (1969) dedicated to the Northern Irish landscape painter T. P. Flanagan. The poem's title mirrors that of a set of 1960s paintings by Flanagan, *Boglands*; and the bog becomes of course an enduring poetic resource for Heaney. Years later, the 'Squarings' sequence in *Seeing Things* (1991) had its origins in a collaborative exhibition with Felim Egan, and twelve poems were separately published as a limited edition with lithographs. In an author's note to the 'special copy' Heaney says that certain images of Egan's and some of his own poems are jointly about 'natural landmarks that had become marked absences', and in a 1992 catalogue note for an Egan exhibition he says that the painter's work gives a sense of 'the exquisite ache which the physical world induces'.[36] Both phrases are, surely knowingly, apposite to 'Squarings' too.

Heaney also dedicates other poems to artists, and some figure significantly in poems: the sculptor Oisin Kelly in 'Glanmore Sonnets' in *Field Work* (1979), for instance, the potter Sonja Landweer in 'To a Dutch Potter in Ireland' in *The Spirit Level* (1996), and

---

[35] Seamus Heaney, 'In Small Townlands', *Death of a Naturalist* (London: Faber, 1966), 41.
[36] See Rand Brandes and Michael J. Durkan, *Seamus Heaney: A Bibliography 1959–2003* (London: Faber, 2008), 75; and http://www.felimegan.ie/review.html.

Barrie Cooke painting 'godbeams' in 'Saw Music' in the sequence 'Out of This World' in *District and Circle* (2006). In *Stepping Stones*, Heaney makes plain his friendship with painters from the 1960s on, and his deeply informed knowledge and appreciation of the visual arts generally also becomes clear.[37] His dealings with contemporary painters include limited-edition collaborations, art criticism, catalogue introductions for, mainly, contemporary Irish artists (but also Howard Hodgkin), and the curatorship of an exhibition in the Ulster Museum in 1982, *A Personal Selection*, for which he wrote a catalogue in which a reiterated term of approbation is 'lyric', as in 'lyric precision'. This is impressionistic as art-descriptive terminology but reveals Heaney's tendency to conflate the visual and the poetic, or to reconfigure artwork in poetic terms.[38]

Heaney has ekphrastic poems too, including 'Grotus and Coventina' in *The Haw Lantern* (1987) on a Roman altar bas-relief; the second section of 'Seeing Things', on an unspecified cathedral facade; ' "Poet's Chair" ' in *The Spirit Level*, on a street sculpture in Dublin by Carolyn Mulholland, which includes a comic allusion to 'Sailing to Byzantium'; and 'The Mud Vision' in *The Haw Lantern*, which is a kind of disguised ekphrastic poem, deriving in part from Richard Long's 'Mud Hand Circle'. In that poem, as elsewhere too, Heaney is inventively exploratory in the inherited genre. Notably, 'To a Dutch Potter in Ireland' is a remarkable instance of the dialogism potentially inherent in ekphrasis. Heaney's meditation on glazes by this artist who grew up in occupied wartime Holland embraces both his own childhood in Northern Ireland and a translation of a poem called 'After Liberation' by the Dutch poet J. C. Bloem. 'To a Dutch Potter in Ireland' opens with an italicized epigraphic section in which words themselves are imagined as having 'come through the fire': so an implicit relation is established between poetry and pottery, and between art and the horrors of modern history, before the potter summoned by title and dedication is addressed.[39] Her life and the poet's are then crossed as the poem moves towards an ekphrastic evocation of her glazes which, in a phrase quoted from her, 'bring down the sun'; and finally the poem includes her history and culture and, in translation, her language too, in addition to a reference to the burning Kuwaiti oilfields of the Gulf War in 1991. The dialogism of ekphrasis, then, promotes here a very rich socializing of the lyric voice, joining poet to potter, potter's voice to poet's, poet to poet, and the Second World War to the Gulf War, in a celebration of what an art that comes through the fire, a survivor's art, might offer in the face of human and historical depredation.

So the subject of Heaney's relationship with the visual arts is a large one. Here I want to think about its impact on *North* (1975) and about a later ekphrastic poem on his portrait by Edward McGuire which was reproduced on the back cover of the original Faber edition.

North opens with 'Mossbawn: Two Poems in Dedication', which set the much fiercer poems of the rest of the volume under the affectionate aegis of recollections of

---

[37] See Seamus Heaney and Dennis O'Driscoll, *Stepping Stones: Interviews with Seamus Heaney* (London: Faber, 2008), especially 333–6.

[38] Seamus Heaney's *A Personal Selection* (Belfast: Ulster Museum, 1982) is unpaginated.

[39] Seamus Heaney, *The Spirit Level* (London: Faber, 1996), 2–4.

Heaney's own childhood Northern home. The first, 'Sunlight', with its evocation of the sun 'against the wall/of each long afternoon' and its portrait of a woman at work in a domestic interior using as a duster an archaic 'goose's wing', seems to have Vermeer in its generation. The second, the sonnet 'The Seed Cutters', summons Breughel to authenticate the truth of its own representation of other 'calendar customs'; which is to define an allegiance to a painter of the North in the same gesture in which Heaney defines one to his own place and first community.[40] The gallery-going contemporary is therefore allied, without strain, to the inhabitant of rural Mossbawn. Although this poet appeals to a validating authority, however, the appeal itself cannot but have an authoritative self-assurance too: in any sonnet less capable in tone it would seem a presumption.

Set under these northern painterly stars, the subsequent poems in *North* frequently include elements of ekphrasis, as they meditate various objects into the precisions of appropriately spare language: quernstones; Viking archaeological finds and 'trial pieces'; the anatomical plates of Baudelaire's 'The Digging Skeleton' (that Baudelaire who was intensely preoccupied with the visual arts and an outstanding ekphrastic poet); and Goya's paintings, in an extended ekphrasis at the end of 'Summer 1969'. Here Heaney situates himself in Madrid as Belfast explodes, listening to advice to return and assume some kind of writerly responsibility but instead 'retreat[ing]' to the Prado and taking instruction from this devastating painter of warfare, violence, and brutality. Heaney names the *Shootings of the Third of May* and evokes *Saturn Devouring his Son*: but it is his description of the *Duel with Clubs* as 'that holmgang/Where two berserks club each other to death/For honour's sake, greaved in a bog, and sinking' which seems most directly to correspond with the situation in the North.[41] One of Goya's Black Paintings, it is an image not only of appalling ferocity but of utter futility, since the bog will claim both men anyway, even if one manages to club the other to death first. The relatively peculiar words 'holmgang' and 'berserk' used as a noun call attention to themselves. The former is the Old Norse for a duel to the death and the latter, from the Icelandic, means a wild Norse warrior. Heaney's foregroundedly Northern vocabulary, in an act of commanding ekphrastic appropriation, tears the image from its original Spanish location and gives it, as it were, a newly relevant topography in the same act in which it gives it a newly contemporary political resonance.

These ekphrastic moments in *North* also bring into relief the act of ekphrasis involved in the 'bog poems' themselves, and in fact this holmgang in a bog makes 'Summer 1969' a bog poem too. These are poems which originated, in 'The Tollund Man' in *Wintering Out* (1972), not with a body retrieved from the bog, but with the photograph of such a body. The promissory dedication of that poem's opening line—'Some day I will go to Aarhus'[42]—has, it seems, been kept by the time of 'The Grauballe Man' in *North*, where 'I first saw his twisted face/in a photograph.../but now he lies/perfected in my

---

[40] Seamus Heaney, *North* (London: Faber, 1975), pp. ix–xi.
[41] Ibid., 63–4.
[42] Seamus Heaney, *Wintering Out* (London: Faber, 1972), 36.

memory'.[43] The ekphrastic moments of *North* all put their weight on Heaney's figuration of himself as an 'artful voyeur' in 'Punishment';[44] and, beyond its immediate context in that poem, the phrase may do duty for the ethical awkwardnesses of some forms of ekphrasis too. Keeping a promise made in a poem about a photograph may be read as a self-validating response to that ethical issue.

Edward McGuire's portrait of Heaney seems almost calculated to emphasize the relationship between the poems and the visual arts. Having the portrait of a poet on the jacket of what was only his fourth collection is unusual; but it was all the more so because, as Heaney says in *Stepping Stones*, 'it was the first time Faber broke with the old house style, which had never featured author photographs or jacket art'.[45] This now extremely well-known image seems exceptionally well attuned to the poetic persona implicit in the volume's many uses of the first person singular. Heaney, wearing a dark polo neck, sits at a small table in front of a window with a book open in his hands but looks forward at his portraitist, appearing clenched, even cornered. There is perhaps something Hamlet-like about the representation; and in one of the poems the poet figures himself as 'Hamlet the Dane,/skull-handler, parablist'.[46] A tree with very large leaves and two large-headed birds in its branches, eerily turned towards each other, fills the window. The table is covered in a white cloth with a geometrical design. This portrait makes its sitter an icon: the solitary, concentrated, dark-clothed figure at a kind of altar seems almost monastically dedicated, both to his book and to the natural world beyond the window which seems his true domain. It is a representation of Heaney as one of his own *North* poems.

In 'A Basket of Chestnuts' in *Seeing Things* Heaney revisits the portrait. The poem's opening stanzas describe swinging a loaded basket in that way Heaney has of almost preternaturally getting into language something we've often experienced but hardly even acknowledged, and then reading out of that delicacy of physical evocation a whole system of value—in this case, of both dismay and ratification. 'Description is revelation!' he quotes from Wallace Stevens in a poem in *North*;[47] and the strength of his work always lies, before it lies anywhere else, in the exactness of recording. Which is one reason why painting means so much to him, presumably; and why 'A Basket of Chestnuts' envies that other art when it says of remembered chestnuts:

> And I wish they could be painted, known for what
> Pigment might see beyond them, what the reach
> Of sense despairs of as it fails to reach it,
> Especially the thwarted sense of touch.[48]

---

[43]   Heaney, *North*, 29.
[44]   Ibid., 31.
[45]   Heaney and O'Driscoll, *Stepping Stones*, 327.
[46]   Heaney, 'Viking Dublin: Trial Pieces', *North*, 14.
[47]   Heaney, 'Fosterage', ibid., 65.
[48]   Heaney, *Seeing Things*, 25.

'Known for what/Pigment might see beyond them': a visionary epistemology is made to depend on the activity of painting here, when it becomes impersonally active, its very medium credited with sight, with 'seeing things'.

But the poem then tells us that Maguire had considered using a basket of chestnuts as 'a decoy or a coffer for the light', but instead chose to reflect it off Heaney's shoes. So 'it wasn't in the picture and is not':

> What's there is comeback, especially for him.
> In oils and brushwork we are ratified.
> And the basket shines and foxfire chestnuts gleam
> Where he passed through, unburdened and dismayed.

In these lines the language of dismay and ratification with which the poem opens is now transferred to Maguire himself, in tributary elegy (he died in 1986). Heaney's descriptive accuracy—'foxfire' couldn't be bettered—matches the painter's; and it is this accuracy which makes for the outlasting capacity of art. 'Especially for him', since he is the maker of this enduring object: but, by implication, for his sitter too, who goes on sitting there for as long as the portrait stays. So these lines join painter and poet in memorial evocation, and in the ambivalent triumph and terror of making. They do so too in a very peculiar form of ekphrasis. 'A Basket of Chestnuts' is both an ekphrastic poem by a poet on his own portrait and a poem evoking a painting which does not exist. Summoning the idea of an alternative composition, the poem holds the relationship between writing and painting in an admiring but interrogative tension. It is tribute but displacement too; and, since it is a self-representation which is being displaced, the competition is, we might think, with an earlier self and poet as well as with a painter. Ekphrasis here aids a motion characteristic of Heaney's oeuvre as it develops: returning on itself in order to move further forward.

CHAPTER 17

POETRY, MUSIC, AND
REPRODUCED SOUND

DAMIEN KEANE

I

The 'music of poetry' is certainly one of the more disenchanting phrases to confront in the literary critical canon, one as ready to dispel close attention to similarities between the two arts as to resolve significant differences through auratic hocus-pocus. Despite the stability of the phrase over time, its referent has been decidedly mutable and its use highly instrumental; its overall durability may indeed depend on its power to overshadow historically dynamic interrelations. Based in classical understandings of music, song, and lyric poetry, a long critical tradition has sought to identify intrinsic affinities between poetry and music, from their unfolding in time (versus extending in space, as visual art forms do) to their reliance on patterns of tone, pitch, and duration ('melody' and 'rhythm'). In turn, these immanent correspondences have frequently been invoked to sanction judgements on extra-aesthetic matters, particularly on relations of artist, artwork, and audience. While this distinction of internal and external relationships has never been as clear-cut in practice as in formulation, the literary symbiosis between the 'musical' and the 'poetic' stands primarily opposed to the referential. In order then to dampen what can feel like an aesthetic echo chamber, this essay will triangulate music and poetry with the non-aesthetic category of reproduced sound as a means of developing a thematic overview of its topic. As such, its alternate title might be 'Irish Poetry After Edison'.

Irish poetry has frequently been held to share a special connection to music, based on anything from the 'musicality' of Irish speech to rhyme and stress patterns in verse to beliefs about the social role of poetry in national life. Indeed, Thomas MacDonagh's conception of a distinctive 'Irish mode' in poetry rests on all three.[1] Poetry itself can be

[1] Thomas MacDonagh, *Literature in Ireland* (Dublin: Talbot Press, 1916).

considered a 'technology' of sound reproduction, although its obvious difference from mechanical and electrical means of reproducing sound should not be subsumed by this characterization. If Patrick Kavanagh could summarize his late, 'casual' style as 'being able to play a true note on a dead slack string'[2] it is requisite to notice the kind of metaphor not suggesting itself in context: tuning-in to the proper wavelength, smoothly dropping the needle. Yet the remark had been made during a Telefís Éireann programme, whose script was then published in conjunction with the release of the album *Almost Everything*.[3] Observing this is not to impugn Kavanagh, but only to recognize that he, iconoclasm and all, worked within a field structured in part by symbolic relations to music. For just as the Irish literary field has developed through cooperative antagonisms with other national and transnational fields, modern Irish poetry has relied on associations with music to measure the effects of modernity, at times to deplore them, at others to explore them. At its most successful, this exchange results in stereophonic reflexivity, as in Pearse Hutchinson's 'Fleadh Cheoil', which describes local and emigrant musicians gathering 'to play an ancient music, make it new'.[4] Signifying closer to practical 'transmission' than pure 'innovation', the Poundian note is here made new through reference to the social history of music, to a process of making rather than a declaration of newness.

The scope of this essay is necessarily at odds with the scale of its topic. Several omissions are especially regrettable—Yeats's renewed interest in vocal timbre in the context of broadside publication and radio broadcasting in the mid-1930s; the various uses of 'music' as an organizing category in anthologies of Irish poetry across the period; the intriguing instances of poets listening to recordings of other poets—but it is hoped these matters might serve as outward horizons for the present undertaking. The essay is arranged in three sections, each one gradually moving away from notions of authenticity and originality that have tended to underpin discussions of the relationship of poetry and music. These notions are certainly germane, and perhaps even central, to the topic, but criticism that leaves them unexamined proceeds with its governing questions already asked and answered.

II

An apposite place to begin is a comparison of two recordings of Louis MacNeice's 'Bagpipe Music' made within several months of each other in 1961. Released on *Louis MacNeice Reads Selected Poems* (Argo) and *Louis MacNeice Reads From His Own Works* (Carillon), the recordings employ distinct technical methods of positioning MacNeice's

---

[2] Patrick Kavanagh, *Self Portrait* (Dublin: Dolmen Press, 1964), 29.

[3] Patrick Kavanagh, *Almost Everything*, Claddagh Records CCT 1, 1964 (LP). The television programme was broadcast in October 1962.

[4] Pearse Hutchinson, *Collected Poems* (Oldcastle: Gallery, 2002), 44.

voice, each one extending the poem's meditation on authenticity and modernization.[5] Less concerned simply to imitate music, 'Bagpipe Music' instead embodies the clash of residual and emergent cultural modes in its play of syllables against beats and use throughout of feminine rhymes to carry images of economic depletion. Like certain slapstick comedies, its antic surface admits to harsher underlying realities. For each recording, MacNeice provides an explanatory gloss, the Carillon introduction being twice as long as that on Argo, perhaps in recognition of its American audience. (Carillon released the Yale Series of Recorded Poets.) It ends with information completely absent from the Argo introduction:

> There are just perhaps one or two things, two minor points, I ought to make clear.... 'Ceilidh' is a Gaelic word for a social get-together, social gathering in the evening, usually with Gaelic songs and fiddling or piping. 'Cran' is a measure of herring, rather a large measure, and the point about this herring fishing, which comes in here, is one of [the] economic paradoxes of the 30s, that when they had a really good year, with lots of herring, half the fishermen went bankrupt, because it became a glut on the market.

As a detail of the recording, this annotation is more than an auditory headnote, for it points to precisely those concerns in the poem that are amplified by the technological medium. Performative variations aside—for example, the breakneck pace of the Argo reading is tempered in the Carillon reading—the most marked difference between the two recordings is in their presentation of MacNeice's voice. Listening to the Argo album, one hears the voice within a defined space, for the microphone had been placed far enough from MacNeice to record the reverberations of his voice in the room in which he was speaking. What one hears is a simulation of the sonic space of a small gathering, in this case at a kind of 'ceilidh'. The Carillon recording, on the other hand, presents a reverb-less, disembodied voice indebted to post-war radio broadcasting, the sound of its close-miked speaker fabricating conversational intimacy outside of any grounded space and an illusion of direct communication with listeners. Each of these techniques attempts to create an impression of instant communication, and, as such, each recording skews the poem's concern with sociality and dislocation. 'Bagpipe Music' ends side one of the Argo album on a boisterous note, whereas on the Carillon album it leads into Section IX of *Autumn Journal* and its sceptical account of the lure of ahistorical identification.

The importance of the positioning of the speaker's voice becomes even clearer in relation to the word 'cran'. As MacNeice had glossed it, the term—derived from the Scots Gaelic *crann*, meaning 'lot' or 'share'—refers to a standardized quantity of herring that had been imposed on the traditional economy, again as the poet notes, to deleterious effect. In 'Bagpipe Music', the word has another echo, for a cran (or crann) is the name of a common ornament in piping, consisting of different grace notes played against

---

[5] Louis MacNeice, *Louis MacNeice Reads Selected Poems*, Argo Records RG196, 1961 (LP), and *Louis MacNeice Reads From His Own Works*, Yale Series of Recorded Poets, Carillon Records YP318, 1961 (LP).

unchanging melodic notes (D e-D f-D g-D). Between economic rationalization and traditional practice, the dissonant interplay of these two meanings of 'cran' perfectly condenses the wider tensions at issue in the poem. However, listening to the two recordings, in which MacNeice's voice is 'Bagpipe Music', the dissonance is 'resolved' by the two variations on simulated immediacy produced in the sound engineer's booth. The social intimacies the tripper of the 1930s could not find and would not counterfeit are instantiated on the albums of the 1960s by the aural 'closeness' of reproduced voice and listener.

Similar issues of the reproduced voice and audience arise in recordings of Richard Murphy's *The Battle of Aughrim* and John Montague's *The Rough Field*. Commissioned for the BBC's Third Programme, the recording of Murphy's sequence uses five speakers and musical accompaniment (arranged by Sean Ó Riada and performed by Ceoltóirí Chualann, soon to become The Chieftains) to achieve its meditation on historical discontinuity; it was later released as an album.[6] Having been produced for broadcast, the recorded voices are close-miked and disembodied, each one as solitary as stanzas on the page; for the listener, there is no sense of the five readers speaking, or even existing, in the same space. This reverb-less isolation is here quite 'literary' and neatly enforces the poem's thematic preoccupations: 'They try to imagine/Exactly what took place, what it could mean,/Whether by will or by chance'.[7] Contrasting this vocal isolation is the intercut playing of the musicians, which often builds from one or two players to full ensemble; indeed, a comparable 'isolation' is instrumentally achieved only when Ó Riada plays unaccompanied baroque music on the harpsichord. Conforming closely to Ó Riada's notions of Irish traditional music as unique bearer of national heritage, this contrast of voice and music also chimes with the poem's understanding of traumatic historical rupture. In the monaural field of the recording, the music remains just behind the voices—this mono is not Phil Spector's contemporaneous 'wall of sound'—a placement that intimates fugitive continuities amid overriding loss.

Influenced by Murphy's work, Montague's *The Rough Field* explores personal belonging and inheritance against a backdrop of historical and political division.[8] On the page, the sequence juxtaposes lines of poetry with found texts, historical quotations, and sixteenth-century woodcuts illustrating colonial expansion in Ulster, resulting in a collage whose features compete for the attention of the reader's eye. On record, however, this visual assemblage becomes 'polyphonic, a long poem with many contrasting voices'.[9] Recorded live in London in 1973, the performance orchestrates voices and music to become what Montague calls a 'traditional symphony', developing a series of contrasts toward resolution in uncertainty. Because it is a live recording, it captures the spontaneous interactions of speakers, musicians, and audience in

---

[6] Richard Murphy, *The Battle of Aughrim*, read by Cyril Cusack, Cecil Day-Lewis, Ted Hughes, Niall Toibín, and Margaret Robertson, Claddagh Records CCT 7, 1969 (LP).

[7] Richard Murphy, *The Battle of Aughrim* (London: Faber, 1968), 62.

[8] John Montague, *The Rough Field* (1972; Oldcastle: Gallery, 1989).

[9] John Montague, *The Rough Field*, read by the author, Seamus Heaney, Benedict Kiely, Tom McGurk, and Patrick Magee, Claddagh Records CCT 19-20CD, 2002 (CD). The quotation is from Montague's liner notes.

context, an of-the-moment quality that, in its way, is quite appropriate to the sequence's collage aesthetic. For part nine of 'Patriotic Suite', a halting reading of each stanza is interspersed with several measures of a jig, resulting in a performance that does not cohere. But the section describes the disorienting clash of inheritance and reality— *'Puritan Ireland's dead and gone,/A myth of O'Connor and O Faoláin'*—witnessed at a *fleadh cheoil*, and the recorded performance successfully dramatizes this disjointed condition. In doing so, it reminds us that 'musical' is not always synonymous with 'euphonious'.

Even so, music remains a potent symbol in Irish poetry for more direct or holistic connections between artist and community, for an interactive immediacy denuded or lost in other spheres of modern life. In this regard, it is difficult to overestimate the importance of Seán Ó Riada, whose attempts to fuse the compositional principles of modern European music with the communal practices of traditional Irish music have had a profound influence, especially on his immediate male poetic contemporaries. (Montague, Thomas Kinsella, Seán Lucy, and Pearse Hutchinson have all written elegies for him, as has the younger Seamus Heaney.) Integral to Ó Riada's vision is the presiding figure of the artist, the organizing authority who brings order to chaotic fragments of contemporary experience; integral to his influence has been the apparent confirmation of this vision in the popular acceptance of his work. As reconciler of artist and audience, his example has been crucial to Montague and Kinsella, although each finally casts Ó Riada as a tragic figure unable to fulfil his potential. Set on the first anniversary of Ó Riada's death, Kinsella's *Vertical Man* stages a ghostly encounter with his friend over bourbon, a recording of Gustav Mahler's *Das Lied von der Erde*, and the wailing sirens of the Philadelphia fire department:

> I lifted the glass, and the furies
> redoubled their distant screams.
> To you: the bourbon-breath.
> To me, for the time being,
> the real thing...[10]

With its play of 'bourbon-breath' and inspiration, the poem focuses its occult sight on 'the real thing', the 'residue' of Ó Riada's spirit that outlasts his passing: 'But a residue in the timidity,/a maturer unsureness, as we/prepare to undergo preparatory error.'[11] For all its personal tenderness, the poem is heavy with aesthetic angst, as cultural despair stands in for autonomous distance. In Heaney's 'In Memoriam Seán Ó'Riada', it is this misrecognition that threatens to drag Ó Riada's art into artfulness: ' "How do you work?/ Sometimes I just lie out/like ballast in the bottom of the boat/listening to the cuckoo." '[12] Possessed of 'the *sprezzatura*', Ó Riada's stance continually risks falling prey to the contradictions of mediation it was meant to resolve. Later in *Field Work*, Heaney responds

---

[10] Thomas Kinsella, *Fifteen Dead* (Dublin: Dolmen Press, 1979), 28.
[11] Ibid., 30.
[12] Seamus Heaney, *Field Work* (London: 1979), 29–30.

to this dilemma in 'Song', with its delicate image of being just behind the beat of immediacy: 'that moment when the bird sings very close/To the music of what happens'.[13]

A strikingly different take on mastery and community can be found in Máire Mhac an tSaoi's 'Sunt Lacrimae Rerum', which mourns Séamus Ennis, the renowned piper, music collector, and broadcaster, who died in 1982.[14] The poem adopts the formal conventions of the keen, or traditional lament for the dead, in order to praise Ennis's consummate playing and record its loss to the world. Given his work collecting and documenting traditional music (and recurrent themes of personal, social, and historical loss in Mhac an tSaoi's poetry), the lament is intricately reflexive about the function of such work, employing a centuries-old form to comment on contemporary conditions in a mode opposed to straight recovery or preservation. Like a keen, it directly addresses the departed Ennis: 'Ach, an ríphíobaire Éireann, clos duit ní dán arís—Choíche!' ('But, King-piper of Ireland, voice is with[h]eld from you—Ever!'). Unlike a traditional keen, however, it does not indict or accuse, but grieves for the world: Ennis's stilled voice has left silence over all. In the reflexive context of the lament, it is nevertheless worth recalling that the title of one of Ennis's best-known recordings, still in circulation, is *The Wandering Minstrel*.

As a form of sociality, this technological 'afterlife' is decisive. In what is a thematic rewriting of 'Bagpipe Music', Derek Mahon's 'In the Aran Islands' opens with an image of a *sean-nós* singer as wireless receiver: 'He is earthed to his girl, one hand fastened/In hers, and with his free hand listens,/An earphone, to his own rendition,/ Singing the darkness into light'.[15] Entranced by this doubled figure of transmission, the outsider-speaker then attempts to 'dream [himself] to that tradition', only to find his idyllic tuning-in jammed by the squawking of a gull. Because both singer and speaker are radio-sets, this failed reception of 'tradition' becomes a technical condition: one radio is not more 'authentic' than any other. Tradition is revealed to be a feature of contemporary modernity rather than its antithesis, one that does not, however, imply easy or equal access for all modern subjects. Yet this recognition does not negate the fact that modernity offers its own simulations of traditional belonging. This point is picked up in Mahon's 'I Am Raftery', in which the blind poet is updated as a university lecturer:

> Is it
> empty pockets I play to? Not on your life,
> they ring with a bright inflationary music—
> two seminars a week and my own place reserved
> in the record library. Look at me now,
> my back to the wall, taking my cue from a
> grinning disc-jockey between commercials.[16]

---

[13] Ibid., 56.

[14] Declan Kiberd and Gabriel Fitzmaurice, eds., *An Crann Faoi Bhláth/The Flowering Tree* (Dublin: Wolfhound Press, 1991), 86–7.

[15] Derek Mahon, *Lives* (Oxford: Oxford University Press, 1972), 5.

[16] Ibid., 32.

III

Grinning or otherwise, the disc jockey embodies a changed perception of community, symbolizing the impersonal social relations structuring modern experience. The spatial distance between modern subjects represented here has its temporal analogue in the ability of recording technology to play back the sounds of the departed: indeed, the iconic logo of His Master's Voice pictures a fox terrier faithfully listening to the sound of his dead master's voice as it issues from a gramophone. While the image allegorizes fidelity, literary responses to the transcendence of past and present that it encapsulates have been anything but uniform, ranging from dogged nostalgia for what is gone to ecstatic celebration of what is to be unleashed in the 'post-contemporary'. Each of these poles idealizes the condition of mastery, a shared trait cogently exposed in Rhoda Coghill's 'Epitaph for a Musician', an eight-line lyric on mastery achieved through practice. Having worked for much of her professional life as lead accompanist at Radio Éireann, Coghill would have been familiar with this unglamorous side of the musician's craft: to be an effective accompanist, a player must have a practised and agile sense of sympathy in order to remain necessarily in the background. In a way, it is possible to understand her poetry—its different formal modes pitched to thematic diversity—in similar terms. 'Epitaph for a Musician' considers the interplay of sensory perception ('this world's sounding instruments/Eye, ear, and hand') and inspiration ('the airs the Spirit breathes') within a total sonic field encompassing both living and dead:

> His eyes are open on our dark;
> Our silence beats about his ears;
> And Spirit's new, mysterious theme
> Only the dead musician hears.[17]

Beginning with the indefinite article in its title, the poem gives no indication of this musician's categorical singularity, instead offering learned skill as the medium between inspiration and sense, as the source of greatness. Mastery comes not from genius, but practice. 'Our silence' is thus a temporary condition, awaiting the manifestation of 'our' changed perception in new music.

A similar awareness of music animates the work of Michael Coady. Writing as player and listener, Coady attends to the uncanny presence of sound (musical performance, recordings, overheard talk) in the quotidian world, gracefully and humorously detailing its powerful effects on the shaping of experience, from 'Tracing a Cracked High B-flat for Posterity' to 'Mozart and the Kiss of Time'. Although his work has been rightly celebrated for its thoughtful investigation of locality, the capaciousness of its scope is only truly limned by acknowledging the sonic contours of Coady's writing. Poetic appeals to music often invoke its intangibility as an elegiac figure for separation and loss, for what

---

[17] Rhoda Coghill, *Time is a Squirrel* (Dublin: Dolmen Press, 1956), 17.

is physically absent; in Coady's work, however, this intangibility is always materialized through an occasion (a festival, a session, a stray remark) or object (a recording, his uncle's trombone), thereby situating what can otherwise be preciously ethereal. In the marvellous prose-piece 'Three Men Standing at the Met', this 'grounding' serves to open up the seemingly fated relationship of past and present. It begins with a live broadcast from the Metropolitan Opera House in New York of Verdi's *La Forza del Destino*, an occasion that raises a fundamental question of creative determination: 'All in a micro-second of transmission from there to here. What has this to do with poetry? With some cosmic harmony of hearts? With the music of what happens?'[18] Bringing together family memory, social history, and aesthetic retrieval through 'the force of destiny', the piece tells of how Coady's father and two uncles, as emigrants to New York in the late 1920s, attended a performance of Verdi's opera at the Met, before tracking the fortunes of each man. These family relations become powerfully resonant at its conclusion, when Coady receives an old 78 of the production his father and uncles had seen decades earlier; for him, the arrival of this random gift reveals the word 'destiny' within 'destination'. Reading the piece as exemplary of his oeuvre, one might stress its simultaneously parabolic and material tracing of the routes to and from the local, by way of the intersections of *La Forza del Destino* and family circumstance. The spread of music is thus less a matter of predestination than of what Coady elsewhere calls a 'presequence',[19] a series of momen-tary junctures within the broad frame of historical flux. Following a programme bill, a gramophone disc, and a radio broadcast, readers catch part of the music of what happened.

An attempt to break with a more traditionally figured sense of the past drives Greg Delanty's 'We Will Not Play the Harp Backward Now, No'. Taking its title from Marianne Moore's 'Spenser's Ireland', where playing the harp backward was to be sentimental about the past, the poem begins with a remarkable image: 'We, a bunch of greencard Irish,/vamp it under the cathedral arches/of Brooklyn Bridge that's strung like a harp.' Located beneath 'this American lyre', it contrasts the liberating anonymity of the United States ('many of us/learned the trick/of turning ourselves into ourselves') with the claus-trophobia left behind in Ireland:

> Nor does this landscape play that unheard,
> but distinctly audible
> mizzling slow air
>   that strickens us with the plaintive notes
> of the drawn-out tragedy
> of the old country's sorry history.[20]

The conjoining of slow air and stunting historical legacy derives from the repertory of post-war film and television soundtracks, an elision at once naturalized and clichéd. Justin Quinn has written that Delanty 'merely replaces one wadge of schmaltz with

---

[18] Michael Coady, *All Souls* (Oldcastle: Gallery, 1997), 39.
[19] Ibid., 88.
[20] Greg Delanty, *The Hellbox* (Oxford: Oxford University Press, 1998), 33–4.

another, as he sentimentalizes the possibilities which America offers a younger genera-
tion. Arguably, he retains the old schmaltz also.'[21] While this judgement is not off the
mark, it is harsh in its inability to read the poem beyond the so-called choice of national
inwardness or worldly openness. Extending the connotations of the American wake—
the title of Delanty's volume preceding *The Hellbox*—the poem has its emigrants 'vamp',
a musical term for a riffing pattern used to hold time behind a solo, which here under-
scores the word's more otherworldly associations. It is this connotation of the undead
that returns at the poem's end:

> No, we'll not play the harp backward
> anymore, keeping in mind the little people's harp
> and how those who hear it never live long enough afterward.

These emigrants find liberating anonymity counterpointed by atomized dispersion and
social isolation.

This account of emigration is familiar, even archetypal. Yet to fault the poem for its
failed emancipation from the nation in the name of an unexamined cosmopolitanism is
to trade in an equally familiar and deeply aestheticized account of modern Irish writing:
bye-bye schmaltz (the Yiddish word for rendered chicken fat), hello extra virgin olive
oil. In these straits, an image of 'greencard Irish' vamping beneath the Brooklyn Bridge
usefully conjures Sonny Rollins's solitary nocturnal practice sessions under the more
prosaic Williamsburg Bridge, about a mile up the East River. Here the saxophonist found
necessary privacy for himself to work out his music, while respecting his neighbours'
ears: such was the practical accommodation available to one of the greatest improvisers
in jazz. Whether one holds a passport from the Republic of Ireland or the republic of let-
ters, the capacity for reinvention, of any sort, always exists in relation to embedded forms
of anonymity in the place of arrival. Sentimentalism and cosmopolitanism are two
means, among others, of forgetting this fact of modernity.

This fact, of course, is one not simply in effect in the places to which the Irish have
gone or continue to go, but informs social and aesthetic belonging on the island itself.
With its telephonic title, Blanaid Salkeld's *Hello, Eternity!* explores states of isolation
through avowals of barrenness, sterility, and the failure to engender any sense of poster-
ity. Its poems use night-visions and dream-logic to offset the incessant course of quotid-
ian reality, even as they remain obliged by a sense of lingering inheritance. Conveying
this experience of embalmed inheritance, 'Even the Carollers' expresses profound dis-
enchantment in the form of a Petrarchan sonnet:

> I hate verse. I have lost faith. To the sky,
> Even the carollers sing cold to-night,
> Precise and stiff—their measure of cold delight.
> I know but emptiness and liberty.
> My craft grown old and crazy, I still ply

---

[21] Justin Quinn, *The Cambridge Introduction to Modern Irish Poetry, 1800–2000* (Cambridge:
Cambridge University Press, 2008), 186.

Unwilling oar. No harbour is in sight.
I shall not ride at anchor off the bright
Innisfail, nor catch the beacon's eye.
Unstable, dark, my rough inheritance—
Mapped out by Fate's insoluble mistrust.
There have been ingrates. How should I affirm
I had been thankful for a genial chance?
Unnecessary, sterile, tortured dust—
Kept—but by uncouth anguish, from the worm.[22]

With its blunt opening, the first quatrain distinguishes the speaker from these songsters, whose devoted propriety and sanctioned pleasure are experienced as 'delight'. Setting the 'old and crazy' craft of the speaker against the 'precise and stiff' singing of the carollers, the second quatrain initially seems to gloss the consequences of this existential difference, holding out against the false hope of celestial hearing the possibility of terrestrial reception in a community to come. Yet the terms of this difference are mediated by 'emptiness and liberty', a relation that negates the possibility of deferred homecoming by suggesting a distended present in place of a future. While 'liberty' rhymes most closely with 'crazy'—a standard, if idealized, image of the outsider to social normativity—the sonnet's rhyme scheme insists on the half-rhyme with 'ply' as the hinge between the two quatrains. If alienation is the problem laid out in the first, the second develops it as a virtue made of necessity, a disposition not quite aligned with agency. This small consolation dissipates in the sestet, however, as the unwillingness to stagnate ('I shall not ride at anchor') is revealed to be the lonely provision of a mummified eternity. 'Uncouth anguish' buoys the speaker's 'craft' on its 'rough inheritance', and gratitude for the 'genial chance' offered by 'Fate's insoluble mistrust' is affirmed. 'I hate verse' becomes a profession of *amor fati*, one doubly plangent for being recognized as such. The sonnet's craft is caught between the verse of national tradition and the poetry of male-defined innovation.

Salkeld's disenchantment of the 1930s is transformed in Moya Cannon's 'Driving Through Light in West Limerick',[23] which engages Wallace Stevens's 'The Man With the Blue Guitar' as the occasion for an almost Benjaminian illumination of modern reenchantment. Stevens's poem responds to debates in the 1930s over competing modes of representing 'things as they are', the phrase that repeats across thirty-three modulating cantos.[24] A study in variation, the poem encompasses not only questions of the relation of poetry to the world, but of the status of poetry in the world; and it does so, critically, through the extended figure of the music of the blue guitar. Cannon takes her epigraph from Stevens: 'Poetry,/surpassing music, must take the place/of empty heaven and its hymns'.[25]

[22] Blanaid Salkeld, *Hello, Eternity!* (London: Elkin Matthews & Marrot, 1933), 55.
[23] Moya Cannon, *Carrying the Songs: New and Selected Poems* (Manchester: Carcanet, 2007), 105–6.
[24] Wallace Stevens, *Collected Poetry and Prose*, eds. Frank Kermode and Joan Richardson (New York: Library of America, 1997), 145.
[25] The line in Stevens reads 'Poetry/Exceeding music must take the place/of empty heaven and its hymns'. See Stevens, *Collected Poetry and Prose*, 136–7. The alteration loses some of the ambiguity of the original and, as a result, loads the dice a bit.

The poem opens by contemplating the nature of light—on a West Limerick landscape, in a Quattrocento painting of an angel viewed in a London gallery—and whether it creates or intensifies the beauty of the things on which it falls. This venerable aesthetic quandary is then recast, as the speaker steps from an Underground train and ascends a stairwell filled not with light, but the sound of 'an accordion tune':

> good music
> brought down to where it was needed,
> music surpassing poetry
> gone down again,
> the busker with a red *Paolo Soprani*
> telling again
> of Orpheus in Connacht.[26]

Prismed through the Quattrocento painter (with the golden patron), the man with the blue guitar, and the busker with the red accordion, the poem encapsulates the disenchanting trajectory of Western cultural production. Yet the poem's modern *mise en scène*—the random metropolitan encounters with gallery, Underground, and busker—endows this accordion music with its potential for re-enchantment, as the poem ends in phantasmagoric sight:

> The escalators ground up and down
> carrying all the people
> up and down a hill
> of saffron light.[27]

Here, Orphic music from the red accordion transmutes an everyday setting into a soundscape made bright in the light of this world.

It is the ability of music both to transform and carry over that holds Cannon's poetic eye and ear. In 'Between the Jigs and Reels', she writes that 'Tunes are migratory/and fly from heart to heart',[28] suggesting that this movement exists in the social world. Again, the two lines echo and ornament Stevens: 'The world about us would be desolate except for the world within us. There is the same interchange between these two worlds that there is between one art and another, migratory passings to and fro, quickenings, Promethean liberations and discoveries.'[29] The change from 'to and fro' to 'heart to heart' marks the difference of accent, one spelled out in the last stanza, in which the effects of the playing of Joe Cooley and John Doherty are conveyed:

> the rhythm of Cooley's accordion
> which could open the heart of a stone,
> John Doherty's dark reels
> and the tune that the sea taught him,

---

[26] Cannon, *Carrying the Songs*, 105–6.
[27] Ibid.
[28] Ibid., 112.
[29] Wallace Stevens, 'The Relations Between Poetry and Painting', *Collected Poetry and Prose*, 747.

> the high parts of the road and the underworlds
> which only music and love can brave
> to bring us back to our senses
> and on beyond.[30]

Whereas the eye passes to and fro across the faces of a crowd or features of a landscape and thereby measures its distance from them, the ear is surrounded by and immersed in auditory phenomena: in varying formulations, this distinction is central to divisions between reason and affect in Western metaphysics. What is fascinating about Cannon's poem is that its last four lines challenge this distinction, by visually focusing on music in the world, rather than in the ear. Its closing lines do not describe anyone's interior experience of listening; on the contrary, they represent the lived environment of aural experience, the contingent ground that gives the act of listening its historical meaning. Because of this, the note of transcendence in the final line is one rooted in the 'world about us', in sound beyond the ear: hence tunes that fly among hearts not like angels of heaven, but migrating birds.

IV

Sound beyond the ear and in the world about us is an apt description of a soundscape, a term R. Murray Schafer defines more precisely as:

> the sonic environment. Technically, any portion of the sonic environment regarded as a field for study. The term may refer to actual environments, or to abstract constructions such as musical compositions or tape montage, particularly when considered as an environment.[31]

While Schafer's notion of the soundscape is limited by its residual insistence on an ideal human scale or acoustic 'size', it nonetheless provides a generative channel for approaching Irish poetry that explores the full dynamic range of the sonic world, from the blackbird's whistle to the tin whistle, from humming wires to wireless chatter. This range encompasses the 'authentic' and 'synthetic', but with the signal virtue of locating both, without distinction, as features of a total and lived auditory field. Michael Longley elegantly registers this environment in 'Bud Freeman in Belfast', the second part of his sequence 'Words for Jazz Perhaps':

> Fog horn and factory siren intercept
> Each fragile hoarded-up refrain. What else
> Is there to do but let those notes erupt
>
> Until your fading last glissando settles
> Among all other sounds—carefully wrapped
> In the cotton wool from aspirin bottles?[32]

---

[30] Cannon, *Carrying the Songs*, 112.
[31] R. Murray Schafer, *The Tuning of the World* (New York: Knopf, 1977), 274–5.
[32] Michael Longley, *Collected Poems* (London: Jonathan Cape, 2006), 28.

With the inverted rhyme scheme of its two tercets (aba bab), the poem formalizes the mixing of performative and ambient sound in a one-to-one signal-to-noise ratio: the audiophile might flinch, but this is the context of the listener's experience. Longley describes an appallingly different soundscape in the two-line 'Terezín', about the death-camp known for the orchestras formed by its prisoners: 'No room has ever been as silent as the room/Where hundreds of violins are hung in unison.'[33] The decorum of the poem inheres in its exact attention to silence, to this 'noise' of aftermath: it is an act of remembrance that remains attuned to the grievous particularity of this soundscape. In both cases, the soundscape serves to hold off idealization without succumbing to a pinched realism.

An interest in the aural relations of the particular and the numinous motivates Leontia Flynn's slyly sublime 'Cyprus Avenue', which takes its title from the fourth cut on Van Morrison's *Astral Weeks*. In the poem, a young couple drive to a parking lot and, with Morrison's song on the car stereo, 'practice at the clutch', a vehicular metaphor with a very respectable pedigree in popular music. It would be incorrect to label the song—and, given the poem's outline of 'the way young lovers do', the entire album—as simply its intertext, for the poem not only couches its backward glance at youthful sexual initiation through the allusion to 'Cyprus Avenue', but presents the song as an aspect of the episode itself. This doubled perspective is, in fact, key to the poem's consideration of desire and maturity, of experience itself:

> An old song plays on the radio
> *I am captured in a car seat.*
> On the points of summer and youth
> the whole world pivots.[34]

That the song is a highly mediated commodity issuing from dashboard speakers must not disqualify the recognition of its ability both to inform and inflect understandings of the course of events. Put another way, a soundscape is at once determinate and contingent. *Astral Weeks* is rightly heard as a Belfast album, but it would not exist as such had it not been recorded in New York. Even this judgement rests on fortuity: would the album's fated musical textures be heard in the same way had Bernard Purdie and Chuck Rainey been hired for the session instead of Connie Kay and Richard Davis? Put yet another way, my own father once said that *Astral Weeks* always evoked for him a scene he once knew on Cypress Avenue in Brooklyn.

Other contemporary auditory environments can be as equally hypnotic, if decidedly less charming. In 'Misunderstanding and Muzak', Dennis O'Driscoll tells of a couple's botched meeting to buy groceries, one partner gone to the 'Super Valu supermarket', the other to the 'Extra Valu supermarket'. This domestic contretemps is revealed to be simultaneity, however, as each does the same things at the same times, the only difference being their respective in-house soundtracks: 'Danny Boy is calling you down special-offer aisles./Johann Strauss is waltzing me down special-offer

---

[33] Ibid., 186.
[34] Leontia Flynn, *Drives* (London: Jonathan Cape, 2008), 44.

aisles./I weigh mushrooms and broccoli and beans./You weigh beans and mushrooms and broccoli.'[35] The varieties of mundane experience this is not: a point the poem substantiates in its split-screen, two-line stanzas that track each parallel non-event, including the return of each muzak-loop to its beginning. Wryness aside, the cold object of this 'muzak of poetry' is the atomized, undifferentiated 'experience' offered up by such aural environments, a relation materialized in the inexorable circularity of the loop. Lost in the supermarket, this is the anomic soundscape of the non-place. Against this streamlined uniformity, O'Driscoll's 'Background Music' presents the polyphonic space of memory, in which sounds heard in the 'real-time' of the present join with recollections of past listening to create something other than cacophony: 'cross-hatched sounds that fuse in memory now,/a Charles Ives symphony improvised on the spot'.[36] Growing up in Danbury, Connecticut, Ives often heard different marching bands practising at the four corners of the town green, their musical elements combining according to his own placement on the square; this aural memory would later inspire his experiments in polytonal and polyphonic composition. Placed 'on the spot' between randomness and agency, then, O'Driscoll makes plain the interplay of experience and improvization.

The sonic density of this exchange is thoroughly intensified in the poetry of Alan Gillis, in which the interpenetration of objective and subjective situatedness functions as both ground and overtone in the ambient crackle of the poems. In a world of limited-edition LPs and proliferating hand-held devices, the poems edgily balance constraint and saturation with a language of quotation, metonymic reference, and ironically deployed euphemism, such that this linguistic condition comes to epitomize their very being. In its way, Gillis's work locates itself squarely amid the disputed etymology of 'persona' (a character or voice in a literary text; originally the mask worn by a dramatic player) in *personare* (to sound through). In 'Don't You',[37] the failed connection of a man and a cocktail waitress is told in two ten-line stanzas: the first is composed entirely of snippets from early-1980s pop songs (Human League, Talking Heads, Eurythmics, Duran Duran, Bruce Springsteen), while the second combines another round of song-quotations with bewildered reported speech. What 'straight' utterance there is in the poem consists of narrative set-up ('I asked for your name, tipped you again and again'), rather than voiced emotional interiority; but this complex of emotional guardedness and incomprehension gains its poignancy precisely to the extent that its language is 'displaced'. Although it is tempting to think of Gillis's procedure here as sampling, the format to which 'Don't You' is most directly indebted seems, in fact, to be the mix tape, that genre of longing and frustration, of hopes expressed and lost.

This subtle 'intermediation' is likewise present in Paul Muldoon's 'The Sonogram'. At first glance, the poem is an ekphrasis, a poetic description of two images of a child *in utero*:

---

[35] Dennis O'Driscoll, *Long Story Short* (London: Anvil Press, 1993), 36.
[36] Dennis O'Driscoll, *Weather Permitting* (London: Anvil Press, 1999), 14.
[37] Alan Gillis, *Somebody, Somewhere* (Oldcastle: Gallery, 2004), 19.

> Only a few weeks ago, the sonogram of Jean's womb
> resembled nothing so much
> as a satellite-map of Ireland:
>
> now the image
> is so well-defined we can make out not only a hand
> but a thumb;
>
> on the road to Spiddal, a woman hitching a ride;
> a gladiator in his net, passing judgment on the crowd.[38]

Like a classical ekphrasis, the final couplet offers interpretations of the second tercet, each one serving as a kind of epigrammatic title to the image. These images are not the typical visual representations of ekphrasic poetry, however, for each is the product of sound-reproduction technology, a graphic 'translation' or depiction of a pattern of ultrasonic reverberations. Given its object, the poem's adaptation of an ancient poetic tradition to the conditions of ultrasound reproduction adroitly represents a futurity in touch with its past. By recognizing the sonic aspects of 'The Sonogram', moreover, the poem comes to echo the later sequence 'Sleeve Notes', in which the poet's autobiography takes shape against the albums—their music and their cover-images—in his collection.[39]

In an essay of this length, it would be impossible to summarize the presence of music and sound in the work of Ciaran Carson, so thorough-going is its engagement with the practical experience of aurality: this essay could, in fact, be thought of as merely glossing dynamics found in his work. From the rhythmic pulses of lines to the structural permutations of forms and themes to particularly vivid descriptions of the noise of intercom boxes, helicopters, and all manner of playback media, Carson's writing presents sound as intangible and protean, yet only insofar as it is produced by an infinite variety of tangible, material sources. In turn, sound itself is antiphonal with the objects and conditions of the world, the world acting as a vast resonator and, in so doing, affecting the act of listening. In the novel *The Pen Friend*, the narrator listens to a song on a Billie Holiday CD and is reminded of the same track on an old love's LP, which is itself a re-mastered version of a gramophone recording:

> The record comes to an end and I think how there seemed to be more hiss and crackle on your vinyl copy, more of the atmospherics of lost time, forty years since Billie had laid the track down and I imagine the dust of 1942 sifting down into the grooves of the recording back then, getting into the voice and the instruments, and making that slight lisp in her enunciation all the more poignant.[40]

This recession through formats illuminates a process of production purposefully obscured by industry-driven discourses of 'improved fidelity'; it is also an imaginative

---

[38] Paul Muldoon, *Poems 1968–1998* (London: Faber, 2001), 342.
[39] Ibid., 410–18.
[40] Ciaran Carson, *The Pen Friend* (Belfast: Blackstaff, 2009), 44.

opening out into an expanded and exuberant receptivity. It is a progression with and through the unexpected, a practice of getting on:

> *The tune*
>
> is what we
> know we think
>
> we know as
> blithely we
>
> begin until
> a stumble
>
> brings us ever
> deeper in
>
> to aftertouch
> resounding[41]

---

[41] Ciaran Carson, *Until Before After* (Oldcastle: Gallery, 2010), 116.

CHAPTER 18

....

'PRIVATE RELATIONS': SELVES, POEMS, AND PAINTINGS—DURCAN TO MORRISSEY

....

RUI CARVALHO HOMEM

IN a preface to his collection *Crazy About Women* (1991), Irish poet Paul Durcan (1944–) refers to 'picture-making' and poetry as 'the two preoccupations of my life', and defines himself, therefore, as an artist with 'two spouses'.[1] The passage shows Durcan's willingness to assimilate the range of his artistic commitments to the private world of his affections, and to extend this equation to the rapport between word and image—in the particular context of a collection that integrally consists of poems about paintings. Durcan's stance on that dual assimilation is possibly epitomized in a line that emerges later in the collection: 'Art is private relations—not public relations'.[2]

Durcan's poetry provides a useful starting point for a study of the importance of painting for contemporary Irish poets, and it does so in three interrelated ways. First of all, his writing shows a persistent and programmatic focus on the visual arts: besides the many pictorially derived poems that punctuate his work, two of Durcan's books were planned as responses to museum collections and indeed published by the institutions in question—the already mentioned *Crazy About Women* (which addressed paintings in the National Gallery of Ireland), and *Give Me Your Hand* (1994, National Gallery, London). Secondly, the particular terms in which Durcan addresses the visual arts in order to develop his poetic fictions of gender and human bonds make his writing a signal example of the much-discussed interest that Irish writers from different backgrounds have taken in family settings and their potential for conflict. (Indeed, as pointedly noted by Edna Longley, 'genealogical obsessions…pervade Irish culture', and even 'Irish history

---

[1] Paul Durcan, *Crazy About Women* (Dublin: The National Gallery of Ireland, 1991), pp. x–xi.
[2] Ibid., 23.

remains…a family affair', reflecting, among other factors, the contributions made by the island's major religious traditions towards a massively patriarchal social culture.)[3] Thirdly, Durcan's work offers clear-cut examples of the tendency for poetic appropriations of pictorial art to acquire a self-referential dimension, highlighting the close mutual implication between the word-and-image relation and the poems' chosen themes—which, in the cases to be discussed, derive from the world of the family and private affections.

Thematically and culturally, this implication has often attracted attention. The 'long-standing system of connections' involving painting and love narratives is a central theme in Wendy Steiner's *Pictures of Romance*, while Norman Bryson has provided arguments for a gendered perspective on the history of looking and narrating—the agency of male ocular and discursive power vis-à-vis the passiveness of female objects.[4] But the very *language* of criticism has foregrounded the implication, since assessments of the fraught relationship between verbal and visual forms of artistic expression have often resorted to tropes of gender, generation, and interpersonal relations. From the Renaissance onwards, one of the most popular metaphors applied to the arts in European culture construed poetry and painting as siblings, the 'sister arts'.[5] The (apparent) stringency of current academic discourse has not prevented the use of similar tropes. The 'protracted struggle for dominance between pictorial and linguistic signs', for which W. J. T. Mitchell claims a prominent position in the history of culture, is construed as analogous to human relations, in particular when 'the central goal of ekphrastic hope' is described as 'the overcoming of otherness'.[6] And erotic analogies underlie James A. W. Heffernan's claim that ekphrasis ('the verbal representation of visual representation') is dominated by 'representational friction'; the allure of metaphors drawn from human bodily experience is even more blatant in his remark that 'ekphrasis is dynamic and obstetric: it typically delivers *from* the pregnant moment of visual art its embryonically narrative impulse'.[7] This use of the trope of pregnancy derives from a foundational text for the theme of word versus image, Lessing's *Laocoön* (1766), the source of a famous notion that underlies Heffernan's remark: that painting is characteristically static, an art of space that represents the single instant, as against poetry, an art of time that can capture the plot-like flux of human experience.[8]

[3] Edna Longley, *The Living Stream: Literature and Revisionism in Ireland* (Newcastle: Bloodaxe, 1994), 152–4.

[4] Norman Bryson, *Word and Image: French Painting of the Ancien Régime* (Cambridge: Cambridge University Press, 1981), 46, 92 and *passim*; Wendy Steiner, *Pictures of Romance: Form Against Context in Painting and Literature* (Chicago: The University of Chicago Press, 1988), 55 and *passim*.

[5] The notion has often been critically explored with regard to various moments in literary and cultural history, as in Jean Hagstrum's classic *The Sister Arts. The Tradition of Literary Pictorialism and English Poetry from Dryden to Gray* (Chicago: University of Chicago Press, 1958). For more recent remarks on its fortune in European culture and thought, see W. J. T. Mitchell, *Iconology: Image, Text, Ideology* (Chicago: The University of Chicago Press, 1986), 42–3, 156.

[6] Mitchell, *Iconology*, 43; W. J. T. Mitchell, *Picture Theory: Essays on Verbal and Visual Representation* (Chicago: University of Chicago Press, 1994), 156.

[7] James A. W. Heffernan, *Museum of Words: The Poetics of Ekphrasis from Homer to Ashbery* (Chicago: University of Chicago Press, 1993), 1, 5, 19.

[8] Gotthold Ephraim Lessing, *Laocoön: An Essay on the Limits of Painting and Poetry*, trans. Edward Allen McCormick (Baltimore: Johns Hopkins University Press, 1984), 78 and *passim*.

This essay will suggest that such approaches to the word-and-image relation prove highly productive when applied to the variously unconventional poetics of Paul Durcan, Paul Muldoon, Ciaran Carson, Medbh McGuckian, and Sinéad Morrissey. It will focus on moments in which their poetic writing seeks the benefit of indirection and derives additional imaginative impulse from representations found in another artistic medium. Such moments yield critical insights into both the nature of the rapport between poetry and painting, and some of the defining tensions in the poet's immediate culture; and those insights may take the form of tentative answers to a few recurrent questions. Does the relation between word and image confront us primarily with instances of conflict and rivalry, or rather with forms of coalescence between verbal and visual resources? Further, in what measure can poetry's ambition to address the visual extend or inflect the traditional description of the lyric as a representation of the 'speaking' self, a space for subjective revelation? The poems considered below prompt such broad critical questions in close connection with culturally more specific issues, such as the (already mentioned) Irish tendency to highlight bonds and emotions associated with family settings, with some emphasis on the position of women. This representational preference deserves to be considered both in the light of specific traits of Irish culture, and with regard to its own intriguing assimilation to the rapport between verbal and visual.

In the poetry of Paul Durcan, the pervasiveness of what he has provocatively described as 'private relations' was already clear from his earlier collections, punctuated by titles that combine the (often very 'public') pictorial reference with the poet's characteristic iconoclasms: 'The Collaring of Manet by a Dublin Architect in the National Gallery', 'Fuckmuseum, Constance'. Both these poems appeared in *Jesus Break His Fall* (1980), and they confirm Durcan's penchant for making the pictures yield narratives that concern troubled familial or conjugal scenes. These range from the necrophiliac delusions of the philistine 'architect' who press-gangs Manet 'to do a portrait of my dead wife' laid out 'nude on the formica topped kitchen table';[9] to a realization of overlooked or ignored identities, troped as a pictorial misreading that combines with an epiphany in a museum setting: 'Then suddenly, after 10 years, I realised she was she/When she mistook me for an abstract painting in Room 3.'[10]

Savage satire overwhelms some of Durcan's picture-based narratives of family, love, and marriage, sometimes running the risk of compromising the denunciation by excessive keenness. Durcan's readiness to equate patriarchal oppression (even male desire) with fascism is certainly striking, but it carries a potential element of overkill: as in 'The Perfect Nazi Family is Alive and Well and Prospering in Modern Ireland'—included in *Jumping the Train Tracks with Angela* (1983)—a humorous but bitter refraction of Adolf Wissel's painting of a *Farming Family from Kahlenberg* (1939). Neither is this strategy limited to poems with such stentorian titles, themselves instances of Durcan's rhetorical strategies; it is also pursued in more conventionally announced ekphrastic pieces, such as those that borrow the painting's own title followed by the 'after' formula that signals

---

[9] Paul Durcan, *Jesus Break His Fall* (Dublin: Raven Arts, 1980), 33.
[10] Ibid., 43.

the poet's indebtedness to his pictorial source. Examples of this include 'The Jewish Bride—*after Rembrandt*' and 'The Vision of St Hubert—*after Breughel*': both from *The Berlin Wall Café* (1985). 'The Jewish Bride' reads a fictionalized piece of twentieth-century history into Rembrandt's seventeenth-century painting, interweaving the Holocaust's murderous anti-Semitism with the voyeuristic violence of the (would-be? potential?) rapist, confessed in the first person: 'my swastika eyes', 'my jackboot silence', 'my gestapo voice'.[11] In Durcan's writing this confessional tone is all the more blatant for its combination with a transparent autobiographical account (a narrative of the dissolution of the family, pervaded by male guilt). The effect of this in 'The Vision of St Hubert' is that Hubert's Pauline tale of redemption, placidly evoked in the painting, is overwhelmed by the poem's scenario of marital mayhem:

> I decided to hunt down my wife:
> Gauleiters of Revenge revved-up in my veins
>
> …
>
> I will put the fear of God the Führer into her
> And smear the walls of her bedroom with the blood of her children[12]

Compared to this, the family narratives that Durcan continued to privilege in his two collections entirely devoted to paintings can be described as serene—despite the continuity of the themes of dysfunction, abuse, and disintegration. Both *Crazy About Women* and *Give Me Your Hand* offer reproductions of the paintings next to the poems that they prompted, which may help explain a relative downtoning of Durcan's departures from his pictorial sources. The poet's 'versions' of the paintings may still be dislocated in time and space, but the fact that the word-and-image relation is supported by a coexistence in the space of the book (rather than by evoking an absent picture) means that Durcan's refigurations of his named and displayed sources are not so radical as to prevent readers from acknowledging the poem as a rendering of the painting.

Some pictorial genres prove especially enticing for Durcan's narrativization of family scenes and women's predicaments. A case in point is the conversation piece: examples include, in *Crazy About Women*, 'Man with Two Daughters', 'An Interior with Members of a Family', or 'Mrs Congreve with Her Children'; in *Give Me Your Hand*, 'A Family Group in a Landscape', 'Mr and Mrs Andrews', and 'The Painter's Daughters Chasing a Butterfly'. To the extent that Durcan's accounts of such pictorial scenes are often humorously outlandish vis-à-vis more conventional readings, his proneness to *iconoclasm* (etymologically and literally 'breaking icons') becomes even more strikingly literal when his pictorial referents are sacred art—as is the case with paintings of the Holy Family.

Durcan's appropriations of the Holy Family tend, as always, to extract them from the temporal and cultural framework of their production and bring them close to the poet's time and concerns—ethically, politically, artistically. 'The Marriage of the Virgin', the opening poem in *Give Me Your Hand*, brings a fourteenth-century painting to bear on

[11] Paul Durcan, *The Berlin Wall Café* (Belfast: Blackstaff, 1985), 41.
[12] Ibid., 69.

the unequal marriage between a young woman and an old man, a standard topic in literature dealing with traditional rural life in Ireland (as portrayed by Patrick Kavanagh, for example, extolled by Durcan as an admired predecessor).[13] However, the poem's emphatic anachronisms also involve construing Christ's sacrifice in the light of present-day politics, economics, and ethics—as diverse as the sinister 'protection' one buys from gangsters, and the issue of gay rights. Further, 'The Marriage of the Virgin' involves a meta-artistic, self-referential challenge: in this verbal figuration of a visual figuration, the white marriage that binds Mary to Joseph is troped as 'abstract'—Mary declares, 'I come to him abstract.'[14] To the extent that 'abstract' opposes 'figurative', the erotic is, by implication, brought to bear again on the representational design by suggesting that figuration (which envelops 'Mary's' intriguing statement), by entailing a focus on the body, involves desire and coupling.

In 'The Marriage of the Virgin', Mary is given the prerogative of appearing as the fictional consciousness through which Durcan appropriates and refigures the painting—a cognitive female point of view and vocal stance which, extracted from an ineluctably patriarchal dispensation, is itself a counter-cultural statement.[15] The most memorable example of this penchant for playing with unexpected perspectives and voices from such a canonical genre is probably 'The Holy Family with St John', a poem in *Crazy About Women* on a late fifteenth-century painting. The speaking voice and the cognitive focus are identified in this case with a peripheral, diminutive male figure in the background, disclosed as an autobiographical projection when he derives his fascination for the family scene from his condition as 'a man without a family' (a predicament that has recurrently characterized Durcan's confessional writing).[16] This figure, who is barely in the picture, has nonetheless the privilege of viewing the scene from the front, like any external onlooker; indeed, this is the only perspective that allows him to note the painting's peculiarities in the light of present-day figurative expectations and attitudinal commonplaces. Ostensibly voiced from the edge of the painting, Durcan's poem plays with yet another shift in focus. Both the appropriated title ('The Holy Family with St John') and the painting's spatial arrangement give central importance to the shared childhood of Jesus and John, their touching hands troping a mystical relay. However, the central and larger part of the poem echoes the curious 'affinity', the apparently meaningful eye contact between Joseph 'and his donkey, conversing with one another' as they approach from the background, along a winding path. The suggestion that man and donkey are engaged in male bonding, 'the husband…confiding about his sensational spouse', daringly brings the erotic implication into the framework of the paradigmatic white marriage, enhanced by the donkey's famed potency. The provocative centrality that Durcan's

[13] See his sequence of poems on Kavanagh (opening with 'Surely My God is Kavanagh') in *Greetings to Our Friends in Brazil* (London: Harvill, 1999), 127–42.

[14] Paul Durcan, *Give Me Your Hand* (London: Macmillan/National Gallery, 1994), 9.

[15] On Durcan's representations of women, their cultural implications, and their relation to feminism(s), see Ruth Padel, 'Spin', in Colm Tóibín, ed., *The Kilfenora Teaboy: A Study of Paul Durcan* (Dublin: New Island 1996), 122; Longley, *The Living Stream*, 214–16.

[16] Durcan, *Crazy About Women*, 11.

poem accords to the animal is confirmed in the *interrogatio* that closes the poem: 'What is it that a donkey sees in a man?' Earlier, Durcan's persona avows, 'I revel/In the human family's animal beauty'; this may be no more than a sobering reflection on the communality of Creation, but it can also suggest that the extension of Durcan's 'private relations' beyond the borders of the species involves a hybridization of aesthetic perception.[17]

(Un)holy families, disturbing erotic insights, hybrid forms: this combination is both recognisable and prominent in the work of Paul Muldoon. Such shared elements in their representational range only enhance the fact that Durcan and Muldoon have been read as epitomizing the 'differing formal procedures' that have come to characterize a postmodern moment in Irish poetry, respectively north and south of the border.[18] In Muldoon's case, a pervasive fascination for hybrid beings and borderline experiences is matched by his formal preferences—such as his taste for quotation, pastiche, and parody—and confirmed in his critical readings of texts that foreground 'the ideas of liminality and narthecality'.[19] Muldoon's interest in equivocal identities found an early focus in his collection *Mules* (1977), where literal reference to the hybrid equines in the title coexisted with a variety of metaphorical approximations, the range of which included family identity and autobiographical implications (e.g. in 'The Mixed Marriage'). Unlike Durcan's rhetoric of confessional candour and emotional intensity, however, the personal layer of reference in Muldoon's poetry tends to be approached only indirectly, and the mediations that characterize his slanted writing have on a few memorable occasions found their formal match in his poems about paintings.

Muldoon's ekphrastic practice has focused, on at least two occasions, on pictures featuring couples of a more or less unusual nature. His collection *Moy Sand and Gravel* (2002) includes 'Anthony Green: *The Second Marriage*', originally commissioned for *A Conversation Piece*, a collection compiling ekphrastic poems and reproductions of the paintings they address. Muldoon takes Anthony Green's faux-naïf wedding scene of a middle-aged couple, posing in their finery against a garish and over-furnished living room, and makes it yield a narrative of transgression and punishment—which denies the couple the status of 'blushing bride and...nervous groom' and reads their worried stiffness as that of 'a pair of con artists summoned before/a magistrate inclined to throw/the book at con artists'.[20] The poet's construction of the scene as courtroom drama makes the poem an arrogation of judicial authority, with ironical implications for the intermedial relation: the verbal appropriator of a pictorial scene—an artist drawing on the figurative resources of another artist—uses the prerogative of poetic utterance to impute an illicit appropriation of goods to the mute subjects of a 'conversation piece', the rather gauche-looking couple that he dubs 'con artists'. The ironical and self-referential import of this narrative of transgressive possession and transmission also relates closely to the *secondariness* (as against originality or singularity) that marks both painting and poem:

---

[17] Ibid.

[18] Longley, *The Living Stream*, 196–7.

[19] Paul Muldoon, *To Ireland, I: The Clarendon Lectures in English Literature 1998* (Oxford: Oxford University Press, 2000), 5.

[20] Paul Muldoon, *Moy Sand and Gravel* (London: Faber, 2002), 32.

the most immediate sense of *The Second Marriage* as the title of Green's painting is only too clear in the bride and groom's lined faces, but Green has consciously painted this (quasi-parodic) wedding scene *after* a hallowed precedent, Van Eyck's *Portrait of Giovanni Arnolfini and his Wife*.[21] Muldoon's poem *after* Green's painting makes his 'Second Marriage' doubly so, but the title acquires a particular resonance in Muldoon's work, both for its congeniality with a poetics that thrives on rewritings, and for a specific precedent in his oeuvre—another poem after a painting that one might call his 'first marriage'.

The poem in question is 'The Bearded Woman, by Ribera', which first appeared in *Mules* and is arguably the collection's 'most powerful family image'.[22] It ostensibly describes the peculiar seventeenth-century painting named in its title: indeed, when a poem appropriates the title of a painting it invites an assumption of equivalence, suggesting that the verbal representation will fully stand in for the pictorial object in the reader's experience. This assumption is particularly forceful when the painting is *not* reproduced next to the poem, although (paradoxically) it may constitute an additional stimulus for the reader to look for a reproduction and assess the supposed substitution. Muldoon's poem on José de Ribera's painting duly describes the woman who sports a 'luxuriantly black' beard and virile face, but also exhibits a 'bared... pap', breastfeeding a baby; and it explores her contrast with a 'willowy and clean-shaven' husband, 'in the shadows'.[23] The painting is construed as surpassing anything else in freakishness, but also as eliciting the informed reaction of the visually cultivated observer who acknowledges the weird appeal of 'this so unlikely Madonna' and provocatively asks: 'Might this be the Holy Family/Gone wrong?'[24] This question certainly sees Muldoon partaking in the 'deconstruction' of 'Catholic Ulster' through a slanted, refracted confrontation with its iconography.[25] At another level, the question interrogates the painting with regard both to object and medium: it postulates a dysfunctional family, as much as a breakdown in representation, a wayward or incompetent attempt at a pictorial genre in sacred art.

This generic dimension alerts us to a strategy that proves surprisingly common in ekphrastic writing: a pluralization of the pictorial referent, as a poem is found to address more paintings (grouped by genre or object of representation) than the one it explicitly acknowledges.[26] Further, the sense of norm that underlies Muldoon's hypothesis of

[21] See the editorial notes in Adrian Rice and Angela Reid, eds., *A Conversation Piece: Poetry and Art* (Newry: The National Museums and Galleries of Northern Ireland/Abbey Press, 2002), 147. For a more detailed reading of this interpictorial relation, see my 'Couplings: Agon and Composition in Paul Muldoon's Ekphrastic Poetry', *Estudios Irlandeses*, no. 0 (Barcelona: 2005): 58–66. http://www.estudiosirlandeses.org/RuiCarvalhoHomem.pdf

[22] Tim Kendall, *Paul Muldoon* (Bridgend: Seren, 1996), 57.

[23] Paul Muldoon, *Poems 1968–1998* (London: Faber, 2001), 57–8.

[24] Ibid.

[25] Longley, *The Living Stream*, 52.

[26] For a more detailed critical reading of 'The Bearded Woman, by Ribera' from this particular perspective, see my 'Of Beards and Breasts, Baldheads and Babies: Muldoon's Mongrel Families', in *Beyond Borders: IASIL Essays on Modern Irish Writing*, ed. Neil Sammells (Bath: Sulis Press, 2004), 178–90.

'wrong[ness]' prompts readers to check the poem's visual source and consider two sets of relations: between Ribera's painting and 'authentic', conventional examples of the Holy Family; and between the painting and Muldoon's verbal rendering. The latter assessment will allow readers to note the poem's deviation from key features of its ostensible object: the husband as depicted by Ribera is admittedly secondary to the painting's title figure, but he is an integral part of the composition, without whom the 'Holy Family' analogy could hardly be offered, and not the effete figure that Muldoon describes as intruding, 'Between mending that fuse/And washing the breakfast dishes', in the space dominated by his full-bearded wife. This shows Muldoon deliberately refiguring Ribera's grotesquerie in the light of late twentieth-century discourses on identity and gender—but he does so with an ambiguity of sense and purpose that brings this ekphrastic exercise into the range of his poetics of parody and pastiche.

In *Mules*, 'The Bearded Woman, by Ribera' was flanked by 'Blemish' (about a woman with 'one brown and one blue eye')[27] and 'The Merman', ensuring a close connection between flawed but celebrated nature, hybridity, and intermediality—a connection above which hovered the rhetorical question that opened the book's title poem: 'Should they not have the best of both worlds?'[28] Muldoon's more recent writing, and in particular his collection *Horse Latitudes* (2006), has confirmed the critical view that, in his poetry, 'states of suspension or indeterminacy…are the logical extension of the concerns of *Mules*',[29] and it has proved that this extension is assisted by the poet's curiously persistent interest in equine imagery and the visual arts. Before dealing with horses verbally, *Horse Latitudes* conjures up the beasts through a pictorial mediation: the book's cover reproduces George Stubbs's *Mares and Foals without a Background* (c.1762).[30] Stubbs's title proves particularly apt: it associates the representational limbo of a blank background with the primary sense of Muldoon's title, as glossed in a blurb: 'an area north and south of the equator in which ships tend to be becalmed, in which stasis if not stagnation is the order of the day, and where sailors traditionally threw horses overboard to conserve food and water'. However, suspension and stasis, combined with a lack of background, are hardly what readers would associate with the book's title sequence, once its rationale is understood. 'Horse Latitudes' is crucially about the terrible dynamics of war through history, since its nineteen sonnets—all beginning with a 'B', but excluding the telltale Baghdad (the Iraq war is the public crisis that prompts and underpins the sequence)—are all named after battles, although any representations of the events evoked by the titles tend to be temporally and spatially dislocated. Against a backdrop of centuries-long slaughter (the common lot of humans and equines on the battlefield), the cryptic, intermittent narrative of a haunted love relation unfolds—beginning with 'Beijing'.

Indeed, in the sequence's first sonnet the male persona awakes 'beside Carlotta' (his lover), views her 'terra-cotta' body and is reminded of the massive artistry of 'those

[27] Muldoon, *Poems 1968–1998*, 57.
[28] Ibid., 67.
[29] Clair Wills, *Reading Paul Muldoon* (Newcastle: Bloodaxe, 1998), 136.
[30] Paul Muldoon, *Horse Latitudes* (London: Faber, 2006).

thousands of clay/horses and horsemen' in Emperor Qin Shihuang's mausoleum, set in a millenial rigor mortis that no 'cajoling…musicians' can break. Paradoxically, the main reason why the stasis of funereal sculpture prompts a comparison with the woman's sleeping body is that she is doomed by an ominously dynamic process: 'Proud-fleshed Carlotta. Hypersarcoma'.[31] Muldoon's peculiar phrasings for referring to the woman's breast cancer are part of the structure of concepts and images that hold the 'Horse Latitudes' sequence together. A sarcoma is a malignant tumour that grows from 'connective tissue' (OED); prefixing it with 'hyper' foregrounds the rampant verbal surfing and conceptual connectivity that energizes Muldoon's poetics—while it mirrors and glosses the phrase that opens the line, since 'proud flesh' is also a form of abnormal growth, a keloid scarring that often affects horses. The human-equine analogy, launched by the allusion to the clay horses and confirmed by this cross-species diagnosis, underpins the sequence's private narrative; gory anticipations of Carlotta's surgical mutilation find an eerie antecedent in the discovery that, against an earlier war scenario, 'Her grandfather's job was to cut/the vocal cords of each pack mule/with a single, swift excision'.[32] Concomitantly, Carlotta's ordeal becomes a trope for a sick world order: when the male persona spots 'on her breast a Texaco star',[33] the denunciation of 'crude oil' deals served by war becomes conflated with the superpower's military emblem; both logo and emblem are mirrored in the star-like expansion of cancerous tissue as visually revealed by medical technology, made into the deathly object of an ekphrasis. In the face of such raging dynamics, the couple's 'highest ambition' can only be 'simply to bear the light of the day/we had once been planning to seize'.[34] Eschewing the active *carpe diem* zest for a passive serenity provides another angle on the analogues sought in art—the emperor's 'horses and horsemen', Stubbs's equines 'without a background'; and it enriches the thematic tension in 'Horse Latitudes' between movement and stasis, while once more defining the range of 'private relations' as the ethical and emotional platform from which the public crisis is approached and represented.

This interpenetration of public and private in fact provides a useful contrast with some of the recent poetry of Ciaran Carson, who has also written about war scenarios by drawing on the shared or analogous fate of humans and horses, while engaging in ekphrastic exercises. In Carson's *Breaking News* (2003), equine imagery epitomizes those battlefield atrocities whose known and represented victims are almost always human. Poems such as 'Horse at Balaklava, 1854' and 'Some Uses of a Dead Horse' derive their rhetorical impact from a tension between the terseness of Carson's clipped-line diction (which in this collection starkly contrasts with the extra-long lines that characterized much of his earlier verse) and images of an *inhumane* evisceration. Curiously, such brutality cannot be represented without resorting to a (*human*) surgical simile, as the horse is 'ripped open by/a shell…as by a/surgeon's knife', in 'Horse at Balaklava, 1854'.[35]

---

[31] Ibid., 3.
[32] Ibid., 21.
[33] Ibid., 9.
[34] Ibid. 3.
[35] Ciaran Carson, *Collected Poems* (Oldcastle: Gallery, 2008), 437.

However, a proper perception and verbal expression of the animal's living energy also requires a human mediation, that of visual art—since it cannot but be troped as 'the picture of life'.[36] This reflects a cultural inevitability (animal beauty construed as such only by resorting to previous human constructions of such beauty), but also, more specifically, the frequency and intensity with which, throughout history, horses became the object of artistic representation. Of the three paintings ekphrastically addressed in *Breaking News*, the one selected for the cover (Théodore Géricault's *The Farrier's Signboard*, aka *The Blacksmith*) depicts a rampant stallion held, with some difficulty, by the farrier.[37] The closing lines of Carson's poem on this painting connect the scene with the turmoil of the Napoleonic Wars, but all that precedes it concerns the artistic process, showing the poet's fascination with human control, through art, over animal power. This fascination is here manifested both with regard to the human figure in the painting and to the artist's hand, which painted the ebullient and dynamic scene onto a notoriously harsh surface:

> roughly carpentered
> gap-jointed
> boards[38]

A yearning for emulation is undisguisable, through the suggested homology between this and the formal austerity of Carson's verse in *Breaking News*. With the exception of this inter-artistic dimension, there is little scope for the representation of 'private relations', and their defining impact on the self, in this book. Instead, it is the aforementioned combination of an intermedial design, the transparency of personal poetic ambition, and the understated rhetoric of Carson's short lines that arguably retains a lyrical quality in *Breaking News*, balanced against the collection's prevalent emphasis on a history of wars, and its memorialization in the Belfast toponymy.

Medbh McGuckian is hardly indifferent to the themes of conflict and remembrance, and yet the range of her representations has sometimes been seen as contained within a 'feminine' world of the domestic space, and of obliquely worded 'private' emotions. As so often is the case, however, such apparent placidity can become a standpoint from which to approach 'public' concerns. This strategy has had its clearest expression in a note appended to the title poem of *Drawing Ballerinas* (2001), dedicated to a 'schoolfellow and neighbour' killed in the Troubles: 'The painter, Matisse, when asked how he managed to survive the war artistically, replied that he spent the worst years "drawing ballerinas".'[39] This is also one of many explicit painterly references in McGuckian's poetry, which includes titles such as 'The Sitting', 'Self-Portrait in the Act of Painting a Self-Portrait', 'Sky Portrait', and 'Picasso's Windows'. This interest is sometimes extended to other ways of visually apprehending and recording the real, as with two poems from *The Face of the Earth* (2002) in which the pictures can be X-ray images: 'Reading the

---

[36] Ibid.
[37] Ciaran Carson, *Breaking News* (Oldcastle: Gallery, 2003).
[38] Carson, *Collected Poems*, 459.
[39] Medbh McGuckian, *Drawing Ballerinas* (Oldcastle: Gallery, 2001), 15.

Earthquake' and 'Studies of Her Right Breast'. They inflect the tendentially erotic charac-
ter of other representations of the body in McGuckian's poetry; when the memory of
'gentle/processions to churchyards' is introduced, the imagery of sickness is com-
pounded by mourning and existential discomfort.[40]

This representational complex, based on a female bodily presence which becomes
visually/pictorially mediated, can be recognized in its wealth of possibilities in 'Hazel
Lavery, The Green Coat, 1926'. The poem, included in *Drawing Ballerinas*, ostensibly
addresses a portrait of the celebrated second wife of the author, the painter Sir John
Lavery. Hazel Lavery was famous as a high-society hostess in early twentieth-century
London, but she also contributed to the conditions that led to the Anglo-Irish Treaty of
1921, by making her husband's studio the setting for some of the negotiations.[41] Her pres-
ence in the Irish historical and (specifically) visual memory was, however, to be best
ensured by a rare and memorably mundane development: one of her husband's portraits
of her was chosen to figure on Bank of Ireland notes.[42] Hazel Lavery thus became a sin-
gular epitome of desire, both amorous and material, in the Irish imagination: having
given herself to famous leading men of contemporary Irish history (Michael Collins,
Kevin O'Higgins—with both of whom she had love affairs),[43] she also lent her face to the
country's new currency.

However, McGuckian's 'Hazel Lavery, The Green Coat, 1926' is an extreme case of
the indirection that tends to characterize the relation between ekphrastic poems and
the paintings' historical or biographical circumstances—or, indeed, their figurative
traits, which readers of the poems may not easily infer. In spite of the descriptive prom-
ise in the poem's borrowed title, even the apostrophic gesture of the opening lines con-
cerns the painting's emotional effect on the poet, rather than the addressee: 'Agreed
image, of your open self, your personhood,/do not put me into a sadness like your
own'.[44] In fact, the poem's second stanza implicitly devalues literalness in representa-
tion by praising the painter's ability to represent 'your inner sun', 'a real hearbeat and a
lucid mind', rather than (just) the death-bound nature of 'a body degrading into matter'.
And this defines the conditions for artistic emulation: the highest ambition of portrait
artists (to depict the inner life of their object) is cited in order to be implicitly equated
with the lyric's vocation to represent a subjectivity—traditionally, through the poet's
self-representation.

McGuckian's enactment of such a design is hardly 'traditional', though, and its particu-
larity is mediated in several ways. The self is approached and represented through a picto-
rial mediation; historical references to which the poet is hardly indifferent are mediated
through the portrayed's implication in them; and (fundamentally) the resources

---

[40] Medbh McGuckian, *The Face of the Earth* (Oldcastle: Gallery, 2002), 36.
[41] Sinéad McCoole, *Hazel: A Life of Lady Lavery 1880–1935* (Dublin: Lilliput, 1996), *passim*.
[42] Indeed, her picture remained the notes' watermark until the euro brought the demise of the Irish
punt. See www.centralbank.ie/data/AnnRepFiles/2001AReport.pdf, 43 (last accessed 28 September
2009).
[43] McCoole, *Hazel, passim*.
[44] McGuckian, *Drawing Ballerinas*, 34.

employed towards representing the self, impacted by the painting and its ballast of memory, consist largely of other texts and images. Critical consideration of McGuckian's work has duly noted her rampant intertextuality, which characteristically operates through glossing and unmarked quotation.[45] Visual (re)sources extend this practice, and (just like the appropriated texts) have their possible meanings altered by partaking in a grid of 'private relations'. In the Lavery poem, McGuckian's range of references can be seen to include a few expected sources—biographical accounts, W. B. Yeats's allusion to 'Hazel Lavery living and dying'[46]—but also highly unexpected incidental references (of a kind that can only be identified in the age of electronic search engines). Thus, the glamour of the socialite's luxury garments is ironically equated with a false mortification, 'the whitish patina of verdigris and rose/carmethian that begging soldiers forge/on the eight hanging days', an allusion to the fairground environment of public executions at Tyburn, in eighteenth-century London.[47] And this ironical view of the 'green coat' from which painting and poem derive their titles also resorts to tropes from military history, when the coat's equation with 'armour' is combined with an obscure allusion to Napoleon's legendary ability to survive his horses—again, an equine, battlefield image: 'it is as though you actually wore armour,/with nineteen horses killed under you'.[48]

Saluting Hazel Lavery's resilience is one of the ways in which sympathy is balanced against strands of irony and a hint of satire throughout the poem, and this also bears on the poet's ability to identify with the subject (in spite—or because—of the apparent dimensions of futility and incoherence in her biography). A passage addressing Hazel Lavery's 'sense of chastity' might appear to be on the side of irony, but the lines in question are in fact about an empathy: 'Your sense of chastity/starts a shape in me attached to life at all/four corners'.[49] These lines are about a creative consequence, an artistic relation troped as engenderment, but they are also about ethics, and this perception becomes more incisive if and when readers are able to realize that the passage includes an unmarked quotation from Virginia Woolf's *A Room of One's Own*.[50] The very inclusion of this remark from a writer who stood for some of the perplexities faced by the intellectually independent woman in predominantly patriarchal environments, acquiring iconic status in women's studies, queries the assumptions of frivolousness that would

[45] See Shane Alcobia-Murphy, *Sympathetic Ink: Intertextual Relations in Northern Irish Poetry* (Liverpool: Liverpool University Press, 2006), 43–91 and *passim*.

[46] W. B. Yeats, *The Variorum Edition of the Poems of W. B. Yeats*, ed. Peter Allt and Russell K. Alspach (Basingstoke: Macmillan, 1956), 602.

[47] McGuckian, *Drawing Ballerinas*, 35.

[48] Ibid. For the Napoleon reference, see http://www.ljhammond.com/notebook/nap-right.htm (last accessed 28 September 2009).

[49] McGuckian, *Drawing Ballerinas*, 34.

[50] Woolf writes: 'Imaginative work…is like a spider's web, attached ever so lightly perhaps, but still *attached to life at all four corners.*…But when the web is pulled askew, hooked up at the edge, torn in the middle, one remembers that those webs are not spun in midair by intercorporeal creatures, but are the work of suffering, human beings, and are attached to the grossly material things, like health and money and the houses we live in'; *A Room of One's Own* [1929] (London: Granada, 1981), 41; my emphasis.

seem to inhere in Lady Lavery's all too public life.[51] This implicit vindication of the socialite's dignity also chimes with the suggestion of guilt on the poet's part that transpires from a passage in the poem's first stanza: 'I am using your heated body with its/ easy mark of beauty'; and some of the poem's imagery comes close to representing Hazel in sacrificial terms, a latter-day saint of sorts.[52] The combination of these traits entails an artistic and ethical purport that seems to counter Clair Wills's contention that '[McGuckian] presents women's experience as unknowable and therefore *useless*'.[53]

A sense of legacy and example binding women writers arguably connects McGuckian and Sinéad Morrissey, the last poet to be considered in this essay. This is crucially manifested by an inclination to pictorialize reality from a perspective that is emphatically female and grounded in a private (often domestic) circumstance. A case in point is provided by Morrissey's *Through the Square Window* (2009). The title alludes to a feature of the former British TV show for children *Play School* (in which the presenter prompted viewers to glimpse what was through a round, square, or arched window); in broader terms, however, it proposes a collection of poems as successive instances of a framed outlook, and draws on an obvious but nonetheless persuasive mutual troping—the window frame vis-à-vis the bounded pictorial space. Further, the title poem equates the poet's locale with the emblematic landscape of Dutch Golden Age painting, itself an epitome of the interface between the private scene and the public gaze: 'The clouds above the Lough are stacked/like the clouds are stacked above Delft.'[54] This equation with the skies of Vermeer or De Hooch might suggest a rather ponderous approach to visual representations, but *Through the Square Window* in fact announces itself visually through an image of girlish irreverence: the book's cover reproduces a 1950s photograph entitled 'Girl about to do a handstand'.[55] The playfulness that this seems to promise is balanced, however, by darker scenarios: one has to progress no further than the book's opening poem, 'Storm', to find a 'Gothic' environment combined with a reference to a 'stranded/ little girl in the photographs/growing sorrowful'.[56] In a variety of tones, indeed, the collection recurrently seeks the mediation of images, proposing the self as a complexity that is visually troped, and visually pluralized in feminine shapes: 'I have been my own kaleidoscope—five winter-bleached girls on a diving board, ready to jump.'[57]

---

[51] The relevance of this has to be considered in the light of McGuckian's sometimes controversial relation to feminism: see Thomas Docherty, 'Initiations, Tempers, Seductions: Postmodern McGuckian', in *The Chosen Ground: Essays on the Contemporary Poetry of Northern Ireland*, ed. Neil Corcoran (Bridgend: Seren, 1992), 191–210; Kimberly S. Bohman, 'Surfacing: An Interview with Medbh McGuckian', *Irish Review* 16 (Autumn/Winter 1994), 95–108.

[52] McGuckian, *Drawing Ballerinas*, 34.

[53] Clair Wills, *Improprieties: Politics and Sexuality in Northern Irish Poetry* (Oxford: Clarendon Press, 1993), 68–9.

[54] Sinéad Morrissey, *Through the Square Window* (Manchester: Carcanet, 2009), 32.

[55] On the critical relevance of the covers of Morrissey's earlier collections, see Elmer Kennedy-Andrews, *Writing Home: Poetry and Place in Northern Ireland, 1968–2008* (Cambridge: D.S.Brewer, 2008), 260–1.

[56] Morrissey, *Through the Square Window*, 9.

[57] Ibid. 19.

Ostensibly placid familial scenarios underlain by an indefinite, sometimes ominous sense of trouble: these are conditions in which both Medbh McGuckian and Sinéad Morrissey have taken an active writerly interest. There is also an additional coincidence in that both McGuckian and Morrissey have written about portraits by John Lavery of women in his household. Morrissey's own poem is about a picture of the painter's daughter, Eileen (born of his first marriage), said to have been rather peripheral to the Lavery household both before and after his father's second marriage (a phrase that has tended to recur throughout this essay).[58] Morrissey's choice to address Lavery's 'Eileen, Her First Communion', and to select the portrait for the cover of her collection *Between Here and There* (2002), therefore brings her ekphrastic poem into a particular layer of self-reference in her writing: that which concerns the formative consequence of the poet's stark perception of exclusion, reflecting biographical data that range from an unusual childhood amid Belfast's sectarian landscape, to the dissolution of the family home and the wanderings of her adult experience.[59] 'Eileen, Her First Communion' carries out the already familiar strategy of thwarting expectations of a close match between the two representations (visual and verbal), and it does so through a dislocation in time and circumstance. This is clearly announced from the surprising opening line—'Years later, after the painting, we planned her wedding'—which makes the *later* moment the object of the poem, and implicitly construes it as symmetrical to the earlier ceremony evoked in the title.[60]

When the poem positions itself 'after the painting', the formula involves more than derivation, announcing rather the ekphrasis of another (yet unpainted) scene. Nonetheless, the conceit of Morrissey's piece may depend on the perception of a calqued pattern: readers are bound to note how closely Eileen, in the actual painting, resembles a child bride—the implication being that the later ceremony (coupled with the first communion in the visual record of a family girl) would somehow be a 'second marriage'. This poem that departs from the portrait of a communion girl to envisage the scene of her wedding, against a background of domesticity and sisterly solidarities (manifest in the 'we' of a plural female persona), has a sacral, liturgical drift, but also an undercurrent of 'old panic' and 'desperate' thoughts.[61] And these various dimensions converge in the Christian but also ghostly trope that Morrissey applies to the fictionalized moment when a wedding dress is prepared for a fitting—also the moment when Eileen connects the two polar events on which the poem hinges:

> On the third day my sister
> and I raised a dress in her absence
> that made her terrified. Too similar,
> was all she said.[62]

---

[58] McCoole, *Hazel*, 37.

[59] See Michael Parker, *Northern Irish Literature, 1975–2006: The Imprint of History*, vol. 2 (Basingstoke: Palgrave, 2007), 157; Kennedy-Andrews, *Writing Home*, 256–7.

[60] Sinéad Morrissey, *Between Here and There* (Manchester: Carcanet, 2002), 15.

[61] Ibid.

[62] Ibid.

Panic is overcome; and yet the wedding day, rather than embraced with the delight of anticipated happiness, seems to be met with the unfaltering 'resolution' that a tragic figure might bring to an inevitable ordeal, providing a bleak ending to this poem about a painting that would seem designed to evoke a response of endearment. These are 'private relations' that spell oppression and malaise, rather than emotional and experiential enablement.

The poems considered above can reasonably be described as epitomizing their authors' characteristic voices—from Durcan's public, iconoclastic mode of address, and Carson's brooding review of dire historical scenarios, to the distinct modes of indirection and understatement that mark Muldoon's ironies, McGuckian's (inter)textualized obscurities, and Morrissey's poignant encounters of self with world and otherness. The various pieces share a fascination with the additional expressive possibilities that the intermedial design brings to their diverse poetics; what is more, they confirm, in the variety of their fictional elaborations, the 'dynamic and obstetric' capacity (nurturing and delivering the pictures' narrative embryo) with which Heffernan has credited ekphrasis.[63] They also offer reiterated examples of the dual process into which W. J. T. Mitchell analyses ekphrasis (a 'conversion' of visual into verbal, followed by 'the reconversion of the verbal representation back into the visual object in the reception of the reader'),[64] the corollary of which is that the painting's visual recomposition in the reader's consciousness is bound to yield a radically different image. Thus, verbal narration does not harness meaning by bringing the stability of rational discourse to bear upon the (possible) ambiguities of the fleeting, visually captured moment; on the contrary, it causes additional instability, by challenging the apparent determinacy of figurative representation. But these instabilities also become closely bound up with recurrent themes in contemporary Irish poetry—family and generation, the difficult borders between intimate and public experience, challenged gender roles, and the perplexities and oppressions faced by women. The doubts and anxieties posed by the 'private relations' that become the object of representation find a correlative in the undecidability of the word-and-image rapport: is it predominantly about contention or composition, agon or 'sisterly' mutuality? It is this conundrum that Peter Wagner has in mind when he refers to the 'Janus face' of ekphrasis: it 'promis[es] to give voice to the allegedly silent image', and yet strives 'to overcome the power of the image by transforming and inscribing it'.[65] Recognizing the productivity of this tension in the work of these five Irish poets, as a distinctive feature of their diverse poetics, is also to acknowledge their active contribution to an age-old rationale for discussing texts that rise to the ceaseless challenge posed by pictures.

[63] Heffernan, *Museum of Words*, 5.

[64] Mitchell, *Picture Theory*, 164.

[65] Peter Wagner, ed., *Icons-Texts-Iconotexts: Essays on Ekphrasis and Intermediality* (Berlin: Walter de Gruyter, 1996), 13.

CHAPTER 19

CONTEMPORARY NORTHERN IRISH POETRY AND ROMANTICISM

PETER MACKAY

TOWARDS the end of Ciaran Carson's 'Ballad of *HMS Belfast*' the speaker claims, when the *aisling* fades, 'We woke, and rubbed our eyes, half-gargled still with braggadocio and garble' (with 'garble' in the poem a mis-rhyme for 'the fog-horn trump of Gabriel').[1] 'Garble' and 'braggadocio' also appear in the second section of 'Opus Operandi' (the previous, penultimate poem in *The Ballad of* HMS Belfast):

> A school of clocks swarmed out from the Underwood's overturned undercarriage,
> Full of alphabetical intentions, led astray by braggadocio and verbiage.
>
> Typecast letters seethed on the carpet, trying to adopt its garbled Turkish
> Convolutions. They were baffled by the script's *auctoritas*.[2]

Braggadochio (from Edmund Spenser's *Faerie Queene*) is invoked for his connotations of empty boasting or arrogant pretension. The linguistic 'garble', meanwhile, is a reworking of the 'gobbledygook' which is uttered by a 'voice box' through the wire grille in 'Night Patrol'[3] and is also associated with the 'squawk-box' of '33333'[4] and the wireless speaking 'through the hiss of static' in 'Dunne':[5] each of these images suggests a listening-in which is also incomprehension, the attempt at and failure of communication and language, a linguistic 'getting lost' which is equivalent to the (at the same time productive and intimidating) labyrinthine landscapes of Carson's poems. In 'Opus Operandi' any attempt towards '*auctoritas*' is undermined by a combination of braggadocio, garbling, bafflement, and verbiage.

---

[1] Ciaran Carson, *The Ballad of HMS Belfast* (Oldcastle: Gallery, 1999), 126.
[2] Ibid., 110.
[3] Ibid., 26.
[4] Ibid., 30.
[5] Ibid., 11.

More specifically the repeated pairing of braggadocio and garble suggests a way of listening into and mistaking literature (and in particular texts, such as *The Faerie Queene*, which implicate the English literary canon in Ireland). The concern of the poems is how to engage with a previous 'script's *auctoritas*' and how to overcome the state of 'half-gargled'-ness, the limiting of voice caused by such engagements. In a 1982 interview with Frank Kinahan, Seamus Heaney also struggles with *auctoritas*:

> I think part of being a poet is precisely this business of having the authority to do your own work—*auctoritas*, yourself as the *auctor* of the work—and there is always of course the quarrel between the deliberately shaping, intending spirit and the other more precious and inviolable thing of knowing that it is all gift. And so one treads warily between the dictates of intelligence, which say 'Look, you can't just sit down and do these wee poems just for pleasure – this has to be a work,' and the knowledge that, on the other hand, the muse in you—whatever that is—must be allowed her unconscious brooding thing.[6]

The terms of the quarrel on which the question of *auctoritas* is based—the shaping intellect and the unconscious muse—appear again and again in Heaney's criticism. In 'Feeling into Words', for example, the shaping (masculine) intelligence is associated with Yeats, the pliable (feminine) unconscious with Wordsworth.[7] This binary opposition does change, however, through Heaney's critical career. Patricia Horton notes how ' "Wordsworth" is a shape-changer in Heaney's prose, prone to metamorphosis depending on Heaney's priorities, agendas and anxieties',[8] and how the Yeatsian and Wordsworthian elements later fuse for Heaney, as 'Wordsworth becomes a fully masculine tradition in which Yeats plays a secondary role'.[9] Poetic authority is a case here of accepting and directing the influence of poetic precursors as well as 'mediating the shaping intellect and the unconscious muse'.[10] Heaney's comments on *auctoritas* are part of a discussion of the shift from the 'narrow…tight line' of *North* (1975) to *Field Work* (1979), where he attempted 'to change the note and to lengthen the line'.[11] At first, Heaney relates, the change was unwelcome:

> Back then I thought that that music, the melodious grace of the English iambic line, was some kind of affront, that it needed to be wrecked; and while I loved the poem ['Glanmore Sonnets III'], I felt at the time that its sweetness disabled it somehow.

---

[6] Seamus Heaney, Interview with Frank Kinahan, *Critical Inquiry* 8, 3 (Spring 1982), 410–11.

[7] Seamus Heaney, *Finders Keepers: Selected Prose 1971–2001* (London: Faber, 2003).

[8] Patricia Horton, ' "A Truly Uninvited Shade": Romantic Legacies in the Work of Seamus Heaney and Paul Muldoon', in *Last Before America: Irish and American Writing*, ed. Fran Brearton and Eamonn Hughes (Belfast: Blackstaff, 2001), 23.

[9] Ibid., 21.

[10] This is not the idea of 'authority' as a contemporary poetic-social power structure critiqued by Peter McDonald; it is closer to the authority achieved by the poetry which McDonald describes as a 'kind of poetry that knows too much to play by these rules, and is not abject in relation to the authority of its time; it accepts form as its *sine qua non*, and puts up with the finally uncontrollable difficulty and complexity of language; it knows that words, not "personality", are what survive or perish'. Peter McDonald, *Serious Poetry: Form and Authority from Yeats to Hill* (Oxford: Oxford University Press, 2002), 14.

[11] Heaney, Interview with Frank Kinahan, 411.

I suppose, then, that the shift from *North* to *Field Work* is a shift in trust: a learn-
ing to trust melody, to trust art as reality, to trust artfulness as an affirmation and not
to go into the self-punishment as much. I distrust that attitude too, of course. Those
two volumes are negotiating with each other.[12]

Alongside the negotiation between volumes and cadences, Heaney here negotiates dif-
ferent poetic traditions, and the 'English' poetic tradition in particular (associated vari-
ously here with the 'iambic line', 'sweetness', 'melody', 'art as reality', and 'artfulness as an
affirmation'). This is, in part, a positive and politically abstracted comment on English
Romantic poetry—it is Wordsworth who is the guiding spirit of *Field Work*, and whose
Grasmere poems underlie and disrupt Heaney's Glanmore; the dynamic it creates of
simultaneous attraction and 'distrust' suggests, characteristically for the Heaney of this
period, a surreptitiously erotic relationship—a trysting—with previous poetry, and with
Wordsworth in particular.

Both Carson and Heaney engage in 'creative misreading' of precursors in their poetry
(and Heaney in his criticism), as Harold Bloom suggests all poets do. They do not, how-
ever, correspond easily to the Freudian model of the family romance through which
Bloom viewed poetic influence, with an Oedipal struggle to the death with a male pre-
cursor and six ratios of poetic misprision.[13] The weight lent to influence by Bloom, and
the shadow cast by Bloom on any subsequent discussions of influence, has tended to
skew the field in poet-centred (rather than text-centred) approaches to the relationship
between poets, to the extent that 'influence' is used to cover a wide and diverse range of
interactions, where a range of nuanced terms (both positive and negative) would be
more informative: apprenticeship, fosterage, emulation, pick-pocketing, 'monstrous
debt', trysting, flirting, and intimidation, for example; notions of intertextuality, appro-
priation, undermining, hybridization and even the (dubious) concept of genetic textual
inheritance also do not fit snugly under the cover of 'influence'. Recent creative misread-
ers of Bloom do treat influence as more positive than anxious, but in the process remove
much of the original energy from Bloom's theory. Michael O'Neill, for example, accepts
the Bloomian notion that the poem is 'a place where the finest and most nuanced read-
ing of a previous poem or poetry occurs', but swerves from Bloom to state that 'the desire
to establish difference and originality is productive not only of anxiety but also of
acknowledgement and admiration'.[14] Lucy Newlyn, meanwhile, identifies the work of
Christopher Ricks as a counterbalance to that of Bloom: Newlyn suggests that Ricks's
work offers a 'benign model of influence', that the 'Ricksian art of resisting generaliza-
tions through close reading' can be 'an antidote to the reductive dogmatism of Bloomian
theory', and that, as a result, it avoids falling—in Barthes' words—into a Bloomian 'myth
of filiation' (and so into the traps of the family romance).[15]

---

[12] Ibid., 412.

[13] Harold Bloom, *The Anxiety of Influence* [1973] (Oxford: Oxford University Press, 1997).

[14] Michael O'Neill, *The All-Sustaining Air: Romantic Legacies and Renewals in British, American,
and Irish Poetry since 1900* (Oxford: Oxford University Press, 2007), 11.

[15] Lucy Newlyn, 'Foreword', *The Monstrous Debt: Modalities of Romantic Influence in Twentieth-
Century Literature*, ed. Damian Walford Davies and Richard Marggraf Turley (Detroit: Wayne State

The rest of this chapter will discuss strategies adopted in some recent Northern Irish poetry to negotiate, undermine, and compete with Romantic texts and poets, whether they seek influence anxiously, appropriate it arrogantly, or—in a post-Bloomian sense—accept its benign glow. The interest in the interplay between Romantic and Northern Irish poets lies partly in the way Northern Irish poets position themselves with regard to the Romantics and to each other. Heaney's work repeatedly engages with Wordsworth as one of his main adopted influences (alongside Yeats, Kavanagh, Hughes, Frost, Lowell, Mandelstam, and Milosz, to name some of the predominant figures), and Heaney's self-identification with Wordsworth offers a stance which has been undermined, deconstructed, troubled, and ironized by successors such as Muldoon and Carson. This has lead to a critical paralleling of the Romantic groups with different 'generations' of Northern Irish poets, which, as Patricia Horton notes, is 'inspired primarily by Muldoon, who turns to a Byronic model precisely because he finds in Byron's parodic relationship to Southey, Coleridge and Wordsworth, a model for his own relationship to Heaney'.[16] The parodic (and inaccurate) nature of the analogy is important: the generational shifts in the respective groups of poets are quite different, and it is part of the parodic element of Muldoon's positioning that he casts them as comparable. There is a much greater degree of dialogue between the Northern Irish generations than the canonical Romantic generations—Heaney is 'influenced' by Muldoon, and Carson by Alan Gillis, for example, in a way that Coleridge was not by Shelley or Wordsworth by Keats—and the Northern Irish poets are not confined to one 'generation' of Romantics: Heaney, for example, writes on Keats and Byron as well as Wordsworth. Similarly, although Horton associates Heaney with Wordsworth and Muldoon with Byron, the neatness of the generational parallels is disrupted by the subsequent association of Mahon and Shelley, and of Paulin with both Shelley and Coleridge.[17] Finally, the antagonism between Southey and Byron is not reflected in the (generally) affectionate ironizations of Northern Irish poetry.

Aside from personal positioning on the part of the poets, interest in the Romantic period tends to be in connections between poetry and the political or social. For Horton, 'Romanticism' (despite the difficulties of definition inherent in the term) offers, like Eastern European poetry, an example of 'a powerful intersection between poetry and politics in which ideas about the role of the poet, the function of poetry, and the relationship of the poet to community, audience and authority, are particularly urgent';[18] for O'Neill, meanwhile, it is the 'doubleness' of Romantic poetry that is important, given that it is 'a movement which implies that art is at once autonomous and shaped by historical circumstance, which licenses transcendental questing while valuing the meanest flower that blows, and which gives a new status to the self even as it frequently investi-

University Press, 2006), p. xiii. Newlyn quotes Roland Barthes's *Image-Music-Text* (New York: Hill & Wang, 1978), 160, for the 'myth of filiation'. See Christopher Ricks, *Allusion to the Poets* (Oxford: Oxford University Press, 2002).

[16] Patricia Horton, 'Romantic Intersections: Romanticism and Contemporary Northern Irish Poetry', PhD thesis, Queen's University Belfast (15 September 1996), 3.

[17] Ibid., 7.

[18] Ibid., 4.

gates the self's relationship with society'.[19] These issues remain relevant because, as Paul de Man comments, we still think (and think of Romanticism in particular) Romantically—the crises and concerns central to Romanticism are still those which determine how we view and recreate 'Romanticism':

> with romanticism we are not separated from the past by that layer of forgetfulness and that temporal opacity that could awaken in us the illusion of detachment. . . . Now it is precisely this experience of the temporal relationship between the act and its interpretation that is one of the main themes of romantic poetry.[20]

That is, we have a relationship with Romanticism that is doubled rather than detached (however illusorily), and any discussion of Romanticism is, in effect, an exploration of its simultaneous presence and absence in the contemporary world. This is reflected in discussions of influence themselves. As Newlyn argues, questions of contemporary relationships with Romanticism seem in particular tied to Bloomian notions of influence, since Bloom is himself 'nothing if not Romantic', building on Keats's claim with regard to Milton that 'Life to him would be death to me':[21]

> Poems, [Bloom] believes, are written by authors, not by anonymous scribes; and authors have psychic compulsions. Romantic authors were preoccupied above all else with *identity*, which they saw as more or less synonymous with originality: 'a poet's stance, his Word, his imaginative identity, his whole being, must be unique to him, and remain unique, or he will perish as a poet'.[22]

Any equation of 'identity' with 'originality' is troubled by the notion of 'authority' or *auctoritas* raised by both Heaney and Carson, especially when 'authority' is seen as being characteristic of the relationship not just between the poet and other poets, but also between the poet and society as a whole, or culture as a whole: authority, that is, as a stance not just within poetry, but in the world. The rewriting of Romanticism in Northern Irish poetry is thus part of the wide-ranging (and often avowedly postmodern) re-evaluation and recreation of Romanticism as a fitting precursor of (as well as troubling presence in) contemporary literature.[23] The Romantic crisis over the role of the poet, and the political implications of this crisis, are also given particular political import in this Northern Irish re-evaluation: for the most part it is a stressed *English* Romanticism, and especially the six traditionally canonical poets, whose identity and authority are re-evaluated (with Byron's Scots-Englishness often elided).[24] Thus, in

---

[19] O'Neill, *The All-Sustaining Air*, 122.

[20] Paul de Man, *The Rhetoric of Romanticism* (New York: Columbia University Press, 1984).

[21] John Keats, 'Letter to George and Georgina Keats, 17–27 September 1819', *Selected Letters* (Oxford: Oxford University Press, 2002), 303.

[22] Newlyn, 'Foreword', viii, quoting Bloom, *The Anxiety of Influence*, 71.

[23] See Edward Larrissy, ed., *Romanticism and Postmodernism* (Cambridge: Cambridge University Press, 1999), 3.

[24] There is, however, awareness of the recent critical excavations and reclamations of oppressed or lost poetic voices: Sinéad Morrissey's PhD thesis, for example, was on 'The Revolution in Action: Servants in British Fictions of the 1790s' (PhD Thesis, Trinity College Dublin, 2004).

Heaney's 'The Ministry of Fear'—which reformulates the Wordsworthian motif of the growth of the poet's mind into a polyphonic matrix of quotations and allusions to the texts that have (in)formed the later poet's mind—the crux is, famously, how the English canon involves and enacts political exclusion: 'Ulster was British, but with no right on/ The English lyric: all around us, though/We hadn't named it, the ministry of fear.'[25]

The polemics of 'The Ministry of Fear' are, however, only one aspect of Heaney's re-reading of Wordsworth. There are clear Wordsworthian echoes or assessments through-out Heaney's oeuvre, from the—in effect—'spots of time' in *Death of a Naturalist* (1966), to 'Wordsworth's Skates' and 'A Scuttle for Dorothy Wordsworth' in *District and Circle* (2006); it is also commonplace now to note how Heaney in his criticism 'not only re-created Wordsworth in his own image, but forged a poetic image of himself out of Wordsworth',[26] and re-created Wordsworth again and again to fit his own changing poetic self-image. This relationship between the poets never once subscribes to Bloomian *agon*; instead, following Heaney's own prompting, it could best be seen as one of ongoing metaphorical 'fosterage'. In the *Prelude* Wordsworth claims how he was 'foster'd alike by beauty and by fear',[27] when describing the period during which he was boarding at Hawkshead Grammar School (the poet's mother had died in 1778, the year before Wordsworth went to Hawkshead, and his father died in 1783 while the boy was still at the school). As the poem makes clear, this fosterage was less from any human fos-ter-parents than from the natural landscape of his 'beloved vale', or more precisely a reli-gio-mystical force within the landscape. This passage appears as epigraph to the 'Singing School' sequence of Heaney's 1975 *North*, which includes 'The Ministry of Fear', and a poem, 'Fosterage', which describes Heaney's relationship with the novelist and short-story writer Michael McLaverty: 'He...fostered me and sent me out, with words/ Imposing on my tongue like obols'; he also advises Heaney to 'Go your own way. Do your own work.'[28] 'Fosterage' is here primarily a process of poetic and literary education, of learning how to work with words. Where it was the Lake District hills that educated Wordsworth, it is Wordsworth himself whom Heaney describes as a 'mountain on the horizon';[29] it is Wordsworth and his poetry that educate and foster Heaney, enlarging his consciousness, encouraging his imagination, enabling him, and making him take 'the measure of [him]self and the world, and [him]self-in-the-world'.[30]

---

[25] Seamus Heaney, *North* (London: Faber, 1975), 65.

[26] Hugh Haughton, 'Power and Hiding Places: Wordsworth and Seamus Heaney', in *The Monstrous Debt*, ed. Davies and Turly, 62.

[27] William Wordsworth, *The Prelude 1799, 1805, 1850*, ed. Jonathan Wordsworth, M. H. Abrams, and Stephen Gill (New York: Norton, 1979), I, 306.

[28] Heaney, *North*, 65. Heaney taught with McLaverty in the St Thomas Intermediate school in west Belfast. A spectral James Joyce gives Heaney similar advice in the final section of 'Station Island'. The Joyce character tells the younger poet: 'What you must do must be done on your own/so get back in harness. The main thing is to write/for the joy of it'. There is no suggestion here, however, that Joyce 'fosters' Heaney. See Seamus Heaney, *Station Island* (London: Faber, 1984), 92–3.

[29] Seamus Heaney, Interview with John Brown, *In the Chair: Interviews with Poets from the North of Ireland* (Salmon Publishing: Cliffs of Moher, 2002), 77.

[30] Ibid., 77.

Fosterage is not just a matter of educational support and emotional succour, however. In medieval Ireland, fosterage was a political as well as an educational institution, which would help form and maintain political alliances between the two families (fostering and fostered); as such, it was also used as a means of assimilating English settlers into Irish life (and as a result was seen as a threat to English political power).[31] And in being 'fostered' by Wordsworth, Heaney also adopts Wordsworth as a political exemplar, thus allowing himself access to the 'English lyric' and unsettling the lyric's exclusive Englishness. In his 1984 lecture 'Place and Displacement', Heaney suggests that the last books of the *Prelude* 'worry and circle and ruminate in an effort to discover what had happened to him in the 1790s when a passion for liberty and human regeneration, embodied for Wordsworth in the fact of the French Revolution, came into conflict with other essential constituents of his being founded upon the land and love of England'.[32] Wordsworth is here a foil for the political tensions of Northern Irish poets, as Heaney claims that 'Like the disaffected Wordsworth, the Northern Irish writers I wish to discuss take the strain of being in two places at once, of needing to accommodate two opposing conditions of truthfulness simultaneously'.[33] Heaney presents no difficulty in appropriating Wordsworth as a radical, doubled, and politically torn figure, despite his later ossified conservatism (similarly, it is a dissenting, radical Wordsworth that features in Tom Paulin's essay 'A Republican Cento: "Tintern Abbey"').[34]

'At Toomebridge' combines the two elements of Heaney's 'foster' relationship with Wordsworth: the emphasis on the natural landscape as an influential and inspirational source; and the ability for what is learned from nature to oppose violence and psychic displacement. The speaker in the poem first develops a sense of freedom and knowledge from the natural landscape ('Where the flat water/Came pouring over the weir out of Lough Neagh/As if it had fallen shining to the continuous/Present of the Bann'). Second, he introduces recent political history, and relates that to a historical precedent: 'Where the checkpoint used to be./Where the rebel boy was hanged in '98'.[35] Finally, Heaney suggests how the combination of landscape and political history can be metamorphosed and 'opened' up into poetry (with a self-reflexive comment on his own earlier transformations of apoliticized natural motifs—the eels in 'The Lough Neagh Sequence'): 'Where negative ions in the open air/Are poetry to me. As once before/The slime and silver of the fattened eel'.[36] Through the reference to 1798 (the iconic year of the United

---

[31] See Peter Parkes, 'Celtic Fosterage: Adoptive Kinship and Clientage in Northwest Europe', *Comparative Studies in Society and History*, 48, 2 (April 2006), 368: 'Longstanding colonial fears of the moral degeneration of fostered Anglo-Irish settlers, and their resultant disloyalty to the English crown were overtly expressed in Clause II of the Statutes of Kilkenny in 1367. This proscribed "fostering of children" (*nurtur de enfantz*) together with alliances by "marriage, gossipred (*compaternitie*)... concubinage or amour" as treasonable offences.'

[32] Seamus Heaney, *Place and Displacement: Recent Poetry of Northern Ireland* (Grasmere, England: Trustees of Dove Cottage, 1984), 2–3.

[33] Heaney, *Place and Displacement*, 4–5.

[34] Tom Paulin, *Crusoe's Secret: The Aesthetics of Dissent* (London: Faber, 2005), 138–63.

[35] Seamus Heaney, *Electric Light* (London: Faber, 2001), 3.

[36] Ibid.

Irish rebellion and the *Lyrical Ballads*) the poem makes English lyric and Irish history coincide, to offer the possibility that an art rooted in the natural landscape can redeem political violence. Once 'distrust' of the English iambic line is overcome, that is, Heaney can find his relationship with Wordsworth liberating, positive, and comforting. Heaney's reading of Wordsworth is generously optimistic; his own repeated turns to rural traditions, pastimes, images, and idylls are in part intended to recreate a bolster against contemporary violence which is necessarily timeless and—in a Schillerian sense—sentimental. It is no less deliberate and crafty a poetic-cultural move for this, however; the self-aware artifice of a poem such as 'The Harvest Bow' is a conscious, shrewd comment on the process of 'creating' naive optimism. Nevertheless, the luminous possibility of peace and hope created in the poem is testament to a belief running through it that there is a benevolent force underlying the landscape, art, and existence, the essence that Wordsworth tended to call 'Nature' and then, latterly, 'God', and which Heaney nowhere names.

It is Heaney's association of poetry with rural traditions and a benign Wordsworthian life force that Carson undermines in 'The Irish for No', his redaction of Keats's 'Ode to a Nightingale' and the Heaney of *Death of a Naturalist* to *North* (1975):

> The border, it seemed, was not yet crossed: The Milky Way trailed snowy brambles,
> The stars clustered thick as blackberries. They opened the door into the dark:
> *The murmurous haunt of flies on summer eves.* Empty jam-jars.
> Mish-mash. Hotch-potch.[37]

The purpose of the disconnected allusions to Heaney and quotations of Keats is, in part, to use Keatsian negative capability to undermine and de-centre a Wordsworthian egotistical sublime associated with Heaney. However, it is also to replace Romantic sublimity with postmodern indeterminacy. As Paul Hamilton comments, 'the Romantic trope of sublimity recasts failures of understanding as the successful symbolic expression of something greater than understanding; Postmodernism recasts this success as indicating only the indeterminacy of meaning'.[38] Where Heaney's poetry maintains the vestiges of 'something greater than understanding', for Carson there can be nothing more than 'mish-mash', 'hotch-potch', and the eternal vacillation between 'yes' and 'no'; there will never arise or emerge a hidden sublime truth out of the mess of flax dams or rotting jam. Rather than creating new truths or supportive fostering, Carson's poem opens and affirms uncertainties, which are themselves new versions of the Romantic crises of the lack of 'correspondence between nature and consciousness' and the parallel (troubled) 'experience of the temporal relationship between the act and its interpretation'.[39] When questions are addressed in 'The Irish for No'—'*Was it a vision, or a waking dream?*', '*The Bank that Answers All/Your Questions*, maybe?', 'What's all this to the Belfast businessman

[37] Ciaran Carson, *Collected Poems* (Oldcastle: Gallery, 2008), 111.
[38] Paul Hamilton, 'From Sublimity to Indeterminacy: New World Order or Aftermath of Romantic Ideology', in *Romanticism and Postmodernism*, ed. Larrissy, 13.
[39] De Man, *Rhetoric of Romanticism*, 59, 49.

who drilled/Thirteen holes in his head with a Black & Decker?'[40]—the answers are endlessly deferred, and the poem itself exists in the gap between the question and the never achieved answer, gesturing towards a future that is only present 'in history… as the remembering of a failed project that has become a menace,'[41] whether that project is Enlightenment progress, Romantic sublimation, or Heaney-esque redemption. 'Auctoritas' is revealed as the empty boasting of a Braggadocchio, in a text where different narratives are garbled together with no hope of disentangling them but instead are left as 'metonymies for an unstated (and, we infer, unstatable) whole.'[42]

In Carson's rewriting of Keats and Heaney there is no 'myth of filiation'; neither of the precursor poets are father figures who need to be slain or supported. Paul Muldoon's rewriting of the Romantics is somewhat different, if only because his poetry returns so frequently to the trope of biographical and poetic fathers, with Heaney prime among the latter. Fran Brearton counsels, however, against accepting Muldoon's presentation of Heaney in this way (or indeed Muldoon's presentation of anything) at face value, and the overly neat reading of Muldoon such a reading provides:

> Muldoon is thus the poet who breaks with tradition, but who, very fortunately, provides within his own poetry a parody of the tradition he disrupts.... Criticism thus replicates the movement laid out autobiographically by Muldoon: from Patrick Muldoon, mushroom-gatherer, to Paul Muldoon, magic mushroom experimenter; from the safe empiricism of a Heaney or a Frost to the unsafe elusiveness and surrealism of a Muldoon.[43]

This is important because Muldoon's most intense engagement with Romantic poetry and myth ('Madoc: A Mystery') is often read—like Carson's—as a distancing and deconstruction of Heaney's optimistic readings of Romanticism. As Brearton comments, the Heaney-as-poetic-father trope offers a relatively 'easy' way in to Muldoon's work; Muldoon's non-committal comment that he is 'not an expert on "the anxiety of influence", but can see the argument for that' characteristically encourages without sanctioning such a way of reading his own poems;[44] Muldoon's response allows both the presentation of meaning (or commitment) and its ironic distancing. This is reflected in 'Madoc: A Mystery', as Heaney is linked to Coleridge and Southey's Pantisocratic plan whereas Muldoon self-associates with Byron, the conjunction of 'The tinkle/of an Aeolian harp./Eels./Elvers.'[45] (The 'Feuerbach' section of the poem, for example, connects Coleridge and Heaney via Heaney's 'Lough Neagh Sequence' which is parodied in 'A Briefcase', the poem immediately preceding 'Madoc.') This association—very much to

---

[40] Carson, *Collected Poems*, 110–1.

[41] De Man, *Rhetoric of Romanticism*, 58–9.

[42] Sean O' Brien, *The Deregulated Muse: Essays on Contemporary British and Irish Poetry* (Newcastle: Bloodaxe, 1997), 192.

[43] Fran Brearton, 'For Father Read Mother: Muldoon's Antecedents', in *Paul Muldoon: Critical Essays*, ed. Tim Kendall and Peter McDonald (Liverpool: Liverpool University Press, 2004), 48.

[44] Paul Muldoon in John Haffenden, *Viewpoints: Poets in Conversation with John Haffenden* (London: Faber, 1981), 134; quoted in Brearton, 'For Father Read Mother', 59.

[45] Paul Muldoon, *Poems 1968–1998* (London: Faber, 2001), 274.

the parodic point of the poem—deliberately flatters Muldoon and not Heaney: grandi-
ose poetic pretensions (his own included) are ironized as truths cede to plot twists and
magic is replaced by MacGuffins.

Unlike Heaney's generous attitude to Wordsworth's politics in 'Place and
Displacement', Muldoon's 'Madoc' exposes the connections between Romantic 'poetry
and the politics of imperialism and nation-building... as the poets' democratic, republi-
can ideals decline to narrow dogmatism'.[46] Muldoon's approach is similar to Carson's in
'The Irish for No'. Carson, in his own words, explores 'how the romantic agony—that
is the Romantic desire to transcend reality, to escape from the awfulness of life, and the
recognition that such transcendence is impossible—fits into a concept of brutality and
political violence';[47] similarly, Muldoon implicates Romantic escapism in systemic and
intercultural abuses of power, as the stately pleasure dome of Coleridge's Xanadu
becomes the corporation 'Unitel, its iridescent dome'.[48] As such, where Carson's poem is
infused with a sense of vacillation, of the indeterminacy of meaning, however, Muldoon's
takes an ethical position towards the Romantic poets' plans for political and historical
involvement (even though this ethical position is made slippery by Muldoon). Much of
the difficulty of the poem is the manner in which the ethical position is structural to the
poem. Poetry is cast as parallel to, implicated in, but separate from both philosophy (the
names of the philosophers used to label, contextualize, and confuse each of the poem's
sections) and the historical process of colonization and imperialization (which the
poem *imagines* rather than presents as fact). The poem takes an ironic angle to and from
philosophy and history, with a consequent lack of access to any notion of truth, and also
to any linear narrative progression (implicitly critiquing the poetic-politics of the
Pantisocratic enterprise, while also undermining poetry's ability to perform any politi-
cal critique). For Clair Wills, this use of irony articulates 'the consciousness of failure,
and of lack of authority. True to the legacy of romanticism, Muldoon's poetry continu-
ally struggles with the desire to transform experience into an aesthetic artefact, while
recognizing the impossibility of fully grasping it'.[49] This 'lack of authority' is, however,
not a cause for anxiety, but an excuse for mischief, and for undermining any pretensions
to authority (since it is everyone, not Muldoon alone, who is trapped in this situation).
Where the speaker in Carson's 'Opus Operandi' states that 'they were baffled by the
script's *auctoritas*', it is the notion of authority, including linguistic authority (witness the
slipping between 'Croatan', 'Croatoan', and 'Crotona'), that is baffled in 'Madoc'.[50]

Muldoon's self-identification with the Byronic 'Satanic' school is germane, since
Satan's challenge to the authoritarian Old Testament God, and his 'swerve' as he falls
from heaven, features in the *clinamen*, the first of Bloom's ratios of poetic influence;[51]

---

[46] Clair Wills, *Reading Paul Muldoon* (Newcastle: Bloodaxe, 1998), 150–1.
[47] Ciaran Carson, interview with Frank Ormsby, *Linen Hall Review* 8:1 (1991), 6, quoted Patricia
Horton, '"Faery lands forlorn"', 1, 62.
[48] Muldoon, *Poems 1968–1998*, 321.
[49] Wills, *Reading Paul Muldoon*, 15.
[50] Muldoon, *Poems 1968–1998*, 320.
[51] Bloom, *Anxiety of Influence*, 45.

and, as Paul Hamilton notes, in the contemporary postmodern era, 'Like Satan in *Paradise Lost*, our journeys are never original, only perverse, and the country into which we travel has already been mapped by a moral orthodoxy we can refract or invert in various ways, but never escape.'[52] It is the refraction of a challenge to overarching tyrannical power and moral orthodoxy that informs Leontia Flynn's 'Washington', a rewriting of Shelley's 'Ozymandias'. Stylistically following Carson's example in 'The Irish for No' (with lines from Shelley's poem interspersed with a tourist's experience of Washington, rather than a flâneur's impressions of Belfast), Flynn's effect is quite different. The United States is cast as the latest in the line of ephemeral (though at the time apparently omnipotent) regimes; more importantly, the perspective of cultural tourism—the 'rapid tourist mode'—which the poem adopts is also implicated and undermined. Shelley's poem is itself a monument to achievement which has—within the poem—fractured: given the pattern of impermanence, the perspective of Flynn's poem is itself exposed as being temporary or ephemeral—its authority will also fade. And central to the poem is a 'Satanic', blaspheming turn which renders authority fluid and impermanent: 'in rapid tourist mode, between/*Who said* the Washington Memorial/and...Jesus fucking Christ...this mausoleum/where Lincoln sits in state, and there in stone/fluent and just his Gettysburg address.'[53] Not only is Christ undermined, but the undermined Christ irrupts into and threatens the narrative thread of the poem, the tourist perspective (which itself breaks through Shelley's words): and once one authority is denied they are all denied. Here all that is left is the image of electronic communication, the 'men with walkie-talkies' 'by the White House', reminding the reader of the repeated images from Carson's poems. In Flynn's walkie-talkies though, there is not even a garbled squawk; all that is left is silent threat. Where Carson's poetic authority depended on the street-smart boasting and garbling flâneur able to live (and play coolly) with indeterminacy, in Flynn's poem even this perspective is undercut and exposed as artistic presumption. Not only will Ozymandias's political authority fade, so too will Shelley's poetic authority, and that of the contemporary poetic voice that misreads and claims influence from the Romantics, however generous, affectionate, agonistic, ironic, or arrogant that misreading may be.

[52] Paul Hamilton, 'From Sublimity to Indeterminacy', 15–6.
[53] Leontia Flynn, *Drives* (London: Jonathan Cape, 2008), 29.

PART VI

ON THE BORDERS: A FURTHER LOOK AT THE LANGUAGE QUESTION

CHAPTER 20

'GHOSTS OF METRICAL PROCEDURES': TRANSLATIONS FROM THE IRISH

AODÁN MAC PÓILIN

TRANSLATIONS from the Irish formed an important bridge between the Anglo-Irish literary renaissance and the early stages of the Gaelic revival. Both had been stimulated, in part, by a rediscovery of the Gaelic literary heritage, and both, for widely differing reasons, hoped to persuade their largely Anglophone audience of the value of that heritage. Douglas Hyde's hastily produced bilingual collection, *Abhráin Grádh Chúige Chonnacht/Love Songs of Connacht*, published in 1893, the year the Gaelic League was founded, was a key text that briefly blurred the distinction between the two movements.

The *Love Songs* provided both metrical and prose translations. In the prose versions and commentary Hyde used an intensified, almost over-literal version of Hiberno-English: a transition dialect, with its Gaelic substratum, that had developed in rural Ireland as the community language changed from Irish to English. It could be an effective means of conveying something of the freshness and naive directness of popular songs in Irish, as in the following verse from Hyde's prose translation of 'A Ógánaigh an Chúil Cheangailte/Ringletted Youth of my Love':

> And I thought, my storeen, That you were the sun and the moon. And I thought after that, That you were snow on the mountain. And I thought after that, That you were a lamp from God, Or that you were the star of knowledge Going before me and after me.[1]

Yeats famously saw in Hyde's experiments with Hiberno-English prose the coming of a new power into literature, and Hyde's approach was to influence Synge and Lady

---

[1] Douglas Hyde, *Abhráin Grádh Chúige Chonnacht or Love Songs of Connacht* (Dublin: Gill & Co., 1893), 43.

Gregory. In the metrical version of this verse, we can see Hyde himself being influenced by J. J. Callanan and Samuel Ferguson, two nineteenth-century translators, as well as by the English-language folk songs of Ireland, which themselves often reflect Gaelic metrics. The Irish is in eight-line stanzas which break naturally into four couplets, each forming a unit of four—sometimes five—stressed and eight or nine unstressed syllables. This high proportion of stressed to unstressed syllables, common in Gaelic songs, gives the metre a long, skipping quality, which is sometimes intensified and sometimes modified by assonance between long broad vowels. A singer would naturally linger on the long vowels, as would an Irish speaker reading the text. Hyde's metrical version shows an easy facility for rhymed verse, an instinct to follow the long, flexible rhythms of the Irish, accentuated by double rhymes ('fountain', 'mountain'; 'find me', 'behind me'—this last echoing 'shining' on the same line), and he reflects the vowel-music of the song by introducing a variety of stressed broad vowels—'thought', 'O', 'love', 'so', 'moon', 'fountain', 'snow', 'cold', 'mountain', 'more', 'God', 'knowledge', 'before':

> I thought, O my love! you were so—
> As the moon is, or sun on a fountain,
> And I thought after that you were snow,
> The cold snow on top of the mountain;
> And I thought after that, you were more
> Like God's lamp shining to find me,
> Or the bright star of knowledge before,
> And the star of knowledge behind me.[2]

Hyde has no compunction about introducing fillers to facilitate either scansion or rhyme. His version differs from its original by having up to seven stresses in each couplet, and the syntax, while simple, is perhaps a shade over-formal, but it does manage to convey to a remarkable extent the feel of the original Irish.

Lady Gregory was the only writer to follow Hyde in translating songs into synthetic Hiberno-English prose, although Patrick Pearse's sensitive non-metrical translations also owed something to him. While some of her versions strike a note of patronizing inauthenticity, she was sometimes highly successful, and her understated version of the powerful love song *Dónall Óg* is, arguably, as affecting as any metrical translation:

> You have taken the east from me; you have taken the west from me;
> you have taken what is before me and what is behind me;
> you have taken the moon, you have taken the sun from me;
> and my fear is great that you have taken God from me![3]

Hyde's metrical translations, with their straightforward diction and relatively natural speech rhythms, were to have a greater influence. Well-known anthology pieces such as

[2] Ibid., 43.
[3] Augusta Gregory, in Donagh MacDonagh and Lennox Robinson, *The Oxford Book of Irish Verse* (Oxford: Oxford University Press, 1958), 108.

Padraic Colum's 'Poor Girl's Meditation' (Colum found the original in Hyde's *Love Songs*), Thomas MacDonagh's 'Yellow Bittern', and numerous other twentieth-century translations owe much to Hyde's example.

The 1890s saw the publication of two other significant books of translations, both by men who had published their first work in the mid-nineteenth century. Standish Hayes O'Grady had published a lively, rhyming version of an eighteenth-century poem in 1855,[4] but for his prose translations of the poetry in *Silva Gadelica* (1892) adopted a ponderously grand manner: 'be not loquacious, nor censorious rashly; be the multiplicity of thy chivalrous qualities what it may, yet have thou not the Ilrachts hostilely inclined to thee.'[5] This style survived into the twentieth century only among academic translators providing parallel texts of the admittedly cryptic Bardic verse.

The other translator, George Sigerson, had perpetrated a book of dull translations of mainly eighteenth-century poetry in 1860.[6] In the muscular versions in his ambitious 1897 publication *Bards of the Gael and Gall: examples of the poetic literature of Erinn done into English after the metres and modes of the Gael*,[7] he undertook to translate verse from every period and every style within the tradition. Before examining the translations, it may be useful to take a brief look at the nature and range of Gaelic poetry.

The extensive corpus of poetry in the Irish language goes back to at least the sixth century AD, 'the earliest voice from the dawn of West European civilisation', as Kuno Meyer put it.[8] Most of what has survived of Gaelic poetry between the earliest period and the first half of the eighteenth century was composed by the learned classes, clerics, lawyers, and professional poets, and preserved by professional scribes or churchmen. Poetry from the earliest phase was in irregular, accentual, alliterative verse. The eighth century saw the emergence of rhyming verse forms based on a syllable count rather than on rhythmic metres, a mode that was to dominate Irish-language verse for nearly a millennium. Of the first period of syllabic verse, a small body of nature poems and dramatic lyrics is deservedly the best-known. Syllabic metres became increasingly more elaborate, until, towards the close of the twelfth century, they developed into what is commonly known as Bardic poetry, produced by a hereditary aristocratic class trained to compose formidably intricate verse in an obscure and dense linguistic register. Except for a handful of personal poems and some political poetry from the end of the period, modern readers, and translators, generally find Bardic poetry pretty turgid, preferring a much smaller body of informal verse, particularly the courtly love poems composed by non-professional poets in simpler syllabic forms and far more accessible language.

---

[4] Discussed in Robert Welch, *A History of Verse Translation from the Irish, 1789–1897* (Gerrards Cross: Colin Smythe, 1988), 138–42.

[5] Standish Hayes O'Grady, *Silva Gadelica*, vol. 2, *Translation and Notes* (London: Williams and Norgate, 1892), 115.

[6] Erionnach (George Sigerson), trans., *Poets and Poetry of Munster*, Second Series (Dublin: John O'Daly, 1860).

[7] George Sigerson, *Bards of the Gael and Gall* (Dublin: Talbot Press; London: T. Fisher Unwin, 1897).

[8] Kuno Meyer, *Selections from Ancient Irish Poetry* [1911] (London: Constable, 1928), p. vii.

During the seventeenth and eighteenth centuries, the learned class, as its traditional patrons were dispossessed or became Anglicized, began to adapt its technique to popular taste and developed highly complex accentual rhyming metres. This class was eventually replaced by a new class of part-time poets and scribes: schoolmasters, priests, tradesmen, farmers, and labourers. Although the learned native tradition had almost disappeared by the latter half of the nineteenth century, some of the earlier verse was preserved by and adapted to the oral tradition, which itself nurtured a rich body of verse, in songs, prayers, and poems, that began to be collected on a large scale when the language revival took off in the 1890s. This over-brief summary ignores some important continuities: accentual, non-rhyming verse continued to be composed during the syllabic period; syllabic verse was still being produced in the eighteenth century; and, in Irish-speaking districts, local poets were still composing songs and poems in traditional modes well into the twentieth.

Sigerson translated poems from the entire range of what was then available to him. Few of his translations have any particular merit, but his approach to syllabic poetry is particularly dubious. The following bathetic version of a lacklustre original is the lament of a man for his wife, Fáil, who died of shame on seeing him naked. Sigerson's translations bristle with vocabulary from a poetic register that was moribund even in the 1890s—'hearken', 'wold', 'yore', 'thou', 'wouldst', 'yon', 'shalt', 'ere', 'neath', 'twain'—and his pursuit of the structures of Gaelic verse is often bought at the cost of both syntax and comprehensibility. Sigerson claimed that his English version reproduces 'the metre and rime-sounds of the original', the first four lines of which could translate as: 'I sit above the strand (stormy the cold). My teeth chatter—great is the tragedy that has come upon me':

> Sate we sole, in cliff-bower—
>   chill winds shower—
> I tremble yet—shock of dread
>   sped death's power
> The tale I tell: fate has felled
>   Fáil most fine.
> She a man, bare, beheld,
>   In sun shine
> Shock of death, death's dread power,
>   Lowered fell fate,
> Bare I came, hence her shame,
>   stilled she sate.[9]

The chief weakness in Sigerson's translations is an enthusiastic and mechanical application of the dense alliterative and rhyming patterns of Gaelic syllabic poetry to accentual English verse with full-blown English rhymes—very different to the Irish system, as we shall see. Robin Flower, writing of syllabic verse in his introduction to his own somewhat mannered translations in *Love's Bitter Sweet*, may have been thinking of Sigerson

---

[9] Sigerson, *Bards*, 96.

when he noted that 'the peculiar effect of the Irish manner with its interlacing rimes and balanced phrasing cannot be reproduced in any English which may hope to give the effect of poetry'.[10] The above poem is not the worst of Sigerson's attempts, as clusters of stressed syllables slow down the lines. Generally, a combination of regular rhythms and full English rhymes turn his translations into a metronomic jingle:

> Blame thy spouse not, without thought,
> Never beat thy hound for naught;
> Never strive with senseless loon –
> Wouldst thou war with a buffoon?[11]

Occasionally Sigerson could try for a more straightforward register, particularly in his versions of the metrically simpler, accentual folk songs, and sometimes almost made it, but the temptation to poeticize and his clunking rhythms always defeated him in the end:

> How pleasant for the small birds
> To waken in the grove,
> And, close upon the same bough,
> To whisper to their love.
>
> Not thus, alas, our fortune
> My very heart's delight!
> 'Tis far apart each morning
> We waken to the light.
>
> She's fairer than the lily,
> Such beauty there is none:
> She's sweeter than the violin,
> More lightsome than the sun;
>
> But better than all beauty
> Her noble heart and free,
> O God, who art in heaven,
> Remove this pain from me![12]

One other translator of this period should be mentioned, although his significant output consists of only one poem. T. W. Rolleston's sonorous anthology piece, *The Dead at Clonmacnois*, was known to Yeats as early as 1888[13] although apparently not published for some years:

> In a quiet water'd land, a land of roses,
> Stands Saint Kieran's city fair:
> And the warriors of Erin in their famous generations
> Slumber there.

[10] Robin Flower, *Love's Bitter Sweet* (1925), quoted in Eleanor Knott, *Irish Classical Poetry* (Dublin: Three Candles Press, 1960), 18.

[11] Sigerson, *Bards*, 117.

[12] Ibid., 327.

[13] W. B. Yeats, *W. B. Yeats, Letters to Catherine Tynan*, ed. Roger McHugh (New York: McMullen Books, 1953), 54.

There beneath the dewy hillside sleep the noblest
Of the clan of Conn,
Each below the stone with name in branching Ogham
And the sacred knot thereon.

There they laid to rest the seven Kings of Tara,
There the sons of Cairbre sleep –
Battle-banners of the Gael, that in Kieran's plain of crosses
Now their final hosting keep.

And in Clonmacnois they laid the men of Teffia,
And right many a lord of Breagh;
Deep the sod above Clan Creide and Clan Conaill,
Kind in hall and fierce in fray.

Many and many a son of Conn, the Hundred-Fighter,
In the red earth lies at rest;
Many a blue eye of Clan Colman the turf covers,
Many a swan-white breast.[14]

The main problem with this mellifluous, atmospheric poem, as a translation, is that in both metre and sense it strays so far from the tightly constructed (and rather dull) fourteenth-century Bardic poem on which it is based that it is difficult to call it a translation. Rolleston, then, like Mangan before him, represents another strand of the translation tradition: the poet with no particular loyalty to his original.

It may be useful at this stage to examine what, for want of a better phrase, could be called the ethics of translation. This essay makes a number of assumptions which are not universally accepted but provide a necessary framework for what follows. It is assumed that the prime purpose of translating is to enable a reader with little or no knowledge of the language of the original to gain some insight into both the meaning and impact of a poem, and that the translator's task is to serve both the original text and the reader. Not every translator shares this view. Ezra Pound's 'Homage to Sextus Propertius' transposed into English felicities that never existed in the original, possibly, as Robert Graves argued, due to his ignorance of Latin,[15] but also because his main interest was in the quality of the English-language version of the poem, as a poem; fidelity to the original was neither his only nor his primary aim. In the heat of the controversy that raged until Pound eventually denied that 'Homage' was a translation, T. S. Eliot produced an admirably loyal if somewhat contorted defence of Pound. Eliot's argument, if I understand it correctly, is that there is really no such thing as translation, but that Pound is a great translator whose translations are translucencies, and who invented Sextus Propertius for the modern age in the same way that he invented Chinese poetry. The translation of 'Homage', he says, is not a translation; it is a paraphrase and a *persona* and a criticism and an interpretation. It is both too little of a translation and too much of a translation to be

---

[14] Justin McCarthy et al., eds., *Irish Literature*, vol VIII (Philadelphia: Morris & Company, 1904), 2,979.
[15] Robert Graves, *The Crowning Privilege* (London: Pelican Books, 1959), 242–4.

intelligible to anyone who is not, firstly, an accomplished student of Pound's poetry (in other words, already a fan), and secondly a classical scholar (in other words, someone who does not need a translator).

Pound's approach is of course completely legitimate as a creative strategy, but for an audience unfamiliar with the original it should come with a health warning. James Stephens, in his aptly named *Reincarnations*, approached his Gaelic originals openly in a spirit of freedom from either the words or intentions of his sources:

> This book ought to be called Loot or Plunder or Pieces of Eight or Treasure-Trove, or some name which would indicate and get away from its source, for although everything in it can be referred to the Irish of from one hundred to three hundred years ago the word translation would be a misdescription.... Some of the poems owe no more than a phrase, a line, half a line, to the Irish, and around these scraps I have blown a bubble of verse and made my poem. In other cases, where the matter of the poem is almost entirely taken from the Irish, I have yet followed my own instinct in the arrangement of it, and the result might be called new poems.[16]

Stephens's stunningly successful plunderings of the seventeenth-century poet Daibhí Ó Bruadair fall well into this category, but, through no fault of his, are often represented in anthologies as translations. Michael Hartnett's approach to Ó Bruadair was precisely the opposite:

> Many would say that I have created an unnecessary and insurmountable barrier between myself and Ó Bruadair in my insistence that a poet who is such a consummate craftsman should be translated with obsessive care, that his techniques should be brought across as faithfully as possible. 'Poetry is that which gets lost in translation' is a widely-held notion: I do not agree with it. A poet/translator, if he loves the original more than he loves himself, will get the poetry across: he may even get the whole poem across or, at second best, force his own version—within the strictures laid down by the original author—as close as possible to poetry.[17]

For this reader, while Hartnett is by far the most trustworthy and least egotistic translator of Nuala Ní Dhomhnaill's contemporary poetry, his experiments with Ó Bruadair's complex and sophisticated seventeenth-century Gaelic verse are more problematic. Verses here and there have some of the intensity and exuberance of the originals, and the fidelity of his modern English to the Irish modes is admirable, but for some reason, as with similar experiments by Austin Clarke, the translations rarely have an independent life of their own.

Ó Bruadair is a difficult poet. It goes without saying that the more dense the language of the original, the more intensely it plays with the texture of the language itself, the more it indulges in wordplay or ambiguity, the more its effects depend on linguistic nuance and unfamiliar cultural references, and the more complex its formal structure, the more difficult it is to transpose into an alien idiom. These problems are even more

[16] James Stephens, *Reincarnations* (New York: Macmillan, 1918), 71–2.
[17] Michael Hartnett, *Ó Bruadair: Translations from the Irish* (Oldcastle: Gallery, 1985), 13.

acute in that poetry which is most distant in function and form from that of our own era, unless the very exoticism of the earlier verse is itself the attraction. Not only does Bardic verse, for example, embody all the above barriers, it could also be valued as much for its indecipherability as for any other quality. As the King of Greece put it in the medieval tale *Oidhe Chloinne Tuireann*: 'That's a good poem, but I do not understand one word of what it means.'[18] It is not surprising, therefore, that little of the enormous body of Bardic verse has entered the canon of translations. Love of obscurity goes back to the oldest dateable poem in Irish, *Amra Choluim Chille/The Elegy of Columba*, composed shortly after the saint's death in 597. This is an extraordinarily opaque text, not simply due to its archaic language and esoteric register, but from a deliberate strategy in which syntax and grammar are mangled and tortured almost out of recognition.

Not all the earliest Gaelic poetry is as impenetrable. Kuno Meyer, the German scholar who unearthed much of this material, was also among its most sensitive translators. This is his version of a poem in an irregular accentual metre which he believed could be dated to the fifth century:

> The fort over against the oak-wood,
> Once it was Bruidge's, it was Cathal's,
> It was Aed's, it was Aillill's,
> It was Conaing's, it was Cuilíne's,
> And it was Maeldúin's:
> The fort remains after each in his turn
> And the kings asleep in the ground.[19]

While the poem would have had an added force for an audience for whom the kings listed in the poem had some resonance (who today knows anything about the Uí Berraidi of Leccach?), it can still, as a meditation on the transience of life and the transience of power, appeal to a modern audience. The litany of names builds up to the climax of the final two lines. Meyer has maintained the feminine endings of lines two to four and the stressed syllable that closes the initial sentence. The final two lines end in stressed mono-syllables, giving a certain apophthegmatic effect to the conclusion that is also in the original, and the final rounded vowels and 'n' in the last three lines echo the rhyme and consonance of the Irish (*Dúin, úair, úir*). There are some deviations from the literal, particularly in the final two lines, which translate as: 'The fort after each king in turn/and the host, they sleep in the clay'. It is not uncommon for academic translators, in the interests of clarity, to add verbs or to smooth out syntax. However, it is clear that Meyer was also aiming to maintain the momentum and dramatic effect of the final lines, so he made other adjustments, sacrificing the word 'host', separating 'each' and 'king', changing 'king' for 'kings' and transposing it to another line, and, finally, turning the verb 'sleep' into an adverb. The deviations from the literal meaning are slight, but the gain in readability, smoothness, and fidelity to the rhythm and impact of the original are immense.

---

[18] Richard J. Duffy, ed., *Oidhe Chloinne Tuireann/The Fate of the Children of Tuireann* (Dublin: Gill & Co., 1888), 38.

[19] Kuno Meyer, *Selections*, 93.

Rhyme barely featured in the original of Meyer's poem, but later came to play a key role in Gaelic poetry. It is also one of the most contested issues among translators of Irish poetry. This essay takes its title from the introduction to the bilingual anthology *An Duanaire 1600–1900: Poems of the Dispossessed*, whose compilers, Seán Ó Tuama and Thomas Kinsella, had initially planned to use available translations and to fill in the gaps with new versions. However, the anthology was intended primarily for readers with some knowledge of modern Irish, and most available translations departed from literalness. They eventually decided that Kinsella would translate all the poems, rejecting the few (non-rhyming) translations which fulfilled their strict criteria 'in the interests of "texture", as well as general usefulness':

> With a great deal of the poetry of the period the effects are bound up with prosody and technique: the syllabic or accentual rhythms, devices of rhyme, assonance, and so on. All of this is untranslatable. The occasional alliterations in the English, the ghosts of metrical procedures, give only a hint of the easeful elaborateness and linguistic elegance of many of the best poems in the book. Likewise with the syllabic 'oddness' that will be felt here and there in the translations of non-accentual poems; these only faintly echo the distinguished effects of bardic 'unrhythmical metre', as the Irish scholar Bergin phrases it. Translators who have worked on this poetry have usually chosen to rhyme their versions, but their rhyming is frequently in a mode that bears little relation to the rhyming of the original. Accepting that there must be losses in translation, it seemed to us that the loss involved in opting for rhyme could be too heavy, especially if the rhymes in English were still to remain an inadequate reflection of the prosodic qualities of the original poems. The translations, therefore, are unrhymed, but indicate the major basic rhythms of the originals.[20]

One fascinating element in the bilingual introduction is that there are some significant differences in emphasis, and sometimes in content, between the Irish and English versions. The hope expressed in the English version (presumably mainly the work of Kinsella), that the translations 'will also interest readers with no Irish at all', was omitted from the Irish.[21] Although the translations concentrated on literalness, it was also hoped that they could be 'read with some naturalness, suggesting some of the poetic quality of the originals'. The Irish summarizes the last phrase in the words 'nádúrtha agus fileata'— 'natural and poetic'—and then adds an additional sentence admitting that it was not always easy to reconcile even these limited aims.

In 1986 Kinsella published his *New Oxford Book of Irish Verse*, in which all but a handful of the scores of translations from the Irish are by him. Echoing *An Duanaire*, he defends his decision to filter one and a half millennia of Irish Gaelic verse through a single poetic sensibility on the not entirely persuasive grounds of 'comparison and general usefulness' (it is not clear what can be compared to what). In another echo of the earlier book, Kinsella defines his aim in translating the poems as an attempt to 'transmit the

---

[20] Seán Ó Tuama, Thomas Kinsella, *An Duanaire 1600–1900: Poems of the Dispossessed* (Dublin: Dolmen Press/Bord na Gaeilge, 1981), pp. xxxvii, xxxix.
[21] Ibid., pp. xxxvi, xxxvii.

essential contents of the originals in their major basic rhythms'.[22] However, the context has completely changed. The English versions of *An Duanaire* were intended primarily as a crib for an audience that could read Irish. *The New Oxford Book of Irish Verse* is a monolingual publication aimed at an Anglophone readership. In the second book, Kinsella's decision to reject rhyme is clearly no longer based on pragmatic criteria. It is now revealed as an aesthetic creed.

As a creed, it is not without justification. It is true that Gaelic rhyme is significantly different to English rhyme. It is true that a rhyming scheme, if it is to be meaningful, must be reasonably consistent, and that, as a result, many translations are distorted by the imperative of finding a harmonious rather than a meaningful word. There is, however, a counter-argument. Rhyme is a key binding element of all the syllabic and most of the accentual verse in the Irish Gaelic tradition. An equally strong case can be made that sometimes even an alien form of rhyme can provide some kind of shadowy approximation to one of the central elements of the original poem.

As Ó Tuama and Kinsella noted, in the compromise that is translation, translators must first identify that which they can never hope to transfer, decide what they wish to keep, and jettison the rest. Not an easy task, but the enormous body of literary (rather than literal) translations made over the last hundred years or so has proved how attractive the challenge is. *The Midnight Court*, an eighteenth-century extravaganza, has more than a thousand lines. It was tackled once by Dennis Wolfe in the early nineteenth century, but more than a dozen times in the post-revival period: by Michael C. O'Shea (1897), Arland Ussher (1926), Frank O'Connor (1945), Lord Longford (1949), David Marcus (1953), Patrick C. Power (1971), Thomas Kinsella (1981), Coslett Quinn (1982), Bowes Egan (1985), Noel Fahey (1998), Yam Cashen (2005), Ciaran Carson (2005), not to mention a fragment translated by Brendan Behan, who claimed to have left the rest of it on a bus, and two sizeable sections by Seamus Heaney. A large number of other established English-language poets have made significant contributions to the genre. Brendan Kennelly, John Montague, and Desmond O'Grady should be added to the list of those already mentioned. Others, not primarily known as poets, have also contributed to the genre; of these, Frank O'Connor was deservedly the best-known and most prolific, but this group includes Seán O'Faoláin and Brian O'Nolan, and the scholars Kenneth Jackson, Gerard Murphy, Eleanor Hull, Eleanor Knott, and James Carney. Others, including Paul Muldoon, have worked on contemporary poetry in Irish. Unfortunately, we do not have space to explore the entirely different set of challenges posed by Irish-language poetry in a modern idiom.

The genre is so large, in fact, that rather than try to provide even a survey of its range, I propose now to look closely at one short syllabic poem which has been translated more than a dozen times, and to examine the gains and losses involved in a number of metrical translations. The ninth-century verse *Int én bec* survived in an eleventh-century metrical tract as an illustration of a particular syllabic metre, *snám súad*. It can be translated as:

---

[22] Thomas Kinsella, *The New Oxford Book of Irish Verse* (Oxford: Oxford University Press, 1986), p. vii.

> The small bird which has whistled from the tip of a bright yellow beak sends out a note over Belfast Lough—a blackbird from a yellow-heaped branch.

Whether this was originally a fragment from a longer poem, a marginal note to a manuscript, or simply a metrical exercise is not known, but its attraction is easy to see. It is short and simple; anyone with a reasonable knowledge of modern Irish can make out all but two words of the original. It is also one of those exquisite nature poems whose qualities were identified by Kuno Meyer in his 1911 *Selections from Ancient Irish Poetry*:

> In nature poetry the Gaelic muse may vie with that of any other nation. Indeed these poems occupy a unique position in the literature of the world. To seek out and watch and love Nature, in its tiniest phenomena as in its grandest, was given to no people so early and so fully as the Celt.…It is characteristic of these poems that in none of them do we get an elaborate or sustained description of any scene or scenery, but rather a succession of pictures and images which the poet, like an impressionist, calls up before us by light and skilful touches. Like the Japanese, the Celts were always quick to take an artistic hint; they avoid the obvious and the commonplace; the half-said thing to them is dearest.[23]

The poem also has the attraction that key images—particularly the final image of the yellow-heaped branch—are strong enough to make it work in even an unadorned prose version, yet even the most loose approximation to its elaborate metrical structure provides a constant challenge. There is one other, iconic attraction, for some of the translators anyway. Place names play an important role in Irish poetry in both languages, and this poem has possibly the earliest reference in poetry to Belfast Lough. The attraction of associating a delicate ninth-century poem with industrialized, strife-torn twentieth-century Belfast should not be overestimated. This image has been used in the logo of the Seamus Heaney Centre for Poetry in Queens University Belfast, and one local group, in a gesture that has nothing of the half-said about it, plans to erect a thirty-foot blackbird in the city. However, although John Hewitt refers to this poem as the first written reference to his native place, the association with Belfast is probably an illusion; the Lough is twelve miles long, and a thousand years ago Belfast was a swamp—for all we know, the blackbird sent out its note from a bush in Bangor.

The poem has been given an interlinear translation by Donald Murray, the Scottish artist who provided the calligraphy for the poem in *An Leabhar Mòr/The Great Book of Gaelic*. Murray is a native speaker of Scottish Gaelic, and his version closely follows the word order of the original. All the words involved in the metrical system are in italics:

> Int én *bec*
> > The wee bird
> ro léic *feit*
> > has let out a whistle—
> do rinn *guip*
> > from the point of a beak

[23] Meyer, *Selections*, pp. xii–xiii.

> *glanbuidi*:
>   bright yellow:
> fo-cheird *faíd*
>   it sends out a call
> ós *loch laíg*
>   above Lough Laig
> *lon* do *chraíb*
>   a blackbird from a branch
> *charnbuidi*
>   yellow-heaped.[24]

The verse has three syllables in each line, twenty-four in all, no fewer than fourteen of which play some part in what Eleanor Knott has described as syllabic poetry's 'complex mosaic of sound'.[25] There is alliteration in the sixth line, between *loch* and *laíg*, as well as binding alliteration between lines three and four, *guip, glanbuidi*, lines six and seven, *laíg, lon*, and lines seven and eight, *chraíb, charnbuidi*. The first three lines end in single-syllable words and the fourth line consists of a three-syllable word, a pattern that is repeated in the next four lines. All line-endings have either rhyme or imperfect rhyme within the Gaelic system in the pattern *aaabcccb*, the fourth and final lines rhyming on all three syllables.

The best summary of the dynamic of syllabic metrics I have found is from the scholar Osborne Bergin, who in his youth composed subtle and complex Gaelic verse that would have been poetry if he had anything to say. Writing of two of the main strategies of syllabic poetry, rhyme and consonance, he says:

> [W]hat Irish poets aimed at was not identity, but similarity combined with variety. Their scheme of rhyme, *comardad*, is based upon a delicate classification of consonants, each of which may correspond to any other in its own group, with a result far more subtle than the rime of other languages. A further similarity combined with variety is attained by the use of *uaithne* or consonance, in which, while the metrical weight of corresponding syllables is equal, the vowels must be different. Then there is the varied rhythm…[26]

The Gaelic rhyme system calls for some explanation. It will be noticed that *faíd, laíg*, and *craíb* have exactly the same vowels, *aí*, one of the requirements of perfect rhyme. Consonants are classified in related groups which often correspond closely to what modern linguistics can identify as, say, spirants, liquids, plosives, and so on. In English prosody, rhymes between voiced stops, say *bad, bag*, and *lab*, would be identified as half-rhymes. In Irish they would be full rhymes: 'In fact,' Professor Carney says, 'what in English would be regarded as full rhyme, in Irish would often be felt as a breach of good style.'[27] But it is more

---

[24] Malcolm Maclean and Theo Dorgan, eds., *An Leabhar Mòr, The Great Book of Gaelic* (Edinburgh: Canongate Books, 2002), 37.

[25] Knott, *Irish Classical Poetry*, 18–19.

[26] Osborn Bergin, 'Metrica', *Ériu: The Journal of the School of Irish Learning*, vol. IX, pt. I (Dublin, 1921), 80–1.

[27] James Carney, *Medieval Irish Lyrics* [1967] (Dublin: Dolmen Press, 1985), p. xi.

complicated than that, as in this case the final consonants of *faíd, laíg*, and *craíb* do not represent voiced stops: the *d* is pronounced similarly to the English *th* in *then*, the *b* is pronounced somewhat like a *v*, and the *g* is a guttural sound that does not exist in English. To find the equivalent of rhymes based on *d, g*, and *b*, we would have to look at the first three lines, where *bec, feit*, and *guip* appear to end in the unvoiced stops *c, t*, and *p*, but are actually pronounced as the voiced stops, *g, d*, and *b*. However, in the first three lines the vowels do not match perfectly, so the rhyme between *bec* and *feit* would be regarded as imperfect rhyme, while *guip*, because its final consonant belongs to the same group and the vowel has equal length, has consonance with both. As Osborn Bergin has noted, such deviations from Gaelic full rhyme are not only permitted but desirable. The overall effect is of a subtle, muted, but dense patterning of associated sounds quite unlike the effect of English full rhyme. This is one of the things that went so badly wrong with George Sigerson's attempts to imitate syllabic metres: instead of reflecting their characteristic delicate pattern of related sounds, he goose-stepped them into English doggerel.

There is some controversy on the place of rhythm in Gaelic syllabic verse. When the fundamental organizing principle of a poem involves a syllable count, the rhythms of syllabic verse can be peculiar to an ear attuned to the rhythms of English poetry, but in some cases rhythm can also, when read with the natural stresses of the language, provide an interesting contrapuntal effect to its syllabic structure. Each of the first three lines of the 'Blackbird' consists of one unstressed and two stressed syllables, and the fourth line of two stressed and one unstressed syllable. This creates a natural caesura in the poem, which then repeats the pattern, except that the stressed, unstressed, stressed rhythm of the second-last line separates it slightly from the preceding lines, and gives a further emphasis to the triumphant image, *charnbuidi*—'yellow heaped'—of the final line.

It is clear that it is extremely difficult to reproduce the metrical apparatus of this poem in English, and even more difficult to do so in a way that would also reflect its meaning. Each translator has chosen a different set of compromises. Surprisingly, none of the poets who provided metrical translations has managed, or wished, to retain what is arguably the poem's most vivid image, the 'yellow-heaped branch', which raises the intriguing question of whether, in this case, a prose version is preferable to a metric one. All the Northern poets in fact have taken the suggestion of the poem's editor, Gerard Murphy, that 'The blackbird would seem to have been singing from a gorse-bush',[28] (it is by no means certain that a blackbird would have taken the risk of whistling from *aiteann gaelach*, the low-growing native gorse). None of them used the word 'gorse' or its alternative 'furze', and all chose the local term 'whin'. For John Hewitt, this was a deliberate gesture. His version, in which he distilled the poem down to seventeen syllables and called a haiku, opens a 1968 poem called 'Gloss, on the difficulties of translation':

> Across Loch Laig
> the yellow-billed blackbird
> whistles from the blossomed whin.

---

[28] Gerard Murphy, *Early Irish Lyrics* (Oxford: Oxford University Press, 1956), 6.

Hewitt goes on to discuss the problems of translating the music of the original:

> I may have matched the images
> but the intricate word-play
> of the original—assonance
> rime, alliteration—
> is beyond my grasp.
>
> To begin with, I should
> have to substitute
> *golden* for *yellow*
> and *gorse* for *whin*,
> this last is the word we use
> on both sides of Belfast Loch.[29]

It is clear that Hewitt was tempted by both the assonance and alliteration offered by 'golden' and 'gorse', but, characteristically, rejected them; 'gorse' on the grounds of his highly self-conscious Ulster regional identity, 'golden', possibly because it was too obviously 'poetic' for his own restrained aesthetic. He does, in fact, have alliteration in every line, and the initial 'l' of Loch Laig is repeated five more times within his seventeen syllables. While he has abandoned the line-breaks of the original, his use of sprung rhythm—a run of three stressed syllables in the first line, and four between the second and third lines (I read the second syllable of 'blackbird' as having more weight in this context than it normally does)—give some sense of the wayward rhythmic effect that syllabic poetry (if not this particular syllabic poem) can have.

All the other poets who translated this poem have followed the line-breaks of Murphy's scholarly edition, and most of them have ensured that their version breaks into two groups of four lines. Kinsella, as might be expected, makes no attempt at rhyme, and uses irregular alliteration:

> The little bird
> Let out a whistle
> From his beak tip
>   Bright yellow.
> He sends the note
> Across Loch Laíg
> —a blackbird, a branch
>   A mass of yellow.[30]

Lines have irregular syllabic length. The main gesture towards the rhythm of the Irish is in emphasizing the fourth and final two lines by both rhythmical and typological strategies. Like Hewitt, Kinsella uses irregular clusters of stressed syllables, such as 'beak tip/ bright yellow', which also deviates from the natural word order of English. As in the interlinear translation quoted above, the inversion of English word order can be justified as an attempt to hint at the linguistic structure of the original in a kind of uber-literal

---

[29] Alan Warner, ed., *The Selected John Hewitt* (Belfast: Blackstaff, 1981), 18.
[30] Thomas Kinsella, *New Oxford Book of Irish Verse*, 30.

translation. However, after Kinsella had set up the expectation of unadorned literalness, the final two lines come as a bit of a shock. He appears to have reinterpreted the final line not as the compound adjective *carnbuidi* but as two words, *carn buidi*, 'a yellow heap' or 'a heap of yellow'. This interpretation is grammatically impossible, as the lenition of *charnbuidi* identifies it as an adjective. While this deviation could be justified if it improved the flow, comprehensibility, rhythm, or imagery of the translation, it does none of these things. Kinsella, then, has given us less than a literal translation and less than a poetic one.

Kinsella left the poem without a title, so that the enormous body of people who do not know that Loch Laíg is Belfast Lough would have no notion of the poem's provenance. Some translators, like Frank O'Connor, got around this problem by incorporating the English name into the title:

> The Blackbird by Belfast Lough
>
> What little throat
> Has framed that note?
> What gold beak shot
>   It far away?
> A blackbird on
> His leafy throne
> Tossed it alone
>   Across the bay.[31]

O'Connor is one of the twentieth century's finest translators of Irish accentual poetry; his versions of O'Rahilly's eighteenth-century poetry are superb, and his 'Midnight Court' has only recently been superseded by Ciaran Carson's version. He tended to be less successful with syllabic poetry, and the 'Blackbird' is a particularly bad example. In this translation, his priorities were to maintain syllabic regularity (four syllables per line) and to reproduce the end-rhyming scheme of the original, with the result that the English pays not much more than a passing nod to the Irish. To his credit, he deviated slightly from English full rhyme ('shot' against the full rhymes of 'throat' and 'note'; 'on' against 'throne' and 'alone'), but this is not enough to modify the thumping rhythm of his version (it is not clear whether the internal rhyme between 'tossed' and 'across', or the binding alliteration between 'alone' and 'across', was deliberate, but neither help the pulse of the translation). O'Connor blamed his failure as an original poet on the thousands of lines of bad poetry he had learned by heart in his late teens: 'though my taste in poetry improved, my memory refused to adapt itself, and when it should have been producing masterpieces, it would suddenly take things into its own hands and produce something frightful by some minor Georgian poet like Drinkwater'.[32] Where the formal constraints of Gaelic accentual metres brought out the best in O'Connor, syllabic poetry sometimes brought out the worst.

---

[31] Frank O'Connor, *Kings, Lords and Commons* (London: Macmillan, 1962), 27.
[32] Frank O'Connor, *An Only Child* (London: Macmillan, 1962), 136.

Whether fidelity to a regular syllabic structure is necessary to a successful translation is an interesting question. It could be argued that rhythm is so basic to English-language poetry that it is almost impossible to adjust the ear to a non-rhythmic mode, and that the challenge of syllable counting benefits the translator more than the reader. Ciaran Carson, whose first language was Irish, follows closely the sense of the original poem, and maintains a strict pattern of two stresses and four syllables per line, this last requiring one archaism, 'o'er'. His most interesting innovation, however, is in his adaptation of the modes of Gaelic rhyme to English:

> the little bird
> that whistled shrill
> from the nib of
>   its yellow bill:
>
> a note let go
> o'er Belfast Lough—
> a blackbird from
>   a yellow whin[33]

In the fourth and eighth lines 'bill' and 'whin' would form a full rhyme in Irish, and 'yellow bill' and 'yellow whin' replicate the three-syllable rhyme of the original *glanbuidi* and *charnbuidi*. The last stressed syllable in lines one to three and five to seven have related, if not regular sounds. In the first three lines, 'bird', 'shrill', and 'nib' have the same short vowel, and involve a subtle double semi-consonance. In Irish prosody, *l* and *r* belong to the same consonant class, and although *d* and *b* technically belong to different classes, they are related sounds in that both are stops, one voiced and one unvoiced. Lines five to seven end in similar but not identical *o* sounds. There are other echoes of Gaelic metrics, such as the assonance between the unstressed second syllable of 'yellow' with 'of' and 'from', and assonance between 'note', 'go', and 'o'er'. However, while the inversion of 'whistled shrill' brings the last stressed syllable of that line into a subtle relationship with the lines on either side of it, its dominating, full English rhyme with *bill* in the fourth line unbalances what should arguably be the strongest rhyme in the poem, that between the fourth and final lines. 'Shrill' is the main deviation from the meaning of the original: 'nib' for what is usually translated as 'point' is less a deviation than might be thought; it not only brings a vivid metaphor into the poem, to balance the loss of 'yellow-heaped branch', but also echoes a secondary meaning of the word *gob* (beak), which can also be a nib.

Seamus Heaney also decided to privilege the syllabic and rhyming structure of the original in the first of two translations of the poem.[34] In discussing the poem he writes that the Irish has twenty-two syllables,[35] a misreading based on the modern pronuncia-

---

[33] This can be found on the website of the Seamus Heaney Centre for Poetry: www.qub.ac.uk/schools/SeamusHeaneyCentreforPoetry/

[34] The later version can be found on the website of the Seamus Heaney Centre for Poetry.

[35] Seamus Heaney, 'The God in the Tree', in *The Pleasures of Gaelic Poetry*, ed. Seán Mac Réamoinn (London: Allen Lane, 1982), 25.

tion of the word *buí* (yellow) as opposed to the Old Irish two-syllable *buidi*. Otherwise, all the lines have three syllables:

> The Blackbird of Belfast Lough
>
> The small bird
> let a chirp
> from its beak:
>   I heard
> woodnotes, whin-
> gold, sudden.
> The Lagan
>   blackbird!

There are no full English rhymes in this version, but every line-ending has some aural relationship with at least one other line, some of which conform to the Irish rhyming system and some of which shadow it: the *p* (unvoiced) and *b* (voiced) of 'chirp' and 'bird', while in different categories in the Irish system, are closely related sounds; the *k* of 'beak' has consonance in Irish metrics with the *p* of 'chirp' and the vowel in 'chirp' has assonance with 'heard'; 'bird', 'heard', and 'blackbird' all have a short vowel and an *rd* sound (and one off-stress rhyme). In syllabic poetry, rhymes between stressed and unstressed syllables are common, and Heaney repeats the stressed *in* of *whin* in the unstressed endings of 'sudden' and 'Lagan', which contain the voiced stops *d* and *g*, bringing them close to full Irish rhyme. There are clusters of stressed syllables throughout the poem, and occasional assonance ('woodnotes', 'gold') and alliteration. Only the first three lines closely follow the sense of the original, but Heaney's self-imposed aim of maintaining syllabic regularity and a high concentration of related sounds has been given priority over literalness. While 'sudden' and 'I heard' are not in the original, 'Lagan' has a particular resonance as an equivalent of *Loch Laíg*, as the Irish for Belfast Lough and the Lagan river that flows through the city are both derived from the word in Irish for 'calf'.

Carson and Heaney, in their versions of the poem, have shown the possibilities of adapting elements of Gaelic prosody to English. By adopting Bergin's principle of creating a soundscape that chooses similarity rather than identity, combining similarity with variety, they have conveyed something of the subtle cadences of the Irish poem, its complex mosaic of sound. In challenging Kinsella's claim that Gaelic metrics are untranslatable, they have pointed the way to a different aesthetic of translation for this important body of poetry.

CHAPTER 21

TRANSLATION AS COLLABORATION: NÍ DHOMHNAILL AND MULDOON

ERIC FALCI

THAT Nuala Ní Dhomhnaill is the most well-known and widely celebrated Irish-language poet of the twentieth century is beyond dispute. That this renown is at least partly connected to the widespread availability of her work in dual-language volumes—with her Irish poem on the left side of the facing page and an English translation on the right—is clear. That her roster of translators includes most of the significant poets in contemporary Ireland—from Hartnett to Heaney to Longley to Mahon to McGuckian to Ní Chuilleanáin to Muldoon to Carson—is, again, quite clear. And that Paul Muldoon has become the main translator of her work and, in many accounts, the most successful, is, finally, apparent.

It is possible, and very useful, to counter all of these assumptions. One might argue that Ní Dhomhnaill's position as the most well-known poet in Irish shouldn't necessarily lead to the conclusion that her work is the most important Irish-language poetry in the modern period. One might follow this up by suggesting that the writings of Máirtín Ó Direáin or Seán Ó Ríordáin, major Irish poets of the mid-century, were actually more significant, both in terms of their linguistic and aesthetic innovations and because of their widespread influence on later poets, including Ní Dhomhnaill. One might then propose that because Ó Ríordáin's work experiments so vigorously with the Irish language and literary tradition it is less inherently amenable to translation, and therefore has not been able to make its way into a literary canon shaped by the ideologies of monoglot English readers and Anglo-American literary and academic institutions. One might make the somewhat related argument that widespread translation into English can dilute the particularities of Irish-language poetry, and actually becomes a way to erase or subdue the Irish texts under the name of translation. Louis de Paor and Biddy Jenkinson have most forcefully articulated such positions, and Jenkinson's 'preference not to be translated into English in Ireland'—what she calls 'a small rude gesture to those who think that everything can be harvested and stored without loss in an English-speaking Ireland'—is the defining statement of this stance.[1] De Paor has powerfully described 'the forgery of the facing page' as what occurs when 'the English translation...replaces the Irish while appearing to replicate it, insisting it has redeemed the original while suggesting itself as a legitimate substitute'.[2] This argument is entirely convincing; and yet translation into English and dual-language publication does continue to occur, and looks to be the most viable mode of publishing poetry in Irish. If this is the case, then the more immediate question becomes not about whether or not such a publication format is best, but how to approach the work that is presented in such a format.

One useful approach might be to judge each translation's fidelity to the original, while also seeking to compare and contrast that poem's translation by different hands. Such an analysis would be undergirded by a theory of translation that, explicitly or not, would fall somewhere on the spectrum of acceptability and adequacy that has been most comprehensively mapped by Lawrence Venuti in *The Translator's Invisibility*. One could suggest that certain translations aren't adequate to the specifics of the language of the source text, and therefore have made themselves too acceptable within the codes and expectations of the target language. In such cases the translations become too readable, and the specific singularity of the text—of the poem in Irish—is erased by the fluency of the translation. A related argument concerns the fidelity of the translation to the original, and again it is important to think of this as a spectrum rather than a binary. A translation that sticks closely to the original, either working word for word, phrase for phrase, or line for line, may be judged to be too 'flat' in the target language. Aiming for adequacy to the source language, or trying to render too closely the original in the target language, might result in a loss of poetic vivacity. On the other hand, a translation that wanders too far from the content, tone, or spirit of the original might be judged to be something more like a version of a text, rather than a translation of it.

In *After Babel*, George Steiner argues that in cases 'where translation takes place at close cultural-linguistic proximity', there is a particular tension between the adequate translation and the acceptable one.[3] Steiner suggests that because there is such a close cultural connection between an original language and a target language—and Irish and English would be an example of such proximity—the tendency would be for the translation to be too fluent, that it would close the gap between itself and the original too tightly. Steiner writes that 'the delineation of "resistant difficulty"', the endeavour to situate precisely and convey intact the "otherness" of the original, plays against "elective affinity", against immediate grasp and domestication'. He continues, 'good translation...can be

---

[1] Biddy Jenkinson, 'Letter to the Editor', *Irish University Review* 21, no. 1 (Spring/Summer 1991), 34.

[2] Louis de Paor, 'Disappearing Language: Translation from the Irish', *Poetry Ireland Review* 51 (Fall 1996), 67, 62.

[3] George Steiner, *After Babel: Aspects of Language and Translation* [1975] (Oxford: Oxford University Press, 1998), 412.

defined as that in which the dialectic of impenetrability and ingress, of intractable alien-
ness and felt "at-homeness" remains unresolved, but expressive. Out of the tension of
resistance and affinity, a tension directly proportional to the proximity of the two lan-
guages and historical communities, grows the elucidative strangeness of the great trans-
lation".[4] Steiner's delineation of the complexities of translation at a 'close cultural-linguistic
proximity' is vital in the context of Irish poetry. An overly acceptable translation would
capitulate to an Anglophonic hegemony and would only further the incorporation of
Irish-language literature into the norms of a canon produced and conducted in English.
Overly adequate translations—which would, at the vanishing point, be equivalent to no
translations at all—would enact their own end, and such an essay as this would have
been neither asked for nor possible.

The translations of Ní Dhomhnaill's poetry have been situated in these various ways,
and her work has been framed by the larger issues of the historical relationship of Irish
and English on the island of Ireland, and the asymmetricality of that relationship in the
modern period. Whether the critical angle of entry is the fact of the translations in the
first place, their mode of appearance, or the particular strengths or weaknesses of any
particular translator, readers of Ní Dhomhnaill's work have had to—and must continue
to—address the conditions and assumptions of their own reading practice, and to read
across the double pages of the dual-language volumes. If the translation doesn't trouble
its own processes in order to produce some sort of readerly estrangement, it is crucial for
readers to evoke and stage such estrangements in order to realize more fully the complex
interactions between the Irish poem and the English translation. This is particularly
important considering the translation history of Ní Dhomhnaill's work, which, as
Michael Cronin has argued, has resulted in the situation in which 'each translator has
his/her unmistakeable form of fluency, so that it is the original poet rather than the
translator who becomes invisible'.[5] I want to posit a reading model that counters such
fluency. The presence of both texts side by side should force a mode of incursive reading,
one that continually uses one side of the double page to upset the unity or naturalness of
the other. This kind of reading has both a hermeneutic and an ethical vector, and should
subtend the kinds of readings we produce, not only of Ní Dhomhnaill's body of work,
but of dual-language editions generally, especially when they feature a minority lan-
guage translated into a majority or hegemonic one, as is surely the case when Irish poems
are paired with their versions in English.

In dual-language formats in which the translations do trouble their own processes by
attempting to register the distortions and transformations inherent to any act of transla-
tion, especially literary translation, it is important not only to mark the differences and
disjunctions between the two sides of the double page, but also to consider the original
and translation as a theoretical tandem. In considering Paul Muldoon's translations of
Ní Dhomhnaill's poetry, then, it is necessary both to mark the moves and swerves that

[4] Ibid., 412–13.

[5] Michael Cronin, *Translating Ireland: Translation, Languages, Cultures* (Cork: Cork University
Press, 1996), 177.

his translations make and to track their effects as they aggregate into an embedded *ars poetica* of translation. It is not only that Muldoon's translations of Ní Dhomhnaill depart from and modify their originals in startling and often zany ways, but that these departures, transpositions, and mutations gesture towards a practical theory of poetic translation within their manoeuvres. That Muldoon's translations of Ní Dhomhnaill are frequently playful and contain all sorts of self-reflexive winks and nods doesn't seem to be the most interesting point (this is, after all, Paul Muldoon). Rather more intriguing is the way such play is deployed and managed within an overall translation practice that is remarkably faithful to the general tone and movement of Ní Dhomhnaill's Irish poems.

Muldoon has become both in practice and reputation Ní Dhomhnaill's main translator. Her first dual-language volume, *Selected Poems/Rogha Dánta* (1986/1988), includes a few translations by Ní Dhomhnaill herself (a practice that she hasn't continued), but the bulk of the book features Michael Hartnett's translations. In an 'Afterword' to a reissue of *Selected Poems/Rogha Dánta* in 2000, Ní Dhomhnaill writes that Hartnett 'came to translate these poems because at the time he was the only English-language poet with good enough Irish that I knew'.[6] In the 'Afterword' she describes the haphazard way in which the poems to be translated were chosen from among those in her first two volumes, *An Dealg Droighin* (1981) and *Féar Suaithinseach* (1984), and mentions that there wasn't a 'particularly close form of collaboration involved in the translation'.[7] For subsequent dual-language volumes Ní Dhomhnaill has provided cribs of the poems for her translators, whose proficiency in Irish ranges from fluency to the proverbial 'cúpla focal'. Judging by the nature of the translations, the various translators must have approached the cribs quite differently, and it is safe to say that the major form of collaboration between Ní Dhomhnaill and her translators is mediated through these cribs. Especially when the collaboration is conducted at long range, transatlantically in the case of Muldoon and Ní Dhomhnaill, the cribs serve Ní Dhomhnaill as a mechanism of authorial control as well as of authorial abdication. Ní Dhomhnaill has stated that she 'is not a poet in English', and has generally maintained a 'laissez-faire' attitude towards the translations.[8] However, the cribs themselves are a considerable authorial intervention, especially considering that all of her translators know less Irish than she does. Recognizing that there exists for each poem a line-by-line translation, prepared by Ní Dhomhnaill and used by a translator either as starting point or guide or sounding board, offers another potential order of readerly and critical activity.

A reader of Ní Dhomhnaill's dual-language volumes—and I would argue that most of her readers, no matter their proficiency in Irish, will read her work in such volumes, simply because those volumes are significantly more accessible on both sides of the

---

[6] Nuala Ní Dhomhnaill, *Selected Poems/Rogha Dánta* (Dublin: New Island Books, 2000), 161.

[7] Ibid., 166.

[8] Nuala Ní Dhomhnaill, *Selected Essays*, ed. Oona Frawley (Dublin: New Island Books, 2005), 200; Ní Dhomhnaill, *Selected Poems/Rogha Dánta*, 166. For Ní Dhomhnaill's descriptions of the processes of translating her work, see Kaarina Hollo, 'Acts of Translation: An Interview with Nuala Ní Dhomhnaill', *Edinburgh Review* 99 (Spring 1998), 99–107.

Atlantic—comes to a given poem and is immediately faced with its double articulation. Both the Irish and the English are visible at once, whether or not the Irish will be readable to whatever degree. Each poem in *Pharaoh's Daughter*, the 1990 dual-language volume with translations by thirteen different poets that initiated her rise to prominence, is headed by Nuala Ní Dhomhnaill's name on the left side of the double page, atop her poem in Irish, and the respective translator's name on the right side, above the translation. There is, in one sense, an overwhelming insistence on authorship. Ní Dhomhnaill is not only the author of the volume, the one whose name is most prominent on the front and back covers, the spine, and the title pages, but she is specified as the author of each poem in Irish. At the same time, each page features an authorial reoccupation, as the translator's name—in the same-size font and in a corresponding position on the page—works in conjunction with, and somewhat against, Ní Dhomhnaill's. In Ní Dhomhnaill's next dual-language volume, *The Astrakhan Cloak* (1992), Muldoon is the sole translator, named below Ní Dhomhnaill on the cover and title page, but the individual poems name neither poet nor translator (obsessively naming Ní Dhomhnaill and Muldoon at the top of every page would, indeed, be somewhat disconcerting). This format is kept for Ní Dhomhnaill's 2007 dual-language volume, again translated entirely by Muldoon, *The Fifty Minute Mermaid*. In her other dual-language volume, *The Water Horse* (1999), each English translation is initialled by one of the volume's two translators, Medbh McGuckian (MMcG) and Eiléan Ní Chuilleanáin (ENíC).

This admittedly tedious catalogue of various paratextual matters in Ní Dhomhnaill's volumes is meant to suggest one point: that for the most part the translations are forcefully marked. They are signalled as such. Even in the Ní Dhomhnaill/Muldoon volumes, where the author's and translator's names aren't included on every page, it is clear that there are two writerly hands. This is made abundantly clear on the back cover of the Gallery Press edition of *The Fifty Minute Mermaid*, which features similar-sized photos of each of the authors—Ní Dhomhnaill's above Muldoon's. None of Ní Dhomhnaill's dual-language volumes include the sort of apparatus (preface, translator's introduction, epilogue, notes, glossary) that would help to situate the premises and intent of the translations, and that would flesh out the translation dynamic at work in the volumes, but this may not be as bad a thing as some have suggested. The effect of this lack of contextualization and explanation is to offload such matters onto the reader. This, I think, is entirely to the good, so long as our readings actually account for the various modes of mediation, distortion, and material transformation that the dual-language volumes encode.

One way of accounting for these mediations is to recognize the presence of a third text, Ní Dhomhnaill's crib, within the matrix of the double page, so that what was a toggling back and forth across a double page becomes a triangulation of the two sides of the page with the elided crib. The point isn't necessarily to try to locate the crib in order to find out what changed from Ní Dhomhnaill's crib to the translator's version. Such a mode of analysis would be locked irrevocably into an untenable notion of an urtext. Material effects and conditions would disappear as analysis reduced to a search for origins. Rather, the notion of the cribs allows for a kind of speculative criticism in which the translation isn't read as simply right or wrong, adequate or acceptable, but rather as a transformative instance, one simultaneously suggested by and distanced from the authored text. The great value of Muldoon's translations of Ní Dhomhnaill is that they manage to surface the notional crib within versions that also transform the text. They are at the same time close to Ní Dhomhnaill's originals, and daring rescorings of them.

In general, Muldoon alternates between a close fidelity to the Irish text and blatant mischief. The five Muldoon translations included in *Pharaoh's Daughter* are emblematic of this dual tendency. He renders the title of Ní Dhomhnaill's 'An Crann' ('The Tree') as 'As for the Quince'. He translates Ní Dhomhnaill's archetypal 'bean an leasa' ('fairy woman') as 'this bright young thing' and then as 'her ladyship' in the same poem.[9] (Though it should be noted that the strangest aspect of this text is that in Ní Dhomhnaill's Irish poem the 'bean an leasa' speaks in English.) He renovates the 'lios', the fairy-fort, in 'Comhairle Ón mBean Leasa', into a pair of nightclubs, 'the *Otherworld Club* or the *Faerie Queen*'.[10] In his translation of what has become Ní Dhomhnaill's signature poem, 'Ceist na Teangan'/'The Language Issue', he fleshes out semantics by means of enjambment. The phrase in Irish, 'taobh na habhann' ('the side of the river'), is set across two lines in the translation so that 'the edge/of a river' is an edge of the poem as well.[11] Muldoon's virtuosic facility for rhyme in his own work carries over into his translations, as in 'Gan do Chúid Éadaigh' ('Nude') when he splits Ní Dhomhnaill's eight-line stanzas into quatrains with typically gaudily inventive rhymes (nude/natty, la-di-da/doe, sinewy/snow). Although Ní Dhomhnaill has written that compared to English 'the Irish language has an abomination of end-rhymes', it isn't only that Muldoon imposes his own penchant for rhyme onto his translations.[12] Muldoon's rhymes often attempt to produce analogous effects in sound or rhyme as appear in Ní Dhomhnaill's Irish. When Ní Dhomhnaill does include end-rhymes, as in the final lines of 'An Crann', which, as I've mentioned, Muldoon translates as 'As for the Quince', these lines describe a tree that is still standing after the 'bean an leasa' ('the woman from the fairy-mound') has taken a Black and Decker chainsaw to it:

> Murab ionann is an crann   As for the quince, it was safe and sound
> a dh'fhan ann, slán.   and still somehow holding its ground.[13]

Muldoon keeps the basic sense of the final lines and reproduces Ní Dhomhnaill's somewhat rare use of a concluding perfect rhyme. But his preservation of the final rhyme is effected through two American colloquialisms, 'safe and sound' and 'holding its ground', that introduce a radically new kind of discourse to the poem. The translation crookedly nods to Ní Dhomhnaill's devoted incorporation of the Irish vernacular by bringing in an

---

[9] Nuala Ní Dhomhnaill, *Pharaoh's Daughter*, rev. ed. [1990] (Winston-Salem, North Carolina: Wake Forest University Press, 1994), 36–7.

[10] Ibid., 145.

[11] Ní Dhomhnaill, *Pharaoh's Daughter*, 154. For further examples of this tactic, see the first six lines of 'Titim i nGrá' ('I Fall in Love') and the final five lines of 'Lá Chéad Chomaoineach' ('First Communion') in Nuala Ní Dhomhnaill, *The Astrakhan Cloak*, trans. Paul Muldoon (Winston-Salem, North Carolina: Wake Forest University Press, 1992), 22–3 and 32–3.

[12] Ní Dhomhnaill, *Selected Essays*, 182.

[13] Ní Dhomhnaill, *Pharaoh's Daughter*, 38–9.

entirely different vernacular register, one that has become increasingly central to Muldoon's own poetic project. The final lines of his translation of 'An Crann' sound so unavoidably like Muldoon parodying 'Muldoon' that they become the marker of their own linguistic intrusion. The larger point is that Muldoon's rhymes, which just as often have no basis in the original poem in Irish, seem less like attempts at fluency and more like ways of signalling readers back to the Irish side of the double page.

A similar tactic occurs at the end of Muldoon's translation of 'Coco-de-Mer', one of the sections of Ní Dhomhnaill's sequence 'Immram'. Ní Dhomhnaill's poem, which describes the myth surrounding the once-yearly sex lives of the trees that produce the eponymous massive island fruits, ends with the speaker and a companion standing still as ghosts as they hear the trees rumbling past them:

D'imigh na crainn tharainn de thruist láidir   as the trees went jumbering past
go tulcanta talcanta talantur.   with their judders and jolts and jostles.[14]

In this case, Muldoon's lines exemplify Ní Dhomhnaill's own wish for her translations: 'It doesn't really matter if the words mean different things. The most important thing is to get the voltage that is behind the words.'[15] Getting the right voltage in this case necessitates a translation that intertwines sonic transposition and semantic transfer, and could be said to exemplify a famous passage from Walter Benjamin's hugely influential essay, 'The Task of the Translator': 'unlike a work of literature, translation does not find itself in the center of the language forest but on the outside facing the wooded ridge; it calls into it without entering, aiming at that single spot where the echo is able to give, in its own language, the reverberation of the work in the alien one.'[16] Muldoon empties the syntax of the original in order to reproduce some of the energy of its sonorities, even though he needs to change the key of Ní Dhomhnaill's lines. The repeated 't-l-c' motive in the original's 'tulcanta talcanta talantur' is transposed in the translation to 'j-t(d)-l' or 'j-l-t'. Ní Dhomhnaill's final line repeats slightly modified forms of the verb *tolgánn*, meaning 'to thrust or jolt', and while Muldoon keeps the broad semantic sense of the original, his version changes the verb forms into what we might call 'moving nouns': 'judders and jolts and jostles'.[17] He jostles the original to show the seams between it and the translation, but also to suggest that these seams have a particular textual magnetism, and so again to force a reading that traverses strangely the gutter of the double page.

Such transmogrifications appear throughout *The Astrakhan Cloak*, and Muldoon's most famous bit of play occurs in his translation of Ní Dhomhnaill's 'Deora Duibhshléibhe'

---

[14] Ní Dhomhnaill, *The Astrakhan Cloak*, 90–1.

[15] Nuala Ní Dhomhnaill, Medbh McGuckian, and Laura O'Connor, 'Comhrá', *The Southern Review* 31, no. 3 (Summer 1995), 600–1.

[16] Walter Benjamin, 'The Task of the Translator', *Illuminations*, ed. Hannah Arendt, trans. Harry Zohn (New York: Schocken Books, 1969), 76.

[17] There is also possibly a severely buried allusion in Ní Dhomhnaill's line to the early Irish story 'Giolla an Fiuga', or 'The Lad of the Ferule', which was published in the first volume of the *Irish Texts Society*, edited by Douglas Hyde (London: David Nutt, 1899). In one part of the story the lad takes a mighty leap, and the phrase used is 'coircéimib tulcanta talcanta tréan-móra', which Hyde translates as 'with vigorous, valorous, mighty-great steps' (*Irish Texts Society*, vol. 1, 18, 19).

('Dora Dooley'). In the poem the speaker describes meeting 'Deora Duibshléibhe', a 'bean sí' or woman of the fairy-mound (Muldoon gives the well-known transliteration 'banshee' in his translation), on her way to keen 'the Fitzgeralds of Murrargane'. Ní Dhomhnaill's original describes the fairy-woman as wearing a green cloak—'chlóca uaithne'—but Muldoon describes the cloak as being made of 'green astrakhan'.[18] Hidden within this seemingly unnecessary, and invented, specification of the cloak's type of cloth is a bilingual pun. The word for translation in Irish is 'aistriúchán', so the woman's cloak is not only a magic cloak (she is, after all, from the otherworld), but it is also a translating cloak. This passage, noted first by Bríona Nic Dhiarmada, can stand as the prototypical instance of Muldoon's translation strategies.[19] It is an imposition into the original text that resonates first in the English (because that's where it first occurs), then back into the Irish where its significance as a pun is registered, and finally back into the English where the pun is activated. The cloak made of astrakhan is also a woven (a textual) translation ('aistriúchán'). Devious and nuanced, this moment of Muldoonery carries significant freight. It requires a reading that, wherever it might start, moves from the English to the Irish back to the English, and one that first finds the bilingual pun in 'astrakhan' and then diffuses that pun through the entire poem (and the entire book, since the phrase is repeated as the volume's title).

Such strategies have been read in a few different ways. Dillon Johnston writes that 'Paul Muldoon acknowledges the otherness of Irish not by striving for Irish effects in English so much as by leaving evidence that the translation distorts, as it attempts to convey, certain distinctively Irish characteristics.'[20] David Wheatley has complicated that basic argument, asserting that by 'filling his version with imported references Muldoon creates an effect of register-shifting and incongruity that identifies the poem as a site of linguistic disturbance... recognizable in its own way as a translation.'[21] It is possible to refine these notions even more by suggesting that the mode of distorted conveyance that Muldoon's translations attempt isn't based on a static binary in which 'Irish' is always other but still assimilable enough so that 'certain distinctively Irish characteristics' can be made available. Or that, as Wheatley suggests, they front their own shifting registers in order to 'identif[y] the poem as a site of linguistic disturbance'. This, while surely right, might imply that Ní Dhomhnaill's poem in Irish isn't already a 'site of linguistic disturbance'. The kind of 'register-shifting' that Wheatley notes is not necessarily a new stylistic strata in Muldoon's translation, but the transposition of a different kind of register-shifting—between the Irish oral vernacular and the literary register—that is already part of Ní Dhomhnaill's project in Irish.

---

[18] Ní Dhomhnaill, *The Astrakhan Cloak*, 46–7.

[19] Bríona Nic Dhiarmada, 'Going For It—And Succeeding', *The Irish Literary Supplement* 12, no. 2 (Fall 1993), 3–4.

[20] Dillon Johnston, *The Poetic Economies of England and Ireland, 1912–2000* (New York: Palgrave, 2001), 173.

[21] David Wheatley, 'The Aistriúchán Cloak: Paul Muldoon and the Irish Language', *New Hibernia Review* 5, no. 4 (2001), 127–8.

Justin Quinn has offered a different line of critique. In *The Cambridge Introduction to Modern Irish Poetry, 1800–2000*, Quinn suggests that Muldoon's translation strategies emerge as a result of dissatisfaction with Ní Dhomhnaill's poetry. He writes that Muldoon 'makes his translations of Ní Dhomhnaill an extension of his own poetry... the liberties he takes elsewhere... display an impatience and lack of interest in the original. This is hardly surprising as Muldoon is a far superior poet, and ultimately his translations amount to a criticism of her limitations.'[22] Just before this passage, Quinn suggests that since Ní Dhomhnaill's poetry is influenced more by models of twentieth-century American free verse than by the 'complex bardic forms of the Irish tradition', its translation into English is a 'type of homecoming'.[23] Hidden within these critiques is perhaps a more important pair of insights, both of which have been anticipated by Johnston and Wheatley.

Whatever we might make of Quinn's arguments, he is absolutely right to suggest that, on the one hand, Ní Dhomhnaill's poetry is deeply influenced by modernist American poetry, and that, on the other, Muldoon's translations function as criticisms. However, their incorporations of twentieth-century American poetry aren't indicative of an abandonment of traditional Irish forms, but rather a reinvigoration of both Irish and American forms. That this exact line of argument has been used against almost every single instance of poetic experimentation in the past two centuries, whether by Keats, Dickinson, Eliot, or Ó Ríordáin, should be enough to give pause. American poetry from Whitman and Dickinson through Berryman and Plath has been a significant influence on poetry in Irish since the 1970s and the emergence of the *Innti* writers at University College, Cork. The central figures in this group—Michael Davitt, Gabriel Rosenstock, Liam Ó Muirthile, and Ní Dhomhnaill—absorbed various aspects of twentieth-century poetry from America, Britain, and Europe as part of a deliberate project to widen the scope of poetry in Irish, which, in their view, had developed (or failed to develop) within an aesthetic and ideological environment that was deeply insulated and, in some ways, stultifying. This does not necessarily lead to the conclusion that Ní Dhomhnaill's poetry is somehow not really in Irish because of its engagement with American poetry. Quinn's further suggestion that Muldoon's poems function as 'criticisms of [Ní Dhomhnaill's] limitations' is at least partially right. They are criticisms, but not at all of Ní Dhomhnaill's poetry. Rather, they function as critiques—both self-critiques and critiques of the activities in which they engage.

The two seemingly contradictory tendencies in Muldoon's translations of Ní Dhomhnaill actually produce a dialectic that constitutes the particular kind of critique embedded within the translations and their originals, one which registers as forcefully at the site of reading as it does at the site of writing. By alternating back and forth between close translations, ones that don't depart all that much from the sense of Ní Dhomhnaill's original, and more adventurous renderings, Muldoon compels a reading that allows

[22] Justin Quinn, *The Cambridge Introduction to Modern Irish Poetry, 1800–2000* (Cambridge: Cambridge University Press, 2008), 150.

[23] Ibid., 149.

neither original nor translation to rest steadily on the page or to feign autonomy. Muldoon's translations are not, emphatically not, all of a piece. Some, such as 'Feis' and many sections of 'The Voyage' from *The Astrakhan Cloak*, and a great majority of the poems in *The Fifty Minute Mermaid*, are very faithful to the originals, and read more like line-by-line translations than versions or reconceptions. Others are close to the original except for a few manifest alterations or additions, such as the bilingual pun in his translation of 'Deora Duibhshléibhe', or the transposition of 'an capall coille' to 'the acrostical capercaillie' in 'The Lay of Loughadoon',[24] a manoeuvre which alludes to Muldoon's own poem entitled 'Capercaillies', collected in *Madoc—A Mystery*, an acrostic poem spelling out the phrase, 'Is this a New Yorker poem or what'.[25] These are the instances of Muldoonery that I mentioned before, and are best seen as local, and loaded, effects.

The other kind of translations that often appear among Muldoon's versions of Ní Dhomhnaill's poems might best be described as restylizations. Such poems, as I've mentioned before, often draw from Muldoon's own poetic practice by incorporating a great deal of rhyme, either taking a cue from rhymes or near-rhymes that appear in Ní Dhomhnaill's poems and reconfiguring them in English, or by structuring translations around rhymes when there were none in the Irish. Related to this is Muldoon's proclivity for rewriting Ní Dhomhnaill's own vernacular tone in Irish into varieties of American vernacular. As in his own poetry, all sorts of American idioms and quasi-slang phrases dot his Ní Dhomhnaill translations. Even limiting examples to the five Muldoon translations in *Pharaoh's Daughter* makes for a sizable list: 'calm and collected', 'topsy-turvy', 'holding its ground', 'the long and short/of it', 'la-di-da', 'icing on the cake', 'talking/the hind leg off a donkey'.[26] Such colloquialisms appear next to idioms that are distinctly closer to British or Irish English: 'he lost the rag', 'the brolly under your oxter', 'his famous motoring-car', 'someone slips me a Mickey Finn'.[27]

At times, such modulations appear in Muldoon's translations for Ní Dhomhnaill's 2007 volume, *The Fifty Minute Mermaid*, but more noticeable is how close Muldoon's versions are to their originals. This is especially the case for the long sequence of mermaid poems that take up the bulk of the volume. First collected in Ní Dhomhnaill's 1998 volume *Cead Aighnis* ('Leave to Speak'),[28] the mermaid poems constitute one of the major projects in her canon, and can be connected to the earlier 'Mór' poems and her rearticulations of Irish mythological material, whether the stories of Cú Chulainn and Medbh in her first two Irish-language volumes, or the *cailleach* or *spéirbhean* sections in *Feis* (1991). In several interviews and essays, Ní Dhomhnaill has noted that one of the major problems of the dual-language volumes is that they dismantle the architectures of the books in Irish.[29] Some poems are left untranslated or are reordered and

[24] Ní Dhomhnaill, *The Astrakhan Cloak*, 67.
[25] Paul Muldoon, *Madoc—A Mystery* (London: Faber and Faber, 1990), 6–7.
[26] Ní Dhomhnaill, *Pharaoh's Daughter*, 37, 39, 91, 105.
[27] Ní Dhomhnaill, *Pharaoh's Daughter*, 37, 91, 105, 145.
[28] Nuala Ní Dhomhnaill, *Cead Aighnis* (An Daingean: An Sagart, 1998).
[29] Ní Dhomhnaill, *Selected Essays*, 200.

recontextualized within the dual-language volumes. Although she has gone on to argue that nonetheless 'the whole act of translation seems to me vitally important' because 'what we gain is still so much greater than what we lose', one of the aims of *The Fifty Minute Mermaid* seems to be to transmit a sense of the more extended schemes that undergird Ní Dhomhnaill's discrete lyrics.[30] For this reason, perhaps, Muldoon fore-goes many of the stylistic tactics that had typified his earlier translations in order to render clearly the architectonics of the mermaid sequence.[31]

Additionally, the mermaid poems are often extended narratives about different aspects of the merpeople that Ní Dhomhnaill shapes out of various parts of the Irish oral tradition and, especially, her extensive research at the Department of Irish Folklore in University College, Dublin. As dependent on the storytelling impulse as the lyric one, the poems in *The Fifty Minute Mermaid* are by turns inflected by mythology, anthropol-ogy, and psychology, and they aggregate a narrative about the history of the merpeople (and one mermaid in particular whose journey from sea to land and back structures the sequence) who have come to land, and the effects of this transmigration. The poems articulate the liminal space between this world and the otherworld (or between the outer world and the interior one) along which almost all of Ní Dhomhnaill's poems are arranged, and which Muldoon has described as the 'world-scrim' particularly crucial in the larger body of Irish literature.[32] Ní Dhomhnaill has described the 'highly elaborate conceptual framework [that] exists in Irish to describe and deal with the "otherworld"' as proof of the fact that 'in Ireland the border between this world and the "otherworld" was never drawn', and further suggests that this framework is 'virtually untranslatable due to an inbuilt bias in the English language against the validity and tangibility of oth-erworldly experience'.[33] Muldoon's relatively straight translation throughout much of *The Fifty Minute Mermaid* is almost like the inversion of his earlier mischief. Having established a set of readerly expectations based on his work in *Pharaoh's Daughter* and *The Astrakhan Cloak*, Muldoon upends those expectations, forcing us—once again—back to the specificities of Ní Dhomhnaill's poems in Irish.

It is significant, then, that one of the most intriguing moments in the volume occurs when such a limen is staged. The central narrative of 'Admháil Shuaithinseach', which Muldoon translates as 'A Remarkable Admission', has to do with an instance when the speaker gets a hint of the traumatic, exilic past of the merpeople, and is given a frame-work for understanding the relationship between this world and the otherworld.

---

[30] Ibid.

[31] The second part of *The Fifty Minute Mermaid*, which consists of the mermaid sequence (the first part collects three poems and translations that had been published previously), doesn't precisely match the sequence as it appears in *Cead Aighnis*, under the title 'Na Murúcha a Thriomaigh'. A few poems drawn from different sections of *Cead Aighnis* appear in *The Fifty Minute Mermaid*'s mermaid sequence, and a few poems that don't appear in *Cead Aighnis* are included in *The Fifty Minute Mermaid*. Translations of many of the other poems in *Cead Aighnis*, apart from the mermaid poems, are included in *The Water Horse*.

[32] Paul Muldoon, *To Ireland, I* (Oxford: Oxford University Press, 2000), 7.

[33] Ní Dhomhnaill, *Selected Essays*, 86, 85, 86.

The speaker, a teenager deep into the complexities of various school subjects like biology and accounting, finds something in the water and brings it to one 'Tomás' to ask him what it is. Tomás, digging for worms on the shore, tells her that it's a catfish, and that everything on land has its equal ('a chomh-maith d'ainmhí') in the sea.[34] He goes on to mention that this includes 'an mhurúch', 'the sea-person', and then immediately turns and leaves (Muldoon writes that he 'disappeared').[35] The speaker is left abandoned:

> D'fhág sé ar snámh mé idir dhá uisce.   He left me hanging there,
> like a drowned man between two seams
> of water.[36]

Literally, Ní Dhomhnaill's final line says, 'he left me swimming between two waters'. Muldoon's expansion of and addition to the line ramifies in several ways.

By factoring out the 'dhá uisce' into two lines, and by translating the phrase as 'two seams of water', Muldoon attempts to explicate Ní Dhomhnaill's final line and, in doing so, undoes its wonderfully impossible grammatical logic. In a poem that hints at a notion of total equivalence between what lies above the water and what lies below it, the radical non-equivalence of this final figure performs more accurately the traumatic break between the realms which seems to cause Tomás's sudden, far-sighted departure. 'Two seams of water' makes clear sense figuratively if we translate the water into stone or shale, or some other 'land-like' substance that could have a seam. In this sense, Muldoon's rescoring of the final line's logic allows it to be read from a terrestrial perspective. Ní Dhomhnaill's line doesn't permit such a point of access. 'Water' is generally not a counted noun. We might speak synecdochically of 'two waters' if we mean two bottles or glasses of water, or collectively of the 'waters of Babylon' if we mean a body of water, but we don't have a literal plural for the substance of water (Ní Dhomhnaill's phrase 'dhá uisce' uses the singular form of the word for 'water'). That a 'highly elaborate conceptual framework' for talking about the otherworld, according to Ní Dhomhnaill, exists in Irish but is 'virtually untranslatable' into English, is made strikingly clear by Muldoon's rendering. In order to think our way through the line, first in the Irish and then in the English and then back in the Irish, we have to metaphorize, another form of translation that necessitates both transfer and distortion. The two waters that are utterly interwoven in the Irish—this world's and the otherworld's, which mirror each other's life-worlds—are carefully separated in the English, into 'two seams' and two lines. Additionally, Muldoon's conversion of 'ar snámh', which primarily means 'swimming' but can also mean something nearer to 'floating', into 'hanging there' adds a deathliness that doesn't register at the end of the original. This deathliness is intensified when the speaker compares herself to a 'drowned man'. First hung and then drowned and then turned into a man, the speaker undergoes a series of traumas analogous to those that the *murúcha*

---

[34] Nuala Ní Dhomhnaill, *The Fifty Minute Mermaid*, trans. Paul Muldoon (Loughcrew, Ireland: Gallery Press, 2007), 86.

[35] Ní Dhomhnaill, *The Fifty Minute Mermaid*, 88–9.

[36] Ibid.

suffer in the exile from the water.[37] If every translation, as the title of Muldoon's translation of Ní Dhomhnaill's earlier poem 'Comhairle Ón mBean Leasa' has it, involves something of a 'heist', then perhaps also necessary is a confession. Muldoon's final lines encode both a crime (metaphorical though it may be) and an admission, but this admission can only be remarked by reading back across the book's gutters, and so the 'heist' becomes bi-directional.

The larger point isn't only that Muldoon wilfully reconfigures the texts, courts anachronism, or engages in rampant code-switching in his translations of Ní Dhomhnaill's poetry: he surely does. Just as Ní Dhomhnaill's poems switch between classical Irish literary registers, modes of traditional Irish vernacular, newer idioms in Irish that might be back-translations from Hiberno-English or American English, and the occasional macaronic phrase. At another level, Muldoon's translations are so clearly ventriloquistic—Muldoon is 'doing' Muldoon translating Ní Dhomhnaill—that his recognition and exploitation of 'the otherness of Irish' goes well beyond distorting what Johnston calls 'certain distinctively Irish characteristics'. By making Ní Dhomhnaill sound so much like 'Muldoon', Paul Muldoon's translations undermine the possibility of the fidelity of translations even as he engages in the act of translating. Both languages are made other to each other even as they are juxtaposed across the gutters of the double page. At times Muldoon gives us poems that are more like cribs of Ní Dhomhnaill's Irish, a scenario that is interestingly complicated by the fact that we know that Ní Dhomhnaill gives her translators cribs of her Irish. At other moments his translations read so much like highly stylized versions of Muldoon that we are made hyper-aware of their status as translations. And throughout we are presented with 'teeny-weeny' keys that adamantly do not open onto the Irish text and so become self-reflexive tokens of their own slanted involvement: a 'quince-tree', a 'cloak of green astrakhan', 'the acrostical capercaillie', or 'two seams of water'.[38] In all of these cases, it isn't that Muldoon is simply taking creative licence, but rather that these additions embed a critique, one that has to be *read*, and which requires a reading that moves back and forth across the double page.

---

[37] Because many of the poems in *The Fifty Minute Mermaid* have a female speaker, and because an uncle of Ní Dhomhnaill's named Thomas Murphy was one of her main sources of lore, I am assuming a female speaker in this poem, hence the significance of the re-gendering triggered by Muldoon's final simile. On Thomas Murphy, see Ní Dhomhnaill's *Selected Essays*, 28–37.

[38] Ní Dhomhnaill, *The Astrakhan Cloak*, 57; *Pharaoh's Daughter*, 37; *The Astrakhan Cloak*, 47 and 67; *The Fifty Minute Mermaid*, 89.

CHAPTER 22

....

INCOMING: IRISH POETRY AND TRANSLATION

....

JUSTIN QUINN

I

....

Translation from languages other than Irish is of marginal interest for the understanding of contemporary Irish poetry written in English. However, there are some exceptions where it is illuminating to consider recent Irish poets' engagements with other languages (Seamus Heaney with Old English; Derek Mahon, Ciaran Carson, and David Wheatley with French; more distantly, Michael Longley with Greek; and Peter Fallon and Derek Mahon with Latin).[1] Many poets translate from cribs, as a kind of exercise 'to keep the engine ticking over,'[2] and thus avoid serious engagement with cultures beyond those of the anglophone world. The lack of interest displayed by many Irish poets is not particular to the country, but is shared by the world of anglophone literature in general. Laurence Venuti, in his history of translation, has remarked on translation's 'marginal status in British and American cultures' at the present time. He points out that the total of translated books published in Britain and America at the beginning of the 2000s is in the range of only 1.4–2.07 per cent; whereas on the continent the figures are significantly higher (Germany, 7–14 per cent; France, 8–12 per cent; and Italy, 22–25 per cent). In conclusion, he states: 'Since World War II, English has been the most translated language worldwide, but it isn't much translated into'.[3]

---

[1] Samuel Beckett, who wrote poetry in French, is a special case and is dealt with by David Wheatley elsewhere in this volume. I would like to mention here that Eamon Grennan's translations of Leopardi, while excellent in themselves, do not make us revise our opinion of his, or other, poetry. In Peter Fallon's case, the connections are mainly to be found between his translation of the *Georgics* (Oldcastle: Gallery, 2004) and his collection *The Company of Horses* (Oldcastle: Gallery, 2007).

[2] Derek Mahon, *Adaptations* (Oldcastle: Gallery, 2006), 11.

[3] Laurence Venuti, *The Translator's Invisibility: A History of Translation* [1995] (London: Routledge, 2008), 7, 11.

With the adoption of English as the first language of the country, Irish writers have been able to partake in perhaps the most important European literary tradition, that of the English language. But they have also adopted the general apathy of the English speaker to what goes on outside the language. One might argue that the writer who is an English monoglot necessarily inhabits a larger linguistic world than the writer who is, say, an Italian monoglot, thus rendering second-language acquisition less necessary. (In the US and UK alone, it is not unusual for over 300,000 books to be published in a year, compared to say over 50,000 in Italy.)[4] The world of anglophone literature is larger and more diverse—both geographically, culturally, and in terms of publications: the sun does not seem to set on the anglophone empire. Certainly, this lack of interest in what goes on outside English has not stunted the language's literary culture.

II

In his memoir of growing up in south Dublin in the 1950s, Hugo Hamilton describes the particular linguistic situation in his house. His father was an Irish-language enthusiast who had married a German woman. While the father had learnt German, the mother never learnt Irish (though she may have had passive knowledge of it). English was forbidden, and the children were beaten for bringing even the briefest phrase through the front door. The degree of the father's linguistic fanaticism is also indicated by the account of his attempt to start an import-export business: it failed because he would 'not sell anything to anyone unless they say his name properly in Irish'—the rather unusual name of Ó hUrmoltaigh, the Irish version of Hamilton.[5] Both Irish and German were spoken in the house, and in the following passage Hamilton describes his awareness of the anglophone world that existed outside:

> When you're small you're like a piece of white paper with nothing written on it. My father writes down his name in Irish and my mother writes down her name in German and there's a blank space left over for all the people outside who speak English. We're special because we speak Irish and German. . . . My mother says it's like being at home again and my father says your language is your home and your country is your language and your language is your flag.[6]

The father was involved in a grand imaginative effort that stemmed from Douglas Hyde's desire to de-anglicize Ireland. But the effort, like his business, fails, as Hamilton's memoir is written neither in Irish nor German, but in English, the language of Ireland. Hamilton's book is of use because it alerts us to the presence of borders around the anglophone world, especially as it exists in Ireland. With general access to English and American culture through newspapers, films, and television over the past few decades,

---

[4] Ibid.

[5] Hugo Hamilton, *The Speckled People* [2003] (London: Harper Perennial, 2004), 108.

[6] Ibid., 3.

Irish people have become unaware of these particular borders around their mother tongue.

I wish to take the Hamilton house in south Dublin as a kind of frame to structure the following discussion of poetry translation by Irish poets from languages other than Irish. With one or two exceptions, these poets are native speakers of English. Their knowledge of foreign languages varies from ignorance to fluency, and when they translate into English, they, like other translators, must decide *what* English is the target language. By this I mean that they must ask themselves whether they wish to translate into a standard conventional literary idiom, let us say, the poetic equivalent of Received Pronunciation; or will they translate into an English that is marked by Irishness (This can range from peppering the translation with Irish usage or vocabulary to a more widespread use of local dialect, though the latter is rare.)?

Irish literature achieves definition at the end of the nineteenth century in part by its claim to difference: it brings new types of knowledge (viz., Yeats's use of folklore, Synge's accounts of the western world) and it transforms the literary idiom by acknowledging the ghost of the Irish language within English (Synge, again, is the obvious example.). How is an anglophone writer to be considered Irish if he or she does not carry some distinguishing marks (both traces and wounds) from the original language of the country? The question causes some anxiety, because of the attendant fear of dissolving into an imagined homogeneous anglophone tradition, or worse still, of being considered English. Many twentieth-century Irish writers have strategically placed these marks within their literary productions in order to define their difference. When poets write their original works in English, the spectral presence of Irish is often a distinguishing characteristic. Of course English, even as written by a poet as notionally 'pure' as, say, Alfred Tennyson, Thomas Hardy, or Edward Thomas, is a language that is full of spectral linguistic presences. The Irish writer, however, privileges a particular set of these traces whose provenance reflects the historical experience of his or her country.

The situation becomes more complex when they translate into English. On the one hand they assert English as their native tongue—for that is the only language they can translate literature into, and it is one of the supreme ways to claim a language as their own. But because, for many, their usual literary practice has involved the orchestration of those spectres above, they employ them again when they translate. This latter gesture would seem to undermine their ownership of the English language. It would seem that it is not quite theirs. (Eiléan Ní Chuilleanáin has remarked that she writes 'English rather as if it were a foreign language into which I am constantly translating'.)[7] It is, in Jacques Derrida's phrase, a kind of prosthesis that imagines a first and more fundamental

---

[7] Leslie Williams, '"The Stone Recalls its Quarry": An Interview with Eiléan Ní Chuilleanáin', in *Representing Ireland: Gender, Class, Nationality*, ed. Susan Shaw Sailor (Gainesville: University Press of Florida, 1997), 31. Medbh McGuckian has also spoken of English in similar terms (Nuala Ní Dhomhnaill, Medbh McGuckian, and Laura O'Connor, 'Comhrá', *The Southern Review* 31: 3 [Summer 1995], 606–7), and Paul Muldoon quotes Octavio Paz with approval when he said that original poems are themselves translations, in *The End of the Poem: Oxford Lectures on Poetry* (London: Faber, 2006, 195).

language.[8] As in the case of the Hamilton house, there are three languages in play here, just as there are when Edwin Morgan translates Jean Racine into Scots vernacular.

'Not quite theirs': in what way does it make sense to say that Irish people, and therefore Irish poets, do not quite own English? They have spoken it for many generations, many have only the vaguest knowledge of Irish, and even if they approach fluency, only a handful can claim it as a native tongue on a par with their English. Their accents are distinctive, but no more so than those of, say, Yorkshire or Lincolnshire. Clearly, they own English. But how then are we to understand those 'spectres' of Irish that appear in Irish poetry and literature? Derrida answers this question thus: no one has a native tongue without such spectres, and turning this answer back to the case of Irish poets, we can view them as poets of the English language, much like Tennyson, Hardy, and Thomas, but with their own set of spectres.

The huge extent of the anglophone world, with a consequent vague awareness of its borders, creates an interesting and special dynamic, in the general culture, and in poetry. If one is a monoglot, it is difficult to comprehend the linguistic, political, ethical, and imaginative barriers that lie between different languages. This ignorance can of course be both enabling and disabling. (On one side, for instance, Yeats's ignorance of Irish fuelled some of his finest writing.) Ignorance can intensify curiosity, and it can foreclose it.

In what follows, I will examine some of the work of Irish poets—both as they translate, adapt, 'version', and as they write poems about translation—through the frame of the Hamiltons' front window. These poets inhabit the 'blank space left over' of English, which is limned by Irish on the one hand and the presence of a foreign language on the other. They are extremely curious about linguistic borders. Even those poets who know no Irish at all, and have not inherited a sense of responsibility towards the language, still evince a concern for it, as manifested in their versions of Irish poetry and occasionally the themes of their own poems (Good examples here are Derek Mahon and Michael Longley.). It is an interesting space, not merely for what it tells us about translation practice in Ireland, but also about contemporary poetic practice.

III

The range of poetry translated by Irish poets, while patchy, is at least broad, and so it is worthwhile introducing categories for distinguishing the salient features. The first is knowledge of the other language. This varies dramatically. For instance, Seamus Heaney, who translated Jan Kochanowski, has no knowledge of Polish, and worked with a scholar, Stanisław Barańczak, to produce *Laments*.[9] Eavan Boland occupies the middle

---

[8] Jacques Derrida, *Monolingualism of the Other; or, The Prosthesis of Origin*, trans. Patrick Mensah (Stanford: Stanford University Press, 1998), 61.

[9] Jan Kochanowski, *Laments*, trans. Seamus Heaney and Stanisław Barańczak (London: Faber, 1995).

ground. In her introduction to an anthology of German poets which she edited and translated, she remarks that German is 'a language I cannot understand but need to hear', but later she says that she 'could feel the poems on the page, could remember the sound of words, could catch the music of the movement';[10] moreover, she heard German spoken around her for a lot of her childhood.[11] A little further on in the middle ground, there is Ciaran Carson who translated some of the sonnets of Arthur Rimbaud, Stéphane Mallarmé, Charles Baudelaire, and has good reading knowledge of French and 'a fairly accurate idea of the originals'.[12] At the other end of the spectrum, there is, for instance, Harry Clifton, whose fluency is consolidated by the fact that he lived for an extended period in France, and so possesses a deep cultural knowledge in addition to linguistic proficiency.

Beyond these considerations, knowledge of the translated language is an important indicator, as it tells us the degree to which the poet-translator has lived—practically, imaginatively—outside English. A monoglot translator is only going to have a hazy idea of the different modes of being that exist in other languages, and of the subsequent difficulty of conveying them into their native tongue. George Steiner describes what is to be gained through such transactions:

> The frontiers between languages are 'alive'; they are a dynamic constant which defines either side in relation to the other but no less to itself. This is the enormously complex topology which lies behind the old tag that knowledge of a second language will help clarify or deepen mastery of one's own. To experience difference, to feel the characteristic resistance and 'materiality' of that which differs, is to re-experience identity. One's own space is mapped by what lies outside; it derives coherence, tactile configuration, from the pressure of the external. 'Otherness', particularly when it has the wealth and penetration of language, compels 'presentness' to stand clear.[13]

For many centuries, for Irish poets, this frontier lay between Irish and English. Much of Michael Cronin's *Translating Ireland* (1996) brilliantly attends to this border in poetry. But this is no longer the case, despite the examples of Michael Hartnett, Seamus Heaney, and Thomas Kinsella; and it is difficult to encounter 'Otherness', whether linguistic or cultural (if there is a difference), in much contemporary Irish poetry.

This loss necessarily creates the above-mentioned anxiety that Irish poetic identity will dissolve into anglophone poetry, and to assuage this there are many poems that proclaim and protest their Irishness (for instance, this is to be found in some poems by John Montague, Seamus Heaney, and Eavan Boland; and is endemic in the standing army of the lower ranks). Raymond Williams remarked that once people start talking about

---

[10] Rose Ausländer et al., *After Every War: Twentieth-Century Women Poets, Translations from the German*, trans. Eavan Boland (Princeton: Princeton University Press, 2004), 2, 13.

[11] E-mail to the author, 26 August 2009.

[12] Ciaran Carson, e-mail to the author, 1 September 2009.

[13] George Steiner, *After Babel: Aspects of Language and Translation* [1975] (Oxford: Oxford University Press, 1998), 381.

organic culture you know it's gone, and the parallel is obvious. Even within the Irish Renaissance itself one can distinguish between Synge, who was closest to the Irish language and yet not drawn to Irishness as a theme, and Yeats, who never learnt Irish and yet made Irishness his great theme.

The second important factor is the proximity of the translated language to English. This can take two forms—linguistic and historic. French is linguistically close, and it is also historically close, by which I mean that there have been many centuries of interaction between the two languages. By contrast, Irish and English are historically close, but linguistically distant. The poet-translator can assume basic knowledge of Irish, French, and, at a stretch, German, Spanish, Italian, or Latin; but can assume no knowledge of Romanian, Dutch, Slovak, or Hungarian, etcetera. This assumption about the reader's basic knowledge of the linguistic and historical background plays an important role in the way the translation is executed and presented.

The third factor is familiarity with the translated work. In his introduction to his translation of Dante's *Inferno*, Ciaran Carson remarked that '[t]ranslating ostensibly from the Italian, Tuscan or Florentine, I found myself translating as much from English, or various Englishes'.[14] Since H. F. Cary's first translation in 1805–06, there have been numerous translations into English, and recently poets such as Robert Pinsky and Sean O'Brien have produced versions. The anglophone reader has a fair idea of what he or she will encounter when picking up the latest translation of the *Inferno*, and this means that the translator aims primarily to distinguish the translation from other translations of this well-known work. A counter-example is Eiléan Ní Chuilleanáin's translation of the contemporary Romanian poet Ileana Mălăncioiu. In contrast with Dante, there is virtually no context for the reception of Romanian poetry, whether contemporary or classic, in English. This obviously gives the translator a lot more freedom, but it also makes her responsible for the creation of, if not a new poetic universe, then certainly a new house on the street. The Romanian poetic tradition is intimately connected with that of Europe, but Romanian poets will know more of, say, French and Italian poets, than vice versa, and this imbalance can create curious stylistic and thematic pressures and challenges within the original work, which are subsequently multiplied for the translator.

I have already discussed the fifth factor, and this is the extent to which the translator introduces Hiberno-English, or elements of Irish culture into the material in order to domesticate or localize it. As far as I know, there is no Irish equivalent to Edwin Morgan, but there is much in the middle ground. For instance, Seamus Heaney introduces the Hiberno-English word 'bawn' into his translation of *Beowulf*, explaining that '[i]n Elizabethan English, bawn (from the Irish *bó-dhún*, a fort for cattle) referred specifically to the fortified dwellings that the English planters built in Ireland to keep the dispossessed natives at bay'.[15] Here the word-choice resonates within the long relationship between Ireland and England, even though that relationship has ostensibly nothing to

---

[14] Ciaran Carson, 'Introduction', *The Inferno of Dante Alighieri*, trans. Ciaran Carson (London: Granta, 2002), p. xx.

[15] Seamus Heaney, 'Introduction', *Beowulf*, trans. Seamus Heaney (London: Faber, 1999), p. xxx.

do with *Beowulf* itself. Heaney makes clear that he inserts the word for his own sake: 'Putting a bawn into *Beowulf* seems one way for an Irish poet to come to terms with that complex history of conquest and colony, absorption and resistance, integrity and antagonism'.[16]

Another instance is Ciaran Carson: 'When I began looking into the *Inferno*, it occurred to me that the measures and assonances of the Hiberno-English ballad might provide a model for translation.'[17] As in the case of Heaney, the introduction of Irish elements to the translation has more to do with the translator than the nature of the work to be translated. It is a valid strategy, but although Heaney and Carson announce such Hiberno elements in their respective introductions, these elements play a relatively minor role in the pages that follow, which adopt a conventional poetic idiom that could have been produced by a poet from any anglophone background.

The sixth factor is form. Should the translator try to replicate the formal aspects of the original? Carson set himself the difficult task of replicating Dante's *terza rima* (though the result is marked by uneasy archaisms, which seem to be employed to get the rhyme). Ní Chuilleanáin replicates Mălăncioiu's rhymes only in places. Derek Mahon's translation of Paul Valéry's 'Le Cimetière marin' is rhymed, but the rhyme scheme differs from the original. Pearse Hutchinson, although he rhymes his other translations occasionally, made no attempt to rhyme his translations of the great Catalan poet Josep Carner.

This brief survey provides a general idea of the varieties of engagement between Irish poets and foreign-language poetry, on the practical level of translation. I now wish to look at the role translation plays, both as method and theme, in the original work of several poets.

IV

For much of the twentieth century, and especially in the second half, poets have included translations and versions in their own collections, occasionally in order to draw attention to another poet, but mostly to orchestrate the foreign material so that it forms an integral part of their own work. To some, such a practice might seem appropriative, yet it can have the salutory effect of extending the poet's acoustic, or bringing a new perspective on a familiar theme. The exemplars are American: mainly Robert Lowell—especially in *Near the Ocean* (1967)—and also Richard Wilbur. Derek Mahon and Seamus Heaney both made this an important element of many of their collections. One index of the device's acceptance is that we can find it in the first collections of many of the next generation of Irish poets, for instance, Conor O'Callaghan (1993), Vona Groarke (1994), David Wheatley (1997), Caitríona O'Reilly (2001), and John McAuliffe (2002); although in Alan Gillis's debut (2004) the practice is beginning to be parodied.

---

[16] Ibid.
[17] Carson, 'Introduction', *The Inferno*, p. xxi.

A special example of this is to be found in the work of Michael Longley: over the last two decades he has been involved in an osmotic relationship with Homer's poetry, whereby lines and images from the ancient Greek are joined seamlessly with his own material. It is something more than allusion, and it is not exactly translation, or versioning, or domestication. Rather it is a type of graft—with the botanical connotations of that word, its etymology in 'writing', and the false etymology of 'craft'.

But an example from one of Mahon's collections will provide the standard practice. *The Hunt by Night* (1982) is typical of his *oeuvre* as it moves from the local to the global. At the outset there are poems set in Portrush, Derry, and on Rathlin Island. 'Tractatus' raises the question of where the edge of the known world is, and Mahon sets out on this journey, eventually arriving at the last poem, which is entitled 'The Globe in North Carolina', with the whole earth indirectly within his purview from outer space ('dim stone where we were reared').[18] Such a global purview is constructed in poems such as 'Another Sunday Morning' and 'The Terminal Bar'. With the same aim, but different means, 'The Earth' is the penultimate poem of the collection. This is a version (Mahon knows no Russian.) of Boris Pasternak's poem. I cannot judge it as translation, but it is clear that it works on several levels within the book. It simulates a confirmation of Mahon's global perspective, that is, it shows that his themes are to be found in other countries and languages. Given the book's date of publication, it is significant that Pasternak is Russian, which is evocative of the Cold War. The world might be divided by politics, but it sings in harmony on other levels. The poem's last lines, which imagine the 'release [of]/ The heart-constraining ice', suggest a thaw both on personal and political levels.[19] These will be combined again in 'The Globe in North Carolina', which is addressed to a lover on the other side of the ocean.

Mahon's version is beautiful. Even though the stanzas are unforgiving rhymed trimeters, the effect of lightness and freedom is intense—the ease of the idiom harmonizing with the sense of spiritual release that the season brings:

> Spring bursts in the houses
> of Moscow. A moth quits
> its hiding place and flits
> into the light of day
> to gasp on cotton blouses;
> fur coats are locked away.

The gasp is that of eros released—the moth is a kind of spokesperson for the people of springtime. Pasternak reveals a more extreme perception of seasonal change than is available to inhabitants of temperate zones such as Ireland. One must simply stay indoors to a greater extent in Russia during the winter, and so the disappearance of the cold erases the iron division of inner and outer:

> Outside and in, the same
> mixture of fire and fear,

---

[18] Derek Mahon, *The Hunt by Night* (Oxford: Oxford University Press, 1982), 62.
[19] Ibid., 60.

the same delirium
of apple blossom at
window and garden gate,
tram stop and factory door.

So why does the dim horizon
weep, and the dark mould
resist? It is my chosen
task, surely, to nurse
the distances from cold,
the earth from loneliness.

Which is why, in the spring,
our friends come together
and the vodka and talking
are ceremonies, that the river
of suffering may release
the heart-constraining ice.[20]

The sharp distinction between seasons in Russia intensifies the physical, or erotic charge, of the emotions; in contrast, Ireland had a winter of Jansenism for several decades. This last remark is not only meant to be flippant, but draws our attention to one of Mahon's great themes: erotic joy. He is drawn to celebrating moments when 'our whole existence [is] one erogenous zone'.[21] But these moments are often blocked, not only by the ranks of nay-saying cassocks, but by Mahon's own considerable pessimism, which has marred not a few of his poems.

One way that leads Mahon to the erotic is ventriloquism, or versioning.[22] He uses a crib of a Latin, German, Occitan, or Russian poem as the occasion to say something he could not otherwise. This strategy became obvious with the publication of *Adaptations* (2006), a book which collected Mahon's translations and versions. It ranks among his finest publications, and one of the themes that he repeatedly searches out is eros. *Adaptations* reminds us of Walter Benjamin's desire to write a book entirely made up of quotations. Of course, Mahon does not merely quote, or suppress his own voice, in order to let others sing through him. The opposite is the case: every poem bears the stamp of his style, and yet he finds a way for that style to accommodate the other poet. This is particularly apparent in his outstanding translation of Valéry's 'Le Cimetière marin', which is like a harmony for two voices. But unless one knows all the languages he versions from, one cannot finally decide whether it is harmony or imposition: on the evidence of the French and Irish, it appears to be the former. The question the title of the book then raises is: who is Mahon adapting? Is he adapting his chosen poets, or is he adapting himself to them?

[20] Derek Mahon, *Adaptations* (Oldcastle: Gallery, 2006), 85–6.
[21] Derek Mahon, *Collected Poems* (Oldcastle: Gallery, 1999), 287.
[22] Rui Carvalho Homem argues that 'Mahon's characteristic sombreness...emerges in a variety of pieces that prominently include translations', thus suggesting that translation provides a very different stimulus to Mahon; See *Poetry and Translation in Northern Ireland: Dislocations in Contemporary Writing* (Houndsmills: Palgrave-Macmillan, 2009), 201.

The harmonies that Mahon finds in poems from a range of languages never raise the question of language itself, in the way, say, Hamilton does in the passage quoted above. Such an awareness is the subject of Paul Muldoon's 'Quoof'. As the poem explains, the title is his family's argot for 'hot water bottle', and he considers the times he has introduced this word to his various lovers. The pace of the poem conveys the way the speaker deliberates on the passage of a word from argot to general use. Not yet the movement between languages per se, but rather a simulation of this. In the sestet of the sonnet, it moves to this level, as the speaker is far from Ireland, in New York, and in a hotel room 'with a girl who hardly spoke any English'.[23] This introduces a person who is outside both the family group and the larger linguistic group of anglophones. The tremulous elegance of the poem derives from the way it stands on the edge of its own language, imagining, we assume, what the phoneme of the title will sound like to this girl:

> ...my hand on her breast
> like the smouldering one-off spoor of the yeti
> or some other shy beast
> that has yet to enter the language.[24]

This is a kind of linguistic sublime, where the poet imagines what lies beyond the bourne of his linguistic competence.[25] The first line quoted here designates that border as intensely physical, and the moment of sexual anticipation is also an anticipation of knowledge to come, both carnal and linguistic (entering the language suggests the image of sexual penetration).

Muldoon has not done as much 'versioning' as Mahon, and in general confines himself to translations of Nuala Ní Dhomhnaill from Irish, a language of which he has a good grasp. However, in his recent books, French has increasingly played an intriguing role. For instance, one forum of 'The Bangle (Slight Return)' from *Hay* (1998) is a restaurant in France, where the waiters enquire of the speaker in French about his next gastronomical wish. This is counterpointed, among other things, with the fantasy that his father never died, but instead made off to Australia. This last raises the ghosts of the Aboriginal spirits in place names such as Wooroonooran. The speaker can't quite distinguish what is going on in all the phonic confusion. The border between languages that was so apparent in 'Quoof' has disintegrated and the poem moves through a nightmarish linguistic chaos.

In *Horse Latitudes* (2006), we find 'At Least They Weren't Speaking French'. This title begins and ends each verse of this ballad-like poem, and seems to be offered as a consolation: no matter what terrible things happen within a family—senseless death, lack of connection between one's own children and one's own parents—at least the people

---

[23] Paul Muldoon, *Quoof* (London: Faber, 1983), 17.

[24] Ibid.

[25] I have discussed this idea in 'Outside English: Irish and Scottish Poets in the East', in *Modern Irish and Scottish Poetry: Comparative Readings*, ed., Peter MacKay, Edna Longley, and Fran Brearton (Cambridge: Cambridge University Press, 2011).

involved were not speaking French.[26] This consolation is so outrageous and inappropriate that it appears to resemble rather the nonsense elements in, say, Mother Goose. But as in Mother Goose, the denotation remains: we still are enraptured by the idea that the 'dish ran away with the spoon', though one knows it is there to rhyme with 'moon'. So too does French linger as a kind of threat and danger, a zone where our communication does not function. The abhorrence is not explained, and is all the more powerful for that.

French, along with German, plays a central role in Ciaran Carson's *For All We Know* (2008). His engagement with the language goes back at least to *The Alexandrine Plan* (1998), in which he translated thirty-four sonnets by Rimbaud, Baudelaire, and Mallarmé. The Baudelaire translations were the book's outstanding achievement, offering an unlikely pairing of poetic sensibilities. As in the case of Mahon, Carson was neither imposing himself on his chosen material (as he sometimes did in the Rimbaud translations) nor was he imposed upon.

Mixing elements of autobiography, *For All We Know* weaves its way through the imaginary lives of a pair of lovers. One of the repeating ideas is that our lives and our things are second hand, that we live most intensely through the lives of others.[27] One of the most important borders that the lovers must cross in order to be together is language: they meet between French and English. Early in the book and the first time the lovers meet, the man remarks to the woman, 'You're not from around here, I said. No, from elsewhere, you said./As from another language, I might have said, but did not.'[28] The man's French is also said to be good, so a strange oneiric commutativity permeates their relationship, as they move between languages and their geographic hinterlands. This connects with the idea of doubles, as people metamorphose ever so slightly when they move into another language. Indeed, both lovers have grown up bilingually, and this leads to the idea of their being different people in different languages: 'It's because we were brought up to lead double lives, I said./Yes, you said, because of the language thing it was one thing/with my father, another with my mother.'[29] So, to shift languages entails profound readjustments, which are sometimes physical:

> I could see you when I shut my eyes, remembering you
> as you were—this wordless annunciation of yourself
>
> clothed momentarily in the body of another,
> thinking in another language had you been spoken to—
>
> as strange to me as when I first saw you in your own flesh,
> as we go with each other as we have done, fro and to.[30]

[26] French is again associated with disaster in Muldoon's translation of Aimé Cesaire's poem 'Earthquake', published in the wake of the earthquake in Haiti in 2010: *New Yorker*, 25 January 2010, 42.

[27] Carson has remarked that the film of that title, *Das Leben der Anderen* (2006), was an inspiration for the poem. E-mail to the author, 13 September 2009.

[28] Ciaran Carson, *For All We Know* (Oldcastle: Gallery, 2008), 25.

[29] Ibid., 66.

[30] Ibid., 46.

The revelation of nakedness for the first time is compared to switching languages. If one is used to speaking a particular language with another person, it is a strange, revelatory, and sometimes subtly embarrassing experience to switch to another that you both have in common. It is as though some part of the other's identity has been withheld up to this point. The passage above catches this bizarre experience, as the lover's thoughts move translingually.

Carson's first language is Irish, his poem is in English, and it engages the linguistic border with French (and some German). In this respect, it fits very neatly into the view from the Hamiltons' front window. There is a strong sense of the lovers being bordered by other languages, but also of their passing over those borders, transforming themselves and their memories in the process. Carson's engagement with French can be profitably placed beside Claudio Guillén's remark, that '[t]he second idiom, not mastered by the poet to the same degree as his own, but with which he holds a dialogue that finally became part of the growth of his spirit, does not imply the same degree of externality or of separation characteristic of the history and atmosphere of modern nation states.'[31] As the notes to For All We Know indicate, one of the impulses of the poem was a French ballad that Carson learnt in childhood. European national literatures tend to elide such interiorization of foreign languages, even as they are founded upon multilingual knowledge. The Irish case is more complex, as the national literature is in large part written in English, and there is thus much anxiety about the degree to which this is dependent on the Irish language and its written culture.

Carson's work deftly sidesteps the issue of the prerogatives of a national literature: the poem's interiorization of French is an index of the way in which, not only in For All We Know, he ranges beyond the linguistic and cultural boundaries of Ireland, and indeed in part thematizes the imaginative work that takes place as one moves across the border of English. It is also of note in this context that the idiom of the poem is extremely bland, something like the deliberately etiolated prose of Kazuo Ishiguro or Ian McEwan. Carson, quite strikingly, does not use any elements of Hiberno-English, or Belfast demotic, as he did to great effect in a book like Belfast Confetti (1989). Indeed, the elements of Irish, and more particularly, Belfast culture, that were so emphatic in earlier books, are just a distant hum on the horizon here. So while the poem thematizes the transformations that take place as one moves between languages, it does so in a somewhat 'internationalized' anglophone poetic idiom. Earlier, I referred the Irish anxiety of disappearing into the great anglophone sea (of poetry, and of the general culture). Neither the characters nor the author of For All We Know harbour any such anxiety.

Unlike Carson, Peter Sirr is not a native speaker of Irish, but he is a professional translator into the language, and knows several other European languages. Nonetheless (2004) ends with a sequence of 'workings, adaptations, versions, "skeleton" translations of poems in Old Irish, Middle Irish and Latin,'[32] and it is striking that he does not draw on

[31] Claudio Guillén, The Challenge of Comparative Literature, trans. Cola Franzen (Cambridge: Harvard University Press, 1993), 260.
[32] Peter Sirr, Nonetheless (Oldcastle: Gallery, 2004), 33.

this material as part of a national discourse, that is, to make remarks about the state of the nation. Unlike the earlier Carson, Sirr has never foregrounded Hiberno-English, or even a Dublin vernacular: his idiom is to a large extent smooth, 'internationalized', and unmarked by any local demotic, like *For All We Know*. But here again we encounter the paradox of the poet's heightened sensitivity to the levies that are paid and the metamorphoses that occur as one moves between languages: this idea also informs many of the poems of Sirr's *Bring Everything* (2000).

'Doktoro Esperanto' from *Nonetheless* is a witty and amusing take on the idea of a language without borders, an 'Internacia Lingvo'.[33] It focuses on L. L. Zamenhof, the language's inventor:

> Wherever he is the words are clear, swung back and forth
> across the valleys. The mountains
> have learned his language,
> gods practise it and the woken come to it again
>
> in a flurry of introductions. *Mi estas*
> *Doktoro Esperanto*...No passports or signposts,
> nothing flourished
> or flagged; whoever is here has travelled far
>
> and remembered
> all sixteen unshakable rules
> of the Internacia Lingvo.
> It leaps from their suitcases,
>
> this language to stay up all night in.
> The guns can't get through,
> the earth articulate with graves
> stays put
>
> and he is back at his schoolboy desk
> counting again
> *Unu, du, tri, kvar*...
> conscripting words from all the old armies,
>
> scraping the uniforms off.
> A world wakes in his notebook:
> rooftop, sun, the streets of the city
> wavering, shifting, then clear again, his hand
> touching the table, the glass trembling *Bonvenon!*[34]

There is a sweet comedy in the idea of gods and mountains having to learn a language, and also of the language itself leaping from a suitcase. The foil for the humour is the idea of languages as autochthonous, arising from particular landscapes and their peoples, and consequently encoded by national movements. But the humour is also at the expense of Zamenhof, who here resembles a somewhat desperate and fanatical

---

[33] Ibid.
[34] Ibid.

travelling salesman. The guns and graves register the more sombre effects of linguistic, and thus national, difference (though peoples with common languages are also able to go to war with each other). Moreover, the comic image of the gods learning the language also indicates that a change in language precipitates a change in religion, or general world view. The phrase 'whoever is here' suggests the ways in which people reinvent themselves in a new language, which picks up on one of the central themes of *Bring Everything*.

Awareness of the borders of English informs the poetry of Muldoon, Carson, and Sirr in different ways.[35] All three are mindful of the traces and marks left by the Irish language in English, but yet they do not rehearse those as part of a post-colonial performance. Irish does not merely become one language among others for them—it clearly occupies a special position—but the bond of cultural nationalism has been broken. In this essay I have shown that one cannot begin to consider the engagement of Irish poets with translation until one acknowledges the mark, the spectre, or the trace of the Irish language. Moreover, to consider the idea of translation, and the relationship with other languages, can help us to understand some of the new directions of Irish contemporary poetry, as several Irish poets, using a globalized English idiom, explore the borders of the English tongue. This does not lead us back to a post-colonial narrative, or if it does, it transforms that narrative to make it unrecognizable, as that narrative's episodes, interludes, and chapters are reassembled into a new story.[36]

[35] I have discussed this idea in connection with the work of Medbh McGuckian in my *Cambridge Introduction to Modern Irish Poetry, 1800–2000* (Cambridge: Cambridge University Press, 2008), 170–1.

[36] I would like to acknowledge the assistance of Michael Cronin, Peter Fallon, Anna Housková, Erik S. Roraback, and especially David Wheatley. Also, Eavan Boland, Ciaran Carson, and Eiléan Ní Chuilleanáin kindly answered enquiries about their work.

CHAPTER 23

....

A STYLISTIC ANALYSIS
OF MODERN IRISH POETRY

....

PAUL SIMPSON

I

....

The title of this chapter may be misleading, simply because it is impossible to produce a definitive account of the broad stylistic praxis of a body of work subsumed by the generic label 'modern Irish poetry'. No chapter-length study of style and composition can place a stylistic cordon around the technical exuberance and linguistic richness of modern Irish poetry. Indeed, in the case of the best poets, it is unlikely, without at least a book-length treatment, that we could even approximate a detailed stylistic analysis of any single writer considered in this volume, given the complex mosaic of interlocking features of language that constitute this or that writer's 'style'. From another perspective, the problem is compounded further by the vast analytic toolkit that serves modern Stylistics. This toolkit, which houses a veritable armoury of language models and frameworks, has seen an almost exponential expansion over the last two decades. The contemporary stylistic method now extends from the micro-analysis of patterns of sound, vocabulary, and grammar, through the study of language as discourse, to, most recently, the 'cognitive-poetic' exploration of the interface between language and literary understanding. In sum, a single stylistic analysis of modern Irish poetry, with the exhaustiveness and descriptive adequacy that such a project would demand, is to all intents and purposes impossible.

So, if not a comprehensive statement about the style of modern Irish poetry, what *is* the present chapter about? Language in its broadest conceptualization is not a disorganized mass of sounds and symbols, but is instead an intricate web of levels, layers, and links. And this intricate web, clearly articulated as a set of analytic tools, is what a stylistic analysis can bring, so to speak, to the literary-interpretative table. The present chapter shows where a stylistic survey begins, and points to the directions it may take. It argues, *pace* most contemporary stylistic research,[1] that a cogent and organized method of analysis, with a clearly set-out palette of descriptive tools, can if needed make for a useful antidote to the sort of textual reading that is based solely on ad hoc observation, crude impressionism, and piecemeal analysis.

Stylistics is interested in what writers do *with* and *through* language, and in the raw materials out of which literary discourse is crafted. For instance, the stylistic analysis of metaphor in poetry does not view such figurative language as somehow special or intrinsic to the genre of poetry; rather, the analysis works from the crucial understanding that metaphor, while endemic to all human communication and understanding, manifests in *special ways* in poetry. It is important therefore that poetic creativity is measured against the more unrefined resources that frame it, against the everyday and the commonplace in language.

The remainder of this chapter follows the basic organizing principles of the stylistic method, developing through a series of sections focusing on different levels and layers in language structure. Each area of language organization is illustrated by examples from the work of modern Irish poets and, following the aims set out above, a tentative analysis is developed through which comparisons may be drawn about composition and method. The chapter is therefore programmatic rather than interpretative, of necessity a survey of patterns in text rather than of literature in its historical context.

II

Every text is organized through several interlocking levels of language, levels which can be identified and teased out in stylistic analysis. With respect to the close linguistic analysis of poetry, the traditional 'starting place' has almost exclusively been with *lexico-grammar* and (interrelatedly) with *sound patterning*. Indeed, this focus on the core building blocks of the language system was the bedrock, in spirit if not in name, of the New Criticism of the 1930s and is implicitly the mainstay of practical criticism courses on many contemporary degree programmes in English.[2]

The label *lexico-grammar* subsumes the term 'lexis', which refers to the vocabulary of a language and to the way words are built from constituent structures, and the term 'grammar', which refers to the ways words combine syntactically with other words to form phrases, clauses, and sentences. The guiding principle in stylistic explorations of this aspect of poems (and other kinds of texts) is that the features of language that appear 'on the page', as it were, must always be seen in the context of other choices from the

---

[1] A representative sample of such work includes Geoff Leech, *Language in Literature: Style and Foregrounding* (Harlow: Longman, 2008); John McRae, *The Language of Poetry* (London: Routledge, 1998); Paul Simpson, *Stylistics* (London: Routledge, 2004); Peter Verdonk, *Stylistics* (Oxford: Oxford University Press, 2002).

[2] Peter Verdonk, 'Introduction', *Twentieth-Century Poetry: From Text to Context*, ed. Peter Verdonk (London: Routledge, 1993), 1–2.

language system. The key question, in short, is: why this pattern over that one? And what particular effects are engendered by a *particular* pattern when so many other linguistic possibilities present themselves? These questions echo Roman Jakobson's concept of the 'poetic function' in language.[3] In a formulation which has stood the test of time in Stylistics, Jakobson argues that a special feature of poetry is the way that a pattern of literary significance (his 'principle of equivalence') can be established because the particular words chosen (the 'axis of selection') can resonate with other words across a poetic line (the 'axis of combination'). It is thus a characteristic of literary discourse that choices in vocabulary and grammar, strategically made from a pool of alternative possibilities, acquire extra significance in the context of the words and grammatical collocations that surround them.

Here is the opening of Louis MacNeice's poem 'Carrickfergus':

> I was born in Belfast between the mountain and the gantries
> To the hooting of lost sirens and the clang of trams:...[4]

MacNeice's textual strategy here is simple: place the Subject element of the sentence first ('I'), and then follow it with the main verbal structure ('was born'). The Subject element can be tested or probed by asking the question 'who' or 'what' in front of the verb, and together the Subject and Verb form the finite grammatical 'hub' of the clause which constitutes the 'arguable' part of its message. In the lines above, the hub is followed by a series of 'trailing constituents' realized through prepositional phrases which pick out focal points in the industrial landscape. These phrases are themselves coordinated into parallel structures: the preposition 'between' governs both the mountain and the gantries, while 'To' embraces parallel noun phrases headed by the onomatopoeic pair 'hooting' and 'clang'.

Overall, this is a pattern where the least complex grammatical elements are placed first, then to be followed by a build-up of more complex units. Compare this style with the opening stanza of Michael Longley's 'The Linen Industry':

> Pulling up flax after the blue flowers have fallen
> And laying our handfuls in the peaty water
> To rot those grasses to the bone, or building stooks
> That recall the skirts of an invisible dancer[5]

In an altogether very different grammatical design, 'anticipatory' elements are built up in advance of the main clause (which is only delivered at the start of the second stanza). The constituents Longley uses are both subordinate and non-finite, embodied by participial forms ('Pulling up...'; 'laying...'; 'building...') and an infinitive ('To rot...'). As such, these forms contain no grammatical Subject—notice how they do not satisfy the test above—and they are not marked for tense, so neither the time reference nor the

[3] Roman Jakobson, 'Closing Statement: Linguistics and Poetics', in *Style in Language*, ed. Thomas Sebeok (Cambridge, MA: MIT Press, 1960), 350–77.
[4] Louis MacNeice, *Collected Poems*, ed. Peter McDonald (London: Faber, 2007), 55.
[5] Michael Longley, *Collected Poems* (London: Jonathan Cape, 2006), 143.

agents involved in the processes are specified. In the absence of this arguable hub in the clause, we must wait for the grammatical indeterminacy to be resolved.

The sequential non-finite clauses that open 'The Linen Industry' act as a kind of grammatical slow-burner, as a drawing-in mechanism. The subordinate clauses are not free-standing but instead point forward to some later resolution in the form of the main Subject-Verb configuration that we know will come... eventually. When provided at the start of the second stanza, the finite element is emphatic: 'We become a part of the linen industry'. And its inclusive first person plural pronoun also confirms the hint in an earlier phrase, 'our handfuls', showing that it has not been an individual speaking voice who has been involved in the processes depicted in the first stanza, but a pair of lovers. Fran Brearton remarks that in this, one of Longley's finest love poems, the act of love is subtly merged with the natural world, a merging that brings cyclical renewal to human relationships.[6] The progression of this stanza, and its representation of lovers as linen-makers, embodies very much the fusion of these strands of meaning.

Two associated issues are worth addressing here and both will serve to open up new areas for discussion as the remainder of this chapter unfolds. Stylistics always considers how a text might otherwise have been, how the stylistic pattern observed might have felt had it been, say, reversed or inverted. Moreover, many stylistic analyses are characterized by 'textual interventions'[7] which take the form of transpositions and rewritings. If, for example, the clausal elements of MacNeice's 'Carrickfergus' had been reversed—'In Belfast, between the mountain and the gantries, to the hooting of lost sirens and the clang of trams, I was born'—it would be a very different kind of text, overly stylized and to my mind one that arguably sounds rather contrived. A similar reverse-transposition of the Longley sequence would lose the 'drawing-in' facility of the original and all of its gradually unfolding inclusiveness in the movement from the first stanza to the second.

Outside Stylistics, this type of textual intervention has often been criticized for its seeming travesty of important works and for its apparent lack of respect for the 'special' language that is literature.[8] The Stylistic riposte is straightforward: far from being (or attempting to be) iconoclastic, transposition probes the fabric of a text's construction and throws into sharper relief the linguistic terrain that supports the writer's craft. Textual intervention does not disrespect writers or writing; quite the opposite, in fact, because in addition to driving home the point of the analysis, it can help distil and crystallize the very essence of the writer's style.

The second issue concerns the way different systems of language interlock and connect. The visual layout (graphology) of a poem makes for a key intersection with the lexico-grammar and can sustain the complex intermixing and playing off of one system against the other. With a strategically placed comma at the end of the first stanza of 'The Linen Industry', for example, Longley anticipates the arrival of the main clause in the

[6] Fran Brearton, *Reading Michael Longley* (Tarset: Bloodaxe, 2006), 153.
[7] Rob Pope, *Textual Intervention: Critical and Creative Strategies for Literary Studies* (London: Routledge, 1994).
[8] Simpson, *Stylistics*, 99.

second—as suggested earlier, pointing forwards to the resolution of the non-finite struc-
tures in the first. By contrast, MacNeice's stanza ends with the line 'Where the bottle-
neck harbour collects the mud which jams' and this structure, a classic enjambment,
demands the grammatical completion in subsequent text of its line-final transitive verb.
This completion is reached through a run-on to the opening line of the next stanza: 'The
little boats beneath the Norman castle'.

This intersection between grammatical structure on the one hand, and stanzaic and
graphological structure on the other, opens up many stylistic-creative possibilities, not
least in its scope for manipulating the reading process and creating controlled ambigui-
ties across poetic lines. The act of reading (and listening) is not to do with the under-
standing of individual words in isolation but is instead a search for overall sense and
meaning. In reading, we anticipate sense units and we search out and process first (what
look like) complete units.

A particularly elegant example is found in Sinéad Morrissey's poem 'On Waitakere
Dam', which plays on the intersection between grammar and graphology. The descrip-
tion is of an upended rowing boat, abandoned beside the lake:

> It was lavish with silverfish and looked
> defeated, humped on its secret
> like a hand. There was nowhere to go to
>
> but the magnet of the middle lake
> where a vapour sat wide as Australia[9]

The enjambment between these verses develops in essence a very simple stylistic tech-
nique, one that allows a creative manipulation of the interface between reading strategy
and stanzaic form. Ending the first verse where she does, Morrissey creates a kind of sty-
listic *trompe l'oeil* through the sequence 'There was nowhere to go to'. This initial, seem-
ingly complete, sense unit requires a conceptual overhaul in the context of subsequent
lines. In a progression where a feeling of restriction gives way to one of release, the mag-
netic draw of the lake reveals that it was not the case, after all, that there was nowhere to
go to.

The stylistic impact of techniques like these can be profound because one initially
held reading disintegrates in the face of a second. Here, the reorientation in interpreta-
tion occurs when we realize, across the verse boundary, that the complement 'but the
magnet of the middle lake' offers a less stark resolution to the suggested constraint
embodied in the structure that precedes it. The reorientation is also accompanied by an
abrupt widening of focus—the narrow focal point of the damaged boat on the shore
gives way to a liberating expansiveness—an expansiveness as wide, indeed, as Australia.
And while the initial sense engendered in the first part of the sentence is displaced by the
grammatical 'revision' that opens the second stanza, the ghost of its meaning somehow
remains.

---

[9] Sinéad Morrissey, *Between Here and There* (Manchester: Carcanet, 2002), 38–9.

Leaving aside for the moment patterns of stanzaic organization, another key stylistic feature of the body of work under scrutiny is sound patterning and sound symbolism. Sound patterning is not only intricately bound up with patterns of vocabulary and grammar, but, as we shall see later, with figurative and related stylistic patterns in poems. This aspect of language organization cannot be ignored in any close reading of a poem, and the study of metre, in particular, has come to represent a major specialism in contemporary Stylistics.[10] *Onomatopoeia* is a feature of sound patterning which is often thought to form a bridge between 'style' and 'content'. It can occur either in a *lexical* or a *nonlexical* form, although both forms share the common property of being able to match up a sound with a nonlinguistic correlation in the 'real' world. Lexical onomatopoeia draws upon recognized words in the language system—as in the words 'clang' and 'hooting' in the lines from MacNeice, whose pronunciation enacts symbolically their referents outside language. Nonlexical onomatopoeia, by contrast, refers to clusters of sounds which echo the world in a more unmediated way, without the intercession of linguistic structure. For example, the mimicking of the sound of a car revving up might involve a series of nonlexical approximations, such as *vroom vroom*, or *brrrrm brrrrm*, and so on.

A productive use of sound symbolism can be seen in the following stanza, from Seamus Heaney's poem 'A Constable Calls', where a policeman's visit is monitored from the perspective of a small boy. Here the final line exhibits lexical onomatopoeia:

> A shadow bobbed in the window.
> He was snapping the carrier spring
> Over the ledger. His boot pushed off
> And the bicycle ticked, ticked, ticked.[11]

In a penetrating study of repetition in poetry, Derek Attridge comments on these very lines from Heaney, suggesting that this stanza's final use of mimetic repetition implies 'an infinity of possible repetitions'.[12] In characteristic stylistic method, Attridge considers how the line might otherwise have been rendered as text (for example 'And the slow bicycle quietly ticked') and he rightly points out how the significance of 'ticked' becomes diminished if used only once. Exact repetition of this sort is therefore 'anti-closural'; it tends to mark time, like the fade-out of a piece of recorded music.

Edward Larrissy has suggested that Attridge's interpretation might be developed further.[13] In the context of the poem as a whole, the sequence 'ticked, ticked, ticked' is more complexly tendentious. It has a particular resonance because in the circumstances of this 1960s-set poem, this stanza-final cadence, suggestive perhaps of a ticking bomb, is a portent of the Troubles to come. A stylistic gloss of these lines would certainly endorse such a reading. For a start, the sequence in question is rhythmically marked out through its pattern

---

[10] Derek Attridge, *The Rhythms of English Poetry* (Harlow: Longman, 1982).
[11] Seamus Heaney, *North* (London: Faber, 1975), 66–7.
[12] Derek Attridge, 'The Movement of Meaning: Phrasing and Repetition in English Poetry', in *Repetition: Special Issue of Swiss Papers in English Language and Linguistics 7*, ed. Andreas Fischer (Tubingen: Gunter Narr Verlag, 1994), 61–83.
[13] Personal communication.

of three consecutive stressed one-syllable words—not at all a common way of ending a stanza of verse. Moreover, while the pattern is anticipated in the penultimate line of the stanza ('...boot pushed off'), the final line foregrounds the design through repetition of the same, single, lexically onomatopoeic word: 'ticked, ticked, ticked'. By lexicalizing the word into a verb in the past tense, Heaney creates a finite structure with Subject-Verb agreement and while this locates the clause in a narrative time frame, there is a kind of phonological price to pay for it. Unlike other morphological possibilities (as in 'tick', or 'ticks'), the past-tense morpheme 'ed' (in spite of its spelling) is realized in pronunciation as the voiceless plosive /t/. This makes the pattern of transition between the consonants in the whole word (/tIkt/) cumbersome and difficult to articulate: moving from an alveolar to a velar, and then back to an alveolar realization. My sense is that this foregrounded pattern in both sound and meaning has a deadening effect, suggestive, as Larrissy and others intimate, of a ticking bomb, and which in its conformation presages imminent conflict.[14] And as Attridge's rewrite confirms, the minutiae of a particular poetic phrasing is significant when considered against the backdrop of other ways of saying. Here, the awkwardness in articulation of this last segment is perhaps a foreshadow, like the 'shadow' that bobs 'in the window' in line one of the stanza, of the Troubles to come.

III

In Stylistics, as in much work in Critical Theory, the term *discourse* describes the job language does, more open-endedly, in its social and cultural context. Stylistics is interested in language as a function of texts in context, and it acknowledges that literary discourse is embodied in a time, a place, and in a cultural and cognitive system. Texts not only allude to or embody other texts and discourses, they also manifest in a particular *sociolinguistic code* (a term covering the cluster of linguistic varieties that both derives from and shapes the sociocultural backdrop to a text). In this regard, accents and dialects are especially important linguistic varieties because they are influenced and shaped by the regional origin and socioeconomic background of speakers. Whereas dialects are distinguished by patterns in grammar and vocabulary, accents are distinguished through patterns of pronunciation, and both are a major index of the organizing resource of the sociolinguistic code in which a (literary) text is framed. Consider this sequence from Alan Gillis's poem 'Last Friday Night':

> ...I
> was fuckin weltered an Victor was ripe
> aff his head cos we'd been round wi Johnny
> like, downin the duty-free fuckin gargle, aye.[15]

---

[14] For instance, Edna Longley refers to the final repetition as evocative of the caller's bike becoming 'an implausibly melodramatic time-bomb', in *Poetry in the Wars* (Newcastle: Bloodaxe, 1986), 147.

[15] Alan Gillis, *Somebody, Somewhere* (Oldcastle: Gallery, 2004), 27.

Here the narrating voice recalls, in almost stream-of-consciousness fashion, a raucous drugs- and alcohol-fuelled Friday night on the town, but key to the recollection is the sociolinguistic code through which this discourse is mediated. Dominant features of urban Belfast vernacular speech are prominent: the word-final 'ing' variable realized in its non-standard form ('fuckin', 'downin'), alongside consonantal elision in grammatical words 'wi' ('with') and 'an' ('and'). The familiar discourse particles of Belfast English are also foregrounded, such as the utterance-final markers 'like' and 'aye', which work in tandem with marked, stereotypical features of the Belfast accent. The spelling 'aff' (for 'off') captures the Ulster-Scots-influenced vowel realization which in Belfast English makes homophones of words like 'pot' and 'pat' or 'impossible' and 'impassable'. The sociolinguistic code is further enriched by 'antilanguage' features[16] where concepts particularly relevant to an urban subculture (often, and unsurprisingly, to do with drink, drugs, and violence) are re-lexicalized into new terms: see 'gargle' in the fragment above, or elsewhere in the same poem, 'skank', 'disco biscuits', 'mill-up', and so on.

Poetry, like all writing, is not created *in vitro* in some kind of social and historical vacuum, but is instead shaped and underpinned by a web of other texts and discourses. Intertextual reference is best conceptualized along a continuum where the allusion may be 'implicit' or 'manifest'. Implicit intertextuality comprises often indirect echoes of other texts and images, while at the other end of the continuum manifest intertextuality incorporates the embodied text more explicitly. Implicit intertextuality inheres in a turn of phrase, a design in composition that recalls a perhaps faintly remembered ballad, proverb, or story. In the following fragment from Seamus Heaney's 'Anahorish 1944', the second line is phrased in a peculiar way:

> Two lines of them, guns on their shoulders, marching.
> Armoured cars and tanks and open jeeps,
> Sunburnt hands and arms. Unknown, unnamed,
> Hosting for Normandy.[17]

The grammatical context around this line is largely asyndetic, which is to say that units are conjoined, list-like, without formal connecting words. In sharp contrast, the second line exhibits marked connectivity with the conjunction *and*, slowing the development of the line to create a discernible alternation between its accentuated and weak syllables. This alternation crystallizes into a regular series of trochaic feet (the 'dum-de' style of metre) to form a rhythmical schema that resembles very much a line of pentameter verse.

In all, Heaney's foregrounded pentameter line is perhaps more than enough to activate an intertextual echo of these lines:

> Armoured cars and tanks and guns
> Came to take away our sons

This couplet is from Barleycorn's Republican song, 'The Men behind the Wire', which was penned by group member Paddy McGuigan and released in response to the British

[16] Simpson, *Stylistics*, 104–5.
[17] Seamus Heaney, *District and Circle* (London: Faber, 2006), 7.

government's introduction of Internment in 1971. Of course, in the song version the scan is an obvious prerequisite of the ballad rhythm, but in Heaney it stands in marked contrast to the largely free-verse patterns around it, patterns that capture more the cadences of spoken language. The resonance is also shrewdly anachronistic: whereas the poem in which it is framed recalls American troops arriving in Northern Ireland towards the end of the Second World War, the insinuation of a ballad from the early 1970s is a grimly prophetic allusion to a conflict yet to come.

Moving towards the opposite end of the continuum of intertextuality, here is a striking use of manifest intertextual reference, from the first part of Alan Gillis's poem 'Don't You':

> I was working as a waitress in a cocktail bar,
> that much is true. But even then I knew I'd find
> myself behind the wheel of a large automobile,
> or in a beautiful house, asking myself, well,
> if sweet dreams are made of these…[18]

Making for a stark (and comic) contrast with the type of framing used by Heaney, this poem embraces a dialogic structure in which a postulated male respondent answers the female voice whose discourse constitutes the first stanza of the poem. Of course, Gillis has fashioned this discourse out of a kaleidoscope of popular song lyrics from the 1980s, in the extract above drawing, respectively, on Human League, Talking Heads, and Eurythmics. Although formed with explicit segments from these notably kitsch pop songs, the poem nonetheless acquires its own narrative momentum, and as is often the case with echoic intertextual reference of this sort, its own form of comic irony.

Exploring poems as discourse is not of course restricted to patterns which inhere in explicit allusions to other texts. The language code subsumes other varieties, which, in addition to accent and dialect, include *idiolect* (the unique speech style of an individual) and *register* (a variety defined according to the particular purpose or activity for which it is used). The full panoply of these resources is perhaps nowhere more evident than in the poetry of Ciaran Carson, whose work embraces many aspects of the language code, from idiolectal coinages to pronounced stylistic movement through vernacular and register. For instance, his poem 'This Device' makes extensive use of vocabulary that marks the paraphernalia of terrorist activity: 'device'; 'three mercury tilt switches', 'trembler switch', and so on. These multi-noun phrases (a hallmark of technical registers) are, however, paralleled by a more informal style, 'it's liable to/explode between/two twitches/of an eyelid', where the alliterative pattern that links 'switches' and 'twitches' connects the two frames of discourse. The poem, in a seeming afterthought of spoken vernacular, concludes thus:

> not that you'd
>   know anything
>   about it[19]

[18] Gillis, *Somebody, Somewhere*, 19.
[19] Ciaran Carson, *On the Night Watch* (Oldcastle: Gallery, 2009), 119.

Elsewhere in the same collection, in 'Over Agincourt', Carson captures the hovering of an army helicopter over South Belfast through a rhythmical scheme which mirrors the pulse of the helicopter engine. Again, a more technical vocabulary ('nimbostratus', 'infrared') is suffused with more idiomatic usages, although this pattern is itself overlain with a striking metaphorical glaze: the helicopter in question ploughs 'infrared furrows' over 'the rain clouds/of starlings/turned to arrows'.[20] With the foregrounding of the resonances and reflexes of language as discourse, Carson's poetry exhibits a delicate 'multi-voiced-ness' through its presentation of the linguistic markers of social, cultural, and historical reference.

IV

In its earlier decades, the practice of Stylistics was mainly involved in developing interpretations of literary texts based on the application of ever more sophisticated models of language and linguistics. However, this emphasis was at the expense of any account of the *cognitive* processes that inform, and are affected by, the way we read and interpret literary texts. By way of redress, recent work in Cognitive Stylistics (or Cognitive Poetics) has, with its main focus on the processes of reading rather than writing, addressed precisely this problem, arguing that literature is perhaps better conceptualized as a way of reading than as a way of writing.[21] At the fore of this 'cognitive turn' in Stylistics has been the study of *conceptual metaphor*, comparatively, in both literature and in everyday language. It needs to be stressed that metaphor is defined strictly and rigidly from this perspective, with a strong theoretical input from research in cognitive linguistics and experimental psychology.[22] So, in advance of looking in detail at examples of this trope in modern Irish poetry, a short account of the model of metaphor is necessary.

A metaphor is a process of mapping between two different cognitive domains, known as the *target* domain and the *source* domain. The target domain is the topic or concept being described through the metaphor while the source domain refers to the 'different' concept drawn upon in order to facilitate the metaphorical construction. Thus, an expression like 'He's sustained by her love' can be captured, following the accepted practice of glossing in small capitals, by the formula LOVE IS A NUTRIENT. Importantly, the relationship between conceptual metaphor and linguistic form is an

---

[20] Ibid., 134.

[21] The Cognitive Stylistic method is embodied in the following work: Peter Stockwell, *Cognitive Poetics* (London: Routledge, 2002); Joanna Gavins and Gerard Steen, eds., *Cognitive Poetics in Practice* (London: Routledge, 2002).

[22] Key relevant work in psychology and cognitive linguistics includes: Ray W. Gibbs Jnr., *The Poetics of Mind: Figurative Thought, Language and Understanding* (New York: Cambridge University Press, 1994); George Lakoff and Mark Johnson, *Metaphors We Live By* (Chicago: The University of Chicago Press, 1980); George Lakoff and Mark Turner, *More than Cool Reason: A Field Guide to Poetic Metaphor* (Chicago: The University of Chicago Press, 1989).

indirect one, which means that the same metaphor can be expressed through a variety of individual linguistic-stylistic constructions. Thus, the LOVE IS A NUTRIENT metaphor can be embraced in alternative patterns such as 'I'm starved of affection' or 'She thrives on his love'. Moreover, the concept of 'love' can itself form the target domain for a range of other source domains, and conventional metaphors with this pattern include LOVE IS A JOURNEY ('Our relationship is going nowhere') or LOVE IS A BATTLE ('They've been at each other's throats for months'), LOVE IS FIRE ('She's an old flame'), and so on.

Another important dimension of conventional metaphors concerns the direction which the cognitive mapping takes. It is often the case that the more abstract or abstruse a target domain, then the more likely it is to be captured through a source domain which is more familiar and recognizable to human experience. This results in metaphors which cast complex ideas in terms of palpable, material, or even visceral facets of human understanding. For instance, the metaphor IDEAS ARE FOOD is relayed through a variety of everyday constructions like 'I can't stomach that idea', 'Your theory's half-baked', or 'His story is pretty hard to swallow', and so on. Replicated in a great many everyday metaphorical patterns, this pattern of mapping between an abstract target domain and a more physical source domain, such as that between IDEAS and FOOD, is known as *concretization*. As such a pattern demonstrates, metaphors are not some kind of frivolous alterative to literal thought, but are often very basic schemes by which people conceptualize their experience of their external world.

Thus far the account has focused, deliberately so, on everyday metaphor rather than on metaphor as manifested in poetry. As a general principle, what arguably sets the use of metaphor in literature apart from the more 'idiomatized' uses we have seen above is that literary metaphors are typically more novel and typically less clear.[23] Poets, in particular, consciously strive for novelty in literary expression and this requires developing not only new conceptual mappings but also new stylistic frameworks through which these mappings can be presented. The idea that a particular metaphor is 'novel' can be understood in a number of ways, informally gathered here into the following shorthand categories: *newness, multiple mapping, compression,* and *elaboration.*

First, newness in metaphor can be captured by, simply, the uniqueness of the conceptual mapping between a source and target domain. Whereas the conceptual metaphors discussed above are a familiar part of everyday discourse, mappings in poetry can be striking, alien, and sometimes disquieting, as in formulae like POTTERY IS A COLD WOMAN, BOREDOM IS A ROCK, FRUIT IS A BURIAL GROUND, MEMORY IS A GRAMMAR, or CONVERSATION IS DAIRY FARMING. These novel mappings happen to be the very structures that underpin, respectively, the five examples below:

> Terracotta vases and teapots
> queue beside their warm kiln

---

[23] Zolton Kövecses, *Metaphor* (Oxford: Oxford University Press, 2002).

> like shivering women
> waiting for the sauna
>
> (Katie Donovan)[24]
>
> Boredom was a rock that rolled between them
>
> (Sinéad Morrissey)[25]
>
> Shoppers steer trolleys
> past cairns of avocadoes
>
> (Mary O'Donoghue)[26]
>
> to forget is
> a common verb
>
> (Ciaran Carson)[27]
>
> Our one-way conversation was like milking
> a mastitic cow who regards you
> reproachfully...
>
> (Catríona O'Reilly)[28]

In stylistic analysis, it is important to differentiate sets of metaphors involving the same target domain from sets of other, unrelated metaphors which develop different target and source domains. Multiple mapping is when the same target domain is played out through plural source domains. Thus, in this sequence from Leontia Flynn's 'What you Get':

> ...where the trucks
> are moored, fed and watered[29]

the verb phrase of the second line activates two source domains in its depiction of the trucks: respectively, A WHEELED VEHICLE IS A SHIP ('moored') and A WHEELED VEHICLE IS A DOMESTICATED ANIMAL ('fed and watered'). By imputation, much multiple mapping in metaphor tends to be *compressed*, as in the lines from Flynn, where the same grammatical unit embraces different metaphorical connections.

Again, the interconnectedness of the levels of stylistic organization is a key principle, where the resources of the lexico-grammar can be exploited to compress multiple metaphorical meanings within short phrasal or clausal units. Here, for instance, are two sets of mappings which develop through a simple arrangement of noun phrases:

> My belly a factory,
> a recycling plant,
> a compost heap.
> My pelvis a girdle,

---

[24] Katie Donovan, 'The Potter's House', in *The New Irish Poets*, ed. Selina Guinness (Tarset: Bloodaxe, 2004), 87–8.

[25] Sinéad Morrissey, 'Street Theatre', *Between Here and There*, 19.

[26] Mary O'Donoghue, 'This is Sunday', in *The New Irish Poets*, ed. Guinness, 256–8.

[27] Ciaran Carson, 'What Then', *On the Night Watch*, 139.

[28] Catríona O'Reilly, 'To the Muse', in *The New Irish Poets*, ed. Guinness, 268.

[29] Leontia Flynn, 'What you Get', in ibid., 99.

> a breeding-ground,
> a nursery.
> (Dorothy Molloy)[30]

Whereas some of the previous examples, through their use of simile in particular, made explicit the pathway for the conceptual mapping, these lines from Molloy pare down the grammatical fabric to its sparsest; lines which, in the absence of any verbal unit, offer three different source domains apiece for the terms 'belly' and 'pelvis'. It is often a feature of compressed metaphors that their design, which lacks explicit indicators to invite comparison between domains, tends to make them, so to speak, almost trip over one another in their delivery.

The term *elaboration* encompasses more loosely a range of innovative devices in the construction of literary metaphor. Elaboration generally describes the capturing of an existing component of the source domain in an unusual or unconventional way. For example, if the source domain of a conceptual metaphor is HOUSE (as in A BODY IS A HOUSE), this offers considerable scope for expansion through expressions which introduce associated schemata from the same domain. Thus, we connect a house with its familiar 'props' like doors (and by further association, keys to open them), windows (and therefore curtains), and stairs (and banisters), and so on.

This type of elaboration is carried through in a bitingly harsh sequence from the poem 'First Blood', again by Dorothy Molloy, in which an innocent encounter turns into a sudden and violent sexual assault:

> Someone
> is opening the door of my house
> with a scalding hot key. There is blood
> on the floor.[31]

In the reference to 'a scalding hot key' a feature of the source domain of the A BODY IS A HOUSE metaphor is elaborated in such a way as to acquire extra signification in the metaphorical mapping. Commenting on this poem, Selina Guinness remarks that the poem's impact stems from the way the man's abuse is directed 'both at body and narrative'. I interpret this remark, with respect to the piece of text above, as a textual strategy which weaves between both literal and metaphorical meaning: the 'blood on the floor', can, after all, be both. Interestingly, of this and other poems by Irish women poets, Guinness suggests that connections between body and poetic psyche are constantly explored and reinvented, a textual connection to perhaps a wider cultural embarrassment about Ireland's body politics.[32]

Thus far this account of poetic metaphor has been supported through a series of short illustrations from a number of modern Irish poets. This is not at all to suggest that any of these writers employ a partial or limited use of literary metaphor, with perhaps only one or two 'trademark' techniques in metaphor composition at their disposal. In fact, it is

---

[30] Dorothy Molloy, 'Envelope of Skin', in ibid., 196–7.
[31] Dorothy Molloy, 'First Blood' in ibid., 194–5.
[32] Guinness, ed., *The New Irish Poets*, 20–1.

normally the case that metaphor is developed expansively and in varied ways by these poets, and even a short passage of text will present a range of novel linguistic-stylistic expressions. Arguably the innovator *sine qua non*, in terms of the richness and complexity of her use of conceptual metaphor, is Medbh McGuckian. The work of this writer epitomizes Kövecses's axiom that metaphors in literature are typically more novel and typically less clear. In very broad stylistic terms, McGuckian's use of figurative language is characterized by its density of linguistic organization, where multiple metaphors, developed through different sets of target and source domains, are often set down early in a poem and are then returned to and elaborated progressively over the remainder of the poem.

Although there is not the scope here to develop these observations on McGuckian in any degree of detail, some illustrations might at least signal where this stylistic exuberance is located in her work. For instance, in the opening line of 'The Flower Master':

Like foxgloves in the school of the grass moon[33]

the simile part of a metaphorical construction is presented first, as the Adjunct element to a main clause that will come later. Yet all four of the line's lexical words—that is, the 'content'-carrying words—have the capacity to activate different metaphorical paths: 'foxgloves', 'school', 'grass', and 'moon'. This is a striking instance of the technique of compression discussed earlier, where latent multiple and interconnected mappings are presented in advance of the main finite 'hub' of the clause.

Similarly, in 'The Aphrodisiac', a woman's recounting of a relationship that has ceased to have a sexual aspect, is elaborated through a complex network of images of houses and places. Rejecting the 'menacings of love' from her former sexual partner, the woman articulates the platonic side of the redefined relationship as wanting 'the bright key to his study', while the former lover is 'banished to his estates'. In a telling final sequence, this highly elaborated metaphorical chain is completed with 'this is not the only secret staircase', a suggestion perhaps that a relationship with a new lover has formed.

Finally, another of the striking methods of metaphorical expression used by McGuckian is *functional conversion*, which is the transposition of a word or phrase into a different (unfamiliar) grammatical class or category. For instance, in 'The Dowry Murder' the decorum required for the wearing of a revealing fabric is addressed by the female voice thus:

...the part
Of my body that deals with it needs churching...[34]

Note in the second line the functional conversion 'churching', where an item from the word class of noun has been shifted to form the present participial of a transitive verb. This is not only an interesting elaboration of the A BODY IS A HOUSE metaphor observed

---

[33] Medbh McGuckian, *The Flower Master and Other Poems* (Oldcastle: Gallery, 1993), 41.
[34] Ibid., 43.

earlier, but it is also, through the novelty of the linguistic expression used to frame it, an ideal exemplum of the principle of creativity in poetic metaphor.

V

This chapter began with a caveat concerning the task at hand; namely, that the linguistic heterogeneity of modern Irish poetry makes an all-embracing stylistic analysis of it impossible. In its entirety, such a collection of work would, as noted, make for a huge stylistic investigation. This is not however to suggest for a moment that we cannot engage in the productive stylistic analysis of modern Irish *poems*. Indeed, the programmatic orientation of this chapter has been to sketch a framework of analysis that might well be pressed into such literary-interpretative service, a framework that moves from patterns in grammar, sound, and vocabulary, through aspects of discourse, to the conceptual and cognitive dimensions of poetic composition.

In the context of these remarks, it is surprising then that genuinely stylistic investigations of modern Irish poems are few and far between. Aside from Attridge's work on sound patterning discussed above, article-length studies include Dan McIntyre's close analysis of Seamus Heaney's 'Mossbawn'.[35] Using the conceptual framework of *deixis*, which is the grammatical encoding of orientation in space, time, and person, McIntyre explores how readers take up different positions in the story world of the poem. Again with the emphasis on Heaney, Peter Verdonk offers a contextualized-stylistic reading of 'Punishment', looking in particular at the relationship between Heaney's rhetorical techniques and the status of the text as discourse.[36] And then there is Paul Simpson and Fran Brearton's detailed literary-linguistic analysis of Michael Longley's poem 'The Comber', which amongst other things demonstrates how this short poem exhibits extremely sophisticated stylistic texturing in its illumination of the themes of memory and time.[37] Beyond these studies, however, there is little work which focuses explicitly on the language of Irish poetry, on what Heaney has described as 'a self-bracing entity within the general flux and flex of language'.[38]

This chapter has also argued throughout that it is the full gamut of the system of language that makes all aspects of a writer's craft relevant in stylistic analysis. At the forefront of this approach has been the theoretical preoccupation with the idea of 'language as choice'. This has meant both considering a text's structuring against its potential

---

[35] Dan McIntyre, 'Deixis, Cognition and the Construction of Viewpoint', in *Contemporary Stylistics*, ed. Marina Lambrou and Peter Stockwell (London: Continuum, 2007), 118–30.

[36] Peter Verdonk, 'Poetry and Public Life: A Contextualised Reading of Seamus Heaney's "Punishment"', in *Twentieth-Century Poetry: From Text to Context*, ed. Verdonk, 112–33.

[37] Paul Simpson and Fran Brearton, ' "Deciphering Otter Prints": Language, Form and Memory in the Poetry of Michael Longley', *The Honest Ulsterman: Special Feature on Michael Longley* 110 (2001), 17–31.

[38] Seamus Heaney, *The Redress of Poetry: Oxford Lectures* (London: Faber, 1995), 15.

alternatives and thinking of the process of composition as strategic selection from the linguistic code that frames it. After all, one only has to look at Heaney's account of the creative path that led him to revise a single verb in the opening line of his poem 'Follower' to see how judicial, central, and far-reaching is the process of stylistic selection.[39] While a description of linguistic structure does not in itself provide the key to a text's 'meaning', a close literary-stylistic analysis of a text's language nonetheless serves to explain why certain types of meaning are at least possible. And if Stylistics is about anything, it is about the far-reaching possibilities of this flux and flex of language.

[39] Ibid., 63–4.

PART VII

POETRY AND POLITICS: THE 1970s AND 1980s

CHAPTER 24

....

BEFITTING EMBLEMS:
THE EARLY 1970S

....

HEATHER CLARK

THE American poet Adrienne Rich once compared poetic form to 'asbestos gloves', writing, 'it allowed me to handle materials I couldn't pick up bare-handed'.[1] Her observation could apply equally well to Irish poets who wrote during the Troubles in Northern Ireland. Derek Mahon's claim that 'a good poem is a paradigm of good politics'[2]—that an orderly poem could serve as a powerful metaphor of an orderly political system— suggests the important role form played in several Irish collections in the early 1970s, particularly John Montague's *The Rough Field*, Thomas Kinsella's *Butcher's Dozen*, Derek Mahon's *The Snow Party*, Seamus Heaney's *North*, and Eavan Boland's *The War Horse*. Despite the poets' aversion to writing 'Troubles poetry', the political situation in the North formed the presiding preoccupation of these collections: Montague, Boland, and Kinsella condemned injustices committed by the British, while Heaney and Mahon alluded to contemporary violence through historical settings and metaphors. Whether they approached the violence obliquely or directly, however, all used formal strategies to create what Yeats called 'Befitting emblems of adversity'.[3] This commitment to form was not unusual in post-war Britain and Ireland, where free verse was sometimes regarded as a distinctly American phenomenon. Yet for Irish poets during the early years of the Troubles, the use of form took on a new urgency. By interrogating the relationship between form and violence, the poets offered meditations not only on their divided society, but the efficacy of poetry itself.

The early 1970s in Northern Ireland were a time of escalating violence and increasing despair within the Protestant and Catholic communities. The years between 1970 and

---

[1] Peter Davison, *The Fading Smile: Poets in Boston from Robert Lowell to Sylvia Plath* (New York: Knopf, 1994), 40.

[2] Derek Mahon, 'Poetry in Northern Ireland', *Twentieth Century Studies* 4 (1970), 93.

[3] W. B. Yeats, 'Meditations in Time of Civil War', *The Variorum Edition of the Poems of W. B. Yeats*, ed. Peter Allt and Russell K. Alspach (Basingstoke: Macmillan, 1956), 420.

1975 were the bloodiest of the Troubles: in 1972, nearly five hundred people died and five thousand were injured; that year alone there were over ten thousand shootings and nearly two thousand explosions.[4] British troops had arrived on Belfast's streets in August 1969, and though Catholics had initially regarded them as protectors against Loyalist aggression, by the time internment without trial was introduced in 1971 the army was seen as foe rather than friend. The political situation deteriorated further in January 1972 when thirteen civil-rights marchers were shot by British soldiers in Derry. Bloody Sunday, as the day came to be known, was a catalyst for IRA recruitment and support.[5] The next month the British Embassy in Dublin was burnt down by an enraged group of protesters, while in March 1972 Britain suspended Stormont and instituted a policy of Direct Rule from Westminster. It would be over twenty-five years before Northern Ireland would take steps towards self-governance.

The increasing sectarian violence meant that Northern Ireland, and Irish poets, were thrust onto an international stage. While the poets wanted to give voice to what Wilfred Owen called 'the pity of war', they were worried about inadvertently cheapening or aestheticizing the violence they wrote about.[6] They knew Theodor Adorno's famous dictum, uttered in the wake of the Holocaust, 'It is barbaric to write poetry after Auschwitz', and must have wondered whether it was also barbaric to write rhyming couplets about Bloody Sunday.[7] Luckily, Irish poets who came of age in the late 1960s and early 1970s had models they could look to as they attempted to chart this perilous terrain: W. B. Yeats and Louis MacNeice. Yeats's 'Meditations in Time of Civil War' was an important text in this respect, as was MacNeice's *Autumn Journal*. There, MacNeice implied that art was too often used as a retreat from the 'responsibility of moral choice' by which he meant engagement with the difficult ethical issues of one's age.[8] Disengagement, whether from life or the looming war against fascism, was cowardly:

> Aristotle was right to think of man-in-action
> As the essential and really existent man
> And man means men in action; try and confine your
> Self to yourself if you can.[9]

Throughout *Autumn Journal*, MacNeice attempts to reconcile the introspective art of poetry with 'action'. His own verse, with its sense of moral duty, falls under this category, but less 'committed' art does not. In Section XV, for example, 'Shelley and jazz and lieder' become emblems of indifference to suffering.[10] MacNeice suggests that form itself is a

---

[4] National Archive of Great Britain (www.nationalarchives.gov.uk).

[5] Marc Mulholland, *Northern Ireland: A Very Short Introduction* (Oxford: Oxford University Press, 2002), 79.

[6] In a draft preface to his poems, Owen wrote, 'My subject is War, and the pity of War. The Poetry is in the Pity.' See *The Poems of Wilfred Owen*, ed. Jon Stallworthy (London: Chatto & Windus, 1990), 192.

[7] This phrase appeared in Adorno's 1951 article, 'Cultural Criticism and Society'.

[8] Louis MacNeice, *Collected Poems*, ed. Peter McDonald (London: Faber, 2007), 146.

[9] Ibid., 143.

[10] Ibid., 135.

type of 'action' that gives a poem coherence and structure. Lack of form, or 'jazz', suggests fracture, chaos, decadence, even subversion of traditional values. This is partly why the Movement poets of the 1950s wrote mostly in form; in the wake of the Second World War, they felt that the wild energy of Romantic and Modernist verse endorsed a sensibility that was more fascist than democratic. Ted Hughes, whose verse challenged the Movement, put it nicely: 'Where I conjured up a jaguar, they smelt a stormtrooper. Where I saw elementals and forces of Nature they saw motorcyclists with machine guns on the handlebars.'[11] Like their literary predecessors, Irish poets writing in the 1970s were also sceptical of art for art's sake, and turned to, or experimented with, formal poetic structures as they attempted to express what at times seemed inexpressible.

John Montague's *The Rough Field* (1972) was the most overtly political collection to appear in Ireland during the early seventies, and the most formally experimental. In both respects, the collection owed much to American influences, as Montague admitted in his preface. His decision to write in 'open-form' was influenced by the verse of William Carlos Williams and Charles Olson, while his 'experience of agitations' in Berkeley and Paris in the late 1960s provided him with a glimpse of the kind of civil disobedience that would soon become part of the political landscape in Northern Ireland.[12] When it came time for Montague to write about his own disinheritance, these American models would help shape his politics and his aesthetic. Montague also pointed out that his work was shaped by a more 'rooted' tradition, and named Hugh MacDiarmid as an important influence.[13]

The mixture of protest and postmodern collage in the pages of *The Rough Field* marked a new direction in Irish poetry. Despite its experimental sensibility, however, the collection made much use of traditional form. The nod to form is appropriate in a collection that reads as a post-colonial elegy for what Montague called the 'shards of a lost tradition'—the old Gaelic culture that had been displaced by the English colonizers.[14] The culmination of these dispossessions, Montague implies, is the present-day violence in Northern Ireland, whose shadow hovers over all the poems in the collection.

Montague mourns the passing of the Irish language and the landscape that nurtured it: he writes in 'A Severed Head' of 'our tribal pain', 'The whole landscape a manuscript/ we had lost the skill to read,/A part of our past disinherited'.[15] In 'Like Dolmens Round my Childhood, the Old People', he describes the villagers of Garvaghey, his childhood home, as 'Gaunt figures of fear and of friendliness' who have passed 'Into that dark permanence of ancient forms'.[16] (The title *The Rough Field* is an English translation of the Irish *garbh acaidh*, or 'Garvaghey' in anglicized form.) Montague makes an explicit connection between colonial aggression and the erosion of Irish Catholic village culture in

[11] Interview with Ekbert Faas, in Ekbert Fass, *Ted Hughes: The Unaccommodated Universe* (Santa Barbara: Black Sparrow Press, 1980), 201.

[12] John Montague, *The Rough Field* [1972] (Oldcastle: Gallery, 2005), p. vii.

[13] Ibid., p. vii.

[14] Ibid., 34.

[15] Ibid., 39.

[16] Ibid., 15.

'A Severed Head', which chronicles the Flight of the Earls and the eventual disappear-
ance of 'the last Gaelic speaker in the parish'.[17] By placing excerpts of seventeenth-cen-
tury British letters and tracts relating to the conquest of Ireland in the margins of this
text, he points to the relationship between past and present violence in Ireland. These
colonial dispossessions, he implies, have led to 'a province in flames'.[18] The poem ends
with a personal meditation on the consequences of dispossession:

> To slur and stumble
> In shame
> the altered syllables
> of your own name...
>
> ....To grow a second tongue, as
> harsh a humiliation
> as twice to be born.[19]

One of the collection's most striking features is visual. Throughout his pages Montague
reproduces woodcuts from John Derricke's *A Discoverie of Woodkerne*, which depicts
Sir Henry Sidney's late sixteenth-century campaign against Irish chieftains in Ulster.
The word 'woodkerne' comes from the Irish *ceithearnaigh*, and refers to Irish soldiers
who were, as Thomas Dillon Redshaw points out, regarded by the English as ' "savages"
or "wild men" who lived beyond the Pale'.[20] Derricke's woodcuts are placed at the begin-
ning of the collection's eleven sections. While many depict British violence against the
woodkerne, others show Irish customs. Montague uses both types of scenes to empha-
size the dual purpose of *The Rough Field*—not only to protest against British colonialism
past and present, and thus draw attention to the root causes of unrest in Northern
Ireland, but to elegize the Gaelic culture in Ulster that the English had nearly erased.

Montague's experiments with traditional form are also visually intriguing. Part One
of the collection's first sequence, 'Home Again', is written in sonnet form, Part Four in
tercets, and Part Five in regular seven-line stanzas with a loose rhyme scheme. Several
other sequences also use regular stanza lengths. Even the more experimental sequences
make use of traditional stanza forms. In 'The Bread God', for example, a Shakespearean
sonnet that describes the significance of a hidden mass rock is placed between excerpts
from a Loyalist propaganda pamphlet and a letter from Montague's uncle about finding
'a way to resolve the old hatreds'.[21] Part One of 'Hymn to the New Omagh Road' does not
follow any traditional form, yet it invokes a formal symmetry in its two sections titled
'Loss' and 'Gain'. On each side, Montague balances an aspect of Gaelic culture in Ulster
that has disappeared with an image of suburbs and motorways. In Part Two, he alter-
nates his own irregular stanzas with the regular aabb quatrains of Patrick Farrell's 'By

[17] Ibid., 35.
[18] Ibid., 38.
[19] Ibid., 39.
[20] Thomas Dillon Redshaw, notes to *The Rough Field*, 90.
[21] Montague, *The Rough Field*, 29.

Glencull Waterside', which describes a flowering landscape about to be destroyed by 'the crustacean claws of the excavator':

> The trout are rising to the fly; the lambkins sport and play;
> The pretty feathered warblers are singing by the way;
> The black birds' and the thrushes' notes, by the echoes multiplied,
> Do fill the vale with melody by Glencull waterside.[22]

Montague counters this with his own bleak depiction of what the vale has become:

> A brown stain
> seeps away from where the machine
> rocks and groans to itself, dis-
> colouring the grass, thickening
> the current of the trout stream
> which flows between broken banks
> —the Waterside a smear of mud—
> towards the reinforced bridge
> of the new road.[23]

Montague counters Farrell's formal reassurances with his own 'open' stanza, filled with flat monosyllables. His verse is purposefully harsh in contrast to Farrell's, whose rhymes allude to the ballad tradition that is itself in danger of disappearing with the landscape that nurtured it. Here, language and landscape are intimately tied: the pleasures of form are linked to the pleasures of the undisturbed waterside, while the defiled landscape is described through dull dissonance.

The most political poem in the collection, 'A New Siege', was dedicated to Bernadette Devlin, a Republican activist who was the youngest female Member of Parliament from 1969 to 1974. The poem's title alludes to the Siege of Londonderry in 1689, in which Protestants attempted to defend the city from Jacobite troops. Montague, however, begins with a reference to present violence in Northern Ireland:

> *Once again, it happens.*
> *Under a barrage of stones*
> *and flaring petrol bombs*
> *the blunt, squat shape of*
> *an armoured car glides*
> *into the narrow streets*
> *of the Catholic quarter*
> *leading a file of helmet-*
> *ed, shielded riot police;*
> *once again, it happens,*
> *like an old Troubles film,*
> *run for the last time...*[24]

---

[22] Ibid., 60.
[23] Ibid., 61.
[24] Ibid., 71.

Montague follows this reflection with sixteen long dimeter stanzas set in two horizontal rows across the page; all allude to either past or present violence in Derry and Northern Ireland. Some stanzas recall the horror of the seventeenth-century siege, in which the city was:

> a spectral garrison
> > no children left
> sick from eating
> > horseflesh, vermin
> curs fattened on
> > the slain Irish
> still flaunting
> > the bloody flag
> of 'No Surrender'.

Others depict contemporary struggle:

> Lines of suffering
> > Lines of defeat
> Under the walls
> > Ghetto terraces
> Sharp pallor of
> > Unemployed shades
> Slope shouldered
> > Broken bottles
> Pubs and bookies
> > Red brick walls
> Falls or Shankill
> > Lecky or Fountain
> Love's alleyway
> > Message scrawled
> Popehead: Tague
> > My own name
> Hatred's synonym[25]

Such stanzas are placed foursquare on each page; the effect is meant deliberately to disorient the reader, who must work hard to distinguish between historical eras. The form emphasizes Montague's point that contemporary and past violence are so intertwined that we cannot easily separate them. History is repeating itself yet again.

Thomas Kinsella's *Butcher's Dozen: A Lesson for the Octave of Widgery* also uses form to make a political message. The poem, written in regular iambic tetrameter and rhyming couplets, decries the killing of thirteen civilians by British paratroopers in Derry on 30 January 1972, and angrily parodies the findings of the Widgery Tribunal that investigated the incident. The findings, which, Kinsella wrote, 'exonerated the troops more or less, and managed to leave a suspicion of conspiracy and covert violence hanging over

---

[25] Ibid., 74.

some of the victims', appeared on 26 April 1972.[26] Kinsella published *Butcher's Dozen* as a pamphlet just a week after the findings appeared. As he later wrote in a postscript to *Fifteen Dead* (1979):

> *Butcher's Dozen* was not written in response to the shooting of the thirteen dead in Derry. There are too many dead, on all sides, and it is no use pitting them hideously against one another. The poem was written in response to the Report of the Widgery Tribunal. In Lord Widgery's cold putting aside of truth, the *n*th in a historic series of expedient falsehoods—with Injustice literally wigged out as Justice—it was evident to me that we were suddenly very close to the operations of the evil real causes.[27]

The long poem was written in the white heat of anger, as Kinsella has acknowledged: 'The pressures were special, the insult strongly felt, and the timing vital if the response was to matter, in all its kinetic impurity'.[28] Despite what Donatella Badin has called its 'rough doggerel and strained rhymes', Kinsella argued that 'it was exactly what was needed'.[29]

Kinsella resurrects the ghosts of the slain victims in *Butcher's Dozen* through an act of prosopopoeia. He allows these victims to tell their side of the story, which differs starkly from the findings of the Tribunal. One section of the report, for example, claimed that British soldiers found nail bombs in the pockets of Gerald Donaghy. In Kinsella's poem, Donaghy responds to this false charge:

> A bomber I. I travelled light
> —Four pounds of nails and gelignite
> About my person, hid so well
> They seemed to vanish where I fell.
> When the bullet stopped my breath
> A doctor sought the cause of death.
> He upped my shirt, undid my fly,
> Twice he moved my limbs awry,
> And noticed nothing. By and by
> A soldier, with his sharper eye,
> Beheld the four elusive rockets
> Stuffed in my coat and trouser pockets.
> Yes, they must be strict with us,
> Even in death so treacherous![30]

The ghosts of several other protesters also point to the treachery of both the British troops and the Widgery Tribunal. Some discuss the root of the violence, and place the blame squarely on the shoulders of British imperialism. As one ghost says, in an image that anticipates Heaney's 'Act of Union':

---

[26] Thomas Kinsella, *Fifteen Dead* (Dublin: Dolmen Press/Peppercanister, 1979), 54.

[27] Ibid., 57.

[28] Ibid.

[29] Donatella Badin, *Thomas Kinsella* (New York: Twayne, 1996), 175; Kinsella, *Fifteen Dead*, 57.

[30] Thomas Kinsella, *Collected Poems* (Oxford: Oxford University Press, 1996), 137–8.

'You came, you saw, you conquered ... So.
You gorged—and it was time to go.
Good riddance. We'd forget—released—
But for the rubbish of your feast,
The slops and scraps that fell to earth
And sprang to arms in dragon birth.
Sashed and bowler hatted, glum
Apprentices of fife and drum,
High and dry, abandoned guards[31]

The poem ends, however, on a note of sympathy for these Protestants. 'Doomed from birth, a cursed heir,/Theirs is the hardest lot to bear', Kinsella writes. The final ghost hopes for a new age of tolerance—'We all are what we are, and that/Is mongrel pure'— yet the speaker's sombre reflections as he stands in the spot where the thirteen were killed belies this hope:

The gentle rainfall drifting down
Over Colmcille's town
Could not refresh, only distil
In silent grief from hill to hill.[32]

Butcher's Dozen upset several critics, who deemed it nationalist propaganda. Edna Longley accused Kinsella of destroying the 'dignity' of the dead by representing them as 'ghoulish', and suggested that he imbued those victims with a 'fascist hysteria'.[33] But Kinsella's language alarmed even normally sympathetic critics such as W. J. McCormack, Conleth Ellis, and Gerald Dawe.[34] The controversy was not unlike that which would surround Heaney after the publication of *North* in 1975. Heaney, in fact, was one of Kinsella's supporters; he praised the poem's 'rage and certitude'.[35] Kinsella defended his work, noting that the magnitude of the event justified the literary protest: 'One changed one's standards, chose the doggerel route, and charged'.[36]

Curiously, both Kinsella and Edna Longley have both referred to the poem as 'doggerel'.[37] Kinsella has pointed out that he used as his model for the poem the traditional Irish *aisling*, as well as the tribunal section of Brian Merriman's *The Midnight Court*. The poem was probably also influenced by the Irish ballad tradition. But its rhyming couplets and iambic tetrameter perhaps owe as much to English predecessors. It is not only

---

[31] Ibid., 141.

[32] Ibid., 141–2.

[33] Edna Longley, 'Spinning through the Void', *Times Literary Supplement*, 19 December 1980, 1446.

[34] Brian John notes that the British and Irish Communist Organization issued a pamphlet titled 'Kinsella's Oversight: A Reply to "The Butcher's Dozen"'. It was meant to call attention to what they felt was the bourgeois emphasis of the original poem. Brian John, *Reading the Ground: The Poetry of Thomas Kinsella* (Washington DC: Catholic University Press, 1996), 144.

[35] Seamus Heaney, 'The Poems of the Dispossessed Repossessed', *The Government of the Tongue* (London: Faber, 1988), 32.

[36] Kinsella, *Fifteen Dead*, 58.

[37] Longley called it 'Broadsheet doggerel' in Longley, 'Spinning through the Void', 1,446.

the spectres of the dead protesters who hover over this poem, but those of canonical English writers who mastered the couplet form, such as John Donne, John Dryden, and Alexander Pope. Kinsella's four-beat line, with its marching, military cadence, emphasizes its bitter irony, but the choice of the couplet itself may also be ironic. In theory, the couplet form allows Kinsella to bring a kind of order to the chaos of Bloody Sunday—at least on the page. But Kinsella does not look to form to assuage, as Heaney does. Kinsella's use of the couplet, whose high point came in the eighteenth century, mocks an Enlightenment sensibility that cherished the values of freedom, tolerance, and order—virtues the British associate with the national character but which, Kinsella implies, have been undermined by imperial greed. Thus the sense of order in the rhymes is ironic; Kinsella satirizes the Tribunal's attempt to bring order to an event that in reality is too complex for simple verdicts. This is why so many of Kinsella's full, monosyllabic rhymes are facile; through them, and the unrelenting drumbeat of the tetrameter, he creates a sense of claustrophobia. The form is meant to sound oppressive, for it impedes a more lyric, natural expression. Thus, when Kinsella calls his verse 'doggerel', he may be suggesting that the form of his poem reflects the false sense of order that the Tribunal sought to bring to the case, and that the soldiers sought to bring to the protest when they killed innocent civilians. The whole concept of 'order' is brutally satirized in *Butcher's Dozen*.

Eavan Boland treats the concept of order differently in her second collection, *The War Horse* (1975). Boland is now best known as a poet who seeks to revise the relationship between woman and nation in Ireland. *The War Horse*, however, preceded her engagement with feminist themes; the collection is more concerned with violence in Northern Ireland than with female experience. It is also more reliant on form than later works, in which her metre becomes looser and her stanzas shorter. Because Boland's voice shifted so radically after *The War Horse*, we might read her reliance on traditional form as simply an early stage in her poetic apprenticeship. Still, several poems in this collection show that Boland, along with her male contemporaries, found form an enabling way to approach artistic representation of violence in the North. For her, orderly artistic expression becomes a manifestation of a hoped-for political order.

Boland's 'Child of Our Time' is perhaps the most interesting example of her attempt to restore a sense of order, through her art, to a nation that had become grievously disordered. The elegy was written in memory of a child who died in the Dublin car bombings of 1974. Through its form, it seeks to reconstruct a 'new language' which will oppose and replace the language of militant nationalism. The first stanza reads:

> Yesterday I knew no lullaby
> But you have taught me overnight to order
> This song, which takes from your final cry
> Its tune, from your unreasoned end its reason,
> Its rhythm from the discord of your murder
> Its motive from the fact you cannot listen.[38]

---

[38] Eavan Boland, *New Collected Poems* (New York: Norton, 2008), 41.

The potential for language to bring order to chaos lies at the heart of this poem. The child's death has 'taught' the poet to 'order/This song', to bring 'reason' to 'your unreasoned end', 'rhythm' to 'discord'. Here, the consoling power of language is not questioned or ironized. In the final stanza, Boland promises the dead child that she will 'find for your sake' 'a new language', one that will be unlike the 'idle talk' that has led to sectarian violence. Boland suggests that this new language will be structured, 'with rhymes for your waking, rhythms for your sleep'. In fact this new language sounds very much like poetry itself. Accordingly, the sestets are written in iambic pentameter, and use an orderly rhyme through variations of an *abc* scheme. Form here is clearly a profound component of Boland's vision of the 'new language' she hopes will help change discourse in Northern Ireland. Other poems that address the conflict, such as 'The War Horse' and 'A Soldier's Son', likewise use traditional form. Although Boland would later distance herself from these 'public' poems, and the use of elaborate form itself, they underscore the appeal of form for yet another major Irish poet approaching the conflict in Northern Ireland during the early 1970s.

Seamus Heaney has written at length about the relationship between form and politics in Northern Irish poetry. After the violence of summer 1969, he wrote that 'the problems of poetry moved from being simply a matter of achieving the satisfactory verbal icon to being a search for symbols adequate to our predicament'.[39] Heaney has gone to considerable lengths to justify the act of composing what he has called 'pure' poetry—that is, poetry that seems to eschew politics for aesthetics—in a time of political turmoil.[40] In an important 1984 essay about poetry in Northern Ireland, 'Place and Displacement', Heaney spoke of the 'profound relation here between poetic technique and historical situation', and tried to dispel the notion that Northern poets' concern with form equalled disengagement from pressing contemporary issues.[41] He argued that poets did bear a 'political responsibility' and that form was a powerful way of fulfilling this responsibility:

> A poetry of hermetic wit, of riddles and slips and self-mocking ironies, may appear culpably miniaturist or fastidious to the activist with his microphone at the street corner, and yet such poetry may be exercising in its inaudible way a fierce disdain of the activist's message, or a distressed sympathy with it.[42]

Form, Heaney wrote, liberated Northern poets from the 'entrapment' they had experienced as members of a sectarian society, where decisions about identity and belonging were rigid and preordained:

> The only reliable release for the poet was the appeasement of the achieved poem. In that liberated moment...when the timeless formal pleasure comes to its fullness and exhaustion...the poet makes contact with the plane of consciousness where he

[39] Seamus Heaney, *Preoccupations: Selected Prose 1968–1978* (London: Faber, 1980), 56.
[40] Seamus Heaney, *Finders Keepers: Selected Prose 1971–2000* (London: Faber, 2002), 118.
[41] Ibid., 118.
[42] Ibid., 119.

is at once intensified in his being and detached from his predicaments. It is this deeper psychological compulsion which lies behind the typical concern of Northern Irish poets with style, with formal finish, with linguistic relish and play.[43]

Here, Heaney equates form with freedom, and argues that 'formal pleasure' need not be divorced from political engagement.

Heaney, in his search for '[b]efitting emblems of adversity', famously turned to the bog bodies that had been excavated in Denmark in the 1950s, which he encountered as images in P. V. Glob's book *The Bog People* (1969). The photographs offered him a glimpse into the rituals of violence that were part of life in Northern Europe during the Iron Age (it appeared that many of the victims were sacrificial), and he immediately began to see the bog bodies as a powerful metaphor for the political situation in Northern Ireland.

The bog poems in *Wintering Out* (1972) and *North* (1975) do not rely on traditional form, but they do share similar formal qualities. Many are written in dimeter and trimeter quatrains that make heavy use of assonance and consonance. Heaney frequently uses section breaks, as Yeats did, and monosyllabic lines. In both 'The Tollund Man' and 'The Grauballe Man', almost every stanza contains at least one completely monosyllabic line. This nod to Anglo-Saxon verse helps conjure a dark world of tribal violence and lends a sombre, almost hypnotic quality to the speaker's observations. Heaney's reverent tone bothered many critics, among them Ciaran Carson and Edna Longley, who accused him of indulging in nationalist sentiment and using inappropriate metaphors.[44] They felt Heaney had drawn false parallels between present-day Northern Ireland and Iron Age Jutland, and worried that his emphasis on martyrdom—the Tollund Man's 'sad freedom'[45]—was politically irresponsible. While the subject matter of the poems ostensibly inspired this controversy, the slow, prayer-like *sound* of the poems contributed to critics' sense that Heaney was not so much condemning tribal violence as he was legitimizing its ritualistic overtones. In 'The Grauballe Man', for example, Heaney's use of sibilance and assonance to describe the body of the murdered victim is almost sensual:

> His hips are the ridge
> and purse of a mussel,
> his spine an eel arrested
> under a glisten of mud.[46]

The horror of the mutilated body with its 'slashed throat' is tempered here by the reassuring repetition of soft vowels and soothing 's' sounds. It was partly this pleasing aural cohesion that led critics to argue that Heaney was aestheticizing the violence he wrote about—elevating the idea of sacrifice and endowing it with a sense of nobility. Later in the poem, as if swayed by his own transformative verse, Heaney writes,

[43] Ibid., 118.
[44] See Ciaran Carson, 'Escaped from the Massacre?', *Honest Ulsterman* 50 (1975), 183–6, and Edna Longley, '"Inner Émigré: or "Artful Voyeur"? Seamus Heaney's North', *Poetry in the Wars* (Newcastle: Bloodaxe, 1986), 140–69.
[45] Seamus Heaney, *Opened Ground* (New York: Farrar, Straus and Giroux, 1999), 63.
[46] Ibid., 110.

> Who will say 'corpse'
> to his vivid cast?
> Who will say 'body'
> to his opaque repose?[47]

This was the kind of sentiment which critics would point to as politically charged; in transforming horror into something beautiful, they felt Heaney had crossed a dangerous line. Presumably for Heaney, however, the poems' formal elements were attempts to bring an imagined order to a world of darkness and violence. This desire, and its attendant risks, is evident in the final two stanzas of 'The Grauballe Man'. Here, Heaney achieves an impressive formal symmetry that mirrors that of the Dying Gaul he is describing. The Grauballe Man, he writes, 'lies/perfected in my memory':

> hung in the scales
> with beauty and atrocity:
> with the Dying Gaul
> too strictly compassed
>
> on his shield,
> with the actual weight
> of each hooded victim,
> slashed and dumped.[48]

Here the speaker seems to doubt the moral authenticity of the Dying Gaul, who lies 'too strictly compassed/on his shield'. Heaney may be suggesting that his own symmetry in the last stanza—the first and last lines each have three syllables, all monosyllabic, while the middle two lines have six syllables—may itself be 'too strictly compassed'. Heaney intimates that such symmetry, while pleasing to eye and ear, might not be adequate to measuring the weight of the actual (as opposed to aestheticized) victims, who have been 'slashed and dumped'. In this line, with its heavy, monosyllabic dimeter and masculine ending, the speaker finally faces the horror that the poem had earlier tried to assuage. Heaney shows us that engaging with 'timeless formal pleasure' liberates, but also has the potential to leave the poet distracted, even 'detached from his predicaments'.[49] Thus the poem is not only about parallels between tribal violence in Iron Age Jutland and Northern Ireland, but the morally ambiguous role of form itself in aesthetic representations of violence.

Derek Mahon's collection *The Snow Party* was published in 1975, the same year as *North*. To some extent, the two collections share similar concerns and approaches to the political situation in Northern Ireland. Like Heaney, Mahon used both formal structures and alternative historical settings to speak about contemporary violence. Unlike Heaney, however, Mahon steered clear of controversy by scrupulously avoiding metaphors that implied an affiliation or sympathy with a particular side. The strongest poems in this collection, such as 'The Snow Party' and 'A Disused Shed in Co. Wexford', suggest

---

[47] Ibid.
[48] Ibid., 111.
[49] Heaney, *Finders Keepers*, 118.

parallels with the present-day situation in the North, but their scope is broader. These poems not only present complex questions about the roots of political violence in society, they ask the reader to consider the potentially voyeuristic role of the artist in mediating such violence. Like Heaney in 'The Grauballe Man', Mahon turns a sceptical eye on his own attempts to bring 'order' to violence.

Mahon has spoken of his 'commitment' to form, a commitment that sustained him while writing *The Snow Party*.[50] There, the relation between form and violence is a central concern. In the title poem of that collection, 'The Snow Party', Mahon questions whether beauty serves as a distraction from violence, or sustenance in the face of violence. The poem imagines a snow party in the city of Nagoya, attended by Basho, the seventeenth-century Japanese master of haiku form. Viewers gather around a window to watch the snow fall as they drink tea and converse. The first five stanzas present the snow party as elegant tradition, yet the speaker regards it more ambiguously in the last three stanzas:

> Elsewhere they are burning
> Witches and heretics
> In the boiling squares,
>
> Thousands have died since dawn
> In the service
> Of barbarous kings;
>
> But there is silence
> In the houses of Nagoya
> And the hills of Ise.[51]

Echoing the haiku, Mahon uses tercets with short dimeter and trimeter lines. He also skilfully uses caesurae to slow the reader; the many pauses reinforce the quiet, meditative tone of the poem. Mahon undermines this formal quietness, however, in the last stanza when he refers to the 'silence' of those at the snow party. The imagery of stillness and coldness serves a double purpose: while these images give the poem a crystalline, Yeatsian clarity, they also emphasize the themes of indifference and inaction. Mahon suggests that these aesthetes have literally turned their backs on violence perpetrated 'Elsewhere'. This violence, Mahon shows, has political roots: 'barbarous kings' have ordered the deaths of 'thousands', many of them ('Witches and heretics') opponents of institutionalized authority. While Mahon may be suggesting that beauty and suffering can coexist, the implication here is more likely that beauty has the potential to distract from, or make one indifferent to, suffering. In his analysis of this poem, Hugh Haughton called those at the snow party 'poetic nature worshippers', a phrase that hints, perhaps, at Mahon's sceptical attitude toward the efficacy of poetry itself.[52]

---

[50] Eamon Grennan, transcript of 'The Art of Poetry LXXXII' with edits by Derek Mahon, typed MS, Box 34, Derek Mahon Papers, Emory University Manuscript and Rare Book Library, p. 39. This excerpt does not appear in the published *Paris Review* interview.

[51] Derek Mahon, *Collected Poems* (Oldcastle: Gallery, 1999), 63.

[52] Hugh Haughton, *The Poetry of Derek Mahon* (Oxford: Oxford University Press, 2007), 99.

Such scepticism is more obvious in Mahon's 'A Disused Shed in Co. Wexford', first published in *The Listener* in September 1973. In a series of ten-line stanzas, Mahon presents a surrealist vision of abandoned mushrooms clamouring for attention 'Deep in the grounds of a burnt-out hotel'.[53] The poem's scope is both local and global: although the mushrooms represent victims of 'Treblinka and Pompeii', Mahon gives the shed an Irish location, and reveals that the mushrooms have been festering there 'since civil war days'. He tells us that a 'half century' has elapsed since the mushrooms were last seen, a span that dates the poem to its year of composition. This detail suggests that the poem is as much about the displacement and dispossession endured by the citizens of Northern Ireland during the Troubles as it is about victims of the Irish Civil War, the Holocaust, imperialism, and natural disaster. Mahon himself has commented upon his oblique approach here: 'It's possible for me to write about the dead of Treblinka and Pompeii: included in that are the dead of Dungiven and Magherafelt. But I've never been able to write directly about it.'[54]

While the poem attempts to elegize those dead, it also makes a broader point about the role of the poet in documenting suffering. In the last stanza, the 'Lost people' beg the journalists who have discovered them 'to speak on their behalf/Or at least not to close the door again'. Finally, the mushrooms address the photographer directly: 'You with your light meter and relaxed itinerary/Let not our naïve labours have been in vain!' The double meaning of 'light meter' points squarely to the poet: Mahon expresses unease about his own attempt to write a poem that memorializes victims whose suffering has rendered them 'wordless'. The lines question whether words are at all adequate to the task at hand, and whether the use of form trivializes the pain endured by those who died. Still, as Terry Eagleton has noted, 'A Disused Shed' 'asserts its control, calmly refusing to lose its head'.[55] Indeed, the poet revels in lyrical wordplay, as in the first stanza, when the 'echo trapped for ever' itself echoes in 'a flutter/Of wild flowers in the lift-shaft,/Indian compounds where the wind dances'. The poem's formal mastery attests to the poet's confidence in his own ability to minister effectively to the silenced victims even as he asks his readers to treat the balm of his words with scepticism. In this way, 'A Disused Shed in Co. Wexford' achieves that frail, elusive balance between 'beauty and atrocity'—without being 'too strictly compassed'—sought by so many Irish poets in the early 1970s. It was, and still is, among the most difficult aesthetic acts to accomplish.

---

[53] Mahon, *Collected Poems*, 89.
[54] Quoted in Haughton, *The Poetry of Derek Mahon*, 118.
[55] Terry Eagleton, *How to Read a Poem* (Oxford: Wiley-Blackwell, 1996), 86.

....

CHAPTER 25

'NEUROSIS OF SAND': AUTHORITY, MEMORY, AND THE HUNGER STRIKE

....

SHANE ALCOBIA-MURPHY

We have asserted that we are political prisoners and everything about our country, our arrests, interrogations, trials and prison conditions show that we are politically motivated and not motivated by selfish reasons or for selfish ends. As further demonstration of our selflessness and the justness of our cause, a number of our comrades, beginning today with Bobby Sands, will hunger strike to the death unless the British government abandons its criminalisation policy and meets our demand for political status.[1]

The statement issued by the prisoners at the outset of the 1981 hunger strike at the Maze Prison, Belfast, not only sought to explain and justify the principled motivation for the escalation of their protest but to reaffirm their authority as political prisoners; as Marc Mulholland argues, '[t]he prisoners' rationale cut clear to their self-perception as a legitimate army'.[2] The gap between their internalized conception of themselves as freedom fighters and the government's perspective at the time was made manifestly clear in an uncompromising speech made by the British prime minister, Margaret Thatcher, in which she reaffirmed her adherence to the official policy that '[t]here is no such thing as political murder, political bombing or political violence. There is only criminal murder, criminal bombing and criminal violence.'[3] Although the prisoners had been incarcerated

---

[1] Prisoners' statement smuggled from the Maze prison cited in Chris Ryder, *Inside the Maze: The Untold Story of the Northern Ireland Prison Service* (London: Methuen, 2000), 233.

[2] Marc Mulholland, *The Longest War: Northern Ireland's Troubled History* (Oxford: Oxford University Press, 2002), 134.

[3] Margaret Thatcher, *The Times*, 6 March 1981, cited in Arthur Aughey and Peter G. Neumann, *Britain's Longest War: British Strategy in the Northern Ireland Conflict, 1969–1998* (Basingstoke: Palgrave, 2003), 111.

for their violent acts rather than for their political beliefs, Thatcher's logic was an example of a convenient doublethink; as Timothy Shanahan has contended, she 'conveniently overlooked the fact that the hunger strikers had been arrested and convicted under legislation stemming from the Prevention of Terrorism Act (1974) that had defined terrorism as "the use of violence for political ends" '.[4] This war of words was but one stage in a long propaganda campaign. Successive British governments sought to delegitimize the activities of the paramilitary organizations by adopting the internal conflict model which proposed that the Northern Irish situation was 'reducible to the intractable sectarianism of two mutually opposed communities';[5] thus, the British government could mask their own involvement in and responsibility for the ongoing conflict. In effect, they became, in the words of one commentator, 'the mediator of good will in a dispute between two communities caught in a time warp of reformation theology and atavistic nationalism, as the disinterested, altruistic government pouring money, men, and arms into the province for the sole purpose of stopping two groups of incorrigible, belligerent Irish from executing their murderous designs on each other'.[6]

As part of this criminalization policy, the decision to end special-category status in Northern Ireland was taken following the Gardiner Report of 1975: those convicted of terrorist offences would no longer be granted political status and would thus lose special privileges (free association, the right to wear their own clothes, the right to refrain from prison work). The government's strategy not only provided 'justification for political containment', but was widely regarded as 'a powerful weapon in the hands of the authorities' since it mobilized 'popular approval and legitimacy behind the state'.[7] Indeed, the construction of the Maze prison (1975–76) was itself a physical manifestation of the new regime: not only did it replace the existing internment camp, its low-rise cellular structure, comprising blocks of cells made from pre-cast concrete, embodied the government's aims. Commenting on its architecture of containment, Louise Purbrick notes that '[w]ithin the controllable cell spaces of the H-block, the prison authorities would hold sway over the prisoners' and that '[i]t was hoped that the design of the Maze (Cellular) would make it possible to operate a conventional prison, to implement the Prison Rules'.[8] Thus, the battle for legitimacy was carried on inside the prison. For the authorities, the strategy 'was characteristically a rigid enforcement of rules and assertion of the powers of staff, the internalisation of what were essentially propagandist positions by staff and managers, a prison culture of brutality, violence and dehumanisation, and constant political "interference" from senior politicians…in the micro-management

[4] Timothy Shanahan, *The Provisional IRA and the Morality of Terrorism* (Edinburgh: Edinburgh University Press, 2008), 172.

[5] Stefanie Lehner, 'The Peace Process as Arkhe-Taintment?', *Irish Studies Review* 15:4 (2007), 508.

[6] Padraig O'Malley, *Biting at the Grave: The Irish Hunger Strikes and the Politics of Despair* (Boston: Beacon Press, 1990), 205.

[7] Laurence McKeown, *Out of Time: Irish Republican Prisoners, Long Kesh, 1972–2000* (Belfast: Beyond the Pale, 2001), 22.

[8] Louise Purbrick, 'The Architecture of Containment', in Donovan Wylie, *The Maze* (London: Granta Books, 2004), 103.

of prisoners';[9] for the nationalist prisoners, however, 1975–80 was a period characterized by continuous protest. On 14 September 1976, Ciaran Nugent, the first prisoner to be sentenced under the new regime, refused to wear the prison uniform and chose instead to wear a single blanket; this marked the beginning of what came to be known as 'The Blanket Protest'. After those on the protest were moved from H1 and H2 blocks to H5 in May 1977, the conflict escalated: those prisoners 'slopping out' were intimidated and assaulted, resulting in a decision by the protesters to initiate a 'no wash' protest. What followed was a period of heightened tension and increasing brutality within the Maze. As Nugent recalls:

> The screws were really starting to step up their harassment and we believe it came from British officials – to step up the harassment to break the protest. During the day they were coming in and kicking your pot over your mattress – the place was completely stinking. The only thing you had was a mattress and a blanket: we couldn't sleep in it – there were maggots running out of the blankets. So to save our beds and blankets…we decided to throw the slops out of the windows. But the screws went round the back and shoved it all back through the window again….So we had no alternative to put it on the walls.[10]

This escalation of the protest, with the refusal to wash or shave and the smearing of faeces onto the cell walls, became known as 'The Dirty Protest'. Following an abortive hunger strike (27 October–18 December 1980) the prisoners began a better planned and more prolonged hunger strike on 1 March 1981, a date of symbolic significance given that it was the fifth anniversary of the removal of special-category status. The prisoners' demands—'[t]o wear their own clothes; to refrain from prison work; to associate freely with one another; to organise recreational facilities and to have one letter, visit and parcel a week; to have lost remission fully restored'[11]—could not be acceded to by the government; in the words of the Northern Ireland Secretary, Humphrey Atkins, to do so 'would be to legitimise and encourage terrorist activity'.[12]

Throughout the different protests the republican battleground emerged in the form of the body-as-text; as Joseph Ruane and Jennifer Todd bluntly state, '[t]he struggle between prisoners and warders, republicans and British state, was symbolically fought out on the prisoners' emaciated bodies'.[13] The refusal to wear prison uniforms, the spreading of faecal matter on cell walls, and the martyrdom by self-starvation constituted the practical means by which the prisoners could distance themselves from British authority. Their nakedness, for example, instigated a 'countertextualisation' of the body whereby the proposed assimilation of political prisoners into the category of Ordinary Decent Criminal was disrupted. In particular, throughout the 217 days of hunger strike,

[9] Peter Shirlow, *Beyond the Wire: Former Prisoners and Conflict Transformation in Northern Ireland* (London: Pluto Press, 2008), 29–30.
[10] Ciaran Nugent cited in Ryder, *Inside the Maze*, 180–1.
[11] Ryder, *Inside the Maze*, 218.
[12] Humphrey Atkins cited in Ryder, *Inside the Maze*, 218.
[13] Joseph Ruane and Jennifer Todd, *The Dynamics of Conflict in Northern Ireland: Power, Conflict and Emancipation* (Cambridge: Cambridge University Press, 1996), 111.

the starving body became 'a text, the living dossier of its discontents' since, following the republican logic, 'the injustices of power [were] encoded in the savage hieroglyphics of its sufferings'.[14]

Poetic responses to the hunger strike often utilize and engage with this corporeal discourse: the body becomes a text in the absence of any other means of communication. In Colette Bryce's '1981', for example, 'a man cowers, says it with hunger,/skin, bone, wrought to a bare/statement',[15] and in John Montague's 'Sands' (named after Bobby Sands, who died on 5 May 1981 after sixty-six days on hunger strike), the speaker proclaims that the poem is 'a song of silence', 'the sound of the bone/breaking through the skin/of a slowly wasting man'.[16] While the body has an expressive function in both texts, the substance or political import of that expression is not brought to the fore; rather than valorize any ideological position, the poems emphasize the human dimension of protest and focus on the body's pained vulnerability.

By contrast, much propagandist verse about the hunger strikes grants the prisoners' body a quasi-mythical status, thereby de-historicizing the conflict. For instance, Criostoir O'Flynn's 'Hunger Strike' equates the starving prisoner with Christ, the presence of whose fasting body is perceived as a threat 'to the body politic'.[17] Set in AD 30, the poem presents the 'fasting Man' as Christ enduring his quarantine:

> The Man went on fasting; but wondered whether
> Death by hunger or by bloody crucifixion
> Would be more to his purpose. Either
> Way he would rise again, and the wilderness
> Could become Eden.

The religious lexis conveniently elides the very real differences between Christ's peaceful spiritual mission and the militant actions of a republican. The text's ideological presumptions are very much in line with nationalist pronouncements at the time which argued that the hunger strike's 'associations with asceticism, penitential fasting, atonement for wrongdoing, asking of forgiveness for transgressions against others, altruistic intercession on behalf of the community...conferred on the hunger strikers a moral stature'.[18] In *Postnationalist Ireland*, Richard Kearney describes how the hunger strikers in the H-Block sought to realign 'their plight with a mythico-religious tradition of *renewal-through-sacrifice*': subscribing to a 'mythic logic', the protesters appealed to 'a "sacred" memory of death and renewal which provided an air of legitimacy for present acts of suffering by grafting them onto paradigms of a recurring past. It thus afforded these acts a timeless and redemptive quality'.[19] Typical of this genre is Micky Devine's 'If

---

[14] Maud Ellmann, *The Hunger Artists: Starving, Writing and Imprisonment* (London: Virago Press, 1993), 16–17.

[15] Colette Bryce, '1981', *The Full Indian Rope Trick* (London: Picador, 2005), 11.

[16] John Montague, 'Sands', *Hunger Strike: Reflections on the 1981 Hunger Strike*, ed. Danny Morrison (Dingle: Brandon, 2006), 112.

[17] Criostoir O'Flynn, 'Hunger Strike', *Hunger Strike and Other Poems* (Dublin: FNT, 1984), 19–20.

[18] O'Malley, *Biting at the Grave*, 109.

[19] Richard Kearney, *Postnationalist Ireland: Politics, Culture, Philosophy* (London: Routledge, 1997) 110.

Jesus',[20] a poem written on the eve of his hunger strike, in which he highlights the pro-
tester's vulnerability and lack of agency, all the while implying a Christ-like status:

> For this day a broken body
> Will live through trial and fear
> And feel the pain of hunger
> And shed a silent tear.
> He'll look around him
> And to Heaven make a plea:
> 'They crucified you, Jesus,
> Now they're doing it to me.'

Such religious symbolism was widespread at the time, featuring on murals in Nationalist
areas. As Kearney states, '[w]hile wall-drawings showed battered and emaciated prison-
ers in Christ-like posture', the wire of Long Kesh was 'transformed into crowns of
thorns'.[21]

Paul Muldoon's 'Aisling',[22] perhaps the most well-known poem which deals with how
the imprisoned body constituted the stage on which the conflict was enacted, takes issue
with the de-historicizing tendency of republican propaganda. The poem's enumeration
of body parts includes 'eyes', 'mouth', 'kidney' (used as an adjective), 'hand' (used as a
verb) and 'Maw'. These are accompanied by references to bodily secretions, such as the
venereal 'lemon stain', 'a lick' and 'spittle'. While focusing on the 'real' body, the poem
repudiates the myth-making tendency. Playing with the conventions of the traditional
Gaelic vision poem, Muldoon transforms 'the traditionally venerated figure of Cathleen
Ni Houlihan (or 'Mother Ireland') into an unidentifiable female who infects her lovers
with disease or...lures them to self-destruction'.[23] In the poem there are three bodies,
two of which are diseased: the first is that of the dream woman (or 'aisling'), usually a
'chaste and virginal figure',[24] who is now represented as an anorexic with venereal dis-
ease; the second is that of the speaker who has been given the 'All Clear' after his carefree
sex with the goddess figure; the third is that of the hunger striker whose 'more commit-
ted relationship with the captivating Cathleen-Anorexia results in near self-destruction'.[25]
Unlike the hunger striker, the text's speaker remains uncontaminated in the face of acute
political events, a claim that the poet may be making for himself. The speaker, of course,
is not Muldoon, nor should the two be equated; however, the absence of a clear
statement of his beliefs has led to harsh condemnation, especially on the part of a
certain strain of nationalist criticism which tends to dismiss Muldoon as an apolitical
trifler who 'plays with politics, but snaps his fingers and disappears, vapour-like, up the

---

[20] Micky Devine, 'If Jesus', *Hunger Strike*, ed. Morrison, 48.
[21] Kearney, *Postnationalist Ireland*, 112.
[22] Paul Muldoon, 'Aisling', *Quoof* (London: Faber, 1983), 39.
[23] Elmer Kennedy-Andrews, 'Heaney and Muldoon: Omphalos and Diaspora', *Paul Muldoon: Poetry,
Prose, Drama*, ed. Elmer Kennedy-Andrews (Gerrards Cross: Colin Smythe, 2006), 109–10.
[24] Clair Wills, *Reading Paul Muldoon* (Newcastle: Bloodaxe, 1998), 94.
[25] Tim Kendall, *Paul Muldoon* (Bridgend: Seren, 1996), 96.

post-modern chimney when any reality knocks at the door'.[26] Such criticism ignores the very real dilemma faced by the poet: how does a creative writer respond to a political event in a non-partisan way? In his lecture 'Getting Round: Notes Towards an *Ars Poetica*', Muldoon defends the position of the poet who 'insists on the freedom not to espouse directly any political position',[27] and it is a stance which is typical of those who, when depicting or referring to the hunger strike, find it necessary to defend the autonomous and ethically unfettered status of poetry in the face of pressures towards political engagement.

The line that is literally central to the poem, found between a stanza evoking both anorexia and venereal disease and a stanza describing a hunger striker off his fast, is the shoulder-shrugging 'It's all much of a muchness.' This isolated line is poised as a bridge, the graphic equivalent of a semantic link between anorectic deity and abortive hunger striker:

> Was she Aurora, or the Goddess Flora,
> Artemidora, or Venus bright,
> or Anorexia, who left a lemon stain on my flannel sheet?
>
> It's all much of a muchness.
>
> In Belfast's Royal Victoria Hospital
> a kidney machine
> supports the latest hunger-striker
> to have called off his fast, a saline
> drip into his bag of brine.

By equating hunger striking with anorexia nervosa, Muldoon might conceivably be accused of constructing a simplistic, depoliticizing analysis of the prison struggle, but what the poet may be trying to foreground in this juxtaposition is the fact that, as in anorexia, the hunger strikes were a symptom of a self-image crisis, a reaction against social pressures to fit into a particular form: in other words, there was a disjunction between how the hunger strikers saw themselves and the way in which they were being represented by the British state. In her analysis, Edna Longley puts the case more forcefully by suggesting that nationalism itself had become a destructive neurosis: 'In blaming the hunger-strikers' emaciation on their idealised cause, the poem equates that cause with a form of physical and psychic breakdown. "Anorexia" is Cathleen Ni Houlihan in a terminal condition.'[28]

In her earlier poetry, Medbh McGuckian briefly flirts with myth and Christological symbolism when, in an elegy for her father entitled 'The Aisling Hat',[29] she establishes a parallel between his death, that of a hunger striker, and Christ's resurrection. In an interview she describes her father's death in the following way: 'he started to die on a

---

[26] Barra O. Seaghadha, 'And Again...', *Graph* 7 (Winter 1989–90), 20.

[27] Muldoon, 'Getting Round: Notes Towards an *Ars Poetica*', *Essays in Criticism* 48:2 (April 1998), 127.

[28] Edna Longley, *The Living Stream: Literature and Revisionism in Ireland* (Newcastle: Bloodaxe, 1994), 109.

[29] Medbh McGuckian, 'The Aisling Hat', *Captain Lavender* (Oldcastle: Gallery, 1994), 44–9.

Sunday and died on the Wednesday. It was like the Crucifixion—the three days.'[30] The poem's first movement consists of twenty-nine stanzas, during which the father is portrayed heroically. McGuckian transforms the gritty realism of a farming life on the River Shesk ('horse-sweat'): the man is an ancient ('Paleolithic'), Romantic ('Promethean head') figure with the personal attributes of courtesy ('handshakes'), cunning ('sliding like a knight's move'), and an intimate connection to the land. Detailing his physical attributes—heart, face, head, arms, lips, eyebrows, thorax, skin, hands, eyes are all mentioned—her first impulse is to transform him into a bird, thereby affirming his ability to transcend human limitations (his face is 'a cognac eagleskin'). Yet she also, gradually, acknowledges his physical decay:

> Twin wings unseverable
> were those enormous eyes, legs of the heron
> reconciled to their uselessness.[31]

Indeed, in a remarkably concise and evocative image, she conflates the fall of Icarus with her father's coffin entering the ground: 'The earth like some great brown/ceiling came rushing at your head'.

The second movement begins with an enigmatic stanza, at once suggestive of past knowledge and future potential:

> Until we remembered that to speak
> is to be forever on the road,
> listening for the foreigner's footstep.[32]

The lines alert the reader to a particular theme running through the poem, one alluded to in its title, namely the promise offered by the Aisling figure of the imminent arrival of a foreign power coming to the aid of a colonized Ireland. That this is not incidental is confirmed by the poem's source. The entire text is a montage of quotations from Osip Mandelstam's prose[33] through which McGuckian encrypts a nationalist narrative.[34] Of particular importance is the following description of a man's dying body, one which is taken from Mandelstam's 'Journey to Armenia':[35]

The body of King Arshak is unwashed and his beard is wild.

The King's fingernails are broken, and wood lice crawl over his face.	His body is unwashed, his beard wild, his fingernails broken,

---

[30] McGuckian, personal interview, The Marine Hotel, Ballycastle, 19 August 1996.

[31] McGuckian, *Captain Lavender*, 46.

[32] Ibid., 47.

[33] Osip Mandelstam, *The Collected Prose and Letters*, ed. Jane Gray Harris, trans. Harris and Constance Link [1979] (London: Collins Harvill, 1991).

[34] See chapter 4 of my *Sympathetic Ink: Intertextual Relations in Northern Irish Poetry* (Liverpool: Liverpool University Press, 2006).

[35] The quotations from 'Journey to Armenia' are on the left and McGuckian's text ('The Aisling Hat', 48) is on the right.

His ears have grown deaf from the silence,
but they once appreciated Greek music.

He controls my hair and my fingernails.
He grows my beard and swallows my saliva, so
accustomed is he to the thought that I am here in the
fortress of Anyush.

his ears deaf from the silence.

He controls my hair, my fingernails, he
swallows my saliva, so accustomed
is he to the thought that I am here.

Within the elegy, McGuckian identifies to such an extent with 'the idealized parental fig-ure'[36] that the boundaries between them become blurred; rather than experiencing healthy mourning, the poet exhibits what Peter Sacks terms secondary narcissism which lies 'at the core of melancholia'.[37] However, the father-daughter boundary is not the only one to be conflated here as the father is figured triply as a dying prisoner: he is King Arshak, Osip Mandelstam, and a dying hunger striker. By omitting specific details ('King Arshak', 'the fortress of Anyush'), McGuckian avoids making the politically loaded con-nection to the hunger strike known to the general reader. Indeed, Nadezhda Mandelstam's account in *Hope Abandoned* provides an insight into how sensitive the image proved dur-ing her own time: 'Caesar Volpe, for example, not only published "Journey to Armenia" in *Zvedzda*, but even included the passage, after it had been forbidden by the censorship, about King Arshak, imprisoned by the Assyrian in a dungeon without a ray of light and from which there was no escape'.[38] The parallel between her father and a republican hero may well be spurious, but it has an emotional value for McGuckian, allowing her to asso-ciate her father with acts of heroic endurance during illness.

In her early poetry, McGuckian tended to approach the hunger strike from an oblique angle not only due to political sensitivity, but also out of confusion concerning what constituted an appropriate response. In an essay entitled 'The Desire for Freedom' she recalls that she once had used the word 'sand' as a coded reference and that she 'was haunted by its associations'. She then cites the 'The Golden Path' as being influenced by '[a] sense of numbed confusion and not knowing where to go'.[39] Made up of phrases taken from Philippe Roberts-Jones's *Beyond Time and Place*, an overview of the tradi-tion of non-realist painting in the nineteenth century, the poem's opening stanzas out-line a necessarily compromised resolution to her dilemma:[40]

---

[36] Peter Sacks, *The English Elegy: Studies in the Genre from Spenser to Yeats* (Baltimore: Johns Hopkins University Press, 1985), 15.

[37] Ibid., 10.

[38] Nadezhda Mandelstam, *Hope Abandoned*, trans. Max Hayward (London: Collins and Harvill Press, 1974), 410.

[39] McGuckian, 'The Desire for Freedom', *Hunger Strike*, ed. Morrison, 192.

[40] McGuckian, 'The Golden Path', *Two Women, Two Shores* (Maryland: The Chestnut Hill Press, 1989), 35. McGuckian's text is on the right; on the left are quotations, with page numbers, from the source text—Philippe Roberts-Jones, *Beyond Time and Place: Non-Realist Painting in the Nineteenth Century* (Oxford: Oxford University Press, 1978).

plucked by the camera (90)	Not like a camera I plucked you;
'the closed eyes' (78); 'in obedience to my Dream' (78); the clearing opens on to another dream (117); the gold of these bodies (101); 'disentangled' (112)	Your eyes closed in obedience to my dream, And opened on a clearing to another dream Which was the gold of your own body disentangled.
The beach [...] remains a place of loneliness and even oppression (96) may feel excluded or enfolded (118) in answer to or as an obstacle (117)	A beach more than a house is a place Of oppression—it feels at once excluded And enfolded, can be both an answer And an obstacle, a path through all the tangle
'all the tangle' (117); one woman's dream (108)	Of an unknown woman's dream.

Unlike in 'The Aisling Hat', here the poet has agency and controls, rather than is controlled by, the prisoner:[41] as an ostensible subject for a poem, she 'plucks' him and his body works in obedience to her 'dream'. The opening line's discounted simile—'Not like a camera'—declares her adherence to a non-realist aesthetic; that which is perceived by the eye is subordinate to its reception and imaginative reconfiguration by the inner eye. McGuckian, then, is seeking (in the words of Seamus Heaney) 'another place where the mind could take shelter from the actual conditions'.[42] The extracts which make up the first stanza refer to Odilon Redon's *Closed Eyes* (1890) and *The Dream* (1904), two paintings that foreground inward meditation, and she cites from Redon's journal, *À soi-même*, in which he writes about the creation of an artistic language with which to engage with the world: 'I have, I think, yielded submissively to the secret laws that have led me to turn out after a fashion, to the best of my ability and *in obedience to my dream*, things I have put my whole self into' [emphasis added].[43] Likewise, in the second stanza she cites from Redon's praise of Rodolphe Bresdin's *Clearing in the Forest* (1880): 'His powers were those of imagination alone. He devised nothing in advance. He improvised with delight or worked up to a stubborn perfection *all the tangle* of that minute, almost imperceptible vegetation that you find in these forests he saw in his dreams' [emphasis added].[44] However, while oblique reference to the hunger strike and a dislocating, imaginative response via dream language may well offer 'a path through all the tangle' in 'The Golden Path', the poet does concede that such a strategy is not without tension: the technique presents 'both an answer/And an obstacle'; the subject is both 'excluded/And enfolded'.

[41] Here 'sand'/Bobby Sands is indicated by the poem's location (the beach).
[42] Seamus Heaney, 'Place and Displacement: Reflections on Some Recent Poetry in Northern Ireland', *Contemporary Irish Poetry*, ed. Elmer Andrews (Basingstoke: Macmillan Press, 1992), 129.
[43] Redon cited in Roberts-Jones, *Beyond Time and Place*, 77–8.
[44] Redon cited in ibid., 117.

Thus, it is unsurprising that in later poems, such as 'Monody for Aghas', she approaches the subject less obliquely by using an historical analogy. In this poem she recalls the example of Thomas Ashe who went on hunger strike with his comrades in Mountjoy Jail demanding to be treated as a prisoner of war.[45] On 25 September 1917 he died due to 'clumsily administered forcible feeding',[46] and the text, borrowing as it does from Sean O'Casey's account of Ashe's death, describes in detail the violence inflicted on his body, focusing in particular on his lips:[47]

his mouth is forced open, and a gag is fixed firmly between the lips (167); a tube of three foot in length […] which had previously been used on ten other sufferers was dipped in hot water (167); the tube was withdrawn and inserted again (167); food clogged the tube, which had then to be withdrawn and cleansed (167)	that were forced open, strapped open, by a sort of meal of a fixed gag, a three-foot tube previously used on ten others, dipped in hot water, and withdrawn and inserted, clogged and withdrawn, and cleansed…

The relation to the 1981 hunger strike is not presented in the text and the textual ventriloquism grants the poet a necessary distance from her subject. It is a strategy which she has deployed on many occasions. In 'The Sands of St Cyprien', a recent poem published in a collection of reflections on the 1981 hunger strike edited by Danny Morrison, McGuckian again seeks out an historical analogy for the experiences of the Maze prisoners, but this time she uses a non-Irish example. The text, made up of nine largely unrhymed tercets, is created by splicing together extracts from *Spanish Culture behind the Wire*, an analysis of oral testimonies and memoirs by Spanish republicans who experienced internment by the French in concentration camps located along the open shorelines of southern France between 1939 and 1945:[48]

frozen sand (21); it looked so innocent (72); Footprints were erased and blood was soaked up like water (72)	Frozen sand: it looked so innocent It erased footsteps and soaked up blood Like water.

[45] See Robert Kee, *The Green Flag: A History of Irish Nationalism* (London: Weidenfeld and Nicolson, 1972), 606–7.

[46] Tim Pat Coogan, *De Valera: Long Fellow, Long Shadow* (London: Arrow Books, 1993), 100.

[47] McGuckian, 'Monody for Aghas', *Drawing Ballerinas* (Oldcastle: Gallery, 2001), 27–9. McGuckian's text is on the right; on the left is the source text, Sean O'Casey, *Feathers from the Green Crow*, ed. Robert Hogan (London: Macmillan, 1963), 167.

[48] McGuckian, 'The Sands of St Cyprien', *Hunger Strike*, ed. Morrison, 196. McGuckian's text is on the right; on the left are quotations, with page numbers, from Francie Cate-Arries, *Spanish Culture behind the Wire: Memory and Representation of the French Concentration Camps, 1939–1945* (Lewisburg: Bucknell University Press, 2004).

behind the barbed-wire perimeter (cover);	Behind the barbed-wire perimeter
'The motley group of huts' (164);	Of that motley group of huts,
fistfuls of (30); his very being was slowly	His very being was fistfuls of hardened sand:
being turned into hardened sand (168)	
'sand running through my veins' (168)	Sand running through his veins.
Sand-neurosis (168); sand-induced fits (168)	Neurosis of sand. Sand induced fits.
'the pull of molecules of sand' (177)	The pull of molecules of sand.
the hated sand-jail (184);	In the sand-jail where consonants burned away,
'The air was filled with particles	The air was filled with particles
of excrement; the discoloured liquid	Of excrement, little L-shaped pieces . . .
from standing pools of urine blew	
in our faces' (239); 'little L-shaped	Discoloured liquid
pieces' (239)	From standing pools of urine
	Blew their imagined wholeness in their faces.

Focusing on the material conditions of imprisonment, the speaker characterizes the inmates' experience as a gradual loss of self, abandoned as they are 'to the alienation of their own abject otherness':[49] 'wholeness' in such an environment is 'purely imagined'. Here, McGuckian is being faithful to the testimonies collected by Francie Cate-Arries since each tends to recreate 'the place of the camp through tropes of the void, as an unnameable nowhere whose dehumanized and demoralized inhabitants are constantly threatened by the brute forces of both Nature and Man'.[50] Hence, the opening stanzas depict three interrelated types of loss, each symptomatic of a radical dehumanizing alterity: physically ('erased footsteps'; 'soaked up blood'), mentally ('sand-neurosis'), and linguistically ('consonants burned away'), the individual is stripped of all that defines him as human. Indeed, that 'His very being was fistfuls of hardened sand' is demonstrated by the third stanza's stultifying repetition of 'sand' and the absence of verbs: the text, like the prisoner, is held in stasis.

However, what concerns both Cate-Arries and McGuckian is not simply loss as immediately experienced due to incarceration; rather, both their texts highlight the more insidious process of othering whereby the events themselves become altered by or erased from historical record, and both authors explicitly seek to recover occluded narratives:

I don't know if I read it in a newspaper	I don't know if I read it in a newspaper,
or if someone told me (48)	Or if someone told me,

---

[49] Cate-Arries, *Spanish Culture*, 238.
[50] Ibid., 22.

twenty-four hours have gone by (156)	Or if I heard it after twenty-four hours had gone by:
Nothing reported could be further from the truth (239)	But nothing reported could have been Further from the truth...

'Truth', of course, is a problematic term, particularly in a poem which explicitly parallels the prison experiences of republicans from wholly disparate locations and time periods, as exemplified by the poem's title—'The Sands of St Cyprien'—which works geologically (the beach environment) as well as patronymically (Bobby Sands). Indeed, the images used from the accounts of the French camps to evoke both the Dirty Protest and the 1981 hunger strike—'skeleton in a blanket'; 'a carcass in manure'—are inaccurate since they conflate the three different phases of the republican struggle within the Maze. Nevertheless, a poem is not a historical narrative: its purpose here serves as a call to remember the suffering endured by the prisoners and to counter the dehumanizing strategies of those who choose not to recognize their humanity. In an accompanying essay, the poet speculates on the lack of commemorative verse for the ten dead hunger strikers: 'Why, we may ask, is there no poem of the stature and resonance of "Easter 1916" for these ten men?... Because these men were merely "the scum of the earth" and deserved no epitaph?'[51] Such questions echo those of Judith Butler; analysing the effects of prohibitions on public commemoration, particularly for those viewed as inherently 'other', she asks: 'Who counts as human? Whose lives count as lives?.... What *makes for a grievable life*?'[52] To commemorate the hunger strikes risks not only reopening old wounds, but also may valorize the actions and beliefs of those whose existence was inimical to the state.

While McGuckian shows few qualms about asserting that a prisoner's life is 'grievable', her contemporary, Seamus Heaney, has been far more circumspect. Indeed, in his final Oxford lecture he records how he refused to go to the funeral of Francis Hughes, the second man to die on hunger strike, despite his being a neighbourhood friend of the family in Bellaghy: 'I would have been wary of the political implication of attendance.'[53] Heaney has repeatedly reflected, both in his poetry and in his prose writing, on the tensions arising from the two opposing pulls that preside over the production of poetry, especially in deeply politicized societies: the need, on the one hand, to engage in a response to the demands of pressing and often violent contemporary events, in the labour towards 'tilting the scales of reality towards some transcendent equilibrium';[54] and, on the other, poetry's defining and liberating compulsion to affirm itself as a self-enclosed, independent space of complete and distinct meaning. In 'The Flight Path', a poem whose very title is suggestive of such a tension between escape and constraint, he describes, in section 1,

---

[51] McGuckian, 'The Desire for Freedom', *Hunger Strike*, ed. Morrison, 192.
[52] Judith Butler, *Precarious Life: The Powers of Mourning and Violence* (London: Verso, 2004), 20.
[53] Heaney, *The Redress of Poetry* (London: Faber, 1995), 187.
[54] Ibid., 3.

a moment from childhood—the shaping of a paper boat by his father—which eventually comes to symbolize the enterprise of poetry itself:

> The first fold first, then more foldovers drawn
> Tighter and neater every time until
> The whole of the paper got itself reduced
> To a pleated square he'd take up by two corners,
> Then hold like a promise he had the power to break
> But never did.[55]

The process of compression and reshaping which characterizes the pleating of the paper boat parallels the exercise of extreme verbal compression which defines poetry. Moreover, this act is described both in its creative, transformational aspect—it presents all the potential of a promise—and as a craft, a work of circumspect and laborious construction. The alliteration in the first line ('first fold first'; 'foldovers') is a rhetorical equivalent of the reiterative action being described, whereas the internal rhyme ('Tighter and neater') of the second line might help suggest poetry's formal self-sufficiency. At the end of this first section, however, the paper boat is described as being 'as hollow/As a part of me that sank because it knew/The whole thing would go soggy once you launched it.' As well as pointing to the inherently artificial nature of the poetic object and its often uneasy relationship with the reality it reproduces, what Heaney may be trying to articulate in this self-defeating image of the launched paper boat are the dangers of an excessive immersion of poetry in the ebb and flow of contemporary events. It is hardly surprising, then, that the next two sections should be densely populated with images of flight and escape, of the 'buzz from duty free', in what Neil Corcoran describes as 'a summary of several of the topographical "translations" of Heaney's own biography'.[56]

Neil Corcoran is certainly correct in his identification of translation as a recurrent theme as well as a formal component of the poem. As an activity which involves both the exercise of restraint—of following another author's path—and of literary re-creation (therefore propitious to creative flight), translation embodies and further illuminates Heaney's concerns and it is central to section 4 of 'The Flight Path', which goes back to the political events of 1979, at a time when Heaney included a translation of the 'Ugolino' episode from Dante's *Inferno* in *Field Work*. Heaney dramatizes an episode that took place in 1979 of an encounter with a Sinn Féin official:[57]

> So he enters and sits down
> Opposite and goes for me head on.
> 'When, for fuck's sake, are you going to write
> Something for us?' 'If I do write something,
> Whatever it is, I'll be writing for myself.'
> And that was that. Or words to that effect.[58]

---

[55] Heaney, *The Spirit Level* (London: Faber, 1996), 22.
[56] Neil Corcoran, *The Poetry of Seamus Heaney: A Critical Study* (London: Faber, 1998), 190.
[57] Heaney relates the particulars of this encounter in an interview by Henri Cole: 'Seamus Heaney: The Art of Poetry LXXV', *Paris Review* 144 (Fall 1997), 111.
[58] Heaney, *The Spirit Level*, 29.

Both the colloquial language and the counterpointed rhythm caused by the caesura in the lines of this dialogue denote a level of impatience and urgency, not just on the part of the political activist, but also on that of the poet in relation to the purpose and account-ability of poetry. The stanza's final sentence, 'Or words to that effect', introduced casually as the conclusion of a narrative, stands also as a reminder of the poet's refusal to write words to any politically predetermined effect. Since this refusal seems to be his 'last word' on the matter, the transition to the following stanza is somewhat puzzling as Heaney confronts the H-block protest, in the figure of Ciaran Nugent, in a striking equi-librium of directness and obliquity:

> The gaol walls all those months were smeared with shite.
> Out of Long Kesh after his dirty protest
> The red eyes were the eyes of Ciaran Nugent
> Like something out of Dante's scurfy hell,
> Drilling their way through the rhymes and images
> Where I too walked behind the righteous Virgil,
> As safe as houses and translating freely:
> *When he had said all this, his eyes rolled*
> *And his teeth, like a dog's teeth clamping round a bone,*
> *Bit into the skull and again took hold.*[59]

The starkly factual assertion which opens the stanza is then followed by increasingly associative and abstract imaginative patterns, so that the 'red-eye special from New York', one other instance of flight and escape, is now transformed into the 'red eyes' of Nugent, and the H-blocks where the dirty protest took place become 'Dante's scurfy hell'. Heaney's awareness of the dangers implicit in this aestheticization is visible in the set-ting of the comparison: the eyes are 'Like something'; the terms remain vague, especially since these are the eyes that can literally *see through* 'the rhymes and images' produced by the poet. Thus, Heaney seems to portray Nugent as an accusatory figure, perhaps in the recognition that the republican prisoner was producing an engaged response (unlike the poet himself). Heaney resorts to a more oblique approach which allows him to address the dirty protest and the hunger strike in his own terms, and this amounts to straying from the path of republican mythology and rhetoric. Rather than bring the stanza and section to a close with a direct statement, Heaney cites three lines from his own translation of the 'Ugolino' episode from Dante's *Inferno*.

The canto centred on 'Ugolino' narrates the tale of Count Ugolino della Gherardesca who, after being imprisoned for treachery alongside his children and grandchildren, eventually resorts to cannibalism. Thus, Heaney might be offering an oblique and dry comparison between Count Ugolino's eating of his own children and the ethics of the republican movement, which fed off its own supporters by offering them up for sacrifice during the hunger strikes (a theme implicitly referred to in Muldoon's 'Aisling'). Moreover, although one could argue that, by only quoting three lines, Heaney refrains

---

[59] Ibid., 30.

from giving voice to Ugolino's distressing narrative, focusing instead upon his vengeful *'fiero pasto'* (bestial meal), Heaney is nonetheless summoning the memory of the origi-nal text, and the line which immediately precedes the quoted passage, 'then hunger killed where grief had only wounded',[60] constitutes a crucial moment in Dante's text, in that it is an elliptic and therefore oblique reference to the heinous act of cannibalism itself. It is not only Dante's subject matter but also his choice of approach that Heaney is espousing in his representation of yet another terrible act in the history of the Troubles.

If representation in 'The Flight Path' is characterized by distance from the hunger strikes, in terms of its temporal production and its recourse to literary allusion, section IX of the longer sequence 'Station Island', published in 1984, moves in the opposite direc-tion as it ventriloquizes the thoughts and feelings of Francis Hughes.[61] The poem's title refers to the site of pilgrimage in Lough Derg where Catholics travel to perform a series of penitential exercises, which include abstaining from food and sleep, so as to attain spiritual purification. Therefore, as the poet 'walks the stations' a first instance of identi-fication is established between poet and hunger striker since part of the republican rhet-oric adopted during the hunger strikes consisted in a justification of their protest in terms of the exercise of the Catholic principle of redemptive suffering.

Whereas in previous sections of 'Station Island' the first-person utterance begins invariably by being that of the poet, in section IX, contrary to what the reader is expect-ing, and although clearly identified by the inverted commas, the speech is that of the fasting Hughes. The first stanza conveys the experience of starvation both through images of the self-consuming body ('My brain dried like spread turf, my stomach/ Shrank to a cinder and tightened and cracked.') and by reproducing the mental disorien-tation which results from starvation (Hughes's voice travels back and forth between reminiscences of his career as hit man for the IRA and as prisoner 'on the blanket'.). When Heaney writes that 'Often I was dogs on my own track/Of blood on wet grass that I could have licked', he is not only referring to the particular manner in which Hughes was captured by the British army,[62] he is also intimating curious tensions that arise from self-inflicted violence:[63] Hughes is both hunter and hunted, perpetrator and victim of violence, a circumstance that also describes the very act of hunger-striking to the death. Therefore, the ominous ambush is described as a 'Stillness I felt safe in' and Hughes is both 'emptied and deadly'. One further image, as Hughes describes himself as a 'white-faced groom', provides a connection with the next movement in the poem in which the poetic voice takes over. This image of innocence is marred by the knowledge that

---

[60] Seamus Heaney, *Field Work* (London: Faber, 1979), 63.

[61] Seamus Heaney, *Station Island* (London: Faber, 1984), 84–6.

[62] After a gun battle with the army, Hughes's gun was found, and near it, a trail of blood which was followed across several fields in Glenshane (County Londonderry).

[63] Moreover, Catherine Byron identifies a Christological parallel in these elements: 'The images of his telescoped narrative half-resonate with images from Christ's passion: the bloody trail of the way to Calvary, the draped blanket of mockery'. See Byron, *Out of Step: Pursuing Seamus Heaney to Purgatory* (Bristol: Loxwood Stoneleigh, 1992), 159.

Hughes, as republican soldier and later as hunger striker, has espoused an ideology that has proven diseased and, ultimately, deadly:

> There he was, laid out with a drift of mass cards
> At his shrouded feet. Then the firing party's
> Volley in the yard. I saw woodworm
> In gate posts and door jambs, smelt mildew
> From the byre loft where he had watched and hid
> From fields that his draped coffin would raft through.... [64]

Here Heaney pursues Hughes's trail but the traces he finds are those of infected nature ('woodworm' and 'mildew') and, as Catherine Byron points out, 'the bog, which should be a wet and boundless centre of fructification and preserving, does not, in the pilgrim's vision, "work" this victim "to a saint's kept body" '.[65] Hughes is also portrayed as a figure at odds with the landscape: 'Unquiet soul, they should have buried you/In the bog where you threw your first grenade'. Both alien and native to his homeland, Hughes is the personification of deadly innocence.

In many respects the ten dead hunger strikers are 'unquiet souls', especially considering the debates surrounding the future of the now empty Maze prison. Despite calls for a museum or interpretative centre to be established on the site, there is anxiety, as Declan McGonagle notes, 'that retaining the H-Block hospital wing [where the hunger strikers died] will inevitably make this a site of Republican pilgrimage and facilitate a Republican ownership of the history of Long Kesh/Maze and, by extension, a wider ownership of the Troubles period as a whole'.[66] There is little desire on the part of the British government to work any of the hunger strikers 'to a saint's kept body'. Indeed, in the aftermath of the Belfast Agreement and the creation of the Northern Ireland Assembly, narratives produced by the media and governmental institutions have been underscored by a pronounced and predominant process of selective forgetting whereby the awkward sectarian complexities of the Troubles have been erased or archived. Thus, as Colin Graham's recent research has documented, a recurrent trope has emerged in Northern Irish culture of 'an ache which notices, knows, but can barely comment on the cauterisation of the dark complexity of the past'; hence, 'the difficult and the embarrassingly recent past, or the irritatingly non-conforming present, is archived'.[67] Poets refuse this archival tendency: while the examples cited above may differ in their ideological position, each seeks to remember, record, and detail imaginative responses to the suffering. By humanizing the hunger strikers rather than rendering them as 'other', the poems recognize that theirs were grievable lives.

[64] Heaney, *Station Island*, 84.
[65] Byron, *Out of Step*, 160.
[66] Declan McGonagle, 'If You Are Not Confused, It Means You Don't Understand: Reflections on the Maze as Political Space', *The Lives of Spaces*, ed. Hugh Campbell et al. (Belfast: IAF, 2008), 196.
[67] Colin Graham, ' "Every Passer-by a Culprit": Archive Fever, Photography and the Peace in Belfast', *Third Text* 19:5 (September 2005), 568.

CHAPTER 26

ENGAGEMENTS WITH THE PUBLIC SPHERE IN THE POETRY OF PAUL DURCAN AND BRENDAN KENNELLY

JOHN REDMOND

WHILE it would be wrong to declare, in the manner of Francis Fukuyama, that we have reached the end of Irish history, nevertheless, the mood of the island, in the first decade of the twenty-first century, is distinctly *fin de siècle*. With the globalization of the Irish economy, the secularization of Irish society, the humiliation of the Catholic Church, the Americanization of Irish culture, and the (messy) conclusion of the Troubles, the modernizing wave which began to roll across Ireland at the beginning of the 1960s has everywhere left its mark. While still in earshot of revisionism's 'long withdrawing roar', both sides of the border might now be characterized as living (to adapt Ted Hughes) 'in the remains'. This quiet, deflationary period in Irish history provides an opportunity, then, to reflect on some of the actors in the island's story of modernization. Here I will discuss the work of two poets who surfed in on the revisionist tide: Paul Durcan and Brendan Kennelly.

Critical surveys of Irish poetry often bracket Durcan and Kennelly together and for understandable reasons. Both are well-known public figures in Ireland, both are memorable performers of their own work, and both command unusual enthusiasm in their audiences. In the sometimes fierce exchanges which, during the 1970s and 1980s especially, dominated the national conversation, both have been keen participants. Hailing from non-metropolitan backgrounds both, after some diversions, have settled in Dublin and both, with this career trajectory very much in mind, closely identify with the example of Patrick Kavanagh. Like all poets from the Republic, both have had to endure the somewhat diminished visibility caused by the overwhelming success of the Northern Irish poets. But if the confessionalism of 1960s American poetry has any literary equivalent in Ireland, then it is to be found in their work (stylistically, both are extremists) rather than in that of the Ulster poets. Both Durcan and Kennelly have faced significant setbacks in their private lives: the former endured a broken marriage, a battle with alcohol, and ongoing depression, while the latter's own epic battle with alcoholism received an equally epic public airing on Irish television and radio. In both cases, the resulting crisis provoked a decisive reorientation of their writing, which was embodied in two pivotal books: for Durcan *The Berlin Wall Café* (1985), and for Kennelly *Cromwell* (1983).

Although the level of their engagement with the public sphere has been high, we cannot say that either poet has been close to exerting political power. They have, however, been close to those who exerted it. In a 1996 book-length tribute to Kennelly, *This Fellow with a Fabulous Smile*, we find various members of the Irish Establishment, including Bono, Gay Byrne, and the then Taoiseach, Charles Haughey, writing in his praise. If, in a notoriously small country, the treatment of the public sphere by both poets has always had some personal basis, then to that extent they are followers of W. B. Yeats. When Yeats wrote in 'The Municipal Gallery Revisited' of the glory of having 'such friends', he lauded an intellectual elite which had decisively shaped the emerging nation. Via his own family history, Durcan is especially closely connected to this aspect of the Yeatsian legacy. The McBride of 'Easter 1916' was Joseph McBride, brother of John McBride, Durcan's grandfather who was, in turn, married to Maud Gonne. As Durcan tells us in *The Laughter of Mothers* (2007), he was always aware of this important connection even if neither he nor his mother were entirely happy about it:

> Maud Gonne was a disloyal wife
> And, therefore, not worthy of Mummy's love.
> For dynastic reasons we would tolerate Maud
> But we would always see through her.[1]

Although it would be surprising if such a pedigree did not confer on Durcan some Lowellesque sense of literary entitlement, the poem at least affects a measure of embarrassment.

While we should not be surprised if the reputations of living poets are still in flux, the place of both these poets in Irish poetic history is far from settled. Reflecting on Durcan's work and its critical reception, Dennis O'Driscoll offers a balanced summary: 'Durcan's work divides critics, some praising it as visionary, comical, satirical, others finding it baggy and verbose, the work of a jester to the middle classes.'[2] With only a slight change of emphasis, the same kind of uncertainty applies to the work of Brendan Kennelly.

The factional nature of Irish cultural debate (documented, for example, by W. J. McCormack in *The Battle of the Books*) provides one source for the competing attitudes towards both poets. We might take as an example the contrasting treatment accorded to Durcan's work by two of Ireland's leading literary critics, Declan Kiberd on the one hand and Edna Longley on the other. While Longley has criticized Kiberd for 'the suppression of [Durcan's] political poetry in *The Field Day Anthology*', she has also

---

[1] Paul Durcan, 'The MacBride Dynasty', *The Laughter of Mothers* (London: Harvill Secker, 2007), 72.
[2] Dennis O'Driscoll, *Troubled Thoughts, Majestic Dreams* (Oldcastle: Gallery, 2001), 70.

written of her first meeting with Durcan as personally important for her own participa-
tion in 'the battle of the books': 'Any later engagement I may have had with North/South
cultural politics probably goes back to 'meeting Paul Durcan on the top deck of a bus in
Cork City.'[3] By contrast, Declan Kiberd has seemed, at least until recently, to be sceptical
about Durcan's poetry. In Kiberd's two most significant and comprehensive critical
books, *Inventing Ireland* and *Irish Classics*, Durcan is only mentioned once, and that is in
the limited context of the poet capturing the country's sour mood in the 1980s.[4]

One could provide a reductive political explanation for these alternative readings, but
the critical uncertainty about Durcan's work reasonably reflects its mix of successes and
failures—and also its mixed successes and mixed failures. Durcan's political poems,
especially those written in the 1980s, are often brutal in their satire. Take for example his
depiction of a nervous priest confronting a sexually voracious woman:

> She—a feminist, would you believe it!—
> Would no more keep out of my bed
> Than say *Au Revoir* to Adam if she met Adam in the garden
> (Her name is Evelyn, by the way, Evelyn MacNamara:
> She had an abortion by Canon Mick Coyle last year
> And, the year before that, an abortion by Bishop Tim Green:
> MacNamara's Band—they call her in Maynooth.)[5]

Given Durcan's considerable gifts as a performer, it is easy to imagine this poem raising
laughter at one of his well-attended readings, but then it is just such easy point-scoring
which lends support to the view of him as 'a jester to the middle classes'. Although subse-
quent sexual scandals surrounding the Catholic Church mean that writing of this sort
might, in retrospect, be re-categorized as documentary rather than as satire, it is scarcely
adequate as poetry. True, the lines generate an electric current of surprise, but that is
mostly because of Durcan's decision to publish them. It is only the overly polarized
nature of Irish criticism which inhibits their just appraisal.

Much of Durcan's early work is informed by a very simple and reductive value system.
Merely to identify a character with one of those institutional targets of politically liberal
Ireland, for example the Catholic Church and the Gaelic Athletic Association, is enough
to damn them. Conversely, to identify a character as an artist or a bohemian or some
other desirable type is enough to elevate them. In the opening of the following poem, the
provocatively titled 'The Perfect Nazi Family is Alive and Well and Prospering in Modern
Ireland', we find a typically extreme example:

> Brillo is the husband and he played county football
> For sixteen years and won every medal in the game:

---

[3] Edna Longley, 'Paul Durcan and the North: Recollections', in *The Kilfenora Teaboy—A Study of
Paul Durcan*, ed. Colm Tóibín (Dublin: New Island Books, 1996), 108, 104.

[4] Declan Kiberd, *Inventing Ireland: The Literature of the Modern Nation* (London: Jonathan Cape,
1995), 609.

[5] Paul Durcan, 'Fr Peadar Party—Third Secretary to the Archbishop', *Jumping the Train Tracks with
Angela* (Dublin: Raven Arts, 1983), 42.

> With his crew-cut hair and his dimpled blue chin
> And his pink, rosée cheeks:
> There is a photo of him on every sideboard in the county.
> He has five children and he hopes to have five more
> And, for convenience, he also has a wife...[6]

This is, at once, crude and startling, startlingly crude perhaps. Nevertheless, even when Durcan is assassinating a stereotype, his poetry tends to be redeemed by other virtues—visual sharpness, brisk authority of voice, and verbal surprises (*blue* chin). In the end, what this reductive poem most reduces is Durcan's own talent, stripping it of its subtlety and flexibility. Indeed, this particular political poem might support some well-known remarks of Edna Longley:

> Poetry and politics, like church and state, should be separated. And for the same reasons: mysteries distort the rational processes which ideally prevail in social relations, while ideologies confiscate the poet's special passport to *terra incognita*.[7]

Kennelly's poetry, like Durcan's, is shot through with extraordinary levels of antagonism. Like Durcan's, it is heavily dependent on the shock treatment which it routinely metes out to stereotypes and clichés. Often this rough handling involves a diachronic element, as in *The Book of Judas* (1991) where Biblical characters are to be found roaming contemporary Dublin, or, in a reversal of the process, recognizable fixtures of Irish life are transported back to Biblical times. In that long poem, the Judas-voice, which speaks through businessmen, bankers, and politicians, is cynically male and tired. The familiarity of the scenarios which he characteristically describes is overlain with jadedness and déjà vu. In interview, Kennelly has elaborated on the deficiencies in Irish society which comprise the targets of his critical long poems:

> I see a lot of people [in Ireland] liking to be told what to think, whether it is the Church or the Leaving Cert or the hoisting of responsibility onto political figures, to be oracles of revelation...the pedestallisation of mindlessness.[8]

The typical antagonism of these remarks—typical of Kennelly and typical of his generation—is formally reflected in his work by its frequent use of dialogue. Many of Kennelly's poems are verbal duels between strongly contrasting types. Typical of this class of poem is 'The Return':

> I feel again a wave of hate
> Begin to drown my mind and there
> In the struggle arena, I rise, I live,
> Amazed at the obscenities scalding my lips,

---

[6] Ibid., 33.

[7] Edna Longley, 'Poetry and Politics in Northern Ireland', *Poetry in the Wars* (Newcastle: Bloodaxe, 1986), 185.

[8] Richard Pine '"The Roaring Storm of Your Words": Brendan Kennelly in Conversation with Richard Pine', in *Dark Fathers into Light: Brendan Kennelly*, ed. Richard Pine (Newcastle: Bloodaxe, 1994), 186.

> Untouched when his great head cowers
> Then lifts—O God, that unforgettable shape—
> Begging the pardon that I will not give.[9]

In this poem, where Kennelly encounters a dysfunctional teacher he knew from boyhood, a number of recurrent themes appear: the arbitrariness of authority, the attraction of cruelty, and the inadequacy of educators. However, one has to point out that the poem is seriously flawed. 'A wave of hate' is a thumping cliché, as is the image of the poet's mind drowning. Although it may not be derivative, the phrase 'struggle arena' is awkward, the kind of unrevised mental shorthand which is widespread in Kennelly's work. The poem is over-dependent on easy intensifications generated by words like 'amazed' and 'unforgettable', while the modifier, 'great', and the verb, 'scalding', are merely obvious. Meanwhile, the ecphonetic aside, 'O God, that unforgettable shape', is clunkily theatrical. Only the last line, which depends on a fairly simple inversion, has any mild resonance.

By becoming celebrities who were willing to speak on topical public issues, Durcan and Kennelly faced another risk: a measure of absorption by Ireland's political class. This is illustrated by their relationships to the man who was Ireland's most significant political figure during the 1980s, Charles Haughey. Though an undoubtedly complex political figure, Haughey was found by the Moriarty Tribunal to have 'devalued democracy', thanks to engaging in various forms of embezzlement. Disliked by large sections of the media establishment, he sought a kind of cultural offset through his patronage of the arts, becoming, as W. J. MacCormack put it, 'managing director of the Culture Industry'.[10] This helps to explain his launching Kennelly's book, *Poetry, My Arse* (1995). In an otherwise warm recollection of his friendship with Kennelly, the Irish journalist Bruce Arnold, wrote sharply on this point:

> What he [Haughey] did, covertly with Des Traynor and his close friends, which was to introduce them to an inside track financially, making them into an elite, he also did more publicly for artists. Not surprisingly, artists revered him for it.[11]

Arnold goes on to criticize Kennelly for having too close a relationship with such a flawed politician.

Meanwhile Paul Durcan's milder association with Haughey has attained a kind of emblematic status, not least because it was used by Colm Tóibín to open his study of the poet, *The Kilfenora Teaboy*. The association sprang from an invitation extended by Haughey—and accepted by Durcan—to read at the official opening of the controversial Knock Airport in 1986. Throughout the poet's own memoir of the event, he describes members of the governing party in glowing, even Yeatsian, terms. While Haughey's personal bearing is described, for example, as 'open' and 'brave', we are afforded various

---

[9] Brendan Kennelly, 'The Return', *Breathing Spaces: Early Poems* (Newcastle: Bloodaxe, 1992), 16.

[10] W. J. McCormack, *The Battle of the Books* (Dublin: Lilliput Press, 1986), 85.

[11] Bruce Arnold, *The Spire and Other Essays in Modern Irish Culture* (Dublin: The Liffey Press, 2003), 80.

vignettes of his courtesy, as in the following case. Before taking off for Knock in a small plane, Durcan and the Fianna Fail leader are in a car, listening to radio reports of bad weather:

> At a roundabout a woman driver obeyed the rules of the roundabout and Mr Haughey leaned forward and saluted her. I was astonished that a man whose day was in ruins before it had even started could be concerned with such chivalry.[12]

Durcan continues in similar vein. Through a milling crowd at the airport, Mr Haughey supportively holds the poet's hand ('who else but he', we are asked, 'would have bothered?') and is finally sketched in near-hagiographical terms as a 'traveller-king' steering his way through the 'open skies of life and death'. Needless to say, this description is, from almost any point of view, unreliable. The playful distortion which is at the heart of Durcan's forceful subjectivity limits its use as *political* discourse. Indeed Durcan's wild bias is a good illustration of why poets *cannot* replace journalists, and why poets, for most purposes, are ineffective in relation to the political sphere.

To balance these reservations, it should be said that Durcan is a remarkably various poet and that his books have brought different *kinds*—as well as different *levels*—of success. We might think, in this context, of the very first poem in his first full-length book, *O Westport in the Light of Asia Minor* (1975):

> I met her on the First of August
> In the Shangri-La Hotel,
> She took me by the index finger
> And dropped me in her well
> And that was a whirlpool, that was a whirlpool,
> And I am very nearly drowned.[13]

Within a short space, Durcan covers an enormous distance. The title introduces a poetic procedure which is notably homophonic. In this casual aisling, the poet meets his beloved on the day of 'Lughnasa', the Celtic Harvest festival, to which 'Nessa' is sonically, if not etymologically, linked. Lugh is the Celtic god of light, and *nasád* refers to a gathering for games or a more general assembly. The poem is centred around swimming ('snámh' in Irish, another near sound-alike), and the lover's swim occurs within a mile of Buck Mulligan's famous immersion in *Ulysses*. The woman's name is a variant on 'Agnes' or 'Vanessa', though its mythological Irish sound may put us in mind of one of Yeats's heroines (perhaps via the monumental red hair of Jane Morris). In the poem, the speaker shows some initial nervousness about joining Nessa, and that suggests a further sonic near miss, one that is closely connected with seasickness: *nausea*.

If this homophonic reading of 'Nessa' is in danger of seeming too Muldoonian (and there are surprising connections between the two poets which remain to be explored), one might balance this by pointing out the skill with which the poem's opening

---

[12] Paul Durcan, *Paul Durcan's Diary* (Dublin: New Island Books, 2003), 158.

[13] Paul Durcan, 'Nessa', *O Westport in the Light of Asia Minor* [1975] (London: Harvill, 1995), 3.

telescopes the action. With a deftly erotic shift, the poet is reduced, so that he disappears like a penny down a wishing well (or a holy well). These still (and deep) waters are immediately agitated by the doubly deployed double-stress of 'whirlpool', which in turn leads to a final phrase that, in its airy colloquialism, is more usually associated with rainfall. Of course, the figure of the whirlpool also alludes to Ulysses and his wanderings, and reminds us how often the movement of a Durcan poem is a kind of swirl, whether centripetal or centrifugal, and so looks forward to the spirals, stone circles, and snail shells, which decorate one of Durcan's most daring and memorable poems, 'A Snail in My Prime'.

Foreign names in Irish poetry are always a potential form of escape—they detonate throughout Durcan's work quite as much as the references to Peru and India in Mahon's 'A Disused Shed in County Wexford'. In 'Nessa', the toponym 'Shangri-La' gives notice of one of Durcan's enduring obsessions with 'the importance of elsewhere', which, as we will see later, informs another of his most important poems, 'Greetings to our Friends in Brazil', and which he himself has characterized as a utopian longing:

> My work as a poet has always been searching for the other place. The notion of 'utopia' is fundamental to something about myself, and I think, about human nature.... All my life I have been looking for a Mont Saint Victoire. And it is no accident that most of my books have the names of places in them.[14]

'Nessa' is as perfect as 'Inversnaid' or 'Canal Bank Walk'—in the sense that one cannot imagine how it could be improved. I emphasize this because even though I am making a case, here, for Durcan's greatest success occurring in a certain kind of poem, I don't want to minimize the *variety* of his achievement. He has succeeded, for example, in blues and ballads, in the polyphony of 'Tullynoe: Tete a Tete in the Parish Priest's Parlour', in the queer refrains of 'The Centre of the Universe', in narratives both real and surreal. In the final part of this essay, though, I will make a case for Durcan's highest achievements coming in a certain kind of casual, self-emptying poem—I am thinking, for example, of 'A Snail in my Prime', 'Greetings to Our Friends in Brazil', and '11 September 2001'—in which he reoriented himself towards the public sphere.

Returning to Kennelly for a moment, it is ironic that a writer whose public pronouncements are so insistently nonconformist became so institutionalized early on. The dark trajectory from Trinity College to St Patrick's Hospital via alcohol dependence has been followed by more than one Irish poet. This kind of institutionalization was one which Durcan, who dropped out of university early on, luckily managed to avoid.

Kennelly did show early promise. In his poems of the 1960s he questions various forms of authority—familial, clerical, and educational—with a simple eloquence. 'To Learn' is a sign of what he was capable:

> There were nine fields between him and the school.
> The first field was deep like his father's frown

---

[14] Paul Durcan, 'Passage to Utopia', in *Across the Frontiers: Ireland in the 1990s*, ed. Richard Kearney (Dublin: Wolfhound Press, 1998), 192.

> The second was a nervous pony
> The third a thistle with a purple crown[15]

At the end of this mildly ironic poem, the boy reaches school, where he buckles down to learn. In poems like 'A Horse's Head' and 'Shell', Kennelly explores the kind of rural territory which was on speaking terms with the work of Kavanagh and Heaney. Those modest successes, like his rapid academic elevation, can partly be explained by the poet's prodigious energy. In a brief memoir of their childhood, his brother Paddy recalls, for example, how hard he would study, even during the summer holidays:

> Though I cannot give his exact timetable, I feel it must have involved up to twelve hours a day study. Perhaps from eight in the morning till nine at night, with breaks for just meals and brief walks.[16]

At the same time such industry ran the considerable risk of over-production. Throughout the 1960s, Kennelly produced collections of poetry with remarkable frequency, a habit which attracted sceptical commentary from Augustine Martin:

> An initial assertion may be risked: that Kennelly was recklessly prolific during those early years; and that his publisher's faith in his precocious talent together with the user-friendly popularity of the poetry itself may have constituted a mixed blessing for his reputation, if not indeed for that talent itself.[17]

This single-minded productivity prevailed up to the publication of his three 'epics', *Cromwell*, *The Book of Judas*, and *Poetry, My Arse*. Here, the experiments with ventriloquism first made in early poems like 'Shell' and 'Lightning' are vastly inflated, and the work becomes crowded with eloquent and audacious dramatic characters:

> Jesus is Oliver's friend, they get on well
> Together despite the occasional
> Tiff concerning the nature of pain
> Inflicted on folk who lack the cop-on
> To comply with Oliver's ironside commands.[18]

While one reason for Kennelly's sudden production of bitter epics may be found in his personal life, another reason may have been that competitive anxiety which, in the wake of the Northern Irish renaissance, was experienced by so many poets in the Republic. As a grandiose state-of-the-nation book, *Cromwell* looks like an attempt to compete with Heaney's *North*, although in the end it more resembles some of Heaney's influences: the Hill of *Mercian Hymns* and especially the Hughes of *Crow*.

---

[15] Brendan Kennelly, 'To Learn', *A Time for Voices: Selected Poems 1960–1990* (Newcastle: Bloodaxe, 1990), 20.

[16] Paddy Kennelly, 'Brotherly Moments', in *This Fellow with the Fabulous Smile: A Tribute to Brendan Kennelly*, ed. Åke Persson (Newcastle: Bloodaxe, 1996), 75.

[17] Augustine Martin, 'Technique and Territory in Brendan Kennelly's Early Work', in *Dark Fathers into Light*, ed. Pine, 36.

[18] Brendan Kennelly, 'Friends', *Cromwell* [1983] (Newcastle: Bloodaxe, 1987), 97.

John McDonagh's study of Kennelly's work identifies 'The Thought-Fox' as a possible influence on *The Book of Judas*, but a more substantial case for Hughes's influence can probably be mounted.[19] The titles and general method of *Crow* are echoed by Kennelly's non-sequential narrative in *Cromwell* as well as by what Terence Brown calls 'the perhaps rather too frequent satiric anachronisms' of that book and *The Book of Judas*.[20] We might compare the flip, understated tone of titles like 'An Example', 'A Condition', and 'Oliver's Prophecies' in *Cromwell* with 'A Disaster', 'A Grin', and 'Crow's Playmates' in Hughes's book. As in *Crow*, the action of *Cromwell* and *The Book of Judas* is cartoonish, space is theatrically distorted, and all three works combine a Manichaean outlook with bursts of grotesque violence. A further possible link: the fifth section of *The Book of Judas* begins with 'An Interview', a poem which is strongly reminiscent of Hughes's 'Examination at the Womb-Door'. In both cases the anti-hero of the book has to pass a flippantly staged exam with a cosmic figure:

> I answered reasonably well on miracles,
> Moses, Abraham, Isaac. I cut
> The balls off false gods. I made a case for whores,
> Murderers and sundry criminal misfortunates.
> At the end, Jesus nodded. He looked me in the eyes,
> 'Congrats, Judas' he said, 'The job is yours.'[21]

In other words, 'Pass, Crow.'[22]

While there may be some who regard these two large books as Kennelly's poetic legacy, in truth, they magnify his weaknesses. In these cases, quantity does not beat quality. To produce a good selection of Kennelly's poems, an editor would need to be extremely selective. In a later collection like *Glimpses*, he shows little in the way of development and what we encounter is essentially a series of drafts of poems, incipient aphorisms:

> Dear Dublin, you sleep tonight in a bed
> of scandal, savage gossip, caricature, hate.
> Is this the legacy of our dead?
> Will the good word be always late?[23]

The title of the poem, like the title of the book, indicates the throwaway nature of this particular creative process. Kennelly remains an industrious maker of half-finished poems. Here and there, though, we encounter something memorable, as in the following three-line poem:

> The spider crawls into the Bible
> comes to rest
> deep in the Book of Genesis.[24]

[19] John McDonagh, *Brendan Kennelly: A Host of Ghosts* (Dublin: The Liffey Press, 2004), 130.

[20] Terence Brown, 'Awakening from the Nightmare: History and Contemporary Literature', *Ireland's Literature: Selected Essays* (Mullingar: Lilliput, 1988), 253.

[21] Brendan Kennelly, *The Book of Judas* (Newcastle: Bloodaxe, 1991), 129.

[22] Ted Hughes, 'Examination at the Womb-Door', *Crow* [1970] (London: Faber, 1972), 15.

[23] Brendan Kennelly, 'Just Another Day', *Glimpses* (Tarset: Bloodaxe, 2001), 86.

[24] Brendan Kennelly, 'Crawler', *Glimpses*, 84.

In an admittedly small way, this has something of the same charge which we get when we read of the juxtaposition between religious ritual and insect life in Robert Frost's 'Design'.

Although his achievements as a poet are questionable, Kennelly remains a significant literary figure. As his career in education might suggest, he is at his best as a teacher, whether at the podium or on a television panel. The strength of his influence can be gauged by an account given by one of his most distinguished students, Declan Kiberd:

> No platform lecturer whom I subsequently heard at Oxford could rival his passion, lucidity, and wit. Some were more learned, many more wise; but none could send auditors sweeping back to the library to fight over possession of the books which the lecturer has just been discussing.[25]

If Durcan's poetry, like Kennelly's, was in danger of becoming a victim of Ireland's inflexible cultural battles, *The Berlin Wall Café* represented a decisive turning point. Throughout that book, Durcan turns the critical spotlight, which he had usually trained on others, squarely on himself. Arising from the ashes of a broken marriage, the book is another example of an Irish poet developing by self-reproof and it joins that select canon of 'inward Midnight Courts' which includes Muldoon's 'Yarrow' and Heaney's 'Station Island'. As Derek Mahon noted about Durcan at the time:

> The role of 'exemplary sufferer', in Susan Sontag's phrase, is one which he has courted, consciously or otherwise, throughout his career, as if obscurely aware that he is temperamentally suited to the role of sacrificial victim...[26]

The Berlin Wall Café, however, is too raw in its grief. There is no doubt that many of its poems, in their embrace of victimhood, are excessive, particularly in their promiscuous use of Nazi imagery. Here, for example, the poet characterizes his relationship with his wife:

> A Jewish Bride who has survived the death-camp,
> Free at last of my swastika eyes
> Staring at you from across spiked dinner plates
> Or from out of the bunker of a TV armchair;
> Free of the glare off my jackboot silence;
> Free of the hysteria of my Gestapo voice[27]

Such work may well have been therapeutic, but only for Durcan. One is even tempted to think of this work as deliberately bad, as if the self-hatred which is so conspicuously on display were spilling over into an orgy of aesthetic self-sabotage. John Goodby has forcefully stated the case against these aspects of the collection:

> There are...many objections to be raised about Durcan's references to Nazism, as there are to his persistent idealisation of women.... Both aspects of the work can be

[25] Declan Kiberd, 'Brendan Kennelly, Teacher', in *This Fellow with a Fabulous Smile*, 82.
[26] Derek Mahon, 'Orpheus Ascending: The Poetry of Paul Durcan' in *The Kilfenora Teaboy*, 167.
[27] Paul Durcan, 'The Jewish Bride', *The Berlin Wall Café* (Belfast: Blackstaff, 1985), 41.

read as tendentious, glib, and self-dramatising, disproportionate to the events being discussed...[28]

Frost wrote that 'the best way out is always through'.[29] In *The Berlin Wall Café*, Durcan may have gone too far but at least he got out. Thereafter his poetry has a new kind of nakedness and it increasingly refuses to accept the default antagonisms of the Irish public sphere.

At a conference in Turin, Durcan tells us, he came across the Italian philosopher (and politician), Gianni Vattimo:

> It was a revelation to me. Vattimo spoke humorously and with energy of the strength to be gained from a recognition of the 'feebleness of one's identity' and of the 'casual role of the self'. These phrases, heard in a foreign place, connected with the thing Patrick Kavanagh had been saying twenty or thirty years ago—and that I've been mulling over for years. In particular, I think of his celebration of what he called the art of 'complete casualness'.[30]

The casual but purposeful wandering which we find in some of Durcan's later poetry might usefully be compared with some of the processes of The New York School. John Ashbery once defined a Frank O'Hara poem as an account of its own creation, and a poem like 'The Day Lady Died' allows its twists and turns to reflect the serendipities of city life, reflecting Nietzsche's phrase that we should let chance be worthy of determining our fate. Durcan's poetics of the casual converges with Vattimo's description of loss of metaphysics by attempting to be at home in an accidental universe.

If Durcan's more reductive early poetry has been guilty of a kind of antagonistic idealism, then his later work embraces a more relational picture of the public sphere and is much less reliant on stereotype. The speaking subject of the poem—usually the poet himself—not only has to admit the presence of competing voices, it has to admit to being formed out of them. Durcan's admiring reference to Vattimo might be suggestively placed beside the meeting of American pragmatism and European hermeneutics which takes place in Rorty and Vattimo's *The Future of Religion*. There Vattimo makes the following case:

> ...postmodern nihilism (the end of metanarratives) is the truth of Christianity. Which is to say that Christianity's truth appears to be the dissolution of the (metaphysical) truth concept itself.[31]

In other words, the dissolution of metaphysics which is, for institutional Christianity, the end, is for Durcan's Christianity, the beginning.

---

[28] John Goodby, *Irish Poetry Since 1950: From Stillness to History* (Manchester: Manchester University Press, 2000), 245.

[29] Robert Frost, 'A Servant to Servants', *The Poetry of Robert Frost*, ed. Edward Connery Latham (London: Vintage, 2001), 64.

[30] Durcan, 'Passage to Utopia', in *Across the Frontiers*, 192–3.

[31] Richard Rorty and Gianni Vattimo, *The Future of Religion*, ed. Santiago Zabala (New York: Columbia University Press, 2005), 51.

Durcan's increasingly relational conception of the public sphere helps to place his fondness for calendar customs. A day in his poetry is not an otherwise undifferentiated period of twenty-four hours but rather one cosmic souvenir out of a possible three hundred and sixty-five. His *Diary* begins, 'Last Saturday, January 6, was the Feast of the Epiphany. I'd been looking forward to it all week.'[32] He goes on to place the Feast Day in a web of social relationships. The Epiphany is important, Durcan avers, because we are the Three Wise Kings, and this revelation prompts a characteristic blitz of proper nouns:

> 'Kings' is just a nickname. It's because we're ordinary folk that they call us 'Kings'. I'm Melchior by the way and, as I say, I've got lodgings in Ringsend and that's Caspar and he lives in Phibsborough—in Great Western Square actually—and the third fellow with the mustard hair is Balthassar and he lives in Westport, Co. Mayo, in the old Protestant rectory.[33]

The later poems are full of repetition and proper nouns, and the repetition of proper nouns. Lucy Collins reminds us that, despite his often critical attitude to Catholicism, Durcan allows 'the linguistic aspects of litany and invocation to permeate the form and style of his work.'[34] In some ways, Durcan sees the world around him as an encyclopedia of social obligations.

We might accept, as a philosophical proposition, the impossibility of a private language, but Durcan's poetry registers this proposition as an emotional fact, as though language and loneliness were polar opposites. As the African proverb has it, a person is a person through persons, and so, in Durcan's work, we encounter others, at first, through their public names. Hence Durcan has an obsession with occupations. Much of the (sometimes too easy) comedy of his early work involves mere juxtapositions of peculiar occupations, a surgeon, as it were, introducing an umbrella-maker to the operator of a sewing-machine:

> He was a goalkeeper and I am a postmistress
> And the pair of us believed—I say 'believed'—in Valentine's Day.[35]

But this concern with unlikely occupations, which are made to seem as comical and unlikely as a bicycle in Flann O'Brien's *The Third Policeman*, is also a commentary on social disconnection, the absurdity of specialization. By way of contrast, Heaney's occupations strike us differently because they imply a pre-industrial or pre-urban setting—a blacksmith meeting a thatcher does not seem so odd. Alongside his reverence for occupations, we can also place Durcan's affection for titles. In his elegy for Cearbhall Ó Dalaigh, for instance, the president is variously referred to as 'Cearbhall of the City Centre and the Mountain Pool', as 'Cearbhall of the Merry Eyes', and 'O Yellow Sun'; and

[32] *Paul Durcan's Diary*, 1.

[33] Ibid., 3.

[34] Lucy Collins, 'Performance and Dissent: Irish Poets in the Public Sphere', in *The Cambridge Companion to Contemporary Irish Poetry*, ed. Matthew Campbell (Cambridge: Cambridge University Press, 2003), 216.

[35] Paul Durcan, 'The Rose of Blackpool', *Jumping the Train Tracks with Angela*, 13.

his burial place of Sneem is 'Sneem of the Beautiful Knot'. As Richard Kearney has put it, 'Durcan pleads for a prelapsarian language which might name without violence, praise without prejudice.'[36]

To conclude the essay I want to look, in extended fashion, at one of Durcan's later successes, 'Greetings to Our Friends in Brazil'. It might be described as a 'short long poem' and recalls Edna Longley's observation that the poetry of Durcan and Kennelly was 'able to capitalise on freedoms won by *The Great Hunger*'.[37] Indeed if Kavanagh had been able to combine the panoramic social insight of 'The Great Hunger' with the psychological balance and mature charity of his Canal Bank Sonnets, then the final result might have been close to Durcan's remarkable poem. Like much of his later work it introduces a kind of revisionary Catholicism which, as it happens, is not far removed from the type of religious feeling favoured by Kennelly:

> The kind of catholicism that interests me is ragged, irrational, probably unjustifiable, but full of interesting little sentences, of faces, of a myth that is, to me, pleasing…[38]

In one sense 'Greetings to Our Friends in Brazil' is, by Durcan's early standards, unusually flat, a long narrative of a weekend, which drifts casually over a myriad of his themes: homelessness, charity, theatricality, religious devotion, community games, verbal performance, learning, toleration, and mercy. Yet all of these are caught by the poem's extravagance, its wanderings over the connections which bind us together, as though in the near-utopian embodiment of religious ritual which the poem itself represents, life would spill over into the Mass as much as the Mass would spill over into life. As is almost customary, the poem begins with a series of proper nouns, a precision which will be hugely displaced by the numerous blurrings of boundary that will follow:

> On the Friday night before the last Sunday in September
> I got a phone call from Father Patrick O Brien CC, in Kilmeena, Co Mayo
> Inviting me to drive over to his house on Sunday afternoon
> And watch the All Ireland Hurling Final on television,
> Mayo against Kerry.[39]

Although this poem does not involve a train, there is something in its opening tone of Philip Larkin's 'That Whitsun, I was late getting away'.[40] Perhaps the vital difference is that Durcan's poem will refuse to be a set-piece, skirting but finally refusing the state-of-the-nation panoramics of Larkin's poem. Events unfold at a leisurely pace—the speaker attends Mass, dines with the priest, and they watch the match.

Although not without its fantastic flights, the level of deliberate realism is high—one feels, as one does not always feel when reading Durcan, that if the events described did

---

[36] Richard Kearney, *Postnationalist Ireland: Politics, Culture, Philosophy* (London and New York: Routledge, 1997), 135.

[37] Edna Longley, *Poetry in the Wars*, 15.

[38] Kennelly, ' "The Roaring Storm of Your Words" ', in *Dark Fathers into Light*, 184.

[39] Paul Durcan, *Greetings to Our Friends in Brazil* (London: Harvill, 1999), 3.

[40] Philip Larkin, 'The Whitsun Weddings', *Collected Poems*, ed. Anthony Thwaite (London: Faber, 2003), 92.

not occur, they might very well have occurred. The characters, too, are three-dimensional. This includes the figure of the priest, Father Patrick O'Brien, who is literate, sensitive, and humane. The poem circles around social issues but not in a fashion which encourages any kind of predictable reaction—one cannot tell where the poem is going, and it maintains its feel for surprise right up to the end.

Speaking about Ireland's 'Culture Wars', W. J. McCormack once described Irish poetry as 'incurably descriptive', a line which rather assumes that not only is there no cure in description, but there is no revelation either.[41] Durcan's poem does put its faith in description, and he explores the landscape in the spirit of Frost's remark that a poem should be 'a happy discoverer of its ends'.[42] The poem is local rather than national in its orientation, with the focus overwhelmingly on a section of Mayo, its secondary focus being the implements of electronic communication, primarily a mixture of television and radio.

In its purposeful drift, Durcan's newly constructed personality roots the poem. In this respect we might compare it with an early poem, 'The Night They Murdered Boyle Somerville' in his first collection, *O Westport in the Light of Asia Minor*. In that early poem, Durcan's encounter with a kind of everyman, representative rural couple is authoritative and compelling, but even so the method which he adopted at the time calls for an inflated description of the elderly man:

> He was a king-figure from out the islands of time,
> A short round-shouldered man with a globe of a skull
> Whose lips were the lips of an African chieftain
> Having that expression from which there is no escape,
> A gaze of the lips,
> Interrupted only by the ritual blowing of an ancient pipe.[43]

This poem attempts to place Ireland in a global relationship, but the gesture of universality seems stunted, broken off by more local priorities. As with other instances in early Durcan, the reader feels provoked, or feels at any rate that provocation is the main point, but the translation is only half-convincing.

Returning to 'Greetings to Our Friends in Brazil', a key moment arises during the broadcast of the game when the radio commentator Mícheál Ó Muircheartaig, well-known in Ireland for his extravagant verbal style, engages in one of his more poetic flights:

> . . . the ball goes to Kenneth Mortimer having a great game for Mayo
> He has a brother doing research work in the Porcupine Bank
> But now it goes to Killian Burns of Kerry
> The best accordion-playing cornerback in football today.
> We hope you're on the astra if you're in outer space.

    [41] McCormack, *The Battle of the Books*, 14.
    [42] See Cleanth Brooks, Robert Frost, Robert Penn Warren et al., *Conversations on the Craft of Poetry* (New York: Holt, Rinehart & Winston, 1961).
    [43] Durcan, *O Westport in the Light of Asia Minor*, 59.

> On my watch it says two minutes and fifty-three seconds left but
> We haven't had time to send greetings to our friends in Brazil
> Proinnsias O Murchu and Rugiero da Costa e Silva.[44]

Like a piece of 'found poetry', the ventriloquized Ó Muircheartaig appears to outdo Durcan in extravagance, a wryly manic reminder of the poet as we have sometimes known him in a poem where the movement is otherwise serene. This casual encounter of Durcan with himself, through the media of radio and television, reads like a self-emptying, out-of-body experience.

Thereafter the poet drives home through appalling weather, meeting in the process a semi-destitute woman who appears to challenge his depressed state of mind. She is initially presented in Joycean terms, though the encounter itself, with its amiably wandering conversation, is like a combination of Samuel Beckett's *All That Fall* and Frost's 'A Servant to Servants'. The poet returns to his spartan accommodation on Achill Island. As the speaker drifts off to sleep, the poem, like Joyce's short story 'The Dead', begins to dilate. Durcan begins to affirm himself by negation and his embrace of contingency leads to a kind of solidarity:

> For the first time in years
> I feel no craving:
> Not for food not for drink not for anything.
> Not for grapes.
> Not for newspaper not for book.
> Not for radio not for television not for telephone.
> I hear the tempest o'er the mountain and the sea.
> I hear the silence of the spheres.
> I see two hundred million pairs of shut eyes
> Of two hundred millions sleeping faces
> Behind two hundred million windows in the warring night.
> Only the dead are not homeless.[45]

Here, I take it the two hundred million eyes belong to the population of Brazil (or perhaps the populations of Ireland and Brazil) and that this prepares the reference to the homeless. If the problem of modern living is the one defined by Brendan Kennelly (himself mentioned in the poem), that is, to be 'at home in homelessness',[46] then this is Durcan's 'solution', however temporary, and however much in need of constant renewal. Here we might recall Fintan O'Toole's remark that Durcan's Ireland is 'a place that has become post-modern without ever becoming really modern, a place in which the global village is still a one-horse town'.[47] If such a condition is a matter of criticism, then this poem implies that it also has potential advantages, as 'Greetings to Our Friends in Brazil' makes of Mayo a global shantytown. The poem ends:

[44] Durcan, *Greetings to our Friends in Brazil*, 7–8.
[45] Ibid., 11.
[46] Kennelly, '"The Roaring Storm of Your Words"', in *Dark Fathers into Light*, 179.
[47] Fintan O'Toole, 'In the Light of Things as They Are: Paul Durcan's Ireland', in *The Kilfenora Teaboy*, 32.

I hear Father O'Brien at my side at my ear:
His exegesis of the word 'mercy'—
Its Aramaic etymology;
'Mercy is by definition exclusively divine.
Mercy is a divine not a human term.'
I feel ready to go to bed.
Let me pray:
Greetings to our friends in Brazil.[48]

---

[48] Durcan, *Greetings to our Friends in Brazil*, 12.

CHAPTER 27

DOMESTIC VIOLENCES: MEDBH McGUCKIAN AND IRISH WOMEN'S WRITING IN THE 1980s

LEONTIA FLYNN

MEDBH McGuckian published her first full-length collection of poetry, *The Flower Master*, in 1982, but her work had already appeared, and attracted attention, in pamphlets and anthologies produced by both English and Northern Irish presses. The pamphlets *Single Ladies: Sixteen Poems*, and *Portrait of Joanna*, which were produced in 1980 by, respectively, Interim Press and Ulsterman Publications, contained many poems reprinted in the later book, and were greeted as the work of a bold and original new voice. What was most striking about these debuts, along with a rich, distinctive style, was a consistent pre-occupation with traditionally feminine activities such as flower-arranging, marriage, and childbirth. It was this pervasive interest in gender that most often struck reviewers: Tim Dooley in the *TLS*, echoing a description from the poem 'Tulips', characterized the poems as embodying 'womanliness', 'an assertive quality, neither traditionally feminine, nor yet feminist in an ideologically straitened way';[1] while in *Encounter* Alan Jenkins considered McGuckian's 'erotic fluency' in relation to her theme, which he described as 'an experience of femininity and feminine activities'.[2] An emphasis was also laid on gender by Paul Muldoon in his introduction to *Single Ladies* in which he welcomed the 'talented poetess': 'I write "poetess" advisedly,' he commented, 'since Medbh McGuckian insists very firmly on her poems having been written by a woman...'.[3]

---

[1] Tim Dooley, 'Soft Cushionings', rev. of *The Flower Master* by Medbh McGuckian, *Times Literary Supplement* (29 October 1982), 1200.

[2] Alan Jenkins, 'Private and Public Languages', rev. of *The Flower Master* by Medbh McGuckian, *Encounter* LIX (5 November 1982), 57.

[3] Paul Muldoon, ed., *Single Ladies: Sixteen Poems* (Devon: Interim Press, 1980), 21. McGuckian frequently uses the description 'poetess' in her work, as in 'Ode to a Poetess' from *Venus and the Rain* (Oldcastle: Gallery, 1984).

In discussing early McGuckian as a way of thinking about women poets more generally, this might be as good a place to start as any. What does it mean for a poet in 1980 to insist that her poems are authored by a woman, or to call herself (or be called) a 'poetess'? In the second half of the twentieth century, this identification is arguably both freighted with negative associations and defiantly hard-won. From Robert Graves's famous characterization of the role of the poet as a male one—'Woman is not a poet: she is either a Muse or she is nothing'—to its corollary, the curtailment of writing by women into a separate category (the caricature of the woman writer as a sentimental dilettante, or dabbler),[4] women writers have tended to be both over- and under-identified with their gender. The American feminist poet Adrienne Rich criticized what she saw as a tendency to retreat from the restrictive associations attached to the 'poetess' into a neutral sexuality. In her essay, 'When We Dead Awaken', Rich describes the patriarchal bias in her education as a young poet which led her to confuse her desire for women poets to be men's equals with thinking they should sound *the same* as men; the sentimentality of the 'poetess' and the neutrality of the male-identified woman poet are named as twin pitfalls:

> Until recently this female anger and this furious awareness of the Man's power over her were not available materials to the female poet, who tended to write of love as the source of suffering, and to view that victimisation by love as an almost inevitable fate. Or, like Marianne Moore and Elizabeth Bishop, she kept sexuality at a measured and chiseled distance in her poems.[5]

For feminists like Rich, the corrective to this was to move 'their experiences as women' to the centre of their writing, or to attempt to discover an authentic female identity. Such a project implies the use of poetic language as a medium for the truth and often *intimacy* of female experience—and these challenges were also being taken up in the Ireland in which Medbh McGuckian began to write. Eavan Boland, a predecessor with whom McGuckian has identified, questioned, in print, the androgynous poetic practice she inherited in Dublin in the early 1960s. 'You are Irish. You are a woman,' she tells her former self in her memoir *Object Lessons*; 'Why do you keep these things at the periphery of the poem? Why do you not move them to the centre, where they belong?'[6] Such self-centring in women's poetry is usually perceived as running parallel with the Women's Movement: the Irish Women's Liberation Movement was established in 1970

---

[4] See for instance Anne Sexton's comments on women 'dabbling in poetry' in response to the question whether she had ever felt at a disadvantage as a woman poet: 'That's a very big subject. Oh terrific. Yes. Definitely... there are so many lady poets and they're almost all so bad.... There are whole clubs of women poets: its all right to be a poet if you're a woman. Therefore you can be a bad one.... Women don't strive to make anything real out of it. They just dabble in it.' Quoted in Deryn Rees-Jones, *Consorting with Angels: Essays on Modern Women Poets* (Tarset: Bloodaxe, 2005), 128.

[5] Adrienne Rich, 'When We Dead Awaken', *On Lies, Secrets and Silence: Selected Prose* (London: Virago, 1980), 168.

[6] Eavan Boland, *Object Lessons: The Life of the Woman and the Poet in Our Time* (Manchester: Carcarnet, 1995), 132.

and the Northern Ireland Women's Rights Movement in 1975. Successive victories in the liberalization of divorce laws and campaigns against pay discrimination and maternity rights (seen to culminate in Mary Robinson's election as Head of State in the Republic of Ireland in 1990) coincided, then, with questions about women in literature. In 1983 the Women's Press conducted a survey of poetry publishing, which found women were 'under-represented' in anthologies of Irish poetry. Feminist publishing houses Attic Press and Salmon Press were established in Dublin and Galway, and produced anthologies of contemporary and historical Irish women's poetry; in Belfast, the Northern Irish Women's Rights Movement published a collection of contemporary Northern Irish Women Writers entitled *The Female Line*.[7] The keynote of these feminist publications was often that of women moving from silence to subjectivity and assertive self-revelation, enshrining in their work a host of previously taboo experiences. An overview of Irish women's poetry in the 1990s summed it up thus:

> As women become more assertive about their voice, less hesitant about a literary life, more confident about their talent, a body of poetry with different emphases began to emerge. Poems about orgasm and masturbation, poems about wombs, childbirth, mastectomies, hysterectomies, anorexia created images of women not embarrassed about their bodies.[8]

Given her 'insistence that her poems are written by a woman', are McGuckian's poems part of this broader representative impulse? The 'only girl' selected for inclusion in Muldoon's *Faber Book of Contemporary Irish Poetry* of 1986, and the only high-profile woman among the generation of Northern Irish poets (Ciaran Carson, Paul Muldoon, Frank Ormsby), who in turn followed poetically strong forefathers (Seamus Heaney, Michael Longley, Derek Mahon), McGuckian nevertheless clearly rejects the poetically 'sexless' voice. Indeed, her preliminary pamphlets suggest, in their very titles, a concern with female authorship ('Portraits') of female subjects ('Joanna', 'Single Ladies'). Her first readers' sense of her 'womanliness' as facilitating 'a hitherto unrepresented view of experience' suggests, then, that she has overcome the problem of creating a female definition for the poet by taking recourse to female identity and experience in the way also advocated by her feminist contemporaries, whatever reservations critics might have had about their 'ideologically straitened' outlook.

This is one way to approach *The Flower Master*, and perhaps in particular those poems which take sexuality as their subject. Indeed several of the poems here might seem to deal with the taboo subject matters of the woman moving her body to 'the centre' of

[7] Ruth Hooley, ed., *The Female Line: Northern Irish Women Writers* (Belfast: Northern Ireland Women's Rights Movement, 1985). See also A. A. Kelly, ed., *Pillars of the House: An Anthology of Verse by Irish Women from 1690 to the Present* (Dublin: Wolfhound, 1987), as well as Ailbhe Smyth, ed., *Wildish Things: An Anthology of New Irish Women's Writing* (Dublin: Attic Press, 1989). The findings of the Women's Press are discussed in Dennis J. Hannon and Nancy Means Wright, 'Irish Women Poets: Breaking the Silence', *The Canadian Journal of Irish Studies* 16 (1990), 57–65.

[8] Patricia Boyle Haberstroh, *Women Creating Women: Contemporary Irish Women Poets* (Dublin: Attic Press; Syracuse, NY: Syracuse University Press, 1996), 23.

poetry. The original edition of the collection opens, for instance, with the poem 'That Year', followed by 'Tulips', 'Problem Girl', and 'The Chain Sleeper':

> That Year
>
> That Year it was something to do with your hands:
> To play about with rings, to harness rhythm
> In staging bleach or henna on the hair,
> Or shackling, unshackling the breasts.
>
> I remembered as a child the red kite
> Lost forever over our heads, the white ball
> A pinprick on the tide, and studied
> The leaf-patterned linoleum, the elaborate
>
> Stitches on my pleated bodice.
> It was like a bee's sting, or a bullet
> Left in me, this mark, this sticking pins in dolls,
> Listening for the red and white
>
> Particles of time to trickle slow, like a wet nurse
> Feeding nonchalantly someone else's child.
> I wanted curtainings, and cushionings;
> The grass is no bed after dark.[9]

'That Year', it seems safe to say, is the year marked by the onset of menstruation. This is a sexual marking which is 'read' back into prepubescence and childhood, and forward, through imagery of further key moments in adult female sexuality. That is, the red and white (bleach and henna) of adolescent awkwardness both look back to the lost innocence of childhood (red kite, white ball), and menarche or expectation of menarche (the trickling 'red and white particles of time') is compared to lactation (a wet nurse breastfeeding). The child's sense of sexual wounding is like 'sticking pins in dolls', which, as with the stitches on her pleated bodice (suggesting a girlish dress, domestic needlework, and caesarean stitches), evokes a combination of girlhood, future maternity, and powerful (voodoo-like) female ritual. The poem ends with curtainings and cushionings and the reference to 'bed', which again are suggestive of sex, 'feminine' soft furnishings, and (curtained) childbirth. 'That Year' could therefore be interpreted as dealing with a whole range of specifically female experiences, rooted in biology and all shrouded in a sense of Nature's powerful mysteriousness. Notably, in the revised edition of *The Flower Master* from 1993 the poem is renamed 'Eavesdropper', and this title makes its concerns strangely both more and less elusive.[10] Eavesdropper now suggests (as well as someone listening in) 'Eve' and the 'drop' into the fallen world of fertility and childbearing brought about by her transgression. On a rather less elevated note, however, an 'eavesdropper' is also (in translation, as it were) someone who has 'fallen off the roof', from the eaves. And as anyone who has read *Lolita* might remember (Humbert Humbert speculates of Lolita:

---

[9] Medbh McGuckian, *The Flower Master* (Oxford: Oxford University Press, 1982), 9.
[10] Medbh McGuckian, *The Flower Master and Other Poems* (Oldcastle: Gallery, 1993), 15. The final line here reads: 'The grass is an eavesdropper's bed'.

'Has she already been initiated by mother nature to the Mystery of the Menarche? Bloated feeling. The curse of the Irish. Falling from the roof. Grandma is visiting…'),[11] 'falling off the roof' is, again, slang for menstruation.

In this vein, Thomas Docherty has written that both 'That Year' and 'Tulips' are 'pubescent initiations'. Euphemistic as 'That Year' is, 'Tulips' is, by a wide margin, the more oblique poem, but Docherty insists that here too we will detect the note of sexual initiation if we listen for it. The first stanza organizes itself around the differences in shape between flowers: the open, receptive bell of the daffodil, and the closed tulip which thwarts the (life-bringing) rain:

> Touching the tulips was a shyness
> I had had for a long time – such
> Defensive mechanisms to frustrate the rain
> That shakes into the sherry-glass
> Of the daffodil, though scarcely
> Love's young dream: such present-mindedness
> To double-lock in tiers as whistle-tight,
> Or catch up on sleep with cantilevered
> Palms cupping elbows. It's their independence
> Tempts them to this grocery of soul.[12]

The second part of the poem appears to take off in the direction prompted by the description of the tulips as 'independent' (and, metaphorically, childless), for now they are 'governesses' who are 'easily/Carried away' and receive their comeuppance. In the sun, the tulips enact 'ballets of revenge' and, in a line omitted from the revised version of the poem (sacrificed to McGuckian's growing obliquity), 'are sacrificed to plot'. Ultimately, then, exposure to the sun proves more damaging than the fertilizing rain. The tulips' 'faces' are:

> Lifted many times to the artistry of light –
> Its lovelessness a deeper sort
> Of illness than the womanliness
> Of tulips with their bee-dark hearts.[13]

Leaving aside, for a moment, this business with governesses, the sexual transgression here lies in the *sound* (especially if said with an American accent) as well as the shape of tulips. Docherty writes:

On the one hand, touching the tulips might suggest an obvious touching of the phallus; but on the other, it also suggests the woman touching her own lips, both mouth and vagina. The poem thus becomes one of covert masturbation, a 'womanliness of tulips'.[14]

[11] Vladimir Nabokov, *Lolita* [1955] (London: Penguin, 1995), 74.

[12] McGuckian, *The Flower Master* (1982), 10.

[13] Ibid.

[14] Thomas Docherty, 'Initiations, Tempers, Seductions: Postmodern McGuckian', *The Chosen Ground: Essays on the Contemporary Poetry of Northern Ireland*, ed. Neil Corcoran (Bridgend: Seren, 1992), 196–7.

To see 'Tulips' as a poem of masturbation in fact links it to later work in *The Flower Master*, such as 'Gentians' and 'The Orchid House' (part I and II of 'The Orchid House' in the revised edition), which appear to draw analogies between female anatomy and flowers (genitals/gentians), and to question an unreproductive female sexuality. The 'Gentians', indeed, are almost graphically sexual: 'all their pleats/And tucks as though they had something precious/Deep inside, the beard of camel-hair/In the throat.' Nevertheless, 'No insects/Visit them, nor do their ovaries swell', and 'They tease like sullen spinsters'.[15] This interpretation also links 'Tulips' with the sequence of poems, in both versions of *The Flower Master*, which focus on moody, masturbatory, or adolescent girls. The 'Problem Girl', in the poem of the same name, is 'a sitter out in a darkened room', and 'The Chain Sleeper' 'sleeps and sleeps', wears 'fussy perfume', and dreams of herself as a 'midnight goddess'. Ultimately, these are 'single ladies' about whose fates McGuckian seems pessimistic:

> Such semi-precious stones the longshore whittles.
> They lie in split-level waste tips, banding in volcanoes,
> Like potatoes; their careers are cut and dried,
> For costume jewellery, for other people's keeping.[16]

The independence of adolescence—like masturbation, characterized by solitude and 'sterile' sexual activity, and like the independence of tulip-governesses—is short lived here. There is even a note of Adrienne Rich's 'female anger' and 'furious awareness of the Man's power' over these 'semi-precious' lives. They are destined for marriage or sexual exploitation: for 'other people's keeping'.

Although the revised edition of *The Flower Master* omits 'Problem Girl' and 'The Chain Sleeper', in fact the structure of the new *Flower Master and Other Poems* intensifies the sense that these poems seek to chart the trajectory of 'a woman's experience of life'. In this collection the reader now encounters the rather more subtle moody, menstrual problem girls of 'Smoke', 'Faith', 'Spring', and 'The "Singer"', and a chronological reading of the poems finds the theme of pubescence gives way to heterosexual union and maternity. As with the flower allegories of 'Tulips' and 'Gentians', arguably this striking organization of the work finds 'mature female sexuality', and the voice of the poet, associated with pregnancy and childbirth or married maternity. At the opening of the revised collection, then, the reader encounters a young speaker whose desires (and line endings) are as volatile as the 'smoke' she describes: 'I am unable even/To contain myself, I run/Till the fawn smoke settles on the earth'.[17] In 'Faith' and 'Spring', other ambiguous epiphanies are experienced by a girl in the female/domestic environment of the family: she burns the 'starry litter' of her grandmother's sloughed-off skin in 'Faith', and—as mysteriously—rises from her sister's bed at night in 'Spring':

---

[15] McGuckian, *The Flower Master* (1982), 25.
[16] Ibid., 11, 12.
[17] McGuckian, The *Flower Master and Other Poems* (1993), 11.

> The curtains slit at my hand,
> My breathing marbled the pane:
> There was my face in the window,
> Frosted, so hard to see through.[18]

'Aunts', in which the speaker participates voyeuristically in her young aunts' romantic courtships, is also echoed thematically by 'The "Singer"', which registers adolescent discontentedness (or masturbatory 'disconnectedness'), and impatience for sexual experience. Here, the adolescent girl sits at the mother's old sewing machine, a symbol of adult, domestic 'womanliness', which of course the speaker is unable to operate:

> In the dark I drew the curtains
> On young couples stopping in the entry,
> Heading home. There were nights
> I sent the disconnected wheel
> Spinning madly round and round
> Till the empty bobbin rattled in its case.[19]

These poems are among the most lucid that Medbh McGuckian has ever written, and an awareness of the subtle narrative progression of the book also allows the reader to use them to unlock the more difficult work here. Via 'The Long Engagement', the 'disconnected' girl can be seen to develop into a speaker engaged in sexual relationships ('Lychees', 'The Hollywood Bed'), and one impatient for 'my power as a bride' ('The Soil Map').[20] These are 'powers' which include the 'curtainings and cushionings' of both domestic arrangement and, in 'The Flitting', rearrangement, and childbearing. Thus, after the 'childless house' of 'Your House', with its sterile lovemaking ('pickled in silence'), and what might be Eve, again, addressing her offspring *in utero* in 'The Sunbench' ('This is not the hardness of a single night,/A rib that I could clearly do without. It is/The room where you have eaten daily...'), events move from the contemplation of maternity to conception and birth.[21] Indeed, so richly interwoven is the imagery of *The Flower Master*, that a 'trout', symbol of fertility in 'Gateposts', makes a glimpsed reappearance at the end of the collection's title poem. This is the 'special guest' summoned 'to our low doorway,/Our fontanelle, the trout's dimpled feet'.[22] As with much of what is veiled or coded in McGuckian's first collection concerning women's regenerative capacities, some ambivalence is registered alongside descriptions of intense lyrical beauty, and in the later poems the reader may sense that with the 'power of a bride' comes a 'power-cut'. In 'Power-Cut', which is structured around images of watery disintegration, the baby is safe in its 'lobster-pot pen', the domestic speaker's sponge, and perhaps sense of self, dissolves like 'A permanent wave gone west' as (widowed) old age is anticipated in the image of lumpy candle wax like a 'dowager's hump'.[23]

[18] Ibid., 12, 13.
[19] Ibid., 14.
[20] McGuckian, The *Flower Master* (1982), 15, 16, 17, 29–30.
[21] Ibid., 32.
[22] Ibid., 35.
[23] Ibid., 47.

Here is another of those girlish lives which has been entrusted to 'other peoples' keeping'. In particular, the final poem of McGuckian's collection, 'The Mast Year', completes the journey which was anticipated by 'That Year', and ends *The Flower Master* with a haunting and mysterious sense of specifically maternal power and powerlessness. Mast is the fruit of forest trees, and it brings the reproductive trees (those trees 'ever eager/to populate new ground') not only their 'Lammas Growth' (Lammas is a harvest festival), but also—with an echo of Larkin's 'Afternoons', in which the young mothers' 'beauty has thickened'—'The thickening of their dreams'.[24]

To summarize *The Flower Master* in this way suggests that the work McGuckian has undertaken as a 'poetess' is indeed the exploration of female experience in its many phases, which might be summed up as the transition from 'Single Ladies' to 'Married Mothers'. However euphemistically the poems guard their sexual secrets, the *intimate truths* of masturbation, female heterosexuality, and maternity are contained within the very form of the work. The progression from problem girl to bride and mother, then, is not only mimetic of a female cycle in the 'fallen world' effected by Eve, but it self-consciously marks McGuckian's departure from a patriarchal poetic tradition. The departure is also from the model of the solitary, male-identified poet described by Adrienne Rich—that of 'Miss' Moore or Miss Bishop who 'kept sexuality at a measured and chiseled distance in [their] poems'. Adolescent girls, after all, are not the only 'single ladies' here. Among the 'sullen spinsters', fossils, and unreproductive plants which suggest McGuckian's preoccupation with sterility, it is possible to see figures for her poetic predecessors. 'Mr McGregor's Garden', for instance, raises the spectre of Beatrix Potter (lady author as genteel unmarried recluse), while in 'Tulips', Thomas Docherty has detected a reference to Henry James's novella 'The Turn of the Screw', an 'ambiguous tale of frustrated sexuality and of a young woman's relations with a "master"'.[25] Readers, however, may think more readily of the famous 'governesses' of Victorian literature: both the heroines who worked to support themselves, yet were so often 'carried away' and 'sacrificed to the plot' of a traditional love story (like Jane Eyre), and also the independent 'Single lady' authors of these works, who (like Charlotte Bronte) were governesses themselves. 'Tulips' is also the title of a well-known poem from 1961 by Sylvia Plath, who herself had something of a horror of 'barren women'. In it the 'little smiling hooks' of the speaker's husband and children weigh against the contrary pull of isolated (sexless and death-bound) artistic creation:

> I watched my teaset, my bureaus of linen, my books
> Sink out of sight, and the water went over my head.
> I am a nun now, I have never been so pure.[26]

Since a further definition of 'tulip' is, as Docherty also notes, 'a showy person: one greatly admired',[27] it is possible to draw all these threads together into a reading of both 'Tulips'

[24] Ibid., 51.
[25] Docherty, 'Initiations', 195.
[26] Sylvia Plath, *Collected Poems*, ed. Ted Hughes (London: Faber, 1981), 161.
[27] Docherty, 'Initiations', 196.

and *The Flower Master* in terms of the definition of 'the poetess' with which McGuckian is engaging. Women who sell their soul (McGuckian condenses this to 'grocery of soul') by publishing are in danger of being 'sacrificed to plot[s]', either of their own making, of literary canon-formation—or even the continuing 'narrative' of the generations, through childlessness or suicide. McGuckian's poetry, while feminist in its awareness of a specifically female line in writing, also gestures to a traditional community of women in the form of aunts, grandmothers, and widows.[28] As such, the poet rejects solitary, disconnected figures in favour of a speaker whose relation to others, as mother, lover, and wife (symbolized in 'Tulips' by the receptive 'sherry-glass/Of the daffodil'), can be accommodated, rather radically, into her poetry.

The novelty of McGuckian's debut pamphlets and first volume, then, is the result of her determination to re-gender the role of the poet in a way which dovetails with contemporary feminist objectives. From masturbation to married relations and maternal loneliness, her themes specifically relate to women. The domestic realm of *The Flower Master* is veiled in a dense, romantic language, but is still recognizably there: to redistribute the emphasis of Alan Jenkins's review, *beneath* that 'erotic fluency' is 'an *experience* of femininity and feminine activities'. It could even be said that, however obliquely, McGuckian has moved her own autobiographical experience to the centre of the poem. The poet married in 1977 and gave birth to her first son in 1980. It was about this time, as Michael Allen records, that 'she was writing a poem a day'.[29] Her creative output clearly coinciding with motherhood, it is unsurprising that the tropes of singleness and dependence should come to the fore, or that with coming to maturity as an artist and woman, the poet should reflect on the frustrations of her adolescence. Indeed, the poet herself has described her work in terms which encourage such impressions. She has specifically said that she feels herself to be going 'against the traditional childless woman-artist grain',[30] and many of the earliest readings of McGuckian's work regarded the mysterious truths enshrined there as directly relating to her own private life. Patricia Boyle Haberstroh, for instance, asserts that the poetry is 'decidedly autobiographical'; as a young wife and mother, it is concerned with 'modelling a woman's struggle to balance dependence and independence, to be connected to others but maintain a course of her own'.[31] As in so many female narratives of progressive enlightenment in the 1980s, in Ireland as elsewhere, through the beautifully crafted organization of the volume the 'single lady' represented and finally outgrown is seen to be McGuckian herself.

* * *

[28] McGuckian, *The Flower Master and Other Poems* (1993) is dedicated 'for my mother without my father', which suggests the poet's mother prior to marriage and without offspring, as well as (as she was by the time of this revised edition) widowed.

[29] Michel Allen, 'The Poetry of Medbh McGuckian', *Contemporary Irish Poetry: A Collection of Critical Essays*, ed. Elmer Andrews (London: Macmillan, 1992), 286.

[30] Kathleen McCracken, 'Interview with Medbh McGuckian', *Writing Irish: Selected Interviews with Irish Writers from The Irish Literary Supplement*, ed. James P. Myers (New York: Syracuse, 1999), 165.

[31] Haberstroh, *Women Creating Women*, 138.

Without *entirely* negating the above reading of Medbh McGuckian's first collection, I want now to suggest that it is inadequate. It is inadequate, first, to the experience of reading these poems—from which few readers will discern anything so representative or personal as the above account suggests; and it is inadequate in a way that might prompt us to look again at the definitions of the 'poetess' with which we began. Even those readers who might wish to discover a straightforward validation of women's experience admit that a full understanding of such experience is always just beyond our reach in McGuckian's early work. Peggy O'Brien writes that at the heart of these poems is a 'content, often erotic, that encompasses what is nearly unsayable', and that they hoard 'knowledge that belongs exclusively to the poet's private life beyond the margins of the poem'[32]—which in fact leaves such 'unsayable content' largely a matter of speculation. The difficulty of McGuckian's poetry, from the very outset, means that often we are not sure that truths from her private life, or about women's experience in general, *are* what's being hinted at—and in fact another impulse throughout *The Flower Master* runs contrary to 'truth' altogether. That is, not only do the poems thematize the withholding of sense (the wariness of 'getting carried away' by exposure in 'Tulips') but rather (and this is noted less often by her readers) they also exhibit an interest in falsehood, fiction, and performance. One of the quietest and most autobiographical poems in the revised edition, 'Aunts' seems to make this very point. In it, the young speaker casts herself in the role of truth-teller, puncturing her young aunts' romantic constructions of themselves:

> My aunts jived their way
> Through the '50s to my teens.
> They lay till noon and called me up
> To listen for their lovers at the gate,
> And paid me for the colour of their eyes –
> 'Grey', I said, or 'Brown', when they wanted
> Blue or hazel, in their giggling,
> Sleeping-together dreams.[33]

Indifferent to the more prosaic, and implicitly *realistic,* 'grey' or 'brown' of their (or possibly their lovers') eyes, the aunts go about continuing with their make-up, which is also a form of romantic make-believe: 'I watched them shading in their lips/From sugar pink to coral, from mulberry to rose'. The poem then concludes with the revelation to the young girl of her aunts without their feminine paraphernalia: naked, un-made up, dishevelled—and rather hairy:

> Once out of the blue
> I caught them dancing on the bed,
> With their undergrowth of hazel,
> And their make-up sweated through.

---

[32] Peggy O'Brien, 'Reading Medbh McGuckian: Admiring What We Cannot Understand', *Colby Quarterly* 28:4 (1992), 239, 244.

[33] McGuckian, *The Flower Master and Other Poems* (1993), 22.

If this were a poem in which the falsehoods or omissions of female experience were redressed by the telling of intimate truths and the revelation of authentic identities, as for instance in Eavan Boland's *In Her Own Image* (1980), the disclosure of these women's bodies would operate as a 'moment of truth' for the young speaker. Instead in 'Aunts' the 'sweated-through' make-up continues to be linked with the layer of fantasy the speaker has tried to puncture: for the words 'blue' and 'hazel' which are used to describe their naked dancing are words associated with the aunts' romantic 'made-up' versions of themselves. Just as the slipperiness of language ('hazel', for instance, is both a colour and a shrub) allows for a magical blurring of fact and fiction, so McGuckian's poem suggests that it is not in the business of telling truth and, furthermore, that what poses as 'the naked truth' is never quite as straightforward as it seems.

The message of 'Aunts' might also be that is a mistake for women (and women writers) to try to cast off their false identities *as* women, and embrace the real versions of themselves. As Patricia Waugh puts it:

> There can be no simple legitimation for feminists in throwing off 'false consciousness' and revealing a true but 'deeply' buried female self. Indeed, to embrace the essentialism of this notion of 'difference' is to come dangerously close to reproducing that very patriarchal construction of gender which feminists have sought to contest.[34]

Who, after all, gets to say where this authenticity lies? The implicit sense in 'Aunts' that what is invented or 'made-up' might be as *real* as that which it conceals, is reinforced elsewhere in *The Flower Master* through McGuckian's interest in theatre and stagecraft. In 'That Year' ('Eavesdropper') the adolescent girl *stages* 'bleach and henna and the hair'. Heterosexual devotion and rivalry is figured as taking place, dramatically, in 'The Hollywood Bed'. Here though marriage and domesticity are represented by a 'narrowing' into increasingly private locations ('the house, the room, the bed'), such privacy doesn't let us see behind the poses being struck on the glamorous 'stage' of the bed: 'You adopt/Your mask...I lie crosswise,/Imperial as a favoured only child'.[35] Even the most intimate of female experiences is somehow *acted*. A poem omitted from the revised edition of *The Flower Master* was in fact entitled 'The Theatre'. 'I throw the window romantically open', claims the speaker, 'Yours is the readership/Of the rough places where I make/My sweet refusals of you, your/Natural violence',[36] and that a concept such as 'natural violence' should be articulated in such a melodramatic, artificial way indicates the ambiguous, ironized place occupied by 'the natural' in *The Flower Master*.

The speakers of McGuckian's poems in this collection, therefore, are rarely straightforwardly *themselves* so much as playing roles or making-up. Even in the apparently autobiographical adolescent poems, what we are offered is never a clear mirror on to female life. Look again at 'Spring', for instance. The final lines of the poem—'There was

[34] Patricia Waugh, 'Modernism, Postmodernism, Gender', *Practising Postmodernism, Reading Modernism* (London: Routledge, 1993), 119, 120.
[35] McGuckian, *The Flower Master* (1982), 17.
[36] Ibid., 46.

my face in the window,/Frosted, so hard to see through'[37]—suggest that the speaker's face, as well as the window, is somehow opaque, inscrutable. This might stand as a metaphor for the failure of transparency that occurs elsewhere here. Rather than artistic self-revelation, what we get throughout *The Flower Master* is reminiscent of John Ashbery's experience in 'Self-Portrait in a Convex Mirror': 'This otherness, this/"Not-being-us" is all there is to look at/In the mirror...';[38] or the discovery, as feminist theorist Judith Butler writes, that 'Language is not an exterior medium or instrument into which I pour a self and from which I glean a reflection of that self.'[39] Like her aunts', the authentic face of the poet/speaker is unavailable, both to herself and her readers.

This leads us back to the issue of how McGuckian defines or redefines the 'poetess'. To use the imagery of 'The "Singer"' (and of course 'singer' could be another word for poet or 'poetess'),[40] McGuckian's disconnected language often spins 'madly round and round' in *The Flower Master*, while something 'empty' rattles inside—a failure of self-presence which runs contrary to any impulse to 'move herself to centre of the poem'. However much one current in *The Flower Master* carries us towards the representation of a personal female history, another pulls against it by hinting at the artificial nature of the personal, openly flaunting the poet's complicity with the posed and stereotyped. For it is precisely *stereotyped* identities that are often at stake as the speakers investigate their 'experience of femininity and feminine experience'. While several of the early poems in *The Flower Master* invite an autobiographical reading, however sketchily we may construct it, it seems to me that others are overtly over-the-top fictions or camp dramas. 'The Dowry Murder', 'The Aphrodisiac', and 'Next Day Hill', in particular signal flagrantly artificial constructions of femininity rather than the private voice of the poet: a glamorous cast of ingénues, brides, and adulteresses. The heroine of 'The Aphrodisiac', for instance, banishes her lover 'to his estates', only to find that 'her books' are as:

> ...frumpish
> As the last year's gambling game, when she
> Would dress in pink taffeta, and drive
> A blue phaeton, or in blue, and drive
> A pink one, with her black hair supported
> By a diamond comb...[41]

The title here, as well as the references to the 'between-maid', a 'secret staircase', and taking to 'rouge again' allude to the conventions of romantic *fiction*: they suggest not only an evasion of subjective experience, but also, one notes, of a specifically *Irish* literary canon (indeed none of McGuckian's single ladies is particularly Irish). 'The Dowry Murder' similarly flags its own complicity in the 'made up'. This poem, with its Romance title, begins like a steamy novelette:

---

[37] McGuckian, *The Flower Master and Other Poems* (1993), 13.
[38] John Ashbery, *Selected Poems* [1986] (London: Penguin, 1994), 202.
[39] Judith Butler, *Gender Trouble: Feminism and the Subversion of Identity* (New York and London: Routledge, 1990), 143.
[40] Eavan Boland, in fact, has a poem about female oral poets in Ireland called 'The Singers'.
[41] McGuckian, *The Flower Master* (1982), 45.

> The danger of biscuit-coloured silk
> Is how it just reveals you, the chill
> Of the balloon material swaying
> In the wind that is not there…[42]

In fact, 'The Dowry Murder' appears to allude to the kind of lowbrow fiction in which such sentiments might appear: 'my railway novel ends/With the bride's sari catching fire/While cooking succotash…'. This kind of second-hand language and elliptical drama can be found everywhere in McGuckian's first collection. Indeed these elevated tones, rather than the quieter, more personal poems like 'That Year', 'Eavesdropper', or 'Spring', will be more familiar to McGuckian's readers, and are more characteristic of the dense style she has subsequently developed.[43]

In *The Flower Master*, then, the overtly 'made up' or fictional weighs against the 'natural' or 'intimate' in a way which prevents the elision of political representation (giving voice to women, implicitly with reference to their 'reality') with artistic representation. Readers, indeed, have been divided on this very issue of McGuckian's self-conscious *literariness*. More than one reviewer has detected a note of parody in McGuckian's heightened style: Alan Jenkins thought that her 'softening and rounding-out of images are too easily caricatured as "conventionally" feminine, and are sometimes disturbingly close to caricature already. Perhaps intentionally so.'[44] Another denounced the poet's refusal to report what's '*really* real, *really* happening', as 'fakery'—in fact, 'pseudo-womanliness'.[45] Yet such 'fakery' suggests something about where McGuckian positioned herself among her literary and feminist contemporaries. For what the excessive and camp voice in *The Flower Master* most resembles is the older voice of the 'poetess' described by Adrienne Rich—the female poet, 'who tended to write of love as the source of suffering…'—or the patriarchal construction of female authorship described by Eavan Boland: the woman writer as 'sentimental confessional dilettante'.[46] That McGuckian does not seek to abolish these definitions but rather writes from *within* this cultural script, animating the stereotype, can perhaps most clearly be seen by looking at one final poem, 'The Sofa':

> Do not be angry if I tell you
> Your letter stayed unopened on my table
> For several days. If you were friend enough

[42] Ibid., 38.
[43] Work on McGuckian's intertextuality by Shane Alcobia-Murphy suggests that a text about Madame de Pompadour may be behind 'The Aphrodisiac', while 'The Sun Trap' is based on McGuckian's early love letters, and 'The Heiress' is based on Antonia Fraser's *Mary Queen of Scots*. See Shane Alcobia Murphy, *Sympathetic Ink: Intertextual Relations in Northern Irish Poetry* (Liverpool: Liverpool University Press, 2006), and *Governing the Tongue in Northern Ireland: The Place of Art/The Art of Place* (Cambridge: Cambridge Scholars Publishing, 2008).
[44] Alan Jenkins, 'Private and Public Languages', 58.
[45] Patrick Williams. 'Save that Tree', rev. of *On Ballycastle Beach* by Medbh McGuckian, in *Honest Ulsterman* 86 (Spring/Summer 1989), 49, 50, 52.
[46] Boland quoted in Dennis J. Hannon and Nancy Means Wright, 'Irish Women Poets: Breaking the Silence', 58.

> To believe me, I was about to start writing
> At any moment; my mind was savagely made up,
> Like a serious sofa moved
> Under a north window. My heart, alas
> Is not the calmest of places...[47]

The opening of 'The Sofa' immediately suggests the literary style of the 'poetess'. There are the mannered, genteel declarations: 'Do not be angry', 'If you were friend enough...', 'alas'. That the persona occupies a space between belle-lettres and high art can also be detected in the ambiguity surrounding the occupation taking place: the 'I' was 'about to start writing' a letter, it seems, rather than a poem, yet the sofa is positioned in such a way (by a north window) as to produce the constant light needed by artists. The emotionalism, the 'savagely made up' mind, and uncalm heart, are also those of the delirious lady-author, and these are reinforced, in the second stanza, as the 'speaker' declares '...my books seem real enough to me/My disasters, my surrenders, all my loss...'. These sentiments are the stuff of stormy romance; as 'real' as the hysterical poetess's books. But poetry does, at this point, make an appearance:

> Since I was child enough to forget
> That you loathe poetry, you ask for some
> About nature, greenery, insects, and, of course,
>
> The sun – surely that would be to open
> An already open window? To celebrate
> The impudence of flowers?

After rejecting a model of poetry curiously similar to McGuckian's own 'flower mastery', the persona or voice of 'The Sofa' in fact explicitly offers something closer to the poetess's *metier*: erotic romance, doomed love, suffering victimhood:

> If I could
> Interest you instead in his large, gentle stares,
> How his soft shirt is the inside of pleasure
> To me, why I must wear white for him,
> Imagine he no longer trembles
>
> When I approach, no longer buys me
> Flowers for my name day...

'The Sofa' ends with a dissolution of the 'I' into domestic chaos, and the final lines, again, blur the distinction between domestic 'curtainings' and the private arena as a 'stage' for performed action. They also, self-consciously, confirm the speaking subject here as provisional or constructed, by 'books':

> Somewhere
> A curtain rising wonders where I am,
> My books sleep, pretending to forget me.

---

[47] McGuckian, *The Flower Master* (1982), 19.

The poem, then, is perhaps the most explicit in the collection in refusing to express *the reality of* female identity as a corrective to false identities, in favour of adopting the mannered voice of a pre-existing construct of the 'lady author'.[48]

This second emphasis I have just laid on the poems of *The Flower Master* now suggests that the single ladies and settled matrons of the collection are less interesting as autobiographical manifestations of the poet's private experience than as ironic deployments of the caricatures into which women writers have too easily been allowed to fall: sullen spinsters, writers of railway novels, gothic tulip-governesses. This, ultimately, seems to me to be what is witty and challenging about McGuckian's debut collection. While she may insist that her poems 'have been written by a woman', this 'woman' in question often seems as much a series of *references* to other types of female identity and women writers as her own subjectively grounded voice. Furthermore, in their theatricality and fictionality, the poems hint that this is actually how such identities are produced in the first place. The feminine 'I' in McGuckian's poems is a product of the drama and narrative that surround it—it is an *effect*. Likewise, the often over-the-top performance of the feminine in McGuckian's work, with all its details of dressing-up, goes some way to suggesting to the reader the level of impersonation and performance involved in 'the real thing'.

This kind of mimicry and referentiality aligns McGuckian's first collection with a poststructuralist feminist position: the poems suggest, as Thomas Docherty puts it, the 'politics of her postmodern questioning of the real',[49] but a feminist point remains. Even in a collection of poems apparently structured by and dealing with 'the facts of a woman's life', the poet suggests, instead of a window onto a non-patriarchal, private female world, we find prior *cultural* representations of femininity. For some readers, again, this lack of authenticity may merely be depressing. Yet a justification of Medbh McGuckian's hesitancy about truth-telling is perhaps found in the fate of some of her contemporaries. In her study of the subject, Clair Wills has argued that women poets are indeed already 'inhabited by meanings', but continues:

> ...once a 'privatisation' of the myths of Mother Ireland...is defined as an attempt to undermine the existing stereotype of Irish femininity by the 'truths' of women's personal experience (in other words, poetry of the expressive voice), it becomes all too easy to fault them for simply creating new stereotypes.[50]

Indeed, in a way, Adrienne Rich's comments at the beginning of this essay demonstrate the very pervasiveness of such 'stereotypes'. Making her point about the taboo nature of poets' status as women, Rich in turn raises female spectres—the dilettante, and, in

---

[48] 'Next Day Hill' (*The Flower Master*, 42–3) seems another example of a poem getting 'carried away', like McGuckian's 'Tulips', by the poetess's idiom. Here, a man is 'turned down/Forever by the only girl', and 'soaks himself in the comfort/Of her name till a kind of mist/Covers the sky that's all exposed,/A gallant white...'. Again, 'mist', 'gallant', an 'exposed sky' all feel like features of a Romance writer's style.

[49] Thomas Docherty, 'Initiations', 194.

[50] Clair Wills, *Improprieties: Politics and Sexuality in Northern Irish Poetry* (Oxford: Oxford University Press, 1993), 54.

relation to Moore and Bishop, the frigid lady author—which are as unhelpful as those she criticizes. Yet, on the other hand, the image of the woman poet writing 'poems about orgasm and masturbation, poems about wombs, childbirth, mastectomies, hysterectomies and anorexia', runs the risk of perpetuating the idea that sex, babies, and the body are women's proper subject matter. Medbh McGuckian's early work can be seen to represent the attraction of Irish women writers in the 1980s to feminist energies, self-witnessing, and the creation of new poetic myths. At the same time, her work registers a general hesitancy about the confinement of their poetry to a separate category this seems to entail. What would the basis of this category be, her poems ask, in history, in terms of *style* or essential identity—when one person's 'womanliness' so easily becomes another's 'pseudo-womanliness'? Indeed these are questions which have not fully been answered to this day.

McGuckian may have sought to evade the question of *what a woman poet is* by drawing attention to the artificiality of her ladies' identities, but one notes, finally, that she herself has not entirely escaped the dangers of being 'sacrificed to plot'. In her book *Consorting with Angels: Essays on Modern Women Poets*, Deryn Rees-Jones echoes Germaine Greer's assertion that ultimately women poets need to see themselves as 'a woman poet, not the woman poet'.[51] Yet for all its ironies, *The Flower Master* has often been read back towards a fairly traditional identity politics. One reader of 'The Sofa', in fact, manages to construct a 'plot' containing a 'wife' who is praised for expressing 'her emotional reality, emotional maturity—the truth...'.[52] Likewise McGuckian has sometimes been received as *the* rather than *a* woman poet, with a popular belief holding (not entirely unencouraged by McGuckian herself) that the poet's linguistic difficulty represents the mystical channelling of deep reserves of femininity.[53] It is almost as though, when she asks us in 'The Sofa', 'If I could/Interest you instead in his large, gentle stares...', we have bought both the romantic wares on offer, and the figure of poetess selling them. At any rate, oblique as her treatment of domesticity and female experience is, *The Flower Master* remains by far the most accessible of McGuckian's collections: retreating behind more widely 'quoted' material and complicated poetic manoeuvres, the poet has never again exposed even so fleeting a glimpse of nakedness.

[51] Greer, quoted in Rees-Jones, *Consorting with Angels*, 26.

[52] Alexander G. Gonzalez, 'Celebrating the Richness of Medbh McGuckian's Poetry: Close Analysis of Six Poems from *The Flower Master*', in *Contemporary Irish Women Poets: Some Male Perspectives*, ed. Gonzalez (Westport, Connecticut; London: Greenwood Press, 1999), 54.

[53] McGuckian has said, for instance, '[m]y work is usually regarded as esoteric or exotic, but only because its territory is the feminine subconscious or semi-conscious, which many men will or do not recognise and many women will or cannot admit'. See *Contemporary Poets*, ed. Tracey Chevalier, 5th ed. (London and Chicago: St James Press, 1991), 629. It is difficult to know in what spirit to take these remarks.

PART VIII

....

CULTURAL
LANDSCAPES

....

CHAPTER 28

CATHOLIC ART AND CULTURE: CLARKE TO HEANEY

GAIL McCONNELL

I

Religious aesthetics in general, and Catholic art and culture in particular, are engaging subjects that point in various directions. They raise questions about aspects of literature and theology that merit critical attention: What is the nature and constitution of religious aesthetics? What is the utility and value of treating theology in Irish literary criticism? Do Catholic artists necessarily make Catholic art? Does 'Catholic' function only as cultural or sociopolitical signifier, or is it inclusive also of theology? Is it necessary or possible for critical investigations to distinguish between orthodoxy and heterodoxy; between doctrinal religion and personal belief (or non-belief)? What is the relationship of orthodoxy and heterodoxy to poetic practice and poetic forms? If theologies are formed, written, and made, might we conceive of poetic form as a displaced theology?

It is beyond the scope of this essay to answer adequately these questions, but in useful ways they frame, inform, and frustrate what follows. This essay approaches Catholic art and culture through the poetry of Austin Clarke, Patrick Kavanagh, and Seamus Heaney: three poets raised in the Roman Catholic Church in Ireland. If its title suggests that a similitude of poetic perspectives can be discerned on a denominational basis, or that lines of influence run primarily on religious tracks, its purpose is an exploration of difference as much as congruity.

This essay identifies three strands of representation: Clarke's topical social critique and satire of Catholic institutions, and the subtle, grammatical resistances of his poetry; the glimpses of God found by Kavanagh in nature and the rural community, and the praise and prayer poems he offers in response; the iconography of Heaney's poetry, which draws on Catholic observance and ritual, as well as New Criticism, to create verbal icons, and to seek Real Presence in poetic form.

Alongside its thematic engagement with Catholicism, the essay considers the transmutations of poetic form: Clarke's variations on Gaelic poetry, narrative poems, and wordplay; Kavanagh's poetic observances and the ways in which 'Prose prayers become/ Odes and sonnets';[1] Heaney's sacramental poetics and the poem as icon. All three modes reflect and affirm the important influence of Catholic culture to poetry: art critiques Catholic culture; art celebrates sacramental presence; art becomes icon.

II

In his introduction to the *Selected Poems* of Austin Clarke, W. J. McCormack entitles part of his discussion 'A Negative Theology'. 'Again and again,' he writes, 'the speakers in these poems confront their own inability to believe and in so doing indicate also their inability to disbelieve.'[2] The religious doubt McCormack sees as central to Clarke's poetry, he describes as 'an intellectual activity which is religious in itself and not merely in its concerns.'[3] Clarke's poems do not necessarily suggest that knowledge of God is acquired through negation, but they do imply that revelation, however small, is to be found within human experience rather than the walls of the Church. His theology is negative rather than apophatic: pessimistic and critical of the Church, but quiet about how knowledge of the divine might be won. Clarke's fervent anti-clericalism shapes his poetic concerns much more immediately than the *Via Negativa*.

This is not to say that he has given up on the knowledge—and love—of God, but he is reluctant to speak directly to this theme. His poetry surveys the injustices of the Catholic Church in Ireland: its collusion with the State; the melding of spiritual and material economies in its practices and relations with the State; sexual oppressiveness, sexism; sectarianism; indifference to the poor. It does so with indignation, his complaint made with relentless fervency. In this, Denis Donoghue writes, 'he was tireless and therefore tiresome,'[4] explaining, in part, the reason for Clarke's relative critical neglect in assessments of modern Irish poetry.

McCormack's description of Clarke's religious practice as an intellectual activity is an accurate one, which contrasts with Catholicism's sensuous appeal for Kavanagh and Heaney (and, indeed, places Clarke closer to Louis MacNeice). His poetry evokes a version of the Gaelic past, 'not with a romantic's nostalgia for a pre-lapsarian medievalism,'

---

[1] Patrick Kavanagh, 'Lough Derg', *Collected Poems*, ed. Antoinette Quinn (London: Penguin, 2005), 104.

[2] W. J. McCormack, '"Beyond the Pale": Introducing Austin Clarke (1896–1974)', *Austin Clarke: Selected Poems* (London: Penguin, 1992), 12.

[3] Ibid.

[4] Denis Donoghue, *We Irish* (Brighton: Harvester, 1986), 245.

writes Terence Brown, 'but with a classicist's sense of norms by which a society might measure its own manifest deficiencies'.[5] Clarke's critical gaze is focused on the collusion of Church and State. But if the Catholic Church motivates the frustrated anger and satire of his poetry, it is also the source of poetic inspiration to which he remains faithful. His poetry resists the sentimentalizing of religion he perceives in his immediate cultural context, but the Church—whether corrupt, covetous, hypocritical, appealing, or dis-established—is still his abiding interest.

Born in 1896, Clarke published his first collection, *The Vengeance of Fionn*, in 1917. He continued to publish until his death in 1974, his poetic career taking shape amidst the seismic shifts in the political, cultural, and psychological conditions of twentieth-century Ireland. R. F. Foster notes the 'strong theocratic implications' of De Valera's 1937 constitution.[6] Divorce was prohibited, and the constitution legislated for a polity it assumed to be Catholic, enshrining the Roman Catholic Church as the guardian of the faith of the majority of its citizens. In 1938 Clarke published *Night and Morning: Poems*, a volume Maurice Harmon describes as 'a book of religious lyrics'.[7] But the publication is followed by a seventeen-year period of poetic silence during which Clarke does not publish. His silence corresponds with the first years of Fianna Fail's attempt to forge a nation through nationalism and a conservative Catholic ethos, the Emergency, and the beginnings of modernization in Ireland.

Clarke breaks his silence in 1955 with *Ancient Lights. Poems and Satires: First Series*. The first poem, 'Celebrations', watches as the treasury buys grace for the city, and crowds 'celebrat[e]/Prosperity of church and state'.[8] Another, 'The Envy of Poor Lovers', considers those 'State-paid to snatch away the folly of poor lovers/For whom, it seems, the sacraments have failed'.[9] Clarke highlights the natural beauty of sexual love against the institutional confinement suffered by those children born outside of marriage and seized by nuns from their parents. Catholic doctrine on premarital sex is shown to have dehumanizing consequences; a newborn baby becomes a sign of sin, failure, and financial profit. But Clarke's critique of the Irish Catholic Church and State is more emphatic than his critique of Catholicism; the sacraments have failed, or so 'it seems'. The disruptive presence of this clause is crucial to the meaning of the poem. The lovers laid only 'as if it were a sin'.[10] Clarke is at pains to forge a linguistic gap between doctrinal truth and an epistemology of love. The distancing of simile suggests that, far from the sacraments failing, love has begotten love.

The final 'veiled/failed' rhyme of 'The Envy of Poor Lovers' points to the headdresses of those nuns living on sin, and the concealment of the Church's collusion with the Irish State. With remarkable brevity, Clarke portrays the melding of sexual and material

---

[5] Terence Brown, 'Austin Clarke: Satirist', *Poetry Ireland Review* 22 (Summer 1988), 113.

[6] R. F. Foster, *Modern Ireland 1600–1972* (London: Penguin, 1989), 544.

[7] Maurice Harmon, *Austin Clarke: A Critical Introduction* (Dublin: Wolfhound, 1989), 89.

[8] Austin Clarke, *Collected Poems*, ed. R. Dardis Clarke (Manchester: Carcanet, 2008), 195.

[9] Ibid., 205.

[10] Ibid.

economies within and between the Catholic Church and the Irish State in a later poem, 'Living on Sin' from *Flight to Africa and Other Poems* (1963). It is the lovers who fund the religious institutions so prized by the State: their 'hasty sin':

> gives many a nun her tidy bed,
> Full board and launderette. God-fearing State
> Provides three pounds a week, our conscience money,
> For every infant severed from the breast.[11]

The economy of Clarke's lines convey the speed and ease by which love is turned to sin, is turned to subsistence, is turned to severance. 'Living on Sin' effaces lovemaking for a cash economy. But although the final rhyme of 'The Envy of Poor Lovers' underscores failure, it is suggestive also of a bridal veil, as though the lovers have, far below those 'institutions mured above', achieved a holy union.[12] The poem holds out faith in the truth and power of love, in which the sacraments find their foundation, even as it denounces the powerful structures managing their meaning and use.

It is not sacramentalism per se but the regulation of the sacraments by the Catholic Church that Clarke's poetry lambasts. In 'Martha Blake at Fifty-One', unlike 'The Envy of Poor Lovers', the final rhyme presents no resistance to the poem's bleak conclusion. It works to bitter, ironic effect: Martha Blake had been 'anointed' by the priest but 'knew no peace:/Her last breath, disappointed.'[13] As in *Mnemosyne Lay in Dust* (1966), Clarke sings the body not electric or vital, but wasting: suffering indigestion, fever, diarrhoea, and death. Martha's faithful attendance at Mass is set against the Mother Superior's judgement, the sisters' wilful neglect, and the institutional regulations forbidding her the daily sacrament.

Clarke's grotesque and empathetic vision of the frailty of the human body does not have a compelling equivalent in Kavanagh's or Heaney's poetry. Perhaps because of his distrust and abhorrence of the regulation of the symbolic and sacramental by the Catholic Church, Clarke's poetic style tends towards realism and dramatization rather than symbolism. Like many of Clarke's poems, 'Martha Blake at Fifty-One' presents its sympathetic life study as a narrative. His depiction of the Church is primarily satirical, contrasting its cruelties with personal narratives of those neglected or bruised by it. Whereas Kavanagh finds God in the Monaghan fields, and Heaney crafts a verbal icon akin to poetic sacrament, Clarke reaffirms the distance and discord of simile and metaphor.

Alongside Clarke's satirical critique of the Christian Church, Catholic and Protestant, is an abiding interest in humanity's redemption, often outside the rites and rituals of established traditions. In 'Ancient Lights', the title poem of Clarke's 1955 volume, the speaker escapes the terror of penance and confession and offers absolution to himself, sheltering from the rain at a locked door. The crucifix at which the speaker shudders,

---

[11] Ibid., 275.
[12] Ibid., 205.
[13] Ibid., 274.

'The feet so hammered, daubed-on blood-drip,/Black with the lip-scrimmage of the damned',[14] recalls the imagery and atmosphere of Louis MacNeice's 'Belfast', while the city's looming Protestant spires return in Derek Mahon's poetry. Similar imagery reappears in 'The Disestablished Church', from *A Sermon on Swift and Other Poems* (1968), in which the speaker declares 'All human-beings will be redeemed.'[15] The means by which such redemption will be delivered, however, remain obscure. In Heaney's estimation, writing poetry is itself a redemptive act—one he compares, famously, to Jesus's writing in the sand in a story recorded in John's Gospel. Jesus's act of writing saves a woman's life, and poetry, writes Heaney, is equally unlimited in its redemptive, governing power.[16] Clarke is more cynical about the redemptive potential of his writing. Punning on his name in this poem, Clarke has the speaker declare 'No clerk will relight the long sixes',[17] and the bells of St Catherine's go unrung. 'Redemption banks on/Our credit',[18] the poem concludes: salvation calculable at an agreed rate. Redemption isn't produced by poetry—or so it seems. In the imagination of the reader, of course, the candles at the altar are lit and the bells rung even as the speaker explicitly negates these options. Clarke's self-conscious wordplay highlights his reluctance to offer false hope through symbols and sacraments, and thereby repeat the Church hypocrisy he critiques.

Since many of his poems were written and published before the Second Vatican Council (1962–5), Clarke is responding to a different strain of Catholicism than that which emerges at the start of Heaney's career. Clarke's poetry comes from the era before the Council's doctrinal liberalization; before the Constitution on the Sacred Liturgy, which authorized the vernacularization of the liturgy and greater lay participation; and before the Pastoral Constitution on the Church in the Modern World, which acknowledged the need for the Church to adapt itself to the contemporary world. It emerges also from the time before the expressed ecumenism of the Second Vatican Council, which reimagined the Church as 'the people of God' instead of only the clergy.

The scale and shock of these theological and ecclesiastical changes—in particular for isolated rural Irish communities—is registered in the imagined future of Brian Moore's novella, *Catholics* (1972). Reviewing Moore's work in 1976, Derek Mahon writes 'The juxtaposition of the real and the ersatz lies ... at the centre of Moore's universe';[19] a juxtaposition central also to Clarke's critique of the hegemony of the Catholic Church in modern Ireland. Clarke may be similarly engaged in 'depicting the last refuge of the sacramental in a world given over to the materialistic and the meretricious',[20] but the gleam of the sacramental is difficult to detect.

---

[14] Ibid., 199.

[15] Ibid., 461.

[16] Seamus Heaney, 'The Government of the Tongue', *The Government of the Tongue* (London: Faber, 1989), 107–8.

[17] Clarke, *Collected Poems*, 463.

[18] Ibid., 464.

[19] Derek Mahon, 'Webs of Artifice', *Journalism: Selected Prose, 1970–1995*, ed. Terence Brown (Oldcastle: Gallery, 1996), 69.

[20] Ibid., 72.

In his often-quoted note about his conversation with Robert Frost, Clarke is said to have described writing poetry thus: 'I load myself with chains and try to get out of them'.[21] Amidst the poems celebrating love and lovemaking, there is also an unease about the human body, and a sense of constraint, both formally and thematically. Clarke's penitential poetic metaphor and his self-chosen chains have much in common with those restraining 'Miss Marnell'. Published in *Too Great a Vine* (1957), 'Miss Marnell' is a sensitively observed portrayal of the self-sacrificing ways of a lonely spinster, finally driven to madness and 'taken away, fingering to the last/Her ivory decades'.[22] The poem mourns Miss Marnell's unnecessary impoverishment: 'Her withered hand was busy doing good' for African missions and local Catholic causes, while her body and investments languished. The poem is a prelude to *Mnemosyne Lay in Dust*, Clarke's account of mental breakdown in St Patrick's hospital in Dublin. In the figure of Maurice Devane, Clarke portrays an exile from modern Ireland who, in the poem's opening stanza, 'Watched from the taxi window in vain/National stir and gaiety/Beyond himself'.[23] Clarke's own breakdown occurred in 1919, during the War of Independence. Devane's physical and psychological isolation and incarceration, though, is as revealing a record of Clarke's experience of Irish modernization and internationalization during the 1960s as it is a recollection of his experience of Ireland at war. Clarke came of age in a version of Ireland that preceded the emergent student radicalism, the international economic initiatives, and the tourist boom of the 1960s. Clarke also suffered a form of 'Straight-jacketing'[24] in his literary career: his three novels were banned by the Irish Censorship Board.

As Augustine Martin observes, for much of *Mnemosyne Lay in Dust* Clarke presents numerous symbols of confinement within a prosodic structure in which only grammar becomes more urgent.[25] Passive verbs give way to present-tense questions—'Was it a trap?'; 'Who was it?'; ' "Where am I?" '—and assonance reinforces the sense of entrapment in 'cage', 'weighed', and 'Straight-jacketed'.[26] Devane is ever watching 'through the bars',[27] contained within garments, rooms, houses, and walled gardens, and within the compressed metre of the poem. Martin highlights 'the fluent rush of trimeters' in the seventeenth section of the poem, celebrating 'the dawning of freedom and release'.[28] The effect of this shift from the stanza units of the preceding sixteen sections is startling, signalling a welcome release as Clarke starts to relieve Devane and reader alike from the claustrophobic conditions created in the poem.

While in institutional exile, Devane still believes in God. In the first section of the poem, Clarke shows Dublin revelling in 'unsaintly/Mirth'.[29] In the seventh, observing

---

[21] 'Austin Clarke's Notes on the Poems', *Collected Poems*, 541.

[22] Clarke, *Collected Poems*, 212.

[23] Ibid., 325.

[24] Ibid.

[25] Augustine Martin, 'Technique and Passion in Clarke's *Mnemosyne*', *Poetry Ireland Review* 22 (Summer 1988), 99.

[26] Clarke, *Collected Poems*, 329, 330, 332, 342.

[27] Ibid., 341.

[28] Martin, 'Technique and Passion in Clarke's *Mnemosyne*', 98.

[29] Clarke, *Collected Poems*, 325.

Devane's solitude, the speaker declares that religion's 'multitudinous torn cloak'[30] fails to provide protection or shelter. The assertion, 'God's likeness died'[31] in the faces of madmen, frames the eighth section. If the refrain pinpoints a rupture in human/divine relations, psychological illness does not seem the cause of such estrangement, but rather the occasion for religious contemplation. The refrain may urge a revision of that theological concept of *Imago Dei*, by inviting the reader to reimagine God in the faces of madmen and women, instead of assuming the knowledge of God and using it to force others into exile.

As the title suggests, Devane's recovery and 'rememorization' is made by means of a reunion with the Greek goddess of memory and mother of the Muses. Clarke's classicism, however, is hardly incompatible with forms of Catholic devotion; the preservation of a pseudo-religious feminine essence is a variation on Marian devotion—one repeated by Kavanagh and, more intensely, Heaney. But through the homonymic play of the final stanza Clarke limits Devane's recovery, making it only a partial redemption. He steps out of the hospital gates, 'his future in every vein',[32] but as his blood pumps around his body Clarke overshadows the future into which Devane believes he is walking by casting it in 'vain'. Against a surface guiding motion; against direction, Clarke pits vanity. It is a silent third rhyme (with 'vein'/'Devane'), but one which shatters the final stanza's optimism by showing it to be empty. Furthermore, it marks a point of return and repetition, as Clarke paired 'Devane' with 'in vain' in the first stanza.[33] Since Clarke is so highly self-conscious about the power structures governing Ireland's political, theological, and economic culture, his poetic techniques are equally reflexive. Clarke's homonymic play turns language in on itself at the moment he seems to release exile and reader from physical, psychological, and prosodic confinement. As homonyms pile up in the stanza, with 'story/storey' and 'site/sight',[34] they create new claustrophobic conditions. Clarke's cynicism about the forms of liberation that religion purports to offer extends to certain poetic techniques. In the penultimate stanza, he satirizes the entire endeavour: 'Poetic Personification:/Hope frowned'.[35] Revealing its means of signalling despair or achieving empathy, the poem becomes an object lesson in its cunning.

John Goodby highlights how Clarke's reputation has suffered from the polarization of Irish culture as critics argue about mythology and modernism. As he points out, Clarke's 'dense and highly-wrought style always seemed artificial and laboured when set against the realist vernacular style championed by Kavanagh and more or less dominant in Irish poetry since the 1960s'.[36] But, as Goodby suggests, Clarke's habit of highlighting the

---

[30] Ibid., 334.
[31] Ibid., 335.
[32] Ibid., 348.
[33] Ibid., 325.
[34] Ibid. 348.
[35] Ibid.
[36] John Goodby, 'From Irish Mode to Modernisation: The Poetry of Austin Clarke', in *The Cambridge Companion to Contemporary Irish Poetry*, ed. Matthew Campbell (Cambridge: Cambridge University Press, 2003), 22.

materiality of his medium—poetic language—is intimately connected to his religious understanding.[37] His poetry does not replicate transcendent or incarnational theologies, and sacramental presence is difficult to perceive, since language itself poses epistemological problems. The kind of sacramental poetics Clarke resists are those later to be found in Heaney's early poetry. While the sacrament remains central to Heaney's poetry at both the level of theme and form, in 'The Hippophagi', from *The Horse-Eaters* (1960), Clarke parodies the sacrament of the Eucharist by presenting it in cannibalistic terms. Clarke wears what the speaker of 'Robert Frost' describes as 'the unholy mantle/Of poetry', 'scant' and continually rent.[38] Not only does poetry fail to provide remedy or consolation, as in Heaney's view, it is a source of suffering—not sacred, but unholy.

Like an Old Testament prophet bringing a message of revelation, Clarke uses a direct mode of address, with titles such as 'The Subjection of Women' and 'How Covetousness Came into the Church'. He is less concerned with crafting a transcendent poetic image than with presenting a critical depiction of Church practices and politics. Through satire, documentary realism, and variations and translations of Gaelic poetry, Clarke achieves this ambition without straying too far from generic forms. His loss of faith in the materialistic, meretricious Irish Catholic Church is rendered in poetic lines bewailing its failings. But Clarke also counters his cynicism by considering religious faith outside institutional structures. While few of his protagonists experience physical and psychological liberation within the narrative of the poem, Clarke's lexical dexterity at times resists and counteracts the constraining institutional pressures described. The wordplay of *rime riche*, acrostics, anagrams, puns, neologisms, and homonyms is often comic in its effect, but occasionally, or cumulatively, such wordplay offers liberation, inviting release and even blessing. In 'The Straying Student', from *Night and Morning*, the speaker surveys the gendered segregation of the Mass before straying into a romantic vision beyond Inishmore and Ireland. But the vision fails as the speaker's fears bring him back to the Mass:

> And yet I tremble lest she may deceive me
> And leave me in this land, where every woman's son
> Must carry his own coffin and believe,
> In dread, all that the clergy teach the young.[39]

The poems ends with this deathly vision; where Inishmore had chimed with 'shore' and 'doorway'[40] in the opening stanza, to create spatial and imaginative deviations, finally the whole of Ireland is condemned in subservience to clerical instruction. But love, and lexical possibilities, remain. The 'deceive/believe' rhyme exhorts the reader to extend the practice of formal, poetic interpretation to theological teaching; to question, doubt, and resist the claustrophobia of State-sponsored religious dogmatism and to imagine things otherwise.

---

[37] Ibid., 39.
[38] Clarke, *Collected Poems*, 359.
[39] Ibid., 189.
[40] Ibid., 188.

'Penal Law', the poem that follows, presents two ways of learning; two routes to knowledge. Lovers will 'learn by heart/All that the clergy banish from the mind', and all that the State sought to censor. But the poem delights also, as Terence Brown describes it, 'in a carnival of clerkly satiric irreverence'.[41] The lovers learn, 'When hands are joined and head bows in the dark'.[42] This final line's double meaning subverts the poem's title with its sudden *joie de vivre*. The singular bowed head marks Clarke's celebration of sexual pleasure and personal autonomy against a backdrop of religious conformity. Against the cycles of abusive power suggested by the title—from Catholic oppression to Catholic censorship—Clarke presents a comic, sexual, and irreverently sincere alternative.

Through these poetic substitutions Clarke importantly distinguishes doctrinal conformity from individual conscience. If not quite an affirmation of 'The drunkenness of things being various',[43] as with MacNeice's pip-spitting epiphany, Clarke's intelligent wordplay is a celebration of things being other than doctrinally decreed. The poems remain at a tangent to the Church from which they seek to distance themselves and, as such, are limited celebrations of variety, both theological and existential. Catholicism endures as the theological frame within which they operate and find their meaning, but Clarke's reflection on the construction and regulation of meaning remains central. Having witnessed and experienced the power of Church and State to govern language use, his poems continually unsettle their forms of signification, circling back on themselves and frustrating any attempt on a reader's behalf to transcend Irish history through poetic symbol.

The influence of such self-conscious wordplay is seen less in the vernacular speech forms of Heaney's dense quatrains than in the intricate metrical and stanzaic patterns of Derek Mahon's highly polished lyrics. Of course Mahon's lyrical forms also respond in important ways to Yeats, and ways that differ significantly from Clarke's poetic negotiations with his forebear. But since Irish poetry criticism tends to treat religious themes along sectarian lines, it is worth noting how poetic influence crosses confessional divisions. Mahon's reasons for cynicism about transcendence, religious and symbolic, are, like Clarke's, shaped by religion. (It is, in this context, instructive to compare Clarke's exposure to 1930s Catholic theology in the South with Mahon's experience of the Church of Ireland and Calvinist cultural context in the North in the 1950s. There is perhaps more common ground here than Clarke shares with Heaney.)

Clarke's miracles are subtle, lexical ones. In 'Martha Blake', he distinguishes the word from the Word and, like her, struggles with the limits of language:

> Afflicted by that love she turns
> To multiply her praise,
> Goes over all the foolish words
> And finds they are the same;

---

[41] Brown, 'Austin Clarke: Satirist', 121.

[42] Clarke, *Collected Poems*, 189.

[43] Louis MacNeice, 'Snow', *Collected Poems*, ed. Peter McDonald (London: Faber, 2007), 24.

> But now she feels within her breast
> Such calm that she is silent,
> For soul can never be immodest
> Where body may not listen.[44]

Clarke proffers a miracle in the form of an anagram. As Christopher Ricks writes, 'When *silent* becomes *listen* before our very eyes, our ears may listen for ever to or for the silent intimation.'[45] Clarke's sleight of hand follows the sacrament of the Eucharist but is set apart from it. The silent peace intimated occurs in the shadow of the institutional structure and, as Ricks observes, leaves the reader listening or waiting, or doing both at once. This is an irresolvable state, as with the effect of Clarke's much-loved homonyms. But his insistence on the value and necessity of plurality in the face of platitudes and dogmatism constitutes the humane and discerning ambit of Clarke's poetic achievement.

III

If in 'The Great Hunger' Patrick Kavanagh sees religion as 'a counter-irritant like a blister', he sees also that 'God is in the bits and pieces of Everyday'.[46] His poetry seeks not only to critique the impoverished imagination of the institutional Church, but to cultivate a sense of sacramentality out of doors. But if this witnessing to the presence of God in Monaghan's fields renders the poet a priestly figure, Kavanagh's poetic observances testify also to the poet's, and poetry's, distance from divine presence. What we might describe as Kavanagh's panentheism (god *in* nature), as opposed to pantheism (god *as* nature), he is wholly willing to mock, and make the subject of parody, as in 'The Paddiad'. Literally playing devil's advocate to Irish Catholic poetry, he says:

> Devil: 'Paddy Connemara gets my vote
> As the expresser of the Catholic note.
> His pious feeling for the body
> And rejection of the shoddy
> Mystical cloak that Conscience trails
> Places him among the greats of the Gaels[47]

Because he attempted to imitate the techniques of Irish-language verse, Austin Clarke was criticized by Kavanagh, both in this poem and 'The Wake of the Books'. Kavanagh had different hopes for Irish poetry in English, but his reaction to Clarke represents a perceived ideological difference about the centrality to poetry of Gaelic mythology—and, concomitantly, the perceived role of such mythology in uniting Catholicism and nationalism in literary form. The speaker of 'Auditors In' turns away from the mythology

[44] Clarke, *Collected Poems*, 185.
[45] Christopher Ricks, 'Introduction', in Austin Clarke, *Collected Poems*, p. xxiv.
[46] Kavanagh, *Collected Poems*, 73, 72.
[47] Ibid., 154.

embedding Irish nationalism and Catholicism in the soil, consciously choosing 'The placeless Heaven that's under all our noses'.[48] The ecumenism and democratic impulse that seem to lie behind such a pronouncement, however, depend upon accepting that the poet is a theologian in possession of an authentic religious voice.

But Kavanagh is in possession of at least two religious voices. As Antoinette Quinn observes, at the same time as he published 'The Great Hunger', a 'devastating…assault on the cherished nationalist fiction of Irish spiritual ascendancy' centred on its peasantry, Kavanagh wrote for a Catholic weekly, the *Standard*, criticizing Yeats, Synge, and Lady Gregory, and 'asserting that, as writers from a Protestant Ascendancy caste, they were outside the mainstream consciousness of the Irish, were not "the voice of the people"'.[49] This duality regarding Catholicism, and its relationship to power, truth, and Ireland, makes Kavanagh's an endlessly compelling, and conflicted, poetry. He is much less vocal than Clarke about the Catholic Church per se, yet he has absorbed its theology to a much greater extent than Clarke's intellectual and ideological battles will allow.

Catholicism lies behind Kavanagh's critique of provincialism and advocation of parochialism. His celebration of poetry's foundation in the particularity of the parish, and of the capacity of vernacular speech to communicate truthfully far beyond its immediate context, finds its template in the local, parochial network expressive of Catholicism's universalism. He writes, 'Parochialism is universal; it deals with fundamentals'.[50] Kavanagh's representation of divine presence reflects this conception of poetry's dealings with the fundamentals through the specificities of local rows and local language.

God is often found (or sought) 'in some fantastically ordinary incog'.[51] In 'The One', from *Come Dance with Kitty Stobling and Other Poems* (1960), 'God is down in the swamps and marshes…breathing His love by a cut-away bog'.[52] It is immanence more so than transcendence that Kavanagh seeks to represent. His God pervades, sustains, and is constrained by the material universe, and he is cynical of perspectives that excise the divine from earthly matter. 'Sensualist' warns against empty abstraction, even as its capitalized terms suggest respect for ideas as well their forms: 'Do not stray/In the abstract temple of love/There are no priests on the altars/Of Metaphysic/…Is the Body not the temple of the Holy Ghost/And flesh eyes have glimpsed Truth'.[53] In the lovely sonnet, 'The Hospital', also from *Come Dance with Kitty Stobling*, Kavanagh expresses a sense of urgency about the need to portray divine love:

> Naming these things is the love-act and its pledge;
> For we must record love's mystery without claptrap,
> Snatch out of time the passionate transitory.[54]

---

[48] Ibid., 182.

[49] Antoinette Quinn, 'Introduction', in Kavanagh, *Collected Poems*, pp. xix, xx–xxi.

[50] Patrick Kavanagh, *Collected Prose* (London: MacGibbon & Kee, 1967), 283.

[51] Kavanagh, 'God in Woman', *Collected Poems*, 185.

[52] Ibid., 229.

[53] Patrick Kavanagh, 'Sensualist', in *No Earthly Estate. God and Patrick Kavanagh: An Anthology*, ed. Tom Stack (Dublin: The Columba Press, 2002), 65.

[54] Kavanagh, *Collected Poems*, 217.

By observing his surroundings—a bridge, a bent gate, a suntrap—and recording specificities, Kavanagh sees poetry as a quasi-religious act of devotion. Naming is a form of loving that transforms 'functional' matter into 'mystery without claptrap'.[55]

Writing in 1964, Kavanagh commented, 'somehow or other I have a belief in poetry as a mystical thing, and a dangerous thing'.[56] His belief is tempered by the threat or temptation that poetic language tends towards mystification. Wary of poetic deception, his early work maintains his faith in poetry's mystical potential as he sets about naming the gates, trees, roads, and bicycles encountered in the Monaghan hills. But if *Ploughman and Other Poems* (1936) is a collection of mystical pastoral lyrics, 'The Great Hunger' marks a decisive shift to antipastoral. Written and published in 1942 and later collected in *A Soul for Sale* (1947), the poem begins, memorably, 'Clay is the word and clay is the flesh'.[57] This pronouncement could signal an incarnational poetic, where language animates the human body to signify divine presence and meaning. But the following line renders the labourers—these unusual Christ figures—'mechanized scare-crows', deflating the incarnational perspective and satirizing the prophetic voice by taking account of the process of change in modern Ireland. Against poverty, sexual repression, and the industrialization of agriculture, Kavanagh measures the pervasive ideology of an idyllic and prosperous rural Ireland, the religious aspects of which he ironizes in the thirteenth section: 'As it was in the Beginning,/The simpleness of peasant life'.[58]

For his protagonist Patrick Maguire, as for Maria in Joyce's 'Clay' from *Dubliners*, clay becomes synonymous with death rather than the Word. But the poem's bleak conclusion rests upon the assumption that the speaker resumes the narrative in the final stanza. Keats's 'Ode Upon a Grecian Urn' ends with the voice of the urn: ' "Beauty is truth, truth beauty",—that is all/Ye know on earth, and all ye need to know'.[59] These final lines are shrouded in ambiguity by dual perspectives, and it is unclear whether the speaker agrees with the aesthetic pronouncements quoted and paraphrased. Similarly, at the end of 'The Great Hunger', the earth speaks, but it is not clear whether the speaker takes over the narrative and offers his own conclusion. In other words, 'the apocalypse of clay'[60] in the final stanza is only one perspective, and points as much to revelation as to destruction. By imagining and describing apocalyptic screams, Kavanagh's poem becomes a source of revelation, the speaker's voice satiric but nonetheless prophetic—notably, in a literary context, of the altered critical perceptions of the practices and significance of rural life for Irish culture, produced in reaction to the poem. Jonathan Allison suggests that with its final lines the poem is 'not only antipastoral but national anti-epic'.[61] In rethinking the Revival, however, Kavanagh inscribed pastoral pieties of his own, to

---

[55] Ibid.

[56] Patrick Kavanagh, 'Author's Note to *Collected Poems* (1964)', in Kavanagh, *Collected Poems*, 291.

[57] Kavanagh, *Collected Poems*, 63.

[58] Ibid., 85.

[59] John Keats, *Selected Poems* (London: Everyman, 1996), 216.

[60] Kavanagh, *Collected Poems*, 89.

[61] Jonathan Allison, 'Patrick Kavanagh and Antipastoral', in *The Cambridge Companion to Contemporary Irish Poetry*, ed. Campbell, 51.

which the natural imagery, nostalgia, memorialization, and mythologizing of other poems in *A Soul for Sale* testify. Allison demonstrates that, as one of the most influential Irish poets since Yeats, Kavanagh is paradoxically the most uneven. He is both a sceptical antipastoral poet and a lyricist of mystical religious epiphany.

Kavanagh's religious aesthetics, then, are charged with complexity. 'The Great Hunger' pierces the romantic mythology of the peasantry's 'little lyrical fields'[62] in which religion and culture find their basis and meaning. Yet of such fields Kavanagh is also the 'Ploughman'. The early poem of this title rhymes 'God' with 'dark sod', and 'art' with the 'heart'[63] that knows Him. Poetry, ploughing, and prayer mingle in the poem's imagery, equally esteemed and interdependent: God is in the dark sod where 'star-lovely art' resides, as well as the heart. But does this place the poet on an equal footing with the deity he seeks to represent? For both Kavanagh and Heaney, religious aesthetics raise the problem of poetic agency. In 'Lough Derg', written in the same year as 'The Great Hunger', 'Prose prayers become/Odes and sonnets'.[64] They become litanies too, as with the stanzas which follow. By mirroring Catholic forms of devotion in poetry, Kavanagh is more like a Catholic priest than a Gravesian priest of the Muses. But his insistence that Christ 'Hears in the voices of the meanly poor/Homeric utterances, poetry sweeping through'[65] is overblown, and reaffirms the problem of poetic agency: the poet authorizes his own godly perspective.

Kavanagh's poetry repeatedly expresses an anxiety about the status and constitution of poetic forms in relation to their treatment of religious themes and personal beliefs. 'Auditors In' begins in self-examination: 'Is verse an entertainment only?/Or is it a profound and holy/Faith that cries the inner history/Of the failure of man's mission?'[66] At times the poem aspires to constitute prayerful worship, but the attempt is a conflicted one, examining the speaker's isolation and his failure to provide a sincere testimony. Like the trees of 'March' (*Ploughman*), the poet is 'listening with an intense/Anxiety for the Word'. But here the silence is interrupted by the blackbird's song; by 'a new poem's violence'.[67] The imagery and rhyme suggest that poetry might be as much an obstacle to religious contemplation as its vessel.

The later poem, 'Prelude', considers whether 'Old cunning Silence might not be/A better bet than poetry' in being 'true to God'.[68] The poem's register—'counterfeit', 'fraud', 'phoney', 'bogus'—expresses Kavanagh's desire for his poetry to give authentic witness to the world as he experiences it, by articulating his dread of 'pretence'.[69] 'Prelude' criticizes fraudulent critics, priests, professors, and journalists, but the 'fraud/God' rhyme of the second stanza highlights the particular difficulty the poet

[62] Kavanagh, *Collected Poems*, 85.
[63] Ibid., 7.
[64] Ibid., 104.
[65] Ibid., 107.
[66] Ibid., 179.
[67] Ibid., 16.
[68] Ibid., 207.
[69] Ibid., 207, 208.

faces in creating images for the divine. Satire may be 'unfruitful prayer', as the speaker claims. But Kavanagh's satires, like Clarke's, demonstrate the relative ease with which contemporary religious, political, and cultural life can be disparaged, and, by contrast, the tremendous difficulty of creating authentic prayer in poetic form. The Blakean imagery of its conclusion, however, underlines the imaginative and revitalizing power of love within political, religious, and cultural life. The imperative mood, repetition, rhyme, and tone of the final lines owe a more local debt to Clarke: 'Ignore Power's schismatic sect/Lovers alone lovers protect'.[70]

Blake's influence is felt in 'Advent', as well as in 'Christmas, 1939' and the final couplet of 'Canal Bank Walk'. Kavanagh sees in the darkness, penance, and unknowing of the advent season an opportunity for imaginative and spiritual redemption, before 'Christ comes with a January flower'.[71] Advent makes possible a return to childlike innocence and an unconstrained imagination that animates stale objects; a return necessitated by the adult experience, where reason leaves no room for wonder. By making this transient return to innocence or childhood, Kavanagh's poems recognize the necessity of a receptive religious posture, if the transfiguring power of love is to be witnessed. Instead of incarnational poems, then, which depend upon the poet role's as mediator between human and divine, Kavanagh's best poems are transfigurations; necessarily transient miracles, in recognition that poetry cannot make flesh of the Word. From the beginning he has insisted that he is only a 'half-faithed ploughman' ('Monaghan Hills'), who needs the canal's redemptive waters to 'Feed the gaping need of [his] senses' ('Canal Bank Walk').[72] Alcoholism leads Kavanagh to a recognition, in 'Personal Problem', that soil, like soul, 'Needs to be revived by a power not [his] own'.[73]

A line from 'The Wake of the Books' summarizes the effects of Kavanagh's poetry: 'clay transfigured in an innocent dream',[74] or, as in 'The Great Hunger', in a nightmare. His poems are transfigurations rather than incarnations: Christ, truth, and love are only glimpsed in his poetry. Cognizant of temporality, Kavanagh's meditations on divine presence are often mediated through childhood, or recognition of poetry's limits. Kavanagh renders the human body broken and weak, but also vital; transfigured, if only momentarily, through the window of the poetic frame. 'To a Child' warns against 'the unholy ones who tear/Beauty's white robe and clothe her/In rags of prayer'. But if this Keatsian celebration of Beauty seems to reject prayerful contemplation in favour of the aesthetic, it quickly, and with a tenderness of tone, offers a means by which to combine them:

> Child, there is light somewhere
> Under a star.
> Sometime it will be for you
> A window that looks
> Inward to God.[75]

[70] Ibid., 209.
[71] Ibid., 111.
[72] Ibid., 17, 224.
[73] Ibid., 259.
[74] Ibid., 148.
[75] Ibid., 10.

Kavanagh's use of external and internal perspectives is remarkable, and wondrously reflexive. The religious gaze is here a reflexive gaze that needs no clerical mediation or regulation. It is more than mere introspection, as the window is actively looking (as well as passively tilted). God is both within the child and, it seems, the source of light forming the window. This reflexive image is an apt description of religious aesthetics in Kavanagh's poetry: the window is the poetic frame looking actively for the God within (the self; the soil; the parish); yet the window/poem is also merely the evidence of a pre-existing source of light it simply seeks not to shadow or obstruct.

IV

In interviews and prose Seamus Heaney often uses Catholic imagery to express ideas about poetry. Themes of inspiration, visitation, catechism, pilgrimage, and Marian devotion are common in his assessment of poetry, and often he represents the figure of the poet in vatic terms. Heaney's Northern Irish context seems to have thrown his Catholicism into relief, both within his poetry and in the popular imagination; it is evidence of his part in the 'minority culture' and, furthermore, a minority culture of which he is deemed its representative voice. Among others, Seamus Deane renders Heaney 'characteristic of his Northern Irish Catholic community'[76] and its spokesperson. But Heaney's Catholicism is constituted theologically as well as culturally and politically. This doesn't mean that Heaney's absorption of Catholicism and recourse to it in poetry is apolitical. But by considering the theology he absorbs, the Catholic context for the images and interpretative strategies of his poetry emerge more clearly.

Since 'Digging' and the poems of *Death of a Naturalist* (1966), earthiness and physicality have been central to discussions of Heaney's poetry. His interest in digging, depth, and an accompanying sincerity in conveying the details of life in a rural, parochial context has been praised, and parodied—the great mass of agricultural objects strewn throughout his collections is a familiar feature of Heaney's poetic landscape. In a line from 'The Harvest Bow', from *Field Work* (1979), Heaney describes his poetic practice thus: 'I tell and finger it like braille/Gleaning the unsaid off the palpable'.[77] This sensuous and sexual image, and metaphor for poetic production, is a familiar one. Many of Heaney's poems linger over bodies and objects that can be touched, tasted, or smelt—sensual experiences which bring about revelation or redemption. In terms of Catholic art, this could be described as sacramentalism, and the religious symbols Heaney uses to describe poetry's power and function are demonstrative of sacramental poetics in the Catholic mode.

---

[76] Seamus Deane, *Celtic Revivals: Essays in Modern Irish Literature 1880–1980* (Salem: Wake Forest University Press, 1987), 175.

[77] Seamus Heaney, *Opened Ground: Poems 1966–1996* (London: Faber, 1998), 183.

To a much greater degree than Kavanagh, Heaney is engaged in producing religious symbols, and he has drawn heavily on Catholic theology throughout his poetic career. Edna Longley underlines the significance of Catholic devotion to the imagery and forms of *North* (1975); in 'The Grauballe Man', as elsewhere, Heaney is 'inclining to rosary beads indeed', in the attention he pays to the broken body, and in the poem's liturgical rhythms.[78] Heaney's 'squat pen'[79] ('Digging') is engaged not only in the work of poetic excavation, but of incarnation, as in the resurrection of the dead in Heaney's bog poems. Litanies of names and places, as in 'The Tollund Man' from *Wintering Out* (1972), further exemplify Heaney's incorporation of Catholicism in his poetic forms; and the themes of consecration, reverence, sainthood, and blasphemy which occupy the poet attest to its significant influence in subject matter.

'Clearances', from *The Haw Lantern* (1987), mingles the speaker's love of his mother with Marian devotion and the Gravesian muse. In the third poem of the sequence, peeling potatoes becomes a silent communion and sacramental act conducted during, but apart from, the Mass. Familiar also are the ways Heaney's poems endow traditional rural farming and labouring practices with sacramental significance. In 'The Forge', the blacksmith, whose workshop is 'an altar/Where he expends himself in shape and music',[80] mirrors Heaney's own poetic craft in *Door into the Dark* (1969).

There are relatively few references to God in Heaney's poems, compared with the number of religious images. God is not named or prayed to, as in Kavanagh's poetry, nor is the Catholic Church represented with anything near the frequency of Clarke's poetry. In *The Spirit Level* (1996), 'The Gravel Walks' imagines 'an absolution of the body' through the river gravel present 'In the beginning' and as a kingdom within.[81] The quantity and variety of Biblical imagery in Heaney's poems is impossible to exemplify thoroughly. But Heaney's intention, and the effect of his poetry, isn't Christian devotion. He is less concerned with addressing a god outside the perimeters of the lyric poem as with the constitution of the lyric poem itself, and its ritualistic and sacramental capabilities.

In *The Government of the Tongue* Heaney states his belief that 'poetry can be as potentially redemptive and possibly as illusory as love'[82] and, as noted earlier, compares poetry to Jesus's writing in the sand. 'The Rain Stick', from *The Spirit Level*, addresses the reader directly: 'You are like a rich man entering heaven/Through the ear of a raindrop'. He thereby presents the poem as a means of salvation: not only aesthetic, but religious. His habit of titling poems by the object of their enquiry underlines his belief in the pseudo-religious power of the individual poem. That the poem is also the rain stick it imagines, 'the music that you never would have known/To listen for' and which leads the way to heaven, places the poet in a powerful position. Indeed he is usurping Christ's role, as with the tone of the poem's final command: 'Listen now again'.[83]

---

[78] Edna Longley, *Poetry in the Wars* (Newcastle: Bloodaxe, 1986), 152.
[79] Heaney, *Opened Ground*, 3.
[80] Ibid., 19.
[81] Ibid., 424, 423.
[82] Heaney, *The Government of the Tongue*, p. xxii.
[83] Heaney, *Opened Ground*, 395.

In so doing, Heaney is at once borrowing from Christian theology and eroding its importance and authority by presenting poetry in its place. This is perhaps the central paradox of the dual influences of New Criticism and Catholicism which Denis Donoghue advocates in 'Notes Toward a Critical Method: Language as Order'. Published in *Studies* in 1955, Donoghue's essay proposes a method for literary criticism by drawing on the work of critics from the United States he identifies as Catholic, among them W. K. Wimsatt, as well as F. R. Leavis and Cleanth Brooks. Poems, in Donoghue's view, are 'forms, entities, things of order with which to oppose the continual flux, change, transience of life'.[84] He sets out a Catholic vision of literary criticism by reverencing the aesthetic artefact and, in so doing, theologizes aesthetics in New Critical fashion. Donoghue writes 'As a Catholic, a believer in the Communion of Saints';[85] Catholicism, therefore, operates theologically as well as culturally in his essay. He draws a line from Catholicism to Communion to unity in the text, and suggests that the organic wholeness of a text functions as its own form of morality. Although Donoghue rejects explicitly the idea of 'a Catholic literary criticism', he chimes agreement with the view that 'all our problems, from literature to politics, are ultimately religious',[86] and speaks as a self-identified Catholic literary critic invested in the idea of developing a Catholic literary criticism.

The lack of specificity in Donoghue's method and the terms of its applicability is, as Colin Graham observes, problematic for the purposes of Irish literary criticism; and, more broadly, for studies examining religious aesthetics.[87] If the poem becomes a verbal icon, as Donoghue suggests it ought, does it disavow religious iconography by replacing it with a poetic one? If so, is poetic production wholly secular? Or are these models of aesthetic production complementary?

The issue upon which these questions of religious aesthetics hinge concerns the role and authority of the poet. In his 1974 essay, 'Feeling into Words', Heaney writes of his search for 'the satisfactory verbal icon and, after the violent summer of 1969, images and symbols adequate to our predicament'.[88] Expressing dismay at religious and political institutions, Heaney presents poetry as an alternative response to the chaos and violence of the Northern Irish conflict—a conflict he sees as religious struggle, both sectarian and mythic. He presents himself as iconographer; in service, seemingly, to religious as well as aesthetic ends.

But Heaney's delineation of the poet's role makes no mention of God, focusing instead on the poem. He is advocating something about the power of poetry, not about religion per se and the distinction is crucial in any assessment of religious aesthetics. Heaney's recourse to poetry represents his schooling in New Criticism, as well as his familiarity with Catholic iconography. But these are competitive rather than complementary modes

[84] Denis Donoghue, 'Notes Towards a Critical Method: Language as Order', *Studies* 44 (1955), 181.
[85] Ibid., 185.
[86] Ibid., 191, 192.
[87] See Colin Graham, ' "We Irish": What Stalks through Donoghue's Irish Criticism', in *Ireland and Transatlantic Poetics: Essays in Honour of Denis Donoghue*, ed. Brian G. Caraher and Robert Mahoney (Newark: University of Delaware Press, 2007), 81.
[88] Seamus Heaney, *Preoccupations: Selected Prose, 1968–1978* (London: Faber, 1980), 56.

of aesthetic production. In New Criticism, the reader's gaze is focused finally and absolutely on the poem, whereas in the operation of Catholic icons and sacraments the viewer's gaze is directed finally towards God. This dual inheritance leaves Heaney with an irresolvable paradox, but one that seems to render his Catholic borrowings secular.

In poems such as 'Blackberry-Picking', 'Damson', and 'Field Work' Heaney takes the sensuous appeal of the Eucharist a step further, by presenting the poem as both verbal icon and Catholic sacrament. 'Damson' (*The Spirit Level*, 1996) meditates on bloody wounds, from a bricklayer's right hand to one remembered fifty years earlier. The speaker compares the bricklayer's 'matte tacky blood' to 'the damson stain/That seeped through his packed lunch'.[89] Catholic theology of transubstantiation can be seen within this transformation, as Heaney turns blood to fruit: a sign of death to a sign of life. The remembered wound he represents as a form of stigmata, the appeal and power of which is universal. Turned to jam, the damsons take on a 'wine-dark taste'.[90] But it is poet, not priest, who presides over this Eucharist. As with 'Blackberry-Picking', to eat the damson is to eat the poem. As a metaphor for poetic consumption, eating has sacramental significance in Heaney's poetry. Making jam becomes a commemorative form of historical memory—indeed, a form of remembering blood sacrifice. Blood becomes fruit and fruit becomes blood, not only within the poetic frame but through it. But the poem's transubstantiation is a dark change, one in which divine presence seems absent, and in which the identities of the dead seem too numerous to fathom. 'Damson' presents a form of commemoration that is sacramental, but Real Presence here is a tragic impossibility.

The poem cannot bring back the dead, although it invites their commemoration in a sacramental form. 'Damson' borrows Catholic modes of signification and remembrance here, but it recognizes the limits of the appropriation. In the poem's refusal to resurrect the dead, Heaney draws on but distinguishes the Eucharist from his own poetic sacrament. 'Field Work IV' (*Field Work*, 1979) enacts another Eucharistic moment through the 'tight slow burn' of sticky currant juice on the back of the hand. Using the currant flower, the speaker anoints the skin and veins of an unnamed female and concludes the poem by intoning, 'you are stained, stained/to perfection'.[91] It is an erotic encounter: the sacrament is sexualized, the diction sensual. Crucially, however, each of these poems is orientated around the poet's hands. In 'Damson', the bricklayer, Heaney's poetic substitute, 'marvelled at his right, held high and raw'.[92] Writing appears as a sacrificial and sacramental practice, but also a conflicted, fraught, and sometimes guilty process, since Heaney's sacramental forms of memorialization are historical and erotic rather than purely religious.

'Blackberry-Picking' (*Death of a Naturalist*, 1966) is both iconic and sacramental, another poem which draws on the Catholic theology of transubstantiation. It expresses Heaney's search for Real Presence in poetry through the blackberry, which is consumed as in the sacrament of the Eucharist:

---

[89]   Heaney, *Opened Ground*, 405.
[90]   Ibid., 406.
[91]   Ibid., 180.
[92]   Ibid., 405.

> You ate that first one and its flesh was sweet
> Like thickened wine: summer's blood was in it
> Leaving stains upon the tongue and lust for
> Picking.[93]

The word becomes flesh, blood, and wine, and the sacrament extends beyond the poetic frame, to the reader consuming the poem. In the thorn-pricked palms of the blackberry pickers, the blackberry is also an icon of natural stigmata. Poetic productivity is thus associated with sacrifice, a Christ-like act meriting reverence and gratitude. Heaney's template for the poet, then, is not only the priest of the Eucharist, but Christ himself. But set against this, in turn, is the figure of Bluebeard and an anxiety about poetic production. Bluebeard's presence in the poem suggests that Heaney's practice of borrowing religious forms for his own poetic ends is overshadowed by guilt.

Manuscripts of 'Strange Fruit' show that the poem was once entitled 'Reliquary', a meditation on *North*'s reverential theme in explicitly Catholic imagery. Unlike the final published version, the speaker implicates the Catholic Church in his contemplation of death and remembrance: 'Church militant and Church triumphant must/Find a niche for this seasoned head'. But here the dead girl is not only blessed; she becomes as Christ in the sacrament of the Eucharist. In an early draft, the poem concludes:

> This was her body.
> This was her blood.
> This is a monstrance
> for her exposition.[94]

In the Roman Catholic Church, the monstrance is an open or transparent receptacle in which the consecrated Host is exposed for veneration. Heaney's wish that the poem become a monstrance for the divine, whether as verbal icon or Catholic sacrament, is at the heart of his poetic endeavour. These poems and many others ask the reader to consider how Catholic theology, as well as Catholic culture, can be incorporated into, or transformed by, poetic form. Heaney's poetry invites us to ask what Catholic art is and whether, or on what terms, it is even possible.

---

[93] Ibid., 8.
[94] 'Strange Fruit' manuscripts, Seamus Heaney Papers, Manuscript, Archives, and Rare Book Library, Emory University.

CHAPTER 29

....

IN BELFAST

....

ELMER KENNEDY-ANDREWS

WHILE nationalist representations of Ireland and Irishness have traditionally depended on a rural ethos and iconography, Ireland/Ulster has undergone rapid fundamental change in recent years, as evidenced by the unprecedented twentieth-century population shifts attendant upon increasing urbanization, the mobility generated by new technology, the growth of travel and tourism, the influx of foreign investment, and the influence of mass communications of TV, film, and the internet. All these developments, in contributing to the creation of 'the global village', have had the effect of eroding traditional cultural values. In the city, the actual multifariousness and heterogeneity of Irish society are visibly concentrated. The city of flux and diversity is not the natural home of traditional religious, political or cultural pieties. The city, says Eamonn Hughes, quoting Roland Barthes, is 'the place of our meeting with the Other'.[1] Opposed to the idea of the rural, 'which always has at its root an allegedly organicist social structure in which relationships are always familiar', Hughes argues, 'the city affronts the sense of the nation as homogenous'.[2] Referring to the city, Raymond Williams draws attention to how 'within the new kind of open, complex and mobile society, small groups in any form of divergence or dissent could find some kind of foothold, in ways that would not have been possible if the artists and thinkers composing them had been scattered in more traditional, closed societies'.[3] City life complicates traditional monolithic nationalisms, whether Irish or Unionist, because it gives a foothold to other forms of struggle—class or gender, for example—which cut across the traditional divisions and oppositions.

In the North, as Edna Longley notes, Louis MacNeice, 'for whom Belfast was the first city', was 'in the vanguard of absorbing the city into English poetry generally'.[4] His exile's

---

[1] Eamonn Hughes, '"What Itch of Contradiction?": Belfast in Poetry', in *The Cities of Belfast*, ed. Nicholas Allen and Aaron Kelly (Dublin: Four Courts Press, 2003), 115.

[2] Ibid.

[3] Raymond Williams, *The Politics of Modernism: Against the New Conformists*, ed. Tony Pinckney (London: Verso, 1989), 44–5.

[4] Edna Longley, *The Living Stream: Literature and Revisionism in Ireland* (Newcastle: Bloodaxe, 1994), 105.

odi atque amo[5] attitude to Belfast and Ireland more generally, and his poetic vantage point of the sceptical, cosmopolitan outsider in whom multiple strains criss-cross in productive tension, have made him an important example for succeeding poets such as Muldoon who have also been interested in exploring hybrid, plural identity in a culture all too prone to fixity and fossilization.

Ironically, for MacNeice it is the countryside which is the site of flux, while Belfast is the site of stasis. Given the poet's fluid and provisional cast of mind, it is therefore no surprise that his attitude to the city should be marked by ambivalence, doubt, and contradiction. The opening line of 'Carrickfergus' establishes the poet's in-between position: 'I was born in Belfast between the mountain and the gantries'.[6] 'Belfast', from September 1931 (and the opening poem in E. R. Dodds's 1966 edition of MacNeice's *Collected Poems*), offers a picture of an urban wasteland, with its images of monolithic fixity and frozen petrifaction, of life corrupted at its source:

> The cold hard fire of the northerner
> Frozen into his blood from the fire in his basalt
> Glares from behind the mica of his eyes
> And the salt carrion water brings him wealth.
>
> Down there at the end of the melancholy lough
> Against the lurid sky over the stained water
> Where the hammers clang murderously on the girders
> Like crucifixes the gantries stand.[7]

'Valediction' contains another picture of oppressive Protestant industrialism, of life hardened into frozen immobility, time and history brought to a deadly standstill:

> See Belfast, devout and profane and hard,
> Built on reclaimed mud, hammers playing in the shipyard,
> Time punched with holes like a steel sheet, time
> Hardening the faces, veneering with a grey and speckled rime
> The faces under the shawls and caps.[8]

The dominant imagery is of changeless, inanimate, unyielding rock, stone, metal: 'Country of callous lava cooled to stone'. Nevertheless, he concedes that Ireland is an intrinsic part of him: 'But I cannot deny my past to which myself is wed,/The woven figure cannot undo its thread'.[9] As Edna Longley notes, 'Even *in extremis*—"Farewell my country, and in perpetuum"—MacNeice attaches the possessive pronoun to Ireland'.[10]

---

[5] Louis MacNeice, 'Autumn Journal XVI', *Collected Poems*, ed. Peter McDonald (London: Faber, 2007), 140.

[6] MacNeice, *Collected Poems*, 55.

[7] Ibid., 25.

[8] Ibid., 8.

[9] Ibid.

[10] Edna Longley, 'Louis MacNeice: The Walls are Flowing', in *Across a Roaring Hill: The Protestant Imagination in Modern Ireland*, ed. Gerald Dawe and Edna Longley (Belfast: Blackstaff, 1985), 105.

A similar ambivalence resurfaces in Canto XVI of 'Autumn Journal', written during the Munich crisis of 1938, when MacNeice was particularly angered by Irish intransigence, North and South, at a time when the whole of Europe was on the brink of cataclysm:

> A city built upon mud;
>   A culture built upon profit;
> Free speech nipped in the bud,
>   The minority always guilty.
> Why should I want to go back
>   To you, Ireland, my Ireland?[11]

Again, bitterness and aggression coexist with Romantic feelings of attachment and nostalgia: 'Such was my country and I thought I was well/Out of it, educated and domiciled in England,/Though yet her name keeps ringing like a bell/In an underwater belfry'.[12] 'Domiciled in England' is a coldly legalistic designation, deliberately withholding any connotation of homely attachment: Ireland is still '*my* country' (as opposed to the more distanced '*This* England' in Canto XVIII).[13]

In reaction against the petrified violence, venality, and vulgarity, he chooses the freedoms of exile, yet, however angry, appalled, or frustrated Irish society makes him feel, Irish landscape is a perennial wonderland. By concentrating on the actual physical world, the miracle of the ordinary, he rises to a pitch of lyrical intensity that carries him beyond the blocked paralysis, stupidity, and intransigence of the social world into a visionary realm of lightsomeness, fluidity, and freedom:

> But I will not give you any idol or idea, creed or king,
> I give you the incidental things which pass
> Outward through space exactly as each was
> ...
> I give you the smell of Norman stone, the squelch
> Of bog beneath your boots, the red bog-grass,
> The vivid chequer of the Antrim hills, the trough of dark
> Golden water for the cart-horses, the brass
> Belt of serene sun upon the lough.[14]

Here even the 'stained water' of the 'melancholy lough' (in 'Belfast') is now bathed in 'serene sun'. Typical of MacNeice, there is no statement which is not challenged, questioned, or undercut, for this is a poetry of unresolved attitudes, of contradictory and dialectical perspectives. Displacement and dislocation are what drive the writing, his sense of ambivalent belonging constituting a valuable creative resource.

---

[11] MacNeice, *Collected Poems*, 140.
[12] Ibid., 139.
[13] Ibid., 144.
[14] 'Train to Dublin', ibid., 17–18.

It is MacNeice's cultural complexity, his sceptical intelligence, his insistence on the primacy of the living word over dogma and abstraction that make him a figure of special relevance to recent debates about identity and 'home' in Northern Ireland. For a number of succeeding Northern Irish poets, MacNeice represents a refreshing and liberating freedom from regional or national definitions of home, a radical challenge to the conventional modes of Irish poetry. He becomes an example of the poetic potential of what Heaney called 'displacement and unrest'.[15]

Like MacNeice, Derek Mahon has been something of a nomad. As citizen of the world, Mahon is as much 'a tourist in his own country' as he said MacNeice was, adding that 'the phrase might stand, indeed, as an epitaph for modern man'.[16] Mahon's is, as Terence Brown opines, 'a peregrine imagination', an 'emigrant sensibility, perhaps most in exile when actually at home'.[17] Or, as Declan Kiberd has it, Mahon is 'a poet of Belfast, but often by way of disavowal'.[18] MacNeice's *amo atque odi* attitude to Ireland is repeated in Mahon's ambivalent feelings about 'roots' and inheritance. Both poets are inheritors of an environment which is inimical to poetry, yet Ireland haunts their imagination. In 'Glengormley', Mahon writes scathingly of the Belfast suburbia where he grew up—'the terrier-taming, garden-watering days'[19]—but deepens the poem's ironies so that apparent admiration of a primitive energy modulates into criticism of romantic distortion of the past. Watching a preacher on a Belfast street corner in 'Ecclesiastes', the poet launches into a savage denunciation of self-righteous puritan rectitude which is itself saved from superiority and self-righteousness by the speaker's bitter acknowledgement that this is part of him and his inheritance: 'God, you could grow to love it, God-fearing, God-/chosen purist little puritan that,/for all your wiles and smiles, you are.'[20] One of his early poems is called 'The Spring Vacation', originally titled 'In Belfast'. The change of title is significant, eliminating as it does the importance of place, shifting the emphasis from the idea of homecoming to tourism:

> Walking among my own this windy morning
> In a tide of sunlight between shower and shower,
> I resume my old conspiracy with the wet
> Stone and the unwieldy images of the squinting heart.
> Once more, as before, I remember not to forget.
>
> ...
>
> One part of my mind must learn to know its place.
> The things that happen in the kitchen houses

[15] Seamus Heaney, 'The Pre-Natal Mountain: Vision and Irony in Recent Irish Poetry', *The Place of Writing* (Atlanta, GA: Scholars Press, 1989), 47.

[16] Derek Mahon, *Journalism: Selected Prose 1970–1995*, ed. Terence Brown (Oldcastle: Gallery, 1996), 250.

[17] Terence Brown, 'Introduction' to Derek Mahon, *Journalism*, 18.

[18] Declan Kiberd, *Inventing Ireland: The Literature of the Modern Nation* (London: Vintage, 1996), 599.

[19] Derek Mahon, *Collected Poems* (Oldcastle: Gallery, 1999), 14.

[20] Ibid., 35.

> And echoing back streets of this desperate city
> Should engage more than my casual interest,
> Exact more interest than my casual pity.[21]

The poem expresses the poet's conflicted and ambiguous relationship with his Protestant Ulster origins. His relationship with 'his own' is a 'conspiracy'—not something warmly embraced. The reference to 'the unwieldy images of the squinting heart' belittles the religious piety of his people. The paradoxical wordplay of 'I remember not to forget' emphasizes his strained relationship with his home place. Though back in Belfast for a spring vacation, he admits he is unable to feel any strong identification with his own people. Like MacNeice, he is both inside and outside, wavering on the threshold of communal belonging. The poem keeps its distance from the human dramas to which it vaguely alludes in the last verse. Only 'one part' of his mind need concern itself with knowing 'its place'—which is the city of Belfast, but also what society expects of him. Either way, he is careful about how much of himself he is prepared to mortgage to place-poetry. Mahon is the displaced, disaffected Northern Protestant, the migrant cosmopolitan for whom ideas of belonging and community are highly problematic. Without a community to which he can feel he belongs, he is drawn to romantic outsiders, bohemians, the forgotten and neglected, and while his models tend to be marginalized figures of the wider European and American world rather than from within his own culture, there are amongst his own tribe individuals such as 'Grandfather' and 'My Wicked Uncle' who represent a kind of outlawry with which he can identity. These figures embody what he regards as some of the more positive elements of Protestant Belfast-idiosyncratic rebelliousness, irrepressible personality.

Unlike Mahon, Michael Longley stayed and worked in Belfast throughout the 'Troubles'. Contrasting with Mahon's stance of disaffected outsider, Longley identifies with the city, with Belfast's shopkeepers, civil servants, and linen workers who represent the economic and civic life of the city. 'Wounds' juxtaposes images of his father's experiences on the Somme in 1916 with the deaths of the nameless victims of the contemporary Troubles on the streets of Belfast: all wounds are the same. In keeping with this analogizing approach, the situation in Belfast is explored through multiple trans-cultural perspectives: the Warsaw ghetto, First and Second World War battlefields, the Jarama valley, scenes from Homeric epic. Longley relates to Belfast not in terms of inherited familial, tribal, or religious affiliation (His family connection with the province dates from 1927 when his parents first arrived in Belfast from Clapham Common.), but through a process of personal, emotional, and imaginative attachment. Though Belfast was where he was born and brought up and where he worked for over twenty years in the Northern Ireland Arts Council, he valued his position as something of an outsider, his MacNeicean combination of Irish and English viewpoints, which allowed him to respond with flexibility and objectivity to the complexities of the North. In his essay on MacNeice, 'The Neolithic Light' (1973), he remarks that for MacNeice life 'had to be organic, open to all

---

[21] Ibid., 13.

the possibilities. No systems could be imposed'[22]—a statement which summarizes Longley's own poetic refusal to align himself with any political, aesthetic, or religious creed, his determination to remain open to the infinite, often surprising, possibilities of life. This MacNeicean openness means that home is always a matter of choice, not simply of origins, always a personal construct which, in Longley's case, continually looks beyond human community to embrace the whole interconnected earthly ecosystem. Home can be anywhere, and there can be any number of homes. In 'The West', he shifts between 'home' in Belfast and his holiday cottage in Carrikskeewaun, County Mayo, his 'home from home':

> Beneath a gas-mantle that the moths bombard,
> Light that powders at a touch, dusty wings,
> I listen for news through the atmospherics,
> A crackle of sea-wrack, spinning driftwood,
> Waves like distant traffic, news from home,
>
> Or watch myself, as through a sandy lens,
> Materialising out of the heat-shimmers
> And finding my way for ever along
> The path to this cottage, its windows,
> Walls, sun and moon dials, home from home.[23]

The balancing phrases that end each stanza—'News from home' and 'home from home'—challenge and complicate any simple understanding of the meaning of 'home'. The speaker, self-consciously listening and observing, attempts to locate himself in relation to two homes. His situation in the West is not an absconding from, or betrayal of, his Belfast home. Rather, 'home' and 'home from home', Belfast and the West, must be read together simultaneously because these categories are mutually constitutive and contingent. Longley's 'homes' have porous walls. Like the concept of home, the concept of self is also a construct, a matter of choice and experience, not simply of origins: the poet's 'home from home' allows him the distance to contemplate new possibilities of identity. A new self materializes out of heat-shimmers, uncertain, forever eluding full definition: he finds his way *for ever* along/The path to this cottage'. This emergent sense of self owes nothing to cultural myth and everything to the concrete particulars of the place he loves: 'its windows,/Walls, sun and moon dials', references which, while existing credibly as ordinary realistic description, also serve to place the cottage in a vast cosmo-logical context far beyond the frames of any particular cultural myth or political ideology.

Another poet closely identified with Belfast, but evincing a similar impatience with totalizing frameworks and stereotypical identifications, is Ciaran Carson. In Carson's work, Neil Corcoran believes, 'it is surely possible to see the ground of a Northern Irish

---

[22] Michael Longley, 'The Neolithic Night: A Note on the Irishness of Louis MacNeice', in *Two Decades of Irish Writing*, ed. Douglas Dunn (Cheadle Hulme: Carcanet, 1975), 99.

[23] Michael Longley, *Collected Poems* (London: Jonathan Cape, 2006), 69.

poetry of the postmodern beginning to prepare itself'.[24] Carson's own poetry, Corcoran continues, is a search for a way of registering 'the full shock of the challenge to recognized modes and forms represented by the realities of post-1968 Northern Ireland, and more particularly post-1968 Belfast'.[25] Carson's poetry emanates from the Belfast epicentre of the Troubles. Where Fiacc, Heaney, Mahon, and other poets tend to view the city in essentialist terms, as unchanging and monolithic, Carson's new urban poetics unsettles fixed versions of the city. By experimenting with discontinuous, decentred, or ungrounded forms, Carson presents a city space that is unstable and unreliable, yet always susceptible to reconstruction and renewal. Exploring these new spaces leads to the creation of new maps, the formulation of new concepts of identity and place, and the relationships between them. Belfast is no longer the place which must be escaped (even if that were possible), but the location of post-national, encyclopaedic, labyrinthine, ever-shifting Northern scenarios.

Carson's work exemplifies the ways in which 'open' or discontinuous or broken forms function to represent epistemological attitudes. His gapped, elliptical poems whose parts refuse to combine into unified wholes constitute a distinctive view of the world, one originating from within a society in the throes of violent breakdown. A broken style reflects a fractured city. As many of the poems demonstrate, discontinuity can place considerable demands on the reader who is left to arrange the elements more or less as he sees fit. Incompleteness and indeterminacy in the poem reflect the incompleteness and indeterminacy, and even the necessity of such incompleteness and indeterminacy, of our knowledge of reality. Whatever knowledge is available takes the form of disjointed facts or observations with no comprehensive explanations to connect them. Rationalistic metaphysics, and the form in which they are usually presented, are rejected because they give a misleadingly coherent picture of our knowledge of reality.

One of his best-known poems, 'Belfast Confetti' from *The Irish for No* (1987), suggests, in its 'stuttering' but powerfully energetic way, a connection between history and poetry, civil disturbance and textual disturbance:

> Suddenly as the riot squad moved in, it was raining exclamation marks,
> Nuts, bolts, nails, car-keys. A fount of broken type. And the explosion
> Itself – an asterisk on the map. This hyphenated line, a burst of rapid fire...
> I was trying to complete a sentence in my head, but it kept stuttering,
> All the alleyways and side-streets blocked with stops and colons.[26]

No longer able to maintain conventional structure, the poem consists of disjointed lists of things presented without subordination, giving the impression of a discourse unmediated by an ordering rational mind, responding directly to the exigencies of the moment. Relying on an accumulating power of perception, the poem, proceeding through a series of alternating staccato bursts and arrests, speaks emphatically of the

---

[24] Neil Corcoran, 'One Step Forward, Two Steps Back', in *The Chosen Ground: Essays on the Contemporary Poetry of Northern Ireland*, ed. Neil Corcoran (Bridgend; Seren Books, 1992), 215.

[25] Ibid., 216.

[26] Ciaran Carson, *Collected Poems* (Oldcastle; Gallery, 2008), 93.

here-and-now. The suggestive image of confetti (lifted from Padraic Fiacc's poem 'The British Connection'), with its ironic connotations of union and celebration, refers to the missiles hurled by the rioting mob, the disrupted text of the poem, and the confusion of the poet's own shredded thoughts. Against this backdrop of violent disturbance, questions of identity ('What is/My name?'), origins ('Where am I coming from?'), and purpose ('Where am I going?') are thrown into confusion. We can't even be sure who is asking the questions. Is the poet questioning himself? Or has he been stopped by the police or the army? Or is this a similar situation to that described in 'Question Time',[27] where he is watched and followed and then interrogated by local Falls Road vigilantes? Place names, which in Heaney provide the reassuring coordinates of home, are here the markers of an alienating imperial past: 'I know this labyrinth so well—Balaclava, Raglan, Inkerman, Odessa Street—/Why can't I escape?'[28] The speaker, though assimilated to the city, cannot dominate the situation but, instead, begins to lose his initial, complacent 'self' in a process which opens the self to the assault of otherness and contingency. The subject that emerges is a provisional, historical figure, composed through its interaction with the 'other', through remaining 'in play', in movement, a harried *flâneur*. Deprived of a sense of centre, the abstract binaries—subject/object, self/city, inner/outer—which usually form the basis of knowledge and certainty, dissolve into each other, and the subject as autonomous agent is relocated within the networks of historical process, deprived of the distance that would enable him to produce a 'grand narrative' that is without gaps or elisions, without stops or stuttering.

Caught up in the complexity—the dangers and excitement—of the city, Carson's persona is rather different from the Baudelairean or Benjaminian *flâneur* who is a detached observer finding refuge in aesthetic contemplation. The *flâneur* is the pedestrian observer of the metropolis, the 'gentleman stroller of city streets', the 'botanist of the sidewalk', first identified by Charles Baudelaire. Since adopted by Walter Benjamin in his accounts of urban life in 'A Berlin Chronicle' (1932) and the unfinished *Arcades Project* on which he worked throughout the 1930s up to his death in 1940, the *flâneur* has come to typify the subjective experience of urban space. The *flâneur*, as reader of the city, transforms the city into text. His readings of the semiotic city are inevitably momentary and fragmentary. Restricted temporally and physically, he is unable to produce any overarching vision of the modern city as a totality, only glimpses of its parts. Being part of the crowd as well as watcher of the world go by, the *flâneur* enjoys no neutral, privileged vantage point. The continual shifting of perspective creates a montage of moving images, fleetingly and impressionistically registered. In this respect, the *flâneur* indicates a transformation of perception in the new metropolitan milieu, and it is this perspective of situatedness, historicity, and fragmentariness that forms the basis of Carson's new urban poetics. For though Benjamin's *flâneur* operated in the streets and arcades of nineteenth-century Paris, the type is immediately recognizable in the Carsonian persona, for whom

---

[27] Ibid., 165–70.
[28] Ibid., 93.

the city of Belfast is also a space of reading, a semiological environment bound up in individual and cultural memory.

Carson's image of the city as labyrinth is a familiar Benjaminian trope, as in this passage taken from 'A Berlin Chronicle', which Carson uses as epigraph in *Belfast Confetti*:

> Not to find one's way in a city may well be uninteresting and banal. It requires igno-
> rance – nothing more. But to lose oneself in a city – as one loses oneself in a forest –
> that calls for quite a different schooling. Then, sign-boards and street names,
> passers-by, roofs, kiosks, or bars must speak to the wanderer like a cracking twig
> under his feet in the forest.[29]

In the labyrinth of the city, self-location and self-affirmation become a struggle. Mastery—intellectual and psychological—is unsettled. Losing one's way results in a deterritorialization of knowledge. Poetic wandering denies the authority of the official maps and resists the systematization of the world. Like Benjamin, Carson surrenders to the spell of the labyrinthine city, attempting to read and decode the meaning of urban space from clues, traces, fragments that present themselves in what often threatens to become an unbearable sensory overload. The resulting poetry is a profusion of instanta-neous, partially registered, swiftly moving images which reflect the key modern experi-ences, not only of the urban voyeur observing the collapsing city, but also, as the proliferation of commodity brand names in Carson's poetry would suggest, of the Benjaminian customer and consumer.

Benjamin collected thousands of seemingly trivial items of nineteenth-century Parisian bourgeois industrial culture, which were published posthumously as a montage of found materials interspersed with occasional comment. The Arcades Project takes its name from a nineteenth-century architectural form, arcades being covered passageways through blocks of buildings with lines of shops on either side. A whole building is made up of connected parts. Similarly, Benjamin's literary form is a structure of fragments. He valued collections as a form of historiography because their fragmentary arrangements resisted the degree of order and control implied by a 'grand narrative':

> [I]t was not the great men and celebrated events of traditional historiography but
> rather the 'refuse' and 'detritus' of history, the half-concealed, variegated traces of the
> daily life of 'the collective', that was to be the object of study, with the aids of methods
> more akin – above all, in their dependence on chance – to the methods of the nine-
> teenth-century collector of antiquities and curiosities, or indeed to the methods of
> the nineteenth-century ragpicker, than to those of the modern historian.[30]

Another kind of 'detritus' which absorbed Benjamin's attention was the ruin. Since the Parisian arcades dated back to the 1820s, many had fallen into ruin by the time he began

---

[29] Walter Benjamin, 'A Berlin Chronicle', *Reflections: Essays, Aphorisms, Autobiographical Writings*, ed. P. Demetz (New York; Schocken, 1986), 8–9.

[30] Walter Benjamin, *The Arcades Project*, trans. Howard Eiland and Kevin McLaughlin (Cambridge, MA; Belknap Press, 1999), p. ix.

his researches. For Benjamin, it was the ruins of a great building, or the historical epoch the building represents, which could awaken in us a true sense of history. Benjamin interprets ruin as the opposite of the urban spectacle. Ruin enables us to see history not as a smooth chain of events in linear time, expressive of the glory of civilization, but as the sign of death and collapse. The city as ruin can be excavated to reveal nightmarish experiences of alienation and displacement, the latent anxiety of death and catastrophe, the metropolitan uncanny which places the homely, the domestic, and the ordered under threat.

So, Carson, idling in the spaces of the city, presents a kind of dream world in which the human subject, entranced by the phantasmagoria of commodity fetishism, street violence, and the technologies of state control, finds itself petrified, disorientated, divested of agency, placed under surveillance. Wandering through the ruins of the chiasmal arcades of Smithfield Market—a microcosm of the city—the poet reflects the sense of life as a myriad of disconnected impressions. 'Smithfield Market' is something of a ragpicker's random collection of material, a series of vivid, intense, disjointed yet fluid images. Like Benjamin, Carson seeks to discover half-hidden energies of history that are slumbering in the depths of the city, which might provide clues for finding a way out of the labyrinth:

> Sidelong to the arcade, the glassed-in April cloud – fleeting, pewter-edged –
> Gets lost in shadowed aisles and inlets, branching into passages, into cul-de-sacs,
> Stalls, compartments, alcoves. Everything unstitched, unravelled – mouldy fabric,
> Rusted heaps of nuts and bolts, electrical spare parts…
>
> Since everything went up in smoke, no entrances, no exits.
> But as the charred beams hissed and flickered, I glimpsed a map of Belfast
> In the ruins: obliterated streets, the faint impression of a key.
> Something, many-toothed, elaborate, stirred briefly in the labyrinth.[31]

Ending on this ambiguous note, the poem awaits an unknown future. Trapped in the labyrinth, the Thesean *flâneur* comes into possession of the key, or at least 'the faint impression of a key', that may unlock the meaning of Belfast—or take him further into darkness and danger. The poet stirs up repressed communal, historical, or revolutionary remembrance within the alienated city spaces, alert to both the disruptive traces of the unconscious and the possibility of recouping neglected, half-buried collective experience. Lost among the discarded, unpromising material of the everyday, he is ready to undertake the hazardous task of opening up a space for alternative histories, myths, and memories.

Underlying Carson's fragmented, temporally and spatially mobile, digressive poetics is his intuition of centrelessness. He radically undermines the idea of a centre capable of providing discursive unity and fixity, and the claims of any culture to possess a pure and homogeneous body of values. Given a world of flux and contingency, and Carson's return to concrete particulars as the basis of knowledge, the great challenge is how to

---

[31] Carson, *Collected Poems*, 99.

give structure to the array of particulars without violating their particularity. While insisting on the stubborn particularity of things, the 'careful drunken weaving' of connections within and among poems represent a countervailing impulse towards unification. Carson's aesthetic is poised between anti-essentialism and organization. His encyclopaedic form, with its discontinuous, apparently arbitrary arrangement of particulars and its artificial patternings, at once proclaims the unity of the whole and undermines that unity. The resulting narrative is historical *and* fragmentary, structured *and* open, continuous *and* discontinuous.

He takes fragmentariness further in *Breaking News* (2003), the first part of which is remarkable for his abandoning the long line for an extremely short-lined, broken format which owes a good deal to William Carlos Williams. The title works on several levels. It alludes to the continuous stream of reportage that brings the most up-to-date news of what is happening around the world, but also refers to the convulsions of war in the poet's home place and around the world, and to the breaking up of conventional poetic form under pressure of violent events. The collection's title is broken across two poems which appear on facing pages. The first, 'Breaking', contains the image of a car 'about to disintegrate' in an eerily silent Belfast street. The second, 'News', concerns the aftermath of the car bomb. The actual explosion falls into the gap between the two poems, unrepresented and unrepresentable. In 'News', the sign above the *Belfast Telegraph* shop now reads '*fast rap*',[32] reminiscent of the situation described in the earlier 'Gate', from *Belfast Confetti* (1989), where a boutique called 'Terminus' has lost its T and r as a result of a bomb, leaving '*e minus*'. Writing, like maps, is never adequate, especially in times of rapid, violent change: 'Difficult to keep track:/Everything's a bit askew....'[33]

The collection opens with 'Belfast', a poem that gestures towards both Wallace Stevens's 'Thirteen Ways of Looking at a Blackbird' and Williams's rhythms of speech and living, in which Belfast is enveloped in an unreal silence—except for the whistling of a blackbird. Carson's poem, with a similar painterly vividness and concrete precision as one finds in Williams's 'The Red Wheelbarrow', emphasizes patterns of colour, the relationship of the parts of the picture to each other. No one thing stands for something else; it is uniquely itself: 'No ideas/but in things'.[34]

BELFAST

east

beyond the yellow
shipyard cranes

a blackbird whistles
in a whin bush

---

[32] Ibid., 435–6.

[33] Ibid., 153.

[34] William Carlos Williams, 'A Sort of a Song', *Selected Poems*, ed. Charles Tomlinson [1976] (London: Penguin, 2000), 133.

> west
>
> beside the motorway
> a black taxi
>
> rusts in a field
> of blue thistles[35]

Here, William Carlos Williams and American Imagism meet early Irish Gaelic nature poetry. Carson's poem, written with haiku-like precision and clarity, exhibits the kind of freshness and directness, the kind of watchfulness towards nature, that we associate with early Irish nature poems. Indeed, 'Belfast' closely echoes the well-known 'The Blackbird of Belfast Lough', written by a seventh-century Irish monk in the margins of an illuminated manuscript. The influence of the Celtic god in the tree, manifest in blackbird and thistle, continues to hover over the modern metropolis with its motorways, black taxis, and shipyard cranes.

If the danger in a localist or particularist focus is that poems might become a series of isolated fragments unable to speak beyond their own moment, it is through the sheer intensity of the poet's concentration and the degree of imaginative responsiveness that he brings to bear, that his detailed vignettes of particular incidents or scenes assume universal dimensions. Small, apparently insignificant details disclose far-reaching insights, parts contain wholes, fragments tell a bigger story. 'Fragment' refers to a bit of a Tupperware lunchbox from which 'they could tell/the bombmaker wore/Marigold gloves',[36] the single word 'Marigold' suggesting a whole conspectus of orders—natural, domestic, and religious—that the bombmaker has violated. Other ways in which Carson seeks to develop an encompassing poetry have to do with notions of structure, narrative, and design. In 'The Ballad of HMS *Belfast*', from *First Language*—a poem comprised of twenty-five long-lined rhyming couplets—Belfast, set loose from her moorings, begins to drift, to enter other places, other stories. The city does not stand for a rational, firm referent, but slips through the predictable circuitry of 'Both Catestants and Protholics'[37] to become a floating signifier, moving through diverse interpretations and narratives. Whether caught in the modes of hallucinatory fantasy, as in 'The Ballad of HMS *Belfast*', or in the mythical half-light of imagined foreign battlefields, as in *Breaking News*, Belfast, in Carson's account, is a more open and extensive place than the one we have been accustomed to reading about. In *Breaking News*, poems about Belfast and the Troubles are interspersed with poems about the Russian Revolution, the Indian Mutiny, and the Crimean War, the depiction of scenes of different wars reverberating against each other. Diverse histories intersect and open up the space of an encounter, a dialogue, in which neither history is reduced to the other. Narrowly focused snapshots of battle scenes and their immediate aftermath convey the dehumanization of entire societies.

---

[35] Carson, *Collected Poems*, 431.
[36] Ibid., 454.
[37] Ibid., 274.

In rewriting the grammar of urban historiography in terms of discontinuity and centrelessness, Carson dissolves the relationship between power and knowledge on which our understanding of what is central and what is marginal has traditionally been founded. By doing away with the centre, the authorizing principle, he does away with those binary oppositions in which one term is always privileged over the other. Instead, he wants to open us to considerations beyond ourselves, beyond the usual hegemonic structures of understanding and representation, to what exists only as trace or echo or shadow. Categories leak and spill; they cast shadows over one another; they interpenetrate each other. Identity is always open, never finite nor resolved. This new urban poetics implies a very different sense of 'home' from that which we find in the older generation of Heaney or Mahon: Carson's 'home' is neither fixed nor closed, but mobile, mutable, constructed in the movement of language that constitutes the sense of place, belonging, and identity. Dwelling is sustained, not by roots but by dialogue with other histories, other places, other people. The sense of place that is constructed is always contingent, in transit, with neither origin nor end.

In the wake of such exemplars, two younger Belfast poets, who first made their mark in the late 1990s and early 2000s, continue the exploration of the city and what it means to live there. The nomadic Sinéad Morrissey, after some years spent in Japan, New Zealand, and other places, opens her second volume, *Between Here and There* (2002), with 'In Belfast':

> I have returned after ten years to a corner
> and tell myself it is as real to sleep here
> as the twenty other corners I have slept in.
> More real, even, with this history's dent and fracture
>
> splitting the atmosphere. And what I have been given
> is a delicate unravelling of wishes
> that leaves the future unspoken and the past
> unencountered and unaccounted for.
>
> This city weaves itself so intimately
> it is hard to see, despite the tenacity of the river
> and the iron sky; and in its downpour and its vapour I am
> as much at home here as I will ever be.[38]

Returning to Belfast, Morrissey has no strong sense of the place—'it is hard to see'; it is just another corner to sleep in. She recognizes the challenge the city offers to traditional ideas of home, and to any notion of home, nation, or identity as homogenous. The city is where our sense of centre is displaced, and our historical, cultural, and subjective being is disrupted. Yet, Belfast is 'more real' with its 'history's dent and fracture/splitting the atmosphere'. The poet sees herself as the inheritor, not of fixed meanings and identity, but of 'a delicate unravelling of wishes'. It is in the unstable, discontinuous city, in its 'downpour and its vapour', that she feels at home, the word 'vapour' suggesting a

---

[38] Sinéad Morrissey, *Between Here and There* (Manchester; Carcanet, 2002), 13.

metaphorical as well as physical manifestation of the legendary Irish mist. The sense of belonging that emerges at the end is resigned and unillusioned, infused with images of dissolution, disintegration, and unreality.

The single, homogenous point of view, epitomized in colonialism, imperialism, and rational modernity, implies a totalizing vision, mastery of the world. In contrast, Morrissey is absorbed by the incoherence, the estrangement, in modern culture and identity, the gaps opened up by the stranger, the tectonic shifts that displace established meanings and force us to confront the stranger in ourselves. This is the message of the next poem, 'Tourism', which welcomes the upsurge in tourists visiting Belfast in the wake of the ceasefires. 'Our day has come', the poem proclaims, ironically re-citing/re-siting the slogan of the Irish Republican movement, *Tiocfadh ár lá* ('our day will come'): the future lies, not in the fulfilment of national destiny, but in replacement of traditional notions of Irish identity with a new vision of openness, pluralism, and multiculturalism. In opposition to the principle of *Sinn Fein* ('ourselves alone'), Morrissey welcomes 'infection' from outside, and pleads for a new post-nationalist, European state in a language and cadence that recall Mahon's importunate mushrooms in a disused shed:

> So come, keep coming here.
> We'll recklessly set chairs in the streets and pray for the sun.
> Diffuse the gene pool, confuse the local kings,
>
> infect us with your radical ideas; be carried here
> on a sea breeze from the European superstate
> we long to join; bring us new symbols,
> a new national flag, a xylophone. Stay.[39]

Deliberately countering older notions of place/home as bounded territory, and traditional concepts of identity as racially pure and homogenous, Morrissey welcomes the stranger, and embraces the idea of home as being always contingent, open to new influence, in perpetual transit. We are back with metaphors of journey and nomadism: existence as a continual confabulation, with no fixed identity or final destination. Belfast is a 'splintered city', 'gapped' and 'holed', but out of the fragments a new future may yet be constructed, despite setback and disappointment. The tours on which the visitors are taken are symbols of the official attempt to create an acceptable post-Troubles narrative out of a place marked by disjunction and disruption. Circulating among the sites of both achievement and failure ('the festering gap in the shipyard/the Titanic made when it sank./Our talent for holes that are bigger/than the things themselves'), the tourists encounter the uncanny truth of ambiguity. The ideas of home, identity, and belonging which Morrissey proposes, like the traditional narrative of the nation (Irish or British), involve the construction of an 'imaginary community', but her fiction is crucially different from traditional conceptions of community in that it is based on the premise that there is no single language in which 'community' or 'identity' can be incontrovertibly asserted, no single narrative that can claim absolute authority.

[39] Ibid., 14.

In the very fine 'An Anatomy of Smell', Belfast, home, and identity are constructed in terms of the intimate language of smell: the smell of her partner's skin ('I would know your skin in the dark: its smooth magnetic film/would bring me home and cease my being separate'); the smells of other people's hallways; the family smells that children bring to school with them ('slipped giveaways/of origin'); the smells of poet and partner that constitute their 'identity' and 'home' ('Now we too have an identity—/the smell of us is through our sheets and wrapped around our home').[40] Smell 'conquers distance'. It is a more intimate and distinctive marker of identity than any of the usual abstract designations such as race or religion: 'any family/forges something wholly themselves and wholly different/and marks each child for life with the hidden nature of their generative act'. The smell of home is made up of many different smells, which are now shared and transformed in the sharing. When she moves house, she is confident that these intimate markers of home and identity will move with them: 'When we move house/such genealogies as these will follow us.' The poet's concept of home depends not on fixity, boundedness, or stability, nor on a sense of belonging to a particular regional, cultural, or political tradition. Building on existentialist, not essentialist or metaphysical premises, Morrissey constructs her 'home' experientially, from the intimacies of the personal life, from mobile personal relationships and the fluctuating data of the senses. The poem is a cleverly devised vehicle for its message. Like the smell which 'is through our sheets and wrapped around our home', various coordinating textual elements, such as the ghostly presence of rhyme (more strongly evident than is usual in Morrissey's relatively free verse) drifting musically through the sheets of the poem, mimic and fulfil the unifying function which the poet attributes to smell.

Alan Gillis's poems also offer an alternative Belfast. Gillis is the laureate of the postmodern, the era of mass communications, rampant commercialization, and popular culture. The poem '12th October 1994' begins, 'I enter the Twilight Zone'[41]—one of a chain of amusement arcades which takes its name from the title of the American 1960s TV show that specialized in dark, eerie tales of fantasy, science fiction, or horror. Since the 1960s, the 'Twilight Zone' series has become the inspiration of numerous comic books, television and film revivals, a Disney theme-park ride, songs by Golden Earring, Iron Maiden, and The Manhattan Transfer, and a Midway pinball game. With the help of the *Oxford English Dictionary* we also learn that, originally, the term referred to the line separating the portion of a planet that is illuminated by the sun and that in shadow (that is, the area between day and night), more officially known as the 'terminator'. Gillis plays on these references and usages, creating his own poetic 'Twilight Zone', that liminal space between fantasy and reality which is also, in Baudrillardian terms, the realm of the simulacrum. In Gillis's poem, the recreational violence of the video games is situated within the context of the actual violence played out every day in the streets of Belfast during the Troubles. The date of 12 October 1994 was the eve of the announcement from the combined Loyalist Military Command (UDA, UVF, and the Red Hand Commandos) of a ceasefire dependent

[40] Ibid., 34.
[41] Alan Gillis, *Somebody, Somewhere* (Oldcastle: Gallery, 2004), 10.

on 'the continued cessation of all nationalist/republican violence', and twelve days after the IRA ceasefire. Less than a year before, an IRA bomb on the Shankill Road, Belfast, had killed eleven people and, a week later, the retaliatory gun attack by the UFF on a pub in Greysteel left seven dead. The poem blurs the line between this actual violence and the virtual violence of the electronic games. The poem's narrator interacts with the figures on the screen, not the actual people who come and go, and who, as their cartoon names ('Frankie "Ten Pints" Fraser', 'Johnny "Book Keeper" McFeeter', 'Terry "The Blaster" McMaster', 'Benny "Vindaloo" McVeigh') suggest, themselves assume iconographic identity. Further reinforcing the sense of media-saturation is the meticulously specified soundtrack—the catalogue of jukebox hits of the pre-Troubles 1960s playing in the background. Despite the narrator's skill at the game, it is he who is controlled by the machine, and integrated into the material process of objectification and commodification. Even his language, like the game he plays, is a virtual reality: for all its violent 'self-presencing', it can do no more than gesture towards actualization while constantly deferring or frustrating it. In the postmodern world of the 'Twilight Zone', signs, surfaces, and everyday life have no reliable ontological reality. Surfaces and appearances are deceptive, seductive, and mystifying manifestations of an underlying existential reality, which, Gillis seems to be saying, is the alienated condition of contemporary life.

The physical reality of the public spaces of the city, like the actual people who inhabit them, cease to have any significance. A recurrent poetic scenario involves a central image of private space—kitchen, living room, bedroom, hotel dining room, car interior—invaded by the global world; and a recurrent persona is that of the individual, located within a network of relations—global, national, local, indigenous, personal— unsettled, disoriented, or exhausted by the multiplicity and dynamic simultaneity of these relations. This complication of the link between place and culture is evidenced in Gillis's 'Saturday Morning'. The poem begins with a picture of a Saturday morning recreated in all its sensuous immediacy:

> The fart and snigger of sausages and free
> range eggs, the beans of a coffee grinder
> and light house music on a Fujifilm CD . . . [42]

When the speaker moves to his living room and 'slab[s]' on his sofa in front of the TV, he enters another Twilight Zone, zapping from one world to another, his own subjective identity swiftly vanishing in the slipstream of the constant procession of images, 'your face swarming/into pixels'.[43] Reference to the 'mortuary white-/yellow shake of your hands' and the 'slab' of the sofa suggest a kind of death-in-life. For the undifferentiated stream of images levels out the extremes of the banal ('teenage models launching their memoirs') and the truly catastrophic ('where a wave hammer-walled/through the coastal village'), producing a feeling of disorientation, a sense of the fragmentation of cultural experience, a loss of internal coherence:

---

[42] Alan Gillis, *Hawks and Doves* (Oldcastle: Gallery, 2007), 18.
[43] Ibid., 20.

> Lie there long enough and you will drown
> in the glut-stream of yourself, or nothing,
> as you dissolve into the screen, its thin lips
> gaping into such a maw you cannot undo
> its babbling hoodoo.[44]

The older sense of 'home' with which the poem opens is soon undermined as the impact of the vast contemporary reorganization of capital, the formation of a new global space, the use of new technologies of communication make themselves felt. Place is no longer equated with community, and is therefore no longer able to provide a stable basis for identity. 'Saturday Morning' elaborates a concept of space which takes the form of simultaneous coexistence of experience at all geographical scales, from the most local (the intimacy of the kitchen) to the wide space of transglobal connections, accessed with a 'click' of the remote control:

> Click. A celebrity chef provides fresh ideas
> for sausages. Click. The merlin falls like a brick
> on a bank vole's head. Click. The President.
> Click. The pop star peels down to his gonads.
> Click. 'Oh my God, look at her kitchen!' Click.
> Janjaweed teenagers patrol the road to Chad.[45]

A particular place—the speaker's living room—becomes a point of intersection of vast numbers of social relations stretched out over space. The home place is no longer singular or bounded, no longer a place of nostalgia. Boundaries between places are dissolved. The global constitutes the local. Distance becomes meaningless. The identity of both individual and place is multiple, shifting. Gillis's insistent 'clicking' undermines any stability of meaning, breaking down conventional boundaries and identities, and producing a subject who, precariously situated at the intersection of these multiple flows of influence, is reduced to the role of entirely passive consumer. The poem, with its intimation of ideas of sped-up, instantaneous world-wide communication, constant global flows, and spatial interconnectedness, certainly marks the end of essentialist definitions of home, but it also signals a demoralizing homogenization of culture which not even the poet's distinctive vernacular can hold at bay. Postmodernity facilitates relations with 'absent' others, but these are relations of a very limited and superficial kind; meanwhile, social life characterized by 'presence', by local activity, is displaced, marginalized, or obliterated.

As the work of the poets surveyed in this essay demonstrates, 'In Belfast' means many different things. The processes of urbanization, globalization, and migration have produced new relations between rootedness and mobility, centre and periphery, local and global. We no longer need to think of places as having single, unique, essential identities, but as processes, as products of global, interconnecting flows of peoples, cultures, economies, and meanings—of routes rather than roots.

---

[44] Ibid.
[45] Ibid., 19–20.

CHAPTER 30

'OUR LOST LIVES': PROTESTANTISM AND NORTHERN IRISH POETRY

PETER McDONALD

In *An Autumn Wind* (2010), Derek Mahon found himself writing poems of address to celebrated (and now elderly) poetic contemporaries: John Montague, Seamus Heaney, and Michael Longley all received elegantly low-key and companionable verses, while one poet, no longer alive to take delivery of Mahon's lines, was the subject of a substantial elegy. 'Art and Reality' is addressed to James Simmons (1933–2001), and is written largely in the tetrameter couplets which Mahon had used in his own early writing for verse-letters (and which others, notably Longley, had employed for the same purpose). The combination of formal tightness with conversational unbuttoning gives the feeling, at least, of candour. In an elegy, certain kinds of candour are easier than others: frankness about one's view of the deceased, for example, is not subject to the implied comeback that a verse-letter to the living always needs to bear in mind. But Mahon, like any elegist, is writing for a living audience that includes himself; and in this respect, candour is not necessarily at a premium: of all that might be said, not all *should* be said, or (art being limited, sooner or later) necessarily can be said. 'Art and Reality' says much, and powerfully; and what it does not say is also both suggestive and difficult, involving as it does religion, politics, and literary history.

Mahon's poem is from one poet to another; but there are inescapable inequalities in the relationship. Not just that overpowering inequality which all elegies have to figure—between the living writer and his dead subject or addressee—but between poets from the same place and cultural situation with strikingly different degrees of contemporary success: two writers who both came to prominence as 'Ulster poets' in the late 1960s, but whose careers diverged dramatically, both in terms of how and what they wrote and of the popularity and international acceptance of their books. Simmons, in fact, was the more 'populist' writer; and Mahon (at least until the 1990s) the chillier, more impersonal and aloof poet of the two: but Simmons's career did not match that of Mahon (nor, of course, those of Longley and Heaney), and this inequality is something which the elegy needs to put into its particular kind of balance. 'Poetically,' Mahon wrote privately to Longley in 1971, 'the only ways are separate ways';[1] yet some ways have more immediately successful destinations than others, and the divergent paths of Simmons and Mahon are to be taken into account in the elegy.

Conventionally enough in terms of elegy, Mahon celebrates Simmons in the poem, and the portrait he gives is true to much of what Simmons tended to celebrate about himself:

> Burning the energy, burning up
> the roads, not knowing when to stop,
> every day was a rave and every
> evening a new discovery.
> Sworn to our tricky art, you chose
> reality over art and pose –
> an 'Honest Ulsterman' although
> a rogue and romantic even so.[2]

There is a fitting combination of registers here: the freewheeling, pop-culture performer of the first half of the stanza is portrayed in slightly wobbly rhymes and devil-may-care enjambment—'stop' rhyming with 'burning up'—and this designedly less than 'tricky' formal medium is corrected by the stanza's second half, with its end-stopped full rhymes, which sobers up the youthful energy into aesthetics and ethics that, Mahon indicates, were always going to be 'tricky' for someone like Simmons to live with, and live up to. The reference to *The Honest Ulsterman*, the journal founded by Simmons (and in which the young Derek Mahon, too, had been published) touches on a point of difference between the two poets. Importantly, this is a matter of register: what for Simmons might feel like a useful phrase, reclaiming perhaps something of the Ulster regionalist self-assertiveness of an earlier generation, is for Mahon a problematic assertion, as the next stanza explains:

> That title always bothered me,
> the 'honest' claim seemed to imply
> others were charlatans or worse:
> we disagreed there at the start
> one evening in the Longleys' house.
> Perhaps reality and art,
> grown disputatious, even thought
> the two of them were poles apart
>
> and not the mates they really are.

---

[1] Derek Mahon, letter to Michael Longley, December 1971, Michael Longley papers, Emory University, quoted in Heather Clark, *The Ulster Renaissance: Poetry in Belfast 1962–1972* (Oxford: Oxford University Press, 2006), 187.

[2] Derek Mahon, 'Art and Reality: for James Simmons, obit 20/6/01', *An Autumn Wind* (Oldcastle: Gallery, 2010), 43.

In some ways, this is a strange turn for any elegy to take: 'always bothered me' is pitched somewhere between the casual sweeping-up of an otherwise easily discarded detail and picking at an unhealed wound. Plainly, 'bothered' is in a past tense with some bearing, still, on the poem's present—even though, naturally, this is a present without Simmons's mortal presence there to answer back. The line 'we disagreed there at the start' acknowledges a split, and in fact a profound divergence, about which the rest of this poem is reticent; in so doing, it recruits the strength of the disagreement for its own elegiac force: this is to allow the inevitable reconciliation of death (it ends the conversation, one way or the other) to lend some feeling of inevitability to the reconciliation of the disagreement itself. Yet art is 'tricky', as Mahon maintains: and it's worth noticing that the poem doesn't quite manage to solve the dispute within the confines of the stanza Mahon devotes to it, so that although art and reality 'really are' 'mates' (the register here working to equate actual friendship between Mahon and Simmons with the conclusion of an abstract problem), it is the phrase 'poles apart' which gains and keeps the prominence of ending a stanza, its denial far away across the stanza-break. An untidiness in the composition, or a point at which art expresses an untidiness in reality?

Isolation is at issue, certainly; and the elegy is attuned not only to the potential isolation of art from reality, but to the comparative isolation of James Simmons. It leaves him, indeed, out on his own, 'to sing on that white stretch of sand/in the distance'. 'Art and Reality' toys with the kind of biographical particulars that Mahon knows have resonance in a literary-historical sense—not least when the site of this aboriginal disagreement with Simmons is specified as 'the Longleys' house'. The poem declares discomfort with the readings given to the lives of its small circle of friends and poets ('We flinch, of course, when someone writes/our story by his different lights'), but it also relies on a biographical dimension, and 'the Longleys' house' is a significant location for what the poem knows is 'disputatious' matter now, as then. Michael and Edna Longley are part of the story therefore, even though Mahon will say nothing beyond this about them: he can be reticent in the knowledge that the poem's readers are likely to be familiar, not merely with the poetry of Michael but—in however indirect a way—with the critical understanding of Northern Irish poetry made current by his wife Edna. There is a pleasing closedness to the circle, for Edna Longley has been a critical advocate of Simmons as well as Mahon, and if the disagreement surfaced in this house, it was well placed to be resolved there too. Art and reality, it might seem for a moment, are as much 'mates', in the end, as Simmons, Mahon, and the Longleys.

If this is something of a sleight of hand in the poem, a minor instance of the trickiness of its own art, Mahon does not allow the difficulties that were—and are—in the reality of many disagreements to evaporate in its social warmth. 'Art and Reality' is enough of a conventional artist's elegy to include an artistic assessment of its dead subject, and in this respect Simmons emerges as the kind of 'rogue and romantic' who is essentially an entertainer. Beyond the affection of lines like 'Oh, you could be a royal pain,/thorn in the side, flea in the ear' (which are really just posthumous joshing), Mahon implicitly judges Simmons as a writer whose fate was to be something other, finally, than a poet: Simmons is presented as a performer, whose role was that of 'transporting the sad heart that longs/

for new space and an open mind', and the poem ends with Mahon affirming that 'I still hum your songs'. This 'longs'/'songs' rhyme tells, in its own way, the whole story of Mahon's complicated elegy: reality (in the Ulster of the elegist and his subject) is deficient, and leaves much wanting which art provides in the way of a spiritual, political, or sexual liberation. For Mahon, Simmons's career embodies these ways of escape. If he calls his subject's 'sexual ethic' 'dodgy', he also celebrates it: 'You cherished girls of every age/and pitied the poor Paisleyite/deprived of your advantages'; this is Protestant Ulster, a place exposed and renounced by Mahon's own art as much as Simmons's entertainment.

So, Simmons escapes it all, ultimately through death. Yet there is another way of looking at this kind of escape—or, as Mahon puts it, transportation—for the 'sad heart' of Ulster Protestant reality. Here, the actual situation of Simmons is relevant, and uncomfortable: for his lack of literary success (in comparison to his Ulster contemporaries) is a factor in the isolation which Mahon's poem ultimately celebrates. How far 'Art and Reality' feels and explores the discomfort of being on the winning side is open to question; but the shape of Mahon's poetic career has been in part a development from the most extreme and uncompromising sense of isolation towards something more culturally sociable, even companionable ('We have been too long in the cold', one poem in *The Hudson Letter* ends, 'Take us in; take us in!').[3] Isolation may be of the brilliant essence in Mahon's earlier work, but it is not something which his later poetry sets out to recommend. Here, the perceived isolation of Protestant Ulster—at least, of the Protestant Ulster of Mahon's (and Simmons's) youth—is very much a part of the story. In some versions of the narrative (which later Mahon appears to endorse) it is art that shows reality the way out of the cold.

Michael Longley, a practised and expeditious elegist, was quicker off the blocks than Mahon with his own elegy for Simmons, 'White Water', which was included in his *Snow Water* volume in 2004. A minimal poem where Mahon's is expansive, this little piece reduces Simmons to the point where he is only the isolation in which he placed himself, so that all of the past has been collapsed into a total silence. The poem's subtitle is 'In memory of James Simmons', but intimacy is exercised in its first word, 'Jimmy'—perhaps only there:

> Jimmy, you isolated yourself
> At the last bend before white water.
> We should have been fat jolly poets
> In some oriental print who float
> Cups of warm saké to one another
> On the river, and launch in paper boats
> Their poems. We are all separated.
> Your abandoned bivouac should be called
> Something like the Orchid Pavilion.[4]

---

[3] Derek Mahon, 'The Hudson Letter XVIII: The Small Rain' (1995), *Collected Poems* (Oldcastle: Gallery, 1999), 222.

[4] Michael Longley, 'White Water', *Collected Poems* (London: Jonathan Cape, 2006), 322.

The poem is formally relaxed, in its rhymeless cadences, but it is also counselling a kind of relaxation: the 'We should have been…' scenario at the poem's heart is implicitly a statement of regret that 'We' were not thus, and its fey, slightly camp orientalism seems to be offering an artistic alternative for a reality that proved unsatisfactory. 'We are all separated' complicates the isolation identified in Simmons, for the separation must include more than the poet and his subject ('all', not both), and its nature seems to rule out the fantasy of 'fat jolly poets' playing with cups of strong liquor as they lounge in the river. (Arguably, that 'river' fails to convince in any case: Longley's image of cup-swapping and floating answers better to an outdoor jacuzzi.) Announcing itself as an elegy, this fulfils few of the generic functions which press in on Mahon's very different poem, and appears to voice instead a regret that it cannot elegize Simmons, who has separated himself not just from the community of 'fat jolly poets' but from the place in the world (implicitly, the artistic world) he should have occupied, the 'abandoned bivouac' which Longley hazards 'should be called/Something like the Orchid Pavilion'.

Longley's phrasing may look casual, but its low key should not be mistaken for something noncommittal. The orientalizing of Simmons is emphatic, and he is being consigned by the poem firmly to the realm of the metaphorical—a successor, in his minor way, to Yeats's Chinamen in 'Lapis Lazuli'. That 'Orchid Pavilion' may be a fancier, more aesthetically respectable version of 'Barry's Amusements' and 'the old Arcadia' dancehall in Portrush in Mahon's poem, a place for entertaining, and being entertained. Longley's poem is—and maybe knows itself to be—no more than a wistful imagining of mutual entertainment, when death, and more than just death, has led to separation. To the poem's credit, it does not set out to elegize Simmons in the terms and detail to which over time, however sadly, it has lost the right.

The loss is not simply the poem's, but in a more complicated way Longley's as well. Here, as with Mahon, the shadows of literary history inevitably begin to close: when the divergent careers of Simmons and Longley are compared, it becomes obvious that Simmons occupied something other than the high ground of critical esteem and literary success to which Longley (at least since his middle years) has had generous access. It may be that the image of the river in 'White Water' has a certain point in this connection: by the time of Simmons's death, as the cliché would have it, a lot of water had flowed under the bridge of his relationship with Longley. This is something more than a personal matter (though it is that), just as the canvassing of difficulties with Simmons in 'Art and Reality' goes beyond the specifically biographical dimension. 'We are all separated' is the phrase that strikes the significant note here, and the resonances of the separation fit problematically into Longley's otherwise too much at ease, and too easy, short poem.

The 'fat jolly poets' engaged in exchanging verses along with cups of strong drink are not exactly the zenith of a Protestant spiritual aspiration. That much is obvious, and might very well be partly the point of Longley's flight of fancy in commemorating Simmons. Even so, 'We are all separated' is in earshot of sterner, and more religiously specific, kinds of separation that have a bearing on the culture from which poets like Simmons, Mahon, and Longley himself emerge. Two separations in particular haunt Protestant vocabulary in Ulster, both of them Pauline:

Wherefore come out from among them, and be ye separate, saith the Lord, and touch not the unclean thing; and I will receive you. (2 Corinthians 6:17)

Who shall separate us from the love of Christ? shall tribulation, or distress, or persecution, or famine, or nakedness, or peril, or sword? (Romans 8:35)

Between them, this pair of texts maps out much in the psychic landscape of the Protestant Ulster from which the poets (like many others) felt the need to be free: the insistence on necessary apartness from 'the unclean thing' has been made to bear specifically political meanings for religious Unionists over the years, while the declaration of inseparability from the love of Christ has been made to stand for other instances of the inseparable, notably the political union with the Protestant Crown.[5] Separation is not a word to be taken, or given, lightly in Protestant Ulster. It is unlikely that 'We are all separated' does anything so definite as make scriptural allusion, and forcing the phrase into being an allusion does something disproportionate in the context of the poem's overall tone; but the religious and cultural context on which—however far in the background—it ultimately draws is that of the place and history in relation to which Simmons, Longley, and Mahon partly shape their artistic identities and careers.

Does it make sense, though, to talk of 'Protestant' aesthetics in Northern Irish poetry? And in what terms, in fact, could such a thing be talked about at all? Undoubtedly, caution is in order. There are few European societies in a better position than Northern Ireland to know the perniciousness of sectarianism; and sectarian thinking—as well as a more straightforwardly unthinking habit of sectarianism—has blighted Northern Ireland from the beginning. Even now, it would be a dangerous kind of complacency that consigned that habit of sectarianism to the past or to the margins. It is only proper to hesitate, then, before importing sectarian categories to the criticism of Northern Irish literature. But in dealing with modern and contemporary poetry, criticism has largely felt itself free either to ignore religious dimensions—dimensions which are necessarily divisions—or to bring them into the picture using far too broad a brush. The result has been a distortion, one which does, it is true, sometimes answer accurately enough to distortions applied by the poets themselves, but which nevertheless makes it finally more difficult to understand the contexts and values of the various poetic achievements involved.

For a great deal of modern poetry from places like Britain and the USA, analysis in terms of religious affiliation or origin makes next to no sense: there are perfectly good historical and cultural reasons for this, and every reason not to press such a perspective in any serious critical reading. Yet in the case of Northern Ireland, things are not so clear-cut, and the natural reluctance of critics to engage with the sectarian energies that have issued so obviously (and so grievously) in sectarian violence has obscured some vital

---

[5] A Latin phrase from the Vulgate version of Romans 8:35, 'Quis separabit' has been, variously, the motto of some Irish regiments, that of the Northern Ireland coat of arms, and the paramilitary UDA. In 1982, in one of his most brilliant early critical performances, Tom Paulin homed in on the centrality of 'separation' in the thought and vocabulary of Ian Paisley: see his 'Paisley's Progress', *Writing to the Moment: Selected Critical Essays 1980–1996* (London: Faber, 1996), 28–47.

aspects of what Northern Irish poetry actually is: what it draws strength from, what it resists, and what it sets itself to achieve. Of course, there has been a considerable amount of attention given to what was once called 'background' in studies of major poets like Seamus Heaney and (to a lesser extent) Paul Muldoon; but this has very seldom been extended to influence formal, stylistic analysis. The idea, for example, that a particular way of putting things, and of putting some things rather than others, might be conditioned by specifically Catholic, and specifically Northern Irish Catholic, habits and reflexes is one effectively alien to the bulk of criticism which poets like these have generated. (That this is so becomes all the more remarkable when one considers how often, and how explicitly, the poets themselves have given critics their cue.)

The 'Protestant' label, however, has often lain more readily to hand, and it has permitted critics (though not just critics) to identify aspects in Northern Irish culture to which poetry offers an alternative, or from which it provides an escape route. It is taken for granted that no poetry could relate to this 'Protestant' culture in anything but broadly antagonistic ways. That assumption is, from a journalistic or casually political point of view, perfectly understandable; undoubtedly, it helps to keep the multiple contexts of religious and cultural dimensions to manageable proportions. Nevertheless, it is a simplification, and one which can encourage a wider—and maybe a more damaging—kind of inaccuracy in the reception of Northern Irish poetry. The literary career of Tom Paulin, who grew up in Belfast, has given a good deal of support to this view of Protestant culture as something cursed by fundamental political error—the Original Sin of Unionism—into which it fell after 1798, and in whose darkness it dwells to the present day. Paulin's collections of the 1980s, *Liberty Tree* (1983) and *Fivemiletown* (1986), along with his literary criticism and his media presence as a cultural commentator in Britain in the 1990s and after, made current a caricature of Ulster Protestantism as politically fallen and scarcely redeemable, artistically philistine and religiously vulgar, and at all events—at all costs indeed—a state to be transcended.[6]

'Protestant aesthetics' might be thought, at best, an oxymoron. In part, that is a legacy of the simplification which requires Protestant Ulster to be characterized by distrust of art, fuelled by extreme religious prejudice enforced with Calvinist rigour. As far as Northern Irish poetry is concerned, it was two Protestants from the North of Ireland, Louis MacNeice and W. R. Rodgers, who did most in the mid-twentieth century to give this image an enduring literary expression. That either of these poets should have been capable of achieving this is, of course, in itself an indication that the stereotype might not be all-encompassing; but their (very different) works were received as evidence of escape from the stifling philistinism of Ulster, rather than imaginative emanations from that very milieu. In MacNeice's case, the arguments about his degree of attachment to Northern Ireland are complex, much-rehearsed, and still continuing; in that of Rodgers, posterity's relative lack of interest makes them now—and perhaps unfortunately—unlikely to happen. But a third Northern Irish poet of this generation, John Hewitt (who

---

[6] For the complexities behind, and in, Paulin's artistic uses of this caricature, see Peter McDonald, *Mistaken Identities: Poetry and Northern Ireland* (Oxford: Clarendon Press, 1997), ch. 4.

died in 1987), continues to occupy a significant position—less, really, as a poet than as a voice for what one might call cultural Protestantism in Ulster. Hewitt's poetry does not deserve the kind of neglect into which it will probably continue to fall (neglect, like success, comes to the deserving and undeserving alike); but his cultural positioning is still taken as important by Northern Irish writers and their observers. In a way, John Hewitt dead has been far more influential than John Hewitt the living writer: a subject of that most potent form of Irish commemoration, the literary and academic summer school, Hewitt has come to represent a prophetic voice from the past in Ulster Protestant culture, urging the dual imperatives of political liberalism and an attachment to place. Hewitt spent many years living in England, in a career move (to become Director of the City Art Gallery in Coventry) which he presented—and others after him accepted enthusiastically—as a kind of forced exile from the forces of establishment bigotry in the Protestant North. His return to Belfast in retirement coincided with the flourishing of poetry there, and his many late volumes were published locally (by the Blackstaff Press) at the same time as Longley, Heaney, Mahon, Muldoon, and others were consolidating their national and international reputations. With MacNeice and Rodgers dead, Hewitt stepped easily into the role of the senior figure for an increasingly successful group of Northern Irish poets throughout the 1970s.

The 'Regionalism' to which Hewitt was affiliated in the 1930s and 1940s in Northern Irish writing left an ambiguous legacy for the poets of the 1960s and after. Hewitt himself felt that regionalism 'failed' but, whatever he might have meant by this, the consequences of this movement were far-reaching. Seamus Heaney's career, like Longley's and Mahon's, drew real benefits from the sense of local worth and literary legitimacy which Regionalism (and Hewitt in particular) promoted: when the 'Ulster Renaissance' made itself apparent at the end of the 1960s, it was on ground which Ulster Regionalism had prepared—even though its publishers were firmly in literary London. The real 'failure' of Hewitt's regionalism had been essentially a political one, for the attempt to make literary capital out of an insistence that the writer 'must be a *rooted* man'[7] at the very least complicated, and perhaps fatally compromised, any espousal of liberalism, since it relied on the kind of allegiance which, in Northern Ireland, is inevitably and unavoidably divisive in political terms. 'Ulster', that is, means different things to a Protestant and to a Catholic in Northern Ireland; and literature could no more transcend that difference than could the politics of British leftism from the 1930s onwards.

After the late 1960s, the political stakes were higher; and the artistic stakes for poets like Longley, Mahon, and Simmons were sufficiently steep to mean that a specifically 'Protestant' strain was something that could not well be announced. Nevertheless, at the level of style (where the real stakes in poetry are always at their highest), all three poets inherited and worked through modes of expression and thinking that came distinctively from a 'Protestant' literary tradition. This can be visible in the literary judgements that

---

[7] John Hewitt, 'The Bitter Gourd: Some Problems of the Ulster Writer' (1945), *Ancestral Voices: The Selected Prose of John Hewitt*, ed. Tom Clyde (Belfast: Blackstaff, 1987), 115.

tend to be made about the poets, as well as in their own work. A thumbnail sketch of Simmons, for example, offers this:

> Wary of rhetoric and what he sees as the élitist assumptions of much modern verse, Simmons adheres to traditional forms and a tough, colloquially based poetic language. His characteristic idiom offers a street-wise counterpart to John Hewitt's Calvinistic neatness. The note of wry melancholy in the selected pieces is typical.[8]

'Wary of rhetoric' opens the door to a guest who is not going to be easily palmed off with warm words, and from whom we are not to expect any florid eloquence in excess of what is required. There is a perfectly good cue for this in Simmons's own work, in a poem dedicated to Michael Longley, much given over to the virtues of that least Calvinist of musical forms, jazz:

> The campus poets used to write of saxophones
> disgustedly and sneer at gramophones;
> but the word of life, if such a thing existed,
> was there on record among the rubbish listed
> in the catalogues of Brunswick and H.M.V.,
> healing the split in sensibility.
> Tough reasonableness and lyric grace
> together, in poor man's dialect.
> Something that no-one taught us to expect.
> Profundity without the po-face
> of court and bourgeois modes. This I could use
> to live and die with. Jazz. Blues.[9]

The slant of the poem, and that of its dedication, indicate some element of the *ars poetica* here: yet what is most revealing about this aesthetic is that it isn't really an aesthetic at all, but a rough and ready equating of aesthetics to the business of living. Simmons's rough couplets are probably to give the feel of improvisation, but the underlying claim for a style is clear enough: 'Tough reasonableness and lyric grace/together'. This might have the ring of self-assessment about it, but Simmons is in earnest both for himself and, by implication, for others too, including his poem's dedicatee. The verbal art's integrity is an ethical matter: the records contain 'the word of life', the music is 'to live and die with'. 'Life' and 'live' were, admittedly, central to the debased coinage of Lawrentian vocabulary in much 1960s criticism (Simmons's poem is not untouched by academia—the 'split' to be healed 'in sensibility' is there to remind readers of what they learned about T. S. Eliot at university.), but in this context they carry a certain defiant charge. Simmons's poem is an Ulster poem of its time, in that it sets its face against 'the po-face' which would deny 'the word of life': here, 'the word' is up against the Word, and all the Word would put a stop to.

[8] Headnote in Patrick Crotty, ed., *Modern Irish Poetry: An Anthology* (Belfast: Blackstaff, 1995), 191.
[9] James Simmons, 'Didn't He Ramble', *Poems 1956–1986* (Dublin: Gallery; Newcastle: Bloodaxe, 1986), 95.

It seems odd to propose Simmons as a type of religious figure; but his version of lived commitment to art and liberalism, and to political individualism and liberalism, issued in a curiously evangelical notion of writing. Somewhere deep in the Ulster Protestant psyche is the desire, if not to be saved, at least to declare oneself saved from perdition; and Simmons embodied this, by his very particular lights, as distinctly as any Free Presbyterian. True, being saved for Simmons meant a conversion to poetry and music, drinking and sex; but his sense of his salvation as relevant and exemplary for his society is central to much of his creative work. This comes to the surface in an essay where Simmons finds the seeds of his individualist faith in some older Northern Irish fiction:

> You get in these novels what you would expect from common Ulster experience: that such human leaps forward as we are likely to have come from individuals, not from any of the Churches. Yet the individuals who bolster and support their weaker brethren have some sort of faith and a belief in something greater than themselves. The Protestant experience offers the best paradigm of this because it is central to the ethos that the individual should reach beyond the Church to God: to some positive image, created by men at the height of their imagination that embodies permanent truth and inspiration, like the life of Christ. In a barbarous time when we have lost touch with our inspirational past, and the way back is barred by dead forms, fallible human beings still stumble forward by instinct, sometimes.[10]

This is not, perhaps, all that wary of rhetoric; but the rhetoric it does employ taps in directly to Protestant fundamentalism; and Protestantism, indeed, is being offered as 'the best paradigm' of the individualism Simmons sees as necessary for personal liberation.

Fran Brearton has written of how 'Mahon, Longley, and Heaney share the sense of art as an alternative spirituality', adding that this makes art 'a mode of subversion all the more telling in a context where sectarianism is rife'.[11] The accuracy of this needs to be complemented by the understanding that 'spirituality' cannot be free from a sectarian interpretation; that both Catholicism and Protestantism inevitably inflect the professedly secular spiritualities which may issue from them, however far from the forms of 'sectarianism' these may appear to be. Simmons's liberationist individualism, for instance, is unmistakably Protestant in its essence and expression, and this is plain too in the form of its address, in its style. That the sentiments are at odds with 'sectarianism' does not make them free from their origins in religious dissent, and from what has followed from such dissent in Ulster. Of all the poets from a Protestant background, Tom Paulin has been the most willing to discuss the relationship between religious dissent,

[10] James Simmons, '"The Recipe for all Misfortunes, Courage": A Study of Three Works by Ulster Protestant Authors: *Apostate* by Forrest Reid, *Castle Corner* by Joyce Cary and *December Bride* by Sam Hanna Bell', in *Across a Roaring Hill: The Protestant Imagination in Modern Ireland*, ed. Gerald Dawe and Edna Longley (Belfast: Blackstaff, 1985), 97–8.
[11] Fran Brearton, 'Poetry of the 1960s: The "Northern Ireland Renaissance"', in *The Cambridge Companion to Contemporary Irish Poetry*, ed. Matthew Campbell (Cambridge: Cambridge University Press, 2003), 109.

written (and spoken) style, and politics: but Paulin's own politics have tended to get in the way of his fully exploring in terms of contemporary work the cultural, religious, and political complexity he identifies in older literature, while his fascination with the implications of style has, curiously, more often short-circuited his own poetry by over-charging it with stylistic self-awareness and self-analysis. It is with Longley and Mahon, then, that the question of Protestantism and literary expression might have its most revealing applications, although (as their two elegies for Simmons show) each poet might have early and late styles that are not necessarily in accord with each other.

In *An Exploded View* (1973), Michael Longley published a series of verse letters to his contemporaries, Heaney, Mahon, and Simmons. The poem to Simmons makes an interesting comparison to Longley's eventual elegy: written more obviously with the presumption of friendship, and generally on more equal terms, it still celebrates Simmons as an entertainer, while perhaps hoping to stand in the light of Simmons's more rakish persona. 'Play your guitar while Derry burns' has a certain defiance of the worthy that expresses solidarity with the other poet's project, and the atmosphere of irreverence is seen (in Simmons-like terms) as socially exemplary:

> Yes, to entertain your buddies
> With such transcendental studies
> Rather than harmonise with hams
> In yards of penitential psalms
> I count among your better turns:
> Play your guitar while Derry burns...[12]

The 'transcendental studies' are those of 'The blue veins in filigree' 'beneath a breast' and 'The millions acting out their last/Collaborations with the past' 'In a discarded French letter'. All this principled escapism, it's worth noticing, does not relinquish its claim on the metaphysical, and its antipathy to those 'penitential psalms' is really a dislike of penitence, and a going one better than the 'hams' trapped in their Calvinistic, psalm-filled gloom.

More substantial, as a poem, is Longley's letter to Mahon, which is more explicit about the Ulster from which any imaginative or spiritual escape is going to be made. The poem has become well-known for the tensions built in to its opening stanzas, where Longley and Mahon are 'Two poetic conservatives/In the city of guns and long knives', and where talk of 1969 and Belfast leads Longley to speak of 'the burnt-out houses of/The Catholics we'd scarcely loved'.[13] It is less often remarked that most of the poem takes place outside Northern Ireland, in Inisheer, in an atmosphere made strongly religious by the poet's retrospect. It is not only because this move to the West prefigures what was to be a major shift of geographical focus in much of the poet's later work that the locale of 'To Derek Mahon' is suggestive: with that move comes a change is spiritual orientation too—or, at least, the thought of such a change. Heather Clark has given this a fairly straightforward

---

[12] Longley, 'To James Simmons', *Collected Poems*, 56.
[13] Longley, 'To Derek Mahon', *Collected Poems*, 58.

reading, speaking of 'a political as well as geographical trajectory', in which 'the journey to the island symbolizes an attempt to refute the narrow cultural confines of the Protestant community in Belfast and to embrace a more fluid identity, free from sectarianism'. Yet this fails to see that the 'community' from which Longley and Mahon are escaping is not one to which they fully belong: even 'the Catholics we'd scarcely loved' halts some way from an admission of sectarianism (and Mahon's vehement objection to the sentiment further maintains his own distance from any such 'narrow cultural confines').[14]

'To Derek Mahon' is, however, a poem about religion: its course from Belfast to the Aran islands involves Longley in a confrontation with some imaginative impulses that would have to wait a good many years for their fullest artistic expressions in his poetry. The poem records a failure of connection—which is religious as much as cultural—without letting go of the impulse to connect. What exactly is (and isn't) being connected with is less than clear, and Mahon's sensitivity to sectarian implications can be explained by the poem's slightly anthropological attitude to the Catholic inhabitants of Inisheer. The conclusions offered by Longley are far from being conclusive, but their provisionality is concerned with religion in a way that is not at all 'sectarian'. 'We were strangers in that parish', Longley writes of himself and Mahon:

> Dank blankets making up our Lent
> Till, islanders ourselves, we bent
> Our knees and cut the watery sod
> From the lazy-bed where slept a God
> We couldn't count among our friends,
> Although we'd taken in our hands
> Splinters of driftwood nailed and stuck
> On the rim of the Atlantic.[15]

All of this on 'Good Friday years ago': the Lenten habits are part of a kind of secular observance, a piety at one remove, which intersects confusingly with the remove of two middle-class Northern Irish Protestants among the Catholic people of Inisheer. Confusingly, because confused: Longley's images of bent knees, a God sleeping like Christ before Easter Day, and the 'nailed and stuck' 'Splinters of driftwood' all feel like religious motifs. 'Feel like' is to the point, though; for the religion here is something that has to be imagined, or for which Longley has to make a willing suspension of disbelief, rather than the real thing.

Longley's imaginative toying with faith is not incompatible with certain culturally Protestant bearings. It is useful to remember that even Ulster Protestantism is far from

---

[14] Heather Clark, *The Ulster Renaissance*, 168. The line was originally 'The Catholics we scarcely loved': Derek Mahon wrote to the *New Statesman* on 10 December 1971, after the poem's appearance there, to declare the line's 'implications... frankly untrue, if not damaging', and also privately to Longley to protest. See Clark, 185–6. See also Fran Brearton, *Reading Michael Longley* (Tarset: Bloodaxe, 2006), 86–92.

[15] Longley, *Collected Poems*, 59.

single-minded, and that there are divisions of class as well as denomination at work in the community from which Longley, like Mahon, effected some kind of escape. Longley's memoir of his childhood is very forthcoming about the distance, as well as the proximity, between himself and the working-class children with whom he went to primary school.[16] This distance was also one between varieties of Protestantism: to simplify somewhat, the working-class inhabitants of one side of South Belfast's Lisburn Road were less likely (on the whole) to be members of the (Anglican) Church of Ireland than the middle and upper middle classes whose addresses (like the Longleys') were on the other side of that road. There is an element of the 'High' and 'Low' Church distinction here—though at times and in places more pronounced than that, for many varieties of evangelical Protestantism with working-class roots in Ulster are profoundly suspicious both of the worship and the presumed politics of the Anglican communion. Longley's 'Letter' to Mahon could be read from such a perspective as typical of an upwardly mobile Anglicanism that pines both for Roman sacramentalism and for an escape into the Irish Republic. That Longley is unable to believe in his religious symbolism separates him from the Catholics, true; but that he wants to bask in its aura, to have the feel of it even if he cannot hold to the substance, makes him (in a dissenting Protestant reading) typical of a certain kind of Anglican.

Needless to say, this angle of approach is next to worthless from any sane critical point of view, yet its feasibility as a sectarian response is not irrelevant for the poem, nor for Longley's work more generally. Mahon's 1971 discomfort has many ingredients; but one may be an awareness of the poem's slightly religiose tone, its affected reverence, which puts 'The Catholics we scarcely loved', as a phrase, into the bracket of socially superior disdain into which *all* those who fail to be moved by the pseudo-religious imagery may fall. 'The back alleys of Belfast' may be too readily and haughtily left behind in all this. It should be conceded at once that Mahon had his own modes and registers of disdain in his early work, and that these were particularly unsparing in relation to Protestant Ulster; but they were thoroughgoing, where Longley's disdain (if that is what it is) is more particular and self-sparing. Mahon's 'The Spring Vacation' (dedicated to Longley) has poet and addressee 'Rehearsing our astute salvations under/The cold gaze of a sanctimonious God':[17] 'astute' is cutting here, and plays against—by seeming at first to play along with—the accepted currency of personal salvation in Protestant religious discourse.[18] In a poem which begins 'Walking among my own this windy morning', such

[16] See Michael Longley, *Tuppenny Stung: Autobiographical Chapters* (Belfast: Lagan, 1994), 24–8.

[17] Derek Mahon, 'The Spring Vacation', *Poems 1962–1978* (Oxford: Oxford University Press, 1979), 4. The poem's title in Mahon's first collection, *Night-Crossing* (1968), was 'In Belfast (for Michael Longley)'. In Mahon's *Collected Poems* (1999) and *New Collected Poems* (2011), the title is 'Spring in Belfast'.

[18] Hugh Haughton, in his *The Poetry of Derek Mahon* (Oxford: Oxford University Press, 2007), revealingly takes 'our astute salvations' not to include the poet (or Longley) at all, writing of Mahon's 'fellow citizens, rehearsing their "astute salvations"' (34): this is so keen to congratulate the young Mahon on his distance from 'a stifling ethos of Protestant self-control' that it fails to notice the word 'our', in which the poet's own brand of self-control is brilliantly manifested.

astuteness is pointed—and it is 'my own' and 'I' in the first stanza of this poem, even though a first-person plural enters later on: as dedicatee, Longley is being shown something, but Mahon is careful not to presume that everything, or all the force of this particular dynamic of salvation, is something that the two can share. The final stanza, in the poem's original form, is emphatic and, again, self-aware:

> Poetry and fluent drivel, know your place –
> Take shape in some more glib environment
> Away from shipyard, gantry, bolt and rivet.
> Elsewhere assess existence, ask to what end
> It tends, wherefore and why. In Belfast live it.[19]

This ending rings false—the rhyme in the last line is to blame mainly—but Mahon's embittered retort on 'Poetry and fluent drivel' does more than just ventriloquize that familiar voice, the philistine Ulster Protestant: the Belfast of 'shipyard, gantry, bolt and rivet' is that of Mahon's family past, and the inheritance it offers consists partly in this ability to turn the intellect back viciously upon itself, so that poetry's distance from, or proximity to, 'fluent drivel' is never a matter about which the poet can be quite certain. This is a long way from Longley's world, and its register is altogether harder and more dangerous.

That habit of aggressive self-challenge is inherited from dissenting Protestantism. There, a continual dissatisfaction with the individual's performance in the business of life and living is countered by the provision of an absolute standard of reliability in words that are the opposite of 'drivel' in that they are the fixed and unchanging words of Scripture. Mahon's contact with fundamentalist Protestantism may or may not have been close (his time as a child singing in the choir for the Church of Ireland does not argue for such intimacy), but it was pervasive even so; partly, this may be a matter of class and geography. The evidence for this comes in poems like 'Matthew V. 29–30' (a Beckettian *reductio ad absurdum* of 'Lord, mine eye offended, so I plucked it out'); in the many poems of apocalyptic extremity and ecological endtime preaching which are to be found in both his early and later career; and in the gravitation towards questions of salvation in terms of 'life' and what it is to 'live' which continues to be notable in Mahon's work.[20] If there is one motif, in fact, which unites earlier and later Mahon, it is the insistence that we must be born again. In the poet's case, which for all his reticence in terms of interviews and reminiscence is in the poetry figured in clearly autobiographical terms, this is a matter of escaping from the perceived restrictions of family and inward-looking community into a wide world of different friends, places, and cultural assumptions. But Mahon has never been in any doubt that in following the way of artistic salvation, the price to be paid is giving up all one has, forsaking father and mother just as surely as any born-again fundamentalist preacher.

---

[19]   *Icarus* 42 (March 1964), 42.
[20]   Mahon's volume titles include *Lives* (1971) and *Life on Earth* (2008).

'"Songs of Praise"', a study of 'The proud parishioners of the outlying parts' on display for 'the outside broadcast cameras', which survives as a two-stanza poem in Mahon's 1999 *Collected Poems*, originally had two further stanzas:

> Never look back, they said; but they were wrong.
> The zinc wave-dazzle after a night of rain,
> A washed-out sky humming with stars, the mist
> And echoing fog-horns of the soul, belong
> To our lost lives. We must be born again,
> As the gable-ends of the seaside towns insist;
>
> And so we were, to look back constantly
> On that harsh landscape and its procreant sea,
> Bitter and curative, as tonight we did,
> Listening to our own nearly-voices chime
> In the parochial lives we might have led,
> Praising a stony god who died before our time.[21]

'Our lost lives' are perhaps lives well lost; and the 'And so we were' response with which the last stanza begins offers a sardonic response to the 'Ye must be born again' injunction that Mahon remembers from the religious graffiti of Northern Ireland. But the poem also admits tacitly that the looking back which being born again, in a fundamentalist Christian sense, absolutely rules out is actually part of the condition of this other kind of spiritual rebirth, as a compulsion 'to look back constantly'. These stanzas are remarkable, in that they bring together the imaginative landscape and weatherscape that is so typical of Mahon with a great degree of frankness about the location of such a thing, and its meaning. 'Our own nearly-voices' are not the same as voices that are nearly our own: for these voices *aren't* our own, but it is 'our own' voices that are 'nearly-voices' in response to them. This is what comes of being unable to resist the compulsion to look back, Mahon suggests, and the poem itself, as it retreats to the judgemental comfort of an adjective like 'parochial', is no more than a near-voicing of what must not, finally, be voiced. For all that, the loss of these stanzas is one of the poet's severest acts of artistic self-mutilation, in an oeuvre which, as a whole, is arguably too much inclined to ruthless self-harm.

Questions of career-long development have been fraught ones in Mahon's critical reception, and will probably continue to be so. In Michael Longley's case, the received narrative of artistic development is something altogether smoother and less problematic: the assured artistic finish and integrity of the early work transforms with an exemplary slowness into an ever more profound moral focus that finds its idiom in precision of detail, pastoral elegance, and a classically underpinned tragic gravity of regard. There is much to be said for this reading of Longley's career, and there can be no arguing with the huge achievements of his best lyric work—which are by no means confined to any particular phase in that career. Yet artistic success can lead also to the distortion of critical understanding and the underestimation of factors which both contribute to the

---

[21] Derek Mahon, *Courtyards in Delft* (Dublin: Gallery, 1981), 17.

work's genesis and loom large in the poems themselves. Protestantism, for Longley's critics, is one such comparative blind spot. If this seems ironic in the light of the treatment Longley received from some American and Southern Irish commentators early in his writing life (when his work, if noticed at all, was read in terms of a bigoted notion of the Protestant North), it is nonetheless true that Longley's Protestant origins are now taken for granted in ways that fail to discriminate the nuances—religious, social, and broadly cultural—that are so important in establishing the pitch of his mature lyric imagination.

It is important to remember that Longley's work is not haunted—as Mahon's is—by the legacy of fundamentalist religion, and that no Calvinist shadows fall across its vistas. One aspect of this is that anxieties about the value of words—their uses, their potential ambiguities, and their real dangers—are not paralleled in his imagination by the long history of inflexible commitment to the Word of Scripture: this is closer to Mahon because Mahon is socially closer to the kind of Protestantism in which it has played so large a role. It might seem a curiosity of Longley's work that his habits of reverence are not matched by any visible anxiety about the adequacy of words to express that reverence. Descriptive fidelity (especially in Longley's nature poetry) can be extreme, but of course it is never in any danger of seeming extremist; still, the significance such a thing possesses for Longley goes far beyond matters of botanical accuracy. In Longley's poetry there is a direct relation between style and reverence; and to ask about the nature and meaning of that reverence is an unusually hard task.

It may be that Longley's increasing tendency to a religiously tinged reverence should be thought of in specifically denominational terms, as an Anglican habit. A broad brush applying itself to this possibility would portray Longley's pastoral poetry as the creation of places with particular religious associations—expressed in terms of intimate family, and lovingly observed flora and fauna—where there is an indirectly devotional function to be played out. It would also see commemoration as a central activity, where private meditation understands and performs with dignity its public meaning: hence, the legacy of the Great War and that of the Northern Irish Troubles are elements in a process of formal collective remembering. All of this makes Longley—in terms of the Protestant spectrum—an established poet who sounds very like the once-established Church. The point could descend readily into caricature, and become merely silly; but the stylistic features of Longley's lyrics do in fact require scrutiny of their commitment to the seriousness of what they perform and voice.

Longley's later work shows a marked increase in the proportion of poems that announce themselves as in one way or another performative: the poet 'names' things repeatedly in this verse, often 'for' an addressee. At the same time, the work from *Gorse Fires* (1991) onwards has a long line that seems to gravitate towards lists of proper nouns, so that it becomes itself an act of naming, pronouncing particular things one after the other in a cadenced (and often very beautiful) way.[22] The effect is more than casually

---

[22] See John Lyon, 'Michael Longley's Lists', *English*, 45:183 (Autumn 1996), 228–46.

liturgical. The brilliance of the aesthetic result might be seen as begging the question of *why* the poet's voice needs to be exercised in quite this way. Similarly, the growing proportion of Longley's lyrics that are very short (with the single-quatrain poem becoming a favourite form) raises difficulties that persist beyond pleasant sensations delivered by the poems themselves: what appears inconsequential can't really be inconsequential, but to discover the meaning a reader has to receive the minimalist voice with the kind of attentive reverence that matches what the poems themselves are generally up to with the natural world. When little poems speak to each other, in common images and angles of perception, across and between whole volumes, something that means to be consequential is certainly going on. But the reverence required can shade into the reverence that is being laid on:

> A Prayer
>
> In our country they are desecrating churches.
> May the rain that pours in pour into the font.
> Because no snowflake ever falls in the wrong place,
> May snow lie on the altar like an altar cloth.[23]

'May the...' is the sign of a certain confidence: the rain will assuredly pour into the font because that is exactly what a poem like this can make happen, and the poet's voice here is officiating in its own ceremonial world. The hushed atmosphere is a function of the poem's brevity: the quatrain has become a special space, sacred to the lyric voice—where else, really, could 'no snowflake ever falls in the wrong place' sound like anything other than cod wisdom? In truth, nothing falls out wrong in the holy places of later Longley, simply because everything is so completely under the performative voice's control.

To a hostile Protestant reading—an unreformedly sectarian one—all of this would be the stylistic proof of a deep-seated Anglicanism in Longley, one which allows him to appropriate religious symbolism and ceremony even though he does not accept the metaphysical claims of Christianity itself. For many generations in Ulster, this has been a dominant dissenting view of Anglicanism (in love with ultimately Catholic rites and procedures, but too timid to say what it really believes, and too firmly buttressed by privilege to have any need to do so). To press this line further, an antagonistic Protestant view of Anglicanism would contend that words are being treated as merely vehicles of the authority that speaks them, and not as having an inherent and unchallengeable authority in themselves: ultimately, though, they may be no more than 'poetry and fluent drivel', which really cannot tell rain where to fall, nor snow where to lie.

We may seem to be back, with this argument, to the philistinism of Protestant Ulster. Yet dismissing it as philistinism risks allowing poetry too generous a licence with reality, and poetic authority too wide a remit. A residual belief in the potency of the Word might be salutary rather than purely debilitating, and might even suggest ways in which poetic achievement can be assessed against the real situations from which it derives. There have

---

[23] Michael Longley, *The Weather in Japan* (2000), *Collected Poems*, 253.

been many poets other than Longley and Mahon for whom the possibilities of personality in verse have been fraught with risk; and one of the riskiest beliefs has always been that since style expresses personality, the right kind of personality will issue in the right kind of style. The terrible dip in Mahon's achievement comes with *The Hudson Letter* (1995) and *The Yellow Book* (1997), volumes which buy in to the notion that poetic personality can be figured as a kind of literary talk-show performance, losing in the process the stylistic tension and compression that had enabled his finest lyrics. Criticize the style, and you criticize the man.[24] One way of understanding this problem is to remember how far James Simmons believed in the direct path between literary expression and human worth. His thoughts on the matter are not of special value because of his own literary eminence (or indeed lack of it), but because they draw from the Protestantism which— at origin, at least—he and Longley have in common. Here is Simmons, for example, on the ethical shortcomings of Modernism:

> The positive side of Modernism is that it tries to involve the whole energy and intellect of a man in the poem; but the negative side is that it permits the arrogant or confused to bully language or to indulge in obscurity. It allows failure to seem challenging when it is the poet who has failed the challenge, not the reader.[25]

Again (from the same piece), 'I make no apology for thinking clarity and cogency to be of the essence of good writing. . . . I have always taken the sensibility of the writer to be what one is after as a reader, to be in touch with interesting people, people of spiritual authority.'[26] These crisply expressed attitudes might easily be aligned with what could be called a Longleyan aesthetic; though the ascription of 'spiritual authority' to 'interesting people' is looser than anything either of the Longleys would deem allowable (even though Simmons is ascribing it, in this case, to none other than Derek Mahon). The ideas might just as easily be seen as a kind of Protestant aesthetic, of commitment to the freedom of conscience as something expressed supremely in the 'clarity and cogency' of a fully functioning written language.

---

[24] Haughton's *The Poetry of Derek Mahon* is the most energetic of the defences of these two volumes. Its value is limited, like that of the book as a whole, by the sense of vocation which comes occasionally to critics devoting themselves to a particular Irish poet: this means that every new volume must contribute to an upwards line of artistic development, and explanation of what the poet *intends* to do stands in for critical evaluation of what is actually achieved. Haughton reacts to objections to these volumes by simply taking offence on behalf of his author: quoting my own objections to Mahon's self-description as 'a recovering Ulster Protestant', Haughton laments that 'it has been hard for critics to grapple with the differences between earlier and later Mahon' (312); yet it seems to have been harder still for Haughton himself, who cannot perceive anything other than a smooth development and steady increase of worth in the work. Haughton's own exploration of Mahon's phrase gives a good sense of his ability to absorb and accept prejudice: '[Mahon's] later intellectual life can be seen as an attempt to recover from—and resist—his early experience of life in Belfast. The mobility, intellectual scepticism, and aesthetic panache of his work offer a concerted protest against his home culture.' (12) In so far as later Mahon shares this kind of complacency, it contributes to a lessening in the quality of his poetry; his early work provides all the evidence needed to undermine its assumptions.

[25] James Simmons, 'The Trouble with Seamus', in *Seamus Heaney: A Collection of Critical Essays*, ed. Elmer Kennedy-Andrews (Basingstoke: Macmillan, 1992), 46.

[26] Ibid., 43, 45.

Those Simmons remarks come in the context of his extended (and sometimes painfully *gauche*) attack on a Seamus Heaney at the height of his international success. Perhaps, in their way, they constitute something approaching sectarian literary criticism: certainly, they are poor criticism of Heaney. For all that, Simmons understood something of the deep distinctions between the different models of authority which are culturally transmitted in Ulster, and have their most obvious manifestations in different kinds of Christianity, and he was willing to find the evidence for this in the literary styles of those who, if asked, would profess no particular attachment to religious belief.

There may, in other words, be 'Catholic' and 'Protestant' kinds of poetry. In the work of Longley and Mahon, the 'Protestant' elements are in different combinations and at different strengths, but are there nevertheless. That aspects of this sectarian inheritance have been disowned by both poets is clear enough, and is often to the good; though some things left behind in the development of both writers' careers have been more valuable, and might have prevented some weaker pieces of each poet's later work. It remains the case that Northern Irish poetry has benefited enormously from the challenges and constraints presented by the verbal and imaginative context of the Protestant experience, while it has not always been the stronger for the loosening of those constraints in lyric poetry's repeated engagements between reality and art. In the best work of these poets, Protestant elements mean that a sceptical view of 'art' can be as productive as a certain disdain for 'reality' in understanding the lives we lead, and might have led.

CHAPTER 31

WALKING DUBLIN: CONTEMPORARY IRISH POETS IN THE CITY

MARIA JOHNSTON

What is it that the Dublin air does to these writers?[1]

'Now here at last the city was being written into poetry', Eavan Boland, then a student at Trinity College Dublin, observed of the changing Irish poetic landscape in the 'new Ireland' of the 1960s as the city moved into view and Irish poets became newly attentive to its 'sights and sounds and streets'.[2] This essay examines not merely the presence of Dublin city in contemporary Irish poetry but, more particularly, the ways in which Irish poets have moved through it on foot, recording its sensational realities, its sights, sounds, streets as they go, and, moreover, how these ambulatory movements have in turn generated mobile poetic forms and innovative aesthetic manoeuvres. Dublin is internationally recognized as a city of literary walks: held up as 'the twentieth-century novel of walking par excellence', James Joyce's *Ulysses* is the supreme example of the prose of walking.[3] But there is a poetry of walking too, and Irish poets have long shown themselves to be inveterate walkers. Imaginatively inhabiting Dublin from far-off Australia in 1979, Vincent Buckley reminisces about how 'Austin Clarke, victim of/Parnassus walked here once,/Building his maze of short moments',[4] and the streets of the city, the poetic

---

[1] Frederick Warburg quoted in James Knowlson, *Damned to Fame: The Life of Samuel Beckett* (London: Bloomsbury, 1996), 343.

[2] Eavan Boland quoted in Jody Allen Randolph, 'A Backward Look', *Colby Quarterly* 35:4 (1999), 294.

[3] Peter I. Barta, *Bely, Joyce, and Döblin: Peripatetics in the City Novel* (Gainesville: University Press of Florida, 1996), 49.

[4] Vincent Buckley, '*Templeogue: a sound bitten*', *Collected Poems*, ed. Chris Wallace-Crabbe (Victoria: John Leonard Press, 2009), 262.

terrain of Ireland, and the world more broadly, are haunted by a host of pervasive liter-ary pacemakers. As we set off to tour Dublin as a walking-ground for contemporary Irish poets, Hazel Smith's musings on the 'walk poem' as poetic genre comprise an instructive guide: 'When you walk the city you are in some senses *writing* it. The advan-tage of the walk poem is that it retains a sensation of mobility, the impression of place never ossifies' as, 'representative of contemporary life', the walk is 'improvised, transient and ephemeral'.[5] For A. R. Ammons a poem *is* a walk: 'not simply a mental activity: it has body, rhythm, feeling, sound, and mind, conscious and subconscious'.[6] Taking as its start-ing point 1958—the year of first major collections by Thomas Kinsella and John Montague that set the tone for a 'new Ireland' of fresh poetic activity—this essay will forge a network of paths through the city's poetry to uncover connections, intersections, and lines of influence in many directions.

In 1958 Michael Longley walked through the gate of Trinity College Dublin to begin his undergraduate career. He would leave five years later, a 'lapsed Classicist' but a devout published poet, having been joined, in 1960, by Derek Mahon who fast became 'inspir-ing company' and an intrepid travelling companion on their shared journey into poetry.[7] These decisive Dublin years had both of them discovering modern and contemporary Irish, European, and American poetry, and, notably for two poets who would become renowned for their use of the singing line, not just reading but listening to poems in their college rooms. Alive to the heartbeat of contemporary Irish poetic formal innova-tion as they studied their elders—Patrick Kavanagh, Austin Clarke, Louis MacNeice—they 'read aloud to each other' new poems by Montague and got Kinsella's 'lilting lines' off by heart.[8] Trinity's broader literary community offered support from established 'col-lege poets' Brendan Kennelly and Rudi Holzapfel, and opportunities for publication in *Icarus*. But poetry was in no way confined to the cloistered spaces of academe. The city's pubs accommodated the inspirational Alec Reid's 'informal tutorials' and Longley 'spent more time exploring Dublin and James Joyce': 'I was inhaling *Ulysses* and got some early sense of Homer...from Bloom's wanderings'.[9] Dublin's poetic culture was flourishing: Longley holds tactile memories of slim volumes of poetry 'beautifully produced' by Liam Miller's Dolmen Press, while the *Irish Times*, *Dublin Magazine*, and *Poetry Ireland* published and promoted new poetry. With its 'family atmosphere',[10] Dublin boasted an enriching poetic community: poets conversed and converged on the streets as pub and poetic cultures intersected. It was in McDaid's pub that Mahon introduced himself to a largely disinclined MacNeice, and Longley memorably boozed with a 'foul-mouthed

---

[5] Hazel Smith, *The Writing Experiment: Strategies for Innovative Creative Writing* (Northam: Allen & Unwin, 2005), 263.

[6] A. R. Ammons, 'A Poem is a Walk', *Epoch* 18 (Fall 1968), 114–19.

[7] Michael Longley, interview with Dermot Healy, *Southern Review* 31:3 (Summer 1995), 558–9.

[8] Longley, 'A Boat on the River (1960–1969)' (1999), repr. in *Flowing Still: Irish Poets on Irish Poetry*, ed. Pat Boran (Dublin: Dedalus, 2009), 55.

[9] Such peregrinations inspired the poems 'Nausicaa', 'Circe', and 'Odyssey'. Michael Longley, interview with Peter McDonald, *Thumbscrew* 12 (1998–9), 5–14.

[10] Michael Longley, *The Poetry Programme*, RTÉ Radio 1 (9 February 2008).

and beatific' Kavanagh.[11] University College Dublin poets Paul Durcan and Michael Hartnett could also be found 'sitting nervously at Kavanagh's table'.[12] Both Northerners bloomed in this vibrant locale and what would prove to be lifelong preoccupations took root. As Longley plots their peripatetics in 'River and Fountain':

> ... O'Neill's Bar, Nesbitt's –
> And through Front Gate to Connemara and Inishere,
> The raw experience of market towns and clachans, then
> Back to Rooms, village of minds, poetry's townland.[13]

This then was poetry's bountiful townland, and it was in Dublin that Longley formulated his long-held definition of poetry as the 'fountain' of Trinity's 'imaginary' Front Square.

Longley felt 'at home as an Ulsterman living in Dublin',[14] while for Mahon it was a 'home from home'.[15] Both sentiments echo one written during the same time about the same city by one of their most revered poetic elders, MacNeice, who declared, in a 1962 essay for the *New Statesman*, that he had 'always found the city a home from home'. What begins as a jaunty, journalistic account of MacNeice's attendance at the opening of the Joyce Museum—satirizing Bloomsday as the 'promoter's dream'—modulates into a journey back through Dublin's past as it has been bound up with MacNeice's own through a series of affecting reminiscences which, as MacNeice himself concedes, though 'trivial' for him, 'add up to a chain which can lower an anchor when [he] need[s] it'. In this unrequited love letter to the city, MacNeice's affection for the 'old Dublin' is keenly felt as he rhapsodizes about its enduring, unique, artistic qualities, all 'gifts for the amateur photographer': 'the astonishing light and the air that caresses ... and the screaming of the gulls and the newsboys ... the paradoxes of the Dubliners themselves'. The word 'paradoxes' goes to the heart of MacNeice's sense of the city. Dublin, as he concludes, 'remains constant and constantly variable'.[16] The city will not be fixed and so it affords no end of possibilities—creative, philosophical, existential—for the thinking poet in transit. What marks Dublin at this time for both Mahon and Longley must be the city as a site of possibilities but also of enlivening, irreconcilable conflicts and divisions. Of his 'subliminal education' at Trinity, Longley remembers 'walking in and out of the Front Gate and being aware of the tensions in myself and within the university'.[17] As

---

[11] Longley, 'A Boat on the River', 55. See also Derek Mahon, 'Eclogues Between the Truculent', in *Incorrigibly Plural: Louis MacNeice and his Legacy*, ed. Fran Brearton and Edna Longley (Manchester: Carcanet, 2012), 101–2.

[12] Derek Mahon, 'Yeats and the Lights of Dublin', in *The Dublin Review Reader*, ed. Brendan Barrington (Dublin: Dublin Review Books, 2007), 45.

[13] Michael Longley, *Collected Poems* (London: Jonathan Cape, 2006), 237.

[14] Longley, interview with Healy, 558.

[15] Derek Mahon, 'A Ghostly Rumble Among the Drums', in *Journalism: Selected Prose*, ed. Terence Brown (Oldcastle: Gallery, 1996), 223.

[16] Louis MacNeice, 'Under the Sugar Loaf' (June 1962), *Selected Prose of Louis MacNeice*, ed. Alan Heuser (Oxford: Clarendon Press, 1990), 250.

[17] Michael Longley quoted in Fran Brearton, *Reading Michael Longley* (Tarset: Bloodaxe, 2006), 17.

immortalized in Boland's backward-looking battle poem 'Belfast vs. Dublin', Mahon also was conscious of his own divided identity as he strained to find his voice: the 'struggle going on between a surly Belfast working-class thing and something…debonair. The *flâneurs* I couldn't help but admire and envy'.[18] Edna Longley has observed how 'Dublin's mongrel genealogy resembles [MacNeice's] own',[19] and it must be precisely the dislocated city's complex hybridity, as an 'incorrigibly plural' flux of historical and cultural multiplicity, that appealed to Mahon and Longley also.

'I remember long smoky afternoons in Rooms beneath cloudy Dublin skies and think of the Yeats line, "The arts lie dreaming of the life to come"', Mahon has nostalgically recalled.[20] For him, 1960s Dublin is akin to Scott Fitzgerald's Jazz Age; a time of youthful possibility and restless excitement.[21] Indeed, Mahon's wistful retrospections remind us that the critical narrative that has himself and Longley becoming poets under Belfast skies only is a severely partial view. 'The more complex truth', as Mahon has clarified, is that 'at least one [of the so-called Belfast "group"] was sitting in Dublin reading Graves, Crane and Beckett'.[22] 'I began writing here in Trinity', he has unequivocally declared.[23] As Hugh Haughton corroborates, 'it was actually in the Bohemian Dublin of the 1960s that Mahon forged his identity as a poet', thus he should also be seen as part of the Dublin Literary Renaissance of the 1960s.[24] In the same way, Fran Brearton has noted how Longley's first collection *No Continuing City* (1969) 'has its roots in [his] experience not of a "troubled" Belfast, but of Dublin in the first part of the decade'.[25] 'Epithalamion', Longley's final contribution to *Icarus*, opens the collection which also includes 'Graffiti' and 'A Questionnaire' from the Dublin period. Moreover, Longley has since 'rescued from oblivion' as he has described, 'the best of these' *Icarus* poems, 'Tra-na-Rossan'—his first love poem and first poem about the West of Ireland—incorporating it into 'After Tra-na-Rossan' in *Snow Water* (2004).[26] Even if for Longley, there would be no 'continuing', no abiding, city in his poetry—for unlike his hero Frank O'Hara, Longley is a botanist, but not of the sidewalk—this formative Dublin experience still affords creative possibilities: a new poem 'Michaelmas, 1958' positions him still 'lodged above a poetry library, all/the Irish poets accumulating on Victor/Leeson's shelves in Dublin's Wellington Road'—testament to this literary city's continuing hold on his writerly imagination.[27]

'Either literally or metaphorically we were following Mahon', Conor O'Callaghan remembers of himself, Vona Groarke, and Justin Quinn, starting out as poets in the

[18] Derek Mahon, interview by John Brown, *In the Chair: Interview with Poets from the North of Ireland* (Cliffs of Moher, County Clare: Salmon Publishing, 2002), 114.

[19] Edna Longley, *Louis MacNeice: A Critical Study* (London: Faber, 1988), 27.

[20] Derek Mahon, 'The Age of Ignorance', *Icarus* 60 (March 2010), 51.

[21] See Mahon, 'A Ghostly Rumble', 223.

[22] Derek Mahon, 'Modernist Poets', *Irish Times* (16 July 1987), 9.

[23] Mahon, interview by Terence Brown, *Poetry Ireland Review* 14 (Autumn 1985), 13.

[24] Hugh Haughton, *The Poetry of Derek Mahon* (Oxford: Oxford University Press, 2007), 21.

[25] Brearton, *Reading Michael Longley*, 13.

[26] Longley, 'Tarnished Buttons', *Icarus* 60 (March 2010), 47.

[27] Longley, 'Michaelmas, 1958', private correspondence with author (31 May 2011).

1990s: adoring disciples, they would 'totter curiously' after him down Baggot Street 'out of awe'.[28] As 'Captain of my nation' Mahon promenades on Sandymount Strand in Durcan's 'A Visitor from Rio de Janeiro',[29] and of the Belfast-Dublin poets it is Mahon who best exemplifies the *flâneur*. Moreover, as 'Imbolc' in *The Hudson Letter* (1995) signals, it is to Dublin's backstreets that this 'recovering Ulster Protestant', an 'exile and a stranger', looks as a point of return: 'I shall walk the Dublin lanes as the days grow shorter,/I who once had a poem in *The New Yorker*'.[30] These lines set the compass point for *The Yellow Book* (1997), composed in Dublin in 1996. Neatly summed up by Haughton as a 'dandified, aleatoric Dublin kaleidoscope',[31] Mahon, as Dublin elegist, improvises an 'urbane, end-of-season, end-of-century Dublin blues'.[32] Dublin becomes a haunted site of literary convergences, with Fitzwilliam Square as a fallen 'Georgian theme park for the tourist', remembering MacNeice's condemnation of the 'commercial vandalism which is prepared to ruin the finest Georgian vista in the world, Fitzwilliam Street'.[33] '[S] hiver in your tenement' recreates the 'demure 1960s' where Mahon forged his poetic identity as Clarke—to whose 'New Liberty Hall' the title looks back—Kavanagh, and other 'European *littérateurs*' enjoy the city's 'unforced pace': 'Gravely they strolled down Dawson or Grafton St.,/thoughtful figures'.[34] Like his predecessor Clarke, Mahon spent time incarcerated in Jonathan Swift's 'home/for "fools and mad"' which in 'Dawn at St. Patrick's' becomes a 'home from home', a place of restoration. For the poet in crisis, walking confirms continuance, formally grounded by the reliability of end-rhyme: 'Light and sane/I shall walk down to the train'.[35] Mahon's intimate engagement with Dublin has been marked by continual returning, and it is when he cannot walk its streets that his sense of homelessness intensifies. 'The Yaddo Letter' opens on a note of poetic and personal failure as the poet locates himself somewhere 'off Route 9P' looking across the Atlantic to the shaky future of the poem's completion. 'Write to me soon in Dublin', the poet-as-father signs off to his distant children as he anticipates a return to that Edenic place of writerly possibility.[36] Poetic fulfilment is always possible in Dublin, but in a city that is aspirational; of the mind if out of view.

The Dublin of 1958 was the 'more cordial atmosphere' to which John Montague, another 'marooned northerner', returned after his formative sojourn in America and with its poetry. Having previously embarked on his literary career in a 'post-Emergency' Dublin inimical to modern poetry—breeding only 'acrimony and insult'—this curative

[28] Conor O'Callaghan, *In the Chair*, ed. John Brown, 305–6.

[29] Paul Durcan, *Greetings to our Friends in Brazil* (London: Harvill, 1999), 35.

[30] Derek Mahon, *Collected Poems* (Oldcastle: Gallery, 1999), 218. *The Hudson Letter* has been retitled *New York Time* in Mahon's *New Collected Poems* (Oldcastle: Gallery, 2011), and 'Imbolc' is now 'St Bridget's Day'.

[31] Haughton, *The Poetry of Derek Mahon*, 274.

[32] Haughton, 'Le Spleen de Dublin', *TLS* (24 April 1998), 24.

[33] MacNeice, 'Under the Sugar Loaf', 250.

[34] Mahon, *Collected Poems* (1999), 230.

[35] Ibid., 171.

[36] Ibid., 182, 185. 'The Yaddo Letter' is retitled 'Yaddo, or A Month in the Country' in *New Collected Poems*, 157–60.

trans-Atlantic 'flight' opened his stirring artistic consciousness to new poetic methods and exemplars.[37] Settling near Brendan Behan on Herbert Street, Montague enjoyed Liam Miller's revitalizing effect on the literary capital with Dolmen Press publishing his own *Forms of Exile* in 1958. Twenty years on, Montague's book-length sequence of moving love poems, *The Great Cloak* (1978), would include not only one of the quintessential Dublin poems, 'Herbert Street Revisited', but another Dublin poem and a walk poem, 'Walking Late'. Interestingly, Montague's own defining role as love poet evolved in reaction to the much-chronicled 'depressing miasma' of 1950s Dublin: 'one of the answers to that... one of the forces that could transform this, would be the power of love', he has explained in response to a question regarding his 'subversive' motives within the Irish context.[38] *The Great Cloak*, as it moves through marital breakdown to the redemption of new love and fatherhood, is strongly reminiscent of Robert Lowell's controversial *Dolphin* of 1973. Although set firmly in Dublin, formally *The Great Cloak* follows the American line. As such it is a fine example of the distinctive elements of Montague's 'formal ingenuity' as discerned by Adrian Frazier: the 'catlike precision of feet' and mode of 'accelerated grace'.[39] Strongly felt are the tracks of the American poet Robert Creeley behind the lines as Montague, in 'Walking Late', reroutes the trajectory of Irish poetry:

> Walking late
> we share night sounds
> so delicate the heart misses
> a beat to hear them[40]

Montague has often professed his 'affinity' with Creeley, and his debt to the 'American models' who 'helped him rein in his Irish loquacity and hone the short line that has been such a feature of his work'.[41] Here Creeley's characteristic broken music, his style of halting at each line-end, is audible as Montague's heart, sensitive to the same 'delicate' pulse of the line, 'misses/a beat'.

Charles Altieri has paid tribute to Creeley's remarkable 'breath control' that 'can make every line-ending an adventure',[42] and Montague shares the same bold impulse towards 'ending lines... to defeat expectation',[43] exemplified here in the poem where the deer are 'still alert':

---

[37] John Montague, Introduction to *Poisoned Lands*, rep. in *The Figure in the Cave and Other Essays* (Dublin: Lilliput Press, 1989), 53–4.

[38] Montague, 'An Interview with John Montague', by Dennis O'Driscoll, *Irish University Review* 19:1 (Spring 1989), 62.

[39] Adrian Frazier, 'John Montague's Language of the Tribe', *Canadian Journal of Irish Studies* 9:2 (1983), 67.

[40] John Montague, *The Great Cloak* (Dublin: Dolmen Press, 1978), 46.

[41] Montague, quoted in David Wheatley, 'Still in the Swim', *Books Ireland* (February 2000), 5.

[42] Charles Altieri, 'What Does *Echoes* Echo?', in *Form, Power and Person in Robert Creeley's Life and Work*, ed. Stephen Fredman and Steve McCaferty (Iowa: University of Iowa Press, 2010), 48.

[43] Montague, 'A Note on Rhythm', in *The Figure in the Cave*, 48–9.

> to unfold
> their knees from the wet grass
> with a single thrust & leap away
> stiff-legged, in short, jagged
> bursts as we approach
> stars lining
> our path through the woods

Alert himself to the sonorous, the sinuous possibilities of movement over and within the flexible poetic line, in active defiance of limiting poetic conventions that regulate the poem by having it 'march as docile as a herd of sheep between the fence of white margins',[44] Montague's own line-break adventures are enacted through sensitive use of enjambment and verbal concision. The poem is a living, dynamic event; Dublin itself throbs with life as a vibrant, resonating continuum as the walkers progress towards the city that:

> with the paling dawn,
>
> will surge towards activity again,
> the bubble of the Four Courts
> overruling the stagnant quays,
> their ghostly Viking prows,
>
> and the echoing archways…

As the walkers 'circle uncertainly/towards a home', the lines are mimetic of their drifting, tentative progress. Walking is thereby the key action in Montague's poetic formal innovation, with Creeley as pace-setting precursor. 'In Creeley's usage the forward movement of walking is also the creative formulation of the word',[45] Kenneth Cox has remarked, and it is no accident that the jazz dance 'Walking the Dog' was chosen as the title for one of Creeley's most rigorous lectures on poetic technique and the imperatives of duration, timing, rhythm, and sound. 'The majority of Irish poets write as though Pound, Lawrence, Williams, had not brought a new music into English poetry', Montague declared in 1973, citing Kinsella's 'Nightwalker' as one such work that is 'muffled by the old-fashionedness of its form: he has discovered a new subject, but not, I feel, a new metric to energize it'.[46] 'Walking Late' may be read as Montague's own response to Kinsella's 'Nightwalker' of ten years' earlier.[47]

Kinsella is unquestionably the pre-eminent poet of modern Dublin: it was his 'fresh and jagged' 'Baggot Street Deserta' that for Boland typified the city's burgeoning

[44] Ibid., 49.

[45] Kenneth Cox, 'Address and Posture in the Early Poetry of Robert Creeley', in *Robert Creeley's Life and Work: A Sense of Increment*, ed. John Wilson (Ann Arbor: University of Michigan Press, 1987), 183.

[46] Montague, 'The Impact of International Modern Poetry on Irish Writing', *The Figure in the Cave*, 219.

[47] In terms of this call and response between the two poets, Brian John notes that 'Montague may have unintentionally influenced *Nightwalker* through his own *Patriotic Suite* (1966)'. See Brian John, *Reading the Ground: The Poetry of Thomas Kinsella* (Washington, DC: Catholic University of America Press, 1996), 97.

presence in the 1960s. Crucial in this is the trope of walking that drives Kinsella's jour-
neying poetics. As Andrew Fitzsimons has shown, 'the motif of the walk in Kinsella is
invariably an occasion for movement through time as well as space'. What is more,
Fitzsimons's pronouncement that 'what was at one stage in its composition called
"Walking at Night" reveals Thomas Kinsella preparing himself to take Irish poetry into,
in Gerald Dawe's phrase, "uncharted territory"'[48] makes explicit the vital connection
between walking and writerly experiment in the groundbreaking 'Nightwalker'.
Famously criticized by Edna Longley for its unprecedented 'meandering' form,
'Nightwalker' remains, above all, a significant poem about poetry itself and the compo-
sitional process, as the first of Kinsella's poems to have 'the act of poetry, the process of
imaginative digestion' as its subject.[49] In terms of setting a precedent, 'Nightwalker' has
also been held up as the first of Kinsella's poems to achieve the 'successful absorption of
Joyce'.[50] As has been much-documented, this Joycean-inspired walking motif continues
through Kinsella's oeuvre in poems that manage more effectively Montague's 'new met-
ric'. In 'St Catherine's Clock' the poet-walker begins by 'divining the energies of the
prowler' while, traversing central Dublin as a site of history, Kinsella's 'The Pen Shop' is,
as Derval Tubridy has remarked, among the poems that continue what Michel de
Certeau has termed 'the long poem of walking': Kinsella 'uses the poet-speaker's journey
through a specifically delineated urban geography to explore the relationship between
place and politics'.[51] Here again the process of writing is the real subject. Indeed, the pen
shop's 'narrow cell' may be seen to embody not merely, as Fitzsimons has noted, the
monk's cell of ancient Irish literature or Kinsella's own 'narrow room' on Baggot Street,
but formally, Wordsworth's sonnet as 'narrow cell'. Thus the recurrence of this replicative
term here tracks the changes, indicating how far Kinsella's organic poetic forms have
developed since the early years of the less liberating, formal enclosures and, what is
more, how this voyage into 'uncharted territory' is made possible by the choreography
of both body and mind—the human foot and the metrical foot—as life and art, past and
present, keep step with and energize each other.

   Kinsella is rightly regarded as the quintessential Dublin prowler-poet and his most
agile younger followers through the city include David Wheatley and Peter Sirr, both
Trinity College alumni. Kinsella has been an important model for Wheatley who has not
only learnt from him stylistically but, as a scholar, has argued for Kinsella's significance
as 'one of the great modern chroniclers of the city' within an international context that
includes Charles Reznikoff, Geoffrey Hill, and Roy Fisher.[52] Sirr too regards Kinsella as
the supreme poet of Dublin; more than that, he goes against reductive critical views that

---

[48] Andrew Fitzsimons, *The Sea of Disappointment: Thomas Kinsella's Pursuit of the Real* (Dublin:
UCD Press, 2008), 184–6.

[49] Kinsella, 'Interview with Thomas Kinsella', by Dennis O'Driscoll, *Poetry Ireland Review* 25 (Spring
1989), 63.

[50] John, *Reading the Ground*, 24.

[51] Derval Tubridy, *Thomas Kinsella: The Peppercanister Poems* (Dublin: UCD Press, 2001), 216.

[52] David Wheatley, '"All is emptiness/and I must spin": Thomas Kinsella and the Romance of Decay',
Irish Studies Review 16:3 (August 2008), 332.

hold up Kinsella's representations of the city as informed by narrow agendas, by 'the imperatives of nationalism'.[53] As Sirr sees it, such easy readings are in fact more complicated as nothing in Kinsella is straightforward or rigid; rather we get an 'intense and multi-faceted relationship with several Dublins'. Because of this, 'you can't say here is the Dublin of personal memory and here is the public entity, or here is the public and here the private voice. The nature of his pursuit is to find a way of writing which incorporates all of these and moves, often disconcertingly, from one to the other'.[54] Like MacNeice's Dublin, Kinsella's Dublins cannot be simplified or made to stand for one thing only, and in this Sirr follows the older poet's pioneering example. Indeed, moving 'disconcertingly' is Sirr's forte. Moreover, this is enhanced by the formal procedures of his poetry. As Peter Robinson has shrewdly identified, 'to get this evolving sound, Sirr had more or less to abandon the stanza as a self-contained apartment, and to strike out into blocks of responsively improvised verse'.[55] Reviewing Mahon's *The Hudson Letter*, Sirr criticized its 'willed formality' as 'more of an external imposition than a truly releasing scheme'.[56] Taking its lead from Kinsella's meandering forms, Sirr's own formal elan is only ever 'truly releasing': exhilarating, dynamic, and exploratory.

Reviewers of Sirr's *Bring Everything* (2000) attributed its critical import to the way that it placed Dublin city centre-stage in new ways. 'Its central character is the city of Dublin itself as it has never before been seen in our poetry,' Justin Quinn observed.[57] Echoing Quinn, Wheatley too lauded this 'younger Southern poet' who 'stands out for his imaginative commitment to urban life... all too rare in the poetry of Celtic Tiger Ireland'.[58] 'Might the new Dublin give rise to a new Dublin poetry?' Colin Graham asked, noting, like Quinn, how, in Sirr's treatment of the city, Dublin 'becomes a character in its own right', with Sirr a '*flâneur* of the new economy'.[59] Sirr's own critical focus regularly fixes on poets who succeed in capturing a city in motion. Michael Smith, whose own walk home through a Dublin where Kavanagh still held court often overlapped with Hartnett's,[60] is celebrated for his attentiveness to the darker aspects of Dublin city: 'characteristically he's prowling the "Old rotten heart of the city" '.[61] But Sirr's readings of the modern city in poetry extend beyond Ireland. Reading Reznikoff, an avid walker-poet, Sirr relishes poems in which 'the city is a continuous living and radiant presence': 'one of the most attractive aspects of his work is precisely his preparedess... to let the city come alive'.[62] The poetics of the city performed by the 'brilliantly adventurous' Jacques Réda as

[53] Justin Quinn, *The Cambridge Introduction to Modern Irish Poetry* (Cambridge: Cambridge University Press, 2008), 203.

[54] Peter Sirr, 'A Poet's Guide to his City', *Irish Times* (12 December 2006).

[55] Peter Robinson, 'Sleeve of Europe', *TLS* (5 August 2005), 26.

[56] Peter Sirr, rev. of *The Hudson Letter*, by Derek Mahon, *Poetry Ireland Review* 48 (Winter 1996), 84.

[57] Justin Quinn, 'O Seasons, O Cities', *Metre* 10 (Autumn 2001), 106.

[58] Wheatley, 'Floating Down Sheep Street', *TLS* (20 July 2001), 25.

[59] Colin Graham, 'Poems of the City', *Irish Times* (20 January 2001).

[60] Michael Smith, 'Remembering Michael Hartnett', *Irish Times* (16 February 2009).

[61] Peter Sirr, 'Writing the Bare Bones, *Irish Times* (22 August 2009).

[62] Peter Sirr, 'Charles Reznikoff', *The Cat Flap* (22 June 2008) <http://petersirr.blogspot.com/2008/06/charles-reznikoff.html>

he 'reinvents the tradition of the *flâneur*' are hailed for their 'densely textured and richly musical' technique, integral to which is rhythm; the momentum of walking: 'Paris is what he writes with, providing subject and technique. The poems are often grounded in the city which he explores obsessively, traversing vast tracts of it on foot.'[63] In this way, Sirr, like Réda, 'sets himself afloat to drink in the sense data of the streets'.

The process of poetic composition has been likened by Sirr to an 'adventure' with 'no real maps, no sure paths'.[64] *Bring Everything* (2000) brings the multifaceted city to life as a constantly shifting, living organism through the wandering, weaving movements of a walking, thinking consciousness. Joyce once professed to being 'more interested in the Dublin street names than in the riddle of the universe', and Sirr's similar interest in street names and Dublin history makes for poems of startling originality and imaginative reach as the ground-level facts of the city unleash other realities. Street names can transform their surroundings, changing the colour of reality itself, as in 'Sráid na gCaorach' (Irish for 'Sheep Street') where the present street name, 'Ship Street', has come about circuitously thanks to the vagaries of spoken language whereby 'sheep' metamorphosed into 'ship'.[65] Thus, the bilingual street sign commemorates the twists and turns of linguistic translation. Sirr's instinctively orchestrated free verse is a liberating force and the soundscape of the city is evoked in the opening lines' assonance where 'street deep' finds its resonance in 'the bells of two cathedrals'.[66] The city, an animated, cognitive presence, 'leans/as if it has remembered something', and the theme of memory, the city as a palimpsest of history, is thereby asserted. 'Startled', the street 'rubs the wool from its eyes/ and casts off...' at the poem's end as 'sheep' and 'ship' are reconnected through the verb 'casts'. The Irish-language title stresses the linguistic, temporal, and spatial crossovers that traversing Dublin necessitates, all of which is conveyed by the fluid runs over the line breaks and in the poem's inconclusive, elliptical ending. As Sirr takes the common 'corruption' of a street name and riffs on its imaginative and symbolic possibilities, De Certeau's theory of 'the magical powers proper names enjoy', and how these create 'a strange toponymy that is detached from actual places and flies high over the city, like a foggy geography of "meanings" held in suspension', seems appropriate.[67] As they move imaginatively over the Dublin cityscape, Sirr's poems are profoundly alive to this airy indeterminacy and multiplicity of meaning.

In 'The Hunt', Sirr continues to transgress boundaries as a concrete Dublin is transmuted into a watery city through a seafaring metaphor and with verbs such as 'dive',

---

[63] Peter Sirr, 'Small Dramas', *Poetry Ireland Review* 101 (Summer 2010), 90–6 (95).

[64] Peter Sirr, 'The Hat on the Chair', in *The Watchful Heart: A New Generation of Irish Poets*, ed. Joan McBreen (Cliffs of Moher: Salmon Publishing, 2009), 173.

[65] Cf. Shakespeare's *Love's Labour's Lost*, Act II:1 where a similar mishearing of 'sheep' for 'ship' occasions a comic moment:

> Maria: Two hot sheeps, marry.
> Boyet: And wherefore not ships?
> Maria: No sheep, sweet lamb.

[66] Peter Sirr, 'Sráid na gCaorach', *Bring Everything* (Oldcastle: Gallery, 2000), 11.

[67] Michel de Certeau, *The Practice of Everyday Life* (Berkeley: University of California Press, 1984), 104.

'adrift', 'plunging' pulling the ground from under us.[68] Although loco-specific—it plots
its way through 'Old Kilmainham', 'Sitric Street', 'Ivar Street'—the reader never feels
grounded as the poem drifts along on the changing gradations of light, particles of dust,
the varying textures of 'Sirr's intimate city'—a phrase which remembers Joyce's Dublin
as 'the last of the intimate cities'.[69] In 'China', a moment out of *Ulysses*, in which a morn-
ing stroll through Dublin's sense-arousing streets transports Bloom to the orient
('Wander through awned streets. Turbaned faces going by'),[70] finds its twenty-first-cen-
tury parallel. Here, a tumultuous, multicultural Dublin becomes richly overlaid tempo-
rally and spatially as the walker, drunk on a myriad of sensations, takes flight
imaginatively and the city is transfigured in the process:

> There's a moment the air will thicken, and the light shift, as if,
> another country has poured itself in, another life
> lent its corona...[71]

Here Sirr's improvisatory free verse conveys the city's disorienting plurality; Dublin's
unending imaginative terrain is matched by expansive, exploratory lines, and propulsive
sound effects of internal rhyme and repetition that carry the words forward as they
move:

> or it will happen like this:
> a sudden, butchery odour on the street
> and the pavement opens, the sky parts, something
> floating back with such clarity it pulls you short

As the walker enters the city's flow, the lines, mimetic of his physical and metaphysical
movement, swerve and spin, conveying the true multiplicity and contingency of experi-
ence as they hurl the reader into a rapid freefall: 'and then it's gone, then a blur, the rest of
the journey/irrecoverable'.[72]

In Sirr's poetry, simplistic theoretical boundaries—between urban and pastoral, per-
son and place, life and death, past, present, future—are revealed as permeable just as
they are in the city itself; and in *The Thing Is* (2009) the fluid city brings forth new life as
it embodies the force of unstoppable change. In the rambling sequence 'The Overgrown
Path', it is by walking 'these few steps...down half the length of Chatham Street' that the
course of life changes irrevocably. A defamiliarizing, life-altering moment—the news of
imminent fatherhood—stops the walker in his tracks in his attempt to stall time: 'and
I want to stop, hold on, loiter'.[73] Later in the collection, following the child's entry into
the world, its development runs concurrently with that of Dublin itself. In 'In the

[68] Sirr, *Bring Everything*, 12.
[69] James Joyce, quoted in Richard Ellmann, *James Joyce* (New York: Oxford University Press,
1982), 253.
[70] James Joyce, *Ulysses* (London: Penguin, 1992), 68.
[71] Sirr, *Bring Everything*, 14.
[72] Ibid.
[73] Peter Sirr, *The Thing Is* (Oldcastle: Gallery, 2009), 24.

Beginning', the birth and growth of the city is charted in a continuous stream of images. 'Eternal as water, endless as air', the city's continuous music goes on forever, its 'mudflats/ singing'.[74] In this rapturous evocation of Dublin across time, the city as life form is linked to the child, building on the preceding 'At the Intersection' where a walk through Dublin becomes the progress of life itself. Here, the critical tendency to pair Sirr with Frank O'Hara seems particularly appropriate. As the father and child undertake their morning excursion to school, the poet-as-father becomes O'Hara-esque in his elegy for the city in its passing and for the synchronous passing of childhood, as he addresses his young companion:

> We're still here, look: the ruins of the city have risen to meet us.
> Raymond Street: you sit in your buggy and flourish the name like treasure.
> I am wheeling you through masonry, clay, endless riddles of detail.[75]

'Everything we know will disappear with us', the speaker says of the mutable world. Yet 'perfectly at home in the scatter', the child, in her reversible dress, accommodates herself to the changing city, and so to the processes of death. The collection ends with an assurance of the paradoxical 'brutal, lovely/persistence of the city' as Catullus is translated to contemporary Dublin.[76] Reviewing Hartnett's *Inchicore Haiku* (1985), Sirr pithily summarized it 'as if Basho had awoken from the slumber of centuries and found himself in a chipper on Emmet Road'.[77] For Sirr, the collection's achievement lies in the way that the always listening, observing poet of daily 'minutiae' incorporates 'chippers, birdsong, plastic bags' into this diminutive Japanese form. The Hartnett of *Inchicore Haiku* has clearly been influential in opening up paths of possibility for Sirr along which he continues to move with boundless formal, intellectual, and imaginative vivacity.

'You could have foregone all your Shangri-las/to pioneer Siberia-sur-Liffey', David Wheatley writes to his nineteenth-century Dublin forebear, James Clarence Mangan, in *Misery Hill* (2000), as he assumes the mantle of present-day *flâneur* or 'nightwalker' in a contemporary Dublin underworld twinned with Dante's Purgatory.[78] *Misery Hill* is haunted by the presiding spirits of Mangan and Beckett. For Wheatley, Beckett is a Dublin poet whose work 'alternates between claustrophobic trampings round Dublin and moments of blissful centrifugal escape', as the younger poet carefully attends to 'Enueg I' as a 'trek around Dublin' that is spoken by a 'walker'.[79] As Wheatley will know, Beckett confirmed that the poem is 'based on an actual walk that he took from the Portobello Private Nursing Home westward along the Grand Canal out of the city then back along the River Liffey'.[80] Thus it is Beckett the trailblazer that Wheatley pursues.

[74] Ibid., 51.

[75] Ibid., 49.

[76] Ibid., 75.

[77] Peter Sirr, 'The Short and the Long', *Irish Times*, Weekend Review (21 September 1985), 11.

[78] David Wheatley, *Misery Hill* (Oldcastle: Gallery, 2000), 21.

[79] David Wheatley, Preface, *Samuel Beckett: Selected Poems, 1930–1989* (London: Faber, 2009), pp. ix, xii. As Marjorie Perloff has pointed out, 'Enueg I', showing its Joycean influence, has a 'tone of documentary veracity' as its 'depicted circular walk can be traced on a map of Dublin'. What is more, it follows the 'promenade structure' of Guillaume Apollinaire's 'Zone'. Perloff, 'Beckett the Poet', in *A Companion to Samuel Beckett*, ed. S. E. Gontarski (Oxford: Wiley-Blackwell, 2010), 213–14.

[80] See Knowlson, *Damned to Fame*, 137.

Indeed, the connection between walking and continuance in Beckett is made explicit in Durcan's 'The Beckett at the Gate'. Fittingly dedicated to Mahon, it has the poet-walker communing with Beckett, his pervasive ambulatory predecessor: 'I keep on walking;/I'll go on, I think, I'll go on', his expanding stomping ground indisputably that of Beckett: 'Past the gasometer and Grand Canal Dock,/Misery Hill, The Gut, The Drain'.[81] Many of the places signposted across Durcan's post-Beckettian nightwalk are weighty locus points for Wheatley, whose own 'claustrophobic trampings' in the manner of Beckett pivot on questions of home and elsewhere; Wallace Stevens's 'that we live in a place/That is not our own' is the epigraph to the title poem of his first collection, *Thirst* (1997).[82] In 'Autumn, the Nightwalk, the City, the River', Wheatley, with a knowing nod to Kinsella and Beckett, walks Dublin's urban and suburban landscapes under the oppressive cover of darkness. Alert to the changing of the seasons, the rhythms of being, this practised walker identifies the different ambulatory style that autumn necessitates ('nervous, brisker now') and, as he follows the river ('the only living thing') towards a destination unknown, the poem moves in a tentative, meandering free verse that is itself mimetic of the edgy rhythm of walking, the stumbling hesitancies, 'dead-ends'; for 'what matter[s] here is 'being lost'.[83] As the final poem of *Thirst*, its concluding lines open out onto an uncertain, yet vast, spectrum of future exploration beyond 'home': 'already forgetting dry land, open sea'.

Misery Hill continues and extends this perambulating poetics as the isolated speaker walks an inscrutable, amnesiac Dublin city where implausible street names signal only lost connections, impairment, and death: 'Blind Alley,/Smock Alley, Hangman's Lane/ Isolde's Tower'.[84] Devoid of signifier, street sign, or marker, 'Misery Hill' is a long-forsaken site of the city's past, existing 'on the map but nowhere else', although readers of Beckett will know it as part of his symbolic geography. Obsolescence is the theme, the scene one of desertion and ruin on 'this grim street' that remains 'featureless and empty besides'. In this there is a hint of the bleak desolation at the end of Shelley's 'Ozymandias', while the symbolic 'letters/for anywhere but this grim street' call to mind the dead letters of Herman Melville's scrivener Bartleby; Melville's scrivener metamorphoses into the scrivener Mangan, the presiding spirit of *Misery Hill* who lives on posthumously in textual form. In a sequence of fourteen sonnets addressed to Mangan, the great Dublin *flâneur*, Wheatley interrogates Mangan, pursuing his 'dizzy paper trail' of selves.[85] Mangan's own poetic project was concerned with reclamation, and here Wheatley reclaims Mangan as an enabling precursor, appealing to him as a similarly conflicted

---

[81]   Paul Durcan, *Life Is A Dream: 40 Years Reading Poems 1967–2007* (London: Harvill Secker, 2009), 168–74. Erik Martiny reads it as symptomatic of Durcan's struggle with Beckett as a 'frightful, invasive creature'. Martiny, 'Demonic Forefather: Portraits of Samuel Beckett in the Works of Paul Durcan', *Nordic Irish Studies* 5 (2006), 149–56.

[82]   David Wheatley, *Thirst* (Oldcastle: Gallery, 1997), 65.

[83]   Ibid., 74.

[84]   Wheatley, *Misery Hill*, 10.

[85]   Ibid., 13.

poet-critic: 'Help me James, to take upon myself/the sins of poets'.[86] Playfully disloca-
tive rhymes include 'Siberia'/'suburbia', 'Offices'/'faeces' as Wheatley superimposes
Mangan's 'landscape of the lost' on contemporary Dublin: 'Fishamble Street, the Civic
Offices/turning the sky a bureaucratic grey'. The design of the poem skilfully creates a
sense of unending motion, the city's own integral processes of creation and destruc-
tion, as the enjambment in its 'turning' repeats, in the opening lines, the unnatural
working of the Civic Offices on the sky, and, across the seventh and eighth lines, orches-
trates the falling and rising of the buildings, Georgian houses giving way to concrete
formations:

> One last buttressed Georgian house holds out
> precariously against the wreckers' ball
> or simply lacks the energy to fall
> and rise again as one more concrete blot.[87]

The pun on concrete 'blot' (instead of block) points up the eyesore that is reconfiguring
the city skyline. The Civic Offices themselves were built on Wood Quay, the site of a
Viking settlement, and are a blight on the city's landscape, a monument to the destruc-
tion of its historical past. The rising and falling of the city's architecture, as history is
erased and replaced with these obdurate, corporate, high-rise edifices, is underscored
by the rising and falling cadences of Handel's sublime 'ghost harmonics'—unheard,
imperceptible—the lost music reverberating in the speaker's mind only and providing a
poignant ground bass to the city's obliteration. There is no music here, only silence, as
the city's history and culture are wiped out: 'Of you Mangan, not a trace'. A poet seeking
out the company of the ghost of another, Wheatley keeps step with the contemporary
city, past and present, walking his disappearing city to create a journeying meditation on
art and on human existence. In the title-sequence of thirty-three sonnets in terza rima
that ends *Misery Hill*, the walker's madcap peregrination through a warped, debased
Dublin becomes a lurid, burlesque version of Dante's *Purgatorio*. Walking is a *via dolor-
osa*; the poem, a dizzying head-rush of sonnet upon sonnet until the whole of Celtic
Tiger Dublin fades and the speaker is hurled back to the dingy reality of a Dublin bedsit.
Wheatley's affinity with Sirr is clear and his poems of the city share the same 'imagina-
tive commitment to urban life'. Although later collections will have him leave Dublin
and put out to sea, it remains the setting-out point for this inexhaustible, peripa-
tetic poet.

The female *flâneur* in Irish literature has received little critical attention, even less so in
Irish poetry. The idea of the *flâneuse* immediately suggests the figure of the street walker
or prostitute, thereby linking the vulnerable female walker to dangerous realities not
known to the *flâneur*. One of the first twentieth-century Dublin poems to star a female
walker must be Stevie Smith's 'Bag Snatching in Dublin' which dramatizes, through deft
metrical shifts, a Liffey-side walk in the 1930s as 'Sisley' meets her end to the drawn-out

---

[86] Ibid., 16.
[87] Ibid., 12.

accompaniment of the river's 'turgid flood'.[88] Present-day Dublin *flâneuses* include Paula Meehan, who grew up in one of the Georgian houses so beloved by MacNeice and Mahon, but one that had been turned into a tenement slum. One of the most streetwise poets, the city forms a backdrop to her investigations of social and familial history. As Elisabeth Mahoney has summarized: 'There are two main narratives of Dublin in her poetry: a childhood Dublin, a city of memory, and an adult city, constantly rediscovered as it develops.'[89] Another nocturnal ambler, she sets out on her own 'Night Walk' in *Pillow Talk* (1994), covering a large part of the city's history and geography as her nocturnal peregrination takes in Fumbally Lane, the Blackpitts to Mount Street and back. The theme is sexual violence as the poem articulates a 'prayer' for 'that poor woman last night/dragged down Glover's Alley, raped there'.[90] Meehan has expressed her commitment to mapping the city of Dublin in her own terms; 'The city was incredibly well-mapped in literary terms. But, yet, *my* city wasn't',[91] and it is partly through walking that she negotiates her way. For a younger poet such as Caitríona O'Reilly, Dublin is both the point of origin and of necessary departure, as rendered in the poem 'Sunday', set on the Liffey's banks, where the circumscribed river's constrictions reflect the walking poet-speaker's entrapment as she stumbles falteringly with her companion. Formally, the narrow two-line stanzas refuse the harmonies of end-rhyme, and stuttering sound effects predominate as the 'stopped world' of the derelict city is underscored by a hard consonantal cacophony— 'wre*c*ked', 'wind-ro*c*ked', '*c*lamp'—with the Liffey's tortured flow menacingly wound through repeated sibilance: 'twi*s*ts in*s*ide *it*s *st*one confin*es*, heedle*ss*.'[92] In terms of poetic confluences, this must be the same abandoned locale of Wheatley's 'Misery Hill' where 'Only the gods that are cranes can see/the wrecker's yard behind one wall',[93] confirming Dublin, even in its unlikeliest spaces, as a fecund poetic meeting ground, a site of constant renewal—the disused Dockland setting of both poems has since been redeveloped—that the poet sets out from and can return endlessly to.

Having travelled so far across the work of a range of the most intrepid and inventive Irish poets writing and walking today, it seems fitting to end with a walk poem by a poet who persists in complicating any stable notions of place, of gender, of tradition, of language; a multilingual poet of exile and indeterminacy who is deeply attentive to the contingencies of world and word, and who has been one of the most enabling senior figures and formidable presences in Irish poetry, as a lecturer in English at Trinity College Dublin and one of the founding editors in Dublin in 1975 of the magazine *Cyphers*. Cork-born Eiléan Ní Chuilleanáin's identities are many; she may be read as both an Irish

---

[88]   Stevie Smith, *Collected Poems* (New York: New Directions, 1976), 47.

[89]   Elisabeth Mahoney, 'Citizens of its Hiding Place: Gender and Urban Space in Irish Women's Poetry', in *Ireland in Proximity: History, Gender, Space*, ed. Scott Brewster (London: Routledge, 1999), 148.

[90]   Paula Meehan, *Pillow Talk* (Oldcastle: Gallery, 1994), 20.

[91]   Meehan, quoted in Luz Mar González-Arias, 'In Dublin's Fair City: Citified Embodiments in Paula Meehan's Urban Landscapes', *An Sionnach* 5:1/2 (2009), 36.

[92]   Caitríona O'Reilly, *The Nowhere Birds* (Tarset: Bloodaxe, 2001), 33.

[93]   Wheatley, *Misery Hill*, 10.

poet—part of the 1970s generation of Munster poets, part too of the post-Kinsella gen-
eration of Dublin poets—and as the most truly transnational of poet-translators, living
as she does 'between Dublin and Umbria'. As Thomas McCarthy has recognized her dual
position: 'She has always spoken from a double province: the Dublin poem, the Cork
poet.'[94] Belonging to no one school, she has situated herself in time as coming 'half a gen-
eration after Kinsella', aligning herself thus 'away from that masculine agenda of rural
description which Heaney somehow continued',[95] and her urban imagination bears this
out, facilitating a poetry of endless scope and resource across time and space. Although
Dublin may be 'home'—arriving in Dublin in 1967 after 'exile' in Oxford, she says she
discovered 'not only home but Bohemia'– her postmodern imagination encompasses an
extensive, constantly shifting ground as, even here, in what should be read as a straight-
forward interview response, one specific place (Dublin) is defined through another
(Bohemia) to effect profound dislocation and semantic deferral.[96]

Among Ní Chuilleanáin's Dublin poems is 'Man Watching a Woman'. Yet were it not
for the fact of the poem's inclusion on the 1998 audio anthology *Dublin 15: Poems of the
City*, one might not recognize the poem's topography as being of that city. 'Strangeness'
is a key condition of being for this poet who has described poetry as essentially 'the
strangeness of words arranged in lines'.[97] This poem is nothing if not strange, ungraspa-
ble, even if its plot may be given as follows: an unnamed man sets out late at night on
foot, and goes, for reasons never divulged, to watch a woman at work in a refectory, then
moving on through the anonymous city to watch girls working late in bars, at which
point the poem ends. As an inconclusive, open-ended imaginative expedition in which
any specifics of meaning are suspended, it typifies Ní Chuilleanáin's elusive strategies.
Indeed, for Sirr, in an astute essay that laments the lack of experimentation in contem-
porary Irish poetry, Ní Chuilleanáin is held up as a necessary alternative to this; a poet
whose subversive approach 'makes us throw away our maps and wander in the danger-
ous and surprising undergrowth of the poem', one of the poets who 'reinvent the lyric
and send it spinning out of its normal orbit'.[98] Sirr's metaphors here lend themselves per-
fectly to a reading of 'Man Watching a Woman', the obliquities of which may, to my mind,
be illuminated if it is read as a poem about poetry itself and one that foregrounds ques-
tions that go to the heart of Ní Chuilleanáin's searching, endlessly disturbing poetics.
The man in the poem is, after all, another nightwalker, and as it is 'sound' and 'sense' that
set him on his venture, he must embody the figure of the poet at work:

---

[94] Thomas McCarthy, ' "We Could Be in Any City": Eiléan Ní Chuilleanáin and Cork', *Irish
University Review* 37:1 (2007), 232.

[95] Eiléan Ní Chuilleanáin, 'An Interview with Eiléan Ní Chuilleanáin' by Leslie Williams, in
Representing Ireland: Gender, Class, Nationality, ed Susan Shaw Sailor (Gainesville: University Press of
Florida, 1997), 39.

[96] Ibid., 33.

[97] Eiléan Ní Chuilleanáin, 'Where is Poetry?', *Poetry Ireland Review* 92 (2007), 63–6.

[98] Peter Sirr, ' "How Things Begin to Happen": Notes on Eiléan Ní Chuilleanáin and Medbh
McGuckian', *Southern Review* 31:3 (1995), 451, 467.

> The sound of everything folding into sleep,
> A sense of being nowhere at all,
> Set him on his way (traffic far off and wind
> In tall trees) to a back gate, a dark yard...[99]

Sirr has praised the 'trajectory of attentiveness and perception' that sets Ní Chuilleanáin's oeuvre apart, qualities that the nightwalker too possesses as 'He stops and watches. He needs to see this.' Concealed in night, unseen yet all-seeing, remaining detached, out in the cold, he studies the woman through the window, the meaningfully positioned 'privet hedge' suggestive of the privacy that he transgresses from his liminal position. 'Comforted' as he is somehow by the nun's activity in the 'refectory' (fittingly, a place of refreshment), the poem proliferates with present particles at this point as, though sedentary, the nun is all activity ('working', 'sewing', 'dropping', 'falling') as she moves in and is bound by time, her immobile 'feet' clamped down by poetic technique as the hard alliteration of their being 'trapped/in toils of cloth' is secured with an adamantine full stop. 'Comforted', having seen 'this' (the specificity usually endowed by deixis denied here), the nightwalker's progress resumes over lines that run on with propulsive force as 'the night combs out/Long rushing sounds into quiet,/On to the scene, the wide cafés –'. Ever attuned to the world as it presents itself at each moment, the walker now scrutinizes the 'faces behind the bar', and here the music of poetry sounds forth to consolidate artistic activity, poetry as process of sound and rhythm:

> Their muscles bracing under breakers of music
> And the weight of their balancing trays, drinks, ice
>   and change.

What carries over is the precarious poise of poetic composition itself; the full-bodied alliteration of 'bracing', 'breakers', 'balancing' balancing the closing two lines which are further supported and matched through assonance as the *ay* of 'bracing' and 'breaker' is carried over into 'weight', 'trays', and 'change', stablizing the entire transaction. The poem oscillates between stasis and motion to show how the act of poetic composition is itself a balancing act, an act of measuring, weighing, counting—Ní Chuilleanáin has revealed how her own compositional process necessitates formal push and pull.[100] As form is mimetic of content, a tension is set up between the poetics of engagement, of being out in the world, and the concealed, circumscribed handwork of the domestic realm. Yet it is the domestic encounter that enables the man to go on. Suitably, for a poet who has identified herself as having 'never been a domestic woman'—'It's a subject I occasionally contemplate from a distance, but I don't feel it really suits me'—the woman in the poem enacts domestic activity while the man 'contemplates from a distance'.[101] 'When I started

---

[99] Eiléan Ní Chuilleanáin, *The Brazen Serpent* (Oldcastle: Gallery, 1994), 38.

[100] 'Interview with Eiléan Ní Chuilleanáin' by Patricia Boyle Haberstroh, *Canadian Journal of Irish Studies* 20:2 (December 1994), 69.

[101] 'Eiléan Ní Chuilleanáin: Interviewed by Deborah Hunter McWilliams', in *Writing Irish: Selected Interviews with Writers from the Irish Literary Supplement*, ed. James P. Myers (New York: Syracuse University Press, 1999), 204–5.

to write, I had to invent strategies for saying "I" in a female persona.... The nuns were a great help there':[102] Ní Chuilleanáin has plotted her own artistic vocation and it cannot be accidental that it is a nun the man attends to and draws sustenance from. Both conditions of artistic being are therefore viable; the poem refuses to choose between them.

Ultimately, Ní Chuilleanáin's transformative poetics of transit and translation equates the force of poetic composition with the natural vigour of 'a person walking'; formally and rhythmically determined by the thinking, shaping consciousness in a process of exploring the unknowable, the indefinable:

> I'm very interested in the idea that every poem should have a shape of its own, and...that [the words] should have a rhythm, that they should have a weight and shift of their own. And it would be sort of natural, like a person walking...[103]

'If you want to talk about it in terms of place, my place is on the move',[104] Ní Chuilleanáin has gestured, and in 'Man Watching a Woman' the poet as indefatigable prowler is reminiscent of the insatiable stalker of Edgar Allan Poe's 'The Man of the Crowd', a tale of the city that impressed itself upon the pre-eminent *flâneur*-poet, Charles Baudelaire. Indeed, when asked in 1998 to identify a poem that has been 'crucial' for her, Ní Chuilleanáin selected Baudelaire's 'Le Cygne' for the way it 'made the mysterious equation between the heart and the city'. Crucially for Ní Chuilleanáin, Baudelaire's poem of the city 'decentres the being and the personality, refuses to be classified, questions any certain human boundaries', the nineteenth- century metropolis compelling for 'the vastness and variety of its modernity'.[105] 'Man Watching a Woman', as it extends the *flâneur* tradition in art, epitomizes the artist as inhabiting more than one place or state, as defiant of convention, endlessly interrogating and crossing boundaries, keeping apart and on the move, and, in the process, moving poetry itself into new, strange territories, beyond the limits of conventional literary maps and markings. For the most daring Irish contemporary poets, walking in the city makes available the same 'vastness and variety' in poems that are alive to formal exploration and experiment, and whose invigorating intellectual probings and journeyings are often profoundly disruptive and disconcerting. The poem itself becomes expansive, shifting territory, open-ended in its thematic and semantic possibilities, transforming the poetic landscape around it. As the poet-walker experiences on foot the city's restless energies and vitalizing tensions, such ambulatory procedures channel poetic events that are, like the boundaryless, changeable city itself, richly complex, kinetic, and multidimensional.

[102] 'An Interview with Eiléan Ní Chuilleanáin' by Leslie Williams, 39.
[103] 'Interview with Eiléan Ní Chuilleanáin' by Kevin Ray, *Eire-Ireland: A Journal of Irish Studies* 31:1/2 (1996), 66.
[104] 'Eiléan Ní Chuilleanáin: Interviewed by Deborah Hunter McWilliams', 205.
[105] 'Eiléan Ní Chuilleanáin', 'Charles Baudelaire', *Poetry Ireland Review* 59 (1998), 25.

PART IX

THE POET AS CRITIC

....

CHAPTER 32

THE IRISH POET AS CRITIC

....

HUGH HAUGHTON

I

....

In Wilde's 'The Critic as Artist', Gilbert asserts that 'Without the critical faculty, there is no artistic creation at all worthy of the name.'[1] According to T. S. Eliot too, 'the critic and the creative artist should frequently be the same person'. More specifically, he said that 'The poetic critic is criticizing poetry in order to create poetry.'[2]

In Ireland the poet and critic of poetry have certainly tended to be the same person, and usually, by the same token, 'criticizing poetry in order to create poetry'. With the exception of W. B. Yeats and Seamus Heaney, however, they haven't generally acquired an international reputation as poet-critics like Ezra Pound, Eliot, Paul Valéry, or Randall Jarrell. In the *Cambridge History of Literary Criticism*, Yeats is the only Irish writer to figure, appearing in the context of 'The Irish Arts Business' in the 1890s and as a walk-on 'poet-critic' who advocated a 'return to the imagination'.[3] In his *Decolonisation and Criticism*, an historical overview of Irish criticism, Gerry Smyth largely omits poets altogether apart from Yeats and Patrick Kavanagh, though he mentions the 'lacklustre' Austin Clarke and casts Seamus Heaney as the exponent of 'collusive, essentialist fantasies *and* the kind of discourse in which these are celebrated'.[4] There have been some important recent studies of Heaney as critic, but the critical prose of Irish poets has

---

[1] Oscar Wilde, *The Works of Oscar Wilde*, ed. Vivian Holland (London: Harper Collins, 1966), 1,020.

[2] T. S. Eliot, *The Sacred Wood*, 2nd ed. (London: Faber, 1928), 15–16.

[3] Lucy McDiarmid, 'The Irish Arts Business' and Lawrence Lipking, 'Poet-critics', *Cambridge History of Literary Criticism: Modernism and the New Criticism* (Cambridge: Cambridge University Press, 2000), 151–6, 464–6.

[4] Gerry Smyth, *Decolonisation and Criticism: The Construction of Irish Literature* (London: Pluto Press, 1998), 31.

generally been treated as a side-effect of their poetry rather than part of the development of criticism or poetics in or outside Ireland.[5]

Pascale Casanova argues in *The World Republic of Letters* that 'the Irish case furnishes a paradigm that covers virtually the entire range of literary solutions', from the problems of contesting colonial domination, and inventing a national literature, to creating a separate 'literary space' for writing in the global marketplace.[6] Since 1890 poets' prose has been an important agent for forging such a space. For obvious reasons, ideas about national identity, the Irish language, and the cultural distinctiveness of Ireland in relationship to Britain, have played an essential—but not necessarily essentialist—part in their critical writing. Pressures on the poet changed drastically within the period, as the struggle for independence was followed by the establishment of the Free State and Partition, and as national consolidation in the middle century gave way to post-colonial, post-national, and trans-national versions of identity. Nevertheless the question of Irishness, whether embraced or resisted, never entirely dissipates.

In 1890, on the crest of late nineteenth-century nationalism, Yeats wrote that 'There is no great literature without nationality' and 'no great nationality without literature'.[7] Commenting on this, Gerry Smyth observes that for Yeats 'literature . . . signifies a specific realm of activity policed by the artist-critics of Anglo-Ireland, entry to which is subject to their criteria'.[8] Smyth's account of 'artist-critics' as 'policing' involves its own critical policing. Nevertheless it reminds us that quarrels over the relationship between political and aesthetic identity are endemic, as poets competitively carve out a space for their own writing within a country trying to forge a political identity before and after the dissolution of the Union. Yeats wrote later that 'I am no Nationalist, except in Ireland for passing reasons', but passing reasons have lasting consequences, and the shifting and conflicted nationalism of Yeats and the other 'artist-critics' of the Revival left a complex legacy.[9] This specifically Irish context is the reason Yeats is not usually thought of as a 'literary critic' like Matthew Arnold or T. S. Eliot, but it is also why he became such a crucial representative of a poet forging a counter-hegemonic poetics in a modern global context.

Introducing his 'critical prose' in 1937, Yeats said: 'A poet is justified not by the expression of himself, but by the public he finds or creates; a public made by others ready to his hand if he is a mere popular poet, but a new public, a new form of life, if he is a man of genius.'[10] During the years leading up to and succeeding the founding of the Irish Free

---

[5] See Michael Cavanagh, *Professing Poetry: Seamus Heaney's Poetics* (Washington DC: Catholic University of America Press, 2009), and David Wheatley, 'Professing Poetry', in *The Cambridge Companion to Seamus Heaney*, ed. Bernard O'Donoghue (Cambridge: Cambridge University Press, 2008).

[6] Pascale Casanova, *The World Republic of Letters*, trans. M. Devoise (Cambridge, MA, and London: Harvard University Press, 2004), 303–23.

[7] W. B. Yeats, 'Browning' (1890), *Letters to the New Island* (Oxford: Oxford University Press, 1934), 103–4.

[8] Smyth, *Decolonisation*, 74.

[9] W. B. Yeats, 'A General Introduction for my Work', *Essays and Introductions* (London: Macmillan, 1961), 526.

[10] 'Introduction', ibid., p. x.

State, poetic self-expression was inevitably bound up with questions of national self-definition and the constitution of that 'new public', and Yeats's protean and prolific prose was designed both to make a case for his own art and to shape the cultural sphere in Ireland during a period of momentous political transformation. 'Now that I have all my critical prose before me', he observed self-critically, 'much seems evasion'. Nonetheless, he noted that, while unsure about the likely reception of a poem, 'if I give a successful lecture, or write a vigorous critical essay, there is immediate effect'.[11] Yeats's lectures and essays certainly had an electrifying effect on cultural debate, and even his evasions helped define the new forms of literary life. In 'Poetry and Tradition' (1907), he spoke of the 'romantic conception of Irish Nationality' on which he and Lionel Johnson 'founded our art and Irish criticism', and said 'It was our criticism' which 'set Clarence Mangan at the head of the Young Irish poets in the place of Davis', and 'our attacks' on the evaluation of poetry for 'its moral or political worth', which opened the way for the Revival.[12]

Yeats here gives 'Irish criticism' a key role in moving the nationalist agenda into a more *literary* key. His own early critical work was driven (and riven) by contradictory aesthetic needs. He wanted on the one hand to develop his own esoteric post-*Symboliste* poetics in essays like 'Autumn of the Body' (1898) and 'Magic'(1901), and on the other to shape public debates about the function, form, and subject matter of art in Ireland. Douglas Hyde sought in 'The Necessity for the De-Anglicisation of Ireland' (1892) to cultivate 'everything that is most racial, most smacking of the soil, most Gaelic', advocating a return to Irish to help the 'race to develop in future upon Irish lines'.[13] By contrast, Lionel Johnson in 'Poetry and Patriotism' (1894) argued for a more inclusive notion of national culture. 'A living literature', he said, 'may feed upon the literature of the past, and of other nations' while bearing 'the sign and seal of its own nationality'. He asked whether Ireland was 'the only nation which influences from without are bound to ruin and unnationalize; the only nation incapable of assimilating to herself, of nationalizing and naturalizing the heritage of art and learning left by other nations?' While endorsing Hyde's drift, Johnson insisted (in 'Empire strikes back' mode) that Irish writers should be able 'to make raids upon other countries, and bring home the spoils'.[14]

In their criticism Johnson and Yeats argue consistently for an internationally informed and *literary* notion of Irish poetry, anticipating both the aesthetic debates of James Joyce's *Ulysses* and arguments about post-colonial identity. Such critical polemics, though countered by D. P. Moran in *The Philosophy of Irish Ireland* (1905), acted as important catalysts for later poets. In 'Anima Hominis' (1917), one of his most esoteric texts, Yeats proposed (rhetorically) that: 'We make out of the quarrel with others, rhetoric, but of the quarrel with ourselves, poetry'.[15] His own critical prose brilliantly plays out his rhetorical quarrel with Irish culture, but also with literary criticism outside Ireland

---

[11] Ibid., p. xi.

[12] Ibid., 246–60.

[13] Hyde, 'The Necessity for the De-Anglicisation of Ireland', in *Poetry and Ireland Since 1800: A Source Book*, ed. Mark Storey (London: Routledge, 1988), 82–3.

[14] Lionel Johnson, 'Poetry and Patriotism', ibid., 93–106.

[15] W. B. Yeats, 'Per Amica Silentia Lunae' (1917), *Mythologies* (London: Macmillan, 1962), 331.

(as in his demolition of Wilfred Owen's 'passive suffering' and critique of the 'rhythmical flatness' of Eliot's realism in his notorious introduction to *The Oxford Book of Modern Verse*).[16] It also clarifies the self-quarrel which provides the dynamic of his poetry. Such prose helped generate 'a new public, a new form of life', and its characteristic dialectic shaped the ways later Irish poets, usually through their quarrel with Yeats, approached the problematic relationship between art, personal biography, and cultural identity. Yeats's overtly critical essays—the pieces on Shelley, Blake, Synge, Mangan, and Ferguson— are only the tip of the iceberg.

Yeats's views of poetry and poetics are hammered out in his autobiographical writing, the esoteric mythology of *A Vision*, and the brilliant mythological poetics of *Per Amica Silentia Lunae* (1917). His most influential single essay, however, is probably 'A General Introduction for my Work', which combines all of these. It opens with the Wildean claim that 'The world knows nothing because it has made nothing, we know everything because we have made everything.'[17] Announcing that a poet 'never speaks directly as to someone at the breakfast table, there is always a phantasmagoria', the essay is a unique combination of personal memoir, review of Irish political and cultural history, and exercise in speculative poetics. Written at the end of his career, after the establishment of the Irish Free State and his Nobel Prize, its vexed combination of *ars poetica* and cultural autobiography embodies very different priorities from his early contributions to debates about cultural nationalism. Its account of the 'great tapestry' lying behind 'all Irish history', 'the scene at the birth of modern Irish literature', and the relation between his movement and 'the firing squads of 1916', as well as its tortured sense of linguistic division ('Gaelic is my national language, but it is not my mother tongue'), its apologia for traditional stanza forms ('all that is personal soon rots; it must be packed in ice or salt'), and even its hatred of the 'electric signs, where modern heterogeneity has taken physical form', have shaped later readings of Yeats.[18] The poetics of conflict and the autobiographical quarrel with his culture embodied in Yeats's immense critical *oeuvre* entered the bloodstream—and critical prose—of almost all later Irish poets.

II

Beside the self-fashioning Yeats, the most influential Irish poet-critic has been the self-fashioned Stephen Dedalus, protagonist of Joyce's *A Portrait of the Artist as a Young Man*. As a young poet from a lower-class Dublin background, educated in Catholic schools and University College Dublin, Stephen Dedalus was not Yeats nor was he meant to be. This proved a huge gift to later writers, a gift compounded by his lack of poetic *oeuvre*.

---

[16] W. B. Yeats, 'Introduction', *The Oxford Book of Modern Verse* (Oxford: Oxford University Press, 1936), pp. xxxiv, xx.

[17] Yeats, 'A General Introduction for my Work', 509.

[18] Ibid., 509–30.

Stephen's complex entanglement in nationalist politics, urban modernity, and Thomist theology offered many later poets a more workable template than that of the theosophical, Protestant, and senatorial Yeats. Indeed Stephen's remarks on epiphanies, tundishes, sows, nets, and a smithy are probably the most decisive intervention in Irish criticism by any single poet. Though Heaney wrote of 'Yeats as an Example', it is Stephen he takes as an exemplar in the final section of *Station Island*, complementing a contemporary essay in which he hails Joyce rather than Yeats as 'the true liberator'.[19] Though Dedalus's solitary villanelle confirms him as a minor *fin-de-siècle* talent, his conversational *aperçus* and diary entries turned him into a major twentieth-century critic.

Joyce's novel dramatized the intimate alliance between art, Catholicism, and linguistic self-consciousness in Ireland during the struggle towards national Independence in which Stephen's struggle for artistic independence against 'home', 'fatherland', and 'church' takes place: 'I will try to express myself in some mode of life or art as freely as I can'.[20] As he moves to forge his post-Thomist aesthetic of 'impersonality', he tells the nationalist Cranly: 'This race and this country and this life produced me...I shall express myself as I am...You talk to me of nationality, language, religion. I shall try to fly by those nets.'[21] 'Fly by' simultaneously suggests avoiding the nets and using them for flight, encapsulating Joyce's Janus-faced attitude towards national and aesthetic identity. When the Dean of Studies assumes the word 'tundish' is Irish, Stephen jokes that it is the word used in 'Lower Drumcondra...where they speak the best English', before musing 'My soul frets in the shadow of his language.'[22] Stephen goes on to call Ireland 'the old sow that eats her farrow' and to insist on 'silence, exile, and cunning', but the novel ends with diary entries which reinsert the aesthetically independent artist as an agent of resistance into the country he needs to escape, as he seeks 'to forge in the smithy of my soul the uncreated conscience of my race'.[23]

Yeats pondered the idea that his 'movement perished under the firing squads of 1916', saying that Patrick Pearse and Thomas MacDonagh, though not his 'school', would have 'attempted in Gaelic, what we did or attempted in English'.[24] MacDonagh, like Dedalus, was a poet and student at UCD, and in his posthumously published *Literature in Ireland* (1916) he celebrated 'the Irish Mode' as a specifically linguistic phenomenon in the place of the 'Celtic genius' of Arnold, whose *On the Study of Celtic Literature* (1867) he called 'a work of fiction'. MacDonagh offers a complex model for an anglophone literature that takes its bearings from Irish and literature in Irish without being based on essentialist nationalist premises or the 'Anglo-Irish tradition' of Yeats.[25]

---

[19] Seamus Heaney, 'A Tale of Two Islands', *Irish Studies* 1 (1980), 17. See also Heaney, 'Yeats as an Example?', *Preoccupations: Selected Prose 1968–1978* (London: Faber, 1980), 98–114.

[20] James Joyce, *A Portrait of the Artist as a Young Man*, ed. J. S. Atherton (London: Heinemann, 1964), 229.

[21] Ibid., 188.

[22] Ibid., 174–5.

[23] Ibid., 253.

[24] Yeats, 'A General Introduction for my Work', 515–16.

[25] Thomas MacDonagh, *Literature in Ireland* (London: T. F. Unwin, 1916), p. vii, 55.

MacDonagh embraced the new literature in Irish represented by Pearse but also the 'Anglo-Irish literature' in English written by 'the Irish people, mainly of Gaelic stock' who are 'now mostly English-speaking' but whose distinctive 'ways of life and of thought' are different from others which have 'found expression in other English literature'.[26] He includes an anthology of examples of the 'Irish Mode' from poets such as Mangan and Ferguson, documenting the influence of Irish music, speech, and verse, as well as Hiberno-English. Welcoming the death of the *aisling*, he also laid down models for poetry in the native language while arguing that through the Irish Mode poets could contribute 'new wealth' to 'the common literature of the English language' while keeping a 'characteristic literature of [their] own'.[27]

MacDonagh's dedication to forging an independent nation led to his execution, and his *Literature in Ireland*, with its sophisticated account of the realities of a bilingual culture, helped construct a distinctive Irish literature. In 'Poetry and Tradition' (1907), Yeats spoke of wanting 'to forge in Ireland a new sword on our traditional anvil', while in *A Portrait*, Joyce invoked a more industrial smithy to 'forge the uncreated conscience of [his] race'.[28] In their different ways both writers root poetics in autobiography (and vice versa), while representing the work of art and the artist as engaging in a quarrel with (and within) a divided, linguistically colonized national culture in a trans-national context. Their intransigent self-forging aesthetics had a profound impact on the way subsequent writers thought and wrote about their own work.

III

Introducing an anthology of Irish verse, Derek Mahon quoted Stephen's remarks about the 'uncreated conscience' before observing that 'Clarke and Kavanagh have done much to forge that conscience'.[29] As with Yeats and Joyce, that 'forging' took place in prose as well as verse.

Poets' prose takes many forms. However, few later Irish poets in the conscience-forming business escape writing one or more or all of the following: 1) an introduction to an anthology (usually of Irish verse); 2) an essay on Yeats and/or Joyce; 3) an account of 'Irish Poetry today'; 4) reviews of other Irish writers; 4) a commentary on poetry and national identity; 5) an autobiographical account of finding their voice. John Montague said 'every poet must dream of an ideal anthology of the poetry of his country', and Yeats was responsible for *A Book of Irish Verse* (1900), based on 'literary' rather than 'patriotic and political value'.[30] Subsequent poet-anthologists include Montague,

---

[26] Ibid., p. viii, 23.

[27] Ibid., 19, 24.

[28] Yeats, *Essays and Introductions*, 249. See also n. 20.

[29] Derek Mahon, 'Introduction', *The Sphere Book of Modern Irish Poetry* (London: Sphere Books, 1972), 13.

[30] W. B. Yeats, 'Preface', *Irish Verse* (London: Methuen, 1900), p. xv.

Brendan Kennelly, Thomas Kinsella, Peter Fallon, Derek Mahon, Michael Longley, Tom Paulin, Thomas MacCarthy, Paul Muldoon, Nuala Ní Dhomhnaill, and Gerald Dawe. Following in the wake of Louis MacNeice's *The Poetry of W. B. Yeats* (1941), poet-commentators on Yeats include Clarke, Boland, Heaney, Mahon, Kinsella, Muldoon, and Paulin. Among early reports on the Irish poetry scene, Samuel Beckett's hugely influential 'Recent Irish Poetry' (1934) stands out for its iconoclastic demolition of the Celtic 'thermolaters' of the Revival and affirmation of young Irish modernists such as Denis Devlin and Brian Coffey, with their modernist awareness of 'the breakdown of the object' and 'rupture of the lines of communication'. Austin Clarke, dismissed by Beckett for purveying 'the fully licensed stock-in-trade from Aisling to Red Branch Bundling', offered a more upbeat exercise in stock-taking in 'Irish Poetry Today' (1935), declaring Ireland to be 'in an extraordinarily interesting stage of self-discovery'.[31] Later instances include Heaney's 'Place and Displacement: Recent Poetry from Northern Ireland' (1984), Dennis O'Driscoll's 'A Map of Contemporary Irish Poetry' (1995), and Nuala Ní Dhomhnaill's overview of contemporary women poets for the Field Day anthology.[32] In addition to devising such poetic maps, most poets have served up prose portraits of the artist, probably the most distinctive prose genre practised by Irish poets, with Yeats's *Autobiographies* followed by influential essays and interviews by Seamus Heaney, and memoirs by John Montague, Eavan Boland, Michael Longley, Gerald Dawe, Nuala Ní Dhomhnaill, Dennis O'Driscoll, Ciaran Carson, and others.[33]

The mid-century poets engaged in most of these genres, with Austin Clarke's *Twice Round the Black Church* (1962), Louis MacNeice's *The Strings are False* (written in the 1940s and published posthumously in 1965), and Patrick Kavanagh's 'Self-Portrait' (1964) offering a trio of culturally diverse prose self-portraits that record the post-Yeatsian, post-Joycean struggle of Irish poets with nationalism and modernism.

Austin Clarke, a prolific reviewer, attacked MacNeice's *The Poetry of W. B. Yeats* on the grounds that MacNeice's 'real object' was 'to classify Yeats among the modernists', 'younger poets', and 'disciples of T. S. Eliot', whereas in fact Yeats was 'completely unacquainted with contemporary English poetry' and moved 'away steadily from English

[31] Samuel Beckett, 'Recent Irish Poetry', *Disjecta: Miscellaneous Writings*, ed. Ruby Cohn (London: John Calder, 1983), 70; Austin Clarke, 'Irish Poetry Today', *Reviews and Essays of Austin Clarke*, ed. Gregory A. Schirmer (Gerrards Cross: Colin Smythe, 1995), 62.

[32] Seamus Heaney, 'Place and Displacement' (1984), repr. *Finders Keepers: Selected Prose 1971–2001* (London: Faber, 2003), 122–45; Dennis O'Driscoll, 'A Map of Contemporary Irish Poetry', *Troubled Thoughts, Majestic Dreams* (Oldcastle: Gallery, 2001), 67–80; Nuala Ní Dhomhnaill, 'Contemporary Poetry', *The Field Day Anthology of Irish Writing: Irish Women's Writing and Traditions* V (Cork: Cork University Press, 2002), 1,290–7.

[33] John Montague, *Company; a Chosen Life* (London: Duckworth, 2001); Seamus Heaney, *Crediting Poetry*, The Nobel Lecture 1995 (Oldcastle: Gallery, 1995), and Dennis O'Driscoll, *Stepping Stones: Interviews with Seamus Heaney*, (London: Faber, 2008); Eavan Boland, *Object Lessons: The Life of the Woman and the Poet in Our Time* (Manchester: Carcanet, 1995); Michael Longley, *Tuppenny Stung: Autobiographical Chapters* (Belfast: Lagan, 1994); Gerald Dawe, *My Mother City: A Memoir* (Belfast: Lagan, 2007); Nuala Ní Dhomhnaill, 'Cé Leis Tú', *Selected Essays* (Dublin: New Island Books, 2005), 97–155; Dennis O'Driscoll, 'Circling the Square: A Thurles Prospect', *Troubled Thoughts, Majestic Dreams*, 17–31; Ciaran Carson, *The Star Factory* (London: Granta Books, 1997).

poetic influence'.[34] For Clarke, in his numerous essays, Yeats was inescapably bound up with the traditional matter of Ireland, and he reflected in 1940 that 'the loss of Yeats and all that boundless activity in a country where the mind is feared and avoided, leaves a silence which it is painful to contemplate'.[35] Clarke's criticism offers clues to his own long silence as a poet. In 1937 he wrote that 'the deliberate removal of poetry from the political and moral sphere during the Parnell split undoubtedly improved our art, but it carried with it the implications that poetry is not strong enough to express or analyse the passions of real life'.[36] When he returned to poetry later, it was to engage directly with the 'political and moral sphere' and 'passions of real life'. In 'Poetry in Ireland today' (1946), he speaks of his conversion to 'literary Home Rule', arguing that 'the very nature of Irish poetry is misunderstood': 'An Irish poet, writing in the medium of the English language, is aware not only of the English poetic tradition but of Anglo-Irish and Gaelic tradition. Far from being provincial, he must be a focal point of many influences.'[37] He goes on to cite the influence of MacDonagh, under whom he had studied at UCD, noting that 'instead of the "wavering rhythms" of the Celtic Twilight School, we now have complex assonantal patterns', implicitly hitching his star to the 'Irish mode' and making the case for his own technical innovations. He concludes by asserting that 'at a time when our critics are timid and depressed, our poetry is vigorous and lively'.[38]

As an instance of poetic vitality Clarke cites Kavanagh's *The Great Hunger* as 'a realistic study of country life, almost Joycean in its intensity'.[39] Kavanagh defined 'A true creative critic' as 'a sweeping critic, who hates certain things because they are weeds which choke the field against the crop which he wants to sow'.[40] On these terms, unlike the more circumspect Clarke, the Monaghan poet was a model critic. He certainly had a ferociously developed awareness of the innumerable weeds in the field of Irish writing, asserting in 1951 that 'with the exception of Yeats practically none of the verse written in Ireland during the present century has had any poetic merit'.[41]

Kavanagh's *Collected Pruse* [sic] (1967) followed close on the heels of his *Collected Poems* (1966). A rag-bag of memoir, fiction, and reviews from *Kavanagh's Weekly* and elsewhere, it included some sweeping critical pieces in which the poet assaults the Dublin literati and sets out his own poetic stall. Though he claimed he was not trying to 'boost his wares', he argues that the 'so-called Irish Literary movement which purported to be frightfully Irish and racy of the Celtic soil was a thoroughgoing English-bred lie' and that Irishness was a form of 'anti-art'.[42] Kavanagh's animus is rooted in his

---

[34] Austin Clarke, *Reviews and Essays of Austin Clarke*, 17–18.

[35] Ibid., 13.

[36] Ibid., 69.

[37] Ibid., 106–7.

[38] Ibid., 110.

[39] Ibid., 109.

[40] Patrick Kavanagh, 'Self Portrait', *Collected Pruse* (London: MacGibbon & Kee, 1967), 241.

[41] Patrick Kavanagh, 'Literature in the University', *A Poet's Country: Selected Prose*, ed. Antoinette Quinn (Dublin: Lilliput Press, 2003), 235.

[42] Patrick Kavanagh, 'Self-Portrait', ibid., 306, 309.

experience of being taken up as 'the authentic peasant' when 'the big thing besides being Irish was peasant quality' and 'Dublin was a literary metropolis and Ireland, as invented and patented by Yeats, Lady Gregory and Synge, a spiritual entity'. The essay offers an explosive assault on this national myth, as it insists on the 'barbaric life of the Irish country poor', claims 'a poet is never one of the people', and maintains 'there is no audience in Ireland' for poetry. Recoiling from his earlier career and reception, he proclaimed that as a poet he was 'born in or about nineteen-fifty-five' on the banks of the Grand Canal. It was there, 'just out of hospital', that he became 'airborne' (like Joyce's flying Dedalus), after escaping the fantasy of having 'roots in the soil'.[43] In the equally autobiographical 'From Monaghan to the Grand Canal', he asserts 'there has never been a tradition of poetry in Ireland', condemns 'the myth of Ireland as a spiritual entity', and notes 'how poor as technicians the Irish school of poets and novelists has been'.[44]

In another essay he argues that 'none of those whom the world thought creative ever thought for a moment about Art' (side-lining Wilde, Yeats, and Joyce), before launching into an inspirational defence of the 'parochial'. Claiming 'parochialism' and 'provincialism' are opposites because the provincial has no mind of his own until he has heard 'what the metropolis … has to say', the poet proclaims 'All great civilizations are based on parochialism', naming Joyce and George Moore as 'great Irish parishioners'.[45] The result is the late poems of *Come Dance with Kitty Stobling* (1960), a collection which includes 'Epic', his most eloquent statement of parochial poetics, with its claim that Homer made the *Iliad* out of 'such a local row' and 'gods make their own importance'.[46]

Collected Pruse helped make Kavanagh's own importance, with its irreverent defiance of the 'formula for literature which laid all the stress on whether it was Irish or not'.[47] More recently *A Poet's Country: Selected Prose* (2003) offers a fuller representation of his critical trajectory, documenting his hatred of 'the pygmy literature' of the Irish Renaissance, his refusal to recognize Irish as 'a badge of nationhood', his dedication to 'naming' as 'part of the poet's function', and his long battle to avoid the Scylla and Charybdis of nationalism and colonialism without succumbing to a vacuous apotheosis of 'Art'.[48] For Eavan Boland, though 'Yeats had made a literature', Kavanagh 'made the single, daring act of protest which pointed the way forward'.[49] Dennis O'Driscoll, on the other hand, notes that 'few … are sufficiently rooted to find Kavanagh's parochialism attainable', affirming instead John Montague's assertion that 'the real position for a poet is to be global-regionalist', 'born into allegiances to particular areas or places and people' but part of 'an increasingly accessible world': 'actually local and international'.[50]

---

[43] Ibid., 305–16.
[44] Patrick Kavanagh, 'From Monaghan to the Grand Canal', ibid., 272–81.
[45] Patrick Kavanagh, 'Parochialism and Provincialism' (1952), ibid., 282.
[46] Patrick Kavanagh, *Collected Poems*, ed. Antoinette Quinn (London: Allen Lane, 2004), 184.
[47] Kavanagh, *A Poet's Country*, 226–7.
[48] Ibid., 232, 230.
[49] Boland, *Object Lessons*, 91.
[50] 'Global Regionalism: Interview with John Montague', *The Literary Review* 22:2 (Winter 1979), cited in O'Driscoll, *Troubled Thoughts*, 84.

MacNeice, who lived in England, was more obviously international and less 'paro-chial', though his father had an actual parish. In works like 'Carrickfergus' and *The Strings are False*, MacNeice grounded his poetic identity in a specific Northern Ireland geography, but not in his critical prose. Working for the BBC, published by Eliot at Faber, and part of the London scene, MacNeice was well placed to become an influential met-ropolitan critic, but chose not to. He wrote a number of essays on modern poetry in the 1930s, was a perceptive bread-and-butter reviewer of poets from Eliot and Robert Frost to W. H. Auden and Dylan Thomas, as well as publishing *Varieties of Parable* (1965), an eclectic commentary on modern literature written in a heavily discursive mode at odds with the parabolic agility of his poetry. In 'Poetry To-day' (1935), he writes that a poet explaining his work is 'less helpful than the mechanic explaining an engine', but it is 'a human characteristic' to explore 'why, how and what [he] writes'.[51] The 'functions of the-ory are propaedeutic, prophylactic, and corrective…as in learning to play tennis', but 'the work is done with the hands'.[52] He observes 'few poets to-day can assume, as Homer and even Shakespeare could' that his public knows the premises upon which they write and 'it is the critic's job to point out to the public what angle a poet is writing from'.[53] Essays like 'Poetry To-day' and 'Subject in Modern Poetry' certainly clarify his own dis-tinctive angle.

'For me,' MacNeice wrote in 1935, 'the history of post-War poetry in England is the history of Eliot and the reaction from Eliot'. He celebrates Yeats as 'the best example of how a poet ought to develop' and a 'fine case of identity in difference', but views him as an 'esoteric' writer, 'further away from the ordinary English reader or writer than Eliot is; not only because of his cabalistic symbols, etc. but even more because of the dominance in him of the local factor'. For MacNeice, Yeats's 'rhythms and the textures of his lines are inextricably implicated with his peculiar past and even with the Irish landscape'.[54] MacNeice's essays offer broad-brush maps of contemporary poetry, making the case for an impure, formally mobile, contemporary idiom such as Auden's or his own. He does not generally address the 'local' Irish factor in his own case, though he celebrates in un-Yeatsian fashion 'the Irish movement, where poetry was healthily mixed up with poli-tics'.[55] For some readers, this may confirm MacNeice's marginality to the development of Irish poetry; for others, his indifference to the passport issue gives essays like 'Poetry To-day' the 'incorrigibly plural' flair of his verse, which expands the field of reference of Irish poetry. The essay is full of memorable dicta that throw light on his art at the time of *Autumn Journal*: 'A poem to be recognizable, must be traditional; but to be worth recog-nizing, it must be something new'; 'The poem, like the idol, is a kind of Alter Ego'; 'The self-contradictory is what is alive'; 'the best poems are written on two or more planes at

---

[51] Louis MacNeice, 'Poetry To-day', *Selected Literary Criticism of Louis MacNeice*, ed. Alan Heuser (Oxford: Clarendon Press, 1987), 10.

[52] Ibid., 11.

[53] Louis MacNeice, 'Poetry, the Public, and the Critic', ibid., 167.

[54] 'Poetry To-day', ibid., 40–1.

[55] Ibid., 15.

once'; 'There is material for poetry everywhere; the poet's business is not to find it but to limit it.'[56]

The bulk of MacNeice's essays and reviews are business-like at best, but *The Poetry of W. B. Yeats* is a masterwork. Published soon after Yeats's death, it is not only one of the earliest studies of the poet but offers a vigorous debate about the nature of modern poetry. MacNeice reads Yeats in the Irish context but also in dialogue with Eliot, Rilke, Auden, and MacNeice's contemporaries at the historical moment of the start of the Second World War ('for war spares neither the poetry of Xanadu nor the poetry of pylons').[57] The book is in large measure a defence of the poet critiqued by Auden in 'The Public vs the late Mr W. B. Yeats': 'It is an historical fact that art *can* make things happen and Auden in his reaction from a rigid Marxism seems ... to have been straying towards the Ivory Tower'.[58] 'Poetry nowadays appears to need defending',[59] he observes at the start, and though not claiming 'to defend poetry itself' against the Marxists and 'realists', his account of Yeats as a 'rich and complex poet' who wrote 'the best poetry of his time' is a defence by other means.[60] It wrestles eloquently with questions of form and subject, politics and history, aestheticism and modernity, art and nationality, that go to the heart of Yeats's work and his own.

MacNeice clarifies his own autobiographical investment. 'Like Yeats, I was brought up in an Irish middle-class Protestant family', he says, Yeats in the 'primitive west' and he in the 'industrial north'; and where Yeats as a boy reading 'Orange songs, fancied himself dying facing the Fenians', MacNeice 'as a little boy among Orange men', imagined himself 'a rebel against England'.[61] MacNeice shows a lively awareness of Young Ireland, the Gaelic revival, and the work of MacDonagh and others, and is as alert to Yeats's highly politicized Irish worlds as to 1930s England. While he celebrates the influence of the 'pantomimic transformation scenes' of the Irish landscape, he also argues that with the Easter Rising, Yeats 'received from Ireland a violent shock, at the same time horrifying and stimulating', and concludes that, though it is 'unsafe to generalize about Ireland', 'the Irish dialectic is best, perhaps, resolved by a paradox: Ireland, like other countries, has obvious limitations; these limitations, if rightly treated, become assets.'[62] After his impassioned review of Yeats's career, MacNeice acknowledges that, like Gerard Manley Hopkins, he was 'a special case' who turned his own limitations into assets: 'If Yeats had been different from what he was, or had different beliefs ... he might not have written at all. The spiritual lesson that my generation (a generation of vastly different outlook) can learn from Yeats is to write according to our lights. His lights are not ours. *Go thou and do otherwise*.'[63] He ends with the assertion that in Yeats's work 'there is nearly always a

---

[56] Ibid., 12, 13, 43.
[57] Louis MacNeice, *The Poetry of W. B. Yeats*, 2nd ed. [1941] (London: Faber, 1967), 18.
[58] Ibid., 192.
[59] Ibid., 17.
[60] Ibid., 30–1.
[61] Ibid., 50.
[62] Ibid., 48–51.
[63] Ibid., 197.

leaping vitality—the vitality of Cleopatra waiting for the asp'.[64] That Yeatsian vitality finds a mirror in MacNeice's turbulent critical wrestling match.

Clarke, who had wanted to write a study of Yeats himself, was not impressed by MacNeice's bracingly international assessment. Noting that MacNeice had 'first attracted attention' in Ireland with 'Valediction', he criticized the 'morbid fascination with Irish matters' typical of 'a certain type of political Irishman', MacNeice's view of 'the Irish literary movement' as a 'side issue' and his ignorance of 'Irish letters as a whole'. Where MacNeice wanted 'to classify Yeats among the modernists', Clarke saw him as 'a traditionalist in temperament', resisting 'the dominating influence of English literary fashions', so that he and other Irish writers could 'express their own minds in their own way'.[65] The two poets' divergent ways of expressing their 'own minds' about Yeats tell us about their different battles to create an autonomous space for their own writing in the face of the figure to whom Kavanagh attributed the 'myth-making quality' that could 'transform a commonplace society into an Olympian one'.[66]

IV

Thomas Kinsella, a poet who took his bearings from both Kavanagh and Clarke, wrote in 1965 that the quarter century since the death of Yeats was 'like no other period before it for poetry in English, one of critical intelligence'.[67] In 1973, nonetheless, he asserted the need for 'a good critic' to deal with the 'few advances' and 'many throwbacks' in contemporary Irish poetry.[68] Kinsella was not interested in such a role himself, but he wrote a series of diagnostic situation reports which cast light on his own distinctive poetics.

'The Divided Mind' (1973), composed the year of his breakthrough *New Poems*, is the most compelling of these. This pivotal essay draws on 'Poetry since Yeats', written eight years earlier, and provides the basis for the overviews in *New Oxford Book of Irish Verse* (1986) and *The Dual Tradition* (1995). 'The Divided Mind' takes its bearings from Yeats's 'General Introduction for my Work', but might be described as a post-colonial version of Eliot's 'Tradition and the Individual Talent'. For Kinsella, whereas 'a modern English poet can feel reasonably at home in the long tradition of English poetry' and 'conscript an Irish or American poet' into it, an Irish poet 'has access to all of this through his use of the English language' but is 'unlikely to feel at home in it. Or so I find in my own case'.[69] Behind the short history of Anglo-Irish poetry, he senses 'a great inheritance' and 'a great loss' represented by 'the course of Irish poetry stretching back for more than a thousand

---

[64] Ibid., 197.

[65] Clarke, *Reviews and Essays of Austin Clarke*, 17–18.

[66] Kavanagh, 'William Butler Yeats', *A Poet's Country*, 180.

[67] Thomas Kinsella, 'Poetry Since Yeats' (1965), *Prose Occasions: 1951–2006* (Manchester: Carcanet, 2009), 16.

[68] Thomas Kinsella, 'The Divided Mind' (1973), ibid., 40.

[69] Ibid., 31–2.

years'. This means an Irish writer feels a 'division' so fundamental as to form his 'actual imaginative substance'. Where for another writer this might have led to an Irish excep-tionalism like Clarke's, Kinsella takes it as the ground of kinship with 'the best pioneer-ing poetry of the twentieth century, that of Yeats, Eliot and Pound', which offered 'the first full articulation of the world as it is now'. Though he notes 'the special mutilations which are part of the Irish experience', he does not find these 'ruinous for poetry'. Indeed he argues that every writer 'has to make the imagination grasp at identity for himself':

> ... every writer in the modern world, since he can't be in all the literary traditions at once, is the inheritor of a gapped, discontinuous, polyglot tradition. But any tradi-tion will do: if one function of tradition is to link us living with the significant past, this is done as well by a broken tradition as by a whole one—however painful, humanly speaking, it may be. What matters for poetry...is the quality of the response.[70]

These terms mirror and reflect the broken, investigative terms of Kinsella's own verse, with its texture of fracture and splinter, and numinous grasping towards shards of a lost cultural identity. Kinsella is severe about most Irish poets, with the partial historical exception of Mangan and the more recent Clarke and Kavanagh ('two talents who have risen above the general level'). Kinsella's most generous essays are on Austin Clarke and Seán Ó'Riada as flawed artists who combine formal inventiveness with total immersion in Irish culture, and on Ezra Pound, whose *Cantos* embody progress through 'juxtaposi-tion' and where 'meaning' is 'a matter of vortices eddying about us as we possess the contents of the poet's mind'.[71]

Kinsella's Draconian view of Irish poetry bears fruit in his elliptically serial lyric *oeuvre*. 'The Divided Mind' offers a theoretical guide to the assumptions behind near-contemporary poems like 'Nightwalker', but also confirms Kinsella's limitations as a guide to the larger 'gapped' and 'discontinuous' cultural situation in Ireland. Such lim-itations are writ large in the equally intransigent overviews embodied in his *The New Oxford Book of Irish Verse*, an anthology largely built around his own mono-vocal translations from Irish, and *The Dual Tradition*, an account of literary history based on his own Manichean nationalist myth, which reads Irish poetry in terms of coloni-alism and dispossession, while dismissing most of his predecessors and competitors as epiphenomena.

John Montague, introducing his more multi-vocal *Faber Book of Irish Verse* (1974), speaks of the Irish poet as being 'in a richly ambiguous position, with the pressure of an incompletely discovered past behind him, and the whole modern world around him'.[72] His concise review of the history of Irish poetry turns on the spectacular stage entry of Yeats ('*Enfin, Yeats vint!*'), a figure who, according to Montague, showed 'how the appar-ent disadvantages of being Irish could all be turned to gains'.[73] He praises Clarke as 'our

---

[70] Ibid., 39.
[71] Ibid., 65.
[72] Reprinted as 'In the Irish Grain', *The Figure in the Cave* (Dublin: Lilliput, 1989), 125.
[73] Ibid., 122.

first completely Irish poet in English', and celebrates both 'the comedy of Kavanagh' and 'gravity of Kinsella', while arguing that 'through our change of language we have access to the English-speaking world—without that protective attitude an English poet might naturally feel towards the language'.[74] For Montague, who countered Kinsella's 'The Divided Mind' with 'The Unpartitioned Intellect' (1985), 'the Irish writer at his best is a natural cosmopolitan'.[75] In his autobiographical essay 'The Figure in the Cave', a prelude to the long prose memoir of *Company,* he chronicles his divided childhood in Brooklyn and Garvaghey, education in UCD and his travels in the United States and France, and uses his own story to criticize Kavanagh's 'narrowing notion of parochialism' as against 'the unselfish generosity of our great father figure, Yeats'.[76] Montague speaks of his 'strong sense of kinship' with American and French literature, and presents his 'natural complicity' in 'American, Irish and French' cultures as 'natural enough in the late twentieth century', as man strives to reconcile 'local allegiances' with 'developing a world consciousness'.[77] Like Kinsella, and later Heaney, Mahon, and Boland, Montague makes much of the influence of American poetry, and his essay on 'The Impact of International Modern Poetry on Irish Writing' criticizes the predominance of 'conventional, non-experimental poetry' in the country. For him, the 'wider an Irishman's experience, the more likely he is to understand his native country', and he floats the idea of 'denationalization', citing the critical importance of Denis Devlin as a model for an internationally as well as nationally grounded *oeuvre.*[78]

V

In his anthology, Montague observes that 'the next generation of poets sprang from that forgotten and history-burdened area, the North'.[79] With the outbreak of the Troubles, and emergence of a new wave of poets, it was also from Northern Ireland that the most influential Irish poet-critic after Yeats emerged.

Seamus Heaney's essays and lectures range across Irish, British, American, and East European poetry from Eliot to Mandelstam, Frost to Plath.[80] They offer generous, nuanced appraisals of an eclectic, international company of poets, who offer him 'cultural ratification' as a poet following in the 'parochialist' footsteps of Kavanagh but

[74] Ibid., 123–4.
[75] Ibid., 126.
[76] Ibid., 9, 15.
[77] Ibid., 17–19.
[78] John Montague, 'The Impact of International Modern Poetry on Irish Writing' (1973), ibid., 217–19.
[79] Ibid., 125.
[80] Heaney has published four volumes of prose, *Preoccupations* (London: Faber, 1980), *The Government of the Tongue* (London: Faber, 1988), *The Place of Writing* (Atlanta: Scholars Press, 1989), and *The Redress of Poetry* (London: Faber, 1995), as well as *Finders Keepers: Selected Prose* (London: Faber, 2002).

taking his bearings from global literature.[81] In their charismatically professorial way, many of Heaney's essays, as Peter McDonald notes, are 'essential items for serious readers of the poets they examine' but they also always bear on the Derry poet's own project.[82] Taken together, Heaney's criticism embodies both an eloquent *apologia pro vita sua* and an *ars poetica* which, as Neil Corcoran observes, is 'self-consciously the product, or off-shoot, or even intellectual ambience, of his own poetry'.[83] At its heart is a sustained updated version of the Romantic defence of poetry, cross-fertilized with the modernist poetics of Eliot, Frost, Lowell, and Mandelstam. The essays on Yeats and Kavanagh, poetry and place, and Northern Irish poetry are of a piece with those which expound his own autobiographical poetics from the early Wordsworthian 'Feeling into Words' (1974) to his Nobel lecture 'Crediting Poetry' (1995).

The inclusion of 'Crediting Poetry' as a prose Coda to *Opened Ground: Poems 1966–1996* mirrors Yeats's 'A General Introduction' and Wordsworth's 'Essay Supplementary', conceived as a complement to his *Collected Poems*. It recognizes that Heaney's criticism, like Wordsworth's, has been crucial in determining the taste by which his poetry is enjoyed. As Professor of Poetry at Oxford, Boylston Professor of Rhetoric and Oratory at Harvard, and Nobel Laureate, Heaney has proved himself a lecturer for all seasons. In 'On Poetry and Professing' Heaney recalls a life of lecturing and teaching—at school, Queen's University Belfast, and Harvard—and acknowledges that, whatever the difference between the audiences, there is always a 'desire...to have the worth and meaning of the art confirmed'.[84] He has not only acted as unofficial poetic ambassador for his country but as a roving ambassador for poetry itself.

Heaney's critical *oeuvre*, like his poetry, offers a response to the Troubles in Northern Ireland, forming part of an extended debate about the relationship between identity, place, and language, in a province torn between allegiance to the island of Ireland on the one hand and Britain on the other. Like the critical reflections on poetry and nationality of Yeats, Kavanagh, Kinsella, and Montague, it dramatizes the dilemmas of a poet caught between the political and the aesthetic, the national and the international, the colonial and post-colonial, the historical and the transcendent. It documents the poet's continually evolving critical balancing act, affirming the rationale of his own writing as a rural Catholic from Derry responsive to his native place as well as responding to poets from very different cultural backgrounds. In his ground-defining 'Place and Displacement' (1974), Heaney establishes terms of reference for poets and critics grappling to comprehend the 'Northern Irish Renaissance' that accompanied the political conflict in Northern Ireland, including the work of Derek Mahon, Michael Longley, and Paul Muldoon. The critical terms he conjures with are very different from the 'Ulster regionalism' advocated earlier by John Hewitt in 'The Bitter Gourd' (1943), explaining the poets' recourse to spectacular historical, spatial, and aesthetic distances from their

[81] Heaney, 'Milocz and World Poetry', *Partisan Review* 66:1 (1999), 37.
[82] See Peter McDonald, 'Appreciating Assets', *Poetry Review* 92:2 (2002), 78.
[83] Neil Corcoran, *The Poetry of Seamus Heaney* (London: Faber, 1998), 209.
[84] Seamus Heaney, 'On Poetry and Professing', *Finders Keepers*, 67.

native place as a way of responding to the wrenching pressure of political violence on home ground.

The best of Heaney's essays, lectures, and interviews combine autobiography and poetic commentary, reflecting on Eliot's 'auditory imagination' in terms of personal history and geography. From sketches like 'Mossbawn', 'Earning a Rhyme', and 'Something to Write Home About', to the epic autobiographical commentary embodied in the extended interview of *Stepping-Stones* (2008), Heaney amalgamates memoir and poetic commentary as he explores the credibility or credit-worthiness of poetry in a time of conflict. In them all Heaney seeks to root poetry in the tongue's pleasures and 'dialect' on the one hand, and the complexities of cultural history on the other, as he evokes Englands of the mind, Irelands of the ear, and a republic of conscience. 'The Redress of Poetry', a lecture delivered at Oxford in 1989, argues that: 'Professors of poetry, apologists for it, practitioners of it, from Sir Philip Sidney to Wallace Stevens, all sooner or later are tempted to show how poetry's existence as a form of art relates to our existence as citizens of society—how it is 'of present use'.[85] In a sense, all of Heaney's criticism, like his poetry, balances between confirming 'the meaning of art' in itself and seeing it as instrumental in civic life. In 'The Redress', Heaney argues that exemplary figures such as the poets of the First World War, Simone Weil, and George Herbert all engage in a complex 'balancing out the forces' in their work, yielding an idea of poetry as 'a mode of redress' in two different senses. In a critical balancing act of his own, Heaney then seeks to identify them with each other. On the one hand the poetry of redress is 'pressed to give voice to much that has been hitherto denied expression in the ethnic, social, sexual and political life', while on the other it seeks 'to redress poetry *as* poetry, to set it up as its own category, an eminence established and a pressure exercised by distinctly linguistic means'.[86]

Over and over in Heaney's criticism we are lured into celebrating poetry as a quasi-transcendent alternative reality, an equivalent of Arnold's poetry as 'intellectual deliverance', while we are simultaneously urged to view it—via poets as different as Dante, Mandelstam, Bishop, and the Herberts (George and Zbigniew)—as a braced act of cultural resistance. The urgency of Heaney's returns to this debate bespeaks the intransigence of his desire to reconcile the aesthetic and the ethical, and turns his critical *oeuvre* into a teleological Odyssey where celebrations of the art of poetry are always represented as part of his long journey home. This is manifested in 'Place and Displacement', which roots the need to balance political and aesthetic responsibilities in his conflicted identification as a Catholic in a predominantly Unionist province. 'Something to Write Home About' typically writes about his childhood home in County Derry, but its real imperative is once more to reconcile the 'place of writing' with the writing of place—and is less about writing home than about identifying the 'home' of writing with a Wordsworthian dream of childhood. Heaney's version of poetics is always in danger of being culturally exclusionary, which is one reason he needs to insist on its being 'representative'. As a critic, Heaney is never less than representative, simultaneously speaking as son of

---

[85] Seamus Heaney, 'The Redress of Poetry', *Finders Keepers*, 258.
[86] Ibid., 259–60.

Mossbawn, Irish poet, and Arnoldian representative of the transcendent province of poetry itself.

VI

Eavan Boland, like Heaney, has used critical prose to elaborate a poetics grounded in biography and bound up with a project of historical redress, in this case based on gender. Like Heaney, Boland converts her own story into a historically representative one, outlining the structural obstacles faced by women poets, and developing a critique of the sexist poetic culture of Ireland. The arguments were first launched in a pamphlet 'A Kind of Scar: The Woman Poet in a National Tradition' (1989) before being developed in her ambitiously entitled autobiographical study, *Object Lessons: The Life of the Woman and the Poet in Our Time* (1995), which opens with the assertion that she 'began writing in a country where the word *woman* and the word *poet* were almost magnetically opposed'.[87]

Boland tells us the book is written 'not as a prose narrative is usually constructed but as a poem might be: in turnings and returnings' that revolve around 'the visionary place, the obstructed moment' which is her female scene of writing, the Dublin suburbs.[88] As in so many Irish instances of *ars poetica*, her earliest sense of poetry is bound up with Yeats, who she praises for opening a door 'in the dark corridor between the fin-de-siècle and modernism' but confesses to being 'troubled' by. From her retrospective female vantage point, Yeats seems privileged:

> Before he even lifted a pen, his life awaited him in poetry. He was Irish. A man. A nationalist. A disappointed lover. Even his aging was recorded. The values were set. I was to learn how hard it would be to set different values.[89]

Using a historically loaded term, she speaks of the 'ascendancy' of poetry in a Dublin haunted by Joyce and Yeats, but also of 'exclusions'. In the world of the Poem, women had been observed, turned into metaphors, similes, and muses, but always treated as the 'object' of the poem rather than the 'subject' of it. The same was true of 'the story of the nation' as a 'narrative of destiny', constructed around an image of 'Ireland, or Hibernia'; it offered 'no female figure' to identify with and the 'heroine' was 'utterly passive'. Boland records feeling increasingly isolated among 'the male poets' in Trinity College, and, after lectures full of names like Keats and Byron, began to feel that 'poetic tradition itself was a house which held out an uncertain welcome to me', as if 'one room remained shut, locked against the air and intrusion of newness'.[90] Whether the locked room was a Bluebeard's

---

[87] Eavan Boland, *Object Lessons: The Life of the Woman and the Poet in Our Time* (Manchester: Carcanet, 1995), p. xi.

[88] Ibid., p. xiii.

[89] Ibid., 25.

[90] Ibid., 63, 66, 109.

chamber or mad woman's attic, Boland gives a powerful account of her initial sense of disempowerment, not unlike that which Heaney describes in 'Feeling into Words', but ascribed to her experience as a woman. As for Heaney, the encounter with Kavanagh was crucial. 'Kavanagh was a countryman; I was a woman,' she says, but he used his life 'to rebuff the expectations and preconceptions of the Irish poem'.

Reflecting on Plath's suicide in 1963 as dramatizing 'the stresses and fractures between a poet's life and a woman's', Boland claims equally dramatically that she wrote 'partly, in the shadow of that act'. Recounting her increasing interest in the problem of 'form', she speaks of it in terms that recall Corkery's 'hidden Ireland' as coming from 'a powerful meeting between a hidden life and hidden chance in language'. Nevertheless she now found 'The public forms of Irish poetry' were 'bleakly exclusive' of her 'unproved sense of a country', language, and sexuality. In this situation the 'Ireland of historic interpretation' became 'a text in which my name had been written merely to serve and illustrate an object lesson'.[91] Recapitulating 'A Kind of Scar', Boland draws on the thinking of Adrienne Rich, Alicia Ostriker, and Hélène Cixous, to narrate an encounter with a woman from Achill before turning her into 'an emblem' of her central contention in the book about 'the relatively short time' in which 'women have moved from being the objects of Irish poems to being the authors of them'.[92] Speaking of how 'the Irish nation as an existing construct in Irish poetry' was unavailable to her, she characterizes it as 'predominantly male', blaming male poets for continuing 'to trade in the exhausted fictions of the nation' which edited out 'ideas of womanhood'. Noting that women poets were rarely regarded as 'an automatic part of national poetic tradition', she had to write 'lacking the precedent' of 'previous Irish women poets' and learn to generate 'a complex self' within her 'own poem'.[93]

In the latter stages of her self-consciously emblematic text, Boland discusses her gradual appropriation of suburban Dundrum and the way it emerged (in a phrase borrowed from Heaney) as 'a country of the mind'. She goes on to argue for redefinition of the 'political poem', modified by 'subversive private experience' and an acknowledgement of a 'sexual identity' which 'the poetic tradition' and 'Irish poem' had 'almost stifled'. She wanted 'to see the effect of an unrecorded life—woman in a suburban twilight under a hissing streetlight', offering a rebuke to the Irish poem, with 'its inherited voice, its authoritative stance, its automatic reflex of elegy', derived from 'the shadow of bardic privilege'. As 'more and more poems by Irishwomen were written, it was obvious that something was happening to the Irish poem,' she claims, before asserting 'I wrote the political poem in Ireland because I was once politicized within it'.[94] Though observing that she is neither 'separatist nor feminist', she ends by asserting that 'women have a destiny in the form' and 'should break down barriers in poetry in the same way that poetry will break the silence of women'.[95]

---

[91] Ibid., 113, 116, 117.
[92] Ibid., 123–5, 126.
[93] Ibid., 127, 134, 137, 151.
[94] See ch. 8, 'Subject Matters', ibid., 178–9, 187, 196, 199.
[95] Ibid., 254.

Boland quotes Kavanagh's 'Self-Portrait', and her own self-portrait is an exercise in a historical feminist poetics in which she forges a persuasive paradigm for understanding her *oeuvre*. Like Heaney's 'Crediting Poetry', her apologia involves assuming immense representative authority. It embodies her appropriation of critical agency to make the case for her poetic agency, making her a poetic equivalent of her father, who was 'a diplomat representing Ireland'.[96] *Object Lessons* is an object lesson in how to change the critical and political climate in which contemporary poetry is read. An implicit critique of contemporary male poets, it also made a space for Boland's own work. More importantly, it helped clear the ground for the other talented women poets, from contemporaries like Eiléan Ní Chuilleanáin to younger poets who were spared the intellectual battle documented in her critical Irish *Prelude*.

If Boland was the first poet to offer a systematic critique of the masculinism of Irish poetic tradition, the great Irish-language poet Nuala Ní Dhomhnaill took this critical work further, writing from the doubly marginalized standpoint of a woman poet writing in Gaelic. Her *Selected Essays* (2003) constitute a subtle and sustained exploration of the personal, political, and cultural dilemmas confronting a contemporary Irish speaker, as well as a passionate autobiographical defence of her poetry in Irish. Her '*An Bhanfile Sa Traidisiun*: The Woman Poet in the Irish Tradition' (1992) followed closely on the heels of Boland's 'A Kind of Scar' and preceded *Object Lessons*. It opens boldly with the claim that 'Irish poetry in the second half of the twentieth century has been forcefully changed by women's writing', and that that this historical 'watershed' involves 'a vital critique of what was going into the Irish poem in earlier days, and what was kept outside it'.[97] More distinctively, she revisits the tradition of poetry in Irish, noting that, though 'whole groups of women weave in and out of Old Irish texts and are described as poets', 'not one single line has come down to us'. She quotes a literary historian saying 'Women have left little mark on the Irish literary tradition', notes the Field Day Anthology's notorious failure to represent women, and laments Kinsella's omission of contemporary women poets in *The New Oxford Book of Irish Verse* (1986), concluding that 'Woman, as woman, has only been accepted in the literary tradition as either Muse or, if she refuses to play that dreary, boring and unpaid role, then as Bitch'.[98] In the absence of literary fore-mothers in Irish, she argues that 'Representation of Ireland as woman amounts to a form of cultural nationalism', which, if not fortified by 'egalitarian and humanitarian values', can 'easily turn into a deeply fascist, sectarian and sexist movement, as happened in Ireland in the twentieth century'.[99]

Ní Dhomhnaill's prose makes a spellbinding case for the modernity of her Irish-language poetry, the centrality of the *Dinnseanchas* tradition, and her investment in 'folklore' and mythology, explored in terms of her own life and familial allegiance to the

---

[96] Ibid., 50.
[97] Nuala Ní Dhomhnaill, '*An Bhanfile Sa Traidisiun*', *Selected Essays* (Dublin: New Island Books, 2005), 43.
[98] Ibid., 47, 48, 54–5.
[99] Ibid., 57–8.

West Kerry *Gaeltacht*. In doing so she mounts a ferocious critique of the self-proclaimed custodians of the Irish language who determined the State's disastrous linguistic policy. In 'Why I choose to Write in Irish, the Corpse That Sits Up and Talks Back', Ní Dhomhnaill 'talks back' to multiple real and imaginary interlocutors in Ireland and beyond, projected once more through the lens of autobiography.[100] She uses her own experience, in West Kerry, Dublin, and Turkey, to define the nature of her art, its roots in Irish language and culture, and establish a poetics embedded in her statistically anomalous investment in the 'first language'. No other writer has made such a passionate case for the survival of Irish, its cultural vitality and poetic potential, or done so much to change its gender politics.

VII

The critical show goes on, with a contemporary cast of poets that includes Derek Mahon, Brendan Kennelly, Tom Paulin, Gerald Dawe, Dennis O'Driscoll, Bernard O'Donoghue, David Wheatley, Justin Quinn, Alan Gillis, and Peter McDonald, who have all helped redefine the ways we read modern poetry from Ireland and elsewhere. They are all poets and critics if not 'poet-critics', representing in different ways Eliot's principle that 'The poetic critic is criticizing poetry in order to create poetry.'[101]

It is Paul Muldoon, however, who, after a long critical virginity, has emerged as the most influential contemporary Irish commentator on poetry. Until quite recently Muldoon's gnomically perverse verse had to stand on its own devices, without the benefit of self-commentary of the kind practised by Heaney and Boland. After his abandonment of the BBC and move to the United States, however, all changed utterly, and a terrible critical beauty was born. With the publication of *To Ireland, I* (2000), his Clarendon lectures, and *The End of the Poem* (2006), his lectures as Professor of Poetry at Oxford, the poet of *Madoc* (1990) and *The Annals of Chile* (1994) transferred his linguistic virtuosity into professorial prose. Riddled with onomastic gymnastics, farfetched puns, and scholastic wit, the result is neither recognizably criticism, poetics, or fiction, while his searching close readings of texts suggest an unlikely cross between *Pale Fire* and *The White Goddess*, or *Seven Types of Ambiguity* and *Finnegans Wake*.

To Ireland, I offers simultaneously an A to Z of Irish literature and a commentary on Joyce's 'The Dead'. Nevertheless it is not a book to which a reader would go for information about anything other than Muldoon. It reads more like a poetic sequence by other means than a critical treatise. It starts (alphabetically) with the proposition that 'the figure of Amergin is crucial to any understanding of the role of the Irish writer as it has evolved over the centuries'. For Muldoon, this is because of his or her 'quite disproportionate sense of his or her own importance', tendency to 'speak on national issues', and

---

[100]   Ibid., 10–24.
[101]   See note 2 above.

'equally strong' urge towards what Robert Graves calls the 'esoteric' or 'pied'. Muldoon defines this as 'the urge towards the cryptic, the encoded, the runic, the virtually unintelligible'.[102] The four lectures that follow mischievously draw on his own 'urge towards the cryptic, the encoded, the runic' and find Muldoonian equivalents in the whole gamut of Irish literature from Amergin to Zozimus, centred around Joyce but notably excluding Yeats. As a result the book reads like a critical equivalent of *The Voyage of Mael Duin*, one of Muldoon's recurrent prototypes, or a secular rewrite of Yeats's *A Vision* in comic mode.

The End of the Poem starts with a meditation on Yeats's 'All Soul's Night' and ends with Heaney's 'Keeping Going', but otherwise moves beyond Ireland, offering close readings of poems by Hughes, Frost, Bishop, Dickinson, Lowell, Pessoa, and Auden, among others. The lectures reveal Muldoon as a self-conscious critical successor to Yeats and Heaney, but also a reader of uncanny brilliance, writing with a high-wire, self-mocking, and self-delighting inventiveness very different to theirs. He presents the texts he performs as esoteric, onomastic, intertextual, and almost infinitely allusive, making them all, whatever their authorship, sound like poems by Paul Muldoon. There are no agonized reflections over the relationship between poet and society, art and violence, national tradition and individual talent, of the kind we find in Heaney, Boland, and the other poets in the critical tradition we have been tracing. Nevertheless *The End of the Poem* is a work of genuine poetic enquiry. Its most outrageous and far-fetched readings reveal new things and renew familiar debates. Like that of most poets since Yeats, Muldoon's is a trans-national poetics that resists the given 'national' agendas, but as it does so, redefines the distinctively Irish tradition.[103] A genuine instance of Wilde's critical faculty for inventing 'fresh forms', Muldoon's Oxford lectures are a dizzying embodiment of the linguistically plural, globally local self-consciousness that fires the best modern Irish writing.

The essays also confirm Muldoon's argument that Irish poets are prone to a 'quite disproportionate sense of his or her own importance'. Playfully they embody the more general truth that in their prose Irish poets tend to offer accounts of the Importance of Being a Poet and Irish even as they foreground the unresolvable linguistic and cultural complexities that, from the late nineteenth to the twenty-first century, go with the territory.

---

[102] Paul Muldoon, *To Ireland, I* (Oxford: Oxford University Press, 2000), 4–5.

[103] Again, conforming to Pascale Casanova's account in *The World Republic of Letters*. See note 6 above.

CHAPTER 33

THE POET AS ANTHOLOGIST

STEVEN MATTHEWS

IRISH poets have typically used the opportunity provided them by publishers to gather poems into anthologies, in order better to define the nature of their own writing, and the stand it takes within the various possible histories and contexts pressing upon it. In the twentieth century, anthology introductions often form key essays by Irish poets, essays which have been written to describe the poetic past out of which the poets' own writing also derives. The selection of poems included by poets in an anthology can also be telling: works which are essential precursors to the later poets' classic pieces, of course, often appear in their pages. But it is also true that surprising inclusions can throw interesting and important sidelights upon the later poets' own work. Anthologies open up further possibilities for thinking through how the later poet has partly derived their work from, or partly in resistance to, certain aspects of earlier Irish and international writing.

Necessarily here, of course, the notion of 'tradition' is itself a matter for contestation. How much Gaelic writing should be included in an anthology of Irish poetry, historical or 'modern'? Should Gaelic poetry appear only in translation? When, historically, should an anthology of Irish poetry begin? What prominence should be given to the Young Ireland poets of the 1840s, as the first consciously 'national' poets? Should an anthology of modern writing include writers who largely lived, or are living, in other countries? Should Yeats form the first poet anthologized in a volume of twentieth-century Irish poetry or not? Should a poet see the anthology as a 'personal selection', or should the selections included in the book aim to be more representative? How far should the poet draw attention to the fact that their selection includes both Protestant and Catholic writing—what is implied by doing so? Should a volume of 'contemporary' verse include only the more internationally recognizable figures, or should it make an attempt to include the myriad small press, newspaper, and pamphlet poems and poets, in an attempt both to be more representative, but also to put some new Irish poets' names 'on the map'? These, and similar questions, have preoccupied all Irish poets seeking to put together anthologies from the outset of the twentieth century, and continue to do so in the most recent examples. It is on these various questions that this chapter, which seeks to provide a chronology of poetry anthologies created by Irish poets across the twentieth century, must centre.

Inevitably, Yeats forms, in relation to such questions, a troubling and illuminating exemplum of the genre at the outset of this survey. Early on in his career Yeats had anthologized folk tales and occult stories in *The Celtic Twilight* (1893), a compendium of source materials for the poetry which he was then engaged upon. In his *A Book of Irish Verse Selected from Modern Writers* [1895] (revised edition 1900), however, Yeats more deliberately sought to locate that recent poetry of his own within, and against, a particular literary and critical context, one which would become increasingly important to him as his own career developed. The polemical intent of *A Book of Irish Verse* is visible from its inception. Writing to F. J. Bigger about the 1895 first edition, Yeats described the volume as 'an attempt to begin that spring cleaning' of which Irish literature was, he felt, to be so in need. But it is Yeats's desire, as expressed to Bigger, for his anthology to escape from a critical understanding of Irish literature that was 'partizan' (sic), and to try to 'win over to Irish things all Irish people no matter what their politics', which is the more striking for Yeats's own work at this period and beyond.[1] Such desire establishes both a common thread through poet-editors' introductions for their anthologies across the twentieth century, but also seeks to establish the worth of the anthology as a genre in Ireland per se. This worth is founded upon a conception of the poetry anthology as a mode, for the modern Irish poet, of demonstrating and representing significant openness to the several traditions within Irish poetry; an openness which in itself might have important cultural and political resonance within broader national debates.

To this end, Yeats's introductory essay on 'Modern Irish Writing', in *A Book of Irish Verse*, shows him striving to navigate the poetic past. But he does so in ways that now read contentiously, whatever their hugely influential significance (an influence which will be taken up across this chapter). In this essay, Yeats drives a space between aesthetics and politics, and between the Gaelic and English traditions of Irish poetry, a space in which his own favoured precursors are made to appear more authoritatively than they might otherwise have done. After a nod towards Gaelic poetry of the eighteenth century, which, Yeats claims, 'made the people, crushed by the disasters of the Boyne and Aughrim, remember their ancient greatness', it becomes clear that Yeats dates 'modern' Irish writing from the establishment of several key major poets' careers. These were poets, inevitably, who were all writing in English, yet poets who have some connection with Ireland, however tenuous. Oliver Goldsmith (whose adult life was spent mostly in England and Europe), and Richard Brinsley Sheridan (whose connection to Ireland came via his parents, not through his adult abode) head Yeats's selection of work in the anthology.

The Young Ireland movement is treated, in Yeats's introductory essay, via praise for Thomas Davis's sincerity and for his 'flexible' mind, but also via dismissal for the

---

[1] *The Collected Letters of W. B. Yeats*, vol. II, 1896–1900, ed. Warwick Gould, John Kelly, and Deirdre Toomey (Oxford: Oxford University Press, 1997), 652–3.

'mechanical nature' of Davis's verse, driven as it is by nationalist ambition, 'and today we are paying the reckoning with much bombast'. As 'Modern Irish Poetry' continues, this prioritization of 'mind', of Romantic self-reflection, over political ambition in poetry, strengthens. James Mangan is in turn dismissed for his being devoid of 'self-knowledge…the harmony of mind, which enables the poet to be its master'. Only Samuel Ferguson, William Allingham, Aubrey de Vere, and, from more recent times, Lionel Johnson, are excepted from this criticism, since, according to Yeats here, they 'work apart from politics'. In his peroration, Yeats makes the implication, for him, of this critical distinction between the traditions of Irish poetry, and between aesthetics and politics, into a statement about the situation of Ireland at the turn of the twentieth century. For him, Ireland is coming now 'to culture', 'ridding herself of incoherence and triviality', but doing so by building a tradition of literature in English 'unlike others'. Douglas Hyde's translations from the Gaelic are acknowledged for their own worth, and for their popularity, but are taken up into a wider point that Ireland is 'communing with herself in Gaelic more and more', but 'speaking to foreign countries in English', and so salving the 'sickness' which, according to Yeats, has daunted Irish poetry to this millennial moment.

Belatedly, then, for Yeats, Ireland is at last arriving at the creation of a unique 'primeval poetry', set apart from England, but also, to an extent, from its own historical inflections.[2] The Gaelic-language movement is granted contemporary relevance by him, as an inward-looking necessity, in the move towards the creation of a national distinctiveness. But, predictably, priority is claimed for that internationally turned (and accepted) version of Irishness, which Yeats would strive to find ways of creating and promoting throughout his life.

These tensions and resolutions in Yeats's thinking found further controversial impetus late in his career, when he put together *The Oxford Book of Modern Verse 1892–1935* (1936). Yeats's 'Introduction' to *The Oxford Book* revels in a swirl of personal recollection relayed through anecdote, *bon mots*, and a rare opinionatedness, concerning the direction in which he felt poetry to be drifting, across the years covered by his survey. Remembering the rise of Socialism and the industrial upheavals of the 1890s, for instance, Yeats remarks that his circle of writers at 'The Cheshire Cheese' inn in London were 'convinced that to take part in such movements would be only less disgraceful than to write for the newspapers'.[3] He elides a passage in praise of recent translations from Gaelic verse into an anecdote about his friend Oliver St John Gogarty's 'daring' escape from a group of political agitators, whose feelings Gogarty had upset.[4] More specifically, Yeats uses the 'Introduction' to register his dissatisfaction with the kind of poetry we would now consider 'modernist', specifically poetry written by the American poet Ezra

---

[2] W. B. Yeats, 'Modern Irish Poetry', *A Book of Irish Verse Selected from Modern Writers*, rev. edn. (London: Methuen, 1900), pp. xvii, xx, xxii, xxxi.

[3] W. B. Yeats, 'Introduction', *The Oxford Book of Modern Verse 1892–1935* (Oxford: Oxford University Press, 1936), p. xi.

[4] Ibid., pp. xiv–xv.

Pound, and by the recently naturalized Englishman, T. S. Eliot. The latter's verse simply reflects the enervations of modern life in Yeats's view, producing work (particularly after *Poems, 1920*) which is 'grey, cold, dry'. Pound is questioned for the incompletion and the obfuscations of his writing in *The Cantos*: 'When I consider his work as a whole I find more style than form; at moments more style, more deliberate nobility and the means to convey it than in any contemporary poet known to me, but it is constantly interrupted, broken, twisted into nothing by its direct opposite, nervous obsession, nightmare, stammering confusion.'[5] What is implicit is a defence by Yeats of traditional form, of the necessity for the poet to seek to control and contain an increasingly distracting and nerveless modern existence, in order to sustain a more heroic and individually defined aesthetic.

Running across the 'Introduction' is Yeats's continuing sense that 'the filthy tide' (as he elsewhere called it) of modern life has been allowed to overwhelm modern poetry; that the confines of the traditional space which poetic form provides have become beaten down by the multiplicity of modern media, as they affect the individual poet's sensibility. The gap which the earlier *A Book of Irish Verse* had wanted to claim there to be, a gap between the aesthetic fastness of the complete poem, and the trends of contemporary history and politics, is under threat now, to Yeats's mind. Hence the perverse decisions taken by Yeats in his selections for *The Oxford Book*, and his tendentious justifications for them in this opening essay. The poets of the First World War are notoriously excluded by Yeats on these very grounds, since he has 'distaste' for them: 'passive suffering is not a theme for poetry'.[6] His decision to include a long work by Herbert Read, one safely written long after the war, as representative of the experience of the years 1914–18, now looks very bizarre. But equally so does Yeats's other editorial work within his selections.

The book opens with his rendering into blank verse, under the title 'Mona Lisa', of a passage from Walter Pater's work on aesthetics, *The Renaissance* (1873), more in confirmation of Yeats's own later view of the cyclical movement of history, than as a marker of the real tonality of modern verse ('She has been dead many times,/And learned the secrets of the grave').[7] Equally notorious was Yeats's inclusion of Oscar Wilde's 'The Ballad of Reading Gaol', but in a version that preserved only 38 out of the 109 stanzas of Wilde's original poem. Seamus Heaney has written largely in praise of Yeats's redaction, claiming that it allows the 'objective tale of a condemned man's last days' to shine through, out of the 'romantic', 'compensatory and confiding' nature of the original (Yeats suppressed the stanza containing Wilde's most famous line, '...each man kills the thing he loves').[8] Yeats's version seems anxious to remove what he considered the genuine poetry of Wilde's work from the taint which surrounded the life (and what he arguably viewed as that life's 'passive suffering'). It is a decision which underlies the many other,

---

[5] Ibid., p. xxv.
[6] Ibid., p. xxxiv.
[7] Ibid., 1.
[8] Seamus Heaney, 'Speranza in Reading', *The Redress of Poetry: Oxford Lectures* (London: Faber, 1995), 83–102; see especially 88–91.

now odd, strategies deployed by him in this *Oxford Book*, which foregrounds the other-worldly and dated verse of his friends, such as W. J. Turner and Dorothy Wellesley, over what we would now think of as the most significant voices in early twentieth-century British, Irish, and American writing. It is a strategy of perversity only leavened by Yeats's praise in his 'Introduction' for the poets emerging in the 1930s, who he clearly sees as returning to the poetic traditions, and structured poetic forms, with which he was more comfortable, whatever their political ambitions. The relatively full selection from Louis MacNeice, towards the end of the volume, clearly sanctions some implicit potential sense of an emerging tradition within Anglo-Irish poetry itself, in Yeats's mind. Yet these many tensions in Yeats's 'Introduction' and selection threw a long shadow, as will become clear, over subsequent Irish poets' acceptance of commissions to make anthologies.

The lack of anthologies of Irish poetry between the death of Yeats in 1939 and the 1970s probably derives from the comparative absence of Irish poets from international prominence across those decades, and therefore from the sense of a comparatively low marketability for Irish writing, from the perspective of international publishers. Robert Greacen and Valentin Iremonger's *Contemporary Irish Poetry* (1949) from London's Faber and Faber publishers (amongst whose editors at the time was T. S. Eliot), is representative of the few such books which did appear in this extended period. Following a brief Preface which simply explains that the book presents selections from poets who have come to notice since Yeats's death, but which does nothing to locate or characterize the work of this recent generation, the anthology gives a few pages of work by thirty-four poets. These include already established and known writers such as MacNeice, Cecil Day Lewis, and Austin Clarke, as well as a couple of poems each by Padraic Fallon and Denis Devlin. There are also selections from early work by John Hewitt and Pearse Hutchinson. Yet the majority of the poets included in the book are now unknown.

The alphabetical arrangement of the poets in the anthology, and the paucity of work offered, presents a picture of the post-Yeats generation as one adrift, in the absence of the difficult master. Whatever the worth of the individual poems included, there is little attempt to build a coherent sense of what the emerging generation of Irish poets might amount to, how they might situate themselves once the Yeatsian presence has disappeared. These are largely decorous poems in standard English with little flavour, even ten years after MacNeice's *Autumn Journal*, of the range or ambition of a potentially different scope of Irish writing (the MacNeice selection in this anthology ranges from 'Dublin', 'The Sunlight on the Garden', to conclude with 'Turf-stacks' from 1932).[9] Most notable, from the perspective of Irish writing later in the twentieth century, is the absence of Patrick Kavanagh, whose *The Great Hunger* (1942) had epically established the consciousness of deprived and inevitably embittered Catholic Ireland as powerful material for poetic meditation.

Once the 'newsworthiness' of Irish history and politics became tragically established again, with the new outbreak of the so-called 'Troubles' in the later 1960s, and a different

---

[9] *Contemporary Irish Poetry*, ed. Robert Greacen and Valentin Iremonger (London: Faber, 1949); the MacNeice selections appear on 117–25.

generation of writers largely based in the North began to come to international notice, the anthologies of poetry edited by Irish poets began to flow again. To an extent, these anthologies represent an intriguing 'catching up' with a generation of Irish poets' work from the 1940s through the 1960s, and an introduction of it to a broader English-speaking audience. The anthologies began to be gathered, therefore, by a mixture of poets from that mid-century generation, and by the new poets, largely writing at that time out of Belfast, who were coming to international notice. What emerges from both perspectives is a ready concern to treat of Gaelic poetry in more considered (if often also in polemical) ways than had Yeats, and a determined editorial openness, at the height of the recent events in the North, to both Protestant and Catholic traditions of Irish poetry in English. Given their temporal distance now, these anthologies are also characterized by a determination to renegotiate the Yeatsian territory and his importance in the light of more recent poetic, political, economic, religious, and cultural shifts across the island of Ireland.

Derek Mahon's *The Sphere Book of Modern Irish Poetry* (1972) is typical of many of these movements forward, in consideration of the twentieth-century inheritance. Mahon's lucid introduction to the anthology begins by looking back to the effective suppression of Gaelic poetry in the late eighteenth century, and seeing a 'difficult period' as having prevailed in what he calls 'Irish poetry' between that and 'the beginnings of the Literary Revival' in the late nineteenth century. 'Modern', in the anthology's title, really begins for Mahon with Yeats (a 'genius'), ten of whose poems open the selection. But, in an interesting, but now *negative*, reprise of Yeats's own separation of aesthetics and politics, Mahon shows discomfort with his non-poetic cultural and spiritual 'activities', where 'the problems begin'. Mahon finds ready praise for Clarke and Kavanagh as 'demystifiers' and 'secularizers' of Yeats's poetic (but also of his nationalist) pieties, seeing these two poets as seeking to redefine the 'national psyche' in other terms. To this end, Mahon further decentres the Yeatsian inheritance by entering praise for the European focus of the diplomat and modernist poet Denis Devlin—before again finding an unease with such earlier work, this time with the typically 'hieratic' and 'involuted' nature of much of Devlin's output.

In a rapid sleight of argument, Mahon shifts from this latter unease into forwarding a plea for a 'group of poets whose ambiguous ethnic and cultural situation extenuates in their work the Anglocentricity Devlin disliked'. This, of course, is Mahon's own Protestant generation from the North, wedded to MacNeice rather than to Kavanagh ('whatever we mean by "the Irish situation," the shipyards of Belfast are no less a part of it than a county town in the Gaeltacht'). What Mahon felt to be emerging from this recent generation of poets, North and South, is a new 'experimental' but liberated work, free from 'the parochial self-content' of previous Irish poetry and of its critics.[10] What emerges, then, from Mahon's advocacy, is interest in work which, like his own (with his

---

[10] Derek Mahon, 'Introduction', *The Sphere Book of Modern Irish Poetry* (London: Sphere, 1972), 11, 13.

translations from the French poet Philippe Jacottet and from numerous other European figures), looks to the poetic traditions of Europe, whilst also being attentive to the significance of all historical inflections upon the home ground.

Mahon claims that he has tried to be 'objective' in his selections for the book; to reflect what has been 'going on'. His anthology is indeed notable amongst those produced from the 1970s onwards for its eclecticism. It includes seemingly unlikely poets and poems from the modernist generations so important for his own poetry (Yeats, Synge, Joyce, MacGreevy, Beckett, Francis Stuart, Devlin), alongside generous selections from Clarke, Kavanagh, and MacNeice. This is also the first anthology edited by an (at the time recently prominent) Irish poet to begin to sketch in the history of Irish poetry from the 1950s, to the later 1960s (Hewitt, Rodgers, Montague, Kinsella), whilst also recognizing the emergent strengths of his own generation North and South (Simmons, Kennelly, Heaney, Longley, Hartnett, Mahon himself, Boland). The selection ends with a poem by Paul Muldoon, 'The Indians at Alcatraz', a prescient intuition by Mahon of what would be 'going on' next in Irish (and British) writing.

The renewed international prominence of Irish poetry allowed, also, from the mid-1970s to the mid-1980s, for something of a revision of the history of that work from its origins, by two poets who had themselves responded both to the wave of translations of Gaelic which had begun in the 1930s *and* to the arrival of international modernist influences in the 1950s, John Montague and Thomas Kinsella. Montague's *The Faber Book of Irish Verse* led the way in 1974, categorizing its historical or Gaelic materials under ready subsections ('A Way of Life', 'A Monastic Church', 'Women and Love', amongst others), before adopting a chronological listing of poets according to dates of birth, from Thomas Moore onwards. Montague, partly unconsciously but also consciously, presumably, opens his introductory essay 'In the Irish Grain', by sounding as if he were an updated Yeats. He writes of the need to 'spring clean' Irish literature, the same metaphor used by Yeats in his private letter to Bigger. And, like the earlier poet, he berates the critical tradition in his country, with its 'tendency to applaud work for its local or international interest which has hampered any consistent attempt to apply poetic standards'.[11]

Montague accommodates, as did Yeats, Goldsmith and Jonathan Swift to an Irish lineage, mainly for their significance, however, to Joyce and Kavanagh, rather than to Yeats himself. More pertinently, Montague, thinking through the issues behind his own poems like 'A Grafted Tongue', which is included in his selection, describes the suppression of the Irish language by the British as a 'mutilation'—a mutilation from which the national poetry did not recover until the advent of Yeats. In a provocative move, Montague echoes earlier opinion on Yeats, including MacNeice's, that Yeats's work was 'saved from the aestheticism of his English contemporaries' by his Irish nationalist interests.[12] In this, Yeats is tacitly credited by Montague for opening the way to subsequent

---

[11] John Montague, 'In the Irish Grain', *The Faber Book of Irish Verse* (London: Faber, 1974), 21.
[12] Montague, 'In the Irish Grain', 34. See also Louis MacNeice, *Modern Poetry: A Personal Essay*, 2nd ed. [1938] (Oxford: Clarendon Press, 1968), 44.

Irish poetry, offering a model of professionalism 'whose primary concern is the human imagination in all its complexity'.[13]

Montague's argument segues, in other words, between emphasis upon the salving nationalism figured in Irish poetry, and a continuing emphasis upon the fastness of a Romantic aesthetic, in which the Irish poet is cast in a uniquely 'ambiguous' position, feeling pressure from an 'incompletely discovered past', which includes the Gaelic poetry he has selected for the anthology, and from 'the whole modern world around'.[14] This is the same bifurcation which had particularly riven the conclusion of Yeats's introductory essay on 'Modern Irish Poetry', over seventy-five years earlier. Montague's historical approach, ironically perhaps, most benefits his selection when it comes to the twentieth century, offering a couple of poems from each of sixty-four poets (although actually few translated from Gaelic) in a notably comprehensive sweep. These include the modernist generation marked out in Mahon (but including Brian Coffey), down to Muldoon once more, whose work is now set alongside that of Ciaran Carson and Gregory O'Donoghue.

The renewed violence on the ground in the North, however, was at this point (and aided by the emergence of publishing houses committed to locally produced poetry, most notably the Blackstaff Press in Belfast) manifesting itself in anthologies dedicated to the review of the poetry related to these events. Padraic Fiacc's *The Wearing of the Black: An Anthology of Contemporary Ulster Poetry* (1974) is the first such selection. Fiacc's introduction provides a model for similar later books, in its acknowledgement of the potential for anthologies of this nature to seem 'cynical exploitation' of the 'hopefully transient situation', a situation which was, by now, prominent in the world's media. Fiacc proclaims the immediacy of his anthology, produced 'at a certain time...in a certain place', yet claims that it makes no 'final statement' on such matters 'as how deeply contemporary violence can enter a poet's inner being, or how far it should'. He sees the book, rather, as 'pos[ing] the question'. But he seems to mitigate the implications of the 'question' by pointing out also that the current violence 'disfigur[ing] the face of Ireland' has deep historical 'roots', and that his anthology's first section seeks to trace something of that history (the section begins with poems about the Bog People, the subject of Seamus Heaney's poems contemporary to the anthology, and includes work whose content runs through to the Second World War and the North).[15]

In line with this seemingly documentary ambition, Fiacc's anthology includes the work of the by now familiar preceding generation (Hewitt, Montague), alongside writing by nearly fifty local poets about particular recent incidents which is often nearer to reportage. An interesting tension is established, however, between such urgency and

---

[13] Montague, 'In the Irish Grain', 34. Montague's arguments in this essay are clearly derived from his own more extended engagement with history and politics in the wake of the renewed violence in the North, as exampled by his book-length sequence *The Rough Field* (1972)—a sequence from which 'A Grafted Tongue' derives.

[14] Ibid., 37.

[15] Padraic Fiacc, 'Introduction', *The Wearing of the Black: An Anthology of Contemporary Ulster Poetry* (Belfast: Blackstaff, 1974), p. vii.

immediacy, and the aesthetic involved in the deployment by Fiacc of his anthologized poems. These, he notes, are arranged 'symphonically', in four movements, with the historical opening followed by two sections founded on place (Derry, and the 'climactic' Belfast), and a quieter last section, containing reflections on the 'bitterness' resulting from the recent violence. A work, in other words, which began with seemingly to-the-moment energies, and which allowed a more communal reach of poetry through its connection to its particular subject, seems, like later work of this nature, to be (as much as Yeats's anthology was) aimed at some sense of catharsis. Fiacc implies that the anthology presents some ability, simply through moving across the reported history and recent experiences in poetry, to reach beyond the 'certain time' and place of its setting. In this, of course, Fiacc's book mirrors the tropological movement of many of the contemporary poems it contains, and particularly those from the internationally recognized recent poets from the North, with their aspiration that poetry might provide a space whereby the disfigurements of the situation on the ground might be reconciled or moved beyond.

If, by the mid-1970s, it was the case that Seamus Heaney was established in British and American minds as the most eminent of those recent poets, it was also becoming clearer that he was (and is) an adherent of the Yeatsian belief in the primary power of the creative imagination, as manifested in the single lyric poem. Heaney's first collaboration on an anthology—one made with the English poet Ted Hughes—*The Rattle Bag*, exemplifies those virtues in striking ways. The very brief Introduction to the book defends its Auden-like adherence to arranging its poems in alphabetical order according to their title by dismissing others' thematic approaches (which 'would have made it feel too much like a textbook'), or the traditional chronological approach to ordering anthologies: 'botched historical survey'. What their approach prizes, Heaney and Hughes argue, is 'unexpectedness... each poem full of its singular appeal, transmitting its own signals, taking its chances in a big, voluble world'.[16] One gain from the approach is that it enables Heaney and Hughes to put forward an unpredictable range of the radical vernacular energies of English-language poetry, from folk songs, to versions of Anglo-Saxon done by Heaney, to Shakespeare, Wordsworth, John Clare, Hopkins, Lawrence, Yeats, and translations from the contemporary poets from Eastern Europe favoured by Hughes and by Heaney in his turn. Amidst this onrush, only a couple of lyrics by Joyce, and a larger selection from Kavanagh, make for the Irish representation. Heaney and Hughes firmly root their sense of the varied enjoyments of the art within a wide-ranging English-language resource. But the emphasis upon the single poem, providing delight in relation to its position in this anthology rather than to its original contexts, stands out here.

At this time, however, in Ireland itself, there was a growing effort to establish the parameters of the recent upsurge of effective poetry in relation to events on the ground, from both North and South. From the Blackstaff Press in Belfast, Frank Ormsby's *Poets from the North of Ireland* (1979) was quickly succeeded by Gerald

---

[16] Seamus Heaney and Ted Hughes, 'Introduction', *The Rattle Bag* (London: Faber, 1982), 19.

Dawe's *The Younger Irish Poets* (1982). Both Ormsby and Dawe notably, at this time, strike a new note in their introductory remarks, by displaying their even-handedness with regard to the background of the work they have chosen to anthologize, and by pointing to the fraught tensions playing upon Irish writers North and South at this point. Ormsby begins his introductory remarks with a brief history lesson, from the Flight of the Earls through the Ulster Literary Theatre, to Yeats and the Literary Renaissance. He then offers a short biography and critical comments, for each of the twenty poets, born after 1900 in the North, that he has included. He concludes by giving some flavour of the pressures upon these writers, particularly those relating to the decision whether to 'speak out' or to 'say nothing', with regard to 'the realities' of recent Irish history:

> It has been said that their imaginative lives have, to an extent, been 'limited by the horizons defined by the colonial predicament' of the North, and, on another level, that too many of them are 'insulated in some university shelter-belt'.[17]

Perhaps wisely, given the potential for poetic achievement which has lain in this very dilemma for many Irish writers, Ormsby hands the responsibility for judgement here over to the reader, who must 'decide' what she or he thinks on the basis of the poems included.[18]

Gerald Dawe, in *The Younger Irish Poets*, outlines a similar sense of the dilemma of how to read this recent work. 'Younger' means, for Dawe, poets born from the end of the Second World War onwards, and he seeks to consider this group as a new, post-Hewitt, post-Kinsella, and post-Montague 'generation'. He also feels that the work of significant writers from the South has been obscured by the newsworthiness of that which had recently emerged from the North. His selections begin with work by Paul Durcan, and his 'Editor's Note' makes much of the mix included of Protestant and Catholic, rural and urban, writing from South and North. When confronting the issue of the relation of this recent work to the eruption of violence on the ground, though, Dawe inevitably turns to the poets from the North, and sees their response as the standard for much that happens elsewhere on the island. What he envisages is, however, a new sense of 'self-awareness' in all of this poetry against the pressure of events, a being thrown back upon their own resources which is in itself liberating:

> ...the poets presented here are finding ways to liberate themselves, their art, and, by implication alone, their readers, from the literary conventions and the literal expec-tations that have been handed down from the past. Present, I feel, in their best work

---

[17] Frank Ormsby, 'Introduction', *Poets from the North of Ireland* (Belfast: Blackstaff, 1979), 13.

[18] Frank Ormsby's later anthology, *A Rage for Order: Poetry of the Northern Ireland Troubles* (Belfast: Blackstaff, 1992), displays a similarly concerted even-handedness, bringing together work from the most well-known poets from both communities with some precursor pieces (Hewitt's 'The Colony', passages from MacNeice's *Autumn Journal*). Ormsby recognizes once again the pressure upon poets from various sources to 'weigh and scrutinize the relationship between art and politics and the nature of artistic responsibility', but, reviewing the poetry he has been able to include in his selection, sees this situation as 'enabling' and as having produced a 'rich body' of recent work. See p. xvii.

is a need to unburden themselves of the past through whatever means, traditional or experimental, that sustains their own imaginative responsibilities.[19]

Dawe's decision to designate all of his poets, from whatever geographical location or religious tradition, 'Irish', becomes somewhat subsumed in this recourse to a belated version of the familiar Romantic tropes of the free (if responsible) imagination, which operates in a paradoxical 'flight' from the past, but which is yet a discovery of 'what matters in this day and age'. What is notable is that this 'flight', as encapsulated within the covers of the anthology itself, is posited by Dawe as being liberating not just for the poets, but also for the readers—a continuation of that quality we noted from Yeats onwards, through which the anthology is made to serve a broader cultural, and ultimately political, purpose, in these circumstances.

The difficult implications of that political reach are contested once more in the trio of anthologies of Irish and other writing which appeared in 1986, the first two of which became immediately notorious—Tom Paulin's *The Faber Book of Political Verse*, Paul Muldoon's *The Faber Book of Contemporary Irish Poetry*, and Thomas Kinsella's *The New Oxford Book of Irish Verse*. Paulin's 'Introduction' was the most contentious part of his anthology, assaulting as it does what he sees as an Arnoldian tradition of criticism, a tradition most concertedly applied in the twentieth century by T. S. Eliot, in Paulin's view. This is a critical tradition whereby poetry is said to be independent of political context, intent, or purpose. Paulin's confrontation with the Arnoldian, or 'Western', view, that 'poems exist in a timeless vacuum', is, as his remarks imply, derived partly from his understanding about the kinds of poetry being written out of the totalitarianism of Eastern Europe. It also speaks out of the radical Protestant heritage of England which so informs Paulin's own poetic and political positions; and from his reading of Irish history, which gets a subsection in the 'Introduction', alongside others outlining the political and geographical traditions he sees operating across history in English writing.

In the section on 'The Irish Tradition', Seamus Heaney earns a favoured position as one opposing the 'historic legitimacy' of the State of Northern Ireland, yet at the same time refusing 'the simplicities of traditional nationalism', and so striving 'to initiate certain imaginative positives and offer a gracious and civil trust'. Heaney's concern to renegotiate the Yeats tradition (Paulin instances his poem 'Casualty', which directly speaks back to Yeats's 'The Fisherman') presents him as a writer alert to the political implications of his imaginative gestures, yet also alert to the biddings and intransigence of the Irish tradition.[20]

Paulin's reading of the Heaney stance is emblematic, in various ways, of his introductory essay's concern to root out the political resonance of any one poetic image, and to demonstrate that even the most seemingly *apolitical* writing has both a political origin in response to its times and also a political implication for its readers, both at the time it is written and subsequently. The 'Introduction' demonstrates also Paulin's liberal

[19] Gerald Dawe, 'Editor's Note', *The Younger Irish Poets* (Belfast: Blackstaff, 1982), p. xi.
[20] Tom Paulin, 'Introduction', *The Faber Book of Political Verse* (London: Faber, 1986), 17, 42.

attentiveness to traditions which might seem antipathetic, yet which reveal poetic strength (this is most notable in his admiring remarks on John Dryden, and inclusion of the whole of 'Absalom and Achitopel' in his selections). But such accommodation of course has implications for Paulin's other activities at this stage, his directorship (along with Heaney and others) of the Field Day Theatre Company, with its concurrent sense that an understanding of the complex traditions informing literature offers a potential for a new understanding of the way ahead socially and politically in Ireland.[21]

Paulin's admirable and combative volubility on these matters was in marked contrast to the way in which Paul Muldoon chose to mediate his selection of *Contemporary Irish Poetry* to its audience, also in 1986. Rather than offer a personal or narrative introduction to his full selections from ten Irish poets, Muldoon surprisingly chose to reprint as 'Prologue' a passage from a radio dialogue of 1939 between F. R. Higgins and Louis MacNeice. Muldoon's editing of the dialogue, which rehearses the old debates between the necessity for poetry to derive from consciousness of a 'racial' 'blood music' (Higgins), or from a liberated conscience (MacNeice), would seem to judge firmly in the latter's court—the final speech being given to MacNeice, and including:

> Compared with you, I take a rather common-sense view of poetry. I think that the poet is a sensitive instrument designed to record anything which interests his mind or affects his emotions.[22]

Taken in itself, MacNeice's statement might be licensed to underpin the often tumultuous variousness of the clutter and bric-a-brac of the world, which finds itself in the contemporary situations of Muldoon's own poetry. But it also aligns, implicitly, Muldoon's aesthetic against a certain brand of theatrical nationalism (exemplified in the dialogue by Higgins's melodramatic rhetoric). It seems once again to presume that the poetry primarily must take care of itself, whatever political significance it later garners.

Muldoon's selection seems purposely designed, thereafter, to acknowledge the two traditions in Irish writing, opening as it does with broad extracts from the work of Kavanagh and MacNeice (both dead for around twenty years when this 'contemporary' volume was produced). Having established his Catholic and Protestant precursors for the more recent work included, Muldoon then puts forward generous portions from eight writers, with notably only two from the South, Thomas Kinsella and Paul Durcan. His own close contemporaries (notably Boland, Carson) are excluded from inclusion amongst what the backcover blurb describes as 'the most consistently impressive Irish poets after Yeats'. The generic 'Irish', again, stands over the selection without explanation

---

[21] Paulin's inherent radicalism is more on display in his companion collection to the political verse anthology, *The Faber Book of Vernacular Verse* (London: Faber, 1990). Raging again against what he perceives as the 'Parnassian official order' of British, American (and presumably Northern Irish) political and cultural life, his book celebrates what Paulin calls in the 'Introduction' the 'springy, irreverent, chanting, quartzy, often tender and intimate, vernacular voice [which] speaks for an alternative community that is mostly powerless and invisible', p. x. Paulin's arguments (and adjectives) here complement those of his 1983 Field Day pamphlet, *A New Look At the Language Question*.

[22] See Paul Muldoon, ed., *The Faber Book of Contemporary Irish Poetry* (London: Faber, 1986), 18.

or pleading. Muldoon's anthology, therefore, remains typically enigmatic and puzzling to many of its readers.[23]

If Muldoon's anthology silently elides its Northern-ness and concurrent silencing of contemporary Gaelic writing, *The New Oxford Book of Irish Verse*, edited by Thomas Kinsella, predictably and meticulously charts what Kinsella calls, here and elsewhere, 'the dual tradition' of Irish poetry, from its origins to twentieth-century work. Expanding upon his input as translator to *An Duanaire: Poems of the Dispossessed 1600–1900* (1981), Kinsella's 'Introduction' points out the unique opportunities for more recent Irish poets from that 'tradition', 'an area of dual responsibility', both towards the 'growing demands of the poetic medium' and 'the demands of a particularly insistent and rewarding past'. Kinsella points to the century of 'retrieval and self-analysis' which the 'oldest vernacular tradition in Europe', the Irish (as he calls it), has now undergone, and to the opportunities which it has opened, therefore, to the generation succeeding Yeats.

It is a generation which he sees as headed by Kavanagh and Clarke; but more insistently, Kinsella points to the knowledge of Irish shared particularly by his own subsequent poetic generation, including Seán Ó Ríodáin, and John Montague. Given this vast historic perspective on the present, and the fracturings which Kinsella sees between the languages of the 'dual tradition' (fracturings which have had immediate impact upon his own poetic forms), it is perhaps unsurprising, although still shocking, to see Kinsella's Yeatsian slur here, on recent poetry from the North: 'The idea of such a [Northern Ireland] renaissance...is largely a journalistic entity. The past, in Northern Ireland, is not.'[24] It is a slur from which only Heaney and Mahon are (partially) excepted—but one that reveals the insistent sense which runs through Kinsella's own poetry, that 'the past' must underwrite that work's 'dispossessed' sense of modernity. It is the sheer yielding before the present of its situation which for Kinsella, as for Yeats with regard to the poets of the First World War, renders such Northern writing merely transient 'surface'.

If, by the mid-1980s, even as the so-called Troubles continued to run their appalling course, Kinsella's impatience with the Northern phenomenon in poetry is partly understandable, it is a feeling which would seem to have become crystallized by 1990. Peter Fallon and Derek Mahon's 'Introduction' to their *Penguin Book of Contemporary Irish Poetry* points to the 'more than twenty-year-old' history of that 'phenomenon', and follows Gerald Dawe's earlier policy (but this time by harnessing the marketing potency of an international publisher), in order to promote the claims of 'first-rate' poets south of the border. The 'Introduction', in arguing this case, seeks to unshackle even the poets from the North from their hitherto comfortable position in international criticism as

[23] Muldoon's later anthology, *The Faber Book of Beasts* (London: Faber, 1997), revels, like Heaney and Hughes's *The Rattle Bag*, in the 'strange' juxtapositions between poems enforced by his alphabetical arrangement of his selected (poems on) 'beasts'. But this *Faber Book* is notable for the introduction's failure to deliver on its promised 'despotic' defence of its anthologizing methodology, as Muldoon mounts a sustained lament for all of the poems which, for one reason or another, he has been forced to leave out. See p. xvi.

[24] Thomas Kinsella, 'Introduction', *The New Oxford Book of Irish Verse* (Oxford: Oxford University Press, 1986), pp. xxviii, xxx.

poets of 'the particular place', with its violent history: instead, these poets are seen to 'commute' between the local place, and highly paid jobs, often in the United States.[25] The poets of Ireland, in other words, are presented as part of a modern global community, one for whom new, and equally complex, allegiances have been set in the place of the former atavistic complicities. The era of the necessarily polemical anthology is, therefore, almost superseded, at least from the ironically polemical perspective of Fallon and Mahon's essay introducing a panoply of writers, known and unknown, to international audiences.

That their sanguine intuition was correct—that Irish poetry did not need the media attention it had been receiving in order for its worth to be proven, as conditions on the ground were increasingly alleviated—seems evident from the relaxed celebration in Michael Longley's avowedly personal selection of *20th-Century Irish Poems* (2002). Longley points to the new, global, challenges which need to be registered by contemporary poets, from urbanization and from the environment. But he also points to 'the extraordinary Irish achievement' across the past century, in which the 'diversity' of poetic form demonstrates the many ways in which 'a poem can be a poem', a demonstration which confirms, in its turn, the equally many ways 'of being Irish or, more precisely, having an imaginative relationship with Ireland'.[26] Longley's assurance is heartening in its lack of prescriptiveness, and striking in the contrast it makes with the fraught, and sometimes tendentious, attempts at accommodation made by earlier Irish poets when acting as anthologists.

[25] Peter Fallon and Derek Mahon, 'Introduction', *The Penguin Book of Contemporary Irish Poetry* (Harmondsworth: Penguin, 1990), pp. xx–xxi.

[26] Michael Longley, 'Preface', *20th-Century Irish Poems* (London: Faber, 2002), p. x.

CHAPTER 34

....

IRISH POETRY AND
THE NEWS

....

JAHAN RAMAZANI

'THE bad news is that I buy a newspaper every day.' So begins Paul Durcan's two-line poem 'Newsdesk' (2007). 'The good news', it humorously concludes, 'is that I do not read it.'[1] This anti-news news report implicitly defines poetry as the opposite of news-writing, although it also concedes the poet's reliance on newspapers. Like much of Durcan's poetry, this short poem encapsulates something of poetry's ambivalent relation to the news media in Ireland. The attraction is surely there. In 'Tribute to a Reporter in Belfast, 1974', Durcan celebrates a reporter for Raidió Teilifís Éireann (RTÉ), Liam Hourican, for scrupulously chip-carving 'each word and report' about the sectarian violence of the Troubles; his 'verbal honesty' is especially welcome 'in a country where words' have been exploited for sectarian ends 'by poets as much as by gunmen or churchmen'.[2] Notwithstanding this tribute, in which the news bests poetry, Durcan more frequently parodies journalism. Many of his poems lead off with wittily contorted headlines for titles, such as 'Wife Who Smashed Television Gets Jail', 'Minister Opens New Home for Battered Husbands', 'Margaret Thatcher Joins IRA', and 'Irish Hierarchy Bans Colour Photography'—this last a mock-news report in which the Irish Hierarchy bans colour pictures because they contradict the 'innate black and white nature of reality'.[3] While ridiculing clergymen and politicians, such poems parrot journalistic technique and slide from realism to surrealism to implicate news stories in the injustice, absurdity, and even violence they sometimes passively and unquestioningly report.

A century after Joyce's Leopold Bloom 'wiped himself' with the story he had been reading in a popular weekly, Irish writers are still puzzling over the relationship between

---

[1] Paul Durcan, *The Laughter of Mothers* (London: Harvill Secker, 2007), 58.
[2] Paul Durcan, *The Selected Paul Durcan*, ed. Edna Longley (Belfast: Blackstaff, 1982), 25.
[3] Durcan, *Selected*, 89.

literature and the news.[4] Novels such as *Ulysses* have often been seen as shot through with journalistic discourse, but little has been said about the vexed to-and-fro between Irish poetry and the news media. *Ulysses*, in Declan Kiberd's view, 'can be read as a slow-motion alternative to the daily newspaper of Dublin for 16 June 1904. Given that most inhabitants of cities by 1922 read only newspapers by the time of its publication in 1922, it might be construed as an artist's revenge, a reappropriation of newspaper methods by an exponent of the threatened novel form.'[5] The novel, from the Latin *novus* or 'new', bears more etymological and generic resemblances with the present-minded prose of newspapers than does poetry; 'poem' is from the Greek *poiein*, 'to make or construct', and so poems are literally works of artistic making or deliberate shaping. Poetry's time horizons are vast, because of its frequent metaphoric abstraction of the mundane, its layering of different moments, and its being imbued with long-lived verse traditions, thematics, and vocabularies, whereas, in Walter Benjamin's words, '[t]he value of information does not survive the moment in which it was new. It lives only at that moment', resulting in what Benedict Anderson has called the 'obsolescence of the newspaper on the morrow of its printing.'[6] The quickly read, easily disposed of, plot-driven newspaper has often been one of the generic others against which modern and contemporary poetry has defined itself. A passage quoted with some frequency in world newspapers is from William Carlos Williams's 'Asphodel, That Greeny Flower':

> Look at
> what passes for the new.
> You will not find it there but in
> despised poems.
> It is difficult
> to get the news from poems
> yet men die miserably every day
> for lack
> of what is found there.[7]

Newspapers ironically remind themselves of their limitations when they cite these lines, alerting themselves to the soul-sustaining stuff they concede to poetry and situate beyond their ken. Williams identifies 'despised poems' with emotional and spiritual nourishment, as against the information unloaded by the more popular newness media.

Many other modern and contemporary poets have contrasted their work with the news, but they have hardly been able to ignore it. Much has been made of the ancient quarrel between poets and philosophers, but since the Industrial Revolution, a no less intense quarrel

---

[4] James Joyce, *Ulysses* (New York: Modern Library, 1961), 70. The paper was *Tit-Bits*, which provided a digest of stories and worldwide news.

[5] Declan Kiberd, '*Ulysses*, Newspapers and Modernism', *Irish Classics* (Cambridge, MA: Harvard University Press, 2001), 463.

[6] Walter Benjamin, 'The Storyteller', *Illuminations*, trans. Harry Zohn (New York: Schocken Books, 1969), 90; Benedict Anderson, *Imagined Communities*, rev. ed. (London: Verso, 1991), 35.

[7] William Carlos Williams, *The Collected Poems of William Carlos Williams*, vol. 2, ed. Christopher MacGowan (New York: New Directions, 1986), 318.

has been under way between poets and journalists. Twentieth- and twenty-first-century Western poetry has been agonistically intertwined with newswriting throughout a period that witnessed the massive burgeoning of the news media. The extraordinary pressure of the news in Ireland, particularly during the Troubles both early and late in the twentieth century, has given this quarrel a special urgency. In a handful of exemplary poems examined for what they reveal about this quarrel, Irish poets from W. B. Yeats and Louis MacNeice to Michael Longley and Seamus Heaney, Paul Muldoon and Medbh McGuckian, illuminate the constant dialogue between poetry and the news media. According to Kiberd, '[w]hat set the Irish modernists off from their Continental counterparts was their marked willingness to engage with newspapers', as instanced by 'Yeats's voluminous journalizing'.[8] After Yeats, major Irish poets such as MacNeice and Muldoon spent significant parts of their careers working for the news media, both MacNeice and Muldoon as employees of the British Broadcasting Corporation. A recent literary editor of *The Irish Times* has even claimed that Irish 'poems are linked to the newspaper's lifeblood: News'.[9] Already by the 1890s in Ireland, according to a historian, the newspaper had entered its golden age as 'an important passport to entry into the modern world',[10] making it a master discourse that poetry had to respond to, questioning, absorbing, and resisting it. Under modernity, writes Christopher Morash, Ireland, was no longer merely 'a geographical entity' but 'an information field', 'part of a modern informational order' made possible by technologies of instant communications and the news media they proliferated.[11] At the head of the media revolution and ever since have been regional and national newspapers, many of them operly sectarian. How have Irish poets echoed and incorporated newswriting? How have they defined and defended themselves against it? What implicit self-understanding can be teased from their poetry in relation to journalism?

Already at the start of the twentieth century, Yeats was deeply involved with newspapers and periodicals, and yet strenuously refused to be dominated by their terms. 'The newspaper is the roar of the machine', he declared in a 1909 diary entry.[12] Machine and mechanization were anathema to Yeats, as they had been for Blake and other first-generation Romantics. The 'roar of the machine' includes the loud rotating drum cylinders that rapidly spun off mass-printed newspapers, in contrast to the painstaking craft of letterpress book publication in his sisters' Dun Emer and Cuala Press. In context, Yeats is distinguishing between the motives behind newspaper and book production, in particular newspapers' loud 'clash of interests' or 'contest of interests', arguments waged or lost on behalf of what are now labelled interest groups, as against what Yeats, implicitly allying himself with Immanuel Kant on the aesthetic, calls books' 'slight separation from immediate interests'.[13] Little wonder that he, as a young man, declined a job at a unionist newspaper.[14]

[8] Kiberd, *Irish Classics*, 464.

[9] Caroline Walsh quoted in Victor Luftig, 'Poetry, Causality, and an Irish Ceasefire', *Peace Review* 113:2 (2001), 163.

[10] Marie-Louise Legg, *Newspapers and Nationalism: The Irish Provincial Press, 1850–1892* (Dublin: Four Courts Press, 1999), 175.

[11] Christopher Morash, *A History of the Media in Ireland* (Cambridge: Cambridge University Press, 2010), 96, 130.

[12] W. B. Yeats, *Memoirs*, ed. Denis Donoghue (London: Macmillan, 1972), 142.

[13] Ibid.

[14] Richard Ellmann, *Yeats: The Man and the Masks* (London: Faber, 1961), 80.

Not that Yeats was aloof from political engagement. During such public controversies as the Hugh Lane affair (whether a bridge gallery should be built for a collection of Impressionist paintings) and the Dublin lockout of 1913 (whether tens of thousands of workers should have been locked out to prevent unionization), Yeats took positions in public speeches, poems, and journalism, sometimes directing his wrath at the newspapers themselves. As quoted by R. F. Foster, Yeats said, during the Lane affair, 'In Ireland we have a most ignorant press & a priest created terror of culture', and during the lockout: 'When I think, however, of the press of Dublin which is owned by one of the parties to this dispute, and remember how the nationalist press has printed open incitements, publishing the names of working men and their wives for purposes of intimidation, and that the Unionist Press—with the exception of one article in the *Irish Times*—has been disgracefully silent, I find no words to express my contempt.' At the time of the lockout, Yeats defends working-class labour rights against incitement by the 'press of Dublin with the plain connivance of the Castle and the Castle police'.[15] Money, imperial and administrative power, and religious sectarianism pervert journalism's disinterestedness. 'The newspaper is an instrument of power', commented Benjamin, and it 'belong[s] to capital'.[16] Still, the newspaper's representational dominance had to be acknowledged. In a note for *Poems Written in Discouragement*, Yeats reflects on the controversies over Parnell, Synge's *The Playboy of the Western World*, and the Lane gallery: 'In the thirty years or so during which I have been reading Irish newspapers, three public controversies have stirred my imagination.'[17] The introductory prepositional phrase concedes that newspapers are a primary arena for engagement in public life. Accordingly Yeats published some signal public poems in their pages, such as 'Mourn—and Then Onward!' (an elegy for Parnell) in *United Ireland* and 'September 1913' (partly about the lockout) in *The Irish Times*.

During the controversies over the Lane pictures and the Dublin lockout, Yeats's principal antagonist was the press baron William Martin Murphy, proprietor of *The Irish Independent* and *The Evening Herald*. In a history of Irish newspapers, Murphy's *Irish Independent* is said to have 'won respect and admiration for its scorning of sensationalism and for the honourable, impartial treatment it gave to every school of thought in Ireland';[18] but Yeats had an entirely different view. Having been attacked in print by Murphy, Yeats reduces him to the synecdoche of 'an old foul mouth' in 'To a Shade', a poem that apostrophizes Parnell and voices Yeats's critique of Murphy in particular and of the press in general.[19] 'To a Shade'

---

[15] R. F. Foster, *W. B. Yeats: A Life.* vol. 1. *The Apprentice Mage, 1865–1914* (Oxford: Oxford University Press, 1997), 482, 500.

[16] Walter Benjamin, *Selected Writings*, vol. 2, trans. Rodney Livingstone et al., ed. M. W. Jennings et al. (Cambridge: Belknap-Harvard University Press, 1996), 369, 772.

[17] W. B. Yeats, *The Variorum Edition of the Poems of W. B. Yeats*, ed. Peter Allt and Russell K. Alspach (Basingstoke: Macmillan, 1956), 818.

[18] Hugh Oram, *The Newspaper Book: A History of Newspapers in Ireland, 1649–1983* (Dublin: MO Books, 1983), 105.

[19] Yeats, *Variorum Poems*, 292.

revolves around the contrast between the freedom and nobility of the arts and the press's ignorance, trickery, and mob mentality. 'A man' of Parnell's 'own passionate serving kind' (Hugh Lane) has offered a gift (his Impressionist paintings) that could have instilled in future generations ('their children's children') an artistic sensibility ('loftier thought,/Sweeter emotion'). The arts and their patrons look toward the distant horizons of the future; the newspapers are fixated on the now. While Yeats's disagreement with Murphy and the press may start in differences of class, politics, and sect (middle class/would-be aristocracy, Catholic/Protestant, etcetera), it also involves fundamentally divergent genre assumptions about time and representation. In other Irish poems—whether Catholic, Protestant, or neither, working class, elitist, or neither—as we'll see, the constricted timescale of the news is a recurrent point of contrast with poetry's wider temporal horizons and its relative freedom from the imperatives of the immediate present. As against the youthful energies of the arts, Murphy's mouth is 'old', and as against the benefactor's singular nobility, Murphy incites the mob like wolves ('the pack'). By superimposing the Lane affair on the Parnell affair (and Murphy had attacked both men), Yeats exploits the reiterative structure of poetry for figures of thought—the type or paradigm of the unappreciated hero recurring across time.

Yeats's 'To a Friend Whose Work Has Come to Nothing' also associates newspapers with the pursuit of power and self-interest, as against the noble disinterestedness of the arts. The synecdochic reduction of Murphy to another organ of speech, a 'brazen throat', again suggests, like 'old foul mouth', journalism's competitive threat to the voice of poetry. Yeats asks a friend (Lady Gregory) how she and other supporters of the arts can 'compete,/Being honour bred, with' a shameless liar. To 'turn away', to be 'secret and exult', is harder than mere 'Triumph' of the kind pursued by the ruthless newspaper magnate.[20] Losing the competition with soulless, sales-driven journalism, friends of the arts are counselled to retreat, their interiority their final defence. Yeats champions poetry's freedom, nobility, interiority, and *longue durée*, as against the newspaper's shallow present-mindedness and its mastery by power and money interests. Although these contrasts are hardly impartial—Yeats was, after all, implicated in systems of patronage and prestige—they signal his struggle to protect a less sectarian, a larger and longer-visioned, discursive alternative to the news, a powerful rival he saw as dangerously divisive and short sighted.

Yeats contends with the news even in poems that don't refer directly to newspapers or their owners, as indicated by occasional poems titled with the dates of current events, such as 'September 1913', 'Easter 1916', and 'Nineteen Hundred and Nineteen'. 'Easter 1916' reports on the most consequential Irish revolt against British rule and the ensuing execution of its leaders, providing names of the Rising's leaders, the date of the event, brief biographies, and political context—information of the sort one could also find in *The Irish Times*, *The Irish Independent*, *The Freeman's Journal*, *The Evening Herald*, and other newspapers (though most Dublin papers were initially shuttered by proximity to

---

[20] Yeats, *Variorum Poems*, 291.

the fighting). It even ventures policy predictions, such as the possibility that England might implement Home Rule. But if Yeats makes some concessions to the age of the newspaper, he also claims alternative procedures for poetry. Instead of representing his text as a day-after report on the event, he dates the poem's composition five months afterwards, even withholding broad publication for four more years, when it could reso- nate with the Irish War of Independence, and printing it not in a Dublin paper but in London's *The New Statesman*. The poem was hardly a newsflash. Moreover, if we approach the poem not already knowing that nearly sixteen hundred Irish Volunteers and two hundred members of the Citizen Army took over buildings and a park in Dublin, that the rebellion was crushed after six days, that fifteen leaders were executed, that four hundred and fifty people died during the insurrection, we would be hard pressed to extract this information from the poem. Despite its names and dates and por- traits and parliamentary politics, 'Easter 1916' functions poorly if read purely for news delivery. Its iterations and inversions ('All changed, changed utterly'), mind-divided oxymorons ('terrible beauty'), demonstrative adjectives ('That woman's', 'This man', 'This other'), embedded pastoral parable ('The stone's in the midst of all'), mixed perfect and slant rhyme (*name/come, death/faith, verse/Pearse*), performative rhetoric ('I write it out'), abrupt mixing of tenses ('He had done', 'I number him'), and other poetic manipu- lations of language are information poor but aesthetically rich.[21] They formally embody as a repeatable linguistic performance a poet's and perhaps a society's complexly ambiv- alent apprehensions of a major historical event.

If the poem doesn't aspire to objective news reporting, as signalled first and foremost by the prominence of the lyric 'I', does it at least resemble an editorial or leader, since both editorials and poems acknowledge being partial? 'Easter 1916' brilliantly internal- izes and articulates multiple conflicting viewpoints—that the heroes were both heroic and antiheroic, both comic and tragic, bathetic and noble; that their sacrifice resulted from both monomaniacal political fixation and something like romantic love; that their actions would issue in the birth of a free Ireland and may have been an unnecessary waste of life. By its tumultuous movement back and forth between these differing view- points, its fracturing and complicating of nationalist and anti-nationalist views of the Rising, the poem inverts the 'opinion' piece, editorial, or leading article, in which room is usually made for one and only one strongly partisan argument, certainly in Irish and English newspapers at the time, such as Murphy's *Irish Independent*, which vehemently denounced the 'insane and criminal' insurrection by 'unfilial ingrates' and endorsed the execution of the rebel leaders.[22] The poet punctures or interrogates or qualifies his views, parading doubts, uncertainties, and internal divisions of the sort seldom heard in edito- rial or opinion journalism. Whether in its role as objective purveyor of information or as partisan rallying cry, the newspaper is—explicitly in 'To a Shade' and 'To a Friend

[21] Yeats, *Variorum Poems*, 391–4.
[22] 'Criminal Madness', *Irish Independent* (4 May 1916), 2. By 13 May, however, the leading article's tone was more cautious, warning against further executions and the indiscriminate 'rounding up' of all 'sympathisers'(2).

Whose Work Has Come to Nothing', implicitly in 'Easter 1916'—a discursive other against which Yeats's lyric poetry defines its complex aesthetic, affective, and political calibrations.

Yeats was hardly alone in his struggle with print journalism. The year of Yeats's death, fellow Irishman Louis MacNeice published *Autumn Journal* (1939), a long poetic meditation on the autumn of 1938, when the world was swamped with news. Two years later, MacNeice published a critical book on Yeats and launched a career as writer and producer for the BBC. A member of the 1930s generation, for which documentary was an important genre, MacNeice might well seem to have been more open to journalism than Yeats was. In *Modern Poetry: A Personal Essay* he lists 'a reader of newspapers' as among the first qualities he expects of the modern poet,[23] and the plainspoken style of *Autumn Journal* veers closer to journalism than does Yeats's more highly wrought verse. But although MacNeice welcomes into poetry modern technologies and urban experiences that Yeats had shunned, the news—in the dual sense of both reporting and new information—is seen in *Autumn Journal* as insidiously pervasive, a threat to human agency. In canto V, people struggle to comprehend news of Hitler's speeches, but 'cannot take it in', going to their 'Jobs to the dull refrain of the caption "War"/Buzzing around us as from hidden insects'.[24] Surrounding and even 'bombarding' people, the news seems to harm human subjects and confine them in both space and time, as suggested by the rhyme of 'War' with 'before'. Another rhyme sonically encodes the invasion of external news into the body:

> No, what we mean is Hodza, Henlein, Hitler,
> The Maginot Line,
> The heavy panic that cramps the lungs and presses
> The collar down the spine.[25]

In this vivid imagery of the body squeezed by the news (Czechoslovakia threatened and annexed by the Nazis), MacNeice shows the modern subject physically and psychologically pressed by globally mediated events. Yet another enjambment of 'presses' links the word's use as verb (i.e., squeezes) with its meaning as noun (i.e., printing machines):

> And when we go out into Piccadilly Circus
> They are selling and buying the late
> Special editions snatched and read abruptly
> Beneath the electric signs as crude as Fate.
> And the individual, powerless, has to exert the
> Powers of will and choice
> And choose between enormous evils, either
> Of which depends on somebody else's voice.
> The cylinders are racing in the presses ...[26]

[23] Louis MacNeice, *Modern Poetry: A Personal Essay* (Oxford: Oxford University Press, 1938), 198.
[24] Louis MacNeice, *Collected Poems*, ed. Peter McDonald (London: Faber, 2007), 109.
[25] Ibid.
[26] Ibid., 109–10.

In this capitalist hell of mechanical buying and selling, newspapers are seen as having the inevitability of classical fate. Overbearing electric signs and demonically whirling cylinders in rotary printing presses represent the impersonal menace of the news as both medium and message. The underworld associations accrue in MacNeice's diction: 'Who can control his fate?' asked Othello, imagining a day in hell when 'fiends snatch at' his soul.[27] Having depicted people as automata, the canto stumbles in search of agency: first the strained moral assertion that the individual 'has to exert' free will, but then, stuttering between 'choice' and 'choose', the concession that the only choice to be found in the newspapers is 'between enormous evils'. Choiceless choice, powerless power, voiceless voice—MacNeice's paradoxes reveal the constraints on the democratic ideal of a free and informed citizenry; here, the news seems to constrict freedom instead of enlarging it. As the speaker tries to fall asleep, listening to the mechanical inevitability signalled by an up-shifting car and a chugging train, he wonders 'what the morning/Paper will say', before realizing it's already morning, 'the day is to-day'.[28] Bracketing life between the late edition and the morning edition, the news relentlessly defines and delimits temporal succession.

But the back-and-forth ruminations of *Autumn Journal*, its looping back to the personal past and the histories of Britain and Ireland, its allusive layering of the present with classical myths and literary intertexts, and its speculations on the future, differentiate the temporal horizons of this poetic journal from those of journalism. The speaker dwells and speaks from within the unfolding present, but as multiplied, echoed, and stretched into the past and future by poetic form and memory, including sonic echoes and figurative twists in rhyme, alliteration, and metaphor. 'Time is a country', writes MacNeice in canto XXIV, 'the present moment/A spotlight roving round the scene'.[29] If newspapers are locked within the narrow-visioned present, the poet must look farther. 'We need not chase the spotlight', he affirms, 'The future is the bride of what has been'.[30] Although the poet must respond to the now, live in touch with historical change, poetry's wit and formal play, rhymes and metaphors cannot merely be chained to the moment; they link it to time past and future, playing across literary memories and inventive possibilities. 'Literature is news that STAYS news', Ezra Pound declared a few years earlier, citing as example how the 'news in the Odyssey is still news'.[31] Although MacNeice incorporates in *Autumn Journal* the news of 1938, he creates news that stays news by hybridising the genres of prose journal and lyric, the syntax of colloquial statement and formal rumination, the tenses of long literary memory and present-awakened commentary. Formally and humanly expansive, poetry permits MacNeice to register how world historical news threatens to narrow time and constrain agency, even as poetry also enables him to push back against these limits.

Just as Yeats, MacNeice, and others in the first half of the twentieth century write into poetry the Easter Rising, the Irish War of Independence, the Irish Civil War, and the

---

[27] William Shakespeare, *Othello*, V.ii: 265, 275.
[28] MacNeice, *Collected Poems*, 111.
[29] Ibid., 162.
[30] Ibid.
[31] Ezra Pound, *ABC of Reading* [1934] (New York: New Directions, 1960), 29, 44.

Second World War, later Irish poets engage or deflect the cataclysmic news of the post-1968 Troubles over several decades, sometimes in newspapers and other media, sometimes against them, often both at the same time. Among the most celebrated examples of news-inflected poems is one that, published in *The Irish Times* on Saturday, 3 September 1994, marked the suspension of hostilities between armed Catholic and Protestant groups in Northern Ireland. That day's newspaper was busy with news of the first assurances and doubts, hopes and suspicions, attacks and political manoeuvrings after the Irish Republican Army ceasefire on 31 August. *The Irish Times* reported on unionist and republican political responses. One article began, 'The IRA will not retaliate against loyalist attacks on Catholics, and the cessation of its campaign will not be broken by provocation, the Sinn Fein president, Mr Gerry Adams, has said.'[32] Another stated: 'The DUP leader, the Rev Ian Paisley, yesterday announced plans to try to organise an alternative pan-unionist convention in the North' and 'launched a vitriolic attack on the Taoiseach', in which he described 'Mr Reynolds as "the petty little Fuhrer in Dublin"'.[33] It was amid these news stories, bifurcated along Northern Ireland's sectarian divide, that Michael Longley's poem 'Ceasefire' appeared. The newspaper marked the work's identity as poetry by sealing it in a box on page eight and printing it in a font larger than that of the book reviews surrounding it, including a splenetic attack on a book about Patrick Pearse.[34]

How does the poem coincide with and diverge from news reports of this momentous event? As in Yeats and MacNeice, Longley's title marks the poem as having a family resemblance to journalistic reports, a textual index of the now. But this is also where the twain part, for the story the poem tells isn't new but one of the oldest in Western literature:

> Put in mind of his own father and moved to tears
> Achilles took him by the hand and pushed the old king
> Gently away, but Priam curled up at his feet and
> Wept with him until their sadness filled the building.

The immediate present is there, but only as seen through the lens of the ancient past. Instead of representing each event, news-like, in its atomistic singularity, the poem understands the now through its resemblances with a story told long ago in another language in a faraway country—parallels that suspend the immediate pressures of sectarianism. Twinning epic with Shakespearean sonnet, though in quatrains limited to one rhyme at most, the poem reanimates an old lyric form's language of physical beauty and erotic love.

Unlike the news reports that day, this poem understands the event through a nexus of resemblances: the poet sees the ending of the Trojan War in the ending of the Irish Troubles, just as the Greek Achilles sees his own father, Peleus, in the Trojan Priam

---

[32] Maol Muire Tynan, 'Adams Says IRA Will Not React to Attacks', *Irish Times* (3 September 1994), 5.
[33] Dick Grogan, 'Paisley to Organise Pan-Unionist Forum', *Irish Times* (3 September 1994), 5.
[34] Michael Longley, 'Ceasefire', *Irish Times* (3 September 1994), 8. See also the slightly revised version in Michael Longley, *Collected Poems* (London: Jonathan Cape, 2006), 225.

(in Longley's Homeric source, Priam repeatedly calls on Achilles to remember his father). Resemblance crosses the divide between enemies, and grief unites the two men in a microcosmic cross-cultural union, signalled by the plural possessive adjective 'their'. Simile generates further resemblances in the next stanza, between Hector's dead body and the gift it has strangely become:

> Taking Hector's corpse into his own hands Achilles
> Made sure it was washed and, for the old king's sake,
> Dressed in uniform, ready for Priam to carry
> Wrapped like a present home to Troy at daybreak.

Having been reimagined as father and son, their physicality highlighted, the protagonists come still closer through their figuration as lovers:

> When they had each eaten together, it pleased them both
> To stare at each other's beauty as lovers might,
> Achilles built like a god, Priam goodlooking still
> And full of conversation, who earlier had sighed.
> 'I get down on my knees and do what must be done
> And kiss Achilles' hand, the killer of my son.'

Whereas the news reports in *The Irish Times* function as transparent windows onto the objectively apprehended reality of the ceasefire, downplaying their identity as texts, the poem foregrounds its linguistic remaking of the story it retells. At the poem's end, the jangling alliteration of 'kiss' and 'killer', braced within the full couplet rhyme of 'done and 'son', sonically and semantically encapsulates the inversion of violence in reconciliation. Even the poem's first lines, rather than objectively report, had peered into Achilles's consciousness as he remembered his own father. The imprinting on the scene of the poet's singular imagination and language, mediating his ancient precursor's, cannot be overlooked.

News reports are said to tell us who, what, when, where, why, and how, a framework that can help us measure the distance between this newspaper poem and the news. Who and what? The poem's ontology is oblique, seemingly about conflict and reconciliation between Greeks and Trojans but ultimately also about Irish Catholics and Protestants. When? The poem's temporality is likewise ambiguous, suspended between ancient Troy and present-day Northern Ireland. Where? The poem is set in ancient Troy, but by its title refers to (and it was printed in) Ireland, floating translocally in between, unmoored in either site. Why? To explain why he humbles himself before Achilles, Priam says he does 'what must be done', turning on its head a phrase sometimes used to justify killing as obligatory. How? The how of the poem, its elegant verbal texture, its intricate play of resemblances, its formal and figurative echoes of Homer and of the sonnet tradition, are as much what it is about as the events it relates. It revitalizes an ancient poem's story of reconciliation, using it both to place the day's news in a larger context and, after so many years of bloodshed, to set an ethical standard of peacemaking against which the ceasefire can be measured. Like Yeats and

MacNeice, Longley makes powerful use of the cross-temporal, transnational, cross-sectarian potentialities of poetry.

Further demonstrating the ongoing entanglements of Irish poetry with the news, another contemporary poet has often been a news subject, and the news has often been a subject of Seamus Heaney's poetry. 'As a journalist', said Olivia O'Leary of the BBC, 'it was wonderful to come across a great poet who thought that what we did was important'. Borrowing poetry's prestige, O'Leary presupposes the genre's difference from the journalism it flatters with attention. But her next sentence assimilates the most public contemporary Irish poet to her profession: 'We were conscious all the time of someone who reads all the papers, who keeps up with the current affairs debates, who's as interested in news as any journalist, because maybe he feels he needs to know constantly the context in which he's writing. And we quickly realised that that attic in Sandymount is no ivory tower.'[35]

Heaney is more circumspect about journalism than journalism has been about him. The bifurcated structure of his most famous and controversial volume, *North* (1975), embodies poetry's long-running ambivalence toward journalism. The collection divides between a first part, intensely lyric poems that could scarcely be less journalistic, and a second part, poems that openly adapt and engage news rhetoric. Heaney conceded that 'Whatever You Say Say Nothing', a poem initially published alongside prose accounts of the Troubles in *The Listener* and later in part 2 of *North*, was 'journalistic, happily and I'd hope unpejoratively so', written in a 'looser, more documentary style' than his 'more inward, brooding' poems,[36] to the extent that, in Blake Morrison's view, some of the lines 'might almost have been taken from the journalistic prose alongside' them in *The Listener*.[37] But the poem can also be seen as evidencing one of *North*'s two different ways of resisting journalism: like other poems in part 2, it incorporates journalism as ambivalent other against which poetry defines itself, whereas the poems in part 1 resolutely exclude journalism from their lyricism, as externalized alter ego.

'I'm writing just after an encounter/With an English journalist in search of "views/ On the Irish thing"', begins 'Whatever You Say Say Nothing', placing its language in a competitive relation with the journalism it implicitly tags as alien, external, and clichéd.[38] Despite claims about Heaney as a would-be journalist, his verbs and verbals associate the news media—'sniff and point', 'coiled', 'Litter'—with dogs, guns, snakes, and pollution. In an implicit ars poetica, the poem affiliates itself with earlier works of literature, implicitly vaunting poetry's deep transnational memory, here by allusion to *Hamlet*, as distinct from the national biases ('an English journalist') and temporal shallowness of the news:

---

[35] Olivia O'Leary as cited by Darragh Doyle, 'Olivia O'Leary Pays Tribute to Seamus Heaney', The Culch, www.culch.ie/2009/06/03/olivia-o-leary-pays-tribute-to-seamus-heaney. See also Dennis O'Driscoll, 'Heaney in Public', *The Cambridge Companion to Seamus Heaney*, ed. Bernard O'Donoghue (Cambridge: Cambridge University Press, 2009), 56–72.

[36] Dennis O'Driscoll, *Stepping Stones: Interviews with Seamus Heaney* (London: Faber, 2008), 123–4.

[37] Blake Morrison, *Seamus Heaney* (New York: Methuen, 1982), 55.

[38] Seamus Heaney, *North* (London: Faber, 1975), 57.

> The times are out of joint
> But I incline as much to rosary beads
>
> As to the jottings and analyses
> Of politicians and newspapermen[39]

Another self-definitional strategy is to link lyric with the ritualistic and recursive performance of prayer, as contrasted with the rapidly written and consumed 'jottings' of journalists, hastily 'scribbled down'—a distinction encapsulated in the contrastive rhyme of news 'leads' with 'beads'. The harsh internal echo of the spondaic ' "Backlash" ' with ' "crack down" ', inverting the phoneme /ka/ in " 'escalate' ", embeds these clichés in a staccato patter that suggests newswriting's depersonalization of suffering and violence. Suddenly breaking free of satire, the poet defiantly reclaims lyric voice: 'Yet I live here, I live here too, I sing'. Jamming three independent clauses into one line, the poet stakes his right to the local and global, to the indexically defined 'here' of Northern Ireland and the transnational lineage of poets from Homer to Whitman. By contrast with journalism's clichés and ephemerality, poetry must try 'To lure the tribal shoals to epigram/And order', a richly condensed and shaped language that will, in the Horatian boast, be more lasting than bronze, 'aere perennius'.[40]

Instead of incorporating the journalistic rhetoric they war against, like poems in the book's second half, poems in the first half cloak themselves in an intense lyricism that largely shuts out news discourse. And instead of writing about the immediate present, quickly recorded for rapid consumption and disposal, Heaney reflects on bodies preserved for thousands of years in the acidic, cold, de-oxygenated water of peat bogs—their preservative qualities akin to poetry's in creating verbal monuments more lasting than bronze. 'The Grauballe Man' concerns an especially well-preserved Iron Age body, first encountered by Heaney in P. V. Glob's archaeological study *The Bog People* (translated from Danish in 1969). The Grauballe man, his throat cut from ear to ear, was deposited in a Danish bog, probably in sacrifice to a fertility goddess to ensure the coming of a fruitful spring, but he was so well preserved that, two thousand years later, he could still be fingerprinted by the police. While the news of killings by loyalist and republican extremists hovers around the poem's edges, this lyrically self-engaged work is both a poem and a metapoem. Its first words, 'As if', announce the poem as poem, an imaginative thought experiment, a speculative excursion stretching beyond the literal: 'As if he had been poured/in tar'. The word 'seems' ('and seems to weep//the black river of himself') also foregrounds the poet's associative work of imaginatively remaking the body, as do the tropes of fluidity—'poured', 'weep', 'river'—that figuratively liquefy the bog man.[41] His body presented as the product of his grief over his sad fate, the bog man is imagined as self-created, and as such, his beauty illustrates the relative autonomy of the aesthetic, his body and the poem's self-returning melancholy body mirroring one another. Instead of suppressing its figurative properties in favour of news-like transparency, the

---

[39] Ibid.
[40] Ibid., 59.
[41] Ibid., 35.

poem runs wild with similes and metaphors, even remaking the blazon tradition that likened the beloved's parts to fruits and flowers and animals. Parts of the dead man's body are 'like bog oak' and 'like a basalt egg', or they're as 'cold as a swan's foot/or a wet swamp root', or they're metaphorized as 'the ridge/and purse of a mussel' and 'an eel arrested/under a glisten of mud', or they're reimagined as 'a visor' and 'the vent' and 'a dark/elderberry place'.[42] Along with its figurative extravagance, the poem's sonic materiality—for example, the consonants *g* and *b* in 'Grauballe' repeated in the word cluster 'black', 'grain', 'bog', 'ball', 'basalt', and 'egg', and 'swan's foot' rhymed with 'swamp root'—call attention to the poem's dense artifice.

Wordsworth defined lyric poetry as 'emotion recollected in tranquility', and Heaney, saying of the Grauballe man 'but now he lies/perfected in my memory', implicitly compares his lyric labour with the bog's preserving, curing, eternizing the object of its reflection. Twice enjambing 'he lies'—a phrase that in context recalls the 'here lies' or *hic jacet* of tombstones—the poem signals its epitaphic function. Just as the bog does violence to the body in effecting its preservation ('twisted', 'bruised'), so too the poem has had to twist and trope the body as various figurative others (another sense of 'he lies'), perhaps even bruising it in the process of lyricization. In so doing, it has made possible the bog man's rebirth into this poem ('bruised like a forceps baby'), but it worries about the cost of its having aesthetically 'perfected' him. The dead man is likened to a famous statue in the Capitoline Museum, and implicitly the poem also considers whether it has cramped the dead man within the aesthetic. He is:

> hung in the scales
> with beauty and atrocity:
> with the Dying Gaul
> too strictly compassed
>
> on his shield,
> with the actual weight
> of each hooded victim,
> slashed and dumped.[43]

The poem has largely resisted news discourse, foregrounding instead of effacing its artifice, commemorating not a contemporary but an ancient killing, and focusing intently not on 'whodunit' but on the dead body. But the words 'arrested', then 'slashed', then 'corpse' and 'body' insinuate a news lexicon into the poem that culminates in the final words about a 'hooded victim,/slashed and dumped'. Such words still appeared years later in news reports, such as the *Irish Times* obituary for a mid-1970s near-victim of the notorious UVF Shankill Butchers: they 'slashed his arms and wrists. Believing him dead, they dumped him in the alleyway', where he was found alive the next day.[44] But when the phrase 'slashed and dumped' appears at the end of Heaney's poem, in

---

[42] Ibid., 35–6.
[43] Ibid., 36.
[44] Obit. for Gerard McLaverty, 'The Last Victim of the Shankill Butchers', *Irish Times* (22 March 2008), 12.

contrast to news reports, it shocks as much because of its thudding sonic materiality as its referential transparency. By virtue of *not* being overtly about the victims of the IRA or the UVF, by dwelling on a preserved ancient body and on its own poetic body spun out of a profusion of figurative similitudes and sonic clusters and syntactic parallelisms, the poem all the more powerfully evokes the specificity of the Troubles' victims— people whose killings exceed the compass of both aesthetic and journalistic representation. Heaney was harshly criticized for mythologizing and archetypifying the victims of the Troubles in *North*. But his indirect approach—evoking contemporary news by modernist mythical analogy with news thousands of years old—is news that stays news because of the eddying resonances between now and then, between poetry's material body and the victim's bodies. Ethically self-scrutinizing, 'The Grauballe Man' well understands the critique that it has 'too strictly compassed' victims of contemporary Northern Irish political violence in an artificial parallel between them and ancient sacrificial Danish bog victims. But its wager is that poetic resemblance, even when transnationally and transhistorically stretched, makes possible forms of attention and understanding occluded by more denotative, newsy forms.

Whereas the news of sectarian violence is unmistakably present as a shaping force in Heaney's poetry, more interpretive labour is required to uncover the Troubles in Paul Muldoon's early verse, lurking in analogies between American Indians and the Irish, in a poem such as 'Meeting the British', or embedded in the psychoanalytic parable of a violently punished schoolboy turned IRA volunteer in 'Anseo'. Muldoon's approach to news of the Troubles is still more oblique than Heaney's, his scepticism toward journalism still deeper. From early on, he was well aware that his poems seemed to have little to do with the news. In 'Lunch with Pancho Villa', he disarms criticism for fiddling while Belfast burns by voicing it within the poem:

> 'Look, son. Just look around you.
> People are getting themselves killed
> Left, right and centre
> While you do what? Write rondeaux?
> There's more to living in this country
> Than stars and horses, pigs and trees,
> Not that you'd guess it from your poems.
> Do you never listen to the news?
> You want to get down to something true,
> Something a little nearer home.'[45]

The Mexican revolutionary-turned-journalist Pancho Villa, whose naively ocular epistemology is encapsulated in the command 'Look', upbraids the poet for writing rondeaux: their formal circularity and pastoralism impede rather than afford access to the news of contemporary urban violence. But Villa subverts his own advice. He deploys the demonstrative 'this' to root his mimetic writing in a specific place, but where is 'this

[45] Paul Muldoon, *Poems 1968–1998* (London: Faber, 2001), 41–2.

country'? Is it Ireland or Mexico? In the writer's back yard or 'a thousand miles away/ From here'?[46] As often in Muldoon, and still more aggressively than in Heaney, place is questioned as stabilizer of identity and truth. Having privileged the immediacy of first-hand sight, Villa reveals that he means mediated second-hand overhearing: 'Do you never listen to the news?' The 'something true' that the poet is supposed to embrace rhymes slant with 'rondeaux', and 'from your poems' with 'nearer home', evidencing how the telling irresistibly mediates and skews the 'true'. After he unveils the poem's narrative as no more than a stage set, a front door that opens 'Directly on to a back yard', the poet is asked, 'When are you going to tell the truth?' But it turns out the naively titled book *How It Happened Here* may not exist, despite Villa's claims to have co-authored it. Perhaps to tell the truth is to admit that the news fabricates its seemingly uncomplicated and unmediated facts, as in Jean Baudrillard's simulacra theory of the news media. In this poem's constructivist account of even supposedly transparent language, Muldoon questions news realism as a sham and implicitly defends the poet's more self-conscious playing with forms and deliberate reimagining of the real, even at a time of large-scale violence.

To trace some of modern and contemporary Irish poetry's engagements with journalism is not to suggest that poetry's news stays news only when it is about current public events. Many poems turn poetry's discursive dial even farther from the news. Medbh McGuckian, a self-described 'threader/of double-stranded words',[47] writes in a note to the poem 'Drawing Ballerinas': 'This poem was written to commemorate Ann Frances Owens, schoolfellow and neighbour, who lost her life in the Abercorn Café explosion, 1972. The painter, Matisse, when asked how he managed to survive the war artistically, replied that he spent the worst years "drawing ballerinas".'[48] During the Troubles in Belfast, to write poems about the body, flowers, and slips of the tongue was McGuckian's equivalent of drawing ballerinas. War is not present in Matisse's ballerina drawings or most of McGuckian's sensuous word paintings, except by virtue of its exclusion. Her poetry's basic operating procedures are the reverse of what we look for in journalism. Action is indefinite or altogether absent. Sentences dilate, continually deferring meaning in interlocking syntactic ambiguities. Pronouns such as 'you', 'she', and 'they' appear and disappear without referents. Objects blend, one person blurs with another, and contrary ideas dissolve into each other. Metaphorical chains of evocation proliferate and interlink. From Yeats to Durcan, as we've seen, many other poets contend with journalistic rhetoric, referentiality, and present-mindedness, but McGuckian's *écriture feminine* is—in its opacity, self-referentiality, and sensuous verbal surfaces—perhaps the poetry least like journalism.

Not that the Troubles are altogether absent. Having been left out of Frank Ormsby's anthology of poems about the Northern Irish Troubles, *A Rage for Order* (1992), McGuckian cited Pablo Picasso's remark about the Second World War for the epigraph

---

[46] Ibid., 42.

[47] Medbh McGuckian, 'The Dream-Language of Fergus', *Selected Poems 1978–1994* (Salem: Wake Forest University Press, 1997), 48.

[48] Medbh McGuckian, note to 'Drawing Ballerinas', *Drawing Ballerinas* (Oldcastle: Gallery, 2001), 15.

of *Captain Lavender*: 'I have not painted the war...but I have no doubt that the war is in...these paintings I have done'.[49] Then, from the mid-1990s on, once the pressures of the Troubles began to recede, war figured more overtly in her poems: as she writes in 'Life as a Literary Convict', 'Signs of the still recent war/creep among the people like a plague,/dressed as Phoebus'.[50] McGuckian implicitly contrasts her art with photojournalism, 'printed black on white'; her role is instead to 'wander about in search of the dead', to mourn those killed in the still-lingering war, though the living emerge as an overwhelming presence.[51] 'Everything that ended in gunshots/and news of massacres/and third-class funerals' has threatened to become routinized and domesticated:

> ...the clockwork life of the unchanging
> street, and the uninterrupted houses in rows
> neutralised the lava of war
> to a normal part of winter
> at an enormous cost.[52]

Amid memories of relentless violence and arbitrary killing, McGuckian wants emphatically not to neutralize the lava of war. The unpredictability and difficulty of her poems, their opaque way of engaging the Troubles, preclude any comfortable domestication. The daily printing of photos and stories in newspapers, the nightly airing of radio bulletins, the relentless production of TV news shows, all were thought to bring the Troubles closer, but McGuckian wonders whether this simulacrum instead led people to think they understood a catastrophe beyond rational comprehension. Unsettling and estranging, McGuckian's poetry forbids our feeling that we can consume and normalize the reality of viciously inflicted death, suffering, and loss.

By characterizing journalism as seen from within a sampling of Irish poems, I have been unfair to it. Despite the newspaper's dominance during much of the twentieth century, it may soon elicit from poetry more nostalgia than resistance, given its precariousness as a form. Like Paul Durcan, I confess to buying newspapers every day, and I consume various other radio and Web-based news services. I grew up with a foreign-policy expert for a father, his office stacked high with clippings and microfilm reels of *The New York Times*, *The Washington Post*, the Iranian *Kayhan* and *Ettela'at*, and other newspapers, so there may be something of an oedipal dynamic in my sympathy for poetry's attraction to, and irritation with, the news. That said, when poetry is examined in relation to a genre that largely defined how we understood living history in the twentieth century, differences emerge. Newspapers are quickly read; poems are slow, difficult, and repeatable. Poems luxuriate in their verbal surfaces and sounds, making their linguistic texture inescapably complicit in their co-creation of reality; newspapers may

[49] Medbh McGuckian, *Captain Lavender* (Winston-Salem: Wake Forest University Press, 1995), 99. See Edna Longley, *Poetry and Posterity* (Highgreen, Tarset, Northumberland: Bloodaxe Books, 2000), 309.

[50] McGuckian, *The Soldiers of Year II* (Salem: Wake Forest University Press, 2002), 18.

[51] Ibid.

[52] Ibid.

allow for wordplay in catchy headline puns, but for the most part they aim the bulk of their representational energy beyond their linguistic surfaces to public events. Newswriting is focused on the now; poems are long memoried, built out of vast transnational storehouses of figure, rhythm, and sound. Many twentieth- and twenty-first-century Irish poets other than those I've been able to discuss—including Thomas Kinsella, Patrick Kavanagh, Derek Mahon, Paula Meehan, Eavan Boland, Seamus Deane, Ciaran Carson, Rita Ann Higgins, and Nuala Ní Dhomhnaill—take various approaches to resisting journalism, sometimes parodying it, sometimes rigorously excluding it, sometimes drawing it within. From Yeats and MacNeice, to Longley and Heaney, to Muldoon and McGuckian, Irish poets have taken an ever more oblique approach to public events, tying the civic tongue in ever more knots. By the time Durcan and Muldoon are writing, in contrast to Yeats's high literary artifice, the high/low, literary/mass media divide has eroded. But despite these and other differences, poetry's engagement and struggle with journalism—'an old foul mouth' and 'brazen throat', 'jottings and analyses', and *How It Happened Here*—has been vigorous, perhaps especially on an island where news of public events has been insistent and ubiquitous. News discourse has been Irish poetry's shadow self, a shaping counterforce. It has pushed poetry to define itself in its difference from the newspapers and other forms of media that many poets, for all their misgivings, 'buy every day'.

PART X

ON POETIC FORM

CHAPTER 35

....

THE MODERN IRISH SONNET

....

ALAN GILLIS

I

....

'I'm up to my bollox in sonnets', says Edmund Spenser. Or, at least, Brendan Kennelly's version of Spenser in *Cromwell* (1983).[1] Reading contemporary Irish poetry, one might empathize with him. Kennelly's book is a special case, sprawling, as it does, with some 224 sonnets (Spenser's own sonnet sequence, *Amoretti*, contained 88.). Yet such profligacy is nevertheless symptomatic of the form's proliferation in Ireland, in the latter half of the twentieth century and onwards. Recent Irish poetry is saturated with sonnets. In one respect, this simply mirrors broader trends. Internationally, in the modern age, the sonnet remains the celebrity of verse forms; indeed, its celebrity has grown. Like moths to a bright light, poets, critics, and anthologists can't seem to keep away. And yet, the sonnet's modishness in contemporary Irish poetry is particularly striking, because relatively new.

Reading through the Irish anthologies, even one as commodious as Patrick Crotty's recent *The Penguin Book of Irish Poetry* (2010), one finds few sonnets before W. B. Yeats, and it seems clear that Irish lack of interest changes with Yeats. He didn't write many, but those he did write still reverberate. Others certainly penned sonnets, but after Yeats, Patrick Kavanagh crucially influenced the Irish mushrooming of fourteen-liners. Many of Kavanagh's greatest hits are sonnets. From thence, through the 1960s and 1970s, Irish fourteeners kept ticking over: one would point, in particular, to the work of Michael Hartnett. But with publications such as Seamus Heaney's 'Glanmore Sonnets' in *Field Work* (1979), Kennelly's *Cromwell*, and Richard Murphy's *The Price of Stone* (1985), Irish sonnets become a category. Indeed, by the 2010s, it might be easier to count the Irish poets who do not write them with regularity. Ciaran Carson has been a notable practitioner, while Heaney has continued to write them compellingly. Leontia Flynn, Michael Longley, John

[1] Brendan Kennelly, 'Master', *Cromwell* [1983] (Newcastle: Bloodaxe, 1987), 81.

Montague, Eiléan Ní Chuilleanáin, and David Wheatley also spring instantly to mind (as do many more, but the list would become interminable). And most conspicuously of all, Paul Muldoon has predominated over this phenomenon.

Muldoon's affair with the form has been spectacular. Beginning with his second collection *Mules* (1977), his initial efforts reached a crescendo with *Quoof* (1983). By the end of *Quoof*, climaxing with the forty-nine fourteen-line stanzas of 'The More a Man Has the More a Man Wants', the sonnet seemed to have been innovated, refined, expanded, enriched, coarsened, cheapened, turned inside-out, upside-down, given the runaround, tickled, tormented, and terminally left in tatters. One would have understood if he'd left them there. But instead he has continued to compulsively explore the limits and possibilities of the form. Sonnet sequences such as 'The Bangle: Slight Return' in *Hay* (1998), or the eponymous sequence that opens *Horse Latitudes* (2006), only begin to indicate the playful reach and voluminous persistence of his ongoing fixation with what might best be called, in his hands, the fourteen-line verse unit. As such, one might say that the recent bloom and flourish of the form in Ireland, at least regarding poets emerging since the mid-1980s, has taken place within a kind of poetic ecosphere dominated by the challenging and changing sonnetary accomplishments of Muldoon. Yet poetry, of course, is always written within some such ecology of influence, and to write a sonnet is always to participate in a tradition that traverses the boundaries of nation and history. The sonnet tradition is like a microcosm, an admittedly enormous microcosm, of T. S. Eliot's idea of literary history.[2] No new sonnet has its complete meaning alone. What we know about the sonnet is comprised from all those that we have read: a simultaneous order modified by each new innovation.

II

The rules of the sonnet are coordinates mapping a terrain, rather than the terrain itself: the edges blur, and the land retains an ability to be strange and surprising when we enter it. Sonneteers will know a sonnet when they see one, but they'll write them because drawn to a more porous realm of possibility, not quite sure what they're doing, or what they'll come up with. And within the broad outline of a sonnet lurks a further, copious wealth of formal malleability. However, as everyone knows, we might normally expect a sonnet to consist of fourteen lines, most likely in iambic pentameter, and to be structured around a 'volta' or turn. The word derives from the Italian *sonetto*, a diminutive of *suono*, which means 'sound'. Thus a sonnet is a little sound, or song. As its etymology suggests, the key feature of a sonnet is that it's short. But if brevity were all, a verse form with fewer or shorter lines would surely be more popular. The secret power of the sonnet is that it is short and, at the same time, when you get down to it, not quite. Michael Spiller

---

[2] T. S. Eliot, 'Tradition and the Individual Talent', in *Selected Essays* [1932] (London: Faber, 1951), 13–22.

writes of fourteen lines: 'This seems to be rather more … than one requires for the simple expression of a feeling or state of mind, but rather less than one would like for a full discussion of that feeling or state of mind.'[3] This anomalous duration, which seems to demand immediacy, yet which subtly undermines it, has self-evidently proved enormously felicitous. The sonnet is poised between image and discourse. On the page, as a spatial grid, it looks like it could be held at once in the mind, yet it can't, it needs to be temporally passed through: the diachronic and synchronic are held in delicious flirtation.

In the classic sonnet, the turn divides the poem into an octave and sestet, providing the form with its paradigmatic structure. John Fuller claims it is this 'peculiar imbalance of parts which is the salient characteristic' of the form. Indeed, he argues, this 'unequal relationship between octave and sestet … is of far greater significance than the fact that there are fourteen lines.'[4] Quite why this arrangement has proved so fecund is a matter of interest.[5] But at the very least, we can say that sonnets are frequently comprised of an inherently dynamic structure, where equality gives way to tantalizing asymmetry, where a latter phase needs to make its way in the aftermath of a larger, just-passed phase, under pressure from the ticking clock of that fourteen-line limit.

The 'Introduction' to *The Cambridge Companion to the Sonnet*, in its first sentence, announces: 'A lawyer invented the sonnet.' The lawyer in question was Giacomo da Lentini, said to have hit upon the form in the mid-1230s, at the Sicilian court of Emperor Frederick II.[6] This claim is probably simplified. But nonetheless it seems germane to keep the sonnet's association with legal discourse in mind. The sonnet provided a small arena for showing off rhetorical ingenuity, for setting forth a putative argument and, crucially, clinching it. Neither mirror nor lamp, the sonnet was a manipulation of reason and emotion, designed to make a persuasive case. The octave would set out a premise or problem, and the sestet would seek to resolve it, or at least develop and probe it further. Nowadays, it is common wisdom to play down any idea that sonnets might be inherently syllogistic. The *volta* remains a crucial shift in the development of the poem, but this is less a turn of thought than a shift of pitch or tone, a change of light or atmosphere in the room. Yet we might venture that even the most louche contemporary sonnet will be implicitly affected by the rhetorical heritage of its form, ghosted by a subliminal pressure to at least grapple with something, to break through, or come to terms. In a similar vein, the sonnet frequently remains ghosted by its classic 8/6 structure, even when it takes pains to shape itself otherwise.

Nevertheless, a further key feature of the sonnet has been its capacity for evolution. Its history has been marked by perpetual change and reinvention. Obviously, this has taken a

---

[3] Michael R. G. Spiller, *The Development of the Sonnet: An Introduction* (London: Routledge, 1992), 4.

[4] John Fuller, *The Sonnet* (London: Methuen & Co., 1972), 1–2.

[5] See, especially, John Frederick Nims, *Western Wind: An Introduction to Poetry* [1974] (New York: McGraw-Hill, 1992), 302–7; an argument later taken up by Don Paterson, in the 'Introduction' to his anthology *101 Sonnets: From Shakespeare to Heaney* (London: Faber, 1999), p. xvi.

[6] A. D. Cousins and Peter Howarth, ed. and 'Introduction', *The Cambridge Companion to the Sonnet* (Cambridge: Cambridge University Press, 2011), 1.

distinctive chronological course, from its origins in thirteenth-century Sicily, across Europe via Dante and Petrarch, into England via Thomas Wyatt, where it became a compulsion for English Renaissance poets, who morphed its internal structure to suit their language. Given the success of the English Renaissance sonneteers, we are generally informed that the sonnet's fourteen lines bifurcate into two dominant conventions: the Italian sonnet, which we've already referred to as the 'classic' sonnet, comprised of an octave and sestet (the default 'Petrarchan' model rhyming ABBA ABBA CDE CDE), and the 'English' sonnet, comprised of three quatrains and a couplet (the default 'Shakespearean' model rhyming ABAB CDCD EFEF GG). Yet this dual 'Italian-English' notion of the sonnet often seems unhelpful. It goes without saying, for example, that the English 4-4-4-2 frequently mirrors the essential 8/6 structure of the Italian sonnet, while English-language sonneteers have freely explored and adapted both default models anyway. The 'Italian-English' binary occludes the influence of a host of other less dramatic developments. In this sense, the *convention of adaptation* established by the English Renaissance giants of the form, in twisting an Italian model to suit their own needs, should perhaps be taken as their most crucial endowment. It is this will to adapt that would be taken up by English-language sonneteers of the future, not least in Ireland. Moreover, the protean reality of the English-language sonnet gives the lie to simplistic ideas of a homogenized English sonnet tradition, against which the Irish sonnet must do battle.

III

Yeats's relationship with the sonnet was abiding, ambitious, and probably game-changing, in terms of future development of the form. Yet it was also carefully considered and initially tentative, almost clandestine. 'When You are Old', first published in *The Countess Cathleen and Various Legends and Lyrics* (1892), is based upon a sonnet by Pierre de Ronsard, 'Quand Vous Serez Bien Vielle'. But Yeats's poem consists of twelve lines, formed of three quatrains.[7] In this, it takes the shape of several other early Yeats poems. In some of these, each four lines are moulded into an enveloped ABBA rhyme (found in the quatrains of a Petrarchan sonnet), while others feature interlaced ABAB rhymes (found in the quatrains of a Shakespearian sonnet). Helen Vendler, who has written authoritatively on Yeats's sonnets, argues: 'In Yeats's hands, the sonnet—whether Petrarchan or Shakespearean in its quatrain-rhyme—is for a long time compressed into twelve lines, three quatrains, of a continuously evolving parabolic arc, with a homogeneity of effect in which the end, though it may intellectually... contradict the beginning, formally mirrors it'.[8] Of course, there is a danger here in that, once we start hunting for sonnets, every

---

[7] W. B. Yeats, *The Variorum Edition of the Poems of W.B. Yeats*, ed. Peter Allt and Russell K. Alspach (Basingstoke: Macmillan, 1956), 120–1.

[8] Helen Vendler, *Our Secret Discipline: Yeats and Lyric Form* (Oxford: Oxford University Press, 2007), 155.

box-like poem will begin to look sonnetesque. But nevertheless, Yeats's version of Ronsard does indeed suggest he was studying sonnets as he learnt his trade: learning how to combine and sequence short stanzas, balancing development with symmetry, dynamism with echo. There's no reason to suggest he was fixated with sonnets, but they were clearly on his radar. And his coyness with the form is intriguing.

'The Fascination of What's Difficult', a poem of thirteen lines from *The Green Helmet and Other Poems* (1910), comes so close to a sonnet that we may legitimately say there's now a game of sorts going on. Describing 'our colt' (Pegasus) shivering 'under the lash, strain, sweat and jolt', the poem concludes: 'I swear before the dawn comes round again/ I'll find the stable and pull out the bolt.'[9] Vendler writes: 'By the "missing" fourteenth line (recognizable…only by applying the sonnet template) Yeats intends to represent, I think, the airborne escape out the unbolted door of poet and Pegasus together. If we do not recognize the poem as a sonnet *manqué*, we miss the fine wit of the close, the "whoosh" of non-verbal air after the thirteenth line.'[10]

In a similar vein, one might well suppose that 'The Cold Heaven', from *Responsibilities: Poems and a Play* (1914), is a great sonnet, apart from the fact that it has only twelve lines. It certainly has a striking turn, midway through its ninth line ('Ah! when the ghost begins to quicken').[11] A sonnet structure is basically in place, and the final section seems all the more burstingly urgent for being shorter. The poem is in hexameters, where conventional pentameters might have created two extra lines, giving this the feel of a sonnet that has been squashed. In 'The Cold Heaven', space and time have been squeezed, and the poem's curtailment generates greater torque.

In an important respect, it doesn't matter a whit whether these poems are, or are not, sonnets. Yet the sonnet template clearly plays a role in their final achievement. In point of fact, these poems make use of the form to such an extent that it seems appropriate to say they *are* sonnets. Only pedantry, at odds with true poesis, would insist otherwise. In approximating the form, while playfully resisting it, Yeats expands its domain. In this sense, he joins Gerard Manley Hopkins as a great enabler for subsequent sonneteers. Don Paterson has argued: 'The truth…is that the sonnet is pretty much in the eye of the beholder. The form has diversified to the point where its definitive boundaries are so blurred that it has effectively ceased to exist. All we can say with any certainty is that sonnets often demonstrate certain characteristics.'[12] The Irish sonnet has fully contributed to this blurring of boundaries, and while experimentation with the form is now synonymous with Muldoon and Carson, it should be clear that the game begins with Yeats.

This is certainly the case with Yeats's actual fourteen-liners. Given the careful quatrain-rhyming of his twelve-liners, it is striking that he also gives us sonnets without rhyme in both 'The Harp of Aengus', originally untitled in *The Shadowy Waters* (1900), and the title poem of *In the Seven Woods* (1903). Both bear the hallmarks of early Yeats,

---

⁹ Yeats, *Variorum Poems*, 260.
¹⁰ Vendler, *Our Secret Discipline*, 164.
¹¹ Yeats, *Variorum Poems*, 316.
¹² Paterson, *101 Sonnets*, p. ix.

their lambent sonority creating a dreamlike but bruised atmosphere, incantatory yet evanescent, sensuously replete but unfulfilled. 'The Harp of Aengus', in particular, flaunts with its exotic use of Irish proper names and relatively opaque myth ('Edain came out of Midhir's hill, and lay/Beside young Aengus in his tower of glass').[13] It is a poem of opiate richness and lulling repetitions, 'hushing us', as Yeats would have it, 'with an allur-ing monotony, while it holds us waking by variety, to keep us in that state of perhaps real trance':[14]

> Where time is drowned in odour-laden winds
> And Druid moons, and murmuring of boughs,
> And sleepy boughs, and boughs where apples made
> Of opal and ruby and pale chrysolite
> Awake unsleeping fires...

Forgoing structured quatrains to create a more liquescent whole, and with a relatively subtle turn at line ten, this feels less a conventional sonnet than many of the above-men-tioned twelve-liners. And this is precisely why it has been quietly influential. That the poem is part of Yeats's developing game with sonnet convention is clear from its last line, which is only half a line: 'from that hour he has watched over none/But faithful lovers'. While it would be wrong to claim that anything about this poem is abrupt, as we are lan-guidly led into that final short line we are nonetheless tripped by its unexpected break into silence. Again, Yeats has deftly resisted the form in the act of using it, exploring what effects might be garnered from toying with expectation.

'In the Seven Woods' is notable for its sly flirtation with a rhyme scheme. We have a few full end-rhymes: 'bitterness'/'commonness', 'bees'/'happy'/'Pair-na-lee'.[15] But where the former chimes strongly, the latter is separated between lines two, nine, and fourteen. That the poem's concluding note reaches so far back to find its end-rhyme creates a tinge of inconclusiveness, which would not happen if there were no end-rhymes at all. The poem gives enough to suggest the sonic patterning of a conventional sonnet, while it simultaneously dissipates it. And this coquettishness with a rhyme scheme within the boundaries of the sonnet will, again, be deeply, if quietly, influential. The compressed space of the sonnet sharpens our ear for echoes, and makes the emergence of a pattern more likely, while it also provides room for play. Yeats manipulates this, in 'In the Seven Woods', letting the poem hinge upon more subtle reverberations: 'Woods'/'away'/'awhile'; 'happy'/'heart'/'hangs'. The technique produces a captivatingly hesitant, distended feel, which, in itself, is counterbalanced by the fullness of the poem's pentameters, and by its broad realization of the sonnet's conventional bipartite structure. Then again, regarding this bipartite structure, the turn in 'In the Seven Woods', as with 'The Harp of Aengus', comes at line ten, and if we put these alongside 'The Cold Heaven', we can see that Yeats

---

[13] Yeats, *Variorum Poems*, 219–20.
[14] W. B. Yeats, 'The Symbolism of Poetry' (1900), *Essays and Introductions* (London: Macmillan, 1961), 159.
[15] Yeats, *Variorum Poems*, 198.

was drawn to a shorter second section, a more constricted space, redolent of time running out.

More conventional sonnets appeared, such as 'The Folly of Being Comforted' and 'Never Give all the Heart' in *In the Seven Woods*,[16] and 'At the Abbey Theatre' in *The Green Helmet*. The former two are rhymed into couplets, while 'At the Abbey Theatre' returns to Ronsard, this time translated into a fully fledged Shakespearean sonnet. That said, according to Vendler, 'the poem, paradoxically, does not in fact feel Shakespearean'.[17] Beginning 'Dear Craoibhin Aoibhin' (the pen name of Douglas Hyde), the poem affects a tone of chatty immediacy, but is squarely aimed at the national public and is avowedly, if lightly, in scorn of its audience.[18] In a similar vein, 'In the Seven Woods' has a grumble against the modern age ('new commonness/Upon the throne and crying about the streets'). Maintaining this begrudging public defiance within the sonnet form is 'While I, from that reed-throated whisperer', the epilogue to *Responsibilities*, which ends by predicting a future when the speaker's 'priceless things/Are a post the passing dogs defile'.[19] But what is striking about this sonnet is the manner in which it rails against the baseness of tabloid culture through a complex and contorted, twisting, halting and implosive, yet continuous single sentence. Such syntax manifests a linguistic sophistication that scores its own points against the cheap-shot bluntness and populist antics against which the sonnet gripes. But while it thus rises against the crudifying tide, the sonnet is also inflected with an alluring vulnerability. Shrill and pugnacious, yet subtle and introverted, this defensive-aggressive poem suggests that the sonnet's power of public argument might well be linked to the fact that it simultaneously provides a sheltered space for intricate self-reflection.

'Leda and the Swan' from *The Tower* (1928), which is Yeats's, and probably Ireland's, most internationally renowned sonnet, raises the form's stakes to a global, even cosmological level. Overfamiliarity with the poem should not blind us to the clairvoyant power with which it balances abrupt immediacy with macrocosmic consequence, nor to the upsetting nature of its trajectory. The full freight of layered significance limned by the exactitude of 'Leda and the Swan' is nothing short of stunning. Yeats uses the restricted space of the sonnet to occasion his naturalistic opening *in medias res*, but also to provide the tight frame which enables the zoom-out vertigo triggered by his audacious ellipses and rhetorical questionings. The first eight lines are in the Shakespearean mould, utilizing the way in which sonnets can work in developmental segments, creating extra movement within the basic 8/6. 'Leda and the Swan' shifts with each stanza break, and also, most dramatically, midway through line eleven. Each shift might well be called a turn, and the spaces they create between the lines are like ruptures, fissures rent by the violence, gaps into which the exact meaning of what is passing seems to fall. The poem leaves no ambiguity about its cause-and-effect narrative: 'A shudder in the loins

[16] Ibid., 199–200, 202.
[17] Vendler, *Our Secret Discipline*, 167.
[18] Yeats, *Variorum Poems*, 264–5.
[19] Ibid., 320–1.

engenders there/The broken wall, the burning roof and tower/And Agamemnon dead.'[20] But at the same time, the poem interrogates the nature of this predestined history. After the Shakespearean octet, the poem's sestet is Petrarchan, deftly avoiding the potential pithiness of a concluding rhyming couplet. We traverse a lot of space and time between 'engenders there' in line nine and 'brute blood of the air' in line twelve. And so, this shift to an Italian sestet, its neatness ripped by that break in line eleven, creates a relative open-endedness, a delay within the sonic certitude, which underlines the poem's move from telling to asking. In this way, the sonnet's taut structure makes the poem a forceful icon of inevitability, while that concluding question ('Did she put on his knowledge with his power…?') also creates an implosive momentum, in which the reader is perpetually pulled into the inherent mystery of the reality so vividly prescribed.

One of the many fascinations with Yeats is that he was one of the last poets to get away with such directly grandiose, vatic poetry. In terms of the sonnet, he was soon at it again, in the very different 'Meru', one of the 'Supernatural Songs' from *A Full Moon in March* (1935), with its all-encompassing vision of 'the desolation of reality', where Egypt, Greece, and Rome evaporate in a line, and where, 'before dawn', mankind's 'glory and his monuments are gone': an uncanny achievement within fourteen lines.[21] But Yeats's career, to generalize wildly, straddled a period of transformation—the epistemological puncture of modernity—that made it increasingly difficult for poets to aspire to such Olympian diction and perspective without risking inordinate pomposity. Yeats himself wilfully negotiated this shifting terrain throughout his career, making the authenticity of his more soaring and magniloquent moments all the more remarkable. But generally, the poetic route to the high ground would henceforward be more circuitous and indirect: a rhetorical downgrading aptly charted in the subsequent course of the modern Irish sonnet.

In fact, the crown of Yeats's sonnets, certainly in terms of Irish influence, addresses precisely this shift, grounded as it is in irony and homeliness. 'High Talk', from *Last Poems and Two Plays* (1939), appears ramshackle, slipshod, and self-undermining. In its laconic rambling it feels like a lapsed sonnet. But its long lines, its rickety diction, its faux-naive daftness, and its 'All metaphor' reflexivity serve to generate an enticing charm, the more beguiling for being affectionately pitched. It is written in rhyming couplets, but the length of Yeats's hexameters makes the end-rhymes unobtrusive, seemingly coincidental. One is caught unawares as 'High Talk' raises its stakes towards its end, and takes flight for the wilds—the swan here replaced by a 'barnacle goose'—to conclude with rhetoric that is high indeed: 'I, through the terrible novelty of light, stalk on, stalk on;/Those great sea-horses bare their teeth and laugh at the dawn.'[22] The poem thus takes a glorious turn, but this is occasioned by a gradual amplification, rather than a singular break, so that the poem slyly sidesteps its way towards the majestic. The poem's sonnet form has been crucial to its effect, but this has also been somewhat submersed,

[20] Ibid., 441.
[21] Ibid., 563.
[22] Ibid., 622–3.

camouflaged beneath the raggedy tone. The poem's relation to its sonnet structure acts in a similar manner to each line's speech rhythm in relation to its metre, in that there is a distinct stretch between the actual poem and its underpinning verse form. Sonnet structure is being used, and remains formative, but in certain respects has been rendered subterranean and, moment by moment, the poem has an improvisatory feel. 'High Talk' is the epitome of Yeats's achievement with the sonnet because, in it, he creates the illusion of breaking free, finding a form of freedom through precision with the form.

IV

In various ways, then, Yeats set a precedent for sonnetary innovation. And it would seem incontestable that several Irish poets have risen to the challenge. But immediately, one must also stress that, in Ireland, many sonnets have been penned whose success derives from a canny use of the form's conventions. Any list of best Irish sonnets, for example, would surely have to include Kavanagh's 'Inniskeen Road: July Evening' and 'Epic';[23] and the second and third sonnets from Heaney's sequence 'Clearances';[24] and 'The Skylight' from Heaney's 'Glanmore Revisited'.[25] Any poem using convention as effectively as these should be considered innovative. Each uses variations of the 8/6 template to order and proportion both their sound-stream and train of thought. Something simply clicks in these poems, which might remind us that the form is popular for a reason: because it works, when in the right hands.

Nevertheless, it is not so much the precise replication of the convention, but the adaptive use of it, which has been enabling for Irish poets. There are many Irish sonnets that tinker with the classic template to a slight but telling degree. For example, Michael Hartnett's elegy 'That Actor Kiss' reverses the structure to 6/8, but counterbalances this by ending with a classic Petrarchan sestet rhyme scheme, while its stunning turn is effectively held off until its final two lines. Beginning 'I kissed my father as he lay in bed/in the ward', the poem muses: 'he willed to me his bitterness and thirst', before casually offering its devastating conclusion: 'Later, over a drink, I realised/that was our last kiss and, alas, our first'.[26]

Michael Longley's 'Ceasefire' takes a Shakespearean structure, but breaks its 4/4/4/2 into formally numbered sections. This has a dual effect, giving a sense of ritualistic inevitability to its proceedings, while, at the same time, also implanting an element of struggle and contingency within its development—fragility in the seams of its narrative—implying the unsure nature of its process. First published in *The Irish Times* to coincide

---

[23] Patrick Kavanagh, *Collected Poems*, ed. Antoinette Quinn (London: Penguin, 2004), 15, 184.
[24] Seamus Heaney, *The Haw Lantern* (London: Faber, 1997), 26–7.
[25] Seamus Heaney, *Seeing Things* (London: Faber, 1991), 37.
[26] Michael Hartnett, *Collected Poems* (Oldcastle: Gallery, 2001), 212.

with the announcement of an IRA ceasefire in 1994, the aptness of the poem's hesitant structure to its theme and context is compelling. Further, Longley holds off from a full Shakespearean rhyme scheme. He end-rhymes the second and fourth line of the first two quatrains, but then drops this for the third. Again, this gives a hint of ritual over-written by a greater sense of naturalism. But the entire poem is inexorably bound by the force of its conclusion, as the poem unexpectedly heightens into full Shakespearean mode to finish: 'I get down on my knees and do what must be done/And kiss Achilles' hand, the killer of my son.'[27]

One thing that links all of these sonnets, and what is often underplayed in discussion of the form, is the impact of their ending. From the droll splendour of 'I am king/Of banks and stones and every blooming thing' ('Inniskeen Road') to the emphatic audacity of 'Gods make their own importance' ('Epic'); from the devastation in Hartnett's last two lines to the more solacing but equally affecting denouement to Heaney's third sonnet from 'Clearances' ('her breath in mine, our fluent dipping knives—/never closer the whole rest of our lives'): the effect of each poem pivots on its culmination.

Critiques of conventional poetic forms often target the idea of closure, insisting that the right degree of open-endedness—presumed as the ideal for verse—cannot be achieved within pre-set forms, especially those that rhyme. And, to be sure, even its greatest admirers must be wary of the trite potential of a final rhyming couplet in a sonnet. It hopefully goes without saying that no sonnet *must* be rhymed. For example, Derek Mahon's 'As it Should Be' and Eiléan Ní Chuilleanáin's 'Swineherd' are stunning sonnets without a straight end-rhyme between them.[28] But equally, it would seem bizarrely remiss if rhyme wasn't acknowledged as one of the form's most formidable and pleasurable elements. The rhetorical momentum and the compressed yet spacious, somewhat anomalous, duration of the sonnet make it particularly responsive to the sonic attraction of concluding rhymes.

The problem with a concluding couplet is that it risks summing up and repeating what's already been said, with an enforced succinctness or banal smugness. But alternatively, it can nail the point of the sonnet and provide its *raison d'etre*, so that the rest of the poem melts into the sonorous pitch of its *coup de grace*, as in Kavanagh's 'In the Same Mood': 'This year, O maiden of the dream-vague face,/You'll come to me, a thing of Time and Space.'[29] Taking Kavanagh again, the ending of 'Come Dance with Kitty Stobling' is not just a synopsis—the poem's abiding tone is not fully voiced until its final lines: 'I had a very pleasant journey, thank you sincerely/For giving me my madness back, or nearly.'[30] The DNA of the sonnet subsists in the musicality unleashed by its final refrain. In a similar vein, what is implied by the title of Peter Fallon's 'Country Music' is withheld until the poem's end: 'their muttered Bollocks, Shits and Fuck its,/a cursed yolk bent beneath a

---

[27] Michael Longley, *The Ghost Orchid* (London: Jonathan Cape, 1995), 39.
[28] Derek Mahon, *New Collected Poems* (Oldcastle: Gallery, 2011), 49; Eiléan Ní Chuilleanáin, *Selected Poems* (Oldcastle: Gallery, 2008), 34.
[29] Kavanagh, *Collected Poems*, 25.
[30] Ibid., 221.

pair of splashing buckets.'[31] The sonnet seems, or is made to seem, the perfect vehicle for such wit: the ability to turn sense and sound on a sixpence is encouraged by the confined space of the form, which puts pressure on the poet to exercise precisely such skill.

Richard Murphy's sequence *The Price of Stone* is made up entirely of straight Shakespearean sonnets, and the measure of each poem's success, or otherwise, is bound up entirely with its concluding couplet. The best poems of the sequence are those in which the final two lines are integral to the sonnet's development, providing both its narrative and musical culmination. More precisely, the best poems are those in which the concluding couplet generates a final turn, a sense of surprise, which simultaneously segues into a sense of ritualistic finish, as happens, for example, in 'Beehive Cell': 'Three days she throve me, suckling the child,/Doing all she had to do, the sea going wild.'[32] Such endings provide closure, to be sure. But the fullness of the epiphany opens up a sense that there has been a development, a working through, which sends one back to explore the refractions between beginning and end: think of the denouement of a crime novel which ramifies backwards and challenges the nature of all, in the narrative, that has led up to it. The sonnet's rhetorical energy moves outwards, but musically and semantically it also turns back in on itself.

V

Throughout his career, Patrick Kavanagh both honoured the conventions of the sonnet and sought to stretch them, and he personally rated a group of his late sonnets as the apex of his oeuvre. Having recovered from an operation for lung cancer, he'd spent the first half of 1957 in New York, where he evidently enjoyed, and felt affiliated with, much new American poetry. Written soon after, the sonnets from Kavanagh's so-called 'noo pomes' are lithe with improvisatory energy: fusions of spontaneity and incantation, sensuality and epiphany, throwaway slackness and form-bound certitude.[33] John Goodby writes: 'There is a continual play between the demands of the form and the improvisatory philosophy which attempts to destabilize and push these to breaking-point through absurd rhyme, distended line-length, hyphenated compounding, stretched syntax and so on.'[34]

For all the difficulties of Kavanagh's relationship with Yeats, the 'noo' sonnets, in their rickety freedom and self-reflexive playfulness, sound deeply influenced by Yeats's 'High Talk'. Certainly, one 'noo' sonnet gives a direct echo: 'my rhyme/Cavorting on mile-high

[31] Peter Fallon, *News of the World: Selected and New Poems* (Oldcastle: Gallery, 1998), 30.

[32] Richard Murphy, *Collected Poems* (Oldcastle: Gallery, 2000), 229.

[33] See Alan Gillis, '"Ireland is Small Enough": Louis MacNeice and Patrick Kavanagh', in *A Companion to Irish Literature*, vol. 2, ed. Julia M. Wright (Oxford: Blackwell, 2010), 166.

[34] John Goodby, '"In Blinking Blankness": The Last Poems', in *Patrick Kavanagh*, ed. Stan Smith (Dublin: Irish Academic Press, 2009), 145–6.

stilts'.[35] As with 'High Talk', the way in which each of Kavanagh's 'noo' sonnets relates to conventional form echoes a highly elastic relationship between speech rhythm and underpinning metric pattern. Sonnet form in these poems is a latent presence, against which the lines banter and dance.

With these 'noo pomes', Kavanagh raised the stakes for what we might call the vernacular sonnet, making it an ambitious form fuelled by high technique. The snakingly complex, ductile, and extended syntax of Yeats's 'While I, from that reed-throated whisperer' is in the mix here, also. But this is counterbalanced by a rhetorical playfulness, a self-delighting thrill with speech and sound: 'No, no, no, I know...'.[36] These two tendencies create a directness and candour, which is artfully interwoven with a guileful savvy. That Kavanagh wished to rejuvenate the sonnet, rather than subvert and attack it, is clear from his continued gusto with big endings: 'beautiful, beautiful, beautiful God/Was breathing His love by a cut-away bog' (almost all of Kavanagh is sounded in the near-palindrome of that God/bog rhyme).[37] But he was also keen to use the sonnet's end-directed consonance to sly effect, especially in 'Winter':

> Yes, there were things in that winter arrival that made me
> Feel younger, less of a failure. It was actually earlier
> Than many people thought; there were possibilities
> For love, for South African adventure, for fathering a baby,
> For taking oneself in hand; catching on without a scare me, or
> Taking part in a world war, joining up at the start of hostilities.[38]

With the musical direction pulling against the sense (the music suggests that 'hostilities' are the apex of 'possibilities'), there's a slight delay before the irony hits—it takes a while before one thinks about 'South African adventure'—which makes it all the more stinging. And thus, while the susceptible and comedic tone of Kavanagh's vernacular sonnet is its greatest merit, this can also turn and bite.

Just as Kavanagh, at his best, cannot be simplified or pigeon-holed, the vernacular pastoralism that he rejuvenates, in the sonnet form, takes on many differing aspects. Michael Hartnett was arguably next in line to do something distinctive with the sonnet in Ireland. A captivating mix of off-kilter angularity and deep consonance, his sonnets are pervasively enigmatic, even while steeped in conventional tropes. One untitled sonnet begins: 'I saw magic on a green country road—/that old woman, a bag of sticks her load'. It ends:

> Some incantation from her canyoned mouth,
> Irish, English, blew frost along the ground,
> and even though the wind was from the south
> the ash-leaves froze without an ash-leaf sound.[39]

---

[35] Kavanagh, 'Come Dance with Kitty Stobling', *Collected Poems*, 221.
[36] Ibid.
[37] 'The One', ibid., 229.
[38] Ibid., 232.
[39] Hartnett, *Collected Poems*, 87.

The familiarity and strangeness of the sonnet perplexingly haunts the mind. What sort of magic is this? Like Kavanagh in 'Winter', Hartnett uses the sound of the sonnet to devilish effect: that this poem's music creates a tone of broad positivity makes its freeze all the more troubling, as Hartnett counterpoints ingrained harmoniousness against inscrutable irony.

Seamus Heaney, meanwhile, laid down a marker, in terms of sonnets, with 'The Forge' and 'Requiem for the Croppies' in *Door into the Dark* (1969),[40] then memorably returned to the form in *North* (1975), particularly in the vividly crisp and easeful ekphrasis of 'The Seed Cutters';[41] but also in the stark and awful self-awareness of 'Strange Fruit';[42] and in the wounded, ritualistic allegory of 'Act of Union': 'No treaty/I foresee will salve completely your tracked/And stretchmarked body, the big pain/That leaves you raw, like opened ground, again.'[43] Thus, for Heaney, the sonnet is made a vehicle for both the beautiful and the sublime. 'The Seed Cutters' exemplifies the clarity and translucence he brings to the form, while, in 'Strange Fruit' and 'Act of Union', the sonnet becomes an atavistic sounding ground, a pastoral nightmare of psycho-sexual-linguistic torment. Here, Heaney's full-bodied plenitude becomes a startled and violated ripeness.

Clearly the sonnet was in Heaney's thoughts when, during the writing of *North*, he spoke of a need to 'take the English lyric and make it eat stuff that it has never eaten before'. This 'stuff' was to be the 'messy and, it would seem, incomprehensible obsessions of the North'.[44] The lyric was to chew on a dyspeptic mouthful indeed. Yet Heaney has spent his career feeding the lyric stuff that has been inordinately good for it, not least in his sonnets. There is, of course, a great deal of continuity throughout his oeuvre, and nowhere is this better exemplified than in his sonnets. Thus, the 'Glanmore Sonnets' sequence from *Field Work* (1979)[45] gives a healing echo back to 'Act of Union': 'Vowels ploughed into other, opened ground,/Each verse returning like the plough turned round.'[46] Throughout this sequence, the sonnet form is again pitched with a striking psycho-sexual-linguistic intensity, but this time infused with spring-seasoned affirmation. Heaney uses the sonnet's compression to press his self-reflective meditations on lyric-sensual plenty into synaesthetic fermentation, in which prosody becomes a sixth sense, conflated with landscape, just as mind and body fuse in word-music: 'Words entering almost the sense of touch';[47] 'It was all crepuscular and iambic'; 'a rustling and twig-combing breeze/Refreshes and relents. Is cadences.'[48] The putrid ripeness of 'Strange Fruit' is not cleansed away. One sonnet begins: 'Outside the kitchen window a

---

[40] Seamus Heaney, *Door into the Dark* (London: Faber, 1969), 7, 12.
[41] Seamus Heaney, from 'Two Poems in Dedication for Mary Heaney', *North* (London: Faber, 1975), p. xi.
[42] Heaney, *North*, 32.
[43] Ibid., 43–4.
[44] Quoted in Neil Corcoran, *The Poetry of Seamus Heaney: A Critical Study* (London: Faber, 1998), 53.
[45] Seamus Heaney, 'Glanmore Sonnets', *Field Work* (London: Faber, 1979), 33–42.
[46] Ibid., 34.
[47] Ibid.
[48] Ibid., 35.

black rat/Sways on the briar like infected fruit'.[49] Negation remains in the order of things, 'a deep no sound', but is now channelled into a positive verdancy, 'Where small buds shoot and flourish in the hush'.[50]

As a self-conscious return to pure lyric resourcefulness, the sequence is comparable to Heaney's earlier 'New Song' poems from *Wintering Out* (1972).[51] Yet it is interesting to see what difference the sonnet form makes. While the 'New Song' poems were deftly sibylline, supple, and quirky, the 'Glanmore Sonnets' are underpinned with a more normative, reassuring steadiness and heft. Nevertheless, it is the way in which the sequence's 'noo' style characteristics (swift wit and quick shifts, invigorated diction, robust but breaking rhythms) jostle and spring against the grid of their sonnet structure that animates their song. Self-aware that such a sequence might be construed as attempted escapism from the Troubles, Heaney uses sonnet tradition to grant himself a broader vista. Fusing the iconicity of 'The Seed Cutters' with the fervour of a more disjunctive immediacy, the sequence is an apotheosis of the Irish sonnet's regeneration of a distinctly modern and vernacular pastoralism. Using the sonnet form's rootedness in tradition to counterbalance the contingencies, inanities, and chaos of the contemporary, these sonnets are anything but an escape: more an exploration of how the lyric might find a renewed means of adequately pushing back against historical abjection.

As already indicated, the impact and grace of some of Heaney's later sonnets from 'Clearances' and 'Glanmore Revisited' make them key achievements in the Irish poetic canon. But yet another striking achievement with the form announced itself in *District and Circle* (2006), a book to which sonnets provide the backbone: particular highlights being 'A Shiver', 'Polish Sleepers', and 'Out of Shot'.[52] 'A Shiver' is about a hammer blow. The first section deals with anticipation of the swing ('Its gathered force like a long-nursed rage/About to be let fly'). Then the poem suddenly shifts to the aftermath ('does it do you good/To have known it in your bones…?'). The way in which the violence of the hit is elided, at the sonnet's turn, suggests the instantaneousness of such a blow. The poem's elision creates an odd vacancy in the pith of itself, an emptiness which uncannily judders. In the last lines, we are told the blow was 'so unanswerably landed/The staked earth quailed and shivered in the handle'. The effect practically sends shivers back up the frame of the sonnet. As such, the poem seems to consist of pure air, yet also generates a palpable solidity, both of which are left shaken. In such sonnets, Heaney has continued to conjure a probing openness, and set off disquieting vibrations within and through the surety of a fourteen-line structure. The known somehow swallows the unknown in sonnets that seek to grasp the impenetrable.

[49] Ibid., 41.

[50] Ibid., 33, 37.

[51] Examples include 'Anahorish', 'Toome', 'Broagh', and 'A New Song'. Seamus Heaney, *Wintering Out* (London: Faber, 1972), 6, 16, 17, 23.

[52] Seamus Heaney, *District and Circle* (London: Faber, 2006), 5, 6, 15.

VI

For a poet, the sonnet's brevity and prescribed shape is enabling. It won't supply an opening but, once started, it will imply the finishing line. The form provides a measure of time, or a tract of space, which can be held in the mind when writing, supplying a sense of where the rise or fall, the twists and turns, might feasibly occur. Banal it may be, but this practicality is a major reason for the sonnet's evergreen durability. Of course, there's a stigma attached to the idea of writing to pre-set forms, deciding what the duration and shape of a poem will be before composition. The argument is that this will lead to empty artifice, the bland fulfilment of automatic pre-packaging, to MacSonnets. The ideal is, rather, that a form such as a sonnet will suggest itself organically, emerging by necessity or serendipity out of amorphous first-drafted lines. A poem's initial sounding will contain within its nucleus a natural bent towards the form it will eventually fulfil. Crucially, in this ideal, the incipient poem has to find its own way. Its eventual shape must be discovered through active process, through taking wrong turns, banging its head off brick walls. Ideally, as it reaches completion, a sonnet should be somewhat surprised, even unaware, that it is a sonnet. And so, the argument runs, mere versification will produce a clone, while poetry will produce the individualized character of an artwork that bears something like the authenticity of experience within itself.

This possibly explains why there are so many bad sonnets, yet it doesn't quite explain why there are so many good ones. Technique and inspiration don't cancel one another out. The organic metaphor for composition occludes the way in which poets actively use the pre-set structure of verse forms. On the one hand, the template gives the conscious mind something to fixate upon, which frees the unconscious to emerge as part of the process. But the template and the material then begin to counterbalance one another and fuse. The poet mostly attempts to naturalize the grid by imprinting upon it the signature of his or her voice. But a check on subjectivity is also keyed back into the poet's register, which is forced to partake of something objective and given, as voice and tone internalize a broad cultural shaping force, the ley lines of a tradition.

The sonnet form, in its abstraction, offers a perfect grid for charting existentialist anxiety. It is all too brief, yet we are compelled to make something of it. At the same time, the form might be taken as a synecdoche for, or microcosm of, a broad symbolic realm of tradition, the stuff of history and ideology, so that, in the sonnet, subjectivity confronts the field of force within and against which it abides. One thing that cannot be avoided, in the writing of a sonnet, is mediation with the pre-given. And arguably, a somewhat one-dimensional view of this has led to some critics and poets equating verse forms, such as the sonnet, uniformly with conservatism. The writing of a sonnet, it is implied, bespeaks a desire for continuity, for a community of tradition, which can be discerned as ideologically suspect. Yet it seems equally viable to suggest that the sonnet's inherent complicity with tradition can, in fact, make it most apt for an ideologically and metaphysically searching form of poesis, free from easy illusions of individuality and progress. If the sonnet always implies a negotiation with tradition, such a thing is rarely straightforward in work that is worthwhile. But even considering the simplified pejoratives commonly used against the form (that it bespeaks a desire for community and continuity): at the time of writing, amid the debris left by neo-liberal capitalism, not least in Ireland, such things may well soon be 'radical'. In any case, when writing a sonnet, the MacSonnet will always be a pervasive threat, as will inane complicity with moribund ideological forms. But the point is that, in poetry, such threats are inescapable anyway, and the sonnet insists that the poet must confront them.

VII

On one level, the huge proliferation of sonnets in Ireland suggests a cultural and aesthetic confidence, a heightening of sophistication and brio. The feats of Paul Muldoon are exemplary in this regard. Through his inexhaustible skill with the sonnet, almost every possible permutation of the form has seemingly been explored. Here is plenty indeed. And if we set his work beside the hallucinatory sonnet-feats of Ciaran Carson, the rambunctiousness of Kennelly's *Cromwell*, the beautiful but audacious twists and turns of Longley's sonnets in and since *The Ghost Orchid* (1995), the ambitious dexterity of David Wheatley, the more directly emotive but equally playful skill of Leontia Flynn (the list could continue): it would surely be churlish not to celebrate the contemporary Irish sonnet.

The Irish vernacularization of the form has certainly continued apace. Heaney's desire to 'take the English lyric and make it eat stuff that it has never eaten before' would soon be well met by others, reaching a kind of climax, or nadir, in 1983, in Kennelly's *Cromwell*: 'The Devil fucked Oliver Cromwell/In a cottage at the edge of Birnam Wood./He fucked his body first, then he fucked his soul/.../Nine months later, gas poured from Oliver's hole';[53] and in Muldoon's *Quoof*: 'you will lie on the bed/of your own entrails,//to be fist-fucked all night/by blewits, or by chanterelles'.[54] While the potential subversiveness of such registers being voiced in a sonnet quickly evaporates, the historical moment of this dragging of the form into the street and sewer, to create a brashly nightmarish fetidness, should nonetheless be acknowledged.

Beyond this broadening of diction, the sonnet has also been made to transgress boundaries of genre: from the po-mo historical-horror cartoonisms of Kennelly ('William of Orange was always worried/About the state of the Gross National Product./"Unless the G.N.P. improves" he said/To a seminar in Listowel, "We're fucked!"');[55] to the noir-soaked paranoia, twitching with rapt but suspect detail, of Carson ('For one word never came across as just itself, but you/would put it over as

[53] Kennelly, 'Gas', *Cromwell*, 100.
[54] Paul Muldoon, 'Blewits', *Quoof* (London: Faber, 1983), 36.
[55] Kennelly, 'Plans', *Cromwell*, 83.

insinuating something else');[56] to the speeding pulp amoralities of Muldoon's 'The More a Man Has' ('Once they collect his smithereens/he doesn't quite add up').[57] That these poets could make the sonnet have fun with the depravities of history was something novel, welcome, and perplexing indeed.

While experimentation with the sonnet's prosodic form has been par for the course since Yeats, the compulsive versatility with which Carson and Muldoon have pursued such enterprise has made this an overt theme of the work. Carson's nine-line poems in *The Irish for No* (1987) and *Belfast Confetti* (1989), with their 5/4 structure, unmistakably feel like sonnets. When he did give us actual fourteeners (called, as if to help us, 'Sonnet' and 'Four Sonnets') in *First Language* (1993), each effectively consisted of fourteen individual poems, a new one in every line ('Prisoners on the roof are dismantling the roof in a desperate bid for freedom').[58] In the same book, he translated Baudelaire's sonnet 'Correspondances' into four lengthy rhymed couplets.[59] The form was thus deeply implicated in his work of this time, even while Carson didn't produce a single conventional sonnet. In turn, this made his eventual publication of two books of immediately recognizable sonnets—*The Alexandrine Plan* (1998), a collection of translations of Baudelaire, Mallarmé, and Rimbaud; and *The Twelfth of Never* (1998), a book of seventy-eight original sonnets in the same rhyme scheme and alexandrine line—seem a natural progression. It was also probably natural that, in *The Twelfth of Never*, all naturalism had been thrown out of the window. The sonnet form was later returned to, but transformed again, in *For All We Know* (2008), in which fourteen-liners, and sometimes twenty-eight-liners, are stretched over a distinctive fourteen-syllable line, which spools around twilit moments of *déjà vu* and departure, in a haunting mirrored sequence of diversions and divulgence. Soon after, Carson then subjected the sonnet form to a startling act of de-creation, presenting poems of seven short-lined couplets that look like precarious ladders on the page, down the slippery syntax of which the reader slides into a night realm of the imponderable: in *On the Night Watch* (2009), entirely comprised of fourteen liners, and *Until Before After* (2010), in which every third poem is a fourteener. Thus the sonnet, with Carson, is never left alone, nor is it ever familiar or settled.

In particular, in *The Twelfth of Never*, the sonnet is purposively felt as an arbitrary grid. Carson reverses the conventional emphasis of the compositional dialectic (whereby the poet mostly seeks to naturalize the verse form), and instead invites the form's pre-given architecture to predominate: a style that was already under exploration in the rhymed couplets of *Opera Et Cetera* (1996), and various poems in *First Language*. Discussing this method, he once wrote: 'I now remember how rhyme was a powerful springboard from which to launch oneself into the unknown. For, each time that I sat down ... I had no idea what I would write; nor would I have any clue about the

---

[56] Ciaran Carson, 'Second Time Round', *For All We Know* (Oldcastle: Gallery, 2008), 15.
[57] Muldoon, 'The More a Man Has the More a Man Wants', *Quoof*, 53.
[58] Ciaran Carson, 'Four Sonnets', *First Language* (Oldcastle: Gallery, 1993), 26.
[59] Ibid., 39.

outcome. But the accident of rhyme, once I hit on one, would provide a narrative thread, and by about the third couplet, one would have some idea as to its direction.'[60] Letting form arbitrate so readily, Carson's sonnets become an investigation of how subjectivity and the imagination are themselves gridded by unseen but systemic assignations. The effect is liberating, to the extent that arbitrariness rips open the confines of the sonnet and the self, making them confront the odd and unexpected. But at the same time, the grid of the sonnet takes on a controlling aspect and becomes a kind of prison of the limitless.

Meanwhile, Muldoon's inability to leave the form alone has been something else again. He has given us blunt sonnets, tender sonnets, weird sonnets, funny sonnets, nonsense sonnets, scorching sonnets, flippant sonnets, gorgeous sonnets, disturbing sonnets, mad sonnets, maddening sonnets, outraged sonnets, outrageous sonnets, and anti-sonnets. Most tease, some swoon, and many hiccup. He is perpetually breaking down then building back up, shuffling and reconfiguring the internal structure of the form, yet a number of persistent traits are worth recounting: his *ambition* with rhyme; his intermixing of rhyme and varied line length for rhythmic and rhetorical effect; his play with ellipses against continuities; his lexical and tonal resourcefulness; his conflation of idiomatic directness with complex and seemingly bottomless subtleties; his variety of subject matter and, within this variety, his indefatigable persistence with recurrent tropes and themes; his increasing obsession with repetition, and with endings that return back to openings.

Overall, there is a great big hole at the heart of Muldoon's sonnets. Frequently overt in their cryptic quality, he tends to shape the form around an abiding enigma. One of his most frequently discussed sonnets begins: 'Why Brownlee left, and where he went,/Is a mystery even now'; while another, from the same collection, ends: 'Whatever it is, it leaves me in the dark.'[61] We have seen how the sonnet mostly effects a dual movement, simultaneously outwards and inwards; and how, in poems such as Yeats's 'Leda and the Swan' or Heaney's 'A Shiver', the form can be designed to lure us into the elliptic inscrutability of its internal abysm. Essentially, Muldoon makes such a ploy his chief business, through a bewildering multiplicity of ingenious technique.

Meanwhile, his multiplicity has led to perpetual play with the sonnet. In one respect, his constant stretching of convention is familiar to other Irish poets. Two of his best sonnets, for example, consist of fifteen lines ('Something Else' and 'Aftermath').[62] Yet while every Irish sonneteer may be essentially up to the same thing, the sheer comprehensiveness with which Muldoon repeatedly returns to shape-shift the form, always the same yet different, gives to his sonneteering a somewhat epic intensity. If the sonnet is a synecdoche for a cultural tradition, Muldoon's deft skill in perpetually warping the form,

---

[60] Ciaran Carson, discussing *Opera Et Cetera* (Oldcastle: Gallery, 1996), in *Don't Ask Me What I Mean: Poets in their Own Words*, ed. Clare Brown and Don Paterson (London: Picador, 2003), 25.

[61] Paul Muldoon, 'Why Brownlee Left' and 'October 1950', *Why Brownlee Left* (London: Faber, 1980), 22, 9.

[62] Paul Muldoon, 'Something Else', *Meeting the British* (London: Faber, 1987), 33; 'Aftermath', *Hay* (London: Faber, 1998), 93.

while fitting it, builds into a deeply sustained examination of pre-given structures and identitarian grids. His technical facility and playfulness with the form becomes the crucial means by which his work thematically explores, as Clair Wills puts it, a 'struggle between arbitrariness and the authenticity of the traditional community (or indeed personal identity)'.[63] In turn, it should be stressed that such work, certainly up to *Meeting the British* (1987), written within the Troubles' stasis of malevolence, had a hugely liberating, electrifying effect. But at the same time, especially through the lens of his later sonnets, Muldoon's obsessive discombobulating of the form ultimately suggests that something about the sonnet is irreparably damaged. If the sonnet implies a cultural tradition, Muldoon is exploring a moment of damage: his sonnets are reconnoitres of an as-yet uncharted site of psychic and cultural infliction.

Much of Muldoon's sonneteering stretches the identity of the form beyond recognition. A fourteen-line verse unit forms the backbone of a long poem such as '7 Middagh Street', for example, but there seems to be nothing sonnetesque about these units, other than that they consist of fourteen lines. Yet, given his experimentation elsewhere, it becomes impossible, or at least meaningless, to attempt to draw a line of distinction between the sonnet and the mere fourteen-line unit. In which case, his relentless perpetual return to fourteen lines takes on a highly arbitrary aspect, similar to that observable in Carson's sequences. As, again and again, we find ourselves within a fourteen-line structure, in Muldoon's work, we increasingly feel bound within an ineluctable grid of historical and psychic circumscription, in the grip of some unspoken numerical superstructure, and his oeuvre begins to take on a vast imprint of the ever-same.

Treated as an arbitrary grid, the sonnet can clearly be taken in many differing directions. In Carson's *For All We Know*, the long fourteen-syllable line has a cumulative effect, and the lines eventually act like tunnels of blue-note musicality, boring into the subconscious, where memory and invention meet in a kind of radical nostalgia. By contrast, Muldoon, in the twenty-first century, has been reluctant to let the grid of the sonnet settle into any form of ambient consistency. As with Carson, rhyme is the hinge, for Muldoon, for connections: a mechanism for departures and returns, which can create a serendipitous state of possibility, but also inevitability. But at least since *Hay* (1998), the sense of inevitability and enclosure has markedly been intensified in Muldoon's work, mostly because of his increasingly manic compulsion with repetition. His poems, especially his sonnets, have become more and more drawn to repeated words, phrases, lines, refrains, stanzas, and identical rhymes. As one poem from *Maggot* (2010) not atypically puts it: 'Only now do we see…How spasm and lull/are mirrored by lull and spasm'.[64] *Horse Latitudes* (2006) and *Maggot*, in particular, are dominated by corona-like effects where the end of a poem returns to its beginning. This latter technique, of course, was

[63] Clair Wills, *Improprieties: Politics and Sexuality in Northern Irish Poetry* (Oxford: Clarendon Press, 1993), 197.

[64] Paul Muldoon, 'Lines for the Centenary of the Birth of Samuel Beckett', *Maggot* (London: Faber, 2010), 59.

central to Eliot's *Four Quartets*, and persisted throughout Yeats's oeuvre. For those two, however, it had a theologically informed apocalyptic trajectory. Muldoon, by contrast, seems highly sceptical that the trajectory has any positive capacity: it simply persists. And as his endings fold into their beginnings with ever-greater regularity, his sonnets become steadily more marked by limitation and stasis. If one can discern, in the classic sonnet's move from octet to sestet, a form of dialectic movement, or process of development, in Muldoon's increasingly prevalent tail-chasing circular structures, this mirage of development is steadily more mocked.

Muldoon's more recent sonnets remain spellbinding, complex, devious, and enormously pleasurable. But something has also, undeniably, altered since the 1980s. His work with the form has become troubling in a new way, maddening to a differing effect. Whatever else might be said of them, Muldoon has purposively made his newer sonnets vehicles for the mimesis of boredom. The enigmatic hole in the heart, the secret missing centre, over and around which the sonnets proceed, is variously associated in his work with pain, betrayal, bereavement, death, and disempowerment; yet these are increasingly pitched together as a great vacuity, a pervasive emptiness, over which the sonnets chatter and repeat. In this manner, Muldoon is arguably making the sonnet confront our contemporary epoch with consummate archness, and his most recent sonnets, crammed with stuff and emptiness, make him the poet laureate of anxiety and loss of agency.

Discussing the sonnet form recently, Muldoon claimed: 'It's a form... that is predisposed to us and, frankly, to the spectacular limitations of our consciousness. The sonnet, like most of us, can just about deal with one or two thoughts at a time.... It's precisely because of what might be construed as its dullness that the sonnet has managed to be so durable.'[65] While we might read this with a raised eyebrow, especially given Muldoon's own kaleidoscopic achievements with the form, his insistence, here, on taking the sonnet down a peg or two is notable. At the very least, it makes one wary of reaching for grandiose and generalized conclusions about the form in Ireland.

Differing modulations of the Irish sonnet might ultimately signify struggles and transformations within the national cultural bloc, or psychic formation, yet any interpretation along such lines is always likely to be suspect. Sonnets remain the same, over time, yet their broad historical horizon and up-close nuances keep changing. While the rise and rise of the Irish sonnet would seem to signify a broadly positive cultural narrative, it might equally be the case, especially if we look through the frame of recent Muldoon sonnets, that it is more ironically symptomatic of a massive cultural anxiety. But then, one would have to say that such a scenario is entirely normal. The sonnet arose out of European turmoil, and has flourished through perpetual crises and stasis. It would be unreasonable to expect the form, in Ireland, not to give voice to the fault lines, local and global, upon which cultural life is grounded. Yet at the same time, we should respect

---

[65] Paul Muldoon, Meg Tyler, Jeff Hilson, and Peter Howarth, 'Contemporary Poets and the Sonnet', in *The Cambridge Companion to the Sonnet*, ed. A. D. Cousins and Peter Howarth (Cambridge: Cambridge University Press, 2011), 10.

how the sonnet has quietly and subtly reconnected Irish poetic culture to international literary culture, especially Britain's, without any element of cultural cringe or overweening cultural exceptionalism. Indeed, the Irish sonnet has brought riches. In concluding her argument about Yeats's sonnets, Helen Vendler imagines Yeats explaining to English readers that, in Ireland, the sonnet was a site for experiment because it was not, as in England, a site of cultural memory.[66] Well, it's both now.

[66] Vendler, *Our Secret Discipline*, 181.

CHAPTER 36

....

IRISH ELEGY AFTER YEATS

....

STEPHEN REGAN

I

....

If modern elegy finds renewal and redirection in the poetry of W. B. Yeats, it does so in a burst of creative energy that also threatens it with extinction. Within fifty years, between the end of the 1880s and the end of the 1930s, Yeats effectively transforms the genre, from a worn-out pastoral lament to an apocalyptic sublime in which traditional elegiac conventions appear redundant. As early as 1912, there is a chilling intensity in Yeats's vision of the afterlife: 'Suddenly I saw the cold and rook-delighting heaven/That seemed as though ice burned and was but the more ice'.[1] Already, the poetry seems to have moved into a realm far beyond conventional elegiac ritual and consolation. As Jahan Ramazani has noted in his exemplary study of Yeats as elegist, death both 'elicits abundant imaginings and marks the limit of the imagination'. What he finds most striking in Yeats's elegiac verse is 'the effort of lyric after lyric to summon up heroic energy in the face of death'.[2] 'In Memory of Major Robert Gregory' achieves its lasting significance in the tradition of elegy, not least because it combines a monumental tribute with a closing confession of near capitulation and collapse: 'a thought/Of that late death took all my heart for speech'.[3] The daring double elegy, 'In Memory of Eva Gore-Booth and Con Markiewicz', decorously flirts with the ritualistic imagery of light and shade and seasonal change, before consuming all human artefacts, including time itself, in its final incandescent blaze. For later elegists, there is an awe-inspiring challenge in the extraordinary scope and intensity of Yeats's elegies. At the same time, as Edna Longley has argued, Yeats enables a new kind of elegiac writing by powerfully

---

[1] W. B. Yeats, 'The Cold Heaven', *The Variorum Edition of the Poems of W. B. Yeats*, ed. Peter Allt and Russell K. Alspach (Basingstoke: Macmillan, 1956), 316.

[2] Jahan Ramazani, *Yeats and the Poetry of Death: Elegy, Self-Elegy, and the Sublime* (New Haven and London: Yale University Press, 1990), 2–3.

[3] Yeats, *Variorum Poems*, 328.

combining Irish and British traditions, redirecting the patriotic, commemorative mode of Thomas Davis and Thomas Moore towards a more interrogative, ambivalent style (as in 'Easter 1916'), and also (despite his declared opposition to 'war poetry') accommodating the language and style of First World War poets such as Wilfred Owen and Charles Sorley, who in their short careers wrote intensely about violence and death in relation to private and public commemoration.[4]

It is perhaps not surprising, then, that Irish elegy in the later twentieth century initially demonstrates the powerful presence of Yeats by veering away from his influence. Denis Devlin's romantic elegy, 'The Tomb of Michael Collins', opens with a glance back at John Keats's sonnet 'On First Looking into Chapman's Homer' and its thrilling account of the imagination as it cuts across space and time ('Much have I travelled in the realms of gold').[5] The insistently repetitive, self-echoing syntax, however, draws on Yeats's elegy for Robert Gregory: 'Much I remember of the death of men,/But his I most remember, most of all'.[6] The mythologizing impulse that prominently parades the Four Green Fields, Wolfe Tone, and Red Hugh O'Donnell also recalls Yeats, but the plangent apostrophizing owes more to Walt Whitman: 'And sad, O sad, that glen with one thin stream/He met his death in'. The poem views the death of Michael Collins from the poet's childhood perspective ('I was twelve years old that time'), but it adopts this innocent viewpoint partly to avoid a more incisive political vision, evasively attributing the assassination to 'murderous angels'. Seamus Deane dismisses the poem as 'a sad failure', but it illustrates his general point about the difficulty that poets had reconnecting poetry and politics after the Civil War.[7] Even so, there is a moving testimony in the poem's closing remembrance of the day of Collins's death and in its thoughts turning to Whitman and another civil war: 'Walking to Vespers in my Jesuit school,/The sky was come and gone; "O Captain, my Captain!"/Walt Whitman was the lesson that afternoon'.

Quiet, stoical acceptance, rather than a thunderous rage against the dying of the light, is a hallmark in the work of the poet who said 'let grief be a fallen leaf at the dawning of the day'.[8] The pastoral was too much a way of life for Patrick Kavanagh to step back and utilize its literary conventions in formal commemorative verse, but he did write an elegy notable for its moving simplicity after the death of his mother, Bridget Kavanagh, on 10 November 1945. 'In Memory of My Mother' foregoes the typical motifs and rituals associated with the elegy, and establishes local talk of cattle and oats in place of any more elaborate pastoral setting. Even so, if elegy, as Seamus Heaney puts it, 'makes the dead walk again in a beautiful, freed way', then Kavanagh's poem conforms exactly to its

---

[4] Edna Longley, 'Northern Ireland: Commemoration, Elegy, Forgetting', in *History and Memory in Modern Ireland*, ed. Ian McBride (Cambridge: Cambridge University Press, 2001), 241–2.

[5] John Keats, *The Complete Poems*, ed. John Barnard (Harmondsworth: Penguin, 1980), 72.

[6] Denis Devlin, *Collected Poems of Denis Devlin*, ed. J. C. C. Mays (Dublin: Dedalus, 1989), 283.

[7] Seamus Deane, 'Irish Poetry and Irish Nationalism', in *Two Decades of Irish Writing*, ed. Douglas Dunn (Cheadle: Carcanet, 1975), 11.

[8] Patrick Kavanagh, 'Raglan Road', *Collected Poems*, ed. Antoinette Quinn (London: Allen Lane, 2004), 130.

requirements.[9] The poem performs its work of mourning in images aptly chosen from the realm of farmyard labour, 'piling up the ricks against the moonlight' on a 'harvest evening' that carries happy associations of completion and fulfilment, and it finds eternity not in any theological certainty of resurrection but in the lasting memory of the mother's smile. Fittingly, she smiles up at the workers on the rick, rather than smiling down from heaven. For all its apparent artlessness, the elegy is skilfully constructed, with the closing word 'eternally' isolated by a dash but rhyming resoundingly with the monosyllabic 'we', while also bringing with it a lingering echo of the earlier 'happily'.[10]

It might be assumed that Louis MacNeice, whose poetry is so pervasively concerned with flux and transience, would have little recourse to the formal elegy. Significantly, it is W. H. Auden, not MacNeice, who writes the great elegy 'In Memory of W. B. Yeats' and so lays claim to a tradition of poems in honour of dead poets, while installing himself as successor. What MacNeice writes instead is 'Elegy for Minor Poets', which seems so obviously an ironic displacement of the labour of writing the expected elegiac tribute to Yeats, both in its unconvincing encomium, 'I would praise these in company with the Great', and in its liberal disavowal of Yeatsian 'scorn' (recalling the address to Irish poets in 'Under Ben Bulben' to 'Scorn the sort now growing up').[11] MacNeice does, however, write a tribute to Yeats in his critical study, *The Poetry of W. B. Yeats* (1941), the first full-length study of Yeats to be produced after his death, though one peculiarly unforthcoming in its treatment of Yeats's elegies, noting in a very brief reference to his 'nostalgic poem', 'In Memory of Eva Gore-Booth and Con Markiewicz', only that it 'reveals his feeling that the recent Irish revolutionaries had prostituted their own personalities'.[12]

Two deaths in 1942 compelled MacNeice to think about the forms that memorial verse might take in the mid-twentieth century. His father's death is recorded with a dignified distance in Section VII of 'The Kingdom'. The poem contents itself with the refrain from the pulpit, 'All is well', while sceptically noting the cracking voice of the preacher. Here, it is T. S. Eliot, rather than Yeats, who appears to provide the appropriate rhetorical address: 'All shall be well, and/All manner of thing shall be well'.[13] Although the memorial tribute to Bishop MacNeice assumes a modest place within the larger commemoration of the 'Kingdom of individuals', it plays inventively with the elegiac trope of one who is 'dead in daffodil time'. The familiar image of the flower's trumpet is extended into a fitting musical celebration, with the 'yellow fanfares in the trench' echoing the phrase 'All is well', before 'the spades get busy'.[14] 'The Casualty (*in memoriam G. H. S.*)' was written for MacNeice's schoolfriend, Graham Shephard, who drowned at sea while serving with Atlantic convoys in the Royal Navy. MacNeice resists the temptation to glorify Shephard through association with other notable deaths at sea in Milton's 'Lycidas' and Tennyson's 'In Memoriam', suggesting that what remains of their friendship is 'articulate silence'. The

---

[9] Seamus Heaney, interviewed by Melvyn Bragg for ITV, *The South Bank Show*, October 1991.
[10] Kavanagh, *Collected Poems*, 129.
[11] Louis MacNeice, *Collected Poems*, ed. Peter McDonald (London: Faber, 2007), 273.
[12] Louis MacNeice, *The Poetry of W. B. Yeats*, 2nd ed. [1941] (London: Faber, 1967), 135.
[13] T. S. Eliot, 'Little Gidding', *Collected Poems 1909–1962* (New York: Harcourt, Brace & World, 1963), 206.
[14] MacNeice, *Collected Poems*, 247–8.

poem is resistant to cliché—the 'faded star' and the 'misty West'—taking its elegiac motifs instead from popular cultural forms, including music ('So now the concert is over, the seats vacated') and photography. The flux of life, the assured sense of 'things being various', is suddenly ended for Shephard in a striking image of fixity and finality that cleverly combines the camera and the kaleidoscope: 'the shutter fell/Congealing the kaleidoscope at Now'.[15] MacNeice's memories are snapshots, but even so there is an ironic nod towards the elegiac convention of the mourned friend as a literary accomplice: 'Here you are, taking Proust aboard your doomed corvette'. MacNeice also adopts the enquiring second-person address familiar in elegies from 'Lycidas' onwards, though he conveniently bypasses any question of Christian Resurrection by invoking Platonic Form instead: 'O did you/Make one last integration, find a Form/Grow out of formlessness when the Atlantic hid you?'[16]

Shephard is given a literary resurrection as Tom Varney, whose ship is hit by an enemy torpedo in the experimental radio play, *He Had a Date* (1944). The play touchingly compresses the cradle sleep of the child and the deathly sleep of the man, but its most impressive achievement is in articulating the voices of the past in the new broadcasting media of the time, aptly providing what MacNeice describes as 'a private news-reel of episodes from one man's life'.[17] Shephard also reappears as Gavin, 'due to meet his death by water', in the stately terza rima of the sadly neglected *Autumn Sequel* (1954). The distance of a decade, added to the dramatic casting of the book, allows MacNeice to be more candid and intimate than before: 'His sister called and came upstairs and stood/Quietly and said quietly "We have lost/Gavin"'.[18] Canto XVIII of *Autumn Sequel* is MacNeice's 'Lament for the Makers', prompted by news of the death in New York of Dylan Thomas in 1953. This time, the opportunity to invoke 'The measured tread/Of Lycidas' is not missed, but the most affecting portrait of Thomas is one that catches him in his natural element: 'Debonair,/He leant against the bar till his cigarette/Became one stream of ash sustained in air'.[19] As well as demonstrating to sceptics how versatile his terza rima verse can be, MacNeice skilfully combines the deathly ash of the Book of Common Prayer with Shelley's 'all-sustaining air'.[20]

Canto XX recalls Thomas's funeral in Wales (more of 'the misty west'), with MacNeice wearing the same shoes that he wore for the re-burial of Yeats at Drumcliffe churchyard in 1948. There is comic relief here, but also a tacit admission of how hard it was to fill the shoes of Ireland's great poet: 'Drumcliff was wet, those new shoes cramped my feet/At Yeats's funeral'. Later, at Thomas's funeral, MacNeice observes the ritual procession, the

---

[15] Ibid., 237.

[16] Ibid., 240.

[17] Louis MacNeice, *Selected Plays of Louis MacNeice*, ed. Alan Heuser and Peter McDonald (Oxford: Clarendon, 1993), 75.

[18] MacNeice, *Collected Poems*, 378–9.

[19] Ibid., 453.

[20] Percy Bysshe Shelley, *The Major Works*, ed. Zachary Leader and Michael O'Neill (Oxford: Oxford University Press, 2003), 277. For a sustained and illuminating study of this Romantic image and its legacy, see Michael O'Neill, *The All-Sustaining Air: Romantic Legacies and Renewals in British, American, and Irish Poetry since 1900* (Oxford: Oxford University Press, 2007).

ceremonial flowers, and the poet's laurel wreath, but pulls away from 'The Resurrection and the Life'. What consolation he finds is in the legacy and survival of poetry: 'what green thoughts this acre still can yield'. The pastoral imagery of Andrew Marvell's 'The Garden' and Yeats's late poem, 'An Acre of Grass', is blended with an echo of Rupert Brooke's sonnet, 'The Soldier': 'What he took/From this small corner of Wales survives in what he gave.'[21]

II

An impassioned belief in the survival of poetry animates Derek Mahon's eloquent tribute to his Northern Irish predecessor, 'In Carrowdore Churchyard (at the grave of Louis MacNeice)'.[22] The finely pitched combination of sombre declaration and ironic subversion skilfully emulates MacNeice's style, though Hugh Haughton perceptively notes an echo of Auden's elegy, 'In Memory of W. B. Yeats': 'All we may ask of you we have; the rest/Is not for publication, will not be heard.'[23] There are strategically placed references to MacNeice's poems, 'Brother Fire' ('the bombed-out town' and 'The all-clear' alluding to the London Blitz) and 'The Casualty' ('the blind poet' recalling the earlier poem's 'blind minstrel...like Raftery or Homer'), but Mahon's vivid imagery and striking use of paradox most obviously recall MacNeice's 'Snow'. A verbal extravagance and excitement reminiscent of early MacNeice fittingly revitalizes elegiac convention in the shaking of headstones, the igniting of flowers, the bursting of rough winds, the burning of hedges, and the rinsing of choked mud. Mahon's deft, ironic wordplay establishes a sophisticated, urbane distance from death, converting grim realities into poetic tropes, as with the play on 'tense' relieving the 'tension' of *rigor mortis*, and the clichés 'down to the ground' and 'hard as nails' reinforcing the undertone of graveyard humour. The punning is so prevalent and so neatly turned as to warrant Stan Smith's description of 'a playful paronomasia'.[24] Such a display is unusual in modern poetry, and even more unusual in elegy, but its function is to celebrate MacNeice's achievements as a poet, as well as mourning his passing in September 1963. The poem also announces the arrival of his prodigiously gifted successor, with the blackbird of Irish Gaelic poetry and the phrase from Euripides suiting Mahon as well as MacNeice.

Although a strongly elegiac mood pervades much of Mahon's work, it includes very few formal elegies, either public or private, and several poems adopt a decidedly

---

[21] MacNeice, *Collected Poems*, 461, 463.

[22] Derek Mahon, *Collected Poems* (Oldcastle: Gallery, 1999), 17. In Mahon's *New Collected Poems* (Oldcastle: Gallery, 2011), 19, the poem is retitled 'Carrowdore' and the second stanza has been rewritten.

[23] See Hugh Haughton, *The Poetry of Derek Mahon* (Oxford: Oxford University Press, 2007), 38.

[24] Stan Smith, 'The Twilight of the Cities: Derek Mahon's Dark Cinema', in *The Poetry of Derek Mahon*, ed. Elmer Kennedy-Andrews (Gerrards Cross: Colin Smythe, 2002), 250.

anti-elegiac outlook. 'A Refusal to Mourn' recalls Dylan Thomas, but the poem draws resolutely on Mahon's own astringent metaphysics. A recurring preoccupation with imagined afterlives informs his refusal to mourn the death of his shipyard worker grandfather. His premonition of a time when the old man's 'name be mud once again' is both an affectionate acknowledgement of his roguish reputation and an unsentimental acceptance of an eventual return to the earth. Mahon's work covers such an expansive historical terrain, from Neanderthal Man to 'the next ice age', that present losses are diminished and dispersed. Even so, there is a notion of survival and a mystical sense of continuity in the poem. The 'secret bred in the bone' endures, 'Persisting for the unborn/ Like a claw-print in concrete/After the bird has flown.'[25] The delicacy of the image is held out here against the overwhelming threat of destruction and displacement, its freshness already appearing like a fossil in the concrete of the industrial world.

Often, the disconcerting perspective of Mahon's poems is that of an afterlife already achieved, so that the strange limbo-like suspension renders the need for elegy obsolete. The opening of 'Going Home (for Douglas Dunn)'—'Why we died/Remains a mystery'—is one of many startling instances of a transmission of voices from 'the other side'.[26] The speculation clearly echoes MacNeice's elegy for Shephard—'How/You died remains conjecture'—but it nevertheless conveys both intrigue and surprise, all the more effective when we realize that the home in the title is Hull and the river to be crossed is Andrew Marvell's unromantic Humber. Often, too, Mahon's irony is so light and deft that it transcends the thought of dying: 'There will be dying, there will be dying,/ but there is no need to go into that.' 'Everything Is Going To Be All Right' finds a moment of epiphany in 'a riot of sunlight' and unfolds with such lyrical ease that we might be persuaded to read it without irony.[27] When Mahon does write a personal elegy, as with 'A Bangor Requiem' (after the death of his mother in October 1996), there is both irony ('Oh, I can love you now that you're dead and gone') and a shocking directness. The poem is, by its own admission, 'a cold epitaph', and its concern is not so much with grieving as with documenting the 'junk chinoiserie and coy pastoral scenes' of the mother's Bangor bungalow, her own 'idea of the beautiful'.[28] Bruce Stewart understandably claims that the poem can 'hardly be called an elegy at all', though Mahon does make a concession to elegiac notions of persistence and to an ideal of the afterlife in the 'blue skies of the republic' as he travels south: 'all artifice stripped away, we give you back to nature/ but something of you, perhaps the incurable ache/of art, goes with me....'[29] Hugh Haughton notes the echo of Yeats's 'artifice of eternity' from 'Sailing to Byzantium', but

---

[25] Mahon, *Collected Poems*, 88.

[26] 'Going Home (for Douglas Dunn)' first appeared in *The Snow Party* (London: Oxford University Press, 1975), 6–7. It was reprinted in *Poems 1962–78* (Oxford: Oxford University Press, 1979), but has not been included in any subsequent version of Mahon's selected or collected poems.

[27] Mahon, *Collected Poems*, 113.

[28] Mahon, 'A Bangor Requiem', *Collected Poems*, 260–1. *The Yellow Book*, the sequence of twenty poems in which it appears (XVIII), is retitled *Decadence* in *New Collected Poems*.

[29] Bruce Stewart, '"Solving Ambiguity": The Secular Mysticism of Derek Mahon', in *The Poetry of Derek Mahon*, ed. Kennedy-Andrews, 77.

these lines also draw on Yeats's dialectical vision in 'The Tower': 'only an aching heart/ Conceives a changeless work of art'.[30]

A casual reading of the poems might suggest that Mahon's ironic recoil from dying— 'there is no need to go into that'—is a fitting summary of how he viewed the role of the poet in relation to the political violence that erupted in Northern Ireland at the outset of his career. In fact, some of his most powerful poems, 'The Last of the Fire Kings', 'The Snow Party', and 'A Disused Shed in Co. Wexford', are those which both adopt an elevated perspective and simultaneously expose their own privileged ideals to a searing critique. For all the intense, self-lacerating ironies that these poems generate, they nonetheless carry a strong undertow of political lament that looks out from the war-torn North to the Irish Civil War, to the death camps of the Second World War, and to Vietnam. Mahon has steadfastly resisted the pressure to write a poetry of appeasement, even while he acutely registers political oppression and voices the cries of its victims: 'Let the god not abandon us/Who have come so far in darkness and in pain'.[31]

III

The poetry of Michael Longley and Seamus Heaney has sought a way of aligning traditional elegiac convention with the overwhelming loss and grief perpetuated by political violence, though the process has been one of difficult and sensitive accommodation, and of careful adjustment in terms of style and technique. The scale of that task has led them, in both their poetry and their critical essays, to consider the problematic role of the war poets, especially Wilfred Owen, Edward Thomas, Francis Ledwidge, and Keith Douglas, as well as the example of Yeats. Longley's 'In Memoriam', published in his first major collection, *No Continuing City* (1969), is very much the foundational elegy in his work. His intimate mourning for his father, one of the many 'broken soldiers' of the First World War, both validates his role as elegist ('Let yours/And other heartbreaks play into my hands') and establishes him as poetic undertaker and restorer of dignity.[32] The initial formality—'These words I write in memory'—is reminiscent of Yeats's declaration in 'Easter 1916', 'I write it out in a verse'—but the invocation of 'pity' and the drawing-down of blinds (recalling the closing line of 'Anthem for Doomed Youth') suggest that Wilfred Owen is also a strong presence in the poem. There are traces of Longley's education in the Classics, both in the allusions to Odysseus and Telemachus in the father-son relationship and in the closing reference to women (followers of Persephone) going 'Underground'. The poet's own vulnerable existence, his own near-annihilation in his father's wounding, is skilfully caught in the sudden chronological collapse in stanza three, and in the purposeful rhyme of 'funeral urn' and 'waiting my turn'. The

---

[30] Haughton, *Poetry of Derek Mahon*, 305.
[31] Mahon, 'A Disused Shed in Co. Wexford', *Collected Poems*, 90.
[32] Michael Longley, *Collected Poems* (London: Jonathan Cape, 2006), 30.

conventional Christian resurrection, accompanied by angels, is displaced by the reappearance of the chorus girls, doubling up as the summoned muses of the poet, while the respectful drawing-down of blinds gives way to the lifting of skirts. At the same time, the poem happily entertains the fantasy of the father's blinding entry into heaven: 'On the verge of light and happy legend/They lift their skirts like blinds across your eyes.'[33]

Three notable elegies appeared in *An Exploded View* (1973), all of them probably written in the spring and summer of 1972, as the political conflict in the North intensified. 'Kindertotenlieder', alluding to Gustav Mahler's song cycle, bluntly asserts that 'there can be no songs for dead children'. There is certainly little room for lyric grace in the brief, unrhymed form of the poem, but the children nevertheless impose themselves on the poet's imagination amidst the unmistakeable imagery of war: 'The crazy circle of explosions,/The splintering tangent of the ricochet'.[34] There is a strong sense of paternal care and responsibility in the poet's acknowledgement of his 'unrestricted tenants'. The domestic metaphor is one of compassionate, imaginative accommodation, but it hints disconcertingly at a crowding in of the dead (unrestricted in number as well as access), just as the seemingly innocent images of 'fingerprints' and 'teethmarks' take on an unsettling forensic exactness.

The plural title 'Wounds' embraces the poet's soldier father and the victims of random sectarian killings, while also acknowledging the hurt felt by those who are left in grief. Memories of the First World War, transmitted from father to son, enter the poem as intimate 'pictures' and 'secrets' in a way that both legitimates the role of the poet as elegist and connects the earlier conflict with the political violence of the 1970s. The grotesque 'landscape of dead buttocks' in 1914–18 finds a parallel in the undignified image of three dead teenage soldiers in the present conflict, with 'bellies full of/Bullets and Irish beer, their flies undone'.[35] At the same time, the military glories of the First World War are undermined by the father's painful admission, 'I am dying for King and Country, slowly.' Going 'over the top' at the Somme in 1916 is contrasted with the killing of a bus conductor whose civilian uniform, like the television and the supper dishes of his home, reminds us of his civic role and his social ordinariness. The apologetic words, 'Sorry Missus,' attributed to 'the shivering boy' who carries out the shooting, are shockingly inadequate, but as an intuition of what he might have said they perhaps carry all too clearly the need for empathy and understanding.

Longley's unshakeable conviction that poetry should honour the dead, even when consolation is hard to find, gives shape and authority to his elegiac triptych, 'Wreaths', published in *The Echo Gate* in 1979. In circumstances where traditional theological reassurances are likely to be met with scepticism, the creative gesture in offering the poem as a wreath of words is, itself, one of the few resources of hope and comfort. Longley's 'Wreaths' are tributes to those victims of sectarian assassination in ordinary, everyday

---

[33] Ibid., 31. Fran Brearton offers a detailed and extensive account of the poem's mythopoeic elements, including the 'skirt-lifting' image in *Reading Michael Longley* (Tarset: Bloodaxe, 2006), 39.

[34] Longley, *Collected Poems*, 61.

[35] Ibid., 62.

occupations: 'The Civil Servant', 'The Greengrocer', 'The Linen Workers'. The poems balance an appalling but respectful truth to the violent events they witness with a determination to fill the void with whatever grace or beauty can still be found in lyric verse. Peter Sacks's excellent point about the 'astonishingly poised and urbane conversation' that flows through Auden's elegies applies equally well to Longley's poems: his voice 'consoles as much by its manner as by what it says'.[36]

As in 'Wounds', the three parts of 'Wreaths' show the violent incursion of sectarian politics into the everyday domestic rhythms of people's lives: 'He was preparing an Ulster fry for breakfast/when someone walked in the kitchen and shot him'.[37] The loss of life entails the loss of all that life's accomplishments and skills: 'The books he had read, the music he could play'. The poem conveys the indignity of death in a grotesque inversion of the customary welcome bestowed on a guest of honour: 'They rolled him up like a red carpet'. It also leaves a question mark hanging over the consolation that art might offer when faced with the terrible derangement of grief. The depiction of psychic disturbance is all the more powerful for its calm and restrained delivery: 'Later his widow took a hammer and chisel/And removed the black keys from his piano'. In 'The Greengrocer' the ethic of service is cruelly violated, and there is a harsh irony in the image of 'holly wreaths for Christmas' on sale in the dead man's shop. The poem answers that violation with a rueful reflection on the Christmas spirit of giving, with seasonal offerings occupying the space traditionally reserved for elegiac ritual and consolation: 'Dates and chestnuts and tangerines'.[38]

'The Linen Workers' opens with a shockingly surrealist image of 'Christ's teeth', abruptly subverting traditional elegiac codes of resurrection and redemption. The bleak and ferocious picture of contemporary Christianity conveyed by the 'exposed canines' is only mildly relieved by the comic but similarly grotesque 'deadly grin' in the false teeth worn by the poet's father.[39] The seemingly bizarre preoccupation with teeth is a psychic pretext, a preparation for imaginatively confronting the massacre of ten linen workers, among whose dispersed possessions on the road where they were killed is 'a set of dentures'. The sacrificial nature of their deaths is implied in the imagery of bread and wine, but the suggestions of the sacramental and the miraculous are displaced by the poet's more immediate concern with the restoration of dignity and composure. To mourn these dead is to open up old wounds, to bury his father 'once again', but before he can do so he must observe the necessary rituals which are both part of a mythologized rite of passage and part of an enduring search for recompense.

Jahan Ramazani has noted how often in elegiac writing, 'the poet becomes a kind of "funeral director"', and how, in certain poems, 'one can discern an uneasy mediation

[36] Peter Sacks, *The English Elegy: Studies in the Genre from Spenser to Yeats* (Baltimore and London: Johns Hopkins University Press, 1985), 304.
[37] Longley, *Collected Poems*, 118.
[38] Ibid.
[39] Ibid., 119.

and conflict between the voices of poet and undertaker'.[40] The point is well made in rela-
tion to the 'parodically hortatory tone' that Wallace Stevens is adept at managing (in
'The Emperor of Ice-Cream', for example); but Michael Longley, though not without
exuberance and opulence, is less likely to glorify the emperor of ice cream than to mourn
the death of the ice-cream man. What makes 'The Ice-cream Man' such a memorable
and imposing elegy is that its extravagant naming of ice-cream flavours and wild flowers
is accompanied by an acute recognition of its own forlorn endeavour to fill the void with
words. A wreath of verse in the form of an elegiac catalogue, the poem is also a moving,
intimate conversation between a parent and a child.[41] The loss of innocence that accom-
panies the child's experience of death is captured in the movement from the easy facility
of the opening lines—'Rum and raisin, vanilla, butter-scotch, walnut, peach:/You would
rhyme off the flavours'—to the tense and more insistent naming of the flowers of the
Burren.[42] The poem both tenders its pastoral emblems of consolation and peers into the
awful emptiness of utter inconsolability. The record of 'flowers seen in one day' is a cele-
bration of nature's profusion, but it might also be read as a lamentation of transience and
decay.

   Longley's love of nature, his acute responsiveness to birdcall and botany, makes him at
once an unlikely war poet and an exemplary elegist. In this respect, the poet he most
resembles is Edward Thomas. The tribute he offers in 'Edward Thomas's Poem' might
well provide his own epitaph: 'The nature poet turned into a war poet as if/He could cure
death with the rub of a dock leaf.'[43] If Thomas has been a reassuring and nurturing pres-
ence throughout Longley's career, so too has the Mayo townland of Carrigskeewaun,
where many of his birds and flowers dwell. In the many elegies written for friends and
fellow poets since the IRA Ceasefire in August 1994, Longley has continued to turn to
the West of Ireland in search of 'a language not to be betrayed'.[44] Recalling the death by
fire of Oisín Ferran in a Dublin flat, 'The Pleiades' turns to the sea for its elegiac images
of quenching and washing, but its imaginative swell keeps pushing westwards to the
Atlantic and upwards to the stars: 'But when I knew that he was dead I found this mem-
ory/For Oisín of stars clustered on Inishbofin or Inishturk'.[45] This sparkling elegy plays
out a familiar response in Longley's work—a generous giving and sharing of the pre-
cious sights and sounds of the still turning world.

   Snow Water (2004) finds fitting emblems for the poet's increasing tendency to elegize
himself amidst the loss of friends in illness and old age. The lapwing and the marsh mar-
igolds of Carrigskeewaun are striking elegiac motifs, as well as living examples of an

---

[40] Jahan Ramazani, *Poetry of Mourning: The Modern Elegy from Hardy to Heaney* (Chicago and
London: University of Chicago Press, 1994), 17.

[41] Fran Brearton records that the poem was written for Longley's youngest daughter after John
Larmour, an off-duty RUC officer who was looking after his brother's ice-cream shop, was shot and
killed by the IRA in October 1988. See *Reading Michael Longley*, 182.

[42] Longley, *Collected Poems*, 192.

[43] Ibid., 307.

[44] Edward Thomas, 'I never saw that land before', *The Annotated Collected Poems*, ed. Edna Longley
(Tarset: Bloodaxe, 2008), 120.

[45] Longley, *Collected Poems*, 231.

intricate and evolving ecology. What immortality might be found in art is measured against the durability of nature, the pitch of poetry against the poignancy of birdsong, as in the finely wrought elegy for Michael Hartnett, 'An October Sun': 'Michael, your/ Poems endure the downpour like the skylark's/Chilly hallelujah, the robin's autumn song.'[46] The heron is an apt elegiac bird for the 'tall and skinny' poet, Kenneth Koch, and 'Heron' gives him due ascendancy as he takes to the air and flies through a poetic locale that encompasses both Carrigskeewaun and Central Park, New York. The imagined negligence, bewilderment, and guilt are all recognizable elegiac tendencies, skilfully registered here in the insistent repetition and in the invocation of Psalm 22: 'I didn't know./I didn't know that you were "poured out like water/And all your bones were out of joint". I didn't know.'[47]

The arrival of swans at Carrigskeewaun sets in train a meditation on the poet's own mortality that clearly acknowledges Yeats but does so in a characteristically relaxed and conversational style: 'Oh, what day is it/This October? And how many of them are there?'[48] The old burial mound at nearby Templedoomore is a salient topographical feature in Longley's poetic landscape. What looks like a poem about place, 'Above Dooaghtry', shifts into self-elegy with the imploring and unexpected line: 'At Carrigskeewaun, bury my ashes.'[49] The closing poem in the collection, 'Leaves', asks stoically but self-consciously, 'Is this my final phase?'[50] Man and work are blended in the poem's consuming imagery of 'foliage on fire', but thought and imagination are fully alive in the brilliance of 'the westering sun's red declension'. The swans carry their elegiac import into A Hundred Doors (2011), in which Longley's inventions of farewell are more pronounced and more intense than ever. The title poem, alluding to the Byzantine church of Our Lady of a Hundred Doors on the Greek island of Paros, recalls an over-zealous sacristan who blows out newly lit candles, and who 'Doesn't care as he shortens my lives'.[51] There is a strong sense of poetic proprietorship here, evident as well in the earlier recital of family names as 'a kind of prayer or poem', but the poet's own slow-burning existence is implicated in the sacristan's affront. More dramatically and more explicitly, 'The Lifeboat' imagines for the poet 'an ideal death' at the end of the bar in Charlie Gaffney's pub, only to find that the dead man is the landlord, leaving him bereft and helpless: 'The pub might as well be empty forever now.'[52] The toy lifeboat that he launches from the charity boxes 'with an old penny' is a whimsical, ineffective emblem, a call for rescue directed towards his struggling, abandoned self.

Longley's treasured images of birdlife, icy water, and dawn light coalesce in the radiant elegy, 'The Holly Bush', for the poet Dorothy Molloy: 'The poets you loved are your consort now./Golden plovers—a hundred or more—turn/And give back dawn-light

[46] Ibid., 292.
[47] Ibid., 323.
[48] 'Arrival', ibid., 288.
[49] Ibid., 289.
[50] Ibid., 324.
[51] Michael Longley, A Hundred Doors (London: Jonathan Cape, 2011), 15.
[52] Ibid., 20.

from their undersides.'[53] There is nothing strained in this consolatory offering, since the elementary imagery traditionally associated with mourning and renewal arises naturally from a familiar and closely observed landscape: 'The edge of the dunes wears a fiery fringe.' Longley's credentials as a love poet and his tender forms of address give his elegies a poignant intimacy: 'When I've left Carrigskeewaun for the last time,/I hope you discover something I've overlooked.'[54] The greenshank's 'estuarial fluting' is the haunting call of a poet who has already imagined his own leave-taking. It sounds like a signing-off, but a lyric fragment tucked away at the end of the book, almost out of sight, reasserts the presence of a poet 'waiting to/cross over/at the end/of my days'.

IV

Growing up on a farm in County Derry was an experience that allowed Seamus Heaney to test the conventions of pastoral poetry against contemporary actualities at an early age. Even so, his elegies have continued to be closely associated with the land. The poems in *Death of a Naturalist* (1966) lament the loss of childhood innocence and trace the awakening of adolescent consciousness through an awed fascination with rotting flax, decaying blackberries, and frogspawn turning into tadpoles. Along with this maturing view of natural processes comes a deepening awareness of the land as a depository of history. The poems of youthful self-elegizing have a feigned naivety, but in their formal craftsmanship reveal the hand of a poet who already knows how to 'dig' with a 'pen' ('Digging'). Two elegies in particular establish Heaney's distinctive handling of the genre and demonstrate his capacity to write movingly about both intimate, personal loss and shared, communal grief. 'Mid-Term Break' is an elegy for Heaney's younger brother, Christopher, who died in a road accident at the age of four in 1953. The painful break in the family is signalled formally in the isolation of the closing line, which is, itself, from the penultimate line 'knocked...clear', but which nevertheless retains connection through its near rhyme, 'A four foot box, a foot for every year.'[55] The deflection of grief into the measurement of things is reminiscent of Wordsworth's description of a thorn tree 'Not higher than a two year's child', but the poem also suggests the early influence of Robert Lowell's *Life Studies* (1959), and its candid, yet precise, articulation of grief.[56] 'At a Potato Digging' shows modern-day agricultural workers in a 'Processional stooping', as if in ritual mourning for the victims of the Famine in the 1840s. There is a ghostly superimposition of the past on the present, with the workers resembling the 'higgledy skeletons' of the previous century and feeling their fingers 'go dead in the cold'.[57] Heaney's

---

[53] Ibid., 22.

[54] 'Greenshank', ibid., 48.

[55] Seamus Heaney, *Opened Ground: Selected Poems 1966–1996* (New York: Farrar, Straus and Giroux, 1998), 11.

[56] Stephen Gill, ed., *William Wordsworth* (Oxford: Oxford University Press, 1984), 59.

[57] Seamus Heaney, *Death of a Naturalist* (London: Faber, 1966), 31–2.

entry into the darkness of the past as a way of illuminating the present anticipates the method of the later bog poems.

A similar exploration of Irish historical experience in relation to present needs and aspirations occurs in 'Requiem for the Croppies' (published in *Door into the Dark* in 1969), this time aided by the formal requirements of the sonnet form. Written in 1966 to commemorate the fiftieth anniversary of the 1916 Rising, the poem also looks back to 1798 and the ideals of the United Ireland Movement. 'Requiem for the Croppies' is ambitious and resourceful in the way that it experiments with voice, marrying the sonnet to the popular folk idiom of ballads like 'The Croppy Boy', and quietly articulating the redemptive ideals of Irish political elegy: 'They buried us without shroud or coffin/And in August the barley grew up out of the grave.'[58] That the voice appears to come from the grave or from the ghost of a fallen rebel makes this early elegy all the more remarkable. As Heaney himself notes, 'Requiem for the Croppies' was to become, unexpectedly, a poem that linked the violent deaths of 1798 and 1916 with the escalating sectarian conflict in the North in the late 1960s, just as *Door into the Dark* was to prove an ominous title for his second volume of poems.[59]

In the bog poems of *Wintering Out* (1972) and *North* (1975), Heaney explores the troubling parallel between sectarian killings in his own North and the ritual sacrifices to the earth goddess in early Ice Age settlements across other parts of northern Europe. Jahan Ramazani has made a bold attempt to read these startling poems as elegies which reactivate the powerful mythic substructure of the pastoral tradition, including 'fertility cults in which ritual death assures rebirth'. At the same time, he concedes that poems like 'Bog Queen' and 'Punishment' appear to offer 'a bleak parody of elegiac resurrection', recoiling from tradition 'in the shock and immediacy of the renewed violence'.[60] Where the poems in *Wintering Out* and *North* most obviously keep a pact with elegiac tradition, however, is in the continuing need for assuaging rituals: 'Now as news comes in/of each neighbourly murder/we pine for ceremony,/customary rhythms'.[61]

In *Field Work* (1979), Heaney adopts a more formal elegiac mode, commemorating the deaths of fellow artists, friends, and relatives, among them victims of sectarian violence. 'The Strand at Lough Beg', written in memory of Heaney's second cousin, Colum McCartney, draws inspiration from Dante's *Purgatorio*, but also from medieval Irish legend. Very few modern elegies observe the conventions of the genre so trustingly, while also reworking those conventions to fit the needs of the present. The waters of Lough Beg and the 'soft treeline of yew' establish a pastoral setting embellished with marigolds and bulrushes.[62] Colum McCartney inhabits the landscape not as the traditional shepherd, but as a peaceful farmhand. The three parts of the elegy work to recover and rehabilitate the dead man within the landscape that he knew, first presenting his death with shocking immediacy, then recalling his youth and his rural surroundings, finally moving

---

[58] Heaney, *Opened Ground*, 23.

[59] Seamus Heaney, *Preoccupations: Selected Prose 1968–1978* (London: Faber, 1980), 56.

[60] Ramazani, *Poetry of Mourning*, 339, 337.

[61] Heaney, 'Funeral Rites', *Opened Ground*, 96.

[62] Heaney, *Opened Ground*, 145.

towards a tentative resolution and resurrection. The loose pentameter and sporadic rhymes support the poem's narrative progression without any sense of strain or artificiality.

Heaney shows immense tact and authority in balancing a depiction of violent death with a consolatory suggestion of redemption. The ghostly reappearance of the dead man, as Lough Beg 'half shines under the haze', is skilfully arranged through a subtle shift in tense and voice: 'I turn because the sweeping of your feet /Has stopped behind me, to find you on your knees/With blood and roadside muck in your hair and eyes'.[63] The imagined ritual washing of the body and the plaiting of rushes stays true to elegiac convention, while the green vestments signify both spiritual and political renewal, recalling the United Ireland ballad, 'The Wearing of the Green', and its memorable quotation at the end of Yeats's 'Easter 1916'. In a startling re-encounter with his dead cousin in *Station Island* (1984), the poet is rebuked for having drawn 'the lovely blinds of the *Purgatorio*' and 'saccharined' his death 'with morning dew'. This is not so much a change of heart about the earlier memorial as an instance of Heaney's continuing quarrel with himself about the role and adequacy of poetry in a time of violence.[64]

'Casualty' was written in the aftermath of the Bloody Sunday killings of thirteen civilians by the British Army in Derry in 1972, though the subject of the elegy is Louis O'Neill (not named in the poem), a fisherman who was 'blown to bits' in the bombing of a public house on the day after the funerals.[65] The poem enters into a sustained dialogue with Yeats, both in refusing 'Easter 1916' as a model of political elegy and in choosing for its meditation an actual fisherman, in contrast to the ideal figure who is Yeats's audience in 'The Fisherman'. It also employs the brisk elegiac trimeter that Yeats adopts for these two poems. The 'turned back' of the fisherman, the solitary independence that has led to his death after ignoring a curfew, suggests to Heaney another, more creative, 'turning back' in the form of poetic revision and reflection. The labour of fishing involves a rhythm, 'the line lifted', and a stirring of the imagination, 'turning/Indolent fathoms white'. If there is a disavowal of Yeatsian rhetoric, there is also a strong indebtedness to his relentless self-questioning, powerfully conveyed by Heaney in the ghostly return of the alert and obstinate fisherman: 'Dawn-sniffing revenant,/Plodder through midnight rain,/Question me again.'[66]

Heaney's distinguished achievements as an elegist include the candid, intimate poems of mourning for his mother and father in *The Haw Lantern* (1987) and *Seeing Things*

[63] Ibid., 146.

[64] For a more extensive discussion of elegiac conventions in 'The Strand at Lough Beg', see Stephen Regan, 'Seamus Heaney and the Modern Irish Elegy', in *Seamus Heaney: Poet, Critic, Translator*, ed. A. B. Crowder and J. Hall (Basingstoke: Palgrave Macmillan, 2007), 9–25.

[65] At the time Heaney wrote the poem, it was thought that the bombing of the Imperial Bar in Stewartstown on 3 February 1972 was the work of the IRA, carried out because the pub had continued to serve customers during the curfew following Bloody Sunday. It is now believed that the attack was carried out by loyalists.

[66] Heaney, *Opened Ground*, 147–50. Edna Longley notes that 'It is a bold move of Heaney's...to step away from memorial commonalities, even represent their constricting as well as bracing force'. See 'Northern Ireland: Commemoration, Elegy, Forgetting', 246.

(1991), and also the deeply felt tributes for fellow poets, Zbigniew Herbert, Ted Hughes, Joseph Brodsky, and Czesław Miłosz, in *Electric Light* (2001) and later volumes. The elegiac sequence, 'Clearances', written after the death of Margaret Heaney in 1984, explores the painful processes of grief and adjustment to loss, giving shape and significance to memory in the tightly compressed form of the sonnet. The third sonnet in the sequence strangely inverts domestic and sacred rituals, so that the shared potato peeling of mother and son takes on religious and sacramental overtones, while the priest performing the last rites goes 'hammer and tongs at the prayers for the dying'. The 'fluent dipping knives' hold togetherness and separation in a happy, painful suspension, as does the long perspective of the final line: 'Never closer the whole rest of our lives'.[67] The simultaneous apprehension of joyful union and sorrowful separation is similarly achieved through deftly placed negatives and a subtle manipulation of tense in 'Seeing Things', as Heaney recalls his father returning 'undrowned' from the river: 'And there was nothing between us there/That might not still be happily ever after'.[68]

The family elegies in *Human Chain* are deeply moving in the way that they light upon the premonition of loss in childhood, imbuing it with a retrospective remorse, as if seeing it 'For the first time'.[69] The memories in 'Album' are prompted by the 'oil-fired heating boiler' as it 'comes to life', its noise recalling the collapse of the chestnut tree at the end of 'Clearances'. The memories are presented as photographs of the child and his parents in an album, but the primary impulse in the poem is to 'imagine them'. As Michael Parker points out, the act of remembering is caught in the shifting verbal tense ('it must have been…Could have been'), while the recollection of childhood ('Shin-deep in hilltop bluebells') is coloured by Heaney's schoolboy reading of Keats.[70] Though it might be too late, the poem nevertheless shares its 'apt quotation' from Antoine de Saint-Exupéry, and it offers another apt quotation (*'A grey eye will look back'*) from Columcille of Iona, who is honoured later in the volume in 'Colum Cille Cecinit'. Columcille's cherishing of Derry is recalled among the memories of St Columb's College, the 'green leaves and acorns' in the college arms contrasting with the cut oaks of Grove Hill. The departing parents in 'Album', leaving the college as 'a couple', are seen again in memory, 'All the more together/For having had to turn and walk away, as close/In the leaving (or closer) as in the getting'.[71] The simultaneous anticipation and recollection of loss, and the pained appreciation of a closeness borne out in separation, play over the poems of childhood and growing up, including 'The Conway Stewart', in which the conventions of letter writing are felt upon the pulses: '"Dear"/To them, next day'.[72] In a later poem, the couple is 'Uncoupled', and the mother and father are seen as unknown shades in the Virgilian

---

[67] Heaney, *Opened Ground*, 285.

[68] Ibid., 317.

[69] Seamus Heaney, 'Album', *Human Chain* (London: Faber, 2010), 4–8.

[70] Michael Parker, 'His Nibs: Self-Reflexivity and the Significance of Translation in Seamus Heaney's *Human Chain*', The Annual Basil Bunting Lecture, Durham University, 28 April 2011.

[71] Heaney, *Human Chain*, 5.

[72] Ibid., 9.

Underworld, though the poem ends with a stinging childhood premonition of loss: 'his eyes leave mine and I know/The pain of loss before I know the term'.[73] Meaning and duration are powerfully combined here, reminding us of how superbly well Heaney, like Yeats, finds words in the very declaration of being at a loss for them.

V

Among Irish elegists after Yeats, Paul Muldoon is the poet who most obviously exemplifies 'the moral doubts, metaphysical scepticism, and emotional tangles that beset the modern experience of mourning'. In Jahan Ramazani's terms, he is clearly at the forefront of those poets who have been 'making the elegy more harshly satiric, ironic, and combative than ever before'.[74] Set against the idealizing, restorative modes of earlier elegies, Muldoon's poems of mourning appear stubbornly recalcitrant, wildly digressive, and deeply ambivalent. They are also bewilderingly experimental in form. It is worth noting that the playful criticism directed at Yeats in the voices of Auden and MacNeice in '7, Middagh Street' takes the measure of his achievements as an elegist. Wystan questions the 'crass, rhetorical//posturing' of 'Easter 1916', puzzling over *certain* men', while Louis notes the extravagant diction and peculiar linguistic slippages in the elegy for Eva Gore-Booth and Con Markiewicz: 'Both beautiful, one a gazebo'.[75] Even so, Yeats is undoubtedly the elegist whom Muldoon has to live up to. A crucial part of Yeats's legacy has been the stoical vision implicit in his self-composed epitaph: '*Cast a cold eye/On life, on death*'.[76]

'Incantata' (suggesting 'enchantment', as well as 'cantata' and 'incantation') was written by Muldoon for the American artist, Mary Farl Powers, after her death in 1992. The opening is both abrupt and intimate, but the manifold allusions to painting, history, and mythology serve as deflections away from the likelihood of all-consuming loss: 'I thought of you tonight, *a leanbh*, lying there in your long barrow/colder and dumber than a fish by Francisco de Herrera'.[77] The Irish *a leanbh* ('child' or 'baby') is both endearing and estranging within a stanza that ranges from ancient burial practices and Inca civilization to submarines and surrealism. Muldoon recalls an early poem by Yeats, 'All Things can Tempt Me' (1909), which ends with the poet's wish to be 'Colder and dumber and deafer than a fish', but he also draws on the elegy 'In Memory of Major Robert Gregory', both in the opening echo ('All, all are in my thoughts to-night being dead') and in the adoption of the eight-line stanza previously used by Abraham Cowley. The mouth 'X-Actoed' from a potato sets up a chain of images to do with printmaking and repetition, but it also alludes to Auden's definition of poetry as 'a way of happening, a mouth'

[73] Ibid., 11.

[74] Ramazani, *Poetry of Mourning*, p. x, 21.

[75] Paul Muldoon, *Poems 1968–1998* (London: Faber, 2001), 178, 189.

[76] Yeats, 'Under Ben Bulben', *Variorum Poems*, 640.

[77] Muldoon, *Poems*, 331.

in his elegy for Yeats.[78] The dying body of the artist is conflated with her work, as in the references to her 'pink/spotted torso' and the 'army-worms' that are both emblems of disease and figures in a work titled 'Emblements'. The poem's erotic suggestiveness ('when you undid your portfolio, yes indeedy') is typical of its candour, but its method also involves writing 'at arm's length'. The long arms of Lugh, the Celtic god of autumn, embrace the poem as it moves through its reflections on destiny and chance.

Intricate patterns of rhyme and rhythm structure the poem's compulsive flow of memories and give shape to its meditations on the 'notion that nothing's random'.[79] Repeatedly, the poem performs a set of elegiac gestures—'I saw you again tonight... You must have known... That's all that's left'—only to pull away towards the welter of images and ideas that both bind and separate poet and lover. The poem's cultural allusions range from the Book of Kells to the Dire Straits song 'The Sultans of Swing', from Vivaldi to Van Morrison, shoring fragments against a pervasive sense of ruin. The literary references run amok as the poem contemplates how art 'builds from pain, from misery, from a deep-seated hurt,/a monument to the human heart/that shines like a golden dome among roofs rain-glazed and leaden'.[80] Yeats's 'Sailing to Byzantium' is pre-eminent here, but there are echoes of Keats and Coleridge as well. The aesthetic objectivity of the rain-glazed red wheelbarrow of William Carlos Williams is conflated with 'The Leaden Echo and the Golden Echo' of Gerard Manley Hopkins and the despairing possibility that 'nothing can be done'.[81]

Stanza 23, at the centre of the elegy, calls on Joyce and Beckett to make sense of *quaquaqua*, before turning to an obsessive, repetitive cataloguing of 'all that's left', cutting across the years of the Troubles, but also gathering together the fleeting memories of a shared existence, sometimes based on no more than the slip of a syllable: 'how you called a Red Admiral a Red/Admirable'. The suspended syntax of the final three stanzas creates a space in which the miraculous might happen: 'that you might reach out, arrah,/ and take in your ink-stained hands my own hands stained with ink'.[82] The old Irish exclamation has a strangely steadying effect at the end of the line, preparing us for the powerful chiasmus at the close. The staining with ink is an enduring image of shared artistic endeavour, even though its more mundane suggestions of mortality turn it decisively away from 'the white radiance of Eternity'.[83]

'Incantata' was included in *The Annals of Chile* (1994), which Muldoon dedicated to the memory of his mother, Bridget Regan. 'Yarrow' distills that memory into an elegiac meditation of over a thousand lines, replaying ninety rhyme words (shared with

---

[78] W. H. Auden, *Collected Poems*, ed. Edward Mendelson (New York: Random House, 1976), 197.

[79] Iain Twiddy offers the most detailed and persuasive account to date of Muldoon's inventive verse forms in his elegies. See *Pastoral Elegy in Contemporary British and Irish Poetry* (London: Continuum, 2012).

[80] Muldoon, *Poems*, 335.

[81] Gerard Manley Hopkins, *The Major Works*, ed. Catherine Phillips (Oxford: Oxford University Press, 2002), 155.

[82] Muldoon, *Poems*, 336, 339, 341.

[83] Shelley, *The Major Works*, 545.

'Incantata'), across a series of short, sestina-like sequences. The formal pattern, with its pervasive sense of circling and returning, has its thematic corollary in the poet's return to his childhood origins in the townland of Moy. 'Yarrow' is the healing herb, *Achillea millefolium*, its overwhelming profusion of flowers corresponding to an overwhelming sense of loss, but the stream that 'fanned across the land' recalls the elegiac 'Yarrow Revisited' in which Wordsworth ambitiously rhymes 'Yarrow' with both 'sorrow' and 'marrow'.[84] As with 'Incantata', the poem seeks to assuage its grief in the rhythmic sway of repetition and refrain: 'All would be swept away... Would that I might... Again and Again...', while remaining ironically disposed towards its own consolatory gestures. Conventional elegiac emblems are swallowed up at the 'zap' of the remote control, with Michael Jackson's moon-suit suddenly becoming an unlikely substitute. Muldoon perfects his own cold style of tragic gaiety, at one point entertaining the prospect of Yeats addressing Sylvia Plath in the voice of Joyce's Citizen: 'How much longer must we Irish vent/Our spleen against their cold, their rook-delighting heaven?'[85] Although the poem refutes the mother's appeal to 'some higher power, some Deo/this or that', it nevertheless acknowledges the possibility of consolation beyond its own rhythmic resources. Matthew Campbell emphasizes the 'little by little' approach of the elegy, claiming that what it values is 'an attachment not just to memory, but to those small things which refuse forgetting or disavowal, which refuse to accept annihilation'.[86]

Muldoon's attachment to small things might explain his continuing interest in the sonnet. The other side of his epic expansiveness is formal compression, and in *Horse Latitudes* (2006) he measures grief in a variety of forms, as he mourns the loss of his sister, Maureen, to whom the book is dedicated. His 'Hedge School' sonnet ruefully reflects on learning and liberty, linking his great-great-grandmother's outlawed Catholic education with his daughter's 'all-American Latin class', and noting how enlightenment is no guarantee of either happiness or freedom.[87] He knows his Shakespeare well enough to cite Luciana's claim in *A Comedy of Errors* that 'headstrong liberty is lash'd/with woe' (2.1.287), but he finds himself stranded like a hedge school pupil, 'sheltered in a doorway' in St Andrews, where 'another Maelduin' was once bishop. Playing with etymology is both a diversion from grief and a genuine quest for knowledge, a point well illustrated in the abnormally long penultimate line containing 'the *New Shorter Oxford English Dictionary*'. The rhyme that frames the sestet of the sonnet, 'Sis' and '*metastasis*', powerfully embodies the distance between intimate, family attachment and the awful, impersonal realization of impending death. It effectively seals the sonnet's preoccupation with tracing roots.

Two longer poems, 'Turkey Buzzards' and 'Sillyhow Stride', come at grief in different ways, one circling around it in a long sweep of a single sentence before closing in decisively, and the other performing a series of jazz riffs in terza rima. The turkey buzzards,

[84] Gill, ed., *William Wordsworth*, 365.
[85] Muldoon, *Poems*, 349, 375–6.
[86] Matthew Campbell, 'Muldoon's Remains', in *Paul Muldoon: Critical Essays*, ed. Tim Kendall and Peter McDonald (Liverpool: Liverpool University Press, 2004), 173.
[87] Paul Muldoon, *Horse Latitudes* (London: Faber, 2006), 94.

hungry for roadkill and hovering above 'the thick scent/of death', turn out, unexpect-edly, to be the representatives of a decadent art, 'two petals... steeped in style', floating on buoyant Swinburnean verse. The poem probes the role of elegy, enquiring sardoni-cally whether it doesn't prey too easily on suffering: 'It's hard to imagine, dear Sis,/why others shrink/from the sight of a soul in bliss'. The closing image of the birds 'stripped of their command' is also one of art chastened and subdued, having been 'so long/above it all'.[88] The turkey buzzards reappear at the end of 'Sillyhow Stride', where the Latin name *Cathartes aura* helps to explain their elegiac function. The question of whether art is ever truly cathartic is left hanging in the air.

'Sillyhow Stride' was written in memory of the rock musician, Warren Zevon, who died in 2003, but it reaches out to the poet's sister. The 'sillyhow' or 'caul', traditionally regarded as a good-luck charm, is now emptied of its mythological significance: 'I knelt and adjusted the sillyhow//of her oxygen mask, its vinyl caul/unlikely now to save Maureen from drowning in her own spit.'[89] The stride of the jazz pianist is emulated in terza rima stanzas embellished with quotations from John Donne, though Muldoon's own artistic power is repeatedly figured through a changing array of guitars and amps ('a Gibson Les Paul/overdriven through a Fender Vibratone'). Zevon's colourful life is celebrated with passing allusions to hit records, but also with images that record catas-trophe on a global scale, and with repeated allusions to widespread suffering (a down-market, down-at-heel Man of Sorrows carries his 'full-length cross' down 42nd Street). Muldoon has an inimitable way of creating new forms (in this case 'the rock elegy') from a sudden collision of different cultural registers: 'Our last few grains of heroin ash stashed in a well-wrought urn'. His manipulation of the pedantic and the pedestrian within a single sentence ensures that there is sufficient artistic distance to allow the pain to sur-face: 'as surely as you knew the mesotheliomata//on both lungs meant the situation was lose-lose'.[90]

To look at the shape and development of the elegy from Yeats to Muldoon is to appre-ciate the many disruptions and redefinitions that the genre has undergone, but it is also to acknowledge the vital role that it has had in mediating between private mourning and public commemoration, breaking down hardened, institutionalized attitudes and creat-ing space for dignified reflection. As Edna Longley suggests, elegy is 'the genre that poets have made most distinctively expressive with reference to the Troubles', as well as 'a genre on which other kinds of poem converge or from which they depart'. In turn, 'Troubles elegy has also contributed to the reinvention of elegy itself.'[91] The contemporary poets considered here have written, and go on writing, with an unusually intense awareness of loss, coupled with an extraordinary versatility in devising the formal means of articulat-ing that loss. Extending Yeats's legacy, they have given elegy a prominent place in the history of modern poetry.

[88] Ibid., 78–81.
[89] Ibid., 99.
[90] Ibid., 106.
[91] Edna Longley, 'Northern Ireland: Commemoration, Elegy, Forgetting', 237.

CHAPTER 37

'REPEAT THE CHANGES CHANGE THE REPEATS': ALTERNATIVE IRISH POETRY

JOHN GOODBY

I

Reviewing the *Oxford Book of Irish Verse* in 1958, W. R. Rodgers noted that 'The Irish have never been bitten by the T.S.E. fly: they are not given to exploring the waste land of the spirit or the private condition of man.'[1] Yet despite his claim, which has been repeated at regular intervals, and in various ways, by almost all leading critics of Irish poetry since, twentieth-century Irish poetry has in fact been threaded through by a distinct, and often distinguished modernist-derived strain (In this essay I shall generally refer to this as 'alternative poetry', the least disputable term available, except when accuracy is better served by another.). The poetry of the 1930s modernists, discussed elsewhere in this book, has in recent years received its critical due; however, the alternative poetry written since the time of Rodgers's claim—apart from that of Thomas Kinsella—is still almost unknown. This has unbalanced the understanding of the nature and history of Irish poetry, and left it looking more conservative, coherent, and introspective than it actually is.

Resistance to poetic avant-gardism and modernism is generally the rule in anglophone cultures, and reflects an empirical bias which has deep cultural and historical roots.[2] That resistance, however, varies from place to place. Few American critics, given

---

[1] W. R. Rodgers, *Threshold* 2:4 (Winter 1958), 63.

[2] As in Britain, most Irish criticism defines poetry in the rather limited terms of the personal lyric. In such poetry, as Andrew Crozier defined it in 1983, an authoritative self discourses in a world of banal, empirically derived objects and relations, employing an elaborate figurative language to draw together the self and its objects. Energy is focused on the invention of figures (this is the poet's 'voice'),

the unignorability of William Carlos Williams, John Ashbery and Rae Armantrout, Pulitzer Poetry prize winners all, can dismiss the modernist legacy as a negligible one. Equally, while the Hardy-Auden-Larkin plain-style tradition has dominated British poetry and its attendant critical discourse for the last half century, there has recently been a general, if grudging acknowledgement of the importance of the likes of Roy Fisher, J. H. Prynne, and Denise Riley. But in Ireland the response is patchier than this, and it is still possible even for otherwise well-informed critics and readers to be unaware of the Irish counterparts of these poets.[3]

This is largely due to the fact that the discourses defining Irish poetry add a particularly acute concern with national and cultural affiliation to the empiricist suspicion of formalist experiment. For decades, it has been assumed that work by Irish poets must either be about Ireland or the condition of being Irish. The fact that Irish identity, or identities, have been so fiercely contested, is one reason for this. From the 1960s onwards this tendency was strengthened by the impact of the Troubles, which encouraged poets to assert the value of the individual in the face of pressures to be communally representative. The kind of self chosen was not the one bequeathed by modernism and modern thought—processual, multiple, self-contradictory—but a coherent, pre-twentieth-century one. In Northern Ireland, too, English ties also recommended pre-modernist poetic form. A further reason for this tendency has been what the *Cambridge Companion to Contemporary Irish Poetry* describes (without necessarily endorsing it) as the appeal of, and the role assigned to, Irish poetry in the global literary economy: 'in a shrinking world... [Irish] poetry still told of the sense of place, voice and community, even from displaced locations'.[4] This global role is not one which good poets, of whatever stripe, have been comfortable with, but it has inevitably grown out of the excellence of post-1960s Northern poetry, its London publication, and a long-standing perception of Ireland as an overwhelmingly rural and (ironically, considering the outcome) non-commercialized society. Taken together, these factors have meant that, even in its dissident mode (that is, in opposing national pieties, or taking anticlerical or anti-patriarchal stances), Irish poetry overwhelmingly presents a stable, expressivist self, using language more or less instrumentally, often to shape a narrative anecdote centred on a clinching

---

and the plausibility with which these rewrite the world is made, in turn, to guarantee the authenticity of that self. For all its invention, and despite ostensibly constituting the nature of the poem (the 'poetic'), language is nevertheless always instrumental, a means for reflecting the object world, conceptually subordinate to the empirical reality of the self. Andrew Crozier, 'Thrills and Frills: Poetry as Figures of Empirical Lyricism', in *Society and Literature 1945–1970*, ed. Alan Sinfield (London: Methuen, 1983), 199–234. For more recent and more comprehensive discussions of the subject, see John Wilkinson, 'Frostwork and the Mud Vision', *The Cambridge Quarterly* (2002), 93–105, and John Matthias, 'British Poetry at Y2K', www.electronicbookreview.com

[3] Thus, Edna Longley: 'Modernism has promoted narrow, abstract readings of twentieth-century poetry... the formalist emphases of Modernism are largely redundant in the presence of a mode where form has always been the *sine qua non*.... the parasitic literariness in Modernism... has hit poetry hard'. Edna Longley, 'Introduction', *Poetry in the Wars* (Newcastle: Bloodaxe, 1986), 13.

[4] Matthew Campbell, 'Ireland in Poetry: 1999, 1949, 1969', in *The Cambridge Companion to Contemporary Irish Poetry*, ed. Matthew Campbell (Cambridge: Cambridge University Press, 2003), 3.

image, gesture, or phrase. As a result, contemporary Irish poets who accept the challenges that modernism poses have for a long time been excluded from the very category of 'Irish poet'. As one of them, Catherine Walsh, has noted: 'You are only supported [in Ireland] if you are part of that tradition... that must celebrate above all else your sense of Irishness and your sense of being part of an ongoing linear tradition of Irish writers, writing out of bondage, almost'.[5]

And yet things are not quite as simple as this suggests. Poetic practice and critical prescription, for a start, are two different things. The work of Derek Mahon and Medbh McGuckian, for example, is hardly innocent of modernism; nor, on the other hand, would alternative poets claim that they formed a counter-tradition utterly distinct from, and opposed to, the mainstream. Moreover, as I have argued elsewhere, Northern Irish poetry in the 1980s to some extent dismantled the well-made lyric it inherited, using experimental form in the process.[6] Too much can be made of this aspect in any case: as one avowed experimentalist, Randolph Healy, has pointed out, 'technique is an unreliable fence if you wish to carve up the landscape of poetry'.[7] Nor is Europe (or the USA) necessarily synonymous with 'advanced', if this means a positivism which is inappropriate to the way poetry actually evolves. Thus, J. C. C. Mays, a champion of alternative poetry, has argued that the Dublin-based Yeats was more radical than Paris-based James Joyce in the 1930s, and that no Irish alternative poets 'parade difficulty as obviously as Paul Muldoon or as eagerly as Ciaran Carson, for both of whom it is the thing on the plate'.[8] 'Thing on the plate' is the sting in the tail—the postmodern flourish is there to 'enliven dull facades'—but Mays takes both to be formal experimentalists who are unafraid of difficulty. Indeed, distinctions blur, without necessarily vanishing, the more closely they are examined. Rather than a conservative-to-radical *spectrum*, the poetic field is better viewed as a *constellation* of practices, the discursive (and market) perceptions of which marginalize alternative poetry, but which contains numerous cases of poets themselves engaging in boundary breaking. It is with the sense of unravelling a complicated skein, then, that I attempt in what follows to trace alternative poetic activity

[5] Peterjon Skelt, ed. *Prospect into Breath: Interviews with North and South Writers* (Twickenham and Wakefield, North and South Press, 1991), 184.

[6] John Goodby, *Irish Poetry since 1950: From Stillness into History* (Manchester: Manchester University Press, 2000). The success of the second-wave Northern Irish poets is one reason why there seem to be no alternative poets currently in Northern Ireland. The Derry-born, Donegal-raised Geoffrey Squires and the Belfast-born OuLiPo writer Philip Terry (b. 1962) both live in England. Terry's poem 'The Movement', which reads simply 'Now wash your hands', may indicate one reason for this. Philip Terry, *Oulipoems 2* (Tokyo/Toronto: Ahadada Books, 2009).

[7] Healy points out: 'The alternation of prose and verse is beautifully handled in Boethius' *The Consolation of Philosophy*. Dense argument flows passionately through Lucretius' *On the Nature of the Universe*. Random methods, whether in divination poems or as part of biology, have an ancient history. Collage was almost *de rigueur* among Renaissance Latinists. The erasure of self was as near complete as it can be among the *Fiannaíochta* poems of the early middle ages.... The surreal has to work hard to beat nursery rhyme, never mind the awesome oddness of the simply literal.' Randolph Healy, 'The Wandering Wood', *Poetry Ireland Review* 73 (Summer 2002), 115–29.

[8] J. C. C. Mays, *N11 A Musing* (Clonmel: Coelacanth Press, 2003), 3, 9.

in Ireland from 1964 to the present in the work of five representative poets—Eugene Watters, Geoffrey Squires, Trevor Joyce, Maurice Scully, and Catherine Walsh.[9]

II

The impulse to work against the dominant Irish poetic grain has been constant, and has outcropped, throughout the twentieth century. However, it is a small-scale, gapped, and sporadic phenomenon, and until the 1960s usually entailed emigration or self-silencing. The one mid-century exception was Eugene Watters, a teacher in Finglas, who was best known in his lifetime as an Irish-language activist and writer by the Irish form of his name Eoghan Ó Tuairisc. Watters's first language, however, was English, and his masterpiece is the now almost forgotten long poem *The Week-End of Dermot and Grace* (1964), an exuberant, knotty, and verbally brilliant 1,300-line renewal of the modernism of Eliot and Joyce which, like Thomas Kinsella's 'Downriver' (1962), attempts to confront early 1960s Ireland with some of the malign aspects of the modern world it had hitherto avoided.

Set in Dublin in August 1945, during the weekend following the destruction of Hiroshima, the poem follows Dermot and Grace, two young lovers attempting to escape Dublin for the seaside town of Castlefinnerty. Watters uses the modernist 'mythical method', mapping Dermot and Grace's flight onto the Irish legend of Diarmuid and Gráinne, together with a series of Near Eastern vegetation and fertility myths derived from Sir James Frazer's *The Golden Bough* via *The Waste Land*. His couple flee not Fionn, but the petty tyranny of Dermot's employer, Mr Finn, as well as memories of Grace's dead husband, Kelly (who was also Dermot's best friend), and the more general boredom of Dublin life. But almost immediately things go disastrously wrong. As their train pulls out of Amiens Street Station, Dermot and Grace find themselves in the company of an old countryman who insists on talking about his gallstone operation. Then, just outside the station, the train crashes in a tunnel, fatally injuring all three.

From line 114 onwards, the poem is a psychodrama, the projection from Dermot's dying brain of the planned weekend. Dermot's consciousness projects himself and Grace arriving at Castlefinnerty. In part two, then, they seem to spend Saturday sea-bathing, walking beside fields, and lying on a golf links watching the moon rise; in reality, Dermot is passing back through the biological and historical origins of human life and society,

---

[9] Poets I cannot discuss in this essay for reasons of space, but who are a crucial part of the mix, are: Mairéad Byrne, Sean Carey, Randolph Healy, James Hogan [Augustus Young], Judy Kravis, David Lloyd, Hugh Maxton [W. J. McCormack], Billy Mills, and Michael Smith. For analysis of the work of Maxton, see Alex Davis, 'The Irish Modernists and their Legacy', in *The Cambridge Companion to Contemporary Irish Poetry*, ed. Matthew Campbell, 86–8. Davis also discusses the work of Mills and Smith in his pioneering account of alternative Irish poetry, *A Broken Line: Denis Devlin and Irish Poetic Modernism* (Dublin: UCD Press, 2000).

symbolically represented by sea and cultivation, the 'links' punningly those of geneal-
ogy. In the third and final section he and Grace wake together in a bed which is also a
tomb. Now at the verge of death, Dermot must choose extinction or rebirth. Grace, Finn,
and Kelly press him to choose life, 'that famous thing', the 'dreaming wine', but Dermot
has had enough of it. Heroic values—all human endeavour it may be—have been ren-
dered worthless by the Bomb:

> Hero?
> He rose?
> Hiroshima.
>
> Hail hole in determinate night,
> O round O,
> By Jove, Leda's only easteregg.
> X marks the out out damned spot.[10]

'Bear us', he repeats, trying to escape, 'Let us alone. The bright day is free.' But as he des-
perately resists life, in the concluding lines, he feels Grace beside him and a last flare-up
of desire: 'Dear heart, do not touch me so', he protests, but it is too late. His love for her
recalls him from oblivion to new existence. The ego dissolves ('the I dispenses/At least
with its dreaming masks... Unthinks itself into birth's wounds') as tomb becomes womb,
and his cry of resistance, still almost against his will, turns into a birth-cry:

> The I cries its whimpering negation,
> Drawing the air in to make blood and voice.
>
> Brethren pray that my sacrifice[11]

The radical unselving of Dermot is to some extent that of the poem itself which, in true
modernist fashion, views historical crisis as one of language and representation, subjec-
tivity and artistic form. The final, Christ-like, un-full-stopped appeal, blurs August 1945
and Easter 1916, offering national as well as individual rebirth, and this is a good exam-
ple of the work's formal adventurousness, its assured interweaving of various voices, lan-
guages, histories, cultures, and legends ranging from Shakespeare's *Venus and Adonis* to
Greek tragedy and Puccini's *Madame Butterfly* (the latter dramatizing gender and colo-
nial conflicts). The sensuous details of Dublin life—'Big Bert [who] swears/Finger and
thumb's the sovereign cure for greenfly', Grace taking 'tea... at Mary-Ann's;/From Uncle
Oscar who fought the Black-and-Tans'—do not humanistically 'ground' Watters's
abstract vision of the sexual life force driving civilization, so much as confirm its exces-
siveness through their sheer linguistic *jouissance*, amounting as they do to a refusal of
the distinction between a given authorial self, and a history and a world somehow unas-
sailably 'out there'.[12]

---

[10] Eugene Watters, *The Week-End of Dermot and Grace*, in *Poetry Ireland Review* 13 (Spring 1985), 31.
[11] Watters, *Week-End*, 71.
[12] Ibid., 31–2.

III

The Week-End of Dermot and Grace looks back to Joyce and Eliot, to produce a late modernist equal of Austin Clarke's *Mnemosyne Lay in Dust* and Patrick Kavanagh's *Lough Derg*. However, it had little impact. In the late 1960s, a new generation of alternative poets appeared who were oblivious to *Week-End*, reflecting the gapped nature of this tradition, or anti-tradition. The new writers took their cue from the 1930s poets and from Europe, and their most important focus was New Writers' Press (NWP), founded in Dublin in 1967 by Trevor Joyce and Michael and Irene Smith. Mike Smith and Joyce opposed the ruralist-traditionalist poetic style dominant at the time, promoting alternatives through NWP and its house journal, *The Lace Curtain* (1969–75).[13] Yet as in Britain at this time, mainstream and alternative poetries were more mutually tolerant than they subsequently became. Mike Smith's *Lace Curtain* editorials savaged kitsch traditionalism—'the lie that Ireland is an incorrigibly literary country...the work of Bórd Fáilte admen [and] an indigenous multitude of tenth-rate non-poets'— rather than traditionalism itself (thus, Kavanagh was valued, but more for his awkward individualism than his verse).[14] Against a poetry defined by 'place, voice and community', Smith sought to establish an alternative genealogy by republishing the 1930s modernists, while in their editorial labours he and Joyce showed remarkably Catholic tastes.[15]

IV

Smith and Joyce apart, the only contemporary alternative poets NWP mustered were Geoffrey Squires and James Hogan (Augustus Young).[16] Squires was initially the most impressive of the four. He had read English at Cambridge, lived in France and Iran, and broadcast work on the BBC before publishing *Drowned Stones* (1975), a collection which

[13] For details of the activities of NWP, see Trevor Joyce, 'New Writers' Press: The History of a Project', in *Modernism and Ireland: The Poetry of the 1930s*, ed. Patricia Coughlan and Alex Davis (Cork: Cork University Press, 1995), 276–306.

[14] Michael Smith and Trevor Joyce, Editorial, *The Lace Curtain* 2 (1970), 2.

[15] NWP confounds the elitist label usually applied to avant-garde presses. Thus, its titles included Paul Durcan's first collection, three collections by Michael Hartnett, as well as the first non-US edition of Jack Spicer. The same can be said of *The Lace Curtain*, which set Derek Mahon beside Asa Benveniste, published more Kavanagh than Beckett, and was more inclusive than the far better-known *Honest Ulsterman* and *Poetry Ireland Review*. Both press and journal were also unusually open to poetry in translation: the former published the first English-language edition of Borges's poetry, for example, while the latter carried work by, among others, Andrade, Bachmann, Benn, Colinas, Desnos, Machado, and Trakl.

[16] Very little has been written on Hogan. Mays offers the only brief account in print in *N11 A Musing*, 20–2. See also Hogan's website: www.augustusyoung.com/links.html

reveals a sophisticated absorption of Black Mountain verse and contemporary French poetics and philosophy. Charles Olson's essay 'Projective Verse', with its attack on 'the lyrical interference of the individual as ego',[17] is an influence, as the opening poem, which decentres its subject by putting it in parentheses, shows:

> (And all the trouble to learn him, the
> strangeness of another, his turnings)
> it was good, it was as it should be, we lived
> two miles from the town, quite isolated, no
> car
>
> didn't get the electric till 1953 and only got
> it then because my mother had the sense to give
> the engineer a cup of tea
>
> well he said we might as well take it up the
> hill when we're at it.[18]

The book combines childhood landscapes with more esoteric matter gleaned from contemporary thinking about the nature of identity, material which increasingly nudges aside the poetic self. As this implies, landscape and childhood events are not, as in the contemporary work of Heaney and Montague, the ground of identity, but rather occasions for existential self-recognition.

In 1976, pursing a similar restriction of the ego, Squires spent a year isolated from English in a remote village in Crete, without media access and almost no reading material. Bolstered by his interest in phenomenological philosophy, this sojourn led him away from a modernism of ellipsis, collage, and the interrogation of language into new poetic territory in *Figures* (1978), *XXI Poems* (1980), and *A Long Poem in Three Sections* (1983). *Figures* is organized around 'complex non-linear/memories/and whispers of composite faces'; that is, a key image, or phrase, loosely anchors a phenomenological matrix. Thus, one poem opens 'Over the other side of the county/that man died', but then turns to its present moment rather than to narrative resolution:

> stillness now
> in the dark
> of the plantation
>
> pitch-pine spruce elder
> sky appearing
> in the gap of a fire-break
>
> short summer nights
> another star and another and another[19]

[17] Charles Olson, *Collected Prose*, ed. Donald Allen and Benjamin Friedlander (Berkeley: University of California Press, 1997), 247.

[18] Geoffrey Squires, *Untitled and Other Poems: 1975–2002* (Bray: Wild Honey Press, 2004), 9.

[19] Squires, *Untitled*, 47.

Coherence in the absence of a clinching symbol or narrative closure is achieved by dissolving the consciousness into a distinct, but unappropriative delineation of the processes of one's surroundings. In *XXI Poems*, however, even the decentred key images are absent; poems move from the external projection of the self to a more internalized representation of self and object world, the difference, according to Squires's own distinction, between 'centrifugal' and 'centripetal' poetry.[20] As in Beckett's later prose and Coffey's major sequences, Squires now emphasized the individual as the poem's organizing centre, not in any confessional sense, but as a provisional, abstract, notating consciousness constituting and constituted by its relationship with its surroundings.

This poetics of perception is extended in *A Long Poem in Three Sections*, which gives the impression of breaking in upon his own thought processes at the moment they rise to a climax of observation, each examining a single subject in turn: trees in a forest; rocks on a hillside; light glancing on buildings. The poem's epigraph—'After all, the world does not confront but surrounds me'—is from Merleau-Ponty's *L'Oeil et L'Esprit*, and posits a self immersed in its environment, not aimed at it in some means-end way. Romantic or modernist depth is eschewed in favour of dissociated complexity; there is no depth, but a recession of surfaces, multiple perspectives, self-interrogatory 'troubled vision', and a language that conveys the impression of straining for ever more accurate renderings of the process of perception.

During the 1990s, in *Landscape & Silences, This, Poem for Two Voices, Littoral*, and *Pastoral*, the presence of landscape diminished; Squires charts how:

> the mind…moves over things
> like a light shadow
> which darkens them for a moment only a moment
> and hardly at all.[21]

Figure and background, subject and object are even more inseparable; nothing is 'purely external out there'. The point (although nothing is goal-oriented in this work) is that nothing in the object world can be assimilated to, or exhausted by, the structures of perception. *Untitled I, Untitled II* (both 2000), and *Untitled III* (2002) continue the attenuation, with the exception of a reprint of *Untitled II* in which Squires cut up and scattered its material over a text just one-third its length. This may have been a response to criticism, such as Yann Lovelock's of 'Poem for Two Voices', that it was 'inert and unoriginal', diluting the 'tang' of the poetic spirit in 'too much chaser' of Merleau-Ponty and philosophy.[22] Whatever the reason, it was a momentary deviation. Recent works, such as *So* (2007), are published only as Adobe documents on the Shearsman website; typically with just one or two lines per page, the pdf format's accentuation of the relation between text and the surrounding bright blankness, and

---

[20] Alex Davis, *A Broken Line*, 156.

[21] Squires, *Untitled*, 121.

[22] Yann Lovelock, review of *Untitled & Other Poems 1975–2002*, *Stride* (November 2004), 3: http://stridemagazine.co.uk/2004/nov/lovelock.squires.htm

the contemplative reverberations this sets up, mimics their renderings of an embodied consciousness moving through the world.[23]

V

By contrast with Squires's dissolutions of the subject, Trevor Joyce's work is always marked by a struggle between a deep suspicion of the imprisoning potentials of form and a fierce desire for achieved and intricate structures. Tropes of imprisonment, metaphysical anguish, and death dominate the early work, collected in *Pentahedron* (1972), which is set in a claustrophobic Dublin of bridges, monuments, vaults, churches, and walls. Trakl, Baudelaire, and early Eliot inform a ghost-ridden, yet depopulated and silent urban wasteland, full of *memento mori* in which 'Speech is a broken bird or stunned wings'.[24] This world is unsettling in its neither fully alive nor dead quality, and the poems are charged with the anxiety that they betray the world because language can never truly mirror it. The morbid and fatalistic qualities have proved too much for some critics, but their excessiveness can be related to a Dublin gothic strain, in which Joyce's predecessors include Maturin, Mangan, and his namesake James Joyce.[25]

Some of these anxieties were overcome in a 'working' of the Middle Irish *Suibhne Geilt* as *Sweeny Peregrine* (1976), which foregrounded the original's lacunae- and interpolation-riddled nature. The effect was intensified by separating the heterogeneous material of the original into a prose narrative and a suite of lyrics, a bicameral structure deployed many times since in Joyce's work. The self-queryings, gaps, and contradictions undermine narrative integrity and authority in the prose section, and emphasize that this is a framed retelling. The lyrics, on the other hand, capture Sweeny's pain, and the bleak beauty of the landscapes he traverses:

> In summertime the blue-grey herons stand
> rigid above sharp waters.
>
> In wintertime the wolfpacks
> thread the snow-glens with their spoor,
> and with their moaning they thread the long wind.
>
> I hear their snow-blurred howling
> as I cross the iron lakes
> and crack the frost from my beard.[26]

---

[23] See: www.shearsman.com/pages/books/ebooks/ebooks_pdfs/So.pdf

[24] Trevor Joyce, 'Chronicle', *With the first dream of fire they hunt the cold: a body of work 1966–2000* (Dublin and Kentisbeare, New Writers' Press/Shearsman Books, 2001), 63.

[25] Andrew Duncan notes 'I counted the words dying/die/death/dead in *Pentahedron* (1972) and came to 30 (in 44 pages)', and he finds in Joyce's early work a 'de-organic quality' and 'a prevailing tone of hypersensitive loathing'. See Andrew Duncan, 'Pale angel exuvial who can mix it with the chicken', *Jacket* 20 (December 2002): http://jacketmagazine.com/20/dunc-r-joyc.html

[26] Joyce, *With the first dream*, 25.

For all its plangent intensity, there is no romantic afflatus here, and the natural world is not aestheticized as a compensation for suffering.[27]

Joyce, who moved to Cork in 1984, found his writing blocked by his aesthetic and linguistic anxiety, and by Irish society's inward turn, and a second collection of his own poetry, *stone floods*, did not appear until 1995. This reflected a decade and more of immersion in Chinese and Japanese writing, and particularly the philosophy of Dogen, as well as Joyce's work as a business systems analyst with Apple. As its punning title suggests, Joyce had developed an interest in paradoxical states, states in which the fixed and solid becomes fluid, the impermeable porous, and transgression and control grow into each other. Sand is a central theme, as a stony substance which flows, as the raw material of the ambiguous solid-liquid, glass, and as the source of the silicon in chips used to store, or petrify information 'flows'. 'The Turlough' offers perhaps the most powerful image for these properties, turloughs being suddenly flooding karstic limestone lakes found in the West of Ireland.[28] Solid-fluid signifying words like 'fast' are favoured, as are those which operate backwards and forwards in the signifying chain, and bring about reversals of sense.[29] The *renga* form, in which three poets alternately contribute lines, makes a structural device of this effect, and in 'Chimaera' Joyce devised a *renga* from material by the Cavalier poet Richard Lovelace, the nineteenth-century French poet Aloysius Bertrand, and the fourth-century BC Daoist Lie-zi to ingeniously dramatize his guilty aestheticism in a manner which did some justice to the dialogic 'incoherence' of the world.

Although narrative is subverted in *stone floods*, Joyce concluded that its lyric forms were still too closed, and in the John Cage-influenced *Syzygy* (1998) he took the incorporation of chaos in tight structures to new lengths. It is built on three found texts, fragments of which run backwards and forwards through 'The Drift', the first section, in arrangements which permit a narrative reading. This is the first of the twelve parts of 'The Drift':

> And then there is this sound
> that starts with a scarcely audible
> rustling inside gold the whisper
> echoing within the diamond
> grows to take in snatches
> from high stars from elsewhere
> the disintegrating actions
> of clocks so that eventually
> you attend to the infinities
> of numbers shattering

---

[27] Joyce's version is a flight from the lyric 'I', unlike Seamus Heaney's better-known *Sweeney Astray* (1983), which offers a unified narrative and takes Sweeney as a romantic figure of the alienated artist.

[28] Joyce, *With the first dream*, 95 and note, 236.

[29] For example, Nate Dorward finds in just three lines of 'Cold Course' 'puns lurking in "bolted down", "still", and "fastness" [all] register[ing] the paradox of static motion'. See Nate Dorward, 'On Trevor Joyce', *Chicago Review* 48:4 (Winter 2002/3), n.p.

the shriek that is the change
of several millions[30]

These parts are then rearranged in a second section, 'The Net', using a computer spread-sheet programme. The result is an extraordinary, dense work in which the 'blind deploy-ment of predetermined procedures carry a force both of lyricism and of narrative', revealing meanings unintended by their author; it showed Joyce how 'densely overde-termined language, functioning in its most intensely personal mode of the lyric, could survive radical disruption and return…a yield which the reader might gather'.[31] Moreover, as Joyce notes, the poem's symmetry was deliberately impaired, in line with its concern with the misalliance between conceptual schemas and the object world.

A wave of new works resulted from the insights yielded by *Syzygy*, among them *Without Asylum* (1998) structured on reversed causality, in which a narrative of blos-soming, fruiting, and nectar-gathering is interwoven with one of deforestation; *Hopeful Monsters* (1998), a prose collage work; and *Trem Neul* (1999), which splices texts in par-allel columns of prose and poetry. A fascination with cyborgs in the first mines Joyce's gothic vein again, while the second develops his interest in boundaries in an 'autobio-graphical essay in prose and verse from which everything personal has been excluded', made of 'the memories and apprehensions of others'.[32]

As this suggests, Joyce's work shares the thrust of much recent avant-garde poetry; namely, a desire to register the depredations of history while avoiding the tendency of a poetry of expression to arrogate the suffering of others to the lyric 'I' through its mastery of poetic language. For Joyce this would amount to complicity with the language of the dominant power structures and media whose messages saturate our world in a language (particularly of advertising and journalism) which enforces passive consumerism, apa-thy, and submission.[33] Poetry's role is to reveal language's compromised engagement with the world, its resistance to totalizing structuration. Yet if to do so requires forms whose levels of manipulation equal those of the forces they oppose, it might be argued that responsibility is being abrogated in another way, and this raises the question posed by Alex Davis of whether Joyce's 'difficulty' is symptomatic of the malaise it interrogates—the problem which Theodor Adorno claimed faced all modernist-derived artworks.[34]

[30] Joyce, *With the first dream*, 136.

[31] Trevor Joyce, 'Why I Write Narrative', personal communication with John Goodby, 16 August 1999. See also J. C. C. Mays, Nate Dorward, and Alex Davis for accounts of 'Syzygy'.

[32] Back cover of Joyce, *With the first dream*.

[33] Joyce expounds these ideas most thoroughly in 'The Point of Innovation in Poetry', in *For the Birds: Proceedings of the First Cork Conference on New and Experimental Irish Poetry*, ed. Harry Gilonis (Sutton: Mainstream Poetry; Dublin: hardPressed poetry, 1998), 18–26.

[34] For Adorno high modernist art, through its dissident and creatively distorted formal structures, was alone able to register the deformations of the spirit created by existence under late capitalism, but was increasingly smothered by the products of the culture industry; even so, both high and low art reflected alienation, being the 'halves of an integral freedom, to which, however, they do not add up'. Theodor Adorno, Letter of 18 March 1936: Ernst Bloch et al., *Aesthetics and Politics*, trans. and ed. Rodney Taylor (London: NLB, 1977), 123. For more on this Adornoesque aspect of Joyce's work, see John Goodby and Marcella Edwards, '"glittering silt": The Poetry of Trevor Joyce and the Myth of Irishness', *Hungarian Journal of English and American Studies* 8:1 (2002), 173–98.

One response is found in Joyce's most recent work, *What's in Store: Poems 2000–2007*. The sheer heterogeneity of this 306-page collection arguably offsets the opacity of any organizing principle; to either side of its mid-point in the prose poem 'STILLSMAN', a pun on stasis and Joyce's father's career in a distillery, fall translations of European folk songs and Chinese and Irish poetry, as well clumps of thirty-six-word lyrics (the remains of a three-dimensional sestina, and another example of the destabilizing impurities Joyce introduces into his works). One of the concerns of the book is simply with historical analogues hinting at 'what's in store': thus, 'Capital Accounts', from *Ch'ang-an: Ku-i* by Lu Chao-lin (AD 638–84), as its title suggests, reflects on a society which resembles that of Ireland before the banking collapse of 2009. In doing so, Joyce also draws on works by his ancestors, P. W. Joyce and R. D. Joyce, folklorists, translators, and historians, who also attempted to 'translate' one period of Irish history into their nineteenth-century present.[35] This can be linked to the book's concern with mortality—'what's in store' for us all—but this sense is just about overborne by yet another, that of language's continuing abundance, or 'store'.

VI

NWP ran out of steam in the increasingly conservative climate of the later 1970s. Slump, political impasse, and emigration all took their toll on a cultural climate, north and south, which had precious little spare space for experiment or novelty. In W. J. McCormack's words, 'Faced with expanding violence in the 1970s...the Irish imagination for the most part opted for an older, more cohesive community. It braced itself for the shock of the new by elegizing and simultaneously inventing an interior order which spoke of..."more supportive parish structures", "the greater warmth of the pre-nuclear family". In this, of course, it relied upon ever-available pastoral images of the past.'[36] Its success beyond Ireland meant that the Northern lyric became the model for many emerging poets in the Republic. Even so, mid-1970s Dublin saw the emergence of a new alternative poetic scene. Much of the credit for this was due to Maurice Scully, a Trinity College graduate, who organized a series of readings and edited two avant-garde journals, *the Belle* (1978– 80) and *the Beau* (1981–84). Other emerging poets associated with the activity included Randolph Healy, Billy Mills, and Catherine Walsh; Mills started hardPressed Poetry in 1985 and was joined by Walsh in 1986.[37] Unlike NWP, hardPressed had no recuperative project, although like Smith and Joyce, Mills and Walsh revere Brian Coffey,

---

[35] See John Goodby, '"Through My Dream": Trevor Joyce's Translations', *Études Irlandaises*, 35:2 (Autumn 2010), 149–64.

[36] W. J. McCormack, *The Battle of the Books* (Dublin: Lilliput Press, 1987), 67.

[37] Others associated with this post-NWP grouping include Mairéad Byrne, Seán Carey, Judy Kravis, and David Lloyd. All but Byrne were anthologized by Scully for the Irish issue of *Angel Exhaust*. Material on hardPressed and Mills and *The Journal* can be found at http://gofree.indigo.ie/~hpp/

whose longevity meant that he was an exemplary figure for several successor generations.

Scully, Mills, and Walsh worked outside Ireland in the 1980s and early 1990s. This was one reason why an encounter with NWP was delayed, and the missed opportunity is typical of the history of Irish alternative poetry. Yet their American influences, and English connections and publications, reflect a greater awareness, by comparison with Smith and Joyce a decade before, of equivalent poetries beyond Ireland. Among others, Scully brought Roy Fisher, Gael Turnbull, and Tom Raworth to read in Dublin, and the choice of figures somewhat maverick in British alternative poetry terms says something about the group's own eclectic, non-programmatic nature. Another difference, reflecting the date of their emergence and the rise of Critical Theory after 1970, was the influence of the US avant-garde tradition of the Objectivists, Charles Olson, and early LANGUAGE poetry. While Joyce's formalism, Smith's recuperations, and Squires's phenomenology mark them out as neo-modernist, the later group, by contrast, owe more to a neo-avant-garde poetics of radical indeterminacy. Scully has testified to the effects of reading Ron Silliman's *In the American Tree* and Charles Bernstein's *Content's Dawn*, and in his words 'poetry (space) "is an activity/not a body of reading" '.[38]

It is symbolic of the gapped nature of Irish alternative poetry that the single most important event in its recent history had nothing to do with the poets themselves, and took place several thousand miles away from Ireland, at the 1996 'Assembling Alternatives' conference organized by Romana Huk at the University of New Hampshire. Huk invited NWP poets (Joyce and Squires) and *Belle/Beau* poets (Scully, Healy, Mills, and Walsh), and so, unknowingly, brought about the first meeting between the two groups. The effect on all concerned was profound. The First Cork Conference on New and Experimental Irish Poetry in 1997 (now an annual event) and Randolph Healy's Wild Honey Press were both outcomes, but the most significant one was simply a delighted sense of the discovery of kindred spirits, and the confidence, enthusiasm, creativity, and solidarity it generated.

The New Hampshire conference also coincided with renewed critical interest. In 1995 the first account, by Joyce, of the activities of NWP was published in an edited volume of essays on the 1930s modernists.[39] The Cork conference proceedings, and critical essays, pamphlets, and articles by Alex Davis, Robert Archambeau, J. C. C. Mays, Harry Gilonis, and others, also appeared, as did an Irish special issue of the English avant-garde journal *Angel Exhaust* in 1999. In 2000 the first extended scholarly account of the history and development of alternative Irish poetry formed the closing section of Davis's monograph, *A Broken Line: Denis Devlin and Irish Poetic Modernism*. With these works, in critical terms the genie was out of the bottle; no reputable anthology or critical account of Irish poetry since has been able to ignore completely the post-1960s alternative poets.

[38] Maurice Scully, *livelihood* (Bray: Wild Honey Press, 2004), 18.
[39] See note 13 above.

VII

Recognition and increased activity continued into the 2000s, which witnessed the completion of what is probably Irish alternative poetry's most ambitious project. Maurice Scully began the *Things That Happen* sequence in 1981, and the last instalment of this 600-page work in eight books and three chapbooks appeared in 2006.[40] Like similar extended, but minimally structured poetic sequences charting a writer's existence— Louis Zukofsky's *'A'* is another example—it is hard to say what Scully's work is 'about'. As he had written in 1984, he desired a poetry that '[doubted] its own importance in a simple world. The world is extremely complex and the most complex poem the mind can conceive... is extremely simple in the world. A poem is beautiful to the degree that it records an apt humility in the face of the complexity it sees but fails to transmit.'[41] A note of 2008 suggests that the 'apt humility' required the eschewal of narrative linearity, or mythic or other imposed structures: '*Things That Happen* in its entirety is written around motifs and sub-motifs. The motifs interlace in waves and eddies which echo and deepen as the reader progresses. [It] is structured radially so that you can dip in almost anywhere and pick up the music of the interlacing motifs. This is the driving impulse of the work.'[42]

What are these 'motifs', and how do they operate? Scully's desire to register the complex flux of the world entails refusal of definition and closure, in a skittering, playful, yet serious style which makes coherent excerption very difficult. Yet readers soon learn to recognize recurring scenes, themes, and strategies. One is the act of painting a door after learning that his five-year-old son, Louis, would recover from a serious fall. Another is the near-apocalyptic onset of the rains, in Lesotho, in a house roofed with corrugated iron. Another is 'the Giant's buckle', an image from a children's story but also a symbol of violent authority. The locations and act of writing also recur continually; one, from when Scully worked as a night watchman on a Dublin building site, is possibly the originating moment for *Things That Happen*:

> And then I woke up. I was at a table in a
> small shed on a building site in Dublin. It
> was 1983 and I'd just written the words: 'Site
> normal. Nothing to report' in the logbook
>   ...I seemed to
> be full of the dream of reading, a sort of noise

---

[40] The component parts are: *Five Freedoms of Movement* (1987); *livelihood* (2004), which collected five books (*The Basic Colours: A Watchman's Log* [1994], *Zulu Dynamite*, *Priority* [1995], *Steps* [1998], *Adherence*, and three linking 'interstices', published separately as *Prelude*, *Interlude* and *Postlude* [1997]); and *Sonata* and *Tig* (both 2006). Scully has since published two chapbooks and a further book-length work, *Humming* (2009).

[41] Maurice Scully, 'As I Like It', *the Beau*, 3 (1983/4), 10.

[42] Maurice Scully, *Doing the Same in English: A Sampler of Work 1987–2008* (Dublin: Dedalus Press, 2008), 200.

> *in itself, I know, inside one's self...*[43]
> It was one of my duties as a night watchman on the site
> to check the site every hour on the hour & enter in
> the site logbook, every hour on the hour, Site normal.
> Nothing to report then to phone HQ to report that there
> was, in truth, nothing to report.[44]

This seems to suggest that there is no such thing as what we lazily call 'nothing'; rather, the world is occurring continually all around us, but because we notice only what is obviously significant we tend to miss this. The first passage I quote is followed by lines beginning: '*The car had once been blue/and the lorry had been brown.... Now all the little cars were grey*'; they come from Enid Blyton's *The Six Little Motor Cars*, and are used to describe the child-like 'certainty', the 'basic colours' approach of the 'Gem school' of finished, rounded poetry—including Scully's own earlier style (GEM=JEM=rural colloquial for 'Seamus'). From this moment on, the quality of attention changes, for now the lyric ego in its standard form is renounced; it ranges from the small-scale—often the activities of insects, following Pound's *Pisan Cantos*—the cosmic ('the sensitive blue balloon of the Earth/in Space, that miracle')—and the Heraclitean flux of the humdrum, astonishing world between; wind in the trees, rain, birdsong, traffic noise, passing clouds, all 'things shimmering and going by'.[45] Immersion does not mean trance; the mind is shown working on the raw data, and, to an extent, embroiled in spinning out its biography. Hence, recurrent asides on family, landlords, life in Italy, Africa, and the West of Ireland (often marked by snatches of Italian, Irish, and Sesotho), making a 'livelihood' teaching ('I wish I had a house, wheedle and whine'), and complaints about the 'repetitive/clones' of official verse culture, 'the Gem school'.[46] Scully insistently uses generic, uninformative titles, such as 'Sonnet', 'Ballad', and 'Song' (as well as others only marginally less lacking in specificity, such as 'Fire', 'Rain', 'Steps', 'Sound'), but in this world of excited yet alert attention, 'sonnets are "sonic nets"' rather than traditional forms. Indeed, the concept of the net is a pervasive one, since recurring titles, scenes, themes, and lines act as a 'lattice' which the writer, spider-like, 'tours' for catches, his desire to capture or reflect existence both hesitant and committed.

The writing is kept alive by the alertness, fluidity, and subtlety with which consciousness is rendered in ejaculation, interrogation, commentary, parody, self-mockery, qualification, ventriloquism, and even lyric afflatus. The introduction to *The basic colours* is characteristic:

> ...I think yes
> I was touring this lattice
> now that all the little cars were grey
> ah yes he said she said
>   hey they said I'm
>   we've got a new book out

---

[43] Scully, *livelihood*, 65.
[44] Ibid., 75.
[45] Ibid., 175, 160.
[46] Ibid., 155, 18, 107.

> have you seen it
> they said
> quick! bus red
> notebooks in your
> pockets I it's about
> it I think they
> said it's about
> disparate/desperate
> the battles of a lifetime
> (love, death & the rentman)
> fading/phasing
> I could barely with great care
> hear then…[47]

Scully's speaking subject is more embattled than Squires's, as the more abrupt lines, shifts of subject, and humorous defensiveness all show. The dialogue with the external world is more frenetic, and while readers are invited to help piece it together, they are not allowed to rest or meditate.[48] If, in Squires, a primary consciousness expresses itself *through* language, patiently plumbing phenomenological depths, the self in Scully is wholly constructed, or improvised, created *from* language (as in the 'disparate/desperate' wordplay), beset and at the same time validated by its involvement in the contingent ('love, death & the rentman').

Things That Happen is still too recent, and too large a work, to assess properly. However, the self-effacing virtuosity with which it negotiates the passage of its provisional ego between everyday existence and linguistic dissolve, its acute notations on parenthood, partnership, work cares, and a self of 'the merest threads//holding "stability" together' in 'patience privacy/doggedness' (a humorous deflation of Stephen Dedalus's credo), its admissions of frustration while avoiding the false foreclosures of 'AW. DAH', all without becoming formless and boring, are hugely impressive.[49] Scully manages to create a lyric 'I' whose discrete identity arises from language's autonomy, rather than being forged in opposition to it like those of many mainstream poets, whose poetic self-projections, for all their superficial dishevelment, are woodenly monologic by contrast.

VIII

Scully's concern with flux is also found in the work of Catherine Walsh, yet Walsh goes further towards a completely written surface of depersonalized textuality, and her fragmentation, parataxis, and collage continually highlight the unworkableness of poetry

[47] Ibid., 17.
[48] See Kit Fryatt, '"Must not attempt escape/from here and now": Maurice Scully Reading Brian Coffey', in *Other Edens: The Life and Work of Brian Coffey*, ed. Benjamin Keatinge and Aengus Woods (Dublin and Portland: Irish Academic Press, 2010), 231.
[49] Scully, *livelihood*, 322, 99.

reliant on image, and a model of language as communication.[50] By contrast to Scully's chaffing, haunted, but ultimately self-mocking consciousness, in Walsh's poetry the autobiographical material (and self) is more radically dispersed across the space of the page, and intercut with other, non-subjective texts. And while she, too, writes out of a domestic scene, all of her books begin with a sense of personal dislocation, of being in transit, and non-belonging, as reflected in a greater interest in the poetics of error, incompletion, and occasional opacity.

Making Tents (or 'tense') introduces the temporary homes of an emigrant life, and the linguistic unease that derives from surviving as a TEFL teacher in Barcelona. Some passages—such as the conflation of a childhood memory with a family myth concerning the Black and Tans, and the song of a wood pigeon—are verbal-visual maps, almost concrete poems:

> take two cows
> Taffy take two
> wood pigeons across the river
> in the orchard
> ka cu coo
> khaki kaku[51]

This separates the contemplation of place from a mythos of rootedness by eliminating obvious affective charges; this quality intensifies in her next work, *Short Stories*, which mixes unattributed quotes, historical material, natural history, and dictionary definitions by way of undercutting 'The constant temptation to indulge in anecdote: narrative'.[52] This prepared the way for a more determined mix of source materials and languages in *Pitch*, in which columns of material on the same page offer separately simultaneous or cross-linked multiple reading paths:

> I used to read her stood 'never rescind' they said
> Well   still collectively denying
>   oh well[53]

Different verbal layers, drawn from overheard speech, ruminations, social reportage, the extasis of lyric reverie, and repetition à la Gertrude Stein, produce a richly dialogic weave of what Walsh calls a 'stratification/of experience' in which no one version of events is 'easy in the mind'.[54] There is an avant-garde urge to explore the communal possibilities of poetry here, but paradoxically it can only be (tentatively) achieved through fragmentation which induces a sense of doubt.

---

[50] I am thinking here of Marjorie Perloff's discussion of the response of US poets to the saturation of late twentieth-century society by the powerful images generated by advertising, news, business, and politics. Marjorie Perloff, *Radical Artifice: Writing Poetry in the Age of Media* (Chicago: University of Chicago Press, 1991, repr. 1994), 92.

[51] Catherine Walsh, *Idir Eatortha* and *Making Tents* (London: Invisible Books, 1996), 80.

[52] Catherine Walsh, *Short Stories* (Twickenham and Wakefield: North and South, 1989), 19.

[53] Catherine Walsh, *Pitch* (Durham: Pig Press, 1994), 11.

[54] Walsh, *Pitch*, 36.

In *Idir Eatortha* ('in between'), this fascination with unbelonging is even more concerned with transient urban land-, sound-, and language-scapes; that it in parts reads like a script, with directions ('[politely, respectfully]') is a reminder of the work's strong performance aspect.[55] The world of *City West* (2005) is also that of suburban Dublin, now shaped by the daily tasks of bringing up a family. As in *Idir Eatortha*, the particulars of existence are fugitive—traffic, a rose, the Dart, washing, a brick wall, sleeping children—and intercut with overheard speech ('how ye? a yeah rih'), songs, news media, and the communings of a hovering, often distracted, consciousness.[56] This can be brilliantly done, using the 'dashing gerund' of present participles to describe children's play, for example, or in giving a powerful sense of the noise and threat implicit in city life, as well the swirling 'inhibitions/reticence//mythical castles' through which it is all filtered and perceived.[57] The final pages of *City West* may mark a break with West Dublin for the West of Ireland, however; a passage in Irish, part of which reads 'focus on the/tension between traditional native ideas/of the world and more modern ways of/looking at things', is followed by another about:

> looking at the map, the details, whatever,
> emerged, without prompting,
> in a natural way...
>   —to think of your public rather than of
> the truth of what you say is, for
> instance, quite common and not
> regarded as a crime—[58]

This presents the writer and the market, mainstream and alternative poetries, in terms which are stark by comparison with Scully's more playful flytings, and the book's telling last words are '(time to go)'.[59]

This suggests that *Optic Verve* is continuous with the move from Dublin and disengagement from aspects of the modern urban world. Certainly, its title plays on 'optic nerve', the conduit by which the image-saturated consumer-capitalist world is delivered to us. But the book's opening is as determinedly non-visual and opaque as anything Walsh has written, reminiscent of Coffey or certain lines (for instance 'Of about to within which') from Ron Silliman's *Tjanting*:

> bird better hurry
> yet meant should change
> in stare whatever pursue
> while repose as ever just
> time separate effect present each way
> of this never need or fulfil
> not only decision it's blinded

---

[55] Walsh, *Idir*, 39.
[56] Catherine Walsh, *City West* (Exeter: Shearsman, 2005), 69.
[57] Ibid., 22, 65.
[58] Ibid., 80.
[59] Ibid., 82.

for chance perfectly allowance
once mind[60]

This both mimics the opacity of the post-contemporary world and resists its visual lingua franca in extreme textuality. After three such paragraphs on separate pages, this material is confined to right-hand pages as short Spanish phrases appear on the left-hand pages, and then erupt in a complex weaving of fragmentary English and Spanish. At the same moment, the right-hand page initiates a narrative in realist prose about Walsh's family, the demolition of Dublin's notorious Fatima Mansions housing scheme. Having broached questions of naming and home, the text reverts to Walsh's characteristic complex open-field verbal weaves, featuring double-and triple-columned parallel narratives, self-contained and yet liable to cross-refer, through which a resistance to 'some/C18the rationalism' and the 'internalised//ideologies/which were/justifying/oppression' periodically emerges.[61] Like *City West*, the constantly varying poetic textures, rhythms, and shapings of *Optic Verve* virtuosically '[peel]/away the middle march' of any Casaubon-like key to experience and prevent the 'repose' of 'impositional narrative'.[62] But it is also much more charged with anger; at deaths of loved ones, at the gombeen depredations of businessmen, politicians, and planners, at the fate of the Irish language, and at postmodernism's 'rabid decontextualizations' of history.[63] This partly reflects the move to Limerick, for the Gaelic and family material increases as the book progresses. Whether the stridency of the political denunciations, in particular, is always contained by the frame established by the book's subtitle, 'A Commentary', is a moot point, it seems to me. However, *Optic Verve* is often more intelligently and provocatively complex, as well as more passionate, than anything Walsh has written, and she is aware of, if not entirely in control of, its excess, signalling at one point that it may be a necessary taking stock ahead of further development: 'if angry so ought/we know/each other'.[64]

IX

The New Hampshire encounter of 1996 fell between the IRA ceasefire in 1994 and the 1998 Good Friday Agreement. The erosion of polarized politics since that date has opened up a newly tolerant cultural space in which alternative poetry has been able to thrive as never before in Ireland. Technical as well as cultural-political changes have expanded its reach and recognition during the last fifteen years. The worldwide web has made it easier for a small number of dispersed poets to form a critical mass and a

---

[60] Catherine Walsh, *Optic Verve: A Commentary* (Exeter: Shearsman, 2009), 7.
[61] Ibid., 28.
[62] Ibid., 73, 54.
[63] Ibid., 107.
[64] Ibid., 129.

supportive network, in Ireland and beyond. It has also allowed a circumvention of official poetry's monopoly of representation: the first item given on a Google search for 'Irish poetry', for example, is a Wikipedia entry containing a paragraph on 'Experiment' that mentions Smith, Joyce, Squires, Young, Scully, and Healy. Cost and distribution difficulties mean that successors to *The Lace Curtain* have been rare and short-lived, although the Galway-based *Burning Bush* (1999–2004), edited by the Irish-American Mike Begnal, was an exception. Begnal, shaped by Beat, African-American, and New York School poetry, had arrived in Ireland in the late 1990s and was shocked by the staidness of its poetic culture; the first issue of *Burning Bush* asked the awkward question 'Is there an Irish underground?' The ensuing debate featured in the *Irish Times*, and Begnal established contact with Joyce, Healy, and others, publishing many of the poets discussed in this essay before eventually returning to the USA. Although it reflected the spread of alternative poetry outside Dublin and Cork, *The Burning Bush* also probably demonstrated the unviability of such a journal in Ireland, while confirming the possibilities of the web: the websites of SoundEye, Wild Honey, and hardPressed, and poets' blogs, perform something of the function of journals, and will inevitably expand in the future. On the other hand, another new technology, print on demand, has strengthened the historically weak Irish small-press scene; Wild Honey, NWP (and the recent Wurm im Apfel Press in Dublin and Default Publishing in Cork) can now match the quality of publications by the majors without being crushed by storage costs, and market and distribute via the web.

Crucially, too, the poets have received recognition outside Ireland: Fanny Howe describes Joyce as a favourite poet, for example, and Peter Riley enthuses about Scully. The SoundEye festival is a regular event on the international alternative-poetry circuit, and is busily being emulated by Wurm im Apfel. Unlike the 1960s and the 1980s, then, Irish alternative poetry today has irreversibly broken with its marginalized condition. This, in turn, has made it more difficult to ignore in Ireland. Thus, Michael Smith held the (rotating) editorship of *Poetry Ireland Review* in 2002, Trevor Joyce has been poet in residence at Galway and Cork universities, and both have been elected to Aosdána. The Irish Writer's Centre has hosted readings by Charles Bernstein and Peter Manson. North-South exchanges have been extremely limited, but Ciaran Carson and Medbh McGuckian have read at the Cork SoundEye Festival, and, with Fran Brearton and Alan Gillis, Carson organized a symposium on alternative poetry at the Seamus Heaney Centre in Belfast.

Against J. C. C. May's observation in 2006 that 'younger people who write [alternative] poems... are largely invisible', and his speculation that interest in such work could become 'as select as that which composes Latin elegiacs or clutches at the Book of Common prayer', it appears to me that alternative Irish poetry has been renewing itself for some time.[65] Inevitably, as what I have already said indicates, in this world the signs of growth or decay register themselves at a very small-scale level, and are therefore difficult to verify; a new small press here, a grant given there, a mainstream anthology including an alternative poet, and so on. But it is, I feel, significant that the SoundEye event in Cork is now run

---

[65] Mays, *N* 11, 26.

not by Trevor Joyce but by arts workers and writers in their twenties and thirties, among them the poets James Cummins, Rachel Warriner, and Fergal Gaynor. It is also significant that Wurm im Apfel has emerged to play a similar role in Dublin, championing the work of Coffey and Scully and organizing readings by alternative poets from Britain and the USA (Its organizers, in their thirties, include the poet Dylan Harris and the critic Kit Fryatt.). In the meantime, international interest and support has continued.

Most important of all is the undeniable quality of the poetry itself. The last fifteen years has seen a huge upsurge in creative energy, evidenced in the appearance of major works by Joyce, Scully, and Walsh, and *Collecteds* from Mills and Squires. It is clear from this work that Irish alternative poetry is not some derivative or willed offshoot of British or American experimental poetries. When it was 'discovered' in the 1990s, there was speculation that one of the most striking features of its poetic ecology—the varied and distinct voices of its practitioners—might be a result of having been unskewed by exposure to external forces, of its isolation from the Irish mainstream and only tangential involvement in North American and British alternative poetries. This has been confirmed, insofar as that distinctiveness has not changed as a result of the greater integration of Irish alternative poetry, over the last decade, into the circuits of the international poetry world beyond.

Moreover, its Irish provenance is inescapable, even though it does not ostensibly concern itself with identity. Maurice Scully, for example, makes extensive use of the Irish language in *Things That Happen*, and his work banters continually with Irish mainstream poetry as 'Beauty Permanence plc'.[66] Billy Mills's clipped lyrics draw on early Irish nature poetry. Randolph Healy's poems are chiefly concerned with logic, science, and the counter-intuitive, but are concerned with things Irish too: one poem, '(The) Republic of Ireland', anagrammatizes its title ('her lie-lined tub of crap/her pallid beef in court') to withering effect.[67] Catherine Walsh uses *dinnseanchas*, Dublin slang, and Irish politics and history. Finally, Trevor Joyce's work is thematically 'Irish' from the imperial deforestation in *Without Asylum* to the recent, as-yet-unpublished *Rome's Wreck*, an 'intralingual translation' of Edmund Spenser's *The Ruines of Rome* into a monosyllabic contemporary English which offers a witty, post-colonial slant on the Planter poet's polysyllabic rhetoric.[68]

In the range of contemporary English-language alternative poetries, Irish poets present an interesting and fruitfully anomalous case. Their work resembles, in some ways, that of the US LANGUAGE poets, being directed against the instrumental use of language. Yet as we have seen, in Scully's case, a residual sense of self stubbornly inheres in this poetry, and is perhaps related to Ireland's history as a colony and its consequent lack, unlike the US and Britain, of imperial guilt and hence of a wholesale renunciation of the sovereign ego. This has arguably been aided by the poetry's democratic, non-elitist

---

[66] Maurice Scully, *Humming* (Exeter: Shearsman, 2009), 31.
[67] Randolph Healy, *Green 532: Selected Poems 1983–2000* (Cambridge: Salt Press, 2002), 40.
[68] Goodby, 'Through My Dream', 162–4.

spirit, and its lack of disfigurement by the 'ruinously competitive or programmatic' aspects of some of its English and US counterparts.[69]

As alternative Irish poetry becomes less ignorable, however, the dialectical relationship with the mainstream in which it exists, and its implicit critique of a marketized poetics, is bound to lead to more soul-searching, forcing all readers of Irish poetry to question the rather self-centred terms in which it has defined itself hitherto. Even if it only exposes critical aporias and serves as a reminder that poetry is what society defines as poetry rather than some timeless essence, alternative Irish poetry will have served a useful purpose in making Irish writing generally, buoyed by the successes of the Irish brand for so many decades, less complacent. Yet even if one should never lose sight of the irony by which the Ireland of Yeats, Joyce, and Beckett now has one of the most conservative poetry cultures in the world, the deeper irony is that Ireland's very precocity in literary innovation—and for Baudelaire the first authentically modern writer was Charles Maturin—derives from a dialectical, rather than purely oppositional, relationship between alternative and conservative mainstream poetries; the marginalized 'failure' of the one is intimately related to the marketized 'success' of the other.[70]

[69] Mays, *N 11*, 11.

[70] As Mays notes, 'The persistent, distinctive strain of alternative writing develops alongside, indeed is irregularly produced by, the striking conservatism (traditionalism) of Irish poets who have proved so successful in the world market and are consequently emulated at home.' Mays, *N 11*, 17.

CHAPTER 38

'THE NOTHING-COULD-BE-SIMPLER LINE': FORM IN CONTEMPORARY IRISH POETRY

FRAN BREARTON

I

In 'The Irish Efflorescence', Justin Quinn argues in relation to a new generation of poets from Ireland (David Wheatley, Conor O'Callaghan, Vona Groarke, Sinéad Morrissey, and Caitríona O'Reilly among them) that while:

> Northern Irish poetry, in both the first and second waves, is preoccupied with the binary opposition of Ireland and England...[t]he youngest Irish poets...are not bounded in the same way by this opposition. The extent of their lack of engagement with this theme is evident when one notices that they do not even go to the trouble to subvert it.... Several of these poets write about experiences abroad, but even this eludes the usual pattern of exile and return which structured so much expatriate Irish poetry in the past. And while none of them is from Dublin, they are not concerned either with the myths of rural culture that animated Patrick Kavanagh's poetry, or, through its subversion, Anthony Cronin's. The extent of this thematic shift should not be underestimated: although the term is a little modish, it seems accurate to say that they are the first genuinely post-national generation.

However, as he goes on to note, '[i]n formal aspects they are more conservative', some learning 'their handling of half-rhyme and stanza from Derek Mahon, some their prosody from Michael Longley'. Most, he says, 'avoid Muldoon at all costs', since his 'tone is so infectious and spreads so rapidly'; and '[a]s for imitating Heaney, they leave that to Americans'. Thomas Kinsella, he concludes, 'has had virtually no impact on them, and they perpetuate the division between conservative mainstream and experimental margins that was present in Irish poetry for most of the twentieth century'.[1] Quinn is not advocating that perpetuation as a willed act necessarily; rather the comment acknowledges a debate that has been at the heart of Irish poetry criticism for decades. Indeed, as Matthew Campbell notes in his essay for this book, it may even be traced back to the nineteenth century: 'Between Mangan and Ferguson', he writes, 'a fissure of a sort opens up in Irish poetry, one that may be seen to this day', between 'an innovative strain in Irish poetry open to international influences' and a 'liberal-conservative development of a self-consciously Hiberno-English poetic diction or prosody'.[2]

My focus here is on three poets from the Republic of Ireland—David Wheatley, Caitríona O'Reilly, and Justin Quinn himself. Identified by Quinn as part of a new 'post-national generation', they have also been loosely (if not always accurately) associated with formal conservatism, even with a new formalism; they worked collaboratively in the 1990s and early 2000s; they have significantly contributed to critical debate about modern poetry in ways that might throw into question some of the labels attached to them and to Irish poetry more generally; and they complicate the 'division' or 'fissure' sometimes traced in Irish literary history. Quinn published his first poetry collection, *The O'o'a'a' Bird*, in 1995, Wheatley's debut, *Thirst*, appeared in 1997, and O'Reilly's *The Nowhere Birds* in 2001. Wheatley and Quinn co-founded *Metre*, a journal of poetry and criticism, in 1996, O'Reilly later joining them on the editorial board; for all three, the journal *Thumbscrew*, founded by Tim Kendall in 1994, and which ran for twenty-one issues, shutting up shop in 2002, provided a lively and often controversial outlet for their poems and poetry reviews; Wheatley and O'Reilly worked collaboratively in a long partnership that resulted in a joint publication, *Three-Legged Dog*, in 2002; and Quinn and Wheatley have had a long (literary) friendship, comparable in its way to the early friendship between Mahon and Longley, one that has involved, over the years, the exchange of poems for comment and critique. All three studied at Trinity College Dublin in the early 1990s. Both Quinn and O'Reilly attended (as did Sinéad Morrissey and Claire Kilroy) the writers' workshops run by Michael Longley, then Writer Fellow at Trinity, from January to April 1993, with Wheatley also closely associated with the group.[3]

In a tribute volume published on the occasion of Michael Longley's seventieth birthday, Caitríona O'Reilly acknowledges both the importance of the Trinity workshops to her own formal development, and the 'higher-than-usual number of participants' in the group who 'persisted with writing and have since published books'. The latter she attributes to Longley's ability to inspire younger poets; the former she describes as the discovery, for the first time, 'that a poem has a ticking heart and lungs, that there is an emotional and rhetorical logic to the way it unfolds in time and space'. The workshops

---

[1] Justin Quinn, 'The Irish Efflorescence', *Poetry Review* 91:3 (Autumn 2001), 46.

[2] See ch. 1, p. 10.

[3] Those who wished to be considered for attendance at the two-hour workshops were required to submit portfolios in advance. Wheatley, as far as Longley recalls, did not do so, hence was not part of the group, although he did meet with Longley to discuss his work during the same period. Michael Longley, interview with the author, July 2011.

presented them with formal challenges in the different modes of the lyric. 'I became', O'Reilly writes, 'obsessed with locating the break in the line, with finding artful symmetry and instinctive balance'.[4] Given the preoccupation with set forms in all three writers (of which more anon), Longley's significance to their development might initially seem counter-intuitive. His preference is not for writing in set forms (the sonnet is the exception) and his oeuvre is free of the villanelles and sestinas essayed by peers such as Mahon, Heaney, and Muldoon. Yet Longley's concentrated lyric style (in contrast to the looser, conversational, and overtly political style and idiom of Durcan and Kennelly, who loomed large on the Dublin scene in the 1980s and 1990s), the quest for 'balance' in the earlier work, where almost every poem is rhymed, and his complex syntactical structures, bear fruit in O'Reilly most evidently, but in Quinn and Wheatley too.

The fascination with form, a fascination worn on the sleeve (as it is in Longley's and Mahon's early work) in the poetry published by O'Reilly, Quinn, and Wheatley in the 1990s and early 2000s, might have begun in, or been nurtured by, the writing workshop. Selina Guinness notes too, in *The New Irish Poets*, that the presence of sestinas and villanelles in Irish poetry of the 1990s is partly to do with 'academe' (MAs in Creative Writing; doctoral study of English literature).[5] But these three poets have done more than produce one or two academic exercises either in the laborious acquisition of technique or in the service of a neo-formalist aesthetic: the interest is evidently more extensive. Along with other formal varieties, O'Reilly has notched up a sestina ('Thin'), more unusually, a pantoum ('Persona'), a poem in terza rima, 'The Mermaid', and some sonnets; Quinn, prose poems, sonnets, several sonnet sequences, villanelles ('A Strand of Hair' and 'Days of 1913'), a poem in terza rima without the rima ('Vesalius and the Soul'); Wheatley, extraordinarily, three sestinas ('Bray Head', 'Landscape with Satellite Dish', and 'Chronicle'), two villanelles ('Poem' and 'Recklessness'), prose poems, sonnets and sonnet sequences, an extended terza rima poem ('Traffic'), a sequence in terza rima ('Misery Hill'), and some haiku ('Whalebone Haiku').

In a recent essay for *Poetry Ireland Review*, surveying the journal's poetry publishing in the first decade of the twenty-first century, Maria Johnston notes that the 'enduring poetry workshop favourite, the sestina', in its various *PIR* appearances, 'ultimately puts one in mind of the final question in Ian Duhig's list of questions that turn bowels to sorbet: "Would you like to see my earwax candles?/Would you like to hear my new sestina?".'[6] Yet if the sestina can be a sometimes unfortunate rite of passage, a poem that, as Paul Fussell observes, 'would seem to be one that gives more structural pleasure to the contriver than to the apprehender',[7] there are exceptions that prove the rule. One such is Leontia Flynn's '26' in her first collection *These Days* (2004); another is O'Reilly's 'Thin' from *The Nowhere Birds*, a poem which in marrying form to subject turns its

[4] Caitríona O'Reilly, 'When in Doubt, Intimidate the Opposition', in *Love Poet, Carpenter: Michael Longley at Seventy*, ed. Robin Robertson (London: Enitharmon Press, 2009), 106–7.

[5] Selina Guinness, 'Introduction', *The New Irish Poets* (Tarset: Bloodaxe, 2004), 30.

[6] Maria Johnston, 'Reading Irish Poetry in the New Century: *Poetry Ireland Review* 2000–2009', *Poetry Ireland Review* 100 (March 2010), 37.

[7] Paul Fussell, *Poetic Meter & Poetic Form*, rev. ed. [1965] (New York: McGraw Hill, Inc., 1979), 145.

self-conscious artificiality into its virtue. Equating the form of the poem, the 'room' of the stanza, with the physical body of the speaker, and with a trapped psyche, O'Reilly turns the discipline of the set form into a comment on the progress of the disease—anorexia:

> It is chill and dark in my small room.
> A wind blows through gaps in the roof,
> piercing even the eiderdown. My skin
> goose-pimples in front of the cloudy glass
> though there was scalding tea for dinner
> with an apple. I'm cold to the bone.

What begins, in both cases, as a willed exercise in control, ultimately ends by controlling its author: power gradually shifts from the anorexic to anorexia itself; the poet's imaginative licence is increasingly subject to the implacable demands of the sestina. Where form obtrudes (as in 'I'm such a bone-/head!') the discomfort, the bits of the poem that stick out, one might say, are themselves an equivalent of the bones that begin to protrude through the speaker's skin: 'My hip-bones/stick in the foam mattress.... My ribs rise like the roof/of a house that's fashioned from glass'. The process of the poem is one of destructive self-discipline, and simultaneous creation of a fragile edifice, a body (like the brittle body of the poem) only just holding itself intact: *'how shatterproof is my skin?'* While the poem records its female speaker's literal shrinking, a negation of self, it also insists on making space for itself, in paradoxically gruesome fashion, against the pressures of a male-dominated environment: the speaker's starved and therefore 'more habitable' skin is a 'ceiling that shatters like glass/over those diners off gristle and bone'.[8] Fitting oneself into the sestina is not exactly the equivalent of slipping into something more comfortable—although that may be precisely the poem's point.

O'Reilly's observance of the demands of a sestina is, as we would expect given her subject, fairly exact, and exacting. Its only slight variations are 'bone/bones', 'room/room's', and, once only, 'skin/skim', 'glass/class'; of its end words, 'dinner' is the unaltered (unconsumed) constant until the envoi, where it mutates into 'diners', at which point 'roof', also a constant through six stanzas, becomes the more politically charged, and shattered, glass 'ceiling'. By contrast, Wheatley's 'Landscape with Satellite Dish' falls rather into Fussell's category above, the pleasure seeming to lie more in the making than the reading, and the rationale for the form (Bart Simpson meets the sestina, 'Doh!') less in evidence.[9] More conventional, and also from his first collection, is 'Bray Head', which paints a landscape of mountain, gorse, and sea, and captures, through the repetitions, a certain tranquillity. But it is the sestina in his second collection, 'Chronicle', that more convincingly earns its form, and it does so, in contrast to O'Reilly's approach, by opening up to a degree of flexibility—first through its hexameter line, giving the poet, in effect, an additional forty-two feet to play with, and lengthening the gap between the appearance of the end-words; second, by a degree of end-word variation in which the linguistic play is not merely born out of necessity, but is part of the poem's effect:

---

[8] Caitríona O'Reilly, *The Nowhere Birds* (Tarset: Bloodaxe, 2001), 20–1.
[9] David Wheatley, *Thirst* (Oldcastle: Gallery, 1997), 38–9.

'Wicklow' mutates, variously, into 'clue', 'claw', and 'loy'; 'van' into 'vain', 'oven', 'even', and 'heaven'; 'roads' into 'roods' and 'raids'; and, in a poem which carries a wry conscious-ness of Heaney and Muldoon, 'father', constant through the first five stanzas, becomes 'fodder' in the sixth. That the father is poetic fodder here (as he has been so productively for Heaney and Muldoon) serves as an acknowledgement that this is both a family 'Chronicle' and a literary one, with echoes of Wheatley's literary forefathers, of Heaney's sestina 'Two Lorries', for instance, or of 'Digging':

> My grandfather is chugging along the back roads
> between Kilcoole and Newtown in his van,
> the first wood-panelled Morris Minor in Wicklow...
>
> ...
>
> The old man never did get to farm like his father,
> Preferring to trundle his taxi along the back roads.

The poem's convoluted syntax brings the chronicle full circle, memory doubling back on itself ('All this coming back to me in the mountains/early one morning'), so that it plays effectively to the form's capacity for linearity and circularity at the same time:

> ...driving on down to Hacketstown with my father
> we find grandfather's grandfather under an even
> gravestone gone to his Church of Ireland heaven,
>
> and his grandfather too, my father maintains,
> all turned, long since to graveyard fodder
> just over the country line from their own dear Wicklow,
> the dirt tracks, twisting lanes and third-class roads
> they would have hauled themselves round while they endured,
>
> before my father and I ever followed the roads
> or my mountainy cousins first picked up a loy,
> or my grandfather's van ever hit that garage door.[10]

In Muldoonian fashion, the poem has its tail in its mouth (compare '7 Middagh Street'), and, with the 'loy' of the envoi irresistibly reminiscent of Christy Mahon's *Playboy of the Western World* 'patricide', a parodic spirit of reverent irreverence towards literary tradi-tion, lineage, and the (vanishing) point of origin.

Wheatley's *Misery Hill* (2000) is dominated by set forms, from the opening 'Sonnets to James Clarence Mangan', through two villanelles and a sestina, to the closing 'Misery Hill', a sequence of thirty-three poems in terza rima.[11] Likewise, Quinn's second collec-tion, *Privacy* (1999), a book preoccupied with (poetic) architecture, is also one in which he tries his hand at a couple of villanelles, a form notoriously difficult to sustain effec-tively in English. As John Lennard observes, 'Perhaps more than any other form specify-ing line repetition, villanelles live or die by what John Hollander calls "one simple

---

[10] David Wheatley, *Misery Hill* (Oldcastle: Gallery, 2000), 39–40.
[11] 'Misery Hill' is the title given both to a shorter lyric in *Misery Hill*, 10–11, and also to the long sequence which closes the book, 60–92.

phenomenon: repeating something often may make it *more trivial*—because more expected and therefore carrying less information, as an engineer might put it—or, because of shifting or developing context in each stanza preceding, *more important*".[12] Unsurprisingly, no more than three twentieth-century villanelles in English have made their way convincingly into the Western canon—Dylan Thomas's 'Do not go gentle into that good night', William Empson's 'Missing Dates', and Elizabeth Bishop's 'One Art'. Heaney's 'Villanelle for an Anniversary', a poem written in 1986 to celebrate Harvard's 350th year, was his first villanelle and, he has said, one that 'should be his last', the form chosen in part for practical reasons.[13] Mahon's own forays into the territory in the early 1980s, indicative of his affinity with French poetry, 'The Andean Flute', 'The Dawn Chorus', and 'Antarctica', never quite lift themselves above the extreme artifice of the form, although the most memorable of them, 'The Andean Flute', has a quality of lyrical enchantment in tension with a controlled 'frenzy', and a musicality that serves its 'ancient theme': 'He dances to that music in the wood./Who said the banished gods were gone for good?'[14] Muldoon, unable to resist the kind of challenges posed by Empson, pulls off a double villanelle in *Horse Latitudes*, a technical triumph.[15]

The villanelle by Wheatley in *Misery Hill*, simply entitled 'Poem', finds memorable repeating lines, as in 'The roof has fallen but the house still stands', with the potential to carry different metaphorical resonance, although the poem itself does not, through the repetitions, gather an incremental significance. The form necessitates that it ends where it began; but as with many villanelles, necessity is not always made into virtue, and the reflection of 'Poem' on its own form—'the house still stands'—tends towards the static.[16] The same is true of Quinn's 'Days of 1913', from *Privacy*, although here that time-warped quality serves the poem's purpose more evidently, in its depiction of Central European small-town certainties in the days before the First World War swept them aside:

> The sun goes down on courthouse and mainstreet.
> The grocer has his borsch and says as often,
> 'This soup the emperor himself could eat.'[17]

---

[12] See John Lennard, *The Poetry Handbook*, 2nd ed. [1996] (Oxford: Oxford University Press, 2005), 52, and John Hollander, *Rhyme's Reason*, 3rd ed. [1981] (New Haven and London: Yale University Press, 2001), 38.

[13] See the *Harvard Gazette*, 3 October 2011: http://news.harvard.edu/gazette/story/2008/10/heaney-catches-the-heart-off-guard/. The poem was delivered in Harvard's Tercentenary Theatre in 1986 and its form was apparently an attempt to answer the question 'How do people listen to a poem over a loudspeaker?'

[14] Derek Mahon, *The Hunt by Night*, 2nd ed. [1982] (Oxford: Oxford University Press, 1995), 13.

[15] See Paul Muldoon, 'Soccer Moms', *Horse Latitudes* (London: Faber, 2006), 28–9. Empson's challenge lies in his own poetic achievement, but also in his criticism, as in for instance his throwing down the gauntlet on the double sestina in Sidney's *Arcadia*: 'limited as this form may be, the capacity to accept a limitation so unflinchingly, the capacity even to conceive so large a form as a unit of sustained feeling, is one that has been lost since that age'. William Empson, *Seven Types of Ambiguity* [1930] (London: Chatto & Windus, 1956), 38.

[16] Wheatley, *Misery Hill*, 46.

[17] Justin Quinn, *Privacy* (Manchester: Carcanet, 1999), 45.

The repetitions become, in the course of the poem, a manifestation of post-war nostalgia for pre-war values, with the setting sun a broader reflection on loss of empire: 'Their words repeat/with longing in their children's children's children,/The sun gone down on courthouse and mainstreet.' Both poets, too, have written villanelles as love poems. Wheatley's 'Recklessness', whose form in one sense belies its title, with its opening line, 'Join me again, love, in the old mistake', is a nod to the 'old mistake' of love, and/or the failures of love, as well as to the unfulfilled 'ache' that is the love poem itself, 'the permanence we aim at and we miss'.[18] Quinn's 'A Strand of Hair' is perhaps the only one of these poems that marries its form perfectly to subject. An epithalamion, obliquely reminiscent of a seventeenth-century metaphysical love poem (as mediated, too, by Longley's own early 'Epithalamion', a poem similarly indebted to the metaphysicals), 'A Strand of Hair' plays on its form as both freedom and restraint. Through its circling and repetition it holds a delicate balance between choices made and choices never to be made:

> And though I never asked you for your hand,
> We will be married, and
> As this, hardly to be felt, twines around my finger,
> So light will be our wedding-band.
> . . .
> And you won't ask me to leave my rain-cursed land
> Forever for your city with its saner weather.
> I'll never ask you too. Give me your hand.
> So light will be our wedding-band.[19]

It may be attributable in part to particular influences (the later 'freer' Plath one of them, MacNeice another) that O'Reilly evidences far less of a compulsion to work in set forms, to 'order' her imagination to this degree. Quinn notes O'Reilly's capacity to give 'an impression of incredible compactness and discipline' whilst still often 'writing in freer modes'.[20] And yet, as in 'Thin', the strict form tests the capacity for freedom within boundaries, proving an effective vehicle for the explorations of self, and for the play of interior and exterior, fixity and fluidity, that characterize her work. A rare outing in English for the pantoum occurs in her second book, *The Sea Cabinet*, in 'Persona'. If it is less assured than Muldoon's venturing into the territory in 'The Mountain is Holding Out',[21] the form is nevertheless suited to her occasionally surreal imaginings and projections of a sometimes trapped and disturbing psyche because of its structurally disorienting effects. As John Hollander observes, in the pantoum, 'a touch of the riddle is preserved in that the first half of each quatrain is about something wholly different from the second half'.[22] The strangeness of 'Persona', the forced nature of its artificiality, its laboured forward movement (four steps forward, two steps back), is both its form and its theme:

---

[18] Wheatley, *Misery Hill*, 54.
[19] Quinn, *Privacy*, 12.
[20] Justin Quinn, 'The Irish Efflorescence', 49.
[21] See Muldoon, *Horse Latitudes*, 87–8.
[22] Hollander, *Rhyme's Reason*, 44.

> The mud-brown river is clotted with debris.
> What can I do with these dark adhesions,
> These unmoored pieces of the night?
> They breathe their black into my day –
>
> What can I do with these dark adhesions?
> If dreams are rooms in which my self accretes,
> They also breathe their black into my day.
> As a manikin, I set myself to work
>
> In dreams or rooms in which my self accretes.
> See me there with the pained carved face.

This 'pained carved' poem is cryptic; its repetitions and knotty accretions are difficult, like the mannikin's 'wooden limbs', to make 'work'. Nevertheless, it does go some way towards creating an atmosphere *of* difficulty too, a form of inward struggle at odds with an outward projection.

II

Beyond the use of set forms, notable is the fascination in Quinn with rhyming couplets, or with triplets in Wheatley—in, for instance, 'Gable End', from *Mocker*, where the mindset explored in the poem is bound up with its dead-end (gable end) end-rhymes:

> ...I too return to prod at the past,
> content if I can be the unnoticed guest
> and drop dead letters to myself in the post,
>
> delivered and thrown away at the gable end
> as I must have been, to end up lost and found
> sharing my postcode with the rain and wind.
>
> I paint myself into the tightest corner
> and, though I could not be a slower learner,
> mouth the slogans on each flag and banner
>
> that I might join the gable end people
> at last, surrendering to their appeal
> and saying a prayer beneath their dreary steeple...[23]

The parodic elements are unmissable here too—of Mahon in 'The Last of the Fire Kings', or 'Day Trip to Donegal'—as is a shared subversive Beckettian sensibility in which, as Mahon puts it, '[h]aving hit rock bottom as you do with him, you know there's nowhere to go but up'.[24] (Like Mahon, Wheatley, it seems, in his twenty-first-century Hull 'exile', is

---

[23] Wheatley, *Mocker* (Oldcastle: Gallery, 2006), 36.
[24] Derek Mahon, 'Each Poem for Me Is a New Beginning', interview by Willie Kelly, *Cork Review*, 2/3 (June 1981), 11.

not actually going 'to die their creature and be thankful'.)[25] With only a handful of exceptions, most of the poems in Quinn's *The O'o'a'a' Bird* and *Privacy* are rhymed. In *Privacy* in particular, rhyme can be expressive of the poet's being landlocked, tower-blocked, and contained, literally it seems, in squares and oblongs; yet the serendipity enjoined on the poet by rhyme can also allow for free play: as 'Bathroom' has it, 'A fight between the gridded immovables/And something that will always hate right angles....'[26] Sometimes the patterns force considerable ingenuity, as in 'Weekend Away', with its seven stanzas rhyming abcdefg with each other. Or in 'Non-Enclave', the obvious visual trick (the poem is right-aligned on the page, capitalizing the final rather than first character of the line) disguises its abba rhymes which, appearing as they do at the start of the line, are not discernible by the ear: 'this is extra ,is what's kept outside thE /door (rhymes clicking shut like locks) when it's rounD / four below and snowstorms swirl in lovelesS /-ness ,in chaos...'.[27] Quinn's interest in rhyme is not, of course, in the creation of a Muldoon-style rhyming grid—his practice in the 1990s shows more affinity with the early Longley, whose poems in his first collection are almost all rhymed, or with early Mahon through to *The Hunt by Night* (1982). But, the disclaimers about Muldoon's influence aside, there is nevertheless, in both Quinn's and Wheatley's work, a lurking fascination with such grand designs, and with the potential to shape their writing in intricate patterns not always immediately visible. Quinn, like Muldoon, is a fairly compulsive sonneteer (sonnets comprise about a third of Muldoon's *oeuvre* to date), with, for instance, a sequence of Onegin stanzas in *Fuselage*,[28] twenty sonnets, 'Prague Elegies', in *Waves and Trees* (2006), or twelve sonnets, of various kinds, making up 'The Months', in his most recent collection *Close Quarters* (2011). Wheatley comes closer to Muldoonian ambitions, perhaps, in the final 'Misery Hill' sequence, which sustains its terza rima through thirty-three poems, and which takes us on a Gallogly-esque narrative journey ('Nemo reappeared, bearing a toothbrush//and soap. "How could you," he began, "even/ imagine I'd leave you?" One of the new arrivals/yanked his jacket and asked, was this a safe haven//or what...').[29]

In an interview, Quinn acknowledges that what he misses most, living as he does in Prague, is the sea.[30] On the one hand his imagination is, of necessity, drawn into an urban landscape, 'these ringing blocks/Laid down upon the whiteness of the page';[31] on

---

[25] See Derek Mahon, 'The Last of the Fire Kings', *The Snow Party* (London: Oxford University Press, 1975), 10.

[26] Quinn, *Privacy*, 16.

[27] Ibid., 59.

[28] The poems are untitled. See *Fuselage*, 42–8. The 'Onegin stanza' is fourteen lines in iambic tetrameter, rhymed ababccddeffegg.

[29] Wheatley, *Misery Hill*, 62. See Muldoon, 'The More a Man Has the More a Man Wants' in *Quoof* (London: Faber, 1983), 40ff.

[30] See 'Justin Quinn: An Irish Poet in Prague' at www.radio.cz/en/section/books/justin-quinn-an-irish-poet-in-prague

[31] 'Apartment', *Privacy*, 15. Living in a tower block in Prague (and in a landlocked country) is, he says, rather like living in a huge machine, a far cry from the leafy suburbs of Dublin where he grew up. See n.30 above.

the other, he returns often to shaped, heterometric poems reminiscent of Mahon's technique in the title poem of *The Hunt by Night*, or of Longley's 'The Hebrides' from *No Continuing City*, poems whose ebb and flow across the page is central to their effect, and latently indicative, it seems, of a seaboard imagination. These experiments in what is close to pure syllabic verse (as Hollander notes, 'an importation into English from other languages')[32] are part of a larger concern in Quinn to work with visual as well as aural effect, characteristic also of Mahon (if one recalls for instance the shape poem 'The Window' in Mahon's *The Snow Party* [1975]),[33] and for both indicative of non-anglophone influences. In 'Clearing', as in other poems which adopt this kind of form (such as 'Childishness' or 'A Shrike'), Quinn's style is an attempt to capture movement, flux, and the natural world, the rhythmical momentum pushing towards clarity and freedom in stanzas whose underlying template is ten, four, eight, six, ten, and four syllables:

> As though we were the first to walk the earth
> And see this place,
> The twilight's flare on grass and wort,
> First to see the slant
> Of sunrays downward, every glance and pause
> Echoed with portent . . . [34]

Quinn closes his first collection, *The O'o'a'a' Bird*, with a sequence of twenty poems, 'Days of the New Republic', each comprising four five-line stanzas, with an ababa rhyme scheme. The sequence tests out stanzaic shapes for a new order. If the five-line stanza offers more room for manoeuvre, the potential for an asymmetrical open-endedness, the rhyme pattern inscribed on each poem by Quinn simultaneously seeks to connect the beginnings and endings that are his thematic concern. In 'Last Poem' he writes: 'You'd like to end with it, that's right?/The nothing-could-be-simpler line', although the poem ends with 'promise/Of new futures limbering up, as I/Full-stopped, step off into whiteness'.[35] The 'nothing-could-be-simpler line' eludes the poet, both as the 'line' to take, and, literally, in the poem itself, where it is spoken, but blacked out on the page and unreadable; yet it is also, in a sense, the in-between space where he finds himself (as in 'A Strand of Hair'). 'Days of the New Republic' is an attempt to structure thought in the uncertainties of the new Czech Republic, post-Velvet Revolution, a sequence carrying (as in 'Ur-Aisling') a consciousness of the Irish Republic's own founding mythologies, setting Quinn's adopted home of Prague alongside the home he left in Dublin. The 'line' of these poems, indeed of Quinn's *oeuvre* as a whole, is a line he identifies in the final poem of the sequence 'Geography', as the 'nothing-

---

[32] Hollander, *Rhyme's Reason*, 23.

[33] Mahon reprinted this, his only shape poem, in *Poems 1962–1978* (Oxford: Oxford University Press, 1979) but not thereafter. *The Snow Party* also contains two prose poems, 'A Hermit' and 'The Apotheosis of Tins', not subsequently reprinted. Cf. Quinn's prose poems in *Privacy*.

[34] Justin Quinn, *The O'o'a'a' Bird* (Manchester: Carcanet, 1995), 37.

[35] Ibid., 67.

could-be-simpler/Line where skies depend on seas'; it is also the borderline between two countries, and between the two (or three) languages in which, variously, he writes, lives, and works.

The five-line stanza, as Lennard notes, is less common than the tercet, quatrain, or sestet.[36] It appears seldom in Heaney's early work, for instance, only twice in *Death of a Naturalist* (1966), in two lesser-known poems, 'The Folk Singers' and 'Poor Women in a City Church', once in *Wintering Out* (1973), in 'Bye-Child', and once in *North* (1975), in 'Belderg'; Heaney's imagination, not untypically, is drawn on the whole into tercets and quatrains.[37] Yet by contrast, the five-line stanza is the form of a number of Mahon's and Longley's early 'signature' poems—Mahon's 'In Belfast' (retitled 'Spring in Belfast'), 'Preface to a Love Poem' (with an ababa rhyme scheme), 'Van Gogh among the Miners', or 'The Forger', all from *Night-Crossing* (1968); Longley's 'Epithalamion' and 'A Personal Statement' (both rhymed ababb), or 'Leaving Inishmore', and 'In a Convent Cemetery' (both ababa), from *No Continuing City* (1969) as well as, amongst others, the later 'Irish Poetry', 'The West', 'Landscape', 'Second Sight', or 'Home Ground'—notably in other words, poems preoccupied with 'home'. Philip Larkin's 'Home is So Sad' (ababa), 'Arrivals, Departures', 'Wants', or 'I Remember, I Remember' with its bleak conclusion '"Nothing, like something, happens anywhere"',[38] offer a precedent here too, not just for Mahon and Longley in the 1960s and 1970s, but later for Wheatley's 'Misery Hill', a retrospect on Dublin from the vantage (or disadvantage) point of Hull:

> Here's a single high-heeled shoe
> posed upright, still wearable,
> and a poster for a concert last year.
> …
> The wind lifts again, a post-office van
> passes silently by with letters
> for anywhere but this grim street
> with its rubble and wire-topped walls,
> featureless and empty besides.[39]

The avoidance of rhyme, and asymmetry here, along with the Larkinesque details knowingly imported across the Irish sea (a reminder that the poet sometimes narrowly associated with England and provincialism can happen anywhere too), are apposite to the rather mundane and 'featureless' landscape of 'Misery Hill'. In contrast, as Paul Fussell notes, '[t]he most attractive kinds of five-line organisation seem to involve the envelope

---

[36] John Lennard, *The Poetry Handbook*, 45. Five-line stanzas, Lennard notes, 'have no agreed name'. Paul Fussell also argues, this time in relation to three-line stanzas, that 'the general rarity of successful English three-line stanzas, suggests that stanzas of even- rather than odd-numbered lines are those that appeal most naturally to the Anglo-Saxon sensibility. We may inquire how well any three-line stanza, regardless of the talent of its practitioner, can ever succeed in English.' *Poetic Meter & Poetic Form*, 132.

[37] They are also generally unrhymed, although there are exceptions: 'Poor Women in a City Church', a poem with its echoes of MacNeice and Larkin, is rhymed aabab.

[38] Philip Larkin, *Collected Poems*, ed. Anthony Thwaite (London: Faber, 2003), 69.

[39] David Wheatley, *Misery Hill* (Oldcastle: Gallery, 2000), 11.

principle, the principle of enclosure and return...where the closure of the final sense is coincident with the sound closure echoing its initial rhymes'.[40] That may be one reason why the form suits those poems which tiptoe around a problematical concept of 'home', as well as those in search of an emotional homecoming. Mahon's 'Preface to a Love Poem', with its delicate circling of its subject, works through structure and rhyme in precisely that way too, as does Longley's 'In a Convent Cemetery': 'Although they've been gone for ages/On their morning walk...Convening out of sight and sound/To turn slowly their missal pages,//They find us here, of all places....'.[41] Others resist enclosure and return, reaching instead for a more syntactically complex and uneven structure, suggestively open-ended—as in Longley's later unrhymed five-line poems, of which he writes several in the 1990s.[42]

In Longley's *Gorse Fires*, the volume which heralds that new 1990s style, with its opening up into the longer, fluid (generally unrhymed) lines of his later work, the poet is, as he describes himself, 'an orphan now', 'making do with what has been left me'.[43] The liberating uncertainty and loss which are in part the impetus for Longley's recovery of poetry in the 1990s after a period of writer's block[44] are also influential in terms of O'Reilly's quest for self-expression. In the free-verse poem which opens her first collection, 'Perdita', she writes: 'I cannot feel found./I filled your absence in me/with all the wrong things, father,/fardels, odd bits, gewgaws...'.[45] 'Perdita' may be read as posing the problem of the 'woman poet' in relation to tradition, the 'father' here a symbolic, and literary figure, who, in the context of *A Winter's Tale*, refuses to, or simply cannot, recognize his daughter and abandons her. 'Perdita' contains the stuff of nightmares— 'trees like lobster claws/and howling. Being chased'; the body of the poem is 'the thin skin over a scream'. Throughout *The Nowhere Birds*, O'Reilly's preoccupation with carving and sculpting an exterior always carries an awareness of the fluidity, or, in 'Perdita', the 'mesh of dark' beneath. It is a concern that carries obvious political resonance in a poem such as 'Ninety Eighty-Four', an indictment of the culture and society which brought about the death of schoolgirl Ann Lovett in the 1980s.[46] In a mischievous opening, 'Saint Laurence O'Toole meant business,/with his...stiff mitre', while 'Mary wore lipstick and no shoes'. As the poem progresses, the iconography, the familiar, unchang-

---

[40] Paul Fussell, *Poetic Meter & Poetic Form*, 139

[41] Michael Longley, *Collected Poems*, 34.

[42] The five-line stanza is habitual to Longley throughout his career; the five-line poem, however, appears only in the early 1990s, often as a single sentence in loose hexameter, and seeming, thus far, unique to *The Ghost Orchid* (1995), where the title poem itself is one of six five-line poems, and *The Weather in Japan* (2000), which has a further five instances of the form.

[43] See Michael Longley, 'Icon' and 'Sea Shanty', *Gorse Fires* [1991] (London: Jonathan Cape, 2009), 1, 36.

[44] See Fran Brearton, ch. 5, *Reading Michael Longley* (Tarset: Bloodaxe, 2006) for further discussion of this point.

[45] O'Reilly, *The Nowhere Birds*, 11.

[46] Ann Lovett, a schoolgirl of fifteen, died, along with her baby boy, from haemorrhage and exposure after giving birth beside a grotto in County Longford in 1984. No one knew she was carrying the child. The event caused a public outcry and debate in Ireland.

ing statues of childhood, and the rigid codes represented by them, begin to destabilize in the face of human tragedy: 'whole crowds of Marys/wept bloody tears in the groves,// making signs with fragmented hands'.[47] Elsewhere, as in the five-line poems 'Atlantic' and 'Watermark', which owe a debt to Longley's 'The Ghost Orchid', where the petals are 'bruised into darkness', and to the fluid gender politics of his later work, the hard/ soft, surface/depth counterpointing of the poems turns, impossibly, absence into presence, the single sentence holding in its form the transient moment that has already gone. In 'Watermark':

> Among the signs that lovers' bodies give
> I loved the slow uncurling of your palms
> like beech-leaves making shadows over water:
> how my skin was awash for days on end
> with the impress of hands on a river.[48]

In the opening poem to *Privacy*, Quinn, the poet not quite in exile but permanently in transit, asks 'Where/Oh where will I unpack?'[49] The question is answered in and by the poems that follow, as he unpacks on the page, balancing his experience of Ireland with a life lived in Central Europe, and with significant international as well as Irish influences permeating his work.[50] For O'Reilly, resident in Dublin, there is a consciousness that the 'contemporary Ireland' she knows 'is almost laughably at odds with the largely fictional but weirdly persistent national construct posited by "strong" (in the Bloomian sense) writers such as Yeats, Joyce and Heaney. It is, to quote Sean O'Brien, an Ireland "where nobody lives"'.[51] If, faced as she is with different problems in terms of self, society, and tradition, she 'cannot feel found' at the opening of *The Nowhere Birds*, she is at home, in the end, in the body of her forms, both 'open' and 'closed'; yet those forms in O'Reilly, like the body, are fragile and deliberately 'uneasy', pushed almost to breaking point, conscious of 'the dark space under the stairs', 'worried' by what is in the 'corner', what one senses but cannot see just off the edge of the canvas.[52] In the final poem of her first book, 'Augury', the implied take-off into a new-found imaginative freedom and confidence might also be the birds (poems) taking off from the page into the 'nowhere' of the title, a process of composition aware of its imminent disappearance: 'For days they practise flying, then they fly'.[53]

---

[47] O'Reilly, *The Nowhere Birds*, 15.

[48] Ibid., 36.

[49] Quinn, *Privacy*, 9.

[50] See 'Justin Quinn: An Irish Poet in Prague' for discussion of the influence of Petr Borkovec, a contemporary whom he translates frequently, and other European writers on his own work.

[51] Caitriona O'Reilly, rev. of *Selected Poems* by Bernard O'Donoghue, *The Guardian*, 19 April 2008.

[52] See Caitriona O'Reilly, 'Burning Pig', 'Anxiety', and 'Thunder over the Humber', *The Nowhere Birds*, 50, 51, 52.

[53] O'Reilly, *The Nowhere Birds*, 63.

III

In *Serious Poetry*, Peter McDonald points out that:

> Form itself is a word long under suspicion in academic circles. However, poets
> themselves are unlikely to worry about the consequences, in the politics of the acad-
> emy, of any supposed 'formalism'. A respect for poems, and a respect for poems'
> workings, negotiations with language and each other, and economies of meaning,
> image, and expression, is the common currency of poetic influence; without these
> things, talk of 'intertextuality' remains mere academic chatter. It may be significant
> that this creative fascination with form is so often combined with a sceptical attitude
> to the received shapes of authority in the literary, cultural, and political spheres, at
> least among the best and most enduring poets. Because of this acceptance of form's
> authority, real poets know (as they have always known) that poetry cannot work to
> extra-poetic agendas...[54]

If a younger generation of poets from the Republic have, as suggested thus far, found
more compelling influences—certainly in terms of form—in the work of poets from the
North whose perceived 'formalism' has itself proved controversial, this is not to under-
play the importance, in other contexts, of poets such as Paul Durcan or Eavan Boland to
a contemporary Dublin scene. As Quinn observes, 'Boland...has cleared a space for
Irish women poets to emerge', even though 'her style has not been taken up by her jun-
iors'.[55] Similarly, he describes Durcan as 'an agent of social change in Ireland', who in the
1980s and 1990s 'stood as a messenger—an angel more properly—bringing news that
things could be otherwise'. Yet he concludes that Durcan's poetry 'seems unlikely to find
a permanent place in the canon. It is as though its energies were completely expended on
its occasions and has none left to move us two decades later.'[56] It is, however, to argue that
their 'creative fascination with form'—a fascination through which Quinn, Wheatley,
and O'Reilly reflect on, and redirect thinking about such tried and tested themes as
place, exile, language, and the politics of gender—owes a greater debt to those poets for
whom the pressure to write to, and therefore the compulsion to resist, extra-poetic agen-
das has informed, often in politically subversive ways, their own observance of form's
'authority'.[57]

That Quinn and Wheatley, or, in a different way, O'Reilly, are so evidently drawn to,
and fascinated by, particular kinds of formal challenge, might also seem at the very least
to affirm their place on one side of that division between 'conservative mainstream and

[54] Peter McDonald, *Serious Poetry: Form and Authority from Yeats to Hill* (Oxford: Clarendon Press,
2002), 15.

[55] Quinn, 'The Irish Efflorescence', 46.

[56] Justin Quinn, 'Containing Multitudes', rev. of Paul Durcan, *Life is a Dream: 40 Years Reading
Poems, Poetry Ireland Review* 100 (March 2010), 134–5.

[57] For further discussion see Edna Longley, *Poetry in the Wars* (Newcastle: Bloodaxe, 1986) and
McDonald, 'Yeats, Form, and Northern Irish Poetry', in *Serious Poetry*, 138–66.

experimental margins'. In her introduction to *The New Irish Poets*, Selina Guinness argues that enterprises such as *Thumbscrew* and *Metre* 'served as the promoters and often the defenders of a "new formalism"'. Changes to Irish life, she suggests, have animated this 'new formalism'; it has also been 'accelerated by academe... [by] an awareness among younger poets of the need to learn the trade as Yeats commanded'.[58] Yet the picture that emerges, in both the poetry and criticism, qualifies the lines of battle sometimes crudely drawn between formalism and experimentalism, traditionalism and modernism, as it also complicates poetry's relation to 'social change'. If anything, the formal preoccupations of these poets suggest not so much a 'formalist' ethos, whether that term carries a positive or negative charge, as a desire, with varying degrees of success, to stretch the limits of formal possibility in response to a rapidly changing social and political environment. This they strive to do in a manner which may be seen as antipathetic to certain new formalist *or* neo-modernist articulations as they have manifested themselves in Irish critical debate. It is, in other words, an obsession not simply with 'form', but with formal and stylistic diversity.

In so far as both *Metre* and *Thumbscrew* had something in common, this may be seen as the desire to step outside commonly accepted (often London-centric) literary judgements; to pay attention to small presses, to lesser known as well as major poetic figures; and, more particularly in the case of *Metre*, to acknowledge poetic dialogue beyond these islands, to enable preoccupations 'to be freely shared across borders'.[59] *Thumbscrew* had from the outset a refreshing scepticism, a propensity to question accepted judgements, and an ability to ruffle feathers. In the last issue of the magazine, Tim Kendall, its founder, notes that he relied at the outset on:

> a wave of upcoming critics and poet-critics, all in their twenties, who shared not so much a program or manifesto as a distaste for the insider dealings of the poetry scene. From Ireland came John Redmond, David Wheatley, Justin Quinn; from England, Ian Sansom; from the States, Stephen Burt; from South Africa, Elizabeth Lowry. I could rely on any of them to state what they thought and to state it intelligently and entertaining; between them, they very soon began to influence for the better the culture of poetry reviewing in this country.[60]

'The great advantage of an independent little magazine,' he concludes, 'is that it need not pander to anyone'. Here are some turns of the screw: Ian Sansom ('Armitage's poetry is a compendium of all that is pseudo, mal-dicted and calloused in the underworld of the English language. And that's his good stuff'); Simon Brittan ('the most irritating [and potentially misleading] aspect of Duffy is her insistence on writing prose as though it were poetry'); Caitríona O'Reilly ('everything Paulin writes labours under the dead hand

---

[58] Guinness, ed., *The New Irish Poets*, 14, 30.

[59] Quinn, 'Of Grids, Flux, and the Patternless Expanse', rev. of Armitage and Crawford, eds, *The Penguin Book of Poetry from Britain and Ireland Since 1945*, in *Contemporary Poetry Review*: www.cprw.com/Quinn/grids.htm

[60] Tim Kendall, 'Editorial', *Thumbscrew* 20–21 (2002), 2–3. Although, as he goes on to say, '*Plus ça change*: the London scene is still cosy, self-savouring and mediocre...'.

of Lit. Crit.'); Justin Quinn ('the abandonment of regular rhyme and meter probably had more to do with Kinsella's own failure to master them than with the times being out of joint, or some such Modernist escape hatch').[61] If *Metre* has ruffled fewer feathers, it has also served to promote a more cosmopolitan view of Irish poetry. Both magazines evidence a willingness to criticize the most mainstream of 'conservative mainstream' poets.

Guinness's 'new formalism' tag, applied either to these journals or to the Irish poets writing and publishing in this generation, is thus misleading, since the term has a particular currency, notably in the US, where 'new formalism' is a kind of rearguard action being fought against a neo-modernist poetics and LANGUAGE poetry. William Baer's introduction to the first issue of *The Formalist*, the US magazine which ran from 1990 to 2004, set out his agenda as follows: '*The Formalist* is dedicated to metrical poetry, which the editors feel is the mainstream of English-language verse. We hope to create a forum for formal poetry and to encourage a renewal of interest in traditional poetic craftsmanship.' It was, for X. J. Kennedy, 'a shining refuge for poets who play the Grand Old Game of rhyme and meter'.[62] It is hard to imagine such overt promotion of poets' interest in rhyme and metre would be felt as necessary in the Irish tradition (even if critics have felt impelled to defend the politics of traditional forms), or that in Ireland an anthology might be published entitled *A Formal Feeling Comes: Poems in Form by Contemporary Women*, an American anthology which, according to the *Yale Review* 'challenge[s] the notion that women today write, or ought to write, primarily in free verse...'. 'Form' here equates with 'traditional form' (otherwise one might ask which poems by women, indeed by anyone, are *not* 'in form'); and the book is embattled in a way we might in Britain or Ireland (where a formal feeling never went away) more usually associate with neo-modernist aesthetics. Its poems, the editor suggests, 'contradict the popular assumption that formal poetics correspond to reactionary politics and elitist aesthetics'.[63] If that criticism has itself, however erroneously, been levelled at Heaney, Longley, and Mahon, their work has not been, in consequence, sidelined in the academy, or pushed to the margins of the publishing world. Indeed, those critics who advocate more extensive attention to neo-modernist writing in Ireland, claim a comparable neglect or misunderstanding in Ireland of experimental forms as they try to make a case for an Irish modernist poetic.[64] And websites devoted to British avant-garde or neo-modernist

---

[61] See *Thumbscrew* 1, 3, 7, 17.

[62] See http://theformalist.evansville.edu/formalist.htm

[63] Annie Finch, ed. *A Formal Feeling Comes: Poems in Form by Contemporary Women* (Ashland, OR: Story Line Press, 1994), 1. The anthology is, of course, specifically concerned with the gender politics of traditional form, recognizing it as a uniquely 'troubled legacy' for women poets, although the links to 'new formalism' more generally are evident in the introduction.

[64] John Goodby, for instance, argues that 'the world of Irish neo-modernist poetry...has intermittently shadowed mainstream poetry since the 1950s', and that their 'relationship' between the two is 'characterised...by ignorance and outright dismissal'. *Irish Poetry since 1950* (Manchester: Manchester University Press, 2000), 301. 'Relationship' here presumably means the attitude he attributes to the 'mainstream'; although one could argue the issue both ways, given his own dismissal of what he calls 'the limitations of the "I" of the Northern Irish lyric'.

poetry tend to be rather embattled too, on a mission to counter an 'anti-modernist and anti-innovative bias within the dominant British literary culture', and dismissive, in the process, of more traditional poets such as Larkin and Hughes (or at least dismissive of those who admire them).[65] In more restrained fashion, the recently established *Journal of British and Irish Innovative Poetry* recognizes that 'the equivalent North American work is well-represented in academic work, but researchers on British and Irish poetry have no dedicated refereed journal'.[66]

Quinn as a critic is alert to, and frustrated by, the polarization of poetry criticism (particularly American poetry criticism) into distinct camps, or movements, which can, he argues, push 'the best readers of literature into unhelpful rearguard actions'. He makes a case instead for 'a criticism which attends to the societal context of poetry without reneging on responsibilities to poetry as a discourse distinct from politics and ideology, one with its own special rhetorical funds and resources', and he attributes to a 'younger generation of critics' the felt need to 'renew our sense of the particularly literary aspects of poems, while also attending to political contexts and the ways in which poetry matters to lives'.[67] When it comes to the battle-lines drawn between 'stylistic differences', the preference for a diversity of style which crosses such boundaries is expressed with a certain frustration:

> Will they ever ask you to write a sonnet at S.U.N.Y., Buffalo? Will something a little disjunctive ever creep into The Formalist? The vigilance with which these borders are patrolled makes for a tedious purism, whose end result is the impoverishment of poetry and not its empowerment.[68]

Since his own interest in traditional forms is bound up with an interest in experimentation too, particularly with typography and layout, Quinn's criticism of a British and Irish culture of publishing and reviewing poetry is of its own tendency to patrol the borders too, rather than testing 'the boundaries of form', or allowing them to be tested: 'the stylistic experiments of poets like John Ashbery and A. R. Ammons have received general acclaim in the U.S., whereas anyone in Britain who so much as fiddles with the syntax or displaces a capital instantly designates their collection to the out-tray of the established publisher'.[69] 'The bottom line', he writes, 'is that there isn't really a plurality of poetic cultures in Britain and Ireland at the present time.... What is different is the demographics of the poets' backgrounds: you don't have to go to Oxford (although it has to be admitted

---

[65] See 'An Introduction to British Innovative Poetry', at www.modernpoetry.org.uk/nrsh.html

[66] www.gylphi.co.uk/poetry/index.php

[67] Justin Quinn, *Gathered Beneath the Storm: Wallace Stevens, Nature and Community* (Dublin: UCD Press, 2002), 1–2.

[68] Quinn, 'Of Grids, Flux, and the Patternless Expanse', www.cprw.com/Quinn/grids.htm

[69] Ibid. One senses that for Quinn, multiculturalism, internationalism, plurality, heterogeneity, are no more than buzzwords in poetry criticism if the arguments for their existence are not proven by a necessary thematic and stylistic diversity. See also his argument in 'The Multicultural Meld' in *Contemporary Poetry Review* where, considering Native American poetry, he argues that 'the gaze of multiculturalism (wielded by the poets as much as the critics) is homogenizing and…identities are erased by the title "Native American"'.

that it still helps), and you don't have to be white and male (positive disabilities these days) if you want to make it. But such diversity has not resulted in any great diversity in poetic style.[70]

Quinn is not here advocating instead an 'innovative' or 'neo-modernist' aesthetic. His own poetry tells a different story; and in any event, stylistic diversity may be no more or less characteristic of the 'experimental margin' than it is of the 'conservative mainstream'. (His interest in Jorie Graham, a poet 'singular in the American context as she is, it seems, capable of learning from most camps', may be revealing in terms of Quinn's own ambitions.[71] Graham's poetry, he says gives the impression of 'a strikingly original intelligence that has taken the lyric form apart and put it back together again according to new blueprints'.)[72] Wheatley, a Beckett scholar, and a poet whose modernist affiliations are the most apparent of the three (to the extent that he is listed as author of one of '21 Worthwhile Contemporary British Innovative Poetry Blogs'),[73] reveals a slightly different frustration, this time with critical readings of that more 'experimental margin'. Reviewing a collection of essays on Brian Coffey, he writes:

> As someone with an abiding love of experimental modernist writing, I find it dispiriting that the desire to have a modernist generation of poets of our own in Ireland, where the faintest pretence of one existed, leads us to see in Coffey the major experimental poet he patently was not. Beside the real thing – beside Montale, Vallejo, Char, Seferis – Coffey is bloodless and secondary.[74]

The 'real thing', in Wheatley's phrase, is not 'home grown'; nor does it need to be. The 'desire' for 'our own' heritage is itself subjected to scrutiny in the ironic and parodic ('conservative') modes of Wheatley's poetry; and in the 2006 collection, *Mocker*, his forays into a more obviously modernist style and his experiments with rhythm, syntax, layout, and fragmentation owe more to the writers he names above, to Beckett and James Joyce, or to his English contemporaries and precursors Peter Riley or Peter Didsbury, than to Coffey or Devlin. In 'Fintan and the Hawk of Achill', the medieval source text becomes the vehicle for an experimental play on the politics of translation and textual fragmentation:

<pre>
        put in the shape   of a salmon each spring
     by the Bann   the Suir   the Liffey   the Shannon
     to suffer   stuck fast   in the ice   of Assaroe of the seals
                             came   the hawk
              that plucked out   my eye[75]
</pre>

---

[70] Quinn, 'Of Grids, Flux, and the Patternless Expanse'.

[71] Ibid.

[72] Justin Quinn, 'Pundits of the Weather', *PN Review* 113 (January–February 1997).

[73] '21 Worthwhile Contemporary British Innovative Poetry Blogs', www.modernpoetry.org.uk/lists.html Wheatley's blog is at http://georgiasam.blogspot.com/

[74] David Wheatley, 'Cloisters, Courtyards, Laneways', rev. of *Other Edens: The Life and Work of Brian Coffey*, ed, Benjamin Keatinge and Aengus Woods, *Poetry Ireland Review* 100 (March 2010), 139.

[75] David Wheatley, *Mocker* (Oldcastle: Gallery, 2006), 57.

If this collection in particular makes him something of a fly in the formalist ointment, that he retains his fascination with traditional forms also makes him a rogue element in the 'Innovative' scene.[76]

From pantoum to postmodern rupture, it seems rather as if anything goes. Quinn, Wheatley, and O'Reilly are, in Wheatley's phrase, 'formalist or experimental as the mood takes them'.[77] If anything goes, not everything works. Yet it is fair to say that they 'offer in their variousness compelling examples of the range and scope of Irish poetry as it enters the twenty-first century'.[78] Anyone placing them too securely on one or other side of the formalist/experimental, mainstream/marginal border is likely to find they have smuggled themselves across it at various points. The stylistic and formal variety in evidence across all three poets (and others of their generation) is indicative of a desire to eschew a simple 'line', in more ways than one, and it suggests a conscious move away from some of the debates—or divisions—that have pervaded Irish poetry criticism in the twentieth century.

[76] For further discussion of *Mocker*, notably of 'Bankside-Wincolmlee by Instamatic', a 'homage to Peter Didsbury', see Maria Johnston, 'Dark Horse Among the Hippos', *Dublin Review of Books*, at www.drb.ie/more_details/08-09-25/Dark_Horse_Among_The_Hippos.aspx

[77] David Wheatley, 'Irish Poetry into the Twenty-First Century', in *The Cambridge Companion to Contemporary Irish Poetry*, ed. Matthew Campbell (Cambridge: Cambridge University Press, 2003), 250–1.

[78] Ibid., 251.

PART XI

ON RECENT POETRY

CHAPTER 39

NEW IRISH WOMEN POETS: THE EVOLUTION OF (IN)DETERMINACY IN VONA GROARKE

CATRIONA CLUTTERBUCK

I

A new generation of Irish poets, which emerged during the 1990s, was the first to inherit an established tradition of female as well as male forebears. Younger men and women poets can now assume the example of an assertive, exploratory, and self-interrogating poetic voice by women as part of their artist's birthright. However, the base value of gender-framed literary traditions remains seriously contested in Ireland. Because of this, the tools needed to register the female voice in Irish poetry are underdeveloped in our critical culture. As a result, for younger women poets especially, the task of claiming their foremothers' legacy and developing it on their own terms is compromised.

This essay holds that the female voice in the Irish poetry tradition reconvenes relations between transcendent vision and sensual material bodily awareness, between free indeterminate existence and grounded subject identity. It argues that Irish women poets at their best celebrate interdependence between these opposite domains as the basis of life renewal in the private and public spheres alike. Arguably, each new generation of women poets responds to the contemporary *zeitgeist* in two main stages: the spirit of the age seeming to demand that they uphold one or the other side of the above equation, they spend their apprenticeships dissolving the bond between determinate and indeterminate forms of identity and understanding—but their poetic maturity remaking that connection.

The voices of the present crop of younger Irish women poets were formed in the context of the publicly fraught sociopolitical and cultural debates on gender and modernity of the 1980s and 1990s, to which the active input of their immediate female predecessors was crucial, yet which largely disenchanted rather than inspired the new generation. That now-senior grouping of contemporary Irish women poets, among whom are found Eavan Boland, Eiléan Ní Chuilleanáin, Nuala Ní Dhomhnaill, Medbh McGuckian, Paula Meehan, Rita-Ann Higgins, and Moya Cannon, themselves emerged during the late 1960s, 1970s, and 1980s—a time when Ireland was exposed to an era-transforming series of political, economic, and cultural crises, most involving open and often bitter conflict. These included the Northern Irish Troubles, the warring priorities of post-colonialism and revisionism as approaches to the study of Ireland, the struggle to incorporate EU social legislation, battles over reproductive rights and marital status, major recession and emigration, the collapse of the Soviet Union, and the impact of directly encroaching globalization. Even though a broad liberationist ethic informed or arose from many of these crises, the movements involved tended to remain reliant on fixed ideas of the female: woman functioned to represent the various principles of freedom concerned, rather than to herself enact, interrogate, and benefit from those freedoms. Not only in spite of its exposure to crisis, then, but also because of it, Irish political and social life remained resistant to the insights of body-centred gender consciousness—that gender awareness which continues to challenge the structures of the Irish body politic today.

The 1970s and 1980s generation of women poets found in this situation at once their nemesis and their motivation. This older grouping recognized almost from the outset that poetic transcendence would be meaningless without acknowledging the claims of the situated body. Their early protest-oriented work responded wholeheartedly to the then-insistent political imperative that poets should honour the claims of Irish women's and men's material, sexual identities. In the face of that practical and communal imperative, however, the equally important but more abstract and ideal task with which they were charged—of exploring women's and men's independent capacity for transcendent vision and free indeterminate being—risked being submerged.

For the women poets who have emerged since the mid-1990s—Vona Groarke, Sinéad Morrissey, Kerrie Hardie, Colette Bryce, Caitríona O'Reilly, Yvonne Cullen, and Leontia Flynn, among others—the situation is different. Most of these poets are of the generation of women for whom 'unquestioned personal independence was...the norm'.[1] The groundwork of protest regarding gender inequality having already been effected by their foremothers, they have been able to take for granted the fact that their female identity can be integrated with their witness to political, social, and personal experience: their major early focus instead has been on accessing, in their different ways, the freedoms of transcendence and indeterminacy.

However—as for the foregoing generation but from an opposite starting point—this early focus has carried the risk of a narrowing of poetic engagement, along with the likelihood of greater accomplishment. The current younger set of Irish women poets

---

[1] Lucy Collins, 'Architectural Metaphors: Representations of the House in the Poetry of Eiléan Ní Chuilleanáin and Vona Groarke', in *Irish Literature since 1990: Diverse Voices*, ed. Scott Brewster and Michael Parker (Manchester: Manchester University Press, 2009), 143–4.

confronted expectations of individualistic self-realization underpinned by habits of political fatalism, integral to the *zeitgeist* of the 1990s and the Celtic Tiger era. The signature of this impulse towards disengagement is the scepticism that their emerging voices have tended to adopt as a dominant mode of dealing with the world: arguably a newly available position for the Irish woman poet. This scepticism has been directed towards stabilizing the swings between doubt, anger, and celebration prevalent in the examples of their predecessors, fluctuations which accompanied the Irish cultural and critical stand-offs that took place between the late 1960s and the early 1990s. More broadly, that stance of scepticism has targeted over-easy assumptions of the possibility of intervention in present-day sociopolitical environments—ones in which freedom of action and conscience are more outwardly guaranteed but more inwardly compromised. The younger poets have emerged in a changed world, one where human lives are subject to seemingly unstoppable forces of globalized markets, technology, and resurgent religious and national fundamentalism, to a point unimaginable in the 1970s and 1980s. In the face of such broader factors, these poets' disengagement from politics has been motivated by the desire to reclaim for the individual the powers of clear-sighted overview and particularized creativity. Such scepticism is in this regard a valid and necessary position. However, that conscious disengagement from issues of public power has been effected in their early aesthetics, to the point of risking the relegation of the body once again to invisibility as co-creative agent of identity and meaningful change.

Unsurprisingly, then, this scepticism among the newer Irish women poets has included in its sights traditional feminist defences of woman-centred ideals of origin and community, agency and understanding. Vona Groarke's formulation 'Women Irish Poets' as subtitle for the special edition of the journal *Verse* she edited in 1999, wherein she concluded that 'the best of Irish women poets are not writing "Irish Women's Poetry"', is indicative.[2] Yet the poets of Groarke's generation are not unaware of the irony that their withdrawal from the terms of traditional feminism is founded upon a confidence in their voices as women bequeathed to them through the challenges already faced by their predecessors. For *both* generations of women poets, after all, women's assumed immersion in sensual bodily life and grounded self-presence has had to be interrogated as a restrictive block to their full self-enablement: for the older group this assumption was proffered through older patriarchal discourses, and for the younger, through newer second-wave feminist ones.

Crucially, however, that same immersion in the body has also had to be reclaimed by each grouping. The maturation of the aesthetics in each generation is recognizable at the point where they begin seriously to attend to the authority of the individual imagination, in specific conjunction with grounded and communally framed sexual identity. This arises through a hard-earned realization that either of these domains—the transcendent and the body-conscious political—becomes disfunctional without the other. The reclamation of the female body on non-essential terms is a task which has demanded of each generation, differently, a revision of their understanding of the claims of that

² Vona Groarke, 'Editorial', *Verse* 16:2 (1999), 8.

power of transcendence. Their challenge here is to understand that the body functions both as anchor and springboard of the sublime, thus operating simultaneously as the point of departure and arrival of their empowerment as poets. The integration of the separate energies of those two loci of empowerment remains for both generations of women poets a problematic quest—a focus of agitation and inspiration at the centre of their writing lives.

The outcome of this process of reclamation of the complex body for both generations is that their maturing work invites reconciliation with as well as disavowal of the exclusive culture in which they first came to poetic consciousness—whether that exclusivity has been suffered more directly in terms of traditional patriarchal constraints, or newer feminist ones. Both groups then, each from a different starting point, are called to enter into trust, not only with the legacy of their dominant predecessors in the poetry tradition, but more broadly with the terms of the delimiting sociopolitical structures of understanding which have formed them. Only by means of this difficult double move of critique and reconciliation, in turn, can the damaged culture to which these writers speak, attain healing.

Poets of any era can only effect a move like this through an aesthetic which models inclusive, self-reflexive engagement. Such a self-aware art requires precision mapping of the liminal zone between the concrete dimensions of experience and the worlds of the purely imagined—an achievement exemplified by the older generation of Ireland's contemporary women poets, and very much sustained by the younger one. These new writers, through their recharging of Irish poetry's signature focus on the theme of fractured inheritance and belonging, attend in a revitalized way to the ghostliness-cum-materiality of history and the self. As the work of their exemplar Vona Groarke testifies, the uneasy yet unbreakable relationships between the body and the spirit, reality and representation, and order and chaos, remain central to this defining preoccupation of Irish art.

II

Perhaps Vona Groarke's clearest theme is the condition of exile as it relates to the ideal of sanctuary. Through this theme she explores the relative ephemerality or continuity of identity and experience: a concern newly relevant to the Ireland of the 1990s and 2000s. Groarke recognizes this nexus of concerns as driven by the order-chaos binary by which tradition and modernity negotiate their complex relationship. From the outset of her first volume, *Shale* (1994), she points out, in 'Lines', how 'We paint, we make a plausible scene'—how, 'With such indifferent passion for order,/we administer the scene.'[3] The illusoriness of such constructed order is seen in the (in)stability not only of the modern autonomous subject, but of the given material domain in which that subject finds itself.

---

[3] Vona Groarke, *Shale* (Oldcastle: Gallery, 1994), 36.

The title symbol of shale—'soft, finely stratified rock that splits easily' (*OED*)—aptly points to this easily fractured potential of the located, self-affirming subject, as this poet's founding preoccupation. It is signalled in her early poetry in the way Groarke equally re-enacts and questions the idealization of romantic isolation and rebellion through self-identification with nature, fluidity, and the lost home—a trope of Irishness identified both with tradition and modernity. Her poetry reveals how traditional are such scripts of modern individualism in the Irish context, and how modern are those of traditional communal identity. In 'The Lighthouse', for example, a poem on rural electrification from her second collection, *Other People's Houses* (1999), the 'overcoated men' who 'cheer for progress and prosperity' following the lead of the parish priest are oblivious to the sophisticated refraction of the known created by the fire and lamp light of an older system, which generated (for women in particular) the affect of home—an affect scattered for ever by the 'clamour of new light' associated with modernity.[4] Crucially, Groarke tests how radical or conventional, enabling or disabling, this interdependence of tradition and modernity in Irish and larger Western culture can be.

Questions of gender index this enquiry throughout. For Groarke, the available forms of inherited order have already collapsed from within, largely as a consequence of the unreflective patriarchal constitution of Irish and larger Western culture in the modern era (Her early diagnosis here follows on from that proffered by older contemporaries including Thomas Kinsella, Derek Mahon, Eavan Boland, Eiléan Ní Chuilleanáin, and Medbh McGuckian.). To summarize that analysis, the order associated with modernity is based upon the position of an over-privileged masculine subject, by which male rationalism leads to the false elevation of the realms of the mind and spirit over that of the body. As a result of this 'rage for order' (to quote Wallace Stevens), the body is falsely converted into the terms of the mind and spirit, whereby both are disabled.

If inherited order is no longer available to the modern Irish man or woman, this lack is itself an inheritance: the broken tradition has itself become a literary, tribal-familial, and philosophical patrimony. Thomas Kinsella has long explored and celebrated this discontinuity as compelling both the freedom to self-create and the responsibility to relate: to reconnect with others and with the past. Groarke in her early work is sceptical as to whether this challenge has yet been, or ever will (or indeed can) be, taken up in Irish culture—a scepticism seen increasingly in the three volumes up to and including *Flight* (2002). She explores the danger of a situation where the rhetoric of the exiled self allows one to claim all the privileges of subject-identity without its responsibilities. In this situation, the alterity associated with the body, as affirmable through the materiality of the speaking voice, becomes increasingly invisible. The body in this economy is blotted out: it is 'Black as the image of the centre of the end, the eye/of darkness that sees only light.' Without that body awareness, this subject's claim to universal perspective—along with the authority of tradition which that claiming of a totalized viewpoint safeguards—can only fail: 'Perhaps there is a forest of light./Perhaps there is one black tree.../but in my house, the vigil of leaves is scattered,/only to begin at the edge of things again'.[5] In this scattering of modernity's claim that man's access to consciousness and knowledge is unbounded, that claim is revealed as a 'gallery/of tricks, delusions, magic, sleight-of-hand,/alchemy, astronomy, old-wives' tales and/even lies'.[6]

In the Irish experience of modernity in particular, the ideal of the autonomous yet grounded subject is a 'house' that we 'always thought . . . would hold us', wherein we had expected to 'come upon a store of memory/that would remind us, call us to ourselves', but which instead 'has been blown open/to a vacant future, bleak as January,//in which no window is lit'.[7] Groarke intimates, however, that the 'lost house' of the fractured and exiled self in Irish culture has itself become an assumed identity that has lent itself to complacency. The desired yet impossible home, as such, is a receding dream which, in 'Going Home', 'shatters my breath' in passing, and exposes us to the void: 'a silence gaining ground behind it'. The result, in 'Daphne as a Modern Theme', is that that notional homeland becomes a prison wherein the individual Irish subject remains bound to the terms of virtual reality: 'a landscape in which/my likeness is set,//a small, false figure/foreshadowing/my life'.[8]

Groarke's initial inquiry into the instability of established systems of order clearly announces her choice to abandon such redundant systems, especially literary and philosophical ones. And yet, this disavowal remains equivocal. Her early voice is one that speaks 'From [the] Disused House' of the deconstructed institution and practice of modernity, wherein she cannot settle but yet remains somehow still trapped: 'I am in the process of not being here./I don't think I will ever leave./After Christmas, I will certainly move on.'[9] In other words, the sophisticated political and philosophical alertness signalled so soon in Groarke's career is also belied by *Shale*'s continuing attachment to a ghostly unified cultural universe expressed in modernist terms, whereby this 'order' is reconvened in the shape of fragments shored of necessity against communal ruin. In the title poem, these fragments make up the 'necklace of shale I made for you/that has grown warm between us', as young lovers opt for the solidity of redundant tradition.[10] Groarke will later directly confront the limitations of such reinvestments in normative order, especially when enacted by women, but this first 1994 volume only goes so far as to signal the irony of the reinforced conservatism they demand.

In 'Figures on a Cliff', for example, Groarke subverts Wallace Stevens's famous celebration of the superiority of human creative power over that of nature in 'The Idea of Order at Key West', through giving voice to the female figure who in his poem merely mediates this concept—yet this subversion finds itself undone. Groarke here questions the older poet's elevation of spirit over body by having her woman speaker assert the crucial impact of context and perspective on the centrality of the self as human subject.

---

[5] Groarke, 'Insomnia', *Shale*, 32, 33.
[6] Groarke, 'Reflections', *Shale*, 29.
[7] Groarke, 'Home', *Shale*, 53.
[8] Ibid., 11, 52, 40.
[9] Groarke, 'From a Disused House', *Shale*, 51.
[10] Ibid., 12.

However, this woman finds that to so question that centrality, is—in typical modernist terms—to invert rather than rebalance that power relationship with nature. In other words, it is to risk eliminating herself altogether, in a movement that dovetails ominously with patriarchy's sidelining of female subject identity—'A slight shift in perspective, and I disappear.'[11] The speaker's self-presence in Groarke's poem remains inherently provisional, dependent as it is on the 'kindness' of the light, which will allow her only temporarily to reassume her own egocentric importance. Here the human individual and external reality subsist in an either/or power relationship: control is claimed either by man or nature, never by both in agreement together, and loss of agency for either, when it occurs, is total.

This figuring of the void beneath modernity's untenable claiming of stability is a measure of Groake's inability, in *Shale*, to conceive any viable alternative to those establishment terms of order—an alternative that could be offered by integrating chaos into such systems and thereby changing them. Order and disorder, instead, tend to be prescribed in either/or relations throughout Groarke's early work, so that 'The thing that is told/is the journey *from* chaos to the burning star' (my emphasis).[12] However, when that burning star is reached, it is strangely devoid of meaning: 'You shout out our names to claim possession./The silence brings a sense of being adrift.'[13] Because of this oppositional understanding of order-chaos relations, early Groarke cannot truly embrace instability, for the void this connotes still threatens too seriously: 'There are nights when she wants to leave a space/so vivid it makes the other pages void./But how then to continue the next night?'[14] But to deflect this void by converting it back into the terms of traditional order—as Groarke effectively opts to do in her apprenticeship stage—is paradoxically to regenerate that emptiness, as she soon comes to realize.

In the shift from *Shale* to Groarke's second volume, *Other People's Houses*, we find this stand-off between order and chaos to be more clearly delineated, but also more open to question. The speaking subjects of these poems begin to align themselves, at least partly by choice, with the pole of disorder, flux, exile, and immateriality. The symbol of the house becomes a focal trope for this process. In 'The Image of the House', for example, the speaker and her child stand unadmitted outside the house of absolute order as its necessary 'flaw', and in 'The Empty House', 'the shape we made in the bed will pucker out' as the 'shadows' of the otherness of the material world—a realm indifferent to human presence—will 'drain what is left of us away'.[15]

There is still no real meeting of terms between order and chaos in this second collection, but there *is* an acceptance of the fact of co-dependent relationship between the provenance of stability and familiarity (associated with the home, the self, consciousness, and history as the story of the past), and that of irreducible strangeness (associated

[11] Ibid., 48.
[12] Groarke, 'If There is a City', *Shale*, 46.
[13] Groarke, 'Rain Bearers', *Shale*, 57.
[14] Groarke, 'First', *Shale*, 44.
[15] Groarke, *Other People's Houses*, 50, 51.

with the larger world, other people's lives, and history understood as the factuality of the past itself). '[F]or all its confinement and poise', Groarke tells us, the house of traditional order 'is, in turn, preoccupied with skies'.[16] Freedom begins to be less equivocally associated with chaos, on the basis of which Groarke begins to let go of her earlier need to have it both ways, 'As though I could keep one hand on the lock/and the other on the handle of the door'. She begins to accept that the individual is fate's plaything, called to recognize its own immateriality: 'What does it matter that we have made a home/where we can draw the curtains and talk of tomorrow', she asks, 'if we are thinking of this: the shapes we made in darkness,/ . . . our faces marooned in stars'.[17]

III

Groarke's third book, *Flight*, marks a notable maturing in her poetic, this in the range and depth of its celebration—but also its interrogation—of her openness to the absent self. On the one hand she announces her disengagement from the governing assumptions of her earlier work regarding the desirability of affirmable subject identity: 'Home. You've gone as far as you care to go/in that direction. Nothing comes of it.'; on the other, '*Your entry*, Last name, First name, *should be here*'.[18] Newly concerned with the application of her insight to the realm of public politics, Groarke's equivocal elevation of evacuated identity follows on from her disenchantment with untenable claims for substance in the project of Irish national achievement: she 'saw through/the most we made of what we'd amounted to:/limbs; nothing in particular; maybe skin', which is the result of a culture infected by 'a fancy for tripping on what [it] might have done'.[19] However, the volume as a whole remains unresolved as to whether the indefinite identity it highlights is part of the problem or the solution, the term 'flight' at once connoting freedom and escapism. As Michael A. Kinsella notes, the collection 'seems to "double back" on itself and on the potential of its title'.[20]

Flight attends recurrently to the unsaid and the superannuated, to slippage towards fluidity of being and the sustaining of unresolved, suspended moments, and generally to 'The drunkenness of things being various', in Louis MacNeice's famous words from 'Snow': a poem in the corner of Groarke's eye throughout this period. Such a condition of MacNeicean openness annotates the ideally indeterminate position of the poet in relation to the potential meaning of their material at the point of writing: 'Something beginning with a slightness/and possibly taken from there . . .//though currently unsure

[16] Groarke, 'House Rules', *Other People's Houses*, 12.
[17] Groarke, 'The Haunted House' and 'Outdoors', *Other People's Houses*, 54, 55.
[18] Vona Groarke, 'The End of the Line', *Flight* (Oldcastle: Gallery, 2002) 29, 28.
[19] Groarke, 'The Magic Touch' and 'The End of the Line', *Flight*, 45, 28.
[20] Michael A. Kinsella, 'Displaced by Flight', rev. of Vona Groarke, *Flight*, in *PN Review* 29:2 (November/December 2002), 61–2.

how to proceed/or to convince'.[21] For Groarke this indeterminate position is one that allows for a richness of existential awareness and creative openness to experience, through which (in theory) the amplified human understanding that poetry tries to capture and enable, can unite with its medium in the material conditions of lived experience, language skills, and the labour of writing: 'Effortless and uninscribed, the sky/has earthed everything outside' so as to '[settle] on this:/the point at which two rumours coalesce,/one to do with vision, one with voice'. The ideal here, in 'Flight', is to combine order and disorder in perfect balance—to generate an effect both 'chaotic and restrained'. Yet this title poem realizes that 'death…/is rattling even in these lines', signalling this volume's attendant awareness of the dangers of that evacuated and indeterminate subject position.[22]

Groarke highlights this danger as especially applying to Irish women, who live in a society where female self-realization has always been compromised. Hence Groarke's deliberate revision of the terms of MacNeice's 'Snow' in her poem 'Shot Silk', in which she registers the politics of gender and nation coded within an elevation of 'the drunkenness of things being various'. This critique is offered through Groarke's exposure inside MacNeice's 'room' of the invisible guarantor of such altereity: a woman who 'works between the fire and the roses in the window', between the everyday and the numinously enlarged real. Trapped in this room as in an aesthetic zone safeguarded from contact with the realities of public political conflict, she registers the earlier poet's celebrated 'incompatibility' of known and unknown, order and chaos, inside and outside, not as a source of sudden richness, but of discomfort and loss: 'Her face is flushed, her back tingles with cold.' This woman is suggested as a sovereignty goddess dressed in silk ' "*Fit for a queen*" ' but also in 'gloves/of skin from an aborted calf which (for all its *tendresse*)/stiffens on her hand'. She testifies to how the offspring of the Droimeann Donn Dílis, the lost heifer of Irish aspiration to visionary political self-determination, becomes sacrificed to ideals of freedom still hung upon a female shape whose bodily reality 'will leave no mark'.[23] Small wonder then that in this room, 'Ashes of roses are spilling at her feet.'[24]

In *Flight*, Groarke demonstrates a far more specific awareness of Irish life as weighed down by its attachment to fantasy completions, being especially alert, in 'White Noise', to the 'brass wishfulness' associated with ideals of political nationalism.[25] This is a realm in which order and chaos are locked in unhealthy relation, 'a landscape/wasted by the fervour of clean lines', and accordingly one based on the exclusion of the female and of material reality more generally.[26] 'Imperial Measure', for example, highlights this exclusion by focusing on the domestic realities of the 1916 Rising. This poem traces the failure

---

[21] Groarke, 'The Verb "to herringbone" ', *Flight*, 13.

[22] Groarke, *Flight*, 16.

[23] For a foundational analysis of such un-self-reflexive deployment of the female form in Irish Studies, see Moynagh Sullivan, 'Feminism, Postmodernism and the Subjects of Irish and Women's Studies', in *New Voices in Irish Criticism*, ed. P. J. Mathews (Dublin: Four Courts Press, 2000), 243–50.

[24] Groarke, *Flight*, 62.

[25] Ibid., 68.

[26] Groarke, 'The Way It Goes', *Flight*, 20.

of the ideals of the Revolution through an imagined history of how the rich food and drink claimed by the insurgents at the start of Easter Week quickly decayed, leaving their appetites 'undiminished'. Images of 'bread that turned to powder in their mouths', rotting vegetables, painfully sacrificial calves and stale pastries offer an extended metaphor of the souring vision of the Irish Republic—its absence of proper sustenance—in the period since Independence: 'biscuits slumped under royal icing./Éclairs with their cream/already turned./ . . . a gross/or two of drinking chocolate, stewed and taken without/sweetener or milk'.[27]

Groarke recognizes as her inheritance an ideal of achieved national autonomy whose false assertions of freedom must be challenged, through exposing as the condition of that ideal's claims to total presence the necessity to dissolve subjectivity. By so highlighting this problem, of course, Groarke calls into question her own leaning towards evacuated, undetermined identity. She begins, in 'Snow in Summer', to see her own approach—one whereby she 'took to being/not easy to pin down'—as a mode which serves rather than resists the appropriative claims of a cultural and political tradition in which the male partner can simply '[call] a halt' to such experimentation and assert its exclusivist underside: 'as though he were all for honesty/and the opposite of sleight of hand'. Unsurprisingly, given this revealed conservative agenda, 'His name//for me was "Rosebud", and I came to picture him/with a flat cap and a stoop and far too many metaphors/for me.' Thus, indeterminate subject identity is challenged as retroactive: 'It was love in a mist./It was what do you call it and what is its name/and how does it go when it comes to be gone?'[28] The poem 'Thistle' offers an apt metaphor for Groarke's dilemma: such indeterminacy is one whose drive for freedom is 'the same hay I last made when I was twelve', but whose embedded and poisonous essentialism remains operative, in the form of 'the same ragwort I discarded, that still thrives'.[29]

IV

In *Flight*, Groarke struggles to find the right balance between acknowledging the efficacy on the one hand, and the danger on the other, of valorizing the non-insistent, unpretentious self. By *Juniper Street* (2006), that missing balance begins to be found. The fourth volume's opening poem, 'Ghosts', models this new coming to terms in its suggestion that a meeting point between solidity and fluidity of presence, between available and absent identity, can simultaneously be a valid *and* an illusory possibility. This poem thus both allows and disallows the reality of ghosts—they are at once how we register the meaning of temporal change—'Something like breath on your cheek/or an aftertaste of summer, years ago', but also how we register the scattering of any such meaning: ghosts

---

[27] Groarke, *Flight*, 64, 63, 64.
[28] Ibid., 46, 47.
[29] Ibid., 18.

are 'silverfish throwing your reflection off a beat./Or a peony petal blown onto your path.' Groarke takes her signature here from her children who—as they embody a future she cannot share—represent both positions: 'They breathe ghosts into January/that stand for the split second it takes/to take us in, and then they're off/ . . . like figments of the air.'[30] In this volume, asserted meaning and denied meaning no longer necessarily cancel each other out. Accordingly, in 'The Annotated House'—a poem in which female sexuality and writing describe each other to radical effect[31]—Groarke configures the point of fore-closure of the poem's achievement, as of the female sexual self's, as also the moment of its delivery: 'my pen, scratching through loose-leaves,/comes to a dead stop at the very moment when/the boiler downstairs, like breaking news,/shunts the here and now into one full clause.'[32]

Juniper Street, unlike Groarke's preceding work, proposes that loss of sustainable coherent meaning can both be acknowledged and recuperated, this by integrating the available remnants of that meaning with lived life as play.[33] '[L]ets skew it with a spray of last night's dreams', the speaker of 'Archaeology' proposes of her unforthcoming creation, the poem she is drafting, so that its 'story told/as if through frosted glass'[34] has the imprimatur of an indeterminacy that may be unavoidable and even mislead-ing, but which is also revealing of the truth. In terms adapted from this volume's title poem, '[T]he heat' of such incomplete yet still-desired meaning needs to be 'felt . . . as something on the turn/that would carry us over the tip of all that darkness/and land us on the stoop of this whole new world.'[35] The order of art is equivalently something to be embraced *through*, not despite, its elisions and escapism, as Groarke suggests in 'The Letter "d"': here her faulty typewriter with 'one key,/shy of impact' that 'won't strike true', is affirmed as producing 'a written life . . . //that compensates for absence,/ . . . forgets itself in coping with just this.'[36]

The specific imperative for this shift towards compromise with and redemption of loss is Groarke's new understanding of chaos as a condition of violence: in *Juniper Street*, immediately and physically, as well as abstractly and psychologically, chaos involves threat—whether we are speaking of the political violence of Irish republican activism or the natural violence of weather extremes in her new home in America. Already in *Flight*, her instinct had begun to turn towards revalorizing the self-present subject along with the idea of order on which that centred identity depends, but the old danger of

[30] Vona Groarke, 'Ghosts', *Juniper Street* (Oldcastle: Gallery, 2006), 11.
[31] See Selina Guinness, 'The Annotated House: Feminism and Form', in *Irish Poetry After Feminism: Princess Grace Irish Library Lectures 10*, ed. Justin Quinn (Gerrards Cross: Colin Smythe, 2008), 72, 74–8.
[32] Groarke, *Juniper Street*, 55.
[33] Lucy Collins notes this development towards playfulness in Groarke. Lucy Collins, rev. of Vona Groarke, *Lament for Art O'Leary*, and Vona Groarke, *Spindrift*, in *Irish University Review* 40:2 (Autumn/Winter 2010), 218, 217–20.
[34] Groarke, *Juniper Street*, 39, 38.
[35] Ibid., 52.
[36] Ibid., 56.

re-embracing essentialism in the act of so resisting chaos, returns as soon as the newer danger of courting essentialism in the act of embracing chaos is seen off—a classically circular problem whose solution would seem to recede the more attention is paid to it. By *Juniper Street*, Groarke intervenes in this downward spiral through consciously defending the idea of order and the notion of 'safe' identity—falsely constructed as this ideal is revealed to be—as a provisional stay against chaos.

Crucially, this order can only offset that chaos by deliberately allowing it in. Groarke's fourth volume follows a similar conceptual path to her first book, except that in *Juniper Street* the inadequacy of the sense of structure so desired is openly rather than covertly recognized. Even more importantly, that same order is now validated precisely through its failures. This is because such flawed, provisional order is recognized as based on the reality of a human being's lived compromise with the assaults of larger, unpredictable experience, as well as being grounded in the achievement of surviving these assaults. In 'We Had Words' the notion that the threat of a hurricane, which makes 'This day, all day, ... hypothetical', can be resisted through the power of language 'to bear the weight of this', is a claim that clearly can be turned inside out by the storm force of that same reality, whereby such assertions of human ordering power become equivalent to 'spineless pines bent double in thin air'. Nevertheless, on the occasion treated in this poem, the actual hurricane 'bypasses us completely', thereby partially validating the 'hours spent on [the] high ground' of this confidence—represented now by 'our new words islanded and arch, to steer us wide of harm'.[37] Such confidence in subject agency is patently contingent and fragile, but is also a poignant reminder that such a search for security and autonomy is a valid human activity.

Groarke in *Juniper Street* explores the links between determinate and indeterminate subject agency, open and closed representative meaning, and concrete and virtual reality, as relationships which are symbiotic rather than oppositional. As a result of seeing them this way, she intimates, these relationships have more positive than negative outcomes. The poem 'To Smithereens'—which deals with the connection between public political history and private domestic recreational activities as associated especially with women—offers an important meditation upon this interdependence. This poem attends to the insistent history of Irish sectarian bloodletting as a near-virtual, ungraspable, 'backward drift' of horror, which can only be pinned down by tracking it to the irreducible materiality of the shattered bodies of its victims. One of these was Lord Louis Mountbatten, murdered by the IRA in 1979. But as Groarke recognizes, the reality of his particular death—representative of the deaths of so many others in the Troubles—is lost in its reverberating consequence, as that dark and multiple effect infiltrates the domestic lives of ordinary people: it is 'news that falls in slanted beats//like metal shavings sprayed from a single,/incandescent point to dispel themselves/as the future tense of what they fall upon'. This issue of the impossibility of truly locating the origin and effect of major public political conflict in terms of real people's lives is addressed rather than refused

---

[37] Ibid., 30.

through the example of the children on the 'sunlit Spiddal beach', seemingly oblivious as they are to Mountbatten's death as the news of it comes through. Like poets writing in the period during and just after the Northern Irish Troubles, children claim the right to concentrate on the task of capturing 'a marvellous haul of foam and iridescent sand/and water that laughs at them as it wriggles free'. They and their mothers are 'lifted clear of the high-tide line' of that public political horror, 'into another order of silence'.[38]

This is not, however, a space of evasion. In that different order, Groarke locates the memory of her mother and herself sitting together in an Athlone cinema watching the film *Gandhi*. The cinema here is a space of enlarged understanding. Mediated by its proximity to the river Shannon—the symbolic boundary between 'civilized' modernity and 'primitive' tradition in Ireland—this cinema makes available for general conscious-ness the link between India and Ireland, Mountbatten's public service in one former British colony and his violent death in another, with the effect of highlighting the co-dependence of political idealism and racist brutality in post-colonial cultures world wide. These links are 'the slipknot/of darkness the river ties and unties in the scenes': everything in this space, including the mother falling asleep against the 'crimson plush' of the seats, leads awareness back to the reality of sectarian death likewise central to that film—but also to the means of overcoming its terrible legacy: 'It's here//that every single thing casts off, or is brightly cast,/into a flyblown, speckled plural that scatters tracks/in the heat and dust of the locked projection room.' In this contained, focused location—approximating in its provisional and make-do nature, the space of the successful politi-cal poem—the language of foreclosed singular meaning can be translated into that of renewable plural meaning. The mother wakes at the dark signal of the Hiberno-English phrase, '"To smithereens"', but instead of connoting violent death, in explaining this phrase to her daughter she alters for good—whether in a manner strictly accurate or not—its provenance and application: '"I'm pretty sure it's Indian. It means/to open (like an Albertine); to flower."' An inheritance of violence is here both misread *and* validly reread as a location of new possibility.[39] 'It is a matter of inflection', as Groarke says in 'The Local Accent', 'of knowing what/to emphasize, and what to let drift away'.[40]

In this collection, therefore, the accelerating pessimism of *Flight* is reversed: *Juniper Street* moves instead towards cautious optimism as the violence of public history is at once foregrounded, offset, and redeemed by the more positive possibilities of personal history and larger history's recoverability. The dream of self-presence begins to be revali-dated in this volume as it is incorporated into the reduced reality of the individual's and the nation's own lack of completion: it is, like the Shannon in Groarke's hometown of Athlone, a 'river...pitched so far from the sea/it announces itself in elision, as though everything/unsaid could still bed down in depth and unison'.[41] In this new understand-ing, dreams lost can still nurture one's sense of being in and embracing the now. This in

[38] Ibid., 15.
[39] Ibid., 15, 16.
[40] Ibid., 18.
[41] Ibid., 18.

turn opens the way towards the recuperation of previously exclusive traditions as potentially inclusive. Such healing is understood here as conditional upon the necessity to validate fantasy worlds, but only insofar as their authority is recognized as provisional rather than absolute.

V

Juniper Street successfully proposes the coterminous and even mutually enabling nature of relations between meaning and meaninglessness, in poems that operate as conceptual snapshots or multi-angled illuminations of this complex claim. In that 2006 volume, individual personae in the poems—the speaker first and foremost among them—function as exemplary representatives of these new relations, but Groarke is not concerned with practical human action arising from that rebalanced, renewed understanding. Already by the end of *Juniper Street* she is identifying this gap, in poems which convey an arising fear that the balance she has so carefully elaborated might merely represent 'the exact blue of a hyacinth/forced out of season', which will not withstand exposure to reality because it is based on an unacceptable level of wish-fulfilment: it may be only 'a door hung up on two bars of folksong,/a swingball flicking in between backhands'.[42] In Groarke's next and latest collection, *Spindrift* (2009), that philosophical accord is put to the test in a sustained manner, as she focuses on how (and if) it can be applied to real life—on whether or not this ideal balance is likely to work in practice as 'an ascending scale that tilted,/over the top, into the ditch'.[43] This larger volume, accordingly, is much more grounded in the gritty everyday world of parenthood, work, physically occupied spaces, encountered artworks, and especially, love relationships: 'Body skin. Kith and kin. Other buckled things' making up the 'noun house' of human experience.[44] Just as Groarke now wants her engagement with the ideal to be tuned to the concrete exigencies of her given reality, she realizes that her earlier-achieved accord can only be sustained by confronting more deeply than ever before 'the fear that discontinuity and meaninglessness lie at the core of human existence, [and] that relationships provide only a temporary stay against these conditions'.[45]

This testing in the real renders Groarke once more suspended between order and disorder, groundedness and ephemerality, as, now, between her old life in Ireland and her new life in America: 'any given morning pins/a swatch of sunlight/to my purple shamrock plant'.[46] This dislocation, and the task of newly coming to terms with the

---

[42] Groarke, 'Ghosts', *Juniper Street*, 59.

[43] Vona Groarke, 'Horses', *Spindrift* (Oldcastle: Gallery, 2009), 19.

[44] Groarke, 'Bodkin' and 'An Teach Tuí', *Spindrift*, 28, 50.

[45] Lucy Collins, '"I will not again": Selfhood and Loss in Vona Groarke's *Spindrift*', unpublished conference paper delivered in April 2010.

[46] Groarke, 'Away', *Spindrift*, 14.

discrepancies it involves, is to the fore. Although exhausted by the unexpected failure to reconcile the differences she also recognizes as structuring her experience, in the volume as a whole she moves beyond such stalemate, allowing the contingency and uncertainty of her own and her loved ones' connection to time, place, and each other, riskily to confirm rather than safely undermine the value of that same connection. Key to this advance is the fact that human choice (if not agency) is foregrounded in *Spindrift* in a new way, channelled as it is through the volume's overarching focus on the 'I' voice's decision to believe or not believe in her place in a basically positive universe, and on the conditions of making that choice. Like the gauntlet which in 'An American Jay' she throws down to the self-mocking escapism of her Alaska-bound students by forcing them to write poems in traditional form yet which treat contemporary events, she challenges herself to engage with the ideal of order as it might be applied to random real life: she discovers herself 'too old' to allow her postmodern awareness that meaning-making operates like a funfair carousel, to block its capacity 'to circulate a sincere song of desire, blaze and arousal'.[47]

In consequence, Groarke here offers a new projection of women's lives as actively, rather than passively, challenging false understandings of the order-chaos binary that still preoccupies this poet. She affirms the 'Finesse' and materiality of women's traditional investment in style as a form of self-knowing positive investment in the possibility of identity—a 'Clutch Handbag' with a 'tear in the satin', through which the woman-centred rosary's 'five decades' of faith in such order 'have slipped' till its possibility has become something 'that nobody, but nobody,/recalls'.[48] To reverse this ignorance requires a further prayer—that the 'lost/father', who represents the established literary and cultural tradition, recognize as the 'catch/of shadow/at [his] back' the daughter he had assigned to a position 'lagging/some short/way behind'. Her wish is that he be 'remind[ed]…/to call/for' that daughter on his 'way home'—in other words, that this tradition realign itself with the feminine in experience, so that father and daughter alike can reach their true destination.[49]

The question of good and bad faith is central to these concerns in *Spindrift*. As a general principle (elaborated by Jean-Paul Sartre), good faith is belief chosen in belief's defining condition of instability, requiring the believer's full awareness that this faith has potential to be undermined by the believer's own developing understanding or by future-revealed circumstance. Good faith is to be clearly distinguished from bad faith—that is, from belief that declares itself secure while secretly holding itself untenable. Crucially, however, good faith is also proven by its partial overlap *with* bad faith. Groarke explores the issue of good and bad faith in her poem 'The Small Hours'. 'I talk too much; give far too much away', she here declares, in reaction to which naive faith she opts to 'mumbl[e] my company'—to resist such affirmation by deploying it only in strategic terms. However, in so 'mumbling' or equivocating with faith, Groarke hopes

[47] Ibid., 16, 18.
[48] Groarke, 'The Clutch Handbag', *Spindrift*, 23.
[49] Groarke, 'By and By', *Spindrift*, 20.

also to renew it: 'I reckon on/a two-fold pay-off: some echo;/being found out, consequence'.[50]

The major pattern operating in this collection is that the earlier poems tend to credit the likelihood of bad faith, while the later poems embrace the possibility of good faith. The struggle out of the dark space of deflected yet absorbed disillusionment forms the main trajectory in *Spindrift*. The symbol of artificially solid ground extending over or into water in the shape of jetties, docks, and piers represents both the bad and the good faith structuring the development of thought in this collection. In an early-positioned poem, 'The Jetty', faith's capacity for certainty 'hardly matters' to the speaker, preoccupied as she is with her own 'fumbling in the thicket' of meaning.[51] However, because every apparent delivery of that meaning must dissolve as 'evening/will soak boat and jetty; eventually, this page', the protagonist-poet has a choice: either (as Sartre would advocate), to come to terms with this provisionality as an inbuilt condition of meaning rather than as proof of its cancellation, or, to evade that uncertainty on the surface level of consciousness, while simultaneously allowing it to proliferate beneath. This latter delimited option is figured in the conclusion to this poem where, by the time evening blots out the jetty, 'I'll have slipped inside a fuchsia bud/of wine and spindle tips of light from a porch/over the lake that answers, very nicely, to our own.'

The nature and cost of such bad faith is more directly identified midway through *Spindrift*, in the Mahon and Rich-influenced poem 'Trapdoor'. Here, 'All day the water has been acquiring serenity/only to.../presume to be on intimate terms/with worldly hills, a knowledgeable sky'; but such surface equanimity 'fools no one'.[52] This is because the speaker witnesses this calm as having 'at its dark heart' a 'practiced and accomplished suffering', accessible only through the act of swimming down through the trapdoor of consciousness until one locates 'the pike,/the undertow, . . .//the former dock that, one night,/simply unhinged itself and drifted back/beyond a superficial gloss/to within the lake'. If the loan of confidence in meaning was already under default in the earlier poem, here it seems all but foreclosed: the dock—representing the speaker's trust that the world can answer to her own condition and understanding, and she to its—is now submerged, and her larger aim of finding a place in the world, of aligning her external and internal realities, is jeopardized. But this very identification of bad faith, because it requires recognition of the depths of alterity through which life proceeds, is the basis by which that same bad faith is overturned. When we come to the poem 'Pier', located towards the end of the collection, we find a more mature good faith clearly in the ascendant. Through the allegory of a lone swimming expedition, the speaker now claims the right to enter life 'Head first', *in* all its uncertainty:

> . . . climb the final steps
> up to the ridge. And then let fly. Push wide,
> tuck up your knees so the blue nets hold you,

---

[50] Groarke, *Spindrift*, 15.
[51] Ibid., 12.
[52] Ibid., 35.

> wide-open, that extra beat. Gulp cloud;
> Enter the tide as if it were nothing,
> really nothing, to do with you. Kick back.
> Release your ankles from its coiled ropes;
> slit water, drag it open, catch your breath.[53]

The shift from the 'Summer-bleached', lichen-seamed jetty of apparent yet already undermined faith, to the unhinged drowned dock of its irrefutable loss, to the elevated jumping point of the pier which represents its renewed functionality, annotates the extraordinary personal and poetic journey recorded not only in *Spindrift* but in Groarke's work as a whole thus far. The destination of that journey is indicated as one where incompletion is also completion, requiring that this poet 'interrupt accomplishment/with creases and the finest cracks/that might be said to breathe'.[54] It is one where to realize the otherness of the basic structures of our lives is to achieve resolution. Neither total optimism nor despair of meaning can suffice. What *will* suffice is the act of embracing '"Joy to the World"' in all its contingency.[55] 'I begin to learn/the simple thing//...that will not be refused', she says towards the end of *Spindrift*, which may be exactly the kind of open faith in 'love//that will not be refused' which is prepared for through her strategy of 'silence/in proportion/to desire'.[56] Only by such means, she intimates, can one come into co-presence with oneself, with one's own place in the Real, so as to discover—in *Spindrift*'s concluding words—that

> It is all a kind
> of love song, really,
> and I am only
> listening to it,
> trying to follow
> the words.[57]

[53] Ibid., 56.
[54] Groarke, 'Cowslips', *Spindrift*, 60.
[55] Groarke, 'The Difficult Poem', *Spindrift*, 54.
[56] Groarke, 'Purism', *Spindrift*, 59.
[57] Groarke, 'Spindrift', *Spindrift*, 73.

CHAPTER 40

··

'A POTTED PEACE/LILY'?[1] NORTHERN IRISH POETRY SINCE THE CEASEFIRES

··

MIRIAM GAMBLE

It is as if every gable end of this most 'unpoetic' of cities has its poetic graffito: the corners of its streets are stiff, not with rhetoric, but with poetry.[2]

In his essay ' "What itch of contradiction?" Belfast in Poetry' Eamonn Hughes focuses on the ability of the city to disturb fixed categories of interpretation: the binaries by which, amongst other things, secure identities are formed and on which they are founded. 'The city,' Hughes remarks, 'affronts the sense of the nation as homogenous' by forcing the individual into perpetual and strange encounters with the 'other'. Belfast, then, as both representational and lived space, has always militated against the 'rustic imperative' of Irish writing, asking more questions than it answers, raising 'contradictions' not as a means of settling hard and fast distinctions but in terse opposition to such distinctions.[3] The 'binaries' of Belfast, primary amongst which remains, at the time of Hughes's writing, the question as to 'whether it is a living city or a necropolis', trouble rather than affirm: '[Belfast] is caught in an endless chain of signification, self-divided and always deferred.' This, Hughes suggests, would be true of any city, but with Belfast it, like every other bothersome aspect of identity formation, has been 'profoundly accentuated by the Troubles'.[4] Three decades of civil war have held Belfast in a vacuum of uncertainty, the capital of a province which, emphatically, cannot see its future.

---

[1] Alan Gillis, *Hawks and Doves* (Oldcastle: Gallery, 2007), 52.
[2] Eamonn Hughes, '"What itch of contradiction?" Belfast in Poetry', in *The Cities of Belfast*, ed. Nicholas Allen and Aaron Kelly (Dublin: Four Courts Press, 2003), 101.
[3] Ibid., 114, 115.
[4] Ibid., 107.

Belfast, as we all know, is now running hard on the heels of that future: the ceasefires of the 1990s were followed in 2007 by the institution of devolved government at Stormont; the Troubles, having passed from lived reality into a saleable product, gleam like 'a staked African wasp' from behind the windows of the tourist bus.[5] There are boat tours, bus tours, walking tours, black taxi tours; you can sign your moniker on the peace wall. Goodwill is everywhere, as is 'progress', and the idea of the city-as-necropolis now seems profoundly dated. Poetry, as well as gracing the gable ends (where they still exist), now crowns the dome of one of Ireland's largest and plushest shopping malls, which itself sits on the erstwhile site of one of the city's oldest and most characterful bars, now revamped in 'beige leatherette'.[6] 'Belfast'—or at least the Belfast of 'mixed grills and whis-keys (cultureless, graceless, leisureless)'—is, in the words of Leontia Flynn, 'finished', and a new Belfast is coming 'under construction', keen to take its place:

> Belfast is finished and Belfast is under construction.
> What was mixed grills and whiskeys (cultureless, graceless, leisureless)
> is now concerts and walking tours (Friendly! Dynamic! Various!).[7]

One might well ask what this means, first for Hughes's sense of the city as challenging space, and second for the art which must now emerge from that reordered civitas, so seemingly fat of cheek, so prosper-placid. Its rebarbative aspects tamed, does Belfast stop posing more problems than it offers solutions? How, following in the wake of three decades of war poetry, will the poets now coming of age define themselves and their role, particularly in relation to the city? It will be the purpose of this essay to engage with and attempt to answer these questions.

I will refer throughout to the work of three poets—Leontia Flynn, Alan Gillis, and Sinéad Morrissey—none of whom had published a collection before the ceasefires of 1994, and all of whom wrestle, at a profound and sustained level, with the problem of representing and interrogating their 'own moment in history'.[8] I will argue that, perhaps contrary to expectation, the peace context renders identity in Northern Irish poetry more, rather than less problematic; that the surface glitter of 'normalization' masks as well as embodies a malaise to which these poets are attuned; that expanded opportuni-ties in terms of, for example, travel, also entail expanded responsibilities; and finally, that fulfilling the role of conscience for a society which does not care to hear is equally essen-tial as, and more difficult than, speaking for and to a populace which audibly demands one's contribution. I assume throughout that 'culture is a debate, an argument' and that the new poetry of this so poetry-bedaubed city takes, as it always has done, a crucial part in that debate.[9] The coordinates have changed; the need for creative responses remains

---

[5] Sinéad Morrissey, *Between Here and There* (Manchester: Carcanet, 2002), 14.

[6] Leontia Flynn, *Drives* (London: Jonathan Cape, 2008), 2.

[7] Ibid., 2.

[8] Aaron Kelly, 'Geopolitical Eclipse: Culture and the Peace Process in Northern Ireland', *Third Text*, 9:5 (September 2005), 553.

[9] Tom Paulin, 'The Vernacular City', in *The Cities of Belfast*, ed. Allen and Kelly, 234.

constant. I hope to show how these three poets offer interrogations of 'our predicament' and tentatively propose solutions that may prove 'adequate to' it.[10]

Belfast, site of an enduring and much-media-covered conflict, has in fact, it could be argued, been for the past few generations an 'identi-city' *par excellence*. The mnemonic quality of the city as represented in, for example, the work of a poet such as Ciaran Carson, is undeniable, and it is precisely those features to which Hughes's essay draws attention that have made it so. The Troubles, rather than problematizing Belfast's identity, have in the past confirmed it: Belfast, like the many other sites with which Carson connects it, has been firmly located on the 'conflict map' since the outbreak of hostilities in 1968. Likewise, the poet has held a prominent place as spokesperson or sage in relation to the conflict. Despite Michael Longley's wholly defensible opposition to the idea of the writer of poems as instant cultural commentator, the fact remains that the genre was unusually buoyant in the North in the late twentieth century, enjoying a cultural centrality from which, in other Western locations, it had long since fallen away.[11] The Belfast of the Troubles was the heyday of the poet, however much we might deny the symbiosis of that relationship: many a great poem was born of the fraught 'binaries' to which Hughes attends (and to which we might add that of artistic freedom versus civic responsibility).

The city, by contrast, is both cheekily and pointedly absented from the list of 'B' battle locations in the title sequence to Paul Muldoon's *Horse Latitudes* (2006), and the general pose of this collection is instructive in terms of how we might begin to probe the 'post-ceasefire' atmosphere, as read in the work of poets both established and new. Outwith the Troubles, Carson takes to probing other conflicts: the Crimean War, the Second World War, the Troubles re-read through the lens of private relationships. Muldoon instead turns his attention to entropy—failed aspirations ('Soccer Moms'), the descent from the sublime to the ridiculous ('A Hummingbird'), the clash between debased urban sprawl and the erstwhile natural world ('Starlings, Broad Street, Trenton, 2003').[12] The revised position of the artist vis-à-vis social commentator or anti-establishment 'rebel' is wearily encapsulated in a poem comparing two appearances by Bob Dylan at Princeton University ('Bob Dylan at Princeton, November 2000'):

> That last time at Princeton, that ornery degree,
> his absolute refusal to bend the knee.
>
> His last time at Princeton, he wouldn't wear a hood.
> Now he's dressed up as some sort of cowboy dude.
>
> That last time at Princeton, he wouldn't wear a hood.
> 'You know what, honey? We call that disquietude.[13]

---

[10] Seamus Heaney, *Finders Keepers: Selected Prose 1971–2001* (London: Faber, 2002), 23.

[11] Michael Longley, Introduction, *Causeway: The Arts in Ulster* (Belfast: Arts Council of Northern Ireland; Dublin: Gill and Macmillan, 1971), 8.

[12] Paul Muldoon, *Horse Latitudes* (London: Faber, 2006), 28, 82; Paul Muldoon, 'A Hummingbird', *Answering Back: Living Poets Reply to the Poetry of the Past*, ed. Carol Ann Duffy (London: Picador, 2007), 21.

[13] Muldoon, *Horse Latitudes*, 24.

Dylan's 'disquietude' may not be palpable, but Muldoon's certainly is: in these poems, he continually disturbs, by assuming, the complacent register of the contemporary, and worries at Francis Fukuyama's notion that we may, indeed, have arrived at the 'end of history'.[14] 'A Hummingbird', written in response to D. H. Lawrence's exuberant rendering of prehistoric grandeur, pits enervated conversational bathos against the 'jabbing, terrifying monster' painted in the original.[15] Lawrence's poem concludes with the assertion that 'We look at [the humming-bird] through the wrong end of the telescope of time'; in Muldoon's, it is almost as though we have walked past the telescope unawares, and blundered on into some flaccid limbo.[16] Lawrence's context pre-dates language, the means by which we understand and rationalize the universe; Muldoon's falls out, with language, at the other end, signifying the natural death point of the system. The poem, a sonnet, is, bar the concluding couplet, entirely comprised of empty conversational tit-bits:

> 'I'm guessing she's had a neck-lift *and* lipo.'
> 'You know I still can't help but think of the *Wake*
> as the apogee, you know, of the typo.'

The couplet sums up: language and its creatures are 'Like an engine rolling on after a crash,/long after whatever it was made a splash'.[17] Muldoon is, needless to say, sticking the boot in here: he opposes, in his courting of it, the slack, dulled language of the age, just as he opposes in Dylan the falling away from political activism to self (and national) parody. 'A Hummingbird' is as ingenious in its choice of model—the spitfire Lawrence— as it is in its mode of response, the way in which it turns the telescope around again. The point, however, is that the territory Muldoon surveys here is 'beyond': beyond action, beyond commitment, beyond even saving, perhaps. There are no big concerns, nothing to latch onto or strive towards: everything has been achieved and, in the achieving, palls sadly into that 'which deadens and endures'.[18]

Admittedly Muldoon now writes from within an American context, but similar tendencies can be observed in many of the earliest poems of the three poets under examination here (all of whom were, at the time, based in Northern Ireland). *These Days* (2004), the first collection from Leontia Flynn, repeatedly addresses the condition of belatedness:

> For 64,000, what's Paris's oldest bridge?
> The Pont Neuf? The Pont Royale? We can't remember which is which.
> And the days are too long, and the nights are too long,
> And life lounges late on the sofa. Not. Flipping. That. Switch.[19]

---

[14] Francis Fukuyama, *The End of History and the Last Man* (London: Penguin, 1992).
[15] D. H. Lawrence, 'Humming-bird', *Answering Back*, 20.
[16] Ibid., 20.
[17] Muldoon, *Answering Back*, 21.
[18] Louis MacNeice, *Selected Poems*, ed. Michael Longley (London: Faber, 1988), 19.
[19] Leontia Flynn, 'Bridges', *These Days* (London: Jonathan Cape, 2004), 31.

The winsomeness of Flynn's voice has tended to distract attention from the seriousness of the matter at hand: what she grapples with in poems like 'Bridges' is, precisely, the sense of having no poetic 'role', no civic function. Like Gillis, Flynn often revisits the poems of the past, both contrasting their contours with the (diminished) contours of her own life, and seeking, through them, for a sure sense of how to proceed. The figure of the parent, whether literary or biological, is of critical significance to Flynn's early poetic: in 'Eeps', the biological father prompts, Heaney-style, the speaker's desire to write, and in 'Acts of Faith' the mother tends a sick daughter who, at twenty-four, still cannot manage to field the world alone.[20] '26', a sestina, contrasts the mother's assumption of responsibility at twenty-six (marriage, setting up house) with the daughter's failure to make any such commitment; it ends inconclusively: 'What will you give up? What will be handed down?'[21] This is not mere ineptitude, however: the opening poem to the collection introduces a subject who, 'preachy with book-learning', has spent years being groomed for greatness, only to find, on reaching maturity, that the expected niche is nowhere to be seen.[22] Flynn's poetic enacts a continuous assault on the pretensions of the individual (and, thus, the lyric voice). In 'The Amazing, Disappearing', the subject is out of focus, lacking sure definition: '"Watch out for that—"'. In 'The Second Mrs de Winter', she forms a poor substitute for the absented 'original'. In 'The Franklin's Tale', the 'amazing' action undertaken by her is the ordinary feat of learning to drive. And in 'It's a Wonderful Life' (#1), the over-dramatically imagined 'apotheosis of our lives' (public suicide) is undercut equally by the backdrop against which it is set (a student flat 'Somewhere between five and seven in the morning/to gauge by the light and inferior type of talk show') and by the fact that, again, the 'inspiration' behind it is derived from a source that pre-dates the self—in this case, the film from which the poem takes its title.[23] The point, however hedged with irony, is clear: Flynn's is a poetic persona both unsure of its own features and 'salivating' for a sense of vocation.[24] *These Days* suggests that she can find nothing satisfactory to write 'about', and that she is chronically unsure of her coordinates, both as poet and citizen.

To some extent, these features mark Flynn's out as an aesthetics of transition—one ghosting the vacuous point at which separate cultures collide and, ultimately, swap control of the vehicle. As Colin Graham suggests, the last ten to fifteen years have marked 'a transitional phase in Belfast's physical and social being': 'the new and the old are juxtaposed', both architecturally and ideologically.[25] As Flynn puts it, 'Belfast is finished and Belfast is under construction'.[26] Similarly, Sinéad Morrissey writes of being 'between here and there' (and Alan Gillis of being 'somebody, somewhere'); she also

---

[20]   Flynn, *These Days*, 3, 2.

[21]   Ibid., 50.

[22]   Ibid., 1.

[23]   Ibid., 12, 13, 30, 35.

[24]   Ibid., 30.

[25]   Colin Graham, '"Every Passer-by a Culprit?" Photography and the Peace in Belfast', *Third Text* 19:5 (September 2005), 571–2.

[26]   Flynn, *Drives*, 2.

encapsulates the precise quality of the transitional moment in a poem from her sequence, 'China':

> One day, China met China in the marketplace.
> 'How are you, China?' asked China, 'we haven't talked in so long'…
> 'It's true,' replied China. 'We have a lot to catch up on.'[27]

This allegorical figuration of separate 'faces' of the same country meeting each other concludes a sequence which has (literally) travelled extensively between the two: composed after a British Council funded trip on the Writers' Train, the 'China' poems pit urban-industrial squalor ('a semaphore of cranes') against vegetable opulence ('Spinach, pak choi, cabbage greens') and ancient symbolic language against contemporary clamour ('the city with a name like the din of a smithy').[28] Morrissey likewise brings this split perspective to the changing face of Belfast. In her poem, 'In Belfast' (which takes its cue from and radically updates Derek Mahon's 'In Belfast', now retitled 'Spring in Belfast'), 'history's dent and fracture' still 'split[s] the atmosphere' but, in conjunction with this, the wheels of consumerist capital begin to turn in earnest:

> The inhaling shop-fronts exhale the length
> and breadth of Royal Avenue, pause,
> inhale again. The city is making money
> on a weather-mangled Tuesday.[29]

The animism of this image—the leviathan maw of the high street sucking in and spitting out the unperceiving subject—strikes chords with the approach of Alan Gillis, who might be said to have replaced Carson as Belfast's lover-laureate. In 'To Belfast', a poem which takes the sestina form but fails to finish it, Gillis celebrates the city's habit of 'getting out of hand', refusing to 'stem/to…cameras'—in effect, that 'off-beat, headstrong, suicidal charm' which Morrissey records with greater scepticism.[30] Gillis's poem, like Flynn's persona, is trapped in the vortex of conflicting trends and attitudes—whilst he wishes to see the city's self-protecting 'bullet-proof knickers drop like rain' (or, in Morrissey's terms, to see it coming into its 'own abundance'), he laments the seemingly inevitable Californication this will entail, the transformation of Belfast into a 'Hollywood film' funded and styled by external influences:

> For Belfast, if you'd be a Hollywood film, then I'd be Grace
> Kelly on my way to Monaco, to pluck the stem
> of a maybell with its rows of empty shells, its head
> of one hundred blinded eyes. I would finger your trace
> in that other city's face, and bite its free hand
> as it fed me, or tried to soothe the stinging of your rain.[31]

[27] Sinéad Morrissey, *The State of the Prisons* (Manchester: Carcanet, 2005), 30.
[28] Ibid., 24–5.
[29] Morrissey, *Between Here and There*, 13.
[30] Alan Gillis, *Somebody, Somewhere* (Oldcastle: Gallery, 2004), 16; Morrissey, *Between Here and There*, 14.
[31] Gillis, *Somebody, Somewhere*, 16.

The substitution for individualist 'grace' of the iconic 'Grace' of the silver screen, the hundred identically 'blind' eyes of the maybell—even the morphing of Hughes's 'hard and soft' binary, identified as characteristic of Belfast in the poems of MacNeice, into mass-produced virtual 'hardware and software': all these bespeak the shift from a city which, however problematically, held fast to its own defining marks ('the tramlines of your cellulite skin') into one that is indistinguishable from anywhere else in the developed Western world.[32] What wafts from the shop-fronts under this new dispensation is not the racket and clatter of localized breath so much as the airy absence of the global market.

Gillis's poem, however, does have a sting in its tail. The abbreviated formal template—the poem has only four stanzas, rather than the requisite six and a three-line envoi—does not indicate failure, or even entropy, so much as the feisty interjection of the dissonant subject. In historical-determinist readings, society moves through an inevitable series of stages before arriving at the 'ideal state': according to theorists such as Fukuyama, liberal democracy (for which read late capitalism) represents this terminal point, and is thus the pinnacle of achieved 'normality' towards which all peoples should strive.[33] The sestina, as form, enacts this very process when taken to completion: although cyclical, in that it repeat-transforms identical terms, it lends itself cleanly to narrative development in a manner eschewed by most set lyric forms (compare, for example, the villanelle as described by Eavan Boland and Mark Strand: 'Its repeated lines, the circularity of its stanzas, become, as the reader listens, a repudiation of forward motion, of temporality and therefore, finally, of dissolution').[34] By sticking a spanner in the works—curbing the propulsive drive—of this formal framework, Gillis both protests against and arrests, however temporarily, the progress of Belfast down the set path from identi-city to identikit-city. On the cusp of Graham's moment of transition he grasps, like the photographers whose work Graham analyses, 'the trace . . . of a city that once was and is now being denied'.[35]

The work of all three poets is ghosted by the traces of that which is 'being denied', though this rarely takes the form of straightforward mourning either for the past itself or for the victims of that past. Whereas the 1990s 'ghost book' focused on the difficulty of coming to terms with the past and finding an acceptable means of moving on (witness, for example, Muldoon's *The Annals of Chile*, Longley's *Gorse Fires*, and Ormsby's *The Ghost Train*), the spectres which haunt the work of Flynn, Gillis, and Morrissey are more likely to be those, on the one hand, of locality, and, on the other, of the individuated self.[36] To these one might add, also, the phantoms of class and of the engaged political subject. Aaron Kelly has written persuasively of the less examined and more egregious

[32] Hughes, ' "What itch of contradiction?" ', 106.
[33] See Fukuyama, *The End of History*.
[34] Mark Strand and Eavan Boland, *The Making of a Poem: A Norton Anthology of Poetic Forms* (New York: Norton, 2001), 8.
[35] Graham, ' "Every Passer-by a Culprit?" ', 572.
[36] See Michael Parker, *The Imprint of History*, vol. 2, *Northern Irish Literature 1975–2006* (Basingstoke: Palgrave Macmillan, 2007), 162.

aspects of the peace process, a process which to some extent at least masks continuing and chronic inequality beneath the veneer of high-level private investment projects. His argument is worth quoting at length, not least for the angered fervour with which it is delivered, and its determination to break the codes of polite written discourse:

> Rather than a new ethical dispensation, Northern Irish society's reconciliation is an economic one, a reconciliation with the dynamics of a world system and the post-modern, an ideology whose only compass is the flow of capital around the globe.... The voguish phrase that inserts itself in all late capitalist discourse about economic development and the supposed benefits of private enterprise, investment and regeneration for everyone – 'the trickledown effect' – should not obscure the fact that working-class communities are being pissed on from a great height. In contrast to a popular will to end sectarian conflict, the state-sponsored aspects of the Peace Process – extending British 'Third Way' capitalism westwards and the Celtic Tiger northwards...aim at establishing a wishy-washy and market-driven postmodern pluralism that actually serves to mask the real socioeconomic divides in our city that threaten ultimately to remove power from people completely.[37]

Also a conscientious objector to the jargon of peace (witness his poem 'Progress'), Gillis likewise makes a point of introducing 'unacceptable' elements into the language of his poems and, at times, allowing these elements to run the show. In an essay on 'The Vernacular City', Tom Paulin argues for the establishment of a 'national literature' conducted through the 'energy and pithy imagery' of Belfast's 'scutching vernacular'.[38] In poems like 'Last Friday Night' and 'Home and Away', Gillis might be seen to take this baton up, giving back to his native city the rallying cry of its spiky dialect, and thus bolstering its quiddity against the threat of normalization.[39] In truth, however, the voices to which Gillis gives airtime in these poems are the ghettoized poor—those who, as Kelly affirms, have been pushed to (or left on) the sidelines of the gentrified city, and whose micro-narrative finds no place in the self-congratulatory blurb of 'wishy-washy...pluralism'. These are ghosts who are still alive, and whom the newly painted city would prefer to ignore. By giving them room in his poems Gillis lends them subjectivity; yet the power with which the poems endow 'wee Markie' etcetera is not wielded triumphantly but rather accusatorily. Their voices form a scathing reminder; they are contemporary Belfast's marginalia, both social and poetic, rather than the centrally printed text.

Gillis, then, does not write dialect poems in his own voice (they serve a different purpose), but his lyric persona does incorporate rebellious streaks, at the level of both image and subject matter. In the sestina 'For What We Are About To Receive', the reader is treated to a stomach-churning binge on rancid pork loins, 'five Belfast baps and twelve green/bottles of beer'.[40] Rather than buying from the popular end of the 'pine-/fresh

---

[37] Kelly, 'Geopolitical Eclipse', 547–8.
[38] Paulin, 'The Vernacular City', 239.
[39] Gillis, *Somebody, Somewhere*, 27; *Hawks and Doves*, 40.
[40] Gillis, *Hawks and Doves*, 16.

mall', Gillis's speaker cussedly opts for the 'snubbed' part and, indeed, in this poem, speaker might be seen as equivalent to city, on the model of 'To Belfast':

> ...you laid down the law that night I brought clear
> spring water and readymade greens
> that I sprinkled with toasted pine
> nuts as you spelled out loud and clear that the odds
> against us keeping faith were five thousand
> to one, and that I needed to get over
>
> the fact that we were over.[41]

In other words, the speaker's attempt to 'gentrify' fools nobody; a purchase from the posh end of the mall doesn't ensure the proverbial leopard has changed its spots. This, like many of the poems in *Hawks and Doves*, Gillis's second collection, is a disgusting poem and a poem of disgust: its remit is by no means limited to shocking via physical revulsion, but the assumption by Gillis of, if one likes, the crossover stigmata of the bingeing-yet-still-tatty city into his own persona is a significant technique, and one that is also adopted, with personal variations, by both Flynn and Morrissey. In 'Poem for Christmas', Flynn brilliantly equates herself with the Belfast depicted by Aaron Kelly, a Belfast economically buoyed but still caught at the political crossroads (it is dated December 2005, before the institution of devolved government):

> To this place of gangsters, double deals and crime rings
> I must belong: both of us like to drive
> if they can love us, men off one by one
> with broken promises. Then *pause* – and seem to thrive
> as words and buzzwords rush to fill the vacuum.[42]

Morrissey too raises questions as to the legitimacy of surface unity and polish: her poems constantly disturb the line between inner and outer, saying things they 'shouldn't' and implicitly marking poetry as the vehicle through which social silencings are challenged, as in 'The Second Lesson of the Anatomists' and '& Forgive Us Our Trespasses':

> *See how the inside belies our skin,*
> say the anatomists,
> after showing us how freakishly we split;
>
> *the outside smooth and assiduous*
> *unto itself, while the inside*
> *baffles and seethes...*[43]

> Accept from us the inappropriate
> by which our dreams and daily scenes stay separate[44]

[41] Ibid., 16.
[42] Flynn, *Drives*, 23.
[43] Morrissey, *State of the Prisons*, 11.
[44] Morrissey, *Between Here and There*, 21.

'The Second Lesson of the Anatomists' goes on to connect the body private with the body socio-civic explicitly, drawing parallels between the epidermis and the fragile 'glass room' of a party boat on the river:

> There is a party going on. There is wine
> and a light fixture being obedient
> unto itself. And then there is this spillage
>
> in the centre
> from somewhere stranger and more extravagant
> which has drawn us all here.

The 'truth', for Morrissey, is always 'stranger and more extravagant' than the 'effortlessly deceptive' nature of what is presented and accepted at face value;[45] the precise nature of the 'spillage' in this poem, though it is clearly linguistic, remains undefined, but it is not an imaginative step too far to conceive of it as being poetry itself: the outburst that spoils the gilded party, the language that refuses 'quiet conformism' in favour of what Gillis calls the 'cockamamie-chorded music' of dissent:

> Long since the burger-eating burghers of bright suburban valleys
> ordered me to lay off this cockamamie-chorded music
> because it disrupted their day's work and upset their night.[46]

One of the values Morrissey prizes most highly is freedom of speech, and in her work the right to speak is frequently associated with the act of bucking dominant trends. In 'Flight', she assumes the voice of a woman who is doomed to sport a scold's bridle for daring to speak her mind, and whose visionary impulse is opposed to her husband's staid (and coveted) rationalism:

> My husband desires a sign.
> But for all his reading of *Revelation*
> I say heaven admits its own
> And it is Him. The jaw-straps tighten.[47]

This is not femininity run wild, however. Morrissey is well schooled in the literature and ideology of the eighteenth century, and her work poses a fruitful dialogue between civic Enlightenment values and the power of that which, outside the framework, continues to exist in a state of subversive potential; likewise, she balances Utopian impulses with the Meliorist recognition that imperfection is not only human, it is a positive good. Unlike Gillis, Morrissey is not inclined to hatchet the establishment directly, but in her bristling defence of personal freedom, her continuing belief in the value of 'prophetic speech',

---

[45] See also 'The Invitation', *Through the Square Window* (Manchester: Carcanet, 2009), 33–5. Morrissey is equally alert to the surrealism of the conventional. See, for example, 'Mother Goose', *Through the Square Window*, 46.

[46] Morrissey, *State of the Prisons*, 11; Graham, ' "Every Passer-by a Culprit?" ', 569; Gillis, *Hawks and Doves*, 57.

[47] Morrissey, *State of the Prisons*, 9.

and, perhaps most importantly, her attitude towards and application of language, she opposes both the flattened media discourse of the day and the 'shadowy' powers-that-be who would dull potentially disruptive responses through manipulation of that discourse.[48] Where Gillis stresses the impact of those forces that would numb or pap out of existence any verbal challenge ('this fall from bustle into soft bubbles/of self-regard where the headless chicken-/like rampage of...days dissolves into easy-/listening nights, while outside are militias,/lead levels, diplomacy and logistics') and, indeed, in his praxis, enacts that very impact, piling information on information so that 'everything glitters for an instant/and then snuffs it', Morrissey simply opposes them by doing otherwise and, primarily, by drawing greedily on the vast resources of language available to her.[49] In her poem 'Matter', she covets not only the eccentric explanations of ancient scientists—theories from a time before science became obsessed with 'gauze instruments and [a] penchant/for boiling'—but the very wealth of phenomena, and words hitched to phenomena, to which they grant her access; likewise, in 'Pearl' she upholds and voices the desire to constantly 'be amazed'.[50] More than either of the other poets discussed here, Morrissey openly values and regards as politically forceful the faculty of imagination on its own terms and in its own right: this, and the duty and right to speak, form the twin axes of her poetic; they are also the points from which she undermines 'the pastiche paradise of the post-modern'.[51]

On the surface of it, few poets have less in common than Morrissey and Leontia Flynn: against Morrissey's joyful exoticism of diction Flynn pitches a smartly streetwise lingo; in place of Morrissey's roving strain, Flynn is short, sharp, and to the formal point; the broadening of horizons that draws Morrissey to literal travel is lambasted by Flynn as a bourgeois fallacy, which leads only to superficial encounters with myriad versions of the same thing. Finally, and perhaps most importantly, the value Morrissey places on originality (and, concomitantly, agency) is rendered deeply suspect in Flynn's *oeuvre*, which goes out of its way to floor any pretensions upheld by the individual voice. *These Days* contains forty-eight poems: twenty-nine of them are single- or two-stanza poems fed through a ten-line framework, as though to suggest that every subject taken on is forced into the same-size factory mould.

Earlier, I suggested that Flynn's brand of anti-epiphany points towards immersion in an aesthetics of transition, and that the means by which she goes about detracting from her own literary value could be linked primarily to a vacuum in Northern Irish culture: the point at which Northern Ireland teeters on the brink of becoming one thing rather than another, without yet having decided (or had decided for it) what will constitute the features of its new 'face'.[52] Colin Graham argues that 'For the last decade or so, Northern Ireland has been strangely without any significant utopian cultural coordinates.

[48] Kelly, 'Geopolitical Eclipse', 546.
[49] Gillis, *Hawks and Doves*, 63, 65.
[50] Morrissey, *Through the Square Window*, 14; *Between Here and There*, 58.
[51] Derek Mahon, *The Yellow Book* (Oldcastle: Gallery, 1997), 19.
[52] Flynn, *These Days*, 18.

Meanwhile the political scene has asked all else to wait for it.'[53] Read alongside Gillis or Morrissey's work this seems unfair, but it adheres almost perfectly to the grim dramatizations of 'waiting' (or even, Generation X-style, patent ignoring) discernible in Flynn's earliest poems—poems which have her 'fiddling/with the radio dial.../While Rome Burns', viewing sociopolitical uproar as a 'festival time'.[54] 'Punch-drunk' and media-savvy, she seems the perfect model of lethargic disengagement. The analogy is, however, too neat—not least because it should never be this easy to map poetry onto the political realm—and there is much in Flynn's work that suggests a deeper interrogation of, and reaction against, her own cultural 'moment', particularly in terms of her exploration of precisely that entity so prized in Morrissey's poems, the individual lyric voice.

In 'Two Crossings', Flynn hatches a tidy metaphor for the Northern Ireland of the late 1990s—a culture in a boat that is pretending 'not to be' one, and thus not to be going any-where. In the process, she also conjures up a convincing depiction of the 'gloomy' Northern Irish, dissatisfied with everything yet too polite to say so:

> One of my miserable neighbours is a gigantic beery man
> with a moustache. He is complaining loudly
> because one of his party didn't receive their free drink.
> He tells them: if you don't complain about nuthin,
> nuthin is ever done...
>
> ...
>
> A waitress dives over to clear up and ask was everything alright?
> The miserables tell her it was, thankyou,
> thankyou very much – [55]

As an observation on agency, this is astute (the Northern Irish never get because they're too embarrassed to ask), but what is perhaps more interesting is the contrast between Flynn's own narrative voice in the poem and the 'leviathan and clattering *accent*' she describes. Not only does Flynn's voice lack this accent—the very premise on which the poem is based and with which its air '*seems to be* alive' (italics mine)—it is in fact positively American in key. The approach is subtle, but clearly evident: 'people *quit* moon-walking the deck'; folk gather 'in the *diner*'; it might be 'snowing over the sea *right now*' (italics mine). If the air in the boat is alive with one kind of accent, the poem's breath is slyly laced with another—or, perhaps more suggestively, 'half asleep with [the] rocking' of it. The phrase 'seems to be alive' thus comes to imply its opposite, for both parties: those with the accent (and without the will to speak) pass into redundancy, whilst the poem's speaker finds herself colonized, not by Standard English (Ireland's oldest linguis-tic grouse), but by the worldwide distributor of popular culture. This is not the language of cool worn lightly but, rather, a critical appraisal of the ubiquitous and all-effacing blanket nature of that language. What Gillis enacts at the level of visual signifier (the landscape branded by confectionery, etcetera) is woven by Flynn into the vocal texture

---

[53] Graham, '"Every Passer-by a Culprit?"', 568.
[54] Flynn, *These Days*, 8.
[55] Ibid., 25–6.

of her poems; both yield lyric personae who, like the city they write about, have been encroached upon and infected by the 'shadowy' powers that be.[56] Gillis's completed sestina, 'For What We Are About To Receive', proffers, in contrast to 'To Belfast', a speaker who is trapped helplessly in the very system he would oppose; likewise Flynn's voice, lauded by the British establishment for its 'basic-wage, take-what-you-get...assurance', is in fact a carapace formed of the Hollywood-esque influences that dictate her fate in 'It's a Wonderful Life'.[57]

This is not to suggest that Flynn is in thrall to a language or a set of mannerisms over which she lacks control; rather, it is to draw attention to the way in which she manipulates language as a form of 'mimicry', and to propose that, rather than showing her hand, she shields jealously an active subjectivity *behind* the winsome frontage of her poems, suggesting their attractive 'personality' has little to do with their underlying thrust.[58] On the one hand, she mocks through embodiment the monoculture of the American Diner World; on the other she protects her true identity from it. The interaction of these tactics is clearly visible in one of her best-known poems, 'The Myth of Tea Boy', in which the characters, keeping their 'secret belie[fs]' to themselves, 'act like [they're] in diners/from everyone's favourite Hopper poster, Nighthawks' and, like the 'fronts on the Golden Mile', depend on this 'pose' to protect their fragile sense of self:

> As the room fills up with 'Eternal Flame': the cover version, on the radio,
> and, floor to ceiling, the last of the summer light, we also know
> for as long as this pose is held we won't spill a single drop.[59]

In other poems, this circumspection is applied directly to the language in which it is iterated. 'On the Third Floor of the Royal Infirmary' compares a girl's fraught response to her new 'face' to the speaker's attitude to the written word: 'Now she can no more look, cold-eyed, in a looking glass/than I at this'.[60] And in 'Poem for Christmas', 'words' are equated with the 'buzzwords' of peace: city and poet both *'pause'*—cease active being— 'and *seem* to thrive/as words and buzzwords rush to fill the vacuum' (italics the author's, then mine).[61]

The emphasis on thriving (or its opposite) in 'Poem for Christmas' flags up a recurrent trope in Flynn's work—that of sickness—which again both highlights and opposes

---

[56] Gillis, *Somebody, Somewhere*, 13–14; Kelly, 'Geopolitical Eclipse', 546.

[57] Gillis, *Hawks and Doves*, 16–17; John Burnside, cover blurb to *These Days*.

[58] For an analysis of the technique of 'mimicry' as applied to photography, see Graham, '"Every Passer-by a Culprit?"', 569–70. Graham argues that the apparently documentary approach of mimicry permits the artist to intervene in and comment upon the image being presented, thus creating 'aesthetic...disturbance' and asserting personal agency. For a direct playing out of this idea in the poems, see 'Personality', where the essence of the poem is described as 'the rictus grin/on a student's practice corpse—that breathes iambically/*between* each line, with their knives parting the skin,/love me, love me, love me, love me...' (Flynn, *Drives*, 10; italics mine). Flynn here inverts the predicted intonation of the final line to lay the stress on the self—'love *me*, love *me*'—rather than on the general concept of 'love'. The distinction between surface and depths is also instructive.

[59] Flynn, *These Days*, 37.

[60] Ibid., 18.

[61] Flynn, *Drives*, 23.

the conditions of the poetry's making. *These Days* performs a whistle-stop tour of contemporary neuroses: anorexia, obsessive compulsive disorder, and depression all make an appearance, and are set against the backdrop of the poet's own long-suffered tryst with eczema. But it is in her second collection, *Drives*, that the subject of illness truly takes hold. The book plays host to a series of poems, mostly in sonnet form, that adopt as their unifying principle the physical and mental affliction of artists, and suggest that (as in Gillis's 'For What We Are About to Receive') the artist lays bare social malaise through both physical and subconscious responses to his or her environment. Dissonance, as in other aspects of Flynn's poetry, seeps through the cracks in the perfect skin, rather than advertising itself upon the surface. For example, 'Alfred Hitchcock' pits Hitchcock's penchant for the 'ice-white blonde,/groomed to perfection'—sure symbol of 1950s wealth and style—against the fact that:

> Hitchcock himself will never learn to drive
> on account of his lifelong, much-debated fear
> that a copper might pull him over – and give
> no warning or reason, but march him from the car
>
> and lock him away in the dark where his terrified cries,
> unheard or unheeded, are the cries of a blubbery child.[62]

The oedipal aspects of the poem aside (the 'much-debated fear' is, as in many of the poems, attributed to the mother), this marks within the artist a point of intersection between the topside and undersides of society: a society in which he succeeds—is indeed viewed as a cultural icon—and of which he yet retains the not-so-irrational fear that boosts and generates his work. (Hitchcock is, after all, the master of the psychological thriller, and was doing his best work during the McCarthy era.) Likewise, in 'Sylvia Plath's Sinus Condition', Flynn highlights 'the channel prone to flood' that links 'the long-limbed, gee-whiz, perfect girl...this blonde self' to 'the darker one,/who breeds an absent father's awful abscess'. As with Hitchcock, Plath straddles the stools of socialite and social dissident, her poetry acting as the 'fistula' through which the one arises to infect (or disinfect) the other.[63] The use of illness-as-dissent might seem a passive construction—one which permits of doing nothing—but can in fact be viewed in the opposite light. By assuming (like Flynn herself) the accepted characteristics of the social paradigm—by, in effect, mimicking—Plath and Hitchcock gain access to positions of power and influence which they would otherwise be denied; by wearing camouflage, they successfully infiltrate the establishment, and are able to criticize it from within. Just so, in one of the most politically forceful poems in *Drives*, Flynn lurks beneath the camouflage of the canon as a means of both shielding and making (or 'driving' home) her point. The poem, 'Washington', shapes itself around Shelley's 'Ozymandias':

> *I met a traveller*, walking in the mall
> in Washington, in April, *from an antique land,*

[62] Ibid., 33.
[63] Ibid., 46.

map-less, in rapid tourist mode, between
Who said the Washington Memorial
and…Jesus fucking Christ…this mausoleum
where Lincoln sits in state, and there in stone
fluent and just his Gettysburg address.
Boundless on either side, are wreaths to war.
Look on my works ye mighty and despair.
And by the White House, men with walkie-talkies.[64]

This poem turns the 'cover version' paradigm round and sees Flynn coming into her 'own abundance', albeit through the means of an incomplete narrative that 'lets [itself] out' carefully, and refuses, with Longley, the journalistic imperative of quick and easily digestible comment; the true poet, as Marianne Moore suggests, 'digesteth harde yron' and demands the same robustness of the reader.[65] 'Washington' also highlights indirectly Flynn's close relationship with the poets of the American pantheon, a relationship opposed to her impish donning of popular culture from the same source: where one feeds the surface, the other feeds the heart of her aesthetic, as is made clear by her engagement with, amongst others, Robert Lowell, Elizabeth Bishop, and, of course, Plath, in the artist poems of *Drives*. Finally, the poem is exemplary in pointing to a Belfast which has undergone radical transformation in relation to its boundaries and, consequently, the limits within which its writers can comfortably rest.

Flynn, Gillis, and Morrissey belong to a city which must now admit of 'frigates gathering for war'—war that happens not on the doorstep, but 'too far/out for us to see'—as part of its ethical purview; a city that is hopelessly entangled with, and must therefore bear responsibility for, the imperialist colossus which is currently, in Morrissey's words, 'Loose in the world. And out of proportion.'[66] This Belfast has shed its binaries, and in their place has taken on not the single hue of the homogenously settled but instead the bizarre, shifting colourations of what Morrissey calls 'Found Architecture'—the product of a kaleidoscope:

that makes its heel-to-toe shapes, not from beads or seeds
or painted, meticulous details, but from the room,

from whatever room I happen to be in[67]

All three poets both depict and challenge this architecture, paying honest attention to its complexity, and continuing to fight the corner of poetry not only as 'a way of happening' but also, crucially, as 'a mouth'.[68] No quiet conformism here; no fear of taking the wheel. Northern Ireland is the land of the lyric, and these three poets continue that trend; they also find new ways of bringing the lyric into forced conjunction with the cosmopolitan

[64] Ibid., 29.
[65] Flynn, *These Days*, 35; Marianne Moore, *Complete Poems* (London: Penguin, 1994), 99–100.
[66] Gillis, *Hawks and Doves*, 12; Morrissey, *The State of the Prisons*, 37.
[67] Morrissey, *Through the Square Window*, 18.
[68] W. H. Auden, *Selected Poems*, ed. Edward Mendelson (London: Faber, 1979), 82.

space of the contemporary city.[69] There is no room in their work for the notion of lyric as a space of rooted tranquillity (or even potted scion). Flynn's 'Airports' captures succinctly the contemporary condition of being everywhere and nowhere at the same time: 'when we return, the airports remain in us./We rock, dry-eyed, and we are not at home.'[70] But they do find innovative means of garnering force from its formal cohesiveness—means related, perhaps, to Aaron Kelly's querying response to the mission statements of postmodernism:

> It is no coincidence that at a moment in History when millions of people previously denied a voice in that historical process...have, at however minimal a level...been able to articulate their oppression and exclusion, the dominant intellectual and political centres of the Western world suddenly decide that truth no longer exists; that narrative must fail to represent since all stories are suspect; that identity... can be dismissed as an oppressively anachronistic essentialism in an era of hybrid flux.[71]

This sounds very much like a command to 'Pull yourself together'—resist ultimate dispersal—which is precisely what the lyric poem does; it is also the imperative-to-self of Gillis's news-and-nonsense besieged speaker in the long poem 'Saturday Morning'.[72] 'N.I.' emphatically does not and cannot stand, these days (if it ever did), for 'N[ot] I[nterested]'; there is, quite simply, too much at stake.[73]

---

[69] See Aaron Kelly, 'Desire Lines: Mapping the City in Contemporary Belfast and Glasgow Poetry', in *Modern Irish and Scottish Poetry*, ed. Peter Mackay, Edna Longley, and Fran Brearton (Cambridge: Cambridge University Press, 2011), 359–63, for an analysis of Gillis's use of the urban lyric.

[70] Flynn, *Drives*, 35.

[71] Kelly, 'Geopolitical Eclipse', 546.

[72] Gillis, *Hawks and Doves*, 21.

[73] Flynn, *Drives*, 22.

Select Bibliography

I. Poetry

Beckett, Samuel, *Selected Poems, 1930–1989*, ed. David Wheatley (London: Faber, 2009).

Berkeley, Sara, *Facts About Water* (Newcastle: Bloodaxe, 1994).

—— *Strawberry Thief* (Oldcastle: Gallery, 2005).

—— *The View from Nowhere* (Oldcastle: Gallery, 2010).

Boland, Eavan, *New Collected Poems* (Manchester: Carcanet, 2005).

—— *Domestic Violence* (Manchester: Carcanet, 2007).

Bolger, Dermot, *Taking My Letters Back: New and Selected Poems* (Dublin: New Island Books, 1998).

Bryce, Colette, *The Heel of Bernadette* (London: Picador, 2000).

—— *The Full Indian Rope Trick* (London: Picador, 2005).

—— *Self-Portrait in the Dark* (London: Picador, 2008).

Campbell, Joseph, *The Poems of Joseph Campbell* (Dublin: Allen Figgis, 1963).

Cannon, Moya, *Carrying the Songs: New and Selected Poems* (Manchester: Carcanet, 2007).

Carson, Ciaran, *Collected Poems* (Oldcastle: Gallery, 2008).

—— *On the Night Watch* (Oldcastle: Gallery, 2009).

—— *Until Before After* (Oldcastle: Gallery, 2010).

Clarke, Austin, *Collected Poems*, ed. R. Dardis Clarke (Manchester: Carcanet, 2008).

Clifton, Harry, *The Desert Route: Selected Poems* (Oldcastle: Gallery, 1992).

—— *Night Train Through the Brenner* (Oldcastle: Gallery, 1994).

—— *Secular Eden: Paris Notebooks 1994–2004* (Salem: Wake Forest University Press, 2008).

Coady, Michael, *All Souls* (Oldcastle: Gallery, 1997).

—— *One Another* (Oldcastle: Gallery, 2003).

—— *Going by Water* (Oldcastle: Gallery, 2009).

Coffey, Brian, *Poems and Versions 1929–1990* (Dublin: Dedalus, 1991).

Colum, Padraic, *Selected Poems*, ed. Sanford Sternlicht (New York: Syracuse University Press, 1989).

Cronin, Anthony, *Collected Poems* (Dublin: New Island Books, 2004).

Davis, Thomas, *Thomas Davis: Selections from his Prose and Poetry*, ed. T. W. Rolleston (Dublin: Talbot Press, 1914).

Davitt, Michael, *Selected Poems/Rogha Dánta* (Dublin: Raven Arts, 1987).

Dawe, Gerald, *Selected Poems* (Oldcastle: Gallery, 2012).

Deane, John F., *Toccata and Fugue: New and Selected Poems* (Manchester: Carcanet, 2000).

—— *Manhandling the Deity* (Manchester: Carcanet, 2003).

—— *The Instruments of Art* (Manchester: Carcanet, 2005).

—— *A Little Book of Hours* (Manchester: Carcanet, 2008).

—— *Eye of the Hare* (Manchester: Carcanet, 2011).

Delanty, Greg, *Collected Poems 1986–2006* (Manchester: Carcanet, 2006).

Devlin, Denis, *Collected Poems of Denis Devlin*, ed. J. C. C. Mays (Dublin: Dedalus, 1989).

Durcan, Paul, *Life is a Dream: 40 Years Reading Poems 1967–2007* (London: Harvill Secker, 2009).

Ennis, John, *Selected Poems* (Dublin: Dedalus, 1996).

Fallon, Padraic, *Collected Poems* (Oldcastle: Gallery, 1990).

Fallon, Peter, *News of the World: Selected and New Poems* (Oldcastle: Gallery, 1998).

—— *The Company of Horses* (Oldcastle: Gallery, 2007).

Fiacc, Padraic, *Ruined Pages: New Selected Poems* (Belfast: Lagan, 2012).

Flynn, Leontia, *These Days* (London: Jonathan Cape, 2004).

—— *Drives* (London: Jonathan Cape, 2008).

—— *Profit and Loss* (London: Jonathan Cape, 2011).

French, Tom, *Touching the Bones* (Oldcastle: Gallery, 2001).

—— *The Fire Step* (Oldcastle: Gallery, 2009).

Gillis, Alan, *Somebody, Somewhere* (Oldcastle: Gallery, 2004).

—— *Hawks and Doves* (Oldcastle: Gallery, 2007).

—— *Here Comes the Night* (Oldcastle: Gallery, 2010).

Gore-Booth, Eva, *Selected Poems* (London: Longmans, Green, and Co., 1933).

Grennan, Eamonn, *Selected and New Poems* (Oldcastle: Gallery, 2000).

—— *Still Life with Waterfall* (Oldcastle: Gallery, 2001).

—— *The Quick of It* (Oldcastle: Gallery, 2004).

—— *Out of Breath* (Oldcastle: Gallery, 2007).

Groarke, Vona, *Shale* (Oldcastle: Gallery, 1994).

—— *Other People's Houses* (Oldcastle: Gallery, 1999).

—— *Flight* (Oldcastle: Gallery, 2002).

—— *Juniper Street* (Oldcastle: Gallery, 2006).

—— *Spindrift* (Oldcastle: Gallery, 2009).

Hardie, Kerry, *Selected Poems* (Oldcastle: Gallery, 2011).

Hartnett, Michael, *Collected Poems* (Oldcastle: Gallery, 2001).

—— *A Book of Strays* (Oldcastle: Gallery, 2002).

—— *Translations* (Oldcastle: Gallery, 2003).

Healey, Dermott, *What the Hammer* (Oldcastle: Gallery, 1998).

—— *The Reed Bed* (Oldcastle: Gallery, 2001).

—— *A Fool's Errand* (Oldcastle: Gallery, 2010).

Healy, Randolph, *Green 532: Selected Poems 1983–2000* (Cambridge: Salt, 2002).

Heaney, Seamus, *Opened Ground: Poems 1966–1996* (London: Faber, 1998).

—— *Electric Light* (London: Faber, 2001).

—— *District and Circle* (London: Faber, 2006).

—— *Human Chain* (London: Faber, 2010).

Hewitt, John, *The Collected Poems of John Hewitt*, ed. Frank Ormsby (Belfast: Blackstaff, 1991).

Higgins, F. R., *Arable Holdings* (Dublin: Cuala Press, 1933).

—— *The Gap of Brightness* (London: MacMillan, 1940).

Higgins, Rita Ann, *Sunny Side Plucked: New and Selected Poems* (Newcastle: Bloodaxe, 1996).

—— *Ireland is Changing Mother* (Tarset: Bloodaxe, 2001).

Hutchinson, Pearse, *Collected Poems* (Oldcastle: Gallery, 2002).

Hyde, Douglas, *Abhráin Grádh Chúige Chonnacht* or *Love Songs of Connacht* (Dublin: Gill, 1893).

Joyce, James, *Poems and Shorter Writings* (London: Faber, 1991).

Joyce, Trevor, *With the first dream of fire they hunt the cold: a body of work 1966–2000* (Dublin: New Writers' Press, 2001).

—— *What's in Store: Poems 2000–2007* (Dublin: New Writers' Press, 2007).

Kavanagh, Patrick, *Collected Poems*, ed. Antoinette Quinn (London: Allen Lane, 2004).

Kennelly, Brendan, *A Time for Voices: Selected Poems 1960–1990* (Newcastle: Bloodaxe, 1990).

Kinsella, Thomas, *Collected Poems, 1956–2001* (Manchester: Carcanet, 2001).

Laird, Nick, *To a Fault* (London: Faber, 2005).

—— *On Purpose* (London: Faber, 2007).

Ledwidge, Francis, *The Complete Poems*, ed. Liam O'Meara (Newbridge, Kildare: Goldsmith Press, 1997).

Longley, Michael, *Collected Poems* (London: Jonathan Cape, 2006).

—— *A Hundred Doors* (London: Jonathan Cape, 2011).

Lysaght, Séan, *Selected Poems* (Oldcastle: Gallery, 2010).

MacDonogh, Patrick, *Poems*, ed. Derek Mahon (Oldcastle: Gallery, 2001).

MacGreevy, Thomas, *Collected Poems of Thomas MacGreevy: An Annotated Edition*, ed. Susan Schreibman (Dublin: Anna Livia Press, 1991).

Mac Lochlainn, Gearóid, *Struth Teangacha/Stream of Tongues* (Connemara: Cló Iar-Chonnachta Teo, 2002).

MacNeice, Louis, *Collected Poems*, ed. Peter McDonald (London: Faber, 2007).

Mahon, Derek, *Poems 1962–1978* (Oxford: Oxford University Press, 1979).

—— *Adaptations* (Oldcastle: Gallery, 2006).

—— *New Collected Poems* (Oldcastle: Gallery, 2011).

—— *Raw Material* (Oldcastle: Gallery, 2011).

Mangan, James Clarence, *Selected Writings*, ed. Sean Ryder (Dublin: UCD Press, 2004).

Matthews, Aidan, *Minding Ruth* (Oldcastle: Gallery, 1983).

—— *According to the Small Hours* (London: Jonathan Cape, 1998).

McAuliffe, John, *A Better Life* (Oldcastle: Gallery, 2002).

—— *Next Door* (Oldcastle: Gallery, 2007).

—— *Of all Places* (Oldcastle: Gallery, 2011).

McCarthy, Thomas, *Mr Dineen's Careful Parade: New and Selected Poems* (London: Anvil, 1999).

—— *Merchant Prince* (London: Anvil, 2005).

—— *The Last Geraldine Officer* (London: Anvil, 2009).

McDonald, Peter, *Biting the Wax* (Newcastle: Bloodaxe, 1989).

—— *Adam's Dream* (Newcastle: Bloodaxe, 1996).

—— *Pastorals* (Manchester: Carcanet, 2004).

—— *The House of Clay* (Manchester: Carcanet, 2007).

—— *Torchlight* (Manchester: Carcanet, 2011).

McFadden, Roy, *Collected Poems: 1943–1995* (Belfast: Lagan, 1996).

McGuckian, Medbh, *Selected Poems* (Oldcastle: Gallery, 1997).

—— *Shelmalier* (Oldcastle: Gallery, 1998).

—— *Drawing Ballerinas* (Oldcastle: Gallery, 2001).

—— *The Face of the Earth* (Oldcastle: Gallery, 2002).

—— *Had I a Thousand Lives* (Oldcastle: Gallery, 2003).

—— *The Book of the Angel* (Oldcastle: Gallery, 2004).

—— *The Currach Requires No Harbours* (Oldcastle: Gallery, 2006).

—— *My Love Has Fared Inland* (Oldcastle: Gallery, 2008).

Meehan, Paula, *Pillow Talk* (Oldcastle: Gallery, 1994).

—— *Mysteries of the Home: A Selection of Poems* (Newcastle: Bloodaxe, 1996).

—— *Dharmakaya* (Manchester: Carcanet, 2000).

—— *Painting Rain* (Manchester: Carcanet, 2009).

Molloy, Dorothy, *Hare Soup* (London: Faber, 2004).

—— *Gethsemane Day* (London: Faber, 2006).

Montague, John, *Collected Poems* (Oldcastle: Gallery, 1995).

—— *Smashing the Piano* (Oldcastle: Gallery, 1999).

—— *Drunken Sailor* (Oldcastle: Gallery, 2004).

—— *Speech Lessons* (Oldcastle: Gallery, 2011).

Morrissey, Sinéad, *There Was Fire in Vancouver* (Manchester: Carcanet, 1996).

—— *Between Here and There* (Manchester: Carcanet, 2002).

—— *The State of the Prisons* (Manchester: Carcanet, 2005).

—— *Through the Square Window* (Manchester: Carcanet, 2009).

Muldoon, Paul, *Poems 1968–1998* (London: Faber, 2001).

—— *Moy Sand and Gravel* (London: Faber, 2002).

—— *Horse Latitudes* (London: Faber, 2006).

—— *Maggot* (London: Faber, 2010).

Murphy, Richard, *Collected Poems* (Oldcastle: Gallery, 1999).

Ní Chiulleanáin, Eiléan, *Selected Poems* (Oldcastle: Gallery, 2008).

—— *The Sun Fish* (Oldcastle: Gallery, 2009).

Ní Dhomhnaill, Nuala, *Selected Poems/Rogha Dánta*, trans. Michael Hartnett (Dublin: Raven Arts, 1988).

—— *Pharaoh's Daughter* (Oldcastle: Gallery, 1990).

—— *The Astrakhan Cloak*, trans. Paul Muldoon (Oldcastle: Gallery, 1992).

—— *The Water Horse*, trans Medbh McGuckian and Eiléan Ní Chiulleanáin (Oldcastle: Gallery, 1999).

—— *The Fifty Minute Mermaid*, trans. Paul Muldoon (Oldcastle: Gallery, 2007).

O'Callaghan, Conor, *The History of Rain* (Oldcastle: Gallery, 1993).

—— *Seatown* (Oldcastle: Gallery, 1999).

—— *Fiction* (Oldcastle: Gallery, 2005).

O Direain, Mairtin, *Dánta 1939–1979* (Dublin: An Clochomhar, 1980).

—— *Beasa an Tuir* (Dublin: An Clochomhar, 1984).

—— *Craobhog Dan* (Dublin: An Clochomhar, 1986).

O'Donoghue, Bernard, *Selected Poems* (London: Faber, 2008).

—— *Farmers Cross* (London: Faber, 2011).

O'Driscoll, Dennis, *New and Selected Poems* (London: Anvil, 2004).

O'Grady, Desmond, *The Road Taken: New and Selected Poems, 1956–1996* (Salzburg: University of Salzburg Press, 1996).

O'Malley, Mary, *The Boning Hall* (Manchester: Carcanet, 2002).

—— *A Perfect V* (Manchester: Carcanet, 2006).

O'Reilly, Caitriona, *The Nowhere Birds* (Tarset: Bloodaxe, 2001).

—— *The Sea Cabinet* (Tarset: Bloodaxe, 2006).

O Riordain, Sean, *Eireaball Spideoige* [1952] (Dublin: Sairseal and Dill, 1986).

—— *Tar Eis Mo Bháis* [1978] (Dublin: Sairseal and Dill, 1986).

—— *Brosna* [1964] (Dublin: Sairseal and Dill, 1987).

Ormsby, Frank, *A Store of Candles* (Oxford: Oxford University Press, 1977).

—— *A Northern Spring* (Oldcastle: Gallery, 1986).

—— *The Ghost Train* (Oldcastle: Gallery, 1995).

—— *Fireflies* (Manchester: Carcanet, 2009).

O Searcaigh, Cathal, *An Bealach 'na Bhaile/Homecoming* (Indreabhan: C16 Iar-Chonnachta, 1993).

—— *Na Buachailli Bána* (Indreabhan: C16 Iar-Chonnachta, 1996).

—— *Out in the Open*, trans. Frank Sewell (Indreabhan: Cló Iar-Chonnachta, 1997).

—— *An Tnuth leis an tSolas* (Indreabhan: Cló Iar-Chonnachta, 2001).

O'Sullivan, Seamus (James Starkey), *Collected Poems* (Dublin: Orwell Press, 1940).

Paulin, Tom, *Selected Poems 1972–1990* (London: Faber, 1993).

—— *Walking a Line* (London: Faber, 1994).

—— *The Wind Dog* (London: Faber, 1999).

—— *The Invasion Handbook* (London: Faber, 2002).

—— *The Road to Inver: Translations, Versions, Imitations 1975–2003* (London: Faber, 2004).

Quinn, Justin, *The O'o'a'a' Bird* (Manchester: Carcanet, 1995).

—— *Privacy* (Manchester: Carcanet, 1999).

—— *Fuselage* (Oldcastle: Gallery, 2002).

—— *Waves and Trees* (Oldcastle: Gallery, 2006).

—— *Close Quarters* (Oldcastle: Gallery, 2011).

Redmond, John, *Thumb's Width* (Manchester: Carcanet, 2001).

—— *MUDe* (Manchester: Carcanet, 2008).

Riordan, Maurice, *A Word from the Loki* (London: Faber, 1995).

—— *Floods* (London: Faber, 2000).

—— *The Holy Lands* (London: Faber, 2007).

Rodgers, W. R., *Poems*, ed. Michael Longley (Oldcastle: Gallery, 1993).

Salkeld, Blanaid, *Hello, Eternity!* (London: Elkin Matthews & Marrot, 1933).

—— *The Fox's Covert* (London: Dent, 1935).

—— *The Engine Is Left Running* (Dublin: Gayfield, 1937).

—— *Experiment In Error* (Aldington: Hand & Flower Press, 1955).

Scully, Maurice, *livelihood* (Bray: Wild Honey Press, 2004).

—— *Doing the Same in English: A Sampler of Work 1987–2008* (Dublin: Dedalus Press, 2008).

Simmons, James, *Poems 1956–1986* (Oldcastle: Gallery, 1986).

Sirr, Peter, *Selected Poems* (Oldcastle: Gallery, 2004).

—— *Nonetheless* (Oldcastle: Gallery, 2004).

—— *The Thing Is* (Oldcastle: Gallery, 2009).

Squires, Geoffrey, *Untitled and Other Poems: 1975–2002* (Bray: Wild Honey Press, 2004).

Sweeney, Matthew, *Selected Poems* (London: Jonathan Cape, 2002).

—— *Sanctuary* (London: Jonathan Cape, 2004).

—— *Black Moon* (London: Jonathan Cape, 2007).

—— *The Night Post: A New Selection* (London: Salt, 2010).

Synge, J. M., *J. M. Synge: Collected Works, Volume I: Poems* (Oxford: Oxford University Press, 1962).

Tynan, Katherine, *The Poems of Katherine Tynan*, ed. Monk Gibbon (Dublin: Allen Figgis, 1963).

Walsh, Catherine, *City West* (Exeter: Shearsman, 2005).
—— *Optic Verve: A Commentary* (Exeter: Shearsman, 2009).
Watters, Eugene, *The Week-End of Dermot and Grace* (Dublin: Allen Figgis, 1964).
Wheatley, David, *Thirst* (Oldcastle: Gallery, 1997).
—— *Misery Hill* (Oldcastle: Gallery, 2000).
—— *Mocker* (Oldcastle: Gallery, 2006).
—— *A Nest on the Waves* (Oldcastle: Gallery, 2010).
Wingfield, Sheila, *Poems* (London: Cresset Press, 1938).
Yeats, W. B., *The Variorum Edition of the Poems of W. B. Yeats*, ed. Peter Allt and Russell K. Alspach (Basingstoke: Macmillan, 1956).

II. Anthologies

Agee, Chris (ed.), *The New North: Contemporary Poetry from Northern Ireland* (Salem: Wake Forest University Press, 2008; London: Salt, 2011).
Barry, Sebastian (ed.), *The Inherited Boundaries: Younger Poets of the Republic of Ireland* (Dublin: Dolmen, 1986).
Brooke, Stopford and T. W. Rolleston (eds.), *A Treasury of Irish Poetry in the English Tongue* (New York: Macmillan, 1915).
Brown, John (ed.), *Magnetic North: The Emerging Poets* (Belfast: Lagan, 2006).
Crotty, Patrick (ed.), *Modern Irish Poetry: An Anthology* (Belfast: Blackstaff, 1995).
—— (ed.), *The Penguin Book of Irish Poetry* (London: Penguin, 2010).
Daiken, Leslie H. (ed.), *Goodbye Twilight: Songs of the Struggle in Ireland* (London: Lawrence and Wishart, 1936).
Davis, Wes (ed.), *An Anthology of Modern Irish Poetry* (Cambridge, MA: Harvard University Press, 2010).
Dawe, Gerald (ed.), *The Younger Irish Poets* (Belfast: Blackstaff, 1982).
—— (ed.), *The New Younger Irish Poets* (Belfast: Blackstaff, 1991).
—— (ed.), *Earth Voices Whispering: An Anthology of Irish War Poetry 1914–1945* (Belfast: Blackstaff, 2008).
Delanty, Greg and Nuala Ní Dhomhnaill (eds.), *Jumping off Shadows: Selected Contemporary Irish Poets* (Cork: Cork University Press, 1995).
Duffy, Noel and T. Dorgan (eds.), *Watching the River Flow: A Century in Irish Poetry* (Dublin: Poetry Ireland, 1999).
Fiacc, Padraic (ed.), *The Wearing of the Black: An Anthology of Contemporary Ulster Poetry* (Belfast: Blackstaff, 1974).
Fitzmaurice, Gabriel (ed.), *Irish Poetry Now: Other Voices* (Dublin: Wolfhound, 1993).
Greacen, Robert and Valentin Iremonger (eds.), *Contemporary Irish Poetry* (London: Faber, 1949).
Guinness, Selina (ed.), *The New Irish Poets* (Tarset: Bloodaxe, 2004).
Heaney, Seamus and Ted Hughes (eds.), *The Rattle Bag* (London: Faber, 1982).
Kennelly, Brendan (ed.), *The Penguin Book of Irish Verse* (Harmondsworth: Penguin, 1970).
Kiberd, Declan and Gabriel Fitzmaurice (eds.), *An Crann faoi Bhláth/The Flowering Tree* (Dublin: Wolfhound, 1991).
Kinsella, Thomas (ed.), *The New Oxford Book of Irish Verse* (Oxford: Oxford University Press, 1986).

Longley, Edna (ed.), *The Bloodaxe Book of 20th Century Poetry from Britain and Ireland* (Tarset: Bloodaxe, 2001).

Longley, Michael (ed.), *20th Century Irish Poems* (London: Faber, 2002).

MacDonagh, Donagh and Lennox Robinson (eds.), *The Oxford Book of Irish Verse* (Oxford: Oxford University Press, 1958).

Mahon, Derek (ed.), *The Sphere Book of Modern Irish Poetry* (London: Sphere, 1972).

—— and Peter Fallon (eds.), *The Penguin Book of Contemporary Irish Poetry* (London: Penguin, 1990).

McBreen, Joan (ed.), *The Watchful Heart: A New Generation of Irish Poets* (Cliffs of Moher: Salmon Publishing, 2009).

Meyer, Kuno, *Selections from Ancient Irish Poetry* [1911] (London: Constable, 1928).

Montague, John (ed.), *The Faber Book of Irish Verse* (London: Faber, 1974).

—— (ed.), *Bitter Harvest: An Anthology of Contemporary Irish Verse* (New York: Scribner, 1989).

Muldoon, Paul (ed.), *The Faber Book of Contemporary Irish Poetry* (London: Faber, 1986).

—— (ed.), *The Faber Book of Beasts* (London: Faber, 1997).

O'Brien, Peggy (ed.), *The Wake Forest Book of Irish Women's Poetry 1967–2000* (Salem: Wake Forest University Press, 2000).

Ormsby, Frank (ed.), *Poets from the North of Ireland* (Belfast: Blackstaff, 1979).

—— (ed.), *A Rage for Order: Poetry of the Northern Ireland Troubles* (Belfast: Blackstaff, 1992).

Ó Tuama, Seán and Thomas Kinsella (eds. and trans.), *An Duanaire 1600–1900: Poems of the Dispossessed* (Dublin: Dolmen Press/Bord na Gaeilge, 1981).

Paulin, Tom (ed.), *The Faber Book of Political Verse* (London: Faber, 1986).

—— (ed.), *The Faber Book of Vernacular Verse* (London: Faber, 1990).

Ryan, Desmond (ed.), *The 1916 Poets* [1963] (Dublin: Gill & Macmillan, 1995).

Yeats, W. B. (ed.), *A Book of Irish Verse Selected from Modern Writers* (London: Methuen, 1896).

—— (ed.), *The Oxford Book of Modern Verse 1892–1935* (Oxford: Clarendon Press, 1936).

III. PROSE

Alcobia-Murphy, Shane, *Sympathetic Ink: Intertextual Relations in Northern Irish Poetry* (Liverpool: Liverpool University Press, 2006).

—— *Governing the Tongue in Northern Ireland: The Place of Art/The Art of Place* (Cambridge: Cambridge Scholars Publishing, 2008).

—— and Richard Kirkland (eds.), *The Poetry of Medbh McGuckian* (Cork: Cork University Press, 2010).

Alexander, Neal, *Ciaran Carson: Space, Place, Writing* (Liverpool: Liverpool University Press, 2010).

Allen, Nicholas and Aaron Kelly (eds.), *The Cities of Belfast* (Dublin: Four Courts Press, 2003).

Allison, Jonathan (ed.), *Yeats's Political Identities: Selected Essays* (Ann Arbor: University of Michigan Press, 1996).

Annwn, David, *Arcs Through: The Poetry of Randolph Healy, Billy Mills & Maurice Scully* (Dublin: Wild Honey Press, 2001).

Archambeau, Robert, *Another Ireland* (Bray: Wild Honey Press, 1998).

Beckett, Samuel, *Disjecta: Miscellaneous Writings and a Dramatic Fragment*, ed. Ruby Cohn (London: John Calder, 1983).

Boland, Eavan, *Object Lessons: The Life of the Woman and the Poet in Our Time* (Manchester: Carcanet, 1995).

Brearton, Fran, *The Great War in Irish Poetry: W. B. Yeats to Michael Longley* (Oxford: Oxford University Press, 2000).

—— *Reading Michael Longley* (Tarset: Bloodaxe, 2006).

—— and Edna Longley (eds.), *Incorrigibly Plural: Louis MacNeice and his Legacy* (Manchester: Carcanet, 2012).

Brown, John, *In the Chair: Interview with Poets from the North of Ireland* (Cliffs of Moher: Salmon Press, 2002).

Brown, Richard Danson, *Louis MacNeice and the Poetry of the 1930s* (Tavistock: Northcote House, 2009).

Brown, Terence, *Louis MacNeice: Sceptical Vision* (Dublin: Gill & Macmillan, 1975).

—— *Northern Voices: Poets from Ulster* (Dublin: Gill & Macmillan, 1975).

—— *Ireland's Literature: Selected Essays* (Mullingar: Lilliput, 1988).

—— *The Life of W. B. Yeats* (Dublin: Gill & Macmillan, 1999).

—— *The Literature of Ireland: Culture and Criticism* (Cambridge: Cambridge University Press, 2010).

—— and Nicholas Grene (eds.), *Tradition and Influence in Anglo-Irish Poetry* (Basingstoke: Macmillan, 1989).

Byron, Catherine, *Out of Step: Pursuing Seamus Heaney to Purgatory* (Bristol: Loxwood Stoneleigh, 1992).

Campbell, Matthew (ed.), *The Cambridge Companion to Contemporary Irish Poetry* (Cambridge: Cambridge University Press, 2003).

Carpenter, Andrew (ed.), *Place, Personality and the Irish Writer* (Gerrards Cross: Colin Smythe, 1977).

Carson, Ciaran, *Last Night's Fun* (London: Jonathan Cape, 1996).

—— *The Star Factory* (London: Granta Books, 1997).

—— *Fishing for Amber* (London: Granta Books, 1999).

—— *Shamrock Tea* (London: Granta Books, 2001).

—— *The Pen Friend* (Belfast: Blackstaff, 2009).

Cavanagh, Michael, *Professing Poetry: Seamus Heaney's Poetics* (Washington DC: Catholic University of America Press, 2009).

Clark, Heather, *The Ulster Renaissance: Poetry in Belfast 1962–1972* (Oxford: Oxford University Press, 2006).

Clarke, Austin, *Twice Around the Black Church* (London: Routledge, 1962).

—— *A Penny in the Clouds* (Dublin: Routledge and Kegan Paul, 1968).

—— *Reviews and Essays of Austin Clarke*, ed. Gregory A. Schirmer (Gerrards Cross: Colin Smythe, 1995).

Corcoran, Neil, *The Poetry of Seamus Heaney: A Critical Study* (London: Faber, 1998).

—— (ed.), *The Chosen Ground: Essays on the Contemporary Poetry of Northern Ireland* (Bridgend: Seren Books, 1992).

—— *Poets of Modern Ireland: Text, Context, Intertext* (Cardiff: University of Wales Press, 1999).

Coughlan, Patricia, and Alex Davis (eds.), *Modernism and Ireland: The Poetry of the 1930s* (Cork: Cork University Press, 1995).

Craig, Cairns, *Yeats, Eliot, Pound and the Politics of Poetry* (London: Croom Helm, 1982).

Cronin, Anthony, *Dead As Doornails, A Chronicle of Life* [1976] (Oxford: Oxford University Press, 1986).

Crosson, Seán, *The Given Note: Traditional Irish Music and Modern Irish Poetry* (Newcastle: Cambridge Scholars Publishing, 2008).

Davis, Alex, *A Broken Line: Denis Devlin and Irish Poetic Modernism* (Dublin: University College Dublin Press, 2000).

Dawe, Gerald, *The Proper Word: Collected Criticism—Ireland, Poetry, Politics*, ed. Nicolas Allen (Omaha: Creighton University Press, 2007).

Donoghue, Denis, *We Irish* (Brighton: Harvester, 1986).

Dorgan, Theo (ed.), *Irish Poetry Since Kavanagh* (Dublin: Four Courts, 1996).

Dunn, Douglas (ed.), *Two Decades of Irish Writing: A Critical Survey* (Manchester: Carcanet, 1975).

Ellmann, Richard, *Yeats: The Man and the Masks* (London: Faber, 1961).

——— *The Identity of Yeats* (London: Faber, 1964).

Fitzsimons, Andrew, *The Sea of Disappointment: Thomas Kinsella's Pursuit of the Real* (Dublin: UCD Press, 2008).

Foster, John Wilson, *Colonial Consequences: Essays in Irish Literature and Culture* (Dublin: Lilliput, 1991).

Foster, Roy, *W. B. Yeats: A Life. Vol. 1: The Apprentice Mage, 1865–1914* (Oxford: Oxford University Press, 1997).

——— *W. B. Yeats: A Life. Vol. II: The Arch-Poet, 1915–1939* (Oxford: Oxford University Press, 2003).

——— *Words Alone: Yeats and his Inheritances* (Oxford: Oxford University Press, 2011).

Garratt, Robert F., *Modern Irish Poetry: Tradition and Continuity from Yeats to Heaney* (Berkeley and Los Angeles: University of California Press, 1986).

Gillis, Alan, *Irish Poetry of the 1930s* (Oxford: Oxford University Press, 2005).

Gilonis, Harry (ed.), *For the Birds: Proceedings of the First Cork Conference on New and Experimental Irish Poetry* (Dublin: hardPressed Poetry, 1998).

Goodby, John, *Irish Poetry since 1950: From Stillness into History* (Manchester: Manchester University Press, 2000).

Grene, Nicholas, *Yeats's Codes* (Oxford: Oxford University Press, 2008).

Grennan, Eamon, *Facing the Music: Irish Poetry in the Twentieth Century* (Omaha: Creighton University Press, 1999).

Haberstroh, Patricia Boyle (ed.), *Women Creating Women: Contemporary Irish Women Poets* (New York: Syracuse University Press, 1996).

——— (ed.), *My Self My Muse: Irish Women Poets Reflect on Life and Art* (New York: Syracuse University Press, 2001).

Harmon, Maurice, *The Poetry of Thomas Kinsella* (Atlantic Highlands, NJ: Humanities Press, 1975).

——— *Austin Clarke: A Critical Introduction* (Dublin: Wolfhound Press, 1989).

Harvey, Lawrence, *Samuel Beckett: Poet & Critic* (Princeton: Princeton University Press, 1970).

Haughey, Jim, *The First World War in Irish Poetry* (London and New Jersey: Associated University Presses, 2002).

Haughton, Hugh, *The Poetry of Derek Mahon* (Oxford: Oxford University Press, 2007).

Heaney, Seamus, *Preoccupations: Selected Prose 1968–1978* (London: Faber, 1980).

—— *The Government of the Tongue* (London: Faber, 1988).

—— *The Redress of Poetry: Oxford Lectures* (London: Faber, 1995).

—— *Finders Keepers: Selected Prose 1971–2001* (London: Faber, 2002).

—— and Dennis O'Driscoll, *Stepping Stones: Interviews with Seamus Heaney* (London: Faber, 2008).

Henn, T. R., *The Lonely Tower: Studies in the Poetry of W. B. Yeats*, 2nd edn. (London: Methuen, 1965).

Hewitt, John, *Ancestral Voices: The Selected Prose of John Hewitt*, ed. Tom Clyde (Belfast: Blackstaff, 1987).

Holdeman, David and Ben Levitas (eds.), *Yeats in Context* (Cambridge: Cambridge University Press, 2010).

Homem, Rui Carvalho, *Poetry and Translation in Northern Ireland: Dislocations in Contemporary Writing* (Houndsmills: Palgrave-Macmillan, 2009).

Howes, Marjorie, *Yeats's Nations: Gender, Class, and Irishness* (Cambridge: Cambridge University Press, 1996).

Jackson, Thomas H., *The Whole Matter: The Poetic Evolution of Thomas Kinsella* (Dublin: Lilliput, 1995).

John, Brian, *Reading the Ground: The Poetry of Thomas Kinsella* (Washington DC: Catholic University Press, 1996).

Johnston, Dillon, *Irish Poetry after Joyce* (Notre Dame: University of Notre Dame Press, 1985).

—— *The Poetic Economies of England and Ireland, 1912–2000* (Basingstoke: Palgrave, 2001).

Joyce, James, *Occasional, Critical, and Political Writing*, ed. Kevin Barry (Oxford: Oxford University Press, 2000).

Kavanagh, Patrick, *Collected Pruse* (London: MacGibbon & Kee, 1967).

—— *A Poet's Country: Selected Prose*, ed. Antoinette Quinn (Dublin: Lilliput Press, 2003).

Keatinge, Benjamin and Aengus Woods (eds.), *Other Edens: The Life and Work of Brian Coffey* (Dublin: Irish Academic Press 2009).

Kelleher, Margaret and Philip O'Leary (eds), *The Cambridge History of Irish Literature*, vol. 2 (Cambridge: Cambridge University Press, 2006).

Kendall, Tim, *Paul Muldoon* (Bridgend: Seren, 1996).

—— (ed.), *The Oxford Handbook of British and Irish War Poetry* (Oxford: Oxford University Press, 2007).

Kendall, Tim, and Peter McDonald (eds.), *Paul Muldoon: Critical Essays* (Liverpool: Liverpool University Press, 2004).

Kenneally, Michael (ed.), *Poetry in Contemporary Irish Literature* (Gerrards Cross: Colin Smythe, 1995).

Kennedy-Andrews, Elmer, *Contemporary Irish Poetry: A Collection of Critical Essays* (Basingstoke: Macmillan, 1992).

—— *The Poetry of Derek Mahon* (Gerrards Cross: Colin Smythe, 2002).

—— *Writing Home: Poetry and Place in Northern Ireland 1968–2008* (Cambridge: D. S. Brewer, 2008).

—— (ed.), *Seamus Heaney: A Collection of Critical Essays* (Basingstoke: Macmillan, 1992).

—— (ed.), *Paul Muldoon: Poetry, Prose, Drama* (Gerrards Cross: Colin Smythe, 2006).

—— (ed.), *Ciaran Carson: Critical Essays* (Dublin: Four Courts Press, 2009).

Kiberd, Declan, *Inventing Ireland: The Literature of the Modern Nation* (London: Jonathan Cape, 1995).

—— *The Irish Writer and the World* (Cambridge: Cambridge University Press, 2005).

Kinsella, Thomas, *The Dual Tradition: An Essay on Poetry and Politics in Ireland* (Manchester: Carcanet, 1995).

—— *Prose Occasions: 1951–2006* (Manchester: Carcanet, 2009).

Kirkland, Richard, *Literature and Culture in Northern Ireland since 1965: Moments of Danger* (London and New York: Longman, 1996).

Larrissy, Edward, *Yeats the Poet: The Measures of Difference* (Hemel Hempstead: Harvester, 1994).

Loftus, Richard J., *Nationalism in Modern Anglo-Irish Poetry* (Madison and Milwaukee: University of Wisconsin Press, 1964).

Loizeaux, Elizabeth Bergmann, *Twentieth-Century Poetry and the Visual Arts* (Cambridge: Cambridge University Press, 2008).

Longley, Edna, *Poetry in the Wars* (Newcastle: Bloodaxe, 1986).

—— *Louis MacNeice: A Study* (London: Faber, 1988).

—— *The Living Stream: Literature and Revisionism in Ireland* (Newcastle: Bloodaxe, 1994).

—— *Poetry & Posterity* (Tarset: Bloodaxe, 2000).

Longley, Michael, *Tuppenny Stung: Autobiographical Chapters* (Belfast: Lagan, 1994).

MacDonagh, Thomas, *Literature in Ireland: Studies Irish and Anglo-Irish* (London: Fisher Unwin, 1916).

Mackay, Peter, Edna Longley, and Fran Brearton (eds.), *Modern Irish and Scottish Poetry* (Cambridge: Cambridge University Press, 2011).

MacNeice, Louis, *Varieties of Parable* (Cambridge: Cambridge University Press, 1965).

—— *The Strings Are False* (London: Faber, 1965).

—— *The Poetry of W. B. Yeats* [1941] (London: Faber, 1967).

—— *Modern Poetry: A Personal Essay* [1938] (Oxford: Clarendon, 1968).

—— *Selected Literary Criticism of Louis MacNeice*, ed. Alan Heuser (Oxford: Clarendon, 1987).

—— *Selected Prose of Louis MacNeice*, ed. Alan Heuser (Oxford: Clarendon Press, 1993).

—— *Letters of Louis MacNeice*, ed. Jonathan Allison (London: Faber, 2010).

Mahon, Derek, *Journalism: Selected Prose 1970–1995*, ed. Terence Brown (Oldcastle: Gallery, 1996).

Matthews, Steven, *Irish Poetry: Politics, History, Negotiation* (London: Macmillan, 1997).

—— *Yeats as Precursor: Reading in Irish, British and American Poetry* (Basingstoke: Palgrave Macmillan, 2000).

Mays, J. C. C., *N 11 A Musing* (Clonmel: Coelacanth Press, 2003).

McCormack, W.J., *Blood Kindred: W. B. Yeats: The Life, The Death, The Politics* (London: Pimlico, 2005).

McCracken, Kathleen, *Radical Vision: Paul Durcan* (Tarset: Bloodaxe, 2003).

McDiarmid, Lucy, *Saving Civilization: Yeats, Eliot and Auden Between the Wars* (Cambridge: Cambridge University Press, 1984).

McDonald, Peter, *Louis MacNeice: The Poet in his Contexts* (Oxford: Clarendon Press, 1991).

—— *Mistaken Identities: Poetry and Northern Ireland* (Oxford: Clarendon, 1997).

—— *Serious Poetry: Form and Authority from Yeats to Hill* (Oxford: Oxford University Press, 2002).

Montague, John, *The Figure in the Cave and Other Essays*, ed. Antoinette Quinn (New York: Syracuse University Press, 1989).

—— *Company: A Chosen Life* (London: Duckworth, 2001).

Moriarty, Dónal, *The Art of Brian Coffey* (Dublin: UCD Press, 2000).

Muldoon, Paul, *To Ireland, I* (Oxford: Clarendon Press, 2000).

—— *The End of the Poem: Oxford Lectures on Poetry* (London: Faber, 2006).

Ní Dhomhnaill, Nuala, *Selected Essays* (Dublin: New Island Books, 2005).

O'Brien, Conor Cruise, *Passion and Cunning* (New York: Simon and Schuster, 1988).

O'Brien, Sean, *The Deregulated Muse: Essays on Contemporary British and Irish Poetry* (Newcastle: Bloodaxe, 1997).

O'Donoghue, Bernard, *Seamus Heaney and the Language of Poetry* (Brighton: Harvester, 1994).

—— (ed.), *The Cambridge Companion to Seamus Heaney* (Cambridge: Cambridge University Press, 2009).

O'Driscoll, Dennis, *Troubled Thoughts, Majestic Dreams* (Oldcastle: Gallery, 2001).

O'Neill, Michael, *The All-Sustaining Air: Romantic Legacies and Renewals in British, American, and Irish Poetry since 1900* (Oxford: Oxford University Press, 2007).

Parker, Michael, *Seamus Heaney: The Making of the Poet* (Iowa City: University of Iowa, 1993).

—— *Northern Irish Literature, 1956–2006*, 2 vols. (London: Palgrave Macmillan, 2007).

Paulin, Tom, *Ireland and the English Crisis* (Newcastle: Bloodaxe, 1984).

—— *Writing to the Moment: Selected Critical Essays 1980–1996* (London: Faber, 1996).

—— *Crusoe's Secret: The Aesthetics of Dissent* (London: Faber, 2005).

Pine, Richard (ed.), *Dark Fathers into Light: Brendan Kennelly* (Newcastle: Bloodaxe, 1994).

Quinn, Antoinette, *Patrick Kavanagh: Born-Again Romantic* (Dublin: Gill & Macmillan, 1991).

—— *Patrick Kavanagh: A Life* (Dublin: Gill and Macmillan, 2001).

Quinn, Justin, *The Cambridge Introduction to Modern Irish Poetry, 1800–2000* (Cambridge: Cambridge University Press, 2008).

—— (ed.), *Irish Poetry After Feminism: Princess Grace Irish Library Lectures 10* (Gerrards Cross: Colin Smythe, 2008).

Ramazani, Jahan, *Yeats and the Poetry of Death: Elegy, Self-Elegy, and the Sublime* (New Haven and London: Yale University Press, 1990).

—— *Poetry of Mourning: The Modern Elegy from Hardy to Heaney* (Chicago and London: University of Chicago Press, 1994).

Ryan, Ray (ed.), *Writing in the Irish Republic: Literature, Culture, Politics* (London: Macmillan, 2000).

Schirmer, Gregory A., *The Poetry of Austin Clarke* (Gerrards Cross: Colin Smythe, 1983).

Sewell, Frank, *Modern Irish Poetry: A New Alhambra* (Oxford: Oxford University Press, 2001).

Shovlin, Frank, *The Irish Literary Periodical, 1923–1958* (Oxford: Oxford University Press, 2004).

Smith, Stan (ed.), *Patrick Kavanagh* (Dublin: Irish Academic Press, 2009).

Stallworthy, Jon, *Louis MacNeice* (London: Faber, 1995).

Symons, Arthur, *The Symbolist Movement in Literature* (London: William Heinemann, 1899).

Tóibín, Colm (ed.), *The Kilfenora Teaboy—A Study of Paul Durcan* (Dublin: New Island Books, 1996).

Tubridy, Derval, *Thomas Kinsella: The Peppercanister Poems* (Dublin: UCD Press, 2001).

Vendler, Helen, *Seamus Heaney* (Cambridge, MA: Harvard University, 1998).

—— *Our Secret Discipline: Yeats and Lyric Form* (Oxford: Oxford University Press, 2007).

Watt, Stephen, *Beckett and Contemporary Irish Writing* (Cambridge: Cambridge University Press, 2009).

White, Harry, *Music and the Irish Literary Imagination* (New York: Oxford University Press, 2008).

Wilde, Oscar, *The Writings of Oscar Wilde*, ed. Isobel Murray (Oxford: Oxford University Press, 1989).

Wills, Clair, *Improprieties: Politics and Sexuality in Northern Irish Poetry* (Oxford: Oxford University Press, 1993).

—— *Reading Paul Muldoon* (Newcastle: Bloodaxe, 1998).

Wood, Michael, *Yeats and Violence* (Oxford: Oxford University Press, 2010).

Wright, Judith M. (ed.), *A Companion to Irish Literature*, 2 vols. (Oxford: Blackwell, 2010).

Yeats, W. B., *Mythologies* (London: Macmillan, 1952).

—— *Autobiographies* (London: Macmillan, 1955).

—— *Essays & Introductions* (London: Macmillan, 1961).

—— *A Vision* [1937] (London: Macmillan, 1962).

—— *Explorations* (London: Macmillan, 1962).

INDEX